Ethics in the Workplace

SELECTED READINGS IN BUSINESS ETHICS

Second Edition

Robert A. Larmer
University of New Brunswick

WADSWORTH

THOMSON LEARNING ™

Australia • Canada • Mexico • Singapore • Spain • United Kingdom • United States

WADSWORTH

THOMSON LEARNING ™

Philosophy Editor: Peter Adams
Assistant Editor: Kara Kindstrom
Editorial Assistant: Anna Lustig
Print/Media Buyer: Robert King
Permissions Editor: Joohee Lee
Production Service: Buuji, Inc

Copy Editor: Linda Ireland/Buuji, Inc.
Cover Designer: Laurie Anderson
Cover Image: Photographer: Daisuke Morita;
  Source: PhotoDisc
Compositor: Buuji, Inc.
Printer: RR Donnelley

Printed in the United States of America
4 5 6 7 8 9   09 08 07

For permission to use material from this text,
contact us by
Web: http://www.thomsonrights.com
Fax: 1-800-730-2215
Phone: 1-800-730-2214

Wadsworth Thomson Learning
10 Davis Drive
Belmont, CA 94002-3098
USA

For more information about our products,
contact us:
Thomson Learning Academic Resource Center
1-800-423-0563
http://www.wadsworth.com

International Headquarters
Thomson Learning
International Division
290 Harbor Drive, 2nd Floor
Stamford, CT 06902-7477
USA

UK/Europe/Middle East/South Africa
Thomson Learning
Berkshire House
168-173 High Holborn
London WC1V 7AA
United Kingdom

Asia
Thomson Learning
60 Albert Street, #15-01
Albert Complex
Singapore 189969

Canada
Nelson Thomson Learning
1120 Birchmount Road
Toronto, Ontario M1K 5G4
Canada

Library of Congress Cataloging-in-Publication Data
Ethics in the workplace : selected readings in business ethics /
[compiled by] Robert A. Larmer.—2nd ed.
    p. cm.
Includes bibliographical references.
ISBN-13: 978-0-534-54659-5
ISBN-10: 0-534-54659-5
   1. Business ethics. I. Larmer, Robert A.
HF5387 .E848 2002
174'.4—dc21   2001026528

To my father, J. Robert Larmer,
with whom I have worked many happy hours

Contents

Part II Business and the Employee

Preface

ETHICS IN THE WORKPLACE is intended to provide an introduction to the field of business ethics for both upper- and lower-division undergraduate students. Its aim is to present, through a series of readings, a reasonably comprehensive examination of the major ethical issues associated with business and the professions. The text begins by demonstrating the relevance of moral theory to business and then structures the practical discussions so that they lead to widening spheres of moral relevance. Organizing the text in this manner helps students realize that ethical problems typically intertwine and must be dealt with at both individual and societal levels. Part I explores the relation of morality to business and introduces the major ethical theories. Part II examines the ethical issues arising from the employer-employee relationship. Part III focuses on the relation between business and the consumer, and Part IV examines the relation between business and society.

The text presents articles that are readily accessible to the nonspecialist, yet reflect the increasing philosophical sophistication of work in this area. Recognizing that students using this text will often have little or no acquaintance with philosophy, I have sought to make the acquisition of the tools of the trade a little easier by providing introductions to the articles found within each chapter. I have also included case studies, review questions, and suggestions for further reading at the end of each chapter. In addition, I have included two appendices. The first offers advice on writing article summaries and critical essays and includes two sample article summaries, one of Albert Carr's "Is Business Bluffing Ethical?" and one of Mary Midgley's "Trying Out One's New Sword." The second lists Latin terms commonly used in philosophical discussions and provides an explanation of their meanings.

With regard to the case studies, I have in most instances chosen actual legal cases. My intention in doing this is not to suggest to students that whatever turns out to be legal is moral, but rather to illustrate the complexity of ethics in real life. That one is not always rewarded for doing the right thing, or that what is legal may in many instances not satisfy the demands of morality is well illustrated by these cases. My intention has been to provoke students to think for themselves rather than simply to accept the *status quo*.

New in This Edition

➤ Over 30 percent new material
➤ A large selection of recent (post-1995) high-quality readings
➤ Additional classic readings
➤ Readings in ethical theory and environmental ethics written specifically for this text
➤ Expanded chapter introductions providing both a general introduction to the topic and specific introductions for each reading
➤ Expanded and updated supplementary reading lists for each chapter topic
➤ InfoTrac College Edition search terms for each chapter topic to help students make use of Web resources

An updated instructor's manual is also available. In it, I have provided sample summaries for each chapter of the text and the outcomes of the legal cases discussed. I have also included other cases and their outcomes to supplement those given at the end of each chapter in the text.

Several expressions of gratitude are appropriate. David Toner from West Publishing originally encouraged me to propose a text in the area of business ethics, and Clark Baxter and Linda Poirier at West provided valuable editorial guidance in producing the first edition. West has subsequently been acquired by International Thomson Publishing. I am grateful to Peter Adams and Kara Kindstrom of the Wadsworth division of Thomson for their help in preparing this second edition. Further thanks are due to the referees who provided a great deal of constructive advice in the production of the second edition. Thanks to the following reviewers of the second edition: Glenn Moots, Northland University; Ralph Forsberg, Delta College; and Claudia McCollough, Coastal Carolina University. The following reviewed the first edition: Gary Cox, SUNY/Geneseo; David B. Fletcher, Wheaton College; Norris Frederick, Queens College; Geoffrey P. Lantos, Stonehill College; Richard N. Lee, University of Arkansas; Anne M. McCarthy, Indiana University; Marcia A. McKelligan, DePauw University; Peter J. Meh, University of Central Arkansas; Steven K. Paulson, University of North Florida; Lena B. Prewitt, University of Alabama; Doran Smolkin, Kansas State University; and Peter K. Steinfeld, Buena Vista College. I would also like to thank Anne Pugh of the University of New Brunswick Philosophy Department for her willingness to provide secretarial services above and beyond the call of duty. Most of all I would like to thank my wife, Lorena Henry, for her continual love and support.

My hope is that the enjoyment and intellectual challenge I have found in selecting and preparing these readings will be shared by students and instructors and that the material I have chosen will prove useful to those endeavoring to act ethically in the workplace.

Robert A. Larmer

Introduction: Philosophy, Ethics, and Business

Why Study Ethics?

IN WRITING THIS INTRODUCTION, I have been reminded of the old joke about the millipede who was asked to describe the process of walking. After giving the question considerable thought, the millipede was unable ever to walk again. The point is that it is one thing to engage in an activity and quite another to give an accurate description of it. Plato long ago reminded his readers that a courageous person may give an inadequate account of what courage is. Similarly, there are many people who are highly ethical, but have little acquaintance with moral theory. It is also true that it is far better actually to be ethical than simply to be able to give an account of morality.

Nevertheless, it is important to reflect on what it means to be ethical. Unlike the millipede's walking, which demands no theoretical knowledge on the part of the millipede, attempts to be ethical pose practical problems that often can be helpfully addressed by appealing to ethical theory. The theory may be held explicitly, or, as is often the case, implicitly, but it influences decision making. Thus, for example, the person who claims that it would have been morally permissible to assassinate Hitler if that would have shortened the war and saved many lives, may not realize that she is appealing to what ethicists call the Principle of Utility, which states that the test of whether an action is moral is whether it produces the greatest good for the greatest number. It is nonetheless a theoretical belief that influences her ethical practice. The advantage of making implicit theoretical beliefs explicit is that we can then examine them in order to determine how they fit with other beliefs we hold and whether we should modify or abandon them altogether. For instance, does the Principle of Utility which seems to justify the assassination of Hitler hold for all ethical decision-making? If it does hold for all ethical decision-making, does it imply that my intuition that I do not have to share my lottery winnings, even if that would make a lot of people happy, is mistaken and needs to be abandoned? If the Principle of Utility does not hold for all ethical decision-making, what are the circumstances in which it should be applied and the circumstances in which it should not? These types of questions are not easy to answer, but neither are they easily avoided.

Making ethical theory explicit is valuable insofar as it helps persons who want to act morally to evaluate their experience and to assess situations they find ethically perplexing. It should be emphasized, however, that ethical theory does not, by itself, produce moral individuals. Understanding this enables us to avoid the naive assumption that taking a course in ethical theory will automatically develop moral character. Aristotle long ago warned that people often

> take refuge in theory and think they are being philosophers and will become good in this way, behaving . . . like patients who listen attentively to their doctors, but do none of the things they are ordered to do. As the latter will not be made well in body by such a course of treatment, the former will not be made well in soul by such a course of philosophy.[1]

In street slang, his point could be put as "You can't just talk the talk, you gotta walk the walk."

A Brief Introduction to Philosophy

It is impossible to discuss ethical theory in any kind of systematic way without at least a nodding acquaintance with philosophy. Unfortunately, those who have never studied philosophy often think of it as a somewhat mysterious discipline. There is a tendency on the part of many to think of it as especially profound or especially silly, or sometimes both. We have a curious respect for philosophers, but we often also picture them as rather strange individuals who have trouble dealing with the practicalities of life. Nor is this view a particularly recent one. Thales, a Greek who lived in the sixth century B.C. and is generally given the title of being the first philosopher, was said to have fallen down a well while trying to observe the stars. The story is probably not true, but it does illustrate the long history of this view of philosophers as being too heavenly minded to be any earthly good.

No doubt part of this ambivalence results from the fact that philosophers study important questions, but what they say in response to these questions is sometimes disturbing. We respect them for inquiring into these issues, but we sometimes fear that we may not be entirely comfortable with what they might tell us. Add to this the sneaking suspicion that, although a lot of intellectual horsepower is being expended, it is not easy or sometimes even possible to connect the abstractions of philosophers to the workaday world and it becomes understandable why many people have mixed feelings toward philosophy.

It must be emphasized, however, that philosophy is not unique in these respects. All disciplines have implications for the important issues of our lives, and it is possible in all disciplines for intelligent persons to expend a lot of time and energy, yet reach incorrect conclusions. Nor is philosophy unique in the sense that it can lose touch with the practicalities of everyday life. It is true that philosophical discussions can become quite esoteric, but then so can a good number of scientific discussions. It may be no easy matter to follow a philosophical discussion of the morality of whistleblowing, but I suspect it is less difficult to understand

[1]Aristotle, *Nicomachean Ethics*, Bk. 2, Ch. 4, Lines 13–18, transl. W. D. Ross in *The Basic Works of Aristotle*, ed. Richard McKeon (New York: Random House, 1941).

than a scientific discussion of "quaternary history of upwelling, paleoproductivity and the oxygen minimum on the Oman margin."[2] At the very least, it is far from clear that this particular scientific discussion is more relevant to the practicalities of life than a philosophic discussion of whistleblowing.

Many people might grant the point I have just made, namely, that disciplines other than philosophy run the risk of becoming so abstract as to lose touch with reality, but they would suggest that philosophy is more apt to fall into this trap than most. The view that the sciences are much more tough-minded than the humanities, that the standards of what constitute good science are clear and concrete, whereas the standards in the arts and especially in philosophy are obscure and soft, is a common one even among academics.

I think this view can be shown to be badly mistaken, and I shall say quite a bit more on the subject in Chapter 2 when we discuss ethical relativism. In the present context, it is enough to observe that many of the specialized disciplines we now distinguish from philosophy were, in the past, considered to be part of it. Psychology, political science, physics, chemistry and biology were all at one time included in the discipline of philosophy. These disciplines are no longer considered part of philosophy, not because philosophers have no interest in these areas or because philosophical questions are not relevant to them, but because the accumulation of knowledge and the development of sophisticated and specialized techniques for studying their subject matter has made it necessary for them to develop into independent areas of study. For these disciplines to be contemptuous of philosophy is like someone insulting the sexual morality and child-rearing practices of his parents; it does not reflect well on one's own origin and history.[3]

With regard to gaining an initial understanding of what philosophy is and what philosophers do, we can begin by noting that the word *philosophy* comes from two Greek words, *philo* and *Sophia,* meaning love and wisdom respectively. Philosophy, then, means love of wisdom and a philosopher is, presumably, a lover of wisdom. It is noteworthy, in the context of discussing business ethics, that for the ancient Greeks who began Western philosophy, wisdom was understood to include not only knowledge but also the practice of virtue.

Philosophers are typically interested in four interrelated areas of study. These are: (1) logic, the study of correct methods of reasoning; (2) metaphysics, the study of what it is that exists; (3) epistemology, the study of how that which exists is known; and (4) axiology, which includes ethics, the study of what is good, and aesthetics, the study of what is beautiful. That these four areas cover, in one way or another, all of reality reveals that philosophy is what we might call an interdisciplinary discipline. Not only do various disciplines such as history, biology, sociology, and business administration, to name only a few, raise particular issues that are of importance for the pursuit of wisdom and hence philosophy, but they also have foundations that are, in the final analysis, philosophical.

[2]I am indebted to John Thorp's excellent article "The Emperor's Clothes" in *The Canadian Federation for the Humanities Bulletin,* Vol. 13, No. 1, Winter 1990, pp. 1-4, for this example.
[3]It is revealing in this regard that it is far easier to get a scholarly article published in a science journal than in a humanities journal. Recent surveys indicate that the typical science journal accepts for publication 65-70% of the manuscripts submitted, whereas the typical humanities journal accepts only 20-30% of the submissions it receives. One Canadian journal in philosophy accepts only 5% of the manuscripts it receives. (See *Bulletin of the Canadian Federation for the Humanities,* Vol. 13, No. 1, Winter 1990, p. 4.) It seems difficult to hold, therefore, that other disciplines, especially the sciences, are inherently more tough-minded than philosophy and have higher standards of objectivity.

Ethical Theory and Its Application to Business

At its most general level, ethical inquiry is an attempt to comprehend the foundations of value and to integrate and systematize the principles of correct moral reasoning. Built into the ethical project of determining what is of value is the view that people ought to pursue that which is valuable. Although for purposes of convenience we often treat ethical questions independently of questions of logic, metaphysics, and epistemology, it is clear that in the long run these questions are intricately interwoven. Questions of what is of value can scarcely be answered independently of answering logical questions concerning what constitutes correct reasoning, metaphysical questions concerning what is real, and epistemological questions concerning how we come to know. Nevertheless, all inquiry must begin somewhere and it would be a mistake to insist that we cannot begin to study ethics until we have studied logic, metaphysics, and epistemology. This said, if we are wise we will realize that the more we study any branch of philosophy, the more its interconnectedness with other branches of philosophy will emerge.

Business ethics involves the practical application of ethical theory. We are familiar with the idea that an engineer wanting to build a bridge must know the principles of physics and chemistry and then creatively apply them to the situation at hand. We are also familiar with the fact that, although there may be many different ways of applying these principles so as to produce a satisfactory bridge, it is not the case that "anything goes." One cannot ignore the principles governing the design of bridges and expect a good result. Similarly, if one wishes to create an ethical company, one must know the principles of ethics and creatively apply them to the situation at hand. There may be many different ways of applying these principles so as to produce an ethical company, but, as in bridge-building, it is emphatically not the case that "anything goes." One can no more ignore ethical principles and expect a moral company than one can ignore the principles of physics and expect a safe bridge.[4]

I have been developing an analogy between engineering and the application of ethical principles in business. An important difference is that, whereas very few of us have to design bridges, most of us are involved with business in one form or another—whether it be as worker, owner, or consumer. As individuals we can often safely ignore the proper principles of design for bridges because we will probably never need to build one. We cannot, however, safely ignore the principles of ethics, since we are all faced with ethical decisions not only in the business environment, but in many other areas of our lives. With this in mind, let us proceed.

---

[4]It is sometimes objected that this analogy is misleading. Engineering, it is suggested, is a science and has an exact methodology; ethics is something other than a science and has no exact methodology. Truth can be arrived at in engineering; it is far from clear that it can be arrived at in ethics.

There is some truth in this objection. Aristotle, in speaking of ethics, pointed out that one must not expect more precision than the subject allows. Arriving at ethical conclusions is quite a different process than solving quadratic equations. This, however, scarcely destroys the analogy. Even in engineering, it is difficult to talk of an optimal design that precludes other approaches, though there is liable to be considerable agreement over what constitutes a good design. Similarly, even though there are different major ethical theories, there is considerable overlap in what they suggest is ethical behavior. If disagreement over design approaches in engineering does not automatically make us skeptical of the ability of engineers to build good bridges, neither should disagreement among ethicists automatically persuade us that they cannot give good advice regarding ethical behavior.

Chapter 1

The Relevance of Morality to Business

Introduction

THE TITLE OF THIS CHAPTER may come as a surprise to some readers. Many people feel that the words *business* and *ethics* do not really go together. We are probably all familiar with the comment that "business ethics," like "square triangle" or "married bachelor," is a contradiction in terms. Underlying such comments is the perception that either in theory or in practice there exists tension between the requirements of business and the claims of morality.

Sometimes all that is meant is that in actual practice, business people frequently act unethically. If this is all that is meant, the claim should scarcely surprise us. The fact that people, whether they be in a business setting or some other environment, often act unethically is hardly news.

Sometimes, however, what is meant is much stronger. Sometimes what is being suggested is that it is in principle impossible to engage in business and to act morally. Implicit in this latter claim is the view that, since it is impossible to be in business and act ethically, we cannot blame those in business for failing to fulfill the requirements of morality.

If the stronger view is taken, we need to ask what are the reasons for believing it. The suggestion that business and morality have little or nothing to do with each other is a radical claim that should not be lightly adopted. The consequences of accepting such a view need to be carefully considered.

What is clear is that the fact that business people often act unethically cannot be taken to support the assertion that "business ethics" is a contradiction in terms. Ethical claims describe not how in fact people act, but rather how people should act. They express not how individuals necessarily behave, but rather how they should behave. When, for example, I claim that people should not steal, I am not claiming that people do not as a matter of fact steal, but that they ought not to.

Our hope and aim is that ultimately people will come to act in the way that they should and that our descriptions of how people in fact act will come to coincide with our claims about how they should act. Thus, to say that business people commonly act unethically in no way demonstrates that ethics is in principle irrelevant to business. On the contrary, if such a claim is true, it indicates that special efforts are needed to bring business practice into line with the requirements of morality.

The view that it is impossible to engage in business and yet act ethically seems a stronger candidate if one wishes to support the idea that "business ethics" is a contradiction in terms. One can scarcely have an ethical duty to accomplish what is in fact impossible. If the conditions of doing business are such that they make acting ethically impossible, then it is hardly rational to insist that those in business must conduct business in an ethical manner.

The problem is that the view that one cannot be in business and act ethically seems clearly false. Not only do many successful business people take ethics very seriously, but it is hard to see how business could occur in the absence of a moral environment. To provide only one of many possible examples, unless those in business recognize the obligation to keep promises and honor contracts, business could not exist. This is not to suggest that business people never break contracts, but if such behavior ever became general, business would be impossible. Just as telling a lie is only advantageous if the majority of people generally tell the truth, shady business practices are only advantageous if the majority of those in business recognize the existence of moral obligations. Immorality in business is essentially parasitic inasmuch as it tends to destroy the moral environment that makes its existence possible.

Generally, those who claim that it is impossible to act morally and engage in business do not really mean to suggest that morality is entirely irrelevant to business, but rather that what it means to act in a morally correct way is quite different in business than in other areas of life. As in the case of the claim that "business ethics" is a contradiction in terms, this can be understood in two ways. It might be taken as suggesting that an individual may have obligations and duties as a private citizen that she does not have as a business person. It could also be taken as making the more radical claim that fundamentally different principles of morality apply to business than to other areas of life, and thus what constitutes ethical behavior in business is completely different than in other activities.

The suggestion that we have obligations and duties as private citizens that we do not have as business persons seems true. I do not treat my family members as business acquaintances, and I have special duties to them that I do not have to my employer. This does not imply, however, that there are no basic principles of morality that apply to all spheres of life. I may have duties and obligations to my wife that I do not have to my administrative assistant, but this scarcely means that I have no common duties to both. The importance of respect for persons generates duties that cross the boundaries of life-activities. I should, for example, no more lightly break a promise to my administrative assistant than I should to my wife.

The more extreme claim that radically different principles of morality apply to business would justify the conclusion that what constitutes ethical behavior in business cannot be judged by the standards we employ in other areas of life. The problem for someone who wishes to hold this position is to make clear what these other principles are and what justifies employing them in business, but not elsewhere. This is no easy matter if for no other reason than there are no watertight divisions between business and other areas of life. How we conduct ourselves in the workplace affects how we conduct ourselves in other environments and vice versa. Attempts to argue that completely different moral principles govern the workplace seem in danger of falling victim to moral schizophrenia.

The selections in Chapter 1 illustrate that it is impossible to separate business from ethical issues and thus set the stage for our discussion of ethical theory in Chapter 2. Albert Carr's well-known article "Is Business Bluffing Ethical?" was an early attempt to make clear the relation between business and morality. Carr has often been interpreted as suggesting that ethical considerations have no place in business, but this is not what he really says. His claim is not that ethics has no place in business, but that radically different standards of right and wrong apply in business. What would be clearly immoral in private life is not, and should not be, considered immoral in business. Carr would not deny that business people should behave ethically and do indeed have moral obligations, but he would insist that we not measure these obligations by the standards of morality relative to private life, but rather by those relative to business.[1]

Carr claims that business is like a game and argues that, since it is like a game, it must be judged by completely different moral standards than those governing other areas of life. This is what is known as an argument from analogy. The insight underlying such arguments is that we should treat similar cases in a similar way. Thus, if two cases are similar in all relevant respects, then they should be treated in a similar manner. For example, if two students from the same class in the same school with the same grade-point average both apply to the same university for the same program, we would expect them to be treated in a similar fashion, that is, they would either both be accepted or both be rejected.

It is essential to realize that arguments from analogy can be either very strong or very weak. The key issue in evaluating arguments from analogy is to examine not only the relevant similarities, but also the relevant dissimilarities. Things that are similar in some respects may be very dissimilar in others and these dissimilarities may provide good reasons for treating them differently. Thus, for example, two students may share a similarity of both being male, but be quite dissimilar in terms of the quality of work they submit to their instructor. It would be an unconvincing argument to suggest that, because they are both male and thus similar in some respects, they should receive the same mark.

It is important, therefore, to examine Carr's suggested analogy between business and games more closely. This is the focus of Daryl Koehn's article "Business and Game-Playing: The False Analogy." After a detailed examination of nine important differences between playing games and engaging in business, she concludes that Carr's analogy is very weak. She suggests that it provides little insight into the nature of business and no reason to think that the ethics of business are like those of a game.

---

[1]Carr's view that the principles of morality are in no sense absolute, but rather relative to different contexts, is a variation of a theory of morality known as moral relativism. Although many people find it initially attractive, deeper inspection reveals that it has grave flaws. The difficulties inherent in moral relativism are explored further in Chapter 2.

Is Business Bluffing Ethical?

ALBERT Z. CARR

A RESPECTED BUSINESSMAN with whom I discussed the theme of this article remarked with some heat, "You mean to say you're going to encourage men to bluff? Why, bluffing is nothing more than a form of lying! You're advising them to lie!"

I agreed that the basis of private morality is a respect for truth and that the closer a businessman comes to the truth, the more he deserves respect. At the same time, I suggested that most bluffing in business might be regarded simply as game strategy—much like bluffing in poker, which does not reflect on the morality of the bluffer. . . .

I reminded my friend that millions of businessmen feel constrained every day to say *yes* to their bosses when they secretly believe *no* and that this is generally accepted as permissible strategy when the alternative might be the loss of a job. The essential point, I said, is that the ethics of business are game ethics, different from the ethics of religion.

He remained unconvinced. Referring to the company of which he is president, he declared: "Maybe that's good enough for some businessmen, but I can tell you that we pride ourselves on our ethics. In 30 years not one customer has ever questioned my word or asked to check our figures. We're loyal to our customers and fair to our suppliers. I regard my handshake on a deal as a contract. I've never entered into price-fixing schemes with my competitors. I've never allowed my salesmen to spread injurious rumors about other companies. Our union contract is the best in our industry. And, if I do say so myself, our ethical standards are of the highest!"

He really was saying, without realizing it, that he was living up to the ethical standards of the business game—which are a far cry from those of private life. Like a gentlemanly poker player, he did not play in cahoots with others at the table, try to smear their reputations, or hold back chips he owed them.

But this same fine man, at that very time, was allowing one of his products to be advertised in a way that made it sound a great deal better than it actually was. Another item in his product line was notorious among dealers for its "built-in obsolescence." He was holding back from the market a much-improved product because he did not want it to interfere with sales of the inferior item it would have replaced. He had joined with certain of his competitors in hiring a lobbyist to push a state legislature, by methods that he preferred not to know too much about, into amending a bill then being enacted.

In his view these things had nothing to do with ethics; they were merely normal business practice. He himself undoubtedly avoided outright falsehoods—never lied in so many words. But the entire organization that he ruled was deeply involved in numerous strategies of deception.

Pressure to Deceive

Most executives from time to time are almost compelled, in the interests of their companies or themselves, to practice some form of deception when negotiating with customers, dealers, labor unions, government officials, or even other departments of their companies. By conscious misstatements, concealment of pertinent facts, or exaggeration—in short, by bluffing—they seek to persuade others to agree with them. I think it is fair to say that if the individual executive refuses to bluff from time to time—if he feels obligated to tell the truth, the whole truth, and nothing but the truth—he is ignoring opportunities permitted under the rules and is at a heavy disadvantage in his business dealings.

But here and there a businessman is unable to reconcile himself to the bluff in which he plays a part. His conscience, perhaps spurred by religious idealism, troubles him. Before any executive can make profitable use of the strategy of the bluff, he needs to make sure that in bluffing he will not lose self-respect or become emotionally disturbed. If he is to reconcile personal integrity and high standards

From Harvard Business Review *46 (1), 1968. Reprinted by permission of* Harvard Business Review.

of honesty with the practical requirements of business, he must feel that his bluffs are ethically justified. The justification rests on the fact that business, as practiced by individuals as well as by corporations, has the impersonal character of a game—a game that demands both special strategy and an understanding of its special ethics.

The game is played at all levels of corporate life, from the highest to the lowest. At the very instant that a man decides to enter business, he may be forced into a game situation, as is shown by the recent experience of a Cornell honor graduate who applied for a job with a large company:

> This applicant was given a psychological test which included the statement. "Of the following magazines, check any that you have read either regularly or from time to time, and double-check those which interest you most. *Reader's Digest, Time, Fortune, Saturday Evening Post, The New Republic, Life, Look, Ramparts, Newsweek, Business Week, U.S. News & World Report, The Nation, Playboy, Esquire, Harper's, Sports Illustrated*."
>
> His tastes in reading were broad, and at one time or another he had read almost all of these magazines. He was a subscriber to *The New Republic,* an enthusiast for *Ramparts,* and an avid student of the pictures in *Playboy.* He was not sure whether his interest in *Playboy* would be held against him, but he had a shrewd suspicion that if he confessed to an interest in *Ramparts* and *The New Republic*, he would be thought a liberal, a radical, or at least an intellectual, and his chances of getting the job, which he needed, would greatly diminish. He therefore checked five of the more conservative magazines. Apparently it was a sound decision, for he got the job.
>
> He had made a game player's decision, consistent with business ethics.

A similar case is that of a magazine space salesman who, owing to a merger, suddenly found himself out of a job:

> This man was 58, and, in spite of a good record, his chance of getting a job elsewhere in a business where youth is favored in hiring practice was not good. He was a vigorous, healthy man, and only a considerable amount of gray in his hair suggested his age. Before beginning his job search he touched up his hair with a black dye to confine the gray to his temples. He knew that the truth about his age might well come out in time, but he calculated that he could deal with that situation when it arose. He and his wife decided that he could easily pass for 45, and he so stated his age on his résumé.
>
> This was a lie; yet within the accepted rules of the business game, no moral culpability attaches to it.

The Poker Analogy

We can learn a good deal about the nature of business by comparing it with poker. While both have a large element of chance, in the long run the winner is the man who plays with steady skill. In both games ultimate victory requires intimate knowledge of the rules, insight into the psychology of the other players, a bold front, a considerable amount of self-discipline, and the ability to respond swiftly and effectively to opportunities provided by chance.

No one expects poker to be played on the ethical principles preached in churches. In poker it is right and proper to bluff a friend out of the rewards of being dealt a good hand. A player feels no more than a slight twinge of sympathy, if that, when—with nothing better than a single ace in his hand—he strips a heavy loser, who holds a pair, of the rest of his chips. It was up to the other fellow to protect himself. In the words of an excellent poker player, former President Harry Truman, "If you can't stand the heat, stay out of the kitchen." If one shows mercy to a loser in poker, it is a personal gesture, divorced from the rules of the game.

Poker has its special ethics, and here I am not referring to rules against cheating. The man who keeps an ace up his sleeve or who marks the cards is more than unethical; he is a crook, and can be punished as such—kicked out of the game or, in the Old West, shot.

In contrast to the cheat, the unethical poker player is one who, while abiding by the letter of the rules, finds ways to put the other players at an unfair disadvantage. Perhaps he unnerves them with loud talk. Or he tries to get them drunk. Or he plays in cahoots with someone else at the table. Ethical poker players frown on such tactics.

Poker's own brand of ethics is different from ethical ideals of civilized human relationships. The game calls for distrust of the other fellow. It ignores the claim of friendship. Cunning deception and concealment of one's strength and intentions, not kindness and open-heartedness, are vital in poker. No one thinks any the worse of poker on that account. And no one should think any the worse of the game of business because its standards of right and wrong differ from the prevailing traditions of morality in our society.

Discard the Golden Rule

This view of business is especially worrisome to people without much business experience. A minister of my acquaintance once protested that business cannot possibly function in our society unless it is based on the Judeo-Christian system of ethics. He told me:

> I know some businessmen have supplied call girls to customers, but there are always a few rotten apples in every barrel. That doesn't mean the rest of the fruit isn't sound. Surely the vast majority of businessmen are ethical. I myself am acquainted with many who adhere to strict codes of ethics based fundamentally on religious teachings. They contribute to good causes. They participate in community activities. They cooperate with other companies to improve working conditions in their industries. Certainly they are not indifferent to ethics.

That most businessmen are not indifferent to ethics in their private lives, everyone will agree. My point is that in their office lives they cease to be private citizens; they become game players who must be guided by a somewhat different set of ethical standards.

The point was forcefully made to me by a Midwestern executive who has given a good deal of thought to the question:

> So long as a businessman complies with the laws of the land and avoids telling malicious lies, he's ethical. If the law as written gives a man a wide-open chance to make a killing, he'd be a fool not to take advantage of it. If he doesn't, somebody else will. There's no obligation on him to stop and consider who is going to get hurt. If the law says he can do it, that's all the justification he needs. There's nothing unethical about that. It's just plain business sense.

This executive (call him Robbins) took the stand that even industrial espionage, which is frowned on by some businessmen, ought not to be considered unethical. He recalled a recent meeting of the National Industrial Conference Board where an authority on marketing made a speech in which he deplored the employment of spies by business organizations. More and more companies, he pointed out, find it cheaper to penetrate the secrets of competitors with concealed cameras and microphones or by bribing employees than to set up costly research and design departments of their own. A whole branch of the electronics industry has grown up with this trend, he continued, providing equipment to make industrial espionage easier.

Disturbing? The marketing expert found it so. But when it came to a remedy, he could only appeal to "respect for the golden rule." Robbins thought this a confession of defeat, believing that the golden rule, for all its value as an ideal for society, is simply not feasible as a guide for business. A good part of the time the businessman is trying to do unto others as he hopes others will *not* do unto him.[1] Robbins continued:

> Espionage of one kind or another has become so common in business that it's like taking a drink during Prohibition—it's not considered sinful. And we don't even have Prohibition where espionage is concerned; the law is very tolerant in this area. There's no more shame for a business that uses secret agents than there is for a nation. Bear in mind that there already is at least one large corporation—you can buy its stock over the counter—that makes millions by providing counterespionage service to industrial firms.. Espionage in business is not an ethical problem; it's an established technique of business competition.

"WE DON'T MAKE THE LAWS"

Wherever we turn in business, we can perceive the sharp distinction between its ethical standards and those of the churches. Newspapers abound with sensational stories growing out of this distinction:

---

[1] See Bruce D. Henderson. "Brinkmanship in Business," HBR March–April 1967, p. 49.

1. We read one day that Senator Philip A. Hart of Michigan has attacked food processors for deceptive packaging of numerous products.[2]
2. The next day there is a Congressional to-do over Ralph Nader's book, *Unsafe At Any Speed*, which demonstrates that automobile companies for years have neglected the safety of car-owning families.[3]
3. Then another Senator, Lee Metcalf of Montana, and journalist Vic Reinemer show in their book, *Overcharge*, the methods by which utility companies elude regulating government bodies to extract unduly large payments from users of electricity.[4]

These are merely dramatic instances of a prevailing condition; there is hardly a major industry at which a similar attack could not be aimed. Critics of business regard such behavior as unethical, but the companies concerned know that they are merely playing the business game.

Among the most respected of our business institutions are the insurance companies. A group of insurance executives meeting recently in New England was startled when their guest speaker, social critic Daniel Patrick Moynihan, roundly berated them for "unethical" practices. They had been guilty, Moynihan alleged, of using outdated actuarial tables to obtain unfairly high premiums. They habitually delayed the hearings of lawsuits against them in order to tire out the plaintiffs and win cheap settlements. In their employment policies they used ingenious devices to discriminate against certain minority groups.[5]

It was difficult for the audience to deny the validity of these charges. But these men were business game players. Their reaction to Moynihan's attack was much the same as that of the automobile manufacturers to Nader, of the utilities to Senator Metcalf, and of the food processors to Senator Hart. If the laws governing their businesses change, or if public opinion becomes clamorous, they will make the necessary adjustments. But morally they have in their view done nothing wrong. As long as they comply with the letter of

the law, they are within their rights to operate their businesses as they see fit. . . .

Violations of the ethical ideals of society are common in business, but they are not necessarily violations of business principles. Each year the Federal Trade Commission orders hundreds of companies, many of them of the first magnitude, to "cease and desist" from practices which, judged by ordinary standards, are of questionable morality but which are stoutly defended by the companies concerned.

In one case, a firm manufacturing a well-known mouthwash was accused of using a cheap form of alcohol possibly deleterious to health. The company's chief executive, after testifying in Washington, made this comment privately:

> We broke no law. We're in a highly competitive industry. If we're going to stay in business, we have to look for profit wherever the law permits. We don't make the laws. We obey them. Then why do we have to put up with this "holier than thou" talk about ethics? It's sheer hypocrisy. We're not in business to promote ethics. Look at the cigarette companies, for God's sake! If the ethics aren't embodied in the laws by the men who made them, you can't expect businessmen to fill the lack. Why, a sudden submission to Christian ethics by businessmen would bring about the greatest economic upheaval in history!

It may be noted that the government failed to prove its case against him.

CAST ILLUSIONS ASIDE

Talk about ethics by businessmen is often a thin decorative coating over the hard realities of the game:

> Once I listened to a speech by a young executive who pointed to a new industry code as proof that his company and its competitors were deeply aware of their responsibilities to society. It was a code of ethics, he said. The industry was going to police itself, to dissuade constituent companies from wrongdoing. His eyes shone with conviction and enthusiasm.
>
> The same day there was a meeting in a hotel room where the industry's top executives met with the "czar" who was to administer the new

[2] *The New York Times*, November 21, 1966.
[3] New York, Grossman Publishers, Inc., 1965.
[4] New York, David McKay Company, Inc., 1967.
[5] *The New York Times*, January 17, 1967.

code, a man of high repute. No one who was present could doubt their common attitude. In their eyes the code was designed primarily to forestall a move by the federal government to impose stern restrictions on the industry. They felt that the code would hamper them a good deal less than new federal laws would. It was, in other words, conceived as a protection for the industry, not for the public.

The young executive accepted the surface explanation of the code; these leaders, all experienced game players, did not deceive themselves for a moment about its purpose.

The illusion that business can afford to be guided by ethics as conceived in private life is often fostered by speeches and articles containing such phrases as, "It pays to be ethical," or, "Sound ethics is good business." Actually this is not an ethical position at all; it is a self-serving calculation in disguise. The speaker is really saying that in the long run a company can make more money if it does not antagonize competitors, suppliers, employees, and customers by squeezing them too hard. He is saying that oversharp policies reduce ultimate gains. That is true, but it has nothing to do with ethics. The underlying attitude is much like that in the familiar story of the shopkeeper who finds an extra $20 bill in the cash register, debates with himself the ethical problem—should he tell his partner?—and finally decides to share the money because the gesture will give him an edge over the s.o.b. the next time they quarrel.

I think it is fair to sum up the prevailing attitude of businessmen on ethics as follows:

We live in what is probably the most competitive of the world's civilized societies. Our customs encourage a high degree of aggression in the individual's striving for success. Business is our main area of competition, and it has been ritualized into a game of strategy. The basic rules of the game have been set by the government, which attempts to detect and punish business frauds. But as long as a company does not transgress the rules of the game set by law, it has the legal right to shape its strategy without reference to anything but its profits. If it takes a long-term view of its profits, it will preserve amicable relations, so far as possible, with those with whom it deals. A wise businessman will not seek advantage to the point where he generates dangerous hostility among employees, competi-

tors, customers, government, or the public at large. But decisions in this area are, in the final test, decisions of strategy not of ethics.

The Individual and the Game

An individual within a company often finds it difficult to adjust to the requirements of the business game. He tries to preserve his private ethical standards in situations that call for game strategy. When he is obliged to carry out company policies that challenge his conception of himself as an ethical man, he suffers. . . .

If an executive allows himself to be torn between a decision based on business considerations and one based on his private ethical code, he exposes himself to a grave psychological strain.

This is not to say that sound business strategy necessarily runs counter to ethical ideals. They may frequently coincide; and when they do, everyone is gratified. But the major tests of every move in business, as in all games of strategy are legality and profit. A man who intends to be a winner in the business game must have a game player's attitude.

The business strategist's decisions must be as impersonal as those of a surgeon performing an operation—concentrating on objective and technique, and subordinating personal feelings. . . .

All sensible businessmen prefer to be truthful, but they seldom feel inclined to tell the *whole* truth. In the business game truth-telling usually has to be kept within narrow limits if trouble is to be avoided. The point was neatly made a long time ago (in 1888) by one of John D. Rockefeller's associates, Paul Babcock, to Standard Oil Company executives who were about to testify before a government investigating committee: "Parry every question with answers which, while perfectly truthful, are evasive of *bottom* facts."[6] This was, is, and probably always will be regarded as wise and permissible business strategy.

FOR OFFICE USE ONLY

An executive's family life can easily be dislocated if he fails to make a sharp distinction between the

---

[6]Babcock in a memorandum to Rockefeller (Rockefeller Archives).

ethical systems of the home and the office—or if his wife does not grasp that distinction. Many a businessman who has remarked to his wife, "I had to let Jones go today" or "I had to admit to the boss that Jim has been goofing off lately," has been met with an indignant protest. "How could you do a thing like-that? You know Jones is over 50 and will have a lot of trouble getting another job." Or, "You did that to Jim? With his wife ill and all the worry she's been having with the kids?"

If the executive insists that he had no choice because the profits of the company and his own security were involved, he may see a certain cool and ominous reappraisal in his wife's eyes. Many wives are not prepared to accept the fact that business operates with a special code of ethics. An illuminating illustration of this comes from a Southern sales executive who related a conversation he had had with his wife at a time when a hotly contested political campaign was being waged in their state:

> I made the mistake of telling her that I had had lunch with Colby, who gives me about half my business. Colby mentioned that his company had a stake in the election. Then he said, "By the way, I'm treasurer of the citizens' committee for Lang. I'm collecting contributions. Can I count on you for a hundred dollars?"
>
> Well, there I was. I was opposed to Lang, but I knew Colby. If he withdrew his business I could be in a bad spot. So I just smiled and wrote out a check then and there. He thanked me, and we started to talk about his next order. Maybe he thought I shared his political views. If so, I wasn't going to lose any sleep over it.
>
> I should have had sense enough not to tell Mary about it. She hit the ceiling. She said she was disappointed in me. She said I hadn't acted like a man, that I should have stood up to Colby.
>
> I said, "Look, it was an either-or situation. I had to do it or risk losing the business."
>
> She came back at me with, "I don't believe it. You could have been honest with him. You could have said that you didn't feel you ought to contribute to a campaign for a man you weren't going to vote for. I'm sure he would have understood."
>
> I said, "Mary, you're a wonderful woman, but you're way off the track. Do you know

what would have happened if I had said that? Colby would have smiled and said. 'Oh, I didn't realize. Forget it.' But in his eyes from that moment I would be an oddball, maybe a bit of a radical. He would have listened to me talk about his order and would have promised to give it consideration. After that I wouldn't hear from him for a week. Then I would telephone and learn from his secretary that he wasn't yet ready to place the order. And in about a month I would hear through the grapevine that he was giving his business to another company. A month after that I'd be out a job."

> She was silent for a while. Then she said, "Tom, something is wrong with business when a man is forced to choose between his family's security and his moral obligation to himself. It's easy for me to say you should have stood up to him—but if you had, you might have felt you were betraying me and the kids. I'm sorry that you did it, Tom, but I can't blame you. Something is wrong with business!"

This wife saw the problem in terms of moral obligation as conceived in private life; her husband saw it as a matter of game strategy. As a player in a weak position, he felt that he could not afford to indulge an ethical sentiment that might have cost him his seat at the table. [This article was written in 1968. It reflects an attitude towards women that has been deservedly criticized in recent thinking.]

PLAYING TO WIN

Some men might challenge the Colbys of business—might accept serious setbacks to their business careers rather than risk a feeling of moral cowardice. They merit our respect—but as private individuals, not businessmen. When the skillful player of the business game is compelled to submit to unfair pressure, he does not castigate himself for moral weakness. Instead, he strives to put himself into a strong position where he can defend himself against such pressures in the future without loss.

If a man plans to take a seat in the business game, he owes it to himself to master the principles by which the game is played, including its special ethical outlook. He can then hardly fail to recognize that an occasional bluff may well be justified in terms of the game's ethics and warranted in terms of economic necessity. Once he clears his mind on this point, he is in a good position to match his strategy against that of the other players. He can then determine objectively whether a bluff in a given situation has a good chance of succeeding and can decide when and how to bluff, without a feeling of ethical transgression.

To be a winner, a man must play to win. This does not mean that he must be ruthless, cruel, harsh, or treacherous. On the contrary, the better his reputation for integrity, honesty, and decency the better his chances of victory will be in the long run. But from time to time every businessman, like every poker player, is offered a choice between certain loss or bluffing within the legal rules of the game. If he is not resigned to losing, if he wants to rise in his company and industry, then in such a crisis he will bluff—and bluff hard. . . .

Business and Game-Playing: The False Analogy

DARYL KOEHN

A NUMBER OF BUSINESS writers have argued that business is a game and, like a game, possesses its own special rules for acting. While we do not normally tolerate deceit, bluffing is not merely acceptable but also expected within the game of poker. Similarly, lies of omission, overstatements, puffery and bluffs are morally acceptable within business because it, like a game, has a special ethic which permits these normally immoral practices (Carr, 1968). Although critics of this reasoning have used deontological and utilitarian arguments (Bowie, 1993) to show that deceit in business is just as immoral as it is in any other realm of human practice, little attention has been paid to the fact that the argument is one of analogy This oversight is unfortunate, given the strong intuitive appeal Carr's argument has to both business persons and to commerce students.

This paper aims to redress this oversight by critically scrutinizing the form, as well as the content, of Carr's argument. The analogical argument for business' special ethic is only as strong as the alleged similarities between business and game-playing. In this paper, I will show that this analogy is quite weak and incapable of either providing much insight into business or of offering a reason to think that the ethics of business are, or even could be, like those of a game. I will also show in passing that we might draw very different conclusions about the right way to act if business is analogized to other playful activities (e.g., a co-operative group treasure hunt) instead of poker. To make my argument, I will describe characteristic traits of a game and consider trait-by-trait whether business shares these features.

Trait One: A game is played to win

All competitive sports and many games are played to win. Of course, both have a social dimension. But the player who does not at least try to play well and to beat her opponents will likely not be much in demand as a golf or bridge partner. Where there are winners there are also losers. Business, however, is not an activity in which one player—management—wins while the other players—customers, employees, suppliers—lose. While some corporations no doubt have an "us versus them" mentality, many routinely aim at "win-win" situations. They do so because they know they cannot stay in business if they aim at defeating those with whom they interact. True, businesses do compete with one another. But their individual survival requires that they try to prosper by accustoming their customers, to predictably satisfactory service and products so that these customers will buy from

From Journal of Business Ethics *16: 1447–1452, 1997.* © *1997 Kluwer Academic Publishers. Printed in the Netherlands. Reprinted with permission from Kluwer Academic Publishers.*

them again. (The word "customer" derives from the verb "to accustom.") Business managers also need the co-operation of their employees. If the employees come to feel that they have lost at the game of business, they may simply refuse to provide a consistent supply of productive work. And once again the company will have trouble prospering.

The recent emphasis on quality management has highlighted the extent to which the good will of a company's customers, employees, and suppliers is a fragile business asset not easily regained once squandered. Yet the business-game analogy places this asset at great risk. Viewing business as a game like poker commits management to seeing its customers, employees, and suppliers as people over whom to score a triumph. While friends who lose at poker usually continue to show up at the weekly game because they enjoy one another's company in general, customers and suppliers are not management's friends. They are not bound by any ties of friendship to continue to play in management's "game" having been once burned. In business, unlike in a game, human relations are likely to be permanently fractured if one or the other party loses.

If business is like any game, it seems more like the team sports of basketball or volleyball where the players have incentives to co-operate with one another and to develop, rather than destroy, trust. Better still, one might compare business practice to a playful activity like a group treasure hunt or a sailing voyage in which the sailors are trying to set a new world record. This latter analogy focuses our attention not only on the cooperative aspects of business practice but also upon ways in which co-operation may generate more ideas and better communication than competition and lead to a more profitable business in the long run.

Trait Two: In games, losers suffer few consequences

The losses suffered by those who are outplayed in a game are rarely life-devastating. Players know that losing is part of playing the game. Boris Becker lost his share of games as a youngster and will lose to ever younger players as he ages and loses agility. Playing a game entails both striving to excel while at the same time learning to lose graciously. The proof that losses in games are not gen-

erally severe is that as the danger an activity poses to life increases, the less likely we are to treat this activity as a game. Russian roulette is a game only in the eyes of a masochist. And poker players who gamble away the money necessary for their health insurance and for feeding their children are more addicts than participants in a game.

By contrast, the stakes in business are consistently very high. If a company tries to deviously one-up the competition by rolling out a new product before it has been thoroughly tested, the product may fail. If it does, employees may lose their jobs and health insurance. The community which is home to this corporation will be hard hit if the manufacturing plant closes. Local government tax revenues will likely fall as a result of this business' misjudged bluff, crippling government's ability to initiate and sustain programs in the general public interest. Even "winning" corporations who gain market share through their successful deceits and bluffs may find themselves very big losers as the larger community's economy reels from the consequences of the bad gambles made by other businesses. In business, unlike in games, there is no "winner-take-all," if indeed there are even "winners" in any conventional sense of the word.

Trait Three: A game is constituted by certain rules

Games do not simply use rules to regulate the actions of players. The rules themselves by and large define the practice. There is no point in a baseball batter arguing that he should be allowed fifteen missed swings at the plate. In baseball, after three missed swings, he is out. If one asks why this is so, the answer simply is: That's the rule in baseball. The player who demands fifteen strikes before retiring from the plate is neither playing baseball nor playing it well. Rules also obviously constitute the various card games. Hearts are always trump in the game of hearts but not in bridge because the rules of each game make it so. While business practice does recognize some conventions, it is far from being constituted by a set of rules. For example, foreign exchange traders typically employ conventions for hand signals and for quoting prices. They also extend one another certain courtesies. A trader generally does not wait until the very end of the trading day to try to unload millions of Swiss francs in the local market. Nevertheless, individual traders can and do evolve their own private guidelines for how and when they will establish positions, with whom they will trade, whether they will trade one currency only against the dollar or do a cross-trade against another foreign currency. There are few explicit rules in business. And what rules there are function as guidelines. So, although a trading firm will likely have a rule limiting the size of a position a trader may assume or carry overnight, exceptions can be and are made to this "rule." Business practice is not, therefore, constituted by a set of rules; and it is of little help to suggest, as Carr does, that the businesspeople, like poker players, can do whatever it takes to win as long as they stay within the rules, given that business lacks the rules poker has.

Trait Four: The rules of the game are fixed

In card games and sports, rules are promulgated in advance of playing the game. They are publicly known, and anyone who wishes to play a particular game must abide by the rules. Occasionally the rules are changed by commissioners or tournament officials. Proposed rule revisions are discussed and, if accepted, are made known. But the rules do not evolve in and through the playing of the game. I cannot start slapping the ten in slapjack and expect my fellow players to allow me to get away with this innovation. Yet, in business, people try new practices all the time, hoping that their changes will improve sales or communication with customers or with employees; alter the product in some desirable way; or make for more efficient production. This kind of evolving approach is not merely tolerated; it is an expected and necessary part of working with suppliers, employees and the larger community to deliver quality goods to customers and to earn a satisfactory return on shareholder investment. So even if there were a business rule that one could deceive competitors or customers, there would be no reason why this rule could not change tomorrow if business practitioners started to trust rather than deceive one another. One is not entitled, therefore, to speak as though business is a settled practice of one-upmanship involving deceit and misrepresentation.

Trait Five: Rules of the game are accepted by all who play the game

All adults who play a game tacitly agree to play by the rules. Moreover, they know they are party to such an agreement. Such knowledge explains why poker players do not complain when they lose a hand to someone who is bluffing. Bluffing is a part of the game and a strategy that all poker players have admitted as permissible. Similarly, outright lying is permitted in the children's game of "I doubt it" because all players comprehend that the game's rules require that players lie. Bluffing and lying in business, though, are problematic in part because all parties to the transaction have not agreed to using deceit and misrepresentation in the conduct of exchange. The young first-time car buyer with his heart set on a particular car; or the Amish merchant who is scrupulously honest with his customers about the ripeness, age, and origin of the fruit he sells is not going to assume that the used car salesman's "final" price is anything but the final price. Nor do all corporate employees understand the deceit connected with "voluntary" giving to the Crusade of Mercy or United Way. The corporate representative who collects donations generally fails to mention that employees who do not give and make the corporation look good will never advance in management ranks. Some employees catch onto the unspoken message. But others never do.

These cases suggest that the deceit or manipulative bluff cannot be excused on the ground that it has caused no harm because all parties know that the salesperson or corporate representative is engaged in a form of deceit. Everyone knows no such thing. Consequently, the analogy between business and a game with its own special ethic is really a variant of the fallacy of assuming the consequent: That all parties to a business exchange have agreed to deceit-allowing rules is exactly what must be shown, rather than presupposed. And establishing this fact will be difficult since it is far from clear that business even has formal fixed rules, much less rules to which all players have agreed to adhere.

Trait Six: Players act intermittently

People play games for recreation. Recreation occupies only a portion of human beings' lives. Working, rearing children, helping friends, and discharging civic duties take up much of our time. Even professional athletes do not play competitively during the off-season, spending this time with their families or on other life projects. Business, though, generally goes on throughout the year. Managers and employees often find it hard to take a vacation because of the press of things to be done. Leaves of absence are still more difficult to obtain. Corporate employees may not want to work for some period, yet businesses (e.g., banking, or food and medical supply distribution) must go on because people's lives depend upon them. The continuing existence and activity of a corporation matters greatly. So it is hardly surprising that a fair amount of a firm's time is devoted to selecting and training successors to senior management. Here again the analogy between business and games breaks down. Bobby Fischer did not have to train the next grandmaster. If the game of chess or poker were to disappear from the world scene, life would go on with little disruption. Life will also continue if Sears or General Motors ceases to exist as a result of bad business decisions. But the dislocation will be severe. The work of business is not play. It is an essentially public activity that must go on if societal functioning is not to be impeded. Comparing business to games like poker irresponsibly trivializes the importance of business and obscures just what is at stake for those who participate in it and are affected by it.

Trait Seven: In games the scope for bluffing is quite narrow and well-understood

Although, in a game such as poker, participants may be dealt quite a large number of different hands, when it comes to bluffing, a player's options are pretty limited. She may pretend either to hold better or worse cards than she in fact has. However, when a person begins to bluff in business, the possibilities are as limitless as human creativity. And precisely because bluffing or misrepresentation can take so many unpredictable forms in business, it is a dangerous course on which to embark. It can lead both the business and other parties into uncharted waters. For example, as a way of raising the stakes during a dispute with a government agency such as the IRS, a bank might threaten to block a pending loan to one of

the former Soviet bloc countries. The action might be legal and thus would qualify as within the supposed "rules" of the business game. It might even lead others in government to pressure the IRS to back down. Yet it might also permanently harm relations between the U.S. government and the fledgling republic that desperately needs the loans and is terribly nervous about any sign that the money might fail to materialize. If the republic has a nuclear arsenal, the bank's "bluff" might even rekindle the arms race. The example is somewhat extreme, but the basic point is not farfetched: Overstatements, deceits and bluffs by business may have far-reaching ramifications for both domestic and foreign policy in a world in which business greatly influences the conduct of each. Poker is played in smoke-filled back rooms. Business acts on the world stage. It is irresponsible, consequently, to suggest that a business corporation is entitled to bluff its way through its interactions with other parties whenever it thinks it might stand to gain a short-term profit or forestall some loss and to do so without any consideration of the long-term and short-term effects of this bluff upon other parties and upon the nation which allows this same corporation to exist in the first place.

Trait Eight: Players in a game risk only what is theirs to risk

When people play sports, they risk injuring their bodies in the case of betting games, people hazard their money. In both cases, what players risk belongs to them. In business, however, if management were to borrow against a firm's assets as part of a bluff to convince a competitor that it was planning a major acquisition, the manager would be jeopardizing assets which are not his or hers. The company is owned by the shareholders who have supplied the equity against which the firm has borrowed. This equity is the shareholders', not management's. Moreover, management's "bluff" may also create a lien on the assets necessary to fund the firm's pension obligations, money on which the employees have a claim. Irrespective of whether the bluff accomplishes its intent of, say, frightening a competitor into a costly, precipitate countermove, the fact remains that neither the shareholders nor the employees have authorized the manager to gamble with their money. Given that no ordinary citizen is morally entitled to speculate with funds belonging to someone else, it is hard to see how business management could be so justified.

Trait Nine: In a game, it is clear to whom any gain belongs

Implicit in the analogy between a game and business is the notion of an agent who develops and executes strategy. Any gains accruing as a result of the game plan belong to the strategizing agent. Losses, too, must be covered by this same agent. If one is going to argue that businesses are entitled to bluff or to shade the truth, then one must be clear about just who is doing this bluffing. The person of a corporation is a legal fiction that does not initiate actions or at least does not do so in any simple sense. Presumably, then, business managers are the persons who are allegedly entitled to feint, trumpet the products in overstated ways, etc. But if business managers are allowed to engage in such maneuvers, there is no reason why, qua gamesters, they cannot execute these strategies in such a way as to maximize their own personal gains. One can well imagine a CEO who intentionally manages matters in such a way that he will be let go from the firm with a golden parachute package far more lucrative than his current salary. The firm may have been driven into the ground under his management. But if corporate ethics are those of the game, the manager is a good player who has played consummately well, availing himself of every legal opportunity to haul in the biggest pot. The problem, of course, is that firms will find it close to impossible to exist if management ceases to consider the larger corporate interest but ponders only how to increase its own income and wealth.

Conclusion

Since business shares few, if any, of the characteristic features of card games or of competitive sports, the assertion that business is like a game and exhibits the ethics of a game is simply that—an assertion not backed by much in the way of argument. Those who would argue for a special business game ethic would do well to consider the types of arguments medical and legal ethicists have offered in defense of special professional ethics. Defenders of a medical ethic, for example, have

understood that they must not only assert the existence of a special ethic but must also account for why actions in accordance with these special ethics are morally permissible (Kass, 1985). Thus, medical ethicists defend the physician practice of protecting patient confidence not by an analogy to the lawyer's practice of keeping client confidences but rather on deontological or utilitarian grounds. Patient confidentiality is justified on the ground that it preserves the trust necessary for patients to be healed or that it respects patient autonomy by allowing the patient control over the extent to which his or her history is made public.

Those who assert that business has the ethics of the game have offered no such arguments in support of the morality of the business ethic. On the one hand, their unstated reasoning appears to be that since business is a game and since the rules of the game simply are the rules, little else needs to be or can be said about the rightness of business action. This reasoning fails to persuade because the above analysis has shown that business bears almost no resemblance to a game understood as a rule-constituted low-risk private practice voluntarily engaged in by parties all of whom know and who have assented to the rules and who risk only what is theirs to risk. On the other hand, the argument may be that business bluffing and misrepresentation are morally permissible because, although such practices are normally harmful, business players know that these deceits are tolerated and can therefore protect themselves from harm. But this line of argument is not promising either. Knowing that people in my neighborhood randomly fire their guns on New Year's Eve, I am able to take measures to avoid being shot. But it does not follow that it is right for drunk people to fire blindly into the night. Moreover, since many of the people hurt by a business bluff gone bad do not know of such practices or are in no position to avoid the evil consequences of them, the conceit that business is no more than a poker game writ large cannot be sustained. Rather than continuing to speak of business as a game, we would be better served if we abandoned entirely the business-game analogy and focussed instead on the practical implications of the genuinely special features of business practice, features such as its corporate structure and dependence on many parties' co-operation. its longstanding partnership with government, and its capacity to greatly affect domestic and foreign policy.

References

Bowie, Norman E.: 1993, "Does It Pay to Bluff in Business?," in Tom L. Beauchamp and Norman E. Bowie (eds.), *Ethical Theory and Business* (Prentice Hall, Inc., Englewood Cliffs, NJ), pp. 460–462.

Carr, Albert Z.: 1968, "Is Business Bluffing Ethical?," reprinted in Tom L. Beauchamp and

Norman E. Bowie (eds.), *Ethical Theory and Business* (Prentice Hall, Inc., Englewood Cliffs, NJ). pp. 449–454.

Kass, Leon R.: 1985, *Toward a More Natural Science: Biology and Human Affairs* (The Free Press, New York, NY), pp. 157–246.

Questions for Chapter 1

1. Carr suggests that as long as a company does not break the law, it cannot be accused of immorality in its pursuit of profit. Does complying with the law guarantee that an action is moral? Explain.
2. Carr suggests that an individual cannot be successful in business unless he or she adopts a radically different moral stance in business than in his or her personal life. Do you agree that this is true? How would you defend your answer?
3. What does Koehn mean when she claims that "in business, unlike in games, there is no 'winner-take-all,' if indeed there are even 'winners' in any conventional sense of the word"?
4. Koehn suggests that "emphasis on quality management has highlighted the extent to which the good will of a company's customers, employees, and suppliers is a fragile business asset not easily regained once squandered. . . . the business-game analogy places this asset at great risk." What does she mean by saying this? Is she raising a moral issue? How do you think Carr would respond to her claim?

Case 1.1   John's Dilemma

John has recently been asked by his boss to deal with the disposal of a manufacturing by-product. Until several months ago, it was legal to dispose of it in state landfills, but new legislation has made it illegal to do so. The new legislation is based on research that suggests serious health risks are associated with the by-product. As far as John can determine, there is no reason to doubt the validity of the research, although it is still in its early stages.

The technology exists to neutralize the by-product, but it is expensive both in its start-up costs and day-to-day operation. Neighboring states have not yet enacted legislation to forbid disposal of this by-product in their landfills, and it

seems clear that they will not do so in the immediate future. The cost of shipping the waste to neighboring landfills is much less than the cost of implementing the technology for neutralizing the by-product.

Two colleagues, Brian and Marjorie, give John quite different advice. Brian suggests that, since it is legal and much cheaper to ship the wastes to neighboring landfills, this is obviously the correct decision. Given the legality of shipping the waste, questions of morality do not arise.

Marjorie argues that, in light of the health risks associated with the by-product, it is immoral to dispose of it landfills. She argues that the morality of different methods of waste disposal should be decided not on the basis of legality or cost, but on whether they pose a health hazard. She claims that, given there is no reason to doubt the scientific research suggesting the by-product poses a health hazard, it would be immoral to dispose of it in neighboring landfills, even though it might be legal.

John is sympathetic to Marjorie's view. He is concerned, however, that adopting the neutralizing technology will leave the company at a competitive disadvantage. He wishes to do what is morally right, but he does not want the company or his future prospects to suffer. Brian points out that the welfare of many employees may rest on his decision and that the scientific evidence,

although suggestive, is not yet conclusive. Marjorie comments that the welfare of the employees should not take precedence over the public good and that it should not be assumed that the scientific evidence will be overturned.

John resolves to think about the issue further, knowing that he must make a decision in the next week.

1. Is Marjorie correct when she asserts that John should not put the welfare of fellow employees above the public good?

2. Should the fact that he may jeopardize his career if he makes an unpopular decision affect John's decisionmaking?

Further Readings for Chapter 1

Eric H. Beversluis, "Is There 'No Such Thing as Business Ethics'?," *Journal of Business Ethics* 6, 1987.

Norman E. Bowie, "Does It Pay to Bluff in Business?" in *Ethical Theory in Business,* ed. Tom L. Beauchamp and Norman E. Bowie (Englewood Cliffs, NJ: Prentice-Hall, 1993), pp. 460–462.

Sir Adrian Cadbury, "Ethical Managers Make Their Own Rules" in *Ethics in Practice,* ed. Kenneth R. Andrews (Boston: Harvard Business School Press, 1989), pp. 70–76.

Joanne B. Ciulla, "Business Ethics as Moral Imagination" in *Business Ethics: The State of the Art,* ed. R. Edward Freeman (Oxford University Press, 1991), pp. 212–220.

Scott Cook, "The Ethics of Bootstrapping," *Inc. Magazine,* September 1992, pp. 87, 90, 95.

Laura L. Nash, "Ethics Without the Sermon" in *Ethics in Practice,* ed. Kenneth R. Andrews (Boston: Harvard Business School Press, 1989), pp. 243–257.

Barbara Ley Toffler, *Tough Choices: Managers Talk Ethics* (New York: John Wiley & Sons, 1986).

INFOTRAC COLLEGE EDITION To learn more about the topics from this chapter, you can use the following words to conduct an electronic search on InfoTrac College Edition, an online library of journals. Here you will find a multitude of articles from various sources and perspectives: *www.infotrac-college.com/wadsworth/access.html*

business ethics

bluffing

Chapter 2

A Brief Introduction to Ethical Theory

Introduction

WE HAVE SEEN in Chapter 1 that moral concerns are inherent in business. Questions of how we ought to act toward others and how they ought to act toward us can no more be escaped in business than in other areas of life. Our goal in this text is to say something useful concerning various practical ethical issues arising from business activities. It is important, however, before proceeding directly to the problems we wish to discuss, to spend a little time examining ethical theory. Just as one cannot successfully build a piece of furniture without at least an elementary understanding of principles of design, it is impossible to resolve practical ethical issues without some understanding of the principles upon which ethical decisions should be made.

The selections in this chapter illustrate diverse theoretical approaches to questions of morality. Mary Midgley's "Trying Out One's New Sword" describes and criticizes the theory of moral isolationism, that is, what we have called cultural relativism—the view that the truth or falsity of moral claims is determined solely on the basis of what society one lives in. She is especially concerned to assess whether this theory provides a basis for respecting and tolerating the views of other cultures. Her conclusion is that, contrary to what is frequently assumed, it does not.

The theory of ethical egoism holds that what is morally correct is determined by whether it is in one's self-interest or not. In his article "Egoism," written especially for this text, George Williamson discusses both why ethical egoism often seems initially attractive and why, upon deeper reflection, it is generally rejected as an inadequate view of what is required if one is to act ethically.

Williamson discusses a number of issues that are involved if one wishes to adopt ethical egoism. One of the most important of these is that it seems difficult to hold that what is ethically correct is what is in my self-interest, yet at the same time recommend to other individuals that what is ethically correct is what is in their self-interest. How, if I am an ethical egoist, can I recognize what someone else does in his or her self-interest as ethically correct if it thwarts what is in my self-interest?

The ethical egoist might be tempted to reply that the rightness or wrongness of an action is relative to whether it serves one's self-interest or not. Thus the same action could be right, inasmuch as it serves one individual's self-interest, and wrong insofar as it does not serve another individual's self-interest.

There are at least two problems with making this response. The first is that it does not really solve the issue of how an ethical egoist can recommend to others that it is ethical to follow their self-interest. If what is ethical is what is in my self-interest, and if it is not in my self-interest that other people simply follow their own self-interest, how can it be ethical for me to recommend that they act in their own self-interest?

Second, the view that the rightness or wrongness of an action is entirely relative to the individual seems to imply subjectivism—an even more extreme version of relativism than cultural relativism. Whereas cultural relativism makes the truth of moral claims relative to the culture, subjectivism makes their truth relative to the individual. In cultural relativism it is impossible to make cross-cultural moral claims; in subjectivism it is impossible to make interpersonal moral claims. Given that morality is intimately associated with interaction between persons, subjectivism seems fatally flawed. If it could be shown that ethical egoism implies subjectivism, this would seem to be a good reason to regard ethical egoism as inadequate.

Our next reading comes from Aristotle's (384–322 B.C.) chief ethical work, the *Nicomachaen Ethics.* Aristotle's ethical theory is important not only in its own right, but also in its influence on both medieval natural law theories and contemporary virtue ethics. Whereas Kant (Kantianism) and Mill (utilitarianism) focus on the rightness or wrongness of specific actions done by a moral agent, Aristotle focuses on the qualities and dispositions of the agent. He emphasizes not the action produced, but the moral character of the agent by which it is produced.

Also characteristic of Aristotle is his emphasis that the good person can be defined as the person who acts according to human nature. For Aristotle, to be virtuous is to fulfill your proper function. The function of a knife is to cut, so a virtuous knife is a knife that cuts well. It should come as no surprise, therefore, to learn that much of the *Nicomachaen Ethics* is devoted to developing a theory of human nature. Whatever the difficulties in defining human nature, and these prove to be many, Aristotle would insist that we can have no idea of what it is to be morally good if we do not first have some idea of the proper function of humans.

Natural law theories are sometimes caricatured as suggesting rigid guidelines concerning every detail of human conduct. Although it is true that proponents of natural law such as Aristotle and the medieval philosopher Thomas Aquinas (1224–1274) think that the fundamental principles underlying proper human behavior are nonnegotiable, they are generally careful to acknowledge that there is room for flexibility and a certain amount of disagreement over how these principles are to be applied in particular situations. What is clear is that, for these thinkers, what is moral coincides with what will most truly fulfill human nature.

It should be noted that contemporary theories of virtue ethics have philosophical roots in Aristotle and the natural law tradition. Like Aristotle and Aquinas, proponents of virtue ethics wish to focus on the qualities of the moral agent, rather than on particular actions. Their emphasis is thus not on the rules and principles to guide specific actions, but rather on the characteristic long-term patterns of behavior from which actions arise. Where they tend to part company with Aristotle and Aquinas is in their willingness to forego grounding the virtues in a metaphysical theory of human nature. Whether or not it is possible to reap the fruits of earlier traditions emphasizing the virtues, without also following their lead in linking metaphysics and ethics remains to be made clear.

We find in Immanuel Kant (1724–1804) great emphasis on the idea that morality is essentially an outworking of applied or practical reason. Kant thinks that the only thing that is inherently good is a good will, a good will being defined as one that acts from duty. If asked what it means to act from duty, Kant would reply that it means to act in accordance with universal law, as determined by reason. If, therefore, one wishes to determine whether a proposed action is truly moral one should ask oneself whether the principle according to which one is acting can be applied universally. If it can, then one's proposed action is morally justified, but if it cannot, then the action is immoral.

We have, then, on Kant's view, a litmus test by which we may determine the rightness or wrongness of our actions. Our actions are to be judged moral or immoral not on the basis of whether they fulfill some fundamental aspect of human nature or on the basis of their consequence, but on the basis of whether the principles underlying them can be universalized. Kant called this test the categorical imperative, formulating it in the following words: "Act only according to that maxim [principle] by which you can at the same time will that it should become a universal law of nature." It is this principle that provides the linchpin of Kant's extensive and complicated ethical system.

John Stuart Mill (1806–1873), along with Jeremy Bentham (1748–1832), is generally regarded as the founder of utilitarianism. Utilitarianism takes its name from its appeal to what Mill called the Principle of Utility or the Greatest Happiness Principle. Whereas for Kant the test of the morality of an action lies in whether the principle motivating it can universalized, for Mill the test of whether an action is moral lies in whether it promotes happiness. To the degree that an action tends to increase the sum total of happiness in the world, it is to be judged moral; to the degree that it tends to decrease the sum total of happiness in the world, it is to be judged immoral. Actions are not intrinsically right or wrong, but rather are judged right or wrong by virtue of their consequences.

As is evident in the selection I have chosen, Mill insisted that the quality of pleasure is as relevant as the quantity of pleasure. Later utilitarians have tended to concentrate simply on the question of quantity. I suspect that the reason for this is that not only does introducing the notion of higher and lower pleasures complicate the notoriously difficult task of quantifying happiness, but any nonarbitrary attempt to distinguish between higher and lower pleasures must make at least an implicit appeal to the notion of what is properly human, that is, a theory of human nature. To do so seems to open the door to a natural law theory of ethics. Mill may have been right to distinguish between higher and lower pleasures, but it is not clear that his theory will permit such a distinction.

Later utilitarians have distinguished between act and rule utilitarianism. Act utilitarianism, sometimes called direct utilitarianism, involves appealing to the Principle of Utility directly to guide actions. On this theory, particular actions are judged moral or immoral by an immediate appeal to whether they satisfy the

Principle of Utility. Rule utilitarianism, sometimes called indirect utilitarianism, involves generating an intermediate rule by means of the Principle of Utility, for example, do not lie, against which particular actions are then judged moral or immoral. On this theory, although the Principle of Utility is still the ultimate sanction of morality, it is not the immediate criterion by which particular actions are evaluated.

The view that there is a distinctively feminist approach to ethics has become increasingly popular. Many feminists have wanted to claim not only that traditional moral theories have been biased in their application, but also that these theories are inherently flawed and must be replaced by a feminist ethic. It is, however, no easy matter to describe or define such an ethic. In the reading I have selected, Alison Jaggar, a leading feminist, begins by saying that feminist ethics are distinguished by their explicit commitment to rethinking ethics with a view to correcting male bias and ends with the observation that feminist ethics, far from being a rigid orthodoxy, is a ferment of ideas and controversy, many of them echoing and deepening debates in nonfeminist ethics.

That male bias has, in many instances, skewed the application of moral theory and that feminists have been instrumental in exposing such bias is evident. Whether this implies not only that there is a distinctively feminist approach to ethics, that is, uncovering male bias in the application of moral theory, but also a distinctively feminist ethical theory is another matter. It is one thing to detect bias in the application of a theory; it is another to suggest the theory is so deeply flawed that it must be replaced with something fundamentally different. Many thinkers would admit the existence of moral bias, yet deny that this necessitates the wholesale rejection of traditional moral theory. All that can safely be said in the context of our present discussion is that Jaggar seems correct in her observation concerning the ferment of ideas and controversy and that, although a number of important feminist thinkers believe in the possibility and necessity of developing a distinctively feminist ethic and are actively working on this project, such an ethic has yet to be articulated and evaluated in detail.

Even so brief a glance at moral theory as that which we are taking reveals deep disagreement. To many this seems a pessimistic conclusion. How, in the midst of such disagreement, can we hope to develop guideposts for determining what is ethically correct?

One way of approaching this question is to note that a theory may contain a good deal of truth and yet fail as a complete or total account of what needs to be explained. This opens up the possibility of a theory subsuming what is true in alternative theories, yet rejecting their claims to completeness. I am not going to undertake this project here, but it does bear emphasis that it is possible to find truth in a theory without thereby accepting it completely. We do not, for example, have to accept Kantianism in its entirety to accept the claim that the notion of duty plays an important role in the moral life. Neither do we have to accept utilitarianism in its entirety to accept that the morality of actions is often evaluated with regard to their consequences. Similar points could be made with respect to most of the theories we are examining. The issue, therefore, is not whether a particular ethical theory contains truth, but whether it gives a complete and comprehensive account of what it is to act morally. Remembering this will help in appreciating the merits of theories that must nevertheless be rejected as comprehensive accounts of morality.

Trying Out One's New Sword

MARY MIDGLEY

ALL OF US ARE, more or less, in trouble today about trying to understand cultures strange to us. We hear constantly of alien customs. We see changes in our lifetime which would have astonished our parents. I want to discuss here one very short way of dealing with this difficulty, a drastic way which many people now theoretically favour. It consists in simply denying that we can ever understand any culture except our own well enough to make judgements about it. Those who recommend this hold that the world is sharply divided into separate societies, sealed units, each with its own system of thought. They feel that the respect and tolerance due from one system to another forbids us ever to take up a critical position to any other culture. Moral judgement, they suggest, is a kind of coinage valid only in its country of origin.

I shall call this position "moral isolationism." I shall suggest that it is certainly not forced upon us, and indeed that it makes no sense at all. People usually take it up because they think it is a respectful attitude to other cultures. In fact, however, it is not respectful. Nobody can respect what is entirely unintelligible to them. To respect someone, we have to know enough about him to make a *favourable* judgement, however general and tentative. And we do understand people in other cultures to this extent. Otherwise a great mass of our most valuable thinking would be paralysed.

To show this, I shall take a remote example, because we shall probably find it easier to think calmly about it than we should with a contemporary one, such as female circumcision in Africa or the Chinese Cultural Revolution. The principles involved will still be the same. My example is this. There is, it seems, a verb in classical Japanese which means "to try out one's new sword on a chance wayfarer." (The word is *tsujigiri*, literally "crossroads-cut.") A samurai sword had to be tried out because, if it was to work properly, it had to slice through someone at a single blow, from the shoulder to the opposite flank. Otherwise, the warrior bungled his stroke. This could injure his honour, offend his ancestors, and even let down his emperor. So tests were needed, and wayfarers had to be expended. Any wayfarer would do—provided, of course, that he was not another Samurai. Scientists will recognize a familiar problem about the rights of experimental subjects.

Now when we hear of a custom like this, we may well reflect that we simply do not understand it; and therefore are not qualified to criticize it at all, because we are not members of that culture. But we are not members of any other culture either, except our own. So we extend the principle to cover all extraneous cultures, and we seem therefore to be moral isolationists. But this is, as we shall see, an impossible position. Let us ask what it would involve.

We must ask first: Does the isolating barrier work both ways? Are people in other cultures equally unable to criticize *us*? This question struck me sharply when I read a remark in *The Guardian* by an anthropologist about a South American Indian who had been taken into a Brazilian town for an operation, which saved his life. When he came back to his village, he made several highly critical remarks about the white Brazilians' way of life. They may very well have been justified. But the interesting point was that the anthropologist called these remarks "a damning indictment of Western civilization." Now the Indian had been in that town about two weeks. Was he in a position to deliver a damning indictment? Would we ourselves be qualified to deliver such an indictment on the Samurai, provided we could spend two weeks in ancient Japan? What do we really think about this?

My own impression is that we believe that outsiders can, in principle, deliver perfectly good indictments—only, it usually takes more than two weeks to make them damning. Understanding has degrees. It is not a slapdash yes-or-no matter. Intelligent outsiders can progress in it, and in some ways will be at an advantage over the locals. But if this is so, it must clearly apply to ourselves as much as anybody else.

Our next question is this: Does the isolating barrier between cultures block praise as well as blame? If I want to say that the Samurai culture has many virtues, or to praise the South American Indians, am I prevented from doing *that* by my outside status? Now, we certainly do need to praise other societies in this way. But it is hardly possible that we could praise them effectively if we could not, in principle, criticize them. Our praise would be worthless if it rested on no definite grounds, if it did not flow from some understanding. Certainly we may need to praise things which we do not *fully* understand. We say "there's something very good here, but I can't quite make out what it is yet." This happens when we want to learn from strangers. And we can learn from strangers. But to do this we have to distinguish between those strangers who are worth learning from and those who are not. Can we then judge which is which?

This brings us to our third question: What is involved in judging? Now plainly there is no question here of sitting on a bench in a red robe and sentencing people. Judging simply means forming an opinion, and expressing it if it is called for. Is there anything wrong about this? Naturally, we ought to avoid forming—and expressing—*crude* opinions, like that of a simple-minded missionary, who might dismiss the whole Samurai culture as entirely bad, because non-Christian. But this is a different objection. The trouble with crude opinions is that they are crude, whoever forms them, not that they are formed by the wrong people. Anthropologists, after all, are outsiders quite as much as missionaries. Moral isolationism forbids us to form *any* opinions on these matters. Its ground for doing so is that we don't understand them. But there is much that we don't understand in our own culture too. This brings us to our last question: If we can't judge other cultures, can we really judge our own? Our efforts to do so will be much damaged if we are really deprived of our opinions about other societies, because these provide the range of comparison, the spectrum of alternatives against which we set what we want to understand. We would have to stop using the mirror which anthropology so helpfully holds up to us.

In short, moral isolationism would lay down a general ban on moral reasoning. Essentially, this is the programme of immoralism, and it carries a distressing logical difficulty. Immoralists like Nietzsche [*Nietzsche* (1844–1900) was a German philosopher who attacked what he called *herd morality*, i.e. conventional morality, and urged that the individual must move beyond good and evil to create his or her own value.] are actually just a rather specialized sect of moralists. They can no more afford to put moralizing out of business than smugglers can afford to abolish customs regulations. The power of moral judgement is, in fact, not a luxury, not a perverse indulgence of the self-righteous. It is a necessity. When we judge something to be bad or good better or worse than something else, we are taking it as an example to aim at or avoid. Without opinions of this sort, we would have no framework of comparison for our own policy, no chance of profiting by other people's insights or mistakes. In this vacuum, we could form no judgements on our own actions.

Now it would be odd if Homo sapiens had really got himself into a position as bad as this—a position where his main evolutionary asset, his brain, was so little use to him. None of us is going to accept this sceptical diagnosis. We cannot do so, because our involvement in moral isolationism does not flow from apathy, but from a rather acute concern about human hypocrisy and other forms of wickedness. But we polarize that concern around a few selected moral truths. We are rightly angry with those who despise, oppress or steamroll other cultures. We think that doing these things is actually *wrong*. But this is itself a moral judgement. We could not condemn oppression and insolence if we thought that all our condemnations were just a trivial local quirk of our own culture. We could still less do it if we tried to stop judging altogether.

Real moral scepticism, in fact, could lead only to inaction, to our losing all interest in moral questions, most of all in those which concern other societies. When we discuss these things, it becomes instantly clear how far we are from doing this. Suppose, for instance, that I criticize the bisecting Samurai, that I say his behaviour is brutal. What will usually happen next is that someone will protest, will say that I have no right to make criticisms like that of another culture. But it is most unlikely that he will use this move to end the discussion of the subject. Instead, he will justify the Samurai. He will try to fill in the background, to make me understand the custom, by explaining the exalted ideals of discipline and devotion which produced it. He will probably talk of the lower value which the ancient Japanese placed on individual life generally. He may well suggest that this is a healthier attitude than our own obsession with security. He may add, too, that the wayfarers did not seriously mind being bisected, that in principle they accepted the whole arrangement.

Now an objector who talks like this is implying that it *is* possible to understand alien customs. That is just what he is trying to make me do. And he implies, too, that if I do succeed in understanding them, I shall do something better than giving up judging them. He expects me to change my present judgement to a truer one—namely, one that is favourable. And the standards I must use to do this cannot just be Samurai standards. They have to be ones current in my own culture. Ideals like discipline and devotion will not move anybody unless he himself accepts them. As it happens, neither discipline nor devotion is very popular in the West at present. Anyone who appeals to them may well have to do some more arguing to make *them* acceptable, before he can use them to explain the Samurai. But if he does succeed here, he will have persuaded us, not just that there was something to be said for them in ancient Japan, but that there would be here as well.

Isolating barriers simply cannot arise here. If we accept something as a serious moral truth about one culture, we can't refuse to apply it—in however different an outward form—to other cultures as well, wherever circumstance admit it. If we refuse to do this, we just are not taking the other culture seriously This becomes clear if we look at the last argument used by my objector—that of justification by consent of the victim. It is suggested that sudden bisection is quite in order, *provided* that it takes place between consenting adults. I cannot now discuss how conclusive this justification is. What I am pointing out is simply that it can only work if we believe that *consent* can make such a transaction respectable—and this is a thoroughly modern and Western idea. It would probably never occur to a Samurai; if it did, it would surprise him very much. It is *our* standard. In applying it, too, we are likely to make another typically Western demand. We shall ask for good factual evidence that the wayfarers actually do have this rather sur-

prising taste—that they are really willing to be bisected. In applying Western standards in this way, we are not being confused or irrelevant. We are asking the question which arise *from where we stand,* questions which we can see the sense of. We do this because asking questions which you can't see the sense of is humbug. Certainly we can extend our questioning by imaginative effort. We can come to understand other societies better. By doing so, we may make their questions our own, or we may see that they are really forms of the questions which we are asking already. This is not impossible. It is just very hard work. The obstacles which often prevent it are simply those of ordinary ignorance, laziness and prejudice.

If there were really an isolating barrier, of course, our own culture could never have been formed. It is no sealed box, but a fertile jungle of different influences—Greek, Jewish, Roman, Norse, Celtic and so forth, into which further influences are still pouring—American, Indian, Japanese, Jamaican, you name it. The moral isolationist's picture of separate, unmixable cultures is quite unreal. People who talk about British history usually stress the value of this fertilizing mix, no doubt rightly. But this is not just an odd fact about Britain. Except for the very smallest and most remote, all cultures are formal out of many streams. All have the problem of digesting and assimilating things which, at the start, they do not understand. All have the choice of learning something from this challenge, or, alternatively, of refusing to learn, and fighting it mindlessly instead.

This universal predicament has been obscured by the fact that anthropologists used to concentrate largely on very small and remote cultures, which did not seem to have this problem. These tiny societies, which had often forgotten their own history, made neat, self-contained subjects for study. No doubt it was valuable to emphasize their remoteness, their extreme strangeness, their independence of our cultural tradition. This emphasis was, I think, the root of moral isolationism. But, as the tribal studies themselves showed, even there the anthropologists were able to interpret what they saw and make judgements—often favourable—about the tribesmen. And the tribesmen, too, were quite equal to making judgements about the anthropologists—and about the tourists and Coca-Cola salesmen who followed them. Both sets of judgements, no doubt, were somewhat hasty, both have been refined in the light of further experience. A similar transaction between us and the Samurai might take even longer. But that is no reason at all for deeming it impossible. Morally as well as physically, there is only one world, and we all have to live in it.

EGOISM

GEORGE WILLIAMSON

EGOISM MAY BE DEFINED as the narrow or even exclusive focus on the individual and his or her concerns. In the context of ethics, egoism may be posed as an ethical *theory* or as a sweeping ethical *problem*. As an ethical theory, it asks how one may justify obligation, and answers that self-interest, the considered regard for one's own good, is the best way to do this. As a problem, it asks why anyone should be good at all, that is, why one should ever recognize obligations to others, rather than simply do as one pleases. As an ethical theory, egoism at least purports to make sense of obligation and even allows duties to others: in this, it claims to enter into competition with other ethical theories as a reasonable determiner of right conduct. But as a problem, it rather seems to undermine the notion of obligation itself, so far as this is distinct from an individual's desires; and in this, it at best can claim to be a personal worldview that one may adopt. Perhaps it can be shown, by examining the success of egoism as an ethical theory, that ultimately egoism as a theory devolves into a merely personal worldview, and further that even as a personal worldview, it is objectionable.

Egoism as a Theory

Egoism, considered as an ethical theory, is consequentialist: that is, it is the sort of theory that determines actions to be right or wrong depending on the consequences they produce. Specifically, the consequences important to the egoist are the effects of acts on self-interest. Those that tend to support or promote self-interest are held to be right or required, and those that tend to undermine self-interest are held to be wrong or forbidden.

What, however, is to count as one's self-interest? Generally, an egoist will have basic needs in common with others and must take care to ensure he is fed and sheltered. But beyond this, it seems to be a matter of individual preferences. Different egoists will choose to actualize different talents and indulge different pleasures. The particular set of preferences of an individual egoist can be summed up as "that which is their Good." But the egoist must also employ some degree of forethought. What really is good for one is not likely to be the satisfaction of immediate desires. If one bases nutritional decisions on immediate cravings, one may well end up with a diet high in salt, fat, and sugar, and this cannot for long be consistent with seriously thought-out self-interest.

A fairly obvious set of duties to oneself may be generated in this manner. But what about duties to others? Are they completely excluded by this standard? Egoists typically protest that this is far from the case, and rather, their standard in fact tells the truth about human relations. I do have duties to others and they can be seen to be required exactly because they promote my own self-interest. Philosophers have occasionally argued that this is indeed the foundation of society.[1] Why do I enter into relation with other human beings? On my own, I am relatively defenceless in the face of adversity and relatively powerless to satisfy my basic needs. But when two or more of us get together, we are more able to defend ourselves and more able to secure food and shelter. The house I build on my own would be a rather sad structure or would be raised rather slowly: with help, I can

---

[1] E.g., Thomas Hobbes.

Reprinted with the permission of George Williamson.

overcome this. There is nothing of concern for others here. I help and share exactly because I see it in my interest to do so. Seen this way, I will have duties to others, but only because these promote my self-interest.

The major philosophical objection to egoism takes off from this point. We can see how I might arrive at duties to others, but will all the duties generated from self-interest be *consistent* with each other? One mark of a good theory is that everything it asserts to be true is mutually compatible. Similarly, if it can be shown that egoism generates two duties that cannot both be performed at the same time, this should indicate its inadequacy as a theory. And this seems to be the case.[2] Consider the following example.

Suppose two egoists arrive in a small town at the same moment. Being both concerned to satisfy their basic needs, they each look around for a business they can open or a service they can provide. Both realize the town is without a donut shop, and such a shop would likely do well. They each see that it is their duty to open that donut shop, and undertake to do so. At that moment they become aware of each other, and of the fact that given the size of the market for donuts, only one donut shop can really be successful. They are in a conflict of interest: only one of them can promote their self-interest by this means. Egoism seems to have generated two duties that cannot both be performed, and seems to offer no way to resolve the conflict.

Why can't the duty generated by the theory, at the point of conflict, just be cooperation for both? It certainly can—but this merely puts the problem off one step. Suppose the two egoists form a partnership: one handles the coffee, the other the baked goods, and they split the profits. This would work well, but for the fact that it seems to be in the interest of each to squeeze out his or her partner, if at all possible, and have the profits for him or herself. If this is not possible, is either partner required to observe honest business practices? Certainly—to the exact extent that it is in his or her interest to do so. Whoever does the books for the partnership may well see embezzlement to be in his or her interest. The conflict seems only to have gone underground.

The claim here is that examples like these show egoism as a theory to be inconsistent. Not every-

thing it requires as a duty is possible in practice. But is the example realistic? Conflicts of interest seem to be a regular feature of human life. The need to resolve conflict seems to be one reason a consistent moral theory is so essential. But where exactly is the inconsistency in the above example? The egoist can point out that the theory only tells each person to pursue his or her self-interest, and so far as the actions of both persons really can promote self-interest, they are doing as the theory requires. The inconsistency arises only when we suppose conflicts of interest are to be resolved by the theory itself The egoist has perhaps already accepted conflict as a part of life. Conflict is to be resolved by the victory of one person over another, not by ethical theory. Inconsistency no longer seems to be a part of the theory itself.

Those who push the inconsistency objection might go further. The inconsistency lies not just in the inability to resolve conflict. It is a *logical* inconsistency, for when egoism generates duties in the above example, it requires the pursuit of self-interest on the one hand and also the undermining of self-interest on the other. It requires competition for basic goods and also the elimination of competition, for part of my pursuit of self-interest is to prevent that which can interfere with that pursuit. Clearly, your pursuit of self-interest is one of the things that interferes with my pursuit But a theory that requires a duty and also requires the prevention of that duty's actualization is logically inconsistent. Imagine a theory that requires us to give to charity and to prevent any charitable actions.

The egoist, however, will reply that we have simply left out mention of to which person's self-interest we are referring. When we see that the required pursuit of self-interest refers to *my* self-interest and the required prevention of the pursuit of self-interest refers to *your* self-interest, it is plain there is no inconsistency here. The inconsistency would arise only if it was my own pursuit of self-interest that I was required to prevent. We might try to object further that the inconsistency now is between whole sets of incompatible duties for each person: since each of these refers to a different person, there is no way egoism as a theory can be a generator of universal duty. All the duties it generates are unique to a given person, but duties are meant to be universal: actions that are required of all. The egoist, however, can simply reject this requirement: all that is required of the theory is

[2]Cf. Kurt Baier.

that it produce a set of duties that can be consistently acted out by the individual. Egoism, of course, takes the individual as its central concern. Why would it start from this point only to succumb to a demand that it focus on all others as well?

At this point, we must ask what is left of egoism *as an ethical theory?* The egoist has forsworn both the resolution of conflict and the generation of universal duties, and argued that these features of some ethical theories can be renounced without loss. The resolution of conflict must be reckoned a major task accomplished by an ethical theory, and a great loss if given up. But the egoist has acknowledged conflict as a part of life and of human nature. A knowledge of duties required of all actors also seems a great advantage to human life, but only under the presumption that the presence of another person has some significance beyond that person's effects on my self-interest, a presumption not shared by the egoist.[3] How much has been given up? These are major jobs that an ethical theory should do for an actor. We might well ask if egoism is any longer of the same species as other ethical theories.

But there are other roles besides moral actor that we must on occasion take up. Sometimes we are simply witnesses to events of moral significance and share our reflections upon them with others. Here we seem to be *moral spectators.* We are not called upon to act or actually adjudicate the events in question, but by exemplifying moral reasoning, we perhaps serve to keep ourselves and others mindful of the importance of our values. And sometimes our role is more proactive than this—sometimes friends call upon us for advice as to what to they should do regarding a situation of moral significance. Here we must play the role of *moral advisor,* and put our moral reasoning to work so that we may give relevant council to our friends.

If egoism works as a moral theory, it should be able to account for these roles as well as our role as a moral actor. But when it comes to the role of moral spectator, the egoist will ask the egoist's standard question, "Do the events I witness have any effect on my self-interest?" And of course, in the role of moral spectator, the answer is "no" since if the events in question do affect one's self-interest, one's relation to them is certainly more than simply "spectator." However, if that is the

case, these events can have no moral significance for the egoist and will not be worthy of remark. Since events have moral significance only by affecting one's self-interest, no event that does not do this is a moral event to the egoist. Hence, egoists can never play the role of moral spectator, unlike those who recognize some moral standard independent of their self-interest.

What about the role of moral advisor? When the egoist's friend comes to ask for advice, the egoist, like anyone else, can try to put his or her moral reasoning into the service of solving another's problems. In general, the egoist's advice will be something like "Do what is in your self-interest." But whose self-interest is this? The egoist's theory only mentions the egoist's self-interest, not his or her friend's. So is the egoist advising the friend to do what is in the egoist's self-interest? This would hardly be helpful, or friendly, advice, and the egoist need not expect his or her friends to come back for further advice on their problems. The notion of "self-interest" does not seem to generalize in quite the way we might expect. We all have our "self-interest," but clearly this concept has a different meaning in each individual case.

Suppose the egoist can overcome this, can recognize what would be in his or her friends' interest and can advise them on what they must do to accomplish it. But now, a new kind of problem comes up. Suppose a friend comes for advice on starting a new business and, unbeknownst to the friend, the egoist has plans for a similar business, such as in the donut shop example. The friend asks if the egoist thinks there is a market sufficient to make the business successful. Having done the market research, the egoist knows the business will be a success, but only if there are not two such businesses. But now the egoist is in a quandary: as a moral actor, the egoist sees it is in his or her interest to be the person starting the new business, but as a moral advisor to the friend, the egoist sees that he or she should recommend starting the new business since it is in the friend's interest, and these are incompatible courses of action. Clearly, to be a moral advisor and undercut one's own self-interest in the advice one gives to friends is not in one's self-interest, so it seems the egoist must choose to "misadvise" the friend and recommend against starting the new business, and then start it him- or herself.

This alone is enough to jeopardize the role of moral advisor, but we can take the situation two steps further and show how much worse it can get. When the friend sees the very business he was advised would fail being constructed under the name of his friend, the egoist, the friend must come to the conclusion that accepting advice from egoists is a bad idea, since you can never be sure that the self-interest to which they refer is really yours or simply the egoist's. So the consequence of egoism seems to be that no one would take the role of moral advisor seriously. That's the first step, and the second is that the egoist, reflecting that competition with the interests of others is probably not ultimately in his or her self-interest —since eventually the egoist will find him- or herself in situations as above where someone's interest has to suffer—will decide that being an *honest* moral advisor is a bad idea. In fact, egoists may wish to throw others "off the scent" by advising publicly that everyone should look out for the good of others, while privately pursuing their self-interests. Rather than being a moral advisor recommending their own egoistic moral theory, it might be in their self-interest to keep it to themselves. But of course, this is the end of the role of moral advisor.

We might also say that it is the end of egoism as a moral theory, for now it is not purporting to account for obligation, since it is not even a public event. Since the egoist now has no serious intention of recommending this as a theory for anyone else to follow (that might not be in his or her self-interest), it seems to be no more than a personal worldview the egoist has adopted. Egoists might try to reply that in fact this is the theory they are recommending to others: they recommend the pursuit of self-interest to all, but the implication of that is that everyone should publicly claim to promote altruism, while privately pursuing their self-interest. But this is nonsense. There is no possible way to recommend a theory the first implication of which is that you should conceal the fact that you hold the theory, and further if this recommendation somehow came about, it would be unlikely to be in the egoist's self-interest anyway. Having everyone put on their altruist face and then pursue their self-interest would be exactly the sort of competition the egoist should seek to avoid. Any way you look at it, the egoist cannot coherently recommend pursuit of self-interest as a general principle for determining conduct, and so effectively has no moral theory at all.[4]

Egoism as a World View

Following the above reasoning, the egoist might simply say, "Fine. And what would be wrong with my taking egoism as my worldview and living my life accordingly?" Now egoism is really more of a problem for all ethical theory, rather than a competing theory. For when egoists ask why not live this way, they are asking why they should recognize any obligation at all, rather than do as they please, never mind the effects on others. Well, why, or why not?

Egoists might support their view by suggesting things already are this way, anyway. If you observe human conduct, is it not the case that the motivation to do anything at all comes from a concern for oneself? To sum this up, are not all actions prudential? I prefer to do what I want and take what I want, but when I cannot do this, I avoid doing what I prefer to escape punishment or I do only what I cannot get away with neglecting. Why do children share? Parental authority enforces it. Why do adults share and seem concerned for each other? They see it as in their interest. All human behaviour is motivated by regard for oneself, so the only reason obligations are recognized at all is self-interest, if not to secure advantage, then to avoid punishment. But just wait until your back is turned.

Is this view correct? As a generalization about human behaviour, it seems to far overstep the evidence, so it should be easy to come up with counterexamples. I cite the example of persons who give money to charity or time to public service. Surely, this reflects a sacrifice of self-interest and a genuine concern for others. But the egoist might point out, with some plausibility, that it is really for the tax receipt that they give to charity and for the heightened community status that the time is given. This must be true some of the time: at the very least, the examples are not unambiguous. So what then of cases such as Gandhi or Mother Theresa? Are not such outstanding examples of dedication to others unambiguous? But the egoist might force the point. Gandhi and Mother Theresa are perhaps only the more egoistic for the excesses to which they will go for self-aggrandizement. Apparently, we must pull out the stops. What about the soldier who throws himself on a live

[4]Discussion based on Paul Taylor

grenade to save his comrades, or the single mother who works three jobs to support her children, essentially sacrificing all enjoyment of her life to their happiness? If the egoist at this point suggests that the proper understanding of these actions lies in the fact that these people acted on their own personal preferences and therefore it is concern for themselves that motivates them, we might throw up our hands. What a strange world in which the greatest egoist is the one who sacrifices himself to others! Apparently, now the egoist is happy to count working myself to death for my family as as much an expression of my self-interest as my indulging in a huge feast while others starve. If so, the egoist can hardly protest the imposition of any obligation to others—this too would be an expression of self-interest.

Egoists' reason why they should adopt egoism as a worldview does not look like it will do them much good. Can we give them a positive reason why they should not hold this worldview? Perhaps we can turn to ancient philosophy for an answer. Through the auspices of two of his characters in the *Republic,* Plato raises this very question. He introduces as a device the myth of the ring of Gyges, which by making the wearer invisible, allows one to do as one pleases and escape the consequences of one's actions. The two characters press the point on Socrates that given the supposition that this would change the wearer's behaviour considerably, clearly the only reason one does accept obligations to others is self-interest—the desire to avoid punishment. This seems to be confirmed in that the life of the person who is able to do wrong with impunity is better than that of the person who has only conformity to the rules to fall back on, and by the fact that in educating children in correct behaviour, we often cite potential punishment as a motivation for following the rules.

Socrates' reply employs another mythic device. He describes the human soul as composed of three different creatures, a human, a lion, and a monster something like a hydra. These three perhaps represent different capacities and tendencies found in human behaviour. The hydra perhaps signifies brute force which is useful when tamed but which runs amok when wild, the lion signifies courage but with a tendency toward savagery and violence, and the human signifies reason but with the tendency to lack discipline. Socrates suggests that to refuse to do good and instead serve one's own

desires is akin to allowing the hydra to run amok and make war on the lion and the human, to which the lion responds with further violence, and the human is completely dominated by the two of them. To do good, by contrast, is to employ reason to tame the lion and master the hydra, so that their strengths can be used to achieve the goals of the human. To recognize our obligations and obey them is to establish a principle of order within ourselves, which allows us to choose what is truly good for us. But to refuse this is to allow our desires to run amok, with no distinction among them as to which serve our good and which have bad consequences. In other words, Socrates' suggestion is that to do wrong, that is, to follow one's own selfish desires when one should follow good rules, is a form of self-destruction.[5]

A fascinating parable, but of course, no one is composed of a hydra, a lion, and a human being. Can the myth be applied to our problem, or must it simply remain a colourful myth with no relevance? Consider this: the egoist clearly has a species of the good in mind when he or she insists on pursuing his or her self-interest. That good is comprised of whatever the egoist perceives to be a part of his or her self-interest. Imagine the egoist with a noble cast of mind including, as part of the egoist's good, a number of traits we would count as virtues, such as dignity, integrity, diligence, and so on. Generally, these traits can be derived from self-interest. If the egoist runs a company producing certain items of quality, diligence in maintaining that quality might be essential to ensuring the success of the egoist's business, which would be in his or her interest. Some employments, however profitable, might be degrading and humiliating: if this is a loss to the egoist's self-interest, the trait that preserves the egoist against this might well be his or her sense of dignity. This is in general—what happens in the case that the benefit of maintaining these virtuous traits is outweighed by the benefit of letting them languish? Remember that the worth of these traits for the egoist comes from their contribution to his or her self-interest. If the egoist wishes to put his or her foot down and maintain these traits, he or she must justify this in terms of his or her self-interest, or give them up for the same reason. When the egoist is offered a cool million, for a rather degrading and humiliating task,

---

[5] *Republic*, Book IX.

and the egoist's dignity otherwise allows him or her only modestly profitable employment, the egoist's personal pursuit of self-interest seems to suggest it is worth it. But is it not a rather undignified dignity that distinguishes itself only by the demanding price at which it can be bought? An integrity that righteously insists "Here I stand and I will go no further—until I get a high enough bid" is no integrity at all. Even if the egoist is never driven to these extremes, these traits are incompatible with self-interest. Dignity maintained out of self-interest is not dignity as we know it.

The important thing about these traits is that they all reflect our choice of ourselves as persons. I insist on my integrity because I insist on being a certain kind of person rather than some other kind. There are "some things I will not do," either for profit or under duress, because to do them would be to become a different sort of person than I wish to be. I count some activities as undignified because the person I wish to be would not stoop to such things. When I choose to dump my toxic waste into the river to avoid the cost of proper disposal, and conceal this from the public, I give up the person who is honest, who values persons over profits, who cares what happens to the environment or future generations, and accept the person who is greedy, shortsighted, and vicious. I become a crawling bug rather than a human being.

Notice that I am not choosing integrity or other virtues solely for the sake of my own self-image—it is not that simple. I choose to be a certain person

not only in respect of concern for myself, as if in a vacuum, but in respect of concern for others. In the toxic waste illustration, the person I chose to be stood or fell with my treatment of others. If I am truthful to others and regard it as my obligation to be so, then I am the honest person; if I feel no binding force in the obligation and lie instead, I am the liar. Choosing myself as a certain kind of person is to choose myself as having a certain value. But the value I seek for myself is bound up with the value I attach to others, and this value is summed up in the obligations I recognize as owed to them.

Now, is this not what Socrates suggests? Choosing to be good, to recognize obligation as binding, is to establish an order within ourselves—I will be *this* and not *that*—and this order is the same thing as being a valuable sort of person. To refuse obligation is to refuse the sort of order that makes that person possible and to undermine the possibility of being valuable at all—it is, in short, self-destruction. This seems to me to be the meaning of ethics in the broadest sense. The fact that human beings can and do relate themselves to norms (obligations, values) is what it means to count human beings as valuable at all. To be a human being is to be open to the force of values, to recognize obligation. If at this point anyone is so great an idiot as to persist in questioning why he or she should want to be a valuable sort of person, one can only present that person with the alternative: it is the difference between walking upright as a human being and crawling as something less—you decide!

From *Nicomachean Ethics*

ARISTOTLE

EVERY ART AND EVERY INQUIRY, and similarly every action and pursuit, is thought to aim at some good; and for this reason the good has rightly been declared to be that at which all things aim. . . . If, then, there is some end [i.e. goal or purpose] of the things we do, which we desire for its own sake (everything else being desired for the sake of this),

and if we do not choose everything for the sake of something else (for at that rate the process would go on to infinity, so that our desire would be empty and vain), clearly this must be the good and the chief good. Will not the knowledge of it, then, have a great influence on life? Shall we not, like archers who have a mark to aim at, be more likely

Reprinted from Aristotle's Nicomachean Ethics, *trans. W. D. Ross,* © *(1925 by Oxford University Press.*

to hit upon what is right? If so, we must try, in outline at least to determine what it is. . . .

Since there are evidently more than one end, and we choose some of these . . . for the sake of something else, clearly not all ends are final ends; but the chief good is evidently something final. Therefore, if there is only one final end, this will be what we are seeking, and if there are more than one, the most final of these will be what we are seeking. Now we call that which is in itself worthy of pursuit more final than that which is worthy of pursuit for the sake of something else, and that which is never desirable for the sake of something else more final than the things that are desirable both in themselves and for the sake of that other thing, and therefore we call final without qualification that which is always desirable in itself and never for the sake of something else.

Now such a thing happiness, above all else, is held to be; for this we choose always for itself and never for the sake of something else, but honour, pleasure, reason, and every virtue we choose indeed for themselves (for if nothing resulted from them we should still choose each of them), but we choose them also for the sake of happiness, judging that by means of them we shall be happy. Happiness, on the other hand, no one chooses for the sake of these, nor, in general, for anything other than itself.

From the point of view of self-sufficiency the same result seems to follow; for the final good is thought to be self-sufficient. Now by self-sufficient we do not mean that which is sufficient for a man by himself, for one who lives a solitary life, but also for parents, children, wife, and in general for his friends and fellow citizens, since man is born for citizenship. [T]he self-sufficient we . . . define as that which when isolated makes life desirable and lacking in nothing; and such we think happiness to be; and further we think it most desirable of all things, without being counted as one good thing among others—if it were so counted it would clearly be made more desirable by the addition of even the least of goods; for that which is added becomes an excess of goods, and of goods the greater is always more desirable. Happiness, then is something final and self-sufficient, and is the end of action.

. . . [T]o say that happiness is the chief good seems a platitude, and a clearer account of what it is is still desired. This might perhaps be given, if we could first ascertain the function of man. For just as for a flute-player, a sculptor, or any artist, and, in

general, for all things that have a function or activity, the good and the "well" is thought to reside in the function, so would it seem to be for man if he has a function. Have the carpenter, then, and the tanner certain functions or activities, and has man none? Is he born without a function? Or as eye, hand, foot, and in general each of the parts evidently has a function, may one lay it down that man similarly has a function apart from all these? What then can this be? Life seems to be common even to plants, but we are seeking what is peculiar to man. . . . [H]uman good turns out to be activity of soul in accordance with virtue, and if there are more than one virtue, in accordance with the best and most complete.

But we must add "in a complete life." For one swallow does not make a summer, nor does one day; and so too one day, or a short time does not make a man blessed and happy.

. . . [N]o function of man has so much permanence as virtuous activities and of these the most valuable are more durable because those who are happy spend their life most readily and most continuously in these; for this seems to be the reason why we do not forget them. The happy man will be happy throughout his life; for always, or by preference to everything else, he will be engaged in virtuous action and contemplation, and he will bear the chances of life most nobly and altogether decorously, if he is "truly good" and "foursquare beyond reproach."

. . . Since happiness is an activity of soul in accordance with perfect virtue, we must consider the nature of virtue; for perhaps we shall thus see better the nature of happiness. . . .

Neither by nature . . . nor contrary to nature do the virtues arise in us; rather we are adapted by nature to receive them, and are made perfect by habit.

. . . [T]he virtues we get by first exercising them, as also happens in the case of the arts as well. For the things we have to learn before we can do them, we learn by doing them, e.g. men become builders by building and lyre-players by playing the lyre; so too we become just by doing just acts, temperate by doing temperate acts, brave by doing brave acts.

. . . [B]y doing the acts that we do in our transactions with other men we become just or unjust and by doing the acts that we do in the presence of danger, and being habituated to feel fear or confidence, we become brave or cowardly. The same is true of appetites and feelings of anger; some men become temperate and good-tempered, others self-indulgent and irascible [i.e. irritable], by behaving in one way or the other in the appropriate circumstances. Thus, in one word, states of character arise out of like activities. This is why the activities we exhibit must be of a certain kind; it is because the states of character correspond to the differences between these. It makes no small difference, then, whether we form habits of one kind or of another from our very youth; it makes a very great difference, or rather *all* the difference.

. . . The question might be asked, what we mean by saying that we must become just by doing just acts, and temperate by doing temperate acts; for if men do just and temperate acts, they are already just and temperate. . . .

Actions . . . are called just and temperate when they are such as the just or the temperate man would do; but it is not the man who does these that is just and temperate, but the man who also does them *as* just and temperate men do them. It is well said, then, that it is by doing just acts that the just man is produced, and by doing temperate acts the temperate man; without doing these no one would have even a prospect of becoming good.

. . . [W]e must consider what virtue is. Since things that are found in the soul are of three kinds—passions, faculties, states of character, virtue must be one of these. By passions I mean appetite, anger, fear, confidence, envy, joy, friendly feeling, hatred, longing, emulation, pity, and in general the feelings that are accompanied by pleasure or pain; by faculties the things in virtue of which we are said to be capable of feeling these, e.g. of becoming angry or being pained or feeling pity; by states of character the things in virtue of which we stand well or badly with reference to the passions, e.g. with reference to anger we stand badly if we feel it violently or too weakly, and well if we feel it moderately; and similarly with reference to the other passions.

Now neither the virtues nor the vices are *passions,* because we are not called good or bad on the ground of our passions, but are so called on the ground of our virtues and our vices, and because we are neither praised nor blamed for our passions (for the man who feels fear or anger is not praised, nor is the man who simply feels anger blamed, but the man who feels it in a certain way), but for our virtues and our vices we are praised or blamed.

Again, we feel anger and fear without choice, but the virtues are modes of choice or involve choice. Further, in respect of the passions we are said to be moved, but in respect of the virtues and the vices we are said not to be moved but to be disposed in a particular way.

For these reasons also they are not *faculties;* for we are neither called good nor bad, nor praised nor blamed, for the simple capacity of feeling the passions; again, we have the faculties by nature, but we are not made good or bad by nature. . . .

If, then, the virtues are neither passions nor faculties, all that remains is that they should be *states of character.* . . .

We must, however, not only describe virtue as a state of character, but also say what sort of state it is. . . .

[Moral] virtue must have the quality of aiming at the intermediate. . . . [I]t . . . is concerned with passions and actions, and in these there is excess, defect, and the intermediate. For instance, both fear and confidence and appetite and anger and pity and in general pleasure and pain may be felt both too much and too little, and in both cases not well; but to feel them at the right times, with reference to the right objects, towards the right people, with the right motive, and in the right way, is what is both intermediate and best, and this is characteristic of virtue. Similarly with regard to actions also there is excess, defect and the intermediate. Now virtue is concerned with passions and actions, in which excess is a form of failure, and so is defect, while the intermediate is praised and is a form of success; and being praised and being successful are both characteristics of virtue. Therefore virtue is a kind of mean, since, as we have seen, it aims at what is intermediate. . . .

Virtue, then, is a state of character concerned with choice, lying in a mean, i.e. the mean relative to us, this being determined by a rational principle, and by that principle by which the man of practical wisdom would determine it. Now it is a mean between two vices, that which depends on excess and that which depends on defect; and again it is a mean because the vices respectively fall short of or exceed what is right in both passions and actions, while virtue both finds and chooses that which is intermediate. Hence in respect of its substance and the definition which states its essence virtue is a mean, with regard to what is best and right an extreme.

From *Grounding for the Metaphysics of Morals*

IMMANUEL KANT

THERE IS NO POSSIBILITY of thinking of anything at all in the world, or even out of it, which can be regarded as good without qualification, except a *good will*. Intelligence, wit, judgment, and whatever talents of the mind one might want to name are doubtless in many respects good and desirable, as are such qualities of temperament as courage, resolution, perseverance. But they can also become extremely bad and harmful if the will, which is to make use of these gifts of nature and which in its special constitution is called character, is not good. The same holds with gifts of fortune; power, riches, honor, even health, and that complete well-being and contentment with one's condition which is called happiness make for pride and often hereby even arrogance, unless there is a good will to correct their influence on the mind and herewith also to rectify the whole principle of action and make it universally conformable to its end. The sight of a being who is not graced by any touch of a pure and good will but who yet enjoys an uninterrupted prosperity can never delight a rational and impartial spectator. Thus a good will seems to constitute the indispensable condition of being even worthy of happiness.

Some qualities are even conducive to this good will itself and can facilitate its work. Nevertheless, they have no intrinsic unconditional worth; but they always presuppose, rather, a good will, which restricts the high esteem in which they are otherwise rightly held, and does not permit them to be regarded as absolutely good. Moderation in emotions and passions, self-control, and calm deliberation are not only good in many respects but even seem to constitute part of the intrinsic worth of a person. But they are far from being rightly called good without qualification (however unconditionally they were commended by the ancients). For without the principles of a good will, they can become extremely bad; the coolness of a villain makes him not only much more dangerous but also immediately more abominable in our eyes than he would have been regarded by us without it.

A good will is good not because of what it effects or accomplishes; . . . it is good only through its willing, i.e., it is good in itself. . . .

The concept of a will estimable in itself and good without regard to any further end must now be developed. . . . Therefore, we shall take up the concept of *duty*. . . .

I here omit all actions already recognized as contrary to duty, even though they may be useful for this or that end; for in the case of these the question does not arise at all as to whether they might be done from duty, since they even conflict with duty. I also set aside those actions which are really in accordance with duty yet to which men have no immediate inclination, but perform them because they are impelled thereto by some other inclination. For in this [second] case to decide whether the action which is in accord with duty has been done from duty or from some selfish purpose is easy. This difference is far more difficult to note in the [third] case where the action accords with duty and the subject has in addition an immediate inclination to do the action. For example,[1] that a dealer should not overcharge an inexperienced purchaser certainly accords with duty; and where there is much commerce, the prudent merchant does not overcharge but keeps to a fixed price for everyone in general, so that a child may buy from him just as well as everyone else may. Thus customers are honestly served, but this is not nearly enough for making us believe that the merchant has acted this way from duty and from principles of honesty; his own advantage required him to do it. He cannot, however, be assumed to have in addition [as in the third case] an immediate inclination toward his buyers, causing him, as it were, out of love to give no one as far as price is concerned any advantage over another. Hence the action was done neither from duty nor from immediate inclination, but merely for a selfish purpose. . . .

[1][The ensuing example provides an illustration of the second case.]

From Immanuel Kant, Grounding for the Metaphysics of Morals, *3rd ed., 1993, trans. James W. Ellington, pp. 7–15, pp. 34–37 (edited). Reprinted by permission of Hackett Publishing Company, Inc. All rights*

To be beneficent where one can is a duty; and besides this, there are many persons who are so sympathetically constituted that, without any further motive of vanity or self-interest, they find an inner pleasure in spreading joy around them and can rejoice in the satisfaction of others as their own work. But I maintain that in such a case an action of this kind, however dutiful and amiable it may be, has nevertheless no true moral worth.[2] It is on a level with such actions as arise from other inclinations, e.g., the inclination for honor, which if fortunately directed to what is in fact beneficial and accords with duty and is thus honorable, deserves praise and encouragement, but not esteem; for its maxim lacks the moral content of an action done not from inclination but from duty. Suppose then the mind of this friend of mankind to be clouded over with his own sorrow so that all sympathy with the lot of others is extinguished, and suppose him still to have the power to benefit others in distress, even though he is not touched by their trouble because he is sufficiently absorbed with his own; and now suppose that, even though no inclination moves him any longer, he nevertheless tears himself from this deadly insensibility and performs the action without any inclination at all, but solely from duty—then for the first time his action has genuine moral worth.[3] . . .

An action done from duty has its moral worth, not in the purpose that is to be attained by it, but in the maxim according to which the action is determined. The moral worth depends, therefore, not on the realization of the object of the action, but merely on the principle of volition according to which, without regard to any objects of the faculty of desire, the action has been done. From what has gone before it is clear that the purposes which we may have in out actions, as well as their effects regarded as ends and incentives of the will, cannot give to actions any unconditioned and moral worth. Where, then, can this worth lie if it is not to be found in the will's relation to the expected effect? Nowhere but in the principle of the will, with no regard to the ends that can be brought about through such action. . . .

An action done from duty must altogether exclude the influence of inclination and therewith every object of the will. Hence there is nothing left

which can determine the will except objectively the law and subjectively pure respect for this practical law, i.e., the will can be subjectively determined by the maxim[4] that I should follow such a law even if all my inclinations are thereby thwarted.

Thus the moral worth of an action does not lie in the effect expected from it nor in any principle of action that needs to borrow its motive from this expected effect. For all these effects (agreeableness of one's condition and even the furtherance of other people's happiness) could have been brought about also through other causes and would not have required the will of a rational being, in which the highest and unconditioned good can alone be found. Therefore, the pre-eminent good which is called moral can consist in nothing but the representation of the law in itself. . . .

But what sort of law can that be the thought of which must determine the will without reference to any expected effect, so that the will can be called absolutely good without qualification? Since I have deprived the will of every impulse that might arise for it from obeying any particular law, there is nothing left to serve the will as principle except the universal conformity of its actions to law as such, i.e., I should never act except in such a way that I can also will that my maxim should become a universal law.[5] Here mere conformity to law as such (without having as its basis any law determining particular actions) serves the will as principle and must so serve it if duty is not to be a vain delusion and a chimerical concept. The ordinary reason of mankind in its practical judgments agrees completely with this, and always has in view the aforementioned principle.

For example, take this question. When I am in distress, may I make a promise with the intention of not keeping it? I readily distinguish here the two meanings which the question may have; whether making a false promise conforms with prudence or with duty. Doubtless the former can often be the case. Indeed I clearly see that escape from some present difficulty by means of such a promise is not enough. In addition I must carefully consider whether from this lie there may later arise far

---

[2][This is an example of case 3.]
[3][This is an example of case 4.]

[4]A maxim is the subjective principle of volition. The objective principle (i.e., one which would serve all rational beings also subjectively as a practical principle if reason had full control over the faculty of desire) is the practical law.
[5][This is the first time in the *Grounding* that the categorical imperative is stated.]

greater inconvenience for me than from what I now try to escape. Furthermore, the consequences of my false promise are not easy to forsee, even with all my supposed cunning; loss of confidence in me might prove to be far more disadvantageous than the misfortune which I now try to avoid. The more prudent way might be to act according to a universal maxim and to make it a habit not to promise anything without intending to keep it. But that such a maxim is, nevertheless, always based on nothing but a fear of consequences becomes clear to me at once. To be truthful from duty is, however, quite different from being truthful from fear of disadvantageous consequences; in the first case the concept of the action itself contains a law for me, while in the second I must first look around elsewhere to see what are the results for me that might be connected with the action. For to deviate from the principle of duty is quite certainly bad; but to abandon my maxim of prudence can often be very advantageous for me, though to abide by it is certainly safer. The most direct and infallible way, however, to answer the question as to whether a lying promise accords with duty is to ask myself whether I would really be content if my maxim (of extricating myself from difficulty by means of a false promise) were to bold as a universal law for myself as well as for others, and could I really say to myself that everyone may promise falsely when he finds himself in a difficulty from which he can find no other way to extricate himself. Then I immediately become aware that I can indeed will the lie but cannot at all will a universal law to lie. For by such a law there would really be no promises at all, since in vain would my willing future actions be professed to other people who would not believe what I professed, or if they over-hastily did believe, then they would pay me back in like coin. Therefore, my maxim would necessarily destroy itself just as soon as it was made a universal law.[6]

Therefore, I need no far-reaching acuteness to discern what I have to do in order that my will may be morally good. Inexperienced in the course of

[6][This means that when you tell a lie, you merely take exception to the general rule that says everyone should always tell the truth and believe that what you are saying is true. When you lie, you do not thereby will that everyone else lie and not believe that what you are saying is true, because in such a case your lie would never work to get you what you want.]

the world and incapable of being prepared for all its contingencies, I only ask myself whether I can also will that my maxim should become a universal law. If not, then the maxim must be rejected, not because of any disadvantage accruing to me or even to others, but because it cannot be fitting as a principle in a possible legislation of universal law, and reason exacts from me immediate respect for such legislation. . . .

[S]uppose that there were something whose existence has in itself an absolute worth, something which as an end in itself could be a ground of determinate laws. In it, and in it alone, would there be the ground of a possible categorical imperative, i.e., of a practical law.

Now I say that man, and in general every rational being, exists as an end in himself and not merely as means to be arbitrarily used by this or that will. He must in all his actions whether directed to himself or to other rational beings, always be regarded at the same time as an end. . . . Rational beings are called persons inasmuch as their nature already marks them out as ends in themselves, i.e., as something I which is not to be used merely as means and hence there is imposed thereby a limit on all arbitrary use of such beings, which are thus objects of respect. Persons are, therefore, not merely subjective ends, whose existence as an effect of our actions has a value for us; but such beings are objective ends, i.e., exist as ends in themselves. Such an end is one for which there can be substituted no other end to which such beings should serve merely as means. . . .

If then there is to be a supreme practical principle and, as far as the human will is concerned, a categorical imperative, then it must be such that from the conception of what is necessarily an end for everyone because this end is an end in itself it constitutes an objective principle of the will and can hence serve as a practical law The ground of such a principle is this: rational nature exists as an end in itself. In this way man necessarily thinks of his own existence; thus far is it a subjective principle of human actions. But in this way also does every other rational being think of his existence on the same rational ground that holds also for me;[7] hence it is at the same time an objective principle,

[7]This proposition I here put forward as a postulate. The grounds for it will be found in the last section. [See below Ak. 446–63.]

from which, as a supreme practical ground, all laws of the will must be able to be derived. The practical imperative will therefore be the following: Act in such a way that you treat humanity, whether in your own person or in the person of another, always at the same time as an end and never simply as a means.[8] . . .

8. [This oft-quoted version of the categorical imperative is usually referred to as the formula of the end in itself.]

From *Utilitarianism*

JOHN STUART MILL

THE CREED WHICH ACCEPTS as the foundation of morals, Utility, or the Greatest Happiness Principle, holds that actions are right in proportion as they tend to promote happiness, wrong as they tend to produce the reverse of happiness. By happiness is intended pleasure, and the absence of pain; by unhappiness, pain, and the privation of pleasure. To give a clear view of the moral standard set up by the theory, much more requires to be said; in particular, what things it includes in the ideas of pain and pleasure; and to what extent this is left an open question. But these supplementary explanations do not affect the theory of life on which this theory of morality is grounded— namely, that pleasure, and freedom from pain, are the only things desirable as ends; and that all desirable things . . . are desirable either for the pleasure inherent in themselves, or as means to the promotion of pleasure and the prevention of pain.

Now, such a theory of life excites in many minds . . . inveterate [i.e. long-standing obstinate] dislike. To suppose that life has . . . no higher end than pleasure—no better and nobler object of desire and pursuit—they designate as utterly mean and grovelling; as a doctrine worthy only of swine, to whom the followers of Epicurus were, at a very early period, contemptuously likened; and modern holders of the doctrine are occasionally made the subject of equally polite comparisons. . . . [Epicurus was an early Greek philosopher (341–270 B.C.) who founded a system of ethics which held that the chief ethical goal was to live a pleasurable life.]

When thus attacked, the Epicureans have always answered, that it is not they, but their accusers, who represent human nature in a degrading light; since the accusation supposes human beings to be capable of no pleasures except those of which swine are capable. If this supposition were true, the charge could not be gainsaid, but would then be no longer an imputation; for if the sources of pleasure were precisely the same to human beings and to swine, the rule of life which is good enough for the one would be good enough for the other. The comparison of the Epicurean life to that of beasts is felt as degrading, precisely because a beast's pleasures do not satisfy a human being's conceptions of happiness. Human beings have faculties more elevated than the animal appetites, and when once made conscious of them, do not regard anything as happiness which does not include their gratification. . . . It is quite compatible with the principle of utility to recognise the fact, that some *kinds* of pleasure are more desirable and more valuable than others. It would be absurd that while, in estimating all other things, quality is considered as well as quantity, the estimation of pleasures should be supposed to depend on quantity alone.

If I am asked, what I mean by difference of quality in pleasures, or what makes one pleasure more valuable than another, merely as a pleasure, except its being greater in amount, there is but one possible answer. Of two pleasures, if there be one to which all or almost all who have experience of both give a decided preference, irrespective of any feeling of moral obligation to prefer it, that is the

From John Stuart Mill, Collected Works of John Stuart Mill, Vol. 10, Essays on Ethics, Religion and Society, *ed. J. M. Robson. Toronto: University of Toronto Press, © 1969.*

more desirable pleasure. If one of the two is, by those who are competently acquainted with both, placed so far above the other that they prefer it, even though knowing it to be attended with a greater amount of discontent, and would not resign it for any quantity of the other pleasure which their nature is capable of, we are justified in ascribing to the preferred enjoyment a superiority in quality, so far outweighing quantity as to render it, in comparison, of small account.

Now it is an unquestionable fact that those who are equally acquainted with, and equally capable of appreciating and enjoying, both, do give a most marked preference to the manner of existence which employs their higher faculties. Few human creatures would consent to be changed into any of the lower animals, for a promise of the fullest allowance of a beast's pleasures; no intelligent human being would consent to be a fool, no instructed person would be an ignoramus, no person of feeling and conscience would be selfish and base, even though they should be persuaded that the fool, the dunce, or the rascal is better satisfied with his lot than they with theirs. . . . A being of higher faculties requires more to make him happy, is capable probably of more acute suffering, and is certainly accessible to it at more points, than one of an inferior type; but in spite of these liabilities, he can never really wish to sink into what he feels to be a lower grade of existence. . . . It is better to be a human being dissatisfied than a pig satisfied; better to be Socrates dissatisfied than a fool satisfied. And if the fool, or the pig, is of a different opinion, it is because they only know their own side of the question. The other party to the comparison knows both sides.

. . . I have dwelt on this point, as being a necessary part of a perfectly just conception of Utility or Happiness, considered as the directive rule of human conduct. But it is by no means an indispensable condition to the acceptance of the utilitarian standard; for that standard is not the agent's own greatest happiness, but the greatest amount of happiness altogether; and if it may possibly be doubted whether a noble character is always the happier for it nobleness, there can be no doubt that it makes other people happier, and that the world in general is immensely a gainer by it. . . .

According to the Greatest Happiness Principle . . . the ultimate end, with reference to and for the sake of which all other things are desirable (whether we are considering our own good or that of other people), is an existence exempt as far as possible from pain, and as rich as possible in enjoyments, both in point of quantity and quality; the test of quality, and the rule for measuring it against quantity, being the preference felt by those who, in their opportunities of experience, to which must be added their habits of self-consciousness and self-observation, are best furnished with the means of comparison. This, being, according to the utilitarian opinion, the end of human action, is necessarily also the standard of morality; which may accordingly be defined, the rules and precepts for human conduct, by the observance of which an existence such as has been described might be, to the greatest extent possible, secured to all mankind; and not to them only, but, so far as the nature of things admits, to the whole sentient creation.

Against this doctrine, however, arises another class of objectors, who say that happiness, in any form, cannot be the rational purpose of human life and action; because in the first place, it is unattainable [and in the second] . . . men can do *without* happiness; that . . . human beings . . . could not have become noble but by learning the lesson of . . . renunciation; which lesson, thoroughly learnt and submitted to . . . [is] the beginning and necessary condition of all virtue.

The first of these objections would go to the root of the matter were it well founded; for if no happiness is to be had at all by human beings, the attainment of it cannot be the end of morality, or of any rational conduct. Though, even in that case, something might still be said for the utilitarian theory; since utility includes not solely the pursuit of happiness, but the prevention or mitigation of unhappiness; and if the former aim be chimerical, there will be all the greater scope and more imperative need for the latter. . . . When, however, it is thus positively asserted to be impossible that human life should be happy, the assertion, if not something like a verbal quibble, is at least an exaggeration. If by happiness be meant a continuity of highly pleasurable excitement, it is evident enough that this is impossible. A state of exalted pleasure lasts only moments, or in some cases, and with some intermissions, hours or days, and is the occasional brilliant flash of enjoyment, not its permanent and steady flame. Of this the philosophers who have taught that happiness is the end of life were as fully aware as those who taunt them. The happiness which they meant was not a life of rapture; but moments of such, in an existence made up of few and transitory pains, many and various pleasures, with a decided predominance of the active over the passive, and having as the foundation of the whole, not to expect more from life than it is capable of bestowing. A life thus composed, to those who have been fortunate enough to obtain it, has always appeared worthy of the name of happiness. And such an existence is even now the lot of many, during some considerable portion of their lives. The present wretched education, and wretched social arrangements, are the only real hindrance to its being attainable by almost all.

. . . In a world in which there is so much to interest, so much to enjoy, and so much also to correct and improve, every one who has . . . [a] moderate amount of moral and intellectual requisites is capable of an existence which may be called enviable; and unless such a person, through bad laws, or subjection to the will of others, is denied the liberty to use the sources of happiness within his reach, he will not fail to find this enviable existence, if he escape the positive evils of life, the great sources of physical and mental suffering—such as indigence, disease, and the unkindness, worthlessness, or premature loss of objects of affection. The main stress of the problem lies, therefore, in the contest with these calamities, from which it is a rare good fortune entirely to escape; which, as things now are, cannot be obviated, and often cannot be in any material degree mitigated. Yet no one whose opinion deserves a moment's consideration can doubt that most of the great positive evils of the world are in themselves removable, and will, if human affairs continue to improve, be in the end reduced within narrow limits. Poverty, in any sense implying suffering, may be completely extinguished by the wisdom of society, combined with the good sense and providence of individuals. Even that most intractable of enemies, disease, may be indefinitely reduced in dimensions by good physical and moral education, and proper control of noxious influences; while the progress of science holds out a promise for the future of still more direct conquests over this detestable foe. And every advance in that direction relieves us from some, not only of the chances which cut short our own lives, but, what concerns us still more, which deprive us of those in whom our happiness is wrapt up. As for vicissitudes of fortune, and other disappointments connected with worldly circumstances, these are principally the effect either of gross imprudence, of ill-regulated desires, or of bad or imperfect social institutions. All the grand sources, in short, of human suffering are in a great degree, many of them almost entirely, conquerable by human care and effort. . . .

And this leads to the true estimation of what is said by the objectors concerning the possibility, and the obligation, of learning to do without happiness. Unquestionably it is possible to do without happiness; it is done involuntarily by nineteen-twentieths of mankind, even in those parts of our present world which are least deep in barbarism; and it often has to be done voluntarily by the hero or the martyr, for the sake of something which he prizes more than his individual happiness. But this something, what is it, unless the happiness of others, or some of the requisites of happiness? It is noble to be capable of resigning entirely one's own portion of happiness, or chances of it: but, after all, this self-sacrifice must be for some end; it is not its own end; and if we are told that its end is not happiness, but virtue, which is better than happiness, I ask, would the sacrifice be made if the hero or martyr did not believe that it would earn for others immunity from similar sacrifices? Would it be made, if he thought that his renunciation of happiness for himself would produce no fruit for any of his fellow creature, but to make their lot like his, and place them also in the condition of persons who have renounced happiness? All honour to those who can abnegate for themselves the personal enjoyment of life, when by such renunciation they contribute worthily to increase the amount of happiness in the world; but he who does it, or professes to do it, for any other purpose, is no more deserving of admiration than the ascetic mounted on his pillar. He may be an inspiriting proof of what men *can* do, but assuredly not an example of what they *should*.

. . . The utilitarian morality does recognise in human beings the power of sacrificing their own greatest good for the good of others. It only refuses to admit that the sacrifice is itself a good. A sacrifice which does not increase, or tend to increase, the sum total of happiness, it considers as wasted. The only self-renunciation which it applauds, is devotion to the happiness, or to some of the means of happiness, of others; either of mankind collectively, or of individuals within the limits imposed by the collective interests of mankind.

I must again repeat, what the assailants of utilitarianism seldom have the justice to acknowledge, that the happiness which forms the utilitarian standard of what is right in conduct, is not the agent's own happiness, but that of all concerned. As between his own happiness and that of others, utilitarianism requires him to be as strictly impartial as a disinterested and benevolent spectator. In the golden rule of Jesus of Nazareth, we read the complete spirit of the ethics of utility. To do as one would be done by, and to love one's neighbour as oneself, constitute the ideal perfection of utilitarian morality. . . . If the impugners of the utilitarian morality represented it to their own minds in this its true character, I know not what recommendation possessed by any other morality they could possibly affirm to be wanting to it; what more beautiful or more exalted developments of human nature any other ethical system can be supposed to foster, or what springs of action, not accessible to the utilitarian, such systems rely on for giving effect to their mandates.

Feminist Ethics: Some Issues for the Nineties

ALISON M. JAGGAR

FEMINIST APPROACHES to ethics are distinguished by their explicit commitment to rethinking ethics with a view to correcting whatever forms of male bias it may contain.[1] Feminist ethics, as these approaches are often called collectively, seeks to identify and challenge all those ways, overt but more often and more perniciously covert, in which western ethics has excluded women or rationalized their subordination. Its goal is to offer both practical guides to action and theoretical understandings of the nature of morality that do not, overtly or covertly, subordinate the interests of any woman or group of women to the interests of any other individual or group.

While those who practice feminist ethics are a shared project, they diverge widely in their views as to how this project may be accomplished. These divergences result from a variety of philosophical differences, including differing conceptions of feminism itself, a perennially contested concept. The inevitability of such disagreement means that feminist ethics cannot be identified in terms of a specific range of topics, methods or orthodoxies. For example, it is a mistake, though one to which even some feminists occasionally have succumbed, to identify feminist ethics with any of the following: putting women's interests first; focusing exclusively on so-called women's issues; accepting women (or feminists) as moral experts or authorities; substituting "female" (or "feminine") for "male" (or "masculine") values; or extrapolating directly from women's experience.

Even though my initial characterization of feminist ethics is quite loose, it does suggest certain minimum conditions of adequacy for any approach to ethics that purports to be feminist.

Within the present social context, in which women remain systematically subordinated, a feminist approach to ethics must offer a guide to action that will tend to subvert rather than reinforce this subordination. Thus, such an approach must be practical, transitional and nonutopian, an extension of politics rather than a retreat from it. It must be sensitive, for instance, to the symbolic meanings as well as the practical consequences of any actions that we take as gendered subjects in a male dominated society, and it must also provide

[1]Many of the ideas in this paper have been developed in the course of long-term discussions with Marcia Lind. This paper has benefitted tremendously from her insistent questioning and from her insightful responses to earlier drafts. Pamela Grath also made a number of helpful comments.

From Journal of Social Philosophy *20 (1–2) (Spring–Fall 1989). Reprinted by permission of the* Journal of Social Philosophy.

the conceptual resources for identifying and evaluating the varieties of resistance and struggle in which women, particularly, have tended to engage. It must recognize the often unnoticed ways in which women and other members of the underclass have refused cooperation and opposed domination, while acknowledging the inevitability of collusion and the impossibility of totally clean hands [Ringelheim 1985; King 1989].

Since so much of women's struggle has been in the kitchen and the bedroom, as well as in the parliamentary chamber and on the factory floor, a second requirement for feminist ethics is that it should be equipped to handle moral issues in both the so-called public and private domains. It must be able to provide guidance on issues of intimate relations, such as affection and sexuality, which, until quite recently, were largely ignored by modern moral theory In so doing, it cannot assume that moral concepts developed originally for application to the public realm, concepts such as impartiality or exploitation, are automatically applicable to the private realm. Similarly, an approach to ethics that is adequate for feminism must also provide appropriate guidance for activity in the public realm, for dealing with large numbers of people, including strangers.

Finally, feminist ethics must take the moral experience of all women seriously, though not, of course, uncritically. Though what is *feminist* will often turn out to be very different from what is *feminine,* a basic respect for women's moral experience is necessary to acknowledging women's capacities as moralists and to countering traditional stereotypes of women as less than full moral agents, as childlike or "natural." Furthermore, as Okin [1987], among others, has argued, empirical claims about differences in the moral experience of women and men make it impossible to assume that any approach to ethics will be unanimously accepted if it fails to consult the moral experience of women. Additionally, it seems plausible to suppose that women's distinctive social experience may make them especially perceptive regarding the implications of domination, especially gender domination, and especially well equipped to detect the male bias that has been shown to pervade so much of male-authored western moral theory.

On the surface, at least, these conditions of adequacy for feminist ethics are quite minimal—although I believe that fulfilling them would have radical consequences for ethics. I think most feminist, and perhaps even many nonfeminist,[2] philosophers would be likely to find the general statement of these conditions relatively uncontroversial, but that inevitably there will be sharp disagreement over when the conditions have been met. Even feminists are likely to differ over, for instance, just what are women's interests and when they have been neglected, what is resistance to domination and which aspects of which women's moral experience are worth developing and in which directions.

I shall now go on to outline some of these differences as they have arisen in feminist discussions of five ethical and meta-ethical issues. These five certainly are not the only issues to confront feminist ethics; on the contrary the domain of feminist ethics is identical with that of nonfeminist ethics—it is the whole domain of morality and moral theory. I have selected these five issues both because I believe they are especially pressing in the context of contemporary philosophical debate, and because I myself find them especially interesting. As will shortly become evident, the issues that I have selected are not independent of each other; they are unified at least by recurrent concern about questions of universality and particularity Nevertheless, I shall separate the issues for purposes of exposition.

Equality and Difference

The central insight of contemporary feminism without doubt has been the recognition of gender as a sometimes contradictory but always pervasive system of social norms that regulates the activity of individuals according to their biological sex. Thus individuals whose sex is male are expected to conform to prevailing norms of masculinity, while female individuals are expected to conform to prevailing norms of femininity. In 1970, Shulamith Firestone began her classic *The Dialectic of Sex* with the words "Sex class is so deep as to be invisible" and, for the first decade of the contemporary women's movement, feminists devoted themselves to rendering "sex-class" or gender visible; to exploring (and denouncing) the depth and extent

---

[2]"Nonfeminist" here refers to philosophers who do not make their feminist concerns explicit in their philosophical work; it is not intended to imply that such philosophers do not demonstrate feminist concern in other ways.

of gender regulation in the life of every individual. Norms of gender were shown to influence not only dress, occupation and sexuality, but also bodily comportment, patterns of speech, eating habits and intellectual, emotional, moral and even physical development—mostly in ways that, practically and/or symbolically, reinforced the domination of men over women.

The conceptual distinction between sex and gender enabled feminists to articulate a variety of important insights. These included recognizing that the superficially nondiscriminatory acceptance of exceptional, i.e., "masculine," women is not only compatible with but actually presupposes a devaluation of "the feminine." The sex/gender distinction also enabled feminists to separate critical reflection on cultural norms of masculinity from antagonism towards actual men [Plumwood 1989].

Useful as the concept of gender has been to feminism, however, more recent feminist reflection has shown that it is neither as simple nor as unproblematic as it seemed when feminists first articulated it. Some feminists have challenged the initially sharp distinction between sex and gender, noting that, just as sex differences have influenced (though not ineluctably determined) the development of gender norms, so gender arrangements may well have influenced the biological evolution of certain secondary sexual characteristics and even of that defining criterion of sex, procreation itself [Jaggar 1983]. Other feminists have challenged the distinction gender and other social categories such as race and class. Recognizing that feminist claims about "women" often had generalized illicitly from the experience of a relatively small group of middle-class white women, feminists in the last ten years have emphasized that gender is a variable rather than a constant, since norms of gender vary not only between but also within cultures, along dimensions such as class, race, age, marital status, sexual preference and so on. Moreover, since every woman is a woman of some determinate age, race, class and marital status, gender is not even an independent variable; there is no concept of pure or abstract gender that can be isolated theoretically and studied independently of class, race, age or marital status [Spelman, 1989]. Neither, of course, can these other social categories be understood independently of gender.

Their increasingly sophisticated understandings of gender have complicated feminists' discussions of many moral and social issues. One of these is sexual equality At the beginning of the contemporary women's movement, in the late 1960s, this seemed to be a relatively straightforward issue. The nineteenth century feminist preference for "separate spheres" for men and women [Freedman 1979] had been replaced by demands for identity of legal rights for men and women or, as it came to be called, equality before the law. By the end of the 1960s, most feminists in the United States had come to believe that the legal system should be sex-blind, that it should not differentiate in any way between women and men. This belief was expressed in the struggle for an Equal Rights Amendment to the U.S. Constitution, an amendment that, had it passed, would have made any sex-specific law unconstitutional.

By the late 1970s and early 1980s, however, it was becoming apparent that the assimilationist goal of strict equality before the law does not always benefit women, at least in the short term. One notorious example was "no fault" divorce settlements that divided family property equally between husband and wife but invariably left wives in a far worse economic situation than they did husbands. In one study, for instance, ex-husbands' standard of living was found to have risen by 42% a year after divorce, whereas ex-wives' standard of living declined by 73% [Weitzman 1985]. This huge discrepancy in the outcome of divorce resulted from a variety of factors, including the fact that women and men typically are differently situated in the job market, with women usually having much lower job qualifications and less work experience. In this sort of case, equality (construed as identity) in the treatment of the sexes appears to produce an outcome in which sexual inequality is increased.

The obvious alternative of seeking equality by providing women with special legal protection continues, however, to be as fraught with dangers for women as it was earlier in the century when the existence of protective legislation was used as an excuse for excluding women from many of the more prestigious and better paid occupations [Williams 1984–5]. For instance, mandating special leaves for disability on account of pregnancy or childbirth promotes the perception that women are less reliable workers than men; recognizing "pre-menstrual syndrome" or post-partum depression as periodically disabling conditions encourages the perception that women are less responsible than men; while attempts to protect women's sexuality through legislation restricting pornography or excluding women from employment in male institutions such as prisons, perpetuate the dangerous stereotype that women are by nature the sexual prey of men. This cultural myth serves as an implicit legitimation for the prostitution, sexual harassment and rape of women, because it implies that such activities are in some sense natural. In all these cases, attempts to achieve equality between the sexes by responding to perceived differences between men and women seem likely to reinforce rather than reduce existing differences, even differences that are acknowledged to be social rather than biological in origin.

Furthermore, a "sex-responsive," as opposed to "sex-blind," conception of equality ignores differences *between* women, separating all women into a single homogenous category and possibly penalizing one group of women by forcing them to accept protection that another group genuinely may need.

Sooner or later, most feminist attempts to formulate an adequate conception of sexual equality run up against the recognition that the baseline for discussions of equality typically has been a male standard. In Catharine MacKinnon's inimitable words:

> Men's physiology defines most sports, their needs define auto and health insurance coverage, their socially designed biographies define workplace expectations and successful career patterns, their perspectives and concerns define quality in scholarship their experiences and obsessions define merit, their objectification of life defines art, their military service defines citizenship, their presence defines family, their inability to get along with each other—their wars and rulerships—defines history, their image defines god, and their genitals define sex [MacKinnon 1987:36].

Having once reached this recognition, some feminist theorists have turned away from debating the pros and cons of what MacKinnon calls the "single" versus the "double standard" and begun speculating about the kinds of far-reaching social transformation that would make sex differences "costless" [Littleton 1986]. In discussions elaborating such notions as that of "equality as acceptance," feminists seem to be moving towards a radical construal of equality as similarity of individual outcome, equality of condition or effect, a conception quite at odds with traditional liberal understandings of equality as equality of procedure or opportunity.[3]

While some feminists struggle to formulate a conception of sexual equality that is adequate for feminism, others have suggested that the enterprise is hopeless. For them, equality is an integral part of an "ethic of justice" that is characteristically masculine insofar as it obscures human difference by abstracting from the particularity and uniqueness of concrete people, in their specific situations and seeks to resolve conflicting interests by applying an abstract rule rather than by responding directly to needs that are immediately perceived. Such feminists suggest that a discourse of responsibility [Finley 1986] or care [Krieger 1987] may offer a more appropriate model for feminist ethics—even including feminist jurisprudence. Both of these suggestions remain to be worked out in detail.

The tangled debate over equality and difference provides an excellent illustration of one characteristic feature of contemporary feminist ethics, namely, its insistence that gender is often, if not invariably, a morally relevant difference between individuals. Given this insistence, the starting point of much feminist ethics may be different from that of modern moral theory; instead of assuming that all individuals should be treated alike until morally relevant grounds for difference in treatment can be identified feminist theorists may shift the traditional burden of moral proof by assuming, until shown otherwise, that contemporary men and women are rarely "similarly situated." This leads into a related and equally crucial question for feminist ethics in the nineties, namely, how to characterize and evaluate impartiality.

Impartiality

In the modern western tradition, impartiality typically has been recognized as a fundamental value, perhaps even a defining characteristic of morality,

---

[3]Feminists moving this direction seem to be paralleling Marx's move, in his *Critique of the Gotha Programme,* towards a society where an emphasis on equality of rights has been abandoned, since the differences between individuals result in its producing inequalities of outcome, and where the principle of social organization is: "From each according to his (*sic*) ability, to each according to his (*sic*) needs."

distinguishing true morality from tribalism [Baler 1958]. Impartiality is said to require weighing the interests of each individual equally, permitting differentiation only on the basis of differences that can be shown to be morally relevant. Impartiality thus is linked conceptually with equality and also with rationality and objectivity, insofar as bias often has been defined as the absence of impartiality.

In the last few years, the preeminence traditionally ascribed to impartiality has been challenged both by feminist and nonfeminist philosophers. Nonfeminists have charged that an insistence on impartiality disregards our particular identities, constituted by reference to our particular projects and our unchosen relationships with others; and that it substitutes abstract "variables" for real human agents and patients. Williams [1973,1981], for instance, has argued that the requirement of impartiality may undermine our personal integrity because it may require us to abandon projects that are central to our identity, and he also suggests that acting from duty may sometimes be less valuable than acting from an immediate emotional response to a particular other. Macintyre [1981] and Sommers [1986] have argued that impartiality fails to respect tradition, customary expectations and unchosen encumbrances, and may require behavior that is morally repugnant.

While some of the moral intuitions that motivate the nonfeminist critics of impartiality certainly are shared by many feminists, other institutions most likely are not. It is implausible to suppose, for instance, that most feminists would join Williams in applauding Gaugin's abandonment of his family in order to pursue his art, or that they would join Sommers in accepting without question the claims of customary morality on issues such as women's responsibilities. Instead, the feminist criticisms of impartiality tend to be both less individualistic and less conventionalist. They are quite varied in character.

Nell Noddings [1984] is one of the most extreme opponents of impartiality and her work has been influential with a number of feminists, even though the subtitle of her book makes it clear that she takes herself to be elaborating a feminine rather than a feminist approach to ethics. Noddings views the emotion of caring as the natural basis of morality, a view that would require impartiality to be expressed in universal caring. Noddings claims, however, that we are psychologically able to care only for particular others with whom we are in actual relationships, i.e., relationships that can be "completed" by the cared-for's acknowledgement of our caring. She concludes that pretensions to care for humanity at large are not only hypocritical but self-defeating, undermining true caring for those with whom we are in actual relationship. Noddings' arguments, if valid, of course would apply indifferently to caring practised either by men or by women, and so the distinctively feminist interest of Noddings work might seem to reside solely in her obviously debatable claim that women are "better equipped for caring than men" (97) and therefore less likely to be impartial. As we have noted already, however, feminist ethics is not committed to reproducing the moral practice even of most women and so feminist (and nonfeminist) moral theorists need to evaluate critically all of Noddings' arguments against impartiality, independently of whether her claims about "feminine" morality can be empirically confirmed.

A different criticism of impartiality has been made by those feminist philosophers who assert that, while impartiality is associated historically with individualism, it paradoxically undermines respect for individuality because it treats individuals as morally interchangeable [Code 1988; Sherwin 1987]. Many, though certainly not all, feminists claim that women are less likely than men to commit this alleged moral error because they are more likely to appreciate the special characteristics of particular individuals; again, however, feminist estimates of the soundness or otherwise of Code's and Sherwin's argument must be independent of this empirical claim.

Finally at least one feminist has extended the claim that women need special protection in the law by recommending that feminist ethics should promote a double standard of morality limiting moral communities on the basis of gender or perhaps gender solidarity. Susan Sherwin writes that feminists feel a special responsibility to reduce the suffering of women in particular; thus, "(b)y acknowledging the relevance of differences among people as a basis for a difference in sympathy and concern, feminism denies the legitimacy of a central premise of traditional moral theories, namely that all persons should be seen as morally equivalent by us" [Sherwin 1987:26. Cf. also Fisk 1980, Fraser 1986 and Hoagland 1989]. However, since women and even feminists are not homogenous groups, as we have seen, this kind of reasoning seems to push the suggested double standard towards becoming a multiple moral standard— which enlightenment theorists might well interpret as the total abandonment of impartiality and thus of morality itself.

A variety of responses seems to be available to the foregoing criticisms of impartiality. One alternative is to argue that the criticisms are unwarranted, depending on misrepresentation, misunderstanding and caricature of the impartialist position [Herman 1983; Adler 1990]. If this response can be sustained, it may be possible to show that there is no real conflict between "masculine" impartialism and "feminine" particularism, "masculine" justice and "feminine" care. Another alternative is to bite the bullet of direct moral confrontation, providing arguments to challenge the intuitions of those who criticize impartiality as requiring courses of action that are morally repugnant or politically dangerous. Yet a third alternative may be to reconceive the concept of impartiality and the considerations appropriate for determining our responsibilities toward various individuals and groups. Feminist ethics must find a way of choosing between those or other options and evaluating the proper place of impartiality in ethics for the nineties.

Moral Subjectivity

Related to the foregoing questions about impartiality are questions about how to conceptualize individuals, the subjects of moral theory. Feminists and nonfeminists alike have criticized the neo-Cartesian model of the moral self, a disembodied, separate, autonomous, unified, rational being, essentially similar to all other moral selves. Marx challenged the ahistoricism of this model; Freud challenged its claims to rationality; contemporary communitarians, such as Sandel and MacIntyre, challenge the assumption that individuals are "unencumbered," arguing instead that we are all members of communities from which we may be able to distance ourselves to some extent but which nevertheless are deeply constitutive of our identities; postmodernists have deconstructed the model to reveal fractured rather than unitary identities.

The gender bias alleged to contaminate each of the traditions mentioned above means that feminists cannot appropriate uncritically existing critiques of the neo-Cartesian moral self. Nevertheless, in developing their own challenges to this model of the self, feminist theorists often have paralleled and/or built on some nonfeminist work. For instance, feminist investigations into the social imposition of gender have drawn on neo-Freudian object relations theory in demonstrating how this central feature of our identity is socially constructed rather than given [e.g. Chodorow 1978]. Code's and Sherwin's previously mentioned accusations that modern moral theory recognizes individuals only as abstract variables, representatives of social types, is reminiscent of communitarian discussions of the encumbered self. And further connections with communitarianism, as well as phenomenology and Marxism, may be seen in the growing philosophical interest among feminists in embodiment and the ways in which it is constitutive of our identity [e.g.. Spelman 1982; Young 1990]. All these theorists offer distinctively feminist grounds for resisting the universalism, essentialism and ahistoricity of the Cartesian model and for refocusing on the need to recognize particularity and difference in conceptualizing the self.

Other feminist critiques of the neo-Cartesian subject concentrate on the common modern construal of rationality as egoism, which "overlooks the fact that millions of people (most of them women) have spent millions of hours for hundreds of years giving their utmost to millions of others" [Miller, 1976]. Others have challenged the frequent modern assumption, (explicit, for instance, in utilitarian revealed preference theory), that expressed or even felt desires and needs can be taken at face value, as givens in moral theory, pointing to the need for feminist ethics to offer an account of the social construction of desire and to suggest a way of conceptualizing the distinction between what the Marxist tradition has called "true" and "false" needs [Jaggar 1983]. Feminist explorations of the power of ideology over the unconscious and the revelation of conflicts within the self have challenged the Cartesian assumption of the self, as well as the assumption that the self is essentially rational (Grimshaw 1988]. Finally, descriptions of women's supposed "morality of caring" [Gilligan 1982] have challenged the assumption of the ontological separateness of the self and reinforced the importance, perhaps even the moral or epistemological priority, of the self as part of a moral and epistemic community.

Given this burgeoning literature, it is evident that a central concern for feminist ethics in the nineties must be to develop ways of thinking about moral subjects that are sensitive *both* to their concreteness, inevitable particularity and unique specificity, expressed in part through their relations with specific historical communities, *and* their intrinsic and common value, the ideal expressed in Enlightenment claims about common humanity, equality and impartiality [Benhabib, 1986].

Autonomy

One aspect of this task is the rethinking of autonomy which, like impartiality (to which it is often conceptually connected), has been a continuing ideal of modern moral theory. (In addition, a closely related concept of autonomy has played a central role in the Cartesian epistemological tradition, which envisions the search for knowledge as a project of the solitary knower.) The core intuition of autonomy is that of independence or self legislation, the self as the ultimate authority in matters of morality or truth. In the Kantian tradition, where the ideal of autonomy is particularly prominent, moral autonomy has been elaborated in terms of disinterest, detachment from particular attachments and interests, and freedom from prejudice and self-deception [Hill, 1987].

Contemporary feminists have had a mixed response to the modern ideal of moral autonomy. On the one hand, they have insisted that women are as autonomous in the moral and intellectual senses as men—as rational, as capable of a sense of justice, and so on; and they have also demanded political, social and economic autonomy for women through political representation, the abolition of sex discrimination and respect for women's choices on issues such as abortion. On the other hand, however, some feminists have questioned traditional interpretations of autonomy as masculine fantasies. For instance, they have explored some of the ways in which "choice" is socialized and "consent" manipulated [MacKinnon 1987; Meyers 1987]. In addition, they have questioned the possibility of separating ourselves from particular attachments and still retaining our personal identity, and they have suggested that freeing ourselves from particular attachments might result in a cold, rigid, moralistic rather than a truly moral response [Noddings 1984]. Rather than guaranteeing a response that is purely moral, freeing ourselves from particular attachments might instead make us *incapable* of morality if an ineliminable part of morality consists in responding emotionally to particular others.

Feminist ethics in the nineties must find ways of conceptualizing moral agency choice and consent that are compatible with the feminist recognition of the gradual process of moral development, the gendered social construction of the psyche, and the historical constraints on our options. This is one area in which some promising work by feminists exists already [Holmstrom 1977; Gibson 1985; Meyers 1987].

Moral Epistemology and Anti-Epistemology

Enlightenment moral theory characteristically assumed that morality was universal—that, if moral claims held, they were valid at all times and in all places. However, the modern abandonment of belief in a teleological and sacred universe rendered the justification of such claims constantly problematic, and much moral theory for the last three centuries has consisted in attempts to provide a rational grounding for morality. At the present time, both the continental European tradition, especially but not only in the form of post-modernism, and the Anglo-American tradition, especially but not only in the form of communitarianism, have developed powerful challenges to the very possibility of the view that morality consists in universally valid rules grounded in universal reason. The inevitable result of these sceptical challenges has been to reinforce normative and meta-ethical relativism.

Feminists are ambivalent about these challenges. On the one hand, many of the feminist criticisms of modern moral theory parallel the criticisms made by communitarianism and postmodernism. On the other hand, however, feminists are understandably concerned that their critique of male dominance should not be dismissed as just one point of view. It is therefore crucial for feminist ethics to develop some way of justifying feminist moral claims. However, moral epistemology is an area in which feminists' critiques are better developed than their alternatives.

Feminist discussions of moral epistemology may be divided into two categories, each distinguished by a somewhat different view of the nature of morality. Feminists in the first category do not explicitly challenge the modern conception of morality as consisting primarily in an impartial system of rationally justified rules or principles, though few feminists would assert that it is possible to identify rules that are substantive, specific and hold in all circumstances. Those in the second category, by contrast, deny that morality is reducible to rules and emphasize the impossibility of justifying the claims of ethics by appeal to a universal, impartial reason. The contrast between these two groups of feminists is not as sharp as this initial characterization might suggest: for instance, both share several criticisms of existing decision procedures in ethics. But feminists in the former group are more hopeful of repairing those procedures, while feminists in the latter group seem ready to abandon them entirely.

Feminists in the latter group frequently claim to be reflecting on a moral experience that is distinctively feminine and for this reason they are often—incorrectly—taken to represent a feminist orthodoxy They include authors such as Gilligan [1982], Noddings [1984], Baier [1987], Blum [1987], Ruddick [1989] and Walker [1989]. While there is considerable variation in the views of these authors, they all reject the view attributed to modern moral theorists that the right course of action can be discovered by consulting a list of moral rules, charging that undue emphasis on the epistemological importance of rules obscures the crucial role of moral insight, virtue and character in determining what should be done. A feminist twist is given to this essentially Aristotelian criticism when claims are made that excessive reliance on rules reflects a juridical-administrative interest that is characteristic of modern masculinity [Blum 1982] while contemporary women, by contrast, are alleged to be more likely to disregard conventionally accepted moral rules because such rules are insensitive to the specificities of particular situations [Gilligan 1982; Noddings 1984]. A morality of rule, therefore is alleged to devalue the moral wisdom of women, as well as to give insufficient weight to such supposedly feminine virtues as kindness, generosity, helpfulness and sympathy.

Some feminists have claimed that "feminine" approaches to morality contrast with supposedly masculine rule-governed approaches in that they characteristically consist in immediate responses to particular others, responses based on supposedly natural feelings of empathy, care and compassion [Gilligan 1982; Noddings 1984] or loving attention [Murdoch 1970; Ruddick 1989]. However, apart from the difficulties of establishing that such a "particularist" approach to morality [Blum 1987] indeed is characteristically feminine, let alone feminist, attempts to develop a moral epistemology based on such responses face a variety of problems. First, they confront the familiar, though perhaps not insuperable, problems common to all moral epistemologies that take emotion as a guide to right action, namely, the frequent inconsistency, unavailability or plain inappropriateness of emotions [Lind 1989]. In other words, they face the danger of degenerating into a "do what feels good" kind of subjective relativism. In addition, it is not clear that even our emotional responses to others are not responses to them under some universal description and so in this sense general rather than particular—or, if indeed particular and therefore nonconceptual, then perhaps closer to animal than to distinctively human responses. It is further uncertain how these sorts of particular responses can guide our actions towards large numbers of people, most of whom we shall never meet. Finally, the feminist emphasis on the need for "contextual" reasoning opens up the obvious dangers of *ad hoc*ism, special pleading and partiality.

Not all feminists, of course, are committed to a particularist moral epistemology. Even some of those who take emotions as a proper guide to morality emphasize the intentionality of emotions and discuss the need for their moral education. Additionally, while most feminists criticize certain aspects of the decision procedures developed by modern moral theory,[4] some believe it may be possible to revise and reappropriate some of these procedures. The main candidates for such revision are the methods by Rawls and Habermas, each of whom believes that an idealized situation of dialogue (which each describes differently) will both generate and justify morally valid principles.

Rawls' decision procedure has been the target of a number of feminist criticisms. Okin, for instance, as noted earlier, has argued that Rawls' procedure

---

[4]Most feminists, for instance, perceive traditional formulations of social contract theory to be male biased in various ways [Jaggar 1983; Held 1987; Pateman 1988].

will not generate moral consensus unless considered judgements of men and women coincide, a coincidence she believes quite unlikely in any society that continues to be structured by gender. She has also attacked Rawls' assumption that the parties in the original position will be heads of households, correctly noting that this precludes them from considering the justice of household arrangements [1987]. Benhabib [1986] has argued that those who reason behind Rawls' veil of ignorance are so ignorant of their own circumstances that they have lost the specific identities characteristic of human agents. She takes this to mean that "there is no real *plurality* of perspectives in the Rawlsian original position, but only a *definitional identity*" [413, italics in original]. Benhabib criticizes what she calls this "monological" model of moral reasoning on the grounds that, by restricting itself to "the standpoint of the generalized other" and ignoring the "standpoint of the concrete other," it deprives itself of much morally relevant information necessary to adequately utilize the Kantian moral tests of reversibility and universalizability In spite of these criticisms, Okin [1989] believes that Rawls' hypothetical contract procedure can be revised in such a way as to incorporate feminist concerns about justice within the household, about empathy and care and about difference.

Benhabib [1986] suggests that a "communicative ethic of need interpretations," based on Habermas' account of an ideal dialogue, is capable of overcoming what she perceives as Rawlsian monologism. It does this by acknowledging the differences of concrete others in ways compatible with the contextualist concerns that Gilligan attributes to women who utilize the ethic of care. Other feminists, such as Fraser [1986] and Young [1986], also seem attracted to such a method, although Young criticizes Habermasian descriptions of ideal dialogue for failing to take account of the affective and bodily dimensions of meaning [395]. In order to genuinely acknowledge the specific situations of concrete others, however, an *actual* rather than hypothetical dialogue seems to be required, albeit a dialogue under carefully specified conditions. But it is hard to imagine how actual dialogue could even approximate fairness in a world of unequal power, unequal access to the "socio-cultural means of interpretation and communication" [Fraser 1986] and even unequal availability of time for moral reflection and debate.

One possible alternative both to an unwelcome relativism and to what many feminists see as the pretensions of moral rationalism may be the development of a moral standpoint that is distinctively feminist. Sara Ruddick claims that such a standpoint can be found in maternal thinking [1989] but her work has been criticized by some feminists as ethnocentric [Lugones 1988] and overvaluing motherhood [Hoagland 1989]. Even if the feminist standpoint were differently identified, however, problems would remain. Standpoint epistemology derives from Marx and, at least in its Lukacian version, it seems to require an objectivist distinction between appearance and reality that is quite alien to the social constructionist tendencies in much contemporary feminism.

The controversy in feminist moral epistemology currently is so sharp that Held [1984] has suggested abandoning the search for a "unified field theory" covering all domains of life activity. However, other authors have pointed to the danger that, if a supposedly feminine "ethic of care" were limited to the realm of personal life, as Kohlberg, for instance, has suggested, it would be perceived as subordinate to the supposedly masculine "ethic of justice," just as, in contemporary society; the private is subordinate to the public.

Conclusion

Even such a limited survey as this should make it evident that feminist ethics, far from being a rigid orthodoxy, instead is a ferment of ideas and controversy, many of them echoing and deepening debates in nonfeminist ethics. The centrality of the issues and the liveliness of the on-going discussions suggest that the nineties will be a fruitful period for feminist ethics—and thus for ethics generally.

References

Adler, Jonathan, "Particularity, Gilligan and the Two-levels View: A Reply," *Ethics* 100:1 (October 1990).

Baier, Annette, "The Need for More Than Justice," *Science, Morality and Feminist Theory,* ed. Marsha Hanen and Kai Nielsen, Calgary: University of Calgary Press, 1987.

Baier, Kurt, *The Moral Point of View: A Rational Basis of Ethics,* New York: Random House, 1958.

Benhabib, Seyla, "The Generalized and the Concrete Other: The Kohlberg-Gilligan Controversy and Feminist Theory," *Praxis International* 5:4 (January 1986).

Blum, Lawrence, "Kant's and Hegel's Moral Rationalism: A Feminist Perspective," *Canadian Journal of Philosophy* 12:2 (June 1982).

Blum, Lawrence, "Particularity and Responsiveness," *The Emergence of Morality In Young Children*, eds. Jerome Kagan and Sharon Lamb, Chicago: University of Chicago Press, 1987.

Chodorow, Nancy, *The Reproduction of Mothering: Psychoanalysis and the Sociology of Gender*, Berkeley: University of California Press, 1987.

Code, Lorraine, "Experience, Knowledge and Responsibility," *Feminist Perspectives in Philosophy*, edited by Morwenna Griffiths and Margaret Whitford, Bloomington & Indianapolis: Indiana University Press, 1988.

Finley. Lucinda M., "Transcending Equality Theory: A Way Out of the Maternity and the Workplace Debate, *Columbia Law Review* 86:6 (October. 1986).

Fisk, Milton, *Ethics and Society: A Marxist Interpretation Value*, New York: New York University Press, 1980.

Fraser, Nancy, "Toward a Discourse Ethic of Solidarity," *Praxis International* 5:4 (January, 1986).

Freedman, Estelle, "Separatism as Strategy: Female Institution Building and American Feminism 1870–1930, *Feminist Studies* 5:3 (1979).

Gibson, Mary, "Consent and Autonomy," *To Breathe Freely: Risk, Consent and Air*, Totowa, NJ: Rowman & Allan-held, 1985.

Gilligan, Carol, *In a Different Voice: Psychological Theory and Women's Development*, Cambridge. MA: Harvard University Press, 1982.

Grimshaw, Jean, "Autonomy and Identity in Feminist Thinking," *Feminist Perspectives in Philosophy*, eds. Morwenna Griffiths and Margaret Whitford, Bloomington and Indianapolis: Indiana University Press, 1988.

Held, Virginia, *Rights and Goods*, New York: The Free Press, 1984.

Held, Virginia, "Non-Contractual Society," *Science, Morality and Feminist Theory*, eds. Marsha Hanen and Kai Nielsen, Calgary: University of Calgary Press, 1987.

Herman, Barbara, "Integrity and Impartiality," *The Monist*, 66:2 (April 1983).

Hill, Thomas E., Jr., "The Importance of Autonomy," *Women and Moral Theory*, eds. Eva Feder Kittay and Diana T. Meyers, Totowa, NJ: Rowman and Littlefield, 1987.

Hoagland, Sara Lucia, *Lesbian Ethics: Toward New Value*, Palo Alto, CA: Institute of Lesbian Studies, 1989.

Holmstrom, Nancy, "Firming Up Soft Determinism," *The Personalist* 58:1 (1977).

Jaggar, Alison M., *Feminist Politics and Human Nature*, Totowa, NJ: Rowman and Allanheld, 1983.

King, Ynestra, "Afterword," *Rocking the Ship of State: Toward a Feminist Peace Politics*, ed. Adrienne Harris and Ynestra King, Boulder CO: Westview Press, 1989.

Krieger, Linda J., "Through a Glass Darkly: Paradigms of Equality and the Search for a Woman's Jurisprudence," *Hypatia: A Journal of Feminist Philosophy* 2:1 (1987).

Lind, Marcia, "Hurne and Feminist Moral Theory," paper read at conference on *Explorations in Feminist Ethics: Theory and Practice*, University of Minnesota-Duluth, October 7–8, 1988.

Lugones, Maria, "The Logic of Pluralism," paper read at the annual meeting of the American Philosophical Association (Eastern Division), Washington, D.C., December 1988.

MacIntyre, Alasdair, *After Virtue: A Study in Moral Theory*, London: Duckworth, 1981.

MacKinnon, Catharine A., *Feminism Unmodified: Discourses on Life and Law*, Cambridge, MA: Harvard University Press, 1987

Meyers, Diana T., "Personal Autonomy and the Paradox of Feminine Socialization," *Journal of Philosophy* LXXXIV:11 (November, 1987).

Meyers, Diana T., "The Socialized Individual and individual Autonomy: An Intersection between Philosophy and Psychology," *Women and Moral Theory*, ed. Eva Feder Kittay and Diana T. Meyers, Totowa, NJ: Rowman & Allanheld, 1987.

Miller, Jean Baker, *Toward a New Psychology of Women*, Boston: Beacon, 1976.

Murdoch, Iris, *The Sovereignty of Good*, London: Routledge & Kegan Paul, 1970.

Noddings, Nel, *Caring: A Feminine Approach to Ethics and Moral Education*, Berkley: University of California Press, 1984.

Okin, Susan Moller, "Justice and Gender," *Philosophy and Public Affairs* 16:1, (Winter 1987).

Okin, Susan Moller, "Reason and Feeling in Thinking about Justice," *Ethics* 99:2 (January 1989).

Plumwood, Val, "Do We Need a Sex/Gender Distinction?" *Radical Philosophy* 51 (Spring 1989).

Ringelheim, Joan, "Women and the Holocaust: A Reconsideration of Research," *Signs* 10:4 (Summer 1985).

Ruddick, Sara, "Maternal Thinking," *Feminist Studies* 6:2 (Summer 1980).

Ruddick, Sara, "Preservative Love and Military Destruction: Some Reflections on Mothering and Peace," *Mothering: Essays in Feminist Theory*, ed.

Joyce Trebilcot, Totowa, NJ: Rowman and Allanheld, 1984.

Ruddick, Sara, *Maternal Thinking: Toward a Politics of Peace*, Boston: Beacon Press, 1989.

Sherwin, Susan, "A Feminist Approach to Ethics," *Resources for Feminist Research* 16:3, 1987. (Special issue on Women and Philosophy").

Somers, Christina Hoff, "Filial Morality," *The Journal of Philosophy* 83:8 (August 1986).

Spelman, Elizabeth V., *Inessential Woman: Problems of Exclusion in Feminist Thought*, Boston: Beacon, 1989.

Walker, Margaret, "Moral Understandings: Alternative 'Epistemology' for a Feminist Ethics," *Hypatia: A Journal of Feminist Philosophy* 4:2 (Summer 1989).

Weitzman, Lenore J., *The Divorce Revolution*, New York: The Free Press, 1985.

Williams, B., "A Critique of Utilitarianism," *Utilitarianism: For and Against*, Cambridge: Cambridge University Press, 1973.

Williams, B., "Morality and the Emotions," *Problems of the Self,* Cambridge: Cambridge University Press, 1973.

Williams B., "Persons, Character and Morality," "Moral Luck," and "Utilitarianism and Moral Selfindulgence," *Moral Luck*, Cambridge: Cambridge University Press, 1981.

Williams, Wendy W., "Equality's Riddle: Pregnancy and the Equal Treatment/Special Treatment Debate, *New York University Review of Law and Social Change* XIII:2(1984–5)

Young, Iris Marion, "Impartiality and the Civic Public," *Praxis International* 5:4 (January 1986).

Young, Iris Marion, "Throwing Like a Girl: A Phenomenology of Feminine Body Comportment, Motility and Spatiality," "Pregnant Embodiment: Subjectivity and Alienation," "Breast as Experience: The Look and the Feeling," *Stretching Out: Essays in Feminist Social Theory and Female Body Experience,* Bloomington: Indiana University Press, 1990.

Questions for Chapter 2

1. If we accept the claim that cultural relativism is true, does it follow that whether or not we should believe it depends on what society we live in?

2. Are people capable of acting unselfishly? If they are not capable of acting of unselfishly, does it make any sense for the ethical egoist to suggest that people ought to act selfishly? If people are capable of acting unselfishly, would this cast any doubt on the theory of ethical egoism?

3. Is there such a thing as human nature? Assuming there is, how would you go about determining what it is?

4. Are all moral actions universalizable?

5. Is it always more moral to act out of duty than out of some other motive, for example, sympathy for one's fellow humans?

6. Utilitarianism judges actions moral or immoral solely on the basis of their consequences. Is this true of any other moral theory? If so, how does that theory differ from utilitarianism.

7. It seems possible that what is considered virtuous might vary from society to society. Would this imply that virtue ethics is a form of relativism?

8. Jaggar says that "feminist approaches to ethics are distinguished by their explicit commitment to rethinking ethics with a view to correcting whatever forms of male bias it may contain." Could a nonfeminist also have an explicit commitment to purifying ethics of male bias?

9. Jaggar suggests "that feminist ethics, far from being a rigid orthodoxy, . . . is a ferment of ideas and controversy, many of them echoing and deepening debates in nonfeminist ethics." Does this in any way count against the possibility of distinguishing a distinctively feminist theory of ethics?

Case 2.1 The Life Boat[1]

On July 5, 1884, the crew of an English yacht, Thomas Dudley, Edward Stephens, Richard Parker, and another sailor surnamed Brooks, were forced to abandon ship 1,600 miles from the Cape of Good Hope during a severe storm. Richard Parker was between seventeen and eighteen years of age; the others were mature adults.

They found themselves in an open lifeboat with no supply of food except for two one-pound tins of turnips and no source of fresh water apart from any rain they could catch in their oilskin capes. For three days they had nothing to eat except for the turnips. On the fourth day they caught a small turtle. By the twelfth day the turtle had been entirely consumed and they were unable to catch any further food. They continued to drift on the open ocean roughly 1,000 miles from land.

On the eighteenth day, July 23, after having been seven days without food and five without water, Dudley and Stephens approached Brooks suggesting that someone, this being understood to be Parker, should be sacrificed to save the rest. Brooks disagreed and Parker was not consulted.

On the nineteenth day, July 24, Dudley suggested to Stephens and Brooks that lots should be cast concerning who should be sacrificed to save the rest. Brooks again refused to consent and Parker was again not consulted. No drawing of lots took place. Later in the day Dudley and Stephens spoke of their families and suggested it

would be better to kill Parker who had no dependents. Dudley proposed that if no help had arrived by the following morning, Parker should be killed.

No help arrived the following day. Dudley told Brooks to take a nap and made signs to Stephens and Brooks that Parker would be killed. Stephens agreed to the act, but Brooks again disagreed. Parker, who at no time had agreed to being killed, was lying at the bottom of the boat, helpless and greatly weakened by famine and the drinking of sea water.

Dudley offered a prayer asking forgiveness for them all if either of them should be tempted to commit a rash act, and that their souls might be saved. Subsequently, Dudley, with the consent of Stephens, went to the boy, and, telling him that his time had come, cut his throat. The three man fed upon Parker's body and blood for four days. On the fourth day they were picked up by a passing vessel.

It is clear that if the men had not fed upon Parker, they would not have survived to be rescued, but would have died of famine. It also seems clear that Parker, being in a much weaker condition, was likely to have died before them.

1. What are the implications of the various theories of morality concerning the morality of what occurred?

2. Was Brooks guilty of any wrongdoing?

3. If it was clear that Parker was going to die no matter what, would this affect the morality of what occurred?

[1]Selected from The Queen v. Dudley & Stephens, 1884, 14 *Law Reports Queen's Bench Division* 273.

Further Readings for Chapter 2

Jonathan Harrison, ed., *Challenges to Morality* (New York: Macmillan, 1993).

Kenneth F. Rogerson, ed., *Introduction to Ethical Theory* (Toronto: Holt, Rinehart & Winston, 1991).

James Sterba, ed., *Contemporary Ethics* (Englewood Cliffs, NJ: Prentice-Hall, 1989).

INFOTRAC COLLEGE EDITION To learn more about the topics from this chapter, you can use the following words to conduct an electronic search on InfoTrac College Edition, an online library of journals. Here you will find a multitude of articles from various sources and perspectives: *www.infotrac-college.com/wadsworth/access.html*

ethical relativism

virtue ethics

natural law ethics

Kantianism

utilitarianism

feminist ethics

Chapter 3

Bargaining, Due Process, and Employee Participation

Introduction

FREEDOM OF SPEECH and conscience are highly valued in Western society, as is the right to due process. This emphasis on civil liberty has not, however, typically extended to the workplace. In the United States, a country in which citizens are guaranteed the right to vote and participate in political decisions, there is in the private sector no universal recognition of employee rights to freedom of speech, due process, privacy, or job security. Although the right to collective bargaining has become more firmly established, there are many who defend the doctrine of employment-at-will, namely, the presumed right of an employer to hire, fire, promote, or demote without cause or notice. The issue of whether the restrictions customarily placed on employees in the workplace are consistent with the emphasis placed on due process and individual freedom in other areas of life is an important one and has begun to receive a great deal of attention.

Those who argue that such restrictions are justified employ several arguments. First, they argue that there is a fundamental difference between constitutional rights and proposed employee rights. The civil rights guaranteed constitutionally concern the public sphere and are largely negative, that is, they guarantee not that one will possess certain goods, but that one will not be unjustly interfered with in how one orders one's life. By contrast, presumed employee rights to job security, due process, and participation in organization of the workplace concern private agreements between individuals and are largely positive, that is, they guarantee not simply noninterference in ordering one's life, but rather entitlement to certain goods. There is then, they argue, no inconsistency in asserting the existence of civil rights, but denying the existence of proposed employee rights.

Second, it is often claimed that if we are to guarantee civil rights, it must be recognized that agreements between employer and employee are essentially private matters. If we are to protect the freedom of the individuals involved, then each must have the right to enter into or terminate the agreement at will. The doctrine of employment-at-will, it is argued, does not threaten but rather guarantees the recognition of civil liberties in the workplace.

Third, it is argued that citizens have a constitutional right to control their property. Recognition of this right seems to suggest control over who enters or works on that property.

Fourth, it is often argued that proposed employee rights are incompatible with the flexibility required for corporate efficiency and economic growth. If business is to prosper and be able to respond to changing market conditions, flexible employment practices are necessary.

None of these arguments is beyond criticism. It is not so easy to draw the public/private, negative rights/positive rights distinction as proponents of these arguments suggest. It can plausibly be argued that the employment-at-will doctrine of being able to fire an employee without notice for no reason violates the constitutional right of not being unjustly interfered with in the process of ordering one's life. Equally, appeals to property rights of employers are suspect. Property rights may justify not hiring someone in the first place, but once a person has been hired, the employment-at-will doctrine cannot be justified on the basis of property rights unless one is prepared to argue for the very implausible view that employees are a type of property. Finally, it is far from clear that rejecting employment-at-will negatively affects economic viability.

Perhaps a more helpful approach, at least in the context of our present discussion, is to step back a pace and ask the more general question of why we take the idea of individuals having rights seriously. Casting light on this more general issue may help in deciding what we should say regarding more specific questions concerning employee rights.

Many thinkers ground rights in the fact that they seem to be a necessary condition of human autonomy. Thus, for example, they argue that we cannot respect the dignity and independence of an individual unless we acknowledge the importance of allowing him or her to speak freely. A consequence of this view is that an individual's freedom of speech is not absolute. One is not, on the basis of freedom of speech, permitted to yell "Fire" in a crowded theater. Given that freedom of speech is only justified insofar as it promotes human autonomy, instances where speaking in a certain way clearly interferes with another individual's ability to order his or her life cannot be justified by appealing to one's right to speak freely.

The question, then, is not whether limits should be put on rights; it is evident they must be if the autonomy of more than one individual is to be recognized and valued. The question, rather, is, How do we balance the apparently competing interests of autonomous individuals? How do we balance the legitimate interests of the employee, conceived as an autonomous agent worthy of dignity and respect, with those of the employer, conceived as an autonomous agent equally worthy of dignity and respect? An employee's right to free speech cannot be conceived in such a way that it allows selling valuable confidential information to a competitor, thus undermining the employer's ability to act autonomously. Neither, however, should an employer's freedom to use or dispose of his or her property be conceived in such a way that it undermines any possibility of employees acting autonomously.

The basic goal is to respect the autonomy of both employer and employee. How this is to be done depends largely on particular circumstances. In general, employees need to beware of emphasizing their rights to a degree where the legitimate interests of employers are not respected. Similarly, employers need to beware of ignoring basic rights that are a condition of treating employees as autonomous individuals.

Although the concept of individuals having rights is important, it tends to have the drawback of encouraging individuals to think egocentrically. Too often "rights talk" is conceived only in terms of what one can legitimately claim from others. Unsurprisingly, this type of focus easily leads to an adversarial relationship. In many instances, it may be more helpful for each party not to focus on his or her rights, but rather to ask what it means to treat the other as a person worthy of respect and consideration. Patricia Werhane puts this point very well when she writes

> Respect for employees as human beings . . . is persuasive for granting employees rights to fair treatment in the workplace. By "fair treatment" I mean the right to be treated as an equal, and to enjoy basic rights such as those of freedom, self-development, and control of one's life. Moreover, and this point, too, is obvious, trust ordinarily flourishes between parties when there is an atmosphere of respect, openness, and the free exchange of ideas. By trust I mean, at a minimum, respect for and belief in the reliability, honesty, competence, and integrity of the party with which one is dealing. Having trust in someone or in an institution entails that being vulnerable or taking risks for that person or institution will be reciprocated, recognized, rewarded, or at least, not betrayed.[1]

The importance of mutual respect and trust between employer and employee is explored in the first two readings of this chapter. In her article "Towards Taming the Labor-Management Frontier: A Strategic Marketing Framework," Susan Higgins argues that labor and management must move beyond their traditionally adversarial relationship. She proposes a relationship based on what is known in service industries as "internal marketing." This model suggests that management should focus on satisfying not only its external customers, that is, those who buy the product, but also its internal customers, that is, its employees who create the product. By focusing on its internal customers and developing a relation of mutual trust, management will be in a position to provide better customer satisfaction for its external customers.

Accepting this model means that labor and management would adopt what Higgins calls the Mutual Trust Principle and the Efficacy Principle. Summarized, the Mutual Trust Principle states that you must give the other person good grounds for trusting you if you ask that person to take a risk, and the Efficacy Principle states that you should not ask another person to take a risk if that risk would only benefit those not willing to take the same risk. These principles are a basis for developing trust between labor and management. Higgins argues that, if implemented, these principles would lead to a climate of trust beneficial to both labor and management.

In our second reading, Frederick Post addresses the issue of employee-employer antagonism that so often influences not only the collective bargaining process, but also the day-to-day working environment. In his article "Collaborative Collective Bargaining: Toward an Ethically Defensible Approach to Labor

1. Patricia H. Werhane, "Justice and Trust," *Journal of Business Ethics,* 21, 1999, pp. 237–249.

Negotiations," Post argues that present methods of collective bargaining are based on an adversarial model that fosters resentment and immoral tactics of bargaining. In its place, he proposes a model of what he calls "collaborative collective bargaining" which fosters a nonadversarial environment and encourages truth and candor in the negotiation process.

Our third reading takes up in a direct way the question of whether the traditional doctrine of employment-at-will (a doctrine that has been rejected in Great Britain, its country of origin) can be justified. In "Employee Rights and the Doctrine of At Will Employment," David Hiley examines the traditional view that an employer has an unrestricted right to terminate employees. He argues that, although this view has a long history in law, it is ethically suspect and the burden of proof rests on those trying to defend it on moral grounds. He examines three arguments that have been employed to support employment-at-will: (1) that it is well grounded in common-law tradition, (2) that it is implied by considerations of contract mutuality between employee and employer, and (3) that it is an extension of an employer's property rights. Of these three, he finds the third most convincing, but he does not feel that, even in this case, it will support the right of an employer to dismiss an employee arbitrarily.

Alternative models of the employee-employer relationship, grounded in the concept of employee participation, are gaining increasing attention and acceptance in business. Although there are different forms and degrees of employee participation, the basic idea in such models is that employees have some sort of share in the businesses that employ them. This, it is suggested, will enable management and labor to move beyond their traditionally adversarial roles to a position of common interest.

In our final reading in this chapter, John Kaler explores the different forms employee participation may take. In his article "Understanding Participation," he defines employee participation as any arrangement under which employees have a share in some aspect of a business. He notes that the concept of employee participation can cover a wide spectrum, ranging from legally entrenched systems of codetermination in which employees have an equal voice in the running of the business to modest and purely voluntary schemes of profit sharing. Given that it can cover such a wide range of options, it is useful to develop a schema of the various models of employment that incorporate employee participation.

Kaler's initial step in developing such a schema is to distinguish between models of employment in which employee participation takes the form of a share in decision making and models of employment in which employee participation takes the form of a share in profits. He terms the first type of employee participation "operational" and the second type "financial." Within operational models, he distinguishes various degrees of employee involvement ranging from weak forms of employee consultation in decision making to very strong forms of employee codetermination in decision making. With financial models of employee participation, he distinguishes between weaker models of shared income and stronger models of shared ownership.

He goes on to distinguish the motive for employee participation from the form employee participation takes. He suggests that, although in principle any form of participation could arise out of any motive, in practice employees will urge participation in the interests of fairness and employers will urge participation in the interests of efficiency.

Kaler also distinguishes employee participation from collective bargaining. He argues for this in two ways. His first argument is that, despite certain similarities, collective bargaining and employee participation are essentially different, inasmuch as collective bargaining presupposes that employer and employee relate as two opposing sides, whereas employee participation presupposes a unity based on a shared interest.

His second argument is that employee participation is organizational, whereas collective bargaining is extraorganizational. Employee participation involves the day-to-day shared arrangements of the management structures and property entitlements whereby a business operates. Collective bargaining, on the other hand, operates outside these shared structures and is therefore extraorganizational and nonparticipatory.

Kaler concludes his article by suggesting that employee participation is different from workers' ownership or control of the workplace. Although both types of employee participation lessen the extent of worker subordination, they both preserve the subordination of workers to managers inherent within management structures, and the subordination of labor to capital inherent in the hiring process. Employee participation's relationship to capitalism, therefore, is reformist rather than revolutionary.

Towards Taming the Labor–Management Frontier: A Strategic Marketing Framework

SUSAN H. HIGGINS

RECENT HEADLINES in the business news taken collectively portend jarring structural changes in nearly every sector of the U.S. Economy. From Sears to May Company in retail, from IBM to aerospace in high-tech, from Babcock & Wilcox to sewing machines in manufacturing, we seem to be hemorrhaging blue collar and managerial jobs. Reasons for the layoffs and plant closings are attributed to diverse causes including years of recessionary pressure, the end of the cold war and diminishing demand for military goods; and new opportunities in Mexico as well as other off-shore locations.

As the dust begins to settle from this massive "reinvention" of the corporation, there is an urgent need for business practitioners and academicians to address the ethical dilemmas posed by the new business landscape. We need to collaborate and find the appropriate mechanisms to ensure that U.S. industries are competing in the global economy in a manner that is both fiscally and socially responsible.

This paper focuses on the examination of current trends at work in the U.S. marketplace and proposes a strategic framework for the ethical conciliation of the traditionally adversarial relationship between big business and labor unions. The underlying premise is that we, as a society, will be better off with both of these institutions—corporations *and* labor unions—than without them.

Current Trends

EMPLOYMENT PRACTICES

The U.S. economy is increasingly services oriented, union membership is declining, and there is a dramatic rise in the use of contingent (part-time, temporary) workers.

According to one source: America's largest employer is no longer GM or IBM, but Manpower, Inc., a temporary employment agency; in 1992,

From Journal of Business Ethics *15: 475–485, 1996.* © *1996 Kluwer Academic Publishers. Printed in the Netherlands. Reprinted with permission from Kluwer Academic Publishers.*

while the U.S. economy was generally stagnant, temp jobs grew 17%; one of the largest financial services companies in the country will soon have fewer than 20% of its employees working full-time (Walljasper, 1993: p. 154). Furthermore, recent statistics show that the hotbeds of job growth between November, 1992 and December, 1993 are health care jobs (up 3.7%), financial services (up 2.8%) and autos and trucks (up 4.0%). While these increases are moderately promising, consider the rise in temporary services in the same period of time: 19.1% (Smart and Gleckman, 1993: p. 35). One author interprets the statistics to issue a rather cynical and bleak warning to policy makers: "Lawmakers who believe that the federal debt is America's biggest problem need to trade in some of their frequent flyer points for a ticket to the real America, where they can taste the despair hanging over city avenues and small town streets. Hopelessness is in the air because people know there's a slim chance of getting a good, steady job that offers health benefits and decent pay" (Walljasper, 1993: p. 155).

Bartkowiak (1993) also examines the trend toward part-time employment as a low wage/high turnover hiring philosophy. She argues that this is a short-run cost-cutting solution that is neither advantageous for the company in the long run, nor societally ethical. The consequence of hiring temporary or part-time workers ultimately will be higher costs to the company (initial training, employee theft, absenteeism) and a lack of employee loyalty inhibiting productivity and quality. Furthermore, the societal consequences of the low wage/high turnover model will be a permanently entrenched core of poor people with little or no savings, retirement benefits or medical insurance. The quality of life for these employees and their children is being severely damaged by this trend and Bartkowiak concludes ". . . that many businesses are willing to ignore the needs of the employee for a short term increase in profits for the company. Thus legislation will be required to alter the business practice of adopting a part-time employment policy" (p. 815).

UNIONISM

A concurrent or perhaps consequential trend in the business environment is the decline in union mem-

bership. Unions represent only 11.5% of the private labor force, down from 16.8% ten years ago and 35% forty years ago (Noble, 1993). The tremendous loss of manufacturing jobs, the traditional union stronghold, has not been viewed as alarming, because of the rapid increase in services-related jobs. The macroeconomic data show a steady decrease in national unemployment, with 18 million new jobs created over the past decade. The Government data mask the fact that most of these new jobs are either part-time, temporary, and/or in traditionally lower-paying service jobs. The problem then, is that ". . . two or even three of those jobs together don't provide the same kind of economic security as one of the old-fashioned, full-time, well-paying union jobs that we're losing in droves" (Walljasper, 1993: p.454). . . .

It should be noted that the decline in union membership reflects the elimination of union-held jobs, rather than the members deserting. The result is that a large number of previously well employed people with highly technical, industry-specific skills are scrambling to find janitorial or odd-job employment simply to keep their families afloat. The once proud, blue-collar elite are being told to cede their pride of place to an ascendent new class—temps or "just-in-time" workers. The workers who can be used when needed and then discarded. Corporations argue that the flexibility afforded by these hiring practices, and not having to deal with the cumbersome restraints of union work rules and collective bargaining is the best way to remain profitable, competitive and adaptable in the turbulent world economy.

From the moral and ethical perspective, however, by adopting the non-union, temporary worker philosophy are we not in danger of polarizing U.S. society into an elite cadre of corporate managers and professionals existing inside a nation of permanently underemployed and disenfranchised workers? As a society, we must consider the reflections of one United Auto Workers member: "[Our local union's] . . . members have decreased in membership over the last two years by over 55%. Many good workers have lost their jobs. The jet engine business calls it downsizing, consolidation, streamlining—but the effects are still the same. Union members are losing jobs. What will become of the working class? Only the Lord knows" (*Solidarity*, 1993: p. 5).

INTERNAL MARKETS

A third trend contributing to the ethical dilemma facing U.S. business, in my opinion, is the surge of importance afforded to the quest for total quality through employee involvement programs. From a marketing perspective, the basic premise is intuitively simple: When *every* employee is actively focused on delivering superior value to its market, customer loyalty will increase and profits will rise. But in order to achieve this self-reinforcing system, employees must be involved, empowered and participative within the organization.

Internal marketing, a concept originally applied to service organizations, involves focusing a company's marketing efforts not only on its external customers, but also on its employees as internal customers. The underlying tenet of the model is that by coordinating the efforts of marketers and human resource managers to identify and address the needs and concerns of employees the work environment and morale will improve and thus service to external customers will also improve (Lovelock, 1992: pp. 29–30).

The importance of the employee-customer relationship in a service setting is critical to building customer loyalty. For example, when a guest encounters a problem at a hotel, how the complaint is handled by the employee behind the front desk is far more important to the guest's overall perception of the hotel than any policy written by the owners/executives. Thus, the internal marketing agenda is represented graphically as a pyramid with management at the top, with internal customers and external customers poised as equal recipients of marketing efforts along the base.

The importance of creating a company that is conducive to employee satisfaction in order to achieve customer satisfaction has given rise to a plethora of employee involvement programs in corporate America. Unfortunately, these have been primarily ad hoc programs rather than evolving as an integral component of a company's basic business strategy (Reichheld, 1993: p. 64).

The tenets of internal marketing have been expanded beyond the services sector to a means of improving new product development and implementing cross-functional integration especially with respect to R&D and marketing (Gupta and Rogers, 1991; Moenaert *et al.,* 1994). Indeed, one author looking to the future of work in our society. feels that any distinction between services marketing and product marketing will become moot: "Truly understanding the emerging economy takes a change of mind-set or, inevitably, of paradigm: from thinking of business as making things or churning out product, to realizing that it consists instead of furnishing services, even within what has traditionally been thought of as manufacturing" (Kiechel, 1993: p. 51).

An Ethical Dilemma

The issue which must be addressed is a growing schizophrenia lurking in the business/academic community. On the one hand, the management and marketing journals are replete with articles espousing the positive impact of employee participation programs, empowerment and interfunctional integration as means of maximizing quality, customer satisfaction and, therefore, business performance. On the other hand, the popular press and business newspapers are daily reporting the corporate rush to downsize, out-source, and hire contingent workers in order to survive and flourish in a fiercely competitive global economy. The demise of labor unions is heralded by many as the last gasp of a "dinosaur" (Wiesandanger, 1994: p. 56).

Taken separately, each of these trends can be seen as sound, logical and ethical results of skillful management decision-making in the wake of changing technology and international competition. However, taken collectively, the premise becomes absurd. Can we, as managers, really expect our remaining work-force to trust us? To trust that, as a laborer on the shop floor, input and participation in meeting quality goals or customer satisfaction goals will be appreciated and rewarded? Or will the workers view management attempts at "teamwork" as a means of increasing productivity in order to eliminate more full-time jobs? The chasm created between management and the hourly employee by the convergence of these trends is certainly exacerbated by years of mistrust and ill-will at the union-management interface.

The moral analogy suggested by corporate America's scramble to change is that of talking marriage and thinking one-night stand. A recent article states, "The rush to downsize and replace long-time employees with temps and part-time workers makes corporate rhapsodies to empowerment, partnership, and teamwork so much sweet talk" (Kuttner, 1993: p. 16).

If the fundamental idea of employee involvement programs is to "unleash the energy, creativity and talents of all employees" (Boone and Kurtz, 1994: pp. 2–26), then it is important both strategically and ethically to extend the focus beyond managerial level integration studies to the labor-management interface.

Strategic and Ethical Considerations

The strategic importance to U.S. businesses and labor alike of conciliation and cooperation is starkly highlighted by the recently published study conducted by the government sponsored Dunlap commission. The study is based on a nationwide series of hearings over the past year (May, 1993–April, 1994), seeking to document the current relationship between American labor and management. As noted in one newspaper account, ". . . the report is expected to declare that the United States will never reach its potential in global economic competition unless it replaces current patterns of labor-management conflict with a more peaceful model" (Everett, 1993: p. 1). The spectre of falling short, of being a mediocre player in the new world order of things, should serve as a clarion call for all of the players in the U.S. workplace to strive for new ways to approach one another. The Dunlap report is expected to set the stage for sweeping changes in U.S. labor laws for the first time in sixty years (*ibid*). Certainly, legislative adjustments to improve workplace relations are needed. But forward-thinking corporate executives and labor-leaders alike must now seize the moment to crush the mental walls that have divided them for decades; or no amount of legislation will be fruitful. . . .

The ethical imperative of labor-management conciliation is simple. Labor unions represent the voice of the American blue-collar middle-class. If we allow that voice to fade, we will be left with the discordant cacophony of individuals struggling to survive. From a utilitarian perspective, U.S. society will be better off with a cooperative equilibrium between labor and management. Lynn Williams argues, "Growing up during the Depression watching things spiral downward has shaped my views. . . . The existence of the labor movement has helped prevent a repeat of the 1930s. Unions provide a reason for companies to grapple with maintaining wages. Left alone, capitalism's natural inclination is to hack away. In fact, capitalism needs the checks and balances that labor provides and that the U.S. system recognizes in so many other areas" (Noble, 1994: p. 120).

One could argue that the social conscience of business executives and the quest for quality through employee participation programs will assure that employees are treated fairly, and that the need for labor unions is obsolete. However, it is the institutional continuity provided by the labor union, that should allow the greatest degree of freedom for each individual to participate fully in the workplace. For example, Sidney Rubinstein, a Princeton, New Jersey consultant who has helped corporations develop labor-management "teams" since the late 1950s, estimates that four-fifths of union-less programs fail. "Without the institutional continuity provided by the labor union, programs depend on the enthusiasm of influential individuals. And as influential individuals tend to come and go, so does support for the participation concept" (Noble, 1994: p. 122). From the individual worker's perspective, "The Union empowers us to say what we feel without having to face repercussions. It helps us build a better product" (*Solidarity*, 1993: p. 19).

The Mutual Trust Perspective

Crossing the "great divide" between labor and management necessitates an understanding of why such intransigence exists on both sides. The use of terms such as "armed camps" and "religious wars" illustrates the traditional war-like posture which has characterized this relationship for decades; and which must now be tempered if we hope to compete most effectively in the global economy.

The current situation in labor relations may be viewed in light of a theory of morality in practice put forward by Dees and Cramton (1991). The premise of this theory is that "shrewd" (or deceptive bargaining occurs, at least in part, because no basis for mutual trust exists between the parties involved. Further, the absence of a basis for trust provides the justification for defensive, self-interested behavior. The Mutual Trust perspective relies on two simple principles, which go a long way in understanding why there is continuing friction rather than cooperation between labor and management. These two principles are: (Dees and Cramton, 1991: p. 144)

> Mutual Trust Principle: It is unfair to require an individual to take a significant risk or incur a significant cost out of respect for the interests or moral rights of others, if that individual has no reasonable grounds for trusting that the relevant others will . . . take the same risk or make the same sacrifice.
>
> Efficacy Principle: It is unfair to require an individual to take a significant risk, or incur a significant cost out of respect for the moral rights of others if . . . it would benefit only those who would not willingly incur the same risk or cost.

Because years of adversarial negotiations (punctuated by strikes, lock-outs, etc.) form the background against which current labor relations exist in many companies, neither side trusts the other. The practical difficulty of creating grounds for mutual trust in this hostile environment creates a "moral frontier," beyond which each party must be concerned first and foremost with self-preservation.

Viewed in light of Mutual Trust theory, the clash between labor and management over the adoption of employee participation teams, for example, is predictable. Management sees the implementation of teamwork as an integral part of improving quality and productivity, reducing waste and contributing to long-run viability and profitability. It should be obvious to the worker on the shop floor that her cooperation in following these initiatives will lead to more job security and higher wages as conditions improve. (Furthermore, if you don't do what we suggest, we'll be forced to lay off more workers and we will all be worse off. Trust us.)

The hourly workers at their machines hear all the exhortations toward quality goals as management propaganda, not communications. Probably just another fad. If we become more productive will we be out of a job? Will we benefit from giving you our best ideas, or will our contributions line *your* golden parachutes? How come if you expect us to trust your vision of quality teams, you didn't trust us to be involved with evaluating and overseeing the process to begin with?

Certainly the negotiations and transactions revolving around these issues constitute the pragmatic reality of the Mutual Trust perspective. Because the foundation of trust is absent between labor and management, there is no moral obligation on either side to take a risk. Self-preservation strategies will prevail

It is interesting to consider anecdotal examples illustrating that when both sides realize that self-preservation strategies *require* honest cooperation between management and labor, positive results can be dramatic. In 1988, Akzo Salt was ready to close a rundown, money-losing plant in Michigan. Labor relations at this site were horrible—and reflected the fact that this plant ranked last in the company for productivity, safety, quality and efficiency. One of the general managers of the company put it simply, "Both sides really hated each other" (Wiesendanger, 1994: p. 52). Given this state of affairs, neither the union nor the managers had anything left to lose by agreeing to a last-ditch new approach to preserve everyone's job—cooperation rather than confrontation. Management was willing to "risk" upgrading the facilities, production machinery and training and to *listen* to employees' suggestions in the process: the union was willing to incur wage concessions and modified work rules to permit greater flexibility and work teams. Results of this teamwork within three years: ". . . lost-time injuries on the job plunged from an average of 21 a year to zero. Customer complaints reduced by over 80%. Formal employee grievances dropped from an average of 40 to 50% a year to just one. And in spite of pay increases and higher prices for raw materials, the plant's operating costs declined by 15%" (*ibid*).

This example serves to illustrate that when both sides share the same irrefutable information and, thus, knowledge about the "state of nature" in which they are operating, cynicism and mistrust may be successfully replaced by cooperative endeavors. From the moral pragmatist's view, the benefits derived from cooperative efforts to improve on the state of nature "provide the impetus . . . for risk-taking in hopes of reducing the undesirable features of the moral frontier" (Dees and Cramton, 1991: p. 157).

The Mutual Trust view allows us to justify, or at least understand, why unions and managers continue to resist one another as partners. It also offers a practical springboard to improve the situation, based on the Trust Building Principle of the theory: "When mutual trust is absent or weak, individuals should be willing to take modest risks or incur modest costs, in an effort to build or reinforce the trust required to secure moral action in the future" (*ibid*).

Practical implications of the Mutual Trust model involve relationship building and development of feelings of group identity through more frequent communications and informal contact. "Sometimes all that is needed is for the parties to get together on a regular basis to share concerns and other information relevant to an upcoming negotiation" (*ibid*, p. 160). Actionable strategies, creating a climate of trust for these things to occur, seems to be the fundamental first step which union leaders and corporate executives must tackle on the way to realizing true labor-management cooperation.

Internal Marketing Strategies

The concept of internal marketing as a strategic competitive advantage in services marketing offers a framework for labor and management to begin creating "climates of trust." After all, one may view the employee-employer relationship as a service transaction: the union machinist is providing her labor services which result in a physical product; the company in exchange is providing employment services which result in a paycheck, health and retirement benefits.

From this perspective, management and labor can view the relationship building process within the structure of the internal marketplace. Just as the relationship between an external (paying) customer and the company is the focus of the "4 Ps" of marketing, the relationship between employee and employer is the focus of an internal marketing mix. Following are suggestions which may provide some actionable strategies for improving management-labor relations, based on the internal marketing mix perspective.

Product. Consider, for example, a company which manufacturers wheels and brakes for aircraft. To management, these parts are sold according to their core benefit (safe and reliable stopping); tangible features (made of steel and titanium); and augmented services associated with the product (quick delivery, replacement guarantees). To the machinist who actually makes the various components of the wheels and brakes, the product is defined by some combination of axes, inside and outside diameters, tooling requirements, and the quantities expected by his supervisor.

Internal marketing suggests that management communication with the machinists and other direct laborers shift, from an emphasis on product quantity expectations to an understanding of the "big picture." That is, give the workers the opportunity to see where this torque tube or clutch assembly fits into the big picture of airline safety— *and* company survival. This requires training programs, on company time, for workers. The result will be an understanding of the importance of efficiency and quality as long-run job security for *all* employees; and ease the mistrust that increased productivity will only lead to more layoffs.

An additional understanding of the product, for both the workers and the customers, may be promoted by worker participation at trade shows. This approach has been tried by some progressive U.S. companies and UAW locals who participated in the 1994 North American Auto Show in Detroit. From a manager's viewpoint, "Who better to explain to the customer the ins and outs of the new vehicles than the people who build them?" (*Solidarity*, 1994: p. 19). From a 20-year union employee, "Being in the plant you don't have a perception of the customer. It makes you feel good to see the connection by meeting the buyers" (*ibid*).

Promotion. The need to effectively communicate new ideas and new processes to internal markets is just as important as advertising new products to external customers. The same care and attention must be paid to promotion strategies targeted to workers, if managers expect them to "buy into" new ways of doing things.

For example, management may want to implement quality initiatives involving employee participation teams. Supervisors then tell the workers how this is going to work, how the teams will be made up, and when the teams will meet. The thrust of this approach is to dictate that workers participate in teams because the boss says you have to. It is no wonder that the workers are cynical and cooperation is minimal. One worker sums it up ". . . I'm aware of management's attempt to force participation in programs that tout 'flexibility' and 'worker participation' with no more participation than to assist in deciding what color to paint the restroom walls" (*Solidarity,* 1993: p. 5).

Taking the internal marketing view, management has the opportunity to win cooperation from the union for the participation program by effectively promoting its benefits. Just as consumers buy products that promise to benefit them in some way, workers will "buy" management proposals if there is an explicit benefit for them to do so. Thus, before trying to implement a participation program, management should get the union involved in the planning process. By making evident the core benefits of successful employee involvement programs—job security and/or potential monetary gains from meeting quality goals—the odds are much greater that workers will accept and embrace the challenge.

Price. To the external market, the price of a good or service serves as a signal of value between buyers and sellers. And when buyers are convinced that the perceived value of the product exceeds the perceived cost, the purchase is made. When the post-use evaluation of the product is positive (e.g. the benefits far outweigh the costs), customers feel that they have received superior value, and will likely tell others and remain a loyal customer. On the other hand, when customers find that the purchase cost more and delivered fewer benefits than expected, they are likely to feel angry and misled. In this case, customers may simply choose not to deal with the supplier again, or seek restitution for being misrepresented. "Ethical managers seek to provide full disclosure of all costs associated with using a service, and carefully scrutinize advertising claims and sales presentations to ensure that customers are not misled" (Lovelock, 1991: p. 237).

Taking an internal marketing view, senior managers seeking to win labor cooperation and enthusiasm for employee participation programs can consider this as a transaction: if the product which management is selling is the concept of participation and teamwork, then in addition to making the core benefits evident to labor, costs must also be considered. Obviously, by maximizing the perceived benefits and minimizing the perceived costs of this transaction, managers will be more likely to win acceptance for the proposals.

What are these "'costs" to workers which must be considered? There is no monetary exchange involved, but there are several other key costs that may be incurred, including time, physical efforts, and most importantly, psychic costs (Lovelock, 1991: p. 236). From a union worker's perspective, the time spent attending team meetings represents an opportunity cost. If the perceived benefit to him of such meetings does not exceed the opportunity cost of working at his machine, then the process will be perceived as a "poor value." Likewise, if the team approach requires the machinist to be responsible for running additional equipment, then he must perceive that the physical effort to do so will be more than outweighed by the benefits which will result.

Perhaps the greatest costs to be considered in the context of labor relations are what Lovelock (1991: p. 236) described as psychic costs: mental effort, feelings of inadequacy or even fear. In asking workers to "purchase" management's view of quality initiatives, efforts must be made to allay many unions' view that any ". . . formal systems that foster direct contact between workers and management are deliberate challenges to their role as go-between" (Wiesendanger, 1994: p. 53). Indeed, having the participation-team approach forced into place caused one local union leader to denounce teams as "un-American" (Noble, 1993: p. 122). While this resistance may be seen by some as a stubborn, close-minded reaction, and an indication that unions prefer adversarial relations to cooperation, there may be a more rational explanation for senior managers to consider: workers simply don't see what they will get in return for what they're asked to give.

One actionable strategy to minimize the psychic costs involved with implementing labor-management cooperation is through information sharing. In many cases, workers have very limited access to their company's financial and production figures. Thus, they are left to wonder and speculate on how the company wastes money, gives huge salaries and bonuses to executives, and whether management is telling the truth about quality goals or has some ulterior motives behind its actions (Noble, 1993: p. 121).

Anecdotal evidence exists that an "open-book" management and worker education approach has positive results. Springfield Re-Manufacturing, located in Springfield, Missouri was recently honored by the Business Enterprise Trust for "marrying skillful management and social conscience"

(Steinfels, 1993: p. 7). This company, which was a failing plant in 1979, has grown to 750 employees from 170, and increased annual sales from $21 million to $73 million in the same time period. The basis for this turnaround, as recounted in the *Wall Street Journal:*

> Instead of using numbers secretly to turn workers into rivals or into machines Mr. Stack [the senior executive] used numbers candidly to let workers educate themselves and participate intelligently in a collective effort.
>
> If knowledge is power, Mr. Stack was willing to share it. Bonuses ceased to be a mysterious instrument of management control and became reasonable incentives once everyone could understand their basis. Productivity soared, and so did cooperation" (Steinfels, 1993: p. 7).

By allowing workers to have access to, really understanding and discussing ". . . all the numbers that measure the company's finances and all the production figures that support them . . ." (*ibid*), the workers will clearly perceive that the benefits of cooperation more than outweigh its costs.

Place. The fourth "P" of external marketing, focuses on the effective and efficient distribution of products and services from manufacturer or service provider to the end user. Translated into the internal setting of the labor-management interface, the focus is on mechanisms for effective and efficient distribution of cooperative programs.

First and foremost, the literature suggests that for cooperative programs to be truly successful, they must have the commitment of time and resources from the very top of the company on down (Noble, 1993; Kohli and Jaworski, 1990; Jaworski and Kohil, 1994). Assuming then that senior managers are seeking ways to "distribute" information and encourage innovative participation formats to the direct labor force, what methods are available? First, internal employee research can help identify worker attitudes and perceptions concerning the current work environment and the way in which work-related tasks are currently performed. From this baseline of information training sessions can be molded to introduce participation concepts in a manner which is responsive to worker concerns.

Beyond formal training sessions, managers may consider more informal channels for "distributing" or communicating commitment to cooperation.

These may include personal conversations, newsletters, direct mail or videotaped presentations (Lovelock, 1991: p. 234).

Methods suggested to enhance cross-functional managerial relations may be equally useful in distributing ideas across the labor-management chasm. Kohli and Jaworski (1990) propose social interaction opportunities such as interdepartmental lunches, and sports leagues that required mixed-department teams. More advanced efforts include the exchange of employees across departments, cross-department training programs, and senior department managers speeding a day with executives in other departments.

By extending these strategies beyond the managerial level to include union leaders at the local level as well as workers on the shop floor, the result will be to "foster an understanding of each others' personalities . . . their culture, and their particular perspectives" (Kohli and Jaworski, 1990: p. 15).

Conclusion

Many questions remain about ways to tame the particular "moral frontier" which exists today at the management-labor interface, particularly in light of current trends toward the use of contingent employees and declining labor union membership.

The rise in the use of part-time, temporary employees with no benefits under the guise of corporate flexibility poses a long-run threat to the fabric of our society. Worker loyalty and allegiance are rapidly being supplanted by cynicism and detachment. The decline in union membership and influence exacerbates the problem, tipping the balance of power precariously away from the needs and concerns of the individual factory worker.

Prevailing labor tensions underlying the domestic economy, coupled with the just-in-time hiring bent of many employers, present challenges which, if ignored, may well relegate the U.S. to minor league player status in world competitiveness. The growing gulf between high-wage and low-wage American workers must be addressed before the blue-collar middle class disappears entirely. Surely labor law reform is appropriate, given the changes that have rocked the U.S. workplace over the past decade.

But over and above the importance of the law, labor and management must find mechanisms to achieve a *partnership* with one another if we are to gain a sustainable global competitive advantage. "In this new world order of labor relations, both sides agree they want more productivity, job security, mutual respect and a safe workplace. Then they sit down together and figure out how to achieve it. Both parties understand that if we're going to survive we have to move beyond sneering at each other" (Hershey, 1993: p. 7).

The Mutual Trust perspective offers a logical foundation for understanding how the adversarial relationship has evolved between labor and management. The Trust Building principle gives us the promise that this particular moral frontier may indeed be tamed. And we have several anecdotal "success stories" that the business performance results of cooperation can be dramatic.

The ethical and practical need for conciliation between labor and management is urgent. Supplanting hostile, arms-length negotiations with cooperation built on mutual trust must be viewed as a realistic achievable goal rather than as utopian, philosophical ravings. The internal marketing framework offered here is, perhaps a workable beginning for ". . . creating a climate of trust in which our moral ideals might stand some hope of being implemented" (Dees and Cramton, 1991: p. 161).

References

Bartkowiak, J. J.: 1993, "Trends Toward Part-Time Employment: Ethical Issues," *Journal of Business Ethics* **12**, 811–815.

Bennett, J. T. and J. T. Delaney: 1993, "Research on Unions: Some Subjects in Need of Scholars," *Journal of Labor Research* **XIV**(2), 95–110.

Boatright, J. R: 1993, *Ethics and the Conduct of Business* (Prentice-Hall, Inc., New Jersey).

Boone, L. E. and D. L. Kurtz: 1994, *Contemporary Marketing, 8e,* mini book (Dryden Press, Texas), pp. 2–26.

Byrne, J. A.: 1994, "The Pain of Downsizing," *Business Week* (May 9), 60–69.

Dees, G. J. and P. C. Cramton: 1991, "Shrewd Bargaining on the Moral Frontier: Toward a Theory of Morality in Practice," *Business Ethics Quarterly* **I**(2), 135–167.

Everett, D.: 1994, "Report Condemns Labor Tensions," *The Beacon Journal* (June 2), 1 and 16.

Farber, H. S.: 1987, "The Present Decline of Unionization in the U.S.," *Science* **238**, 915–920.

Gupta, A. K. and E. M. Rogers: 1991, "Internal Marketing: Integrating R&D and Marketing Within the Organization," *Journal of Consumer Marketing* **8**(3), 5–18.

Hershey, W.: 1993, "Union Head Talks New Tone for New Times," *The Beacon Journal* (July 19), A7.

Jarley, P. and S. Kuruvilla: 1994, "American Trade Unions and Public Approval: Can Unions Please All of the People All of the Time?," *Journal of Labor Research* **XV**(2), 97–116.

Kennedy, E. J. and L. Lawton: 1993, "Ethics and Services Marketing," *Journal of Business Ethics* **12**, 785–795.

Kiechel, W: 1993, "How We Will Work in the Year 2000," *Fortune* (May 17), 38–52.

Kochan, T.: 1979, "How American Workers View Labor Unions," *Monthly Labor Review* **102**(4), 23–31.

Kohli, A. K. and B. J. Jaworski: 1990. "Market Orientation: The Construct, Research Propositions, and Managerial Implications," *Journal of Marketing* **54**, 1–18.

Kohli, A. K. and B. J. Jaworski: 1993, "Market Orientation: Antecedents and Consequences," *Journal of Marketing* **57**, 53–70.

Kuttner, R.: 1993, "Talking Marriage and Thinking One Night Stand," *Business Week* (Oct. 18), 16.

Lovelock, C. H.: 1991, *Services Marketing* (Prentice-Hall, Englewood Cliffs, New Jersey).

Lovelock, C. H.: 1992, *Managing Services* (Prentice-Hall, Englewood Cliffs, New Jersey).

Moenaert, R. K., W. E. Sounder, A. DeMeyer and D. DeSchool-Meester: 1994, "R&D-Marketing Integration Mechanisms, Communication Flows, and Innovation Success," *Journal of Product Innovation Management* **11**, 31–45.

Narver, J. C. and S. F. Slater: 1990, "The Effect of a Market Orientation on Business Profitability," *Journal of Marketing* **54**, 20–35.

Noble, B. P.: 1993, "Reinventing Labor: An Interview with Union President Lynn Williams," *Harvard Business Review* (July–August), 115–125.

Reichheld, F. A.: 1993, "Loyalty Based Management," *Harvard Business Review* (March–April), 64–73.

Schmidt, D. E.: 1993, "Public Opinion and Media Coverage of Labor Unions," *Journal of Labor Research* **XIV**(2), 152–264.

Shapiro, B. P.: 1988, "What the Hell Is 'Market Oriented'?," *Harvard Business Review* (Nov. –Dec.), 119–125.

Smart, T. and H. Gleckman: 1993, "O.K., Back to Work," *Business Week* (Dec. 20), 34–35.

Solidarity: 1993 (January–February), International Union, UAW, Detroit, Michigan.

Solidarity: 1994 (April–May), International Union, UAW, Detroit, Michigan.

Sonnenberg, F. K.: 1994, "Trust Me . . . Trust Me Not," *Journal of Business Strategy* **15,** 14–16.

Stark, A.: 1993, "What's the Matter with Business Ethics?," *Harvard Business Review* (May–June), 38–48.

Steinfels, P.: 1993, "Beliefs: Honoring Businesses for Marrying Skillful Management and Social Conference," *Wall Street Journal* (Nov. 13), 7.

Walljasper, J.: 1993, "We Can Work it Out," *Utne Reader* (60), 154–255.

Wattenberg, M.: 1984, *The Decline of American Political Parties, 1952–1980* (Harvard University Press, Cambridge, Massachusetts).

Wiesendanger, B.: 1994, "The State of the Unions," *Journal of Business Strategy* **15**(2), 52–56.

Collaborative Collective Bargaining: Toward an Ethically Defensible Approach to Labor Negotiations

FREDERICK R. POST

I. *Introduction*

THE PRESENT LEGAL and moral environment of current U.S. labor management relations can best be understood through the lens of history. Prior to the enactment of federal labor legislation in 1935, unions had no protection under the law. With a strident employer opposition to unionization coupled with an authoritarian management style, the predictable reaction was a militant labor movement. This produced a state of industrial warfare. As anyone familiar with labor history knows, the employers won almost all the battles.

Only under the umbrella of legal protection, consisting of the original Wagner Act[1] and its subsequent amendments,[2] collectively referred to as the National Labor Relations Act (The Labor Act), have unions and the collective bargaining process been legitimated. While free (meaning minimal governmental interference) collective bargaining is often applauded as the building block of our labor management relations system, it has been criticized recently from a moral and economic perspective.[3] Because the legal framework controlling the collective bargaining process was erected in response to a history of employer hostility towards and exploitation of employees to satisfy utilitarian ends, the legislature, in enacting the Labor Act, tried to balance the power between the two groups. However, the Labor Act does not encourage direct cooperation between an employer and employees; it merely prescribes a legal framework within which the employee representative bargains about the working conditions of represented employee groups.[4] Furthermore, both the administrative agency directed by congress to oversee the Labor

[1]The National Labor Relations (Wagner) Act 49 Stat. 449 (1935), as amended, 29 U.S.C. Sections 141–97 (1958), as amended, 29 U.S.C. Sections 153–87 (Supp. 1, 1959).

[2]The Labor Management Relations (Taft-Hartley) Act, 61 Stat. 136 (1947), 29 U.S.C. Sections 141–97 (1958) and The Labor-Management Reporting and Disclosure (Landrum-Griffin) Act 73 Stat. 519 (1959), 29 U.S.C. Sections 153–87 (Supp. 1, 1959).

[3]Bowie, "Should Collective Bargaining and Labor Relations Be Less Adversarial?" *Journal of Business Ethics,* Vol. 4. 1985, p. 283; Koehn, "Commentary Upon Should Collective Bargaining and Labor Relations Be Less Adversarial," *Journal of Business Ethics,* Vol. 4, 1985, p. 293; Carson, Wokutch & Murrmann, "Bluffing in Labor Negotiations: Legal and Ethical Issues," *Journal of Business Ethics,* Vol. 1, 1982, p. 13.

[4]Section 8(a)2 makes cooperation between most informal or formal employee groups and the employer an unfair labor practice under certain circumstances. If an employer is "cooperating" through certain types of assistance or preferential treatment, the Labor Board may find illegal domination since the definition of a "labor organization" in Section 2(5) is so general that most such groups would qualify.

From Journal of Business Ethics 9, 1990. *Reprinted by permission of Kluwer Academic Publishers.*

Act, the National labor Relations Board (The Labor Board), and reviewing federal courts consistently issue decisions that perpetuate an adversarial labor management environment.

While history provides both an explanation and an excuse for the present legal framework governing labor management relations, the present adversarial system may be less appropriate than the participatory management forms available for dealing with this critical internal business relationship. This is especially true for that aspect of the system which results in the labor contract. Since labor negotiations happen at least every three years, because the law only protects the incumbent relationship for that time period, any movement toward a more peaceful process would be advantageous for all concerned. Because the present system does not provide an optimal solution for this fundamental building block of labor management relations, it is time to consider an alternative approach.

This paper will explain the present adversarial collective bargaining process (ACB) and critique it on legal and ethical grounds. A new speculative methodology that I describe as the collaborative collective bargaining process (CCB) will then be explained and similarly critiqued. I will argue that replacing the present model with the CCB model will result in better long-term results for all parties concerned, those at the table and others whose lives are influenced by the outcome of bargaining.

Section II will examine the ACB model and describe strategies and tactics employed by the parties emblematic to ACB. Section III will contain a critique of ACB as a process on both legal and ethical grounds. In Section IV, I will propose a model for CCB that on both legal and ethical grounds can better accomplish both the tasks and needs of all parties influenced by both the process and the outcome of bargaining. In Section V, I will defend CCB on both legal and ethical grounds, respond to the anticipated arguments against it, and demonstrate that not only is it ethically defensible, but it may be the only viable alternative available for consensually harmonizing conflicting needs within the work places of today.

II. The Current Adversarial Collective Bargaining Process (ACB)

ACB is comparable, in many respects, to the adversarial process used in litigation. There, two parties with a dispute as to the "true" facts and how the law would apply to whatever they are found to be, present their respective versions of the facts to a judge or a jury. This is accomplished by presenting witness testimony and exhibit evidence. Direct and cross examination of witnesses constitutes the method of identifying and clarifying perceptions of events. Technical, largely exclusionary, evidentiary rules, testing relevance, materiality and competency, are applied to the evidence to determine its admissibility for review by the fact finder. This adversarial process is designed to uncover the "true" facts. Ultimately, the goal is to achieve justice.

A similar search for the "true" value of the employees' services and the quality of their working conditions is attempted during ACB but without the judge or jury as fact finder. The "safeguard" of the impartial fact finder used to search for the truth in litigation is foreclosed because there is no comparable safeguard in ACB. The efforts of the parties are directed solely toward concluding an agreement most favorable to their self interests based exclusively on their relative bargaining power. Not only is there no impartial decision maker like the judge or jury, but there are also no meaningful evidentiary rules determining the propriety of witness testimony or of offered documentation. So structured, ACB does not uncover any truths—either the value of employee services or the quality of their working conditions. Finally, the expressed goal of ACB, as articulated in the Labor Act, is not justice or labor and management just but labor peace. So, the announced goal of the process is not the same as the goal in litigation. Furthermore, the Labor Act gives no indication of what labor peace is. With no direction as to what represents achieving this announced goal, how can the participants be expected to find it? I will elaborate on these flaws of ACB and show how CCB corrects them.

Since the much discussed 1968 article "Is Business Bluffing Ethical?" by Albert Carr,[5] which analogizes the game of poker with many types of business negotiations, including labor negotiations, several authors have agreed that Carr's poker game model is an accurate model for describing conventional collective bargaining.[6] I, however,

---

[5]Carr, "Is Business Bluffing Ethical?" *Harvard Business Review*, Jan.–Feb. 1968, at 143.
[6]Carson *et al.*, supra, n.3.

find this analogy inadequate. ACB is more than the poker game analogy suggests. Though bluffing and deception do represent a portion of the behaviors, I will demonstrate that additional morally unsuitable behaviors are commonplace, thus making the picture represented by the poker game incomplete. If anything, it is too kind.

In their article, "Bluffing in Labor Negotiations: Legal and Ethical issues," Carson *et al.*,[7] give a definition of lying as ". . . a deliberate false statement which is either intended to deceive others or foreseen to be likely to deceive others."[8] This definition of lying is encompassed within the broader concept of deception which is defined as "intentionally causing another person to have false beliefs"[9] although the authors point out that "only deception which involves making false statements can be considered lying."[10] With these contextually useful definitions of both deception and lying, which I agree are accurate descriptions of some of the actions of the parties, a definition of the process of ACB as seen by each party is necessary.

The goal of management within the framework of ACB is to negotiate terms and conditions of employment that will

a. restore or improve control over the employees,
b. reduce the labor costs of the employees, and
c. increase the productivity of the employees so that there will be an increase in profitability.

The employer seeks to achieve this goal through the skillful exercise of either actual or perceived power over the union. Management must demonstrate that it has the will and ability to wage a successful battle against the union during a strike to achieve an acceptable settlement. If the union recognizes the employer's will and ability to win such an economic battle, the employer will usually achieve its objectives without a strike.

Conversely, the goal of the union subjected to ACB is to obtain contract language by proposals made at the table that will

a. wrest away employer control over its members,
b. obtain wage and fringe benefit increases for its members, and
c. protect its members from zealous management efforts to increase productivity by demanding rigid job classifications, increases in paid non-work time, and other methods.

I use the word "subjected" because the employer is normally the pro-active party and sets the tone for the negotiations. This will also be true for CCB, as I describe it in Section IV.

With the parties having such clearly contradictory goals, the structure of ACB is a combat model. It makes the battle lines clear, and it grants victory to the more convincing display of power, but it leaves casualties. Indeed, it cannot operate except upon the casualties of the opposing party, and those casualties are the basis for ever-renewed combat.

The legal framework within which the parties do battle is controlled by three deceptively simple sections of the Labor Act. Section 8(a)(5) and Section 8(b)(3) describe the respective duties of the employer and the union to meet and negotiate an agreement that will govern their relationship for the next three years. Failure to reach agreement can trigger the filing of unfair labor practice charges by either party against the other. The loose definition of collective bargaining is contained in Section 8(d) which specifies the type of conduct necessary:

> [Collective bargaining entails] the performance of the mutual obligation of the employer and the representatives of the employees to meet at reasonable times and confer in good faith with respect to wages, hours, and other terms and conditions of employment, or the negotiation of an agreement . . . incorporating any agreement reached if requested by either party. . . .

The Labor Board and reviewing federal courts have repeatedly held that the question of whether either party has met its statutory duty will be determined by the facts of each individual case. These three sections alone establish the parameters of the legality of ACB. There are no guiding regulations such as those employed by other federal regulatory agencies, for example OSHA, EPA, or SEC, Accordingly, whether or not conduct alleged to

---

[7]Ibid.
[8]Ibid. at 17.
[9]Ibid. at 18.
[10]Ibid.

be illegal is found to be a violation of the law is a legal conclusion drawn by the Labor Board after analyzing the facts of the particular case. The decision will seldom be based upon one particular aspect of negotiations, but will be based upon "the totality of circumstances."[11]

After compliance with the strike notice provisions required by the Labor Act,[12] the process of ACB typically begins with the union submitting a written proposal to the employer containing requests for changes in the existing labor agreement. The employer follows with a similarly structured written proposal which reacts to some of the subjects raised by the union and requests other changes in the labor agreement. The negotiation process continues with several additional sessions during which the parties orally present proposals and counter-proposals covering the subject areas raised in their respective initial written proposals.

Both parties must participate in the process to comply with Section 8(d) of the Labor Act. Furthermore, each party must compromise some of its initial positions if it is to convince the Labor Board that it has engaged in good faith collective bargaining. When agreement is reached on subjects that have not been withdrawn, the parties must agree to execute a written contract incorporating any agreement reached if either party requests such a signed document. Written agreements are standard procedure.

Within this minimal statutory framework involving the interplay of only three sections of the Labor Act, the fabric of the law of collective bargaining has developed. Changes in how the Labor Board interprets the law are the by-product of unfair labor practice charges filed alleging that conduct by a party violates the "intent" of the legislature (55 years earlier in 1935) as represented by the statutory language. With the Labor Board makeup determined politically, "intent" does shift back and forth—to the advantage or detriment of the parties. In spite of this further instability in the interpretation of the Labor Act, certain bargaining tactics do represent *per se* violations of the duty to bargain.[13] These acts are so obvious that avoiding

---

[11]Other than in instances where there has been a failure of one party to meet even the minimum requirements of good faith bargaining, or a specific *per se* violation, (see Note 13, *infra*) the Labor Board will investigate all conduct or the "totality of conduct" of a party which is the standard of conduct that determines whether a violation has occurred based upon a cumulation of actions. The original doctrine developed from the U.S. Supreme Court case of *NLRB v. Virginia Elec. & Power Co.,* 314 U S 469 (1941). Recent cases where the Labor Board has found violations under this standard include *Hyatt Regency New Orleans,* 281 NLRB No. 42 (1986) and *Walter A. Zlogar, Inc.,* 278 NLRB No. 149 (1986). To demonstrate the severity of bargaining misconduct required to violate this standard, a review of the recent case of *Roman Iron Works, Inc.,* 275 NLRB 449 (1985) is instructive. During bargaining management engaged in such hard bargaining tactics as reducing its wage offer from the initial proposal, denied a union request for employee addresses, demanded a subcontracting provision, and demanded significant economic concessions. In spite of these several tactics, because management also held several meetings with the union, made complete contract proposals, and offered its own concessions, the Labor Board found no violation of Section 8(a)5 of the Labor Act.

[12]Section 8(d) of the Act was added as one of the Taft-Hartley Amendments, The Labor Management Relations (Taft-Hartley) Act, 61 Stat. 36 (1947), 29 U.S.C. Section 158(d) (1958).

[13]Illustrative examples of *per se* violations of the Labor Act from the cases in which they occurred include: the refusal to bargain at all with the other party, which is considered tantamount to a refusal to even recognize the union, *NLRB v. Insurance Agents International Union,* 361 U.S.:477, (1960); to agree to bargain, but to insist that the bargaining be on subjects outside the scope of mandatory subjects, *NLRB v. Katz,* 369 U.S. 736 (1962); to unilaterally change some aspect of wages, hours, and the conditions of employment during the course of negotiations, without reaching a valid impasse and bypass the union, *Gas Machine Co.,* 221 NLRB No. 129, (1975); insistence on the presence of a court reporter to record all of the negotiating sessions, as a precondition to contract negotiations, *Barlett-Collins Co. v. NLRB,* 237 NLRB No. 106, (1978); insistence upon union bargaining committees' submission of the employer's last offer to the full union membership for a ratification vote as a condition precedent to employer reaching an agreement. *American Seating,* 176 NLRB 850, (1969); employer imposition of an absolute time limit on negotiations, for example, two hours per week, *A.J. Belo Corp. v. NLRB* 411 F.2d 959 (5th Cir. 1969) *cert. den.* 396 US 1007; insistence upon an illegal provision, *NLRB v. Reed and Prince Mfg. Co.,* F.2d 874 (1st Cir. 1941) *cert. den.* 313 US 595; refusal to incorporate matters previously agreed to by a party with no valid justification, *Amalgamated Clothing Workers v. NLRB* 324 F.2d 228 (2d Cir., 1963); intentional misrepresentations at the bargaining table which cause the other party to alter its position to its disadvantage, *Architectural Fiberglass,* 165 NLRB 238, (1967); and refusal to execute a written agreement between the parties prepared at the conclusion of negotiations, *Standard Oil Co. v NLRB* 322 F.2d 40 (6th Cir. 1963).

them still leaves a great amount of latitude for manipulation and exploitation of the other party. Legally permissible deceptive behaviors include: padding proposals, proposing and then withdrawing unreasonable demands to pressure concessions, negotiating noneconomic proposals (language) extensively before ever addressing economic proposals to frustrate and delay, inundating the other party with lengthy confusing written proposals, extending bargaining sessions long into the evening, establishing negotiation locations which involve inconvenience, and reserving secret separate rooms for long caucuses to wear out the other party. These and other tactics are geared to make the negotiating process a thoroughly unpleasant and unrewarding experience for the recipient party.

Although such tactics are legal, there is some point at which the law can be violated if, based upon the totality of circumstances, the Labor Board determines that combinations of these types of conduct make out a violation. However, because of the minimal sanctions for a violation, there is little incentive for an employer to be concerned about where that point is. And, there is even less incentive for the union to be concerned because, practically speaking, there is no meaningful sanction for union violations. And, because both parties are very aware of this, few unfair labor practice charges are ever filed. As to the effectiveness of the law,

> [u]nion officials have contended that the lack of significant remedies makes correction of good faith bargaining violations a farce. Since [The Labor Board] decisions can be appealed to the courts, it might take three or more years for a final determination.[14]

Considering the nature of the practices used in ACB, it would seem that bad faith bargaining charges would be frequently filed, but statistics show just the opposite. For example, in 1984, there were more than 190,000 separate labor contracts in the U.S.[15] Because of the customary

three year duration, approximately one third or, 63,000, are re-negotiated each year. The Labor Board's own statistics in 1983 reveal that 42 percent (12,211 of 28,995) of the charges of employer violations involved employer refusals to bargain in good faith.[16]Therefore, out of approximately 63,000 negotiations, there were 12,211 charges of employer violations or about 19 percent of employers were alleged to have violated Section 8(a)(5) of the Labor Act. 5.6 percent (697) of 11,526 charges of union violations involved union refusals to bargain in good faith.[17] So, in these same number of negotiations, only 0.0009 percent of unions were alleged to have violated Section 8(b)(3) of the Labor Act. Only 19 percent of the time did unions file charges, and employers filed charges against unions less than 1 percent of the time. With little threat of charges being filed and the knowledge that there are no real sanctions anyway, the urge to do whatever is necessary to win is ever present. With the law so toothless, it has only nuisance value.[18]

III. *Legal and Ethical Problems with ACB*

Many of the following criticisms of ACB have been presented before, specifically by Norman Bowie in his 1985 article "Should Collective Bargaining and Labor Relations Be Less Adversarial?"[19] However, I assert that there are additional criticisms that deserve attention and I will begin with them.

While the general nature of the adversarial system imposed by the Labor Act has been much

---

[14]W. Holley and K. Jennings, *The Labor Relations Process* 230 (3rd ed. 1988).
[15]T. Kochan and T. Barocct, *Human Resource Management and Industrial Relations* 20 (1985).

[16]National Labor Relations Board, *Forty-Eighth Annual Report,* Government Printing Office: Washington, D.C. (1986), p. 167.
[17]Ibid.
[18]"Nuisance value" in legal jargon represents the situation where potential liability is so remote for a defendant that the only real financial exposure is the cost of the defense. Therefore, if the plaintiff will accept an amount of money to settle the case that is less than the projected defense cost, the plaintiff should be paid that nuisance value to end the litigation. These types of settlement offers normally insult plaintiffs.
[19]Bowie, *supra* n. 3, at 283.

discussed,[20] it is curious that no criticism has been made about the inability of the current system to accomplish what it has been asked to do. In an adversary setting, bargaining success is determined by combat. The party that best employs its power through skillful, and often deceptive, tactics wins. While the search for truth in a courtroom in the presence of a judge or jury may make sense, it is not logical to suggest that such combat has any way of accurately determining either the *value* of employees services or the *quality* of their working conditions. In fact, it does not. These goals are not the outcome of simply who has (or who pays for) the best advocate. How can such a combat model determine these valued goals? It simply cannot.

[20]See the following books, as illustrative of the literature describing the traditional adversarial model: B. Gray, *Collaborating* (1989); C. Heckscher, *The New Unionism* (1988); W. Ury, J. Brett and S. Goldberg, *Getting Disputes Resolved* (1988); L. Susskind and J. Cruikshank, *Breaking The Impasse* (1987); N. Chamberlain and J. Kuhn, *Collective Bargaining* (3rd ed. 1986); C. Craypo, *The Economics of Collective Bargaining* (1986); T. Kochan, H. Katz and R. McKersie, *The Transformation of American Industrial Relations* (1986); J. Atleson, *Values and Assumption in American Labor Law* (1983); H. Raiffa, *The Art and Science of Negotiation* (1982); S. Bacharach and E. Lawler, *Bargaining* (1981); R. Fisher and W. Ury, *Getting to Yes: Negotiating Agreement Without Giving in* (1981); R. Walton and R. McKersie, *A Behavioral Theory of Labor Negotiations* (1965); T. Schelling, *The Strategy of Conflict* (1960). Illustrative of the several articles appearing in journals discussing ACB and adversarial negotiations in general within the context of American law are: Hyman, "Trial Advocacy as an Impediment to Wise Negotiation," *Negotiation Journal,* Vol. 5, 1989, p. 237; Hyman, "Trial Advocacy and Methods of Negotiation: Can Good Trial Advocates be Wise Negotiators?" *UCLA Law Review,* Vol. 34, 1987, p. 863; Lax & Sebenius, "Three Ethical Issues in Negotiation," *Negotiation Journal,* Vol. 2, 1986, p. 363; Fisher, "Beyond Yes," *Negotiation Journal,* Vol. 1, 1985, p. 67; McCarthy, "The Role of Power and Principle in Getting to Yes," *Negotiation Journal,* Vol. 1, 1985, p. 59; Schuster, "Models of Cooperation and Change in Union Settings," *Industrial Relations,* Vol. 24, 1985, p. 382; Menkel-Meadow, "Toward Another View of Legal Negotiation: The Structure of Problem Solving," *UCLA Law Review,* Vol. 31, 1984, p. 754; Laventhal, "A General Theory of Negotiation: Process, Strategy and Behavior," *U. Kansas Law Review,* Vol. 69, 1982, p. 107; Scobel, "Business and Labor—From Adversaries to Allies," *Harvard Business Review,* Nov.–Dec., 1982 p. 129; White, "Machiavelli and the Bar: Ethical Limitations on Lying in Negotiations." *A.B.F. Res. J.,* 1980, p. 926.

Furthermore, as has been noted above, ACB is a largely unenforceable system. Remedies for employer misconduct at the bargaining table are minimal; remedies for union misconduct at the table are meaningless. Both parties know that bargaining violations will usually go unpunished because neither party ordinarily bothers to file charges. From the parties' perspective, filing charges only further complicates bargaining by introducing government investigators and creating additional disputed issues. The statistics suggest that only the party who is in a desperate condition and believes there has been egregious misconduct will make the effort. Therefore, each party is normally tempted to ignore the law in the effort to achieve its goals. As a result, both unethical and illegal behavior is rewarded.

Another seldom acknowledged yet typically experienced problem with ACB is an existing, often externally caused, bargaining power imbalance between the parties resulting in unfair combat *ab initio*. Often there are many variables beyond the control of one party which prevent it from entering bargaining on a "level playing field." Such variables often so imbalance power that one party begins with a decided advantage and easily exploits the other. Such types of imbalances often persist over time because of the particular relationship resulting in one party being gored continually.

Examples of employer problems placing it at a disadvantage include: a highly leveraged debt condition, a poor cash flow generating capability, inadequate inventory build-up capability, highly skilled irreplaceable employees, a high percentage of employed employee spouses, substantial prior business commitments, short seasonal demand for products, other dependent facilities, or a highly competitive market for the product line.

Similar problems a union may face placing it at a disadvantage include: a small strike fund, a low percentage of employed employee spouses, a high unemployment rate in the geographical area, low skill levels among the employees, a winter month contract expiration date, or alternate employer production facilities.

If any number of these illustrative variables disadvantages one party, the negotiations start out imbalanced and the other party will easily exploit the situation under the ACB model. The predictable outcome is a negative ending to ACB.

There is a winner and a loser or both parties believe they are losers. How can such a system have any moral value for the long-term relationship between the parties when precisely the wrong relationship is fostered and perpetuated?

In addition to my criticisms of ACB, there are other, equally significant criticisms outlined by Bowie,[21] which I will now review briefly to place them within the context of the overall destructive picture of ACB.

The subjects emphasized during the negotiations result in a distortion in favor of the extrinsic job conditions:[22] wages, fringes, seniority provisions, and grievance procedures. This occurs at the expense of possibly more important intrinsic job conditions[23] such as: job responsibility, recognition for work, advancement potential, personal growth, and job content. Often, the payback for emphasis upon extrinsic variables is that no attention is given to the intrinsic variables. This can result in a workplace of well paid but miserable employees who hate the job, and of subtle employer retribution through neglect of intrinsic conditions. In the short term, ACB is a zero sum game, and an embittered loser will seek to avenge those losses somehow.

Such a system frustrates the fundamental principle of commitment to quality that is deemed necessary for company success. The result is economic inefficiencies for the employer since the hostility that remains after the bargaining process is completed spills over into the workplace. Employees will seek recompense if they feel they lost. With such attitudes, how can employees be expected to make the effort to meet the quality standards necessary to compete with foreign competition? Too often they do not, and with predictable results. In fact, much of the recent literature on corporate management[24] has emphasized the necessity of working together. An internally divided employer cannot produce as a team.

Additionally, ACB frequently ignores the remaining stakeholders' interests due to its inherent myopia, and often even ignores stockholders' interests because the control of bargaining strategy is lodged in top management. This small group has much to gain by obtaining results directed to its specific short-run interests. Thus the management negotiating team is often compelled to advance positions that are irresponsible from a long-term perspective in order to satisfy short-term gains. For example, in the recent best seller *Iacocca: An Autobiography,* the author confesses:

> Gradually, little by little, we gave in to virtually every union demand. We were making so much money that we didn't think twice. We were rarely willing to take a strike, and so we never stood on principle.
>
> Our motivation was greed. The instinct was always to settle quickly, to go for the bottom line. In this regard, our critics were right—we were always thinking of the next quarter.
>
> "What's another dollar an hour?" we reasoned. "Let future generations worry about it. We won't be around then."
>
> But the future has arrived, and some of us are still around. Today we're all paying the price for our complacency.[25]

This shortsighted view by management almost destroyed the U.S. auto industry. Ironically, only when at the brink did these employers reconsider their approach to labor negotiations. However, these changes remain an anomaly now.

Ultimately, ACB undermines the importance to society of truth as a moral value. By promoting, and in effect, condoning deception, bluffing and lying as a function of the ACB process, it teaches the participants and other affected parties that truth and honesty as values are irrelevant in labor negotiations. While there is language in court decisions espousing the need for honesty, there are no sanctions for most forms of dishonesty in the bargaining process.[26]

---

[21]Bowie, *supra* n. 3, at 283.

[22]A. Szilagyi and M. Wallace, *Organizational Behavior and Performance,* 110 (2nd ed., 1980).

[23]Ibid.

[24]Illustrative of the numerous examples of contemporary management literature which emphasize participatory management, employee involvement, and empowerment in the workplace include: R. Waterman, Jr., *The Renewal Factor,* 71 (1987); T. Peters, *Thriving on Chaos,* 281 (1987); R. Kanter, *The Changemasters,* 180 (1983); W. Ouchi, *Theory Z,* 97 (1982); T. Peters and R. Waterman, Jr., *In Search of Excellence,* 235 (1982).

[25]L. Iacocca, *Iacocca: An Autobiography,* 304 (1984).

[26]A good example of this phenomenon is the case of *NLRB v. Truitt Manufacturing Co.,* 351 U.S. 149, 38 Lrrm 2024 (1956) where the Supreme Court stated that implicit in the meaning of "good faith bargaining" is honesty. The decision

ACB also assaults, because of the resentment, distrust and confusion it produces among employees, a basic human need for friendship among people. Employees simply do not know where their allegiances are. Do they work for the employer or the union? If they are pro-employer, that must make them anti-union; if they are pro-union, then they must be anti-employer. All of this creates an unsettling division of loyalty among employees and violates a basic human need for friendship and compatibility among both one's peer group and one's superiors in the work place.

Carson *et al.*,[27] argue that this state of affairs may be unavoidable "given the exigencies and harsh realities of economic bargaining in our society."[28] However, they continue, "competitive economic arrangements do not usually *cause* people to become dishonest or treacherous, etc."[29] Rather, they claim "that most of the 'undesirable moral effects' attributed to our economic institutions involve actualizing pre-existing disposition, rather than causing any fundamental changes in character."[30] I disagree. Even if some participants derived such tendencies from prior experiences, I contend that, in ACB labor negotiations, *the arrangements themselves* dictate that the parties act in morally unacceptable ways to survive. My proposed CCB model changes *the arrangements* and eliminates the necessity to become, as Carson *et al.*, state, "dishonest" or "treacherous." . . .

IV. The Proposed Collaborative Collective Bargaining Process (CCB)

The goal of parties who jointly elect to use CCB is to reach an agreement regarding the terms and conditions of employment for the employees represented by the union that *harmonizes* both the legitimate capitalist driven needs and wants of the employer as well as the needs and wants for economic justice of the employees. The process is nonadversarial. There is no power manipulation between the parties involving efforts to win a battle and, through combat, defeat the other side. The CCB process contains five distinct stages. These are

a. the commitment stage,
b. the explanation stage,
c. the validation stage,
d. the prioritization stage, and
e. the negotiation stage.

Each stage builds upon every prior stage. While the process is now speculative, I submit that it represents a workable format because it is predicated upon an agreement made in advance to be candid and open; the use of the focusing influence of a mediator; and the value of a time format that, through structured intensity alone, greatly enhances the potential for reaching agreement.

The initial commitment process is critical because CCB cannot function without the voluntary consent between both parties to reject ACB and, instead, exercise candor, openness, and honesty in the negotiation process. Due to the political nature of every union, the leadership must firmly advocate CCB and sell the concept to the membership. Unless there is membership commitment, the union leadership will be chancing political suicide by advocating such an approach. For this reason, considerable effort must be expended by management to convince the union leadership that there are mutual benefits to be gained by the use of CCB.

A. THE COMMITMENT STAGE

The commitment stage will begin by jointly convened meetings of management and union leadership one year before the expiration date of the labor agreement and again six months closer to the date. At these meetings, the new approach will be discussed in detail with emphasis on the benefits to both parties of collaborating on a new labor agreement. The many problems of ACB, reviewed in Section III of this paper, should be frankly discussed to emphasize the superiority of CCB because those problems are largely obviated through its use. The parties should discuss performance targets for both management and the employees necessary for the proper growth of the company and ways in which

---

does not stand for that proposition, however, but for the principle of law that if an employer "pleads poverty" by basing its rejection of a union's economic proposals upon an inability to pay, the employer must allow the union's auditors access to the corporate financial records to substantiate the position. For this reason, an employer can say "NO" to union economic proposals, but better not claim inability to pay as the reason unless it is prepared to open its books.

[27]Carson, *et al.*, supra, n.3.

[28]Ibid at 20.

[29]Ibid at 21.

[30]Ibid.

gains beyond those targets may be shared. Documentation to support the basis for positions is available in our information intensive business world. A summarization of each of these meetings will be disseminated among the employees.

To ensure a legally binding commitment, a CCB agreement will be prepared and executed by the parties at their second meeting. This document will acknowledge that CCB will be the process used, prescribe a timetable for the five stages, contain a "collaboration compact," acknowledge the mediator selection mechanism to be used, indicate the scope of authority of the mediator, and designate sanctions for noncompliance. If the union will not (or cannot) commit to the use of CCB, then the parties will resort to the conventional ACB as before.

The collaboration compact will consist of a jointly determined list of goals that the parties seek to accomplish during their labor negotiations. The preparation of this list is the initial phase of openness. These shared aspirations form the basis for the mediator's evaluation of the merit of positions expressed. Previously declared written goals will focus the mediator's efforts to push the parties toward an agreement.[31]

The mediator selection mechanism will be determined by the language already contained in the labor agreement that provides for arbitrator selection in the grievance procedure. This typically commences by providing for the parties to informally agree upon an arbitrator. Absent agreement, either the offices of the Federal Mediation and Conciliation Service (FMCS) or the American Arbitration Association (AAA) is contacted, with a request for a list of potential arbitrators from which the parties select an arbitrator. For use in the CCB process, either FMCS or AAA will also be capable of providing qualified persons from which the parties can select a mediator.

The mediator's authority will be designated in the CCB agreement. It will be limited to the authority to use mediating skills to aid the parties in achieving whatever common goals they have established in their collaboration compact. This will not include authority to decide between any two disputed positions, imposing one party's position upon the other party. The mediator will never assume the judicial function of an arbitrator. The CCB process is not a disguised form of the interest arbitration that is sometimes practiced in public sector labor negotiations.

B. THE EXPLANATION STAGE

The next stage is the explanation stage which will consist of the first face-to-face bargaining meeting held one month before the contract expiration date. This will occur at what used to be the first negotiation meeting in ACB. The employer will present all noneconomic and economic proposals with different package options within financially plausible ranges stated as possible objectives. The employer will explain noneconomic language proposals as well as anticipated supportable economic positions presented as ranges. The union will likewise explain its economic proposals as well as changes envisioned as necessary in noneconomic language.

C. THE VALIDATION STAGE

Subsequent to this meeting, the validation stage will begin which will cover the time period between two to four weeks before the contract expiration date. The employer and union representatives will jointly prepare a questionnaire covering the ranges of all possible issues raised by each party. This questionnaire will be administered to the employees during company time. The content of the questionnaire will be determined by the specific proposals that were made by each party during the explanation stage. It will summarize all proposals presented in a forced-choice ranking format that will require the employees to evaluate proposals so that a collective consensus of prioritization will be evident. The exact content of the questionnaire will always be unique to the particular relationship. Generally, however, employer proposals can be expected to be geared toward expanding management rights to achieve increased flexibility and control over employee assignment choices. These goals are presumed to contribute to

---

[31]An analysis of the process by which the parties structure common goals that can direct them toward consensus through the drafting of the collaboration compact is beyond the scope of this article. This process will be analyzed, referencing approaches based upon utilitarian, contractarian and deontological ethical theories, in another article entitled *Toward Consensual Labor Negotiations: Formulation of the Collaboration Compact* (forthcoming).

the ultimate objective of keeping wages and fringes as cast items in line in order to maintain profitability. Generally, union proposals will seek to structure mechanisms for either codetermination of or at least a voice in management decisions controlling its members as well as the typical proposals seeking improvements in wages and fringe benefits.

The greater the extent of harmony between the parties, the greater probability that the proposals of both parties will be directed toward decisions determined either jointly or made only after input from the union. The parties naturally come to the table with somewhat different agendas—the employer negotiating to maintain an acceptable level of profitability and the union negotiating to maintain an acceptable level of member acceptance. If both parties respect each other's goals and the role that the other party can have in better realizing those goals through harmonizing their aspirations, the CCB process can aid them in working together for the benefit of each of them.

Once the questionnaires have been filled out and turned in, the results will be tabulated by computer to obtain mean, median, and average scores for all responses where appropriate. These will then be posted for employee review to demonstrate an awareness of their need for involvement. Because employees have selected between different choice options available, the responses to employer and union proposals will provide important data for both parties. For example, responses to the employer proposals will enable the management negotiating team to better assess the level of dissatisfaction in the group toward certain language proposals or economic modification requests. Likewise, responses given to the union proposals will serve to better inform the union negotiating team as to the strength or weakness of its positions. And, by the posting process, the employee group will learn about its collective consensus on all of the issues placed on the table. Concurrently, each party will obtain any documentation requested during the prior explanation stage and obtain answers to questions raised during that stage.

D. THE PRIORITIZATION STAGE

The next meeting, held two weeks before the contract expiration date after the parties have obtained requested documentation and have enjoyed the benefit of separately assessing the results of the employee questionnaire, will mark the beginning of the prioritization stage. These proceedings will be conducted in the presence of the mediator they have selected. At this meeting, which is the second face-to-face meeting between the parties, they will again present their positions with the supporting documentation which has been obtained so that the mediator can not only understand what is being proposed but also understand the rationale for the proposals.

The mediator will then evaluate the merit of positions expressed based upon the respective presentations gauged with reference to the criteria appearing in the collaboration compact. The technique employed by the mediator will be the Socratic method of uncovering the bases for positions expressed, exposing their merit or lack thereof. For example: Why do you need that? Where else has that proposal been agreed to? Whose idea was that? What problem does that solve? How will implementation of that process increase productivity? How will the work group benefit by introducing that change? And similar inquiries seeking to expose the relative overall importance of each position to the party offering it. Through aggressive questioning by the mediator, and each party of the other, a frank and open discussion of the prioritized supportable needs and wants of each party will be possible. Further, supporting documentation will be scrutinized for its accuracy and relevance.

E. THE NEGOTIATION STAGE

The final stage of CCB is the negotiation stage. This stage will begin between seven to ten days before the contract expiration date. Once the stage begins, strict time guidelines will govern each meeting in order to maximize work efforts and minimize any dilatory tactics or the customary posturing of traditional ACB. The meetings will be held during successive days. The negotiations will commence at 8:00 A.M. and will include breakfast together to start the session in a pleasant setting. This meeting will last for two hours. At 10:00 A.M. there will be a two hour caucus during which each party will discuss separately the position alternatives proposed. The mediator will circulate between the parties' rooms and facilitate by asking questions and probing into the respective positions of each party. The parties will reconvene at 12:00 noon and meet again for two hours over lunch to discuss issues raised during the morning caucus. Precisely at 2:00 P.M., the parties will break for another two hour afternoon caucus. This process will continue with alternating two hour meetings and caucuses with the parties concluding their final meeting at 10:00 P.M. that evening, resulting in eight hours of face-to-face negotiation meetings and six hours of separate caucus meetings. The parties will resume the process the next morning and repeat the same schedule.

The mediator will continue the Socratic questioning about the basis for and necessity of each position proposed by a party. Further, to demonstrate the extent of progress, the mediator will prepare and maintain two lists, the "agreements agenda" and the "disagreements agenda." These two lists will serve as visual guidelines that structure the topics for discussion. The disagreements agenda represents unresolved proposals that remain to be negotiated to agreement. The agreements agenda contains all other proposals that have been already accepted as proposed, accepted as modified, or withdrawn. Posturing and procrastinating will be minimized when the agendas are kept in front of each party, especially during caucus meetings where, to prevent any private pontificating, the mediator can separately challenge each party's positions on all remaining unresolved proposals. And, by such challenges, the mediator can push the parties to compromise and consensus.

On the third day, the length of each type of meeting will be reduced by one hour, resulting in seven hours of face-to-face meetings and seven hours of separate caucus meetings. This should facilitate the progress of negotiations since the often necessary decisions about compromising or withdrawing positions are possible only during the privacy of the separate caucus. This one hour alternating time period process will continue each successive day until the parties decide upon a new tentative labor agreement, subject to the ratification vote of the membership, or the expiration date is reached. Absent agreement at that time, the parties may either agree upon a new later expiration date and continue negotiating or exercise their respective economic weapons such as a strike or a lockout, having failed to reach a satisfactory settlement.

The essence of CCB is to foster by commitment, structure, and format an environment which encourages open and frank discussion with the assistance of a skilled mediator to keep the parties' efforts properly directed much as a judge acts in a court of law. In this new environment, ranges of positions can be openly discussed and package options truly considered on their actual merits. Employee needs and wants, which have already been identified in the questionnaire, will be discussed between the parties and used as a form of prioritization. Employer positions, as supported by requested documentation, will be discussed to determine its priorities. As the negotiations progress, positions will be presented on a package basis. By structuring package proposals, the parties will be pressured to further prioritize options available and less important proposals will be exposed and compromised or withdrawn. The purpose of these intense continuing daily schedules is to lessen the incentive to engage in gamesmanship and tactical posturing, center energy on properly directed negotiations, and build the necessary team environment so the parties can collaborate together in good faith to complete the process before the expiration date. Mediator facilitation can enhance the parties' articulation of needs, wants, and frustrations with candor by drawing out reasons for positions advanced.

A model, illustrating the five-stage structure of the CCB process is given in *Figure 1*. As Figure 1 shows, the progressive movement through each stage narrows, specifies and prioritizes the respective positions. This will contribute to a harmonizing of the many initial conflicting needs and interests of the parties. The resulting labor contract will be truly indicative of both the employees' demonstrated wants and needs (as identified in the questionnaire and further presented and supported by the union) and the employer's supportable wants and needs (as presented by the employer and demonstrated through the validated documentation) so that both parties can leave bargaining with a feeling that each of them won because all positions proposed were debated, justified and considered in the process that led to the new labor agreement. The effect of full participation and consideration of one's views subjected to open debate cannot be overemphasized as a positive element of CCB.

Commitment Stage: 12 & 6 months before contract expiration date

Initial planning meeting convened
Follow-up planning meeting held
Collaboration compact goals determined
Mediator selection process completed
CCB Agreement drafted and executed
Summary of each meeting posted

Explanation Stage: 1 month before contract expiration date

First bargaining meeting held
Initial management proposal presented
Initial union proposal presented
Position basis questioning initiated
Support documentation inquiries raised
Timetable for remaining meetings determined

Validation Stage: 2 to 4 weeks before contract expiration date

Joint employee questionnaire prepared
Joint employee questionnaire administered
Questionnaire results calculated and posted
Requested support documentation assembled
Questionnaire results summaries analyzed
Position validation documentation obtained

Prioritization Stage: 2 weeks before contract expiration date

Second bargaining meeting held
Mediator CCB process facilitation initiated
Prioritized validated management proposal presented
Prioritized validated union proposal presented
Mediator position questioning commenced
Position validation documentation critiqued

Negotiation Stage: 1 week before contract expiration date

Continuous daily bargaining meetings commenced
CCB process daily timetable established
Mediator position questioning continued
Agreements and disagreements agendas drafted and updated
CCB process continued until settlement reached
Settlement agreement drafted and executed

NEW LABOR CONTRACT

Figure 1 Collaborative collective bargaining

V. CCB Is an Ethically Defensible Approach to Labor Negotiations

I will begin by addressing my choice of the word "collaborative" to describe the new model. This word was chosen as opposed to "cooperative" because it more accurately describes the nature of the CCB relationship, one that has evolved between former enemies to what now involves working together for a common shared goal. "Collaborate" is a broader term. It contains within it all of the operative elements of cooperate which, according to *Webster's New Universal Unabridged Dictionary, Deluxe Second Edition,* include: "to act or operate jointly with another or others, to the same end; to work or labor with mutual efforts to promote the same object . . . to practice economic cooperation," but goes further by accurately defining the *historical nature* of the specific relationship, namely, "cooperation with the enemy." For this reason, the descriptive label "collaborative" gives a more complete and contextual meaning to CCB.

What is it about CCB that is ethically justifiable? The process strips away the use of tactics such as bluffing, misrepresentation and lying. The parties cannot state their ranges on particular issues, address the justifications for their positions, and defend their positions in the presence of a skilled mediator and the other party, both of whom will ask probing questions, without openness and honesty. Also, being required to produce supporting documentation for positions will require sober reflection about the basis for positions initially contemplated. The CCB process will preclude any effective use of the most frequently criticized aspects of ACB. Due to the resulting free exchange of positions and ideas, the all too common hostility and distrust that permeates ACB will be eliminated or at least minimized. Because of employee awareness through the questionnaire and knowledge that such a process is being used on their behalf, there should be improved attitudes among employees since their input makes them a part of the CCB process. Consequently, their commitment to employer goals should improve. Better product quality can be anticipated as employees should no longer perceive themselves as separate and isolated from both the bargaining process and the employer.

Furthermore, because most bargaining table dishonesty is not punishable under the present legal framework, a voluntary policy of honesty through the whole CCB process sends a powerful message to the employees. This message should result in reciprocation on their part due to the example that has been set by the employer. Dissemination of the policy, as one important element of the overall corporate mission, will enhance the image of the employer as having moral values that represent the best in corporate citizenship.

Use of the CCB process also underscores the value of the teamwork so needed in our competitive world marketplace. Use of the word "collaborate" defines the working together process. As the current literature emphasizes, the same collaboration in all other aspects of corporate endeavors is necessary to compete effectively and CCB can set the tone for both management style and overall corporate policy.

In addition, CCB satisfies a basic human need for friendship in the workplace. Through the involvement of the employees, a desirable joint allegiance to employer and union *raison d'etre* [reason for being] is now understandable which can eliminate the current unsettling feelings of divided loyalties among employees.

Through the openness of CCB, the inclination to ignore stakeholders' interests is sharply reduced also. Justifications for positions taken will be debated in the presence of a mediator who will probe both parties as to the basis for their wants and needs. This will prevent the management group from prioritizing positions geared to their employment self-interest at the expense of the longer term interests of both stockholders, stakeholders, and the employees as one component of the stakeholder group.

Another value of the process is that intrinsic job variables, traditionally left unaddressed, may become a part of the negotiations. This will be to the distinct advantage of the affected employees. Elements of the job such as employee responsibility, opportunity for personal growth, recognition for good performance, and job content need more bargaining table discourse. This does not occur in ACB. The opportunity to consider these needs exists to a much greater degree under CCB.

As to the question of the value to be placed upon employees' services, there can be more meaningful comparisons made with wage rates of competitors, and a more thoughtful evaluation of cost of living concerns. The result will be that the union can more ably defend the need for wage and benefit increases. In the CCB process, the employer will have to make a better effort to understand whether there is merit to position advanced by the union. While it is difficult to determine the value of any group of employees' services, an open and frank discussion can certainly do more to promote understanding than having such matters determined by power and combat skills under ACB. Outcomes reached in that manner have little, if any, relation to the value of employees' services, as I have related earlier.

Finally, by the use of CCB, resort to the Labor Board for assistance against a wrongdoer's actions will normally be unnecessary. The parties will self-police their behaviors by compliance with the voluntarily agreed upon CCB process, monitored further by an impartial mediator selected by the parties to facilitate their negotiations.

VI. *Conclusion*

The legal system has fostered an adversarial collective bargaining process as an attempt to balance the power relationship between management and employees. This power relationship was out of balance due to the substantial changes in the economy brought about by the industrial revolution and the imbalance led to an exploitation of employees. ACB was an outgrowth of the adversarial search for the truth used in litigation. While the adversarial system did initially advance the economic well-being of employees, it also undermined their intrinsic worth by placing them continually at odds with their employer. It further sanctioned bluffing, deception, intimidation, coercion and other immoral conduct exercised as part of the power manipulation process needed to succeed.

The employer is also exploited because the problems caused by ACB impact directly on its competitiveness and profitability. ACB normally imposes losses on both sides. The workplace becomes a divided camp because of this internal combat. The outcome is economic inefficiency and a destruction of the intrinsic value of the employees.

An article[32] co-authored by several faculty in different disciplines of the Massachusetts Institute of Technology, from among a larger group who had formed the M.I.T. Commission on Industrial Productivity, has concluded that there are "five interconnected imperatives" that the U.S. must implement to achieve competitive industrial performance in the global marketplace of today. Two of these five imperatives reflect what I propose in the CCB process. One imperative is "to develop a new 'economic citizenship' in the marketplace."[33] The authors stress the need for increased employee involvement and responsibility and they emphasize that employees can no longer be treated as expendable parts of the production process but should be treated as long term assets to be nurtured and developed. Employees should become full participants in the destiny of the company.[34] Another imperative is to "strive to combine cooperation and individualism."[35] The authors note that the individualistic spirit that characterizes our culture is often counterproductive in the work places of

today. It is largely absent in the most productive U.S. companies where, in its place," group solidarity, a feeling of community and a recognition of interdependence have led to important economic advantages.[36] These imperatives, the product of an extensive two year study involving 200 companies, 150 plant sites, and nearly 550 interviews in the U.S., Europe and Japan,[37] represent an indictment of the ACB process and graphically illustrate the need for several changes, including what is proposed in the CCB process.

The substitution of CCB can enable the parties to reorient their perspectives on labor negotiations. It should be clear by now that the value of employee services is not a predictable outcome of the combat model of ACB. By following the CCB model, the parties can avoid the negative and self-defeating elements of ACB and, in the process, work together to make the company an internally solidified entity, working toward mutually beneficial common goals, through the use of an ethically defensible approach to labor negotiations.

[32]Berger, Dertouzos, Lester, Solow & Thurow, *Toward a New Industrial America*, 260 SCI. AM. 39 (1989).
[33]Ibid.
[34]Ibid
[35]Ibid.

[36]Ibid.
[37]Ibid at 40.

Employee Rights and the Doctrine of At Will Employment

DAVID R. HILEY

IN A RECENT ISSUE of *Management Review*, the president of the American Management Association described the erosion of the practice of "at will" employment and the employer's right to fire employees for whatever reason. He acknowledged that poor management practices were partly responsible for the increased legislation and litigation limiting the employer's right to fire, but he warned that the trend away from termination at will should concern all employers. The question he

raised was how to balance the employer's need to terminate an employee against the need to treat employees fairly and responsibly. He concluded: "An organization must have the right to terminate incompetent personnel. Indeed, it has the obligation to its stockholders to do so. It must have the right to reduce its workforce in hard times if that is what it needs to do to survive. But the organization behaves self-destructively when it tells its employees that it values the right to treat them

From Business and Professional Ethics *4, 1985. Reprinted by permission.*

capriciously."[1] The problem raised is how to balance an employer's right to terminate against an employee's right to be free from intimidation, retaliation, or caprice.

The erosion of the employer's right to terminate has become a common theme in business periodicals and management and supervision journals[2] as a result of a growing number of legal challenges to the common-law doctrine of employment at will that has allowed employers to terminate an employee without considerations of due process or just cause.[3] Employment at will is a uniquely American doctrine having its source in the common-law principle that where the employment relationship is not bound by a contract specifying the period of employment, the relationship is considered "at will" and can be terminated without cause by either party.[4] Currently, approximately 70 percent of workers in America are considered "at will" employees. Until relatively recently, courts have upheld the employer's right to terminate without cause or notice. In one frequently cited decision a court ruled that employers may dismiss their employees "for good cause, for no cause, or even for causes morally wrong, without being thereby guilty of legal wrong."[5]

Courts are increasingly finding in favor of employees, however. In a number of recent cases of wrongful discharge there have emerged three general grounds for exception to the "at will" doctrine:

1. when discharge violates explicit public policy or statute;
2. when discharge is a result of malice or bad faith; and
3. when discharge violates an implied contract between employer and employee.

With the first sort of exceptions, for example, courts have found that employers are not free to dismiss an employee for serving on a jury or for refusing to commit perjury. The second class of exceptions protects employees from retaliation from employers in such circumstances as sexual harassment or whistle-blowing, or in cases of discharge to avoid fulfilling an agreement on the part of the employer. The third category of cases is the latest legal development. Courts are finding that oral agreements, personnel policy manuals, and employee handbooks are implied contracts between employers and employees and that employers are not free to discharge employees in violation of these implied contracts.

Despite the fact that the employment-at-will doctrine has been the subject of considerable legal attention, it requires ethical analysis because the law in this area is unstable as a result of recent significant challenges. More important, however, the law begins with the acceptance of the common-law tradition and the burden of proof is to justify exceptions to the employer's right to terminate at will; ethical analysis, however, must call the doctrine of employment at will, itself, into question and evaluate its justification in light of a commitment to more general ethical principles of fairness and due process. My initial thesis, then, is that the burden rests with those who defend the employer's unrestricted right to terminate. From a defense of this initial thesis, I will examine arguments that favor an employer's unrestricted right to terminate.

The burden-of-proof thesis rests on a series of claims supporting a *prima facie* right on the part of

---

[1]Norman R. Horton, "Dear New Hire: WE reserve the right to fire you . . .," *Management Review*, August, 1984, p. 3.

[2]See, for example, Jeffrey C. Pingpank and Thomas B. Mooney, "Wrongful Discharge: A New Danger for Employers," *Personnel Administrator*, March 1981, pp. 31–35; Anthony T. Oliver, Jr., "The Disappearing Right to Terminate Employees at Will," *Personnel Journal*, December 1982, pp. 910–17; Maria Leonard, "Challenges to the Termination-at-Will Doctrine," *Personnel Administrator*, February 1983, pp. 49–56; David W. Ewing, "Your Right to Fire," *Harvard Business Review*, March–April 1983, pp. 32–42; "Curtailing the Freedom to Fire," *Business Week*, March 19, 1984; and Charles G. Bakaly, Jr., and Joel M. Grossman, "How to Avoid Wrongful Discharge Suits," *Management Review*, August 1984. pp. 41–46.

[3]For reviews of recent court cases see Lawrence E. Blades, "Employment At Will vs. Individual Freedom: On Limiting the Abusive Exercise of Employer Power," *Columbia Law Review* 67 (1967): pp. 1405–35; John D. Blackburn, "Restricting Employer Discharge Rights: A Changing Concept of Employment At Will," *American Business Law Journal* 17 (1980): pp. 467–92; and Brian Heshizer, "The Implied Contract Exception to At-Will Employment," *Labor Law Journal* 35 (1984): pp. 131–41.

[4]The source of the common-law doctrine of employment at will is H. G. Wood, *A Treatise on Law of Master and Servant* (New York: John D. Parsons, 1887).

[5]*Payne v. Western & A.R.R.,* 81 Tennessee 507 (1884) pp. 519–20.

employees to be free from unfair or arbitrary dismissal and a defeasible right to job security in exchange for satisfactory job performance. It needs to be made clear initially, however, that my burden-of-proof argument requires only the minimal claim of a right to be free of unfair and arbitrary dismissal. These claims, themselves, require extended defense but for my present purpose it is necessary only that they provide a plausibility argument. The most general claim is that in a society that values and protects the rights we have as citizens—not the least of which are fair treatment and due process—it is unreasonable to think that we should not have these rights as workers.[6] Many recent arguments for employee rights are based on the idea that civil rights extend to the workplace. David Ewing, for example, has characterized American corporations as "the black hole of civil rights" and he argues against the idea that the rights we have as citizens should be left in the parking lot with our automobiles.[7] What makes this argument more compelling is the realization that American business is increasingly dominated by large corporate structures that exercise power over the lives of workers comparable to the power governments have over citizens. Lawrence Blades, in the most significant law article on the issue of employer right to terminate, begins his argument for the protection of worker freedom by stating that "large corporations now pose a threat to individual freedom comparable to that which would be posed if governmental power were unchecked."[8] The claim that employees should have the right to fairness and due process, then, is part of the more general claim that employees have rights in the workplace.

In the context of our general commitment to fairness and due process, current practices in the United States regarding the right to be free from wrongful dismissal are all the more inconsistent. Thirty percent of the workforce is protected by collective bargaining agreements, civil service procedures, or tenure policies that prevent the employer from exercising an unrestricted right to terminate. It is implausible to think that the presence or absence of a contract alone entails the presence or absence of a right to fairness and due process.

Two other claims support my burden-of-proof thesis. First, an employee is not bound to his or her job simply through economic dependence. Some legal theorists are claiming that employees acquire a property right with respect to their jobs, thus as a property right, employment requires protection from wrongful or arbitrary violation.[9] The basis for this claim derives from a changing concept of property and from the realization that through seniority, pension plans, life-insurance benefits and the like, employees become "vested" in their employment. Charles Reich, in his influential article "The New Property," has argued that as the role of government has expanded, traditional forms of private wealth and private property are being transformed because we become dependent, as citizens and as businesses, on what he calls "government largess"—unemployment insurance, social security, government contracts, licensing regulations and so on. On Reich's analysis:

> The significance of government largess is increased by certain underlying changes in forms of private wealth in the United States. . . . [T]oday more and more of our wealth takes the form of rights or status rather than tangible goods. An individual's profession or occupation is a prime example. To many others, a job with a particular employer is a principal form of wealth. A profession or a job is frequently far more valuable than a house or a bank account.[10]

If it is plausible to consider a profession or job as property, then workers acquire a right in their jobs that requires protection against wrongful dismissal or caprice.

[6]Patricia Werhane has made this the basis for her argument against the employer's unrestricted right to terminate in "Individual Rights in Business," in *Just Business: New Introductory Essays in Business Ethics,* ed. Tom Regan (New York: Random House, 1984), pp. 107f.

[7]David Ewing, *Freedom Inside the Organization* (New York: Dutton Publishing Co., 1977).

[8]Blades, "Employment At Will vs. Individual Freedom," p. 1409, cited in note 3.

[9]See, for example, Mary Ann Glendon and Edward R. Lev, "Changes in the Bonding of the Employment Relationship: An Essay on the New Property," *Boston College Law Review* 20 (1979): pp. 457–84.

[10]Charles Reich, "The New Property," *Yale Law Journal* 73 (1964). Citation is from reprint in *Property, Profits, and Economic Justice,* ed. Virginia Held (Belmont, CA: Wadsworth Publishing Co., 1980), p. 48.

Finally, perhaps the most important reason employees should be secure from wrongful and arbitrary termination is that such protection is a fundamental enabling right, constituting a condition for the protection of other employee rights. If employees are to be protected in the right of privacy in matters unrelated to their employment, or in their right of conscience or political liberty, then they must be protected from termination growing out of their possession or exercise of these and other important worker rights.

My thesis is that, because of these considerations, the burden of proof rests with those who maintain an employer's unrestricted right to terminate an employee at will. In turning to an examination of arguments that support the employer's rights, I must first point out that the claim that an employer has a right to terminate must be approached from a consideration of rights claims generally, as well as from consideration of the justification of this particular right. Obviously, rights claims must be grounded and the plausibility of the claim depends on the plausibility of the considerations upon which the right is grounded. Furthermore, the possession of a right entails claims on others—minimally the claim of noninterference—and it entails conditions of responsible exercise on the part of the one who possesses the right. My right to drive an automobile involves your obligation not to prevent me from exercising my right, and it involves an obligation on my part that I will exercise it within conditions described by the law and by considerations of safety What is problematic about earlier legal precedents for the employer's right to terminate at will is that courts have supported the right as absolute and unconditioned. That is, the right has been assumed to be unrestricted and without conditions of responsible exercise. The effect of recent court decisions is that the right to terminate is increasingly treated as a defeasible right with both external and internal conditions for exception. Externally, public policy considerations can override the employer's right to terminate. Internally, employer irresponsibility through malice or breach of good faith are grounds for exception.

The employer's right to terminate at will has been grounded in three ways. First, of course, it is grounded historically in the common-law tradition of "at will" employment. That, however, does not constitute an adequate basis for meeting ethical challenge to the employer's right to terminate because the law itself is in the process of significant modification and, more obviously, because of the nonidentity of legality and morality.

Second, the right is grounded in considerations of mutuality between employee and employer drawn from contract theory. Since an "at will" employee has the right to resign at will, it is claimed that the employer has the corresponding right to terminate at will. It is argued that the employer's right to terminate is justified because both parties enter the relationship freely and both are equally free to terminate at will. In a frequently cited ruling, one court found that since "an employee is never presumed to engage his service permanently . . . if the contract of employment be not binding on the employee for the whole term of such employment, then it cannot be binding upon the employer; there would be lack of 'mutuality.'"[11]

This mutuality argument is problematic in two ways. First, applying the notion of "mutuality" from contract theory to the employment relationship assumes that the relationship is symmetrical in the relevant sense necessary to claim that whatever binds or fails to bind one party must bind or fail to bind the other. While there may be an abstract equality and freedom in the employer-employee relationship, there is a significant material inequality and lack of comparable freedom. Synoeyenbos and Roberts have pointed to the fact that there is an inequality of possible harm that slants in favor of the employer. "In times of high unemployment, or in fields of specialization or industries where there is a labor surplus, it will probably be more difficult for the discharged employee to find a new position than for the firm to hire a new employee, consequently, the harm to the employee, in terms of economic hardship and psychological disruption, is often greater than the harm to the firm."[12] In addition to the differential harm resulting from the general condition of the economy, an employee has an investment in his or her job in terms of economic dependency, benefit programs,

[11]*Pitcher vs. United Oil and Gas Syndicate Inc.,* 174 Louisiana 66 at 69, 139 So. 750 at 761 (1932).
[12]Milton Snoeyenbos and John Wesley Roberts, "Ethics and the Termination of Employees," in *Business Ethics* (New York: Promoetheus Books, 1983), p. 249.

pension plans and the like, and these, along with considerations of age, mobility, and family circumstance, imply a lack of mutuality. One might reasonably argue that a clerk's resignation without notice poses comparable harm to a mom and pop market, but the idea of mutuality of harm is simply implausible when comparing the harm to a fired head of household and Exxon Corporation. Work situations in the United States today are more like the latter than the former.

Besides consideration of differential harm, there is also an important asymmetry in relations of power and authority that affects the balance of freedom in the employment relationship. The growing defense of the idea that employees have rights in the workplace roughly parallel to civil rights is grounded, in part, by consideration of the way power is used and abused in organizations. This concern results from the realization mentioned above that large corporate organizations exercise power over workers similar to that of governments over citizens and from obvious abuses of employer power where termination is used as retaliation. Furthermore, differences in authority can exercise indirect coercive influences at the expense of employee rights. The use of polygraph tests as a condition of employment is a case in point. According to one line of argument, since a potential employee is always free to submit to the test or not, the use of a polygraph is not an abridgment of privacy. However, given that the potential employee and the employer do not meet as equals in the hiring setting because of differences in authority and control, and given that the potential employee's decision not to submit to the test is a decision not to be considered for the job, there is a fundamental lack of freedom. A similar situation is emerging in response to recent judgments in favor of employees for unfair dismissal. As one way of avoiding challenges to the right to terminate, some attorneys are advising employers to require employees to sign an "acknowledgment of waiver" agreeing that employment may be terminated without cause or notice. The assumption is that since the employee freely assents to the waiver, the employer will be protected from litigation. Apart from the fact that this response is rather like a restaurant posting a sign that it "reserves the right to refuse service to anyone" in response to desegregation laws, it is not obvious that a potential

employee is any more free to refuse to sign such a waiver than he or she would be to refuse a polygraph test as a condition of employment.

The second problem that mutuality arguments raise for an employer's right to terminate is that mutuality considerations might reasonably be used as a defense *against* the claim that the employer can terminate without cause or notice. It has recently been argued that contract theory implies an obligation of good-faith dealings on the part of the contracting parties and that redress for wrongful discharge might be argued on the basis of a breach of good faith.[13] It is not my purpose to enter the legal issue of applying contract-theory considerations to wrongful dismissal, but rather to suggest that the mutuality argument provides dubious support for the claim that an employer has an unrestricted right to terminate.

The most promising basis for grounding the employer's right to terminate is the claim that it is an extension of private property rights. This argument is implied by the concern among businesspeople about the intrusion of government or the courts in the employment relationship. Although some of these concerns are clearly bad-faith defenses and special pleading, since government involvement is not opposed when it serves business interests—in price supports, protectionist policies concerning foreign trade, corporate bail-outs, for example—there is an important underlying argument that must be considered on its own terms. The most general form of the argument is that in a free economy of privately held businesses, employers have property rights entitling them—in the same way any owner of property is entitled—to do with, dispose of, or make decisions affecting the use of one's property free from interference. There are a pair of issues I do not want to engage in connection with this argument: I do not wish to consider whether free markets or private property are themselves morally justified; and I do not wish to debate the degree to which our economic system conforms to the model of free markets and private ownership. Rather, I am interested in examining the strongest possible case for the claim that the employer's right to terminate at will derives from the right of private

---

[13]See Blackburn, "Restricting Employer Discharge Rights," pp. 482ff., for a review of this issue, cited in note 3.

ownership or private property on the methodological assumption that if it is not justified in the strongest case, then it will not be justified on the basis of whatever modified view of our current economic system one wants to maintain.

It is important to realize that this justification of the employer's right to terminate does not rest simply on the claim of private property rights. As is usually noticed, there is an important connection between rights and interests.[14] Support for the employer's right to terminate must rest not only on claimed property rights but on the claim that maintenance of the employer's unrestricted right fulfills important social interests. Thus this argument is coupled with the utilitarian justification that society's interests are best fulfilled by maintaining the employer's right to terminate at will. Less abstractly, this is the point of concern about the "erosion" of the employment-at-will doctrine in business and management periodicals. The assumption is that if employers are not free to fire, fear of litigation will bring about an increasing reluctance on the part of employers to terminate an employee even when there is just cause. The result, it is argued, is decreased efficiency, productivity, and profitability. Positively stated, the claim is that society has an interest in employers retaining the right to terminate since this right would contribute to a company's ability to maximize efficiency, productivity, and profitability—all of which contribute to social utility.

In examining this grounding of the employer's right to terminate, we must keep in mind that the property-rights argument cuts both ways. Given growing support for the idea that a worker can acquire a property right in his or her job, the issue is, at best, one of conflicting property-rights claims. Further, it is worth noticing that protecting the employer's property right cannot be defended on the basis of general claims about the efficiency of a system of private property. Frank I. Michelman has argued, for example, that the presumption that a system of private property is more efficient than any other system requires justification of the claim that any property system that is otherwise equivalent is less efficient. After considerable analysis, Michelman concludes that such a claim is unsup-

portable and that the justification of a system of private property must rest on noneconomic considerations.[15] More is required to defend the claim that the employer's unrestricted right to terminate serves the interests of efficiency than the argument that it is an extension of private property rights.

The burden rests on the following question: Is efficiency, productivity, and profitability diminished in proportion as an employer's right to terminate is modified? In approaching this question, we must distinguish a range of cases in order to sharpen the issue. First, no one could plausibly argue against an employer's right to terminate an employee for inadequate job performance or for gross misconduct related to job performance. Much of the argument in the "at will" controversy has turned on whether employers have the right to terminate at the other extreme of cases—for bad cause or for no cause at all. The most problematic cases for those who wish to limit the employer's right to terminate, however, fall between the extremes of termination for cause and termination from malice or caprice. Three sorts of cases seem particularly problematic: cases where job performance is adequate, but only minimally so; cases where job performance is adequate, but future growth and productivity is unlikely; and cases where performance and potential contribution are satisfactory, but other factors such as personal incompatibility disrupt efficiency and productivity. The question that must be considered is this: Will the limitation of the employer's right to terminate in the clearly irresponsible cases have the effect of restricting the employer's right to terminate in these more problematic cases? If the answer is yes, then there is plausibility to the claim that a restriction of the employer's right to terminate will constitute a social disutility since it will restrict that area of management judgment and foster mediocre employee performance.

This question can be approached from two directions. First, it could be argued that there are compelling counterexamples one way or the other. Second, the answer could turn on a consideration of whether an unrestricted right to terminate would be more beneficial than the policies and

---

[14]See, for example, Virginia Held's recent book, *Rights and Goods* (New York: Free Press, 1984), chap. 10, where she connects property rights with interests of society.

[15]Frank I. Michelman, "Ethics, Economics, and the Law of Property," *Ethics, Economics, & the Law,* Nomos XXIV, ed. J. Roland Pennock and John W. Chapman (New York: New York University Press, 1982), pp. 3–40.

procedures required of an employer to demonstrate responsible judgment.

The United States is unique in its support of the doctrine of employment at will. One might look to other countries—West Germany or Japan, for example—where employees have security against termination without cause and consider whether the result has been reduced efficiency, productivity, or profitability. Norman Horton, in the article cited at the beginning of this paper, has appealed to the example of West Germany. He writes: "In West Germany, the law against unjust dismissal protects the employee rather than the employer. Although it doesn't prevent employers from firing for just cause, it has effectively created a corporate culture that avoids termination. A manager from a major German chemical company told me he envied the freedom American firms have to fire incompetents. 'You wouldn't believe some of the deadwood we support,' he said."[16] Managers in other countries may envy American employers' freedom to fire, but that is beside the point. The issue is solved neither anecdotally nor by appealing to management preference. Does the practice foster a social disutility? At best, counterexamples are inconclusive. On the one hand, recent literature on declining productivity in America has compared employer-employee relations in the United States unfavorably to those in West Germany and Japan and has placed at least part of the blame for the superior economic performance of Germany and Japan, when compared with that of the United States, on superior management. On the other hand, it is unclear to what extent the success of West German and Japanese business depends on the difference between free market economies and command economies. I am not in a position to enter either debate. It is enough, however, to see that the claim of social disutility will not be justified from obvious counterexamples. The most promising argument, then, must be that an employer's unrestricted right to terminate is more beneficial than the measures required of an employer to show cause and responsible judgment when terminating an employee.

Two different approaches have been recommended in the literature to assure the employer's right to fire and protection against wrongful-dismissal law suits. The defensive strategy is for employers to eliminate possible grounds for liability. Since, for example, courts are treating employee handbooks as binding contracts between employer and employee, some attorneys are recommending the elimination of anything in policy manuals or employee handbooks that could be construed as a commitment to job security that the employer does not intend. In addition, it is recommended that employers carefully document employee misconduct or inadequate job performance and provide the employee with notice of poor job performance. The affirmative strategy is to develop and implement clearly formulated personnel evaluation and review procedures, grievance procedures, and human resources development plans.[17] It seems plausible to expect that clarity of intention and responsibility in employee evaluation will, itself, contribute to efficiency and productivity—or at least it does not seem likely that it will diminish productivity. It also seems plausible to expect that within a framework of clearly articulated personnel policies and grievance procedures, managers would remain free to make personnel judgments for the good of the company—or at least the burden rests with employers to demonstrate why sound personnel policies and the need to show cause restricts their ability to deal effectively with their employees and produces a disutility that overrides an employee's right to fairness and due process.

I have argued that because employees have the right to be free from unfair and arbitrary dismissal, and because there is at least plausibility to the extended claim that they have a defeasible right to their jobs so long as satisfactory job performance is provided, employers do not have an unrestricted right to terminate an employee at will. The arguments most frequently given for the employer's right to fire, do not justify the claimed right against a greater need to protect employees. Though certainly it is essential that employers have the right to make responsible personnel judgments, and though those judgments need not always turn simply on considerations of satisfactory job performance, the burden should rest with the employer to show either that termination is for just cause or that it is justified in terms of considerations of responsible business and personnel policy.

---

[16]Horton, "Dear New Hire," p.3.

[17]See, for example, Leonard, "Challenges to the Termination-at-Will Doctrine," and Charles G. Bakaly, Jr., and Joel M. Grossman, "How to Avoid Wrongful Discharge Suits," cited in note 2.

Understanding Participation

John Kaler

1. *Preliminary distinctions*

(A) PARTICIPATION IS EMPLOYEES SHARING IN THE BUSINESSES WHICH EMPLOY THEM

IF IT IS TO RETAIN any sort of coherent meaning, use of the word "participation" will, in any context, have to retain its root signification of "sharing" or "partaking." More specifically, within business or organizational context it will, unless explicitly qualified in some way, almost always refer to participation by *employees*. Within that context then, the word is strictly speaking an abbreviation for "employee participation" and this is how it will be used here. (Though I shall generally just talk about "businesses" rather than organizations in general.)

It follows that "participation" refers to a situation in which employees have some sort of share in the businesses which employ them. Beyond this it is probably not advisable to be more prescriptive, for what we find is a wide range of situations being referred to which may have little else in common beyond the fact that they can be described in terms of employees "sharing in the business." What they share in and the way in which they share is left open. "Participation" can be anything from the complex and legally entrenched German system of co-determination to some modest and purely voluntary scheme of profit sharing. We have to conclude then, that participation is any arrangement under which employees have some sort of share in some aspect of a business.

(B) PARTICIPATION IS NOT A SPECIFIC KIND OF EMPLOYEE INVOLVEMENT

It is, of course, always possible to be more prescriptive than suggested above. One might, for example, confine the term to just arrangements in which, as in co-determination, there is some sort of joint decision making between management and labour. Arrangements such as profit sharing which might otherwise be spoken of as "participation" would be put into the more general category of "employee involvement." The term "participation" is therefore reserved for a very specific kind of employee involvement.[1]

There are, I think, at least three reasons for rejecting this restriction. Firstly, it does not accord with ordinary usage. In terms of ordinary usage, "participation" is any sort of sharing and not just sharing in decision making. Secondly, even at the level of a specialized business usage, this restriction runs counter to an at least common use of the term. It is at least common, and perhaps even usual, for the term to be applied to many more sorts of arrangements within business than just joint decision making. Thirdly, and most importantly, not to use "participation" of those other sorts of arrangements is to lose sight of that common element, namely *sharing,* which connects these otherwise disparate phenomena not just with each other, but also with joint decision making. To describe them all simply as "involvement" tells us nothing about the nature of the involving. "Participation" does. It tells us it is involvement through sharing. Moreover, it does this while covering just about anything—or perhaps even anything at all—which might be describable as "employee involvement." Consequently, talk of "involvement" would seem redundant. It tells us nothing which "participation" does not do in a more informative yet not too restrictive way.

2. *Participation requires a two sides of industry division*

While certainly rejecting any confinement of the word "participation" to just joint decision making,

---

[1]See Cotton, J. L.: 1993, *Employee Involvement* (Sage, Newbury Park), p. 14, for this reduction of "participation" to a sub-category of "involvement." (Though on p. 3 he rather confusingly makes use of a definition of involvement which describes it as a *"participative* process" [my italics].)

From Journal of Business Ethics *21: 125–135, 1999. © 1999 Kluwer Academic Publishers. Printed in the Netherlands. Reprinted with permission from Kluwer Academic Publishing.*

I can allow that this might be its primary significa-tion. The reason that it might is the very obvious yet (as I will later argue) crucially important fact of participation being very much a matter of indus-trial relations. Put another way (and this is where the crucial importance comes in), it is all about there being "two sides of industry." This is so not just because participation requires at least one other side to participate with, but also because that side must somehow stand in contradistinction from employees for the word to have what I have acknowledged to be its usual sense of *employee* par-ticipation. Most obviously then, that contradistinc-tive side will be employers or, to use economic rather than legal terms, capital as opposed to labour. Alternatively, where managerial representa-tives act on behalf of employers or the issue is one of control rather than ownership (see section 7). then the contradistinctive side takes the organiza-tional form of managers as opposed to the man-aged.[2] As on a day-to-day basis the two sides of industry division largely manifests itself as a dis-tinction between those in control and those being controlled, there is a perhaps understandable ten-dency to see the division largely in this third, specifically organizational form. It is therefore understandable if, as something predicated upon that division, participation gets to be chiefly asso-ciated with that form and therefore seen as mostly to do with joint decision making between man-agers and managed. However, even granting that it has some kind of primary claim to the title, joint decision making cannot, for the reasons I have given, be granted sole claim. There are other ways for employees to share in the busi-nesses they work for and therefore other ways for them to participate—however less than primary they might seem.

3. Forms of participation

I shall speak of different ways of participating as "forms." What determines their classification as this or that "form" is the particular aspect of the business which the participating arrangement allows employees to share in. Thus, for example,

co-determinatory mechanisms are one form of par-ticipation in virtue of giving employees a share in decision making, while profit sharing arrangements are another and quite different form in virtue of giving employees a share in profits.

What these two examples also demonstrate is a categorical division into which, I take it, all estab-lished forms of participation can be fitted and, per-haps, all possible forms as well. It is the division between participation which gives employees a share in running the business they work for as opposed to participation which gives them a share in its financial proceeds. Accordingly, the first fun-damental category of participation might, for want of a better word, be described as "operational," while the second can have no other description but "financial."[3]

Even within the operational category there is more to participation than just joint decision mak-ing. There is also what might be called "delegatory participation," along with the sort of participation involved in transfers of information from managers to managed ("informing" for short), as well as what goes on when managers engage in consulta-tion with staff.

In delegatory participation, managers hand over the running of certain areas to the workforce. It includes such things as quality circles, self-managed work teams, as well as schemes of job enrichment or enlargement to the extent that they provide greater scope for the exercise of discretion by employees. All these things are instances of par-ticipation, and of operational participation in par-ticular, in that they give employees a share in running the businesses they work for. What they are not though, are instances of operational partic-ipation in the form of joint decision making. In delegatory participation, managers transfer deci-sion making powers to employees. They do not, as

---

[2]I shall, as convenience warrants, glide between and across legal, economic, and organizational ways of expressing the two sides of industry divide.

[3]See section 6 for an explanation of why in practice and per-haps in principle all forms of participation are either opera-tional or financial. See also Chryssides, G. and J. Kaler: 1996, *Essentials of Business Ethics* (McGraw Hill, Maidenhead), pp. 99–101, for the origin of the classificatory scheme being offered here. Note that, as I shall indicate by my references, there are many different classificatory schemes for participation. If mine has any advantage it is, I hope, by constructing a more or less sequential scheme through a process of continual sub-categorization (see Figures 1 and 2) and by marking distinctions that might be overlooked (see sections 1(b), 4, 5, and 6).

they must for joint decision making, effect decisions in conjunction with employees.[4]

With informing, it is simply a matter of employees being told of decisions which managers have already made or are going to make, along with possibly being told the reasons for those decisions as well as being kept abreast of developments affecting the business. But regardless of what they are told (or how they are told it), this is employees sharing in something relating to the business, namely information, which is essential to the process of running it. Informing is therefore not just participation, but a specifically operational form as well. But again, what it is not is joint decision making. To be merely told of decisions or to be kept generally informed will not, of itself, involve employees in making decisions together with managers. Informing is, at best, a process which might precede joint decision making.

The place of consultation within operational participation is decidedly ambiguous. In consultation, employees are being asked their opinions before management goes on to make a unilateral decision. It is therefore not joint decision making in any straightforward sense. It is, at most, an opportunity for employees to influence decision making through persuasion. To that extent it is joint decision making of kind—though of an admittedly very weak kind. It is also to some extent informing of one particular sort in that consulting with employees requires telling them of decisions that are going to be made. What consultation is not though, is participation in its own right. Take away the possibility of influencing management decisions through persuasion along with the informing element, and we are left with consultation as nothing but the responses of employees to management proposals. It becomes the mere voicing of opinions by employees; which is not something that can, in itself, constitute participation because it is not something which gives employees any sort of share in the business. (On the contrary, it is the employees giving something *to* the business—even if it is only a piece of their mind.) Thus,

it is only in so far as it overlaps with joint decision making through the possibility of persuasion and with informing through a necessary transfer of information that consultation counts as participation and, moreover, a specifically operational form.

The upshot of all this is that joint decision making emerges as just one form of operational participation alongside the delegatory and informing varieties, with consultation taking its place as a fourth form in so far as it is distinguishable from joint decision making and informing. So whatever primary status it might have, we have to acknowledge joint decision making as just one form of (operational) participation among several, and this can be done by calling it "co-determinatory participation."[5]

In so far as it overlaps with joint decision making, consultation does so, as I noted, only in the very weak sense of allowing employees to influence management decisions. Clearly, what I have now identified as co-determinatory participation is capable of being much more than this. Stronger instances are possible. In recognizing this, we differentiate on the basis of relative strength and weakness: a more or less commensurable characteristic which I shall call "degree." This is though, only one of at least four such commensurable or at least contrasting characteristics attributable to co-determinatory participation. They are all contained within that most developed of co-determinatory systems, the German. What it demonstrates is not just differences of degree, but also what might be called "level," "mode" and "weighting." (A similar analysis—perhaps even using the same or similar terms—can be made for delegatory

---

[4]Most of what goes on under the heading of "empowerment" is delegatory as distinct from co-determinatory participation. (See Kaler, J.: 1999, "Does Empowerment Empower?," in P. Davies and J. Quinn (eds.), *The Ethics of Empowerment* (Macmillan, London).)

[5]This analysis of informing, consulting, and co-determination as more or less operating alongside each other can be contrasted with those that place them in a kind of continuum of increasing employee influence on decision making. (See Marchington, M. et al.: 1992, *New Developments in Employee Involvement* (Department of Employment, London), pp. 7–8, for such a continuum model. See also Knudsen, J.: 1995, *Employee Participation in Europe,* Sage, London), pp. 9–10, for an analysis which is perhaps closer to mine.) There is, I go on to allow, something of a continuum of increasing employee influence *within* co-determination and possibly also, in so far as involves such influencing, *within* consultation. (See the discussion of "degree," "level," and "weighting" in the rest of this section.) But this is not the same as ascending graduations of influence holding *between* informing, consulting, and co-determination.

participation, informing, and consultation but I will not, for reasons of space and tedium, attempt it here—the analogies are, in any case, obvious.)

I have already recognized that the weakest degree of co-determinatory participation is provided by consultation. The strongest degree, call it "full co-determination," is when employees have an equal right with managers to both initiate and veto proposals. A somewhat weaker degree but still way ahead of mere consultation, call it "partial co-determination," is when employees can veto but not initiate proposals.

With differences of level, the dimension is, so to speak, height. It is most obviously represented by the distinction between operational matters to do with more or less day-to-day issues as opposed to those concerning overall policy and direction: call the lower level "procedural," the higher "strategic." A procedural level for co-determinatory participation is exemplified in German works councils: employee elected bodies with different degrees of co-determinatory rights over a range of day-to-day issues.[6] The strategic level is exemplified in the election of employee as well as shareholder representatives on to the supervisory boards of German companies: bodies with overall responsibility for overseeing the running of a company by its managers.

Differences of mode are nothing more than the distinction between employees co-determining through elected representatives (as in works councils and supervisory boards) rather than doing this in person (as a body or individually). It is a contrast which can be denoted by talking of representational and non-representational ways of engaging in co-determinatory participation as "indirect" and "direct" respectively.

There is likewise a numerical aspect to the fourth and final characteristic of weighting. This is usually specific to indirect modes and is nothing more than a measure of the relative voting strength of employee and employer sides in joint decision making. So, for example, on German supervisory boards, employee representatives can have one third of the total votes relative to shareholder representatives, or one half minus one, or fully equal

voting strength subject to the casting vote of a neutral chairperson.[7] (Note that weighting differs from degree in being simply a matter of the number of votes possessed rather than the more complicated matter of grading on the basis of powers to influence, veto, and initiate. Note too the possibility, if not the actuality, of weighting involving a direct rather than indirect mode through the use of referendums allocating different shares of the total vote to employees and shareholders.)

Classification is simpler for those forms of participation that fall into the financial as distinct from operational category. They fall broadly into two sub-categories: those to do with ownership and those to do with income. The first will typically include various schemes for employee share ownership: offering shares at a discount, employee share option plans, employee share ownership plans (operating through trusts) and the like. With financial participation by way of income, we have the linking of pay to profits. Employees are either given a fixed percentage of profits, or else paid profit-related bonuses of some kind.[8] Either way, employees are participating through sharing in the profits aspects of the business; just as in schemes of share ownership they are participating through sharing in its ownership aspect. (See Figure 1 for a summary of section 3.)

4. Source and motive distinct from form

It is, of course, possible to classify participatory arrangements on a basis other than their form; that is to say, on a basis other than the particular aspect of the business which the arrangement gives employees a share in. This is a possibility which is realized when, as sometimes happens, participatory arrangements are categorized in terms of their source or the motive behind them.

[6]See Knudsen, pp. 35–38, for the differing degrees of co-determination in German works councils (along with rights to be informed and consulted).

[7]See Knudsen, pp. 43–44, for differences of weighting in relation to German supervisory boards.
[8]The position of schemes that pay bonuses on the basis of productivity rather than profit is somewhat ambiguous. I am inclined to view them as profit-related in that the point of increases in productivity is presumably to increase profits. (This view is apparently endorsed by Marchington et al., p. 8. But see Cotton, p. 96, for a rather sharper but not entirely convincing distinction between productivity schemes and profit sharing.)

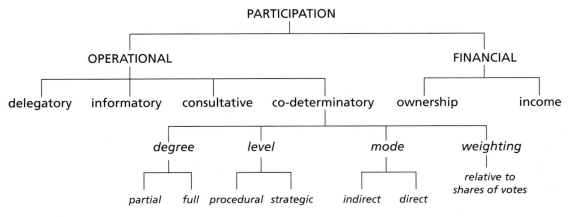

Figure 1 Forms of participation

In the first case, this means distinguishing between arrangements which originate in legalisation and those which do not. For those which do not, there is further distinction between arrangements granted or imposed by management and those which stem from negotiation between the two sides of industry or even, in rare instances, imposed on management by the workforce.

In terms of motive the divisions are potentially vast but in practice probably come down to two very broad and easily recognizable options which, for my purposes, need only minimal explanation. They are considerations of equity as opposed to considerations of efficiency. When the motive is equity, then participation is seen as a means to the end of giving employees a greater share in the operational and/or financial aspects of the business. It is an essentially moral motive which sees the share which employees have without participation as unfair. (For the reason why participation increases that share, see section 7.) When the motive is efficiency, participation is seen as means of improving the performance of employees *through* giving them a greater share in operational and/or financial aspects. (The assumption is that the greater share brings about this improvement through increasing the commitment and/or contentment of staff.) It is, unlike equity, not an essentially moral motive. (Why efficiency can be desired is left open.) However, it can well have a moral dimension to it in so far as increases in efficiency are seen as a means of increasing overall welfare within the business and/or wider society. Also, of

course, the two motives can be combined. It can be accepted that participation increases *both* equity and efficiency. (Add to this a belief in the welfare benefits of efficiency, and participation has *two* specifically moral justifications.) If, on the other hand, it were accepted that participation has no effect on efficiency or even a detrimental effect, then considerations of efficiency can either be safely ignored when the motive is one of equity or else be balanced against the supposed improvements in fairness achieved through participation.

Motive is not, of course, independent of source. All things being equal, a particular motive is likely to have a particular source. So, for example, considerations of efficiency are likely to be to the fore when participatory arrangements have a purely managerial source.[9] Conversely, it is more likely to be equity when the employee side is the source; and perhaps a mixture of equity and efficiency when the source is legislative. The link is not, however, a necessary one. In principle, any motive can spring from any source. A management could, for example, be motivated purely by considerations of equity in establishing some particular set of participatory arrangements—idealism is possible even here.

[9]Both Cotton, p. 3, and Marchington et al., p. 7, define "involvement" through a combination of equity motive and managerial source. (Though for the latter such "involvement" is a sub-category of "participation" that is perhaps close to my "delegatory participation," whereas for the former—as pointed out in note 1—a reverse relationship holds and "participation" is a sub-category of "involvement.")

What is also true is that there is no necessary link between either source or motive and any particular *form* of participation. Any particular form of participation can, in principle, have any particular source and/or motive. Even when there is a strong causal link between motive and source, it does not *necessarily* follow that any particular form of participation is going to be implemented. It all depends on what is believed about any particular form of participation. So, for example, a management motivated by considerations of efficiency might implement a far-reaching programme of co-determinatory participation if it believed that this was the way to maximize efficiency. Conversely, a workforce motivated solely by considerations of equity might, if it were in its power, totally reject such a programme if it believed that the only result would be to increase the burden of responsibility on already overburdened workers. They would, in other words, be rejecting it as inequitable.

The lack of any necessary link between source, motive, and forms of participation means that schemes of classification based on any one of them are, in principle, independent of each other. The three classifications must run in parallel with each other, with any linkage between them operating on a purely contingent basis. (See Figure 2 for a summary of section 4.)

5. Participation distinct from bargaining

For what appears to be very good reasons collective bargaining is often regarded as a form of participation. The apparently good reasons are that it too is a way of relating the two sides of industry and that what emerges from it is a kind of joint decision making between them (in the shape of negotiated settlements). Consequently, or so it seems, collective bargaining has to be regarded as a variant on what I have labelled "co-determinatory participation."[10] (This argument could just as well apply to that performance based bargaining with individual employees presently favoured by managers as it does to trade union based collective bargaining and so to cover both I will refer only to "bargaining.")

Despite these undoubted similarities, bargaining ought not to be regarded as a variety of co-determinatory participation or even as at all participatory in nature. It is, I would argue, a very different and even contrary way of relating the sides of industry as compared to participation. It lacks the element of sharing essential to participation. In bargaining the two sides of industry reach a joint decision but they are, by definition, relating to each other as *opposing* sides. Otherwise there is nothing to bargain over: nothing to pit opposing interests against, be it those of buyer and seller or, as in the industrial relations sort of bargaining, employer and employee. By contrast, in being based on sharing, participation is, by definition, a process in which what may well be opposing interests are brought together in some way. This does not of course mean that differences of interest are abolished—there is at the very least always going to be scope for a disagreement about the precise share going to each side under participatory arrangements. But simply from the fact it is based on sharing, a participating arrangement is always going to be one which establishes a common

[10]See Wallace Bell, D.: 1979, *Industrial Participation* (Pitman, London), p. 10, and possibly Marchington et al., p. 7, for endorsements of the view that collective bargaining is a form of co-determinatory participation. See Knudsen, pp. 24–25, for a rejection and the citing of two other endorsements.

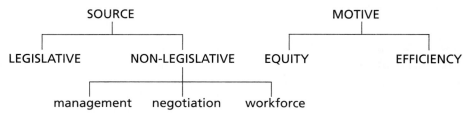

Figure 2 Sources and motives for participation

interest over and above the still separate interest of the parties involved. Where there is participation in the form of profit sharing, for instance, then although there is still scope for disagreement over the share of the proceeds going to each side, there is a common interest in total profits being as high as possible in order to ensure that the amount being received under each share is as high as possible. Likewise, where there is co-determinatory participation then there is a common interest in the joint decision being the right decision—albeit that each side might have wished for the power to vest rather more of its still separate interests in that decision.

With bargaining, on the other hand, there is none of this subsuming of interests within an over-arching common interest. What common interests there might be can play only an extrinsic role. With bargaining there is, for example, nearly always going to be a common interest in having an outcome that permits the organization wherein it takes place to survive and prosper. But any such common interest is, at most, part of the background against which bargaining takes place. It cannot, as it is under participatory arrangements, be intrinsic to the process itself.

Bargaining starts from opposing interests and seeks, at best, their accommodation. However constrained by a background of *common* interest, it remains if not adversarial then at least competitive. In contrast, however constrained by a background of *opposing* interests, in being based on sharing, participation is essentially co-operative in character. Within the scope of the participatory arrangement it establishes what is, in effect, a joint venture between management and labour. Thus, in so far as they are both mechanisms for joint decision making between management and labour, bargaining and participation are alike in what they do (though participation does far more), but more or less total opposites in the way they do it. Bargaining cannot, therefore, be regarded as a form of participation of any kind, co-determinatory or otherwise.

6. *Participation as organizational, bargaining as extra-organizational, and being organizational as the key to understanding participation*

This contrast between participation and bargaining is only partly accounted for by the fact that one is

based on sharing and the other is not. There is a deeper reason which not only accounts for the presence and absence of that factor but also explains the underlying character of participatory arrangements. This deeper reason is that, in a very particular but none the less very fundamental sense, participation is a strictly *organizational* way of handling the relationship between the two sides of industry whereas in that same very particular but fundamental sense, bargaining figures as an *extra*-organizational way.

In saying this of bargaining I am specifically contrasting it with participation. What I am not doing is suggesting that bargaining takes place totally outside an organizational context. Clearly it does not. The two sides of industry engage in bargaining precisely because of an organizational context which constitutes them as "two sides." (They have to be the two sides of something and that something is the organization to which they both belong.) More particularly, bargaining can also be built into organizational structures through such mechanisms as joint negotiating committees (for collective bargaining) or appraisal procedures (for individual bargaining). Nothing I am saying denies such ways of being organizational to bargaining. I am making the very restricted claim that bargaining falls outside the organizational in a sense that is both intrinsic to participation and, though this is a subsidiary matter, fundamental to businesses as organizations.

The fundamental sense in question is the business as a combination of management structure and property entitlements. The first element in this combining is nothing more than the familiar reality of the business organization as lines of managerial authority and responsibility running from top to bottom in some more or less hierarchical fashion (the sort of thing represented by organizational diagrams). The second is the equally familiar reality of the business as an organization based upon ownership and the resulting division into employer as opposed to employee and capital as opposed to labour which gives the one a right to profits and the other a right to wages. That this system of property entitlements operates in combination with managerial structures is, of course, because as a matter of generally prevailing legal fact (and not withstanding a sometimes present separation of ownership and control), managerial authority is ultimately derived from ownership. This then, is a combination of organizational principles that is very clearly fundamental to businesses (as generally constituted) and, quite possibly, definitive. It is, moreover, essentially distributive. This is clearly the case with regard to the property entitlements factor as it very obviously forms the basis for a distribution of financial rewards between the two sides of industry. But it is almost as obviously the case with the management structures element. For what, at bottom, this is all about is the distribution of authority and accountability (as well as power and prestige) between different organizational levels and, more generally, between management as opposed to labour.[11] So judged in relation to these two undeniably fundamental and perhaps even definitive organizational principles, a business is essentially a mechanism for distributing rewards and responsibilities between the two sides of industry. However, whether definitive or not, and no matter to what extent they are fundamental, it is specifically in relation to management structures and property entitlements that I want to say that participation is "organizational" and bargaining "extra-organizational."

What makes participation a strictly organizational process in relation to these two elements is that it always operates through them. In all its different forms it is, in fact, nothing but a way of arranging one or other of these two organizational elements. This is demonstrated by the already noted division of all forms of participation into either operational or financial categories (section 3). For what this amounts to is a division between arrangements involving management structures and those involving property entitlements. When schemes for delegation, informing, consulting, or co-determination are introduced, then it is management structures that are being rearranged. When it is schemes for employee share ownership or profit sharing, then property entitlements are being rearranged. So granted that, as a matter of established practice, all participatory arrangements fall into either the operational or financial categories, then in practice all participatory arrangements involve one or other of those two organizational elements. However, even without reference to that prior categorization we can recognise that this is going to be so simply on the basis that these two organizational elements are, as I have pointed out, essentially distributive in character and, moreover, distributive in relation to

the two sides of industry division. As, therefore, participation is always about employees sharing in some aspect of the business with the employing side, it is difficult to see how it could be anything other than a particular way of arranging one or other of these two organizational elements. By what other means *could* it function? (If, as I am here suggesting, there is no way for there to be distribution between the two sides of industry which does *not* involve managerial structures or property entitlements, then it is a necessary and not merely contingent fact that participation is always an arrangement involving one or other of these two organizational elements.)

Conversely, it is precisely because it does not operate through these two organizational factors that bargaining does not involve sharing and so, despite overlapping with participation in what it does (joint decision making), functions in an entirely different way: competitively rather than cooperatively. Certainly bargaining is very much *about* management structures and property entitlements in that as a negotiation concerning the working and financial conditions of employees, it is those two organizational elements that are being bargained over. But forming the subject matter of a deliberative process is a very different matter from being the mechanism through which the process operates. In recognizing that the latter is the case for participation, we recognise not just what fundamentally distinguishes it from bargaining, but also its underlying character: not just something giving employees a share in the businesses they work for but, more precisely, a means of giving them a share which operates through the specifically organizational elements of managerial structures and property entitlements. Essentially then, the key to understanding participation lies in its contrast with bargaining as a way of ordering the relationship between the two sides of industry and, consequently, of ordering industrial relations in general.

7. Explanatory consequences: understanding why participation presupposes employee subordination, is relative to normal sharing, and is a reforming middle way

What we can now also see is just why participation is viewed with suspicion by those that would

[11]See Chryssides and Kaler, pp. 73–75, on the hierarchical distribution of responsibilities within business organizations.

regard it as a "management tool" for exercising control over workers and undermining their capacity for collective action.[12] In being a way of ordering relations between the two sides of industry that is not only essentially co-operative but also organizational, participation is all about integrating employees with the business. It not only makes the area covered by the participatory arrangement something, as I said, of a joint venture between management and labour, it is also a way of handling industrial relations through strictly organizational arrangements. In this last regard, therefore, it is a way of ordering relations between the two sides of industry which preserves both the subordination of workers to managers contained within management structures (managers give the orders) *and* the subordination of labour to capital contained within property entitlements (capital hires labour). In contrast, though clearly not independent of either sort of subordination, bargaining does at least escape it to the extent that it does not operate through mechanisms which incorporate them. In bargaining there is an element of equality to the relationship in the fact that no matter how unequal their bargaining power, the two sides of industry do at least face each other with a mutual status as bargainers rather than in the subordinating and subordinate roles of managing and managed or employer and employee.

Having said that, it is undoubtedly true that participation modifies the relationship in a way which because it involves employees sharing in operational or financial aspects of the business can be very properly said to *lessen* the extent of subordination in either case. It does this because it must, to some extent, *increase* the share going to the worker side. Why it must is because otherwise there is nothing to distinguish participatory arrangements from any other way of arranging managerial structures and property entitlements. Simply from working within a business and being paid to do so an employee is going to have a share in running it and in its financial proceeds. It is, as I have pointed out, in the nature of managerial structures and property entitlements that they dis-

tribute responsibilities and rewards between the two sides of industry. Consequently, there is no way of arranging either of these two organizational elements without them granting some kind of share in control and financial proceeds to employees—however minimal or meagre. Even the most command-based management has to assign some responsibility to employees; and even the most unfavourable set of property entitlements gives employees some share in rewards. If then, participatory ways of arranging these two things are to be distinguished from non-participatory ways, it can only be on the basis that the former grant a larger share than the latter.

What constitutes a larger share is, of course, infinitely variable. It all depends what is normal: either as between departments, firms, industries, or businesses as a whole. All that can be said is that any arrangement of managerial structures or property entitlements *designed* to give the employee side a greater share in the operational or financial aspects of the business than some prevailing norm is to be regarded as participatory. (The qualification "designed" allows for situations where norms are exceeded in incidental ways that only mimic participation. For example, where there is an above average employee share in control because of lax management, or above average employee remuneration because of labour shortages or simple employer generosity.)

Although participatory arrangements must give employees a greater share than normal, there has to be limits to the size of that share for the arrangement to count as "participatory." Most clearly, it cannot amount to total possession. A situation in which employees have total control, or total ownership, or are in receipt of all profits, is not one in which participation is possible in any area whatsoever. There can only be participation with respect to any aspect of a business when employees are in less than total possession of that aspect. If, for example, it is a totally employee owned business with all profits going to employees but control is in the hands of a separate class of managers, then participation in operational matters is possible. (Though it is perhaps not necessary given that as owners the workers can sack the managers!)

The exact degree to which employee possession must be less than total for participation to be

[12]See Marchington et al., p. 10, for reference to what they label a "control/labour process" model which sees participation as a merely "cosmetic" device for obscuring and extending managerial control.

possible is a moot point. Arguably, it must not exceed equality. If it does then it is perhaps the other side, the managers and/or employers, that are being granted the participation; which given that the term is short hand, for "*employee* participation" (see section 1(a)), means this is not "participation" in the sense relevant here. Arguably then, this is a sense which not only requires a two sides of industry division, but a division in which the employee side can be never more than equal.

If so, then those who talk of workers' control (or for that matter worker ownership) as an ultimate form of participation are probably mistaken.[13] (They are undoubtedly mistaken if they mean total control or ownership.) On a more positive note, given they probably want the worker share to be more than equal, those who denounce participation as a "management tool" must surely have their suspicions confirmed by the finding that participation can never give employees a more than equal share. As against them, however, those who denounce participation as a threat to (any or all of) management's "right to manage," or property rights, or efficiency, must have *their* suspicions confirmed by the finding that it can be anything up to equality.[14] (A contrast of half full as opposed to half empty perhaps?) Unsurprisingly, therefore, support for participation is essentially reformist in character.[15] For reasons of equity and/or efficiency (see section 4), there is seen to be a need to increase the employee share; but only up to a possible half share, and in a way which not only preserves a two sides of industry division but also acts through specifically organizational structures. In so acting, participation provides an alternative to bargaining as a way of relating the two sides of industry and conducting industrial relations in general: an organizational as opposed to extra-organizational way and, more particularly, a cooperative as opposed to competitive way. In contrast, those who oppose participation endorse bargaining as the proper basis for industrial relations: though for those opposing participation because it gives employees too much, this endorsement is because bargaining reflects an essentially benign existing order; while for those who oppose it for giving employees too little, it is because bargaining has the virtue of at least honestly reflecting a harsh prevailing reality.

[13]Wallace Bell, p. 14, allows the possibility of workers' control being an ultimate form of participation. Marchington et al., pp. 7–8, appear to positively endorse this contention. Knudsen, p. 10, cites two apparent endorsements, but rejects it.

[14]See Northrup, H. R.: 1990. "Worker Participation: Industrial Democracy or Union Power Enhancement?," in J. R. DesJardins and J. J. McCall (eds.), *Contemporary Issues in Business Ethics,* 2nd edition (Wadsworth, Belmont), pp. 173–177, for opposition to participation as a threat to the "right to manage."

[15]See McCall, J. J.: 1990. "Participation in Employment," in DesJardins and McCall, pp. 165–173, for a defence of participation illustrating its reformist character.

Questions for Chapter 3

1. Higgins suggests that the distinction between services marketing and product marketing is not nearly so great as is sometimes believed. Her model of "internal marketing" was developed in the context of service industries. Is it so easily transferred to what have traditionally been viewed as product industries as she suggests?

2. Higgins suggests that the "4 Ps of marketing" can be applied to the relationship between labor and management. What are these "4 Ps"? Do you agree that they can be applied to the labor-management relationship? Why or why not?

3. Is the duty to bargain in good faith consistent with the "bluffing" that takes place during negotiations? Explain. Do you agree with Post that present negotiating practices typically foster ill-will? How would you defend your view?
4. Do you think that collaborative collective bargaining could be made to work? Why or why not?
5. Hiley mentions the worry of many employers that if the doctrine of employment-at-will is eroded, the fear of litigation will bring about an increasing reluctance to terminate an employee, even when there is just cause. Is such a fear well-grounded? If it is, how would you suggest remedying the situation?
6. If we take seriously the claim that employers should not be able to terminate arbitrarily and without notice, must we also revise our views about whether an employee has the right to resign arbitrarily and without notice? Why or why not?
7. Kaler suggests that "the place of consultation within operational participation is ambiguous." What does he mean by saying this, and why does he say it?
8. What arguments are there for suggesting that collective bargaining is a form of employee participation? Why does Kaler reject these arguments?

Case 3.1 The Terminated Employee[1]

Ms. Laverty and Mr. Johnson lived together in a common-law relationship. They were both friends of Mr. Cooper who ran a small metal-plating business. In 1980, Cooper hired Laverty as his only salesperson. She had many key responsibilities, including costing, pricing, and keeping customer accounts. By all reports, she was an effective employee and at least partially responsible for the prospering of Cooper's company.

A year of so after hiring Laverty, Cooper permitted Johnson the use of part of his premises to start a chemical-mixing business complementary to Cooper's metal-plating. In 1984, Johnson moved his business to other premises.

In 1985, Cooper accidentally discovered that Johnson's business was no longer complementary, but had become a competitor. Although Cooper had no evidence that Johnson, either through Laverty or by other means, had taken any business from him, Cooper dismissed Laverty without notice. Laverty sued Cooper for wrongful dismissal. During the course of the proceedings, it became clear that, although there was no evidence that Laverty in any way directed existing or potential customers away from Cooper, she was aware that Johnson's new venture was in competition with Cooper's business.

1. Would you agree that Laverty's knowledge of Cooper's business, together with her responsibility as sales manager, were incompatible with her continuing relationship with Johnson and that her dismissal without notice was therefore justified?
2. Would it have been more fair for Cooper to have dismissed Laverty with notice?
3. Did Johnson act ethically?
4. Did Laverty have any obligation to inform Cooper of the new status of Johnson's business? If she had so informed him, should Cooper have then demanded her notice?

[1]Based on Laverty v. Cooper Plating Inc., 17 *Canadian Cases in Employment Law* 44 (1987).

Case 3.2 Successive Employers and the Duty to Bargain[2]

In 1982, Sterlingwale Corporation, which had operated a textile dyeing and finishing plant in Fall River, Massachusetts, for over thirty years, went out of business. The reason for this lay in a combination of poor economic conditions and increased foreign competition. During the period of Sterlingwale's decline in the late seventies and early eighties, the union representing employees met with company officials regarding layoffs and Sterlingwale's failure to pay premiums on group-health insurance. The union expressed its interests in keeping the company operating and in meeting with prospective buyers. The union also agreed in 1980 to extend the expiration date of the collective agreement, due to expire April 1, 1981, for one year without any wage increase and to improve labor productivity.

Shortly after the plant's closing, Herbert Chase, former vice-president in charge of sales for Sterlingwale, and Arthur Friedman, president of one of Sterlingwale's major customers, formed the Fall River Dyeing and Finishing Corporation, and acquired the plant and its assets. Their plan was to use Sterlingwale's former assets and workforce to engage in the commission-dyeing business.

In September 1982, Fall River Dyeing and Finishing began operating the plant and hiring employees. Their initial hiring goal was one full shift of workers. They achieved this goal by mid-January 1983, at which time the large majority of their workers were former Sterlingwale employees. By mid-April 1983, they were hiring two shifts of workers and, for the first time, former

Sterlingwale employees did not constitute the majority of their employees, though this was true only by the slimmest of margins. Working conditions for employees continued to be the same as under Sterlingwale and over half of the new company's business came from former Sterlingwale customers.

In October 1982, the union requested that Fall River recognize it as the bargaining agent for employees and begin collective bargaining. Fall River refused, stating that the request had no legal basis. The union subsequently filed an unfair labor practice charge with the National Labor Relations Board.

1. Do you agree with the union's demand that Fall River should recognize it as the employee's bargaining agent? Why or why not?

2. Whether or not the original union should be recognized as the employees' bargaining agent depends on its continuity, and this in turn depends on whether the majority of employees were ex-Sterlingwale workers. Fall River insisted that the question of whether the majority of workers were ex-Sterlingwale workers should not be asked prior to its hiring a "full complement of workers," that is, mid-April when it put on two shifts of workers and at which time new employees outnumbered ex-Sterlingwale employees. The union insisted that the question should be asked as soon as the employer hired a "substantial and representative" complement of employees, that is, mid-January at which time ex-Sterlingwale employees outnumbered new employees. With whom do you agree and why?

[2]Based on Fall River Dyeing & Finishing Corp. v. N.L.R.B., 107 *Supreme Court Reporter* 2225 (1987).

Further Readings for Chapter 3

Richard D. Arvey and Gary L. Renz, "Fairness in the Selection of Employees," *Journal of Business Ethics* 11, 1992, pp. 331–340.

Stephan Cludts, "Organization Theory and the Ethics of Participation," *Journal of Business Ethics* 21, 1999, pp. 229–236. (This volume of the *Journal of Business*

Ethics is devoted to the topic of employee participation and has a number of worthwhile articles.)

Gertrude Ezorsky, ed., *Moral Rights in the Workplace* (Albany, NY: State University of New York Press, 1987).

Mary Gibson, *Worker's Rights* (Totowa, NJ: Rowman & Allanheld, 1983).

F.A. Reichheld, "Loyalty Based Management," *Harvard Business Review* (July–August) 1993, pp. 115–125.

Patricia Werhane, "Individual Rights in Business" in *Just Business,* ed. Tom Regan (New York: Random House, 1984).

INFOTRAC COLLEGE EDITION To learn more about the topics from this chapter, you can use the following words to conduct an electronic search on InfoTrac College Edition, an online library of journals. Here you will find a multitude of articles from various sources and perspectives: *www.infotrac-college.com/wadsworth/access.html*

worker rights   due process

employment at will   participation

Chapter 4

Privacy in the Workplace

Introduction

IT IS NOT AS EASY as one might first think to define what privacy is or amounts to. There is general agreement that privacy involves a degree of control over information about oneself and a degree of control over how one interacts with others. The problem is that it is not easy to say how much control it involves. Any given piece of information or specific interaction might be considered private in one context, but not in another. This is so because what is considered private depends on the relation one has to the other person. Thus, what is private in relation to one's spouse is quite different than what is private in relation to one's employer. One's spouse might legitimately ask whether one finds a certain brand of underwear comfortable, but it would be inappropriate for one's employer to ask the same question.

It seems clear that what is rightfully considered private depends on the relation to the other person. The hard question is, How do we move beyond this very general observation to specifics? In the context of our present discussion, how do we determine what should be considered private in the relation between employer and employee? What information is an employer or an employee entitled to, what uses may be made of that information, and what methods may be employed in gathering information? The importance of these questions is highlighted by the emergence of powerful new techniques of gathering and processing information. As is frequently the case, the development of new technologies raises concern over their possible abuse.

A standard suggestion is that employers, and presumably employees, should be entitled to gather information that is relevant to a freely agreed-upon contract. Though this suggestion of limiting information disclosure to what is job-relevant seems practical and helpful, it is not without problems. Those who advocate this approach do not wish to include information concerning sexual orientation, marital status, and political or religious beliefs as job-relevant, yet these may all conceivably affect how an individual interacts with others and hence that individual's job performance. Further, this suggestion tells us nothing about what means may be used to gather information. It also fails to address the question of whether in practice there typically exists an equal balance of power between the contracting parties and hence whether the disclosure of information was freely agreed to by the weaker party.

It seems that, useful though it may be, the notion of job relevance will not stand on its own. What is needed is a way of linking job relevance to moral value. Limiting information to what is job-relevant is done because we view privacy as morally valuable. But why do we view privacy as morally valuable?

One very plausible answer is that we value privacy because it is a condition of autonomy, that is, the capacity to make genuine choices about one's goals and activities. Inasmuch as the inability to control information about oneself makes one more vulnerable to manipulation by others, lack of privacy tends to destroy autonomy. This suggests that the fundamental issue is that of respecting the autonomy of individuals. The problem, of course, is that an individual's autonomy is always qualified by the autonomy of other individuals. The legitimate interests of the employee are invariably conditioned by the legitimate interests of the employer, and vice versa. On this understanding of the value of privacy, the notion of job relevance serves as a useful, but scarcely complete, guide to the information employer and employee are entitled to in the context of their relationship.

Our four readings explore concerns raised by the technologies of drug testing and genetic screening. In our first reading, "Drug Testing in Employment," Joseph DesJardins and Ronald Duska examine the issue of whether drug testing violates employee privacy. They ground employee privacy in a contractualist view which holds that an employer is only entitled to information about an employee that is relevant to job performance or safety. They go on to argue that the knowledge of whether an employee is using drugs is not relevant to job performance and only rarely relevant to the issue of safety.

With respect to job performance, they argue that the issue is not whether an employee is taking drugs, but whether the employee is doing his or her job satisfactorily. If the employee is performing satisfactorily, there exists no reason to test him or her; if the employee is not, then one may terminate his or her employment regardless of the cause of nonperformance. In neither case is there any need to test for use of drugs.

With respect to safety, they are willing to agree that testing for drug use may sometimes be appropriate. They suggest that in jobs where the potential for harm is clear and present, and if the employee has given reason to doubt his or her reliability, and if the drugs being tested for really pose a hazard, then testing is appropriate if there exist no equally effective, less intrusive means of acquiring the information needed to ensure safety. They think, however, that such instances are very few in number.

In our second reading, "Drug Testing and the Right to Privacy: Arguing the Ethics of Workplace Drug Testing," Michael Cranford argues that drug testing can be justified as long as the personal information it reveals is collected and used in a way that is relevant to the contractual relationship between employer and employee. His argument for this is that knowledge of drug abuse is relevant to determining whether an employee is fulfilling the terms of the employment contract, or, in the case of a prospective employee, can reasonably be expected to fulfill the terms of the employment contract. Just as an employer is entitled to know an employee's or prospective employee's educational background in order to judge whether that person can fulfill the terms of the employment contract, an employer is entitled to know of drug abuse.

Cranford is very clear that his acceptance of the legitimacy of drug testing does not imply there are not strict limitations on when and how it is permissible for employers to drug-test. In addition to the requirement that the information obtained be relevant to evaluating whether the terms of employment are being met, he sets out three further requirements for drug testing. These are: (1) it must not be unnecessarily harmful or intrusive, (2) it must be efficient and specific, and (3) it must be accurate and precise or at least capable of being checked for accuracy and precision.

After setting out his position, Cranford goes on in the latter part of his paper to defend his argument against possible criticisms. Of particular interest is his reply to the position developed by DesJardins and Duska in our preceding reading. He agrees with them that an employer does not have a right to expect optimal performance from an employee. He argues, however, that drug testing, properly understood, is not directed at obtaining optimal performance from individual employees but rather at ensuring a workplace free from the abuse of drugs. His position is that drug abuse is correlated not with any given employee's performance, but rather with a negative impact on workplace productivity in general. It is thus relevant to determining whether employees will be in a position to honor their contractual obligations.

In our third reading, David Resnik takes up the issue of genetic screening. In his article "Genetic Privacy in Employment," he attempts to specify the general criteria by which an employer is entitled to information he or she would not otherwise be entitled to. The development of such criteria permits their application to situations involving genetic information to determine the morality of genetic screening. Unlike some writers who reserve the term *invasion of privacy* for the wrongful gathering of information, Resnik is prepared to talk of legitimate "invasions" of privacy. Whether or not a particular "invasion" of privacy is justified will depend on whether the employer is entitled to the information that was acquired. This, in turn, will depend on whether the information is relevant to the employee's ability to perform the job.

He concludes that, although many other questions must be answered before implementing any policy concerning the disclosure of genetic information to employers, it is possible to develop genetic-privacy guidelines. These would place strong restrictions on what information employers could legitimately demand, but they would allow some instances in which employers could gain access to genetic information concerning employees.

Our fourth and final reading, "Genetic Information: Consumers' Right to Privacy Versus Insurance Companies' Right to Know," presents arguments both for and against the disclosure of genetic information to insurance companies. The authors, Shaheen Borna and Stephen Avila go on to relate these arguments to a survey of public opinion and to suggest different public policy options.

Arguments for the disclosure of genetic information appeal to what is known as the principle of fair discrimination. Put simply, this principle amounts to the claim that individuals with low-risk factors should pay lower premiums than individuals with high-risk factors. In order to implement this principle, insurance companies routinely collect medical information in order to assess risk. They argue that access to genetic information should be treated no differently than access to other health-related information.

They further argue that to restrict insurance companies' access to such information would permit individuals who have prior knowledge of genetically based future health problems to buy comprehensive insurance at a premium that does not reflect their true risk factor. They suggest that in the long run this would force premiums up to the point where those at low risk would not consider it worthwhile to purchase insurance, leaving only those at high risk to purchase insurance. This process would tend to repeat itself with the possible final result that no insurance would be offered at any price.

Those resisting the disclosure of genetic information to insurance companies express several concerns. The first is that those at higher risk may be forced to pay higher premiums or be denied insurance altogether. Given an increasing reliance upon health insurance, such a denial amounts to a denial of health care for certain individuals.

A second concern is that once genetic information is obtained it becomes part of a patient's permanent medical record. Releasing this information increases the danger that it can be used for purposes other than underwriting an insurance policy. Medical records are routinely shared through the Medical Information Bureau and are also subject to subpoena.

A third concern is that many people may not wish to know their genetic makeup. Finding that one carries a defective gene that means there is a great probability that one will develop an incurable disease in the future might very well be information that an individual has no desire to uncover.

These are legitimate concerns. How strongly they should count against the argument from fair discrimination will depend on how we conceive the nature of health insurance and its relation to a national health care system. If, as is presently the case, health insurance companies operate as private for-profit organizations, then it seems unfair that they should be expected to provide quasi-public health services. If, on the other hand, insurance companies become increasingly subsidized by government funding and function as a component of the national health care system, then the argument from fair discrimination will count for less.

Borna and Avila go on to note that there are several models of how health insurance should operate. Unfortunately, there is little public understanding of the complex and difficult issues involved in balancing the strengths and weaknesses of various models. Their survey reveals that people typically are against the use of genetic testing for underwriting purposes and oppose rejecting any applicants because of their genetic makeup. At the same time, however, these respondents typically oppose higher premiums and any increase in taxes to cover the health care costs of individuals with defective genes. We thus seem faced with the very human tendency to try to have our cake and eat it too.

Drug Testing in Employment

JOSEPH DESJARDINS AND RONALD DUSKA*

ACCORDING TO ONE SURVEY, nearly one-half of all Fortune 500 companies were planning to administer drug tests to employees and prospective employees by the end of 1987.[1] Counter to what seems to be the current trend in favor of drug testing, we will argue that it is rarely legitimate to override an employee's or applicant's right to privacy by using such tests or procedures.[2]

Opening Stipulations

We take privacy to be an "employee right" by which we mean a presumptive moral entitlement to receive certain goods or be protected from certain harms in the workplace.[3] Such a right creates

a *prima facie* obligation on the part of the employer to provide the relevant goods or, as in this case, refrain from the relevant harmful treatment. These rights prevent employees from being placed in the fundamentally coercive position where they must choose between their job and other basic human goods.

Further, we view the employer-employee relationship as essentially contractual. The employer-employee relationship is an economic one and, unlike relationships such as those between a government and its citizens or a parent and a child, exists primarily as a means for satisfying the economic interests of the contracting parties. The obligations that each party incurs are only those that it voluntarily takes on. Given such a contractual relationship, certain areas of the employee's life remain their own private concern and no employer has a right to invade them. On these presumptions we maintain that certain information about an employee is rightfully private, i.e. the employee has a right to privacy.

The Right To Privacy

According to George Brenkert, a right to privacy involves a three-place relation between a person A, some information X, and another person B. The right to privacy is violated only when B deliberately comes to possess information X about A, and no relationship between A and B exists which could justify B's coming to know X about A.[4] Thus, for

*Versions of this paper were read to the Department of Philosophy at Southern Connecticut State University and to the Society of Business Ethics. The authors would like to thank those people, as well as Robert Baum and Norman Bowie, the editors of *Business and Professional Ethics Journal* for their many helpful comments. Professor Duska wishes to thank the Pew Memorial Trust for a grant providing released time to work on this paper.

[1] *The New Republic,* March 31, 1986.
[2] This trend primarily involves screening employees for such drugs as marijuana, cocaine, amphetamines, barbituates, and opiates (e.g., heroin, methadone and morphine). While alcohol is also a drug that can be abused in the workplace, it seldom is among the drugs mentioned in conjunction with employee testing. We believe that testing which proves justified for controlled substances will, *a fortiori,* be justified for alcohol as well.
[3] "A Defense of Employee Rights," Joseph DesJardins and John McCall, *Journal of Business Ethics,* Vol. 4, (1985). We should emphasize that our concern is with the *moral* rights of privacy for employees and not with any specific or prospective *legal* rights. Readers interested in pursuing the legal aspects of employee drug testing should consult: "Workplace Privacy Issues and Employee Screening Policies" by Richard Lehe and David Middlebrooks in *Employee Relations Law Journal* (Vol. 11, no. 3) pp. 407–21; and "Screening Workers for Drugs: A Legal and Ethical Framework" by Mark Rothstein, in *Employee Relations Law Journal* (vol. 11, no. 3) pp. 422–36.

[4] "Privacy, Polygraphs, and Work," George Brenkert, *Business and Professional Ethics Journal,* vol 1, no. 1 (Fall 1981). For a more general discussion of privacy in the workplace see "Privacy in Employment" by Joseph DesJardins in *Moral Rights in the Workplace* edited by Gertrude Ezorsky, (SUNY Press, 1987). A good resource for philosophical work on privacy can be found in "Recent Work on the Concept of Privacy" by W. A. Parent, in *American Philosophical Quarterly* (Vol. 20, Oct. 1983) pp. 341–56.

From Business and Professional Ethics Journal *6(3), 1986. Reprinted by permission.*

example, the relationship one has with a mortgage company would justify that company's coming to know about one's salary, but the relationship one has with a neighbor does not justify the neighbor's coming to know that information. Hence, an employee's right to privacy is violated whenever personal information is requested, collected and/or used by an employer in a way or for any purpose that is *irrelevant to* or *in violation of* the contractual relationship that exists between *employer and employee.*

Since drug-testing is a means for obtaining information, the information sought must be relevant to the contract in order for the drug testing not to violate privacy. Hence, we must first decide if knowledge of drug use obtained by drug testing is job-relevant. In cases where the knowledge of drug use is *not* relevant, there appears to be no justification for subjecting employees to drug tests. In cases where information of drug use is job-relevant, we need to consider if, when, and under what conditions using a means such as drug testing to obtain that knowledge is justified.

Is Knowledge of Drug Use Job-Relevant Information?

There seem to be two arguments used to establish that knowledge of drug use is job-relevant information. The first argument claims that drug use adversely affects job performance thereby leading to lower productivity, higher costs, and consequently lower profits. Drug testing is seen as a way of avoiding these adverse effects. According to some estimates twenty-five billion dollars ($25,000,000,000) are lost each year in the United States because of drug use.[5] This occurs because of loss in productivity, increase in costs due to theft, increased rates in health and liability insurance, and such. Since employers are contracting with an employee for the performance of specific tasks, employers seem to have a legitimate claim upon whatever personal information is relevant to an employee's ability to do the job.

The second argument claims that drug use has been and can be responsible for considerable harm to the employee him/herself, fellow employees,

the employer, and/or third parties, including consumers. In this case drug testing is defended because it is seen as a way of preventing possible harm. Further, since employers can be held liable for harms done both to third parties, e.g. customers, and to the employee or his/her fellow employees, knowledge of employee drug use will allow employers to gain information that can protect themselves from risks such as liability. But how good are these arguments? We turn to examine the arguments more closely.

The First Argument: Job Performance and Knowledge of Drug Use

The first argument holds that drug use leads to lower productivity and consequently implies that a knowledge of drug use obtained through drug-testing will allow an employer to increase productivity. It is generally assumed that people using certain drugs have their performances affected by such use. Since enhancing productivity is something any employer desires, any use of drugs that reduces productivity affects the employer in an undesirable way, and that use is, then, job-relevant. If such production losses can be eliminated by knowledge of the drug use, then knowledge of that drug use is job-relevant information. On the surface this argument seems reasonable. Obviously some drug use in lowering the level of performance can decrease productivity. Since the employer is entitled to a certain level of performance and drug use adversely affects performance, knowledge of that use seems job-relevant.

But this formulation of the argument leaves an important question unanswered. To what level of performance are employers entitled? Optimal performance, or some lower level? If some lower level, what? Employers have a valid claim upon some *certain level* of performance, such that a failure to perform up to this level would give the employer a justification for disciplining, firing or at least finding fault with the employee. But that does not necessarily mean that the employer has a right to a maximum or optimal level of performance, a level above and beyond a certain level of acceptability. It might be nice if the employee gives an employer a maximum effort or optimal performance, but that is above and beyond the call of the employee's

---

[5] *U.S. News and World Report,* Aug. 1983; *Newsweek,* May 1983.

duty and the employer can hardly claim a right at all times to the highest level of performance of which an employee is capable.

That there are limits on required levels of performance and productivity becomes clear if we recognize that job performance is person-related. It is person-related because one person's best efforts at a particular task might produce results well below the norm, while another person's minimal efforts might produce results abnormally high when compared to the norm. For example a professional baseball player's performance on a ball field will be much higher than the average person's since the average person is unskilled in baseball. We have all encountered people who work hard with little or no results, as well as people who work little with phenomenal results. Drug use in very talented people might diminish their performance or productivity, but that performance would still be better than the performance of the average person or someone totally lacking in the skills required. That being said, the important question now is whether the employer is entitled to an employee's maximum effort and best results, or merely to an effort sufficient to perform the task expected.

If the relevant consideration is whether the employee is producing as expected (according to the normal demands of the position and contract), not whether he/she is producing as much as possible, then knowledge of drug use is irrelevant or unnecessary. Let's see why.

If the person is producing what is expected, knowledge of drug use on the grounds of production is irrelevant since, *ex hypothesi* the production is satisfactory. If, on the other hand, the performance suffers, then, to the extent that it slips below the level justifiably expected, the employer has *prima facie* grounds for warning, disciplining or releasing the employee. But the justification for this is the person's unsatisfactory performance, not the person's use of drugs. Accordingly, drug use information is either unnecessary or irrelevant and consequently there are not sufficient grounds to override the right of privacy. Thus, unless we can argue that an employer is entitled to optimal performance, the argument fails.

This counter-argument should make it clear that the information which is sub-relevant, and consequently which is not rightfully private, is information about an employee's level of performance and not information about the underlying causes of that level. The fallacy of the argument which promotes drug testing in the name of increased productivity is the assumption that each employee is obliged to perform at an optimal, or at least quite high, level. But this is required under few, if any, contracts. What is required contractually is meeting the normally expected levels of production or performing the tasks in the job-description adequately (not optimally). If one can do that under the influence of drugs, then on the grounds of job-performance at least, drug use is rightfully private. If one cannot perform the task adequately, then the employee is not fulfilling the contract, and knowledge of the cause of the failure to perform is irrelevant on the contractual model.

Of course, if the employer suspects drug use or abuse as the cause of the unsatisfactory performance, then she might choose to help the person with counseling or rehabilitation. However, this does not seem to be something morally required of the employer. Rather, in the case of unsatisfactory performance, the employer has a *prima facie* justification for dismissing or disciplining the employee.

Before turning to the second argument which attempts to justify drug testing, we should mention a factor about drug use that is usually ignored in talk of productivity. The entire productivity argument is irrelevant for those cases in which employees use performance enhancing drugs. Amphetamines and steroids, for example, can actually enhance some performances. This points to the need for care when tying drug testing to job-performance. In the case of some drugs used by athletes, for example, drug testing is done because the drug-influenced performance is too good and therefore unfair, not because it leads to inadequate job-performance. In such a case, where the testing is done to ensure fair competition, the testing may be justified. But drug testing in sports is an entirely different matter than drug-testing in business.

To summarize our argument so far: Drug use may affect performances, but as long as the performance is at an acceptable level, the knowledge of drug use is irrelevant. If the performance is unacceptable, then that is sufficient cause for action to be taken. In this case an employee's failure to fulfill his/her end of a contract makes knowledge of the drug use unnecessary.

The Second Argument: Harm and the Knowledge of Drug Use to Prevent Harm

Even though the performance argument is inadequate, there is an argument that seems somewhat stronger. This is an argument based on the potential for drug use to cause harm. Using a type of Millian argument, one could argue that drug testing might be justified if such testing led to knowledge that would enable an employer to prevent harm. Drug use certainly can lead to harming others. Consequently, if knowledge of such drug use can prevent harm, then, knowing whether or not one's employee uses drugs might be a legitimate concern of an employer in certain circumstances. This second argument claims that knowledge of the employee's drug use is job-relevant because employees who are under the influence of drugs can pose a threat to the health and safety of themselves and others, and an employer who knows of that drug use and the harm it can cause has a responsibility to prevent it. Employers have both a general duty to prevent harm and the specific responsibility for harms done by their employees. Such responsibilities are sufficient reason for an employer to claim that information about an employee's drug use is relevant if that knowledge can prevent harm by giving the employer grounds for dismissing the employee or not allowing him/her to perform potentially harmful tasks. Employers might even claim a right to reduce unreasonable risks, in this case the risks involving legal and economic liability for harms caused by employees under the influence of drugs, as further justification for knowing about employee drug use.

This second argument differs from the first in which only a lowered job performance was relevant information. In this case, even to allow the performance is problematic, for the performance itself, more than being inadequate, can hurt people. We cannot be as sanguine about the prevention of harm as we can about inadequate production. Where drug use can cause serious harms, knowledge of that use becomes relevant if the knowledge of such use can lead to the prevention of harm and drug testing becomes justified as a means for obtaining that knowledge.

As we noted, we will begin initially by accepting this argument on roughly Millian grounds where restrictions on liberty are allowed in order to prevent harm to others. (The fact that one is harming oneself, if that does not harm others is not sufficient grounds for interference in another's behavior according to Mill.) In such a case an employer's obligation to prevent harm may override the obligation to respect an employee's privacy.

But let us examine this more closely. Upon examination, certain problems arise, so that even if there is a possibility of justifying drug testing to prevent harm, some caveats have to be observed and some limits set out.

Jobs With Potential to Cause Harm

To say that employers can use drug testing where that can prevent harm is not to say that every employer has the right to know about the drug use of every employee. Not every job poses a serious enough threat to justify an employer coming to know this information.

In deciding which jobs pose serious enough threats certain guidelines should be followed. First the potential for harm should be *clear* and *present*. Perhaps all jobs in some extended way pose potential threats to human well-being. We suppose an accountant's error could pose a threat of harm to someone somewhere. But some jobs like those of airline pilots, school bus drivers, public transit drivers and surgeons, are jobs in which unsatisfactory performance poses a clear and present danger to others. It would be much harder to make an argument that job performances by auditors, secretaries, executive vice-presidents for public relations, college teachers, professional athletes, and the like, could cause harm if those performances were carried on under the influence of drugs. They would cause harm only in exceptional cases.[6]

---

[6] Obviously we are speaking here of harms that go beyond the simple economic harm which results from unsatisfactory job performance. These economic harms were discussed in the first argument above. Further, we ignore such "harms" as providing bad role-models for adolescents, harms often used to justify drug tests for professional athletes. We think it unreasonable to hold an individual responsible for the image he/she provides to others.

Not Every Person Is to Be Tested

But, even if we can make a case that a particular job involves a clear and present danger for causing harm if performed under the influence of drugs, it is not appropriate to treat everyone holding such a job the same. Not every job-holder is equally threatening. There is less reason to investigate an airline pilot for drug use if that pilot has a twenty-year record of exceptional service than there is to investigate a pilot whose behavior has become erratic and unreliable recently, or than one who reports to work smelling of alcohol and slurring his words. Presuming that every airline pilot is equally threatening is to deny individuals the respect that they deserve as autonomous, rational agents. It is to ignore previous history and significant differences. It is also probably inefficient and leads to the lowering of morale. It is the likelihood of causing harm, and not the fact of being an airline pilot *per se,* that is relevant in deciding which employees in critical jobs to test.

So, even if knowledge of drug use is justifiable to prevent harm, we must be careful to limit this justification to a range of jobs and people where the potential for harm is clear and present. The jobs must be jobs that clearly can cause harm, and the specific employee should not be someone who is reliable with a history of such reliability. Finally, the drugs being tested should be those drugs, the use of which in those jobs is really potentially harmful.

Limitations on Drug-Testing Policies

Even when we identify those jobs and individuals where knowledge of drug use would be job-relevant information, we still need to examine whether some procedural limitations should not be placed upon the employer's testing for drugs. We have said that in cases where a real threat of harm exists and where evidence exists suggesting that a particular employee poses such a threat, an employer could be justified in knowing about drug use in order to prevent the potential harm. But we need to recognize that as long as the employer has the discretion for deciding when the potential for harm is clear and present, and for deciding which employees pose the threat of harm, the possibility

of abuse is great. Thus, some policy limiting the employer's power is called for.

Just as criminal law places numerous restrictions protecting individual dignity and liberty on the state's pursuit of its goals, so we should expect that some restrictions be placed on an employer in order to protect innocent employees from harm (including loss of job and damage to one's personal and professional reputation). Thus, some system of checks upon an employer's discretion in these matters seems advisable. Workers covered by collective bargaining agreements or individual contracts might be protected by clauses on those agreements that specify which jobs pose a real threat of harm (e.g., pilots but not cabin attendants) and what constitutes a just cause for investigating drug use. Local, state, and federal legislatures might do the same for workers not covered by employment contracts. What needs to be set up is a just employment relationship—one in which an employee's expectations and responsibilities are specified in advance and in which an employer's discretionary authority to discipline or dismiss an employee is limited.

Beyond that, any policy should accord with the nature of the employment relationship. Since that relationship is a contractual one, it should meet the condition of a morally valid contract, which is informed consent. Thus, in general, we would argue that only methods that have received the informed consent of employees can be used in acquiring information about drug use.[7]

A drug-testing policy that requires all employees to submit to a drug test or to jeopardize their job would seem coercive and therefore unacceptable. Being placed in such a fundamentally coercive position of having to choose between one's job and one's privacy does not provide the conditions for truly free consent. Policies that are unilaterally established by employers would likewise be unacceptable. Working with employees to develop company policy seems the only way to ensure that the policy will be fair to both parties. Prior notice of

[7]The philosophical literature on informed consent is often concerned with "informed consent" in a medical context. For an interesting discussion of informed consent in the workplace, see Mary Gibson, *Worker's Rights* (Rowman and Allanheld, 1983) especially pp. 13–14 and 74–75.

testing would also be required in order to give employees the option of freely refraining from drug use. It is morally preferable to prevent drug use than to punish users after the fact, since this approach treats employees as capable of making rational and informed decisions.

Further procedural limitations seem advisable as well. Employees should be notified of the results of the test, they should be entitled to appeal the results (perhaps through further tests by an independent laboratory) and the information obtained through tests ought to be kept confidential. In summary, limitations upon employer discretion for administering drug tests can be derived from the nature of the employment contract and from the recognition that drug testing is justified by the desire to prevent harm, not the desire to punish wrongdoing.

Effectiveness of Drug Testing

Having declared that the employer might have a right to test for drug use in order to prevent harm, we still need to examine the second argument a little more closely. One must keep in mind that the justification of drug testing is the justification of a means to an end, the end of preventing harm, and that the means are a means which intrude into one's privacy. In this case, before one allows drug testing as a means, one should be clear that there are not more effective means available.

If the employer has a legitimate right, perhaps duty, to ascertain knowledge of drug use to prevent harm, it is important to examine exactly how effectively, and in what situations, the *knowledge* of the drug use will prevent the harm. So far we have just assumed that the *knowledge* will prevent the harm. But how?

Let us take an example to pinpoint the difficulty. Suppose a transit driver, shortly before work, took some cocaine which, in giving him a feeling of invulnerability, leads him to take undue risks in his driving. How exactly is drug testing going to contribute to the knowledge which will prevent the potential accident?

It is important to keep in mind that: (1) if the knowledge doesn't help prevent the harm, the testing is not justified on prevention grounds; (2) if the testing doesn't provide the relevant knowledge, it is not justified either; and finally, (3) even if it was justified, it would be undesirable if a

more effective means for preventing harm were discovered.

Upon examination, the links between drug testing, knowledge of drug use, and prevention of harm are not as clear as they are presumed to be. As we investigate, it begins to seem that the knowledge of the drug use even though relevant in some instances, is not the most effective means to prevent harm.

Let us turn to this last consideration first. Is drug testing the most effective means for preventing harm caused by drug use?

Consider. If someone exhibits obviously drugged or drunken behavior, then this behavior itself is grounds for preventing the person from continuing on the job. Administering urine or blood tests, sending the specimens out for testing and waiting for a response, will not prevent harm in this instance. Much drug testing, because of the time lapse involved, is equally superfluous in those cases where an employee is in fact under the influence of drugs, but exhibits no or only subtly impaired behavior.

Thus, even if one grants that drug testing somehow prevents harm an argument can be made that there might be much more effective methods of preventing potential harm such as administering dexterity tests of the type employed by police in possible drunk-driving cases, or requiring suspect pilots to pass flight simulator tests.[8] Eye-hand coordination, balance, reflexes, and reasoning ability can all be tested with less intrusive, more easily administered, reliable technologies which give instant results. Certainly if an employer has just cause for believing that a specific employee

---

[8]For a reiteration of this point and a concise argument against drug testing see Lewis L. Maltby, "Why Drug Testing is a Bad Idea," *Inc.* June, 1987, pp. 152–153. "But the fundamental flaw with drug testing is that it tests for the wrong thing. A realistic program to detect workers whose condition puts the company or other people at risk would test for the condition that actually creates the danger. The reason drunk or stoned airline pilots and truck drivers are dangerous is their reflexes, coordination, and timing are deficient. This impairment could come from many situations —drugs, alcohol, emotional problems—the list is almost endless. A serious program would recognize that the real problem is workers' impairment, and test for that. Pilots can be tested in flight simulators. People in other jobs can be tested by a trained technician in about 20 minutes—at the job site." p. 152.

presently poses a real threat of causing harm, such methods are just more effective in all ways than are urinalysis and blood testing.

Even were it possible to refine drug tests so that accurate results were immediately available, that knowledge would only be job-relevant if the drug use was clearly the cause of impaired job performance that could harm people. Hence, testing behavior still seems more direct and effective in preventing harm than testing for the presence of drugs *per se*.

In some cases, drug use might be connected with potential harms not by being causally connected to motor-function impairment, but by causing personality disorders (e.g. paranoia, delusions, etc.) that affect judgmental ability. Even though in such cases a *prima facie* justification for urinalysis or blood testing might exist, the same problems of effectiveness persist. How is the knowledge of the drug use attained by urinalysis and/or blood testing supposed to prevent the harm? Only if there is a causal link between the use and the potentially harmful behavior, would such knowledge be relevant. Even if we get the results of the test immediately, there is the necessity to have an established causal link between specific drug use and anticipated harmful personality disorders in specific people.

But it cannot be the task of an employer to determine that a specific drug is causally related to harm-causing personality disorders. Not every controlled substance is equally likely to cause personality changes in every person in every case. The establishment of the causal link between the use of certain drugs and harm-causing personality disorders is not the province of the employer, but the province of experts studying the effects of drugs. The burden of proof is on the employer to establish that the substance being investigated has been independently connected with the relevant psychological impairment and then, predict on that basis that the specific employee's psychological judgment has been or will soon be impaired in such a way as to cause harm.

But even when this link is established, it would seem that less intrusive means could be used to detect the potential problems, rather than relying upon the assumption of a causal link. Psychological tests of judgment, perception and memory, for example, would be a less intrusive and more direct means for acquiring the relevant information

which is, after all, the likelihood of causing harm and not the presence of drugs *per se*. In short, drug testing even in these cases doesn't seem to be very effective in preventing harm on the spot.

Still, this does not mean it is not effective at all. Where it is most effective in preventing harm is in its getting people to stop using drugs or in identifying serious drug addiction. Or to put it another way, urinalysis and blood tests for drug use are most effective in preventing potential harm when they serve as a deterrent to drug use *before* it occurs, since it is very difficult to prevent harm by diagnosing drug use *after* it has occurred but before the potentially harmful behavior takes place.

Drug testing can be an effective deterrent when there is regular or random testing of all employees. This will prevent harm by inhibiting (because of the fear of detection) drug use by those who are occasional users and those who do not wish to be detected.

It will probably not inhibit or stop the use by the chronic addicted user, but it will allow an employer to discover the chronic user or addict, assuming that the tests are accurately administered and reliably evaluated. If the chronic user's addiction would probably lead to harmful behavior of others, the harm is prevented by taking that user off the job. Thus regular or random testing will prevent harms done by deterring the occasional user and by detecting the chronic user.

There are six possibilities for such testing:

1. regularly scheduled testing of all employees;
2. regularly scheduled testing of randomly selected employees;
3. randomly scheduled testing of all employees;
4. randomly scheduled testing of randomly selected employees;
5. regularly scheduled testing of employees selected for probable cause; or finally,
6. randomly scheduled testing of employees selected for probable cause.

Only the last two seem morally acceptable as well as effective.

Obviously, randomly scheduled testing will be more effective than regularly scheduled testing in detecting the occasional user, because the occasional users can control their use to pass the tests, unless of course tests were given so often (a practice economically unfeasible) that they needed to stop together. Regular scheduling probably will detect the habitual or addicted user. Randomly selecting people to test is probably cheaper, as is random scheduling, but it is not nearly as effective as testing all. Besides, the random might miss some of the addicted altogether, and will not deter the risk takers as much as the risk aversive persons. It is, ironically, the former who are probably potentially more harmful.

But these are merely considerations of efficiency. We have said that testing without probable cause is unacceptable. Any type of regular testing of all employees is unacceptable. We have argued that testing employees without first establishing probable cause is an unjustifiable violation of employee privacy. Given this, and given the expense of general and regular testing of all employees (especially if this is done by responsible laboratories), it is more likely that random testing will be employed as the means of deterrence. But surely testing of randomly selected innocent employees is as intrusive to those tested as is regular testing. The argument that there will be fewer tests is correct on quantitative grounds, but qualitatively the intrusion and unacceptability are the same. The claim that employers should be allowed to sacrifice the well-being of (some few) innocent employees to deter (some equally few) potentially harmful employees seems, on the face of it, unfair. Just as we do not allow the state randomly to tap the telephones of just any citizen in order to prevent crime, so we ought not allow employers to drug test all employees randomly to prevent harm. To do so is again to treat innocent employees solely as a means to the end of preventing potential harm.

This leaves only the use of regular or random drug testing as a deterrent in those cases where probable cause exists for believing that a particular employee poses a threat of harm. It would seem that in this case, the drug testing is acceptable. In such cases only the question of effectiveness remains: Are the standard techniques of urinalysis and blood testing more effective means for preventing harms than alternatives such as dexterity tests? It seems they are effective in different ways. The dexterity tests show immediately if someone is incapable of performing a task, or will perform one in such a way as to cause harm to others. The urinalysis and blood testing will prevent harm indirectly by getting the occasional user to curtail their use, and by detecting the habitual or addictive user, which will allow the employer to either give treatment to the addictive personality or remove them from the job. Thus we can conclude that drug testing is effective in a limited way, but aside from inhibiting occasional users because of fear of detection, and discovering habitual users, it seems problematic that it does much to prevent harm that couldn't be achieved by other means.

Consider one final issue in the case of the occasional user. They are the drug users who do weigh the risks and benefits and who are physically and psychologically free to decide. The question in their case is not simply "will the likelihood of getting caught by urinalysis or blood testing deter this individual from using drugs?" Given the benefits of psychological tests and dexterity tests described above, the question is "will the rational user be more deterred by urinalysis or blood testing than by random psychological or dexterity tests?" And, if this is so, is this increase in the effectiveness of a deterrent sufficient to offset the increased expense and time required by drug tests?[9] We see no reason to believe that behavioral or judgment tests are not, or cannot be made to be, as effective in determining what an employer needs to know (i.e., that a particular employee may presently be a potential cause of harm). If the behavioral, dexterity and judgment tests can be as effective in determining a potential for harm, we see no reason to believe that they cannot be as effective a deterrent as drug tests. Finally, even if a case can be made for an increase in deterrent effect of drug testing, we are skeptical that this increased effectiveness will outweigh the increased inefficiencies.

In summary, we have seen that deterrence is effective at times and under certain conditions allows the sacrificing of the privacy rights of innocent employees to the future and speculative good of preventing harms to others. However, there are many ways to deter drug use when that deterrence is legitimate and desirable to prevent harm. But random testing, which seems the only practicable means which has an impact in preventing harm, is the one which most offends workers'

---

[9]This argument is structurally similar to the argument against the effectiveness of capital punishment as a deterrent offered by Justice Brennen in the Supreme Court's decision in *Furman v Georgia*.

rights to privacy and which is most intrusive of the rights of the innocent. Even when effective, drug testing as a deterrent must be checked by the rights of employees.

Illegality Contention

At this point critics might note that the behavior which testing would try to deter is, after all, illegal. Surely this excuses any responsible employer from being overly protective of an employee's rights. The fact that an employee is doing something illegal should give the employer a right to that information about his private life. Thus, it is not simply that drug use might pose a threat of harm to others, but that it is an *illegal* activity that threatens others. But again, we would argue that illegal activity itself is irrelevant to job performance. At best *conviction* records might be relevant, but, of course, since drug tests are administered by private employers we are not only exploring the question of conviction, we are also ignoring the fact that the employee has not even been arrested for the alleged illegal activity.

Further, even if the due process protections and the establishment of guilt is acknowledged, it still does not follow that employers have a claim to know about all illegal activity on the part of their employees.

Consider the following example: Suppose you were hiring an auditor whose job required certifying the integrity of your firm's tax and financial records. Certainly, the personal integrity of this employee is vital to the adequate job performance. Would we allow the employer to conduct, with or without the employee's consent, an audit of the employee's own personal tax return? Certainly if we discover that this person has cheated on his/her own tax return we will have evidence of illegal activity that is relevant to this person's ability to do the job. Given one's own legal liability for filing falsified statements, the employee's illegal activity also poses a threat to others. But surely, allowing private individuals to audit an employee's tax returns is too intrusive a means for discovering information about that employee's integrity. The government certainly would never allow this violation of an employee's privacy. It ought not to allow drug testing on the same grounds. Why tax returns should be protected in ways that urine, for exam-

ple, is not, raises interesting questions of fairness. Unfortunately, this question would take us beyond the scope of this paper.

Voluntariness

A final problem that we also leave undeveloped concerns the voluntariness of employee consent. For most employees, being given the choice between submitting to a drug test and risking one's job by refusing an employer's request is not much of a decision at all. We believe that such decisions are less than voluntary and thereby would hold that employers cannot escape our criticisms simply by including within the employment contract a drug-testing clause.[10] Furthermore, there is reason to believe that those most in need of job security will be those most likely to be subjected to drug testing. Highly skilled, professional employees with high job mobility and security will be in a stronger position to resist such intrusions than will less skilled, easily replaced workers. This is why we should not anticipate surgeons and airline pilots being tested, and should not be surprised when public transit and factory workers are. A serious question of fairness arises here as well.

Drug use and drug testing seem to be our most recent social "crises." Politicians, the media, and employers expend a great deal of time and effort addressing this crisis. Yet, unquestionably, more lives, health, and money are lost each year to alcohol abuse than to marijuana, cocaine and other controlled substances. We are well-advised to be careful in considering issues that arise due to such selective social concern. We will let other social commentators speculate on the reasons why drug use has received scrutiny while other white-collar

---

[10]It might be argued that since we base our critique upon the contractual relationship between employers and employees, our entire position can be undermined by a clever employer who places within the contract a privacy waiver for drug tests. A full answer to this would require an account of the free and rational subject that the contract model presupposes. While acknowledging that we need such an account to prevent just any contract from being morally legitimate, we will have to leave this debate to another time. Interested readers might find "The Moral Contract between Employers and Employees" by Norman Bowie, in *The Work Ethic in Business,* edited by Hoffman and Wyly (Oelgeschlager and Gunn, 1981) pp. 195–202, helpful here.

crimes and alcohol abuse are ignored. Our only concern at this point is that such selective prosecution suggests an arbitrariness that should alert us to questions of fairness and justice.

In summary, then, we have seen that drug use is not always job-relevant, and if drug use is not job-relevant, information about it is certainly not job-relevant. In the case of performance it may be a cause of some decreased performance, but it is the performance itself that is relevant to an employee's position, not what prohibits or enables him to do the job. In the case of potential harm being done by an employee under the influence of drugs, the drug use seems job-relevant, and in this case drug testing to prevent harm might be legitimate. But how this is practicable is another question. It would seem that standard motor dexterity or mental dexterity tests, immediately prior to job performance, are more efficacious ways of preventing harm, unless one concludes that drug use invariably and necessarily leads to harm. One must trust the individuals in any system in order for that system to work. One cannot police everything. It might work to randomly test people, to find drug users, and to weed out the few to forestall possible future harm, but are the harms prevented sufficient to override the rights of privacy of the people who are innocent and to overcome the possible abuses we have mentioned? It seems not.

Clearly, a better method is to develop safety checks immediately prior to the performance of a job. Have a surgeon or a pilot or a bus driver pass a few reasoning and motor-skill tests before work. The cause of the lack of a skill, which lack might lead to harm, is really a secondary issue.

Drug Testing for Prospective Employees

Let's turn finally to drug testing during a pre-employment interview. Assuming the job description and responsibilities have been made clear, we can say that an employer is entitled to expect from a prospective employee whatever performance is agreed to in the employment contract. Of course, this will always involve risks, since the employer must make a judgment about future performances. To lower this risk, employers have a legitimate claim to some information about the employee. Previous work experience, training, education, and the like are obvious candidates since they indicate the person's ability to do the job. Except in rare circumstances drug use itself is irrelevant for determining an employee's ability to perform. (Besides, most people who are interviewing know enough to get their systems clean if the prospective employee is going to test them.)

We suggest that an employer can claim to have an interest in knowing (a) whether or not the prospective employee *can* do the job and (b) whether there is reason to believe that once hired the employee *will* do the job. The first can be determined in fairly straightforward ways: past work experience, training, education, etc. Presumably past drug use is thought more relevant to the second question. But there are straightforward and less intrusive means than drug testing for resolving this issue. Asking the employee "Is there anything that might prevent you from doing this job?" comes first to mind. Hiring the employee on a probationary period is another way. But to inquire about drug use here is to claim a right to know too much. It is to claim a right to know not only information about what an employee *can* do, but also a right to inquire into whatever background information *might* be (but not necessarily *is*) causally related to what an employee *will* do. But the range of factors that could be relevant here, from medical history to psychological dispositions to family plans, is surely too open-ended for an employer to claim as a *right* to know.

It might be responded that what an employee is entitled to expect is not a certain level of output, but a certain level of effort. The claim here would be that while drug use is only contingently related to what an employee *can* do, it is directly related to an employee's *motivation* to do the job. Drug use then is *de facto* relevant to the personal information that an employee is *entitled* to know.

But this involves an assumption mentioned above. The discussion so far has assumed that drugs will adversely affect job performance. However, some drugs are performance *enhancing* whether they are concerned with actual *output* or *effort*. The widespread use of steroids, painkillers, and dexadrine among professional athletes are perhaps only the most publicized instances of performance enhancing drugs. (A teacher's use of caffeine before an early-morning class is perhaps a more common example.) More to the point, knowledge of drug use tells little about motivation. There are too many other variables to be considered. Some users are motivated and some are not. Thus the motivational argument is faulty.

We can conclude, then, that whether the relevant consideration for prospective employees is output or effort, knowledge of drug use will be largely irrelevant for predicting. Employers ought to be positivistic in their approach. They should restrict their information gathering to measurable behavior and valid predictions (What has the prospect done? What can the prospect do? What has the prospect promised to do?), and not speculate about the underlying *causes* of this behavior. With a probationary work period always an option, there are sufficient non-intrusive means for limit-

ing risks available to employers without having to rely on investigations into drug use.

In summary, we believe that drug use is information that is rightfully private and that only in exceptional cases can an employer claim a right to know about such use. Typically, these are cases in which knowledge of drug use could be used to prevent harm. However, even in those cases we believe that there are less intrusive and more effective means available than drug testing for gaining the information that would be necessary to prevent the harm. Thus, we conclude that drug testing of employees is rarely justified, and mostly inefficacious.

Drug Testing and the Right to Privacy: Arguing the Ethics of Workplace Drug Testing

MICHAEL CRANFORD

DRUG TESTING is becoming an increasingly accepted method for controlling the effects of substance abuse in the workplace. Since drug abuse has been correlated with a decline in corporate profitability and an increase in the occurrence of work-related accidents, employers are justifying drug testing on both legal and ethical grounds. Recent estimates indicate that the costs to employers of employee drug abuse can run as high as $60 billion per year.[1] Motorola, before implementing its drug testing program in 1991, determined that the cost of drug abuse to the company—in lost time, impaired productivity and health-care and workers compensation claims—amounted to $190 million in 1988, or approximately 40% of the company's net profit for that year.[2] . . .

While admitting that drug testing could mitigate potential harms, some CEOs have elected not to follow the trend set by Motorola and an estimated 67% of large companies,[3] and instead argue that drug testing surpasses the employer's legitimate sphere of control by dictating the behavior of employees on their own time and in the privacy of their own homes.[4] Recent arguments in favor of a more psychologically-sensitive definition of employee privacy place employer intrusions into this intimate sphere of self-disclosure on even less certain ethical grounds.[5] The ethical status of workplace drug testing can be expressed as a question of

[1]According to SAMHSA (Substance Abuse and Mental Health Services Administration), cited in Ira A. Lipman, "Drug Testing Is Vital in the Workplace," *U.S.A. Today Magazine* **123** (January 1995), 81.
[2]Dawn Gunsch, "Training Prepares Workers for Drug Testing," *Personnel Journal* **72** (May 1993), 52.

[3]According to the U.S. Bureau of Labor Statistics, cited in Rob Brookler, "Industry Standards in Workplace Drug Testing," *Personnel Journal* **71** (April 1992), 128.
[4]See Lewis L. Maltby, "Why Drug Testing Is a Bad Idea," *Inc.* (June 1987), 152.
[5]On this point see Michele Simms, "Defining Privacy in Employee Health Screening Cases: Ethical Ramifications Concerning the Employee/Employer Relationship," *Journal of Business Ethics* **13** (1994), 315–325.

From Journal of Business Ethics *17: 1805–1815, 1998. © 1998 Kluwer Academic Publishers. Printed in the Netherlands. Reprinted with permission of Kluwer Academic Publishers.*

competing interests, between the employer's right to use testing to reduce drug-related harms and maximize profits, over against the employee's right to privacy, particularly with regard to drug use which occurs outside the workplace.

In this paper I will attempt to bring clarity to this debate and set the practice of workplace drug testing on more certain ethical grounds by advancing an argument which justifies workplace drug testing. I will begin by showing that an employee's right to privacy is violated when personal information is collected or used by the employer in a way which is irrelevant to the contractual relationship which exists between employer and employee. I will then demonstrate that drug testing is justified within the terms of the employment contract, and therefore does not amount to a violation of an employee's right to privacy. After responding to a battery of arguments to the contrary, I will propose that while drug testing can be ethically justified under the terms of an employment contract, it still amounts to treating employees as a means to an economic end, and is therefore fundamentally inconsistent with a substantive valuation of human worth and dignity.

Privacy and Performance of Contract

Legal definitions of privacy inevitably rely on the 1890 *Harvard Law Review* article "The Right to Privacy" by Samuel Warren and Louis Brandeis. This article offered an understanding of privacy for which a constitutional basis was not recognized until the 1965 case *Griswold v. Connecticut* (381 U.S. 479). In both instances, privacy was understood as an individual's right "to be let alone," with the Griswold decision according citizens a "zone of privacy" around their persons which cannot be violated by governmental intrusion. This definition, utilized by the Court in numerous decisions since the 1965 ruling, will not be adequate for describing the employee's claim to privacy in an essentially social and cooperative setting like the workplace. In such a condition an absolute right "to be let alone" cannot be sustained, and it may well prove impossible for an employee to maintain a "zone of privacy" when the terms of employment entail certain physical demands. This is not to argue that a right to privacy does not exist in this setting; rather, we must conclude that the aforementioned conditions are not necessary components in such a right.[6]

A more useful definition begins with the idea of a person's right to control information about herself and the situations over which such a right may be legitimately extended. For example, information to the effect that an individual possesses a rare and debilitating disease is generally considered private, but a physician's coming to know that a patient has such a disease is not an invasion of privacy. One might also note that while eavesdropping on a conversation would normally constitute an invasion of privacy, coming to know the same information because the individual inadvertently let it slip in a casual conversation would not. These and other examples demonstrate that the right to privacy is not violated by the mere act of coming to know something private, but is instead contingent on relationship between the knower and the person about whom the information is known.

George Brenkert formulates this understanding as follows: Privacy involves a relationship between a person A, some information X, and another individual Z. A's right of privacy is violated only when Z comes to possess information X and no relationship exists between A and Z that would justify Z's coming to know X.[7] Brenkert notes that what would justify Z coming to know X is a condition in which knowing X and having a certain access to A will enable Z to execute its role in the particular relationship with A. In such a case, Z is entitled to information X, and A's privacy is in no way violated by the fact that Z knows. Thus, a physician is jus-

---

[6]DesJardins further argues that these conditions are not sufficient to constitute a right to privacy. In the example of subliminal advertising, if it was effective, one's right "to be let alone" would be violated, but without any clear violation of one's privacy (Joseph R. DesJardins, "An Employee's Right to Privacy," in J. R. DesJardins and J. J. McCall (eds.), *Contemporary Issues in Business Ethics* [Wadsworth, Belmont, CA, 1985], p. 222).

[7]George G. Brenkert, "Privacy, Polygraphs, and Work," *Business and Professional Ethics Journal* 1 (1981), 23. In agreement see DesJardins, "An Employee's Right to Privacy," p. 222; Joseph DesJardins and Ronald Duska, "Drug Testing in Employment," *Business and Professional Ethics Journal* 6 (1987), 3–4.

tified in coming to know of a patient's disease (say, by running certain diagnostic tests), since knowing of the disease will enable her to give the patient medical treatment. One cannot be a physician to another unless one is entitled to certain information and access to that person. Conversely, one can yield one's right to privacy by disclosing information to another that the relationship would not normally mandate. To maintain a right to privacy in a situation where another would normally be entitled to the information to enable them to fulfill the terms of the relationship is, quite simply, to violate the terms of the relationship and make fulfillment of such terms impossible. In the case of our earlier example, to refuse a physician access to the relevant points of one's health status is to make a physician-patient relationship impossible. Similarly, to refuse an employer access to information regarding one's capability of fulfilling the terms of an employment contract is to violate an employer-employee relationship.

The argument advanced at this point is that drug testing involves access to and information about an employee that are justified under the terms of the implicit contractual agreement between employer and employee. An employer is therefore entitled to test employees for drug use. This statement relies on at least two important assumptions. First, a contractual model of employer-employee relations is assumed over against a common law, agent-principal model. It as not the case that employees relinquish all privacy rights in return for employment, as the common law relationship may imply, but rather that the terms of the contract, if it is valid, set reasonable boundaries for employee privacy rights consistent with the terms and expectations of employment. The argument offered here is that drug testing does not violate those boundaries. I am also assuming that drug abuse has a measurable and significant impact on an employee's ability to honor the terms of the employment contract. Employers are entitled to know about employee drug abuse on the grounds that such knowledge is relevant to assessing an employee's capability to perform according to the terms of the agreement. Without arguing for the connection between drug abuse and employee performance at length, the reader's attention is directed to studies which, if not absolutely incontestable in

their methodology, are nonetheless reasonably set forth.[8]

In support of this argument I would first direct attention to other types of information about an employee that an employer is entitled to know, and in coming to know such information does not violate the employee's privacy. Employers are entitled to information about a current or prospective employee's work experience, education, and job skills—in short, information relevant for determining whether or not the employee is capable of fulfilling her part of the contract. More critically, the employer is not only entitled to such information, but is entitled to obtain such information through an investigatory process, both to confirm information the employee has voluntarily yielded about her qualifications, as well as to obtain such relevant information as may be lacking (i.e., inadvertently omitted or, perhaps, intentionally withheld).

Brenkert further adds that an employer is entitled to information which relates to elements of one's social and moral character:

> A person must be able not simply to perform a certain activity, or provide a service, but he must also be able to do it in an acceptable manner— i.e., in a manner which is approximately as efficient as others, in an honest manner, and in a manner compatible with others who seek to provide the services for which they were hired.[9]

Again, the employer is entitled to know, in the case of potential employees, if they are capable of fulfilling their part of the contract, and, in the case of existing employees, if they are adhering to the terms and expectations implicit in the contract. While this latter case can often be confirmed by

[8]See for example U.S. Department of Health and Human Services, *Drugs in the Workplace: Research and Evaluation Data*, ed. S. W. Gust and J. M. Walsh (National Institute on Drug Abuse Monograph 91, 1989), and National Research Council/Institute of Medicine, *Under the Influence? Drugs and the American Work Force*, ed. J. Normand, R. O. Lempert and C. P. O'Brien (Committee on Drug Use in the Workplace, 1994). For example, a prospective study of pre-employment drug testing in the U.S. Postal Service showed after 1.3 years of employment that employees who had tested positive for illicit drug use at the time they were hired were 60% more likely to be absent from work than employees who tested negative (*Drugs in the Workplace*, pp. 128–132; *Under the Influence*, p. 134).

[9]Brenkert, "Privacy, Polygraphs, and Work," 25.

direct observation of the employee's actions at the work site, on occasion the employer is entitled to information regarding behavior which can be observed at the workplace but originates from outside of it (such as arriving at work late, or consuming large quantities of alcohol prior to arriving). As all of these actions may be in violation of the term of employment, the employer is entitled to know of them, and in coming to know of them does not violate the employee's privacy.

My point in offering these examples is to suggest that drug testing is a method of coming to know about an employee's ability to fulfill the terms of contract which is analogous to those listed. An exploratory process, in seeking to verify an employee's ability to do a certain job in connection with reasonable expectations for what that job entails, may also validly discover characteristics or tendencies that would keep the employee from performing to reasonable expectations. Drug testing is precisely this sort of process. As a part of the process of reviewing employee performance to determine whether or not they are fulfilling the terms and expectations of employment satisfactorily, drug testing may be validly included among other types of investigatory methods, including interviews with coworkers, skills and proficiency testing, and (in some professions) medical examinations. The fact that an employee may not want to submit to a drug test is entirely beside the point; the employee may just as likely prefer not to include a complete list of personal references, or prefer that the employer not review her relations with other employees. In all these cases, the employer is entitled to know the relevant information, and in coming to know these things does not violate the employee's privacy. The employee may withhold this information from the employer, but this action is tantamount to ending the employer-employee relationship. Such a relationship, under the terms of employment, includes not only each party's commitment to benefit the other in the specific way, indicated, but also entitles each to determine if the other is capable of performance according to the terms of contract. In this way, each retains the free ability to terminate the relationship on the grounds of the other's nonperformance.

Of course, not just any purpose of obtaining information relevant to evaluating performance under the terms of contract can automatically be considered reasonable. For instance, an employer cannot spy on a prospective employee in her own home to determine if she will be a capable employee. I offer the following criteria as setting reasonable and ethical limits on obtaining relevant information (though note that the requirement of relevancy is in each case already assumed).

1. THE PROCESS WHEREBY AN EMPLOYER COMES TO KNOW SOMETHING ABOUT AN EMPLOYEE (EXISTING OR PROSPECTIVE) MUST NOT BE UNNECESSARILY HARMFUL OR INTRUSIVE

The information may not result from investigatory processes which are themselves degrading or humiliating by virtue of their intrusiveness (e.g., strip searches, spying on an employee while they use the bathroom, interviewing a divorced spouse, or searching an employee's locker) or which may prove unhealthy (e.g., excessive use of x-rays, or torture). (Note: Degrading processes of securing information must be distinguished from processes of securing information which is itself degrading. The latter is not necessarily in violation of this or successive criteria.)

2. THE PROCESS WHEREBY AN EMPLOYER COMES TO KNOW SOMETHING ABOUT AN EMPLOYEE MUST BE EFFICIENT AND SPECIFIC

The information must result from an efficient and specific process—i.e., a process which is the most direct of competing methods (though without compromising point 1 above), and should result in information which corresponds to questions of performance under the terms of the employment contract, and should not result in information that does not so correspond. For example, detailed credit checks may help a bank decide whether a prospective employee is a capable manager of finances, but not directly (only inferentially), and it would also provide a great deal of information that the employer is not entitled to see. Consulting the employee's previous employer, on the other hand, may provide the relevant information directly and specifically.

3. THE PROCESS WHEREBY AN EMPLOYER COMES TO KNOW SOMETHING ABOUT AN EMPLOYEE MUST BE ACCURATE, OR IF NOT ITSELF PRECISE, THEN CAPABLE OF CONFIRMATION THROUGH FURTHER INVESTIGATION

The information must result from a dependable source; if a source is not dependable and is incapable of being verified for accuracy, the employer is not justified in pursuing this avenue of discovery. Thus, the polygraph must be excluded, since it is occasionally inaccurate and may in such cases result in information that cannot be verified. In addition, disreputable sources of information, or sources that may have an interest in misrepresenting the information being sought, should not be used.

Having outlined these, I offer my argument in full: Drug testing is not only a method of coming to know about an employee's ability to fulfill the terms of contract which is analogous to those listed earlier, but which also is reasonable under the criteria listed above.

1. DRUG TESTING IS NOT HARMFUL OR INTRUSIVE

In the Supreme Court case *Samuel K. Skinner v. Railway Labor Executives' Association* (489 U.S. 602), the Court determined that both blood and urine tests were minimally intrusive.[10] While the Court acknowledged that the act of passing urine was itself intensely personal (ibid., p. 617), obtaining a urine sample in a medical environment and without the use of direct observation amounted to no more than a minimal intrusion (ibid., p. 626). The Court justified not only testing of urine but also testing of blood by focusing on the procedure of testing (i.e., "experience . . . teaches that the quantity of blood extracted is minimal," ibid., p. 625) and pointing out that since such tests are "commonplace and routine in everyday life," the

tests posed "virtually no risk, trauma, or pain" (ibid., p. 625). The Court's findings on this case are compelling, and are consistent with my contention that drug testing is not unnecessarily harmful or intrusive. While such testing does amount to an imposition upon an employee (i.e.. by requiring her to report to a physician and provide a urine sample) in a way that may not be commonplace for many employees, the Court ruled that since this takes place within an employment context (where limitations of movement are assumed), this interference is justifiable and does not unnecessarily infringe on privacy interests (ibid., pp. 624–625).

2. DRUG TESTING IS BOTH EFFICIENT AND SPECIFIC

In fact, drug testing is the most efficient means of discovering employee drug abuse. In addition to providing direct access to the information in question, the results of drug testing do not include information that is irrelevant. The test targets a specific set of illegal substances. It can be argued (and has been) that drug testing is not efficient because it does not test for impairment—only for drug use. But this point ignores the fact that the test is justified on a correlation between drug abuse and employee productivity more generally; impairment is itself difficult or impossible to measure, since the effects of a given quantity of substance vary from individual to individual and from one incidence of use to another. The fact that impairment is an elusive quantity cannot diminish the validity of testing for drug abuse. This criticism also ignores the fact that the test is an effective means of deterring impairment, providing habitual users a certain expectation that their drug use will be discovered if it is not controlled.

3. DRUG TESTING CAN BE CONDUCTED IN A WAY WHICH GUARANTEES A HIGH DEGREE OF PRECISION

It is well known that the standard (and relatively inexpensive) EMIT test has a measurable chance of falsely indicating drug use, and is also susceptible to cross-reactivity with other legal substances. But confirmatory testing, such as that performed using

---

[10]While the legal opinion itself only summarizes and does not in and of itself justify a moral argument, it does in this case demonstrate a broad consensus and both rational and intuitive appeals to the matter at hand.

gas chromatography/mass spectrometry, can provide results at a high level of accuracy. This confirmatory testing, as well as a host of other stringent safeguards, is required of all laboratories certified by the National Institute on Drug Abuse.[11]

In summary, my contention is that an employer is entitled to drug test on the grounds that the information derived is relevant to confirm the employee's capacity to perform according to the terms of employment, and that such testing is a reasonable means of coming to know such information. Other points in favor of drug testing, which are not essential to my preceding argument but congruent with it, include the following two items.

First, drug testing is an opportunity for employer beneficence. Testing permits the employer to diagnose poor employee performance and require such individuals to participate in employer-sponsored counseling and rehabilitative measures. Employers are permitted to recognize that drug abuse is a disease with a broad social impact that is not addressed if employees who perform poorly as a result of drug abuse are merely terminated.[12] Second, a specific diagnosis of drug abuse in the case of poor employee performance might protect the employer from wrongful termination litigation, in the event that an employee refuses to seek help regarding their abuse. The results of drug testing might confirm to the court that the termination was effected on substantive and not arbitrary grounds.

Drug Testing and Questions of Justification

A number of arguments have been offered which suggest that drug testing is not justified under terms of contract, or is not a reasonable method by which an employer may come to know of employee drug abuse, and therefore amounts to a violation of employee privacy. These arguments include a rejection of productivity as a justification for testing, charges that testing is coercive, and that it amounts to an abuse of employee privacy by controlling behavior conducted outside the workplace. I will respond to each of these in turn.

First, some have charged that arguing from an employer's right to maximize productivity to a justification for drug testing is problematic. DesJardins and Duska point out that employers have a valid claim on some level of employee performance, such that a failure to perform to this level would give the employer a justification for firing or finding fault with the employee. But it is not clear that an employer has a valid claim on an optimal level of employee performance, and that is what drug testing is directed at achieving. As long as drug abuse does not reduce an employee's performance beyond a reasonable level, an employer cannot claim a right to the highest level of performance of which an employee is capable.[13]

DesJardins and Duska further point out the elusiveness of an optimal level of performance. Some employees perform below the norm in an unimpaired state, and other employees might conceivably perform above the norm in an impaired state. "If the relevant consideration is whether the employee is producing as expected (according to the normal demands of the position and contract) not whether he/she is producing as much as possible, then knowledge of drug use is irrelevant or unnecessary."[14] This is because the issue in question is not drug use *per se*, but employee productivity. Since drug use need not correlate to expectations for a given employee's productivity, testing for drug use is irrelevant. And since it is irrelevant to fulfillment of the employment contract, testing for drugs is unjustified and therefore stands in violation of an employee's privacy.

While I agree that it is problematic to state that an employer has a right to expect an optimal level of performance from an employee, I would argue that the employer does have a right to a workplace free from the deleterious effects of employee drug

---

[11]See Brookler, "Industry Standards in Workplace Drug Testing," 129.

[12] *Contra* DesJardins and Duska, who state, "Of course, if the employer suspects drug use or abuse as the cause of the unsatisfactory performance, then she might choose to help the person with counseling or rehabilitation. However, this does not seem to be something morally required of the employer. Rather, in the case of unsatisfactory performance, the employer has a prima facie justification for dismissing or disciplining the employee" ("Drug Testing in Employment," 6–7).

[13]DesJardins and Duska, "Drug Testing in Employment," 5.

[14]Ibid., 6.

abuse.[15] Drug testing, properly understood, is not directed at effecting optimal performance, but rather performance which is free from the effects of drug abuse. Since the assessment which justifies drug testing is not based on the impact of drug abuse on a given employee's performance, but is correlated on the effects of drug abuse on workplace productivity more generally, drug testing does measure a relevant quantity.

It is also overly simplistic to state that employers need not test for drugs when they can terminate employees on the mere basis of a failure to perform. Employers are willing to tolerate temporary factors which may detract from employee performance; e.g., a death in the family, sickness, or occasional loss of sleep. But employers have a right to distinguish these self-correcting factors from factors which may be habitual, ongoing, and increasingly detrimental to productivity, such as drug abuse. Such insight might dramatically impact their course of action with regard to how they address the employee's failure to perform. It is therefore not the case, as DesJardins and Duska suggest, that "knowledge of the cause of the failure to perform is irrelevant."[16]

A more critical series of arguments against basing drug testing on an employer's right to maximize productivity has been leveled by Nicholas Caste. First, Caste attacks what he identifies as "the productivity argument":

> The productivity argument essentially states that since the employer has purchased the employee's time, the employer has a proprietary right to ensure that the time purchased is used as efficiently as possible. . . . [T]he employer must be concerned with "contract enforcement" and must attempt somehow to motivate the employee to attain maximal production capacity. In the case of drug testing, the abuse of drugs by employees is seen as

diminishing their productive capacity and is thus subject to the control of the employer.[17]

From this argument, Caste states, one can infer that any manipulation is acceptable as long as it is maximizing productivity and he defines manipulation as an attempt to produce a response without regard for that individual's good, as he or she perceives it.[18] Caste goes on to give two examples of hypothetical drugs which, assuming the productivity argument, an employer would be justified in requiring employees to take. The first drug increases employee productivity while also increasing pleasure and job satisfaction. The second drug increases productivity while inflicting painful side-effects on the employee. The fact that the productivity argument appears to sanction the use of both drugs, and in fact cannot morally distinguish between them, seems to argue for its invalidity. Since the productivity argument cannot distinguish between causing an employee pleasure or pain, by adopting its logic one would be forced to the morally unacceptable conclusion that an employee's best interests are irrelevant.

Caste points out that what is wrong with the second drug is not that it causes pain "but that it is manipulatively intrusive. It establishes areas of control to which the employer has no right."[19] He concludes that what is wrong with the productivity argument is that it is manipulative. And what is wrong with manipulation is not the effects it produces (which may, coincidentally, be in the subject's best interests) but rather that it undermines the subject's autonomy by not allowing their desires to be factored into the decision making process[20] Since drug testing is justified by appeal

---

[15]Implicit in this statement is the assumption that employees do not have an absolute right to abuse drugs. This is a point I am neither able (for lack of space) nor interested in taking up at this point, but would instead appeal to a broad societal consensus on drug abuse, legislation against the use of illicit substances (and abuse of legal substances), and various negative social correlates to drug use. Thus, I am convinced that drug abuse can be distinguished from other legitimate (but potentially deleterious) behaviors, such as poor dietary habits.

[16]Ibid.

[17]Nicholas J. Caste, "Drug Testing and Productivity," *Journal of Business Ethics* 11 (1992), 301.

[18]Ibid., 302.

[19]Ibid., 303.

[20]As a side note, I should point out that Caste has gone wrong in assessing his own definition of manipulation (understood as an attempt to produce a response without regard for that individual's good, as they perceived it). What is wrong with manipulation is not that it undermines autonomy, since undermining autonomy is neither a necessary nor a sufficient component in manipulation as he defines it (i.e., I can undermine your autonomy in a way which is in complete accord with your good as you perceive it, and this would not qualify as manipulation). If the subject willingly embraces the act in question, and is in complete agreement with a policy mandating the action, it

to productivity arguments, it also is fundamentally manipulative and results in a morally unacceptable degree of employee control. Drug testing is therefore unethical, and should be rejected.

One could point out that our system of modern law regulates behavior in a way that would also have to be considered manipulative, according to Caste's definition, but he avoids this counterexample by stating that in a democratic system, citizens have a chance to participate in the legislative process. Since their desires participate through the election of representatives who make the laws, Caste argues that our legal system does not destroy autonomy the way mandatory drug testing does, by dictating behavior without any room for autonomy.[21] Before I address the critical oversight here, I should point out that one might rescue drug testing from the charge of being manipulative by using the same argument that Caste did to rescue our legal system. One can exercise the same degree of autonomy with respect to drug testing legislation as one currently does with legislation generally by participating in our electoral system. Since employees have an ability to elect representatives who can limit the use of drug testing, one could argue that drug testing also "does not destroy the individual's autonomy in that he or she retains the capability of input into the governing process."[22] In point of fact, individual autonomy is limited in both cases, as it must necessarily be in any contractual obligation, making any expressed distinction here trivial.

The failure of Caste's argument becomes clear when we realize that, if he is correct, virtually every action required of an employee at a work site would qualify as manipulative—whether the action in question was in her best interests or not, and whether or not she desired to comply, since Caste defines manipulation as a function of restricting autonomy. Dress codes, starting times, and basic performance expectations all may be similarly justified by appeal to the productivity argument—but most of us are not prepared to count these things as manipulative or unjustified. Requirements of this sort are not instances of manipulation, but are

justified expectations which honor a contractual agreement. Similarly, an employee who demands a paycheck of her employer is engaging in manipulation, according to Caste's definition—but this cannot be correct. In the contract, each party is apprised that the other has a right to benefit from the arrangement, and each has a commensurate responsibility to uphold their part. Accountability to the terms of the contract does not amount to manipulation when the accountability in question is reasonable. In agreement with Caste's original criticism, it is not true that an employer has a right to ensure maximal productivity. But an employer does have the right to hold an employee accountable to the terms of the contract, which express reasonable expectations of productivity. From this it cannot be inferred, however, that just any activity to maximize (or even minimally ensure) productivity is justifiable, since the contractual model expressly allows that the employee has certain morally justified claims that cannot be bargained away in return for employment. Since the productivity argument, as Caste depicts it, is in fact not a justification for drug testing under a contractual model, it is not the case that drug testing must be rejected.

In a similar vein, some argue that any testing which involves coercion is inherently an invasion of employee privacy. Placing employees in a position where they must choose between maintaining their privacy or losing their jobs is fundamentally coercive. "For most employees, being given the choice between submitting to a drug test and risking one's job by refusing an employer's request is not much of a decision at all."[23] While Brenkert's arguments against the use of the polygraph are directed at that device's inability to distinguish the reason behind a positive reading (which may not, in many instances, indicate an intentional lie), his argument that the polygraph is coercive is pertinent to the question of drug testing as well.

Brenkert notes that if an employee

did not take the test and cooperate during the test, his application for employment would

---

would still be manipulative under Caste's definition, since manipulation turns not on the effect, nor on the victim's will, but on the motivation of the agent behind the act.
[21]Ibid., 302.
[22]Ibid.

[23]DesJardins and Duska, "Drug Testing in Employment," 16–17. This is also implied in DesJardins, "An Employee's Right to Privacy," p. 226, but in neither case is the argument fully developed.

either not be considered at all or would be considered to have a significant negative aspect to it. This is surely a more subtle form of coercion. And if this be the case, then one cannot say that the person has willingly allowed his reactions to the questions to be monitored. He has consented to do so, but he has consented under coercion. Had he a truly free choice, he would not have done so.[24]

Brenkert's point is surprising, in that his own understanding is that A's privacy is limited by what Z is entitled to know in order to executive its role with respect to A. If Z (here, the corporation) is entitled to know X (whether or not the employee abuses drugs) in order to determine if A (the employee) is capable of performing according to the terms of employment, then the employee has no right to privacy with respect to the information in question. While this does not authorize the corporation to obtain the information in just any manner, the mere fact that the employee would *prefer* that the employer not know cannot be sufficient to constitute a right to privacy in the face of the employer's legitimate entitlement. The employee can freely choose to withhold the information, but this is not so much invoking a right to privacy as it is rejecting the terms of contract.

If Brenkert's criticism of employer testing were valid, then potentially all demands made by the employer on the employee—from providing background information to arriving at work on time—would count as coercive, since in every case where the employee consents to the demand there is a strong possibility that she would not have consented if she was offered a truly free choice. But these demands are reasonable, and the employer is entitled to demand them under the terms of employment, just as the employee is entitled to profit by acceding to such demands.

The final argument considered here is the charge that drug testing is an attempt to "control the employee's actions in a time that has not actually been purchased."[25] Even if we assume that an employer has the right to maximize profitability by controlling the employee's behavior during normal work hours, the employer has no right to control what an employee does in her free time. To attempt to do so is a violation of employee rights. This argument also falls flat, (however, when we realize that the demands of a standard employment contract inherently place limitations on an employee's free time. In a sense, the employment contract demands priority, requiring the employee to organize her free time around her employment schedule in a way that permits her to honor the contractual obligation. For instance, time traveling to and from work occurs during an employee's "free time," and is dependent on the employee's own personal resources, but is rightfully assumed within the terms of the contract. Time and money spent shopping for work attire also falls outside the normal time of employment, but is essential for honoring a mandatory dress code. These are not normally considered violations of an employee's private life, or unethical "controls" placed on an employee by an employer, but are justified, again, under the terms of contract. Drug testing is justified similarly.

Reservations and Policy Recommendations

At least one troubling aspect of drug testing remains to be considered prior to recommendations on policy; and that is the ethics of profit maximization as a justification for including employee testing under the terms of an employment agreement. As Caste correctly observed, the fact that drug testing may be in the best interests of employees is ancillary to the employer's productivity goals.[26] While drug testing may turn out to further the interests of employees by forcing them to confront self-destructive behavior, this correlation between employee's interests and the financial goals of the corporation is merely fortuitous. If drug testing were not perceived as being in the best interests of the company from a financial point

---

[24]Brenkert, "Privacy, Polygraphs, and Work," 28–29.
[25]Caste, "Drug Testing and Productivity," 303. See also Maltby, "Why Drug Testing is a Bad Idea," 152.

[26]Caste, "Drug Testing and Productivity," 302. Caste goes too far when he attributes to corporations following the productivity argument an "absence of concern for the individual employee" (p. 303), but I am in agreement that employer beneficence is, in the case of drug testing, at best an afterthought.

of view, then drug testing would not be the issue it is today.

In counterpoint, one could argue that the financial status of the company is inherently intertwined with the good of employees; as the corporation becomes increasingly profitable, employees are increasingly benefited. One might even argue that, in light of such a framework, profit maximization is central to society and therefore inherently consistent with its values.[27] This model is overly simplified, however; we can easily envision a situation where a corporation, attempting to maximize its profits, does so in a way that is inconsistent with a substantive social ethic but is not otherwise limited by market values. Appealing to profit maximization as a social ethic does not alleviate these tensions.

It is the position adopted in this article that a corporation is entitled to drug test its employees to determine employee capacity to perform according to the terms of the employment contract. That drug testing is not, however, in the large majority of cases, directed at maximizing the employee's best interests, suggests that employers should avail themselves of their right to drug test within reasonable limits. In light of this conclusion, the following policy recommendations are directed at employers, with the goal of balancing the employer's right to drug test with a more substantive regard for the dignity and privacy of employees.

1. TESTING SHOULD FOCUS ON A SPECIFICALLY TARGETED GROUP OF EMPLOYEES

In the case of employers who are testing without regard for questions of safety, I would strongly urge that testing only be done when probable cause exists to suspect that an employee is using controlled substances. Probable cause might include uncharacteristic behavior, obvious symptoms of impairment, or a significantly diminished capacity to perform their duties. Utilizing probable cause minimizes the intrusive aspect of testing by yielding a higher percentage of test-positives (i.e., requiring probable cause before testing will inherently screen out the large majority of negatives). Even with this

stipulation, a drug program may provide a reasonable deterrence factor at the workplace.

It should be noted that this qualification does not apply in cases of job applicants. Employers who insist on testing potential employees will typically do so under a general suspicion of drug use, and may in that cause assume a condition of probable cause.

2. WHEN TESTING IS INDICATED, IT SHOULD NOT BE ANNOUNCED AHEAD OF TIME

Regularly scheduled testing runs the risk of losing its effectiveness by providing an employee sufficient time to contrive a method of falsifying the sample. Drug testing, if it is to be used at all, should be used in a way which maximizes its effectiveness and accuracy.

3. EMPLOYEES WHO TEST POSITIVE FOR DRUG ABUSE SHOULD BE PERMITTED THE OPPORTUNITY TO RESOLVE THEIR ABUSIVE TENDENCIES AND RETURN TO WORK WITHOUT PENALTY OR STIGMA

Employees should only be terminated for an inability to resolve their abuse, once early detection and substantial warning have been made. Employers can mitigate the dehumanizing aspect of this technology by using it as an opportunity to assist abusive employees with their problems, and permitting them to return to their old positions if they can remedy their habitual tendencies. Toxicological testing should therefore be accompanied by a full range of employee assistance interventions.

Acknowledgments

I would like to thank Prof. Bill May at the University of Southern California and the anonymous second reader for their suggestions and detailed criticism in regard to the points raised in this paper (without implicating either of them in the position adopted herein).

[27]See Patrick Primeaux and John Stieber, "Profit Maximization: The Ethical Mandate of Business," *Journal of Business Ethics* **13** (1994), 287–294.

Genetic Privacy in Employment

DAVID B. RESNIK

I. Introduction

RECENT AND PROJECTED ADVANCES in molecular genetics and in genetic screening technology will bring us a wealth of information regarding genetic diseases, abnormalities, and predispositions. This new knowledge will most certainly have positive effects on medicine and health care, but it could also have detrimental consequences for privacy. Employers, insurance companies, governments, and other agencies will try to gain access to genetic information in order to increase profits and efficiency and decrease liabilities and risks. In order to ensure that these advances in genetics do not compromise privacy, it is important to formulate a policy regarding the use of genetic information before our brave new science and technology gets out of control. In this paper, I shall take some steps toward that goal by proposing some guidelines for the disclosure of genetic information in employment. I shall argue that the moral right to privacy allows employees to restrict their employers' access to genetic information in most situations, but that employers may invade an employee's genetic privacy[1] *only if* such an invasion meets criteria for a legitimate (or justified) invasion.

II. The Right to Privacy

It is not my aim in this paper to defend a definition of privacy or explore the moral basis of privacy. Instead, I shall adopt W. A. Parent's approach to privacy and apply it to the issues at hand. I recognize that some readers may disagree with Parent's views, but they do provide a clear and cogent framework for thinking about genetic privacy.[2]

According to Parent, the right to privacy depends on a prior conception of privacy. Privacy, for Parent, "is the condition of not having undocumented personal knowledge about one possessed by others."[3] The key notions in this definition of privacy are "personal knowledge" and "documentation." Parent characterizes personal knowledge as information about an individual that most individuals choose to reveal only to family members and close friends, if they reveal it to anyone at all. What counts as personal knowledge may vary from culture to culture and from person to person. Not all personal knowledge is private, however, because some personal information belongs to the public record; it is information one can find in newspapers, court proceedings, and other public documents.[4]

Given this conception of privacy, Parent defines the moral right to privacy as a "right not to become the victim of wrongful invasions [of privacy].[5] The moral right to privacy is not the right to not have privacy invaded, since there are legitimate invasions of privacy; it is a right not to have privacy *wrongly* invaded. If one assumes that moral rights imply moral obligations, it follows that we have an obligation to avoid wrongfully invading privacy So what counts as a wrongful invasion of privacy? For the purposes of this paper, I shall define a wrongful invasion as one that is not legitimate (or justified). A legitimate invasion is an invasion of privacy which meets all of the following

---

[1] By "genetic privacy" I mean privacy relating to genetic information.

[2] This paper will focus on moral, not legal aspects of privacy. The points I make in this paper should not be affected by metaethical disputes concerning the foundation of moral rights. Although I am using the term "rights" in this paper,

I do not appeal to a theory of natural rights. It should make no difference to my discussion if its turns out that rights are derived from other moral concepts, such as duties or obligations.

[3] W. A. Parent, "Privacy, Morality, and the Law," *Philosophy and Public Affairs*, vol. 12 (1983), p. 269.

[4] This point brings up some interesting questions about documentation. For instance, should we consider information that appears in *The National Enquirer* to be properly documented?

[5] Parent. *op. cit.*, p. 273.

From Public Affairs Quarterly *7(1), 1993. Reprinted by permission.*

criteria (or necessary conditions); a wrongful one does not:[6]

a.   *Justification.* Good reasons or purposes justify the invasion.
b.   *Relevancy.* The information obtained by the invasion is relevant to the reasons or purposes of the invasion.
c.   *Intrusiveness.* The invasion uses the least intrusive means of obtaining the information.[7]
d.   *Specificity.* The invasion is discriminate and has procedural restraints and safeguards.[8]
e.   *Secrecy.* The invasion has post-invasion safeguards to prevent the unwarranted disclosure of information.

III. Privacy in Employment

Given that we have a right to privacy how does employment affect this right? This question raises a number of issues concerning employee rights and the employee-employer relationship. Again, I will not enter a lengthy discussion of these issues, but I will adopt an influential view in order to posit a conceptual framework for addressing the question of genetic privacy in employment. To this end, I shall utilize a contractarian model of the employee-employer relationship and employee rights.[9] In many respects my views will resemble George Brenkert's discussion of the use of polygraph tests in employment, since he also employs a contractarian model.[10]

According to the contractarian model, the employee-employer relationship is a business contract between consenting adults. In the contract, the employee agrees to provide the employer with goods and services in return for money, goods, or other forms of compensation. In addition, the employer may entrust the employee with tools, property, information, and various goods in order to enable her to do her job. This contract will be valid only if a) both parties are responsible and autonomous; and b) both parties respect the rights claims of other contractees. People do not lose their right to privacy when they gain or seek employment; on the contrary people cannot become employees unless they have rights and these rights are respected.

Employers can legitimately gain access to personal information about their employees (or prospective employees), according to the contractarian approach, in order to ensure the validity of the employee-employer contract. Employers need to have this information in order to determine whether their employees will be able to satisfactorily fulfill the duties and responsibilities outlined by the employee's job description in the contract. Employers can legitimately gain access to certain kinds of information about their employees, provided that they continue to respect their employees' privacy rights. In other words, employers can invade employee privacy only when this invasion would qualify as a legitimate invasion of privacy according to the criteria listed above. On the other hand, if an employee (or prospective employee) refuses to disclose certain kinds of information to her employer (or prospective employer), and this disclosure would qualify as a legitimate invasion, then her employer is justified in refusing to hire her (or in firing her).

Having established a conceptual framework for discussing privacy in employment, I am in a better position to answer the central question of this paper: what are the conditions for an employer's legitimate invasion of an employee's genetic privacy? Before answering this question, I need to discuss some facts about genetic information and how it is acquired, since these facts will help us determine what constitutes a legitimate invasion of genetic privacy.

IV. Genetic Information

Nature vs. Nurture. Some traits, such as sex, are determined entirely by our genes, but most traits

---

[6]I have derived these criteria from Parent's position; these are not his exact words.

[7]I will not attempt to define "intrusive" but I shall assume that we can judge whether some technique is more or less intrusive than another technique.

[8]I will also not attempt to define the word "discriminate" but I will assume that we can tell the difference between discriminate and indiscriminate methods. Indiscriminate methods yield much more information than is desired or needed, while discriminate methods can pinpoint specific types of information.

[9]See Norman E. Bowie, "The Moral Contract Between Employer and Employee," in Tom Beauchamp and Norman Bowie (eds.), *Ethical Theory and Business* (Englewood Cliffs, NJ: Prentice-Hall, 1983), pp. 150–161.

[10]George Drenkert, "Privacy, Polygraphs, and Work," *Business and Professional Ethics Journal,* vol. 1 (1981), pp. 19–35.

are determined by both genetic and environmental factors. Although one might claim that possession of a certain gene gives individuals a predisposition for developing a disease (or trait), whether this predisposition is realized depends on environmental factors.[11]

Causal vs. Statistical Connections. The causal pathway from genetic information, encoded in DNA, to an adult human being is incredibly complex, involving thousands of different genes and millions of different chemical reactions.[12] Most traits are not determined by one gene or one environmental factor, but by many different genes and environmental factors. Given this complex interplay of genes and the environment, we can rarely establish a strong causal connection between possessing a genetic characteristic and developing a phenotypic trait; more often than not we must settle for a statistical connection. We may be able to show that possessing a gene gives one a high probability or risk of developing a trait, but it is very difficult to show that a gene causes or determines a trait.

Timing. Although many genes produce their effects throughout a person's entire life, other genes produce their effects during specific times in a person's life span.[13] The important consequence of this fact is that a piece of genetic information might indicate that a person is likely to develop a disease at some time in their life, but this period may not coincide with their period of employment.

Treatment. We can use genetic information to cure or help people, rather than to stigmitize them or seal their fate. As we learn more about human genetics, we also learn how to treat (or prevent) genetic disease. In the future, we may be able to diagnose and treat a wide variety of genetically based illnesses, such as heart disease, diabetes, and cancer.[14]

Testing. In the past, the only way to acquire genetic information about a person would be to do a pedigree analysis of their family tree. However, pedigree analysis is unreliable and limited because it is an indirect method of detecting the presence of genes.[15] Due to advances in biotechnology, we now have a more reliable and powerful method for determining an individual's genetic constitution, genetic screening. Genetic screening is more reliable and powerful than pedigree analysis because it allows scientists to directly examine an individual's genetic material through microscopy or biochemical analysis. In principle, one can give genetic screening tests during any stage of an individual's development, including the fetal stage. Genetic screening is still in its infancy, and it is not perfectly reliable or accurate, but in the foreseeable future it should be possible to use this technology to produce an entire genetic blueprint for any individual—the total gene screen.[16]

V. Legitimate Invasions of Genetic Privacy

Given this brief discussion of genetic information, I am in a position to apply my conceptual framework to the issue of genetic privacy in employment. My main thesis in this section is that invasions of genetic privacy are legitimate *only if* they meet all five of the criteria for invasion discussed in section II. If an invasion of genetic privacy fails to meet any one of these criteria, then it is a wrongful invasion. In order to defend my main thesis, I shall discuss each criterion in the context of human genetics.

(1) JUSTIFICATION

The first criterion that an invasion needs to meet is that it must be done for good reasons or purposes. An employer's primary reason for invading genetic privacy is to validate the employee-employer contract. An employer may need to acquire information about an employee's genetic constitution in order to ensure that she is able to satisfactorily fulfill her duties and obligations outlined in the job description. Since this reason already justifies the disclosure of many types of information to employers, such as education, work record, and so on, it could also be used to justify the disclosure of genetic information, provided that other

---

[11]David Suzuki and Peter Knudson, *Genetics* (Cambridge, MA: Harvard University Press, 1989), pp. 25–45.
[12]Ibid., pp. 48–70.
[13]Ibid., pp. 70–94.
[14]Ibid., pp. 167–68.

[15]Ibid., pp. 164–165.
[16]Ibid., pp. 165–176.

conditions are met. This primary justification for invading genetic privacy can be strengthened by added concerns about worker health and safety, the welfare of others, and health care costs. However, concerns about worker health and safety or health care costs, cannot, by themselves, serve as good reasons for invading privacy; they must be combined with other reasons for to provide a sound justification for invading privacy. (I will provide more argument for this position in section VI.)

(2) RELEVANCY

Assuming that the primary justification for invading genetic privacy is validation of the employee-employer contract, then the information sought must be relevant to this purpose. In other words, invasions of genetic privacy are legitimate provided that the information sought is job-relevant. Can genetic information ever be job-relevant? My preliminary answer to this question is "sometimes yes," although I hasten to add that the concept of "job-relevancy" is extremely context-dependent: it varies according to the job-description and the type of information sought.

Despite these misgivings, I do not think we must settle for a case-by-case approach to relevancy. My earlier discussion of genetic information should be useful in formulating some guidelines for determining whether a piece of genetic, information is job-relevant. Genetic information is job-relevant if and only if the following conditions are met:

1. Possessing the genetic characteristic in question gives one a statistically significant task of not satisfactorily performing duties outlined by the job-description.
2. The characteristic is likely to produce its phenotypic effects during the employee's period of employment.
3. The characteristic's effects cannot be satisfactorily altered, modified, or treated through medicine or therapy.

The conditions are based, in large part, on the nature of genetic information. Condition (1) requires that there be a sound scientific basis for seeking the genetic information. As discussed in section IV, it is rarely the case that one can establish a strong causal connection between possessing a genetic characteristic and manifesting a certain trait. But given the current state of molecular genetics, we can frequently establish at least a statistical connection (or risk) between possessing a genetic characteristic and developing a trait.

The next question that naturally arises is, "what is a statistically significant (or relevant) connection (or risk)?" Since one cannot answer this query without more information about the job and the genetic characteristic in question, I will not answer it here. But I will make a few remarks about statistical significance and genetic risk factors. In evaluating genetic risk factors, we should treat them no differently than other risk factors, such as lifestyle, attitude, and health. We are justified in focusing on genetic risk factors only when they carry a higher risk than other factors which might also be job-relevant. If we do not treat all risk factors equally, we will be unjustly discriminating against people on the basis of genetic characteristics.

Condition (2) is important because genetic characteristics that do not manifest themselves during an employee's period of employment should not be considered job-relevant. For example, scientists have speculated that Alzheimer's disease may have a genetic basis. But since this disease usually does not manifest itself until most employees have retired, employers are not justified in screening for an Alzheimer's gene (if there is such a gene).

Condition (3) is important because if the effects of a genetic characteristic can be treated (i.e. prevented, ameliorated, or satisfactorily overcome), then the characteristic should not be job-relevant. Often people who have genetic diseases can lead healthy, normal lives with proper care and treatment. People who may have treatable genetic diseases may wish to voluntarily participate in genetic screening to protect their own health, but employers are not justified in invading genetic privacy in order to find out about treatable diseases.

(3) INTRUSIVENESS

This condition for a legitimate invasion can be easily satisfied, since employers can use genetic screening, a technique which is the least intrusive (available) means of gaining genetic information.

(4) SPECIFICITY

Although this condition is not as easily satisfied as condition (3), it can be met provided that appropriate safeguards are in place. In performing a genetic screening test on an individual, the screener will have access to a wealth of genetic information. Employers can make their genetic screening discriminate by instructing testers to ignore the excess information and focus on the information in question.

(5) SECRECY

This condition, like condition (4), can also be met, provided that appropriate safeguards are in place. While no one can prevent all information leaks, employers can minimize leaks by enacting policies to protect the secrecy of genetic information. Information from genetic tests should be distributed on a need to know basis, and those who do not need the information should not have access to it. The people who should have access to the genetic information include people who make personnel decisions, and especially the person who has been tested. If you submit to a genetic test, then you have the right to know the results of the test, since these results may provide you with important health information.

VI. Discussion of Hypothetical Cases

The following hypothetical cases serve to illustrate my views on genetic privacy and allow me to address some pertinent objections.

Case 1: The Narcolepsy Gene. Suppose it is discovered that a small percentage of the population possess a gene, gene *X,* that makes them highly susceptible to narcolepsy People with gene *X* have a significant risk of falling asleep during normal waking hours, and there is no effective treatment for this disorder. A major airline company, Safe Air, has had some trouble with pilots falling asleep, and narcolepsy has become an important safety concern. The company decides to require its pilots (and prospective pilots) to submit to a genetic screening test for gene *X.* The test will focus only on gene *X,* and the company will provide safeguards to protect the secrecy of the results.

In this case, Safe Air's invasion of privacy is legitimate since the invasion meets all the criteria for legitimacy. The airline has a strong justification for genetic screening: it wants to validate the employee contract and ensure the safety of its employees and customers. The information sought is relevant to the purpose of the invasion: people with gene *X* run a high risk of succumbing to narcolepsy, and narcoleptics cannot satisfactorily pilot airplanes.

Case 2: The Cancer Gene. In the second case, suppose that a chemical company, Acme Industries, exposes its workers to a small amount of carcinogenic substance, carconine, during the production of plastics. Most people run a very small risk (0.1% chance) of contracting lung cancer when exposed to a small amount of carconine, but a small percentage of the population possesses a gene, gene *Y,* which gives them a significant risk (33% chance) of developing lung cancer after being exposed to carconine. Also suppose that Acme Industries has taken all reasonable steps to avoid exposing its employees to carconine; in order to further reduce carconine exposure it would have to stop producing plastic, its most profitable operation. Acme Industries decides to institute a genetic screening program for gene *Y* in order to protect its employees and reduce health care costs. The program focuses only on gene *Y,* and steps are taken to maintain secrecy

Although this case is not as clear-cut as the first one, it still meets the criteria for a legitimate invasion of privacy Relevancy, intrusiveness, specificity, and secrecy would not seem to be at issue in the case, but the justification would appear to be controversial. The problem with the justification is that the invasion is not done for the purpose of validating the employee-employer contract, assuming that lung cancer does not affect one's job performance until it reaches its final stages.[17] The two stated reasons for invading genetic privacy are to protect employees and to reduce health care costs. Although neither of these reasons, by itself, could justify an invasion of privacy, taken together, they form a good justification for invading privacy in this case.

Some might object that Acme Industries should improve the safety of the workplace instead of screening its employees, but we have already

---

[17]If lung cancer does significantly affect job performance, then Acme Industries' justification would be stronger.

supposed that it has done its best to minimize exposure to carconine. In this example, the only way Acme Industries can reduce carconine exposure is to completely shut down one of its important operations, which could be considered an unreasonable cost. (Given the enormous cost of genetic screening, it is likely that most companies will try to improve the work environment before resorting to genetic screening.)

Some might object that Acme Industries is adopting a paternalistic policy: employees, being autonomous decision-makers, should be able to decide whether they want to expose themselves to dangers or harms. However, one might argue that autonomy can be restricted in this case because employees who do not submit to a genetic screening tests are not fully informed, and hence, not fully autonomous.[18] A person who is not fully autonomous with respect to a certain kind of decision loses the right to make that decision for themselves. Furthermore, one might argue that autonomy can be restricted in this case because the employee who refuses a test is not the only person who could be harmed: the company (as whole) and other employees could be harmed. If an employee gets lung cancer, she could create enormous health care costs for the company, and she might even bring a lawsuit against the company. These costs will result in diminished profit for the company and fewer benefits for other employers.

Case 3: The Heart Attack Gene. Suppose we discover that individuals with gene Z run a high risk of having a heart attack by the time they are 40 years old, but their risk is not significantly greater than the risk run by individuals without gene Z who lead an unhealthy lifestyle (smoke, drink, eat meat, etc.). Nevertheless, a toy manufacturer, Fun Industries, decides to screen potential employees for gene Z for the purpose of avoiding health care costs and maximizing its investment in training costs. It will make sure that its screening program is discriminate and protects secrecy.

Can Fun Industries legitimately request individuals to take a test for gene Z? My answer is a definite "no." Fun Industries' main reason for invading privacy in this case is to minimize health care and training costs. Information about gene Z could not be considered necessary to validate the employment contract or protect employees. Employees with gene Z should be able to do their work as well as people without gene Z, and they will impose no significant risks or hardships on others.

One might object that health can be part of a person's job description and that the purpose of invasion is to validate the employment contract. However, allowing health to be a part of a person's job description would create a slippery slope that would eventually lead to discrimination and bias against the unhealthy.[19] Allowing genetic screening in this case opens the door to a broad range of cases in which employers seek to discriminate against individuals deemed "health risks." Allowing genetic screening in cases 1 and 2, on the other hand, would not result in such disastrous consequences. In cases 1 and 2 the screening is done for highly specific reasons directly related to job performance or genuine safety concerns, while in case 3 the screening is done for more general reasons relating to cost minimization and profit. Screening in cases 1 and 2 is not based on reasons which could also justify screening in a wide range of cases, while screening in case 3 is based on reasons which could justify screening in a wide range of cases. Hence, allowing screening in cases 1 and 2 would probably not lead us down a "slippery slope" toward unjust discrimination and stigmatization.[20]

VII. Conclusion: Genetic Privacy Guidelines

Given this analysis of privacy, genetic information, and hypothetical cases, I draw the following general conclusions (or guidelines) for genetic privacy in employment. Employers may legitimately gain

---

[18]Gerald Dworkin, *The Theory and Practice of Autonomy* (New York: Cambridge University Press, 1988), pp. 17–20.

[19]One of the ironies of this case (and others like it) is that the employment discrimination would result from a particular way of allocating health care resources, i.e. via employer-provided health insurance. This type of discrimination probably would not occur in countries that have socialized medicine.

[20]For more on slippery slope arguments, see Leon Kass, *Toward a More Natural Science: Biology and Human Affairs* (New York: The Free Press, 1985).

access to genetic information *only if* all of the following conditions are met:

1. The information is sought to (a) validate the employment contract, or (b) to protect employees and minimize costs (or both a and b).
2. There is a sound statistical connection between possessing the genetic characteristic in question and manifesting a disorder/trait relevant to the purpose of the invasion.
3. The disorder/trait in question manifests itself during the employee's period of employment.
4. The disorder/trait in question is not currently treatable.
5. A scientifically valid and non-intrusive kind of test is used, e.g., genetic screening.
6. The employers adopt safeguards to ensure that the tests are discriminate and to protect secrecy.

Many other questions need to be answered before we can establish a sound policy regarding the disclosure of genetic information in employment, such as "When is information statistically relevant?," "What counts as taking reasonable measures to improve the work place?," "How can ____ protect secrecy?," and so on. I will not explore these questions in much depth here, but I think these guidelines serve as a good first step toward a sound policy on genetic privacy in employment.[21]

[21]I would like to thank Ed Sherline and an anonymous referee for *Public Affairs Quarterly* for helpful comments. Research for this paper was supported, in part, by a grant from the University of Wyoming.

Genetic Information: Consumers' Right to Privacy Versus Insurance Companies' Right to Know

SHAHEEN BORNA AND STEPHEN AVILA

Introduction

SINCE JAMES WATSON and Francis Crick first identified the molecular structure of DNA in 1953 scientists have been trying to understand more about human genetic possibilities (Genetic Testing, 1992). The research developments suggest the possibility of identifying patterns of genes that raise a person's susceptibility to heart attacks, juvenile diabetes, and certain rare cancers (McAuliffe, 1987).

Information pertaining to an individual's genetic make-up is of great interest to many parties especially to insurance companies. Consumer groups are concerned that genetic information can be used to exclude an individual or an entire family from health or life insurance coverage eligibility. The individual with an indicator trait may also be subject to a significant adverse premium rating, long before the appearance of any eventual symptom. In the extreme, an individual who never becomes symptomatic may be excluded on the basis of his or her being at risk to develop a disorder.

PURPOSE OF THE STUDY

The main purpose of this study is to assess public opinion concerning access to genetic information for underwriting purposes and alternatives available to cover the health insurance costs of individuals who carry genetic materials which predispose them to certain illnesses. The implications of the research findings are discussed and should be of interest to government agencies and private companies involved with the health care system.

From Journal of Business Ethics *19: 355–362, 1999. © 1999 Kluwer Academic Publishers. Printed in the Netherlands. Reprinted with permission of Kluwer Academic Press.*

INSURERS' ARGUMENTS IN FAVOR OF DISCLOSURE OF GENETIC INFORMATION

The argument advanced by the insurance industry is in favor of disclosing genetic information. The cornerstone of this argument is based on the concept of "fair discrimination." The fair discrimination concept holds that insurers should try "to measure as accurately as practicable the burden shifted to the insurance fund by the policyholder and to charge exactly for it, no more and no less. To do so is 'fair discrimination.' . . . Not to do so is unfair discrimination" (Wortham, 1986, p. 361). Therefore, individuals with different risk factors will bear different costs for their insurance. Obviously, applicants associated with low risk factors, both environmental and personal, will be assessed lower premiums than individuals with higher risk factors.

Insurance companies are interested in any type of information which will assist them in properly assessing the risk they underwrite. Genetic information, from an insurer's point of view is, like any other medical information essential for predicting both mortality and morbidity costs.

Insurers point out that the idea of obtaining medical information from their clients and families is not a new one. They routinely collect health related information either through direct questioning (client filling out a questionnaire) or through statements from attending physicians for risk assessment. Insurers see no reason why they can obtain one type of health related information but not the other. Insurers argue that if they are barred by some legislative actions from gaining access to genetic information for risk assessment, the consequences would be bankruptcy for many companies and higher costs for customers. These two points are elaborated below.

GENETIC INFORMATION AND THE CONCEPT OF ADVERSE SELECTION

Adverse selection in insurance literature refers to "the exercise of an option by a person in his own favor and against the interest of the insurer in a case where his and the insurer's interests are not the same" (Long, 1990, p. 34).

Applied to genetic information, individuals who have prior knowledge of their future health problems, will buy the most comprehensive coverage they can in order to cover their future health related costs. Insurance companies accepting these applicants without having knowledge of their potential health problems will offer them policies with premiums which do not reflect true risk. Therefore, people who are likely to buy insurance will be those who are increasingly certain that they will need insurance. The consequence will be higher mortality and morbidity costs for insurance companies. Insurers, in order to cover their costs, will raise their premiums. "As the premiums go up, the better risks will no longer buy insurance, leaving a higher proportion of poor risks to share the costs of benefit payments. But with only poor risks in the pool the premiums must rise. This further squeezes out the better risks and premiums must rise again. The process continues, and the final result may be that no insurance is offered at any price." (For a detailed and numerical example of this process, see Denenberg et al., 1974, p. 27.) It is also possible that as insurance companies spread the cost among all their clients they may become vulnerable to unfair discrimination law suits. (For more detailed discussion, see Cushing, 1993.)

The carriers' concerns are analogous to the risk of writing coverage for the person who is HIV positive. The test results may be known to the applicant years before he or she becomes symptomatic. Testing for the illness may have been performed anonymously so that the information is known with certainty by the applicant but remains unknown to the prospective insurer.

ARGUMENTS AGAINST INSURERS' USE OF GENETIC INFORMATION

Although the fair discrimination argument posed by the insurance companies seems to be credible, there are also persuasive arguments made by right to privacy advocates against the use of genetic testing by insurers. These arguments may be classified into three groups:

The first argument is that insurance will only be afforded by those people deemed to have "healthy" genes and the rest of the population will either be deemed "uninsurable" or will be forced to pay a higher premium because they are considered a higher risk. Because of escalating costs of medical care (for some medical cost figures see, for example, Easterbrook, 1987) and increasing reliance of U.S. population upon health insurance, a denial of health insurance may be tantamount to denial of health care, which in some cases can be the difference between life and death (Wortham, 1986).

Insurance companies do not deny the possibility that when genetic testing becomes both reliable and accurate, individuals who carry defective genes may be subject to higher premiums or at worst be denied insurance coverage. They defend their position on the ground that the main goal of an insurance company like any other for-profit organization is to maximize the return of their shareholders' investment. Insurers are not and should not be expected to provide quasi-public health service.

The second argument against disclosure of genetic information to insurance companies is that of the right to privacy. Once any medical test is performed it becomes part of a patient's permanent medical record and if the applicants are forced to disclose this information to the insurance companies, it also will be more readily accessible to other insurance companies[1] (insurance companies exchange medical information about applicants through the Medical Information Bureau,[2] a databank containing information about insurance applicants) and eventually to a number of other interested parties such as potential employers. Medical records are subject to subpoena, and thus may be used for purposes other than insurance underwriting. (For a discussion of potential abuse of genetic data in context of employment discrimination see Schatz, 1987, and Strudler, 1994.)

Insurance companies argue that the individual's privacy interest may be best protected by refusing to consent to certain tests or refraining from purchasing insurance policies. Once an individual consents to such procedures, his or her ability to control the dissemination of that information may diminish. Insurance companies point out, the applicant for health or life insurance is, by definition, placing his or her health status at issue. As such he or she is implicitly waiving the physician-patient privilege and right to privacy.

The third argument is that people are very wary of genetic testing [and] are not sure if they really want to know whether or not they are carriers of certain defective genes. It would be very hard to cope with the information that an individual is going to develop an incurable disease in the next 10 years or so with almost one hundred percent certainty and he is unable to do something about it. Again, insurance companies argue that due to the voluntary nature of insurance transaction, individuals can avoid emotional trauma by refusing to consent to such procedures.

The above arguments demonstrate the complex nature of the debate related to the genetic testing and the use of genetic test results by the insurance companies. The arguments also point out the fact that these debates are mainly academic in nature and there is almost no mention of public opinion on this important issue which is likely to affect the majority of Americans who increasingly rely on health insurance to cover their medical expenses.

In the absence of a definitive study related to public opinion, it is relevant to have information on this subject from the users of the service, that is, ultimate consumers in the United States. The needed information is whether consumers are willing to share their genetic information with insurance companies and their view on different methods available to cover the health insurance costs of individuals with suspect genes. This information has implications related to resource allocation and public policy alternatives. With this in mind, a consumer survey was conducted during the fall of 1995 in a Midwestern city of the United States.

THE SURVEY

A mail survey of 3,000 households was completed during the fall of 1995 in Muncie, Indiana. The town of Muncie is considered to be very representative of Midwest values and culture and has been used in major sociological studies (Hoover, 1990).

---

[1]When a client completes a questionnaire related to his family health history or submits himself to a simple blood cholesterol test [he] is in fact revealing genetic information to the insurers. (For more on this point see Pokorski, 1990.)
[2]For a detailed discussion of Medical Information Bureau, see Stern, 1974.

Table I. Survey Findings

	Strongly Agree	Agree	No Opinion	Disagree	Strongly Disagree
Insurance companies should be able to require genetic information from their applicants for underwriting purposes.	2.7%	14.9%	6.8%	30.4%	44.75%
Insurance companies should be allowed to reject an applicant for health insurance on the basis of genetic information.	1.4%	6.5%	3.8%	34.6%	53.3%
Insurance companies should be allowed to charge higher premiums on the basis of genetic information.	2.0%	15.6%	4.1%	29.8%	47.8%
Individuals with a defective gene(s) should bear the cost of their insurance in the form of higher premiums.	2.3%	15.4%	7.3%	31.3%	43.1%
If an applicant with a defective gene(s) is not able to afford the cost of his/her insurance, government should bear the expense.	11.5%	27.0%	19.1%	20.2%	20.6%
The health-care cost of individuals should be covered by:					
Special taxes (such as user fees on certain items)	7.6%	27.8%	12.6%	17.1%	16.0%
General taxes (for examples, one percent increase in federal income taxes)	5.1%	22.1%	10.4%	23.6%	19.6%
Individual or group insurance plans Other sources (please specify)	20.1%	47.3%	10.6%	6.0%	3.7%
The government, through legislative action, should prohibit insurance companies from having access to applicants' genetic information.	37.5%	31.5%	8.9%	15.7%	6.0%
The United States should have a national health-care plan that insures everyone regardless of an individual's genetic makeup.	32.8%	31.4%	8.7%	13.6%	13.0%
With a national health-care plan, government should have access to an applicant's genetic information for administrative purposes such as budgeting, health-care facility planning, etc.	10.0%	28.6%	12.6%	24.1%	24.1%

In answering the following question, please keep in mind that it is possible for an individual to request genetic information for financial gain (for example obtaining increased amounts of life insurance or more comprehensive health coverage). Such practices may have an adverse financial impact on insurance companies.

	Strongly Agree	Agree	No Opinion	Disagree	Strongly Disagree
Insurance companies should be allowed to have access to genetic information if and only if an individual acknowledges having a genetic test.	7.2%	39.6%	12.2%	21.1%	18.0%

Table II. Demographic Characteristics of Respondents

Sex of Respondents	male 59.9%	female 34.4%
Age of Respondents	18–21 years	14.5%
	22–29 years	15.3%
	30–39 years	13.6%
	40–49 years	16.1%
	50–59 years	14.0%
	60–69 years	12.6%
	70–79 years	9.5%
	80 years and over	2.6%
Educational Attainment of Respondents	8th grade or less	0.3%
	attended high school	3.0%
	completed high school	16.0%
	attended vocational school	9.8%
	attended college	38.9%
	completed college	12.3%
	post graduate	18.0%
Respondents' Income Before 1995 Taxes	$0–9,999	10.2%
	$10,000–19,999	10.2%
	$20,000–29,999	12.2%
	$30,000–39,999	13.0%
	$40,000–49,999	11.5%
	$50,000–59,999	10.8%
	$60,000–69,000	8.8%
	$70,000 and over	18.4%

A sample of 3,000 households was mailed a questionnaire. Six hundred and sixty two (662) usable questionnaires were returned, a response rate of 22 percent. Tables I and II summarize the demographic characteristics of the respondents and their responses.

It is evident from the data in Table I that the majority of respondents are against:

- Genetic testing for underwriting purposes (75.15%);

- Allowing insurance companies to reject an application on the basis of genetic information (85%);

- Charging higher premiums on the basis of genetic information (77.6%).

On the issue of who should pay the higher costs associated with having defective genes, the respondents are against:

- Individuals with defective genes being responsible for higher premiums;

- Imposition of new taxes to cover the higher costs associated with having defective genes.

Sixty-four percent of the respondents favor having a national health-care plan that insures everyone regardless of an individual's genetic makeup. The irony of this response lies in the fact that the majority of the respondents, as mentioned before, disagree with covering the health care-cost of individuals with defective genes through special taxes.

Policy Alternatives

ALTERNATIVE 1: MAKING GENETIC INFORMATION INACCESSIBLE TO INSURERS

If findings of this research could be generalized to the entire population of the United States, one may expect a good prospect for the passage of laws forbidding insurance companies from requiring genetic tests for underwriting purposes. Although this alternative has good political appeal, it may not be a successful one because the insurers have a strong argument with regard to the fair discrimination principle and how this principle may be defected by adverse selection.[3]

Unless one invokes the idea that health insurance *is* a quasi-public service[4] and insurance companies must offer it to the public, government does not have a compelling reason to prevent insurers from making a profit, a behavior congruent with the principles of a capitalistic society. On the other hand if health insurance is considered a quasi-public service and insurance companies are forced to offer it to the public, two outcomes may ensue: first, insurance companies may discontinue underwriting health insurance policies because it is deemed to be unprofitable, or they may be driven into bankruptcy over time by the claims of insureds who have adversely selected against insurers (Cushing, 1993). Under either scenario individuals with suspect genes will not have an insurance policy.

ALTERNATIVE 2: ALLOWING INSURANCE COMPANIES TO HAVE ACCESS TO GENETIC INFORMATION

A review of state and federal laws by Miller (1989) indicates that with few exceptions, federal and state laws allow insurance companies to have access to genetic information. With regard to the federal laws, the United States Supreme Court in 1868 precluded the federal government from regulating the insurance industry. The Supreme Court reversed its decision in 1944 but the following year Congress enacted the McCarran-Fergurson Act and once again the power of regulating insurance was relegated to the states.

According to Miller only California, Florida, Louisiana, Maryland, and North Carolina, have laws that impose some restrictions on the use of genetic information in setting insurance rates. However, the scope of these state laws are very limited. For example, Louisiana, Maryland, and North Carolina ban the use of only one or two specific traits. The other two states ban the use of genetic information if such ban does not affect the carrier adversely (Miller, 1989).

At the present time insurance companies do not require genetic information mainly because such tests do not pass certain criteria[5] and in general they are very expensive and not very accurate. If new diagnostic and predictive medical tests become accurate and inexpensive, insurance companies in all likelihood will demand these tests from their applicants and very likely they will be able to obtain them. This view was echoed in a survey of major British health and life insurers. "The companies agreed that their underwriting procedures would eventually take account of new diagnostic tests, provided that they proved to be both accurate and reliable" (Cooper and Barefoot, 1987, p. 11).

Under this policy alternative, two scenarios are worth considering. First, with direct gene probe tests it would be possible to tell in advance with *certainty* the consequences of having a defective gene. (For a discussion of a direct gene probe, see for example, Joice, 1987.) Since the basic tenant of insurance is risk management, under the certainty scenario individuals with defective genes either will be denied insurance coverage or their insurance

---

[3]One should not forget the lobbying power of the insurance industry. This lobbying power explains why politicians are very receptive to the voice of the insurance industry. (For more information on the power of insurance industry see, for example, Brooks, 1985.)

[4]Miller makes a reference to insurance as "a vitally important public service" (Miller, 1989, p. 738). See also Miller footnote 60 with regard to insurance as a vital service labeled quasi-public in nature.

[5]Test criteria are: a) Sensitivity; b) Specifity; c) Predictive Value; d) Affordability, Safety, Convenience; e) Status of the test in the medical community; and f) Ease of Performance. For a discussion of these criteria see Pokorski, p. 22; see also U.S. Congress, Office of Technology Assessment, Medical Testing and Health Insurance, OTA-H-384 (Washington, D.C.: U.S. Government Printing Office, 1988).

premiums will be equal to the morbidity and mortality costs plus administrative costs. This scenario is analogous to the situation when an individual knows that approaching flames will engulf his house within a few hours. An insurance company having knowledge of the owner's predicament will either deny the insurance coverage on the house or will set a premium equal to the value of the house plus administrative costs. The difficult questions facing policy makers under the certainty model are enormous. For example: Who should be responsible for health care costs of individuals who cannot afford these costs? What are the social and economic impacts of redistribution of risk, that is, shifting the economic burden entirely from the group to the individuals with defective genes?

The second scenario is the uncertainty model. In this situation genetic tests will indicate the *probability* that an individual may develop certain health disorders in the future. Obviously insurance rates will be adjusted for the high risk categories. Although the outcome for individuals in high risk categories may not be as traumatic as it would be under the certainty model, the question remains the same: who should be responsible for the health care costs of individuals who cannot afford higher premiums?

ALTERNATIVE 3: NATIONAL HEALTH CARE SYSTEM

A majority of respondents favor having a national health care plan that would insure everyone regardless of individuals' genetic makeup. The positive contributions of a national health care could include: less worry and fear about the possibility of being denied insurance coverage or becoming uninsurable, and greater mobility for employees if a person was continuously covered after changing employers. The preexisting condition clause (health conditions that are present would be excluded from coverage under a plan with a new employer) would also have to be eliminated to keep everyone continuously insured.

The main question is how would such a plan be financed? If insurers had to insure all applicants and/or employers were mandated to pay for the plan, the evaluation and pricing of risk would be compromised. The pricing of risk could increase under such a plan for each insured. The fair dis-

crimination for evaluating risks would be violated. (For a general discussion on merits of different national health care systems see, for example, Rich, 1994.)

Conclusion

Based on our survey findings, respondents were against the use of genetic testing for underwriting purposes and rejecting applicants because of their genetic makeup. Ironically respondents were also against higher premiums and an increase in taxes to cover the health care cost of individuals with suspect genes. These conflicting opinions indicate little public understanding of difficult issues such as the limits of individual rights in a free market system, economic and social consequences of shifting the burden of risk from one group to another. Educating consumers on these and other related issues should contribute to a better understanding of the potential benefits and limits of genetic testing. Education and public policy issues regarding genetic testing and how health care can best be managed and financed will continue to be an important challenge into the twenty-first century.

References

Brooks, Jackson: 1985, "Insurance Industry Boosts Political Contributions as Congress Takes Up Cherished Tax Preferences," *Wall Street Journal* 1 (October 10), 64.

Cooper, David and Michael Barefoot: 1987, "Can You Buy Insurance for Your Genes?," *New Scientist* 115 (1569) (July 16), 51.

Cushing, T. H.: 1993, "Should There Be Genetic Testing in Insurance Risk Classification?," *Defense Counsel Journal* 60(2) (April), 249–263.

Denenberg, Herbert S., Robert D. Eilers, Joseph J. Melone and Robert A. Zelten: 1974, *Risk and Insurance*, 2nd edition (Prentice-Hall, Inc. Englewood Cliffs, NJ).

Easterbrook, Gregg: 1987, "The Revolution in Medicine," *Newsweek* 109(4) (January).

"Genetic Testing": 1992, *HR Magazine* 37(10) (October), 111–112.

Hoover, Dwight W.: 1990, *Middletown Revisited* (Ball State University Press, Muncie, IN).

Joice Christopher: 1987, "Genes Reach the Medical Market," *New Scientist* 115(1569) (July 16), 45–47 and 50–51.

Long, John D.: 1990, *Ethics, Morality, and Insurance* (The Bureau of Business Research, Graduate School of Business, Indiana University).

McAuliffe, Kathleen: 1987, "Predicting Diseases," *U.S. News & World Report* **102** (May 25), 64–69.

Miller, Joseph M.: 1989, "Genetic Testing and Insurance Classification: National Action Can Prevent Discrimination Based on the 'Luck of the Genetic Draw'," *Dickinson Law Review* **93** (Summer), 729–757.

Pokorski, Robert: 1990, "Genetic Testing in Private Insurance—Bridging the Gap Between New Knowledge and Its Application," *American Academy of Actuaries* (September–October), 20–25.

Rich, Robert F.: 1992, "National Health Care Reform: Comparing Four Alternative Plans," *Illinois Business Review* **51**(1), 3–4.

Schatz, Benjamin: 1987, "The AIDS Insurance Crisis: Underwriting or Overwriting?" *Harvard Law Review* **100**(7) (May), 1782–1805.

Stern, Lawrence C.: 1974, "Medical Information Bureau: The Life Insurer's Databank," *Rutgers Journal of Computers and Law* **4**(1), 1–41.

Strudler, Alan: 1994, "The Social Construction of Genetic Abnormality: Ethical Implications for Managerial Decisions in the Workplace," *Journal of Business Ethics* **13**(11) (November), 839–848.

U.S. Congress, Office of Technology Assessment: 1988, Medical Testing and Health Insurance, OTA-H-384 (U.S. Government Printing Office, Washington, DC).

Wortham, Leah: 1986, "Insurance Classification: Too Important to Be Left to Actuaries," *University of Michigan Journal of Law Reform* **19**, 349–423.

Questions for Chapter 4

1. DesJardins and Duska argue that one of the necessary conditions of drug testing being justified is that there exists the potential for clear and present harm. How would you define the "potential for clear and present harm"? Could an impaired worker on an auto assembly line conceivably present the potential for clear and present harm?

2. Drug testing might be viewed not primarily as a means of detecting impaired behavior, but rather as a way to verify its occurrence. If drug testing can be made accurate, might it be legitimately used as a means to verify what might otherwise be regarded as the subjective and perhaps unreliable impression of a manager or supervisor? Explain.

3. On what grounds does Cranford hold that "the fact that an employee may not want to submit to a drug test is entirely beside the point"? Do you agree that he is correct in asserting this?

4. In criticizing DesJardins and Duska, Cranford says that "it is . . . overly simplistic to state that employers need not test for drugs when they can terminate employees on the mere basis of a failure to perform." Why does he think this is overly simplistic on their part? Is he correct?

5. Resnik claims that genetic information is job-relevant if and only if the following conditions are met:
   (a) Possessing the genetic characteristic in question gives one a statistically significant risk of not satisfactorily performing duties outlined by the job description.
   (b) The characteristic is likely to produce its phenotypic effects during the employee's period of employment.
   (c) The characteristic's effects cannot be satisfactorily altered, modified, or treated through medicine or therapy.
   Suppose that conditions (a) and (b) obtain but that the characteristic's effect is treatable through medicine or therapy. Suppose further that although the characteristic can be satisfactorily treated, the treatment is very expensive, so much so

that the potential employee cannot afford it. How ought the company conduct itself in deciding whether or not to hire the potential employee?

6. Resnik argues in Case 2 that an individual who refused to submit to a test to reveal whether she possesses a genetic disposition for lung cancer could be viewed as infringing on the autonomy of fellow employees, inasmuch as she could create enormous health costs they would have to help bear. In Case 3 he argues that health is not relevant to a person's job description, since it would create a slippery slope that would lead to discrimination and bias against the unhealthy. Are these two statements consistent? How would you defend your view?

7. What is "adverse selection"? How does this concept relate to the "argument from fair discrimination"?

8. Should insurance companies be allowed to employ diagnostic tests to obtain genetic information if such tests are both accurate and reliable? If so, what restrictions, if any, would you put on the use of such information?

Case 4.1 Drug Testing and the Refuse Collector[1]

In the spring of 1990, Mr. Halischuk had been employed as a refuse helper by the City of Winnipeg for approximately five and a half years. As part of a crew consisting of a driver and one or two helpers, his job was to pick up refuse and load it into a rear collector, which had a compactor in the back of the hopper. In performing this job, it was important that the helper exhibit good judgment, since the potential for harm was great if individuals were not clear of the compactor during operation.

On the morning of May 1, 1990, Halischuk was driven by another employee, in the city refuse truck, to Halischuk's home where they picked up three bottles of beer. While in the truck, they consumed the beer and smoked two marijuana cigarettes. Upon this incident coming to light, Halischuk confirmed a lengthy history of marijuana use and that he had previously used marijuana during working hours and before starting work.

Halischuk was suspended pending a disciplinary hearing on June 4, 1990. During the intervening five weeks, he attended a three-week outpatient rehabilitation program for drug use.

He also apologized to his district supervisor and made clear his intention to stay away from drugs.

G. K. Stewart, director of operations at the city, was impressed with Halischuk's sincerity and cooperation, but was concerned by the issue of workplace safety. Unlike alcohol, drug usage is difficult to detect and is often not apparent until there is a serious addiction. Without revealing Halischuk's identity, Stewart consulted with Dr. William Davis, a PhD in psychology, and manager of the employee occupational safety and health unit.

Davis was of the view that the facts indicated a drug dependence, if not an addiction. He recommended random testing, in order to eliminate the possibility of the user planning around the testing. He suggested that mandatory testing was a "win-win" situation for both parties, since it gave the employee an opportunity to retain his job, yet addressed the employer's legitimate concerns over safety.

Stewart decided that he would require Halischuk to submit to random drug testing for a period of one year and that Halischuk's continuing employment would be contingent upon not testing positive for drug use. The test involved would only indicate the presence of drugs; it would not indicate whether Halischuk was impaired at the time of testing. Periodic usage on

[1] Selected from City of Winnipeg and Canadian Union of Public Employees, Local 500 as found in *Labour Arbitration Cases*, 4th series, Vol. 23, 1991, pp. 441–444.

weekends or outside work hours could cause a positive result at the time of testing.

The union grieved this decision, maintaining that the intrusion into Halischuk's privacy was not justified. It argued that not only was the process of taking urine samples a violation of privacy, but that the nature of the test illegitimately regulated Halischuk's private life for the period he was subject to testing.

1. Should Halischuk's voluntary participation in a rehabilitation program have any bearing on Stewart's decision? Why or why not?

2. Should Halischuk's admission of other delinquent incidents have any bearing on Stewart's decision? How would you defend your view?

3. Was it right for the union to protest Stewart's decision? How would you argue in support of your view?

Case 4.2 Public Safety and the Right to Privacy[2]

James Hennessey worked for Coastal Eagle Point Oil Company in Westville, New Jersey, as an at-will employee in its oil refinery. His job was what is known as a lead pumper. It consisted in supervising the "gaugers" who blend gasoline with various additives and manage the flow of petroleum products through the refinery. The gaugers take their directions from the lead pumper who translates orders and instructions into gauge levels the gaugers then set. The job of lead pumper carries a high degree of responsibility, since there is little direct supervision of the lead pumper and misjudgment on his or her part can result in spills with the potential for major explosions and environmental damage.

When Coastal Eagle acquired the refinery in 1985, it conducted physical examinations, including drug tests, on all employees. At this time, Hennessey tested negative for drug use. Coastal Eagle also issued a written policy in which it prohibited the on-premise use of alcohol, drugs, and controlled substances. It also required that employees advise their supervisors if they had occasion to use medication that could impair judgment or job performance. Further, it notified employees that they might be required, at any time, to give a urine or blood sample to determine compliance with the policy. Part of

Coastal Eagle's policy at this time was that it would help employees who voluntarily disclosed drug problems.

After discovering evidence of on-site marijuana use, Coastal Eagle decided, in January 1986, to conduct random urine testing in the spring. It chose urine testing on the basis that it would be less intrusive than blood testing. It also took steps to ensure that the testing was truly random, that the samples would not be counterfeited, that the samples would not be tested for physiological characteristics other than those indicating drug use, and that positive results would be confirmed by a separate test. It did not, however, notify employees that the tests would be conducted or describe the methodology that would be used. Neither did it directly notify nonmanagement employees that it was rescinding its informal policy of allowing those who tested positive to avoid termination through entering a rehabilitation program. Apparently its expectation was that nonmanagement employees would learn of this change in informal policy through the chain of command.

Hennessey was randomly chosen for testing and his urine tested positive for marijuana and diazepam, the active ingredient in Valium. He neither challenged the accuracy of the results nor suggested he had medical reasons justifying the use of diazepam. Coastal Eagle dismissed him.

Hennessey brought suit against Coastal Eagle. He alleged that the company had violated his

[2]Based on Hennessey v. Coastal Eagle Point Oil Co., 609 *Atlantic Reporter*, 2nd Series, 11 (N.J. 1992).

constitutional right of privacy under New Jersey law. He also argued that urine tests detect only drug use, not degree of impairment, and that some other means of testing by either observation or performance would be both more effective and less intrusive.

1. Hennessey's immediate supervisor evaluated Hennessey's work as "above average," stating that his job "always got done well." Given this, should Hennessey have been dismissed or simply reprimanded?

2. Do you think the claim that drug tests detect only the use of drugs and not actual impairment is relevant to the question of whether drug tests should be allowed?

Further Readings for Chapter 4

George G. Brenkert, "Privacy, Polygraphs and Work," *Business and Professional Ethics Journal* 1(1), 1981, pp. 19–35.

T. H. Cushing, "Should There Be Genetic Testing in Insurance Risk Classification?," *Defense Counsel Journal,* 60(2), April 1993, pp. 249–263.

Gertrude Ezorsky, ed., *Moral Rights in the Workplace* (Albany, NY: State University of New York Press, 1987).

Julie Inness, "Information, Access, or Intimate Decisions About One's Actions? The Content of Privacy," *Public Affairs Quarterly* 5(3), July 1991, pp. 227–242.

Jeffery L. Johnson, "A Theory of the Nature and Value of Privacy," *Public Affairs Quarterly,* 6(3), July 1992, pp. 271–288.

Richard Lippke, "Work Privacy and Autonomy," *Public Affairs Quarterly,* 3(2), April 1989.

Alan Westin, *Privacy and Freedom* (New York: Atheneum Publishers, 1976).

INFOTRAC COLLEGE EDITION To learn more about the topics from this chapter, you can use the following words to conduct an electronic search on InfoTrac College Edition, an online library of journals. Here you will find a multitude of articles from various sources and perspectives: *www.infotrac-college.com/wadsworth/access.html*

privacy

mandatory drug testing

genetic privacy

genetic screening

Chapter 5

Sexual Harassment

Introduction

WHEN WE FIRST THINK of sexual harassment we probably think of what seem to be clear-cut examples, for example, a male supervisor threatening a female subordinate with dismissal if she does not grant him sexual favors. At least initially, we may think, on the basis of such examples, that it will prove an easy task to define sexual harassment and formulate just and effective policies to deal with it. Unfortunately, this is not the case. Defining sexual harassment is far from simple, and designing policies that are effective, yet fair to all parties involved, is extremely difficult.

A good metaphor for constructing a definition is that of trying to weave a net that will catch only the size of fish one desires. A good definition should be neither too narrow, excluding what should be included, nor too broad, including what should be excluded. We do not want a definition of sexual harassment that catches too little, but neither do we want a definition that catches too much. A danger that lurks in focusing only on dramatic incidents that are easily recognized as sexual harassment is that of constructing a definition that is too narrow. Equally, a danger that lurks in labeling as sexual harassment any objectionable action that has sexual content is that of constructing a definition that is too broad. What is needed is a definition of sexual harassment that not only will make clear the grounds on which we judge obvious cases of sexual harassment to be such, but will provide guidance in cases we find difficult to resolve.

With regard to the workplace, the context within which our discussion of sexual harassment arises, the courts have treated sexual harassment as a form of discrimination and distinguished two types. The first, *quid pro quo* (this Latin phrase literally means something for something), occurs when sexual favors are made the condition of employment opportunities. The second occurs when a sexually hostile environment affects an employee's ability to function effectively.

The *quid pro quo* form of sexual harassment is easiest to define, though even here the courts have insisted that it must be shown that the victim suffered a tangible economic loss. It is a far more difficult task to define what constitutes a sexually hostile environment and establish its effect upon an employee.

It is useful to consider the legal issues surrounding sexual harassment, but such consideration cannot serve as a device to leapfrog over the difficult task of defining sexual harassment. At best such an examination serves as a useful starting point for discussion. The law will always employ one or more definitions of sexual harassment, whether the definition(s) be implicit or explicit. The issue of whether the law's understanding of sexual harassment is adequate must be raised, and, if the law is to be just and fair in both theory and application, hard questions of what constitutes an implicit threat must be answered—questions such as, to name only a couple, whether sexual harassment can be judged to have occurred only if the victim has suffered a tangible loss, and whether one can unintentionally sexually harass another.

The readings I have selected for this chapter reveal the diversity of views that exists as regards sexual harassment. Edmund Wall, in his article "The Definition of Sexual Harassment," defends the view that sexual harassment is to be defined primarily in terms of intention. He is concerned with refuting the view that sexual harassment can be defined in terms of behavior. His argument for this is that we distinguish between physically identical actions on the basis of motive. A "sensual touch" might be physically indistinguishable from a "friendly touch," yet one might constitute sexual harassment and the other not. Wall would admit that, especially in more extreme instances, behavior can often be an indicator of motive, but he would insist that motive is the essential element in judging the morality of an action.

For Wall, sexual harassment amounts to violating a person's privacy rights. What is immoral in sexual harassment is not what is proposed, but the inappropriateness of the approach. The sexual harasser engages in intimate communication in a manner and context that do not respect the dignity and autonomy of the victim.

Anita Superson takes quite a different approach in her article "A Feminist Definition of Sexual Harassment." She defines sexual harassment as "any behaviour (verbal or physical) caused by a person, A, in the dominant class directed at another, B, in the subjugated class, that expresses and perpetuates the attitude that B or members of B's sex is/are inferior because of their sex, thereby causing harm to either B and/or members of B's sex." Underlying this definition is the conviction that instances of sexual harassment must be viewed not primarily in terms of harm to the immediate victim, but rather as attacks upon all women.

A consequence of this definition, and in sharp contrast to Wall's view, is that the question of motive is not central. According to Superson, a man may sexually harass a woman without ever intending to. Also irrelevant is the question of whether the victim finds the behavior in question offensive. A woman may be so unaware of her oppression that she does not find harassing behavior offensive. A further implication of this definition, and one to which Superson is careful to draw attention, is that, assuming men are dominant in society, it is impossible for women to sexually harass men.

Most ethical issues involve a balancing of legitimate concerns. It is important not to neglect victims of sexual harassment, but it is equally important to protect individuals from unjust accusations of sexual harassment. A charge of sexual harassment, even if unsubstantiated and subsequently dismissed, can seriously harm a person's career. In his article "Sexual Harassment and the Rights of the Accused," Stephen Griffith addresses the issue of how we can protect people against unjust accusations of sexual harassment.

In Griffith's view, sexual harassment is generally defined much too broadly. He feels that to define anything from rape to "inappropriate innuendo" as sexual harassment not only is confusing, but also has the "doubly unfortunate effect of not only making relatively trivial offenses seem more serious than they are but also of trivializing more serious offenses." He distinguishes sexual harassment from discrimination based on gender on the grounds that sexual harassment should be seen as involving inappropriate sexual activity, while discrimination on the basis of gender does not necessarily involve inappropriate sexual activity. He also distinguishes sexual harassment from other forms of sexual misconduct such as sexual assault, sexual coercion, sexual offers, and sexual boorishness. This is not to say that gender discrimination or these other forms of sexual misconduct are not serious issues, only that it is not helpful to view them as sexual harassment.

Griffith's definition of sexual harassment is that it involves behavior that is sexual or could reasonably be construed as sexual, but that such behavior does not fall into the categories of sexual coercion, sexual assault, or morally unjustified sexual offers. The person exhibiting this behavior must have good reason to believe that the person to whom the behavior is directed regards it as sexual and does not welcome it. Finally, the person exhibiting the behavior must continue to behave in the same manner, even though he or she has realized the behavior is offensive.

Griffith concludes with the recommendation that sexual harassment policies must be widely publicized and must clearly state what constitutes an offense. Such policies should be designed primarily to educate, rather than to investigate and prosecute. He further recommends that no action or mode of behavior should be regarded as sexual harassment unless there is a wide consensus that it does in fact constitute sexual harassment. He concludes by suggesting that accused persons should be told exactly what they are accused of and have the right to have their accuser(s) cross-examined to ascertain whether there exist ulterior motives in bringing charges of sexual harassment.

The Definition of Sexual Harassment

EDMUND WALL

As IMPORTANT AS current managerial, legal and philosophical definitions of sexual harassment are, many of them omit the interpersonal features which define the concept. Indeed, the mental states of the perpetrator and the victim are the essential defining elements. In this essay arguments are presented against mere behavior descriptions of sexual harassment, definitions formulated in terms of the alleged discriminatory and coercive effects of a sexual advance, and the federal legal definition

From Public Affairs Quarterly *5(4), 1991. Reprinted by permission.*

which omits reference to relevant mental states. It is argued that sexual harassment is essentially a form of invasive communication that violates a victim's privacy rights. A set of jointly necessary and sufficient conditions of sexual harassment are defended which purport to capture the more subtle instances of sexual harassment while circumventing those sexual advances that are not sexually harassive. [If X is a *necessary condition* of Y then the absence of X guarantees the absence of Y. Note, however, that the presence of X does not guarantee the presence of Y. For example, in humans a necessary condition of being a mother is being female, but being female does not guarantee that one is a mother. If X is a *sufficient condition* of Y then the presence of X guarantees the presence of Y. Note, however, that the absence of X does not guarantee the absence of Y. For example, in humans a sufficient condition of being male is being a father, but not being a father does not guarantee that one is not male.]

There are many types of behavior that may be classified as instances of sexual harassment, and some people, such as Kenneth Cooper, have proposed that managers explain the concept to their employees primarily through descriptions of various behavior patterns. Cooper addresses the sexual harassment of female employees by male managers in an essay which describes what he terms "six levels of sexual harassment." He seems to order these levels according to what he assumes to be two complementary considerations: a third party's ability to identify the perpetrator's behavior as sexually harassive and the severity of the infraction. The categories are presented in ascending order with the first category ostensibly representing the least flagrant type of behavior, the sixth category representing the most flagrant type of behavior. He writes that "obvious and blatant harassment may be decreasing, but borderline harassment behavior has never let up."[1] He takes the first four categories to be accounts of "borderline" cases.

He refers to the first type of behavior as "aesthetic appreciation." This refers to comments which "express a non-aggressive appreciation of physical or sexual features." For example, an alleged perpetrator says to a coworker: "Gee . . . sigh . . . you're looking better every day!"[2] Cooper refers to such examples as the most "innocent" type of sexual harassment, but believes that these examples, nevertheless, constitute sexual harassment. In such cases the harassment is concealed.

Does managerial behavior which falls under "aesthetic appreciation" necessarily constitute sexual harassment? Cooper argues that "regardless of how harmless these appreciative comments may seem, they are put-downs which lower the group stature of the target." The offender, he tells us, is in a "superior position" from which to judge the employee's physical attributes.[3]

Comments of "aesthetic appreciation" made by male managers to female employees may not be appropriate, but all such comments are not, as Cooper suggests, necessarily instances of sexual harassment. Cooper argues that managerial comments of "aesthetic appreciation" made to employees are sexually harassive because they are "put-downs which lower the group stature of the target." There is a problem here. Such comments are not necessarily a reflection of any group differential.[4] Of course, the manager is in a "superior position" in relation to his employee, but only with respect to her corporate duties—not with respect to her physical attributes. The manager may try to use his corporate authority in order to force his employee to listen to his assessment of her physical attributes. Furthermore, the employee may feel as though she must submit to the manager's remarks, even if he does not openly attempt to coerce her. However, his sexually harassive behavior need not inherently be an exercise of corporate authority. It could simply be misguided human behavior which utilizes his corporate authority.

The second type of behavior which, according to Cooper, constitutes sexual harassment is "active mental groping." Under this heading Cooper places "direct verbal harassment," which evidently includes sexual jokes about the employee, and also the type of staring that may leave an employee feeling as though managers are "undressing them with

---

[1]Kenneth C. Cooper. "The Six Levels of Sexual Harassment." *Contemporary Moral Controversies in Business,* ed. A. Pablo Iannone (New York: Oxford University Press, 1989), p. 190.

[2]Ibid.
[3]Ibid.
[4]See especially pp. 381ff. for a detailed discussion of sexual harassment and discrimination.

their eyes."[5] This is followed by "social touching." Cooper maintains that, along with the first two categories of behavior, this type of behavior is "borderline," since the offender remains "within normal social touching conventions." In other words this behavior misleadingly appears "totally innocent" to a "third party."[6]

As far as "social touching" is concerned, he distinguishes an innocent "friendly touch" from a "sensual touch." He does not provide an example of a "friendly touch," but an example of a "sensual touch" would be "a caressing hand laid gently on the [employee]," or the movement of the manager's hand up and down his employee's back.[7] Unfortunately, Cooper offers no defense of his distinction between two types of touching. Neither does he clearly relate this distinction to his account of sexual harassment, although he seems to assume that a manager's "friendly touch" does not constitute sexual harassment, whereas his "sensual touch" would. He merely warns managers against any "social touching."

The reason why the distinction between an innocent "friendly touch" and a "sensual touch" makes sense is also the reason why behavior descriptions are not central to the definition of sexual harassment. The basis for the distinction lies in the manager's mental state. A sincerely "friendly touch" would depend, among other things, upon the manager's motive for touching his employee. Sexual harassment refers to a defect in interpersonal relations. Depending upon the manager's and employee's mental states, it is possible that some examples of managerial behavior which satisfy Cooper's first, most "innocent" category (i.e., "aesthetic appreciation"), would actually be more objectionable than his second and third categories (i.e., "active mental groping" and "social touching," respectively). Indeed, depending upon the manager's and employee's mental states, cases which fall under any of Cooper's first three categories of sexual harassment could be characterized as "innocent."

Consider the case in which a manager finds that one of his employees strikingly resembles his mother. He has managed this employee for three years without incident, and one day in the corporate dining room they begin to discuss their parents. He may tell her of the resemblance between her and his mother. He may stare at her for a long while (this would constitute "active mental groping" on Cooper's view). He may tell her that her cheek bones are as pretty as those of his mother (an example of "aesthetic appreciation" according to Cooper). Finally, he may put his hand on her shoulder (i.e., an example of friendly "social touching" on Cooper's view) and say "Oh well, I must be getting back to my desk." Given this scenario, it is obvious that at least some employees would take no offense at the manager's behavior. Such a case need not involve sexual harassment, even though mere behavior descriptions would lead up to the opposite conclusion.

Cooper refers to his fourth and final "borderline" category as "foreplay harassment." Unlike "social touching," the touching here is not "innocent in nature and location," although its inappropriateness is still concealed.[8] Examples of "foreplay harassment" include a manager noticing that a button on an employee's blouse is undone. Instead of telling her about it, he buttons it. Another example would be brushing up against her "as if by accident."[9]

Cooper suggests that the "scope, frequency, and feel" of the touching "shows an obvious intent on the part of the offender to push the limits of decency. . . ."[10] In this description of sexual harassment Cooper alludes to the importance of the manager's motive, but does not make its importance explicit. He does not express it as one of the essential descriptions of sexual harassment. Accidental physical contact between a manager and his employee is not, of course, sexual harassment. When the manager deliberately makes contact with his employee from a certain motive or due to his negligence, then he becomes an offender. Whether or not he makes physical contact, he may still be an offender. Indeed, as Cooper recognizes, an employee could be sexually harassed without *any* physical contact between her and her manager.

Cooper overlooks the possibility that what appears to be "foreplay harassment" of an

---

[5]Cooper. *op. cit.,* p. 191.
[6]Ibid.
[7]Ibid.

[8]Ibid.
[9]Cooper, *op. cit.,* pp. 191–92.
[10]Cooper, *op. cit.,* p. 192.

employee may not be. Even when a manager is sexually "petting" an employee in his office, as inappropriate as this behavior could be, he is not necessarily sexually harassing her. Consider the case in which a manager and an employee form an uncoerced agreement to engage in such inappropriate office behavior.[11] This is not sexual harassment. The general problem with behavior descriptions of sexual harassment can be seen when we attempt to construct examples of sexual harassment. The application of any of Cooper's four "borderline" categories to our examples may yield false determinations, depending upon the mental states involved.

Cooper's fifth and sixth categories are not "borderline," but involve flagrant sexual advances. They are "sexual abuse" and "ultimate threat," respectively. The latter which refers to a manager's coercive threats for sexual favors will be discussed later.[12] The former obviously involves sexual harassment.

Probably any behavior which constitutes sexual harassment (i.e., which satisfies certain descriptions of the manager's and employee's mental states) would probably constitute sexual abuse—whether physical or verbal. When an individual is maliciously or negligently responsible for unjustified harm to someone, it would seem that he has abused that person. Abuse can be subtle. It may include various ways of inflicting psychological harm. In fact, there is a more subtle form of sexual harassment accomplished through stares, gestures, innuendo, etc. For example, a manager may sexually harass his employee by staring at her and "undressing her with his eyes." *In light of this and the other limitations of behavior descriptions we need a set of jointly necessary and sufficient conditions of sexual harassment capable of capturing all subtle instances of sexual harassment while filtering out (even overt) sexual behavior which is not harassive.*

Wherein X is the sexual harasser and Y the victim, the following are offered as jointly necessary and sufficient conditions of sexual harassment:

1. X does not attempt to obtain Y's consent to communicate to Y, X's or someone else's purported sexual interest in Y.

[11]See pp. 377ff. for a discussion of coercion and sexual harassment.
[12]Cooper, *op. cit.,* p. 192; see pp. 379–81.

2. X communicates to Y, X's or someone else's purported sexual interest in Y, X's motive for communicating this is some perceived benefit that he expects to obtain through the communication.
3. Y does not consent to discuss with X, X's or someone else's purported sexual interest in Y.
4. Y feels emotionally distressed because X did not attempt to obtain Y's consent to this discussion and/or because Y objects to the content of X's sexual comments.

The first condition refers to X's failure to attempt to obtain Y's consent to discuss someone's sexual interest in Y. X's involvement in the sexual harassment is not defined by the sexual proposition that X may make to Y. If the first condition was formulated in terms of the content of X's sexual proposition, then the proposed definition would circumvent some of the more subtle cases of sexual harassment. After all, Y may actually agree to a sexual proposition made to her by X and still be sexually harassed by X's attempting to discuss it with her. In some cases Y might not feel that it is the proper time or place to discuss such matters. In any event *sexual harassment primarily involves wrongful communication.* Whether or not X attempts to obtain Y's consent to a certain type of communication is crucial. What is inherently repulsive about sexual harassment is not the possible vulgarity of X's sexual comment or proposal, but his failure to show respect for Y's rights. It is the obligation that stems from privacy rights that is ignored. Y's personal behavior and aspirations are protected by Y's privacy rights. The intrusion by X into this moral sphere is what is so objectionable about sexual harassment. If X does not attempt to obtain Y's approval to discuss such private matters, then he has not shown Y adequate respect.

X's lack of respect for Y's rights is not a sufficient condition of sexual harassment. X's conduct must constitute a rights violation. Essentially, the second condition refers to the fact that X has acted without concern for Y's right to consent to the communication of sexual matters involving her. Here X "communicates" to Y that X or someone else is sexually interested in Y. This term includes not only verbal remarks made by X, but any purposeful conveyance such as gestures, noises, stares, etc. that violate its recipient's privacy rights. Such behavior can be every bit as intrusive as verbal remarks.

We need to acknowledge that X can refer to some third party's purported sexual interest in Y and still sexually harass Y. When he tells her, without her consent, that some third party believes she is physically desirable, this may be a form of sexual harassment. Y may not approve of X telling her this—even if Y and the third party happen to share a mutual sexual interest in each other. This is because X's impropriety lies in his invasive approach to Y. It does not hinge upon the content of what he says to Y. X may, for example, have absolutely no sexual interest in Y, but believes that such remarks would upset Y, thereby affording him perverse enjoyment. Likewise his report that some third party is sexually interested in Y may be inaccurate but this does not absolve him from his duty to respect Y's privacy.

X's specific motive for communicating what he does to Y may vary, but it always includes some benefit X may obtain from this illegitimate communication. X might or might not plan to have sexual relations with Y. Indeed, as we have seen, he might not have a sexual interest in Y at all and still obtain what he perceives to be beneficial to himself, perhaps the satisfaction of disturbing Y.[13] Perhaps, as some contemporary psychologists suggest, X's ultimate motive is to mollify his feelings of inferiority by controlling Y's feelings, actions, environment, etc. Yet another possibility is that X wants to conform to what he believes to be parental and/or peer standards for males. The proposed first and second conditions can account for these various motives. The point is that, whatever the perceived benefit, it is the utility of the approach as perceived by X, and not necessarily the content of his message, that is important to the harasser. Furthermore, the "benefit" that moves him to action might not be obtainable or might not be a genuine benefit, but, nevertheless, in his attempt to obtain it, he violates his victim's rights.

The third condition refers to Y's not consenting to discuss with X, X's or someone else's purported sexual interest in Y. Someone might argue that the

first condition is now unnecessary, that X's failure to obtain Y's consent to the type of discussion outlined in the third condition will suffice; the provision concerning X's failure to *attempt* to obtain Y's consent is, therefore, unnecessary. This objection would be misguided, however. The first condition ensures that some sexual comments will not be unjustly labelled as "harassive." Consider the possibility that the second and third conditions are satisfied. For example, X makes a sexual remark about Y to Y without her consent. Now suppose that the first condition is not satisfied, that is, suppose that X *did attempt* to obtain Y's consent to make such remarks. Furthermore, suppose that somewhere the communication between X and Y breaks down and X honestly believes he has obtained Y's consent to this discussion when, in fact, he has not. In this case, X's intentions being what they are, he does not sexually harass Y. X has shown respect for Y's privacy. Y may certainly *feel* harassed in this case, but there is no offender here. However, after X sees Y's displeasure at his remarks, it is now his duty to refrain from such remarks, unless, of course, Y later consents to such a discussion.

The case of the ignorant but well-intentioned X demonstrates the importance of distinguishing between accidents (and merely unfortunate circumstances) and sexual harassment. The remedy for avoiding the former is the encouragement of clear communication between people. Emphasis on clear communication would also facilitate the identification of some offenders, for some offenders would not refrain from making sexual remarks after their targets clearly expressed their objections to those remarks. The above case also reveals that the alleged victim needs to clearly express her wishes to others. For example, when she wishes not to discuss an individual's sexual interest in her, it would be foolish for her to make flirting glances at this individual. Such gestures may mislead him to conclude that she consents to this communication.

The first three conditions are not jointly sufficient descriptions of sexual harassment. What is missing is a description of Y's mental state. In sexual harassment cases the maligned communication must distress Y for a certain reason. Let us say that X has expressed sexual interest in Y without any attempt to obtain her consent. She, in fact, does not consent to it. However, perhaps she has

---

[13]Some sociologists would disagree with me. They believe that the offender must have set himself a "sexual goal" in order for sexual harassment to occur. See K. Wilson and L. Kraus, "Sexual Harassment in the University." This paper was presented at the annual meetings of the American Sociological Association (Toronto, 1981).

decided against the discussion because she finds X too refined and anticipates that his sexual advances will not interest her. Perhaps she welcomes crass discussions about sexual matters. In this case she might not be sexually harassed by X's remarks. As the fourth condition indicates, Y must be distressed because X did not attempt to ensure that it was permissible to make sexual comments to Y which involve her, or because the content of X's sexual comments are objectionable to Y. Yet another possibility is that both the invasiveness of X's approach and the content of what X says cause Y emotional distress. In this case, however, it would appear that Y would neither object to the content of X's sexual remarks nor to the fact that X's sexual remarks nor to the fact that X did not attempt to obtain Y's consent to make these remarks to her. Due to Y's views concerning sexual privacy this case is similar to one in which X does not attempt to obtain Y's consent to discuss with Y how well she plays tennis, or some other mundane discussion about Y.

You may recall that we postponed a discussion of the relation of sexual harassment to coercion and discrimination against women. Let us now explore this relation.

The fact that male employers and managers represent the bulk of the reported offenders has caused some legal theorists and philosophers to conclude that sexual harassment necessarily involves discrimination against women as a class. This approach is unacceptable. The proposed description of sexual harassment in terms of interpersonal relations is incompatible with this account, and, it seems that sexual harassment is not necessarily tied to discrimination or to coercion.

In an essay entitled "Is Sexual Harassment Coercive?" Larry May and John C. Hughes argue that sexual harassment against women workers is "inherently coercive"—whether the harassment takes the form of a threat or an offer. They also maintain that the harm of sexual harassment against women "contributes to a pervasive pattern of discrimination and exploitation based upon sex."[14] They begin by defining sexual harassment

as "the intimidation of persons in subordinate positions by those holding power and authority over them in order to exact sexual favors that would ordinarily not have been granted."[15]

May and Hughes recognize that male employees may be sexually harassed, but choose to limit their discussion to the typical case in which a male employer or manager sexually harasses a female employee. They choose this paradigm because it represents the "dominant pattern" in society and because they believe that, as a class, women have been conditioned by society to acquiesce "to male initiative."[16] According to May and Hughes women represent an injured class. The fact that men dominate positions of authority and status in our society renders women vulnerable to sexual harassment. Furthermore, the sexual harassment of female employees by male employers and managers sparks a general increase in the frequency of the crime, since such behavior reinforces male stereotypes of women as sexual objects[17]

Even if May's and Hughes' social assumptions are accepted, that would not entail that their definition of sexual harassment is adequate. Their definition includes a power differential between the offender and the victim. Unhappily, this circumvents the sexual harassment between employees of equal rank, capabilities and recognition. Suppose that X and Y are co-workers for some company X makes frequent comments concerning Y's sexual appeal and repeatedly propositions Y despite Y's refusals. Authority and rank are superfluous here. Y may be sexually harassed regardless of X's or Y's corporate status. As argued above in the critique of Cooper's article, the harassment at issue is not an extension of X's corporate authority, nor is the harassment essentially explained by the exercise of his authority. Rather, it is essentially explained by X's lack of respect for Y's right to refuse to discuss sexual matters pertaining to Y. If Y chooses not to enter X's discussion or is upset by X's refusal to recognize Y's privacy rights, then sexual harassment has occurred. X's and Y's mental states are essential, not some power differential between them.

Although the law vaguely recognizes the significance of Y's mental state in its sexual harassment

[14]Larry May and John C. Hughes, "Is Sexual Harassment Coercive?," *Moral Rights in the Workplace,* ed. Gertrude Ezorsky (Albany, NY: State University of New York, 1987), pp. 115–22.

[15]May and Hughes, *op. cit.,* p. 115.
[16]Ibid.
[17]May and Hughes, *op. cit.,* p. 118.

definitions, the same is not true of X's mental state. For example, the California Department of Fair Employment and Housing (DFEH) completely omits the alleged perpetrator's mental state in their brief definition. Acknowledging that sexual harassment can occur between co-workers, they define it as "unwanted sexual advances, or visual, verbal or physical conduct of a sexual nature."[18] The difficulty with the DFEH's omission can be seen in the following counter-example. Y may be a paranoid individual who believes that any social advance by a member of the opposite sex somehow harms her. Perhaps X asks Y for a date and Y feels sexually harassed. Let us say that X is not yet planning to discuss with Y anyone's sexual interest in Y and that X terminates the discussion as soon as he notices Y's displeasure. On their definition the DFEH would be forced to consider this sexual harassment when clearly it is not. Although it involves an "unwanted sexual advance," X's mental state points to the innocence of his proposal.

Many of the examples that the DFEH use to illustrate their definition are also ambiguous. Unwanted "touching" is one example. In this case the commission might be referring to unwanted "sensual touching," but they offer no way of distinguishing a sensual from a merely friendly touch. Suppose that Y works in the sales office of some company and X works in the maintenance department. Y may object to X's touching her, but only because she does not want to stain her clothing. She knows that her friend, X, is not sexually interested in her and, if his hands were clean, she would have no objections to his occasional "friendly touch." This is not a case of sexual harassment, although it may, if it persists, show a lack of consideration on X's part. By ignoring the importance of mental states, the DFEH not only fails to identify the perpetrator's lack of respect for Y in genuine sexual harassment cases, but also fails to acknowledge the importance of Y's concerns. In this example Y did not feel sexually harassed, although she may have been upset because of her friend's inconsideration. In this subtle way California law does not do justice to the concerns of this alleged victim.

May's and Hughes' inaccurate definition of sexual harassment skews their inquiry. Their main objective is to illustrate the coercive nature of sexual harassment; more specifically, the coercive nature of sexual threats and offers made to women employees by male corporate authorities. They focus on the type of sexual advances that are tied to hiring, promotions or raises.[19] They briefly refer to a third type of sexual advance, one which is "merely annoying" and one which is "without demonstrable sanction or reward."[20] However, after introducing this third category the authors circumvent it. This oversight is a serious one. The essence of sexual harassment lies not in the content of the offender's proposal, but in the inappropriateness of his approach to the victim. It lies in the way he violates the victim's privacy. This is the "annoying" aspect of his approach which needs elucidating. May and Hughes could not pursue this third type of sexual advance because they had defined sexual harassment in terms of someone in authority acquiring some sexual favor from his employee. They set themselves the task of proving that sexual harassment is necessarily coercive. Their definition thereby hinged on the alleged coercive effects of the harasser's proposal, rather than on his mental state.

We still need to examine May's and Hughes' position that all sexual threats and offers made by male employers or managers to female employees are sexually harassive as well as coercive. They describe a conditional sexual threat from the employer's position: "If you don't provide a sexual benefit, I will punish you by withholding a promotion or raise that would otherwise be due, or ultimately fire you."[21] According to their "baseline" approach "sexual threats are coercive because they worsen the objective situation the employee finds herself in." Before the threat the retention of her job only depended upon "standards of efficiency," whereas, after the threat, the performance of sexual favors becomes a condition of employment.[22] Presumably, these same "baseline" considerations also render the threat sexually harassive.

May and Hughes acknowledge that their "baseline account" of coercive threats is essentially Nozickian. Elsewhere, I have defended an

[18]Pamphlet entitled "Sexual Harassment" (1990), distributed by the California Department of Fair Employment and Housing.

[19]May and Hughes, *op. cit.,* pp. 116–17.
[20]May and Hughes, *op. cit.,* p. 117.
[21]May and Hughes, *op. cit.,* pp. 116–17.
[22]May and Hughes, *op. cit.,* pp. 117–18.

interpersonal description of coercive threats against "baseline accounts."[23] According to my description X issues Y a coercive threat (in his attempt to get Y to do action "A") when X intentionally attempts to create the belief in Y that X will be responsible for harm coming to Y should Y fail to do A. X's coercive threat is described primarily in terms of his intentions. His motive for attempting to create this belief in Y is his desire to bring about a state of affairs in which Y's recognition of this possible harm to himself influences Y to do A. May and Hughes are correct that every conditional sexual threat issued by a male superior to a female subordinate is a coercive threat. (Indeed, a conditional sexual threat issued against anyone is a coercive threat.) The male employer would be trying to create the belief in the female employee that he will be responsible for harm coming to her (i.e. her termination, demotion, etc.) should she fail to comply with his sexual request. He would do this because he wants the prospect of this harm to motivate her to comply. Nevertheless, it is not true that every conditional sexual threat *as May and Hughes describe these threats* would be coercive. If, for example, the employer and the employee are playfully engaging in "banter" when he tells her that without her compliance he will fire her, then she is not being threatened. He does not intend to create the belief in her that harm will come to her. In this scenario she would not be sexually harassed either because the employer has a good faith belief that she consents to this "banter." Therefore, May and Hughes need a more rigorous description of coercive threats which includes the intentions of the person making the threat.

May and Hughes argue that if the employee wants to provide sexual favors to her employer regardless of the employer's demand, she is still coerced. They maintain that her objective baseline situation is still made worse, for now it would be very difficult for her to cease a sexual relationship with her employer should she choose to do so.[24] May and Hughes do not tell us who or what would specifically be making the coercive proposal if the *employee* propositioned the employer. After all, on their view, her offer would worsen her objective situation for the same reason his threat would.

Perhaps they would refer to this as a coercive situation, or would find the employer's consent to the sexual relationship to include some sort of a coercive stance, but, nevertheless, their external analysis overlooks the mental state of the individual who is supposedly victimized. Depending upon her values and personal outlook she may, without reservation, accept her employer's demand as a "career opportunity." By excluding the employee's mental state in their "baseline analysis" they overlook the fact that her situation may improve after the demand and that, to her, the prospect of a permanent sexual relationship with her employer is no problem. According to this "baseline account" she would not be coerced or harassed. Unlike May's and Hughes' account, the proposed interpersonal account of sexual harassment maintains that an employee who receives a sexual threat from her employer is not necessarily sexually harassed. Let us say that he told her she must have sex with him or else be demoted. Still, she may welcome his demand as a "career opportunity." If she is not offended by his demand, then she is not sexually harassed by the threat.

As we have seen May and Hughes maintain that the sexual harassment of a female employee by a male corporate authority is coercive because it worsens the employee's employment situation. They say that sexual harassment by an employer erects an unfair employment condition against women as a class. May and Hughes therefore believe that the discriminatory nature of sexual harassment against female employees is tied to these "coercive" dimensions. They argue that, in general, men do not have to endure the maligned "job requirement" generally foistered upon women and that when men make sexual threats to their female subordinates they "establish a precedent for employment decisions based upon the stereotype that values women for their sexuality. . . .[25] Because the sexual harassment of female employees by male employers worsens the employment situation of women by stereotyping them, we supposedly have a necessary relation between ("coercive") sexual harassment and discrimination.

May and Hughes are not alone in their belief that sexual harassment and discrimination are necessarily related. When they describe their

[23]"Intention and Coercion," *Journal of Applied Philosophy*, vol. 5 (1988), pp. 75–85.

[24]May and Hughes, *op. cit.*, p. 118.

[25]May and Hughes, *op. cit.*, pp. 118–19.

arguments for the coercive-discriminatory effects of a male employer's sexual threat on a female employee, they refer to such a threat as an "instance of discrimination in the workplace."[26] Here they follow federal law by claiming that sexual threats in the workplace fall under the rubric of Title VII of the Civil Rights Act of 1964. They are relying on the fact that in 1980 the Equal Employment Opportunity Commission (EEOC) set a precedent by finding that sexual harassment is a form of sex discrimination.[27]

The prevailing belief that the sexual harassment of women is a form of sex discrimination is ill-founded. Even if we follow May and Hughes and limit our discussion to the sexual harassment of female employees by male employers, something that the EEOC cannot do, a male employer's sexual threat is not necessarily an "instance" of sex discrimination. For a given sexual harassment case, gender may not be a consideration at all. Picture the bisexual employer who is not in control of his sexual desires. He might indiscriminately threaten or proposition his employees without giving consideration to the gender of his victims. The additional "job requirement" referred to by May and Hughes would, in this case, apply to all employees male and female. Indeed, since, as argued above, sexual harassment is primarily a matter of communication which infringes on basic privacy rights, there is no presumption of gender. Now, the EEOC does make reference to a candidate losing a job because another candidate who is less qualified has acquiesced to an employer's sexual threat, but this is not necessarily a case of sex discrimination as May and Hughes contend. Gender need not be the motive behind the employer's sexual threat. If the qualified candidate has been discriminated against, this may occur for a variety of reasons. Although the proposed interpersonal account is compatible with the assumptions that sexual harassment against women generally *contributes* to discrimination against women and that prejudice against women *may* be the motive of most male employers when they sexually harass female employees, we should avoid *defining* sexual harassment in terms of these assumptions.

Of course, the possibility that federal authority was misdirected when the EEOC set policy for sexual harassment in the workplace, does not entail that the EEOC's definition is incorrect. They maintain that: unwelcome sexual advances, requests for sexual favors, and other verbal or physical conduct of a sexual nature constitute sexual harassment when

1. submission to such conduct is made either explicitly or implicitly a term or condition of an individual's employment,
2. submission to or rejection of such conduct by an individual is used as the basis for employment decisions affecting such an individual, or
3. such conduct has the purpose or effect of unreasonably interfering with an individual's work performance or creating an intimidating, hostile, or offensive working environment.

The EEOC'S conditions of sexual harassment not only appear to capture sexual threats and offers, but, also, "annoyances" and other more subtle violations. The EEOC's definition thereby avoids May's and Hughes' mistake. Their third condition also allows for sexual harassment between employees, something also lacking in May's and Hughes' account. Unfortunately, the EEOC's first two conditions seem to suggest that all sexual threats and offers made by employers to employees are sexually harassive. As argued above, not all sexual threats made by employers to employees must be sexually harassive, their inappropriateness notwithstanding. The EEOC's definition of sexual harassment is too inclusive because it fails to capture precisely the victim's mental state and the way that she reacts to the threat. In omitting a description of her mental state the EEOC's definition encourages the FDEH's oversight in allowing a paranoid "victim" to claim sexual harassment against a well-intentioned employer. Moreover, the EEOC makes no provision for the intentions of the employer.

Some states such as California maintain that sexually explicit materials which disturb employees are sexually harassive. This stance seems to be in line with the EEOC's definition. According to the EEOC the employer or employee who, for example, displays a sexually explicit poster may exhibit "physical conduct of a sexual nature" which creates an "offensive working environment." This is a difficult example, but it seems that an employee's mere

---

[26]May and Hughes. *op. cit.,* p. 118.
[27]Equal Employment Opportunity Commission, *Federal Register,* vol. 45, no. 219 (10 November, 1980), Rules and Regulations, 74676–7.

disapproval of such materials does not entail that she is sexually harassed. Even if the disgruntled employee disapproves of the poster's explicit sexual representations, this does not mean that the person displaying the poster is intending to communicate anything to her and about her. Of course, in many cases he may be making a subtle statement to her about her sexual appeal. For example he may be using the poster in order to communicate his or someone else's sexual interest in her. According to the interpersonal account these cases would involve sexual harassment. If he is merely displaying the poster for his own benefit, however, then his behavior is rude, but not sexually harassive. There is a difference between the disrespect involved in rudeness, which indicates poor taste or a breach of etiquette, and the disrespect involved in sexual harassment. In the latter case the privacy of some specific individual has not been respected.

If May's and Hughes' position that all conditional sexual threats by male employers to female employees are sexually harassive and discriminatory in nature has successfully been overturned, their contention that the same considerations also apply to sexual offers collapses. They describe a sexual offer from the male employer's position: "If you provide a sexual benefit, I will reward you with a promotion or a raise that would otherwise not be due."[28] Since the benefit would ostensibly improve the employee's baseline situation, she is made an offer by her employer. Without the offer, she would not get the promotion or raise. Interestingly, May and Hughes argue that such offers actually worsen the employee's baseline situation and are, therefore, coercive offers. They do not explain how the employee's situation is simultaneously improved and worsened, but perhaps they have the following in mind: the employer's proposal is an offer because it may improve the employee's strategic status, whereas his offer is coercive because of certain social considerations. May and Hughes tell us that the employer's sexual offer changes the work environment so that the employee "is viewed by others, and may come to view herself, less in terms of her work productivity and more in terms of her sexual allure." Moreover, they say that, since women are more "economically vulnerable and socially passive than men," they are inclined to "offset [their] diminished status and to

protect against later retaliation" by acquiescing to employer demands. Thus, according to May and Hughes, they are necessarily coerced by a male employer's sexual offer.[29]

May and Hughes argue that there is usually an implicit threat concealed in an employer's sexual offer and that this makes the offer coercive. Of course, here it may be the threat that is coercive and not the offer. What we are interested in is their argument that the employer's sexual offer itself is coercive because it reduces the female employee's self-esteem, and also raises the spectre of some future threat (should the employee fail to comply or otherwise fall victim to the employer's "bruised" ego). Even if May and Hughes are correct and these are the general social effects of these sexual offers, this does not entail that a sexual offer made by a male employer to a female employee is coercive in nature. It would be unreasonable to suggest that every female employee would experience these hardships following a male employer's sexual offer. As mentioned in the discussion of sexual threats, the employee's values and personality contribute to the effects of an employer's presumably coercive proposal. Moreover, May's and Hughes' claim about the coercive effects of these sexual offers hinges upon their "baseline account" of coercion (which has been criticized above).

There is a more plausible alternative to a "baseline account" of coercive offers. An interpersonal account is possible. X makes Y a coercive offer when X intends to create the belief in Y that he will not prevent harm from coming to Y unless Y complies with his request. A genuine offer, on the other hand, would be limited to a mutual exchange of perceived benefits, or it may be a gift. This offer could become coercive if X attempts to cause Y to believe that her rejection of his request will result in some harm to her. Essentially, the coercive element is that X makes his proposed assistance in preventing this harm conditional upon Y's agreement to his request. He tries to use her belief that harm will occur as a way of controlling her. Not all offers by male employers to female employees are like this. Thus, on this interpersonal account, a male employer's offer is not coercive by nature.

We still need to address May's and Hughes' account of the implications of an employer's sexual offer to an employee. We are told that a non-

[28]May and Hughes, *op. cit.*, p. 117.

[29]May and Hughes. *op. cit.*, p. 120.

compliant employee may worry that a disgruntled employer may threaten or harm her at some future date. This is certainly possible. However, such proposals are not coercive unless they involve the relevant intentions. The proposed account does acknowledge that an employer's non-coercive sexual offer might be sexually harassive. As argued above this depends upon the legitimacy of his approach to the employee and upon the employee's

wishes. Moreover, the fact that, according to the proposed view, some of these sexual offers are not coercive or sexually harassive does not alter the fact that an employer who is both considerate and prudent would avoid any behavior that could be construed as sexually harassive.[30]

[30]I am grateful to Burleigh Wilkins for helpful comments on this paper.

A Feminist Definition of Sexual Harassment

ANITA M. SUPERSON*

1. Introduction

BY FAR THE MOST PERVASIVE form of discrimination against women is sexual harassment (SH). Women in every walk of life are subject to it, and I would venture to say, on a daily basis.[1] Even though the law is changing to the benefit of victims of SH, the fact that SH is still so pervasive shows that there is too much tolerance of it, and that victims do not have sufficient legal recourse to be protected.

The main source for this problem is that the way SH is defined by various Titles and other sources does not adequately reflect the social nature of SH, or the harm it causes all women. As a result, SH comes to be defined in subjective ways. One upshot is that when subjective definitions infuse the case law on SH, the more subtle but equally harmful forms of SH do not get counted as SH and thus not afforded legal protection.

My primary aim in this paper is to offer an objective definition of SH that accounts for the

group harm all forms of SH have in common. Though my aim is to offer a moral definition of SH, I offer it in hopes that it will effect changes in the law. It is only by defining SH in a way that covers all of its forms and gets at the heart of the problem that legal protection can be given to all victims in all circumstances.

I take this paper to be programmatic. Obviously problems may exist in applying the definition to cases that arise for litigation. In a larger project a lot more could be said to meet those objections. My goal in this paper is merely to defend my definition against the definitions currently appealed to by the courts in order to show how it is more promising for victims of SH.

I define SH in the following way:

Any behavior (verbal or physical) caused by a person, A, in the dominant class directed at another, B, in the subjugated class, that expresses and perpetuates the attitude that B or members of B's sex is/are inferior because of their sex, thereby causing harm to either B and/or members of B's sex.

II. Current Law on Sexual Harassment

Currently, victims of SH have legal recourse under Title VII of the Civil Rights Act of 1964, Title IX

*I would like to thank John Exdell and Lois Pineau for helpful discussions and many insightful comments on an earlier draft of this paper.
[1]Rosemarie Tong, "Sexual Harassment," in *Women and Values,* Marilyn Pearsall, ed., (Belmont, CA: Wadsworth Publishing Company, 1986), pp. 148–166. Tong cites a *Redbook* study that reported 88 percent of 9,000 readers sampled experienced some sort of sexual harassment (p. 149).

From Journal of Social Philosophy *24(1), 1993. Reprinted by permission of the* Journal of Social Philosophy.

of the 1972 Education Amendments, and tort law.

The Civil Rights Act of 1964 states:

a) It shall be an unlawful employment practice for an employer—
   (1) to fail or refuse to hire or to discharge any individual, or otherwise to discriminate against any individual with respect to his compensation, terms, conditions, or privileges of employment because of such individual's race, color, religion, sex, or national origin. . . .[2]

Over time the courts came to view SH as a form of sex discrimination. The main advocate for this was Catharine MacKinnon, whose book, *Sexual Harassment of Working Women,*[3] greatly influenced court decisions on the issue. Before it was federally legislated, some courts appealed to the Equal Employment Opportunity Commission (EEOC) *Guidelines on Discrimination Because of Sex* to establish that SH was a form of sex discrimination. The *Guidelines* (amended in 1980 to include SH) state that

Harassment on the basis of sex is a violation of Sec. 703 of Title VII. Unwelcome sexual advances, requests for sexual favors, and other verbal or physical conduct of a sexual nature constitute sexual harassment when (1) submission to such conduct is made either explicitly or implicitly a term or condition of an individual's employment, (2) submission to or rejection of such conduct by an individual is used as the basis for employment decisions affecting such individual, or (3) such conduct has the purpose or effect of unreasonably interfering with an individual's work performance or creating an intimidating, hostile, or offensive working environment.[4]

In a landmark case,[5] *Meritor Savings Bank, FSB v. Vinson* (1986),[6] the Supreme Court, relying on the EEOC *Guidelines,* established that SH was a form of sex discrimination prohibited under Title VII. The case involved Mechelle Vinson, a teller-trainee, who was propositioned by Sidney Taylor, vice president and branch manager of the bank. After initially refusing, she agreed out of fear of losing her job. She allegedly had sexual relations with Taylor 40 or 50 times over a period of four years, and he even forcibly raped her several times, exposed himself to her in a restroom, and fondled her in public.[7]

Sexual harassment extends beyond the workplace. To protect students who are not employees of their learning institution, Congress enacted Title IX of the Education Amendments of 1972, which states:

No person in the United States shall, on the basis of sex, be excluded from participation in, be denied the benefits of, or be subjected to discrimination under any educational program or activity receiving federal financial assistance.[8]

Cases of litigation under Title IX have been influenced by Meritor so that SH in educational institutions is construed as a form of sex discrimination.[9]

The principles that came about under Title VII apply equally to Title IX. Under either Title, a person can file two different kinds of harassment charges: *quid pro quo,* or hostile environment.

---

[2]Civil Rights Act of 1964, 42 U.S.C. Sec. 2000e-2(a) (1982).

[3]Catharine A. MacKinnon, *Sexual Harassment of Working Women: A Case of Sex Discrimination* (New Haven: Yale University Press, 1979).

[4]EEOC *Guidelines on Discrimination Because of Sex,* 29 C.F.R. Sec. 1604.11(a) (1980).

[5]The case was a landmark case because it established (1) federal legislation that SH is a form of sex discrimination, (2) that just because the victim "voluntarily" submitted to

advances from her employer, it did not mean she welcomed the conduct, (3) that victims could appeal on grounds of emotional harm, not merely economic harm. For an excellent discussion of the history of the case as it went through the courts, see Joel T. Andreesen, "Employment Discrimination—The Expansion in Scope of Title VII to Include Sexual Harassment as a Form of Sex Discrimination": *Meritor Savings Bank, FSB v. Vinson, The Journal of Corporation Law,* Vol. 12, No. 3 (Spring, 1987), pp. 619–638.

[6]*Meritor Savings Bank, FSB v. Vinson,* 477 U.S. 57 (1986).

[7]Joyce L. Richard, "Sexual Harassment and Employer Liability," *Southern University Law Review,* Vol. 12 (1986), pp. 251–279. See pp. 272–275 for an excellent discussion of the case.

[8]Title IX of the Education Amendments of 1972, 20 USC. Sec. 1681 (1982).

[9]For a very good discussion of the case law regarding Title IX, see Walter B. Connolly, Jr., and Alison B. Marshall, "Sexual Harassment of University or College Students by Faculty Members," *The Journal of College and University Law,* Vol. 15 (Spring, 1989), pp. 381–403.

Quid pro quo means "something for something."[10] *Quid pro quo* harassment occurs when "an employer or his agent explicitly ties the terms, conditions, and privileges of the victim's employment to factors which are arbitrary and unrelated to job performance."[11] Plaintiffs must show they "suffered a tangible economic detriment as a result of the harassment."[12] In contrast, hostile environment harassment occurs when the behavior of supervisors or co-workers has the effect of "unreasonably interfering with an individual's work performance or creates an intimidating, hostile, or offensive environment."[13] Hostile environment harassment established that Title VII (and presumably Title IX) were not limited to economic discrimination, but applied to emotional harm, as well. The EEOC *Guidelines* initiated the principle of hostile environment harassment which was used by the courts in many cases, including *Meritor.*

For each kind of SH (*quid pro quo* or hostile environment), courts can use one of two approaches: disparate treatment, or disparate impact. *Black's Law Dictionary* defines disparate *treatment* as "[d]ifferential treatment of employees or applicants on the basis of their race, color, religion, sex, national origin, handicap, or veteran's status."[14] The key is to establish that the person was harassed because of her sex, and not because of other features (e.g., hair color). Disparate *impact,* in contrast, "involves facially neutral practices that are not intended to be discriminatory, but are discriminatory in effect. . . ."[15] Disparate impact came about because the facts did not always show that an employer blatantly discriminated on the basis of

sex,[16] but the employer's practices still worked to the disadvantage of certain groups. Allegedly, "[f]or both *quid pro quo* and hostile environment sexual harassment, courts use disparate treatment theory."[17]

For women who are harassed other than in an employment or an educational setting, tort law [A *tort* is a private or civil, as opposed to public, wrong. We thus speak of civil as opposed to criminal offenses in the law.] can offer legal remedy. Also, torts can accompany a claim invoking Title VII (and presumably, Title IX).[18] Criminal suits apply only if the victim of harassment "is a victim of rape, indecent assault, common assault, assault causing bodily harm, threats, intimidation, or solicitation,"[19] and in these cases the suit will usually be for one of these charges, not harassment. To be taken seriously, the action requires police charges, a difficulty in SH cases.

Civil torts are a more promising way to go for victims of SH, though with limitations. The battery tort prohibits battery which is defined as "an intentional and unpermitted contact, other than that permitted by social usage."[20] The intent refers to intent to contact, not intent to cause the harm that may result from the contact. The assault tort prohibits assault, which is defined as "an intentional act, short of contact, which produces *apprehension* of battery."[21] The defendant must have intended to arouse psychic apprehension in his victim.[22] Victims can also appeal to the tort of intentional infliction of emotional distress. According to Section 46 of the *Restatement of Torts,*

> Liability has been found only where the conduct has been so outrageous in character, and so extreme in degree, as to go beyond all

---

[10]*Black's Law Dictionary,* 6th Ed. (St. Paul, MN: West Publishing Co., 1990), p. 1248.

[11]Michael D. Vhay, "The Harms of Asking: Towards a Comprehensive Treatment of Sexual Harassment," *The University of Chicago Law Review,* Vol. 55 (Winter, 1988), p. 334.

   In the case of students, *quid pro quo* harassment can take the form of a professor threatening the student with a lower grade if she does not comply with his demands.

[12]Ellen Frankel Paul, "Sexual Harassment as Sex Discrimination: A Defective Paradigm," *Yale Law & Policy Review,* Vol. 8, No. 2 (1990), p. 341.

[13]EEOC *Guidelines, Op.cit.,* at Sec. 1604.11(a).

[14]*Black's Law Dictionary, Op.cit.,* p. 470. It cites *Rich v. Martin Marietta Corp.,* D.C.Colo., 467 F.Supp. 587, 608.

[15]*Topical Law Reports.* (New York: Commerce Clearing House, Inc., 1988). p. 3030.

[16]John C. Hughes and Larry May, "Sexual Harassment," *Social Theory and Practice,* Vol. 6, No. 3 (Fall, 1980), p. 260.

[17]Frankel Paul, *Op.cit.,* p. 337.

[18]See Frankel Paul, *Ibid.,* pp. 359–360, for a list of cases invoking torts along with Title VII claims.

[19]Rosemarie Tong, *Women, Sex, and the Law.* (Savage, MD: Rowman & Littlefield Publishers, Inc., 1984), p. 71.

[20]Frank J. Till, *Sexual Harassment: A Report on the Sexual Harassment of Students.* (Washington, D.C.: National Advisory Council on Women's Educational Programs, 1980), pt. II, p. 13.

[21]*Ibid.,* p. 14.

[22]Tong, *Women, Sex, and the Law, Op.cit.,* p. 73.

possible bounds of decency, and to be regarded as atrocious, and utterly intolerable in a civilized community. Generally, the case is one in which the recitation of the facts to an average member of the community would arouse his resentment against the actor, and lead him to exclaim, "Outrageous."[23]

"[M]ere insults, indignities, threats, annoyances, petty oppression, or other trivialities" will not result in tort action because a person must be "hardened to a certain amount of rough language."[24] The *Restatement of Torts* invokes the reasonable man standard, claiming that the emotional distress must be "so severe that no reasonable man could be expected to endure it."[25] Moreover, the conduct must be done intentionally or recklessly.

Despite major advances made in the last few decades in the law on SH, I believe the law is still inadequate. The main problem in my view is that the law, reflecting the view held by the general public, fails to see SH for what it is: an attack on the group of *all* women, not just the immediate victim. Because of this, there is a failure to recognize the group harm that all instances of SH, not just the more blatant ones, cause all women. As a result, the law construes SH as a subjective issue, that is, one that is determined by what the victim feels and (sometimes) what the perpetrator intends. As a result, the burden of proof is wrongly shifted to the victim and off of the perpetrator with the result that many victims are not legally protected.

For instance, victims filing complaints under Title VII (and presumably Title IX) are not protected unless they have a fairly serious case. They have to show under hostile environment harassment that the behavior unreasonably interfered with their work performance, and that there was a pattern of behavior on the defendant's behalf. Regarding the latter point, the EEOC *Guidelines* say that:

In determining whether alleged conduct constitutes sexual harassment, the Commission will look at the record as a whole and at the totality of the circumstances, such as the nature of the

sexual advances and the context in which the alleged incidents occurred.[26]

It seems unlikely that the victim of isolated incidents of SH could have her complaint taken seriously under this assessment. Under *quid pro quo* harassment, the victim must show she suffered a tangible economic detriment. Disparate treatment cases might be difficult to show because not *all* members of the victim's class (e.g., the group of all females) are likely to be harassed by the defendant. This makes it unlikely that the victim will be able to show she was harassed because of her sex, and not because of some personal feature she has that others lack. Victims who are harassed outside of the workplace and educational institutions have to rely on tort law to make their case, but under it, defendants have a way out by claiming innocence of intention. Under the tort of intentional infliction of emotional distress, victims must have an extreme case in order to get protection.

Victims not protected include the worker who is harassed by a number of different people, the worker who suffers harassment but in small doses, the person who is subjected to a slew of catcalls on her two mile walk to work, the female professor who is subjected to leering from one of her male students, and the woman who does not complain out of fear. The number of cases is huge, and many of them are quite common.

To protect all victims in all circumstances, the law ought to treat SH as it is beginning to treat racial discrimination. In her very interesting paper, Mari Matsuda has traced the history of the law regarding racist speech.[27] Article 4 of the International Convention on the Elimination of All Forms of Racial Discrimination which was unanimously adopted by the General Assembly December 21, 1965, prohibits not only acts of violence, but also the "mere dissemination of racist ideas, without requiring proof of incitement."[28] Apparently many states have signed and ratified the signing of the Convention, though the United States has not yet done so because of worries about freedom of speech protected by the First

[23]*Restatement (Second) of Torts* Sec. 46 (1965) comment a.
[24]Ibid.
[25]Ibid., comment j.
[26]EEOC *Guidelines,* 29 C.F.R., Sec. 1604.11(b) (1985).
[27]Mari J. Matsuda, "Public Response to Racist Speech: Considering the Victim's Story," *Michigan Law Review,* Vol. 87, No. 8 (August, 1989), pp. 2320–2381.
[28]Ibid., pp. 2345, 2344.

Amendment.[29] Aside from the Convention, the United Nations Charter, the Universal Declaration of Human Rights, the European Convention for the Protection of Human Rights and Fundamental Freedoms, the American Declaration of the Rights and Duties of Man, as well as the domestic law of several nations, have all recognized the right to equality and freedom from racism. In these and other codes, racist ideas are banned if they are discriminatory, related to violence, or express inferiority, hatred, or persecution.[30] On my view, some forms of SH are related to violence, and they *all* express inferiority whether or not they express hatred. At the root of the standard on racism that is gaining world-wide recognition is the view that racist speech "interferes with the rights of subordinated-group members to participate equally in society, maintaining their basic sense of security and worth as human beings."[31] Sexual harassment has the same effect, so it, too, should be prohibited. But I think SH can be afforded the best legal protection under antidiscrimination law instead of tort law, as this misses the social nature of SH. The world-wide standard against racist speech recognizes the group harm of racism by realizing that racist speech expresses inferiority; a similar standard against SH should be adopted.

III. *The Social Nature of Sexual Harassment*

Sexual harassment, a form of sexism, is about domination, in particular, the domination of the group of men over the group of women.[32] Domination involves control or power which can be seen in the economic, political, and social spheres of society. Sexual harassment is not simply an assertion of power, for power can be used in beneficial ways. The power men have over women has been wielded in ways that oppress women. The power expressed in SH is oppression, power used wrongly.

Sexual harassment is integrally related to sex roles. It reveals the belief that a person is to be rel-

egated to certain roles on the basis of her sex, including not only women's being sex objects, but also their being caretakers, motherers, nurturers, sympathizers, etc. In general, the sex roles women are relegated to are associated with the body (v. mind) and emotions (v. reason).

When A sexually harasses B, the comment or behavior is really directed at the group of all women, not just a particular woman, a point often missed by the courts. After all, many derogatory behaviors are issued at women the harasser does not even know (e.g., scanning a stranger's body). Even when the harasser knows his victim, the behavior is directed at the particular woman because she happens to be "available" at the time, though its message is for all women. For instance, a catcall says not (merely) that the perpetrator likes a woman's body but that he thinks women are at least primarily sex objects and he—because of the power he holds by being in the dominant group—gets to rate them according to how much pleasure they give him. The professor who refers to his female students as "chicks" makes a statement that women are intellectually inferior to men as they can be likened to non-rational animals, perhaps even soft, cuddly ones that are to serve as the objects of (men's) pleasure. Physicians' using Playboy centerfolds in medical schools to "spice up their lectures" sends the message that women lack the competence to make it in a "man's world" and should perform the "softer tasks" associated with bearing and raising children.[33]

These and other examples make it clear that SH is not about dislike for a certain person; instead, it expresses a person's beliefs about women as a group on the basis of their sex, namely, that they are primarily emotional and bodily beings. Some theorists—Catharine MacKinnon, John Hughes and Larry May—have recognized the social nature of SH. Hughes and May claim that women are a disadvantaged group because

---

[29]Ibid., p. 2345.
[30]Ibid., p. 2346.
[31]Ibid., p. 2348.
[32]This suggests that only men can sexually harass women. I will defend this view later in the paper.

[33]Frances Conley, a 50-year-old distinguished neurophysician at Stanford University, recently came forward with this story. Conley resigned after years of putting up with sexual harassment from her colleagues. Not only did they use Playboy spreads during their lectures, but they routinely called her "hon," invited her to bed, and fondled her legs under the operating table. *Chicago Tribune*, Sunday, June 9, 1991. Section 1, p. 22.

1. they are a social group having a distinct identity and existence apart from their individual identities,
2. they occupy a subordinate position in American society, and
3. their political power is severely circumscribed.[34]

They continue:

> Once it is established that women qualify for special disadvantaged group status, all practices tending to stigmatize women as a group, or which contribute to the maintenance of their subordinate social status, would become legally suspect.[35]

This last point, I believe, should be central to the definition of SH.

Because SH has as its target the group of all women, this *group* suffers harm as a result of the behavior. Indeed, when any one woman is in any way sexually harassed, all women are harmed. The group harm SH causes is different from the harm suffered by particular women as individuals: it is often more vague in nature as it is not easily causally tied to any particular incident of harassment. The group harm has to do primarily with the fact that the behavior reflects and reinforces sexist attitudes that women are inferior to men and that they do and ought to occupy certain sex roles. For example, comments and behavior that relegate women to the role of sex objects reinforce the belief that women *are* sex objects and that they *ought to* occupy this sex role. Similarly, when a female professor's cogent comments at department colloquia are met with frowns and rolled eyes from her colleagues, this behavior reflects and reinforces the view that women are not fit to occupy positions men arrogate to themselves.

The harm women suffer as a group from any single instance of SH is significant. It takes many forms. A Kantian analysis would show what is wrong with being solely a sex object. Though there is nothing wrong with being a caretaker or nurturer, etc., *per se,* it is sexist—and so wrong—to assign such roles to women. In addition, it is wrong to assign a person to a role she may not want to occupy. Basically women are not allowed to decide

for themselves which roles they are to occupy, but this gets decided for them, no matter what they do. Even if some women occupy important positions in society that men traditionally occupy, they are still viewed as being sex objects, caretakers, etc., since all women are thought to be more "bodily" and emotional than men. This is a denial of women's autonomy, and degrading to them. It also contributes to women's oppression. The belief that women must occupy certain sex roles is both a cause and an effect of their oppression. It is a cause because women are believed to be more suited for certain roles given their association with body and emotions. It is an effect because once they occupy these roles and are victims of oppression, the belief that they *must* occupy these sex roles is reinforced.

Women are harmed by SH in yet another way. The belief that they are sex objects, caretakers, etc., gets reflected in social and political practices in ways that are unfair to women. It has undoubtedly meant many lost opportunities that are readily available to men. Women are not likely to be hired for jobs that require them to act in ways other than the ways the sex roles dictate, and if they are, what is expected of them is different from what is expected of men. Mothers are not paid for their work, and caretakers are not paid well in comparison to jobs traditionally held by men. Lack of economic reward is paralleled by lack of respect and appreciation for those occupying such roles. Certain rights granted men are likely not to be granted women (e.g., the right to bodily self-determination, and marriage rights).

Another harm SH causes all women is that the particular form sex stereotyping takes promotes two myths: (1) that male behavior is normally and naturally predatory, and (2) that females naturally (because they are taken to be primarily bodily and emotional) and even willingly acquiesce despite the appearance of protest.[36] Because the behavior perpetuated by these myths is taken to be normal, it is not seen as sexist, and in turn is not counted as SH.

The first myth is that men have stronger sexual desires than women, and harassment is just a natural venting of these desires which men are unable to control. The truth is, first, that women are

[34]Hughes and May, *Op.cit.,* pp. 264–265.
[35]Ibid., p. 265.

[36]These same myths surround the issue of rape. This is discussed fruitfully by Lois Pineau in "Date Rape: A Feminist Analysis," *Law and Philosophy*, Vol. 8 (1989), pp. 217–243.

socialized *not* to vent their sexual desires in the way men do, but this does not mean these desires are weaker or less prevalent. Masters and Johnson have "decisively established that women's sexual requirements are no less potent or urgent than those of men."[37] But second, SH has nothing to do with men's sexual desires, nor is it about seduction; instead, it is about oppression of women. Indeed, harassment generally does not lead to sexual satisfaction, but it often gives the harasser a sense of power.

The second myth is that women either welcome, ask for, or deserve the harassing treatment. Case law reveals this mistaken belief. In *Lipsett v. Rive-Mora*[38] (1987), the plaintiff was discharged from a medical residency program because she "did not react favorably to her professor's requests to go out for drinks, his compliments about her hair and legs, or to questions about her personal and romantic life"[39] The court exonerated the defendant because the plaintiff initially reacted favorably by smiling when shown lewd drawings of herself and when called sexual nicknames as she thought she had to appease the physician. The court said that "given the plaintiff's admittedly favorable responses to these flattering comments, there was no way anyone could consider them as 'unwelcome.'"[40] The court in *Swentek v. US Air*[41] (1987) reacted similarly when a flight attendant who was harassed with obscene remarks and gestures was denied legal recourse because previously she used vulgar language and openly discussed her sexual encounters. The court concluded that "she was the kind of person who could not be offended by such comments and therefore welcomed them generally."[42]

The idea that women welcome "advances" from men is seen in men's view of the way women dress. If a woman dresses "provocatively" by men's standards, she is said to welcome or even deserve the treatment she gets. One explanation harassing professors give for their behavior is that they are bombarded daily with the temptation of physically desirable young women who dress in what they take to be revealing ways.[43] When the case becomes public, numerous questions arise about the attractiveness of the victim, as if she were to blame for being attractive and the consequences thereof. Catcallers often try to justify their behavior by claiming that the victim should expect such behavior, given her tight-fitting dress or shorts, low-cut top, high heels, etc. This way of thinking infests discussions of rape in attempts to establish that women want to be raped, and it is mistaken in that context, too. The myth that women welcome or encourage harassment is designed "to keep women in their place" as men see it. The truth of the matter is that the perpetrator alone is at fault.

Both myths harm all women as they sanction SH by shifting the burden on the victim and all members of her sex: women must either go out of their way to avoid "natural" male behavior, or establish conclusively that they did not in any way want the behavior. Instead of the behavior being seen as sexist, it is seen as women's problem to rectify.

Last, but certainly not least, women suffer group harm from SH because they come to be stereotyped as victims.[44] Many men see SH as something they can do to women, and in many cases, get away with. Women come to see themselves as victims, and come to believe that the roles they *can* occupy are only the sex roles men have designated for them. Obviously these harms are quite serious for women, so the elimination of all forms of SH is warranted.

I have spoken so far as if it is only men who can sexually harass women, and I am now in a position to defend this controversial view. When a woman engages in the very same behavior harassing men engage in, the underlying message implicit in male-to-female harassment is missing. For example,

---

[37]MacKinnon, *Op.cit.*, p. 152, is where she cites the study.

[38]*Lipsett v. Rive-Mora*, 669 F.Supp. 1188 (D. Puerto Rico 1987).

[39]Dawn D. Bennett-Alexander, "Hostile Environment Sexual Harassment: A Clearer View," *Labor Law Journal,* Vol. 42, No. 3 (March, 1991), p. 135.

[40]Lipsett, Ibid., Sec. 15.

[41]*Swentek v. US Air,* 830 F.2d 552 (4th Cir. 1987).

[42]*Swentek v. US Air,* Ibid., 44 EPd at 552.

[43]Billie Wright Dziech and Linda Weiner, *The Lecherous Professor: Sexual Harassment on Campus.* (Boston: Beacon Press, 1984), p. 63.

[44]This harm is similar to the harm Ann Cudd finds with rape. Since women are the victims of rape, "they come to be seen as in need of protection, as weak and passive, and available to all men." See Ann E. Cudd, "Enforced Pregnancy, Rape, and the Image of Woman," *Philosophical Studies,* Vol. 60 (1990), pp. 47–59.

when a woman scans a man's body, she might be considering him to be a sex object, but all the views about domination and being relegated to certain sex roles are absent. She cannot remind the man that he is inferior because of his sex, since given the way things are in society, he is not. In general, women cannot harm or degrade or dominate men *as a group,* for it is impossible to send the message that one dominates (and so cause group harm) if one does not dominate. Of course, if the sexist roles predominant in our society were reversed, women *could* sexually harass men. The way things are, any bothersome behavior a woman engages in, even though it may be of a sexual nature, does not constitute SH because it lacks the social impact present in male-to-female harassment. Tort law would be sufficient to protect against this behavior, since it is unproblematic in these cases that tort law fails to recognize group harm.

IV. Subjective v. Objective Definitions of Sexual Harassment

Most definitions of "sexual harassment" make reference to the behavior's being "unwelcome" or "annoying" to the victim. *Black's Law Dictionary* defines "harassment" as a term used "to describe words, gestures and actions which tend to annoy, alarm and abuse (verbally) another person."[45] The *American Heritage Dictionary* defines "harass" as "to disturb or irritate persistently," and states further that "[h]arass implies systematic persecution by besetting with annoyances, threats, or demands."[46] The EEOC *Guidelines* state that behavior constituting SH is identified as "unwelcome sexual advances, requests for sexual favors, and other verbal or physical conduct of a sexual nature."[47] In their philosophical account of SH, Hughes and May define "harassment" as "a class of annoying or unwelcome acts undertaken by one person (or group of persons) against another person (or group of persons)."[48] And Rosemarie

Tong takes the feminists' definition of noncoercive SH to be that which "denotes sexual misconduct that merely annoys or offends the person to whom it is directed."[49]

The criterion of "unwelcomeness" or "annoyance" is reflected in the way the courts have handled cases of SH, as in *Lipsett, Swentek,* and *Meritor,* though in the latter case the court said that the voluntariness of the victim's submission to the defendant's sexual conduct did not mean that she welcomed the conduct.[50] The criterion of unwelcomeness or annoyance present in these subjective accounts of harassment puts the burden on the victim to establish that she was sexually harassed. There is no doubt that many women *are* bothered by this behavior, often with serious side-effects including anything from anger, fear, and guilt,[51] to lowered self-esteem and decreased feelings of competence and confidence,[52] to anxiety disorders, alcohol and drug abuse, coronary disturbances, and gastro-intestinal disorders.[53]

Though it is true that many women are bothered by the behavior at issue, I think it is seriously mistaken to say that whether the victim is bothered determines whether the behavior constitutes SH. This is so for several reasons.

First, we would have to establish that the victim was bothered by it, either by the victim's complaints, or by examining the victim's response to the behavior. The fact of the matter is that many women are quite hesitant to report being harassed, for a number of reasons. Primary among them is that they fear negative consequences from reporting the conduct. As is often the case, harassment comes from a person in a position of institutional power, whether he be a supervisor, a company-president, a member of a dissertation committee, the chair of the department, and so on.

[45] *Black's Law Dictionary, Op.cit.,* p. 717.
[46] *American Heritage Dictionary of the English Language.* (New York: American Heritage Publishing Co., Inc., 1973), p. 600.
[47] EEOC *Guidelines, Op.cit.,* Sec. 1604.11(a).
[48] Hughes and May, *Op.cit.,* p. 250.

[49] Tong, *Women, Sex, and the Law, Op.cit.,* p. 67.
[50] *Meritor, Op.cit.,* at 1113–16.
[51] MacKinnon, *Op.cit.,* p. 83.
[52] Stephanie Riger, "Gender Dilemmas in Sexual Harassment Policies and Procedures," *American Psychologist,* Vol. 46 (1991), pp. 497–505.
[53] Martha Sperry, "Hostile Environment Sexual Harassment and the Imposition of Liability Without Notice: A Progressive Approach to Traditional Gender Roles and Power Based Relationships," *New England Law Review,* Vol. 24 (1980), p. 942, fns. 174 & 175.

Unfortunately for many women, as a review of the case law reveals, their fears are warranted.[54] Women have been fired, their jobs have been made miserable forcing them to quit, professors have handed out unfair low grades, and so on. Worries about such consequences means that complaints are not filed, or are filed years after the incident, as in the Anita Hill v. Thomas Clarence case. But this should not be taken to imply that the victim was not harassed.

Moreover, women are hesitant to report harassment because they do not want anything to happen to the perpetrator, but just want the behavior to stop.[55] Women do not complain because they do not want to deal with the perpetrator's reaction when faced with the charge. He might claim that he was "only trying to be friendly" Women are fully aware that perpetrators can often clear themselves quite easily, especially in tort law cases where the perpetrator's intentions are directly relevant to whether he is guilty. And most incidents of SH occur without any witnesses—many perpetrators plan it this way. It then becomes the harasser's word against the victim's. To complicate matters, many women are insecure and doubt themselves. Women's insecurity is capitalized upon by harassers whose behavior is in the least bit ambiguous. Clever harassers who fear they might get caught or be reported often attempt to get on the good side of their victim in order to confuse her about the behavior, as well as to have a defense ready in case a charge is made. Harassers might offer special teaching assignments to their graduate students, special help with exams and publications, promotions, generous raises, and the like. Of course, this is all irrelevant to whether he harasses, but the point is that it makes the victim less likely to complain. On top of all this, women's credibility is very often questioned (unfairly) when they bring forth a charge. They are taken to be "hypersensitive." There is an atti-

tude among judges and others that women must "develop a thick skin."[56] Thus, the blame is shifted off the perpetrator and onto the victim. Given this, if a woman thinks she will get no positive response—or, indeed, will get a negative one—from complaining, she is unlikely to do so.

Further, some women do not recognize harassment for what it is, and so will not complain. Sometimes this is because they are not aware of their own oppression, or actually seem to endorse sexist stereotypes. I recall a young woman who received many catcalls on the streets of Daytona Beach, Florida during spring break, and who was quite proud that her body could draw such attention. Given that women are socialized into believing their bodies are the most important feature of themselves, it is no surprise that a fair number of them are complacent about harassing behavior directed at them. Sandra Bartky provides an interesting analysis of why every woman is not a feminist, and I think it holds even for women who understand the issue.[57] Since for many women having a body felt to be "feminine" is crucial to their identity and to their sense of self "as a sexually desiring and desirable subject," feminism "may well be apprehended by a woman as something that threatens her with desexualization, if not outright annihilation."[58] The many women who resist becoming feminists are not likely to perceive harassing behavior as bothersome. It would be incorrect to conclude that the behavior is not harassment on the grounds that such victims are not bothered. What we have is a no-win situation for victims: if the behavior bothers a woman she often has good reason not to com-

---

[54]See Catharine MacKinnon, *Feminism Unmodified: Discourses on Life and Law.* (Cambridge: Harvard University Press, 1987), Chapter Nine, for a nice discussion of the challenges women face in deciding whether to report harassment. See also Ellen Frankel Paul, *Op.cit.,* for an excellent summary of the case law on sexual harassment.

[55]MacKinnon, *Sexual Harassment of Working Women, Op.cit.,* p. 83.

[56]See Frankel Paul, *Op.cit.,* pp. 333–365. Frankel Paul wants to get away from the "helpless victim syndrome," making women responsible for reporting harassment, and placing the burden on them to develop a tough skin so as to avoid being seen as helpless victims (pp. 362–363). On the contrary, what Frankel Paul fails to understand is that placing these additional burdens on women *detracts* from the truth that they *are* victims, and implies that they deserve the treatment if they do not develop a "tough attitude."

[57]Sandra Bartky, "Foucault, Femininity and the Modernization of Patriarchal Power," in Sandra Bartky, *Femininity and Domination: Studies in the Phenomenology of Oppression.* (New York: Routledge, Chapman, and Hall, Inc., 1990), pp. 63–82. See especially pp. 77–78.

[58]Ibid., p. 77.

plain; and if it does not bother her, she will not complain. Either way, the perpetrator wins. So we cannot judge whether women are bothered by the behavior on the basis of whether they *say* they are bothered.

Moreover, women's *behavior* is not an accurate indicator of whether they are bothered. More often than not, women try to ignore the perpetrator's behavior in an attempt not to give the impression they are encouraging it. They often cover up their true feelings so that the perpetrator does not have the satisfaction that his harassing worked. Since women are taught to smile and put up with this behavior, they might actually appear to enjoy it to some extent. Often they have no choice but to continue interacting with the perpetrator, making it very difficult to assert themselves. Women often make up excuses for not "giving in" instead of telling the perpetrator to stop. The fact that their behavior does not indicate they are bothered should not be used to show they were not bothered. In reality, women are fearful of defending themselves in the face of men's power and physical strength. Given the fact that the courts have decided that a lot of this behavior should just be tolerated, it is no wonder that women try to make the best of their situation.

It would be wrong to take a woman's behavior to be a sign that she is bothered also because doing so implies the behavior is permissible if she does not seem to care. This allows the *perpetrator* to be the judge of whether a woman is harassed, which is unjustifiable given the confusion among men about whether their behavior is bothersome or flattering. Sexual harassment should be treated no differently than crimes where harm to the victim is assessed in some objective way, independent of the perpetrators beliefs. To give men this power in the case of harassment is to perpetuate sexism from all angles.

An *objective* view of SH avoids the problems inherent in a subjective view. According to the objective view defended here, what is decisive in determining whether behavior constitutes SH is not whether the victim is bothered, but whether the behavior is an instance of a practice that expresses and perpetuates the attitude that the victim and members of her sex are inferior because of their sex. Thus the Daytona Beach case counts as a case of SH because the behavior is an instance of a practice that reflects men's domination of women in that it relegates women to the role of sex objects.[59]

The courts have to some extent tried to incorporate an objective notion of SH by invoking the "reasonable person" standard. The EEOC *Guidelines,* as shown earlier, define SH partly as behavior that "has the purpose or effect of *unreasonably* interfering with an individual's work performance. . . ."[60] The *Restatement of Torts,* referring to the tort of intentional infliction of emotional distress, states that the emotional distress must be "so severe that no *reasonable* man could be expected to endure it."[61]

In various cases the courts have invoked a reasonable man (or person) standard, but *not* to show that women who are not bothered still suffer harassment. Instead, they used the standard to show that even though a particular woman *was* bothered, she would have to tolerate such behavior because it was behavior a reasonable person would not have been affected by. In *Rabidue v. Osceola Refining Co.*[62] (1986), a woman complained that a coworker made obscene comments about women in general and her in particular. The court ruled that "a reasonable person would not have been significantly affected by the same or similar circumstances,"[63] and that "women must expect a certain amount of demeaning conduct in certain work environments."[64]

But the reasonable man standard will not work, since men and women perceive situations involving SH quite differently. The reasonable person standard fares no better as it becomes the reasonable man standard when it is applied by male judges seeing things through male eyes. Studies have shown that sexual overtures that men find flattering are found by women to be insulting. And even

---

[59]This case exemplifies my point that the behavior need not be persistent in order to constitute harassment, despite the view of many courts. One catcall, for example, will constitute SH if catcalling is shown to be a practice reflecting domination.

[60]EEOC *Guidelines, Op.cit.,* Sec. 1604.11(a), my emphasis.

[61]*Restatement (Second) of Torts,* Sec. 146, (1965), comment j, my emphasis.

[62]*Rabidue v. Osceola Refining Co.,* 805 F2d (1986), Sixth Circuit Court.

[63]Ibid., at 622.

[64]Ibid., at 620–622.

when men recognize behavior as harassment, they think women will be flattered by it.[65] The differences in perception only strengthen my point about the group harm that SH causes all women: unlike women, men can take sexual overtures directed at them to be complimentary because the overtures do not signify the stereotyping that underlies SH of women. A reasonable man standard would not succeed as a basis upon which to determine SH, as its objectivity is outweighed by the disparity found in the way the sexes assess what is "reasonable."

Related to this last topic is the issue of the harasser's intentions. In subjective definitions this is the counterpart to the victim's being bothered. Tort law makes reference to the injuror's intentions: in battery tort, the harasser's intent to contact, in assault tort, the harasser's intent to arouse psychic apprehension in the victim, and in the tort of intentional emotional distress, the harasser's intent or recklessness, must be established in order for the victim to win her case.

But like the victim's feelings, the harasser's intentions are irrelevant to whether his behavior is harassment. As I just pointed out, many men do not take their behavior to be bothersome, and sometimes even mistakenly believe that women enjoy crude compliments about their bodies, ogling, pinching, etc. From perusing cases brought before the courts, I have come to believe that many men have psychological feelings of power over women, feelings of being in control of their world, and the like, when they harass. These feelings might be subconscious, but this should not be admitted as a defense of the harasser. Also, as I have said, many men believe women encourage SH either by their dress or language, or simply by the fact that they tolerate the abuse without protest (usually out of fear of repercussion). In light of these facts, it would be wrongheaded to allow the harasser's intentions to count in assessing harassment, though they might become relevant in determining punishment. I am arguing for an objective definition of SH: it is the attitudes embedded and reflected *in the practice*

the behavior is an instance of, not the attitudes or intentions *of the perpetrator,* that makes the behavior SH.

Yet the idea that the behavior must be directed at a certain person in order for it to count as harassment, seems to suggest that intentions *do* count in assessing harassment. This feature is evident both in my definition, as well as in that found in *Black's Law Dictionary,* which takes harassment to be conduct directed against a specific person causing substantial emotional distress. If conduct is directed at a particular individual, it seems that the person expressing himself must be intentionally singling out that individual, wanting to cause her harm.

I think this is mistaken. Since the harasser can subconsciously enjoy the feeling of power harassing gives him, or might even consider his behavior to be flattering, his behavior can be directed at a specific person (or group of persons) without implying any ill intention on his part. By "directed at a particular individual," I mean that the behavior is in some way observed by a particular person (or persons). This includes, for example, sexist comments a student hears her professor say, pornographic pictures a worker sees, etc. I interpret it loosely enough to include a person's overhearing sexist comments even though the speaker has no idea the person is within earshot (sometimes referred to as "nondirected behavior"). But I interpret it to exclude the bare knowledge that sexist behavior is going on (e.g., female employees knowing that there are pornographic pictures hidden in their boss's office). If it did not exclude such behavior it would have to include knowledge of *any* sexist behavior, even if no person who can be harmed by it ever observes it (e.g., pornographic magazines strewn on a desert island). Though such behavior is sexist, it fails to constitute SH.

V. *Implications of the Objective Definition*

One implication of my objective definition is that it reflects the correct way power comes into play in SH. Traditionally, SH has been taken to exist only between persons of unequal power, usually in the workplace or an educational institution. It is believed that SH in universities occurs only when

---

[65]Stephanie Riger, "Gender Dilemmas in Sexual Harassment Policies and Procedures," *American Psychologist,* Vol. 46. No. 5 (May 1991), p. 499 is where she cites the relevant studies.

a professor harasses a student, but not *vice versa*. It is said that students can cause "sexual hassle," because they cannot "destroy [the professor's] self-esteem or endanger his intellectual self-confidence," and professors "seldom suffer the complex psychological effects of sexual harassment victims."[66] MacKinnon, in her earlier book, defines SH as "the unwanted imposition of sexual requirements in the context of a relationship of unequal power. "[67]

Though it is true that a lot of harassment occurs between unequals, it is false that harassment occurs *only* between unequals: equals and subordinates can harass. Indeed, power is irrelevant to tort law, and the courts now recognize harassment among coworkers under Title VII.

The one sense in which it is true that the harasser must have power over his victim is that men have power—social, political, and economic—over women as a group. This cannot be understood by singling out individual men and showing that they have power over women or any particular woman for that matter. It is power that all men have, in virtue of being men. Defining SH in the objective way I do allows us to see that *this* is the sense in which power exists in SH in *all* of its forms. The benefit of not restricting SH to cases of unequal institutional power is that *all* victims are afforded protection.

A second implication of my definition is that it gives the courts a way of distinguishing SH from sexual attraction. It can be difficult to make this distinction, since "traditional courtship activities" are often quite sexist and frequently involve behavior that is harassment. The key is to examine the practice the behavior is an instance of. If the behavior reflects the attitude that the victim is inferior because of her sex, then it is SH. Sexual harassment is not about a man's attempting to date a woman who is not interested, as the courts have tended to believe; it is about domination, which might be reflected, of course, in the way a man goes about trying to get a date. My definition allows us to separate cases of SH from genuine sexual attraction by forcing the courts to focus on the social nature of SH.

Moreover, defining SH in the objective way I do shifts the burden and the blame off the victim. On the subjective view, the burden is on the victim to prove that she is bothered significantly enough to win a tort case, or under Title VII, to show that the behavior unreasonably interfered with her work. In tort law, where the perpetrator's intentions are allowed to figure in, the blame could easily shift to the victim by showing that she in some way welcomed or even encouraged the behavior thereby relinquishing the perpetrator from responsibility. By focusing on the practice the behavior is an instance of, my definition has nothing to do with proving that the victim responds a certain way to the behavior, nor does it in any way blame the victim for the behavior.

Finally, defining SH in a subjective way means that the victim herself must come forward and complain, as it is her response that must be assessed. But given that most judges, law enforcement officers, and even superiors are men, it is difficult for women to do so. They are embarrassed, afraid to confront someone of the same sex as the harasser who is likely not to see the problem. They do not feel their voices will be heard. Working with my definition will I hope assuage this. Recognizing SH as a group harm will allow women to come to each other's aid as co-complainers, thereby alleviating the problem of reticence. Even if the person the behavior is directed at does not feel bothered, other women can complain, as they suffer the group harm associated with SH.

VI. *Conclusion*

The definition of SH I have defended in this paper has as its main benefit that it acknowledges the group harm SH causes all women, thereby getting to the heart of what is wrong with SH. By doing so, it protects all victims in all cases from even the most subtle kinds of SH, since all cases of SH have in common group harm.

[66]Wright Dziech and Weiner, *Op.cit.,* p. 24.
[67]MacKinnon, *Sexual Harassment of Working Women, Op.cit.,* p. 1. It is actually not clear that MacKinnon endorses this definition throughout this book, as what she says seems to suggest that harassment can occur at least between equals. In her most recent book, she recognizes that harassment "also happens among coworkers, from third parties, even by subordinates in the workplace, men who are women's hierarchical inferiors or peers." Catharine A. McKinnon, *Feminism Unmodified: Discourses on Life and Law.* (Cambridge: Harvard University Press, 1987), p. 107.

Of course, as with any definition, problems exist. Though space does not allow that I deal with them, a few are worth mentioning. One is that many behaviors will count as SH, leading perhaps to an unmanageable number of claims. Another is that it will still be a matter of interpretation whether a given behavior meets the criteria for SH. Perhaps the most crucial objection is that since so many kinds of behavior count as SH, the right to free speech will be curtailed in unacceptable ways.[68]

I believe there are at least partial solutions to these problems. My proposal is only programmatic, and a thorough defense of it would include working through these and other problems. Such a defense will have to wait.

---

[68]For an excellent analysis on sexist speech and the limits of free speech as guaranteed by the Constitution, see Marcy Strauss, "Sexist Speech in the Workplace," *Harvard Civil Rights and Civil Liberties Law Review,* Vol. 25 (1990), pp. 1–51. She cites the relevant case law concerning sexist speech that is not protected by First Amendment rights. She defends the view that the Constitution can prohibit speech demanding or requesting sexual relationships, sexually explicit speech directed at the woman, and degrading speech directed at the woman, but not sexually explicit or degrading speech that the woman employee knows exists in the workplace, even though it is not directed at her. (p. 43) She employs an interesting and useful distinction between speech that discriminates, and speech that merely advocates discrimination, recognizing that the state has an interest in regulating the former, given the harm it can cause.

Sexual Harassment and the Rights of the Accused

STEPHEN GRIFFITH

MUCH OF AMERICA sat transfixed before their television sets during the Supreme Court confirmation hearings for Judge Clarence Thomas while Anita Hill accused him of sexual harassment. The main topic of debate for most people following the hearings was whether it was Anita Hill or Clarence Thomas that was telling the truth, since their testimony was directly contradictory and there was essentially no independent evidence on either side. From a philosophical point of view, however, the most important issue illustrated by this whole affair concerns the nature of sexual harassment in itself. What is sexual harassment anyway, and why is it wrong, if it is? Even if Clarence Thomas did everything Anita Hill says he did, was his behavior seriously immoral, so much so as to justify denying him a seat on the Supreme Court? Opinions on this subject seem to range from saying that behavior of the sort alleged is the moral equivalent of rape to saying that it is simply a bit rude and inappropriate in the context within which it supposedly occurred. More recently, the President of the United States himself has been accused of sexual harassment. Although many people have reacted differently to this case than to that involving Justice Thomas, the wide variety of reactions to both of these cases and the vehemence of many of those reactions suggest that there is considerable confusion concerning the broad issue of sexual harassment which a careful philosophical analysis might help to alleviate.

Sexual misconduct of various sorts has become an increasingly serious problem in our society and must be dealt with both carefully and effectively whenever and wherever it occurs. All too frequently, individuals are sexually abused or assaulted by spouses, lovers, or total strangers, coerced into unwanted sexual activity by superiors, or subjected to unwanted sexual attention or embarrassment.[1] In response to these problems, a just society must have just and effective legislation;

---

[1]Although it seems obvious that the vast majority of victims of these offenses are women, the moral dimensions of the problem are gender-neutral and will be treated as such wherever possible in this paper.

From Public Affairs Quarterly *13(1), 1999. Reprinted with permission.*

public and private institutions and corporations must have effective and fair policies and procedures; both this legislation and these policies and procedures must be consistent with the basic principles of justice, morality and fairness. The case for developing and implementing such legislation and policies has been made often and well, much progress along these lines has been made, and much more still needs to be done. Unfortunately, however, as is often the case in situations involving deeply felt causes, the understandable zeal for dealing with these problems has produced definitions of sexual harassment and attendant legislation and policies which contain the potential for serious abuse of human rights, especially the rights of the accused, and judging from various reports appearing in the media, the implementation of such policies and procedures has actually resulted in such abuse in some cases, especially in the groves of academe. The problem has been well expressed by a character in *Disclosure*, Michael Crichton's novel about sexual harassment:

> the problem is that there's that third category, somewhere in the middle, between the two extremes," Fernandez said. "Where the behavior is gray. It's not clear who did what to whom. That's the largest category of complaints we see. So far, society's tended to focus on the problems of the victim, not the problems of the accused. But the accused has problems, too. A harassment claim is a weapon, Bob, and there are no good defenses against it. Anybody can use the weapon—and lots of people have.[2]

With regard to the problems of the accused, Maatman says the following:

> Many times the accused harasser must prove a negative: that harassment never took place. Putting aside legal liability, the mere charge of unwelcome sexual conduct itself can oftentimes destroy a career or stamp the accused as being of suspect morals and deficient judgment. Not surprisingly, sexual harassment complaints have the potential for malicious use,

whereby an employee falsely asserts the charge as a weapon of retaliation, extortion, or to prevent or insulate a critical review of their own job performance.[3]

Although abuses of this sort may happen and continue to happen in only a small percentage of cases, the fact that any one instance of such abuse can deprive an innocent person of a livelihood, a career, or a good name suggests that we should be mindful of such possible abuses and take steps to minimize this possibility. My purpose in this paper is to suggest the adoption of a more precise definition of sexual harassment than those usually given and to illustrate how some of the abuses which are possible in the implementation of typical existing policies and procedures might thereby be avoided without significantly weakening the legitimate protections afforded by such policies.

The definition of sexual harassment given by the Equal Employment Opportunity Commission illustrates many of the problems referred to above. According to the EEOC,

> Unwelcome sexual advances, requests for sexual favors, and other verbal or physical conduct of a sexual nature constitute sexual harassment when
>
> (1) submission to such conduct is made either explicitly or implicitly a term or condition of an individual's employment;
>
> (2) submission to, or rejection of, such conduct by an individual is used as the basis for employment decisions affecting such individual; or
>
> (3) such conduct has the purpose or effect of substantially interfering with an individual's work performance or creating an intimidating, hostile, or offensive working environment.[4]

The forms of conduct referred to in (1) and (2) fall under the rubric of what will be referred to in this paper as sexual coercion, a serious sexual offense which must be dealt with firmly and effectively whenever and wherever it occurs. Clause (3), on the other hand, taken at face value, could in prin-

---

[2]Michael Crichton, *Disclosure* (Knopf, 1994), p. 397. For a realistic fictional account of the abuse of sexual harassment policies in academe, see *Oleanna*, a play by David Mamet (New York: Pantheon, 1992).

[3]Gerald R. Maatman, Jr., "Primer on the Law of Sexual Harassment," *Federation of Insurance & Corporate Counsel Quarterly* 42, no. 3 (1992): 320.

[4]Michele A. Paludi and Richard B. Barickman, *Academic and Workplace Sexual Harassment: A Resource Manual* (Albany: SUNY Press, 1991), p. 3.

ciple be interpreted so as to apply to a wide variety of behaviors, some of which might not even be offensive to most normal people. This definition thus illustrates a regrettable tendency on the part of those most concerned with the issue of "sexual harassment" to define it much too broadly, so that all sorts of behavior, ranging from such serious sexual misconduct as rape to such relatively inconsequential behavior as the use of "inappropriate innuendo," are placed on a continuum and regarded as different forms of sexual harassment.[5] Thus, for example, gender harassment, seductive behavior, sexual bribery, sexual coercion, and sexual assault are all regarded by some writers as forms of sexual harassment.[6] Defining sexual harassment this broadly not only confuses the issue, but also has the unfortunate consequence that persons who have been accused of relatively minor offenses, often involving behavior which is not even morally blameworthy, are painted with the same accusatory brush as those accused of relatively serious crimes.[7] This has the doubly unfortunate effect of not only making relatively trivial offenses seem more serious than they are but also of trivializing more serious offenses.

There are several other problems with the EEOC definition of sexual harassment. In the first place, the crucial term "sexual" is left undefined, which leaves the entire scope of this definition unacceptably vague, as does the use of the term "substantially" in clause (3). In addition, its use of such subjective terms as "intimidating," "hostile," and "offensive" allows the accuser to define the offense, and the use of the expression "or effect" encourages us to ignore the intentions of the

accused. Neither of these tendencies seems consistent with sound jurisprudence.

All of the above-mentioned defects in the EEOC definition of sexual harassment can be (and to a certain extent have been) substantially mitigated in courts of law. Some of the vagueness has been removed by precedent, and much potential abuse of the EEOC guidelines has doubtless been avoided by fair and experienced judges, impartial juries, rules of evidence, and all the other protections afforded the accused in our legal system. Unfortunately, however, the EEOC definition has also been used as a guideline for many corporate and institutional policies which are implemented in the absence of any of these protections, and it is here that most abuses have occurred.

I. *Narrowing the Scope*

The use which the term "sexual harassment" has come to have in both legal contexts and in scholarly work on this topic has probably become too entrenched to permit any hope that a narrower meaning can be given to the term at this time, but we can at least hope to distinguish more clearly among the wide variety of behaviors which are currently listed together under this heading. In particular, we can distinguish between those forms of behavior which ought reasonably to have been regarded as sexual harassment *per se* and other forms of sexual misconduct which have inappropriately come to be regarded as such.

A. DISCRIMINATION BASED ON GENDER

As a first step, we can distinguish sexual misconduct in general from those offenses which involve unjustifiable discrimination on the basis of gender. Although most discrimination based on gender cannot be justified and should be eliminated whenever and wherever possible, a person's gender and sexual orientation must obviously play a differentiating role in that person's social interaction with other persons. Even if we find it prudent or necessary to limit the types of interaction which are permitted or encouraged in academic or workplace settings, it is not reasonable to stigmatize someone by accusing that person of sexual harassment simply in virtue of the fact that that person treats men and

[5]Cf. F. M. Christensen, "'Sexual Harassment' Must Be Eliminated," *Public Affairs Quarterly* 8, no. 1 (1994).
[6]Cf., e.g., Fitzgerald et al., *Journal of Vocational Behavior* 32, pp. 152–175.
[7]Behavior which is not morally blameworthy may sometimes be justifiably prohibited and thus regarded as an "offense" in appropriate institutional or corporate settings. In particular, it may be prohibited when it seriously detracts from institutional or corporate goals and when this prohibition is not itself a violation of the rights of those engaging in the behavior in question. The point here is thus not that only morally blameworthy behavior may be prohibited, but rather that those who engage in behavior which is not morally blameworthy, even when it is contrary to some morally justifiable policy, ought to be treated differently than those whose behavior is clearly and seriously immoral or illegal.

women differently in some respects in situations where this could reasonably be expected. Chivalry, for example, may be dead, and it is certainly "sexist," but its vestigial remnants are not offensive to reasonable people and can hardly be regarded as immoral.

What is more important, however, is that even unjustifiable discrimination on the basis of gender should not be regarded as an instance of "sexual" misconduct. It is simply an accident of the English language that the word "sex" and its cognates can refer either to sexual activity or to gender. It is perniciously discriminatory, for example, to prohibit women from pursuing certain careers on morally irrelevant grounds, but a person who does this is not thereby guilty of immoral sexual activity, and might in fact lead a morally exemplary life in that respect, despite having "sexist" views. It could be argued, of course, that there are in many cases important sociological and psychological links between discrimination on the basis of gender and what is here being referred to as sexual misconduct, and this is surely why they are so often regarded as different forms of the same thing (i.e., sexual harassment), but a similar point could be made concerning alcohol abuse. There are strong links of an even more obvious sort between alcohol abuse and sexual abuse, but that is no reason to regard alcohol abuse as a form of sexual misconduct or harassment. For most people, the term "sexual misconduct" and the term "discrimination" both have negative connotations, and appropriately so, but the former has a sort of "sleaziness" to it that the latter lacks. They imply completely different sorts of character flaws on the part of those to whom they can truthfully be applied, and this alone is reason enough to regard them as significantly different sorts of offenses. "Sexual" misconduct, including sexual harassment, ought to be defined as involving, either directly or indirectly, sexual activity of some sort, and discrimination on the basis of gender is not necessarily sexual in this sense.

B. OTHER FORMS OF SEXUAL MISCONDUCT

Having distinguished discrimination based on gender from sexual misconduct, we must now distinguish various forms of sexual misconduct from each other. It will be useful to comment briefly upon those forms of sexual misconduct which have inappropriately become regarded as forms of sexual harassment before attempting to define sexual harassment *per se* more precisely.

1. Sexual Assault. The most serious and most obviously immoral type of sexual offense is sexual assault. This would apply not only to forcible rape as traditionally understood, but also to any form of clearly sexual behavior involving the use of physical force against a person without that person's consent. This is sometimes called "sexual imposition," especially in connection with less physically invasive forms of assault. Forcible rape, the most serious type of sexual assault, has long been regarded as a serious crime, and rightly so. It is clear that we must continue to develop and improve laws and institutional policies which deal effectively not only with forcible rape but also with other forms of sexual assault. Although the EEOC definition does not regard sexual assault as a form of sexual harassment, there is a tendency among writers on this topic to list it as such, which may be motivated by an understandable desire on the part of those enraged by sexual harassment to taint it with the opprobrium commonly occasioned by instances of rape. Unfortunately, this runs the risk of having the opposite effect of making sexual assault seem less serious than it is, especially since the vast majority of behaviors commonly regarded as sexually harassing are clearly less serious than sexual assault.

2. Sexual Coercion. The most serious type of sexual misconduct encompassed (inappropriately, according to our present argument) by the EEOC definition of sexual harassment is sexual coercion. It would be beyond the scope of this paper to attempt to define coercion *per se* in any detail. It will be sufficient for our present purposes simply to say that we are being coerced to do something if and only if (1) we are doing something which we would prefer not to do, and (2) we are doing that thing primarily or entirely because someone else has unjustifiably threatened to harm us in some way if we do not. One is then guilty of sexual coercion if and only if one has coerced someone into engaging in sexual activity. In other words, sexual coercion is coercive for the same reasons that other forms of coercion are coercive, and its coercive nature is sufficient in itself to make it wrong, whether or not there are additional reasons for so regarding it.

To the extent that coercion in general involves the threat of harm, the threatened harm may be either physical or nonphysical in nature. Sexual coercion involving the threat of physical harm thus differs from sexual assault as defined above in that the victim of sexual coercion has a "choice," in an admittedly perverse sense, whether to accede to the offender's demands or run the risk of suffering the threatened harm, whereas a victim of sexual assault has no choice in any sense of the term.

It is important to note that successful sexual coercion involving the threat of physical harm can often be more harmful to the victim than the corresponding form of sexual assault, since the victim must suffer not only the indignity of compliance with the offender's demands but also the psychological trauma of feeling partially responsible for the outcome, which trauma often occurs despite assurances to the victim that resistance should not have been expected given the nature of the threats involved and the unlikelihood that the resistance would have been successful. This may help to explain why coercing persons to engage in sexual intercourse by threatening them with physical harm has traditionally been regarded as a form of rape, even if no overpowering force is used and no physical harm of the sort threatened ensues.

Whether the threatened harm is physical or nonphysical, it is important to note that coercion takes place only when it is both reasonable for the purported victim to believe that a threat has been made and unreasonable for the purported offender to deny that a threat has been made. The mere fact that a potential offender is in a position to inflict harm upon a potential victim clearly does not imply that the potential victim has been threatened with this harm. Moreover, the mere fact that a potential victim *feels* threatened, and thus fears that harm will occur unless sexual favors are granted, does not imply that a threat has occurred, even if the potential victim subsequently engages in unwanted sexual activity solely as a result of this fear.

It is important to point out that this can be true even in some cases where the fear in question is perfectly reasonable. If Smith knows or reasonably believes that persons answering some particular description often inflict harm upon persons like him in certain sorts of circumstances, and if he encounters Jones, a person of this description, in

these circumstances, it is perfectly reasonable for Smith to fear Jones. Unless, however, Jones or these circumstances are described in such a way as to be inherently threatening (e.g., "a man brandishing a knife" or "during an armed robbery"), Jones cannot be accused of coercing Smith simply because Jones makes a request of Smith that Smith grants only or primarily because of this reasonable fear. In other words, Jones cannot be held responsible for the fact that persons like Jones sometimes or even often harm others in similar circumstances. This is a perfectly general point that applies to any situation involving encounters between persons of different general descriptions who have been stereotyped in some way.[8]

The point here is not that threats must be explicitly stated in order to be coercive. Brandishing a weapon is clearly a threat of physical harm, and threats can often be subtle and covert but nonetheless conveyed and received. The point here, once again, is that a person is not guilty of sexual coercion unless that person's behavior is truly threatening, which implies not only that the purported victim can reasonably regard the purported offender's behavior as threatening, but also that the purported offender realizes (or is at least in such a position that he or she can reasonably be faulted for not realizing) that this behavior is likely to be regarded as threatening. Thus, engaging in sexual activity with someone who is in a position to inflict some sort of harm, even if one does so solely because one is fearful that this harm will otherwise ensue, does not by itself entail that one is a victim of sexual coercion. One is coerced only when one

---

[8] I have a gainfully employed, law-abiding, African-American male friend who once walked into a convenience market on a very cold day wearing a ski mask. The female clerk, who was alone in the store at the time, saw him and immediately started to hand him the contents of the cash register. Given her own past experience and her knowledge of crime statistics in that neighborhood, it could be argued that her fear of my friend was quite reasonable, and she certainly acted as she did because of this reasonable fear. My friend, however, could certainly not have been accused of coercion. He would not, of course, have been justified in keeping the contents of the cash register in these circumstances, and would probably have been prosecuted for doing so, since it was obvious that the clerk acted out of fear in this case. Suppose, however, that he had simply approached a stranger on the street and asked for a simple favor. If the stranger, without showing any fear, nevertheless granted the favor for this reason, could my friend have been accused of coercion?

is actually threatened with harm.

Unlike sexual assault, which has always been regarded as a serious offense, sexual coercion has traditionally been recognized as such only when the victim has been threatened with bodily harm. One positive development in recent years has been that legal and institutional protection, largely under the rubric of the first two clauses in the EEOC definition of sexual harassment, has been extended to potential victims of sexual coercion involving threats of other types of harm, such as harm to their educational or professional careers. Sexual coercion of this sort is the most serious offense typically regarded as a form of sexual harassment. As is true, albeit to a lesser extent, in the case of sexual assault, there are both conceptual and practical difficulties involved in trying to decide how to handle sexual coercion. Suppose, for example, that a spouse or lover threatens to break off a relationship unless sexual favors are granted, as often happens. Breaking off a relationship could often be regarded as potentially harmful to the threatened person, and threatening to do so for this reason might be morally opprobrious, but it is nevertheless difficult to see how we could justify making such behavior illegal. Laws and policies concerning sexual coercion are most easily justified in cases where there is an institutional or corporate "power differential" between potential offenders and victims, and there would now be at least a rough consensus that this form of behavior is morally unacceptable and should be dealt with effectively when it occurs within this sort of context. It would also appear that there would be no insuperable difficulties involved in reaching a consensus as to how these offenses should be defined.[9] The seriousness of this offense, and the relative ease with which a consensus could be reached concerning not only how to define it but also that it is morally unacceptable, provide ample justification for regarding sexual coercion as a specific type of sexual offense, differing both from the equally serious offense of sexual assault and from less serious forms of sexual misconduct, including sexual harassment *per se*.

3. Sexual Offers. Another sort of behavior sometimes regarded as a form of sexual harassment might be called a "sexual offer." Sexual offers are of two sorts. The first sort of sexual offer is one in which a person offers to confer an otherwise undeserved benefit in exchange for sexual favors. The second sort of sexual offer is one in which a person offers to confer sexual favors in exchange for an otherwise undeserved benefit. Since the refusal to confer sexual favors or undeserved benefits cannot be regarded as "harmful" in the relevant sense, sexual offers do not constitute coercive threats and cannot be regarded as a special case of sexual coercion. There is a clear moral difference between using or threatening to use one's power to harm someone, which is *prima facie* immoral, and using or offering to use one's power to benefit someone, which is not. Moreover, the so-called power differential which looms so large in most cases of sexual coercion is not so clearly relevant here. Any situation in which a person who has the "power" to confer an undeserved benefit in exchange for sexual favors is likely to make such an offer is also a situation in which the person to whom such an offer is made has the "power" to offer sexual favors in exchange for these benefits. It cannot be assumed that the lure of undeserved benefits to someone in a position to confer sexual favors is any more "powerful" than the lure of sexual favors to someone in a position to confer undeserved benefits, so the "power" in such cases is reciprocal. Finally, if *making* a sexual offer is to be regarded as an offense, it is presumably because the relationship that would ensue if the offer were accepted would be in some way illicit or inappropriate. It therefore follows that if making such an offer is to be regarded as an offense, accepting one should also be so regarded, and for the same reason. Thus, other things being equal, making or accepting either sort of sexual offer must be equally offensive, and any policy which mandates sanctions for making one sort of offer must mandate similar sanctions for making the other and for accepting either sort of offer as well.

Sexual offers as here defined are commonly referred to in sexual harassment literature as "sexual bribery." Referring to them in this way is problematic for several reasons, some of which are inherent in the concept of bribery itself. In general, bribery is regarded as an offense primarily in a political context. It occurs when a public official

---

[9]The interpretation of the first two clauses of the EEOC statement is continually being refined in the courts, and even though there is no comparable refining process in academe, reasonable people could probably reach a consensus as to how such cases could be resolved there as well.

who is in a position to confer benefits as a result of holding the position that she holds confers unmerited benefits on someone in exchange for personal gain. It is regarded as an offense partly because it is unjust to those who actually deserve but do not receive the benefits thus conferred and also because it contradicts the purpose for which the official has been given the authority to bestow the benefits in question. Suppose, however, that an elected public official exercises her legitimate authority in such a way that it happens to benefit certain constituents more than others, and suppose that those particular constituents contribute heavily, but in accordance with (admittedly nonexistent) campaign financing laws generally regarded as fair, to the reelection campaign of that official. This would not constitute bribery unless there was an explicit or tacit understanding between the official and her constituents that the benefits in question were to be conferred in exchange for the contributions. The mere fact that benefits have been conferred and contributions made does not imply that bribery occurred or was even attempted. Finally, it could be argued that any law which flatly prohibits public officials from benefiting their constituents or flatly prohibits those constituents from contributing to the campaigns of the elected officials of their choice is at least an infringement, if not a violation, of their rights.[10]

Similar considerations apply in the case of so-called sexual bribery. Offering sexual favors, even to someone in a position to confer undeserved benefits, may be immoral for some reason, but does not necessarily constitute attempted bribery. Neither does requesting such favors from persons one is in a position to benefit constitute soliciting a bribe, even if it is immoral for some other reason. It is only when granting the benefit or favor is made conditional on granting the other that something resembling bribery has occurred or been attempted. Unless this condition is stated explicitly, which is not often the case, any allegation of bribery would have to be based on the contention that the condition was somehow implicit in the context in which the behavior took place. In cases of this sort, the motives and intentions of the parties involved are of paramount importance, and these are often not entirely clear, even to the persons themselves. A person may convince himself that he is acquiescing to a request for sexual favors from his superior because he is in love with her when he really just wants a promotion, and a person may convince herself that an underling who has acquiesced to her request for sexual favors really deserves a promotion, when she is really just in love with him. Great care must therefore be taken in attempting to adjudicate a situation in which someone is accused of sexual bribery. Sexual offers of either sort may be immoral for a variety of reasons, and it may be prudent for institutions to develop policies which attempt to regulate and monitor such behavior, but it could be argued that any policy which flatly prohibits competent adults from making or accepting unconditional sexual offers or requests is an infringement if not a violation of their rights, even if making or accepting such offers or requests is often morally opprobrious in many cases.

4. Sexual Boorishness. Sexual boorishness is nonthreatening, expressive behavior of a sexual nature which is patently offensive to a morally decent and psychologically normal adult of either gender. Obscene gestures, the public display of obscene or pornographic photographs or drawings, the use of obscene language, and otherwise rude sexual comments can all be examples of sexual boorishness in a wide variety of circumstances. Sexual boorishness is most appropriately regarded as sexual misconduct under two circumstances. The first is when it is directed against a particular person and constitutes an instance of sexual harassment *per se,* as will

---

[10]The problem here has been expressed fairly well in a form letter written by U.S. Representative Barney Frank to his contributors, which I will quote at length. "Writing a thank-you note to campaign contributors in today's climate forces me to emulate Rube Goldberg without pictures. That is, I have to write something that reflects (1) my deep genuine gratitude on a personal level for your sending me a contribution to help me stay in Congress, counterbalanced by (2) my concern that someone reading this might infer something disparaging about your motives in engaging in the sinister process of "campaign finance," itself counterbalanced by (3) my interest in keeping you sufficiently happy with me—or insufficiently unhappy—so that you will continue to contribute, in turn counterbalanced by (4) my fear that the media will denounce me for accepting campaign contributions and thereby subjecting myself to improper influence, albeit from proper people." Reprinted in *Harper's,* August 1994, p. 17.

be explained later. The second is when it creates what is sometimes misleadingly referred to as a "hostile environment."[11] This typically refers to a situation in which a person cannot participate in some particular educational experience or engage in some particular mode of employment without being subjected to what has been defined above as sexually boorish behavior. The point of referring to an "environment" here is to emphasize the fact that the behavior in question need not be directed at any one individual in particular. If it seems to be directed toward or primarily offensive to persons of some particular sexual orientation or gender, it can be regarded as a form of discrimination and treated as such. The term "hostile," however, is misleading in this context, because it can refer either to the motives of those responsible for the environment or to those aspects of the environment which render it harmful independently of their source. It is appropriate to hold someone morally responsible for a hostile environment only if they themselves have hostile motives or are indifferent to various consequences of their behavior which they know to be harmful to others. Human beings often express hostility toward one another in a wide variety of ways and for a wide variety of reasons, having to do with race, religion, politics, and moral beliefs, as well as sex and gender, and those who do so can be held morally responsible for the consequences of their actions, but we are understandably reluctant to impose sanctions on persons who engage in such behavior except in highly specific circumstances. For one thing, various persons might unknowingly contribute to a "hostile" environment by unintentionally bringing about certain physically or psychologically harmful aspects of that environment. There is no evidence, other than pseudo-Freudian generalizations of various sorts, that persons who indulge in sexual innuendo or humor, for example, are necessarily expressing hostility toward members of the opposite sex, or realize that their behavior is offensive or harmful in any way, even if, as a matter of fact, it is. The remedy in this case is communication, not punishment, and not "counseling" of a sort which implies that the accused person is somehow mentally ill. Some people are brought up using ethnic slurs without even realizing that they are

doing so.[12] The same is true of at least some sexual boorishness. In both cases, the persons in question are often unaware that their behavior is even offensive.

Although sexual boorishness can be morally opprobrious even when of it does not constitute a sanctionable offense, any attempt to legislate it, either legally or through corporate or institutional policy, must take both cultural differences and the right to freedom of expression into account. Respect for cultural and personal differences is especially important in connection with comments concerning a person's sexual attractiveness, since comments of this sort which are enthusiastically welcomed by some persons may be offensive to others. It is a plain and simple fact, for example, that some persons are pleased and flattered when someone describes them as "sexy," whereas others are embarrassed or even deeply offended. This does not imply that we must tolerate behavior of the extreme sort common in the most sexist societies, but it does imply that we must avoid adopting sexually repressive codes of behavior favored only by those at the opposite end of the spectrum, who have no more right to impose their values on others than anyone else does.

II. *Sexual Harassment* Per se

Sexual coercion and sexual assault are clearly unacceptable and ought to be dealt with effectively and fairly whenever and wherever they occur. Sexual boorishness and sexual offers are more problematic. It would be beyond the scope of this paper to attempt the difficult task of deciding exactly when such forms of behavior are justifiably sanctionable and when they are not, but with appropriate and important qualifications, we might be able to justify laws and policies which regulate or prohibit these sorts of behavior in certain circumstances With regard to sexual harassment *per se*, the challenge is to define it in such a way as not only to distinguish it from unjustifiable discrimination based on gender and the various sorts of sexual misconduct discussed above, but also in such a way as to

---

[11]Cf. clause (3) of the EEOC statement.

[12]My first landlord, an immigrant from Greece, informed me that the term "Greek" is an ethnic slur (the proper term is "Grecian"), but that it did not offend him, since the people that use this term are all "barbarians" anyway.

enable us to determine, at least in principle, whether someone is or is not guilty of this offense. Unless we are able to do this, it is difficult to justify either legal or institutional sanctions concerning sexual harassment.

It would seem that the proper place to begin in an attempt to define sexual harassment would be to say that it must be both clearly sexual in nature and clearly a form of harassment.[13] It would thus be useful at this point to discuss both what it means to say that a form of behavior is sexual in nature and what it means to say that it is a form of harassment.

A. SEXUAL BEHAVIOR

With regard to the term "sexual," there is both a broad and a narrow use of the term. In the broad sense of the term, psychologists and others constantly remind us that almost any form of behavior can be regarded as sexual in some context or other. Since, in cases of alleged sexual harassment, the question as to whether a particular bit or pattern of behavior constitutes an offense so often hinges on whether that behavior is or is not "sexual" in nature, it is especially important for the purpose of crafting a policy statement concerning sexual harassment to adopt, at least at the outset, a more narrow definition. Otherwise, we run the risk of being forced to regard far too many different sorts of behavior as instances of sexual harassment, especially if we give the term "harassment" an equally broad or vague definition. Any law or policy which is sufficiently vague so as to enable us to regard almost anything as an offense is obviously both unwise and unjustifiable. (Cf. the charges brought against Socrates in Athens.)

It will thus be useful at this point to distinguish among (1) behavior which is *prima facie* sexual in nature, (2) behavior which is *prima facie* nonsexual, and (3) behavior which is neither. To say that a bit of behavior is *prima facie* sexual is simply to say that, due to some inherent features of the behavior in itself, it is sexual *unless* there are contextual circumstances which render it nonsexual.

Thus, for example, behavior involving physical contact with genitalia is ordinarily sexual in nature, but would not ordinarily be considered sexual in those cases in which it occurred in connection with some justifiable medical procedure. Similarly, behavior is *prima facie* nonsexual if there is nothing inherent in that behavior which renders it sexual. It can therefore be presumed to be nonsexual in nature *unless* there is something extraordinary about the circumstances in which it occurs which renders it sexual. Such things as playing chess or reading a novel, for example, could be regarded as sexual activities only in highly extraordinary circumstances. Finally, and most importantly within the present context, there are bits of behavior which cannot be *presumed* to be either sexual or nonsexual independently of the context in which they occur. On being told, for example, that X kissed Y, we are not justified in presuming either that X's behavior was sexual or that it was nonsexual unless we know something about the context. Kissing is often a sexual activity, but parents kissing their children on the forehead are seldom if ever engaged in sexual activity, unless we define the term "sexual" much too broadly to be useful in the present context. The foregoing distinctions are applicable to all forms of sexual misconduct, but will be seen to be especially important in the context of sexual harassment.

B. HARASSMENT

With regard to harassment, *Black's Law Dictionary* defines it as a "petty misdemeanor" which involves the use of "words, gestures, and actions which tend to annoy, alarm, and abuse (verbally) another person."[14] It does not ordinarily refer to any form of coercion or assault. If I attempt to coerce someone or strike them in such a way as to physically harm them, I am guilty of something significantly more serious than harassment. Moreover, offering to reward someone for doing something they would not otherwise do, or to do something of this sort in exchange for a reward, even in cases where it is morally unacceptable to do so, would not ordinarily be considered a form of harassment. In general terms, harassment refers only to behavior

---

[13]One virtue of the EEOC definition is that it does at least make it clear that only behavior which is sexual in nature can be regarded as a form of sexual harassment, although it unfortunately leaves the term "sexual" undefined.

[14]*Black's Law Dictionary*, fifth edition, West, St. Paul, p. 645.

which is annoying or offensive, not to behavior which is seriously harmful, threatening, or tempting in a morally pernicious manner. It also seems clear that typically A is harassing B only if A is engaged in behavior toward B which is unwanted by B, is known by A to be unwanted by B, and which is nevertheless repeated by A. Thus, for example, if I tap someone on the shoulder and ask a reasonable question, this would not ordinarily be regarded as harassment. If, however, I continue to do so even after the person in question has made it clear that he would prefer that I not do so, this might constitute harassment, even though my behavior in this instance is not inherently immoral. We might add that a bit of behavior would not ordinarily be regarded as a form of harassment unless it is of a sort which a reasonable person might find objectionable or annoying. If I regularly say "good morning" to my neighbor as I drive off to work in the morning and he is offended by this, I can hardly be accused of harassment, especially if he does not indicate that he is offended by it. Moreover, if I regularly wear a blue shirt and he is offended by this, I cannot be accused of harassing him even if he *does* tell me it offends him. In fact, any attempt on his part to discourage or prevent me from wearing blue shirts might constitute harassment on *his* part, or even worse.

C. SEXUAL HARASSMENT

It would seem that similar considerations should apply to sexual harassment. Roughly speaking, sexual harassment is simply harassment in which the offending behavior is sexual in nature. In other words, to parallel what was said above about harassment in general, the term "sexual harassment" should not be applied to sexual coercion or sexual assault, nor should it be applied to situations in which persons are tempted to voluntarily engage in sexual behavior for morally inappropriate reasons. It should be applied only to sexual behavior which is merely annoying or offensive, not to behavior which is seriously harmful, threatening, or tempting in a morally pernicious manner. A person (A) should be said to be sexually harassing another person (B) only if A is engaged in sexual behavior toward B which is unwanted by B, is known by A to be unwanted by B, and which is nevertheless repeated by A. Finally, a bit of behavior would not

ordinarily be regarded as a form of sexual harassment unless it is of a sort which a reasonable person might find objectionable or annoying.

Since the more intimate forms of sexual activity are those in which consent is clearly called for, it would be inappropriate to refer to any such behavior as sexual harassment. If consent is not given, a person who initiates such activity is guilty of sexual assault. If consent *is* given, initiating such behavior might be immoral for a variety of reasons, but cannot be a clearly sanctionable offense unless it involves a morally unjustifiable sexual offer or is coercive. Since none of these three types of offenses are properly regarded as types of sexual harassment, it follows that sexual harassment cannot involve intimate sexual activity, but must involve sexual activity of a less intimate sort. It must, in other words, involve behavior which is clearly sexual in nature, but not especially intimate.

We are now in a position to see why sexual harassment is so difficult to define, much less adjudicate. Most behavior which is *prima facie* sexual in nature is fairly intimate. Although, as mentioned above, intimate sexual behavior might sometimes involve morally unjustifiable sexual offers or constitute a form of sexual coercion or assault, it seldom if ever constitutes sexual harassment. Typical cases of sexual harassment involve behavior which is *not prima facie* sexual in nature, but is sexual due to its context, if at all. Most often, behavior which is not *prima facie* sexual in nature is clearly sexual only when it constitutes a sexual advance, but behavior of this sort which constitutes a sexual advance in one set of circumstances might not do so in another. Moreover, in many cases of purported sexual harassment, both parties will agree that certain behavior has occurred, but will strongly disagree as to how that behavior should be interpreted or described. For example, a purported victim of sexual harassment (A) may claim that a purported offender (B) has persisted in making "unwanted sexual advances" toward A by engaging in behavior toward A which A, but not B, regards as sexual in nature. If the behavior of B is *prima facie* sexual as defined above, the burden of proof will be on B to show that it was not sexual, and if this behavior is *prima facie* nonsexual, the burden of proof will be on A to show that it is sexual. But what if, as is often if not usually the case, it is neither? Since many types of sexual advance involve behavior which is not *prima facie* sexual in nature, there is often considerable disagreement between purported victims and purported offenders in such cases concerning whether the behavior of the purported offender was in fact a sexual advance. It thus becomes problematic whether any such bit of behavior satisfies one of the necessary conditions which such a bit must satisfy in order to be an instance of sexual harassment.

There are several logically possible ways of resolving this difficulty. One way would be to allow the precise nature of the purported offender's behavior to be subjectively determined by the purported victim. In other words, we might simply say that if the purported victim regards the purported offender's behavior as a sexual advance, then that settles the matter. The problem with this procedure, of course, is that there does not seem to be any *a priori* reason to prefer the subjective opinions of the purported victim to those of the purported offender. For one thing, the latter is surely in a better position to know the inherent nature of his or her motives or intentions.[15] In addition, since the guilt or innocence of the purported offender might well hinge on our determination of whether his or her behavior is sexual in nature, the principle that an accused person is innocent until proven guilty clearly implies that we should give the benefit of the doubt to the accused. But to accept the subjectively determined opinions of accused persons concerning their own behavior as definitive in such cases is to leave potential victims essentially unprotected, since accused persons will almost always describe their own motivations in such a way as to support a claim of innocence.

What is clearly called for here is some objective basis for determining whether a person's behavior is sexual in the relevant sense. Since we are now discussing behavior which is not *prima facie* sexual in nature, any determination must be based on contextual considerations. Among things to be considered will be the intention and other psycho-

logical states of the accused and various social conventions pertaining to interpersonal relationships. In an increasingly multi-cultural world, however, there must be a wide variety of interpretations of what is to constitute a sexual advance, and a correspondingly wide variety of socially acceptable behaviors. Judas, for example, was not making or even pretending to make a homosexual advance when he betrayed Jesus with a kiss, and even today, Arab men often kiss and hold hands with no implication of homosexuality. Similarly, in most cultures and subcultures, including those of the United States, there are many social contexts in which heterosexual embracing, kissing, and other forms of physical affection are not ordinarily considered to be sexual advances, even though there are some persons who seem to regard almost any sort of physical contact whatsoever as a sexual advance. As mentioned previously, we need not tolerate the sorts of behavior which would be regarded as acceptable in the most extremely sexist societies, but we also need not adopt a code of behavior so sexually repressive that we are required to regard all forms of unconsented-to physical contact or affection as sexual advances. No one narrow segment of society should be permitted to impose its interpretation of what constitutes a sexual advance or its views concerning what is socially acceptable on the rest of society. For all these reasons, great care must be taken in formulating legislation or institutional policies according to which a sexual advance can sometimes be a sanctionable offense. In particular, the term "sexual advance" cannot be defined in such a way as to automatically apply to bits of behavior which are often nonsexual in nature. Moreover, persons chosen to exercise judgment concerning whether a given bit of behavior constitutes a sexual advance in some particular context must be sufficiently broad-minded so as to instill confidence in all parties that such judgments will reflect an understanding of all the considerations referred to above.

D. DEFINING THE TERM

We are now in a position to attempt a more precise definition of sexual harassment. As a first approximation, consider the following:

(1) Person A is guilty of sexually harassing person B iff [if and only if]:

---

[15]Many chronic sex offenders, of course, are subject to various types of self-deception concerning their own motives and behavior, but to the extent that this is true, it would seem to render them less responsible for their behavior and to make it more difficult to justify using sanctions against them.

(a) A's behavior toward B is clearly sexual in nature, but does not involve a morally unjustifiable sexual offer or constitute either sexual coercion or sexual assault.

(b) A's behavior toward B is clearly unwanted by B.

The difficulty with this definition is that, depending on what we mean by "clearly" in (b), a person might be guilty of sexual harassment without having any way of being aware of that fact. It might be clear to any number of people that A's behavior is unwanted by B, but unless it is (or at least should be) clear to A, it is difficult to see how A's behavior can be morally sanctionable, unless, of course, it is inherently so for some reason.

Consider now the following substitute for (1), which is derived by substituting (b*) for (b) in (1):

(1*) Person A is guilty of sexually harassing person B iff:

(a) A's behavior toward B is clearly sexual in nature, but does not involve a morally unjustifiable sexual offer or constitute either sexual coercion or sexual assault.

(b*) A's behavior toward B is known by A to be unwanted by B.

A good case can be made for the view that if A's behavior satisfies both of these conditions, A's behavior is morally objectionable. It is perfectly reasonable to claim that there is something morally objectionable about engaging in sexual behavior toward a person when we know that that person does not want us to do so. The difficulty with this definition is that it excludes too much. Suppose, for example, A does not *know* that the behavior in question is unwanted by B, but has good reason to *believe* that it is. A's lack of *knowledge* of B's feelings would certainly not excuse A's behavior in this instance.

Perhaps, then, we can revise our definition again, by substituting (b**) for (b*):

(1**) Person A is guilty of sexually harassing person B iff:

(a) A's behavior toward B is clearly sexual in nature, but does not involve a morally unjustifiable sexual offer or constitute either sexual coercion or sexual assault.

(b**) A has good reason to believe that A's behavior toward B is unwanted by B.

Condition (b**), however, is still too strong. Suppose that A and B are total strangers, that they meet in circumstances in which it would ordinarily be thought inappropriate to make sexual advances (e.g., in a supermarket), and that A makes a sexual advance toward B which is *prima facie* sexual in nature. Unless it is argued (implausibly) that no one ever wants to be propositioned by a total stranger, A might truthfully claim that although she has no good reason to believe that her behavior is wanted by B, she also has no good reason to believe that her behavior toward B is unwanted. We might nevertheless argue that A's behavior in this case might constitute at least a mild form of sexual misconduct. One way of doing so is to point out that such behavior is offensive to most people, whether or not it is offensive to everyone, and that it is morally unacceptable to behave in a way which is offensive to most people in this respect, even if there may be some people who do not find this behavior offensive.

This suggests a further modification in our proposed definition, as follows:

(1***) Person A is guilty of sexually harassing person B iff:

(a) A's behavior toward B is clearly sexual in nature, but does not involve a morally unjustifiable sexual offer or constitute either sexual coercion or sexual assault.

(b***) A has no reason to believe that A's behavior toward B might be wanted by B.

This definition clearly applies to behavior of the sort described above, but instead of excluding too much, it suffers from the opposite defect. Social conventions being what they are, there are many situations in which behavior satisfying both of these conditions would be perfectly acceptable. In the first place, if A and B know each other well enough, a sexual advance which is *prima facie* sexual in nature might be perfectly appropriate. In the second place, if A and B do not know each other well, sometimes the most appropriate way to determine whether a sexual advance is or is not wanted is simply to make one, especially if it is one which is *not prima facie* sexual in nature. There is clearly something amiss in our attempt to define sexual harassment so far.

Sexual relationships cannot exist unless they are initiated by someone. If doing something to initiate a sexual relationship is regarded as "making a sexual advance," it follows that sexual relationships cannot exist unless someone makes a sexual advance. Moreover, the first person to make such an advance in a sexual relationship must do so without knowing whether such an advance is wanted by the other person. The reason for this is that anything the other person did which would suffice to indicate that a sexual advance *was* wanted (or was even not unwanted) could be regarded as a sexual advance on the part of the other person, in which case, contrary to hypothesis, the person in question could not be the first person to make such an advance. Moreover, given this understanding of what constitutes a sexual advance, asking permission to make one is also tantamount to making one. Thus, sexual relationships cannot exist unless someone makes a sexual advance without knowing whether it is wanted.

What follows from this is that making sexual advances, even when it is not known whether they are or are not wanted, cannot be *prima facie* morally unacceptable, so that sexual harassment, if it is to be regarded as morally unacceptable, cannot be defined simply in terms of unwanted sexual advances. Many sexual advances which seem to be morally unacceptable, such as the example given above involving total strangers in the supermarket, are best regarded as instances of mere sexual boorishness, and not as forms of sexual harassment. In order to define sexual harassment correctly we must once again attend to the meaning of the term "harassment."

As we have seen, to harass someone is to *repeatedly* engage in behavior toward that person despite our knowledge or belief that the behavior is unwanted. The fact that the behavior is repeated is especially important in the case of sexual harassment. In the first place, since the only reasonable way to ascertain that a sexual advance is unwanted is often to make it, there are many cases in which one cannot be blamed for making one unless one has already made one and been rebuffed. In the second place, sexual harassment occurs most often among people who know each other but are not involved in a serious romantic or sexual relationship. Since it is considered excessively crude to attempt to initiate such a relationship by making sexual advances which are *prima facie* sexual in nature, people typically do so by making sexual advances which are *not prima facie* sexual in nature. This enables those who wish to reject such an advance to do so by simply responding to it as if it were not such an advance, and it enables those whose advances have been rebuffed to save face by pretending that they were not really making such an advance. The intent in these cases is not to deceive, but simply to minimize hurt feelings and embarrassment. Since, however, sexual advances of this kind are by hypothesis patterns of behavior that need not be regarded as sexual advances at all, it follows that people must often engage in the same patterns of behavior without intending to make any sexual advances. For this reason, it often happens that one person will interpret another person's behavior as a sexual advance when no such advance was intended. This alone is sufficient reason for not defining sexual harassment in terms of such ambiguous behavior.

It also explains, however, why it is so important that the behavior be repeated. Suppose that person A engages in behavior toward person B which A does not regard as sexual in nature but B does. As previously implied, the burden of proof will be on A if the behavior in question is *prima facie* sexual and on B if it is *prima facie* nonsexual. Moreover, even when it is neither, and regardless of what A or B claim to believe about the behavior in question, the context can sometimes make it clear whether this behavior is or is not sexual in nature. The problem is that, even when the context is completely specified, there are many cases in which there may be no clear consensus as to whether the behavior should be regarded as sexual or not. In a single instance of this sort, the benefit of the doubt must be given to the accused. Since, however, by hypothesis, the behavior in question is not *prima facie* nonsexual it could under some conceivable circumstances be regarded as sexual. Thus, if A knows that B regards it as sexual, whether or not A also so regards it, A cannot continue to engage in this behavior toward B without presupposing that B will interpret A's behavior as sexual. Thus, unless A has sufficient reason to believe that B desires or at least has no objection to A's engaging in sexual behavior toward B, A's continuing to engage in the behavior in question shows disrespect toward B of a very serious sort.

We are now in a position to try once again to define sexual harassment. Consider the following:

> (2) Person A is guilty of sexually harassing person B iff:

> (a) A has engaged in behavior toward B which is either *prima facie* sexual in nature or is such that B could reasonably regard it as such, but which does not constitute either sexual coercion, sexual assault, or a morally unjustifiable sexual offer.

> (b) A knows or has adequate reason to believe that B reasonably regards A's behavior as sexual in nature.

> (c) A knows or has adequate reason to believe that B does not want A to continue behaving in this manner toward B.

> (d) A continues to behave in the same manner toward B.

There are several noteworthy aspects of this definition. The first is that condition (a) is necessary but not sufficient. A single, isolated instance of sexual coercion, sexual assault, or a morally unjustifiable sexual offer constitutes a sexual offense, but no isolated bit of behavior can constitute an instance of sexual harassment. Sexual harassment does not involve behavior which is inherently immoral. It occurs only when persons engage in sexual behavior or behavior which could reasonably be interpreted as such toward persons whom they know or have reason to believe may not want them to engage in such behavior. No one can reasonably be expected to continually provide each person they encounter in their daily lives with a detailed description of all those forms of behavior which they regard as sexual, nor can they provide each person with a list of those forms of behavior which they would prefer the person in question not exhibit toward them. For this reason, it often happens that persons engage in such behavior without realizing that it is offensive to others. If those others never indicate in any way that they are offended, or if the behavior in question is such that no reasonable person would be offended by it, the person engaging in it cannot be regarded as having committed an offense.

E. APPLICATIONS, PROBLEMS, AND REMEDIES

Those who justifiably feel that they have been sexually harassed are often reluctant to complain or express their displeasure. Sometimes they are simply too polite and do not want to upset those that are offending them, and sometimes they are simply afraid to complain for fear of reprisal. These fears are sometimes justified, which is precisely why we need sexual harassment policies, but these policies must be such that those who have offended cannot be justifiably accused of an offense unless they have explicitly been made aware that their behavior has been offensive and they have nevertheless continued to engage in it.

Special problems obtain in cases in which the accuser and the accused have previously been involved in an admittedly consensual relationship. Sexual advances made within such relationships are often rebuffed, with no implication that future advances will also be unwanted. For this reason, all the conditions of our definition might be satisfied in such cases even when it is obvious that no sanctionable offense has occurred. For cases of this sort, some further condition would have to be developed which would enable us to determine when one party has made it sufficiently clear to the other party that a sexual relationship no longer exists, so that the conditions spelled out in our definition would once again apply. The point here is not that "anything goes" within a relationship; the point is rather that the remedy for intolerable behavior which occurs within a relationship is to end (or attempt to end) the relationship.

It is sometimes argued that sexual harassment typically involves a "power differential" between perpetrator and victim, in the sense that those who are guilty of it typically occupy positions which give them some sort of authority over their victims. There is an element of truth in this, but it must be stated very carefully. In cases of sexual assault, of course, the perpetrator typically overpowers or threatens to overpower the victim, but it is possible for a less powerful person to sexually assault a more powerful one, especially if the more powerful person does not resist the assault. Differences in power and authority are most prevalent in cases of sexual coercion, especially those in which the threatened harm is nonphysical in nature, since the ability of the perpetrator to issue meaningful threats in these cases depends on the power invested in the perpetrator by his or her position. It is important to point out, however, that in cases of sexual coercion, it is the illegitimate use or threatened use of this power and not its mere possession that is relevant, and the same is true in cases of sexual harassment. Suppose, for example, that Abercrombie occupies a position of power or authority with respect to Fitch, but that Smith does not occupy a corresponding position with respect to Wesson. It is nevertheless the case that if the behavior of Abercrombie toward Fitch is exactly the same as the behavior of Smith toward Wesson and does not involve any threats or offers to use this power or authority, Abercrombie cannot be guilty of sexually harassing Fitch unless Smith is guilty of sexually harassing Wesson. More specifically, suppose that Abercrombie and Smith both request or accept offers of identical sexual favors from Fitch and Wesson respectively, and there is no difference in the observable behavior of Fitch and Wesson. It may be, of course, that Fitch and Wesson have different motives for making these offers or responding as they do to these requests. Fitch may be attempting to curry favor with Abercrombie in the hope that Abercrombie's power will be used to Fitch's benefit, or Fitch may fear that Abercrombie's power will be used against Fitch, whereas Wesson cannot reasonably have either of these motivations with respect to Smith. Since, however, Abercrombie has not, by hypothesis, given Fitch any reason to think that this power and authority will be used in either of these ways, Abercrombie is not responsible for Fitch's hopes and fears, nor for the behavior that flows from them. The most that one can say about Abercrombie in this case is that Abercrombie ought to be sensitive to the possibility that Fitch has these motivations, and should take this possibility into account, whereas Smith has no such obligation with respect to Wesson.

Suppose, however, that Abercrombie has taken this possibility into account, and has, with adequate reason, rejected it. Suppose that, as a matter of fact, Fitch has no such motivations but responds enthusiastically, for morally appropriate reasons, to Abercrombie's request. Further suppose that, at some later date, Fitch becomes angry with Abercrombie, for some reason having nothing to do with Abercrombie's request, and decides to accuse Abercrombie of sexual harassment. Should we countenance a policy which would support such an accusation simply on the grounds that Abercrombie occupies a position of power or authority over Fitch? Having power or authority over others sometimes puts persons in a position which enables them to commit offenses which they would otherwise be unable to commit, but engaging in sexual behavior with someone over whom one has such power and authority does not necessarily constitute an abuse of one's position. The abuse of such power or authority cannot be tolerated, but neither can a policy which permits sanctions against individuals for engaging in otherwise acceptable behavior simply because they engage in this behavior with those with respect to whom they have this power or authority.

The above considerations are not intended to obviate the principles of professional ethics. When the position of power or authority entails professional responsibilities, as opposed to mere supervisory authority, for example, one must obviously carry out these responsibilities in an ethical manner. One reason for this is that professionals often have even more actual power over those whom they serve than that which attaches to their office *per se*. Students, for example, are usually younger than their mentors and often overly impressionable if not awestruck by them, which makes them especially vulnerable to exploitation, and similar considerations apply to those who seek the advice and assistance of physicians, psychologists, attorneys, and other professionals. Institutions and professional organizations therefore have a right if not an obligation to establish and enforce appropriate standards of professional behavior on the part of their employees or members. Policies concerning sexual misconduct of various kinds, including sexual harassment as properly defined, can play an important role in publicizing and enforcing these standards, but must also be designed and implemented in such a way as to respect the rights of the professionals involved. As long as special consideration is given for those who are especially vulnerable to exploitation, any policy which prohibits affectionate or intimate relationships between truly consenting adults is reminiscent of laws against miscegenation.

One seldom noticed effect of sexual harassment policies on many college campuses is that the so-called power differential is actually reversed on these campuses. College professors do seem to have considerable power over their students. They have considerable if not total control, especially in those disciplines where most of the grading is necessarily discretionary, over the assignment of grades to students who might sometimes be academically required to successfully complete courses taught only by some particular member of a faculty. Students also depend on their professors for letters of recommendation both for employment and for future study, as well as for advice and assistance in other matters of some import, and most of these factors are amplified in graduate or professional school. On the other hand, undergraduates are seldom required to complete more than one course with any particular professor, and it is even less likely that a student is significantly dependent on any one professor for a letter of recommendation. In addition, even though most academic deans and department chairs are extremely reluctant to overrule an individual faculty member in the assignment of a student's grades, students who receive uncharacteristically low grades from professors and credibly complain to an appropriate college official that their professor attempted to coerce them into engaging in sexual activity usually receive a fair hearing, even in the absence of a sexual harassment policy.

With the advent of sexual harassment policies, however, students have acquired a great deal of essentially unchecked power over their professors. Any student who is ever alone with a professor, for example, can easily accuse that professor of making unwanted sexual advances or of attempted sexual coercion, whether or not any such accusation is true, and the accusation is likely to be taken seriously, if only because we have now collectively become sensitive to the fact that even true allegations of this sort were not always taken seriously in the past. We are especially likely to take such accusations seriously if there is more than one accuser bringing charges against the same faculty member, which is taken to imply that there has been an offensive "pattern of behavior" on the part of the accused. What we might fail to take into account in such cases is the possibility that the same sort of "herd mentality" that sometimes inclines students to give false testimony in defense of a friend who has been accused of violating some sort of campus pol-

icy might also incline some students to give false testimony to "support" a friend who has convinced them of the accused's guilt. There is even some anecdotal evidence that students have sometimes been encouraged to bring such charges by politically motivated faculty members who disapprove of a specific colleague's behavior and wish to engage in a sort of "ethnic cleansing" of the faculty. The aforementioned "power differential," after all, gives politically motivated faculty members just as much power and influence over budding radical feminists as sexual harassers have over theirs, if not more, and due to their strong feelings on this issue, they may be just as likely to abuse this power. Although examples like this are surely atypical, it would be exceedingly naive to think they do not, much less cannot, occur, especially given the politically supercharged atmosphere afflicting many college campuses.

Situations like that described above are neither typical nor common, but many harassment policies are designed (inadvertently, we can hope) in such a way as to make them more likely.[16] In many cases, for example, students are permitted or even encouraged to make anonymous accusations, on the grounds that requiring them to identify themselves would make them vulnerable to reprisal or embarrassment. In some cases, secret files detailing such allegations are maintained without the knowledge of the accused until such time as sufficient "evidence" has been accumulated to bring charges. When charges are brought, they are sometimes deliberately vague, in order to conceal the identities of the accusers, and are sometimes not given in writing, and accusers are usually not required to face the accused. The accused seldom has the right to cross-examine either the accuser or witnesses that appear on the accuser's behalf, and is often not entitled to counsel that could perform this service on behalf of the accused. Few if any institutions, of course, attempt to dismiss tenured faculty on the basis of such a process alone. There is usually an additional step in the official dismissal process which does afford the accused with due process, but before this stage is reached, there is often an attempt on the part of the administration

[16]It is beyond the scope of this paper to present an exhaustive purvey of sexual harassment cases and policies. The following examples are all based on the author's personal knowledge of actual cases and policies.

to intimidate the accused into resigning in order to avoid a spectacle which would be embarrassing both to the accused and to the institution. This is often effective, since accusations of this kind, even if proven false, do considerable harm to a faculty member, especially if they become publicly known, so that some persons would rather resign than suffer such harm. As Plato perspicuously points out in the *Apology,* people generally think that anyone accused of something vaguely nasty must have done *something* wrong in order to even be accused of such a thing. There is always the suspicion, gladly nourished by most accusers, as well as by administrators in cases where there has been a determination, justified or unjustified, of guilt, that there is more to the story than has been publicly revealed, and even the friends of the accused begin to question his or her character.

Another problem with many sexual harassment policies is that, based loosely on the EEOC statement (especially clause [3]), but without the refining process of the courts, offenses are ill-defined. It is seldom clear what constitutes an "unwanted sexual advance," and it is even less clear what contributes to the creation of an allegedly "hostile environment." This has a "chilling effect" on academic freedom, since faculty members never know when the positions that they take on controversial issues, the examples that they use as illustrations in class, the reading materials that they assign, or even some of the words that they use may prove to be offensive to someone and cost them their career. In some cases, action has been taken against a faculty member even when a clear majority of those students who should presumably be offended are not, and are even willing to testify that they are not, and this action has been taken on the grounds that even if these students are not offended, they should be. What this amounts to is that a small, nonrepresentative but vocal minority is being permitted to establish a strict code of conduct for everyone else.

Other problems are more subtle and thus more difficult to substantiate. There is a tendency, for example, to regard the accused as guilty until proven innocent. The reasonable position that accusations of this nature ought to be given a fair hearing is taken to mean that unless the accused can prove that the accuser is lying, the accusations must be believed. The burden of proof is on the accused, and any attempt to discredit the accuser or the accuser's witnesses is taken to be additional harassment or a form of reprisal. The entire process is all too often reminiscent of the Salem witch trials.

What needs to be done to enable sexual harassment policies to do their job without violating the rights of innocent people is implicit in what has already been said. Policies must be widely publicized and must clearly state what constitutes an offense. No action or mode of behavior should be regarded as a sanctionable offense unless there is a fairly wide consensus within the community that it ought to be so regarded. Accused persons must be told exactly what they have been accused of and who has accused them. They must have the right to cross-examine their accusers, or must at least have the right to have their accusers cross-examined by someone whom they have chosen to represent them. They must also be given the opportunity to determine such things as whether their accusers have any ulterior motives in accusing them, such as disappointment with a grade, feelings of rejection, strong ideological disapproval of the accused's position on controversial issues, desire to impress or please a deeply admired mentor who strongly disapproves of the accused, etc. Accused persons must also be given the opportunity to attempt to determine whether their accusers have previously been harassed or abused by someone with respect to whom they have no possibility of redress, whether they are emotionally disturbed, or whether they have been persuaded to bring charges by someone else who may or may not have a legitimate grievance against the accused.

It is not reasonable to expect sexual harassment policies to incorporate all the rights that would be afforded to the accused in a court of law. For one thing, sexual harassment policies should be primarily designed not to investigate, prosecute, and punish offenders, but to educate people and to work out differences between them in a mutually satisfactory manner. To the extent, however, that sexual harassment policies can have such dire consequences as dismissal and the termination of a career, accused persons should be afforded many of the same rights and privileges afforded them in a court of law, and for the same reasons. To do otherwise is a serious miscarriage of justice.[17]

---

[17]I am deeply indebted to David Lyons, whose strong disagreement with the overall tone of this paper has helped to make his comments and criticisms of several earlier versions of it extremely valuable to me.

Questions for Chapter 5

1. Consider Wall's example of a woman employee who receives a sexual threat from her employer that she will be demoted if she does not have sex with him. The woman, far from being offended, welcomes the opportunity, convinced that it provides her with opportunities for career advancement. Wall maintains that such a woman has not been sexually harassed. Do you agree? Why or why not? How would Superson respond to Wall's claim?

2. Wall argues that if there exists no intent to harass, there can be no sexual harassment, even though the "victim" may feel sexually harassed. Explain why you agree or disagree.

3. Superson argues that in society as it presently exists women cannot sexually harass men. She suggests that "any bothersome behavior a woman engages in, even though it may be of a sexual nature, does not constitute sexual harassment because it lacks the social impact present in male-to-female harassment." Suppose a female superior threatens a male employee with dismissal if he refuses to have sex with her. Do you agree with Superson that such behavior does not deserve to be called sexual harassment? How would you defend your answer?

4. Superson claims that a person's overhearing sexist comments even though the speaker has no idea the person is within earshot constitutes sexual harassment. How would you define sexist comments, and do you agree that this constitutes sexual harassment?

5. Griffith says gender discrimination (sexism) and sexual harassment should be distinguished. He claims that "they imply completely different sorts of character flaws on the part of those to whom they can truthfully be applied, and this alone is reason enough to regard them as significantly different sorts of offenses." On what grounds does he distinguish gender discrimination from sexual harassment? Do you agree that they imply different kinds of character flaws?

6. Griffith says that sexual harassment cannot be defined simply in terms of unwanted sexual advances. What does he mean by saying this, and what is his argument in support of this claim?

Case 5.1 Sexual Harassment and an Employer's Responsibility[1]

In the fall of 1986, Elizabeth Paroline applied for a job as a word processor at Unisys. She was interviewed by Charles Peterson, who had overall responsibility for the office and Edgar Moore. Unknown to Paroline, Peterson had already received complaints that Moore, as well as other men in the office, had made sexually suggestive remarks to and engaged in unwelcome touching of female employees. In response to these complaints, Peterson had convened a staff meeting in which he warned male workers not to engage in behavior that could be construed as sexual harassment and had met privately with Moore to caution him concerning his inappropriate behaviour.

[1] From Paroline v. Unisys Corp., 879 *Federal Reporter* 2d series, 100 (4th Cir. 1989).

During Paroline's interview, Moore asked her what she would do if subjected to sexual harassment. Although Peterson thought the question inappropriate, he never criticized or reprimanded Moore for asking it. Moore recommended Paroline for the job and she was subsequently hired.

Shortly after her hiring, Moore started to make sexually suggestive remarks to Paroline that she found offensive. A little while later, in December of 1986, Moore approached Paroline as she was working and started rubbing his hands on her back. He continued, even though she indicated she wished him to stop.

On January 22, 1987, a severe snowstorm forced the early closing of the office in which Paroline worked. Since she had no ride home, Paroline accepted Moore's offer of a ride. During the ride home, Moore made remarks she interpreted as sexually suggestive, kissed her, and repeatedly tried to hold her hand. When they reached her apartment, he insisted on coming in despite her objections. After several minutes in the apartment, he grabbed Paroline and began kissing her and rubbing his hand up and down her back, despite her demands that he stop. Initially, he refused to remove his hands from her body, but she eventually persuaded him to leave.

The next day, Paroline reported the incident to Peterson. According to Paroline, Peterson indicated there had been previous reports of sexual harassment in the office and promised to eliminate such behavior. Subsequently, Unisys launched a formal investigation of Moore's conduct. As a result, it warned Moore that any recurrence of sexual harassment, or any retaliation against female employees, would be grounds for immediate termination. Unisys also insisted that Moore seek counseling and limit contact with female employees to official company business. It also terminated his access to the company's Sensitive Compartmented Intelligence Facility (SCIF).

On January 29, 1987, Unisys notified Paroline of its disciplining of Moore. Paroline, having learned of Moore's alleged sexual harassment of other female workers and the failure of previous warnings to deter Moore, considered the actions of Unisys inadequate. She also expressed concern that banning Moore from the SCIF area would increase her contact with him because she had not yet obtained a security clearance to enter the SCIF and would thus be forced to remain in the same part of the office where Moore would be working. There is no evidence that Moore made any inappropriate remarks or sexual overtures toward Paroline after she complained to Peterson.

Knowing she was upset, company officials offered Paroline two weeks off. Although Unisys officials asked her not to quit, she submitted her resignation on February 15, 1987, and later filed suit against Moore and Unisys.

1. Unisys argued that it should not be held liable for Moore's actions because it took prompt and adequate remedial steps once Paroline complained to try to deter Moore from further harassment. Explain why you agree or disagree.

2. Evidence exists that after Peterson's staff meeting in which he warned male employees not to engage in behavior which could be construed as sexual harassment, a number of men, including Peterson himself, began joking about the women's complaints of sexual harassment. In court it was argued that this casts doubt on the effectiveness and sincerity of the warnings. Do you agree? Why or why not?

3. To succeed in a hostile environment claim, a plaintiff must show that he or she was not unreasonably sensitive to the working environment and that the harassment interfered with his or her ability to perform the work or significantly affected his or her psychological well-being. If Moore's behavior had not escalated and if Moore had not been in a position of authority over Paroline, could she have reasonably claimed that she was sexually harassed? Why or why not?

Case 5.2 Sexual Harassment and Conflicting Reports[2]

Brenda Purdy began working for Marwick Manufacturing Company early in March 1984 as an assembler of wallpaper sample books. In a complaint to the Ontario Human Rights Commission, she alleged that on April 23, 1984, she was sexually harassed by two coworkers, Paul Arthur and Don Bianco. Purdy alleges that Arthur grabbed her "rear end" when he walked by the workstation at which she and coworkers were assembling sample books and commented that if she would go to bed with him he would suggest to his brother-in-law, the foreman, that she be moved to a better job. Purdy states that she rejected Arthur's advance. She reports that Arthur and Bianco a little later called her back to the remote area of the plant where they worked to show her something. She claims that, upon her arrival, they showed her a book of naked women. She reports that she told them she found it uninteresting and returned to her station. She further reports that Bianco a little later walked by her table and grabbed her rear end.

She alleges that a short time afterward Arthur again asked her to come to the remote area where he and Bianco worked. She claims that when she arrived Bianco pulled down his pants in front of her, upon which she turned around and returned to her work area. According to Purdy, Arthur and Bianco passed her table a few minutes later, at which point Bianco commented that he had won the bet. Purdy understood him to mean that he had bet Arthur he would pull down his pants in front of her.

Purdy complained to the foreman who advised her to talk to the company president. She did so and, after talking with him, was moved to a separate company in the same building with which the president was also associated. She quit after two days, complaining that the work was boring.

Arthur and Bianco denied that any of the events took place as Purdy described them. They admit that Purdy did come to the remote area where they worked, but insisted that it was she who brought and displayed a pornographic magazine. They denied grabbing her posterior, and Bianco denied dropping his pants.

A subsequent investigation revealed that female employees reported finding Purdy in the washroom, visibly upset, on the afternoon in question. When questioned as to the cause of her distress, she reported that Bianco had exposed himself to her. It also revealed that Purdy was correct in her assertion that Bianco was wearing yellow underwear that day. Less in keeping with Purdy's account, however, is that the investigation also revealed that young girls who worked on the premises complained that Purdy had shown them pornographic materials. Also disturbing was the fact that Purdy made no attempt to have fellow workers at her workstation corroborate her story of Arthur and Bianco grabbing her posterior.

1. How would you attempt to determine whether Arthur and Bianco were guilty of sexual harassment? Does the difficulty of determining who is telling the truth have any bearing on what punishment should be contemplated?

2. If the reports of Purdy showing pornographic material to young girls are true, is she guilty of sexual harassment?

[2]Based on *Purdy v. Marwick Manufacturing Co.* as reported in *Canadian Human Rights Reporter*, Vol. 9, Decision 757, Paragraphs 37425-37461, July 1988, pp. D4840-D4845.

Further Readings for Chapter 5

Jan Crosthwaite and Christine Swanton, "On the Nature of Sexual Harassment," *Women and Philosophy: Australasian Journal of Philosophy* 64 (Supp.), 1986, pp. 91-106.

Natalie Dandekar, "Contrasting Consequences: Bringing Charges of Sexual Harassment Compared with Other Cases of Whistleblowing," *Journal of Business Ethics* 9(2), February 1990, pp. 151–158.

Susan M. Dodds, Lucy Frost, Robert Pargetter, and Elizabeth W. Prior, "Sexual Harassment," *Social Theory and Practice* 14, Summer 1988, pp. 111–130.

Iddo Landau, "On the Definition of Sexual Harassment," *Australasian Journal of Philosophy* 77, June 1999, pp. 216–223.

Iddo Landau, "Is Sexual Harassment Research Biased?," *Public Affairs Quarterly* 13, July 1999, pp. 241–254.

Loann S. Lublin, "Thomas Battle Spotlights Harassment," *Wall Street Journal,* October 9, 1991, pp. B1, B5. Also see his article "Harassment: Views in the Workplace," *Wall Street Journal,* October 10, 1991, p. B1.

Catherine MacKinnon, *Sexual Harassment of Working Women* (New Haven, CT: Yale University Press, 1979).ww

INFOTRAC COLLEGE EDITION To learn more about the topics from this chapter, you can use the following words to conduct an electronic search on InfoTrac College Edition, an online library of journals. Here you will find a multitude of articles from various sources and perspectives: *www.infotrac-college.com/wadsworth/access.html*

sexual harassment

gender discrimination

sexism

Chapter 6

Safety
in the Workplace

Introduction

THE ISSUE OF SAFETY in the workplace is obviously an important one. Employees in many professions routinely work with hazardous materials and dangerous machinery. Even when this is not the case, there remain legitimate concerns with regard to the environment in which employees work. The health of a clerical worker may be just as much at risk due to a poorly ventilated office building or an improperly shielded video terminal as that of a worker in what seems to be a more dangerous job. It is essential, therefore, to examine how occupational safety and health are best protected, and how workers' rights are to be construed in relation to issues of safety and health.

The selections in this chapter deal with questions of the rights of employees with regard to the materials with which they work and the conditions under which they work. In "The Employer-Employee Relationship and the Right to Know," Anita Superson argues that, although it has not been commonly recognized, employers have the duty to inform employees and prospective employees of all safety and health hazards associated with their workplace. She argues that, just as a patient has a right to know the risks involved in medical procedures, so an employee has a right to know the risks in his or her workplace. This is not to suggest there are not important dissimilarities between the physician-patient relationship and the employer-employee relationship; rather, it is to claim that whether an individual is in the role of patient or employee, respect for that individual's autonomy implies the right to give informed consent to any risks or hazards with which the individual will be faced.

Superson further argues that the reason employees' right to such information has not been generally recognized lies in the fact that the employer-employee relationship is nonfiduciary, that is, there exists little or no trust on behalf of each party in the actions of the other. There exists, therefore, a strong tendency for employer and employee to treat each other merely as means to an end. Although she recommends reconceiving the employer-employee relationship so that it becomes fiduciary in nature, she thinks a fiduciary employer-employee relationship is consistent with retaining a capitalist system.

Robert Sass, in his article "The Workers' Right to Know, Participate and Refuse Hazardous Work: A Manifesto Right," broadens the discussion. He believes that not only do employees have the right to be informed of hazards in the workplace, but they also have the right to participate in designing and controlling the work environment and process. He argues that the present legal concept of risk should be broadened to apply to work environment matters such as organization and pace of work, scheduling, and job cycle, to name only a few. He suggests that in conventional factories, although lip service is paid to the importance of safety rules, there is pressure on workers to place production before safety. He also comments that "accident proneness" is far less likely to be the result of careless workers than the result of improper management. In his view, workers' lack of control over their work environment is a major cause of accidents. Although he does not explicitly address the issue, his recommendations seem to require considerable modification of any theory of a free market of labor.

Quite a different point of view is expressed by Tibor Machan in his article "Human Rights, Workers' Rights, and the 'Right' to Occupational Safety." In contrast to Sass, who contends that the employer-employee relationship involves special duties owed by employers to employees, Machan argues that there do not exist special workers' rights. He holds that workers possess the same basic rights as other human beings and defends a free labor market. He denies that a free labor market need lead to the exploitation of workers. In his view, taking seriously the basic rights that all human beings possess is sufficient to address the evils that motivate many to invoke the notion of workers' rights. Thus, for example, an employer knowingly or negligently subjecting workers to hazards at the workplace can be seen as fraud. Without claiming any special rights as employees, but simply appealing to their basic right to liberty, workers could press their case in court.

Machan goes on to claim that the moral force of most attacks on the free labor market theory is a result of the fact that many presumed examples of the free labor market really constitute violations of that theory. He argues that a strict and consistent interpretation of taking basic human rights seriously yields all the protection that is needed in the workplace.

The Employer-Employee Relationship and the Right to Know

ANITA M. SUPERSON*

I

DANGERS LURK in the workplace. It has been reported that more than 2,200,000 workers are disabled, and more than 14,000 are killed annually as a result of accidents on the job.[1] The causes include safety hazards such as fires, explosions, electrocution, dangerous machinery, as well as health hazards such as loud noise, harmful dusts, asbestos particles, toxic gases, carcinogens, and radiation.[2] The fact that these and other dangers exist is problem enough; but even more problematic is that an employee's awareness of such dangers, prior to being exposed to them, is often minimal, at best. If an employee is to have any say in what happens to his person, what needs to be established—at least more firmly than it is currently—is an employee's[3] right to know about the presence of health and safety hazards in the workplace.

In what follows, I shall first examine the current status of an employee's right to know. I shall argue that it is the very nature of the employer-employee relationship that gives rise to an employee's limited awareness of on-the-job hazards. Next, I shall offer what I think are the philosophical justifications for an employee's right to know. Finally, in light of these justifications, I shall argue that establishing

an employee's right to know will, in fact, benefit both the employee and the employer, and be one step toward achieving a fiduciary relationship.

Throughout this essay, I compare the employer-employee relationship to that of the physician and patient. Although there are some disparities between the two, the comparison is helpful in that it points out that the moral basis for establishing a right to know for a patient is the same as for an employee, yet the two are not accorded the same recognition by the law. To show that the right to know for patients is not recognized as being the same for employees, yet that it is based on the same philosophical foundation for the same reasons, only strengthens the argument for establishing a right to know in the workplace.

II

In the medical setting a person's right to know about risks involved in different kinds of treatment has been recognized under the guise of informed consent. Recently, there have been many attempts in the law and in various health codes to ensure that patients have given informed consent to medical treatments or experimentation. In *Canterbury v. Spence*, 1972, Circuit Court Judge Spotswood W. Robinson III rules that since "every human being of adult years and sound mind has a right to determine what shall be done with his own body," a physician has a "duty of reasonable disclosure of the choices with respect to proposed therapy and the dangers inherently and potentially involved."[4] Similarly, the American Hospital Association's *Patient's Bill of Rights* (1973) states that "The patient has the right to receive from his physician information necessary to give informed consent prior to the start of any procedure and/or

---

*I am greatly indebted to George Brenkert for his initial suggestion to write this paper, for his very helpful comments on earlier versions, as well as for his encouragement to send it out.

[1] Manuel G. Velasquez, *Business Ethics: Concepts and Cases* (Englewood Cliffs, NJ: Prentice-Hall, Inc., 1982), p. 311.

[2] See Nicholas A. Ashford, *Crisis in the Workplace: Occupational Disease and Injury* (Cambridge, MA: The MIT Press, 1976), pp. 68–83, for a thorough and interesting description of these hazards.

[3] Although I shall use the term "employee" throughout this essay, my arguments shall apply also to the prospective employee since he is faced with a similar choice, that is, whether or not to accept a job in a hazardous work environment.

[4] *Canterbury v. Spence*, US Court of Appeals, District of Columbia Circuit, May 19, 1972, 464 Federal Reporter, 2nd Series, 772.

From Business and Professional Ethics Journal *3(4), Fall 1983. Reprinted by permission.*

treatment."[5] Again, the Nuremberg Code, which focuses on guidelines used in human experimentation carried out in Nazi Germany, specifies that the human subject "should have sufficient knowledge and comprehension of the elements of the subject matter involved as to enable him to make an understanding and enlightened decision."[6] These and other such examples show that through informed consent, a patient's or research subject's right to know about the risks and hazards involved in medical procedures is firmly entrenched. We shall see later that this right is protected by the law. Though the amount of information given to patients may vary among physicians, consent forms must be signed by the patient or by his next of kin. This is true for all patients undergoing most invasive forms of treatment (e.g., surgery).

But the headway that has been made in the medical setting is, unfortunately, unparalleled in the workplace. It was not until 1980 that the Occupational Safety and Health Administration (OSHA) of the United States Department of Labor established the legal right of an employee to "access to employer maintained exposure and medical records relevant to employees exposed to toxic substances and harmful physical agents."[7] In 1983, OSHA issued a final rule requiring

chemical manufacturers and importers to assess the hazards of chemicals which they produce and import, and all employers having workplaces in the manufacturing division . . . to provide information to their employees concerning hazardous chemicals by means of hazard communication programs including labels, material safety data sheets, training, and access to written records. In addition, distributors of hazardous chemicals are required to ensure that containers they distribute are properly labeled, and that a material safety data sheet is provided to their customers. . . .[8]

On the same note, the National Institute for Occupational Safety and Health (NIOSH) reported that workers had the right to know whether or not they were exposed to hazardous chemical and physical agents regulated by the Federal Government.[9] Finally, the National Labor Relations Act (NLRA) recognizes a labor union's right to information that is relevant to a collective bargaining issue, including safety rules and practices.[10] Although these regulations are a step in the direction of securing a worker's right to know, they are insufficient.

First, though the OSHA rulings recently have been expanded from simply permitting access to an employer's exposure and medical records to requiring assessment of the hazards of chemicals and providing information about such chemicals to an employee by means of labels and material safety data sheets, they fail to extend protection through information to many workers. The 1983 regulation applies only to employees in the manufacturing division, yet does not apply to employees in other divisions such as mining, construction, trade, etc. The reasoning underlying OSHA's restriction to manufacturing is that it has determined that the employees in this division "are at the greatest risk of experiencing health effects from exposure to hazardous chemicals."[11] The agency thus hoped to regulate that sector in which it could be most effective for the greatest number of employees. So, although warning labels and safety data sheets, as well as the assessment of hazards which they necessitate, certainly are positive steps toward securing a worker's right to know, they apply to about only fifty percent of all workers.[12]

[5]"A Patient's Bill of Rights," American Hospital Association, reprinted in Mappes & Zembaty (eds.), *Biomedical Ethics* (New York: McGraw-Hill, Inc., 1981), pp. 87–89.

[6]"Declaration of Helsinki," World Medical Association, reprinted in Mappes & Zembaty, ibid., pp. 145–147.

[7]*Federal Register,* Vol. 45 no. 102, Friday, May 23, 1980, Rules and Regulations, Dept. of Labor, Occupational Safety and Health Administration, 23CFR Part 1910, 35212.

[8]*Federal Register,* Vol. 48 no. 228, Friday, November 25, 1983, Rules and Regulations, Dept. of Labor, Occupational Safety and Health Administration, 29CFR Part 1910, 53280.

[9]Ruth R. Faden and Tom L. Beauchamp, "The Right to Risk Information and the Right to Refuse Health Hazards in the Workplace," in *Ethical Theory of Business* (2nd Ed.), Tom L. Beauchamp and Norman E. Bowie (eds.), (Englewood Cliffs, NJ: Prentice-Hall, Inc., 1983), pp. 196–206.

[10]Time D. Wermager, "Union's Right to Information vs. Confidentiality of Employer Trade Secrets: Accommodating the Interests Through Procedural Burdens and Restricted Disclosure," 66 *Iowa Law Review,* 1333–51, July, 1981.

[11]*Federal Register,* Vol. 48 no. 228, Friday, November 25, 1983, Rules and Regulations, Dept. of Labor, Occupational Safety and Health Administration, 29CFR Part 1910, 53284.

[12]Ibid., Table 1, p. 53285.

Second, the OSHA rulings apply only to employees which the agency defines as "a current employee, a former employee, or an employee being assigned or transferred to work where there will be exposure to toxic substances or harmful physical agents."[13] The rulings exclude provision of information regarding hazards to the *prospective* employee. This is problematic because the prospective employee is faced with a similar choice, that is, the choice of whether or not to take on a job which entails working in hazardous conditions. Yet providing this information to prospective employees may raise problems in itself. Employers may find this too time-consuming a task to perform for *each* person contending for a position; or, they may feel an obligation to provide this information only to employees since it is this group of persons which has pledged some degree of loyalty to the company. These problems, though, should be worked around for the sake of the prospective employee who will avoid the trouble of committing himself to a job if he knows in advance that the hazardous working conditions outweigh the benefits of taking on the job.

Third, the OSHA rulings do not apply to all safety and health hazards. The 1980 ruling regulates "toxic substances and harmful physical agents," and the 1983 ruling regulates "hazardous chemicals." Clearly, these rulings do not account for a whole spectrum of on-the-job hazards, some of which were mentioned at the outset of this essay. A worker's right to know of these hazards has yet to be firmly established.

This is not to imply that an employer has no responsibility to keep his workplace safe. In fact, in 1970, the Occupational Safety and Health Act (OSHAct) was passed, establishing safety and health standards for all workers other than those employed by federal, state, and local governments. The Act requires an employer to ensure that his workplace is "free from recognized hazards that are causing or likely to cause death or serious physical harm."[14] But this act, too, is insufficient. It has been reported[15] that the Act protects against only

"recognized hazards," defined as those which "can be detected by the common human senses, unaided by testing devices, and which are generally known in the industry to be hazards." Indeed, this leaves many hazards unaccounted for. It is those hazards not prohibited by law about which the employee may not be informed.

The NIOSH report is inadequate in similar ways. The Institute recognizes a worker's right to know only whether or not they were *exposed* to hazardous chemical and physical agents regulated by the Federal Government. Its inadequacies are that it does not recognize a right to know of hazards prior to exposure to them, and that like the OSHA rulings, it applies only to chemical and physical agents, rather than all on-the-job hazards.

Finally, the National Labor Relations Act accords some protection to employees who belong to labor unions but is also limited. It established that labor unions had a right to "information that is in the hands of the employer and is relevant to bargainable issues."[16] An employee's right to know about hazardous working conditions is usually recognized as being "relevant to bargainable issues." But what sometimes occurs is a conflict between the employee's right to know and the company's right to keep trade secrets. A trade secret has been defined under the *Restatement of Torts* as "any formula, device, or information, used in a business which gives its holder a competitive advantage over those without the secret."[17] Now if a labor union requests information about job hazards, but this information will expose an employer's trade secrets, thereby jeopardizing his competitive advantage, the employer need not necessarily release this information. And in different cases, the law has favored both sides.

In *Borden Chemical,* an administrative law judge of the National Labor Relations Board determined that Borden had refused to bargain in good faith when it failed to release information to the labor union. It was then ordered to supply the information to the union. The reason behind the ruling was that Borden failed to show that disclosure of

---

[13]Ibid., Vol. 45, p. 35215.

[14]The Occupational Safety and Health Act of 1970 (Public Law 91-596), Section 5(a)(1), reprinted in Ashford, pp. 545–75.

[15]Robert Stewart Smith, *The Occupational Safety and Health Act: Its Goals and Its Achievements* (Washington, D.C.:

American Enterprise Institute for Public Policy Research, 1976), p. 9.

[16]Wermager, *op. cit.,* p. 1333.

[17]David Carey Fraser, "Trade Secrets and the NLRA: Employee's Right to Health and Safety Information," 14 *University of San Francisco Law Review,* 495–524, Spring, 1980.

the information would damage its competitive position.[18] Essentially, Borden failed to show how its trade secrets would reach its competitors.[19] In *Colgate-Palmolive,* however, an administrative law judge ruled that the employer was obliged to reveal a list of chemicals in the workplace *except* those constituting trade secrets.[20] Colgate-Palmolive apparently showed how it would be disadvantaged were its trade secrets to be revealed. We can surmise from these two cases and from the OSHA and NIOSH rulings that an employee's right to know is not accorded full protection by the law, and, in fact, may be denied by the law.

III

Why is the right to know in the workplace not firmly grounded? It is the argument of this section that protection of such a right is limited because of the very nature of the employer-employee relationship.

This relationship can be best defined as a non-fiduciary one, meaning that there is little or no trust on behalf of each party in the actions of the other party. This lack of trust stems from the expectations each party has for forming a personal relationship. In most cases, the expectations dictate a non-personal interaction. The employee often feels the same; he views himself as a person for hire, whose function is to perform a certain job for the company or institution in exchange for wages and perhaps a few fringe benefits. If the employee does not like his job for whatever reason, he is free to leave. The employer is also free (for the most part) to fire any employee who is not performing his job in what the employer judges to be a favorable way. As a result, many employees remain with a certain company for only a short period of time, thus making it difficult to come to know their employer personally, if this be at all possible.

Both the employer and employee normally do not enter into their relation thinking that they can trust each other to look out for the other's best interests. Probably the only form of trust existent between the two parties is that the employer will pay the employee a wage that at least matches the work he puts out, and that the employee will perform the job he is asked to do in a way that is normally expected. These are the roles both the employer and employee expect each other to take on. It would be difficult to establish a fiduciary relationship under such expectations. What adds to the difficulty is that often the employer and employee do not even know each other at any kind of personal level. I ask rhetorically: How can a fiduciary relationship be established if no relationship has been established?

Another feature of the employer-employee relationship which adds to its nonfiduciary nature is the reasons both the employee and the employer have for entering into their relationship. The employee enters a relationship with his employer primarily for monetary reasons; he seeks employment in order to earn wages with which he can secure the goods he needs to live. The employer, on the other hand, enters a relationship primarily for the sake of profit-making. His position in respect to that of the employee is one of power. It derives its power from the fact that the employer offers the employee a benefit—wages—if he accepts and performs a job. The employer stands to benefit directly from his employee. He needs a certain job to be done; the company's profits depend upon whether the task is accomplished. And the financial success of the company is directly related to the employer.

Both the expectations of the employee and employer, as well as the reasons for each entering into the relationship, make it likely that an employer would use his employee merely as a means to his own end, to borrow a notion from Kant. That is, the employer, seeking to augment his profits (the end), may use the employee merely as a means to achieve that end. One way in which he could do this is to fail to inform an employee about hazardous work conditions. Failure to inform an employee about these hazards is to deny him information that may affect his decision to stay on the job. And by remaining on the job, the employee works in part for the employer's benefit, that is, to increase the company's profits. In this way, the employee is used as a means to the employer's end.

More specifically, if the expectations of both the employer and employee of each other are as I have described, it is easy for the former to use the latter as a means to an end because being so far removed on a personal level from the employee, he does not

[18]Wermager, *op. cit.,* pp. 1335–36.
[19]Wermager, *op. cit.,* pp. 1343.
[20]Wermager, *op. cit.,* pp. 1345.

feel a sense of obligation towards the employee's welfare. All he has invested in the relationship is that the job gets done. And since the employee does not view the relationship as a fiduciary one, he has no basis for trusting the employer to ensure that the workplace is free from hazards, or at least to inform him of the hazards that do exist. Indeed it would be nice for the employer to do either; yet the employee probably does not expect it, and certainly cannot trust his employer to do so.

And, if the reasons the employer and employee have for entering their relationship are as I have described, this is another reason why an employer may use his employee merely as a means to his own end. If the employer is aware of the power he holds over his employee, that is, that he to a large extent controls the employee's means of livelihood, he may feel no obligation to inform the employee about on-the-job hazards. In fact, somewhat ironically, the employer may even go so far as to view the employee as using *him,* the *employer,* as a means to an end. This belief is based upon the fact that the employee may take on a job solely for the purpose of obtaining money, perhaps with minimum effort put forth, and that the employee is free to leave when he so desires. If the employer has this attitude toward his employee, it becomes easier for him not to inform the employee of hazards in the workplace.

The nature of the employer-employee relationship differs from that of the physician-patient in these two respects. Specifically, the expectations of the physician and patient are of a much more trusting nature. Oftentimes, the physician and patient have established a personal relationship; they, for example, know somewhat about each other's lifestyles, values, etc. Patients generally expect and trust their physician to act in their best interests. They expect that physicians will inform them of the hazards and risks involved in various medical treatments, and that together they will arrive at a decision about what is the best course of action to take. And if the physician fails to inform his patient about these hazards and risks, the patient usually assumes that the information was withheld for his, the patient's, own benefit.

Furthermore, the reasons for the patient and physician entering a relationship are different from that of the employer and employee. Patients seek the advice of a physician because, simply put, they want to be treated for an illness. They expect that the physician will do this, and will give the patient information on forms of treatment. This is what the patient pays for, and thus expects to receive. The physician, in turn, should feel that he has an obligation to provide this information to the patient, unless he can justify withholding it.

The physician's reasons for entering the relationship are different from the employer's. Rather than being solely, or at least primarily, profit-motivated, physicians often view their role as one of benefitting the sick. Certainly there are many physicians who enter the profession for monetary reasons: I do not wish to deny this. Yet, as any physician would admit, there are easier ways to make money. Still, the physician, like the employer, is in a power position. But the source of the physician's power is different. He does not stand to benefit from performing a certain therapy on any *particular* patient (unless, of course, the patient is indeed unique), for it is likely that another patient will choose to undergo that treatment. And, more importantly, physicians will always have patients seeking their services because persons will always get sick. Unless a physician is so inadequate, he can rest assured that he will be in business for a long time. This gives him less reason to deny patients information they need concerning the hazards of treatment. Thus, a physician's power position is not as threatened by loss of profit as is an employer's. He therefore has less reason than an employer to use a person merely as a means to his own end.

Moreover, an employer's reasons for withholding information are often different from those of the physician. While the physician may feel he is acting in the patient's best interests (whether or not he is certainly is open to debate) when he withholds information concerning the risks of treatment, this is not often the case with the employer. The employer withholds information about on-the-job hazards not because he wishes to protect the employee, or to act in the employee's best interests, but because he wants to protect his *own* interests. He wants the company to profit, and this may be possible only if certain hazardous assignments are made. The employer may feel that he is justified in withholding information about risks from the employee. After all, the employee does not have to stay on *this* job; he is free to leave. The employer's reasons for withholding information are thus, unlike those of most physicians, self-interested.

It is these features of the employer-employee relationship, namely, the expectations of both parties, their reasons for entering into the relationship, and the employer's reasons for withholding information, which all contribute to the nonfiduciary nature of this relationship. These features may, of course, all be a result of the capitalist system. If this be so, some persons may argue that the very nature of the employer-employee relationship can be changed only by changing the socio-economic system. I believe this is false, and in Section V I will argue that establishing an employee's right to know will, in fact, make headway in changing the relationship into one that is fiduciary in nature.

IV

We have seen that the nature of the employer-employee relationship is such that it is difficult to establish an employee's right to know. Employers, on the one hand, find little or no reason to give their employees information about hazards in the workplace. In turn, employees find little or no reason to expect to receive this information. The differences in the nature of the relationship are, in all probability, responsible for the dissimilarities in the establishment of the right to know. But should this difference exist? Is there a difference in the choices faced by a person as patient versus a person as employee that will justify the difference in the recognition of the right to know?

I suggest that there is not. Although many disparities exist between the relationships, an important similarity grounds the right to know. It is this: in both cases, the person wants to know the dangers involved for the *same* reasons. He wants to know the risks that may be incurred to his body so that he can decide whether or not to expose himself to those risks. The information is needed for him to make a reasonable choice.

In both situations, the moral basis of the right to know lies in the principle of autonomy. Much talk has been generated about this principle since Mill and Kant recognized its importance. Although the literature offers a variety of definitions, this principle is usually defined in such a way as to include the notion of making one's own decisions affecting one's own life without coercion from others. In order for one to make a responsible decision, he must be informed about the choices with which he is faced. Just as a patient must be informed about the risks involved in a certain treatment in order for him to decide if he wants that treatment, an employee, too, must be informed about the hazards involved in working under certain conditions if he is to make a responsible, autonomous choice about whether or not to subject his person to such risks. In either case, if such information is not disclosed, the person's autonomy has been placed in jeopardy.

The choice faced by both the patient and the employee is one of whether or not to subject one's person to risk of harm. It may be objected that the harms which may be incurred in the workplace are less serious than those which may be incurred in the medical setting. But this is simply not true. The harms incurred in the workplace may be just as serious, and may not be as immediate as those incurred in the medical setting. For example, side-effects from an operation or from taking certain drugs are often known by the patient and/or his physician soon after they are incurred. Harms resulting from on-the-job hazards, however, often take considerable time to manifest themselves, and often require long-term exposure to take effect. For example, chronic berylliosis, constituted by coughing, dyspnea, and anorexia, may appear years after exposure to beryllium.[21] And cancer may take years to manifest itself after exposure to coal tar, paraffin, asbestos, vinyl chloride, and benzene. Other toxic materials do not produce side-effects in the exposed person, but instead in his or her children. These are either mutagenic in nature, in which case they change the genetic makeup of the offspring, or teratogenic in nature, in which case they are capable of causing birth defects in the offspring.[22] This is not to imply that all harms incurred in the medical setting are immediate, and those incurred on the job are made manifest years after exposure; instead, the point is that many do follow this pattern.

Because the harms incurred in the workplace often are made manifest years later, it is more difficult for an employer to face liability charges. In the medical realm, patients can be awarded damages either in battery or in negligence. Traditionally, patients can sue physicians for damages in battery if they are touched, treated, or researched upon

[21]Ashford, *op. cit.*, pp. 76.
[22]Ashford, *op. cit.*, pp. 78.

without consent.[23] In a British Columbia case, it was reported[24] that a patient who suffered loss of smell and partial loss of taste after surgery was awarded damages in battery because she was unaware of these risks at the time of her consent. In America, failure to disclose risks to patients "is considered a breach of the physician's general duty to care to give reasonable information and advice to his patient."[25] To be awarded damages in battery, the patient need only establish that "what was done differed substantially from that to which he assented."[26]

Patients can sue also for damages in negligence. In Canada, it is reported that the physician should inform the patient of the nature and seriousness of treatment lest he be held negligent. The duty in negligence "is based on the nature of the physician-patient relationship as a trust," thus imposing a "basic requirement of honesty upon the physician."[27] In order for a physician to be found negligent, the patient must show that there was a breach of the duty of disclosure and that he, the patient, would not have consented had the required disclosure been given, and that he suffered a loss as a result.[28]

Although a patient can sue for damages in either battery or negligence, an employee has no such privilege. Establishment of workmen's compensation has prevented the right to sue in tort.[29] Prior to the establishment of workmen's compensation, employees could settle under tort law and receive payments for both loss of income as well as for "pain and suffering." Workmen's compensation statutes, however, include payment for loss of income, but only limited payment for "pain and suffering."[30] One source reports that *no* payment for pain and suffering is included.[31] Thus, employers do not have to pay for the full consequences of their negligence. Employees themselves must shoulder most of the burden of costs for employer negligence. This seems especially unjust when we are reminded of the fact that an employee's right to know is not firmly established.

One basis, then, for establishing a right to know in the workplace is that it ensures that an employee is given information necessary for him to be able to make a choice which may significantly affect his life. Informing an employee of workplace hazards puts him in the position of deciding whether or not he wants to be exposed to hazards, and thereby is one step in the direction of promoting his autonomy. Establishment of a right to know is especially important for the workers since he does not have much recourse against his employer if damages ensue.

Another basis for establishing this right lies in the notion of fairness of contract. When a person is hired for a job, there is an implicit contract made between the employer and employee, the terms of which spell out that person X will do job A and will be paid by person Y. This contract requires, like any fair contract, that both parties know what they are contracting to. It is insufficient that an employee know he is consenting to do a certain job in a certain way at a certain pace, and so on. If hazards which may produce harm to his person are involved, he should be made aware of them before he enters the contract. If he is not made aware of the hazards, and enters the contract with the employer, he is not giving fully informed consent to the relevant terms of the contract. The contract is thus unfair.

A third basis for establishing an employee's right to know is partly economic, partly moral. It lies in Milton Friedman's notion of business' social responsibility, namely "to use its resources and engage in activities designed to increase its profits so long as it stays within the rules of the game, which is to say, engages in open and free competition, without deception or fraud."[32] The moral

[23]Karen Lebacqz and Robert J. Levine, "Informed Consent in Human Research: Ethical and Legal Aspects," in *Encyclopedia of Bioethics,* Vol. 2, Warren T. Reich, ed.-in-chief, (New York: The Free Press, 1978), pp. 754–762.

[24]Gilbert Sharpe, LLM, "Recent Canadian Court Decisions on Consent," *Bioethics Quarterly,* Vol. 2 No. 1 (Spring, 1980), 56–63.

[25]Sharpe, ibid., p. 58.

[26]Sharpe, ibid., p. 61.

[27]Janice R. Dillon, "Informed Consent and the Disclosure of Risks of Treatment: The Supreme Court of Canada Decides," *Bioethics Quarterly,* Vol. 3 No. 3&4, (Fall/Winter, 1981), 156–162.

[28]Dillon, ibid., p. 160.

[29]Ashford, *op. cit.,* p. 350.

[30]Ashford, *op. cit.,* p. 392.

[31]"Occupational Health Risks and the Worker's Right to Know," 90 *Yale Law Journal,* 1792–1810, July, 1981.

[32]Milton Friedman, *Capitalism and Freedom* (Chicago: The University of Chicago Press, 1962), p. 133.

justification for the right to know, using Friedman's terms of business' social responsibility, lies in his normative judgment that business should not engage in deceptive practices. Though Friedman does not spell out what this entails, surely withholding information from the prospective employee—information which is likely to influence his decision—is a deceptive practice, prohibited even on Friedman's libertarian analysis of business in the free market system.

An economic justification for the right to know also can be found in Friedman and other free market advocates. It is this: in order to ensure that the free market really *is* free, persons should be able to enter the occupation of their choosing (at least insofar as they meet the qualifications). This choice must be informed. If information about job hazards is withheld, the choice will not be fully informed. And if the choice is not fully informed, it is not truly free. Thus, ignoring the right to know, besides violating moral principles such as autonomy and fairness of contract, violates one of the fundamental economic bases of the free market system.

V

If an employee's right to know becomes firmly established, certain implications are likely to follow. On the negative side, the employer will be faced with the difficult task of determining how much and what kind of information ought to be given to the employee. The employer will have to devote time and effort to find out just what hazards exist, and to convey the results of his findings to the employee. And if the risks involved in taking on a certain job are very high, or very serious, the employer may have difficulty in hiring someone for the job. Also, the company's trade secrets undoubtedly will sometimes be revealed.

While I do not wish to diminish the inconvenience these implications bring to the employer, none is too important to override the employee's right to know. Indeed, there certainly are ways to lessen the inconvenience while still bringing about the desired effects.

More importantly though, it is reasonable to assume that both parties are likely to benefit by establishing an employee's right to know.

It benefits the employee in several ways. First, since the employer will have to ascertain what are hazards in the workplace, he may eliminate at least some of them for the sake of attracting employees. Thus, the environment may be safer for the employee. Second, if the employee is presented with the relevant information about on-the-job hazards, it places into the hands of the *employee* the informed decision of whether or not to accept a position. The employee can then make his *own* choice of whether or not to expose himself to those hazards. Moreover, informing the employee of hazards in the workplace ensures him that the contract made with his employer is fair and not based upon deception. In these ways, it establishes trust in the employer.

The employer, too, benefits. Once he has given such information to his employee, if the employee willingly accepts the job knowing that to which he has consented, and is in some way harmed, the employer would decrease his liability in many cases. After all, it was the employee's decision to expose himself to the hazards. He knew what to expect, and is responsible for his decision. The employer, in many cases, will avoid paying compensation.

Most important is that the right to know may go so far as to establish a fiduciary relationship between employer and employee, much the same as that existent between many patients and their physicians. Part of what is involved in such a relationship is that both parties trust each other to look after each other's best interests. The employer can accomplish this by improving his work environment, by informing his employee of existent hazards, and the like.

The employee, also, can look out for his employer's best interests by unifying his goals with the goals of his employer. If the employee is made aware of risks involved in taking on a certain job, and yet he consents to taking on that job (assuming, of course, that he understands the risks and is not coerced into the job perhaps by another person or because he is unable to find an alternative), he has invested a part of himself into that relationship. He admits his willingness to work for an employer to achieve his employer's goals. The goals of the employer are then shared with the employee. And since the employee knows he is not being deceived about the conditions under which he works, he may have more incentive to do his job well. This, too, is likely to benefit the employer.

It is interesting to note, in conclusion, that the very nature of the employer-employee relationship which makes it difficult to secure an employee's right to know can, in fact, be changed into one of a fiduciary nature through the establishment of a right to know. We have seen that though the philosophical basis for securing a right to know in the workplace is the same as in the medical setting and that the harms which may possibly be incurred are similar, this right is more firmly grounded in the medical setting than in the workplace. What needs to be firmly established for the benefit of both the employer and employee in order to make headway in achieving a fiduciary relationship is an employee's right to know.

The Workers' Right to Know, Participate and Refuse Hazardous Work: A Manifesto Right

ROBERT SASS

I. Introduction

WORKER RIGHTS in workplace health and safety is crucial in bringing about necessary reforms in working conditions, especially their right to know about the chemicals they work with, and to participate on a daily basis regarding work environment matters—both quantitative (noise, dust, etc.) and qualitative (work organization and job design questions), and their right to refuse a job believed (not known) to be dangerous to their well-being.

It can also be argued that existing worker rights (to know, participate and refuse) should be extended and deepened to legally permit workers in industry to deal with work organization (as a social concept) and job design (individual relation to machine) matters, including pace of work, monotony, scheduling, sexual harassment, job cycle, etc., as well as those work environment matters which are important to workers (i.e. daily punishments and humiliations). The extension of the present-day legal concept of "risk" to ensure worker involvement and increased control of their working conditions can also be argued as a moral right derived from a "fundamental need" (health and safety) in the same way arguments were made on behalf of universal medical care. The extension of present-day limited or partial worker rights in occupational health and safety statutes and regulations ought to be "stretched" to deal with greater worker control over work environment matters and the work process.

While this development can be argued as a practical consideration, we must, nonetheless classify this cluster of proposed right as *manifesto rights* for the obvious reason that they are not generally accepted at the present time.

Presently, management and corporate *interests* go beyond what is necessary to maximize efficiency in production with equity. What is, therefore, desirable is the extension of certain civil rights into industry. And by increasing worker rights, we also increase productivity and efficiency, and, more importantly ensure greater justice in industry. This paper will specifically focus on the need to increase worker rights in regard to work environment matters. That is the right of the worker to participate in work environment issues, and to have greater control over the work process. After all, if you neglect and debase workers in order to increase efficiency, you will in the end decrease productivity and make our society poorer. Present-day worker "punishments" and humiliations cannot be justified by appeals to increased productivity and economic "law." An individual worker is more than a "hand," commodity or factor of production only, but something greater, more precious and sacred than material wealth.

A. PRODUCTIVITY VERSUS EQUITY

While it is morally necessary to increase production and equitable distribution of wealth in a world where there is enormous impoverishment and

From Journal of Business Ethics 5: 129–136, 1986. © 1986 by Kluwer Academic Publishers. Reprinted by permission of Kluwer Academic Publishers.

wide-spread starvation, there is no reason why this wealth should be based upon the commodification of labour. Especially, when this form of production and organization of industry results in the de-skilling and dehumanizing of a large part of the workforce.

Current employment relations evolved during the transition from feudalism to capitalism (from simple to composite production. In jurisprudential terms, from a status to a contract society). This development by the law is based upon a "relationship of services"[1] (in contrast to commitment or obligation). According to H. Glasbeek:

> This accords with the notion that an entrepreneur in a competitive society should be free to invest and to dispose of his capital as he sees fit and to be subjected to as little external noneconomic restraint as is consonant with social needs. The upshot of legal acquiescence with this approach is the imposition of onerous duties on the employee as compared with those which burden the employer.
>
> . . . even under collective bargaining regimes all the initial decisions remain an employer's to make. Thus, how much to invest, where to do so, what products shall be made, what amount, what quality, what processes are to be used, what *substances* are to be employed, and so on, are all decisions left to the employer.[2] [Emphasis mine].

In essence, employer freedom of disposition with respect to capital ownership is the supreme legitimizing principle of private ownership. This includes the right not to use, to destroy, to alienate capital ("flight of capital") and the right to buy, to organize, and to control the labour of others, as well as to make decisions concerning the goals of production and the use of surplus value.

While collective agreements and regulation may limit these rights, private ownership remains essentially undisturbed. In Canada today, it is generally accepted by arbitrators that the rights to "manage and operate the enterprise, assign work, determine work methods, procedures and equipment, schedule production, and direct the workplace" are reserved to management.[3] It is "not unusual for unions to withdraw entirely from management decisions at this level."[4]

In a recent study entitled "The Limits of Trade Union Power in Organizational Decision Making," the authors conclude that

> Despite the popular image of powerful unions, such tangential evidence that does exist suggests that the actual power of trades unions over organizational level decisions is relatively low, irrespective of desired or actual participation in the decision making process.[5]

The prevailing residual or reserved rights theory is different from the "status quo" approach which supports the view that the *status quo* should prevail if workers or their bargaining agent oppose or disagree with a management decision until the matter is mutually resolved,[6] even though the contract is silent.

Management's rights under the common law explicitly vested the employer with sole control over the business and management of its affairs, infusing the employment contract with the traditional law of "master-servant." This, in effect, divests the employer of any sense of duty, obligation and responsibility toward those he employs. The employment contract in law emphasizes the *limited* nature of the parties to each other while reserving full authority of direction and control to the employer. The result is, of course, the *limited* rights of workers.

In effect, the employment contract is in large part a legal device for guaranteeing to management

---

[1]Glasbeek, Harry J., "The Contract of Employment at Common Law," in Anderson and Gunderson, *Union-Management Relations in Canada* (Addison-Wesley, 1982), p. 73.

[2]Ibid., p. 73–74.

[3]Swan, Kenneth P., "Union Impact on Management of the Organization: A Legal Perspective," in Anderson and Gunderson, *op. cit.,* p. 280.

[4]Ibid., p. 280.

[5]Wilson, David C., Butler, Cray, Hickson and Mallory, "The Limits of Trade Union Power in Organizational Decision Making," *British Journal of Industrial Relations XX*, No. 3 (November 1982), p. 323.

[6]A leading proponent of this approach was Bora Laskin, former Chief Justice in Canada. See: Re Peterboro Lock Mfg. Co. Ltd. (1953), 4 L.A.C. 1499, at p. 1502 (Laskin). Also see Freedman, S., *Report of Industrial Inquiry Commission on Canadian National Railway "Run-Throughs,"* (Ottawa: Queen's Printer), 1965.

the unilateral power to make rules and exercise discretion. Thus, ownership carries with it the right of "freedom of contract."[7]

This "market theory" of labour incorrectly assumes an approximate *equality* of individuals to function in the market environment, which "is an inappropriate assumption on which to base the actual right to participate."[8] The contract law of employment is partially based upon a fundamental and "empirically absurd" understanding of equality.[9]

Secondly, a major underlying assumption supporting the buying and selling of labour and management's "excessive" prerogatives under common law is our socially accepted conception of work as instrumental rather than self-fulfilling, enabling the worker to sustain status and self-respect. The acceptance of hierarchy and privilege in the organization of production reinforces the "cycle of inequality" in society."[10]

Within a prevailing class structure, the privileged view ordinary blue-collar, manual workers as "fit" for dirty work, Harry Glasbeek states that

in as much as the argument is that the contract of employment doctrines display an assumption that a *superior-inferior relationship* is to be accepted, and that collective bargaining regimes do not share this assumption, it is also of dubious merit. This characterization of the common law is justified on the basis that employers could (and can) treat their employees as servants, as commodities, as a matter of law.[11] [Emphasis mine]

Finally, the acceptance of inequality, the instrumentality of work, and a prejudice towards ordinary workers as having "strong backs and weak minds" reinforces the present dehumanizing organization of industry and judicial and legal constructs pertaining to the employment relationship.

The further acceptance of this situation is positively argued by the social value of the freedom of contract doctrine which construes the relationship between employee and employer as a *voluntary* agreement. The "lack of parity cannot be adduced as a reason for questioning this doctrine in behalf of worker rights, unless one is prepared to question it in all instances where parity is lacking."[12]

Critics of increased worker rights also argue that the establishment of such rights:

. . . will generate gross inefficiency since it will ensnarl simple employee proceedings with procedural red tape. With special rights, no employee can simply be fired or demoted; he must be given a formal hearing; and to ensure that due process is realized, complicated organizational mechanisms must be established, mechanisms that will require time and effort that might otherwise contribute to productive activities.[13]

Clearly, as Donaldson correctly observes,

such critics envision a straightjacketed corporation management, working in an environment in which penalizing and firing workers is all but impossible. The result, presumably, will be lower working standards, lazier employees, and *widespread inefficiency.*[14] [Emphasis mine]

and so equity must be sacrificed by a supposedly greater good: efficiency.

B. PARTICIPATION AND PRODUCTIVITY

To this argument one can reply that worker rights and participation might enhance efficiency. After an extensive review of the literature on this issue, Bruce Stokes states that "ample experience exists to quell most fears that employee involvement in day-to-day company decisions leads to declining economic efficiency."[15] Further, Stokes reported that:

[7]See Alan Fox, *Beyond Contract: Work, Power and Trust Relations,* (Faber, London) 1974, especially pp. 181–190.
[8]Beatty, David M., "Labour is Not a Commodity" in Reiter and Swan *Studies in Contract Law,* 1980, p. 316.
[9]Ibid., pp. 340–1. See also R. H. Tawney, *Equality* (London: Unwin Brooks), 1964.
[10]Fox, Alan, "The Meaning of Work," in *The Politics of Work and Occupations,* edited by Geoff Island and Graheme Salaman (University of Toronto Press), 1980, pp. 172–173.
[11]Glasbeek, H., *op. cit.,* p. 74.

[12]Thomas Donaldson, "Employee Rights," Ch. 7, in *Corporations and Morality* (Prentice-Hall, Inc., Englewood Cliffs, New Jersey), 1982, p. 138.
[13]Ibid., p. 138.
[14]Ibid., p. 138.
[15]Stokes, Bruce, "Worker Participation—Productivity and the Quality of Work Life," *Worldwatch Paper* 25 (December, 1978), p. 33.

A 1975 National Science Foundation survey of 57 field studies of worker participation experiences in the United States found that four out of five reported productivity increases. A 1977 study by Dr. Raymond Katzell of New York University of 103 U.S. worker productivity experiments confirmed these findings. Karl Frieden, in a 1978 study for the National Center for Economic Alternatives, concluded that, "the scientific rigor of many of the studies on workers' participation is less than ideal. However, a clear pattern emerges . . . supporting the proposition that increases in workers' participation results in improvements in productivity.[16]

Even The Trilateral Commission's Task Force on Industrial Relations, an important management research body, admitted that "nothing in the literature suggests that participation significantly harms productivity."[17]

There is a vast body of literature which confirms the positive correlation between worker involvement and productivity. Nonetheless, strong resistance exists against the widening of existing "partial" worker rights in industry.

During my ten year tenure as Associate Deputy Minister of Labour in the Province of Saskatchewan, I sat on a number of Boards of Directors which included union and/or worker representation. The contribution of workers and their representatives was of enormously high quality, and in regard to the bi-partite Work Environment Board of the Potash Corporation of Saskatchewan, of which I was chairperson, the worker and union contribution was, in my opinion, of greater practical and intellectual merit than that of the senior management. This might be because the terms of reference of the Work Environment Board centered upon working conditions with which management was less familiar. This applies to the worker members of the mandatory joint occupational health and safety committees in Saskatchewan.[18]

Consequently, I believe that worker rights should be extended by statute in all areas of production, but full rights be accorded in matters relating to workplace health and safety. This paper will argue the necessity to "stretch" the present legal concept of risk covering dust, chemicals, lighting and other quantifiable and measurable aspects of the workplace to all work environment matters including: how the work is organized, the design of the job, pace of work, monotony, scheduling, sexual harassment, job cycle and similar work environment matters which matter to workers.

II. Worker Participation and Occupational Safety

A. INTRODUCTION

Lack of worker "rights" to control work processes is a major contributor to both increased adverse stress and a worsening of accident rates. Whereas, meaningful participation and greater control has a positive effect on worker health and safety. While worker participation is viewed as a "political" goal, it is also a means to come to grips with bad working conditions.

B. MANAGEMENT PREROGATIVES AND THE IMPOVERISHMENT OF JOB CONTENT

Trade unionism represents a collective act of protecting and improving living standards by people who sell their labour power against people who buy it. This protective function is performed in various ways, but primarily through a method of determining conditions of employment by negotiations or collective bargaining between representatives of the employer and union representatives of the employees. The results of the bargaining are set forth in a written agreement covering "wages, hours and working conditions."

Historically, "working conditions" have come to mean overtime provisions, holiday pay, vacations, and other issues which generally deal with

---

[16]Ibid., p. 33.
[17]Ibid., p. 33.
[18]In 1972, the Government in Saskatchewan passed an *Occupational Health and Safety Act* which required a joint labour-management committee to be set up in places of employment with ten or more employees (Section 20). As former Executive Director of the Occupational Health and

Safety Branch within the Department of Labour from 1973 to 1982, I met with many of these committees and reviewed the Occupational Health and Safety Committee *Minutes* meetings throughout my tenure in government.

the *extrinsic* nature of work, or time away from work as opposed to the *intrinsic nature* of work, or time-in-work. The latter refers to the intensity of work which includes: the length of the work cycle, task variety, skills demanded, the rhythm of work, machine pacing, monotonous and repetitive work which activates only a limited part of the workers' capabilities. When these conditions are part of an authoritarian work setting and a severe structure of command, workers experience a feeling of powerlessness and alienation. They have a limited degree of self-control over their methods of work, and are even restricted in their possibilities for leaving their work station without a stand-in. The "partial" rights of labour limit workers in their involvement in decision-making at the shop-floor level. These job characteristics deny workers control over planning and work methods and are the substantive issues that define the *intrinsic nature* of work which is part of managements' rights and prerogatives. Unfortunately, neither collective agreements nor existing government statutes have pierced this impenetrable fortress. The result adversely effects both worker health and safety.

C. WORKER PARTICIPATION AND SAFETY

In 1971 a British researcher, I. B. Cronin published an article, "Cause and Effect Investigations into Aspects of Industrial Accidents in the United Kingdom."[19] Studying the accident rates of 41 factories, which were essentially alike in most respects, he found that "the 'worst' factory had an accident ratio ten times that of the 'best.'" Of the 41 factories, six were selected—three pairs which were very similar in plant and size and very different in accident ratio—for more careful study. Cronin found that "there was clearly no relationship in the factories concerned between the standard of compliance with the Factories Act and the accident ratio."[20] What was the operant factor then? The results of the study "appeared to indicate some sort of direct relationship between

good safety record and successful joint consultation."[21] Cronin further concluded, "Such indications as there are show the accident rate to be a function of industrial relations. What is more, of a special aspect of industrial relations: communications and participation."[22]

In the mid- 1970's, as Executive Director of the Occupational Health and Safety Branch in the Saskatchewan Department of Labour I wrote a letter to Mr. Cronin seeking further empirical information in support of his thesis. On March 15, 1976, I received a response stating:

I gave up research in this field many years ago now because I found it totally impossible to get cooperation from employers once they realized the lines on which I was working. So far as they were concerned "investigation into the causes of accidents" meant bigger and better statistics and closer and closer examination of working conditions. Once they realized that I was concerned with attitudes and management methods they would have nothing of it. Revans has had much the same experience. It is much the same with publication. The editorial board of the ILR had to have a special meeting before they could pluck up courage to print that little article!

Some time ago Otto Kahn-Freund, of whom you must have heard, was anxious that Penguin Books should publish a short book on the whole of my work. But even with all the weight of Otto's reputation behind it, and that—as they say out here—is quite something, they would not touch it. And I don't think it was the writing. Similarly with Sweet and Maxwell who actually went back on the contract.

The last meaningful thing that I was able to do was with a large local firm in Southampton which, the exception that proves the rule, was interested in what I was trying to do. I was able to do quite a complicated attitude survey of a ten per cent weighted random sample of their employees and found a quite astonishing correlation between the employees who had suffered more than one reportable accident and what might be described as "anti-social" attitudes. Indeed, the link-up was almost embarrassingly complete from a statistical point of view—made

[19]J. B. Cronin, "Cause and Effect? Investigations into Aspects of Industrial Accidents in the United Kingdom," *International Labor Review 103*, 2 (Feb. 1971), pp. 99–115.
[20]Ibid., p. 106.

[21]Ibid., p. 108.
[22]Ibid., p. 115.

even me wonder if the computer had cooked the results![23]

In 1971 the British researchers Philip Powell, Mary Hale, Jean Martin, and Martin Simon published a study entitled, "2,000 Accidents: A Shop Floor Study of Their Causes Based on 42 Months' Continuous Observation."[24] This exhaustive study exposed many of the myths accepted by "safety professionals" today. I will quote just one of their conclusions:

> . . . A general social pressure to do something about risks might embarrass industrial management because it can see itself as the executive of the action required. If the management of a factory sets up a training programme which teaches people that certain of the systems in the factory involve risk of injury, it lays itself open to allegations that it is not doing enough to re-design the systems and eliminate the risks. This might be a root of the apathy we observed. In some cases, it may need strong governmental and public pressure to overcome it.[25]

Another British study, *Safety or Profit*,[26] was published by researchers Theo Nichols and Pete Armstrong in 1973. They found that there exists a fundamental conflict in conventional factories between safety and profit, and that, despite lip-service to safety rules, there is tremendous pressure on workers to place production ahead of safety:

> . . . each of the accidents we have reviewed occurred in context of a process failure and whilst the men concerned were trying to maintain or restore production. In every case the dangerous situation was created in order to make it quicker and easier to do this. In every case the company's safety rules were broken. The process failures involved were not isolated events. Nor were the dangerous means used to deal with them. The men acted as they did in order to cope with the pressure from foremen and management to keep up production. This pressure was continual, process failures were fairly frequent and so the short-cutting methods used to deal with them were repeatedly employed. In each case it was only a matter of time before somebody's number came up.[27]

They further concluded:

> . . . All this suggests that what is needed is some way of counteracting the *pressure for production* on the shop floor. It was just because management were not prepared to relax this pressure that men did not believe their propaganda; for in the long run such propaganda can only be effective to the extent that management *does* put safety before production.[28]

These and other studies indicate that the working conditions for every job are determined totally by the organization of work and the degree of control (or lack of control) that workers have over the means of work and the process of work. The prevailing ideology describes working conditions as a miscellaneous collection of the "physical" and "social" features of a particular job. The reality of the situation is just the opposite: the social organization of work produces both each job and its environment. What is important is the *control* over the work process.

Further it is work organization and the social relations—more particularly the power relations—within the workplace that determine the work environment with which the individual worker is faced, within which he must work—and all too often, which he must endure and suffer.

Once the power relations are seen for what they are, and once it is admitted that the preponderance of power, by far, lies with management, then it follows that "accident proneness"[29] is far more likely to lie, not with an individual worker whose power is very limited, but with a supervisor or manager, whose power is much greater.

For example, I was informed of an experiment conducted in two maintenance departments in the

---

[23]Letter from John B. Cronin to Robert Sass dated March 14, 1976.

[24]Philip Powell, Mary Hale, Jean Martin and Martin Simon, *2,000 Accidents: A Shop Floor Study of Their Causes Based on 42 Months' Continuous Observation.* (London: National Institute of Industrial Psychology, 1971).

[25]Ibid., p. 37.

[26]Theo Nichols and Pete Armstrong, *Safety or Profit: Industrial Accidents and the Conventional Wisdom.* (England: Falling Wall Press, 1973).

[27]Ibid., p. 20.

[28]Ibid., p. 25.

[29]Carelessness and Accident proneness are false accident causation theories which blame the victim, the worker, for accidents and deflect attention from unsafe conditions.

Vancouver Transit Company They were five miles apart. In one department they had a high percentage of accidents while in another there was a low percentage. They switched the supervisors, and found out that the accident rates switched also. The accident rate followed the respective supervisors. Perhaps the supervisor whom the high accident rate followed should be called an "accident prone" supervisor! In all technical questions there is a social dimension.

D. THE CONVENTIONAL WISDOM OF ACCIDENT CAUSATION

The present widely-held management view of accident causation implies a tacit assumption that workers are primarily responsible for accidents through their "carelessness," "accident proneness," or "bad attitudes"—and that they can therefore stop accidents from happening merely by resolving to "be careful," to "obey their superiors," or to "have a positive attitude towards safety." Such an assumption is either naive or perverse. It is naive to believe that workers willingly suffer accidents and injuries, that they seek out dangerous situations just to spite management. There is no valid reason to believe that workers are any more childish, silly, or self-destructive than are accountants, bureaucrats, doctors, lawyers, scientists, managers, safety professionals—or any other group in society. On the other hand, it is perverse to avoid spending money on needed safety improvements in the plant by dogmatically adopting a victim-blaming ideology.

I want to emphasize the fact that unsafe act theories of accident causation are ideology not science. I have been at pains over a number of years to refute these ideologies. I realize, of course, that any number of articles by me will not succeed in eradicating a myth which has become so ingrained in management ideology over the better part of century. However, I would like to quote in full the abstract of an article by me published in the *International Journal of Health Services:*

> The "accident proneness" thesis has been with us since the early 1900s. The early statistical studies that reputedly provided the scientific basis for this notion are examined and found to be lacking due to methodological errors and fragmented view of industrial life. Accident proneness, as originally envisioned, has no empirical foundations. It has, however, become part of the tactical armamentarium [i.e. weaponry] used in "blaming the victim" for industrial accidents. It focuses on the personal characteristics of workers in relation to accident causation, while de-emphasizing the role of dangerous work environments. In this respect, it has acted as a barrier in the development of preventive occupational health and safety principles and practices. The notion has endured not only because it is tactically advantageous, but also because many members of the professions that deal with workplace accidents have accepted it without reservation and lent it credence. For the purpose of industrial accident prevention, however, it would be more appropriate to discard this notion in favor of a more integrated and broader understanding of the nature of the interaction between workers and their socio-technical work environment.[30]

In rejecting the prevailing management ideology on safety I do not want to leave the impression that I am "tearing down" and not "building up," that I can see what is wrong but cannot offer something better. On the contrary, I believe there is a need to emphasize, in regard to accident prevention, worker rights—the right to know, the right to participate, and the right to refuse as a sound theoretical foundation.

---

[30]Robert Sass and Glen Crook, "Accident Proneness: Science or Non-Science?" *International Journal of Health Services* Vol. 11, No. 2 (Nov. 1981), p. 175.

Human Rights, Workers' Rights, and the "Right" to Occupational Safety

TIBOR R. MACHAN

Introduction

I TAKE THE POSITION of the nonbeliever.[1] I do not believe in special workers' rights. I do believe that workers possess rights as human beings, as do publishers, philosophers, disc jockeys, students, and priests. Once fully interpreted, these rights may impose special standards at the workplace, as they may in hospitals, on athletics fields, or in the marketplace.

Human Rights

Our general rights, those we are morally justified to secure by organized force (e.g., government), are those initially identified by John Locke: life, liberty, and property. [*John Locke* (1632–1704), an English philosopher, was the first systematic theorist of *liberalism*, the view that the state's purpose is to preserve the natural rights of its citizens to life, liberty and property.] That is, we need ask no one's permission to live, to take actions, and to acquire, hold, or use peacefully the productive or creative results of our actions. We may, morally, resist (without undue force) efforts to violate or infringe upon our rights. Our rights are

1. absolute,
2. unalienable, and
3. universal:
   a. in social relations no excuse legitimizes their violation;
   b. no one can lose these rights, though their exercise may be restricted (e.g., to jail) by what one chooses to do; and
   c. everyone has these rights, whether acknowledged or respected by others or governments or under different descriptions (within less developed conceptual schemes).[2]

I defend this general rights theory elsewhere.[3] Essentially, since adults are rational beings with the moral responsibility to excel as such, a good or suitable community requires these rights as standards. Since this commits one to a virtuously self-governed life, others should respect this as equal members of the community Willful invasion of these rights—the destruction of (negative) liberty —must be prohibited in human community life.

So-called positive freedom—that is, the enablement to do well in life—presupposes the prior importance of negative freedom. As, what we might call, self-starters, human beings will generally be best off if they are left uninterfered with to take the initiative in their lives.

Workers' Rights

What about special workers' rights? There are none. As individuals who intend to hire out their skills for what they will fetch in the marketplace, however, workers have the right to offer these in return for what others (e.g., employers) will offer in acceptable compensation. This implies free trade in the labor market.

Any interference with such trade workers (alone or in voluntary cooperation) might want to engage in, with consent by fellow traders, would violate both the workers' and their traders' human rights. Freedom of association would thereby be abridged. (This includes freedom to organize into trade associations, unions, cartels, and so forth.)

[1] I wish to thank the Earhart, Jon M. Olin, and Reason Foundations for making it possible, in part, for me to work on this project. I also wish to thank Bill Puka and Gertrude Ezorsky for their very valuable criticism of an earlier draft of this essay, despite their very likely disapproval of my views.

[2] This observation rests, in part, on epistemological insights available, for example, in Hanna F. Pitkin, *Wittgenstin and Justice* (Berkeley, Calif.: University of California Press, 1972).
[3] Tibor R. Machan, "A Reconsideration of Natural Rights Theory," *American Philosophical Quarterly 19* (January 1980): 61–72.

From *Moral Rights in the Workplace*, ed. Gertrude Ezorsky (Albany: State University of New York Press, 1987). *Reprinted by permission. All rights reserved.*

Workers' rights advocates view this differently. They hold that the employee-employer relationship involves special duties owed by employers to employees, creating (corollary) rights that governments, given their purpose, should protect. Aside from negative rights, workers are owed respect of their positive rights to be treated with care and consideration.

This, however, is a bad idea. Not to be treated with care and consideration can be open to moral criticism. And lack of safety and health provisions may mean the neglect of crucial values to employees. In many circumstances employers should, morally, provide them.

This is categorically different from the idea of enforcible positive rights. (Later I will touch on unfulfilled reasonable expectations of safety and health provisions on the job!) Adults aren't due such service from free agents whose conduct should be guided by their own judgments and not some alien authority. This kind of moral servitude (abolished after slavery and serfdom) of some by others has been discredited.

Respect for human rights is necessary in a moral society—one needn't thank a person for not murdering, assaulting, or robbing one—whereas being provided with benefits, however crucial to one's well being, is more an act of generosity than a right.

Of course moral responsibilities toward others, even strangers, can arise. When those with plenty know of those with little, help would ordinarily be morally commendable. This can also extend to the employment relationship. Interestingly, however, government "regulation may impede risk-reducing change, freezing us into a hazardous present when a safer future beckons."[4]

My view credits all but the severely incapacitated with the fortitude to be productive and wise when ordering their affairs, workers included. The form of liberation that is then vital to workers is precisely the bourgeois kind: being set free from subjugation to others, including governments. Antibourgeois "liberation" is insultingly paternalistic.[5]

Alleging Special Workers' Rights

Is this all gross distortion? Professor Braybrooke tells us, "Most people in our society . . . must look for employment and most (taking them one by one) have no alternative to accepting the working conditions offered by a small set of employers—perhaps one employer in the vicinity."[6] Workers need jobs and cannot afford to quibble. Employers can wait for the most accommodating job projects.

This in part gives rise to special workers' rights doctrines, to be implemented by government occupational safety, health and labor-relations regulators, which then "makes it easier for competing firms to heed an important moral obligation and to be, if they wish, humane."[7]

Suppose a disadvantaged worker, seeking a job in a coal mine, asks about safety provision in the mine. Her doing so presupposes that (1) she has other alternatives, and (2) it's morally and legally optional to care about safety at the mine, not due to workers by right. Prior to government's energetic prolabor interventions, safety, health, and related provisions for workers had been lacking. Only legally mandated workers' rights freed workers from their oppressive lot. Thus, workers must by law be provided with safety, health care, job security, retirement, and other vital benefits.

Workers' rights advocates deny that employers have the basic (natural or human) private property rights to give them full authority to set terms of employment. They are seen as nonexclusive stewards of the workplace property, property obtained by way of historical accident, morally indifferent historical necessity, default, or theft. There is no genuine free labor market. There are no jobs to offer since they are not anyone's to give. The picture we should have of the situation is that society should be regarded as a kind of large team or family; the rights of its respective parts (individuals) flow not from their free and independent moral nature, but from the relationship of the needs and usefulness of individuals as regards the purposes of the collective.

By this account, everyone lacks the full authority to enter into exclusive or unilaterally determined and mutual agreements on his or her terms. Such

[4]Peter Huber, "Exorcists vs. Gatekeepers in Risk Regulations," *Regulation* (November/December 1983), 23.
[5]But see Steven Kelman, "Regulation and Paternalism," *Rights and Regulation*, ed. T. R. Machan and M. B. Johnson (Cambridge, Mass.: Ballinger Publ. Co., 1983), 217–248.

[6]David Braybrooke, *Ethics in the World of Business* (Totawa, NJ.: Rowman & Allanheld, 1983), 223.
[7]Ibid., 224.

terms—of production, employment, promotion, termination, and so on—would be established, in line with moral propriety, only by the agency (society, God, the party, the democratic assembly) that possesses the full moral authority to set them.

Let us see why the view just stated is ultimately unconvincing. To begin with, the language of rights does not belong within the above framework. That language acknowledges the reality of morally free and independent human beings and includes among them workers, as well as all other adults. Individual human rights assume that within the limits of nature, human beings are all efficacious to varying degrees, frequently depending upon their own choices. Once this individualist viewpoint is rejected, the very foundation for rights language disappears (notwithstanding some contrary contentions).[8]

Some admit that employers are full owners of their property, yet hold that workers, because they are disadvantaged, are owed special duties of care and considerateness, duties which in turn create rights the government should protect. But even if this were right, it is not possible from this position to establish enforcible *public* policy. From the mere existence of *moral* duties employers may have to employees, no enforcible public policy can follow; moral responsibilities require freely chosen fulfillment, not enforced compliance.

Many workers' rights advocates claim that a free labor market will lead to such atrocities as child labor, hazardous and health-impairing working conditions, and so forth. Of course, even if this were true, there is reason to think that OSHA-type regulatory remedies are illusionary. As Peter Huber argues, "regulation of health and safety is not only a major obstacle to technological transformation and innovation but also often aggravates the hazards it is supposed to avoid."[9]

However, it is not certain that a free labor market would lead to child labor and rampant neglect of safety and health at the workplace. Children are, after all, dependents and therefore have rights owed them by their parents. To subject children to hazardous, exploitative work, to deprive them of normal education and health care, could be construed

as a violation of their individual rights as young, dependent human beings. Similarly, knowingly or negligently subjecting workers to hazards at the workplace (of which they were not made aware and could not anticipate from reasonable familiarity with the job) constitutes a form of actionable fraud. It comes under the prohibition of the violation of the right to liberty, at times even the right to life. Such conduct is actionable in a court of law and workers, individually or organized into unions, would be morally justified, indeed advised, to challenge it.

A consistent and strict interpretation of the moral (not economic) individualist framework of rights yields results that some advocates of workers' rights are aiming for. The moral force of most attacks on the free labor market framework tends to arise from the fact that some so-called free labor market instances are probably violations of the detailed implications of that approach itself. Why would one be morally concerned with working conditions that are fully agreed to by workers? Such a concern reflects either the belief that there hadn't been any free agreement in the first place, and thus workers are being defrauded, or it reflects a paternalism that, when construed as paternalism proper instead of compassion, no longer carries moral force.

Whatever its motives, paternalism is also insulting and demeaning in its effect. Once it is clear that workers can generate their own (individual and/or collective) response to employers' bargaining power—via labor organizations, insurance, craft associations, and so on—the favorable air of the paternalistic stance diminishes considerably. Instead, workers are seen to be regarded as helpless, inefficacious, inept persons.

The "Right" to Occupational Safety

Consider an employer who owns and operates a coal mine. (We could have chosen any firm, privately or "publicly" owned, managed by hired executives with the full consent of the owners, including interested stockholders who have entrusted, by their purchase of stocks, others with the goal of obtaining economic benefits for them.) The firm posts a call for jobs. The mine is in competition with some of the major coal mines in the country and the world. But it is much less prosperous than its competitors. The employer is at present not equipped to run a highly-polished,

---

[8]For an attempt to forge a collectivist theory of rights, see Tom Campbell, *The Left and Rights* (London and Boston: Routledge & Kegan Paul, 1983).

[9]Huber, "Exorcists vs. Gatekeepers," 23.

well-outfitted (e.g., very safe) operation. That may lie in the future, provided the cost of production will not be so high as to make this impossible.

Some of the risks will be higher for workers in this mine than in others. Some of the mineshafts will have badly illuminated stairways, some of the noise will be higher than the levels deemed acceptable by experts, and some of the ventilation equipment will be primitive. The wages, too, will be relatively low in hopes of making the mine eventually more prosperous.

When prospective employees appear and are made aware of the type of job being offered, and its hazards they are at liberty to

a. accept or reject,
b. organize into a group and insist on various terms not in the offing,
c. bargain alone or together with others and set terms that include improvements, or
d. pool workers' resources, borrow, and purchase the firm.

To deny that workers could achieve such things is not yet to deny that they are (negatively) free to do so. But to hold that this would be extraordinary for workers (and thus irrelevant in this sort of case) is to

1. assume a historical situation not in force and certainly not necessary,
2. deny workers the capacity for finding a solution to their problems, or
3. deny that workers are capable of initiative.

Now suppose that employers are compelled by law to spend the firm's funds to meet safety requirements deemed desirable by the government regulators. This increased cost of production reduces available funds for additional wages for present and future employees, not to mention available funds for future prospect sites. This is what has happened: The employee-employer relationship has been unjustly intruded upon, to the detriment not only of the mine owners, but also of those who might be employed and of future consumers of energy. The myth of workers' rights is mostly to blame.

Conclusion

I have argued that the doctrine of special workers' rights is unsupported and workers, accordingly, possess those rights that all other humans possess, the right to life, liberty, and property. Workers are not a special species of persons to be treated in a paternalistic fashion and, given just treatment in the community, they can achieve their goals as efficiently as any other group of human beings.[10]

[10]Ibid. Huber observes that "Every insurance company knows that life is growing safer, but the public is firmly convinced that living is becoming ever more hazardous" (p. 23). In general, capitalism's benefits to workers have simply not been acknowledged, especially by moral and political philosophers! It is hardly possible to avoid the simple fact that the workers of the world believe differently, judging by what system they prefer to emigrate to whenever possible.

Questions for Chapter 6

1. Explain why you find Superson's analogy between a doctor and a patient and an employer and an employee either persuasive or unpersuasive.
2. How should an employee's right to know if he or she is working with hazardous materials be balanced with an employer's right to protect trade secrets?
3. What does Sass mean by the term "manifesto right"?
4. Do you agree with Sass's claim that employees have the right to participate in designing their jobs? Why or why not?
5. Machan claims that "from the mere existence of *moral* duties employers may have to employees, no enforcible public policy can follow." Do you agree or disagree? How does Machan support his claim?
6. Why does Machan think that worker rights imply paternalism? Do you agree? Why or why not?

Case 6.1 Safety and Significant Risk[1]

In 1979, producers of benzene filed petition for review of a new health standard put forth by the Occupational Safety and Health Administration (OSHA) limiting occupational exposure to benzene. Under the Occupational Safety and Health Act of 1970, the Secretary of Labor, through the agency of OSHA, is to ensure safe and healthy working conditions. Where toxic materials are concerned, the act directs setting "the standard which most adequately assures, to the extent feasible, on the basis of the best available evidence, that no employee will suffer material impairment of health or functional capacity." With regard to carcinogens, OSHA has held that no safe exposure level can be determined and that the exposure level should thus be set at the lowest technologically feasible level that will not impair the viability of the industry in question. In the present instance, having determined a causal connection between benzene and leukemia, OSHA reduced the permissible exposure limit to airborne concentrations of benzene from ten parts per million to one part per million and prohibited skin contact with benzene solutions.

Producers of benzene protested the imposition of this new standard on the grounds that OSHA had not shown that the one part per million exposure level was "reasonably necessary or appropriate to provide safe and healthful

employment." They further argued that a safe workplace is not the equivalent of a risk-free workplace and that OSHA had exceeded its authority in seeking a risk-free workplace regardless of cost to the industry.

1. OSHA's decision to lower the exposure standard was based not on an empirical study indicating that leukemia is caused by exposure to ten parts per million of benzene, but on a series of assumptions that some leukemia might result from exposure to ten parts per million and that the number of cases would be reduced by lowering the exposure level to one part per million. Would OSHA's decision be justified if the evidence plausibly suggested a link between benzene exposure at the level of ten parts per million and leukemia, even though firmly documented proof was lacking?
2. Do you agree that a safe working environment is compatible with an environment in which there are risks? How would you define a safe working environment?
3. The Occupational Safety and Health Act was not designed to require employers to provide risk-free workplaces whenever it is technologically feasible to do so, as long as the cost is not great enough to destroy the entire industry, but to eliminate, when feasible, significant risks of harm. Do you think its mandate should be strengthened?

[1]Based on *Industrial Union v. American Petroleum* as found in 100 *Supreme Court Reporter* 2844 (1980).

Case 6.2 Risk and the Normal Conditions of Employment[2]

In 1987, John Walton was a corrections officer employed at Kingston Penitentiary. At that time,

correctional officers rotated through different assignments, one of these being hospital duty. On May 19, 1987, Walton, along with a colleague, was assigned to work in the hospital. Part of the officers' hospital duties was to escort inmates who were kept in isolation cells with no

[2]Based on *Walton v. Treasury Board (Correctional Services Canada)* as found in *Canadian Cases of Employment Law,* Vol. 16, pp. 190–200.

modern plumbing facilities to the washroom each morning and to there empty the contents of the portable toilets kept in inmate's rooms. These wastes often contained semen because of the incidence of masturbation among inmates. Three of the inmates were suspected of having AIDS or Hepatitis B.

Walton and his colleague, out of concern that they might contract one of these diseases through these three inmates throwing their waste upon them, refused to open these inmates' cells. Walton and his colleague also felt that the protective equipment of lightweight surgical gloves covering only hands and wrists and lightweight paper gowns covering only the torso, issued to guards to prevent infection, was not sufficient protection from contracting these diseases through being bitten or spat upon by infected inmates. They requested that they be issued equipment that better protected them and that they be vaccinated against Hepatitis B. They also requested that the practice of storing protective equipment in areas accessible to prisoners be discontinued.

1. Our knowledge of AIDS has increased and we now know that it can be contracted in more ways than was formerly thought. Was Walton's request a reasonable one, given the knowledge available at the time?
2. Should an employee have the right to refuse work that is extremely unpleasant, as opposed to unsafe? At the time, should Walton's work have been characterized as unsafe or simply as extremely unpleasant?

Further Readings for Chapter 6

Carl F. Cranor, "Some Moral Issues in Risk Assessment," *Ethics* 101, October 1990, pp. 123–143.

Gertrude Ezorsky, ed., *Moral Rights in the Workplace* (Albany, NY: State University of New York Press, 1987).

Theodore S. Glickman and Michael Gough, ed., *Readings in Risk* (Washington, DC: Resources for the Future, 1990).

INFOTRAC COLLEGE EDITION To learn more about the topics from this chapter, you can use the following words to conduct an electronic search on InfoTrac College Edition, an online library of journals. Here you will find a multitude of articles from various sources and perspectives: *www.infotrac-college.com/wadsworth/access.html*

workplace safety

employee rights

right to know

informed consent

Chapter 7

Whistleblowing and Employee Loyalty

Introduction

WHISTLEBLOWING can be defined in various ways, but it is basically an attempt by someone on the inside, or formerly on the inside, to bring a wrongful practice to the attention of those who have power to publicize or remedy the situation. Whistleblowing can be done for a number of reasons, including personal gain and revenge. In the United States, the Federal False Claims Act, which applies to anything sold to the government, allows whistleblowers to collect up to 15 percent of any settlements arising out of their whistleblowing. Even in cases where there is no possibility of financial gain, a disgruntled employee may wish to cause trouble for a past or present employer.

In many instances, however, whistleblowers act not out of a desire for personal gain or a vendetta against a disliked employer, but a concern for public welfare and the integrity of the company for which they work. A number of studies report that whistleblowers are typically above-average employees who are highly loyal to their employers. On this basis, it seems we might expect that whistleblowers are admired and respected by their employers. Unfortunately, this is not the case. Typically, whistleblowers are ostracized by fellow workers and are subject to lowered evaluations by supervisors, demotions, punitive transfers, loss of jobs, and blacklisting in their profession. One of the best-known examples is what happened to Roger Boisjoly, a senior engineer at Morton Thiokol, who strongly recommended that the space shuttle *Challenger* not be launched and testified to that effect before the Rogers Commission. Boisjoly found that he was unable to continue working at Morton Thiokol because of alienation from his coworkers and that other companies were unwilling to hire a known whistleblower. It is not uncommon for an employee to lose his or her career as a result of blowing the whistle.

We have, then, something of a mystery. Given that whistleblowers are typically loyal, highly motivated employees, and that it is better to learn about a problem sooner rather than later, and that it is easier to address a problem internally than to involve an external authority, why are whistleblowers reviled rather than admired? Would it not be more rational on the part of employers to encourage whistleblowing rather than attempt to suppress it?

Our three readings explore why whistleblowers typically experience opposition and what is required if a more rational view of whistleblowing is to emerge. In our first reading, "Avoiding the Tragedy of Whistleblowing," Michael Davis argues that a good deal of the persecution whistleblowers undergo lies in the fact that "the rationality of formal organization is an ideal never more than partially achieved." Inasmuch as employees find it necessary to go through outside channels, whistleblowing inevitably points to the fact of organizational dysfunction. Irrational though it may be, even experienced managers are not immune from the very human tendency to blame the messenger for bad news.

Davis argues that whistleblowing typically exacts a high price not only from whistleblowers, who suffer the most severe consequences, but also from employers and fellow employees. In his view, whistleblowing seems to be analogous to major surgery. Although it may in certain circumstances be necessary, it takes a high toll on those undergoing it and if there exists a way of preventing the condition that necessitates it, this should be vigorously pursued. Like an individual, an organization should pursue a healthy lifestyle that will prevent problems from growing to the point where radical measures such as whistleblowing are necessary. At best, whistleblowing is the lesser of two evils.

Davis is correct in his observation that there is a tendency to blame the messenger who brings bad news, but it seems clear there are deeper roots of the persecution whistleblowers face. Whistleblowing is often described by employers and fellow employees as a betrayal of trust—a lack of loyalty where loyalty is owed. It is this feeling of betrayal that best explains the depth of feeling typically aroused by whistleblowing. They have failed, it is felt, to function as team players.

Whether this view, so often held by employers and fellow workers, that the whistleblower is lacking in loyalty and is thus morally deficient, is correct, is discussed by Robert Larmer in "Whistleblowing and Employee Loyalty." Larmer argues that whistleblowing is consistent with loyalty to one's employer and fellow employees. The view that whistleblowing involves a betrayal of loyalty is based on the assumption that to be loyal to someone is to act in a way that accords with what that person believes to be in his or her best interests. This implies that if a whistleblower's employer or fellow employees do not believe whistleblowing to be in their best interests, the whistleblower acts disloyally. In Larmer's view, this common assumption is mistaken. To act loyally toward someone is not necessarily to act in a manner which that person believes to be in his or her interest, but rather to act in a manner that is genuinely in that person's interest, whether he or she believes so or not. Larmer goes on to argue that, to the degree that an action is genuinely immoral, it is impossible that it is in the agent's best interests. It follows that an employer or fellow worker is acting immorally in not ultimately acting in the best interests of either the company or him- or herself and that the whistleblower does not act disloyally in blowing the whistle.

Demonstrating that whistleblowing is compatible with loyalty to one's employer and fellow employees is an important step in changing how whistleblowing is viewed, but it does not, in itself, resolve the many practical difficulties faced by whistleblowers. Whistleblowers often find themselves in the embarrassing position of questioning superiors who would ordinarily be regarded as persons of good will and sound moral judgment. Ethical issues are not always recognized as such, even by persons of acknowledged moral competency in other matters.

What is required, if the common view of whistleblowers as organizational traitors is to change, is not simply argument at a theoretical level, but practical ways of changing the institutional culture that gives rise to this view. It is to this issue that James Benson and David Ross turn their attention in their article "Sundstrand: A Case Study in Transformation of Cultural Ethics."

Sundstrand, a Fortune 500 company that does most of its business as a defense contractor to the government, was charged with ethical violations in the mid-eighties by Pentagon officials. These charges resulted in a huge penalty settlement of $222.3 million and Sundstrand's possible disbarment as a future supplier. Faced with this situation, Sundstrand decided that it was time to pay special attention to fostering ethical conduct as part of its organizational culture. In particular, it decided to encourage internal whistleblowing as a means to detect harmful or illegal activities that needed to be corrected.

In order to accomplish this, Sundstrand had to demonstrate both its genuine commitment to developing a new organizational culture and its willingness to provide the training and resources necessary for employees to function effectively in such a culture. It also had to develop ways to monitor whether it was being effective in its attempt to encourage internal whistleblowing. Benson and Ross discuss the specific steps that Sundstrand took to meet these goals. They go on to investigate whether Sundstrand's program could serve as a model for other organizations wishing to encourage internal whistleblowing. They conclude that, although there are significant differences between the resources that Sundstrand can bring to bear in changing its organizational culture and the resources that smaller companies can bring to bear, many elements of Sundstrand's model are transferable. One of the most important of these is that there be transparency in determining whether the goal of encouraging internal whistleblowing is being met. It is absolutely crucial to the success of such a program that employees be satisfied that they are empowered to make ethical decisions and that encouraging whistleblowing is a genuine goal of the organization, rather than something to which the organization merely pays lip service.

Avoiding the Tragedy of Whistleblowing

MICHAEL DAVIS*

[T]he strength of the pack is the Wolf, and the strength of the Wolf is the pack.
—Rudyard Kipling, "The Law of the Jungle"

MOST DISCUSSIONS OF WHISTLEBLOWING seek to justify whistleblowing or to distinguish justified from unjustified whistleblowing; or they report

who blows the whistle, how, and why; or they advise on how to blow the whistle or how to respond to

College, Grand Rapids, Michigan, September 21, 1989; and at the Mechanical Engineering Bi-Weekly Seminar Series, Western Michigan University, Kalamazoo, Michigan, October 3, 1989. I [Michael Davis] should like to thank those present, as well as my colleague, Vivian Weil, for helping me to see the many sides of whistleblowing. I should also like to thank the editor of this journal for his helpful comments and some useful references.

*Versions of this paper were presented at the Neil Staebler Conference, Institute of Public Policy Studies, University of Michigan, Ann Arbor, February 17, 1988; at Aquinas

From Business and Professional Ethics Journal, 8(4), 1988. Reprinted with permission.

an employee about to blow the whistle or what to do once she has; or they make recommendations for new laws to protect whistleblowers. In one way or another, they treat whistleblowing as inevitable. I shall not do that. Instead, I shall try to help individuals and organizations *avoid* whistleblowing.

That purpose may suggest that I oppose whistleblowing. I do not. I think whistleblowing is, on balance, at least a necessary evil (and sometimes even a good thing). I certainly think whistleblowers should have legal protection.[1] They should not be fired for their good deed or punished for it in any other way. But I doubt that much can be done to protect them. I shall use much of this paper to explain why.

That explanation will bring out the destructive side of whistleblowing, making it easier for most of us to see ourselves in the role of those who mistreat whistleblowers. Insofar as it does that, it will give the organization's case for mistreatment. The explanation will, however, also show the importance of avoiding whistleblowing. We should try to get the benefits of whistleblowing without making people and organizations pay the enormous price whistleblowing typically exacts.[2]

This paper is addressed *both* to those who have a substantial say in how some organization runs *and* to those who could some day have to blow the whistle on their own organization. These groups overlap more than most discussions of whistleblowing suggest.[3] That, however, is not why I have

chosen to address both here. My reason runs deeper. I believe that, even if those two groups did not overlap, they would still share an interest in making whistleblowing unnecessary; that both groups can do much to make whistleblowing unnecessary; and that each will be better able to do its part if it understands better what the other group can do.

I. The Informal Organization Within the Formal

Let us begin with the obvious. No matter how large or small, every formal organization includes one or more informal groups. An academic department, for example, is a network of poker buddies, movie buffs, cooks, and so on. Departmental conversation is not limited to what must be said to carry on departmental business. Ordinary life, ordinary attitudes, permeate the formal structure. Much of what makes the formal organization succeed or fail goes on within and between these informal groups. Who likes you is at least as important in most organizations as what you are. Success is not simply a matter of technical skill or accomplishment. You must also have enough friends properly placed—and not too many enemies. Perhaps only at hiring time do academics talk much about personality but every academic knows of a department that fell apart because certain members did not get along and others that survived financial troubles, campus disorders, and tempting offers to individual members in part at least because the faculty got along so well together.

Though my example is an academic department, nonacademics will, I think, confirm that much the same is true of corporate offices and even of government bureaus. Most of what makes such organizations work, or fail to work, can't be learned from the table of organization, formal job descriptions, or even personnel evaluations. Thinking realistically about whistleblowing means thinking about the informal aspects of formal organization as well as the formal. I shall focus on those informal aspects here.[4]

[1]For a good summary of what is (or could be) offered, see Martin H. Malin, "Protecting the Whistleblower from Retaliatory Discharge," *Journal of Law Reform* 16 (Winter 1983): 277–318. For some suggestion of how ineffective that protection is, see Thomas M. Devine and Donald G. Aplin, "Whistleblower Protection—The Gap Between the Law and Reality," *Howard Law Journal* 31(1988): 223–239; or Rosemary Chalk, "Making the World Safe for Whistleblowers," *Technology Review* 91 (January 1988): 48–57.
[2]The literature describing the suffering of whistleblowers is, of course, large. For a good scholarly summary, see Myron Peretz Glazer and Penina Migdal Glazer, *The Whistleblowers: Exposing Corruption in Government and Industry* (Basic Books: New York, 1989). There is, in contrast, very little about how the organization suffers (or benefits). Why?
[3]The holder of a "professional position" is much more likely to become a whistleblower than an ordinary employee is. See, for example, Marcia P. Miceli and Janet P. Near, "Individual and Situational Correlates of Whistle-Blowing," *Personnel Psychology* 41 (Summer 1988): 267–281.
[4]Compare Chester A. Barnes, *The Function of the Executive* (Harvard University Press: Cambridge, Mass., 1938).

II. Blaming The Messenger

"Whistleblower" is a capacious term. Whistleblowers can, it seems, be anonymous or open, internal or external, well-intentioned or not so well-intentioned, accurate or inaccurate, justified or unjustified. Perhaps strictly speaking, some of these are not whistleblowers at all.[5] But I have no reason to speak strictly here. For my purposes, "whistleblower" may refer to any member of a formal organization who takes information *out of channels* to try to stop the organization from doing something he believes morally wrong (or to force it to do something he believes morally required).[6]

Most organizations will fire a whistleblower if it can, whether she was right or not; will ruin her job prospects if it can; and, if it can do neither, will still do what it can to make her life miserable. Otherwise humane organizations can treat a whistleblower savagely.[7] Why?

The most common answer is that those who mistreat whistleblowers do so because they expect to benefit from having fewer whistleblowers. The self-interest of individuals or their organization explains the mistreatment.

Though no doubt part of the truth, this explanation is, I think, only a small part. We are in general far from perfect judges of self-interest. Our judgment does not improve simply because we assume an organizational role. We can still be quite irrational. Recall how Shakespeare's Cleopatra responds to her messenger's report that Antony has married Octavia:

> . . . Hence,
> Horrible villain! or I'll spurn thine eyes
> Like balls before me; I'll unhair thy head:
> Thou shalt be whipp'd with wire and stew'd in brine . . .
> . . . let ill tidings tell
> Themselves when they be felt.[8]

Though Cleopatra had ordered him to spy on Antony, the messenger will hear more harsh words, receive hard blows, and have a knife angrily put to his throat before he is allowed to leave with a small reward.

Today's formal organizations can treat the bringer of bad news much as Shakespeare's lovesick Cleopatra did. So, for example, in a recent book on corporate life, Robert Jackall grimly recounts what happened to several executives with bad news to tell their respective organizations. Though each discovered wrongdoing it was his duty to discover; reported it through channels, and saw the wrongdoer punished, though none of them was responsible for the wrong reported, and though the organization was better off for the report, the lucky among Jackall's executives had their part in the affair forgotten. Some paid with their careers.[9]

We generally think of information as power—and it is. But thinking of information that way is no small achievement when the information wrecks our plans. Even experienced managers can find themselves telling subordinates, "I don't want to hear any more bad news."

The rationality of formal organization is an ideal never more than partially achieved. We must keep that in mind if we are to understand what happens to so many whistleblowers. An organization that would "whip with wire and stew in brine" the simple bringer of bad news is not likely to respond

---

[5]For a good discussion of the problems of defining "whistleblowing," see Frederick Elliston et al., *Whistleblowing Research: Methodological and Moral Issues* (Praeger: New York, 1985), esp. pp. 3–22 and 145–161.

[6]Even this definition should be read liberally. In most organizations, there are "ordinary" channels the use of which gives no offense and "extraordinary" channels the use of which will give offense. Sometimes one can only determine that a channel is extraordinary by using it. Those using an extraordinary channel will be treated as whistleblowers (and, indeed, will often be so labeled even when they are not whistleblowers according to this—or any other standard—definition). Similarly, the dispute between a whistleblower and her organization may in part be over whether her objection is a moral rather than a technical one (everyone agreeing that *if* the objection is moral, she would be justified). But, since they think the objection is not a moral one, they consider her a "disgruntled employee," not a whistleblower. I do not intend what I say here to turn on how we resolve such difficult cases. For a good summary of the recent literature of definition, see Marian V. Heacock and Gail W. McGee, "Whistleblowing: An Ethical Issue in Organizational and Human Behavior," *Business & Professional Ethics Journal* 6 (Winter 1987): 35–46.

[7]I have in mind especially the response to whistleblowers within academic institutions such as my alma mater: see, for example, Bruce W Hollis, "I Turned in My Mentor," *The Scientist* 1 (December 14, 1987): 1–13.

[8]William Shakespeare, *Antony and Cleopatra* Act II: Sc. 5.

[9]Robert Jackall, *Moral Mazes* (Oxford University Press: New York, 1988). esp. 105–112 & 119–133.

well to the whistleblower—even if, as often happens, the whistleblower serves the organization's long-term interests. The whistleblower is, after all, not only a bearer of bad news; he *is* bad news.

III. *Whistleblowing as Bad News All Around*

Discussion of whistleblowing tends to emphasize the undeniable good the accurate whistleblower does. The incidental harm tends to be overshadowed, perhaps because so much of it seems deserved. The harm done by inaccurate whistleblowing has received much less attention. Why?[10]

Whatever the reasons for ignoring the bad news about whistleblowing, the fact remains that much of it is ignored and, for our purposes, the bad news is crucial. So, let us recall how much bad news there is.

Whistleblowing is always proof of organizational trouble. Employees do not go out of channels unless the channels at least seem inadequate.

Whistleblowing is also proof of management failure. Usually several managers directly above the whistleblower will have heard his complaint, tried to deal with it in some way, and failed to satisfy him. However managers view the whistleblower's complaint, they are bound to view their own failure to "keep control" as a blot on their record.

Whistleblowing is also bad news for those on whom the whistle is blown. What they were peacefully doing in obscurity is suddenly in the spotlight. They will have to participate in "damage control" meetings, investigations, and the like that would not otherwise demand their scarce time. They will have to write unusual reports, worry about the effect of publicity on their own career, and face the pointed questions of spouse, children, and friends. And they may have to go on doing such things for months—or even years.

Insofar as whistleblowing has such effects, no one within the organization will be able to hear the whistleblower's name without thinking unpleasant thoughts. No manager will be able to make a decision about the whistleblower without having bad associations color her judgment. The whistleblower not only makes conscious enemies within his organization, he can also create enormous biases against himself, biases very hard to cancel by any formal procedure.

And that is not all the bad news. What must the whistleblower have become to blow the whistle? At the very least, he must have lost faith in the formal organization. If he had kept faith, he would have accepted whatever decision came through formal channels—at least once he had exhausted all formal means of appeal.

For anyone who has been a loyal employee for many years, losing faith in the organization is likely to be quite painful—rather like the disintegration of a marriage. My impression is that few whistleblowers take their job thinking that they might some day have to blow the whistle. They seem to start out as loyal employees—perhaps more loyal than most. One day something happens to shake their loyalty. Further shocks follow until loyalty collapses, leaving behind a great emptiness. While managers tend to think of whistleblowers as traitors to the organization, most whistleblowers seem to feel that, on the contrary, it is the organization that has betrayed them.[11]

This bad news implies more. Before the whistleblower was forced to blow the whistle, she trusted the formal organization. She took its good sense for granted. That is no longer possible. Faith has become suspicion. Since what we call

---

[10]One reason may be that inaccurate whistleblowing is less likely to make news. Newspapers, police departments, and senior managers are constantly receiving "tips" that don't pan out. These are not news. Another reason inaccurate whistleblowing has received little attention may be that reliably determining that a particular whistleblower is inaccurate can be quite difficult. The whistleblower's evidence may establish only a presumptive case against an organization. The organization may not be able to reply in full without revealing proprietary information or violating the privacy of other employees, leaving outsiders no way to know that the whistleblower is mistaken. Even the organization in question may not be able to make such a determination without great expense—and may therefore never bother. Much whistleblowing seems enveloped in the organizational equivalent of what Clausewitz called "the fog of battle." If we knew more about cases of inaccurate, mistaken, or otherwise flawed whistleblowing, perhaps our assessment of the overall good effect of whistleblowing would change. Perhaps whistleblowing, like tyrannicide. is so likely to hit the wrong target that it cannot in practice be justified. This is a subject about which we need to know more.

[11]See, for example, Dick Polman, "Telling the truth, paying the price," *Philadelphia Inquirer Magazine,* June 18, 1989, pp. 16ff.

"organizational authority" is precisely the ability of the organization to have its commands taken more or less on faith, the "powers that be" now have as much reason to distrust the whistleblower as she has to distrust them.[12] She no longer recognizes their authority. She is much more likely to blow the whistle than before. She is now an enemy within.

Something equally bad has happened to relations between the whistleblower and her coworkers. Whistleblowing tends to bring out the worst in people. Some friends will have become implacable enemies. Others will hide, fearing "guilt by association." Most, perhaps, simply lose interest, looking on the whistleblower as they would someone dying of cancer. These desertions can leave deep scars. And even when they do not, they leave the whistleblower an outsider, a loner in an organization in which isolation for any reason makes one vulnerable.

All this bad news suggests some hard questions: How can a whistleblower work as before with people whose loyalty he no longer shares? How can coworkers treat him as they did before when he is no longer quite one of them? How can he hope for promotion, or even retention, in an organization in which he can put no trust, in which he has no friends, and for which he is likely to make further trouble? These, I think, are plainly not questions a law can answer.

IV. Helping the Whistleblower and the Organization

What then can be done for the whistleblower? One option is to find her another job. That is not easy Potential employers generally shun known whistleblowers. That alone makes finding a new job hard. Then too, the whistleblower may not be as good an interviewee as before. Many whistleblowers seem to signal the bad news even when they do their best to conceal it. They may, for example, sound emotionally exhausted, ask questions that suggest distrust, or just seem prickly. They are like people going through a bad divorce.

Since few potential employers want someone else's troubles, we must draw this paradoxical con-

clusion: the whistleblower's best hope for continuing her career may be her old employer. That the old employer may be her best hope is the chief reason to support laws protecting whistleblowers. Though a law can offer the whistleblower little direct protection, it can prod the organization to think about making peace with the whistleblower.

This, however, is still a slim hope. The organization can make peace with the whistleblower *only if* it can reestablish his loyalty to the organization and his trust in those with whom he must work. That is not easy.

Clearly, the formal organization itself must change enough for the whistleblower to have good reason to believe that he will not have to go out of channels again. The changes will probably have to be substantial, something most organizations automatically resist. But formal changes alone will not be enough to reestablish the whistleblower's informal relations with superiors, subordinates, and coworkers. What is needed in addition is something like marriage counseling, some sort of group therapy to expose and resolve all the feelings of betrayal, distrust, and rejection whistleblowing inevitably generates. The whistleblower will not be safe until he is reintegrated into the formal organization.

Some government agencies have required employees involved in a whistleblowing case to participate in such group therapy. The results so far have not been good. Managers, especially, seem to view such therapy as just one more hoop to jump through on the way to the inevitable.[13] To work, the therapy probably needs to be voluntarily undertaken by all participants, something not easily legislated.

That is why even this best hope for the whistleblower, reconciliation with the organization, is so slim. We need to find better ways to protect whistleblowers. In the long run at least, peace between the whistleblower and the organization is as good for the organization as for the whistleblower. The whistleblower is not really an enemy. An organization that has whistleblowers needs them. The whistleblower is like the knock at the door that wakes one in a house on fire—unwelcome, but better than sleeping till the fire reaches

---

[12]For an interesting analysis of this traditional view of organizational authority (and related issues), see Christopher McMahan, Managerial Authority," *Ethics* 100 (October 1989): 33–53.

[13]I owe this observation to Thomas Devine. I have found no research to confirm it.

the bed. An organization that punishes its whistle-blowers blinds itself to troubles better faced.

To say that is not to deny the disadvantages of whistleblowing described earlier but to explain why we should try to make whistleblowing unnecessary rather than try to prevent whistleblowing in other ways. It is to the chief means of making whistleblowing unnecessary that I now turn.

V. How Organizations Can Avoid Whistleblowing

If whistleblowing means that an organization has trouble using bad news, one way for an organization to avoid whistleblowing is to improve the organization's ability to use bad news. We may distinguish three approaches.

One approach, what we might call the "procedural," builds invitations to report bad news into the ordinary ways of doing business. These procedures can be quite simple, for example, a space on a form for "disadvantages" or "risks." Such a blank almost forces the person filling out the form to say something negative. Those above him are also likely to treat bad news reported in this way as part of "doing the job" than they would the same bad news reported without that specific invitation.[14]

The first approach also includes more complicated procedures, for example, "review meetings" the purpose of which is to identify problems. The review meeting works like a blank space. Where the emphasis is on revealing bad news, more bad news is likely to come out. Revealing bad news is more likely to seem part of the job.

Of course, how things will seem is in part a matter of the mental set the people involved bring to the procedure. That set will be determined in large part by what has happened in the organization before. Organizational atmosphere can turn any procedure into a mere formality. If, for example, people who fill in the disadvantage blank or speak up at a review meeting are commonly treated like

Cleopatra's messenger, the procedures will bring in little bad news. Part of making procedures work is making sure those involved think about them in the right way. This is especially important when the procedures are new and patterns of response have not yet developed.[15]

In a way, then, my first approach, the procedural, presupposes others. Those participating in various procedures need to understand how important bad news can be. They also need regular reminders, because everyday experience tends to teach them how much bad news hurts. Education can provide one reminder; a structure of formal incentives can provide another.

I intend "education" to be understood broadly (so broadly in fact that the line between education and formal incentives all but disappears). Training sessions in which superiors or special trainers stress the importance of hearing the worst is only part of what I have in mind. Everyday experience is also part of education. Subordinates are more likely to take the formal training to heart if they are regularly thanked for giving superiors bad news, if they see that bringing bad news is treated much as bringing good news is, and so on.

Superiors are, of course, more likely to treat well subordinates who bring bad news if the organization makes it rational to do so. But treating such subordinates well will generally be rational only if the organization routinely uses bad news in ways that encourage reporting it—or, at least, do not discourage reporting it. An organization's ability to do this routinely depends on its structure.

For example: Suppose that an organization holds a manager responsible only for what gets reported "on her watch." Suppose too that her subordinate informs her that her predecessor improved the division's profits by skipping routine maintenance and now much of the machinery is in poor condition. The manager will *not* want to report this to her superiors. She would be bringing news that will threaten everyone who must pass it on. She will therefore not want to hear the bad news herself. She will have good reason to tell her subordinate, "Let sleeping dogs lie." Perhaps the dogs will not howl until her successor takes over.

---

[14]For a procedure I doubt will do much good, see Theodore T. Herbert and Ralph W. Estes, "Improving Executive Decisions by Formalizing Dissent: The Corporate Devil's Advocate," *Academy of Management Review* 2 (October 1977): 662–667. Dissent is likely to be more effective if the dissenter is not viewed as "just going through the motions" and likely to be more common if not the job of just one person.

[15]Compare James Water, "Catch 20.5: Corporate Morality as an Organizational Phenomenon," *Organizational Dynamics* 6 (Spring 1978): 3–19.

Now, suppose instead that the organization has routine ways of assigning responsibility to a manager for what she does while in a position even if the bad consequences only become apparent later. In such an organization, a manager has good reason to want subordinates to report the bad news about her predecessor's work as soon as they learn of it. She need not fear such "sleeping dogs." They will not wake to howl for her blood. And, if she lets them lie, she may later have to explain how *she* could have missed them.

Most organizations tend to treat the person in charge as responsible for whatever bad news he must report. Few have any routine for assigning responsibility to anyone else (perhaps because such a routine would be quite expensive).[16] Hence, in that respect at least, most organizations have structures tending to discourage bad news. Leaving managers in charge for long terms, say, ten or twenty years, would probably compensate for this tendency. Few problems lie dormant that long. Today, however, managers seldom stay in one position for even five years. If they do not rise quickly within an organization, they are likely to move to another. This mobility means that most organizations must rely on other means of giving managers reason to welcome bad news.

The most common approach these days is to create alternative channels for bad news so that no one in an organization is in position to block its flow upward. The most traditional of these alternative channels is the regular outside audit. Another is an "open door" policy allowing subordinates to go directly to a senior official, bypassing several layers of management. Another is changing the traditional chain of command into something much more like a lattice, so that subordinates have less to fear from any particular superior and have routine access to more than one. Such arrangements give a manager reason to be thankful that he has heard the bad news from a subordinate rather than from a superior and reason to try to respond in a way likely to satisfy the subordinate. The subordinate has saved the manager from being "blindsided." Such arrangements tend to make whistleblowing unnecessary.

That, I think, is enough for now about how organizations can make whistleblowing unnecessary. We are ready to consider how individuals can avoid becoming whistleblowers.

VI. How to Avoid Having To Blow the Whistle

The simplest way to avoid having to blow the whistle may seem to be joining an organization in which whistleblowing will never be necessary. Unfortunately, things are not that simple. Organizations are human contrivances; none is perfect.

Still, organizations do differ quite a bit. By choosing the right organization, one can reduce substantially the chance one will have to blow the whistle (much as one can reduce substantially the chance of divorce by not "marrying in haste"). The question is how the organization handles bad news. The answer will be found in the organization's procedures, educational programs, and structure, not the ones "on paper" but the ones actually in effect. The difference can be crucial. For example, if the organization has an open door policy, is the door ever used? Since organizations always work imperfectly, an open door that is never used is probably a channel no one dare use, not an unnecessary channel. Using such a channel will probably be treated as whistleblowing.

Any organization described as "one happy family" should be examined with special care. Organizations, like families, generally have arguments, tensions, and the like. That is how they grow. The organization that recalls only good times is not the one that had no bad times but the one that has no use for bad news. It is exactly the kind of organization in which whistleblowing is most likely to be necessary. Personally, I would prefer an organization in which old battles are recalled blow by blow and the general happiness must be inferred from the fact that all participants survived to work together again.[17]

Having chosen the right organization, can one do anything more to reduce the chance he will some day have to blow the whistle? Certainly, but he will have to think in strikingly political terms.

---

[16]*Moral Mazes,* for example, pp. 105–112.

[17]These are, of course, matters of what is now often called "culture." For a good discussion, see Charles O'Reilly, "Corporations, Culture, and Commitment: Motivation and Social Control in Organizations." *California Management Review* (Summer 1989): 9–25.

He will, first of all, want to develop his own informal channels to augment formal channels. So, for example, a new employee W officially reports to A. But if B carries more weight with their common superior, W might want to get to know B. Perhaps they share an interest in chess. Once W is friends with B, W is in position to pass information around A should A try to suppress it. A can hardly object to W playing chess with B. Yet, once A knows W and B are chess buddies, A will be less likely to suppress information W wants passed up. A knows W has a channel around him.

Second, one should form alliances with colleagues and subordinates, people who share one's responsibilities. One should not have to stand alone against a superior. Whenever possible, the superior should have to respond to a common recommendation. Managers are likely to treat a group concern much more seriously than a single individual's. One should try to work through groups as much as possible.

But, third, not any group will do. The group should be sensitive to the moral concerns likely to force one to blow the whistle. The organizations most in need of whistleblowers are also most likely to be so organized that employees become morally less sensitive the longer they work for the organization.[18] So, one will probably need to cultivate the moral sensitivity of potential allies. There are many ways to do this. The simplest is to bring in items from the newspaper raising problems similar to those the organization could face and pass them around at lunch, asking how "we" could handle them. If potential allies share the same profession, one might try getting the local professional society to host discussions dealing with the ethical problems that come up in work they do.[19]

Last, but not least, one needs to cultivate one's own ability to present bad news in a way most likely to get a favorable response. Part of doing that is, of course, presenting the information clearly, with enough technical detail and supporting evidence. But there is more to it than that. Some people have, I think, become whistleblowers for lack of a pungent phrase.[20] A master of words is less likely to have to blow the whistle than someone who, though understanding a peril, has trouble communicating it.

And that is not all. Presenting bad news in a way likely to get a favorable response also includes what used to be called "rhetoric." A little sugar helps the medicine go down. Is there a good side to the bad news? If so, why not present that first? If there is no good side, how about presenting the bad news in a way likely to bring out the personal stake the decision-maker has in responding favorably. Such tactics are usually not mentioned in a discussion of whistleblowing. Yet, it seems to me, many people end up as whistleblowers because they did not pay enough attention to the feelings of their audience.

Those who have substantial say in how an organization runs might, then, want to consider some educational programs our earlier discussion of education may not have suggested. In particular, they might want to consider training employees in such political skills as how to present bad news effectively and how to maneuver it through channels. They also might want to review their hiring practices. For example, will the personnel office reject an applicant who asks whether the company has an open door policy, treat such a question with indifference, or consider it as a plus? Any organization that does not treat such questions as a plus will not select *for* people with the skills needed to make whistleblowing unnecessary.

[18]This claim is defended in: Michael Davis, "Explaining Wrongdoing," *Journal of Social Philosophy* 20 (Spring/Fall 1989): 74–90. See also M. Cash Matthews, "Ethical Dilemmas and the Disputing Process: Organizations and Societies," *Business & Professional Ethics Journal* 8 (Spring 1989): 1–11.

[19]Michael Davis, *One Social Responsibility of Engineering Societies: Teaching Managers About Engineering Ethics,* Monograph #88-WA/DE-14 (The American Society of Mechanical Engineers: New York, 1988).

[20]Perhaps the best example of such a person would be Roger Boisjoly (if his required testimony before Congress was whistleblowing at all). The warnings Boisjoly gave on the night before the *Challenger* exploded were (though technically accurate) in the bloodless language in which engineers generally communicate. He never said anything like "This decision could kill seven human beings." How might things have gone had Boisjoly (or anyone else present) said something of that sort when NASA pressured Thiokol to approve a launch? A hard question, to be sure, but one that at least suggests the potential power of language at the moment of decision. For details, see *The Presidential Commission on the Space Shuttle Challenger Disaster* (Washington, DC: June 6, 1986).

VII. Concluding Remarks

The world can be a hard place. One can do everything in her power and still end having to choose between blowing the whistle on her organization and sitting by while innocent people suffer harm she can prevent. The whistleblower is a tragic character. Her decency pushes her to bring great suffering on herself and those about whom she cares most. Her only alternative, sitting by, would save those she cares about most from harm—but at an incalculable cost (failing to do what she has a duty to do). Her organization will probably be better off in the long run—if it survives. But, in the short run, it too will suffer.

When events leave only this choice, most of us—at least when we are not directly involved—would hope the person upon whom that choice is forced will find the strength to blow the whistle. Heroism is the best we can hope for then. But, looking up from this chain of unhappy events, we can see how much better off everyone would have been had heroism been unnecessary. That is why I have focused on making whistleblowing unnecessary.

Whistleblowing and Employee Loyalty

ROBERT A. LARMER

WHISTLEBLOWING BY AN EMPLOYEE is the act of complaining, either within the corporation or publicly, about a corporation's unethical practices. Such an act raises important questions concerning the loyalties and duties of employees. Traditionally, the employee has been viewed as an agent who acts on behalf of a principal, i.e., the employer, and as possessing duties of loyalty and confidentiality. Whistleblowing, at least at first blush, seems a violation of these duties and it is scarcely surprising that in many instances employers and fellow employees argue that it is an act of disloyalty and hence morally wrong.[1]

It is this issue of the relation between whistleblowing and employee loyalty that I want to address. What I will call the standard view is that employees possess *prima facie* duties of loyalty and confidentiality to their employers and that whistleblowing cannot be justified except on the basis of a higher duty to the public good. Against this standard view, Ronald Duska has recently argued that employees do not have even a *prima facie* duty of loyalty to their employers and that whistleblowing needs, therefore, no moral justification.[2] I am going to criticize both views. My suggestion is that both misunderstand the relation between loyalty and whistleblowing. In their place I will propose a third more adequate view.

Duska's view is more radical in that it suggests that there can be no issue of whistleblowing and employee loyalty, since the employee has no duty to be loyal to his employer. His reason for suggesting that the employee owes the employer, at least the corporate employer, no loyalty is that companies are not the kinds of things which are proper objects of loyalty. His argument in support of this rests upon two key claims. The first is that loyalty, properly understood, implies a reciprocal relationship and is only appropriate in the context

---

[1]The definition I [Robert A. Larmer] have proposed applies most directly to the relation between privately owned companies aiming to realize a profit and their employees. Obviously, issues of whistleblowing arise in other contexts, e.g., governmental organizations or charitable agencies, and deserve careful thought. I do not propose, in this paper, to discuss whistleblowing in these other contexts, but I think my development of the concept of whistleblowing as a positive demonstration of loyalty can easily be applied and will prove useful.

[2]Duska, R: 1985, Whistleblowing and Employee Loyalty," in J. R. DesJardins and J. J. McCall, eds., *Contemporary Issues In Business Ethics* (Wadsworth, Belmont, California), pp. 295–300.

From Journal of Business Ethics, *11, 125–128, 1992. Reprinted by permission of Kluwer Academic Publishers.*

of a mutual surrendering of self-interest. He writes,

> It is important to recognize that in any relationship which demands loyalty the relationship works both ways and involves mutual enrichment. Loyalty is incompatible with self-interest, because it is something that necessarily requires we go beyond self-interest. My loyalty to my friend, for example, requires I put aside my interests some of the time. . . . Loyalty depends on ties that demand self-sacrifice with no expectation of reward, e.g., the ties of loyalty that bind a family together.[3]

The second is that the relation between a company and an employee does not involve any surrender of self-interest on the part of the company, since its primary goal is to maximize profit. Indeed, although it is convenient, it is misleading to talk of a company having interests. As Duska comments,

> A company is not a person. A company is an instrument, and an instrument with a specific purpose, the making of profit. To treat an instrument as an end in itself, like a person, may not be as bad as treating an end as an instrument, but it does give the instrument a moral status it does not deserve. . .[4]

Since, then, the relation between a company and an employee does not fulfill the minimal requirement of being a relation between two individuals, much less two reciprocally self-sacrificing individuals, Duska feels it is a mistake to suggest the employee has any duties of loyalty to the company.

This view does not seem adequate, however. First, it is not true that loyalty must be quite so reciprocal as Duska demands. Ideally, of course, one expects that if one is loyal to another person that person will reciprocate in kind. There are, however, many cases where loyalty is not entirely reciprocated, but where we do not feel that it is misplaced. A parent, for example, may remain loyal to an erring teenager, even though the teenager demonstrates no loyalty to the parent. Indeed, part of being a proper parent is to demonstrate loyalty to your children whether or not that loyalty is reciprocated. This is not to suggest any kind of anal-

ogy between parents and employees, but rather that it is not nonsense to suppose that loyalty may be appropriate even though it is not reciprocated. Inasmuch as he ignores this possibility, Duska's account of loyalty is flawed.

Second, even if Duska is correct in holding that loyalty is only appropriate between moral agents and that a company is not genuinely a moral agent, the question may still be raised whether an employee owes loyalty to fellow employees or the shareholders of the company. Granted that reference to a company as an individual involves reification and should not be taken too literally, it may nevertheless constitute a legitimate shorthand way of describing relations between genuine moral agents.

Third, it seems wrong to suggest that simply because the primary motive of the employer is economic, considerations of loyalty are irrelevant. An employee's primary motive in working for an employer is generally economic, but no one on that account would argue that it is impossible for her to demonstrate loyalty to the employer, even if it turns out to be misplaced. All that is required is that her primary economic motive be in some degree qualified by considerations of the employer's welfare. Similarly, the fact that an employer's primary motive is economic does not imply that it is not qualified by considerations of the employee's welfare. Given the possibility of mutual qualification of admittedly primary economic motives, it is fallacious to argue that employee loyalty is never appropriate.

In contrast to Duska, the standard view is that loyalty to one's employer is appropriate. According to it, one has an obligation to be loyal to one's employer, and consequently, a *prima facie* duty to protect the employer's interests. Whistleblowing constitutes, therefore, a violation of duty to one's employer and needs strong justification if it is to be appropriate. Sissela Bok summarizes this view very well when she writes

> the whistleblower hopes to stop the game; but since he is neither referee nor coach, and since he blows the whistle on his own team, his act is seen as a violation of loyalty. In holding his position, he has assumed certain obligations to his colleagues and clients. He may even have subscribed to a loyalty oath or a promise of confidentiality. Loyalty to colleagues and to

---

[3]Duska, p. 297.
[4]Duska, p. 298.

clients comes to be pitted against loyalty to the public interest, to those who may be injured unless the revelation is made.[5]

The strength of this view is that it recognizes that loyalty is due one's employer. Its weakness is that it tends to conceive of whistleblowing as involving a tragic moral choice, since blowing the whistle is seen not so much as a positive action, but rather the lesser of two evils. Bok again puts the essence of this view very clearly when she writes that "a would-be whistleblower must weigh his responsibility to serve the public interest *against* the responsibility he owes to his colleagues and the institution in which he works" and "that [when] their duty [to whistleblow] . . . *so overrrides loyalties to colleagues and institutions,* they [whistleblowers] often have reason to fear the results of carrying out such a duty."[6] The employee, according to this definition of whistleblowing, must choose between two acts of betrayal, either of her employer or the public interest, each in itself reprehensible.

Behind this view lies the assumption that to be loyal to someone is to act in a way that accords with what that person believes to be in her best interests. To be loyal to an employer, therefore, is to act in a way which the employer deems to be in his or her best interests. Since employers very rarely approve of whistleblowing and generally feel that it is not in their best interests, it follows that whistleblowing is an act of betrayal on the part of the employee, albeit a betrayal made in the interests of the public good.

Plausible though it initially seems, I think this view of whistleblowing is mistaken and that it embodies a mistaken conception of what constitutes employee loyalty. It ignores the fact that

> the great majority of corporate whistleblowers . . . [consider] themselves to be very loyal employees who . . . [try] to use "direct voice" (internal whistleblowing), . . . [are] rebuffed and punished for this, and then . . . [use] "indirect voice" (external whistleblowing). They . . . [believe] initially that they . . . [are] behaving in a loyal manner, helping their employers by

calling top management's attention to practices that could eventually get the firm in trouble.[7]

By ignoring the possibility that blowing the whistle may demonstrate greater loyalty than not blowing the whistle, it fails to do justice to the many instances where loyalty to someone constrains us to act in defiance of what that person believes to be in her best interests. I am not, for example, being disloyal to a friend if I refuse to loan her money for an investment I am sure will bring her financial ruin, even if she bitterly reproaches me for denying her what is so obviously a golden opportunity to make a fortune.

A more adequate definition of being loyal to someone is that loyalty involves acting in accordance with what one has good reason to believe to be in that person's best interests. A key question, of course, is what constitutes a good reason to think that something is in a person's best interests. Very often, but by no means invariably, we accept that a person thinking that something is in her best interests is a sufficiently good reason to think that it actually is. Other times, especially when we feel that she is being rash, foolish, or misinformed we are prepared, precisely by virtue of being loyal, to act contrary to the person's wishes. It is beyond the scope of this paper to investigate such cases in detail, but three general points can be made.

First, to the degree that an action is genuinely immoral, it is impossible that it is in the agent's best interests. We would not, for example, say that someone who sells child pornography was acting in his own best interests, even if he vigorously protested that there was nothing wrong with such activity. Loyalty does not imply that we have a duty to refrain from reporting the immoral actions of those to whom we are loyal. An employer who is acting immorally is not acting in his or her own best interests, and an employee is not acting disloyally in blowing the whistle.[8] Indeed, the

---

[5]Bok, S: 1983, Whistleblowing and Professional Responsibility," in T. L. Beauchamp and N. E. Bowie, eds., *Ethical Theory and Business,* 2nd ed. (Prentice-Hall Inc., Englewood Cliffs, New Jersey), pp. 261–269, p. 263.

[6]Bok, pp. 261–2, emphasis added.

[7]Near, J. P. and P. Miceli: 1985, "Organizational Dissidence: The Case of Whistle-Blowing," *Journal of Business Ethics* 4, pp. 1–16, p. 10.

[8]As Near and Miceli note "The whistle-blower may provide valuable information helpful in improving organizational effectiveness . . . the prevalence of illegal activity in organizations is associated with declining organizational performance" (p. 1).

The general point is that the structure of the world is such that it is not in a company's long-term interests to act

argument can be made that the employee who blows the whistle may be demonstrating greater loyalty than the employee who simply ignores the immoral conduct, inasmuch as she is attempting to prevent her employer from engaging in self-destructive behaviour.

Second, loyalty requires that, whenever possible, in trying to resolve a problem we deal directly with the person to whom we are loyal. If, for example, I am loyal to a friend I do not immediately involve a third party when I try to dissuade my friend from involvement in immoral actions. Rather, I approach my friend directly, listen to his perspective on the events in question, and provide an opportunity for him to address the problem in a morally satisfactory way. This implies that, whenever possible, a loyal employee blows the whistle internally. This provides the employer with the opportunity to either demonstrate to the employee that, contrary to first appearances, no genuine wrongdoing had occurred, or, if there is a genuine moral problem, the opportunity to resolve it.

This principle of dealing directly with the person to whom loyalty is due needs to be qualified, however. Loyalty to a person requires that one acts in that person's best interests. Generally, this cannot be done without directly involving the person to whom one is loyal in the decision-making process, but there may arise cases where acting in a person's best interests requires that one act independently and perhaps even against the wishes of the person to whom one is loyal. Such cases will be especially apt to arise when the person to whom one is loyal is either immoral or ignoring the moral consequences of his actions. Thus, for example, loyalty to a friend who deals in hard narcotics would not imply that I speak first to my friend about my decision to inform the police of his activities, if the only effect of my doing so would be to make him more careful in his criminal dealings. Similarly, a loyal employee is under no obligation to speak first to an employer about the employer's immoral actions, if the only response of the employer will be to take care to cover up wrongdoing.

Neither is a loyal employee under obligation to speak first to an employer if it is clear that by doing so she places herself in jeopardy from an employer who will retaliate if given the opportunity. Loyalty amounts to acting in another's best interests and that may mean qualifying what seems to be in one's own interests, but it cannot imply that one take no steps to protect oneself from the immorality of those to whom one is loyal. The reason it cannot is that, as has already been argued, acting immorally can never really be in a person's best interests. It follows, therefore, that one is not acting in a person's best interest if one allows oneself to be treated immorally by that person. Thus, for example, a father might be loyal to a child even though the child is guilty of stealing from him, but this would not mean that the father should let the child continue to steal. Similarly, an employee may be loyal to an employer even though she takes steps to protect herself against unfair retaliation by the employer, e.g., by blowing the whistle externally.

Third, loyalty requires that one is concerned with more than considerations of justice. I have been arguing that loyalty cannot require one to ignore immoral or unjust behavior on the part of those to whom one is loyal, since loyalty amounts to acting in a person's best interests and it can never be in a person's best interests to be allowed to act immorally. Loyalty, however, goes beyond considerations of justice in that, while it is possible to be disinterested and just, it is not possible to be disinterested and loyal. Loyalty implies a desire that the person to whom one is loyal take no moral stumbles, but that if moral stumbles have occurred that the person be restored and not simply punished. A loyal friend is not only someone who sticks by you in times of trouble, but someone who tries to help you avoid trouble. This suggests that a loyal employee will have a desire to point out problems and potential problems long before the drastic measures associated with whistleblowing become necessary, but that if whistleblowing does become necessary there remains a desire to help the employer.

In conclusion, although much more could be said on the subject of loyalty, our brief discussion has enabled us to clarify considerably the relation between whistleblowing and employee loyalty. It permits us to steer a course between the Scylla of Duska's view that, since the primary link between employer and employee is economic, the ideal of employee loyalty is an oxymoron, and the Charybdis of the standard view that, since it forces

---

immorally. Sooner or later a company which flouts morality and legality will suffer.

an employee to weigh conflicting duties, whistle-blowing inevitably involves some degree of moral tragedy.[9] The solution lies in realizing that to

whistleblow for reasons of morality is to act in one's employer's best interests and involves, therefore, no disloyalty.

[9]In Greek mythology Scylza and Charybdis were two sea monsters living in caves on opposite sides of the narrow straits of Messina separating Italy and Sicily. Reference to the myth is often made by those attempting to steer a middle course between equally unpleasant extremes.

Sundstrand: A Case Study in Transformation of Cultural Ethics

JAMES A. BENSON AND DAVID L. ROSS

AN ORGANIZATION'S CULTURE, which Harris describes as "its distinct identity" (1993, p. 64), has a profound impact upon the lives of both the employer and their employees. For example, at the outset of the employee's association with the organization, culture "punctuates their experiences" and "provides access to . . . shared reality with others in the organization" (Pacanowsky and Trujillo, 1992, pp. 107–116). As their association with the organization develops, the organization's culture is instrumental in transforming individuals into group members (Barnett and Goldhaber, 1993), and in instilling two important attitudes: acceptance of the organization's basic values and creation of awareness of what will happen to them if they refuse to abide by the organization's cultural rules (Fisher, 1993).

Surveys have revealed that members of many organizations feel that the ethics of their organizational culture have deteriorated:

30.6 percent of the respondents felt that ethics had deteriorated within their organization in the last two years. Even though 48.6 percent indicated that their employer had a written code of ethics to guide employee behavior, 37.2 percent said that the subject of ethical behavior is never discussed in the context of their work, and 30.6 percent claim to have been asked by a supervisor to act in an unethical manner on the job. Nearly 2/3 of these felt that they had to follow the order or risk losing

their job. Moreover, 70 percent claim to have witnessed unethical behavior by others in the company, but discovered that, when they informed their supervisor about the behaviour, it often backfired: the boss became angry at *them* (Modic, 1987).

A later survey, of 725 executives and managers, produced similar findings:

65 percent of the managers claimed to have personally seen or had direct evidence of fraud, waste, or mismanagement within their organizations. Of these people, however, only 50 percent reported what they had seen to the appropriate authorities (Keenan and Krueger, 1992).

Societal and legal forces have prodded many organizations to attempt to create or enhance cultural climates which promoted ethical behavior. Barnett (1992) suggests three legal imperatives which have influenced these efforts: increasing federal protection for whistleblowers (parties who report wrong-doing to persons who have the power to correct the problem); the increasing number of state whistleblower protection laws; and the increasing erosion of the employment-at-will doctrine (p. 38). Other reasons have prompted these efforts, as well. One of them is an increasing use of whistleblowing by employees—something which Near and Miceli (1995) predict will increase in the future, due to consumerist attitudes and legal changes which will encourage whistleblowing

From Journal of Business Ethics *17: 1517–1527, 1998. © 1998 Kluwer Academic Publishers. Printed in the Netherlands. Reprinted with permission.*

(p. 703). Other reasons include the various types of corporate damage which can result from whistleblowing, especially if the whistle is blown to an external source (Street. 1995): possible extended and costly litigation, negative publicity, loss of business (Ettorre, 1994); loss of eligibility to bid on certain types of government contracts, regulatory investigation, a need to restore a tarnished public image—even the loss of a valuable employee. As Vinton notes:

> Research on whistleblowing demonstrates that the average whistleblower could be considered a model employee in all other respects, and it would be a shame for the company to lose his or her service (1992).

Graham (1993) agrees:

> Among the research findings that may surprise many readers is that whistleblowers are typically above-average performers who are highly committed to the organization, not disgruntled employees out for revenge (p. 683).

Indeed, uncontrolled whistleblowing is a threat to the very authority structure of an organization, as Miceli and Near's survey of 409 directors of internal auditing suggests (1994). One reason for this may be that employees are seldom encouraged to think of constructive whistleblowing as part of their job responsibility. As Victor, Trevino and Shapiro observe, "Peer reporting is frequently considered an extra-role behavior in that it is generally not a required part of the job" (1993, p. 254). In their relevant study of nearly 300 private-sector employers, Barnett, Cochran and Taylor (1993) found that there was a significant increase in the number of internal disclosures in the organizations which had implemented internal disclosure policies/procedures (IDPP). They also discovered that the level of internal (as opposed to external) whistleblowing disclosures was significantly higher in organizations with IDPP's than in organizations without them, which led them to conclude, "Employers must find more effective and more ethical ways to cope with whistleblowing . . . [and] take steps to encourage *internal* disclosures of suspected wrongdoing" (p. 128).

Unreported employee theft is providing an economic incentive for many organizations to become interested in promoting ethical conduct and internal disclosing of unethical behavior in the workplace. Victor, Trevino and Shapiro (1993) report that the U.S. Chamber of Commerce estimates that workplace theft costs U.S. businesses up to $40 billion each year and that employees are thought to be responsible for much of this unethical behavior (p. 253). Greenberger et al. (1987) discovered that a cultural factor—work group norms—often discourages reporting of this type of unethical behavior.

Another economic factor which is encouraging organizations to develop programs to facilitate internal reporting of unethical conduct is the spreading use of the federal False Claims Act and similar state statutes which are encouraging some employees to avoid notifying management about wrongdoing (Sims, 1994) and, instead, waiting until a problem mushrooms into a sizeable law suit, in the hopes of collecting 10–15% of the final settlement. Gilbert (1994) offers the example of Douglas Keeth:

> The Federal False Claims Act, which covers anything sold to the government, legally institutes whistleblower windfalls. Douglas Keeth, a former vice-president at United Technologies, sued the firm under the Federal False Claims Act over accounting irregularities at its Sikorsky division. Keeth's reward was 15 percent of the $150 million that United paid to the government in settlement. Such potential windfalls have blurred the distinction between whistleblowing and bounty-hunting (pp. 30–31).

One more reason raising concern about the role of ethical conduct in the culture of organizations is an increasing expectation of organizational responsibility. This attitude is reflected by at least "27 federal statutes . . . provid[ing] protection to employees who have 'blown the whistle' on their employer's activities. A whistleblower who has been suspended, demoted or discharged may seek remedies including compensatory damages, punitive damages and attorneys fees" (Costa-Clarke, 1994–1995). Hamilton (1991) provides two recent examples of such protection:

> . . . after an employee of the entertainment company MCA notified his supervisor of a possible kickback scheme, he was fired. The employee filed a wrongful discharge suit, alleging that he was fired because of his attempt to stop the scheme. He recently received a favorable ruling in a California appellate court. In another

California case, a jury awarded a former employee of a large drug company $17.5 million when he was fired after expressing concerns about product safety (pp. 138–139).

A similar type of attitude is demonstrated by an increasing number of state laws intended to protect the employees who blow the whistle. As Egler and Edwards (1992) observe:

> Whistleblowing laws are part of a growing trend toward increasing protection of individual employees rights and the erosion of the traditional "at-will" employment doctrine (p. 24).

In short, organizations are finding themselves facing changes in society's expectations of their responsibility and in society's willingness to protect those who blow the whistle. Increasing recognition of the ethical obligations which society expects of organizations and increasing awareness of the benefits of maintaining healthy workplace climate (to foster internal reporting of wrongdoing), then, are two additional reasons why organizations ought to make ethical conduct an important part of their culture. Barnett et al. (1993) explain why:

> . . . whistleblowing is . . . a difficult ethical issue for employers. They must ensure that the rights of all employees are protected, including those who may be charged with wrongdoing by whistleblowers. They must ensure that the work environment does not degenerate into an atmosphere of mistrust. But if employers do nothing to encourage the internal disclosure of questionable behavior, or if they suppress employee dissent, organizational wrongdoing may go uncorrected and the ethical climate of the business may suffer (p. 128).

Although whistleblowing research has verified substantial effects upon members of organizations, Graham (1993) and Miceli and Near (1992) note little research of the impact of whistleblowing upon the culture of organizations.

Having established the far-reaching effects of organizational culture upon ethical conduct and the potential and actual influences which whistleblowing may impose upon organizations, the remainder of our analysis will address four topics: inadequate legal protection for whistleblowing; statutory pressure for external, rather than internal, whistleblowing; a description of a successful model for encouraging internal whistleblowing; and a prescription for organizations which desire to emphasize ethical conduct as part of their culture and to encourage internal, rather than external, reporting of misconduct.

Inadequate Legal Protection

Especially if done externally, but also if done internally, whistleblowing often leads to unpleasant consequences. In fact, many who write about whistleblowing caution employees to think about the possible consequences before they call misconduct to someone's attention. Typical is the warning of Dandekar (1991):

> Whistleblowers . . . who expose wrongdoing by their organizations often meet with harsh consequences, including dismissal and harassment, for performing what is arguably a social good (p. 89).

Barnett et al. (1993) indicate that a survey of whistleblowers undertaken by Jos et al. found that 95 percent indicated that they suffered reprisals for reporting misconduct. Sixty-one percent lost their jobs; 18 percent were harassed or transferred to another job; and 11 percent had their job responsibilities or their salaries reduced (1989, pp. 552–561). Dismissal from one's job is a form of retaliation which many whistleblowers have experienced in finance (Longo, 1996), science ("Hungry," p. 88), and medicine (Dunkin, 1991).

Often the response of an employer to a whistleblower is psychological harassment. When Inez Austin, an engineer at the Hanford Nuclear Reservation, alerted her supervisors about the possibility of explosions of ferrocyanide, a powerful chemical stored in aging tanks, she was told to keep quiet. She then took her concern to the press (Safram, 1992, 78–83). Her harassment has been extraordinary: she was reprimanded by her supervisor for "inappropriate behavior in the workplace," ordered to see a psychiatrist, and her office was moved, initially, into a closet, and later, into a dusty trailer. Her office furniture, telephone and computer have been taken away, she has received many obscene phone calls at home, and her house has been broken into 13 times. For the past two years, Inez has been reduced to working at clerical jobs (Franklin, "It's only," 1991, pp. 18–19).

Other common retaliations whistleblowers experience include blacking-listing in their occupation, invalid complaints about the quality of their work, relocation, re-assignment to unsympathetic co-workers or supervisors, withholding of benefits, orders to undergo psychological examination, investigation of their finances and personal life, and harassment of friends and family (Ettorre, 1994). Often those who blow the whistle are ostracized by co-workers and treated like a pariah (Dunkin, 1991); sometimes they are set up to fail: being appointed to solve the problem they have reported, but then being denied access to necessary information, and being blamed when the wrongdoing persists (Ettorre, 1994).

Pseudo-concern about the problem is another common retaliation of organizations: supervisors feign interest in learning about the complaint—but they do nothing to correct the problem (Near and Miceli, 1995). Ettorre (1994) indicates that this is the case in more than half of the instances of whistleblowing.

To avoid being blacklisted by their employer, whistleblowers are often induced or coerced into signing silence agreements. If a whistleblower has begun legal action to win back their position, they have probably accumulated substantial debt. Thus, they are often vulnerable to such an enticement.

Although federal and state statutes seem to suggest adequate protection for whistleblowers, the inconsistencies among these laws create a loose patchwork of protection, at best. Although at least 27 federal statutes ostensibly protect the whistleblower, the levels of protection are not consistent. For example, while the Age Discrimination in Employment Act and the Equal Employment Opportunity Act specifically protect a whistleblower against employer retaliations like suspension and demotion and enable a whistleblower to collect compensatory damages, punitive damages and attorney's fees, the Civil Service Reform Act of 1978 does not afford such protections if the employee does not bring the alleged misconduct to the attention of their supervisor before making any disclosure outside the agency (Costa-Clarke, 1994–1995). Egler and Edwards (1992) note another shortcoming in federal laws—there is currently no comprehensive federal whistleblower statute that protects all private employees. Hasselberg (1993), citing Prof. Terry Dworkin of

Indiana University, notes similar problems with state and local laws.

Of 35 state statutes pertaining to whistleblowing, only eleven protect both private-sector as well as governmental/public employees; in the other 24 states, only government employees are protected (Costa-Clarke, 1994–1995). There is also great variation in the level of protection afforded whistleblowers by the various state laws (Dunkin, 1991).

Awareness of the potential for abuse of whistleblower protection has caused states like Alaska, Indiana, Maine, Utah and Wisconsin to require whistleblowers to first disclose their complaints internally before "blowing the whistle" to third parties (Costa-Clarke, 1994–1995).

Now, having demonstrated that external whistleblowing and existing mechanisms provide inadequate safeguards for most whistleblowers, we will examine how some federal and state laws may actually encourage employees to blow the whistle externally in order to collect a portion of the fine or settlement to which their employer agrees.

Encouraging External Whistleblowing

Ettorre (1994) makes an important observation about external whistleblowing:

> If [an] . . . employee has blown the whistle . . . by taking the case outside to other authorities or to the media, the harsh truth is that this represents a failure on everybody's part (p. 19).

Near and Miceli (1995) draw an equally valid conclusion about whistleblowing:

> . . . whistleblowing—in and of itself—is not an unqualified good; its benefits are gained only when the complaint is valid and is effectively handled, resulting in positive change. . . . Therefore, we define the effectiveness of whistleblowing as the extent to which the questionable or wrongful practice (or omission) is terminated at least partly because of whistleblowing and within a reasonable time frame up (pp. 679, 681).

Both federal and state laws pertaining to whistleblowing offer incentives to employees and companies which may encourage them to opt to report misconduct externally, in the hopes of collecting a share of any penalties assessed.

The oldest federal legislation is the False Claims Act. The act offers 10–30 percent of the penalty as bounty for the client and attorney who successfully blow the whistle. By 1987, there were approximately 40 whistleblower cases pending against government contractors ("Revisions," 1987).

Whistleblowers are employing this legislative avenue profitably. From 1986 to 1991, settlements via False Claims Act suits hit $70 million, with $9 million of that going to the plaintiffs (Smart and Schine, 1991). In one such case, whistleblower A. David Nelson received about $1.18 million of the $5.9 million settlement his employer, CSX Transportation, paid after Nelson blew the whistle externally (Machalaba, 1995).

Because of settlements like Nelson's the False Claims Act has been criticized as counterproductive because it provides monetary incentives to employees to bypass internal reporting paths (Ettorre, 1994).

The increasing use of such laws by whistleblowers has led some firms to petition Congress for relief:

> . . . weapons contractors are waging a battle in Congress to make it more difficult for whistle blowers to press their cases and collect huge awards. The contractors claim that multimillion dollar awards encourage unfounded suits and discourage employees from alerting management about wrongdoing (Sims, 1994).

Successful Ethical Cultural Change

We will be discussing our model of successful cultural change in two parts: changing the organization's culture and the impact of these changes upon ethical conduct by employees.

CHANGING THE CULTURE

Certain conditions which organizations may experience or create would seem to foster emphasis upon ethical conduct as an important part of the organization's culture:

1. When the organization has been punished for actual or alleged ethical violations (when the legal costs of disputing alleged ethical violations would exceed the cost of a fine, for example);

2. When management strongly endorses ethical conduct as the expected way to do one's job and encourages employees to ask questions if they aren't certain whether an act they are contemplating is ethical;

3. When management creates a formal program to encourage internal whistleblowing (so that it can be dealt with in-house), including effective measures to protect the identity of the whistleblower.

We suggest that a viable model of such a program is that of Sundstrand Corporation, a Fortune 500 company, headquartered in Rockford, Illinois. Sundstrand's program grew out of charges of ethical violations by Pentagon officials in the mid-1980s. Those charges resulted in an eventual penalty settlement of $227.3 million, the largest financial judgment ever sought against a defense contractor ("Sundstrand Admits," 1988, p. 37). There was also a substantial drop in the worth of the company's stock (from $64 to $48 a share), and a tarnished image, both in its headquarters city and among potential customers. In addition, the company faced disbarment by the Department of Defense—a harsh penalty for a corporation which obtained 62 percent of its sales and 87 percent of its profits from their aerospace division (McKenna, "Sundstrand Faces," 1987, p. 2).

Although the future looked grim for Sundstrand in 1987, the organization decided to embark upon a program to emphasize ethical conduct in its culture, including encouragement of internal whistleblowing by its employees, so that any illegal or harmful activities might be detected and corrected early.

Our study of Sundstrand's successful attempt to change its culture drew upon a variety of sources from 1989–1994. Background information from national newspaper and magazine accounts were consulted to balance local media input. Several candid interviews were conducted with the Director of Human Resources and both Directors of Business Conduct and Ethics for Sundstrand, and company publications provided insight into the communication styles of presentation of new policies. Finally, two independent federal government audits of the Sundstrand whistleblowing program among employees provided measures of program success, and phone logs of Business Conduct and Ethics Department communication with employees provided additional verification.

An essential first step was to demonstrate management's commitment to the new cultural elements. Sundstrand allocated resources to create the position of Corporate Director, Business Conduct and Ethics. It was determined that this director would serve not only as a person to whom unethical conduct could be reported, but that this person would also serve as a resource person to be contacted whenever an employee was unsure whether a proposed action was illegal. Critical to the success of the program was the selection of the initial Corporate Director, Robert Carlson, who was a veteran of 45 years with the company and whose positions in graphics and public relations had made him well-known and respected by many of the organization's employees. One other very important aspect in the choice of Carlson needs to be emphasized. Since he was at the peak of his career, nearing retirement, he was not subject to manipulation on the basis that a decision he made might be risking a promotion; he was immune to manipulation. Mr. Carlson was also people-oriented, a very important trait for management of the many phone calls he would receive and phone inquiries he would make in the process of investigating any complaint. Mr. Carlson had a direct line to the CEO and he was in a position to tell management what they needed to hear (Genovese, 1993).

Second, management needed to take tangible steps to demonstrate an expectation of employees to abide by the new cultural elements. In Sundstrand's case, this involved construction of a Code of Business Conduct and Ethics booklet. Sundstrand also set up an initial ethics training program for all employees of the organization, conducted by 8–10 hired consultants (Genovese, 1993). Just getting the program off the ground, then, required a considerable investment of resources and time from Sundstrand. A strong orientation into the ethics culture is also now a part of Sundstrand's hiring process. When a new employee arrives at Sundstrand, he/she is initially shown a 5-minute orientation film which is followed by a talk by the Director of Business Conduct and Ethics. Then they are given a copy of the *Sundstrand Corporation Code of Business*

Conduct and Ethics. Enclosed in the Code Book is a card for the employee to sign, indicating that they have read the book, understand it, and realize they are obligated to follow the code. They are given 30 days to read the book, then formally asked whether they have read the book and have any questions. Then, as a condition of employment, they are asked to sign and return the card. After 50–90 days on the job, they participate in a 4-hour training session on ethics.

Third, management needed to invest in the necessary training to make certain that employees understood the new cultural elements. Carlson enlisted the services of the Ethics Resource Center, which advises organizations in aerospace and defense, finance, manufacturing, transportation, health care, public utilities and government agencies concerning ethics policies (Ethics Resource Center, 1993). The ERG offers a five-stage process for establishing an ethical philosophy and working procedures tailored to specific organizational needs. Phase One is an assessment of the areas of vulnerability to ethical infractions. Phase Two creates ethics workshops conducted initially by staff professionals and then delegated to corporate trainers. Phases Three through Five involve development of a formal Code of Conduct, implementation and program evaluation (Ethics Resource Center, 1993). Of particular interest to Sundstrand was the purchase of training videos which included such titles as "Conflicts of Interest in the Workplace," "Ethical Issues in Government Contracting" and "It's Up to You: A Management Accountant's Decisions."

The values expressed in the video series were foundational in writing an ethics manual. Written by staff attorneys, the 15-page document adopted an efficient style of language to summarize legal precepts for contract pricing and negotiation, gratuities, conflicts of interest, asset management, and compliance with antitrust, securities, and environmental regulations, as well as the hotline phone number of the Business Conduct and Ethics office (Sundstrand Corp.).

When Robert Carlson retired in 1989, Mr. Vito Genovese assumed the position of Corporate Director of Business Conduct and Ethics, and added a fourth strategy: a substantial effort to ensure consistent high quality of clear information and training pertaining to the new cultural elements. Having noticed inconsistencies in the quality of training which had been done by the consultants he observed, Vito designed a training program and set out to train the firm's 8,000 aerospace employees himself. Working with groups of 50, he developed a format of 35–40 minutes, in which he would present the ethical subject, explain any rules, and then apply the information to situations the employees might encounter on the job, emphasizing the relevance of the ethical concept and rule to the specific audience. Following this, he would open up the session for questions. Ultimately, Vito trained 6,000 of the firm's aerospace workers; Human Resources personnel trained the remaining 2,000 workers in make-up sessions.

FACILITATING HIGH ETHICAL CONDUCT BY EMPLOYEES

Sundstrand effectively empowers its employees in its ethics program to promote personal ownership. An Ethics Awareness Committee has been created at each facility, consisting of someone from management (usually the plant manager), someone from Human Resources, and someone who is nonmanagerial (a shop or clerical worker), with representatives elected or appointed according to each facility's wishes. Each facility's Ethics Awareness Committee meets at least every other month. Minutes of Ethics Awareness Committee meetings are sent to the Director of Business Conduct and Ethics. When problems are brought to the committee, they are empowered to solve minor issues on the spot, but call the Director if the issue is a major one.

A second ingredient in successful implementation of an ethics program is to make the program visible. One is by having several posters, with photographs of the facility's committee head and the corporate Director displayed prominently in each work facility; new posters are put up each month. The purpose is not only to publicize the program, but to help employees feel more acquainted with the person(s) they might call when they have a question or a problem. Meeting this goal involved one of the most difficult parts of Mr. Genovese's job in setting up the program: *visiting every shift at every Sundstrand facility* at least once a year, so employees working on the 2:30 shift in San Diego

or the 7:30 evening shift in Rockford may find themselves shaking hands with this executive, who tells them what his job is and encourages them to call him if they have a question or a problem (they can do so on an 800-line).

A third way to implement a major cultural change as Sundstrand did is to make sure that employees are aware that the program is working, what Mr. Genovese calls "Always Close the Loop," meaning that every call on the hotline needs to be treated as important and each caller must be kept informed of the status of their concern. Even trivial calls receive a response within 24 hours.

Perhaps the most important ingredient in instituting a program to emphasize high ethical conduct and to encourage whistleblowing is to ensure the privacy and protection of any employee willing to use the program. At Sundstrand, when an employee calls the Director, it is not necessary for the employee to reveal his or her name. Immediately after greeting the caller, the Director inquires whether it is safe for the employee to talk from their location (if not, they will be called at home). They are then asked for their work and home phone numbers. Whenever a call is made to the employee's work number, only a return call number is left, not the Director of Business Conduct and Ethics' office. To protect employees who visit the office, drapes are drawn, doors are closed.

The success of Sundstrand's program to date has been measured by two government audits, with government attorneys interviewing employees about their awareness of the program, whether they have made a call on the hotline or knew someone who did, how satisfied they were with the results of their contact with the program, and whether they had experienced any retaliation from participating in the program. The first audit was of 10–15 percent of all aerospace workers and resulted in a 92–93 percent satisfaction rate; the second audit was of 5 percent of the aerospace workers in San Diego, Seattle, and Rockford and achieved a 95–96 percent satisfaction rate (Genovese, 1993)

Perhaps just as important as the audit findings are these other indices:

1. The total number of calls received each year (approximately 550) indicates that employees are aware of the program and seem to trust it.
2. About 400 of the 550 calls are self-conduct checks by employees about proprietary matters

(they are following their training advice: "Ask before you act").

3. About 35–40 of the calls involve ethical issues, which allows Sundstrand to begin an investigation immediately.

4. The number of hotline callers who remained anonymous decreased from 40% in 1989 to 8% in 1992. Anonymous mailers to the Ethics Office declined slightly from 60% in 1989 to 50% in 1992. The increase in numbers of employees willing to identify themselves as whistleblowers suggests that they developed increasing trust in the program. After four years, over 9 in 10 callers felt sufficiently in identifying themselves over the hotline (Business Conduct and Ethics, 1993).

5. The level of credibility achieved by the ethics program is further substantiated by an investigation of motives for contact. Over the four-year period, the company had determined that roughly 50% of the ethics inquiries did not relate to ethics issues, but to Human Resources issues (such as smoking and attendance violations, benefits issues and staff relations). A survey revealed that the promise of anonymity, coupled with sufficient protection, constituted over 50% of the stated reasons for preferring to call the Ethics Office rather than Human Resources. Thus, employees felt more secure dealing with a program which could guarantee protection from retaliation and cut through perceived red tape to obtain a rapid—and satisfactory—response (Gruenwald, 1991, pp. 2–6).

The whistleblowing program has yielded substantial rewards. The 1992 summary of investigations into allegations by employees confirmed the program's value. Seventy-four percent of the cases identified valid company concerns, while 26 percent were groundless. Of the 74 percent of valid cases, half were Human Resources issues and 24 percent involved legitimate ethical violations. Six percent of the violators were terminated; 7 percent attended ethics retraining classes, and 11 percent received a reprimand (Gruenwald, 1991, pp. 2–6).

Model Ingredients

Several ingredients in Sundstrand's ethical conduct program may serve as models for other organiza-

tions which are contemplating the implementation of such a program. The extent to which an organization may choose to incorporate all or some of the Sundstrand model's key ingredients will vary depending upon the size and type of organization, as well as the resources available. Sundstrand is a Fortune 500 company and was the nation's 100th largest defense contractor at the time of the government investigation into misconduct charges (Orr, 1988). The organization clearly possessed the financial resources which enabled them to invest in setting up an ethics department, hiring a full-time Ethics Director and staff, and funding a long-term training program. Further, as a defense contractor, Sundstrand faced "a tangle of complex Pentagon procurement regulations which were turgid and difficult to comprehend" (Burton, 1990, p. 5), prompting an exhaustively prescriptive written code of conduct and a level of oversight which was pervasive and strict. Not only did this organization have the resources and machinery in place to enforce fundamental bureaucratic changes, but the stimulus of paying embarrassingly large fines—$227.3 million—made sweeping changes in Sundstrand's cultural orientation perhaps easier to make: a crisis atmosphere justified wholesale reforms.

Perhaps the most critical ingredient is management's commitment and funding of the necessary cultural change to foster ethical conduct and encourage internal whistleblowing. Implicit in this commitment is what Near and Miceli (1995) suggest is the most important element: creation of a climate that emphasizes shared values regarding wrongdoing. For Sundstrand, this meant funding a new position, Director of Business Conduct and Ethics, hiring the Ethics Resource Center for initial assistance in establishing an ethical philosophy and procedures for implementation, and hiring consultants who did the initial training. The importance of this commitment is suggested by a study done by Barnett, Cochran and Taylor (1990): formal whistleblowing policies encourage more open communication about sensitive ethical and moral issues in an organization.

A second crucial ingredient is demonstrating a strong expectation of ethical conduct by each employee. Sundstrand does this by the pledge that they ask each new hire to make (previous hires made this pledge during their training). This approach accomplishes four important objectives: 1) It emphasizes internal whistleblowing, the value of which is indicated by Barnett et al.'s study of 295 Human Resources executives (1993): when organizations implemented formal internal disclosure policies, there was a significant increase in internal disclosures, the level of internal disclosures was greater among organizations with IDPPS, and there was more internal communication about sensitive issues; 2) It clarifies the procedures and channels for internal whistleblowing; 3) It broadens the concept of whistleblowing to include asking questions about ethics *before* an employee undertakes an act; and 4) It uses a *Code of Business Conduct and Ethics,* as well as training, to emphasize that ethical conduct is a job expectation of every employee. There is an abundance of research to support this portion of Sundstrand's approach. Rogers (1994) notes that the mere existence of a code of ethics encourages ethical behavior; Victor et al. (1993), who studied 159 employees in 18 corporate-owned fast food restaurants, found that *inclination to report wrongdoing* is significantly associated with the perception that it is the employee's *responsibility* to report such conduct, as was actual behavior of *reporting* the wrongful act. This was similar to the finding of Trevino and Victor: employees were more willing to report misconduct if such reporting was a clearly defined job responsibility (Schellhardt, 1993). Barnett et al. (1993) report that "studies of public-sector employees suggest that internal disclosures are more likely when employees are highly aware of established communication channels" (p. 129).

Third, Sundstrand makes certain that employees know how to use their program, both by the *Code Book* and in training. They also post photos and the phone numbers of the Ethics Awareness Committee members and of the Director of Business Conduct and Ethics in prominent locations of each work facility. Barnett (1992) indicates that the wisdom of this is borne out by studies of federal employees, which found a significant association between an employee's knowledge of appropriate internal channels and the likelihood of reporting perceived wrongdoing.

Fourth, Sundstrand uses several aspects of their program to communicate two important messages: that appropriate action will be taken and that whistleblowers will be protected. Miceli and Near

indicate the importance of the first message: "What does deter whistle-blowing is the belief that no one will act to correct the problem" (Graham, 1993). Barnett et al. (1993) cite four studies which found that external disclosures are likely when employees believe that the organization will ignore their complaint. Sundstrand addressed this concern by careful choice of respected employees who were unlikely to be intimidated to head their program, continual promotion of the program, employee empowerment, and continuing on-site visitations. Consequently, employees feel protected. Again, research supports this approach. Barnett (1992) reports that "Whistleblowing studies suggest that employees who believe [they are not protected] . . . may be more likely to blow the whistle outside the organization—a finding in the studies of Near and Jensen (1983), Miceli and Near (1985), Near and Miceli (1986), and Jos et al. (1989).

The final crucial ingredient which is related to ensuring that Sundstrand's program is a success is that of periodic self-examination to determine whether the program is functioning as intended. Crucial data, like employee satisfaction with the program, is gathered by an external agency, while other data is gathered and analyzed internally.

References

Barnett, G. and G. Goldhaber: 1993, *Organizational Communication,* 6th ed. (William C. Brown, Dubuque).

Barnett, T.: 1992, "Why Your Company Should Have a Whistleblowing Policy," *Advanced Management Journal* 57 (Autumn), 38.

Barnett, T., D. S. Cochran and G. S. Taylor: 1993, "The Internal Disclosure Policies of Private Sector Employers: An Initial Look at Their Relationship to Employee Whistleblowing," *Journal of Business Ethics* 12, 127–136.

Burton, T.: 1990, "Sundstrand Pentagon Fraud Case Ends," *Wall Street Journal* (19 Oct.), 5.

Business conduct and ethics: 1993, *Annual Report for Sundstrand Corporation.*

Costa-Clarke, R. J.: 1994–1995, 'The Costly Implications of Terminating Whistleblowers," *Employment Relations Today* (Winter), 447–454.

Dandekar, N.: 1991, "Can Whistleblowing Be Fully Legitimated?," *Business and Professional Ethics Journal* 10 (Spring), 89–108.

Dunkin, A.: 1991, "Blowing the Whistle Without Paying the Piper," *Business Week* (3 June), 138–139.

Egler, T. D. and E. L. Edwards: 1992, "Retaliating against the Whistleblower," *Risk Management* (August), 24–29.

Ethics Resource Center: 1993, Advisory Services.

Ettorre, B.: 1994, "Whistleblowers: Who's the Real Bad Guy?," *Management Review* (May), 18–23.

Fisher, D. F.: 1993, *Communication in Organizations,* 2nd ed. (West Publishing, St. Paul).

Franklin, K.: 1991, "It's Only Plutonium," *Progressive* (October), 15–20.

Genovese, V.: 1993, Personal interview (August).

Gilbert, N.: 1994, "Toot Toot for the Jackpot," *Financial World* (16 August) (163), 30–31.

Graham, J. W: 1993, "Blowing the Whistle (Book Review)," *Administrative Science Quarterly,* (December) (38), 683–685.

Greenberger, D. B., M. P. Miceli and D. Cohen: 1987, "Oppositionists and Group Norms: The Reciprocal Influence of Whistleblowers and Co-workers," *Journal of Business Ethics* **6,** 527–542.

Gruenwald, S.: 1991, *Talking Paper: Sundstrand Corporation PAR-ethics Program* **8,** 2–6.

Hamilton, J.: 1991, "Blowing the Whistle Without Paying the Piper," *Business Week* (3 June), 138–139.

Harris, T. E.: 1993, *Applied Organizational Communication* (Lawrence Erlbaum Associates, Hillsdale, N.J.).

Hasselberg, J. M.: 1993, "Book Review," *Journal of Business Ethics* **12,** 642.

Hungry for justice: 1993, *Economist* (19 June), 88–89.

Jos, P. H., M. E. Tompkins and S. W. Hays: 1989, "In Praise of Difficult People: A Portrait of the Committed Whistleblower," *Public Administration Review,* 552–561.

Keenan, J. P. and C. A. Krueger: 1992, "Whistleblowing and the Professional," *Management Accounting* **74** (Aug.), 21–24.

Longo, T.: 1996, "The Cost of Rebuilding a Career," *Kipplinger's Personal Finance Magazine* (Feb.), 140.

Machalaba, D.: 1995, "CSX Unit to Settle Ex-employee's Suit for $5.9 Million," *Wall Street Journal* (2 Oct.), B6.

McKenna, M.: 1987, "Sundstrand Faces Fines," *Rockford Register-Star* (4 March), 2.

Miceli, M. P. and J. P. Near: 1985, "Characteristics of Organizational Climate and Perceived Wrongdoing Associated with Whistle-blowing Decisions," *Personnel Psychology* **38,** 525–544.

Miceli, M. P and J. P Near: 1992, *Blowing the Whistle: The Organizational and Legal Implications for Companies and Employees* (Lexington Books, New York).

Miceli, M. P. and J. P. Near: 1994, "Whistleblowing: Reaping the Benefits," *Academy of Management Executive* **8**(3), 65–72.

Modic, S.: 1987, "Forget Ethics—and Succeed?," *Industry Week* (19 Oct.), 17–18.

Near, J. P. and T. C. Jensen: 1983, "The Whistle-blowing Process: Retaliation and Perceived Effectiveness," *Work and Occupations* **10,** 3–28,

Near, J. P. and M. P. Miceli: 1995. "Effective Whistleblowing," *Academy of Management Review* **20**(3), 679–708.

Orr, K.: 1988, "Sundstrand Charges On," *Rockford Register-Star* (18 Sept.), 6.

Pacanowsky, M. E. and N. Trujillo: 1992, "Organizational Communication as Cultural Performance," in K. L. Hutchison (ed.), *Readings in Organizational Communication* (W. C. Brown, Dubuque).

Revisions to fraud statute aid suit against Raytheon: 1987, *Aviation Week and Space Technology* (9 Nov.), 27.

Rogers, D. P.: 1994, "Book Review," *Journal of Business Communication* **31**(3), 235–243.

Safram, C.: 1992, "We Dared to Blow the Whistle!," *Good Housekeeping* (April), 78–83.

Schellhardt, T. D.: 1993, "To Prevent Theft, Make Ratting Part of the Job," *Wall Street Journal* (2 April), B1.

Schmitt, R. B. and M. Geyelin: 1994, "Court Overturns Attorney's Fees in Whistleblowing Case," *Wall Street Journal* (1 Dec.), B2.

Sims, C.: 1994, "Trying to Unite the Whistleblowers," *New York Times* (11 April), D1.

Smart, T. and E. Schine: 1991, "The 1863 Law That's Haunting Business," *Business Week* (21 Jan.), 68.

Street, M. D.: 1995, "Cognitive Moral Development and Organizational Commitment: Two Potential Predictors of Whistleblowing," *Journal of Applied Business Research* **11** (Fall), 103–110.

Sundstrand admits guilt: 1988, *Aviation Weekly and Space Technology* (17 Oct.), 37.

Sundstrand Corporation: 1988, *Code of Business Conduct and Ethics.*

Victor, B., L. K. Trevino and D. L. Shapiro: 1993, "Peer Reporting of Unethical Behavior: The Influence of Justice Evaluations and Social Context Factors," *Journal of Business Ethics* **12,** 253–263.

Vinton, G.: 1992, Whistleblowing: Corporate Help or Hindrance?," *Management Decision* **30**(1), 44–48.

Questions for Chapter 7

1. Davis suggests certain procedural and structural strategies to reduce the necessity of whistleblowing on the basis that an ounce of prevention is worth a pound of cure. Given that it is unlikely that the necessity for whistleblowing can ever be entirely removed, what recommendations would you make to help reduce the problems associated with whistleblowing?
2. Is Davis correct in his claim that whistleblowing must inevitably exact high costs both from employee and employer? Why or why not?
3. What is Larmer's argument for suggesting that "blowing the whistle may demonstrate greater loyalty than not blowing the whistle"?
4. Do you agree with Larmer's claim that, to the degree an action is genuinely immoral, it is impossible that it is in the agent's best interests? Defend your answer.
5. What indicators of the success of Sundstrand's program to encourage internal whistleblowing are mentioned by Benson and Ross?
6. Discuss the ways in which Sundstrand encourages its employees to take personal ownership of their ethics program.

Case 7.1 The Challenger *Disaster*

Morton Thiokol, an aerospace corporation, manufactured the solid-fuel booster rocket used to propel the space shuttle *Challenger*. This booster rocket was constructed in segments which progressively burn away during a launch and which need to be sealed from one another to prevent unburned fuel from exploding and destroying the shuttle. Research showed that the seals had a significantly higher failure risk at low temperatures, and Thiokol's contract with NASA specified that the boosters should not be operated at temperatures under 40°F.

The *Challenger's* launch, which had already been delayed several times, was scheduled for January 28, 1986. NASA, under funding pressure, and needing a successful mission to help justify its program, was anxious to avoid the bad publicity associated with another aborted launch. Unfortunately, January 28 turned out to be a cold cloudy day. NASA, wishing the launch to proceed, contacted Thiokol and pressured them to approve a launch, despite the cold weather. Although themselves engineers, Thiokol executives were anxious to accommo-

date an important customer. They overruled the warnings of their engineers working on the project and approved a launch at 30°F. The launch took place, even though the temperature was below 30°F, with disastrous results.

Roger Boisjoly, the chief engineer, testified to a presidential commission that he had made his opposition to the launch known to both Thiokol executives and NASA officials. He was subsequently "reassigned to other responsibilities" and isolated from NASA. He experienced alienation from his coworkers and, despite his experience and former high position at Thiokol, was unable to find a job with other engineering companies. He later took medical leave for post-traumatic stress disorder and subsequently left the company.

1. Does NASA or Thiokol bear the greater degree of blame for allowing the launch to go forward? Explain your answer.
2. Suppose you were Roger Boisjoly and you knew the consequences of whistleblowing. Would you whistleblow? Why or why not? What were Boisjoly's other options?

Case 7.2 Company Suspicion and Changed Working Conditions[1]

Charles G. Oxford worked for the National Laboratories Division of Lehn and Fink Industrial Products Division Inc., a division of Sterling Drug Inc., from 1963 to October 31, 1983, under a contract for an indefinite term. In the late seventies and early eighties, Sterling was prosecuted for submitting false information to the General Services Administration during contract negotiations. As a result of these pricing violations, Sterling eventually had to pay $1,075,000 to the federal government. Ray Mitchell, president of the Lehn and Fink Division, expressed, in October 1981, his belief that Oxford was responsible for reporting Sterling's pricing violations.

In October 1981, Oxford was advised that his position as manager of contract sales would be eliminated effective January 1, 1982, as a result of company restructuring. Oxford was offered, and accepted, a new position as a district sales manager, the lowest position in the National Laboratories Division hierarchy. Coincident with his accepting this new position, Oxford received an "EEO" letter from his supervisor, this being the nickname for a letter used to set an employee up for termination. This letter detailed Oxford's new responsibilities, one of which included conducting floor-care demonstrations five nights a week after business hours.

Oxford's supervisor, who repeatedly criticized Oxford's performance of these new duties, later testified that he had been asked to write the EEO letter by Bill Milliron, a Lehn and Fink executive, and that his repeated criticism of Oxford followed the company procedure outlined by Milliron to document an employee's termination. The supervisor also testified that he had only written two other EEO letters in his career, one to a district manager and one to a regional manager, and that both men had resigned under pressure.

Oxford, who consistently denied reporting Sterling to the General Services Administration, maintained that his supervisor also reprimanded him for performing acts he had not done and that he failed to receive stock he had won in a company sales contest. He left his territory in August 1983 without approval from Sterling and did not return to work. Sterling officially discharged him on October 31, 1983. In 1984, Oxford brought a suit against Sterling, alleging that it had engaged in a systematic campaign to force his resignation.

1. Do you have a duty as a citizen to inform the government if it is being cheated of large sums of money by your employer? Does the government have a duty to protect citizens who do this from retaliation by their employers?

2. Supposing Oxford had asked you if he should blow the whistle on Sterling, and if so, how. What advice would you have given him?

3. If you were a fellow employee of Oxford and he had asked you to support him in his whistleblowing, how would you have replied?

[1]Based on Sterling Drug Inc. v. Charles G. Oxford as described in 743 *Southwestern Reporter,* 2nd series, pp. 380–389.

Further Readings for Chapter 7

Sissela Bok, "Whistleblowing and Professional Responsibility," *New York Education Quarterly* 4, 1980, pp. 2–7.

Natalie Dandekar, "Can Whistleblowing Be Fully Legitimated?," *Business and Professional Ethics Journal* 10, Spring 1991, pp. 89–108.

Richard T. De George, "Ethical Responsibilities of Engineers in Large Organizations: The Pinto Case," *Business and Professional Ethics Journal* 1(1), 1981, pp. 1–14.

Ronald Duska, "Whistleblowing and Employee Loyalty" in *Contemporary Issues in Business Ethics,* 2nd ed., eds. Joseph R. Des Jardins and John J. McCall (Belmont, CA: Wadsworth, 1990), pp. 142–146.

Myron Glazer, "Ten Whistleblowers and How They Fared," *Hastings Center Report* 13(6), 1983, pp. 33–41.

M. P. Miceli and J. P. Near, "Effective Whistleblowing," *Academy of Management* 20(3) 1995, pp. 679–708.

INFOTRAC COLLEGE EDITION To learn more about the topics from this chapter, you can use the following words to conduct an electronic search on InfoTrac College Edition, an online library of journals. Here you will find a multitude of articles from various sources and perspectives: *www.infotrac-college.com/wadsworth/access.html*

whistleblowing

public interest

informers

Chapter 8

Insider Trading

Introduction

INSIDER TRADING can be defined as the buying or selling of stocks on the basis of privileged information available only to a select few. It is widely regarded as unethical and is illegal in the United States and Canada, as well as a large number of European and Asian countries. Nevertheless, some economic and ethical theorists have insisted that insider trading is morally acceptable and ought not, therefore, be illegal.[1] They argue that insider trading can in many instances be viewed as good for the economy, the corporation whose shares are traded, and the insiders who trade the shares, and that it does not necessarily involve defrauding investors. They also note that many countries that either do not have laws or do not enforce laws against insider trading nevertheless function as effective business cultures. The challenge they pose to defenders of the traditional view is to make clear exactly why insider trading should be regarded as unethical.

In "The Ethics of Insider Trading," Patricia Werhane defends the traditional view. She claims that insider trading is both immoral and economically inefficient. She argues that it violates standards of fairness and undermines competition which is the very basis of any free market. In her view, and, she argues, in Adam Smith's view, the free market should not be conceived as permitting the operation of unrestrained self-interest, but rather self-interest qualified by reason, moral sentiment, and human sympathy. Put a little differently, her point is that it is an error to think of Smith's appeal to self-interest as an endorsement of greed. Smith's famous "invisible hand"[2] is not to be conceived as acting independently of the

---

[1]See, for example, Henry Manne, *Insider Trading and the Stock Market* (New York: The Free Press, 1966), and William Shaw, "Shareholder Authorized Insider Trading: A Legal and Moral Analysis," *Journal of Business Ethics*, Vol. 9, 1990, pp. 913–928.

[2]Adam Smith (1723–1790), the founder of modern economics, argued that, although those in business primarily seek their own benefit, a free market produces, "as if by an invisible hand," the overall good of society.

requirements of morality. One's pursuit of self-interest, even within a totally free market, always presupposes the constraints of morality.

Indeed, if self-interest does not operate within the constraints of morality, it will undermine the condition of competition which, along with self-interest, makes possible the operation of a free market. Insofar as insider trading adversely affects the possibility of free competition, or is even generally perceived to adversely affect it, it is detrimental to the system of trade upon which it depends. In Werhane's view, insider trading is not simply a complication in the free market mechanism, but rather thwarts free competition, the life blood upon which free markets depend.

In his article "What Is Morally Right with Insider Trading," Tibor Machan defends the view that there need be nothing morally wrong with insider trading. In saying this, he is not condoning the immoral activity by which inside information is sometimes obtained, for example, by theft or by an employee being bribed to violate a fiduciary duty to keep certain information private. He insists, however, that the question of whether certain information was obtained legitimately is a separate issue from the question of whether it is ever morally appropriate to make use of inside information. In Machan's view, assuming there was no immorality in how one obtained inside information, there need be no immorality in making use of such information.

An objection frequently made is that it is not fair that some people be allowed to make use of information that others do not possess. Machan is not impressed by this objection. He points out that in many other areas of life people routinely make use of special information for their own benefit, for example, the knowledge that an especially desirable house is about to be put up for sale at an attractive price, yet no one regards this as immoral. Assuming there is no immorality in how one comes by knowledge of special opportunities, taking advantage of such opportunities should be regarded as a sign of good judgment, not of unfairness or deceit.

Richard Lippke, in "Justice and Insider Trading," takes up the issue of fairness on both a narrow and broad front. On the narrow front, it may be true that as long as there is no immorality in how insider information is obtained, there can be little objection to its use. To say this, however, does not come to grips with the objection that it is immoral that insiders be allowed to trade on the basis of information to which noninsiders lack access.

Proponents of insider trading often reply that there is nothing morally problematic in this. Carpenters may have knowledge that noncarpenters lack, but no one complains when they use that knowledge to their own advantage. Why then should we regard corporate managers using their specialized knowledge to their advantage, that is, through insider trading, as morally problematic?

Lippke acknowledges that assessing this argument is not an easy matter. It is an argument from analogy, and the strength of such an argument depends on the strength of the analogy employed. Just how similar is the situation of a carpenter using to his or her advantage his or her knowledge of how to build a deck, to the situation of a corporate manager using to his or her advantage inside information to make a profitable trade? At least initially, there seem to be some important differences that weaken the analogy. The carpenter might well employ his or her knowledge to advantage, even if the techniques of building a deck are public knowledge. It is far more questionable whether the corporate manager could employ his or her inside information to advantage should it become public knowledge.

On a broader front, Lippke argues that the morality of insider trading must be evaluated in the context of discussing the principles of justice that should be adopted by society and the degree to which existing institutions instantiate these principles. He claims that, once this is done, the arguments held to justify insider trading are revealed as deficient, inasmuch as they beg the question of whether the existing structures of wealth and power are morally defensible. Discussions of whether insider trading is morally problematic in terms of being unfair must take into account that the ability to profit from the trading of stocks, much less to profit from inside knowledge, is limited to those who are relatively affluent.

The Ethics of Insider Trading

PATRICIA H. WERHANE

Insider trading is the reverse of speculation. It is reward without risk, wealth generated—and injury done to others—by an unfair advantage in information. . . . [T]he core principle is clear: no one should profit from exploitation of important information not available to the public.[1]

INSIDER TRADING in the stock market is characterized as the buying or selling of shares of stock on the basis of information known only to the trader or to a few persons. In discussions of insider trading it is commonly assumed that the privileged information, if known to others, would affect their actions in the market as well, although in theory this need not be the case. The present guidelines of the Securities and Exchange Commission prohibit most forms of insider trading. Yet a number of economists and philosophers of late defend this kind of activity both as a viable and useful practice in a free market and as a practice that is not immoral. In response to these defenses I want to question the value of insider trading both from a moral and an economic point of view. I shall argue that insider trading both in its present illegal form and as a legalized market mechanism violates the privacy of concerned parties, destroys competition, and undermines the efficient and proper functioning of a free market, thereby bringing into question its own raison d'etre [i.e., reason for being]. It

[1]George Will, "Keep Your Eye on Guiliani." *Newsweek*, March 2, 1987, p. 84.

does so and therefore is economically inefficient for the very reason that it is immoral.

That insider trading as an illegal activity interferes with the free market is pretty obvious. It is like a game where there are a number of players each of whom represents a constituency. In this sort of game there are two sets of rules—one ostensive set and another, implicit set, functioning for some of the players. In this analogy some of the implicit rules are outlawed, yet the big players manage to keep them operative and actually often in control of the game. But not all the players know all the rules being played or at least they are ignorant of the most important ones, ones that determine the big wins and big losses. So not all the players realize what rules actually manipulate the outcome. Moreover, partly because some of the most important functioning rules are illegal, some players who do know the implicit rules and could participate do not. Thus not everyone in a position to do so plays the trading game the same way. The game, then, like the manipulated market that is the outcome, is unfair—unfair to some of the players and those they represent—unfair not only because some of the players are not privy to the most important rules, but also because these "special" rules are illegal so that they are adopted only by a few of even the privileged players.

But suppose that insider trading was decriminalized or not prohibited by SEC regulations. Then, one might argue, insider trading would not

From Journal of Business Ethics 8: 841–845, 1989. Reprinted by permission of Kluwer Academic Publishers.

be unfair because anyone could engage in it with impunity. Although one would be trading on privileged knowledge, others, too, could trade on *their* privileged information. The market would function more efficiently since the best-informed and those most able to gain information would be allowed to exercise their fiscal capabilities. The market itself would regulate the alleged excesses of insider trading. I use the term "alleged" excesses because according to this line of reasoning, if the market is functioning properly, whatever gains or losses are created as a result of open competition are a natural outcome of that competition. They are not excesses at all, and eventually the market will adjust the so-called unfair gains of speculators.

There are several other defenses of insider trading. First, insider information, e.g. information about a merger, acquisition, new stock issue, layoffs, etc., information known only to a few, *should* be and remain private. That information is the property of those engaged in the activity in question, and they should have the right to regulate its dissemination. Second and conversely, even under ideal circumstances it is impossible either to disseminate information to all interested parties equally and fairly, or alternately, to preserve absolute secrecy. For example, in issuing a new stock or deciding on a stock split, a number of parties in the transaction from brokers to printers learn about that information in advance just because of their participation in making this activity a reality. And there are always shareholders and other interested parties who claim they did not receive information of such an activity or did not receive it at the same time as other shareholders even when the information was disseminated to everyone at the same time. Thus it is, at best, difficult to stop insider trading or to judge whether a certain kind of knowledge is "inside" or privileged. This is not a good reason to defend insider trading as economically or morally desirable, but it illustrates the difficulties of defining and controlling the phenomenon.

Third, those who become privy to inside information, even if they take advantage of that information before it becomes public, are trading on probabilities, not on certainties, since they are trading before the activity actually takes place. They are taking a gamble, and if they are wrong the market itself will "punish" them. It is even argued that brokers who do not use inside information for their clients' advantage are cheating their clients.

Finally, and more importantly, economists like Henry Manne argue that insider trading is beneficial to outsiders. Whether it is more beneficial than its absence is a question Manne admits he cannot answer. But Manne defends insider trading because, he argues, it reduces the factor of chance in trading both for insiders and outsiders. When shares are traded on information or probabilities rather than on rumor or whim, the market reflects more accurately the actual economic status of that company or set of companies. Because of insider trading, stock prices more closely represent the worth of their company than shares not affected by insider trading. Insider trading, then, actually improves the fairness of the market, according to this argument, by reflecting in stock prices the fiscal realities of affected corporations thereby benefitting all traders of the stocks.[2]

These arguments for insider trading are persuasive. Because outsiders are allegedly not harmed from privileged information not available to them and may indeed benefit from insider trading, and because the market punishes rash speculators, insider trading cannot be criticized as exploitation. In fact, it makes the market more efficient. Strong as these arguments are, however, there is something amiss with these claims. The error, I think, rests at least in part with the faulty view of how free markets work, a view which stems from a misinterpretation that derives from a misreading of Adam Smith and specifically a misreading of Smith's notions of self-interest and the Invisible Hand.

The misinterpretation is this. It is sometimes assumed that the unregulated free market, driven by competition and self-interest, will function autonomously. The idea is that the free market works something like the law of gravity—autonomously and anonymously in what I would call a no-blooded fashion. The interrelationships created by free market activities based on self-interested competition are similar to the gravitational relationships between the planets and the sun: impersonal, automatic interactions determined by a number of factors including the distance and competitive self-interest of each of the market

[2]See Henry Manne, *Insider Trading and the Stock Market* (The Free Press, New York, 1966), especially Chapters X and XI.

components. The free market functions, then, despite the selfish peculiarities of the players just as the planets circle the sun despite their best intentions to do otherwise. Given that picture of the free market, so-called insider trading, driven by self-interest but restrained by competitive forces, that is, the Invisible Hand, is merely one gravitational mechanism—a complication but not an oddity or an aberration in the market.

This is a crude and exaggerated picture of the market, but I think it accounts for talk about the market *as if* it functioned in this independent yet forceful way, and it accounts for defenses of unrestrained self-interested actions in the market place. It allows one to defend insider trading because of the positive market fall-out from this activity, and because the market allegedly will control the excesses of self-interested economic activities.

The difficulty with this analysis is not so much with the view of insider trading as a legitimate activity but rather with the picture of economic actors in a free market. Adam Smith himself, despite his 17th century Newtonian background, did not have such a mechanical view of a laissez-faire [i.e., to let do. In the present context it refers to the principle of non-interference by government in commercial enterprise.] economy. Again and again in the *Wealth of Nations* Smith extols the virtues of unrestrained competition as being to the advantage of the producer and the consumer.[3] A system of perfect liberty he argues, creates a situation where "[t]he whole of the advantages and disadvantages of the different employments of labour and stock . . . be either perfectly equal or continually tending to equality.[4] Yet for Smith the greatest cause of inequalities of advantage is any restrictive policy or activity that deliberately gives privileges to certain kinds of businesses, trades, or professions.[5] The point is that Smith sees perfect liberty as the necessary condition for competition, but perfect competition occurs only when both parties in the exchange are on more or less on equal grounds, whether it be competition for labor, jobs, consumers, or capital. This is not to imply that Smith favors equality of outcomes. Clearly he does

not. But the market is most efficient and most fair when there is competition between equally matched parties.

Moreover, Smith's thesis was that the Invisible Hand works because, and only when, people operate with restrained self-interest, self-interest restrained by reason, moral sentiments, and sympathy, in Smith's case the reason, moral sentiments, and sympathies of British gentlemen. To operate otherwise, that is, with unrestrained self-interest, where that self-interest causes harm to others would "violate the laws of justice"[6] or be a "violation of fair play,"[7] according to Smith. This interferes with free competition just as government regulation would because the character of competition, and thus the direction of the Invisible Hand, depends on the manner in which actors exploit or control their own self-interests. The Invisible Hand, then, that "masterminds" the free market is not like an autonomous gravitational force. It depends on the good will, decency, self-restraint, and fair play of those parties engaging in market activities.[8] When self-interests get out of hand, Smith contends, they must be regulated by laws of justice.[9]

Similarly, the current market, albeit not Smith's ideal of laissez-faire, is affected by how people operate in the marketplace. It does not operate autonomously. Unrestrained activities of insider traders affect competition differently than Smithian exchanges which are more or less equal exchanges between self-interested but restrained parties. The term "insider trading" implies that some traders know more than others, that information affects their decision-making and would similarly affect the trading behavior of others should they become privy to that information. Because of this, the resulting market is different than one unaffected by insider trading. This, in itself, is not a good reason to question insider trading. Henry Manne, for example, recognizes the role of insider trading in influencing the market and finds that, on balance, this is beneficial.

---

[3]Adam Smith, *The Wealth of Nations,* ed. R. A. Campbell and A. S. Skinner (Oxford University Press, Oxford, 1976), I.x.c, II.v.8–12.

[4]*Wealth of Nations,* I.x.a.1.

[5]*Wealth of Nations,* I.x.c.

[6]*Wealth of Nations,* IV.ix.51.

[7]Adam Smith, *The Theory of Moral Sentiments,* ed. D. D. Raphael and A. L. Macfie (Oxford University Press, Oxford, 1976), II.ii.2.1.

[8]See Andrew Skinner, *A System of Social Science* (Clarendon Press, Oxford, 1979), especially pp. 237ff.

[9]See, for example, *The Wealth of Nations,* II.ii.94, IV, v.16.

Insider trading, however, is not merely a complication in the free market mechanism. Insider trading, whether it is legal or illegal, affects negatively the ideal of laissez-faire of *any* market, because it thwarts the very basis of the market: competition, just as "insider" rules affect the fairness of the trader even if that activity is not illegal and even if one could, in theory, obtain inside information oneself. This is because the same information, or equal information, is not available to everyone. So competition, which depends on the availability of equal advantage by all parties, is precluded. Insider trading allows the insider to indulge in greed (even though she may not) and that, by eschewing stock prices, works against the very kind of market in which insider trading might be allowed to function.

If it is true, as Manne argues, that insider trading produces a more efficient stock market because stock prices as a result of insider trading better reflect the underlying economic conditions of those companies involved in the trade, he would also have to argue that competition does not always produce the best results in the marketplace. Conversely, if competition creates the most efficient market, insider trading cannot, because competition is "regulated" by insiders. While it is not clear whether outsiders benefit more from insider trading than without that activity, equal access to information would allow (although not determine) every trader to compete from an equal advantage. Thus pure competition, a supposed goal of the free market and an aim of most persons who defend insider trading, is more nearly obtained without insider trading.

Insider trading has other ethical problems. Insider trading does not protect the privacy of information it is supposed to protect. To illustrate, let us consider a case of a friendly merger between Company X and Company Y. Suppose this merger is in the planning stages and is not to be made public even to the shareholders for a number of months. There may be good or bad reasons for this secrecy, e.g., labor problems, price of shares of acquired company, management changes, unfriendly raiders, competition in certain markets, etc. By law, management and others privy to knowledge about the possible merger cannot trade shares of either company during the negotiating period. On the other hand, if that information is "leaked" to a trader (or if she finds out by some

other means), then information that might affect the merger is now in the hands of persons not part of the negotiation. The alleged privacy of information, privacy supposedly protected by insider traders, is now in the hands of not disinterested parties. While they may keep this information a secret, they had no right to it in the first place. Moreover, their possession of the information has three possible negative effects.

First, they or their clients in fact may be interested parties to the merger, e.g., labor union leaders, stockholders in competing companies, etc., the very persons for whom the information makes a difference and therefore are the objects of Company X and Y's secrecy. Second, insider trading on privileged information gives unfair advantages to these traders. Even if outsiders benefit from insider trading, they are less likely to benefit as much nor as soon as insider traders for the very reason of their lack of proximity to the activity. Insider traders can use information to their advantage in the market, an advantage neither the management of X or Y nor other traders can enjoy Even if the use of such information in the market makes the market more efficient, this is unfair competition since those without this information will not gain as much as those who have such knowledge. Even if insider trading does contribute to market stabilization based on information, nevertheless, one has also to justify the fact that insider traders profit more on their knowledge than outsiders, when their information becomes an actuality simply by being "first" in the trading of the stock. Do insider traders deserve this added profit because their trading creates a more propitious market share knowledge for outsiders? That is a difficult position to defend, because allowing insider trading also allows for the very Boeskyian greed that is damaging in any market.

Third, while trading X and Y on inside information may bring their share prices to the value most closely reflecting their real price-earnings ratio, this is not always the case. Such trading may reflect undue optimism or pessimism about the possible outcome of the merger, an event that has not yet occurred. So the prices of X and Y may be overvalued or undervalued on the basis of a probability, or, because insider traders seldom have all the facts, on guesswork. In these cases insider trading deliberately creates more risk in the market since the stock prices or X or Y are manipulated for not altogether solid reasons. So market efficiency, the end which allegedly justifies insider trading, is not guaranteed.

What Henry Manne's defenses of insider trading do show is what Adam Smith well knew, that the market is neither independent nor self-regulatory. What traders do in the market and how they behave affects the direction and kind of restraint the market will exert on other traders. The character of the market is a product of those who operate within it, as Manne has demon-strated in his defense of insider trading. Restrained self-interest creates an approximation of a self-regulatory market, because it is that that allows self-interested individuals and companies to function as competitively as possible. In the long run the market will operate more efficiently too, because it precludes aberrations such as those exhibited by Ivan Boesky's and David Levine's behavior, behavior that created market conditions favorable to no one except themselves and their clients.

What Is Morally Right with Insider Trading

TIBOR R. MACHAN

Introduction

INSIDER TRADING per se is obtaining information from non-public sources—private acquaintances, friends, colleagues—and using it for purposes of enhancing one's financial advantage. As Vincent Barry explains, "Insider dealings refers to the ability of key employees to profit from knowledge or information that has not yet become public."[1] Sometimes such a practice can be conducted fraudulently, as when one who has obtained the information has a fiduciary duty to share it with clients but fails to exercise it, or in some other criminal fashion, as when the information is itself stolen. These are not, however, features of insider trading as such, as understood in the context of the discussion of business ethics. Never mind that in the enforcement of government regulations it is in fact fraud that is cited that makes the conduct illegal when referred to as insider trading.[2] (This suggests that the bulk of the relevant law does not concern itself so much with what many in the business ethics community worry about, namely, "justice as fairness," but with "justice as honoring of contracts.")

What makes the insider trading business ethics discussions focus upon distinctive is that the information on which trade is based is not known to others within the interested trading community aside from the insider. Insider trading is dealing with the aid of what is not so called "public knowledge" and, thus, it gives the trader an advantage over the rest of the market participants who are on the outside.

---

[1] Vincent Barry, *Moral Issues in Business* (Belmont, CA: Wadsworth Publishing Company, 1983), p. 242.

[2] Rule 106-5 of Securities Exchange Act of 1934. See, also, SEC v. Texas Gulf Sulpher (1968); U.S. v. Chiarella (1980), and U.S. v. Newman (1981). Both definitions and sanctions vary somewhat from state to state and case to case. *Black's Law Dictionary* states that "Insider trading . . . refers to transactions in shares of publicly held corporations by per-sons with insider or advance information on which the trading is based. Usually the trader himself is an insider with an employment or other relation of trust and confidence with the corporation" (St. Paul, MN: West Publishing Company. 1991). p. 547. Pub. L. 100-704. Sec. 7, Nov. l9, 1988, 102 Stat. 4682, provides that there be a study and investigation of, among other things. "impediments to the fairness and orderliness of the securities markets. . . ."

While the language of securities law does mention the fairness that is most often the concern of those discussing insider trading in the field of business ethics, it seems that the main focus of the law and the regulatory bodies fine tuning and enforcing it has to do with fraudulent trading in insider information or its misuse by those who have fiduciary duties not to disclose and use it until it is made available to the general trading public.

From Public Affairs Quarterly *10(2), 1996. Reprinted with permission.*

Against the common view of insider trading presented in business ethics discussions, I want to argue that it may be one's achievement or good fortune to learn of opportunities ahead of others and there is nothing morally wrong with this. In fact, acting on such information can be prudent, exhibiting good business acumen, whenever it does not involve the violation of others' rights. The conventional view rests on the belief that others have a right to one's revealing to them information one has honestly obtained ahead of them. But there is no sound general moral principle that requires this.

We clearly make morally unobjectionable use of special information for our own benefit, despite the fact that others might also benefit were it available to them: as when we are first to learn of the presence of a potential dating partner, a good buy on a used car, or a house coming up for sale in a highly preferred neighborhood. To take advantage of such special opportunities is a sign of good judgment, not of unfairness or deception.

Those who claim otherwise as regard insider trading confuse the marketplace with a game in which rules are devised or set down with the special purpose of giving everyone an even chance—e.g., when in golf or steeple chasing handicaps are assigned, or when in pro football the lowest ranked team gains first choice in the player drafts. The market is more akin to life itself, in which different persons enter with different assets—talents, looks, genetic make up, economic and climactic circumstances—and they must do their best with what they have. In life, apart from occasionally benefiting from the generosity or charity of others, all one has is a fighting chance. Children of musically proficient parents will probably benefit "unfairly" as far as obtaining musical opportunities are concerned. Those born in Bombay, to poor parents, will face harder times than those born in Beverly Hills to movie star parents. No general moral requirement exists for strangers to even this out, only to abstain from imposing obstacles on others, from violating their rights to liberty. The marketplace, too, is a setting wherein different persons face different circumstances. People do not have a natural obligation to perform involuntary service to strangers. In competing with others for opportunities that the market provides by way of demands one can fulfill in return for voluntary compensation, one is treating all other agents with the respect they deserve as the potential traders

they mostly are in such a context. Exceptions exist, of course, as when one trades with friends or family, which raises some moral complications. But the norm is where people treat each other as seeking to find opportunities for trade, nothing more. Other human relationships can obtain side by side, of course, but we can keep the commercial ones distinct enough to understand the ethics that ought to govern us as we embark upon trade. Let me now develop some of these points.

What Is Insider Trading?

The concept "insider trading" employed in business ethics discussions has a broader meaning: it includes anyone's ability to make deals based on not yet publicized knowledge of business opportunities. Insider trading as such, apart from what it may be related to in some cases (such as fraud or the violation of fiduciary duty), involves making financial investments on the basis of knowledge others do not have and may not be able to obtain in ordinary ways. *A* knows the president of a firm who tells *A* that they are thinking of expanding one of their divisions or have struck oil in a new field, so *A* buys a block of stock in anticipation of the increase of value once the deal is done or the knowledge becomes public. *A* is not deceiving anyone, nor is *A* defrauding anyone. *A* is not taking anything from others that *A* wasn't freely given. *A* is acting on special, "insider," information, that is all.

It is conventional wisdom to treat this version of insider trading as morally wrong because it is supposed to affect others adversely by being unfair. As one critic has put it, "What causes injury or loss to outsiders is not what the insider knew or did, rather it is what they themselves [the outsiders] did not know. It is their own lack of knowledge which exposes them to risk of loss or denies the an opportunity to make a profit."[3] By the fact that these others do not know what the insider does know,

---

[3]John A. C. Hetherington, "Corporate Social Responsibility, Stockholders, and the Law," *Journal of Contemporary Business,* Winter (1973), p. 51; quoted In *op. cit.,* Barry, *Moral Issues,* pp. 242–43. One feature of the business ethics discussions of insider trading and other normative topics is that there is hardly any attention paid to the distinction between ethics and public policy. Thus, even if there were something ethically objectionable about some business practice, this does not ipso facto warrant rendering it illegal or subject to government regulation. An analogy might help

they are harmed since they are not able to make use of opportunities that are in fact available, knowable to us.

But what kind of causation is it that fails to make a difference when it does not exist? If someone's knowing a good deal has no impact on what another does, it cannot be said that any harm upon another had been caused by that someone. Certainly, had the other known what the insider knew, he or she could have acted differently. By not acting differently, he or she could easily have failed to reap advantages the insider did reap. But nothing here shows that the insider *caused* any harm, only that he or she had a better set of opportunities. Unless we assume that valuable information known by one person ought, morally—and perhaps legally—be distributed to all interested parties—something that would beg the most important question—there is no moral fault involved in insider trading nor any causation of harm.[4]

Because of the widespread but mistaken view that insider trading is morally wrong, it is conventional wisdom to support its legal prohibition. Of course, even if morally wrong, it may not follow that it should be morally prohibited. Yet there is reason to think that the moral objections are wrongheaded. Because of this we may suspect that the opposition to insider trading is more likely the result of widespread, strong prejudice against gaining economic prosperity without sharing it. Clearly there is a lot of thinking afoot in our era to the effect that a level playing field is morally mandatory when people embark upon commercial or business endeavors.[5]

Why Insider Trading Is Right

Certainly I am at an advantage when I possess information others lack. Nearly everyone in the marketplace is in that position to a certain extent. One might even wish to call this "unfair" in the sense in which any kind of good fortune may be to some people's but not to others' advantage. More precisely, though, the concept of fairness does not apply in this context, even though many believe otherwise. For someone to act fairly requires some prior obligation to distribute burdens or benefits among a given number of people in some suitable proportion or in line with certain specified procedures. But to act fairly does not amount to a primary moral duty—for example, thieves can fairly enough distribute their loot and yet are morally delinquent. Only when one ought to treat others alike, which may occur in special circumstances such as paying attention to all the students in one's class or feeding all of one's children equally well, does fairness count for something morally important.

As this applies to insider trading, if I have a prior obligation to share my information with others, that is, a fiduciary duty to clients or associates, then it is not that the information is "from the inside" but that it is *owed to others* that makes my dealings morally and possibly legally objectionable. It is only in such cases that fairness is obligatory, as a

---

here: when we discuss journalistic ethics, it is clear enough that journalists may engage in unethical behavior that should not be made illegal. This same distinction is not generally observed when it comes to the profession of business. For an exception, see Tibor R. Machan, ed., *Commerce and Morality* (Lanham, MD: Rowman & Littlefield, 1988), especially "Ethics and Its Uses." For a business ethics perspective hospitable to viewing business as a morally honorable profession, see Tibor R. Machan, "Professional Responsibilities of Corporate Managers," *Business and Professional Ethics Journal*, vol. 13 (1994).

[4]If someone does not do what he or she ought to do, the causation involved may be the kind that consists in taking away of a supporting feature of an action: Someone who steals a part of my car engine causes it to fail to operate properly by removing what such operation needs. That is how stealing can cause the ensuing harm. Fraud produces harm similarly: something one owns, namely, what another has legally committed to one, is in fact withheld. But without such commitment, nor even a moral duty to provide, no causation of the lack of desired advantage can be identified. For more on this, see Eric Mack, "Bad Samaritanism and the Causation of Harm," *Philosophy and Public Affairs*, vol. 9 (1980).

[5]The most prominent is, of course, John Rawls, *A Theory of Justice* (Cambridge, MA: Harvard University Press, 1971). One main problem in Rawl's defense of "justice as fairness" is that Rawls believes that no one can deserve his or her advantages or assets in life—it's all a matter of luck. As he puts it, "No one deserves his greater natural capacity nor merits a more favorable starting point in society." The reason? Because even a person's character (i.e., the virtues he or she practices that may provide him with ways of getting ahead of others) "depends in large part upon fortunate family and social circumstances for which he can claim no credit" (104). If one rejects this deterministic account of virtues, then a trader's prudence cannot be discounted as one assesses whether he or she deserves to gain from how trade is conducted.

matter of one's professional relationship to others, one established by the promise made or contract one has entered into prior to the ensuing duty to be fair. It is only then that one can cause injury by refusing to do what one has agreed to do, namely, divulge information prior to using it for oneself. Accordingly, Hetherington's objection to insider trading is without moral force. What he should have objected to is the breaching of fiduciary duty, which may occur on occasion by means of failing to divulge information (possibly gained "from the inside") that has been—perhaps even contractually—promised to a client.

Furthermore, if I have stolen the information—spied or bribed for or extorted it—again the moral deficiency comes not from its being inside information but from its having been ill gotten.

What if the information was come by accidentally? I overhear some people talking in the lavatory or at a bar after they've had too much to drink and have loose tongues. Am I wrong to make use of it?

Here again the issue is just what I owe others. Do I have a natural obligation to share my good fortune with other people?

In emergency situations, when others are in dire need or have met with some natural disaster, virtues such as generosity and charity are usually binding on those who are able to assist. Yet these are not obligations in the sense of something the law must enforce. Indeed, enforcing generosity or charity is impossible—the moral significance of a virtue is destroyed if it is practiced at the point of a gun! Furthermore, in the context of the normal hustle and bustle of life, no such virtues are called for toward strangers, only toward those one is related to by prior commitments, intimacy, and love. Instead, in the ordinary course of life one ought to strive to live successfully, to prosper, to make headway with one's legitimate projects, not embark upon the tasks of emergency crews during an earthquake. Unless one is specifically suited for those professions that address those in special need, one has no business to meddle in the lives of others and ought to carry forth without compunction in those tasks that advance the lives of those one has freely embarked upon to promote.

From the viewpoint of common sense ethics, the idea that there is something morally amiss with insider trading has little to support it. One clearly has no moral, let alone legal, obligation to share information with strangers that may benefit one in other familiar circumstances.

Imagine, for example, that an appealing eligible single woman moves into a neighborhood in which several eligible men would like to meet her. I, one of these men, obtain (insider) information about her impending arrival before others and approach her before other men in my position learn of the fact that she will be part of the community. Have I done wrong? Isn't the prospect of successful romance even more important to people than the prospect of successful investment? Suppose, again, that I learn of a very good violin teacher who is moving to our town and I am first in line to take lessons from him. Am I doing something morally wrong? Nothing supports such a view.

Of course, were I someone who is in no great hurry with finding a mate and had a friend who is, I might generously tell him about the impending arrival of the lady. This would be generous but not obligatory. The same would hold if I had a friend of whose musical ambitions with the violin I am well aware and I learned of the opportunity for taking lessons from a new master in our neighborhood. Were I to forget about my friends in these cases, this might well be justly held against me. But the same does not apply when it comes to strangers.

In fact, there are areas of commerce in the USA not to mention in other societies where insider trading is not prohibited (e.g., Japan), where the type of conduct insider trading exhibits is not only accepted but praised. Consider news reporting. When a news reporter scoops the competition, no one considers this legally actionable, nor, indeed, morally insidious. On the contrary, it is a mark of professional savvy and achievement. Why does this not apply in the case of insider trading? I'll turn to this next.

The Bad Reputation of Commerce

The reason these situations, as distinct from insider trading, do not invite widespread moral rebuke is that we tend to consider objectives such as finding the right mate or learning a musical instrument something benign, morally untainted. When it comes to making economic or financial gains, in many quarters there is an initial moral discomfort about it. The shadow of greed looms very large and tends even to overwhelm prudence, which is, after all, the first of the cardinal virtues.

Why Insider Trading Seems Wrong

Indeed, the intellectual source of moral disdain for insider trading is the more general disdain for economic or commercial self-enhancement, at least among moral philosophers and others in the humanities. There seems to be no end to how fiercely commercial success is demeaned among many of those who preach and reflect upon morality. Yet this seems to me to be utterly misguided.

Becoming prosperous can be a means toward the attainment of numerous worthy goals and should, thus, itself be deemed to be a worthy goal. Not that riches cannot be pursued obsessively, but it need not be done so at all. Any other goal can also be pursued *to a fault*. An artist can be over ambitious vis-a-vis being an artist and, thereby, neglect family, friends, polity. Even truth can be pursued too fanatically. The chances for corruption through the pursuit of economic advantage are no greater than through other pursuits. The disdainful attitude toward commercial professionals is entirely unjustified, a prejudice that deserves as much study as prejudices toward racial, religious or ethnic groups.

What about the fact that we encourage fairness in athletic competition, such as imposing handicaps in golf and horse racing? What about the way baseball and football leagues utilize the player draft to even out the advantages of teams? Does this not indicate that we stress fairness more than I have allowed? Don't we find fairness heavily stressed in the allocation of chores in families and fraternities, not to mention teams?

Bad Analogies

These examples are misleading. It isn't fairness *per se* that's stressed in golf and horse racing; what appears as such is actually an effort to foster games and races that capture and keep the interest of spectators. The same holds for the policy on player drafts. If a team wins repeatedly, interest will begin to wane and the sport will lose its fans.

As to families, there exists a prior obligation to share burdens and benefits among the members, if not equally then at least proportionately. Parents have invited their children into the family, as it were, and when benefits (or burdens) are reaped, all those invited should share them.

Among people who are not in such relationships no fairness principle operates. No doubt, sometimes we make a mistake and transfer the attitudes we have acquired for how to handle matters in the family to other areas of our lives, but that is an illogical extrapolation. And this is evident enough by considering that if I am born to a family with musical talents or good genes, it is not my duty to make sure that those born to families without them somehow share my advantages. Nor am I doing the right thing in imposing my burdens on members of families who do not suffer as mine does. That sort of policy would be more appropriately associated with envy and resentment, not with moral decency.

The Moral Merit of Insider Trading

Accordingly, seeking to benefit through ingenuity and shrewdness is good business, and good business is as important a professional trait as good medicine, good law, good education, etc. Professional ethics, in turn, cannot condemn that which is in accord with ethics in general, such as fortitude and prudence. Competence and skill, even excellence, at managing the material progress one might be able to make in life ought not to be treated as less important than competence and skill at managing artistic, scientific, educational or other types of progress.

There are those who defend insider trading because it contributes to the overall efficiency of market transactions. They argue that those trading from the inside send signals to others whose reactions then help propel the market to its new level of efficiency.

There may be something to this line of defense, although it comes perilously close to arguing that the end justifies the means. Unless the actions of the individuals who engage in insider trading can themselves be shown to be justified, such arguments do not do much good. One can show benefits to society at large based on theft, even murder, yet these are by no means justified based on such reasoning.

Insider trading, moreover, is held to be morally suspect not because its overall value to the society is denied but because many regard fairness, equality, a level playing field, the most important criteria for a morally decent marketplace. The fact is that those are actually not what counts most for the morality of trade. That place is occupied by the respect for individual rights. Within the framework of such respect, insider trading is entirely unobjectionable. In addition, it can be perfectly ethically commendable to act based on such information; it is a matter of prudence and commercial savvy, both of which should be encouraged from those who work for a living.[6]

[6]I wish to thank Professor Clif Perry, the editors of *Public Affairs Quarterly*, and George Childress for the help I received from them in the preparation of this paper. I am, of course, fully responsible for the use I made of this help.

Justice and Insider Trading*

RICHARD L. LIPPKE

LONG ILLEGAL in the United States, insider trading in securities markets is increasingly being legally proscribed in European and Asian countries. France led the way in prohibiting insider trading, outlawing it in 1970, but the United Kingdom, Italy, Sweden, Norway, Spain, Greece, and others have since followed suit.[1] Pressure from the European Community has recently forced Germany to enact laws against such trading, and even Japan and Hong Kong have taken steps to limit its occurrence in their formerly wide-open securities markets.[2]

Meanwhile, the morality of insider trading remains a hotly contested topic in a variety of scholarly journals. Many scholars enthusiastically defend it, and some, while not wholeheartedly defending it, seek to debunk the many arguments against it. The focus of this paper will be on the fairness arguments against insider trading. The underlying idea behind these arguments is that to permit insider trading would be to set up stock market trading rules that are unfair to non-insiders, individuals who do not possess or have access to the sorts of material, non-public information that insiders do. These arguments have been widely discussed. I will lay bare the largely unstated assumptions about fairness behind these discussions and then attempt to show that these assumptions yield, at best, a truncated conception of justice. At worst, these assumptions legitimise, without argument, the political and economic *status quo* in countries with large inequalities. I argue that a defensible treatment of the fairness of insider trading requires both a complete conception of justice and its thoughtful application to existing political and economic institutions.

The discussion is in three main sections. In the first, I summarise the fairness debate about insider trading as that debate has been presented in the recent scholarly literature. In the second section, I reveal the assumptions about fairness implicit in that debate and argue that these assumptions cannot be defended independently of a larger conception of justice. In the third section, I briefly summarise and then use an egalitarian conception of justice to analyse insider trading. By doing so, I hope to illustrate how a more systematic approach to the analysis of insider trading, one that invokes

*I am grateful to Sharon O'Hare for many helpful comments on an earlier draft of this paper.
[1]Pierre Lemieux, "Exporting the Insider Trading Scandal," *The Wall Street Journal*, October 13, 1992.
[2]For developments in Germany, see "Behind the Times," *The Economist*, July 13, 1991, p. 86; for developments in Japan, see "Over to the Men in Uniform," *The Economist*, May 19, 1990, pp. 91–2; for developments in Hong Kong, see Michael Taylor, "Lifting the Veil," *Far Eastern Economic Review*, November 28, 1991, pp. 63–4.

From Journal of Applied Philosophy *10(2), 1993. Reprinted by permission of Society for Applied Philosophy, 1993. Blackwell Publishers, 108 Cowley Road, Oxford, 0X4 IJF. UK and 3 Cambridge Center, Cambridge, MA 02142, USA.*

a complete theory of justice, transforms the debate about the fairness of insider trading. I should add that the conception I employ is one that most commentators would find unappealing. However, one of the points I wish to make is that their discussions do little more than beg the question against such a conception.

Before proceeding further, let me clarify two matters. First, the insiders with which I will most concern myself throughout the paper are corporate managers. They are the individuals most likely to have inside information, and as such, their actions are the principal focus of most discussions of the fairness of insider trading. I won't say much about the other individuals who might come to possess inside information, referred to in the literature as tippees and misappropriators.[3] Second, I will use the term "non-insiders" to refer to those individuals who do not possess any inside information relevant to a particular stock purchase or sale. Non-insiders might be insiders with regard to some stock transactions. And, of course, non-insiders might be and often are corporate employees.

I

As long as insider trading is legally proscribed, there is a fairly simple argument that shows how its existence is unfair to non-insiders.[4] Insiders who trade on material, non-public information, rather than disclosing the information or abstaining from trading as the rules typically prescribe, will be doing little more than cheating. They will be acting in a manner that violates the social expectations fostered by the rules. It is not convincing to argue, as some do, that since non-insiders "know" insider trading takes place, they realise that the official (legal) rules are not the actual rules; therefore their participation in the investing game must condone insider actions. First, it is likely that not all non-insiders know that insider trading takes place or how frequently it occurs. Second, the fact that insider trading is legally prohibited and socially disapproved surely muddies the waters for those who maintain that non-insiders "know" it occurs. At best, non-insiders may be confused about how insiders actually behave. At worst, they may assume that most insiders will abstain from trading or disclose material information.

The more interesting question is whether, morally speaking, insider trading should be legally proscribed. In particular, is there something unfair about such trading such that it ought to be a legitimate target of state action? Now the debate begins in earnest.

The most plausible case to be made that there is something unfair about insider trading emphasis the notion of "equal access to information."[5] It seems a mistake to hold that all parties to a market transaction must have equal information. To require this would be, in effect, to deprive persons of informational advantages they may have acquired through diligent effort. What seems bothersome about insider trading is that non-insiders lack *access* to the information on which insiders are trading. The informational advantage that insiders have is not "erodable" by the diligence or effort of non-insiders. No matter how carefully or exhaustively non-insiders study the available public information about firms in which they invest, they cannot really compete against those insiders who have access to material non-public information.[6]

A typical scenario described by opponents of insider trading is as follows: insiders known of an impending takeover bid for another firm by their firm. In anticipation of the rise in stock prices that usually results from such bids, they purchase shares of the target firm's stock. Often, such insider trading activity will send the target firm's stock price

---

[3]Tippees are individuals who are typically not corporate employees but who are given inside Information by corporate employees. Misappropriators are individuals who are typically not corporate managers but who come across inside information (e.g. financial printers temporarily employed by corporations).

[4]For a useful summary of the legal status of insider trading in the United States, see Bill Shaw, "Shareholder Authorized Inside Trading: A Legal and Moral Analysis," *Journal of Business Ethics*, Vol. 9 (1990): 913–928.

[5]Victor Brudney was one of the first to articulate the equal access argument. See his "Insiders, Outsiders and Informational Advantages Under the Federal Securities Laws," *Harvard Law Review*, Vol. 93 (1979): 322–376.

[6]Also, Patricia Werhane argues that if we value competition on the assumption that it will lead to the most socially beneficial results, then we should favour those rules which promote more vigorous competition. It we allow insiders to trade on their informational edge, competition will be systematically diminished because non-insiders will predictably lose out to insiders. See her "The Ethics of Insider Trading," *Journal of Business Ethics*, Vol. 8 (1989): 841–845.

up slightly. Non-insiders who hold stock in the target firm, believing there is no plausible reason for the rise in the share price, may decide to cash in by selling their stock. Though the non-insiders were able to sell their stock at a higher price than they would have received had the insiders not been active, opponents of insider trading argue that the non-insiders lose out on the further gains that typically result once a takeover bid is publicly announced. Non-insiders, because they lacked access to the information about the takeover bid prior to the public announcement, lose out on the opportunity to receive the additional gain.[7] Instead, the gain goes to insiders and this, opponents argue, is unfair to the non-insider.

Some commentators argue that insider trading is not likely to result in such losses (or unrealised gains) for non-insiders.[8] Yet none of these arguments seems to address the equal access objection head on. It seems likely that there will be some occasions where non-insiders do sell in response to a price rise caused by insider trading activity The fact that this may not necessarily happen or happen often seems beside the point. If insider trading is legally permitted, non-insiders can reasonably complain that the rules are set up in ways that are unjustifiably advantageous to insiders and so likely to the disadvantage of non-insiders. The possibility that the informational advantages insiders have and might use work out to the advantage of non-insiders does not explain why insiders should be allowed to have and use those advantages.[9]

Frank Easterbrook and Jennifer Moore contend that non-insiders really cannot justifiably complain—that they do (or did) not have equal access to this information.[10] Non-insiders could have made career choices to become corporate executives, choices that would have given them access to inside information. Such information is, on this view, one of the perquisites of being a corporate insider. Moore draws an analogy. Plumbers have access to certain kinds of information that non-plumbers do not have (or to which they have more difficult access). Yet, no one complains when plumbers use their informational advantages to their own benefit by charging non-plumbers for their services. Similarly, non-insiders should not complain when insiders use informational advantages to their benefit. Easterbrook maintains that the different costs of access to information are simply a function of the division of labour: "A manager (or a physician) always knows more than a shareholder (or patient) in some respects, but unless there is something unethical about the division of labour, the difference is not unfair."[11]

This is a dubious argument for a number of reasons. Critics of insider trading who rely on the equal access argument clearly have in mind a different point of equal access than the one proffered by Moore and Easterbrook. The critics have in mind equal access via the typical ways in which corporations make information about themselves matters of public record—press releases, trade journals, reports to shareholders, etc. They might argue that there is a great deal of difference between saying that non-insiders should have researched their investment decisions more carefully and saying that non-insiders should have made different career choices.

Still, Easterbrook and Moore may simply be challenging the critics' conception of equal access

[7]Cf. Richard DeGeorge, "Ethics and the Financial Community," in Oliver Williams, Frank Reilly, and John Houck, *Ethics and the Investment Industry* (Savage, MD: Rowman and Littlefield, 1989), p. 203.

[8]For instance, Jennifer Moore argues that insider trading can sometimes actually benefit non-insiders by enabling them to avoid losses, and so is not systematically harmful to non-insiders. See her "What is Really Unethical About Insider Trading?" *Journal of Business Ethics,* Vol. 9 (1990): 171–182. For arguments that insider trading is not likely to harm non-insiders, see Deryl W Martin and Jeffrey H. Peterson, "Insider Trading Revisited," *Journal of Business Ethics,* Vol. 10 (1991): 57–61.

[9]Bill Shaw points out that the current rules with regard to insider trading already give insiders an edge in relation to non-insiders. If nothing else, insiders with material, non-public information know when not to trade, and the disclose-or-abstain rule permits this. See his "Shareholder Authorized Inside Trading: A Legal and Moral Analysis," p. 916. Still, allowing insiders to trade on such information

might tilt things even more in their favour, so the equal access argument could be modified to say that insiders should not be given any more advantages than they already have.

[10]Frank H. Easterbrook, "Insider Trading, Secret Agents, Evidentiary Privileges, and the Production of Information," *Supreme Court Review,* (1981): 309–365, especially pp. 323–330. Moore, "What Is Unethical About Insider Trading?" pp. 172–4.

[11]Easterbrook, "Insider Trading, Secret Agents, Evidentiary Privileges, and the Production of Information" p. 330.

and offering a substitute. However, there are problems with this substitute. What the non-insiders need is not simply the sort of knowledge that comes with the career choice of becoming a corporate manager. After all, some non-insiders (with respect to particular trades) might indeed be corporate managers and so they presumably have that kind of knowledge. Non-insiders need the specific information insiders have enabling them to deal on the stock market with an advantage over others. The claim that non-insiders cannot reasonably complain about the fairness of particular transactions because they too "could" have chosen to become corporate managers is not to the point. It is not insiders' career skills that non-insiders need but the insiders' information about particular business events.[12]

Also, the informational advantages insiders have over non-insiders have no clear analogue in the case of plumbers and non-plumbers. What non-plumbers pay plumbers for is plumbers' knowledge about plumbing. What shareholders pay managers for is managers' knowledge about managing. But plumbers do not seem to have an additional way of gaining an advantage over non-plumbers as do insiders in relation to non-insiders if insider trading is permitted. Insiders are already being compensated for their labour by the shareholders. Insider trading would give them something extra. If that something extra is "taken" without the shareholders' knowledge and consent, then it seems that the shareholders would have two different grounds for complaint. They could complain about their lack of equal access to information, or they could complain that the managers who take advantage of them via insider trades are failing to live up to their fiduciary responsibilities, which are to promote shareholder interests.

Still, both grounds for complaint can be undermined *if* insider trading is authorised by the shareholders. In effect, the shareholders would give their consent to an arrangement whereby corporate managers would be allowed, under certain conditions, to take advantage of their superior access to information.[13] Remember, we are no longer assuming that insider trading is illegal. Instead, we are trying to determine what set of rules regarding insider trading would be fair to all interested parties. Advocates of insider trading contend that it should be up to the shareholders to decide whether insider trading is to be permitted. After all, the information that is being traded on is their property. They should be allowed to determine how this information will best be put to use.

This leads to the question of why the shareholders would ever agree to permit managers to take advantage of the information to which they are privy, especially when the resultant trades might lead to losses (or failures to gain) by shareholders. Also, why would potential investors in a company purchase shares if they knew that the company permitted insider trading? Wouldn't investors be inclined to steer clear of such firms?

The boldest response to these questions is provided by Henry Manne and his followers.[14] Manne argues that if firms allowed insider trading as part of the management compensation package, this would enable them to attract managers who are likely to be more creative, productive, risk-takers. Allowing managers to trade on inside information would provide them the incentive to undertake riskier ventures, try out innovative production techniques, develop new products or services—in general, to engage in those activities that would create more value, in the long run, for the shareholders. Insider trading would allow these managers to reap the benefits of the new information they create and firms would save money by having to pay managers less base compensation. Of course, shareholders would not know precisely when insiders of their own firm were trading based on material non-public information, so shareholders might occasionally lose out in trades where insiders are involved. However, this is something the shareholders might consent to in the hopes of

---

[12]Indeed, the reason why tippees, free riders, and misappropriators can make use of inside information to their advantage is precisely that its usefulness has little to do with having made the career choice to become a corporate manager. Such information is thoroughly "detachable" from the division of labour.

[13]For the most explicit presentation of the shareholder authorisation argument, see Shaw, "Shareholder Authorized Inside Trading: A Legal and Moral Analysis," pp.920–1.

[14]Henry G. Manne, *Insider Trading and the Stock Market* (New York: The Free Press, 1966); see also Dennis W. Carlton and Daniel R. Fischel, "The Regulation of Insider Trading," *Stanford Law Review*, Vol. 35 (May 1983): 857–895.

finding managers who will increase the long-term value of their shares.[15]

Consistent with Manne's argument, others have suggested that as long as a firm's rules about insider trading are a matter of public record, individuals who invest in such firms will have voluntarily assumed the risk of trading in situations where insiders may be operating. Indeed, some argue that investors will react to this prospect by altering their own behavior. They may try to compensate for the possibility of future losses to insiders by paying less for stocks initially.[16] Or, when they see a stock's price rising, anticipating that insiders may know something, they may demand a higher price to induce them to sell. Moreover, most investors seek to reduce their risks by diversifying their stock portfolios. As Kenneth Scott points out, such investors will be less interested in the details of the buying and selling of particular stocks than in the overall performance of their portfolios.[17]

This general line of argument is both limited in its scope and has been subjected to withering criticism by various commentators. Its scope is limited because it seems to justify insider trading only by those employees who have a role in creating the information. It would not justify such trading by tippees or misappropriators. Also, some have suggested that since insiders can profitably trade on negative information, the shareholders would have to be careful to limit any incentives for managers to create such information.[18] Criticisms of the argument have focused on whether there are not other, more effective ways shareholders might use to provide incentives to managers to create value; on

whether there are ways to ensure that managers do not derive "too much" compensation from insider trading; and on whether managers themselves are likely to find the prospect of cashing in on inside information attractive enough to agree to compensation packages that permit such trading.[19]

As Easterbrook and Shaw both note, it is no easy task to weigh all of the pros and cons that have been unearthed by the various commentators.[20] In large part, this is due to the debate turning on the answers to a variety of empirical questions about the effects of firms permitting insider trading versus the effects of their not doing so—questions about which we have little evidence to go on. In any case, there seems a great deal to be said at this point for allowing shareholders to experiment with permitting insider trading if that is what they so desire. After all, it is their property, and the costs and benefits to third parties seem pretty speculative at this point. Investors who wish to steer clear of firms that permit forms of insider trading will presumably be able to do so, at least as long as corporate policies on the subject are made clear. In short, the debate about whether insider trading is fair seems to have been transformed into one about what it is reasonable for shareholders and their hired managers to negotiate amongst themselves.

II

In the preceding section, I explicated the logic of the fairness debate about insider trading as that debate has been recently carried on by scholars in various fields. In this section, I will highlight the assumptions about fairness that seem implicit in that debate and show how they are, if not problematic, at least controversial.

The place to begin is by noting that none of the commentators referred to in the previous section

[15]In response to Werhane's argument that insider trading undermines competition (*supra* note 6), Manne might argue that permitting it may reduce competitiveness in one area but heighten it in others. The market for corporate managers will heat up as firms that permit insider trading compete for those individuals who will take more risks and be more innovative. Also, within firms, allowing managers to profit from insider trading may spur them to try to outdo one another so that they can trade on any information "created."

[16]See Kenneth E. Scott, "Insider Trading: Rule 10b-5. Disclosure, and Corporate Privacy," *The Journal of Legal Studies,* Vol. 9 (1980): 801–818.

[17]Ibid., p. 809.

[18]Negative information might include such things as news of an impending major lawsuit against the corporation, news of poor earnings, or news of a product failure.

[19]There is also considerable speculation about the effects of insider trading on the efficiency of the stock market. However, the concerns with efficiency is different from the concern with fairness.

[20]Easterbrook, "Insider Trading, Secret Agents, Evidentiary Privileges, and the Production of Information," p. 338, see also his "Insider Trading as an Agency Problem," in John W. Pratt and Richard J. Zeckhauser, *Principals and Agents: The Structure of Business* (Boston Harvard Business School Press, 1985) 81–100 Shaw, "Shareholder Authorized Inside Trading: A Legal and Moral Analysis," pp. 921–2.

raises any questions about the fairness of the distribution of wealth, income, opportunities, and power that is the broader social context for decisions about what the rules regarding insider trading will be. Their discussions are simply divorced from the larger and more difficult questions that have been raised by moral and political theorists about the nature of social justice. They are also divorced from the implications the various theories offered have for an analysis of existing political and economic institutions. The existing distribution of property and other goods is taken as given and so, implicitly at least, legitimised.

One point at which this assumption of the legitimacy of the *status quo* is most clearly revealed is in Moore and Easterbrook's contention that non-insiders do have access to inside information at the point when they make their career choices. As we saw, this is a poor argument as a response to the equal access objection to insider trading. It is also an argument that seems rife with assumptions about the justice of the political and economic system in which people in countries like the United States live. I say "seems rife" because it is not altogether clear what Moore or Easterbrook are assuming. Are they assuming, for instance, that no questions of fairness can be raised about the existing division of labour which distributes income, wealth, opportunities, and prestige in certain ways? Or, are they assuming that all peoples' career paths are, in a meaningful sense, matters of choice, such that coal miners could just as easily have "chosen" to be lawyers or investment bankers? Are they assuming that everyone in society has equal access to insider information, at least at the point at which they "choose" their careers?

Again, it is not apparent which, if any, of these assumptions Moore or Easterbrook are making, though their willingness to defend insider trading by invoking the division of labour and the career choices with which it presents individuals certainly suggests that they do not see anything problematic about either notion. If so, their assumptions are obviously at odds with the views of welfare liberals and radical egalitarians about the justice of institutions that tolerate significant disparities in peoples' income, wealth, and life-prospects. Moore and Easterbrook's underlying assumptions about justice or fairness seem quite controversial given the current state of discussion of these matters by moral and political theorists.

However, since their argument is of scant value in the debate about insider trading, perhaps we should turn our attention to the argument that seems to command more respect. That argument holds that as long as insider trading is consented to by the shareholders, there is nothing unfair about the unequal access to information had by insiders. It might seem that such a notion is not in the least controversial, that regardless of one's theory of justice, one will endorse the idea that these sorts of transactions between people are paradigms of fairness. What could be more fair than an informed exchange between parties none of whom is in any way forced to participate in the exchange or accept terms they find unreasonable? Doesn't this show that we can separate the debate about insider trading from the larger, more contentious debates about social justice?

Not really. I suspect that the notion of "voluntary informed consent" will play some important role in almost any plausible theory of justice. However, part of what distinguishes theories of justice is that they say very different things about the conditions that must be satisfied if a voluntary exchange is to be regarded as fully fair. Judgments about the fairness of particular transactions between or among persons are, I would argue, always defeasible in light of judgments about the extent to which the relevant conditions are satisfied. For moderate egalitarians like John Rawls, the focus will be on the extent to which the basic structure of the society in question satisfies his two principles of justice, especially the Difference Principle.[21] To the extent that the two principles are not satisfied, judgments about the fairness of particular transactions between or among persons are problematic. Moderate egalitarians like Rawls will emphasise that exchanges between parties vastly unequal in bargaining power (owing to wealth or social status) are likely to be fair in only a qualified sense even if they involve no overt deception or force.

In contrast, for libertarians, the conditions that must be satisfied if a voluntary informed exchange between persons is to be deemed just are less

[21]John Rawls, *A Theory of Justice* (Cambridge, MA: Harvard University Press, 1971). See also his essay "The Basic Structure As Subject," in Alvin I. Goldman and Jaegwon Kim, *Values and Morals* (Boston: D. Reidel, 1978): 47–71.

structural and more historical in character.[22] To the extent that a particular distribution of property holdings came about in ways that violate libertarian principles of property acquisition and transfer, reference to the fairness of voluntary informed exchanges among individuals whose holdings depend on that distribution is problematic. For instance, suppose that recently released slaves, individuals who have been forcibly deprived of the fruits of their labour, reach wage-labour agreements with their comparatively wealthy former owners, the terms of which greatly favour the former owners. Even libertarians might acknowledge that because of the historical conditions leading up to them, these wage-labour agreements are not paradigms of fairness.

Now, if it is true that judgments about the fairness of voluntary informed exchanges amongst persons cannot meaningfully be separated from theory-dependent judgments about the extent to which certain other conditions are satisfied, what implications does this have for the debate about the fairness of insider trading? It is not that those who have written about insider trading all seem to favour one larger theory of justice over another, or that they do so without really arguing for their preferred theory. It is rather that none of them appears to be operating with any such theory at all—or if they are, it is one that rather simply implies that the social and economic *status quo* in countries like the United States is unproblematically just. I know of no plausible theory that implies this. My hunch is that the commentators wish to avoid delving into the difficulties that discussions of these larger theories of justice inevitably raise. Yet, by avoiding these difficulties, they deprive themselves of the sort of theoretical framework which can alone make an analysis and evaluation of insider trading maximally well-grounded and coherent.[23]

In the next section, I will show how an analysis of insider trading grounded in a larger theory of justice might look. I hope this will further develop and illuminate the points I have made in this section.

III

Egalitarian theories of justice are a diverse lot, ranging from the moderate types like that of Rawls to the more radical types like that of Kai Nielsen.[24] All, however, share certain features, the most important of which for our purposes I will briefly summarise.

First, egalitarian theories generally hold that inequalities in things like income, wealth, power, opportunities, the social conditions for self-respect, etc., ought to be limited. Egalitarians are concerned that people's life-prospects should not differ too significantly along these dimensions affected by humanly alterable institutions and practices. Inequalities can be constrained by the designing of political and economic institutions that maintain certain structural features in society. For instance, while egalitarians may believe competitive markets can play important roles in a just society, they are reluctant to let markets wholly determine the distribution of goods like income and opportunities. Hence, they will favour state involvement in ensuring for all persons not only traditional civil liberties but also goods like subsistence, education and medical care. Or, to take another example, egalitarians are likely to be concerned about the ways in which social and economic power can be exercised to the detriment of some peoples' interests. Thus, they are likely to favour rather strict limits on the extent to which wealth can be transferred between generations and on the extent to influence democratic political decisions. Also, some egalitarians favour extending democratic decision-making structures into the economic sphere. This would entail the institutionalisation of schemes of worker participation, if not control.

Obviously, the preceding depiction of egalitarianism rather brutally oversimplifies it and leaves a great deal of the conception unexplained and undefended. However, I think it will serve to introduce an egalitarian analysis of insider trading.

First, egalitarians would attempt to gauge the extent to which the basic institutional structures of societies accord with their favoured principles of justice. Obviously, different egalitarians will

---

22Cf. Robert Nozick, *Anarchy, State, and Utopia* (New Basic Books, 1974).

23For more on the tendency of those who write about business ethics to avoid the problems raised by competing theories of justice, see my "A Critique of Business Ethics," *Business Ethics Quarterly,* Vol. 1 (October 1991): 367–384.

24Rawls, *A Theory of Justice;* Kai Nielsen, *Equality and Liberty: A Defense of Radical Egalitarianism* (Totowa, NJ: Rowman and Allanheld, 1984).

employ slightly different principles, and even among egalitarians who are in rough agreement about principles of justice, there will be room for disagreement about what these principles imply about the justice of actual societies. In any case, I think it is fair to say that most egalitarians would be greatly dismayed by the distribution of income, wealth, opportunities, and power in many advanced capitalist societies.[25]

Consider the United States, for instance. The existence of significant segments of the population that cannot satisfy their basic needs for subsistence and health care; of large disparities in access to quality education and meaningful work; the ability of those with wealth and economic power to exercise inordinate political and cultural power; and the evidence that the gap between rich and poor is growing, with many in the middle class slipping into poverty, would, for egalitarians, be among the most disturbing features of U.S. society.[26]

Second, egalitarians might note that both corporate insiders and shareholders are likely to be among the most advantaged members of advanced capitalist societies. Corporate executives, those most likely to be in a position to have access to inside information, are handsomely paid and enjoy other perquisites such as prestigious work, power over others, and access to political influence. Those who invest in stocks, corporate executives among them, are also likely to be quite well off. Recent studies of wealth in the U.S., for instance, suggest that approximately 80% of families own no stocks.[27] These studies also suggest that about 95% of all stocks are owned by families with incomes of more than $96,000 per year—that is, by about 3% of all families. Thus, those who are in the top income-bracket are also those able to invest in stocks and accumulate even more wealth.

Egalitarians will note the many attendant effects of this concentration of stock ownership, and with it, legal control of corporations. Though actual control over the day-to-day operations of corporations is typically ceded to hired managers, these managers will generally seek to advance the shareholders' interests. Historically, managements' attempts to do this have resulted in "costs" being passed onto other members of society. For instance, corporations have often sought to evade or weaken environmental regulations, with the result that the costs of pollution, hazardous wastes, and the depletion of scarce resources fall on those with less economic power and influence (including members of future generations). Or, to take another example, corporations have often resisted attempts to provide employees with clearer and safer working environments because doing so would increase costs of production. The result, however, is that employees then bear greater costs owing to the resulting injuries and illnesses.

Supporters of the current scheme of property rights might respond by saying that corporations are answerable to a much broader constituency than the shareholders. First, they must conform to laws and regulations that are, directly or indirectly, democratically enacted. These laws and regulations constrain corporate decision-making in ways that make it more conducive to the interests of all in society. Second, corporations are answerable to the public in other ways. They must produce goods and services that the public is willing to buy—that is, they must be responsive to consumer "votes." Also, corporations are vulnerable to consumer boycotts if their actions are perceived by many as socially irresponsible. The fact that such boycotts are rare suggests that corporations are generally perceived as acting in the interests of all members of society. Finally, supporters of the *status quo* will argue that the stock market performs an invaluable service to society, generating capital funds for businesses that provide jobs and goods and services for many people.

Let me indicate, briefly, what I believe would be the egalitarian response to this line of argument. First, they would repeat their concerns about the extent to which wealth and economic power influence democratic decision-making in advanced capitalist societies. This influence significantly dilutes the actual democratic control that ordinary citizens have over large corporations, arguably to the

[25]Of course, advanced capitalist societies differ from one another in some of their structural features. Any egalitarian analysis will have to take these differences into account in assessing the impact of various insider trading rules.

[26]On the last point, in particular, see Denny Braun, *The Rich Get Richer* (Chicago: Nelson-Hall Publishers, 1991), pp. 137–197.

[27]See the three wealth studies analysed by Richard T. Curtin, F. Thomas Juster, and James N. Morgan, "Survey Estimates of Wealth: An Assessment of Quality," in Robert E. Lipsey and Helen Stone Tice, *The Measurement of Saving, Investment, and Wealth* (Chicago: The University of Chicago Press, 1989): 473–548.

detriment of those citizens. Second, they will argue that it is naive to think that corporations simply respond to consumer "votes." Instead, they actively seek to shape consumer attitudes, preferences, and values through massive persuasive advertising. It is at least an open question whether the resulting consumer "votes" reflect consumers' autonomous beliefs and preferences (those they would have if the conditions for critical reflection on them were not undermined by massive persuasive advertising) or whether they reflect the economic interests of large corporations. Also, corporations are very active in their efforts to shape public perceptions about their character and conduct as economic enterprises. It is no easy matter for the average consumer to get accurate information about the actual conduct of large corporations, even assuming that the average consumer had the time or inclination to engage in the monitoring of corporate conduct. Last, while the current scheme of stock ownership does generate investment funds for economic enterprises, the point of the egalitarian critique of that scheme is to raise the question whether there might be a more desirable alternative scheme. In particular, might there be a scheme that does not rest on and so reflect the influence of considerable inequality, one that would generate investment funds in ways that better advance the interests of *all* members of society?

In the light of the preceding discussion, it might be suggested that egalitarians would view the debate over insider trading as one of little significance—that the 'negotiations" between management and shareholders that proponents of insider trading favour are little more than ways for unjustly advantaged members of society to determine how best to divide, or perhaps increase, the spoils of their advantages.

However, it seems to me that egalitarians could offer more than this to the insider trading debate. They could point out that most who have written about insider trading simply presuppose that those most directly affected by the rules about insider trading are managers and shareholders. Occasionally, in discussions of insider trading, reference is made to its broader effects on the efficiency of the market. But typically, the focus of most analyses is on the motivations, interests, expectations, and behaviour of managers and shareholders. Yet this leaves out of the reckoning

how other' interests are potentially affected by whatever agreements are reached by managers and shareholders. In particular, employees of corporations, especially those not in the top managerial classes, may be affected by those agreements.

For instance, suppose that the shareholders are convinced by Manne's arguments that insider trading will offer valuable incentives to managers to be less risk-averse and so they agree to allow managers to take advantage of the information they "create" through their activities by engaging in insider trading. There are risks here, to be sure, for the shareholders, for their less risk-averse managers may undertake ventures that ultimately cost the shareholders money. Still, the shareholders, at least, take this chance with their eyes open. But what of the other employees of the corporation who lose their jobs or have their wages and benefits cut when the inevitable belt-tightening occurs as a result of failed ventures? Or, to take another possible scenario, what of the employees who lose their jobs or have them downgraded when top management decides to "create value" by taking over another company only then to cut the target's labour costs by eliminating mid-level management positions? These examples make clear that what top managers and shareholders negotiate with regard to insider trading can affect other members of the organisation, not to mention members of the surrounding communities. Less risk-averse managers may be a boon to the shareholders, but not necessarily to other employees or members of society.

Perhaps the interests of other employees are ignored in the debate over insider trading because analysts simply assume that another, independent set of negotiations takes place between corporations and their non-executive employees. Corporations that permit insider trading by their top-level managers could make this clear to other prospective employees, and the latter could be understood to give their consent to the risks involved by agreeing to work for the corporation. Or perhaps most analysts are simply assuming that whatever the negative effects on employees due to the incentives created by insider trading, they are, in principle, no different from the ones that might occur because of other ways of compensating top-level managers. All compensation schemes for top-level managers may contain incentives that lead to decisions that adversely affect certain other employees. What is the difference, it might be asked, between top-level decisions to close plants based on the usual profit-considerations and decisions to lay off employees due to risky ventures (spurred by the lure of insider trading profits) gone sour?

Neither assumption is likely to be seen as defensible from an egalitarian perspective. Egalitarians will regard the claim that employees "consent" to whatever rules corporations have about insider trading (and so to the decisions that may adversely affect them resulting from those rules) as insensitive to the lack of bargaining power most employees find themselves with in relation to large corporations. The inability of prospective employees to do anything but simply accept what the shareholders and managers have negotiated will be seen as especially severe where the alternatives to gainful employment are few and unattractive. Most workers are not as mobile as shareholders who can easily take their investments elsewhere if they do not like the rules regarding insider trading that corporations adopt. Also, if many corporations decide to permit insider trading, the options open to many workers will be greatly limited.

Moreover, it seems that most analysts are simply assuming that employees are to have no say in whether the businesses for which they work permit insider trading. The claim that the possible negative effects of corporate policies permitting insider trading are no different from other policies designed to keep businesses operating efficiently, and at a profit, rests on this assumption. The traditional powers and prerogatives that go with the ownership of property in many advanced capitalist societies are thereby simply reaffirmed. Yet many egalitarians regard the current distribution of power in the workplace as deeply suspect morally because it fails to affirm the autonomy of workers and results in business decisions that fail to advance impartially the interests of all affected. To assume the legitimacy of this distribution without argument is simply question-begging.[28]

It may seem that discussion in the preceding section strays quite a way from the simpler question about the fairness of insider trading with which we began this paper. However, the point I have attempted to make throughout this paper, illustrated in the preceding section, is precisely that the simpler question is too simple. It presupposes that we can intelligently discuss what the rules for insider trading should be independent of a discussion of the broader principles of justice that should be adopted and the extent to which existing institutions realise those principles. If my argument is correct, it points the discussion away from the simple question about the fairness of insider trading to the more complex and contested questions discussed by theorists of social justice. Current analyse of the fairness of insider trading simply beg all of these questions, and to that extent are philosophically facile.

[28]Of course, this extension of democratic decision-making into the economic sphere that many egalitarians favour may seem unattractive if divorced from the other, collateral changes urged by egalitarians. These changes will include better education for many workers, along with the enforcement of due process and the protection of free speech in the workplace.

Questions for Chapter 8

1. Is Werhane correct in her claim that since insider trading undermines competition, it undermines an efficient market? Why or why not?
2. Werhane claims that competition is a precondition of an efficient market. She also claims that competition declines as inequality between individuals increases and that the market is most efficient when there is competition between equally matched parties. What are the implications of this as regards market regulation?
3. Would Machan defend the claim that as long as one does not engage in deception, there is nothing unethical in buying an item for $75 knowing that one can, with little expense or effort, resell it for $2,500? Do you agree? How do you think Lippke would respond to this claim?

4. One frequent objection to insider trading is that it is unfair because the advantage the insider possesses is "unerodable," that is, it could not be overcome by the hard work and ingenuity of an ordinary investor. Critics dismiss this argument on the grounds that, just as one could have chosen to become a plumber and hence possess information not possessed by nonplumbers, so one could have chosen to become a corporate insider and thus possess information not possessed by the ordinary investor. In neither case, they argue, is the possession and use of specialized information unfair. How persuasive do you find this analogy? How do you think Werhane would respond to this analogy? What is Lippke's response to this analogy?

5. Critically assess Lippke's claim that insider trading can only be evaluated in the context of a comprehensive theory of justice.

Case 8.1   The Vengeful Tippee[1]

In the mid-eighties, Carl F. Berner sought damages against Bateman Eichler, Hill Richards, Inc. Berner alleged that he had suffered substantial trading losses because a security broker employed by Bateman Eichler, Hill Richards, in collusion with the officer of a corporation, fraudulently induced Berner to purchase stock in the corporation by revealing false and materially incomplete information about the company and claiming it was accurate inside information.

1. Are tippees, that is, those receiving inside information, less blameworthy than tippers, that is, those divulging inside information? Why or why not?

2. Should tippees be allowed to bring suit against defrauding tippers? Explain your answer.

[1]Based on Berner v. Bateman Eichler, Hill Richards Inc., as found in 105 *Supreme Court Reporter* 2622 (1985).

Case 8.2   Friendship and Insider Trading[2]

In the late 1980s, Plastic Engine Technology Corporation (PETCO) was a small firm listed on the Toronto Stock Exchange, attempting to exploit promising technology in the area of producing small plastic engines. PETCO had received orders for hundreds of thousands of these engines, but needed venture capital to

[2]Based on Regina v. Plastic Engine Technology Corporation, as found in *Canadian Criminal Cases*, 3rd series, Vol. 88, pp. 287–333.

meet costs associated with filling so large a demand. Gerald McKendry, president and CEO of PETCO, approached Woods, a director in PETCO, and president of Head Start Capital Corporation, a company in the business of venture capital for start-up companies.

In October 1988, Woods approached James Richardson, a long-time business associate, for a bridge loan of $500,000 to help PETCO in trying to deal with its chronic cash shortage. Richardson loaned PETCO the money, his loan being secured by a fixed charge on PETCO's assets. PETCO, in the midst of negotiations for equity financing with Samuel Manutech Inc., the Middlefield Capital fund, and a group of individual investors, arranged for the sale and leaseback of substantially all its equipment. With the money obtained from the sale of its equipment, PETCO repaid Richardson's loan in late November 1988.

On December 21, 1988, Manutech, Middlefield, and the group of individual investors signed a letter of intent with PETCO to provide equity financing of $11.25 million. Around the same time, Woods arranged for a second bridge loan from Richardson, to be repaid by PETCO by mid-January 1989. As before, the loan was to be secured by a charge on the assets of PETCO. Woods did not reveal, however, that PETCO was now leasing the equipment it had formerly owned and that Richardson's loan was therefore at much greater risk.

On January 19, 1989, one day prior to the proposed equity financing taking effect, Middlefield advised PETCO it could not proceed. Manutech and the group of individual investors were able to interest Davidson Tisdale Mines Ltd., but the new financial package they put together was conditional on PETCO receiving a federal government grant of approximately $2 million. Initially, it looked probable that the federal government would provide assistance, and the deal closed in escrow on February 7, 1989, with PETCO issuing a press release to that effect. By February 17, 1989, however, it became clear that the federal government would not provide aid and the new financing package collapsed.

Desperate for funds, PETCO asked Woods to propose to Richardson that Richardson convert his bridge loan into equity. On February 22, 1989, Richardson agreed but, on Wood's recommendation, instructed Woods to arrange to short-sell some PETCO shares in order to hedge his risk. (A short sale takes place when someone sells shares prior to owning them by selling shares borrowed from a broker. If the shares decrease in value, allowing the seller to pay a lower price to the broker from whom they were borrowed than what he or she sold them for, the seller will realize a profit.)

On February 24, 1989, PETCO issued a press release stating that although no formal agreement had been reached, it had tentative commitments for approximately $8.5 million in equity financing. Unfortunately for investors, this was simply false. Woods, aware of the misleading nature of the press release, and with full knowledge of PETCO's precarious situation, arranged further short-selling of PETCO shares on Richardson's behalf to minimize Richardson's loss on his loan in the event of PETCO failing. This was done without consulting Richardson.

1. Woods argued that he was not guilty of insider trading, since he received no personal financial benefit from his activities. How would you respond to his argument?

2. Perhaps part of Woods's reason for short-selling stock on Richardson's behalf was that Richardson had originally been misled to believe that his second loan to PETCO was as fully secured as the first. Would this in any way excuse Woods's actions? Why or why not?

3. Was Richardson guilty of any wrongdoing?

Further Readings for Chapter 8

William B. Irvine, "Insider Trading: An Ethical Appraisal," *Business and Professional Ethics Journal* 6(4), 1986, pp. 3-33.

Gary Lawson, "The Ethics of Insider Trading," *Harvard Journal of Law and Public Policy* 11(3), 1988, pp. 727-783.

Panagiotis Lekkas, "Insider Trading and the Greek Stock Market," *Business Ethics* 7, 1998, pp. 193-199.

Henry Manne, *Insider Trading and the Stock Market* (New York: The Free Press, 1966).

Steven Salbu, "Insider Trading and the Social Contract," *Business Ethics Quarterly* 5, 1995, pp. 313–328.

William Shaw, "Shareholder Authorized Inside Trading: A Legal and Moral Analysis," *Journal of Business Ethics* 9, 1990, pp. 913–928.

Patricia Werhane, "The Indefensibility of Insider Trading," *Journal of Business Ethics* 10, 1991, pp. 729–731.

INFOTRAC COLLEGE EDITION To learn more about the topics from this chapter, you can use the following words to conduct an electronic search on InfoTrac College Edition, an online library of journals. Here you will find a multitude of articles from various sources and perspectives: *www.infotrac-college.com/wadsworth/access.html*

insider trading

fraud

Chapter 9

Intellectual Property

Introduction

MOST OF US HAVE, at one time or another, copied a favorite cassette or compact disc in order to have a copy not only in our home, but also in our car. Many of us have photocopied magazine or journal articles to give to a friend or colleague. We are familiar with the fact that it is cheaper to buy a clone computer than the famous brands they so closely imitate, and we probably know people who use pirated software on their computers. These activities, among a host of others that could be mentioned, raise questions concerning copyrights, patents, trademarks, and trade secrets that are becoming increasingly important and complex as our ability to copy, distribute, and process information grows at an exponential rate.

Traditionally, such questions have been addressed in the context of appealing to intellectual property and the rights of property owners to control how their property is used. This raises at least two very complex issues. The first is how we are to conceive of ownership or property. The notion of physical property often proves difficult—do I, for example, own the water in the aquifer below my farm?—but the concept of intellectual property seems even more puzzling. How can I be said to own a certain arrangement of machine parts, for example, their design, and how does someone arranging machine parts in an identical or very similar way violate my property right, since it in no way prohibits my continuing to use that design? Often it is suggested that we must distinguish between an idea and its expression and that, whereas an idea cannot be intellectual property, that is, copyrightable, its expression can be. Unfortunately, this distinction frequently breaks down; in many instances style and content, application and general principle, interpenetrate one another and cannot be easily distinguished.

Second, even if we can make clear the notion of intellectual property, the issue of how such property rights are qualified by public utility or the rights of others arises. Pharmaceutical companies, for example, spend large sums to research and develop new drugs. On this basis, they argue that their patents should extend over large periods of time in order for them to recoup their development costs and finance further research. This argument should not be too quickly dismissed, but there seems little question that, in many instances, long patent periods result in huge profits and keep drug prices much higher than they would otherwise be. Granting the existence of intellectual property rights in such instances does not resolve the question of whether such long patent periods can be justified.

Whether traditional justifications of intellectual property rights are firmly grounded is the subject of Edwin C. Hettinger's article "Justifying Intellectual Property." He argues that because intellectual property is nonexclusive in nature, that is, unlike physical property its possession and use does not hinder its possession and use by others, we should not attempt to develop a theory of intellectual property analogous to theories of exclusive and private ownership of physical property. He further argues that it is far from clear that the concept of intellectual property is consistent with the value society places on the freedom of thought and expression. He thinks that the most persuasive argument in support of intellectual property is one based on social utility, but suggests that even this argument is weak, since it is not obvious that the current system provides the best means of ensuring the availability and dissemination of knowledge.

Lynn Sharp Paine replies to Hettinger in her article "Trade Secrets and the Justification of Intellectual Property: A Comment on Hettinger." In Paine's view, Hettinger's failure to find a justification for intellectual property rights lies in the fact that he tries to treat intellectual property as analogous to physical property and thus focuses his attention on the traditional arguments for private property. She argues that intellectual property rights are best justified not on the grounds of a dubious analogy with tangible property, but rather by virtue of the essential role they play in defining personality and social relationships. Their foundation lies in the right of a person to keep his or her ideas to him- or herself, disclose them to a select few, or disseminate them widely. In contrast to Hettinger's focus on social utility, Paine focuses on the autonomy of the individual and its implications as regards control over his or her ideas. She also suggests that Hettinger ignores the possibility that different intellectual property institutions may be justified in different ways. What justifies one intellectual property institution, for example, copyright, need not be construed as the only possible means of justifying another institution, for example, trade secrets.

Mark Alfino, in "Intellectual Property and Copyright Ethics," takes the position that any adequate theory of intellectual property will have to take into account both the historical circumstances that gave rise to the concept and the present circumstances in which it is applied. He argues that current fair use guidelines, which attempt to operate on the basis of distinguishing between individual and systematic use, are increasingly *ad hoc* in view of the fact that emerging technologies make this distinction difficult to maintain. For example, libraries, through new technologies, are increasingly making use of interlibrary loans and cooperative acquisitions to reduce costs, yet maximize resources available to users.

Alfino sees the problem in terms of tension between individual and social values. On the one hand, there is a legitimate concern to respect private property, and on the other, a legitimate desire to further the availability of knowledge. His approach is to try to develop a *via media* by which information producers recognize an obligation to employ technologies that facilitate wide distribution of their work and by which consumers recognize an obligation to consider the effect of these technologies upon information producers.

In our final selection, "Intellectual Property Rights and Computer Software," John Weckert discusses the morality of copying software. He begins by examining the concept of tangible property—things like cars, houses, television sets, and so on—and justifications of its ownership. He goes on to distinguish tangible property from intellectual property that is intangible. He suggests that, at least *prima facie,* the idea of ownership of intellectual property seems harder to justify than the ownership of tangible property. In the case of tangible property, my use of it is not consistent with unlimited use of it by others, but this is not true in the case of intellectual property. Thus, for example, my ability to use my car is lessened if someone else is allowed to use it, but my ability to sing a song that I wrote or use a computer program I created is not lessened by someone else's use of it.

With regard to the issue of unauthorized copying of commercial software, Weckert suggests that the use that will be made of the copy must be taken into account. Copying that is done solely with the purpose of testing the product, with the intention of buying it if it proves satisfactory, seems unproblematic. Equally, it is difficult to say what is wrong with an individual copying a program that he or she would never consider buying, but considers worthwhile having if it is free. In the latter case, the question of rationalization and self-deception arises, but assuming it is genuinely the case that one would have no interest in purchasing the product, even if free copies were not available, then it is hard to see why such copying should be considered immoral.

Far more questionable is the case where the copied software will be used for commercial gain and where, if it could not be copied, it would be purchased. The main reason for thinking such copying immoral is that it seems clearly to harm the developer of the copied software, inasmuch as it deprives him or her of profits he or she might otherwise generate. It is also argued that such copying harms society, inasmuch as it undermines incentive for people to develop new software.

Weckert feels this argument has force, but he is not convinced that it is conclusive. In his view, it is far from clear that programmers only develop new software because of financial rewards. It might also be argued that if copying were freely allowed, there would be many more people working on modifying and improving software so that overall society would gain rather than lose. Further, it could be claimed that the large sums spent on litigation and copy protection would be better utilized under a system in which widescale copying were permitted. Weckert's conclusion is not that he has proven that such copying should be permitted, but that it is much more difficult than is generally recognized to make a strong case for the ownership of computer software and hence a strong case for restrictions on its copying.

(For further discussion on this topic as it arises in an international context, students should consult Paul Steidlmeier's article "The Moral Legitimacy of Intellectual Property Claims: American Business and Developing Country Perspectives" found in Chapter 17, Business and the International Community.)

Justifying Intellectual Property

EDWIN C. HETTINGER*

PROPERTY INSTITUTIONS fundamentally shape a society. These legal relationships between individuals, different sorts of objects, and the state are not easy to justify. This is especially true of intellectual property. It is difficult enough to determine the appropriate kinds of ownership of corporeal objects (consider water or mineral rights); it is even more difficult to determine what types of ownership we should allow for noncorporeal, intellectual objects, such as writings, inventions, and secret business information. The complexity of copyright, patent, and trade secret law reflects this problem.

According to one writer "patents are the heart and core of property rights, and once they are destroyed, the destruction of all other property rights will follow automatically, as a brief post-script."[1] Though extreme, this remark rightly stresses the importance of patents to private competitive enterprise. Intellectual property is an increasingly significant and widespread form of ownership. Many have noted the arrival of the "post-industrial society"[2] in which the manufacture and manipulation of physical goods is giving way to the production and use of information. The result is an ever-increasing strain on our laws and customs protecting intellectual property.[3] Now, more than ever, there is a need to carefully scrutinize these institutions.

As a result of both vastly improved information-handling technologies and the larger role information is playing in our society, owners of intellectual property are more frequently faced with what they call "piracy" or information theft (that is, unauthorized access to their intellectual property). Most readers of this article have undoubtedly done something considered piracy by owners of intellectual property. Making a cassette tape of a friend's record, videotaping television broadcasts for a movie library, copying computer programs or using them on more than one machine, photocopying more than one chapter of a book, or two or more articles by the same author—all are examples of alleged infringing activities. Copyright, patent, and trade secret violation suits abound in industry, and in academia, the use of another person's ideas often goes unacknowledged. These phenomena indicate widespread public disagreement over the nature and legitimacy of our intellectual property institutions. This article examines the justifiability of those institutions.

Copyrights, Patents, and Trade Secrets

It is commonly said that one cannot patent or copyright ideas. One copyrights "original works of authorship," including writings, music, drawings, dances, computer programs, and movies; one may not copyright ideas, concepts, principles, facts, or knowledge. Expressions of ideas are copyrightable; ideas themselves are not.[4] While useful, this notion of separating the content of an idea from its style of presentation is not unproblematic.[5] Difficulty in

*The original research for this article was completed while I worked for the National Telecommunications and Information Administration of the United States Department of Commerce. I am grateful to Roger Salaman and the Department of Commerce for stimulating and encouraging my work on intellectual property. I wish to thank Beverly Diamond, Margaret Holmgren, Joseph Kupfer, Martin Perlmutter, Hugh Wilder, and the Editors of *Philosophy & Public Affairs* for valuable assistance.
[1]Ayn Rand, *Capitalism: The Unknown Ideal* (New York: New American Library, 1966), p. 128.
[2]See, for example, John Naisbitt's *Megatrends* (New York: Warner Books, 1982), chap. 1.
[3]See R. Salaman and E. Hettinger, *Policy Implications of Information Technology*. NTIA Report 84–144, U.S. Department of Commerce, 1984, pp. 28–29.

[4]For an elaboration of this distinction see Michael Brittin, "Constitutional Fair Use," in *Copyright Law Symposium*, no. 28 (New York: Columbia University Press, 1982), pp. 142ff.
[5]For an illuminating discussion of the relationships between style and subject, see Nelson Goodman's *Ways of Worldmaking* (Indianapolis: Hackett, 1978), chap. II, esp. sec. 2.

From Philosophy and Public Affairs *18 (1989), 31–52.* © *The Johns Hopkins University Press. Reprinted by permission of The Johns Hopkins University Press.*

distinguishing the two is most apparent in the more artistic forms of authorship (such as fiction or poetry), where style and content interpenetrate. In these mediums, more so than in others, *how* something is said is very much part of *what* is said (and vice versa).

A related distinction holds for patents. Laws of nature, mathematical formulas, and methods of doing business, for example, cannot be patented. What one patents are inventions—that is, processes, machines, manufacturers, or compositions of matter. These must be novel (not previously patented); they must constitute nonobvious improvements over past inventions; and they must be useful (inventions that do not work cannot be patented). Specifying what sorts of "technological recipes for production"[6] constitute patentable subject matter involves distinguishing specific applications and utilizations from the underlying unpatentable general principles.[7] One cannot patent the scientific principle that water boils at 212 degrees, but one can patent a machine (for example, a steam engine) which uses this principle in a specific way and for a specific purpose.[8]

Trade secrets include a variety of confidential and valuable business information, such as sales, marketing, pricing, and advertising data, lists of customers and suppliers, and such things as plant layout and manufacturing techniques. Trade secrets must not be generally known in the industry, their nondisclosure must give some advantage over competitors, and attempts to prevent leakage of the information must be made (such as pledges of secrecy in employment contracts or other company security policies). The formula for Coca-Cola and bids on government contracts are examples of trade secrets.

Trade secret subject matter includes that of copyrights and patents: anything which can be copyrighted or patented can be held as a trade secret, though the converse is not true. Typically a business must choose between patenting an invention and holding it as a trade secret. Some advantages of trade secrets are

1. they do not require disclosure (in fact they require secrecy), whereas a condition for granting patents (and copyrights) is public disclosure of the invention (or writing);
2. they are protected for as long as they are kept secret, while most patents lapse after seventeen years; and
3. they involve less cost than acquiring and defending a patent.

Advantages of patents include protection against reverse engineering (competitors figuring out the invention by examining the product which embodies it) and against independent invention. Patents give their owners the *exclusive* right to make, use, and sell the invention no matter how anyone else comes up with it, while trade secrets prevent only improper acquisition (breaches of security).

Copyrights give their owners the right to reproduce, to prepare derivative works from, to distribute copies of, and to publicly perform or display the "original work of authorship." Their duration is the author's life plus fifty years. These rights are not universally applicable, however. The most notable exception is the "fair use" clause of the copyright statute, which gives researchers, educators, and libraries special privileges to use copyrighted material.[9]

Intellectual Objects as Nonexclusive

Let us call the subject matter of copyrights, patents, and trade secrets "intellectual objects."[10] These objects are nonexclusive: they can be at many places at once and are not consumed by their use. The marginal cost of providing an intellectual object to an additional user is zero, and though

[6]This is Fritz Machlup's phrase. See his *Production and Distribution of Knowledge in the United States* (Princeton: Princeton University Press, 1962), p. 163.

[7]For one discussion of this distinction, see Deborah Johnson, *Computer Ethics* (Englewood Cliffs, N.J.: Prentice-Hall, 1985), pp. 100–101.

[8]What can be patented is highly controversial. Consider the recent furor over patenting genetically manipulated animals or patenting computer programs.

[9]What constitutes fair use is notoriously bewildering. I doubt that many teachers who sign copyright waivers at local copy shops know whether the packets they make available for their students constitute fair use of copyrighted material.

[10]"Intellectual objects," "information," and "ideas" are terms I use to characterize the "objects" of this kind of ownership. Institutions which protect such "objects" include copyright, patent, trade secret, and trademark laws, as well as socially enforced customs (such as sanctions against plagiarism) demanding acknowledgment of the use of another's ideas. What is owned here are objects only in a very abstract sense.

there are communications costs, modern technologies can easily make an intellectual object unlimitedly available at a very low cost.

The possession or use of an intellectual object by one person does not preclude others from possessing or using it as well.[11] If someone borrows your lawn mower, you cannot use it, nor can anyone else. But if someone borrows your recipe for guacamole, that in no way precludes you, or anyone else, from using it. This feature is shared by all sorts of intellectual objects, including novels, computer programs, songs, machine designs, dances, recipes for Coca-Cola, lists of customers and suppliers, management techniques, and formulas for genetically engineered bacteria which digest crude oil. Of course, sharing intellectual objects does prevent the original possessor from selling the intellectual object to others, and so this sort of use is prevented. But sharing in no way hinders *personal* use.

This characteristic of intellectual objects grounds a strong *prima facie* case against the wisdom of private and exclusive intellectual property rights. Why should one person have the exclusive right to possess and use something which all people could possess and use concurrently? The burden of justification is very much on those who would restrict the maximal use of intellectual objects. A person's right to exclude others from possessing and using a physical object can be justified when such exclusion is necessary for this person's own possession and unhindered use. No such justification is available for exclusive possession and use of intellectual property.

One reason for the widespread piracy of intellectual property is that many people think it is unjustified to exclude others from intellectual objects.[12] Also, the unauthorized taking of an intellectual object does not feel like theft. Stealing a physical object involves depriving someone of the object taken, whereas taking an intellectual object deprives the owner of neither possession nor personal use of that object—though the owner is deprived of potential profit. This nonexclusive feature of intellectual objects should be kept firmly in mind when assessing the justifiability of intellectual property.

Owning Ideas and Restrictions on the Free Flow of Information

The fundamental value our society places on freedom of thought and expression creates another difficulty for the justification of intellectual property. Private property enhances one person's freedom at the expense of everyone else's. Private intellectual property restricts methods of acquiring ideas (as do trade secrets), it restricts the use of ideas (as do patents), and it restricts the expression of ideas (as do copyrights)—restrictions undesirable for a number of reasons. John Stuart Mill argued that free thought and speech are important for the acquisition of true beliefs and for individual growth and development.[13] Restrictions on the free flow and use of ideas not only stifle individual growth, but impede the advancement of technological innovation and human knowledge generally.[14] Insofar as copyrights, patents, and trade secrets have these negative effects, they are hard to justify.

Since a condition for granting patents and copyrights is public disclosure of the writing or invention, these forms of intellectual ownership do not involve the exclusive right to possess the knowledge or ideas they protect. Our society gives its inventors and writers a legal right to exclude others from certain uses of their intellectual works in return for public disclosure of these works. Disclosure is necessary if people are to learn from and build on the ideas of others. When they bring

---

[11]There are intellectual objects of which this is not true, namely, information whose usefulness depends precisely on its being known only to a limited group of people. Stock tips and insider trading information are examples.

[12]Ease of access is another reason for the widespread piracy of intellectual property. Modern information technologies (such as audio and video recorders, satellite dishes, photocopiers, and computers) make unauthorized taking of intellectual objects far easier than ever before. But it is cynical to submit that this is the major (or the only) reason piracy of information is widespread. It suggests that if people could steal physical objects as easily as they can take intellectual ones, they would do so to the same extent. That seems incorrect.

[13]For a useful interpretation of Mill's argument, see Robert Ladenson, "Free Expression in the Corporate Workplace," in *Ethical Theory and Business*, 2d ed., ed. T. Beauchamp and N. Bowie (Englewood Cliffs, N.J.: Prentice-Hall, 1983), pp. 162–69.

[14]This is one reason the recent dramatic increase in relationships between universities and businesses is so disturbing: it hampers the disclosure of research results.

about disclosure of ideas which would have otherwise remained secret, patents and copyrights enhance rather than restrict the free flow of ideas (though they still restrict the idea's widespread use and dissemination). Trade secrets do not have this virtue. Regrettably, the common law tradition which offers protection for trade secrets encourages secrecy. This makes trade secrets undesirable in a way in which copyrights or patents are not.[15]

Labor, Natural Intellectual Property Rights, and Market Value

Perhaps the most powerful intuition supporting property rights is that people are entitled to the fruits of their labor. What a person produces with her own intelligence, effort, and perseverance ought to belong to her and to no one else. "Why is it mine? Well, it's mine because I made it, that's why. It wouldn't have existed but for me."

John Locke's version of this labor justification for property derives property rights in the product of labor from prior property rights in one's body.[16] A person owns her body and hence she owns what it does, namely, its labor. A person's labor and its product are inseparable, and so ownership of one can be secured only by owning the other. Hence, if a person is to own her body and thus its labor, she must also own what she joins her labor with—namely, the product of her labor.

This formulation is not without problems. For example, Robert Nozick wonders why a person should gain what she mixes her labor with instead of losing her labor. (He imagines pouring a can of tomato juice into the ocean and asks whether he thereby ought to gain the ocean or lose his tomato juice.)[17] More importantly, assuming that labor's fruits are valuable, and that laboring gives the laborer a property right in this value, this would entitle the laborer only to the value she added, and not to the *total* value of the resulting product. Though exceedingly difficult to measure, these two components of value (that attributable to the object labored on and that attributable to the labor) need to be distinguished.

Locke thinks that until labored on, objects have little human value, at one point suggesting that labor creates 99 percent of their value.[18] This is not plausible when labor is mixed with land and other natural resources. One does not create 99 percent of the value of an apple by picking it off a tree, though some human effort is necessary for an object to have value for us.

What portion of the value of writings, inventions, and business information is attributable to the intellectual laborer? Clearly authorship, discovery, or development is necessary if intellectual products are to have value for us; we could not use or appreciate them without this labor. But it does not follow from this that all of their value is attributable to that labor. Consider, for example, the wheel, the entire human value of which is not appropriately attributable to its original inventor.[19]

The value added by the laborer and any value the object has on its own are by no means the only components of the value of an intellectual object. Invention, writing, and thought in general do not operate in a vacuum; intellectual activity is not creation *ex nihilo*. Given this vital dependence of a person's thoughts on the ideas of those who came before her, intellectual products are fundamentally social products. Thus even if one assumes that the value of these products is entirely the result of human labor, this value is not entirely attributable to *any particular laborer* (or small group of laborers).

Separating out the individual contribution of the inventor, writer, or manager from this historical/social component is no easy task. Simply identifying the value a laborer's labor adds to the world

[15]John Snapper makes this point in "Ownership of Computer Programs," available from the Center for the Study of Ethics in the Professions at the Illinois Institute of Technology. See also Sissela Bok, "Trade and Corporate Secrecy," in *Ethical Theory and Business,* p. 176.

[16]John Locke, *Second Treatise of Government,* chap. 5. There are several strands to the Lockean argument. See Lawrence Becker, *Property Rights* (London: Routledge and Kegan Paul, 1977), chap. 4, for a detailed analysis of these various versions.

[17]Robert Nozick, *Anarchy, State, and Utopia* (New York: Basic Books, 1974), p. 175.

[18]Locke, *Second Treatise,* chap. 5, sec. 40.

[19]Whether ideas are discovered or created affects the plausibility of the labor argument for intellectual property. "I discovered it, hence it's mine" is much less persuasive than "I made it, hence it's mine." This issue also affects the cogency of the notion that intellectual objects have a value of their own not attributable to intellectual labor. The notion of mixing one's labor with something and thereby adding value to it makes much more sense if the object preexists.

with the market value of the resulting product ignores the vast contributions of others. A person who relies on human intellectual history and makes a small modification to produce something of great value should no more receive what the market will bear than should the last person needed to lift a car receive full credit for lifting it. If laboring gives the laborer the right to receive the market value of the resulting product, this market value should be shared by all those whose ideas contributed to the origin of the product. The fact that most of these contributors are no longer present to receive their fair share is not a reason to give the entire market value to the last contributor.[20]

Thus an appeal to the market value of a laborer's product cannot help us here. Markets work only after property rights have been established and enforced, and our question is what sorts of property rights an inventor, writer, or manager should have, given that the result of her labor is a joint product of human intellectual history.

Even if one could separate out the laborer's own contribution and determine its market value, it is still not clear that the laborer's right to the fruits of her labor naturally entitles her to receive this. Market value is a socially created phenomenon, depending on the activity (or nonactivity) of other producers, the monetary demand of purchasers, and the kinds of property rights, contracts, and markets the state has established and enforced. The market value of the same fruits of labor will differ greatly with variations in these social factors.

Consider the market value of a new drug formula. This depends on the length and the extent of the patent monopoly the state grants and enforces, on the level of affluence of those who need the drug, and on the availability and price of substitutes. The laborer did not produce these. The intuitive appeal behind the labor argument—"I made it, hence it's mine"—loses its force when it is used to try to justify owning something others are responsible for (namely, the market value). The claim that a laborer, in virtue of her labor, has a "natural right" to this socially created phenomenon is problematic at best.

Thus, there are two different reasons why the market value of the product of labor is not what a laborer's labor naturally entitles her to. First, market value is not something that is produced by those who produce a product, and the labor argument entitles laborers only to the products of their labor. Second, even if we ignore this point and equate the fruits of labor with the market value of those fruits, intellectual products result from the labor of many people besides the latest contributor, and they have claims on the market value as well.

So even if the labor theory shows that the laborer has a natural right to the fruits of labor, this does not establish a natural right to receive the full market value of the resulting product. The notion that a laborer is naturally entitled as a matter of right to receive the market value of her product is a myth. To what extent individual laborers should be allowed to receive the market value of their products is a question of social policy; it is not solved by simply insisting on a moral right to the fruits of one's labor.[21]

Having a moral right to the fruits of one's labor might also mean having a right to possess and personally use what one develops. This version of the labor theory has some force. On this interpretation, creating something through labor gives the laborer a *prima facie* right to possess and personally use it for her own benefit. The value of protecting individual freedom guarantees this right as long as the creative labor, and the possession and use of its product, does not harm others.

But the freedom to exchange a product in a market and receive its full market value is again something quite different. To show that people have a right to this, one must argue about how best to balance the conflicts in freedoms which arise when people interact. One must determine what sorts of property rights and markets are morally legitimate. One must also decide when

---

[20]I thank the Editors of *Philosophy & Affairs* for this way of making the point.

[21]A libertarian might respond that although a natural right to the fruits of labor will not by itself justify a right to receive the market value of the resulting product, that right plus the rights of free association and trade would justify it. But marketplace interaction presupposes a set of social relations, and parties to these relations must jointly agree on their nature. Additionally, market interaction is possible only when property rights have been specified and enforced, and there is no "natural way" to do this (that is, no way independent of complex social judgments concerning the rewards the laborer deserves and the social utilities that will result from granting property rights). The sorts of freedoms one may have in a marketplace are thus socially agreed-upon privileges rather than natural rights.

society should enforce the results of market interaction and when it should alter those results (for example, with tax policy). There is a gap—requiring extensive argumentative filler—between the claim that one has a natural right to possess and personally use the fruits of one's labor and the claim that one ought to receive for one's product whatever the market will bear.

Such a gap exists as well between the natural right to possess and personally use one's intellectual creations and the rights protected by copyrights, patents, and trade secrets. The natural right of an author to personally use her writings is distinct from the right, protected by copyright, to make her work public, sell it in a market, and then prevent others from making copies. An inventor's natural right to use the invention for her own benefits is not the same as the right, protected by patent, to sell this invention in a market and exclude others (including independent inventors) from using it. An entrepreneur's natural right to use valuable business information or techniques that she develops is not the same as the right, protected by trade secret, to prevent her employees from using these techniques in another job.

In short, a laborer has a *prima facie* natural right to possess and personally use the fruits of her labor. But a right to profit by selling a product in the market is something quite different. This liberty is largely a socially created phenomenon. The "right" to receive what the market will bear is a socially created privilege, and not a natural right at all. The natural right to possess and personally use what one has produced is relevant to the justifiability of such a privilege, but by itself it is hardly sufficient to justify that privilege.

Deserving Property Rights Because of Labor

The above argument that people are naturally entitled to the fruits of their labor is distinct from the argument that a person has a claim to labor's fruits based on desert. If a person has a natural right to something—say her athletic ability—and someone takes it from her, the return of it is something she is *owed* and can rightfully demand. Whether or not she deserves this athletic ability is a separate issue. Similarly, insofar as people have natural property rights in the fruits of their labor, these rights are

something they are *owed*, and not something they necessarily deserve.[22]

The desert argument suggests that the laborer deserves to benefit from her labor, at least if it is an attempt to do something worthwhile. This proposal is convincing, but does not show that what the laborer deserves is property rights in the object labored on. The mistake is to conflate the created object which makes a person deserving of a reward with what that reward should be. Property rights in the created object are not the only possible reward. Alternatives include fees, awards, acknowledgment, gratitude, praise, security, power status, and public financial support.

Many considerations affect whether property rights in the created object are what the laborer deserves. This may depend, for example, on what is created by labor. If property rights in the very things created were always an appropriate reward for labor, then as Lawrence Becker notes, parents would deserve property rights in their children.[23] Many intellectual objects (scientific laws, religious and ethical insights, and so on) are also the sort of thing that should not be owned by anyone.

Furthermore, as Becker also correctly points out, we need to consider the purpose for which the laborer labored. Property rights in the object produced are not a fitting reward if the laborer does not want them. Many intellectual laborers produce beautiful things and discover truths as ends in themselves.[24] The appropriate reward in such cases is recognition, gratitude, and perhaps public financial support, not full-fledged property rights, for these laborers do not want to exclude others from their creations.

Property rights in the thing produced are also not a fitting reward if the value of these rights is disproportional to the effort expended by the laborer. "Effort" includes

1. how hard someone tries to achieve a result,
2. the amount of risk voluntarily incurred in seeking this result, and

---

[22]For a discussion of this point, see Joel Feinberg, *Social Philosophy* (Englewood Cliffs, N.J.: Prentice-Hall, 1973), p. 116.

[23]Becker, *Property Rights,* p. 46.

[24]This is becoming less and less true as the results of intellectual labor are increasingly treated as commodities. University research in biological and computer technologies is an example of this trend.

3. the degree to which moral consideration played a role in choosing the result intended.

The harder one tries, the more one is willing to sacrifice, and the worthier the goal, the greater are one's deserts.

Becker's claim that the amount deserved is proportional to the value one's labor produces is mistaken.[25] The value of labor's results is often significantly affected by factors outside a person's control, and no one deserves to be rewarded for being lucky. Voluntary past action is the only valid basis for determining desert.[26] Here only a person's effort (in the sense defined) is relevant. Her knowledge, skills, and achievements insofar as they are based on natural talent and luck, rather than effort expended, are not. A person who is born with extraordinary natural talents, or who is extremely lucky, *deserves* nothing on the basis of these characteristics. If such a person puts forward no greater effort than another, she deserves no greater reward. Thus, two laborers who expend equal amounts of effort deserve the same reward, even when the value of the resulting products is vastly different.[27] Giving more to workers whose products have greater social value might be justified if it is needed as an incentive. But this has nothing to do with giving the laborer what she deserves.

John Rawls considers even the ability to expend effort to be determined by factors outside a person's control and hence a morally impermissible criterion for distribution.[28] How hard one tries, how willing one is to sacrifice and incur risk, and how much one cares about morality are to *some extent* affected by natural endowments and social circumstances. But if the ability to expend effort is taken to be entirely determined by factors outside a person's control, the result is a determinism which makes meaningful moral evaluation impossible. If people are responsible for anything, they are responsible for how hard they try, what sacrifices they make, and how moral they are. Because the effort a person expends is much more under her control than her innate intelligence, skills, and talents, effort is a far superior basis for determining desert. To the extent that a person's expenditure of effort is under her control, effort is the proper criterion for desert.[29]

Giving an inventor exclusive rights to make and sell her invention (for seventeen years) may provide either a greater or a lesser reward than she deserves. Some inventions of extraordinary market value result from flashes of genius, while others with little market value (and yet great social value) require significant effort.

The proportionality requirement may also be frequently violated by granting copyright. Consider a five-hundred-dollar computer program. Granted, its initial development costs (read "efforts") were high. But once it has been developed, the cost of each additional program is the cost of the disk it is on—approximately a dollar. After the program has been on the market several years and the price remains at three or four hundred dollars, one begins to suspect that the company is receiving far more than it deserves. Perhaps this is another reason so much illegal copying of software goes on: the proportionality requirement is not being met, and people sense the unfairness of the price. Frequently, trade secrets (which are held indefinitely) also provide their owners with benefits disproportional to the effort expended in developing them.

The Lockean Provisos

We have examined two versions of the labor argument for intellectual property, one based on desert, the other based on a natural entitlement to the

---

[25]Becker, *Property Rights,* p. 52. In practice, it would be easier to reward laborers as Becker suggests, since the value of the results of labor is easier to determine than the degree of effort expended.

[26]This point is made nicely by James Rachels in "What People Deserve," in *Justice and Economic Distribution,* ed. J. Arthur and W. Shaw (Englewood Cliffs, N.J.: Prentice-Hall, 1978), pp. 150–63.

[27]Completely ineffectual efforts deserve a reward provided that there were good reasons beforehand for thinking the efforts would pay off. Those whose well-intentioned efforts are silly or stupid should be rewarded the first time only and then counseled to seek advice about the value of their efforts.

[28]See John Rawls, *A Theory of Justice* (Cambridge: Harvard University Press, 1971), p. 104: "The assertion that a man deserves the superior character that enables him to make the effort to cultivate his abilities is equally problematic; for his character depends in large part upon fortunate family and social circumstances for which he can claim no credit." See also p. 312: "the effort a person is willing to make is influ-

enced by his natural abilities and skills, and the alternatives open to him. The better endowed are more likely, other things equal, to strive conscientiously."

[29]See Rachels, "What People Deserve," pp. 157–58, for a similar resistance to Rawl's determinism.

fruits of one's labor. Locke himself put limits on the conditions under which labor can justify a property right in the thing produced. One is that after the appropriation there must be "enough and as good left in common for others."[30] This proviso is often reformulated as a "no loss to others" pre-condition for property acquisition.[31] As long as one does not worsen another's position by appro-priating an object, no objection can be raised to owning that with which one mixes one's labor.

Under current law, patents clearly run afoul of this proviso by giving the original inventor an exclusive right to make, use, and sell the invention. Subsequent inventors who independently come up with an already patented invention cannot even personally use their invention, much less patent or sell it. They clearly suffer a great and unfair loss because of the original patent grant. Independent inventors should not be prohibited from using or selling their inventions. Proving independent dis-covery of a publicly available patented invention would be difficult, however. Nozick's suggestion that the length of patents be restricted to the time it would take for independent invention may be the most reasonable administrative solution.[32] In the modern world of highly competitive research and development, this time is often much shorter than the seventeen years for which most patents are currently granted.

Copyrights and trade secrets are not subject to the same objection (though they may constitute a loss to others in different ways). If someone inde-pendently comes up with a copyrighted expression or a competitor's business technique, she is not prohibited from using it. Copyrights and trade secrets prevent only mimicking of other people's expressions and ideas.

Locke's second condition on the legitimate acquisition of property rights prohibits spoilage. Not only must one leave enough and as good for others, but one must not take more than one can use.[33] So in addition to leaving enough apples in the orchard for others, one must not take home a truckload and let them spoil. Though Locke does not specifically mention prohibiting waste, it is the concern to avoid waste which underlies his proviso prohibiting spoilage. Taking more than one can use is wrong because it is wasteful Thus Locke's concern here is with appropriations of property which are wasteful.

Since writings, inventions, and business tech-niques are nonexclusive, this requirement prohibit-ing waste can never be completely met by intellectual property. When owners of intellectual property charge fees for the use of their expressions or inventions, or conceal their business techniques from others, certain beneficial uses of these intellec-tual products are prevented. This is clearly wasteful, since everyone could use and benefit from intellec-tual objects concurrently. How wasteful private ownership of intellectual property is depends on how beneficial those products would be to those who are excluded from their use as a result.

Sovereignty, Security, and Privacy

Private property can be justified as a means to sov-ereignty. Dominion over certain objects is impor-tant for individual autonomy. Ronald Dworkin's liberal is right in saying that "some sovereignty over a range of personal possessions is essential to dignity."[34] Not having to share one's personal pos-sessions or borrow them from others is essential to the kind of autonomy our society values. Using or consuming certain objects is also necessary for sur-vival. Allowing ownership of these things places control of the means of survival in the hands of individuals, and this promotes independence and security (at least for those who own enough of them). Private ownership of life's necessities lessens dependence between individuals, and takes power from the group and gives it to the individual. Private property also promotes privacy. It consti-tutes a sphere of privacy within which the individ-ual is sovereign and less accountable for her actions. Owning one's own home is an example of all of these: it provides privacy, security, and a lim-ited range of autonomy.

But copyrights and patents are neither necessary nor important for achieving these goals. The right to exclude others from using one's invention or copying one's work of authorship is not essential to

---

[30]Locke, *Second Treatise,* chap. 5, sec. 27.

[31]See Nozick, *Anarchy,* pp. 175–82, and Becker, *Property Rights,* pp. 42–43.

[32]Nozick, *Anarchy,* p. 182.

[33]Locke, *Second Treatise,* chap. 5, sec. 31.

[34]Ronald Dworkin, "Liberalism," in *Public and Private Morality,* ed. Stuart Hampshire (Cambridge: Cambridge University Press, 1978), p. 139.

one's sovereignty. Preventing a person from personally using her own invention or writing, on the other hand, would seriously threaten her sovereignty. An author's or inventor's sense of worth and dignity requires public acknowledgment by those who use the writing or discovery, but here again, giving the author or inventor the exclusive right to copy or use her intellectual product is not necessary to protect this.

Though patents and copyrights are not directly necessary for survival (as are food and shelter), one could argue that they are indirectly necessary for an individual's security and survival when selling her inventions or writings is a person's sole means of income. In our society, however, most patents and copyrights are owned by institutions (businesses, universities, or governments). Except in unusual cases where individuals have extraordinary bargaining power, prospective employees are required to give the rights to their inventions and works of authorship to their employers as a condition of employment. Independent authors or inventors who earn their living by selling their writings or inventions to others are increasingly rare.[35] Thus arguing that intellectual property promotes individual security makes sense only in a minority of cases. Additionally, there are other ways to ensure the independent intellectual laborer's security and survival besides copyrights and patents (such as public funding of intellectual workers and public domain property status for the results).

Controlling who uses one's invention or writing is not important to one's privacy. As long as there is no requirement to divulge privately created intellectual products (and as long as laws exist to protect people from others taking information they choose not to divulge—as with trade secret laws), the creator's privacy will not be infringed. Trying to justify copyrights and patents on grounds of privacy is highly implausible given that these property rights give the author or inventor control over certain uses of writings and inventions only after they have been publicly disclosed.

Trade secrets are not defensible on grounds of privacy either. A corporation is not an individual and hence does not have the personal features privacy is intended to protect.[36] Concern for sovereignty counts against trade secrets, for they often directly limit individual autonomy by preventing employees from changing jobs. Through employment contracts, by means of gentlemen's agreements among firms to respect trade secrets by refusing to hire competitors' employees, or simply because of the threat of lawsuits, trade secrets often prevent employees from using their skills and knowledge with other companies in the industry.

Some trade secrets, however, are important to a company's security and survival. If competitors could legally obtain the secret formula for Coke, for example, the Coca-Cola Company would be severely threatened. Similar points hold for copyrights and patents. Without some copyright protection, companies in the publishing, record, and movie industries would be severely threatened by competitors who copy and sell their works at lower prices (which need not reflect development costs). Without patent protection, companies with high research and development costs could be underpriced and driven out of business by competitors who simply mimicked the already developed products. This unfair competition could significantly weaken incentives to invest in innovative techniques and to develop new products.

The next section considers this argument that intellectual property is a necessary incentive for innovation and a requirement for healthy and fair competition. Notice, however, that the concern here is with the security and survival of private companies, not of individuals. Thus one needs to determine whether, and to what extent, the security and survival of privately held companies is a goal worth promoting. That issue turns on the difficult question of what type of economy is most desirable. Given a commitment to capitalism, however, this argument does have some force.

The Utilitarian Justification

The strongest and most widely appealed to justification for intellectual property is a utilitarian

---

[35]"In the United States about 60 per cent of all patents are assigned to corporations" (Machlup, *Production,* p. 168). This was the case twenty-five years ago, and I assume the percentage is even higher today.

[36]Very little (if any) of the sensitive information about individuals that corporations have is information held as a trade secret. For a critical discussion of the attempt to defend corporate secrecy on the basis of privacy see Russell B. Stevenson, Jr., *Corporations and Information* (Baltimore: Johns Hopkins University Press, 1980), chap. 5.

argument based on providing incentives. The constitutional justification for patents and copyrights—"to promote the progress of science and the useful arts"[37]—is itself utilitarian. Given the shortcomings of the other arguments for intellectual property, the justifiability of copyrights, patents, and trade secrets depends, in the final analysis, on this utilitarian defense.

According to this argument, promoting the creation of valuable intellectual works requires that intellectual laborers be granted property rights in those works. Without the copyright, patent, and trade secret property protections, adequate incentives for the creation of a socially optimal output of intellectual products would not exist. If competitors could simply copy books, movies, and records, and take one another's inventions and business techniques, there would be no incentive to spend the vast amounts of time, energy, and money necessary to develop these products and techniques. It would be in each firm's self-interest to let others develop products, and then mimic the result. No one would engage in original development, and consequently no new writings, inventions, or business techniques would be developed. To avoid this disastrous result, the argument claims, we must continue to grant intellectual property rights.

Notice that this argument focuses on the users of intellectual products, rather than on the producers. Granting property rights to producers is here seen as necessary to ensure that enough intellectual products (and the countless other goods based on these products) are available to users. The grant of property rights to the producers is a mere means to this end.

This approach is paradoxical. It establishes a right to restrict the current availability and use of intellectual products for the purpose of increasing the production and thus future availability and use of new intellectual products. As economist Joan Robinson says of patents: "A patent is a device to prevent the diffusion of new methods before the original investor has recovered profit adequate to induce the requisite investment. The justification of the patent system is that by slowing down the diffusion of technical progress it ensures that there will be more progress to diffuse. . . . Since it is rooted in a contradiction, there can be no such thing as an ideally beneficial patent system, and it

is bound to produce negative results in particular instances, impeding progress unnecessarily even if its general effect is favorable on balance."[38] Although this strategy may work, it is to a certain extent self-defeating. If the justification for intellectual property is utilitarian in this sense, then the search for alternative incentives for the production of intellectual products takes on a good deal of importance. It would be better to employ equally powerful ways to stimulate the production and thus use of intellectual products which did not also restrict their use and availability.

Government support of intellectual work and public ownership of the result may be one such alternative. Governments already fund a great deal of basic research and development, and the results of this research often become public property. Unlike private property rights in the results of intellectual labor, government funding of this labor and public ownership of the result stimulate new inventions and writings without restricting their dissemination and use. Increased government funding of intellectual labor should thus be seriously considered.

This proposal need not involve government control over which research projects are to be pursued. Government funding of intellectual labor can be divorced from government control over what is funded. University research is an example. Most of this is supported by public funds, but government control over its content is minor and indirect. Agencies at different governmental levels could distribute funding for intellectual labor with only the most general guidance over content, leaving businesses, universities, and private individuals to decide which projects to pursue.

If the goal of private intellectual property institutions is to maximize the dissemination and use of information, to the extent that they do not achieve this result, these institutions should be modified. The question is not whether copyrights, patents, and trade secrets provide incentives for the production of original works of authorship, inventions, and innovative business techniques. Of course they do. Rather, we should ask the following questions: Do copyrights, patents, and trade secrets increase the availability and use of intellectual products more than they restrict this

[37]U.S. Constitution, sec. 8, para. 8.

[38]Quoted in Dorothy Nelkin, *Science as Intellectual Property* (New York: Macmillan, 1984), p. 15.

availability and use? If they do, we must then ask whether they increase the availability and use of intellectual products more than any alternative mechanism would. For example, could better over-all results be achieved by shortening the length of copyright and patent grants, or by putting a time limit on trade secrets (and on the restrictions on future employment employers are allowed to demand of employees)? Would eliminating most types of trade secrets entirely and letting patents carry a heavier load produce improved results? Additionally, we must determine whether and to what extent public funding and ownership of intellectual products might be a more efficient means to these results.[39]

We should not expect an across-the-board answer to these questions. For example, the production of movies is more dependent on copyright than is academic writing. Also, patent protection for individual inventors and small beginning firms makes more sense than patent protection for large corporations (which own the majority of patents). It has been argued that patents are not important incentives for the research and innovative activity of large corporations in competitive markets.[40] The short-term advantage a company gets from developing a new product and being the first to put it on the market may be incentive enough.

That patents are conducive to a strong competitive economy is also open to question. Our patent system, originally designed to reward the individual inventor and thereby stimulate invention, may today be used as a device to monopolize industries. It has been suggested that in some cases "the patent position of the big firms makes it almost impossible for new firms to enter the industry"[41] and that patents are frequently bought up in order to suppress competition.[42]

Trade secrets as well can stifle competition, rather than encourage it. If a company can rely on a secret advantage over a competitor, it has no need to develop new technologies to stay ahead. Greater disclosure of certain trade secrets—such as costs and profits of particular product lines—would actually increase competition, rather than decrease it, since with this knowledge firms would then concentrate on one another's most profitable products.[43] Furthermore, as one critic notes, trade secret laws often prevent a former employee "from doing work in just that field for which his training and experience have best prepared him. Indeed, the mobility of engineers and scientists is often severely limited by the reluctance of new firms to hire them for fear of exposing themselves to a lawsuit."[44] Since the movement of skilled workers between companies is a vital mechanism in the growth and spread of technology, in this important respect trade secrets actually slow the dissemination and use of innovative techniques.

These remarks suggest that the justifiability of our intellectual property institutions is not settled by the facile assertion that our system of patents, copyrights, and trade secrets provides necessary incentives for innovation and ensures maximally healthy competitive enterprise. This argument is not as easy to construct as one might at first think; substantial empirical evidence is needed. The above considerations suggest that the evidence might not support this position.

Conclusion

Justifying intellectual property is a formidable task. The inadequacies of the traditional justifications for property become more severe when applied to intellectual property. Both the nonexclusive nature of intellectual objects and the presumption against allowing restrictions on the free flow of ideas create special burdens in justifying such property.

We have seen significant shortcomings in the justifications for intellectual property. Natural rights to the fruits of one's labor are not by themselves sufficient to justify copyrights, patents, and trade secrets, though they are relevant to the social

---

[39]Even supposing our current copyright, patent, and trade secret laws did maximize the availability and use of intellectual products, a thorough utilitarian evaluation would have to weigh all the consequences of these legal rights. For example, the decrease in employee freedom resulting from trade secrets would have to be considered, as would the inequalities in income, wealth, opportunity, and power which result from these socially established and enforced property rights.

[40]Machlup, *Production,* pp. 168–69.

[41]Ibid., p. 170.

[42]See David Noble, *America by Design* (New York: Knopf, 1982), chap. 6.

[43]This is Stevenson's point in *Corporations,* p. 11.

[44]Ibid., p. 23. More generally, see ibid., chap. 2, for a careful and skeptical treatment of the claim that trade secrets function as incentives.

decision to create and sustain intellectual property institutions. Although intellectual laborers often deserve rewards for their labor, copyrights, patents, and trade secrets may give the laborer much more or much less than is deserved. Where property rights are not what is desired, they may be wholly inappropriate. The Lockean labor arguments for intellectual property also run afoul of one of Locke's provisos—the prohibition against spoilage or waste. Considerations of sovereignty, security, and privacy are inconclusive justifications for intellectual property as well.

This analysis suggests that the issue turns on considerations of social utility. We must determine whether our current copyright, patent, and trade secret statutes provide the best possible mechanisms for ensuring the availability and widespread dissemination of intellectual works and their resulting products. Public financial support for intellectual laborers and public ownership of intellectual products is an alternative which demands serious consideration. More modest alternatives needing consideration include modifications in the length of intellectual property grants or in the strength and scope of the restrictive rights granted. What the most efficient mechanism for achieving these goals is remains an unresolved empirical question.

This discussion also suggests that copyrights are easier to justify than patents or trade secrets.

Patents restrict the actual usage of an idea (in making a physical object), while copyrights restrict only copying an expression of an idea. One can freely use the ideas in a copyrighted book in one's own writing, provided one acknowledges their origin. One cannot freely use the ideas a patented invention represents when developing one's own product. Furthermore, since inventions and business techniques are instruments of production in a way in which expressions of ideas are not, socialist objections to private ownership of the means of production apply to patents and trade secrets far more readily than they do to copyrights. Trade secrets are suspect also because they do not involve the socially beneficial public disclosure which is part of the patent and copyright process. They are additionally problematic to the extent that they involve unacceptable restrictions on employee mobility and technology transfer.

Focusing on the problems of justifying intellectual property is important not because these institutions lack any sort of justification, but because they are not so obviously or easily justified as many people think. We must begin to think more openly and imaginatively about the alternative choices available to us for stimulating and rewarding intellectual labor.

Trade Secrets and the Justification of Intellectual Property: A Comment on Hettinger

LYNN SHARP PAINE

IN A RECENT ARTICLE Edwin Hettinger considers various rationales for recognizing intellectual property.[1] According to Hettinger, traditional justifications for property are especially problematic when applied to intellectual property because of its nonexclusive nature.[2] Since possessing and using intellectual objects does not preclude their use and

[1] Edwin C. Hettinger, "Justifying Intellectual Property," *Philosophy & Public Affairs* 18, no. 1 (Winter 1989): 31–52.

[2] Thomas Jefferson agrees. See Jefferson's letter to Isaac McPherson, 13 August 1813, in *The Founder's Constitution,* ed. Philip B. Kurland and Ralph Lerner (Chicago: University of Chicago Press, 1987), 3:42.

From Philosophy and Public Affairs *20, (1991) 247–263. The Johns Hopkins University Press. Reprinted by permission of The Johns Hopkins University Press.*

possession by others, there is, he says a "strong prima facie case against the wisdom of private and exclusive intellectual property rights." There is, moreover, a presumption against allowing restrictions on the free flow of ideas.

After rejecting several rationales for intellectual property, Hettinger finds its justification in an instrumental, or "utilitarian,"[3] argument based on incentives.[4] Respecting rights in ideas makes sense, he says, if we recognize that the purpose of our intellectual property institutions is to promote the dissemination and use of information. To the extent that existing institutions do not achieve this result, they should be modified.[5] Skeptical about

the effectiveness of current legal arrangements, Hettinger concludes that we must think more imaginatively about structuring our intellectual property institutions—in particular, patent, copyright, and trade secret laws—so that they increase the availability and use of intellectual products. He ventures several possibilities for consideration: eliminating certain forms of trade secret protections, shortening the copyright and patent protection periods, and public funding and ownership of intellectual objects.

Hettinger's approach to justifying our intellectual property institutions rests on several problematic assumptions. It assumes that all of our intellectual property institutions rise or fall together—that the rationale for trade secret protection must be the same as that for patent and copyright protection.[6] This assumption, I will try to show, is unwarranted. While it may be true that these institutions all promote social utility or well-being, the web of rights and duties understood under the general heading of "intellectual property

---

[3]Hettinger uses the term *utilitarian* in a very narrow sense to refer to a justification in terms of maximizing the use and dissemination of information. Some utilitarians might see intellectual property institutions as promoting objectives other than information dissemination. My discussion of the roots of trade secret principles is perfectly consistent with a utilitarian justification of those principles. Indeed, a utilitarian could argue (as many economists do) that giving people certain rights in ideas they generate through their own labor advances social well-being by promoting innovation. See, e.g., Robert U. Ayres, "Technological Protection and Piracy: Some Implications for Policy," *Technological Forecasting and Social Change* 30 (1986):5–18.

[4]In Hettinger's paper and in mine, the terms *justification, goal, purpose, rationale,* and *objective* are used loosely and somewhat interchangeably. But, of course, identifying the purpose or goal of our intellectual property institutions does not automatically justify them. Some further legitimating idea or ultimate good, such as the general welfare or individual liberty, must be invoked. A difficulty with Hettinger's argument is that he identifies an objective for our intellectual property institutions—promoting the use and dissemination of ideas—and concludes that he has justified them. However, unless maximizing the use and dissemination of ideas is an intrinsic good, we would expect a further step in the argument linking this objective to an ultimate good. Hettinger may think this step can be made or is self-evident from his terminology. However, it is not clear whether he calls his justification "utilitarian" because of its consequentialist form or because he means to appeal to social well-being or some particular good he associates with utilitarianism.

[5]Hettinger seems to think that he has provided a clear-cut objective against which to measure the effectiveness of our intellectual property institutions. Yet, a set of institutions that maximized the "dissemination and use of information" would not necessarily be most effective at "promoting the creation of valuable intellectual works" or promoting "the progress of science and the useful arts." A society might be quite successful at disseminating information, but rather mediocre at creating valuable intellectual works.

There is an inevitable tension between the objectives of innovation and dissemination. The same tension is present in other areas of law concerned with rights in information—insider trading, for example. For discussion of this tension, see Frank H. Easterbrook, "Insider Trading, Secret Agents, Evidentiary Privileges, and the Production of Information," *1981 Supreme Court Review,* p. 309. While we struggle to piece together a system of information rights that gives due consideration to both objectives, we must be wary of the notion that there is a single optimal allocation of rights.

Indeed, the very idea of a "socially optimal output of intellectual products" is embarrassingly imprecise. What is a socially optimal output of poems, novels, computer programs, movies, cassette recordings, production processes, formulations of matter, stock tips, business strategies, etc.? How we allocate rights in ideas may affect the quality and kinds of intellectual products that are produced as well as their quantity and dissemination. Hettinger seems concerned primarily with quantity. The use of general terms like *intellectual product* and *socially optimal output* obscures the complexity of the empirical assessment that Hettinger proposes.

[6]Hettinger mentions trademark as another of our intellectual property institutions, along with our social sanction on plagiarism, but his central discussion focuses on copyright, patent, and trade secret concepts. Neither trademark principles nor the prohibition on plagiarism fits comfortably with his justification in terms of increasing the dissemination and use of ideas. Both are more closely related to giving recognition to the source or originator of ideas and products.

rights" reflects a variety of more specific rationales and objectives.[7]

Second, Hettinger assumes that the rights commonly referred to as "intellectual property rights" are best understood on the model of rights in tangible and real property. He accepts the idea, implicit in the terminology, that intellectual property is like tangible property, only less corporeal. This assumption leads him to focus his search for the justification of intellectual property on the traditional arguments for private property. I will try to show the merits of an alternative approach to thinking about rights in ideas—one that does not depend on the analogy with tangible property and that recognizes the role of ideas in defining personality and social relationships.

The combined effect of these assumptions is that trade secret law comes in for particular serious criticism. It restricts methods of acquiring ideas; it encourages secrecy; it places unacceptable restrictions on employee mobility and technology transfer; it can stifle competition; it is more vulnerable to socialist objections. In light of these deficiencies, Hettinger recommends that we consider the possibility of "eliminating most types of trade secrets entirely and letting patents carry a heavier load." He believes that trade secrets are undesirable in ways that copyrights and patents are not.

Without disagreeing with Hettinger's recommendation that we reevaluate and think more imaginatively about our intellectual property institutions, I believe we should have a clearer understanding of the various rationales for these institutions than is reflected in Hettinger's article. If we unbundle the notion of intellectual property into its constituent rights,[8] we find that different justifications are appropriate for different clusters of rights.[9] In particular, we find that the rights recognized by trade secret law are better understood as rooted in respect for individual liberty, confidential relationships, common morality, and fair competition than in the promotion of innovation and the dissemination of ideas. While trade secret law may serve some of the same ends as patent and copyright law, it has other foundations which are quite distinctive.[10]

In this article, I am primarily concerned with the foundations of trade secret principles. However, my general approach differs from Hettinger's in two fundamental ways. First, it focuses on persons and their relationships rather than property concepts. Second, it reverses the burden of justification, placing it on those who would argue for treating ideas as public goods rather than those who seek to justify private rights in ideas. Within this alternative framework, the central questions are how ideas may be legitimately acquired from others, how disclosure obligations arise, and how ideas become part of the common pool of knowledge. Before turning to Hettinger's criticisms of trade secret principles, it will be useful to think more broadly about the rights of individuals over their undisclosed ideas. This

---

[7]It may be helpful to think of two levels of justification: (1) an intermediate level consisting of objectives, purposes, reasons, and explanations for an institution or practice; and (2) an ultimate level linking those objectives and purposes to our most basic legitimating ideas such as the general good or individual liberty. Philosophers generally tend to be concerned with the ultimate level of justification while policymakers and judges more frequently operate at the intermediate level. Hettinger has, I think, mistaken an intermediate-level justification of patents and copyrights (promoting the dissemination and use of ideas) for an ultimate justification of intellectual property institutions.

[8]Hettinger, of course, recognizes that various rights are involved. He speaks of rights to possess, to personally use, to prevent others from using, to publish, and to receive the market value of one's ideas. And he notes that one might have a natural right to possess and personally use one's ideas even if one might not have a natural right to prevent others from copying them. But he does not consider the possibility that the different rights involved in our concept of intellectual property may rest on quite varied foundations, some firmer than others.

[9]It is generally accepted that the concept of property is best understood as a "bundle of rights." Just as the bundle of rights involved in home ownership differs substantially from the bundle of rights associated with stock ownership, the bundle of rights involved in patent protection differs from the bundle of rights involved in trade secret protection.

[10]Today we commonly speak of copyright protection as providing incentives for intellectual effort, while at the same time ensuring widespread dissemination of ideas. As Hettinger notes, the effectiveness of copyright protection in achieving these aims may depend partly on the period of the copyright grant. Historically, at least before the first English copyright act, the famous 1710 Act of Anne, it appears that the dissemination of ideas was not so central. The common law gave the author an exclusive first right of printing or publishing her manuscript on the grounds that she was entitled to the product of her labor. The common law's position on the author's right to prohibit subsequent publication was less clear. See generally *Wheaton v. Peters*, 8 Pet. 591 (1834), reprinted in *The Founders' Constitution* 3:44–60.

inquiry will illustrate my approach to thinking about rights in ideas and point toward some of the issues at stake in the trade secret area.

The Right to Control Disclosure

If a person has any right with respect to her ideas, surely it is the right to control their initial disclosure.[11] A person may decide to keep her ideas to herself, to disclose them to a select few, or to publish them widely. Whether those ideas are best described as views and opinions, plans and intentions, facts and knowledge, or fantasies and inventions is immaterial. While it might in some cases be socially useful for a person to be generous with her ideas, and to share then with others without restraint, there is no general obligation to do so. The world at large has no right to the individual's ideas.[12]

Certainly, specific undertakings, relationships, and even the acquisition of specific information can give rise to disclosure obligations. Typically, these obligations relate to specific types of information pertinent to the relationship or the subject matter of the undertaking. A seller of goods must disclose to potential buyers latent defects and health and safety risks associated with the use of the goods. A person who undertakes to act as an agent for another is obliged to disclose to the principal information she acquires that relates to the subject matter of the agency. Disclosure obligations like these, however, are limited in scope and arise against a general background right to remain silent.

The right to control the initial disclosure of one's ideas is grounded in respect for the individual. Just as a person's sense of herself is intimately connected with the stream of ideas that constitutes consciousness, her public persona is determined in part by the ideas she expresses and the way she expresses them. To require public disclosure of one's ideas and thoughts—whether about "personal" or other matters—would distort one's personality and, no doubt, alter the nature of one's thoughts.[13] It would seriously interfere with the liberty to live according to one's chosen life plans. This sort of thought control would be an invasion of privacy and personality of the most intrusive sort. If anything is private, one's undisclosed thoughts surely are.[14]

Respect for autonomy, respect for personality, and respect for privacy lie behind the right to control disclosure of one's ideas, but the right is also part of what we mean by freedom of thought and expression. Frequently equated with a right to speak, freedom of expression also implies a *prima facie* right not to express one's ideas or to share them only with those we love or trust or with whom we wish to share.[15] These observations explain the peculiarity of setting up the free flow of ideas and unrestricted access as an ideal. Rights in ideas are desirable insofar as they strengthen our sense of individuality and undergird our social relationships. This suggests a framework quite different from Hettinger's, one that begins with a strong presumption against requiring disclosure and is in favor of protecting people against unconsented-to acquisitions of their ideas.[16] This is the moral backdrop against which trade secrecy law is best understood.

Consequences of Disclosure

Within this framework, a critical question is how people lose rights in their ideas. Are these rights forfeited when people express their ideas or communicate them to others? Surely this depends on

---

[11]Hettinger recognizes a right not to divulge privately created intellectual products, but he does not fit this right into his discussion. If the right is taken seriously, however, it will, I believe, undermine Hettinger's own conclusions.

[12]We would hope that the right to control disclosure would be exercised in a morally responsible way and that, for example, people with socially useful ideas would share them and that some types of harmful ideas would be withheld. But the potential social benefits of certain disclosures cannot justify a general requirement that ideas be disclosed.

[13]Here, I am using the term *personal* to refer to ideas about intimate matters, such as sexual behavior.

[14]The right to control disclosure of one's thoughts might be thought to be no more than a reflection of technical limitations. Enforcing a general disclosure requirement presupposes some way of identifying the undisclosed thoughts of others. Currently, we do not have the technology to do this. But even if we did—or especially if we did—respect for the individual would preclude any form of monitoring people's thoughts.

[15]On the relation between privacy and intimate relationships, see Charles Fried, "Privacy," *Yale Law Journal* 77 (1968):475–93. Below, I will argue that confidentiality is central to other types of cooperative relationships as well.

[16]Whether the presumption is overcome will depend on the importance of the objectives served by disclosure, and the degree of violence done to the individual or the relationship at stake.

the circumstances of disclosure. Writing down ideas in a daily journal to oneself or recording them on a cassette should not entail such a forfeiture. Considerations of individual autonomy, privacy, and personality require that such expressions not be deemed available for use by others who may gain access to them.[17]

Likewise, communicating an idea in confidence to another should not render it part of the common pool of knowledge. Respect for the individual's desire to limit the dissemination of the idea is at stake, but so is respect for the relationship of trust and confidence among the persons involved. If *A* confides in *B* under circumstances in which *B* gives *A* reason to believe she will respect the confidence, *A* should be able to trust that *B* will not reveal or misuse the confidence and that third parties who may intentionally or accidentally discover the confidence will respect it.[18]

The alternative possibility is that by revealing her ideas to *B, A* is deemed to forfeit any right to control their use or communication. This principle is objectionable for a couple of reasons. First, it would most certainly increase reluctance to share ideas since our disclosure decisions are strongly influenced by the audience we anticipate. If we could not select our audience, that is, if the choice were only between keeping ideas to ourselves and sharing them with the world at large, many ideas would remain unexpressed, to the detriment of individual health as well as the general good.

Second, the principle would pose an impediment to the formation and sustenance of various types of cooperative relationships—relationships of love and friendship, as well as relationships forged for specific purposes such as education, medical care, or business. It might be thought that only ideas of an intimate or personal nature are important in this regard. But it is not only "personal" relationships, but cooperative relationships of all types, that are at stake. Shared knowledge and information of varying types are central to work relationships and communities—academic departments and disciplines, firms, teams—as well as

other organizations. The possession of common ideas and information, to the exclusion of those outside the relationship or group, contributes to the group's self-definition and to the individual's sense of belonging. By permitting and protecting the sharing of confidences, trade secret principles, among other institutions, permit "special communities of knowledge" which nurture the social bonds and cooperative efforts through which we express our individuality and pursue common purposes.[19]

Of course, by disclosing her idea to *B, A* runs the risk that *B* or anyone else who learns about the idea may use it or share it further. But if *B* has agreed to respect the confidence, either explicitly or by participating in a relationship in which confidence is normally expected, she has a *prima facie* obligation not to disclose the information to which she is privy.[20] Institutions that give A a remedy against third parties who appropriate ideas shared in confidence reduce the risk that *A*'s ideas will become public resources if she shares them with *B*. Such institutions thereby support confidential relationships and the cooperative undertakings that depend on them.

Yet another situation in which disclosure should not be regarded as a license for general use is the case of disclosures made as a result of deceit or insincere promises. Suppose *A* is an entrepreneur who has created an unusual software program with substantial sales potential. Another party, *B*, pretending to be a potential customer, questions *A* at great length about the code and other details of her program. *A*'s disclosures are not intended to be, and should not be deemed, a contribution to the general pool of knowledge, nor should *B* be permitted to use *A*'s ideas.[21] Respect for *A*'s right to disclose her ideas requires that involuntary disclosures—such as those based on deceit, coercion, and theft of documents containing expressions of those ideas—not be regarded as forfeitures to the common pool of knowledge and information. In

---

[17]Technically, of course, others have access to ideas that have been expressed whereas they do not have access to undisclosed thoughts. But ease of access is not the criterion for propriety of access.

[18]This is the fundamental principle behind the prohibition on insider trading.

[19]The phrase "special communities of knowledge" comes from Kim Lane Scheppele, *Legal Secrets* (Chicago: University of Chicago Press, 1988), p. 14.

[20]In practice, this *prima facie* obligation may sometimes be overridden when it conflicts with other obligations, e.g., the obligation to prevent harm to a third party.

[21]An actual case similar to this was litigated in Pennsylvania. See *Continental Data Systems, Inc. v. Exxon Corporation*, 638 F. Supp. 432 (D.C.E.D. Pa. 1986).

recognition of *A*'s right to control disclosure of her ideas and to discourage appropriation of her ideas against her wishes, we might expect our institutions to provide *A* with a remedy against these sorts of appropriation. Trade secret law provides such a remedy.

Competitive fairness is also at stake if *B* is in competition with *A*. Besides having violated standards of common morality in using deceit to gain access to *A*'s ideas, *B* is in a position to exploit those ideas in the marketplace without having contributed to the cost of their development. *B* can sell her version of the software more cheaply since she enjoys a substantial cost advantage compared to *A*, who may have invested a great deal of time and money in developing the software. Fairness in a competitive economy requires some limitations on the rights of firms to use ideas developed by others. In a system based on effort, it is both unfair and ultimately self-defeating to permit firms to have a free ride on the efforts of their competitors.[22]

Problematic Issues

Respect for personal control over the disclosure of ideas, respect for confidential relationships, common morality, and fair competition all point toward recognizing certain rights in ideas. Difficult questions will arise within this system of rights. If *A* is not an individual but an organization or group, should *A* have the same rights and remedies against *B* or third parties who use or communicate information shared with *B* in confidence? For example, suppose *A* is a corporation that hires an employee, *B*, to develop a marketing plan. If other employees of *A* reveal in confidence to *B* information they have created or assembled, should *A* be able to restrain *B* from using this information to benefit herself (at *A*'s expense)? Does it matter if *A* is a two-person corporation or a corporation with 100,000 employees? What if *A* is a social club or a private school?

Hettinger seems to assume that corporate *A*'s should not have such rights—on the grounds that they might restrict *B*'s employment possibilities. It is certainly true that giving *A* a right against *B* if

she reveals information communicated to her in confidence could rule out certain jobs for *B*. However, the alternative rule—that corporate *A*'s should have no rights in ideas they reveal in confidence to others—has problems as well.

One problem involves trust. If our institutions do not give corporate *A*'s certain rights in ideas they reveal in confidence to employees, *A*'s will seek other means of ensuring that competitively valuable ideas are protected. They may contract individually with employees for those rights, and if our legal institutions do not uphold those contracts, employers will seek to hire individuals in whom they have personal trust. Hiring would probably become more dependent on family and personal relationships and there would be fewer opportunities for the less well connected. Institutional rules giving corporate *A*'s rights against employees who reveal or use information given to them in confidence are a substitute for personal bonds of trust. While such rules are not cost-free and may have some morally undesirable consequences, they help sustain cooperative efforts and contribute to more open hiring practices.

Contrary to Hettinger's suggestion, giving corporate *A*'s rights in the ideas they reveal in confidence to others does not always benefit the strong at the expense of the weak, or the large corporation at the expense of the individual, although this is surely sometimes the case.[23] Imagine three entrepreneurs who wish to expand their highly successful cookie business. A venture capitalist interested in financing the expansion naturally wishes to know the details of the operation—including the prized cookie recipe—before putting up capital. After examining the recipe, however, he decides that it would be more profitable for him to sell the recipe to CookieCo, a multinational food company, and to invest his capital elsewhere. Without money and rights to prevent others from using the recipe, the corporate entrepreneurs are

---

[22]For the view that fair and honest business competition is the central policy underlying trade secret protection, see Ramon A. Klitzke, "Trade Secrets: Importing Quasi-Property Rights," *Business Lawyer* 41 (1986):557–70.

[23]It appears that Hettinger is using the term *private company* in contrast to individuals rather than to public companies—those whose shares are sold to the public on national stock exchanges. If one wishes to protect individuals, however, it might be more important to distinguish small, privately held companies from large, publicly held ones than to distinguish individuals from companies. Many individuals, however, are dependent on large, publicly held companies as their livelihood.

very likely out of business. CookieCo, which can manufacture and sell the cookies much more cheaply, will undoubtedly find that most of the entrepreneurs' customers are quite happy to buy the same cookies for less at their local supermarket.

Non-Property Foundations of Trade Secret Law

To a large extent, the rights and remedies mentioned in the preceding discussion are those recognized by trade secret law. As this discussion showed, the concept of property is not necessary to justify these rights. Trade secret law protects against certain methods of appropriating the confidential and commercially valuable ideas of others. It affords a remedy to those whose commercially valuable secrets are acquired by misrepresentation, theft, bribery, breach or inducement of a breach of confidence, espionage, or other improper means.[24] Although the roots of trade secret principles have been variously located, respect for voluntary disclosure decisions and respect for confidential relationships provide the best account of the pattern of permitted and prohibited appropriations and use of ideas.[25] As Justice Oliver Wendell Holmes noted in a 1917 trade secret case, "The property may be denied but the confidence cannot be."[26] Trade secret law can also be seen as enforcing ordinary standards of morality in commercial relationships, thus ensuring some consistency with general social morality.[27]

[24] *Uniform Trade Secrets Act with 1985 Amendments,* sec. 1, in *Uniform Laws Annotated,* vol. 14 (1980 with 1988 Pocket Part). The Uniform Trade Secrets Act seeks to codify and standardize the common law principles of trade secret law as they have developed in different jurisdictions.
[25] See Klitzke, "Trade Secrets." Different theories of justification are discussed in Ridsdale Ellis, *Trade Secrets* (New York: Baker, Voorhis, 1953). Kim Lane Scheppele is another commentator favoring the view that breach of confidence is what trade secret cases are all about. See *Legal Secrets,* p. 241. In their famous article on privacy, Warren and Brandeis find the roots of trade secret principles in the right to privacy. Samuel D. Warren and Louis D. Brandeis, *Harvard Law Review* 4 (1890):212.
[26] E. I. DuPont de Nemours Powder Co. v. Masland, 244 U.S. 100 (1917).
[27] One commentator has said, "The desire to reinforce 'good faith and honest, fair dealing' in business is the mother of the law of trade secrets." Russell B. Stevenson, Jr., *Corporations and Information* (Baltimore: Johns Hopkins University Press, 1980), p. 19.

It may well be true, as Hettinger and others have claimed, that the availability of trade secret protection provides an incentive for intellectual labor and the development of ideas. The knowledge that they have legal rights against those who "misappropriate" their ideas may encourage people to invest large amounts of time and money in exploring and developing ideas. However, the claim that trade secret protection promotes invention is quite different from the claim that it is grounded in or justified by this tendency. Even if common law trade secret rights did not promote intellectual labor or increase the dissemination and use of information, there would still be reasons to recognize those rights. Respect for people's voluntary disclosure decisions, respect for confidential relationships, standards of common morality, and fair competition would still point in that direction.

Moreover, promoting the development of ideas cannot be the whole story behind trade secret principles, since protection is often accorded to information such as customer data or cost and pricing information kept in the ordinary course of doing business. While businesses may need incentives to engage in costly research and development, they would certainly keep track of their customers and costs in any event. The rationale for giving protection to such information must be other than promoting the invention, dissemination, and use of ideas. By the same token, trade secret principles do not prohibit the use of ideas acquired by studying products available in the marketplace. If the central policy behind trade secret protection were the promotion of invention, one might expect that trade secret law, like patent law, which was explicitly fashioned to encourage invention, would protect innovators from imitators.

The fact that Congress has enacted patent laws giving inventors a limited monopoly in exchange for disclosure of their ideas without at the same time eliminating state trade secret law may be a further indication that trade secret and patent protection rest on different grounds.[28] By offering a limited monopoly in exchange for disclosure, the patent laws implicitly recognize the more

[28] Support for this interpretation is found in Justice Thurgood Marshall's concurring opinion in *Kewanee Oil Co. v. Bicron Corp.,* 416 U.S. 470, 494 (1974). The court held that the federal patent laws do not preempt state trade secret laws.

fundamental right not to disclose one's ideas at all or to disclose them in confidence to others.[29]

Reassessing Hettinger's Criticism of Trade Secret Law

If we see trade secret law as grounded in respect for voluntary disclosure, confidential relationships, common morality, and fair competition, the force of Hettinger's criticisms diminishes somewhat. The problems he cites appear not merely in their negative light as detracting from an ideal "free flow of ideas," but in their positive role as promoting other important values.

RESTRICTIONS ON ACQUIRING IDEAS

Hettinger is critical, for example, of the fact that trade secret law restricts methods of acquiring ideas. But the prohibited means of acquisition—misrepresentation, theft, bribery, breach of confidence, and espionage—all reflect general social morality. Lifting these restrictions would undoubtedly contribute to the erosion of important values outside the commercial context.

How much trade secrecy laws inhibit the development and spread of ideas is also open to debate. Hettinger and others have claimed that trade secrecy is a serious impediment to innovation and dissemination because the period of permitted secrecy is unlimited. Yet, given the fact that trade secret law offers no protection for ideas acquired by examining or reverse-engineering products in the marketplace, it would appear rather difficult to maintain technical secrets embodied in those products while still exploiting their market potential. A standard example used to illustrate the problem of perpetual secrecy, the Coke formula, seems insufficient to establish that this is a serious problem. Despite the complexity of modern technology, successful reverse-engineering is common. Moreover, similar technical advances are frequently made by researchers working independently. Trade secret law poses no impediment in either case. Independent discoverers are free to exploit their ideas even if they are similar to those of others.

As for nontechnical information such as marketing plans and business strategies, the period of secrecy is necessarily rather short since implementation entails disclosure. Competitor intelligence specialists claim that most of the information needed to understand what competitors are doing is publicly available.[30] All of these considerations suggest that trade secret principles are not such a serious impediment to the dissemination of information.

COMPETITIVE EFFECTS

Hettinger complains that trade secret principles stifle competition. Assessing this claim is very difficult. On one hand, it may seem that prices would be lower if firms were permitted to obtain cost or other market advantages by using prohibited means to acquire protected ideas from others. Competitor access to the Coke formula would most likely put downward pressure on the price of "the real thing." Yet, it is also reasonable to assume that the law keeps prices down by reducing the costs of self-protection. By giving some assurance that commercially valuable secrets will be protected, the law shields firms from having to bear the full costs of protection. It is very hard to predict what would happen to prices if trade secret protection were eliminated. Self-protection would be more costly and would tend to drive prices up, while increased competition would work in the opposite direction. There would surely be important differences in morale and productivity. Moreover, as noted, any price reductions for consumers would come at a cost to the basic moral standards of society if intelligence-gathering by bribery, misrepresentation, and espionage were permitted.

---

[29]Congress may have realized that trying to bring about more openness by eliminating trade secret protection, even with the added attraction of a limited monopoly for inventions that qualify for patent protection, would be inconsistent with fundamental moral notions such as respect for confidential relationships, and would probably not have worked anyway.

[30]See. e.g., the statement of a *manager* of a competitor surveillance group quoted in Jerry L. Wall, "What the Competition Is Doing: Your Need to Know," *Harvard Business Review* 52 (November–December 1974):34. See generally Leonard M. Fuld, *Competitor Intelligence: How to Get It—How to Use It* (New York: John Wiley and Sons, 1985).

RESTRICTIONS ON EMPLOYEE MOBILITY

Among Hettinger's criticisms of trade secret law, the most serious relate to restrictions on employee mobility. In practice, employers often attempt to protect information by overrestricting the postemployment opportunities of employees. Three important factors contribute to this tendency: vagueness about which information is confidential; disagreement about the proper allocation of rights to ideas generated by employees using their employers' resources; and conceptual difficulties in distinguishing general knowledge and employer-specific knowledge acquired on the job. Courts, however, are already doing what Hettinger recommends, namely, limiting the restrictions that employers can place on future employment in the name of protecting ideas.[31] Although the balance between employer and employee interests is a delicate one not always equitably struck, the solution of eliminating trade secret protection altogether is overbroad and undesirable, considering the other objectives at stake.

HYPOTHETICAL ALTERNATIVES

Hettinger's discussion of our intellectual property institutions reflects an assumption that greater openness and sharing would occur if we eliminated trade secret protection. He argues that trade secret principles encourage secrecy. He speaks of the "free flow of ideas" as the ideal that would obtain in the absence of our intellectual property institutions. This supposition strikes me as highly unlikely. People keep secrets and establish confidential relationships for a variety of reasons that are quite independent of any legal protection these secrets might have. The psychology and sociology of secrets have been explored by others. Although much economic theory is premised on complete information, secrecy and private information are at the heart of day-to-day competition in the marketplace.

In the absence of something like trade secret principles, I would expect not a free flow of ideas but greater efforts to protect information through contracts, management systems designed to limit information access, security equipment, and electronic counterintelligence devices. I would also expect stepped-up efforts to acquire intelligence from others through espionage, bribery, misrepresentation, and other unsavory means. By providing some assurance that information can be shared in confidence and by protecting against unethical methods of extracting information and undermining confidentiality, trade secret principles promote cooperation and security, two important conditions for intellectual endeavor. In this way, trade secret principles may ultimately promote intellectual effort by limiting information flow.

The Burden of Justification

We may begin thinking about information rights, as Hettinger does, by treating all ideas as part of a common pool and then deciding whether and how to allocate to individuals rights to items in the pool. Within this framework, ideas are conceived on the model of tangible property.[32] Just as, in the absence of social institutions, we enter the world with no particular relationship to its tangible assets or natural resources, we have no particular claim on the world's ideas. In this scheme, as Hettinger asserts, the "burden of justification is very much on those who would restrict the maximal use of intellectual objects."

Alternatively, we may begin, as I do, by thinking of ideas in relation to their originators, who may or may not share their ideas with specific others or contribute them to the common pool. This approach treats ideas as central to personality and the social world individuals construct for themselves. Ideas are not, in the first instance, freely available natural resources. They originate with people, and it is the connections among people, their ideas, and their relationships with others that provides a baseline for discussing rights in ideas. Within this conception, the burden of justification is on those who would argue for disclosure obligations and general access to ideas.

---

[31]See e.g., John Burgess, "Unlocking Corporate Shackles," *Washington Business*, 11 December 1989, p. 1.

[32]Hettinger speaks of ideas as objects, and of rights in ideas as comparable to water or mineral rights. Indeed, according to Hettinger, the difficulty in justifying intellectual property rights arises because ideas are not in all respects like tangible property, which he thinks is more easily justified.

The structure of specific rights that emerges from these different frameworks depends not only on where the burden of justification is located, but also on how easily it can be discharged.[33] It is unclear how compelling a case is required to overcome the burden Hettinger sets up and, consequently, difficult to gauge the depth of my disagreement with him.[34] Since Hettinger does not consider the rationales for trade secret principles discussed here, it is not clear whether he would dismiss them altogether, find them insufficiently weighty to override the presumption he sets up, or agree that they satisfy the burden of justification.

One might suspect, however, from the absence of discussion of the personal and social dimension of rights in ideas that Hettinger does not think them terribly important, and that his decision to put the burden of justification on those who argue for rights in ideas reflects a fairly strong commitment to openness. On the assumption that our alternative starting points reflect seriously held substantive views (they are not just procedural devices to get the argument started) and that both frameworks require strong reasons to overcome the initial presumption, the resulting rights and obligations are likely to be quite different in areas where neither confidentiality nor openness is critical to immediate human needs. Indeed, trade secrecy law is an area where these different starting points would be likely to surface.

The key question to ask about these competing frameworks is which is backed by stronger reasons. My opposition to Hettinger's allocation of the burden of justification rests on my rejection of his conception of ideas as natural resources and on different views of how the world would look in the absence of our intellectual property institutions. In contrast, my starting point acknowledges the importance of ideas to our sense of ourselves and the communities (including work communities) of which we are a part. It is also more compatible with the way we commonly talk about ideas. Our

talk about disclosure obligations presupposes a general background right not to reveal ideas. If it were otherwise, we would speak of concealment rights. To use the logically interesting feature of nonexclusiveness as a starting point for moral reasoning about rights in ideas seems wholly arbitrary.

Conclusion

Knives, forks, and spoons are all designed to help us eat. In a sense, however, the essential function of these tools is to help us cut, since without utensils, we could still consume most foods with our hands. One might be tempted to say that since cutting is the essential function of eating utensils, forks and spoons should be designed to facilitate cutting. One might even say that insofar as forks and spoons do not facilitate cutting, they should be redesigned. Such a modification, however, would rob us of valuable specialized eating instruments.

Hettinger's train of thought strikes me as very similar. He purports to examine the justification of our various intellectual property institutions. However, he settles on a justification that really only fits patent and, arguably, copyright institutions. He then suggests that other intellectual property rights be assessed against the justification he proposes and redesigned insofar as they are found wanting. In particular, he suggests that trade secret principles be modified to look more like patent principles. Hettinger fails to appreciate the various rationales behind the rights and duties understood under the heading "intellectual property," especially those recognized by trade secret law.

I agree with Hettinger that our intellectual property institutions need a fresh look from a utilitarian perspective.[35] The seventeen-year monopoly granted through patents is anachronistic given the pace of technological development today. We need to think about the appropriate balance between employer and employee rights in ideas developed jointly. Solutions to the problem of the unauthorized copying of software may be found in alternative pricing structures rather than in

---

[33]The Editors of *Philosophy & Public Affairs* encouraged me to address this point.

[34]His argument from maximizing the production and dissemination of ideas suggests that the presumption in favor of free ideas is not terribly strong: it can be overridden by identifying some reasonable objective likely to be served by assigning exclusive rights.

[35]That is, we should look at the effects of these institutions on social well-being in general and select the institutions that are best on the whole.

fundamental modifications of our institutions. Public interest considerations could be advanced for opening access to privately held information in a variety of areas. As we consider these specific questions, however, I would urge that we keep firmly in mind the variety of objectives that intellectual property institutions have traditionally served.[36] If, following Hettinger's advice, we single-mindedly reshape these institutions to maximize the short-term dissemination and use of ideas, we run the risk of subverting the other ends these institutions serve.

[36]A utilitarian assessment will also include consideration of the various interests that would be affected by alternative allocations of intellectual property rights. For example, denying authors copyright in their works may increase the power and profit of publishers and further impair the ability of lesser-known writers to find publication outlets. One scholar has concluded that America's failure to recognize the copyrights of aliens before 1891 stunted the development of native literature. For fifty years before the passage of the Platt-Simmonds Act, publishing interests vigorously and successfully opposed recognition of international copyright. This is understandable since the works of well-known British authors were available to publishers free of charge. Publishers were not terribly concerned with the artistic integrity of these works. They sometimes substituted alterative endings, mixed the works of different authors, and edited as economically necessary. There were few reasons to take the risks involved in publishing the works of unknown and untested American writers who might insist on artistic integrity. See generally Aubert J. Clark, *The Movement for International Copyright in Nineteenth Century America* (Westport, Conn.: Greenwood Press, 1973).

Intellectual Property and Copyright Ethics

MARK ALFINO*

PHILOSOPHERS HAVE GIVEN relatively little attention to the ethical issues surrounding the nature of intellectual property in spite of the fact that for the past ten years the public policy debate over "fair use" of copyrighted materials in higher education has been heating up. This neglect is especially striking since copyright ethics are at stake in so many aspects of academic life: the photocopying of materials for classroom use and scholarly work, access to electronic texts, and the cost and availability of single-source information technology such as *Dialogue,* library card catalogues, the *Oxford English Dictionary,* and a variety of other print and electronic resources. Of course, the ethics of copyright are not only an issue for those of us in the business of education: recent allegations of copyright infringement by Texaco, which regularly photocopied articles from scientific and technical journals for its employees, suggests that questions about copyright ethics may arise regularly for every corporation and business. While the recent lawsuits against Kinko's Copies[1] and Texaco may settle some public policy questions in the short run, the legal discourse on fair use depends upon competing ethical institutions which are not likely to be resolved soon.

The ethical quandaries surrounding fair use will not be resolved by appealing to well known principles of property rights. One reason for this is that copying a book involves an act of labor which, one

*The author would like to acknowledge the assistance of Mead Data Central's LEXIS research service.

[1]The *Kinko's* suit (*Basic Books, Inc. v. Kinko's Graphics Corporation*) was recently decided by U.S. District court in New York. The court ruled for the plaintiff, rejecting Kinko's argument that because its clients are educators, its service is protected under the fair use guidelines. As this article goes to press the judge's ruling is not available, but news reports indicate that the decision against Kinko's was based in part upon the fact that Kinko's "Professor's Publishing" service is commercial. This leaves open the question of whether nonprofit university run copy centers could operate within the fair use exemption.

From Business & Professional Ethics Journal *10(2), Summer 1991. Reprinted with permission.*

might allege, creates property in the copy. Unlike the act of labor involved in theft, copying does not, in any obvious way, involve the removal of someone else's property or the violation of their privacy. In the course of our discussion, I will show that there are strong counter arguments to this argument. But here, at the outset, a labor theory of property offers no decisive answer. Second, the electronic transmission of data throws the whole notion of what a "copy" is into confusion: Is text from a database on a terminal a copy? Is an electronic copy of a data file analogous to a paper copy of a printed work? Third, the development of computer software threatens to blur the distinction between a copyright and a patent. Traditionally, patents protect processes or products of processes which show genuine technical innovation. In return for registering (and making public) the process, society grants a limited monopoly to the inventor. Copyrights involve similar protections (though of a longer duration) for the novel expression of ideas. Computer software is a hybrid, combining both novel expressions of old ideas (e.g. displaying a print spreadsheet on a video terminal) and new processes for doing things (e.g. the transformation of a calendar into an algorithm for displaying and printing calendars). There is no escaping the fact that computer software and hardware is transforming the distinction between processes of production (candidates for patents) and expressions of ideas (candidates for copyright).

Finally, new developments in scholarship such as the growth of film studies and the development of video technology as an instructional medium, raise difficult problems for handling copyrights to videotapes and video broadcasts. Typically the more "commercial" a product is the more the courts have been willing to protect copyright holders. When a commercial object such as a movie or documentary becomes an object of study, a confusion arises as to whether fair use should be determined by looking at the motives for its production or the demands of education and scholarship. The 1978 copyright law is far more generous in exempting from protection classroom texts rather than video and broadcasts.

It took several centuries for public discourse to evolve a coherent way of balancing the property claims of print publishers with the society's legitimate claim to have access to cultural works and knowledge. In little more than three decades, the discourse on copyright has been challenged in ways in which the first writers of copyright laws and the most prominent philosophers of property rights could not have imagined. It is hard to imagine John Locke responding to *droit morale* [i.e., moral right] issues such as the artist's right to prevent colorization of films, the reinstallation of contemporary sculptures, or the effect of remodeling a building on the architect's reputation. All of these cases involve copyright issues.

My central contention in this paper is that settling intellectual property questions requires us to attend to the development of the technology of intellectual production and to an ongoing social discourse about the production and value of knowledge and culture. I think these two social processes, technology and discourse about the status of knowledge, are always at work in the emergence of ethical problems and copyright[2] and I think they are also the place to look for solutions. If I am right then policy arguments which proceed primarily by a retrieval of abstract thought on the metaphysical principles of property are inadequate. I will demonstrate my thesis first by showing that our basic understanding of copyright is itself a product of clashes between technological development and social discourse about the value of knowledge and culture. Then I will discuss efforts which focus either exclusively or primarily on a retrieval of property rights talk. I find Edwin Hettinger's work particularly important in this regard, because I think he has a keen sense of the inadequacy of traditional arguments about property rights. Finally, I will show how new copyright policy can be forged by attending to the actual social process (both technological and conversational) which create our difficulties in the first place.

I. Historical and Critical Studies of Copyright and Authorship

In order to show how policy questions arise and are settled, I would like to recount a significant episode in the history of the development of modern

---

[2]To give a simple example, the dilemma over film colorization doesn't occur until the technology for colorizing film develops. Also, the question about how to treat videos in educational contexts doesn't emerge until educators place a value on them as instructional media.

copyright law. My specific claim in relating this history is that social values about technology, knowledge, and culture are the real determinants of our thinking about copyright. Of course, a mere history does not tell us that these *should* be the determinants of our thinking. I will not be prepared to make that claim until I show the inadequacy of some other approaches, which I will do in section II. Still, I think the story I am about to tell goes some way toward *showing* the reasonableness of my general claim.

The best general history of the development of copyright in England remains Lyman Patterson's *Copyright in Historical Perspective,* which traces the development of copyright from the origin of the printing press to the refinement of the modern copyright statutes as a result of the 18th century "Battle of the Books." Copyright began as a royal prerogative granted to the main publishing guild, the Stationers Company. The granting of a license to control copy was originally motivated by the crown's desire to control the spread of potentially threatening religious or political ideas.[3] Until the first modern copyright statute, the 1709 Statute of Anne, the Stationers Company enjoyed an unlimited monopoly over copy, including at times, the right to search buildings and seize copy.[4]

Modern copyright laws, which recognize, as a matter of moral principle, a limit to the monopoly which control of copy entails, begin with the Statute of Anne in 1709, subtitled "An Act for the Encouragement of Learning, by Vesting the Copies of Printed Books in the Authors or Purchasers of such Copies, during the Times herein mentioned." The act first gave legal expression to the idea that the social value of disseminating information and culture was great enough to justify limiting the property interests of publishers. The act also prepared the way for an author's copyright.

The Stationers argued for and received extensions to the statutory limits of copyright in the act.

They continued to charge exorbitant prices for classics of English literature and editions of the Bible, to which they owned the copyright. The "Battle of the Books" took place during the first three quarters of the 18th century[5] as independent publishers, in sympathy with the "Society for the Encouragement of Learning," challenged copyright holders by producing unauthorized editions of popular English literature. In the celebrated case of *Donaldson v. Beckett* (1774), a lasting precedent against perpetual copyright was established.

Mark Rose[6] rightly takes the *Donaldson* case as a turning point in our thinking about copyright. He shows, quite successfully, that behind the *Donaldson* case lay a variety of changes including a new attitude toward authorship, the development of a market for intellectual labor, and the application of the justification of private property to intellectual labor.

In the *Donaldson* case, owners of the copyright to James Thompson's *The Seasons* sued Alexander Donaldson for producing unauthorized copies of the popular work. The defense argued that the statutory period of monopoly granted by the Statute of Anne had run out and that the copy was therefore not protected. The plaintiff argued that copyright is a common-law property right and that statutes merely supplement, but do not absolutely limit, the enjoyment of the right. After a three week hearing before the House of Lords, which featured packed galleries and daily attention from the press, the defense won and the statutory basis of copyright was never again challenged in either England or the United States.

The legal principle at stake in the *Donaldson* case has significant ethical implications. If copyright is a form of limited monopoly granted through statute, based on policy considerations, and not an absolute common-law right, the ethical burden of proof shifts to copyright holders to show that their property interests are more important than the public good of having access to

---

[3]The first three major copyright acts, the *Star Chamber Decrees of 1586 and 1637,* the *Ordinances of 1643 and 1647,* and the *Licensing Act of 1662* were all primarily censorship acts. Lyman Patterson, *Copyright in Historical Perspective* (Nashville, TN: Vanderbilt UP, 1968) 82.

[4]The right to copy remained with the individual guild member who registered it. It was his property in perpetuity. The copyright could be transferred to widows of Guild members, but if the widow remarried outside the Guild, she lost the copyright and it reverted to the company. Patterson 111.

[5]The Statute of Anne (1709) and its extension in 1734 set the stage for the *Donaldson* case (1774), described below. In addition to traditional stationers and renegades like Donaldson, groups like the Society for the Encouragement of Learning (1734) played a part in the "battle."

[6]Mark Rose, "The Author as Proprietor: *Donaldson v. Beckett* and the Genealogy of Modern Authorship," Representations 23 (1988) 51–85.

information. The ethical issue takes a metaphysical turn when we ask, as we shall in section II, just what it is that constitutes the intellectual property protected by copyright. Again, if the "substance" of intellectual property is constituted by statutory fiat, then the limitations of the right are not analogous to limitations of natural rights.

Two kinds of arguments for perpetual copyright were offered during the 18th century. First, the Stationers alleged, especially with regard to literature, that authors are entitled to a perpetual property right because their work is an original invention. Second, many claimed that intellectual property is analogous to real estate and that the right of ownership derives from a right of "occupation." William Blackstone argued in his *Commentaries* (1765–1769) that in publishing a book one is not offering something for public use, as when land is given for use as a highway. Rather, "In such a case, it is more like making a way through a man's own private grounds, which he may stop at pleasure; he may give out a number of keys, by publishing a number of copies; but no man who receives a key, has thereby a right to forge others, and sell them to other people."[7] Thus, Blackstone asserted an analogy between intellectual property and real property over which one has a right of occupation. If Blackstone is right then public access to copyrighted works is not a public right but a kind of visitation right. Copyright infringement is thus not so much theft as trespassing.

The argument from invention, on the other hand, identifies the production of the text with the person of the author. The text is uniquely tied to its origin in the personality of the author. As an extension of the person of the author, the expression embodied in the printed text is quintessentially [essentially] personal property. The argument from occupation satisfies a similar intuition in a different way. It harkens back to a notion of original appropriation. Prior to its expression by the author, the work was like unowned property. Expression is a way of "staking out" or "homesteading" a territory. The peculiar strength to this argument is that it doesn't have to explain how appropriation remains legitimate once all land is

originally occupied. As long as there are infinitely many ways to express something, the author's occupation of his intellectual estate cannot be considered an unjust monopoly.

If these seem like metaphysically extravagant arguments we should look briefly at how great a burden of proof is assumed in any argument for copyright as a natural property right. While there is no question that the physical text is a piece of physical property, the proponent of copyright as a common-law right must claim that a right exists in the ownership of the ideal expression which lies "behind" the text. The argument will not succeed without an appeal to some metaphysical entity which is related to the personality of the author in some way that is relevant to the author's most fundamental interests. In the following passage, William Enfield, a contemporary of Blackstone's, identifies that interest as the profitability of the work. Intellectual property is justified because it is as real a means of making a livelihood as cultivating land:

> In this various world different men are born to different fortunes: one inherits a portion of land; he cultivates it with care, it produces him corn and fruits and wool: another possesses a fruitful mind, teeming with ideas of every kind; he bestows his labor in cultivating *that;* the produce is reason, sentiment, philosophy. It seems but equitable, that a fair exchange should be made of these goods; and that one man should live by the labor of his brain, as well as another by the sweat of his brow.[8]

Ultimately, the argument from invention and the argument from original appropriation dovetail, since behind both lie the intuition that through intellectual labor one makes an original acquisition of a profitable object. The difficult part of the justification is to show that one is morally entitled to the profit which can be made from regarding the ownership of the expression of ideas as an exclusive entitlement. The claim of a just property interest in the potential distribution of the object depends upon *first* regarding that object as an abstract metaphysical entity, but neither argument really justifies the existence of such an entity. The form of

---

[7]William Blackstone, *Commentaries on the Laws of England* 4 vols. (Oxford, 1765–1769) 2:406.

[8]William Enfield, *Observation on Literary Property* (London, 1774) 21–22.

the argument is: If we regard intellectual property as an ideal object, then it is analogous to productive land. Alternatively, we could hold to the view that the production of a book is like the (production of any other object which requires some ingenuity and labor to produce. Then the form of the argument would be: If we regard intellectual property as the objects produced by the joint labor of authors and printers, then it is analogous to the sale of a commodity. In the case of a book, the commodity happens to be reproducible, whether by copying the book longhand or by printing or photocopying. We can compare the book's reproducibility to the reproducibility of any other object. Of course, these alternatives don't tell us which way we should frame the argument, but they show that we could think quite coherently of intellectual property without the metaphysical abstraction which Blackstone's argument entails. We either need a way of choosing between the two ways of framing the argument or we need to recognize that the general argument itself is based on a consideration of social and personal interests extrinsic to the nature of intellectual activity itself.[9]

Before moving to a philosophical consideration of copyright ethics, we should identify some of the specific virtues of critical historical research on this topic. It is a commonplace of much work in ethics that the historical justifications for our ethical intuitions do not settle ethical issues in any ultimate way. The arguments put forward by Blackstone and others during the "Battle of the Books" have a kind of historical interest, but do they reveal the direction which philosophical argumentation should take?

While it is surely naive to suppose that history simply reveals fundamental ethical principles (at least without the interpretive activity of the historical philosopher), it is also unreasonable to suppose that ethical norms which *have histories* are always justifiable apart from the actual social practices to which their histories refer. At a minimum the history of a norm reveals the changing needs to which the norm responds. We may decide that it was historically accidental that certain values were not recognized as fundamental long before they were in fact recognized, but in other cases we cannot help but feel that the value itself is largely motivated by historical circumstance, even if it is logically related to other, more "primary" values which seem less contingent.

In the case of copyright, this tension between *a priori* justification and historical contingency is particularly acute. In the context of the history of the West, it is significant that the ethical values which underlie copyright law emerge alongside the development of economic markets for intellectual labor, the decline of the patronage system, a change in the correlation between literacy and membership in an upper class or clerical class, and the development of a new explanation of intellectual production which emphasized "invention" and "original genius."

The connection between the rise of the modern understanding of copyright and the decline of older more traditional ways of thinking about the credit one deserves for intellectual achievement and the social reward system for the same is well documented.[10] Doubtless, we are a long way from Martin Luther's warning to printers not to be covetous of the proceeds from distributing intellectual works. Luther argued, "I have freely received, freely do I give and expect nothing in return."[11] However, an awareness of the variety of ways of thinking about the values and obligations associated with intellectual production cannot help but persuade the reader that there may be no unique, ahistorical formula for understanding copyright ethics. Rather, a coherent and justified ethical understanding of copyright will have to take into account the actual historical practices governing intellectual production and the value of intellectual activity. This includes an analysis of the technological, political, and economic conditions under which copyrights are claimed. While I certainly do

[9]To set this argument in context one should read Kenneth Vandevelde's "The New Property of the Nineteenth Century: The Development of the Modern Concept of Property," *Buffalo Law Review* 29.2 (1980):325–367, in which he argues that the conceptual difficulties of extending natural property rights to non-physical objects requires an appeal to the public policy benefits of recognizing such property. Thus, in the interest of logical coherence, the argument for natural property rights shifts in character to an argument about social utility.

[10]Martha Woodmansee, "The Genius and the Copyright: Economic and Legal Conditions of the Emergence of the Author," *Eighteenth Century Studies* 17 (1984) 425–448.
[11]Woodmansee 434 (19n), from Martin Luther's "Warning to Printers."

not think that current practices are "self-justifying," I do believe that the justifiability of our ethical intuitions about copyright are so closely connected to current institutional practices that no adequate analysis of the former can ignore the latter. That is why my own position in section III is constructed in relation to concrete problems posed by the institutional practices of publishers, libraries, and educators.

In the next section, I consider two efforts by philosophers to give abstract justifications for positions in copyright ethics. In my criticisms of these efforts I will give further support to the claim made above, that no coherent understanding of copyright can be achieved which does not consider the actual historical conditions under which intellectual labor takes place.

II. Philosophical Approaches to Copyright Ethics

Selmer Bringsjord[12] argues on purely logical grounds that since we have strong intuitions that some forms of copying are permissible and since we cannot make a logical distinction between various forms of copying, therefore all forms of copying are morally permissible.[13]

When scholars think about whether it is morally permissible to photocopy a text, they cannot help but be struck by how much of their everyday activity involves copying in the general sense of the word. Even without considering copying technology (which really includes everything from the pencil to the text scanner), mental activity itself seems to be a form of copying. Surely no one believes that when I jot down a few notes to aid my memory, I am violating any ethical norm. Even if I make several longhand copies of a lengthy passage[14] and distribute them to my friends, it is hard to identify, at first glance, a

moral harm. The introduction of copy technology, it might be alleged, doesn't introduce any new logical features. After all, at one level of use, the copying machine merely replaces the laborious work of copying text longhand. At another level, it merely obviates the need to lug large bound journals back to one's study. Apart from the speed and efficiency of the copying, there seems to be little difference between:

a.   reciting from memory a long poem for several friends on different occasions;
b.   sending them longhand copies; and
c.   sending them photocopies.

If we consider enough cases, we may come to the same conclusion which Bringsjord does that it is morally permissible to copy anything that is in public circulation as long as you don't plan to sell the copy. Because his argument, like the one above, depends upon a gradation of similar cases, I will call such arguments *gradation arguments*. While gradation arguments show us some interesting features of the activity of copying, I think they are fundamentally inadequate as a means of deciding any ethical issues concerning copyright.

The actual argument schema for Bringsjord's argument is a little different from the example above. The basic idea is to argue from a case in which we have no qualms about copying through a series of cases which are not different in any obvious logical or moral sense to a case, finally, which most people (including the framers of the copyright law) would consider unethical. Since there are no logical differences among the particular cases, the conclusion is that the judgement that the last case is unethical is unjustified. The presupposition of this approach is that there can be no differences in our moral appraisal of two cases of copying unless there is a logical difference between the two cases. To illustrate the argument schema, Bringsjord considers twelve cases of "renting a video" beginning with a person who watches the video and "replays" the events in memory, moving through cases in which the viewer has more and more vivid recollections and more and more fantastic abilities to reproduce the movie for friends, ending finally with a case in which the viewer has devised a machine for replaying the movie. It is perhaps relevant that in the fantasy of the thought experiment, we are requested to imagine that the machine has made its recording directly from the brain of the well-situated viewer.

---

[12]Selmer Bringsjord, "In Defense of Copying," *Public Affairs Quarterly* 3 (1989) (1989) 1–9.

[13]I realize that this simple reconstruction is perhaps not as sympathetic as it could be; however, I think this is an accurate representation of the structure of Bringsjord's argument.

[14]For the sake of this argument, suppose I copy more than 250 words from a long poem, thus exceeding the copyright guidelines for photocopying associated with the current U.S. copyright law.

This makes the ultimate copy much like the spontaneous reproduction from memory with which the gradation of cases began.

Bringsjord's argument is quite clever and really does capture our feeling that different cases of copying really don't have different morally relevant logical features. One striking example of this concerns the distinction between fair use in scholarly research and fair use in classroom distribution of copyrighted materials. Current guidelines governing the former are much more liberal than those governing the latter. If someone were to challenge my distribution of a packet of readings, I could place the readings on reserve and require each student to copy them individually But is there really a moral principle at issue here? We could imagine a gradation of cases between purely spontaneous individual copying, which is protected, and systematic copying, which is not, and not find a single step in the succession of cases in which a morally relevant logical difference occurred. As long as we focus on the copying activity itself, the bottom line is that a copy is a copy is a copy

But this is just where the limitation of Bringsjord's argument becomes apparent. He assumes uncritically that the issue of the moral permissibility of copying is to be decided by looking at the logical structure of the copying activity itself. This approach ignores the fact that the same activity performed in different situations may have different moral implications. If the goal of copyright law (and with it copyright ethics) is to promote invention, discovery and intellectual achievement within the context of a free market, then some copying (e.g. systematic copying, even if not for sale) might be judged immoral even though it is no more or less an instance of copying which under other circumstances is judged moral. For example, suppose that one day I am copying from Plato's *Sophist* and, being scrupulous, I determine that there are no living relatives of the copyright owners (in this case the translator). The next day I copy the complete text of a new best selling novel by an up and coming young author. The two cases are logically equivalent, yet there are morally relevant contextual differences.

Bringsjord also makes a rather weak defense against an objection to the logical apparatus behind the argument. One might object, drawing on a paradox from Plato, that by the addition of incremental features, none of which by itself is morally objectionable, one can conclude, fallaciously, that the whole sum of these increments introduces no morally objectionable feature. To use Bringsjord's example, if I claim that a one inch tall man is short and that after adding one billionth of an inch to him he is still short, I might deduce from these premises that a 500 foot tall man is short. The "paradox" is that the argument "is formally valid and has apparently obviously true premises, yet the conclusion is absurd."[15] The author excuses his own argument from this fallacy because he feels the conclusion (that copying is morally permissible) is not absurd. Of course, one's choice of words in an argument is almost always crucial. The fallacy occurs not only when the conclusions are "absurd" but also when they are simply not necessarily true. While the author's conclusion is not absurd, it may or may not be true. Therefore, I think it does commit the fallacy.

But the more serious flaw in the argument was the first one. We cannot assume that moral questions about copying can be resolved without considering the substantive moral issues which underlie our intuitions. In the case of copyright ethics these issues include respect for the author's achievement, respect for property interests, and a recognition of the social claim to fruits of intellectual activity and the social right of free access to information.

Since many of these values are incorporated into natural rights and utilitarian arguments for property we might have better luck with Edwin Hettinger's consideration of such arguments.[16] Hettinger gives a critical assessment of two traditional justifications of copyright:

1. Copyrights are justified as personal property rights; and
2. Copyrights provide incentives to produce knowledge and cultural works and are justified on utilitarian grounds.

The first claim needs to be discussed because one of our principal texts for the justification of property rights, Locke's *Two Treatises,* is remarkably

[15]Bringsjord 6.
[16]Edwin Hettinger, "Justifying Intellectual Property," *Philosophy and Public Affairs* 18 (1989) 31–52.

silent about intellectual property. One possible reason for this is that Locke lived and wrote in an age in which authorship was not proprietary. Intellectual labor was motivated by the independent production of a leisure class or a production sponsored by that class. Locke himself disclaimed authorship and property interests in the very text justifying private property. He is reported to have found the entire book selling industry objectionable on aesthetic, if not moral, grounds.[17] Because proprietary authorship, and with it the very notion of intellectual property, is a more recent notion than private property, a question naturally arises over the possibility of justifying intellectual property with traditional arguments for private property.

Hettinger argues that natural rights arguments justifying intellectual property are weaker than one might suppose, for the following reasons: 1. Intellectual objects are "nonexclusive"; they are not consumed by their use. Since sharing them in no way hinders one's personal use of the object, the burden of proof falls on those who would justify their exclusivity. As Hettinger puts it, "Why should one person have the exclusive right to possess and use something which all people could possess and use concurrently?"[18] 2. There is a fundamental and longstanding ethical tradition recognizing the social value of free (or at least affordable) access to information. 3. Property rights guarantee people an interest in the value added to an object by their acts of labor. But in intellectual objects it is impossible to determine in what portion of the object the author deserves a property interest. "A person who relies on human intellectual history and makes a small modification to produce something of great value should no more receive what the market will bear than should the last person needed to lift a car receive full credit for lifting it."[19] 4. In a market economy driven in part by information, one might argue that copyrights are a means by which individuals provide for their survival and security. But since most copyrights are owned by institutions, Hettinger finds this argument unpersuasive. In addition to these argu-

ments, he argues that copyrighted works may violate Locke's proviso against waste and spoilage (if the copyright holder charges an excessive fee, for instance), but since that argument depends upon argument 1 above, we do not need to address it specifically.

In arguing against the claim that recognizing an *absolute* (perpetual and unrestricted) copyright is necessary to guarantee an individual's human dignity, Hettinger is quite persuasive. But some of the arguments above are not very persuasive. While I agree that the nonexclusivity of intellectual objects is an important logical feature of them, it does not follow from their nonexclusivity that the widespread availability of a copyrighted work would not limit the uses its author *might* make of the work if he *were* entitled to exploit the profitability of the work. Of course, that is not an argument that the author is so entitled, but Hettinger's argument is only valid if one has already excluded "earning money" as one of the legitimate uses of the object.[20] The question of whether limiting the profitability of the object is justified is still open. Therefore, we would do well not to base our arguments on a conception of nonexclusivity which begs the answer to that question.

The second argument is right on the mark and correctly identifies the ethical tension between individual arid social values which lies at the heart of copyright ethics. It also supports Hettinger's basic intuition, with which I also agree, that justifying intellectual property by appeal to the natural rights tradition is not as simple a matter as some would have us believe.

However, I do not think the third argument is very strong. On the traditional view, we are entitled to whatever we get through original appropriation and as a result of adding value to an appropriated object through our labor. The nonexclusivity of intellectual objects guarantees, ideally,[21] that every individual can make an appropriation of his or her intellectual tradition.

---

[17]Peter Laslett, Introduction, *Two Treatises of Government,* John Locke (Cambridge: Cambridge UP, 1988) 7.
[18]Hettinger, p. 35.
[19]Hettinger, p. 38.

[20]This is why it is not adequate, for example, for educators to base claims to fair use solely on the notion that their use is "not for profit." Such arguments ignore the fact that widespread photocopying *does* diminish potential returns to rights holders.
[21]I recognize that if basic opportunities for education and advancement are not available then this counterargument will not succeed.

Thus, we are not giving undeserved credit to individuals who make an innovation in some intellectual endeavor precisely because we do not normally need to take credit away from someone else to do so. Only an absolutist agenda for intellectual property, which no one but an Objectivist[22] would argue for, would result in a wholly proprietary intellectual tradition in which even lending rights were not recognized.

The fourth argument, that the security interests people have in copyright might not be sufficient to justify intellectual property rights, is especially weak. The fact that institutions own many copyrights and patents does not show that individuals do not derive a livelihood from intellectual property. Also, I think a good case can be made that individual proprietary authors *do* depend for their livelihood upon the ability to control the distribution of their work for a limited period of time. The very emergence of proprietary authorship is tied to the growth of economically independent writing careers.[23] I certainly agree that security interests do not justify *unlimited* copyright, but again, who is really trying to justify that position?

In discussing utilitarian justifications for copyright, which are by far the most persuasive, Hettinger claims that he finds it paradoxical that a right which restricts access to intellectual property could actually promote intellectual production. I agree that there is nothing necessary about this relationship. Historically, great intellectual production occurred in the absence of any notion of copyright whatever. However, in the context of a market economy, it is not at all paradoxical that incentives, which may require copyright protection, might promote activity. If people are indeed motivated by the prospect of gain, and if gain is only possible through a control of copying, then a restriction of some uses of intellectual property might really promote production.

Hettinger concludes by arguing for greater government funding of intellectual activity and by urging that public ownership of intellectual property might replace private ownership. I think this proposal makes a certain amount of sense in some areas: for instance, if a company gained exclusive rights to a database which, because it was constantly changing, could in effect become perpetually copyrighted, we might make a strong argument that the monopolistic effect of such a system justified its regulation. This is in fact what occurred in the case of the copyright clearinghouses for the recording industry. Also, I think the government might be too uncritical (or just not business wise) in disclaiming rights to the results of the research which it currently finances.

A government program for funding intellectual and artistic production shares some features with the older patronage system under which authors worked for centuries. Government patronage might be abusive or liberating, depending upon the circumstances. If the funds are given to professionals with a tradition of academic freedom, like the university professors or independent artists, perhaps the results would be good. Of course, governments have interests that may be expressed in funding decisions no matter who the recipient is and governments may have to observe restrictions in funding decisions that private patrons do not (consider the recent controversies over government funding of the arts). But the general claim that private copyright should be weakened by reintroducing a patronage system for intellectual production is quite reactionary. After all, the traditional system for intellectual production was based on such a patronage system (variously controlled by guilds, aristocracies, church and state). Whatever the dangers of proprietary authorship, it emerged in the 17th and 18th centuries partly because intellectuals wanted to be free from the constraints of a patronage system.[24]

While I have been somewhat critical of Hettinger's arguments, I should add that they become quite persuasive if one takes them as arguments against a perpetual and unrestricted copyright. Also, he correctly locates one of the

---

[22]See for example the Objectivist position as it is articulated in "What is the Objectivist position in regard to patents and copyrights?" *The Objectivist Newsletter,* May, 1964, 19–20.
[23]Samuel Taylor Coleridge, William Wordsworth, and Charles Dickens were among the first great English language authors to attempt to earn their living from the relatively new "author's copyright" which the 1834 revision of the Statute of Anne gave expression to. Dickens was especially vocal in his defense of the value of an independent profession of authorship. This trend is also noted in Rose's and Woodmansee's articles.

[24]Of course, this is not to deny that any particular market may be structured in a way that imposes oppressive constraints also.

major philosophical tensions in the copyright ethics debate—the tension between a social ethic which values the availability of knowledge and the ethical foundations of private property. Still, his approach is too divorced from social practices to provide an adequate analysis of the direction which copying practices should take in the future. The interesting question for a philosopher of public policy is whether philosophy can go any further in providing an analysis of this tension which is also sensitive to the role of technology and the social values embodied in marketplace incentives. I think that it can, but not by going back to the general tenets of a theory of private property written at the dawn of the capitalist era and prior to the emergence of contemporary information technology. If the history of proprietary authorship holds any lessons, one is that our ethical intuitions need to be worked out in relation to the concrete social circumstances which pose the ethical problem in the first place. In the 18th century and again in the 20th century the changing economics of the book industry were a guide to courts and legislators trying to weight the harmfulness to information producers of liberalizing copyrights against the harm to society of restricting them. In the late seventies, U.S. copyright reform had to contend with the additional complications of new technologies (e.g. inexpensive copying, video and computer technology) and new uses of older media (e.g. educational uses of visual media and musical recordings). In order to get past the general thesis that neither society nor rights holders have an absolute claim on each other, we shall have to look at concrete social practices affecting the copyright debate today. That is what the next section of this paper proposes to do.

III. Property Rights, Public Access, and the Task of a Future-Oriented Copyright Ethic

Like most ethical controversies, copyright ethics emerges in its contemporary form because of the breakdown of a traditional social structure or matrix of social practices within which ethical questions have either been resolved or lack a motivation. Faced with such a breakdown, we try alternately to retrieve insights from the ethical traditions which precede us and to develop new ways of formulating our justified intuitions for the future. Philosophical work on copyright ethics has so far done the former without sufficient attention to the latter. In copyright ethics, a future-oriented ethical analysis requires some familiarity with the technology and legal thinking within which many of our practices and ethical intuitions are embodied. Future-oriented copyright policy requires further the articulation of *obligations to move toward those technologies which allow us to meet competing demands.*

Current legal and public policy controversy over intellectual property have their origin in the development of xerography and electronic information technology during the sixties and seventies. Prior to that, the most serious area of dispute concerned the fair handling of copyrights to music. Radio broadcasting and sound recording technology made possible social practices similar to the broadcasting of information through telecommunications networks and the duplication of printed works through photocopying.

We might expect, therefore, that the music industry offers a model for handling problems in other areas. Two clearinghouses for collecting copyright royalties, ASCAP and BMI, emerged in the fifties and sixties and soon became recognized as the means for radio stations, bar owners and any public performer of copyrighted music to satisfy their legal (and ethical) obligations to copyright holders. As a result of monopolistic practices in the setting and collecting of royalty fees, both associations were forced by courts to adopt flat-fee pricing schemes and fair rules for imposing and collecting those fees. The flat fee format has had a generally positive impact on the availability of music to a listening public.

No such structure currently exists for the print publishing industry, although the fledgling Copyright Clearance Center is hoping to establish itself in this capacity. However, before discussing this and other approaches to resolving copyright issues in information technology, we should look more closely at the ways in which recent technology is breaking down the traditional approaches to print and information copyrights.

The social value of free access to information is embodied in public lending practices developed during the free public library movement and in "fair use" guidelines which emerged through court cases since the turn of the century[25] and which are currently embodied in section 107 of the current U.S. copyright law (U.S. 17) passed in 1978. They allow specific exemptions for the use of copyrighted material for personal and educational purposes provided such uses pass three tests:

1. Brevity;
2. Spontaneity; and
3. Cumulative Effect.

The point of the tests is to distinguish the occasional and narrowly focused *individual* use of materials from uses which are *systematic* in the sense that they create a significant impact on the market for the copyrighted works. A similar test underlies the provisions of the same copyright law governing fair use in interlibrary loan agreements which libraries use to share resources. Interlibrary loan schemes are more prone to copyright infringement as they become systematic means of avoiding the purchase of books and journals and less infringing as they merely provide a means for individual users to request materials which the local library cannot afford to maintain. Curiously, the fair use guidelines do not apply directly to videotapes, broadcast transmissions, and software, even though the increase in educational use of these media would seem to demand some articulation of the doctrine for them.[26]

The philosophical justification for focusing on the distinction between individual and systematic use is obvious. The more systematic the use, the less one can reasonably claim that the purpose of the use is to gain personal access to information. At one extreme, the individual who systematically copies tapes and books and distributes them for sale is doing more than securing his or her own right to gain access to information. At the other extreme,

the individual who photocopies even a fairly lengthy text for personal study has no intent to infringe on the original market for that text. The fair use test of "cumulative effect" suggests that as long as the cumulative effect of *that individual's* activity is not materially detrimental, then the use is fair. Current discussions of fair use are therefore directly connected to the historical tension between property interests and the social utility of information. A direct line can be traced from the original limitations on perpetual copyright during the "Battle of the Books" to the current exemption allowing individuals to photocopy from books for personal use.

From a philosophical (as well as public policy) point of view, fair use guidelines are interesting because they try to preserve a distinction which is clearly vanishing in the face of current and emerging technology. The distinction between individual and systematic use is increasingly *ad hoc* in the following cases.

1. Interlibrary loan schemes are essentially systematic. Libraries are increasingly using "cooperative acquisitions" programs[27] to reduce spending and increase the range of texts available to users. In a related development, the great number and diversity of scientific and technical journals has led many hospital libraries to use low cost document supply houses, which provide information on a per document basis. These highly efficient behaviors cannot help but affect the market for print materials. It seems regressive to allow property considerations to slow down an inevitable and desirable shift to a system of production which depends less on the sale of hard copies of texts than on the sale of access to texts through networks. On the other hand, by merely shifting to a fee-for-use system, the notion of free access is imperiled. New means of satisfying producers' interests may need to be developed but that cannot occur by continuing to tie fair use to an outdated paradigm in which individual users retrieve individual texts without involving a complex system of distribution.

2. While fair use offers extensive protections to individual scholars, it does not address the reasonable needs of communities of scholarship (including classroom instruction, seminars and professional scholarly societies), which can only function by systematically distributing texts. By orienting fair use

---

[25]Leo Raskind traces the development of the U.S. fair use doctrine from the mid-19th century. However, detailed legal opinion does not emerge until cases involving the use of copyrighted material on radio, television, and film. For an excellent review of the case history, see Leo Raskind, "A Functional Interpretation of Fair Use," *The Journal of the Copyright Society of the USA* (1984) 601–639.

[26]A recent bill before the Senate (S. 198, 101st Congress) addressing software copyrights contained a fair use exemption allowing libraries to lend software to patrons. The exemption was justified by the need to combat illiteracy and promote education, especially in rural and impoverished communities (see S. Rept. 101–265). Cited in *ALA Washington Newsletter*, April 30, 1990, 7–8.

[27]Under cooperative acquisitions schemes libraries agree to supplement rather than duplicate each others' holdings.

to individual scholarly activity, we perpetuate the myth that scholars are not working more and more in community through conferences and telecommunications. Again, what seems like an inevitable and desirable social trend may be retarded by confused and increasingly outdated distinctions between individual and systematic use.

Current legal challenges to "professor's publishing"[28] schemes are based on the notion that such activity systematically undermines the property interests of producers of anthologies and texts for the college market. Clearly, publishers have a right not to have the market for their products systematically eroded by the activities of infringing (if well intentioned) scholars. On the other hand, by limiting an instructor's ability to assemble the best available texts in an affordable and convenient form we compromise our commitment to the social value of free access to learning.

The optimal ethical balance will not be struck merely by setting arbitrary limits to the use of photocopied anthologies, as currently copyright guidelines do.[29] It is important to realize that the ethical conflict itself is exacerbated by the practice of some publishers who hold to a marketing strategy which packages educational materials in costly anthologies. To their credit, some publishers are promoting "custom publishing" services through which they offer to assemble anthologies to suit the customer's needs. The publisher may then collect the royalties lost to the local copy center.

The existence of professor's publishing schemes is evidence of an unmet need in the market and the "custom publishing" program may be a good effort to satisfy that need while preserving author's royal-ties. If we focus on the places in the market at which copyright conflict emerges, I think we will see that the problem lies in the conflict between the technologies of information production and information use or consumption. The solution to these conflicts does not involve a rereading of Locke; rather, it involves a transition to new technologies and marketing practices and a recasting of our traditional intuitions in the terms of the new technologies. Only by looking forward to a future arrangement of technologies and practices in which producers receive a nominal fee for use of copyrighted materials can we overcome the current stalemate in fair use thinking. Thus, an arrangement similar to the copyright clearance houses for the recording industry may be the best future solution to the current controversy.

The Copyright Clearance Center, which operates a growing clearinghouse for print works (primarily from journals), is one part of the solution. However, its approach is fatally flawed because it collects whatever fees producers set for their works. While at first glance this practice appears entirely consistent with the ethics of the marketplace, it provides no room in the new equation for fair use or public access. If the free market pricing structure of the CCC is upheld in court, the notion of fair use on a practical level will be left further and further behind as information technology advances. As libraries and educational institutions increasingly rely on systematic practices (e.g. electronic media, library networking, faxing, and photocopying) which take us away from the traditional domain of fair use, the practical value of free or affordable access to information will be eroded.

The challenge in copyright ethics is, on the one hand, not to hold on to traditional practices when change is immanent and desirable, and, on the other hand, to reconstruct the traditional values in the new technological configuration. The move to an absolutely proprietary information system would represent a failure to meet the second challenge, and the retrenchment of the publishing industry and traditional fair use advocates would represent a failure to meet the first challenge. A flat-fee clearinghouse for photoduplicating of print materials appears to be a good solution because it would add a nominal charge to users (which would be more than offset by likely decreases in the cost of duplication) while allowing producers to recover costs at a high margin of profit (because they would not actually have to produce the copies). A computerized billing service

---

[28]"Professor's publishing" is a term coined, as far as I know, by Kinko's Copies to describe its service of duplicating packets of readings for college course instruction.

[29]Current guidelines allow professors not more than 9 copyrighted works per classroom anthology and prohibit the repeated use of the same anthologies semester after semester. Since no individual article or essay may exceed 2500 words, many packets in use today do in fact violate the guidelines. These guidelines are not part of the actual legislation of *1978 Copyright Act* (PL 94–553, U.S. 17), but were published as a House report (H. Repts. 94–1476 and 94–1733). Excerpts of the reports are available in the American Library Association's *Librarian's Guide to the New Copyright Law* (Chicago, 1978) or from Copyright Information Services, *The Official Fair-Use Guidelines: Complete Texts of Four Official Documents Arranged for Use by Educators,* 3rd edition (Friday Harbor, Washington) 1987.

could be established in major copy centers (such as Kinko's Copies stores, corporate copying facilities, and university copy centers) while leaving alone incidental copiers such as individual library patrons.

I think a similar arrangement could be made for videotapes and software, though these media do have special characteristics which affect our concern for producers' interests. Where production overhead for major software packages and major movie and documentary works is high, more concern might be shown for the market for these products. Economic modelling of producers' rates of return for various types of electronic media might govern decisions to include such media in a flat-fee clearinghouse.

In general then, I recommend that information producers see themselves as socially obligated to move toward technologies which facilitate the wide distribution of their works. At the same time, consumers should allow that the new information technologies they use obligate them to consider the effect of their use on information producers.

IV.   Conclusion

In addition to providing a general introduction to the subject of copyright ethics, I hope I have shown that thinking about copyright cannot be divorced from the history of social practices which originally constituted it. We cannot begin to understand the competing claims of private property owners and society, unless we look at the tension between these competing interests in historical detail. On the other hand, such a history is in no way prescriptive or prospective. Philosophical approaches to copyright are needed and I considered two: Bringsjord's and Hettinger's. However, we will not succeed by merely attending to the logical features of copying (as Bringsjord does). Our ethical intuitions do not possess such precision or generality. Failing that, we might hope that the philosophical tradition justifying property will guide us in thinking about intellectual property. But Hettinger successfully shows that the tradition cannot do this. I suggest the reason for this is, in part, that abstract justifications are too divorced from actual social practices to arbitrate between competing ethical values. In the case of copyright ethics we need to look at current and emerging technology and try to understand how our best intuitions about rewarding personal achievement and allowing public access can be satisfied.

Intellectual Property Rights and Computer Software

JOHN WECKERT*

THE UNAUTHORISED COPYING of computer software is generally considered to be theft and therefore morally wrong.[1] Even just a casual browse through the literature on computer ethics shows that this is the presumption of most discussions of the issue. These discussions tend to focus on the damage caused by this activity and on ways, either legal or technical, to make it more difficult. Rarely is the claim that it is wrong examined, although it is questioned by some not in the mainstream of the computer industry. In this paper it will be argued that it is not at all as obvious as is commonly assumed that unauthorised software copying is morally wrong (except insofar as it is morally wrong to act illegally).

That we have a moral right to own things is a generally unquestioned assumption. It is taken for

*The author wishes to acknowledge the contribution to this paper of Douglas Adeney of the University of Melbourne.
[1]For a good discussion of legal issues and cases, see Galler, Bernard A. *Software and Intellectual Property Protection: Copyright and Patent Issues for Computer and Legal Professionals.* Westport, CT: Quorum Books. 1995.

From Business and Professional Ethics Journal 6, 1997, pp. 102–109. *Reprinted with permission.*

granted that cars, houses, television sets, computers and so on can be owned. In order to set the scene for an examination of computer software, we will begin by briefly considering the arguments for ownership of tangible property, and then move on to the more intangible intellectual variety, of which software is one type.

Tangible Property

Why do we think that private property is justified and a good thing? Probably the most famous justification of property in general comes from John Locke[2] who argued that if one "mixed one's labour" with something then one had a legitimate claim to it. He did, it must be said, place some restrictions on the right to appropriation. There had to be, for example, enough and as good left for others. The basic thrust of this justification of property is that if I construct a shed, it is mine because my labour is mixed with it. A part of me is in the shed. The main weakness of this argument, as Nozick[3] points out, is that it is not obvious why we should gain what we mix our labour with, rather than simply losing our labour. If I poured a can of tomato juice, which I owned, into the sea, clearly I would not thereby own the sea. I would merely become juiceless.

Another argument frequently used today is the utilitarian one that private ownership is necessary as an incentive to work. This dates back to David Hume, who argued that a person's creations should be owned by him or her to encourage "useful habits and accomplishments." This is the argument most often appealed to in support of intellectual property, and in particular, computer software.

A third justification is based on desert. A producer or creator deserves reward for his or her production or creation. If I create something I deserve something in return for my effort. Nothing follows necessarily of course about ownership, but ownership is often thought to be a just reward. It might in some cases be a just reward, but it is not the only one and perhaps not the best one or the one that

the creator wants. The creator may prefer gratitude or recognition to ownership.[4]

Intellectual Property

The Universal Declaration on Human Rights says in Article 27 (2) that "Everyone has the right to the protection of the moral and material interests resulting from any scientific literary or artistic production of which he is the author."[5] The ACM Code of Ethics also endorses the right to intellectual property. It states that a member will "Honour property rights including copyrights and patents."[6] No justification is given by either as to why there are intellectual property rights.

Intellectual property is interestingly different from other property in at least three ways. First, owning an idea, or something abstract, is not simply like owning a physical object. Ownership of a physical object involves the right to continued use and enjoyment of it; if it is a car, for instance, and I take it from you, my theft of it consists in my violation of that right, because you are no longer able to have that use and enjoyment. Taking intangible things like ideas, however, does not exclude their use and enjoyment by the owner. I can take your software by copying it, and we both can use and enjoy it. Intellectual property is non-exclusive. (Strictly speaking, it is expressions or implementations of ideas which are protected by law, and not the ideas themselves. Without wanting to argue the point here, I have some reservations about this distinction, but fortunately the argument of this paper does not depend on it.)

A second interesting aspect of intellectual property is in what sense or to what extent is an idea mine? If I build or buy a shed, I know what is mine. If I either provide all of the labour and materials, or pay for everything myself, it is my shed, other things being equal. But an idea is not like this, even if the article, painting or software which is its manifestation, was written or painted by me. Ideas come from anywhere, and probably any idea

[2]Locke, John, *Second Treatise of Government* (1698). Edition of Laslett, Peter (ed), *John Locke, Two Treatises of Government. A Critical Edition with an Introduction and Apparatus Criticus.* New York: New American Library. 1965.
[3]Nozick. Robert, *Anarchy, State, and Utopia.* Oxford Blackwell, 1980. pp. 174–175.

[4]Hettinger, Edwin C., "Justifying intellectual property," *Philosophy and Public Affairs,* 18 1989, pp. 40–43.
[5]"The Universal Declaration of Human Rights," *Human Rights Manual,* Canberra: Australian Government Publishing Service, 1993, p. 141.
[6]*ACM Code of Ethics and Professional Conduct.* 1992, [1.5]. Retrieved via Netscape gopher://ACM.ORG:70/00%5Bthe_files.constitution%5Dbylaw17.txt

that we have is not ours alone. Most of my ideas come from someone else. At best, when I am "original," I express an idea in a new way, I see associations between ideas not noticed before, I see the relevance of an idea in some situation or I combine ideas in a new way. While these can all be significant, in all of them anything creative that I achieve is the adding of something to preexisting ideas which I have obtained from others. So to what extent is the new idea really mine? Given that I contributed only a little, why should I claim ownership? If I contribute a little to your shed, perhaps I can claim that I own a little, morally anyway, but certainly not that I own the whole building. Similarly, if I write a paper, most of the ideas will have come from elsewhere (most of the ideas in this paper came from elsewhere), so why should I be able to claim sole ownership?

A third difference is the distinction which can be drawn between *moral* rights and *commodity* rights to intellectual property. In this context a moral right is the right to acknowledgement as the author or creator. A commodity right is the right to sell or otherwise profit financially from the property *qua* a commodity. It is one thing to say that we deserve to be acknowledged as an author or creator of something we have produced. It is quite another to maintain that we should have the right to control its access to others.

What then is involved in the ownership of intellectual property such as computer software? If you create software and I steal it by copying it onto my disk or into my area of the computer, you still have it. What I now have is simply a copy of what you still have. This, as already seen, is an important difference between intellectual property and other property. Intellectual property rights do not grant exclusive use and enjoyment of that owned. They are concerned more with control of who can use and enjoy the property, and who gets acknowledgement and financial reward from that use and enjoyment. So the main issue is not taking something from the owner or creator and thereby depriving him or her of access to it. The main issue is *copying*.

What is wrong with the unauthorised copying of the work of another? One answer is simply that it is an infringement of ownership rights. While this violation of rights might be spelt out in terms which have nothing to do with consequences, say in a Lockean manner, more typically it would be

cashed in terms of harm or potential harm to the owner. The owner loses in some way as a result of the copying, just as owners lose in normal theft. Copying is seen as a kind of theft; the theft of an idea. We will first consider grounds for intellectual property which are not utilitarian (that is, not based on harm or incentive), and then look at those which are.

Is there anything wrong with copying where no harm is involved, for example the copying of material that one would never buy? Here the owner is not harmed. There is no financial loss because there was no question of the text or software being purchased. The owner may in fact benefit, given that he or she gets more exposure. But we are still reluctant perhaps to say that this copying is moral. Why? We might try a Lockean justification and say that the owner has rights simply because his or her labour was put into the original. So if anyone copies the work without permission, they are violating his or her rights. Whether copying is moral or not has nothing to do with consequences. It is immoral even if the consequences are good.

While this type of justification is not universally accepted, it is *prima facie* a reasonable account of why we have intellectual property rights. There is always enough and as good left over for others. It does of course have the problem mentioned in the general discussion of property, that is, why do we gain that with which we mix our labour? An alternative justification is that the creator just *deserves* some reward for having an idea and developing it. This has some intuitive appeal, but it does not justify ownership. There are many ways in which one could be rewarded for creating or producing something without being given ownership over it. One could be paid in money, or given a long holiday!

Both of these justifications appear stronger if *moral* rights and not *commodity* rights are considered. It seems more plausible to argue that I have a moral right to what I have created, or that I deserve recognition as the creator, than it does to argue that I own the creation.

Now the utilitarian argument. An owner of intellectual property is deemed to lose if the property is copied, in terms of the ability to sell the idea or perhaps in terms of prestige or promotion. If I have a good idea, paint a good picture, take an interesting photograph, or develop good and novel software, I want people to know that it is mine, and so, perhaps, gain in one or more of the ways just mentioned. If copying were freely allowed, there would be no money to be made, and profits must be available or nobody will make the effort to develop their ideas. Or at least that is the idea. So the issue is essentially one of harm, both to the individual owner, and to the society in general. Again of course, the moral/commodity right distinction is important. Some of the issues, like prestige and promotion, can be addressed by safeguarding moral rights alone.

Before commenting further on this, we will consider the question in another way; when might it be legitimate to copy the work of another without explicit permission? At one end of the spectrum lies the case where a work is copied and passed off as the work of another, for commercial gain. At the other end it might be the scanning of an image from a magazine solely for the purposes of experimenting with morphing. Or it might be using "clip art" to create a new image or copying software purely to see how it works, with the intention of buying if it is suitable. What are the main differences between the two ends of the spectrum? (What I have placed at the legitimate end is not uncontroversially legitimate.) In the first, the copier gains financially at the expense of the owner, and there is deceit involved. In the second case, no financial gain is made from the copying, or if there is, none which affects the owner of the work. And no deceit is involved. The copier can quite happily acknowledge the source of the work or software if the need arises. Perhaps in some cases like this, "fair use" will apply. At the illegitimate end of the spectrum harm, particularly financial, is again seen to be an issue, and so is deceit.

Financial harm caused to the owner is at least one reason, then, why copying is wrong. But it is not so simple. That harming anyone unnecessarily and intentionally, either physically or emotionally, is unethical, is generally accepted. But harming someone financially is not so obviously wrong, even though theft and robbery are not usually considered to be desirable activities. The possibility of financial harm, in fact, is built into the free market system. It is frequently argued that having a free market is better overall than not having one, even though some people will suffer. So harming someone financially in itself is not generally considered unethical. But financial harm does play a part in the argument, as we saw a moment ago. The generation of new ideas is necessary for a society to prosper. It can be time-consuming and costly to generate and develop ideas, so there must be reward for those who do. If there is not, nobody will bother to create. And the most important reward is financial. Without financial reward, society's supply of new ideas will dry up. Therefore there must be some system of copyright and patent regulations which protect intellectual property. So one argument against copying, then, from the perspective of harm, is the harm caused to society at large if there were no restrictions on the practice.

It could be argued, on the other side of the ledger, that if ideas were all in the public domain, and if anyone could work on and develop anything, regardless of where the idea originated, we would all be better off because more would be developed. That the source of new and innovative ideas would dry up without copyright and patent laws to facilitate financial reward is little more than an article of faith. Artists, academics and scientists frequently create without such reward. Perhaps acknowledgement is enough. Or perhaps creation is its own reward. It must be pointed out that this is not an argument against moral rights to intellectual property, only against commodity rights.

The most that this discussion questions, of course, is whether society in general suffers from copying of the work of others, not whether individuals will be harmed by having their works copied. This can certainly happen in our present social structure. This individual harm must be taken into account even if society as a whole would be better off with no restrictions on copying. But it is not an overriding consideration. As we have already noted, some individuals suffer in a free market economy, but the current wisdom is that such an economy is still better than its competitors.

Software Piracy

It has been estimated that software piracy costs United States software producers around $12 billion U.S. annually.[7] This financial loss is the most

[7]See Forester, T. and Morrison, P., *Computer Ethics: Cautionary Tales and Ethical Dilemmas in Computing.* Cambridge, MA: MIT Press, 1995, p. 52, and Bently Systems, "Software piracy: what you should know," 1995. Retrieved via Netscape http://www.bentley.com/anti.piracy.html

commonly cited reason for having strict laws on software copyright and patents.

Software piracy is often thought of as simply the unauthorised copying of computer software. But copying software is not all of a kind. It can mean a number of different things, including the copying of actual code, the copying of the "look and feel" of a program, and the copying of an algorithm. We will consider these in turn, in the light of our earlier discussion of property.

COPYING SOFTWARE

First, by the copying of actual code, we are referring to the making of electronic copies of commercial computer software. We are not interested in one student copying another student's programming assignment. That is just cheating, and there is not much interesting to say about that. But even electronic copying of commercial software comes in a variety of forms, and not all of the moral issues are the same, or necessarily have the same answers. The main differences concern the use to be made of the copy. This might sound odd. After all, surely theft is wrong regardless of the use that is made of the stolen goods. But, as we have already seen, "stealing" intellectual property is a little different from stealing other property. If I "steal" your software by copying it, I am not depriving you of its use. If I steal your car, I am.

Before considering the rightness or wrongness of unauthorised copying of software, we will look at some of the various uses made of the copies, going from the least to the most controversial. (a) The first case concerns copying purely for testing, with the intention of buying if it proves to be satisfactory. (b) A second case is that in which an individual copies, say, a game, which he would never bother buying, but thinks it worth having if free. Here the owner is almost certainly not harmed. No sale has been lost. (c) Finally there is copying where the software is to be used for commercial gain, and where, if it could not be copied, it would be purchased. In this case the owner is certainly harmed.

There are obviously variations on these cases. For example, a group of students might share the cost of the software, and make copies, in a situation where they cannot afford to buy individual copies. Or again, a university might copy some software that it requires for teaching, because it cannot afford the payment that the owner wants for mul-

tiple copies. (No university in its right mind would do this, of course, even if for legal reasons alone.) We will now look at the above three cases in more detail.

(a) The *first case* definitely seems not to be immoral, even if it is illegal. If I copy software purely for testing it, with the intention of buying if it satisfies my needs, I would be doing the owner a good turn. Buying without testing in most cases is just silly. Testing a copy is saving the owner the expense of providing me with a special copy for testing, a service provided by some. The owner has nothing to lose and something to gain by this activity of unauthorised copying for testing. There is perhaps a risk that I will keep the pirated copy rather than buying it, but if I do that then I fall foul of the harm principle. One way of avoiding any copyright problems here would be to allow this as an instance of fair use.[8]

(b) The *second case*, while normally condemned by the computer industry, almost certainly causes no harm at all. If someone copies software that they would never have bought, even if it were inexpensive, the owner suffers no loss. And perhaps more importantly, the "but what if everyone did this" objection carries no weight. If everyone *who would never have bought the software* copied it, the owner is still not harmed. Still no sales are lost. So no case can be made here that the copying is wrong on the grounds that it causes harm. The situation is different if we mean "everyone" to include those who otherwise would have bought it. In this case the owner is harmed, so there is a ground for condemning *that* copying. But if the former kind of copying is wrong, that is, where the software would *not* have been bought, then it must be on the grounds of something like the owner having the right to stop others from using his work, perhaps on the basis of desert. Pushing this line, however, makes the objection of the owner look a little petty. It amounts to saying that even though your using my work without payment is not doing me any harm at all, and is probably doing you some good, I do not want you to do so, "because it is mine." We would probably want to scold a child for behaving like this! There is also another, not implausible, argument, that the

[8]Samuelson, Pamela, "Computer programs and copyright's fair use doctrine," *Communications of the ACM*, 36 September 1993, pp. 19–25.

computer industry actually benefits from this type of copying. It might well be that more hardware is sold because software can be obtained at little or no cost. It is one thing for someone to invest in a computer; it is another for them to continually invest in software. It is surely better for the industry for people to invest in hardware and copy software than not even to buy the hardware. Those without hardware are certainly never going to buy any software. Forester and Morrison[9] give figures to show how little software is sold for each personal computer sold. Their interpretation is that this reveals how much software companies are losing. An alternative interpretation is that it shows how good it is for hardware companies.[10]

(c) Finally, what about the *third case,* copying for commercial use? This does *seem* to be unjustifiable in general. It does deprive the owners of profit, and possibly harms them, although if they are very wealthy the harm may be minimal. It is arguable, of course, that the real harm would be to society in general if this practice were too widespread, because less new software would be created if profits were low. And profits made from software sales would be low if software were not bought.[11] We saw earlier that the argument based on incentive is not always convincing, but it has some plausibility in this case. This is perhaps because in some ways software is more like a tool or a machine than like a novel, a work of art or a research or scholarly article. In those latter cases the creative act in itself is some reward. Perhaps this is less so in the case of developing software. The creative act is in the design. The development, which includes testing, is much more tedious.

It is worth, however, looking at this incentive argument a little more closely, because it is the main one used against copying software. The argument, to recapitulate, is that copying lowers profits, and with low profits there will be little or no incentive to develop new software, and hence society will be the loser. Therefore copying software is not a good thing. But is this really true?

First, the protection of intellectual property is a relatively new phenomenon. People did create and develop all sorts of things before there was any

protection, so one might ask why could not this happen again? It is difficult to believe that painters only paint, musical composers only compose and writers only write because of the financial rewards. Academics, to name just one group, regularly produce scholarly and research works without any financial reward, and did this long before the "publish or perish" mentality was upon us. It is difficult to believe that all programmers only develop new software because of financial rewards. Some people genuinely like programming.

This leads to a second issue. Programmers need to eat, an obvious, but important, point made by Forester and Morrison.[12] But this does not have much to do with the copying of software. Programmers can earn income by selling their services as well as by selling software. It might be objected here that we are concentrating on the wrong group, and that it is the companies which develop software who must be protected. They will not invest money in software development if there are no, or only small, profits to be made. There are two things to be said about this. One is that there are other ways that software companies can earn money. Dyson,[13] for example, argues that with copying and distribution of software being so inexpensive and easy, it would be better if companies used the software to advertise other goods and services. The second point here is that it would not matter so much if companies did not invest large amounts in software development if copying were freely allowed. There would almost certainly be many more people working on modifying and improving software, so it is doubtful that society in general would lose.[14]

[9]Forester, T. and Morrison, P., pp. 52–53.
[10]Dead Addict, "In defence of piracy," 1996. Retrieved via Netscape http://www.15.com/daddict/piracy.html
[11]Forester, T. and Morrison, P. (note 7), p. 71.

[12]Forester, T. and Morrison, P., p. 67.
[13]See Dyson, Esther, "Intellectual value," 1995. Retrieved via Netscape http://www.nlc-bnc.ca/documents/infopol/copyright/dyson.htm, and Eslava, Carlos and Jaime Nubiola, "Hacia una transformacion de la responsabilidad en el mercaco del software: servicio frente a prodicto," ETHICOMP96, III International Conference Values and Social Responsibilities of the Computer Science, Madrid, November 1996. Proceedings Volume 1, pp. 175–180.
[14]See Stallman, Richard, "The GNU Manifesto," 1993. Free Software Foundation Inc. Retrieved via Netscape http://prep.ai.mit.edu/pub/gnu/GNUinfo/GnuManifesto.

For an alternative approach to the perceived problem of software copying, see Davis, R., Pamela Samuelson, Mitchell Kapor and Jerome Reichman, "A new view of intellectual property and software," *Communications of the ACM* 39 March 1996, pp. 21–30.

A third point, related to the issue of easy copying and distribution, is the high cost of preventing copying. Vast sums are spent on litigation. Admittedly, considerable amounts are also made when cases are won, but it is surely doubtful that spending resources on this sort of activity is good for the industry.[15] A related point is that with this increasingly inexpensive copying and distribution it will become ever more difficult to curb unauthorised copying without draconian laws, or at least laws which inhibit creativity and development.

Given what has just been said, it is doubtful at best that society is better off because copying software is severely restricted. The case *for* copying has certainly not been proven, but that is really beside the point. The case *against* copying ought to be firmly established before restrictions are put in place. The burden of proof must be on those who want restrictions.

"LOOK AND FEEL" COPYING

We turn now to a different case; copying the "look and feel" of a programme. Here it is primarily the look of the user interface, and perhaps the important functions of a programme, which are being copied. While the icons, the screen design and so on, may be identical, or nearly so, the code may be quite different. This does seem to be much like copying an idea of someone else, where the idea would normally be protected by a patent. Such "theft" does seem to be much like cheating, and, as such, perhaps ought to be condemned. The owner of the original product will quite likely be harmed if someone else develops similar software. There is no theft of code, but there is the taking of an idea. As well as harm to the owner, it could also be argued that without protection of "look and feel" there will also be broader harm. Creators would be less willing to spend time, effort and money on developing novel ideas if others can then develop similar products and so reduce the profits of the originators of ideas.

The situation, however, is different from that in which the code is copied. There the copying is achieved with little more than the pressing of a few keys or a few clicks of a mouse button. In the look

and feel case, the programme must still be developed. It must be designed, programmed and tested. So the copier must invest time, effort and money into the project, perhaps as much as the originator. Another relevant point is that it is beneficial to computer users if different software packages have similar user interfaces. These make programmes "friendlier" and so easier to learn and use. Once one software package has been learnt, learning another is not too difficult. One has at least some idea of what to look for when learning something new. A third point is that if look and feel is protected, it will almost certainly slow down progress. So it would seem that the disadvantages of copying "look and feel" in the shape of disincentives to develop new products are more than outweighed by the advantages of having some standardisation and consistency among products. Again in this case, then, no very strong argument can be mounted for the immorality of copying on the grounds of harm and utility.

The basic objection to the copying of the look and feel of software seems to be that it is morally reprehensible to take someone else's idea and use it for commercial gain, thereby depriving him or her of income. (That the law may distinguish between ideas on the one hand, and their expressions or usable developments on the other, is largely irrelevant.) This principle, however, is applied very selectively. You might spend large amounts of time and money researching into the best place to build a restaurant. You build it and it is successful. I see your success and decide to build another across the road. I have more money than you, so mine is better, and in a short time I put you out of business. Here I have taken your idea and the fruits of your research and profited by them. This, of course, is quite reasonable in a capitalist system. It might be argued that this example is quite different from the software case. But it is not clear that it is in relevant aspects. In both cases effort and money have been invested in the development of an idea, and in both cases another party has profited from that investment.

COPYING AN ALGORITHM

Finally, is there anything wrong with copying a programme algorithm? This issue is sometimes thought to revolve around the difference between discovery on the one hand and manufacture and

[15]Forester, T. and Morrison, P., *Computer Ethics: Cautionary Tales and Ethical Dilemmas in Computing*. Cambridge, MA: MIT Press, 1995. p. 59.

creation on the other. The law reflects the view that we can, in some sense, own what we make or create, but not what we discover. As has been pointed out by Hettinger,[16] it seems more plausible to say "I own it because I made it" than to say "I own it because I discovered it." There are exceptions, of course. Ownership of geographical territory has traditionally gone with discovery, where "discovery" is used in a very broad sense. But this is not generally applied. Discovering a law of nature does not give one ownership rights over it, and the same applies to mathematical formulae. Other cases are quite problematic. If I develop a recipe for a new drink, should I own that recipe? Did I create the new drink or did I discover it? In a sense I discovered it. All of the ingredients already existed. In another sense I created it, by combining those ingredients in a way not done before.

What has this to do with the right to own programme algorithms? If algorithms are like laws of nature or like mathematical formulae, then they are discovered and so not able to be owned, or so the argument might go. But they are really more like recipes, where the distinction between discovery and creation is much less clear. We certainly discover ways of doing things, and an algorithm is essentially a way of doing something, but there is also a sense in which we create or develop a way of doing things. What seems strange about claiming ownership for an algorithm is that it is saying that I should be the only person who is allowed to do something this way, or if anyone else does it this way, they ought to pay me, simply because I thought of it first. Perhaps a few people will spend less time and effort trying to find new ways of doing things if these new ways cannot be owned. But surely this will be far outweighed by the fact that when new methods are found, everyone will be able to benefit by using them, and perhaps in some cases further develop them themselves.

Patents for programme algorithms are perhaps the most controversial protections for software developers, on purely utilitarian grounds. There are a number of problems apart from those already mentioned. One is that if a new algorithm is discovered, its use will be restricted, regardless

of its value to the community. The reply here will be that if it is valuable, people will be prepared to pay for it, but this leads to another problem. What if someone else, quite independently, discovers the same algorithm and uses it in a programme, oblivious to the fact that it has been patented? Is it really fair or just to make that person pay for the privilege of using something he or she discovered and developed? And perhaps more importantly, should a software developer need to spend time and money searching for patents every time they think of and use a new algorithm, just in case it has been patented? This situation will almost certainly harm everyone except a few who were lucky enough to get patent protection for their algorithms. It is very difficult to see how patent protection for algorithms could possibly assist innovation in software, and, in addition, it is unfair.[17]

Conclusion

We have considered arguments for intellectual property, and found that the justifications are not very strong; certainly not as strong as one would assume from popular discussions. Nothing much follows from the desert argument or the Lockean one for commodity rights, although both do give support to moral rights. In the case of software it is not obvious that society is better off because of copyright and patent laws. The argument based on harm and incentive contains a large portion of faith. The onus should be on those who want these laws to demonstrate clearly that society would be worse off without them. Given the low cost, ease and speed of copying, and the kinds of laws necessary to police them, and their possible consequences, this may not be easy. It is much more difficult than is often admitted to make a strong case for the ownership of computer software.

[16]Hettinger, Edwin C. (note 4), pp. 31–52.

[17]See Samuelson, Pamela, "Should program algorithms be patented?," *Communications of the ACM,* 33 August 1990, pp. 23–27; Epperly, Tom, "Against software patents," The League for Programming Freedom, February 28, 1991 (Updated 1994). Retrieved via Netscape http://osnome. che.wisc.edu/%7Epperly/patents.html; Garfinkel, Simson, "Patently absurd," 1994. Retrieved via Netscape http://www.nlc-bnc.ca/documents/infopol/copyright/gars1.htm

Questions for Chapter 9

1. What is Hettinger's argument for claiming that trade secrets are undesirable in a way in which copyrights or patents are not?
2. Do you agree with Hettinger's claim that the goal of private intellectual property institutions is to maximize the dissemination and use of information? Explain your answer.
3. Paine claims that "even if common law trade secret rights did not promote intellectual labour or increase the dissemination and use of information, there would still be reasons to recognize those rights." What reasons does she mention?
4. How does Paine's framework for addressing the issue of intellectual property rights differ from Hettinger's?
5. What does Alfino mean when he claims that, with regard to intellectual property, "policy arguments which proceed primarily by a retrieval of abstract thought on the metaphysical principle of property are inadequate"? Do you agree?
6. Do you agree with Alfino's claim that the fair use guidelines cannot be maintained in the face of current and emerging technology? Why or why not?
7. Weckert distinguishes between moral rights and commodity rights. What does this distinction amount to? Do you agree that it is easier to justify moral rights than commodity rights?
8. Weckert says,

   The case *for* copying has certainly not been proven, but that is really beside the point. The case *against* copying ought to be firmly established before restrictions are put in place. The burden of proof must be on those who want restrictions.

   Do you agree that the burden of proof should be on those who want restrictions on copying of computer software? Why or why not?

Case 9.1 The Contested Statue[1]

In the fall of 1985, the Community for Creative Non-Violence (CCNV) approached James Earl Reid, a sculptor, to produce a statue dramatizing the plight of the homeless. During the time Reid worked on the statue, CCNV officials visited him several times to monitor progress and to coordinate CCNV's construction of the sculpture's base. In the process of the statue's construction, CCNV members made a number of suggestions and directions concerning the statue's appearance which Reid, in the main, adopted. Upon completion and delivery of the statue, Reid and CCNV, neither of whom had ever discussed copyright of the sculpture, filed competing copyright registration certificates.

CCNV argued that the sculpture was a "work made for hire" and that hence they possessed copyright. This would entitle them to reproduce and sell copies of the statue without Reid receiving any royalties. Reid argued that the statue was

[1]Based on Reid v. Community for Creative Non-Violence as found in 109 *Supreme Court Reporter* 2166 (1989).

not created by an employee within the scope of employment, but rather as the work of an independent contractor and that hence he possessed copyright. Any right to reproduce and sell copies of the statue was his alone.

1. Is Reid morally entitled to copyright on the statue?

2. Does CCNV have a valid claim to joint copyright?

3. Should the distinction between an employee and independent contractor make a difference in regard to who is entitled to copyright?

Case 9.2 Software and Hardware[2]

In 1981, Omnitech Graphics Systems Ltd. sold computer-aided drafting equipment to Cadco Graphics Ltd. This hardware required specific software, owned by Omnitech, to be of any use. Omnitech agreed to provide the necessary software, in the form of floppy disks, on the conditions that Cadco recognize the software remained the exclusive property of Omnitech, that it was nontransferable, and that Cadco would ensure its employees did not copy or permit unauthorized use or disclosure of the software.

In 1985, Perry Engineering acquired the assets of Cadco. Perry transferred the information on the floppy disks Cadco had acquired from Omnitech to the hard drive of the drafting equipment. This was done without Omnitech's consent.

[2]Based on Perry Engineering Ltd. v. Farrage *et al.;* Cadco Graphics Ltd. *et al* (third parties) as described in *Canadian Intellectual Property Reports,* Vol. 26, 1990, pp. 89–95.

Perry subsequently sold the hardware into which it had integrated Omnitech's software to Farrage Ltd. Part of the conditions of the sale was that Perry would transfer to Farrage the title to possess and use Omnitech's software. Upon learning that Perry had integrated the software into the drafting equipment without Omnitech's consent, Farrage refused to pay the balance owing. Perry sued Farrage for breach of contract.

1. Perry argued that since the hardware in question could not be used without the software, Omnitech's prohibition on transfer should not be allowed, inasmuch as it constituted an illegitimate restraint of trade. Do you agree or disagree and why?

2. Do you agree that Perry's contract with Farrage should be enforceable in the circumstances described? Why or why not?

3. Does Omnitech have any moral obligation to allow Farrage access to the necessary software? Explain your reasoning.

Further Readings for Chapter 9

S. M. Besen and L. J. Raskind, "An Introduction to the Law and Economics of Intellectual Property," *Journal of Economic Perspectives* 5(1), 1991, pp. 3–27.

Bernard A. Galler, *Software and Intellectual Property Protection: Copyright and Patent Issues for Computer and Legal Professionals* (Westport, CT: Quorum Books, 1995).

Selmer Bringsjord, "In Defense of Copying," *Public Affairs Quarterly* 3, 1989, pp. 1–9.

Russell B. Stevenson, Jr., *Corporations and Information* (Baltimore: Johns Hopkins University Press, 1980).

INFOTRAC COLLEGE EDITION To learn more about the topics from this chapter, you can use the following words to conduct an electronic search on InfoTrac College Edition, an online library of journals. Here you will find a multitude of articles from various sources and perspectives: *www.infotrac-college.com/wadsworth/access.html*

intellectual property

copyright

fair use

Chapter 10

Bribery

Introduction

WE FOCUS IN THIS CHAPTER on the difficult issues surrounding the topic of bribery. As in the case of sexual harassment, we are liable to think we have a clear idea of what constitutes bribery, only to find on closer analysis that arriving at an adequate definition is more complicated than we first realized. For example, if a salesperson sends a Christmas present to a valued customer, is she offering a bribe? Is a company offering a bribe if it holds a promotional seminar at a popular Caribbean resort and pays the travel costs for the sales representatives of those whom it hopes to persuade to carry its product? Is one guilty of taking a bribe if he or she accepts such a Christmas present or expense-paid seminar?

Further, the acceptability of bribery varies widely from culture to culture. Despite the fact that virtually all cultures officially condemn bribery, there are many societies in which bribery is an informally accepted commercial tradition. We cannot, on pain of lapsing into an untenable relativism, suggest that a company should simply follow the practices of whatever culture it finds itself in, but it is no easy matter to give practical advice to companies trying to operate in cultures where bribery is an established part of doing business.

In our first selection, "Improper Payments and Gifts," Robert Larmer discusses how bribery is best defined and assesses its morality. He defines bribery as the intentional and willing alienation of agency by the employee and a third party, without ever informing the original employer that the employee is no longer working as his or her agent. This allows bribery to be distinguished from a practice such as tipping, where although the employee acts on behalf of a third party, the employee continues to work as a loyal agent of his or her employer. It also allows bribery to be distinguished from extortion, inasmuch as extortion involves the coerced rather than willing alienation of employee agency.

This definition also permits an understanding of how what properly counts as bribery may vary from country to country, without thereby implying the truth of cultural relativism as an ethical theory. It is possible to recognize that the official duties of employees may vary from culture to culture, so that behavior that in one society would constitute taking a bribe should not be so regarded in another, yet accept this definition of bribery. The key question in deciding whether bribery occurs is not the variability of employee behavior, but whether the employee acts as a loyal agent for his or her employer.

As regards the morality of offering or accepting bribes, Larmer holds that such activity is *prima facie* immoral, inasmuch as it involves the violation of the acquired role duties of an employee. This is consistent, however, with recognizing that there can be instances in which the *prima facie* duty of not offering or accepting a bribe can be legitimately overridden on the basis of more fundamental duties.

In "Gift Giving, Bribery and Corruption: Ethical Management of Business Relationships in China," Paul Steidlmeier discusses the complexity of doing business in China. Steidlmeier notes that, although the exchange of gifts in business transactions is well accepted in Chinese culture, there are moral parameters within the culture that distinguish appropriate gifts from bribes. This is not to say that the giving and taking of bribes is not widespread in China. It is to acknowledge that Chinese society recognizes bribery as a moral problem and clearly distinguishes bribery from the social practice of exchanging gifts.

This suggests that, with regard to bribery, there are two issues that need to be addressed by foreign companies wishing to do business in China. First, it is important to understand the culture well enough to be able to distinguish bribery from legitimate social practices such as tipping, commissions, and the exchange of gifts. Second, it is essential to develop strategies of how to deal with genuine instances of bribery and extortion.

With regard to the first issue, Steidlmeier notes the importance of understanding the core values and beliefs that underlie social practice. Thus, for example, coming to an understanding of the emphasis Chinese society places on reciprocity and relational ties and loyalty to the group will greatly aid in comprehending the internal logic that underlies and grounds social practice.

With regard to the second issue of developing strategies of how to deal with genuine instances of bribery and extortion, Steidlmeier notes that this is a difficult and complex task. He suggests eight practical guidelines to help in choosing a Chinese partner firm and four general considerations to be aware of in the negotiation process. One of the most important points he makes is that it is very difficult for a company to deal with bribery entirely on its own. The fact that competitors are often willing to pay bribes in order to facilitate business points to the fact that effective change in this area is hard to achieve without a common code of conduct to which all foreign companies operating in China agree to adhere.

Many North Americans tend to think of bribery as primarily a problem that occurs in conducting business in other cultures. That this is a somewhat myopic view is pointed out in Robert Aalberts's and Marianne Jennings's article, "The Ethics of Slotting: Is This Bribery, Facilitation Marketing or Just Plain Compensation?". The practice of slotting involves manufacturers paying fees to retailers for the display and sale of their products. Thus, for example, retail grocery chains typically will not sell a product unless slotting fees are paid and large book chains generally require high fees for the prominent display of books.

The practice of slotting first became prevalent in the retail grocery sector in the late eighties, where it has been common since then. Defenders of the practice point out that in this sector there is a very low profit margin and that retail grocers must absorb the cost of warehousing, inventory accounting, bar coding, and shelf stocking. They suggest that, given these costs and limited shelf space, stocking a new product is a high-cost risk that justifies the retailer in charging a fee.

That this proposed justification carries some weight cannot be denied. That it entirely warrants either the practice of slotting or the methods by which it is implemented is far from evident, however. The practice of slotting has moved well beyond the retail grocery sector and the methods by which it is implemented are often suspect. In many instances, slotting fees do not seem to depend on a low profit margin, do not typically come down over time even if the product sells well, and tend to be nonuniform and paid in cash. Thus, Aalberts and Jennings note that "market entry rights are unclear, [smaller competitors often cannot afford the fees necessary to get their products displayed], fees change, not everyone is permitted to buy into the system and the use and declaration of revenues is unknown." If the proposed justification of slotting is not simply a rationalization of what looks suspiciously like instances of bribery and extortion, then a uniform and public fee structure that can be clearly related to the actual costs of stocking product needs to be in place.

Improper Payments and Gifts

ROBERT LARMER

I. Swaying Judgments
II. Bribery, Undue Influence, and Extortion: Definitional Issues
III. Bribery, Undue Influence, and Extortion: Moral Issues

Glossary

bribe A gift or consideration offered with the explicit intention of causing an employee or official to violate her role duties to her employer.

duty That which a particular person is bound morally or legally to do.

extortion To cause someone by illegal force or threat to act in a way he would otherwise not wish to act.

prima facie duty A presumptive duty one has in the absence of a more basic duty that would override it.

tip A gift or consideration offered by a third party to obtain services from an employee in his or her official capacity but without the intention of causing that employee to violate her role duties to her employer.

undue influence A gift or consideration that, without any explicit intention on the part of the giver or receiver to violate the role duties of the employee, may nevertheless lead to the employee failing in his role duties by improperly favoring the giftgiver.

IMPROPER GIFTS AND PAYMENTS are by definition to be avoided. Three categories of improper payments and gifts must be distinguished. These are undue influence, bribery, and extortion. How each is defined and why each is prima facie immoral is explored. Also explored is the question of how judgments concerning improper gifts and payments can be made cross-culturally.

I. Swaying Judgments

A. UNDUE INFLUENCE

In thinking of improper payments and gifts, the initial tendency is to think of bribery. Instances of bribery may provide us with paradigm examples but the category of improper payments and gifts is considerably broader than the category of bribery. Thus, for example, an expensive Christmas gift from a supplier to an ordering clerk in a large business might be considered improper, yet not constitute an attempt on the part of the supplier to bribe the clerk or an implicit acceptance of a bribe by the clerk.

The impropriety of such a gift, even though it can scarcely be described as a bribe, lies in the fact that it might unduly influence the clerk's decisions. Rather than evaluating products from competing suppliers on their own merits, the clerk may come to let her personal liking for the supplier who has given her an expensive gift sway her decision regarding who gets the order. The clerk, possibly without realizing it, may come to act in her own interests, rather than in the interests of her employer. Innocent of any intention to act improperly, she nevertheless acts improperly inasmuch as she has let her duty to act in the best interests of her employer be compromised.

B. THE APPEARANCE OF UNDUE INFLUENCE

I have suggested that a sufficient condition of a gift being improper is that it might unduly influence an employee's decisions. Might the clerk in our example argue that she is able to accept the expensive gift without it affecting her ability to fulfill her duties to her employer, and hence that there is nothing wrong in accepting the gift? Leaving aside the very real danger of self-deception, it might still be improper for the clerk to accept the gift. It is important not only that she be able to assure herself that she has not been unduly influenced, but that she be able to assure others of this. She must refrain, therefore, from accepting gifts that, by their nature or the context in which they are given, make it reasonable for others to believe she has been unduly influenced—even if this is not in fact the case. Thus, for example, even if the clerk could know beyond a shadow of a doubt that accepting an expensive trip around the world as a gift from the supplier would not influence her ordering decisions, it would still be improper for her to accept such a gift. Her employer, as well as rival suppliers, have legitimate concerns about whether the acceptance of the gift might illegitimately influence her decisions and, unless she is in the unlikely situation of being able to demonstrate that this will not happen, she is not in a position to do justice to these concerns and hence should not accept the gift. In such matters it is important not only that justice be done, but that it be seen to be done.

C. APPROPRIATE GIFTS

In our example, we have focused on the impropriety of the clerk accepting an expensive gift from the supplier. What can be said as regards the impropriety of the supplier offering such a gift? It is tempting to suggest that the supplier should in no circumstances offer the clerk a gift. This seems too strong, however, inasmuch as it ignores that business transactions take place in a social context and that it is appropriate for the supplier to seek to be on good terms with the clerk. We would not, for example, accuse the supplier of any immorality if he adopts a friendly manner in their business dealings and is careful to remember the clerk's birthday by sending a card. Neither are we likely to consider it inappropriate for the supplier to send a gift of a calendar or a box of chocolates to the clerk as a Christmas gift, because such a gift, unlike an expensive trip around the world, is scarcely liable to compromise, or to be perceived as compromising, the clerk's duty and ability to act in the best interests of her employer. The impropriety of the supplier in proffering an expensive gift lies not in the giving of a gift, but in the giving of a type of gift that has the potential, or is liable to be understood as having the potential, to undermine the proper functioning of the clerk as her employer's agent.

The issue, then, is whether, in a particular relationship involving the performance of professional or official duties, the giving and receiving of a gift is appropriate, and, if so, what type of gift is appropriate. This is hardly a question that can be handled in a purely mechanical manner and there can be no substitute for good will. Certainly, it is wise for the individuals involved to err on the side of caution and for the organizations they represent to provide general guidelines for employees concerning what is acceptable in this regard.

II. Bribery, Undue Influence, and Extortion: Definitional Issues

A. BRIBERY DEFINED

Instances of bribery provide paradigm examples of improper gifts and payment. Unfortunately, this does not mean that defining bribery is a simple task. Uncomplicated though it is to say what constitutes bribery in some instances, it is far from easy to provide a universal definition. We have already suggested that care must be taken to distinguish bribery from gifts and payments that, although inappropriate, could not properly be termed bribes. In addition, we must distinguish bribes from instances of extortion. Also to be considered is the fact that many practices that would be considered bribery in one culture would not only be accepted, but would be expected in other cultures.

Returning to our example of the purchasing clerk, let us suppose that the supplier offers her a large sum of money if she will order supplies from him rather than a rival supplier, and the clerk willingly agrees. This, we will probably agree, constitutes a clear case of bribery. But what makes it such? What are the key elements that enable us to recognize it as an instance of bribery?

Several factors seem relevant. First, it is clearly the intention of the supplier to cause the clerk to violate her duties to act in the best interests of her employer. Second, the clerk is a willing participant; she is in no way forced to violate her duties, yet she agrees to do so in exchange for the reward offered. Third, the duties she is being asked to violate are acquired duties, that is, they are duties she has acquired by virtue of a previous agreement to act in a role of faithful agent for her employer.

Generally, an act of bribery will involve an employee or official, under the influence of a third party offering a reward, illegitimately subverting a prior agreement to act as agent for an employer, thus failing to fulfill the role duties acquired under that agreement. Typically, then, an instance of bribery involves three parties: the person offering the bribe, the employee or official to whom the bribe is offered, and the employer for whom the employee previously agreed to act as an agent. This suggests that bribery essentially involves an intentional and willing alienation of agency by the employee and a third party, without ever informing the original employer that the employee is no longer working as her agent.

Having said this, we do well to recognize that not all bribes are successful. They nevertheless remain bribes, because a bribe, like a gift, is defined not by whether it is accepted, but by the intention of the giver. A bribe remains a bribe whether it is accepted or not but the act of bribery can only occur when the employee consents to take the bribe. Until then we would speak not of bribery, but rather an attempt at bribery.

B. BRIBERY DISTINGUISHED FROM UNDUE INFLUENCE

This understanding of bribery provides conceptual clarity in several ways. First, it helps explain what we have already noted, namely, that not all improper gifts or payments should be considered bribes. We have suggested that for bribery actually to occur there must be an agreement both on the part of the person offering the reward and the person accepting it, to subvert an existing contract. For an employee to accept a gift even though it might unduly influence him, is quite different than to accept the gift with the explicit intention of violating his duties.

C. BRIBERY DISTINGUISHED FROM EXTORTION

Second, this understanding of bribery allows us to distinguish instances of bribery from instances of extortion. Several key differences are clear. One is that whereas bribery involves the willing participation of the person bribed, extortion involves unwilling participation under duress. We do not speak of the person receiving a bribe as a victim, but we would describe someone as a victim of extortion. Adopting a metaphor, we can say that bribery resembles adultery, extortion rape.

Another difference is that bribery essentially involves the alienation of agency, but extortion does not. One cannot accept a bribe and remain a loyal employee, but it is possible to act under duress, yet remain a loyal employee. For example, an employee told by a corrupt inspector that a shipment of goods up to standards will not be passed unless the inspector receives an expensive "gift" might justifiably regard himself as a loyal agent of his employer in acceding to the inspector's demands, even though he in his role as agent of his employer is a victim of extortion. On the other hand, extortion may involve an alienation of agency, as in the case of an employee, say a night watchman, who under threat does not perform his proper role duties and allows the building he is guarding to be burgled.

Yet another difference is that, whereas bribery always involves the subversion of role duties, extortion does not. One can only be bribed if one is acting as an agent for another, but this is not a necessary condition for being a victim of extortion. One may be a victim of extortion both in instances where one is free to act on one's own behalf and where one has acquired duties to act on the behalf of one's employer.

D. BRIBERY AND CULTURALLY RELATIVE PRACTICES

Third, this understanding of bribery provides guidance in assessing practices that would be considered bribery in one culture but are accepted and expected behavior in other cultures. It avoids the conclusion that our definition of bribery must be culturally relative, yet recognizes that what properly counts as bribery may vary from culture to culture. Bribery, we have said, essentially involves an intentional and willing alienation of agency by the employee and a third party, such that the employee illegitimately subverts a prior agreement to act as agent for an employer, thus failing to fulfill the role duties acquired under that prior agreement. This understanding, although not culturally relative, is capable of recognizing that the official duties of employees may vary from culture to culture, so that behavior that in one society would constitute taking a bribe should not be so regarded in another. The key question is not the variability of employee behavior, but whether the employee acts as loyal agent for her employer. This is not to say that if a practice is culturally accepted it does not

constitute bribery, but rather that what counts as the official duties of an employee may be culturally relative.

III. Bribery, Undue Influence, and Extortion: Moral Issues

Our discussion of bribery has allowed us to distinguish between instances of undue influence, bribes, and extortion. It has also led us to conclude that, although there is no need to define bribery in a culturally relative manner, employee duties may be understood differently in different cultures, so that what counts as taking a bribe may differ from culture to culture. What we must now examine is whether there are circumstances in which one could legitimately exert what we would normally call undue influence, offer a bribe, or extort. Additionally, we must examine whether there are circumstances in which one could legitimately accede to what we would normally call undue influence, accept a bribe, or pay extortion.

A. UNDUE INFLUENCE AND MORALITY

We have said that undue influence occurs when an employee is swayed, or in danger of being swayed, from his duty to act in the best interests of his employer. How then could it ever be morally correct either to exert undue influence or to allow oneself to be unduly influenced? The answer that must be given is that, although there exists a prima facie obligation not to exert undue influence or to allow oneself to be unduly influenced, it seems possible to conceive of situations where this obligation would fail to hold. What if the result of the undue influence is that a great harm would be prevented from occurring or that a great good would be brought about?

It deserves emphasis in this regard that contractual obligations are acquired and cannot legitimately conflict with the more general obligations one has simply by virtue of being a human person. For example, one could never have an acquired duty on the basis of a contract to perform murder, because this would violate one's general duty not to kill. Given that there are general obligations that, in unusual circumstances, would necessitate the suspension of what we would otherwise regard as the legitimate role duties of an employee, it seems permissible in such circumstances to exert, or to allow oneself to be influenced by, what in other circumstances would constitute undue influence.

Suppose, for example, the manager of a shoe store has been instructed by its owner not to extend credit. She is approached by a customer, well known for his honesty and for keeping his word, who in the past has frequently bought shoes for his children and has always paid her cash. The customer informs her that, although he knows she has been instructed not to extend credit, could she nevertheless make an exception in this instance. He tells her that his family recently had a house fire in which they lost all their possessions. The insurance check will cover their losses, but will not be issued for a couple of days, and meanwhile his children require winter footwear. He promises that if she will extend the credit he will not let the fact that she has done so become public knowledge and also that he will provide her with free car washes at his service station. Concerned for the welfare of the children, she agrees to extend the credit and, not wanting to offend or embarrass the customer, promises that she will come in for the free car washes he insists on offering her. In such an instance, although we might say that the manager has a prima facie duty to follow the instructions of her employer and that the customer has a prima facie duty not to seek to cause her to violate her duty to her employer, neither has acted immorally, inasmuch as these prima facie duties are trumped by the more general duty of avoiding a considerable but easily preventable harm to the customer's children. To be noted, of course, is the fact that the manager's motive for extending the credit was based on concern for the customer's children and not on the special treatment she would receive as a result of her decision.

B. BRIBERY AND MORALITY

Similarly, in the case of bribery, there exists a prima facie obligation for someone in an official position to fulfill her official duties. There exists, therefore, a prima facie obligation not to subvert the fulfillment of positional duties by offering or receiving a bribe. How seriously this prima facie obligation ought to be taken will depend in large part on the institutional and social context in which one finds oneself. Again, the controlling principle is that role or positional duties generated by contractual obligations cannot legitimately conflict with the more general obligations one has simply by virtue of being a human person. It would seem strange, for example, to suggest that in a politically and judicially corrupt regime, someone who bribed a guard to let an innocent prisoner condemned to a lengthy jail sentence escape, was acting immorally. The prima facie duty of the guard not to let the prisoner escape, and the prima facie duty of citizens not to endeavor by means of bribery to cause the guard to fail in his duty are to be respected to the degree that the institutional and social context generating these positional duties is fair and just.

It might be objected that an example such as I have just given demonstrates only that it is morally permissible under some circumstances to offer a bribe, not that it is morally permissible to take a bribe. Would we not want to say that the prison guard should not require a bribe if his action is genuinely morally motivated? To suggest this is to ignore the possibility that, unless the guard receives enough of a bribe to flee the country, his action of letting the prisoner escape will result in his being executed. We could scarcely suggest the guard is morally required to forfeit his own life to prevent an innocent prisoner from serving a lengthy prison sentence, but it does seem clear that in such a situation the guard could morally accept a bribe that enables him, without having to forfeit his own life, to let the prisoner escape.

C. EXTORTION AND MORALITY

In the normal course of events, extorting someone will be even harder to justify than bribing someone, inasmuch as the person suffering the extortion is a victim rather than an accomplice. Again, any justification of the practice in specific instances will depend on challenging the moral legitimacy of the institutional or social context in which the extortion takes place.

Conversely, paying extortion seems much easier to justify than receiving a bribe. In many instances of extortion one is not acting as an employee or official and thus there are no positional duties to an employer to complicate the question of whether to meet the extortion demands. This is not to suggest that one should automatically give in to the demands of a blackmailer or extortionist in such instances, because one has a prima facie duty to resist the immoral actions of others. There may well, however, be considerations that are capable of overriding this prima facie obligation.

In instances where meeting extortion demands would necessitate failing in positional duties, the question arises as to how greatly the victim or others will suffer if one carries out these duties. For example, we can scarcely fault a clerk for failing in his positional duty by handing over the contents of a cash register to an extortionist if he is faced with the genuine and immediate threat of his home being blown up by a bomb planted by the extortionist. This is not to say that one could never illegitimately subvert one's role duties as an employee by paying extortion. For example, the clerk would not be justified in handing over the contents of the cash register if the threat was only that his windows would be soaped. But supererogatory acts of moral heroism are not implicit in the contractual agreement by which one acquires role duties.

D. CULTURAL DIFFERENCES AND MORALITY

I have suggested that, although the definition of bribery is not culturally relative, what constitutes the official duties of an employee frequently is. This implies that behavior that in one society would count as offering or taking a bribe, that is, behavior that would involve subverting one's official duties, might not so count in another society. In other words, the same behavior might be perfectly consistent with one's official duties. Thus, behavior that in some countries might be construed as offering or demanding a bribe, might in other countries be construed as offering or demanding a tip. The term *tip,* originally an acronym for the phrase "to insure prompt service," implies no alienation of agency, but rather recognizes that an employee can remain faithful to her employer, even though she is independently receiving payment for service to her employer's customers. In such instances, payment to the employee takes place with the implicit or explicit approval of her employer and tends to become simply a cost of doing business, much as tipping a waitress should be included in estimating the cost of a meal at a restaurant.

Equally, however, it implies that the question of whether certain practices constitute bribery is not to be settled by whether the culture in which they occur considers them bribery, but rather whether in fact these practices are consistent with fulfilling one's official duties. This will also hold true in the case of undue influence and extortion. If we think that undue influence, bribery, and extortion are prima facie immoral we must, in the absence of special circumstances justifying these practices, be prepared to criticize the social environments in which they are condoned.

Even more importantly, we must also be prepared to raise the issue of whether the way a particular culture or society conceives official duties is in accord with the general duties we have simply by virtue of our humanity. As I have argued earlier, role or positional obligations cannot legitimately conflict with these more general obligations. The implication of this is that if a particular society conceives professional duties in such a way that these duties conflict with our more basic human duties, then we must be prepared to raise larger moral issues regarding that society's structuring of its institutions and contractual agreements.

References

Anechiarico, F., & Kuo, L. (1995, Spring). The justified scoundrel: The structural genesis of corruption. *Journal of Social Philosophy,* **25,** 1, 147–161.

Berleant, A. (1982, August). Multinationals, local practice, and the problem of ethical consistency. *Journal of Business Ethics,* **1,** 3, 185–193.

Carson, T. (1985, Winter). Bribery, extortion, and the foreign corrupt practices act. *Philosophy and Public Affairs,* **14,** 1, 66–90.

D'Andrade, K. (1985). Bribery. *Journal of Business Ethics,* **4,** 239–248.

Danley, J. Toward a theory of bribery. *Business and Professional Ethics Journal,* **2,** 3, 19–39.

Fadiman, J. (1984, July/August). A traveler's guide to gifts and bribes. *Harvard Business Review,* **4,** 122–136.

Philips, M. (1984). Bribery. *Ethics,* **94,** 621–636.

Gift Giving, Bribery and Corruption: Ethical Management of Business Relationships in China

P. STEIDLMEIER

GIFT GIVING is a prevalent social custom in China in all areas of life: in family and in significant relationships (*guanxi*), as well as in dealing with political authorities, social institutions and business people. For all that, from an ethical perspective, it is very difficult to know when it is proper to give or receive a gift, what sort of gift is appropriate, or what social obligations gift giving imposes (de Menthe, 1990).

Anyone who has lived in a foreign culture knows how difficult it is to successfully adapt to the local way of doing things. One can spend many months learning how to behave, only to find it all too easy to still commit tremendous *faux pas*. For foreigners, the cultural logic and social practices of gift giving present one of the most difficult lessons in learning how to "do business right" in China. Not surprisingly, many Westerners unfamiliar with Chinese culture often make the easy identification of gifts with bribes and allege that the Chinese are promiscuously corrupt in their business practices (*Economist*, 1995a, 1995b). Such an easy identification is, however, incorrect. The Chinese themselves are well aware of the differences. There is hardly an issue that has so preoccupied the Chinese media and incited debate over the past years as bribery and corruption (Levy, 1995). Within Chinese culture itself, there are, indeed, moral parameters to distinguish morally proper gift giving from bribery and corruption.

In this paper I assess the cultural and moral differences between gift giving, bribery and corruption and set forth guidelines for managing business relations in China. I begin with a cultural framework of analysis and then proceed to analyze transactions based upon reciprocity in terms of 1) the action itself and 2) the moral intention of the agents. I conclude with moral guidelines for ethical management.

Developing a Cultural Framework for Reciprocity

John Noonan (1984, p. 3) observes: "Reciprocity is in any society a rule of life, and in some societies at least it is *the* rule of life." China is one of those societies where reciprocity is a foundational pillar of social intercourse. To approach another and bring nothing is unusual, to say the least. To accept a gift and not reciprocate is perceived as morally wrong.

A social custom such as gift giving expresses deeper socially embraced behavioral ideals and norms of mutuality and "right relationships" between people. Practices of gift giving in China include visual behavioral patterns (*organizational artifacts*), which are enshrined in *rites (li)* of proper conduct. Such rites themselves are rooted in normative and prescriptive canons of righteousness (*yi*) and benevolence (*ren*), which express why such actions are culturally meaningful or logical. In general terms, *cultural logic* underscores the numerous socio-cultural values and beliefs that are embedded within organizations and function as a sort of internal gyroscope, which governs the social behavior of people. It is, nonetheless, difficult to discern when it is proper to give a gift, what its nature should be and to whom it should be given. Such discernment is ultimately a matter of *social knowledge*. Proper social knowledge represents the ability to align behavioral patterns with cultural logic.

In the area of business, a manager needs to gather and correlate such cultural information and its supporting ethical data in ways that make sense and render it usable. The three principal aspects of the cultural data base—artifacts, social knowledge and cultural logic—are summarized in Table I. In daily practice companies require a concrete understanding of acceptable business behav-

From Journal of Business Ethics *20: 121–132, 1999.* © *1999 Kluwer Academic Publishers. Printed in the Netherlands. Reprinted with permission.*

Table I. Cultural Databases

Artifacts	Artifacts represent those things that can be seen or heard, e.g. what gifts are given to whom and under what circumstances; artifacts also include such things as how offices are laid out, how people run meetings, how honorifics are used in situations of interaction and so forth. This level of the data base includes the "who-what-where-when" part of the story.
Social Knowledge	Social knowledge includes the social processes and values that people can offer as reasons when questioned, e.g. why and how people should act as they do. It provides the reason why it is proper to give a particular person a particular gift at a particular time, as well as the contrary. In this section of the data base the "how" and "why" of gift giving is covered.
Cultural Logic	Cultural logic provides the worldview which grounds social behavior and knowledge. This part of the data base provides the ideals, values and principles which serve as society's internal gyroscope. It provides a vision of the most fundamental relationships people have to others, to their environment, to truth and reality, to understanding human nature, to time.

ior patterns and an appreciation of why people do things in a certain way. To be successful business practices must be grounded in an accurate reading of these three levels of social meaning (Hofstede, 1980).

While cultural logic represents the transcendental values and worldview that underlie a culture, such as harmony, justice and right relations, artifacts represent the empirically observed behavior of people as they interact with one another, such as exchanging gifts, taking a certain place at table, or greeting a visitor at the airport. Social knowledge mediates between these two levels in determining what is appropriate. For example, if a visitor is coming from abroad, who is the proper person to meet him or her at the airport and what type of gift would be correct.

While the underlying traditional Chinese cultural logic provides the fundamental ethos of business practices, social knowledge provides a clearer map of "the rules of the game," through the mechanisms of routinely expected behavior patterns. The "rules of the game" reflect what people collectively, through social consensus and organizational will, find desirable. They provide specific ways of doing things within the overall structure of normative ethical parameters. Gift giving, for example, is expected behavior, which shows respect to another person and strengthens relationships. The practice is also bounded by rules of moral

legitimacy, which may in the end lead to defining some gifts as illegitimate forms of corruption. Chinese sources themselves are well aware of this (He, 1994; Liu and Xiong, 1994).

In China, gift giving forms part of a larger picture: belonging to a network of personal relationships (*guanxi*). That these relationships be "right" is a matter of utmost moral and practical concern. Gift giving is one of the ways of nurturing such relationships and strengthening the trust, caring, reciprocity and commitment between the parties. In practical terms, the quality of such relationships emerges as a universal primary reference point in judging what one ought to do. In day to day business, these realities lead to patterns of choice and the determination of priorities that are expressed in concrete deeds, such as favoring in commercial deals those people with whom one has close relationships or *guanxi*.

Interacting with Others in China

Chinese culture exhibits a very nuanced social philosophy of *relationships*. These embody both the *respect* one person owes another in terms of face (*myan dz*) as well as obligations of mutual rights and duties (*quanli yu yiwu*), which bind people together. The predominant social structures of Chinese society are found in the web of significant relationships (*guanxi*), based upon family, geographic origin school mates and so forth. A person's *guanxi* outlines who matters and how much they matter and provides the primary basis of moral claims for one person upon another (Gargan, 1996).

Such relationships in China are not uni-dimensional. In fact, they embrace many different levels of intensity. Most generally, they are ranked in order of importance as follows: family, friends or fellows (school mates, colleagues, distant relatives, friends of friends), other Chinese, and the outside world. This ordering is also reflected within a business enterprise: the business itself is a quasi-family and evokes primary loyalties, followed by ties with the enterprises's principal alliances (with banks, suppliers, traders, customers), other Chinese businesses and economic agents, and then the outside world. The principal challenge for a foreign corporation is to insert itself as closely as possible within the inner circles.

In dealing with the Chinese, it is very important to be aware of such things as practices of gift giving and receiving, the proper role for host organizations and guests, correct ways to handle introductions, etiquette in eating and drinking, proper decorum with superiors, peers and inferiors in the workplace, how to handle and express disagreements, proper dress and so forth.

Chinese social behavior has traditionally been quite prescriptive in terms of rites (*li*) and forms of courtesy, manners, politeness, and correct decorum (*li mao*). "*Li*" is highly ritualistic and expresses the proper public manner of relating to a superior, an equal or inferior in extending greetings, speaking, taking a seat, drinking or any expression of self towards another. As pointed out in the previous section, "*Li*" rests upon a broader normative ethic of "right relations," which, for instance, express the heart of ethical concerns in the Confucian tradition (de Bary, 1991, pp. 332ff.). In China, position within the group, rather than over the group or in distinction to it, is far more important than independence from the group. Likewise, respect for others ("face") is of paramount importance and is manifested through gift giving, deference, not publicly disagreeing, public honors within a group, and so forth. Both relationship networks (*guanxi*) and the social stature of face (*myan dz*) are enshrouded in public rituals (*li*), which express status, respect and bonding in formal terms.

Attention must first be paid to instrumental organizational dynamics of structure, control, incentives and time. Chinese organizations tend to emphasize high-status definition and follow the rules of *guanxi* and familial structures. U.S. organizations are more low-status and more rule-based, closely following formal rules and regulations rather than "following relationships." Control mechanisms in the former tend to be more cooperative and based on personal trust, and incentives take forms that emphasize loyalty and security. In the West, control is often more conflictive and regulatory, with incentives based upon individual achievement and merit. In the West, time is a precious commodity as the slogan "time is money" suggests; in China time is put to the service of relationships.

Further, one must consider a central dynamic of personal organizational interaction that stands out: individualism versus group identity. In the West people often define themselves as standing out from the group, emphasizing individual creativity, achievement, reward and status. In China people are more at pains to define their place within a group. This becomes more evident when applying the cultural process to doing business in China.

According to William de Bary (1991, pp. 3–4):

> Reciprocity, then becomes the basis of self-cultivation. One defines ones "self" in relation to others and to the Way which unites them. Thus is constructed the web of reciprocal obligations or moral relations in which one finds oneself, defines oneself. Apart from these one can have no real identity. And yet these relations alone, it is equally important to recognize, do not define one totally.
>
> . . . for Confucius the individual exists in a delicate balance with his social environment, reconciling his own self respect with respect for others, his inner freedom with the limiting circumstances of his own situation in life.

For Chinese, gift giving is a natural dynamic of any relationship: it shows a relationship is valued and is a means of expressing respect and honor for the other person. Gifts express good will and gratitude and, in many ways, can be considered a dynamic form of "social contracting." The difficult aspects of gift giving have more to do with assessing the proper proportionality between persons and the implied sense of obligation or reciprocity that is entailed in giving or receiving a particular gift. For example, in dealing with a Chinese delegation, the leader should receive a better gift than subordinates. One often must proceed by trial and error; however, exchanging equivalent gifts is not a bad rule of thumb: a meal for a meal, a pen for a pen. To avoid bribery, it is important to focus upon whether, through the gift, one is asking one party or other to engage in behavior that is not an integral or legitimate part of the set of transactions at hand, which form the backdrop for meeting in the first place (Clinard, 1995). For example, depositing 1% of a multi-million dollar transaction's value in a Swiss bank account in order to get an official to sign off on a deal could not be construed as a gift.

From Gift Giving to Bribery and Corruption: Present Practices Within China

Gift giving is one of the most pleasant and also one of the most difficult of Chinese customs to understand; however, the lines between gifts and corruption are often blurred.

Business and political corruption are by no means unique to China (Jacoby et al., 1977; Borrus, 1995; Clarke, 1990; Husted, 1994; Kristoff, 1995; Melloan, 1995; Pearce and Snider, 1995). American business people are often wary, because the U.S. "Foreign Corrupt Practices Act" (FCPA) as well as company codes of conduct often prohibit any exchange of gifts between a company representative and a supplier or customer (Greanis and Windsor, 1982). Originally set into law in 1977, the FCPA underwent significant legislative changes in 1988 (Bliss and Spak, 1989) in view of the practices of other countries. In 1994 the OECD (Organization for Economic Cooperation and Development) passed its own "Antibribery Recommendation" and urged member states to follow up with appropriate legislation (Earle, 1996).

One of the most famous business ethics cases of the seventies was the Lockheed payments scandal in Japan (Boukon, 1978). It involved major companies as well as political figures in staggering sums of money. Eventually it led to the United States' "Foreign Corrupt Practices Act" (Young, 1978; Greanis and Windsor, 1982) which focused

attention on the practice of giving gratuities—a seeming necessity at every level of a transaction if one were to be successful at doing business in Japan.

It is important to realize that the Chinese literature itself is full of condemnations of corruption on the part of officials, where alleged "gifts" are actually forms of extortion and bribery (Cheng, 1994; Kolenda, 1990; Gong, 1993; Hao and Johnston, 1995; Jiang, 1995; Liu, 1995). Chinese culture itself has a sense of proper proportionality and reciprocity between those who exchange gifts (Schwartz, 1985, pp. 109–112; 322–327; Rocca, 1992; Legal Research Institute, 1994; Faison, 1995).

Many observers assert that one of the principal motives for the Tiananmen outburst in June, 1989, was the overriding disgust with the corruption of Party officials and their families (Chen, 1995). Since then, the Chinese themselves have been increasingly preoccupied with corruption, internally prosecuting over 167,000 cases from 1993 through September 1995 (Li, 1996; Cao, 1996; Tyler, 1994, 1995). Top officials, including the mayor of Beijing, and their families and cronies have been toppled from power. The word "power" sounds a note of caution, as anti-corruption drives have become intertwined with power struggles among leadership factions following the death of Deng Xiaoping (Barnathan, 1995; Engardio, 1995).

In response to pressure for vast political change, a number of reforms have been introduced to root out corruption and fraud and to stem the widening gap in economic development between the rich and poor (Embassy of the PRC, 1993; Cao, 1996; Kristoff, 1993; Brauchli, 1993a; Barnathan, 1994).

In recent years, according to Chinese sources, the burden of the peasantry has grown to be intolerable and, comparatively speaking, their living standards have declined. A number of issues are involved: rigged prices for agricultural inputs and outputs, corruption of local officials, lack of investment and jobs in the rural sector, and farmers being paid in government "I.O.U.'s" rather than currency (Xinhua Domestic Service, 1993; Brauchli, 1993b; Barnathan, 1993). There are numerous appeals for reform, some from official circles (Xinhua Domestic Service, 1995), some from dissidents (Barmé and Jaivin, 1992).

Moral Analysis of Reciprocity

How is reciprocity, as a general type of moral action, to be analyzed? To call what is empirically a transfer of resources between parties 1) giving a gratuity, or 2) bribery, or 3) a commission involves interpreting the meaning of the empirically observed event. Such interpretation draws upon core human values, respect for local traditions, and an appreciation of context (Donaldson, 1996).

To label it "bribery" is already to make a moral judgment. For in ordinary English (or Chinese) the word bribery itself (*huilu*) connotes a wrongful transfer of resources between parties. Wrongful because the gift giver and receiver apparently strike a deal, which puts their own interests above other parties, who have legitimate prior claims in the transaction and on whose behalf the agents are acting. It not only breaks down trust between people and their agents (d'Andrade, 1985) but also undermines the legitimacy of social institutions (Turow, 1985).

It is just this action which I wish to scrutinize before we characterize it with a label. In Table II I outline the elements of analysis of reciprocity in resource transfers. The moral analysis of such a resource transfer can be exceedingly difficult to carry out. The resource transfer itself can be termed the "empirical part" of the action. It is empirically descriptive of what takes place and, in this sense, is morally neutral. Moral judgment about the action, however, is not neutral.

ANALYSIS OF RECIPROCITY AS A "TYPE OF MORAL ACTION"

In objective categories moral understanding of an existential kind of action demands clarification of values as well as concrete knowledge of ends, means and consequences. Moral judgment then seeks to decide:

1. whether as a type of action "X" is right or wrong
2. whether as a specific instance a particular action "x" is good or bad, and
3. whether the parties (agents) involved are to be praised or blamed

The paying of a commission is ostensibly the least troublesome resource transfer. Morally, it is embedded in a freely undertaken and fair contract framework and represents remuneration in a transaction of mutually beneficial exchange. As a type of action the ends sought, means taken and consequences which ensue are usually justified in terms of instrumental values (efficiency, utility) and self-interest. Such an action is only morally correct if it is consistent with fundamental values of justice and basic moral virtues. Furthermore, the intentions of the parties must be honorable and neither their consciences nor freedom are impaired. However, all of this can be easily suborned. Values of self-interest can be transformed into raw selfishness and expediency replace justice. Some would argue that commissions have become the favorite form of bribery in the United States, because they offer the cloak of legality (Jacoby et al., 1977; Clinard, 1995).

Giving a gratuity, such as a tip, is a bit more difficult to analyze (Philips, 1984; Udoidem, 1987). If it altruistically expresses gratitude—a bonus for a job well done and performance exceeding expectations—it is a sign of generosity and esteem for the other. But if the tippee somehow indirectly communicates that such remuneration is a precondition for good service, then it becomes coercive and a form of extortion. The problem is not with a 15% service charge announced as a matter of policy, but with coercive behavior. Such coercive behavior, in fact, is a partial breach of the contract which is implied when one buys a meal, takes a cab, or gets a haircut: the service promised for a certain price will not, in fact, be delivered for that rate. In giving gratuities, people may respond immediately that there is both a commonly known socio-cultural expectation and approval of tipping in general. The "gratuity portion" of the tip is then reserved to the rate: whether 12% or 20%. In fact, tipping is usually considered part of the tippee's ordinary income. In that sense it represents a suitable means to a good end with beneficial consequences. It may be considered both a "right" type of action as well as a "good" action in the context of a particular tip.

The latter judgment could be altered, however, depending upon the subjective intentions of those involved and the degree of coercion. Tipping may, in fact, mask either bribery or extortion. In coercive tipping, the tippee extorts extra payments for a service. In bribery, the tipper may seek special con-

Table II. Moral Analysis of Reciprocity

	Bribery	Gratuity	Commission
A. *As a Type of Moral Action*			
Social purpose (end)	Gain acquiescence	Express gratitude	Pay for services
Values	Utilitarian	Utilitarian and/ or altruistic	Mutual benefit and reciprocal fairness
Means	To give something the other would appreciate	To give something the other would appreciate	To give what was agreed upon
Consequences	Double-effect	Helps the others and build rapport	Fair mutual benefit
B. *From the Perspective of Moral Agents*			
Individual intention	Success of transaction	Gratitude and future good will	Fairness in contract
Degree of freedom	Condition of success	Voluntary, but there may be social pressure (tip)	Free contractual obligation
Conscience	No one hurt; lesser of two evils	Those with abundance should be generous	Honesty and promise keeping

sideration—the best table without having to either make reservations or wait. In the end, the overall analytical framework of *values-end-means-conse- quences* remains ambiguous. As with commissions, the phenomenon of giving gratuities can either be morally uplifting or an expression of corruption.

Bribery itself emerges as extremely complex. Defined as a *type of action* it is clearly wrong. However, as noted above, to say bribery is wrong is to utter a tautology. That is, bribery (*huilu*) defines a wrongful type of action. To use an exam- ple from Kant, we describe a type of action and its conditions (end, means, values, consequences), name it bribery, and then ask: would one want to make this action universal? The answer is "no." The previous discussion of epistemology and worldview are very important here. For if we asked the question in terms of Mill's utilitarianism (does it produce the greatest happiness for the greatest number?) the answer may well be quite different, whether considering bribery as an individual act or as a rule of behavior. To say that bribery is always wrong can only be established in the context of a specific worldview and a specific value set that one takes as universal and absolute. Subjectively, it is necessarily relative.

ANALYSIS OF RECIPROCITY IN TERMS OF MORAL AGENTS

It is important to move from the analysis of bribery as a *type of action* to a concrete situation. When one asks whether a particular instance of bribery may be good or bad or whether the parties involved may be praiseworthy or blameworthy, the analysis becomes considerably more nuanced because of the complexity of the concrete situation. In this context, the analyst must be particularly careful of ethnocentrism. To the point, to what degree does what appears to be bribery fulfill the conditions set forth in the abstract definition of bribery as a *type of action*?

This is further complicated when, in addition to grasping all the details of a situation, one tries to understand the moral agent him/herself: subjec- tive factors of conscience, intention and degrees of freedom are factored in. In actions of reciprocity, where resources are exchanged between parties, the level of development of each party's conscience may enter in to mitigate circumstances. Bribery in the face of intractably corrupt officials and the cer- tain closing of a plant due to a lost contract, differs from bribery to enrich oneself so as to build a third villa estate. Indeed, officials involved in the Lockheed case, argued the former case and that, in the end, they chose the lesser of two evils. In such cases one may arrive at different judgments of the agents being praiseworthy or blameworthy.

Attention must be paid to the social situation and context. I am not at this point arguing a situational ethics where a *type of action* is right or wrong according to the particular circumstances. Rather, the very concrete definition of the action taking place (i.e. of what is actually happening) derives from the socio-historical context in the first place. That is, the question is not whether "bribery" is all right in Shanghai but not in Kansas City. Rather, is this manner of reciprocity and resource transfer in Shanghai a bribe? This point is crucial to understanding the social purpose and consequences of the transaction and to judging whether this instance is good or bad and whether and to what degree the agents are morally blameworthy or praiseworthy. In many parts of the developing world what a Western observer would call a bribe is, in fact, closer to a tip or the socially expected form of the tippee's remuneration (Tsalakis, 1991; Tsalakis and LaTour, 1995). That does not mean that "anything goes." The former Lockheed scandal and the recent "Recruit scandal" in Japan as well as many instances of corruption cited in the Chinese press have clearly exceeded such bounds (Rosett, 1989; Weisman, 1990).

Even if the *end* or purpose of the transaction is good—the firm is engaged in selling a product very good for the people—the analyst must also ask whether the *means* adopted are suitable and whether the *intentions* of the parties are honorable. Phenomenologically, it is difficult to distinguish a bribe from a tip or a commission or consulting fee. In the end, moral judgment depends upon the social understanding of the meaning of the action as derived from analysis of ends and means, consequences and intentions.

Provided the end or purpose is good, the key difference seems to reside not in the phenomenology of the transaction itself in terms of *means* and *consequences,* but in the *intention* of those who are involved, conditioned by *conscience* and *effective freedom.* The essence of bribery is conflict of interest between self and one's publicly accepted fiduciary duties. Secondly, it affects the *means* a person employs to fulfill his or her fiduciary duty. The

appropriateness of the resource transfer in a particular case and the praiseworthiness or blameworthiness of the parties depends upon the overall social consequences of the action and the intentions of the agents. What if the intentions of the briber are actually good with reference to the project and fulfilling his or her fiduciary duties but those of the bribee are greed? Even then, the action may not be completely bad. Enter the *principle of double effect:* one may make the judgment that the success of the project is impossible without the bribe *and* the good consequences of the project clearly outweigh the evils of the bribe.

Some Guidelines for "Doing Business Right" in China

The guidelines I suggest below are based upon two sets of beliefs: 1) the moral ambiguity one experiences in differentiating bribes from gratuities and commissions and 2) the present situation in China with respect to political and business corruption.

From the above sections, it is clear that it is impossible to clearly distinguish gratuities, bribes and commissions on an empirical basis. Bribes can easily be dressed in the garb of "legitimate commissions" or gratuitous expressions of esteem. Furthermore, in analyzing whether a transaction is morally right or wrong and whether the agents are praiseworthy or blameworthy pivotal elements such as conscience, effective freedom, the determinative dynamics of the situation, and cumulative consequences are often beyond measurement. In the end, these facts attest to the reality that moral probity is ever a matter of discernment of what, in the Socratic tradition, is called wisdom: figuring out how to be excellent at being human.

From Chinese voices themselves, we know the following:

1. corruption is endemic, especially since the reforms of the last decades
2. corruption reaches the highest levels of the ruling elite
3. corruption flies in the face of Chinese (as well as Marxist) tenets and traditions of public morality and the moral dimensions of a public official's responsibility
4. the "corruption debate" among the Chinese also functions as cover for a power struggle or,

perhaps more accurately, for multiple power struggles between factions in the post-Deng Xiaoping era

5. Chinese "rules of the game" lack transparency as well as universality across both a) regions and b) factions—leaving local officials with tremendous discretionary power

If the above observations regarding both ethical judgments, in general, and the Chinese social milieu, in particular, are substantially correct, what is a company doing business in China to do? In part, the answer depends upon the company's intentions: does it wish to behave ethically? or merely legally? or to do "whatever it takes" to make money without getting caught?

The answer to the last of the above questions is simply try to implement "applied Machiavellianism," realizing, however, that the Chinese have developed traditions that in many ways outdo *The Prince!* At present, the atmosphere is ambiguous and opportunistic situations abound.

Simply aiming for legal compliance can be more difficult, but still it is not too formidable. For a U.S. multinational, the rules of the game from the American side are fairly clear, as expressed in numerous regulations, ranging from the FCPA in 1977, the Omnibus Trade and Competitiveness Act of 1988, government agency directives and legal rulings. At the same time, strategies to circumvent them through third parties and holding companies have been developing at a rapid rate. The main problem for foreign multinationals is found on the Chinese side, where, they claim, there is no real *transparency* in the applicable laws and regulations. Regulations vary across ministries and are interpreted differently in different regions. People can be caught and held liable without even knowing their transgressions. As a simple example, it is very dangerous to pay a "commission" to someone whose power base is eroding and who is about to be deposed. The main strategy a foreign company should adopt in order to achieve simple legal and regulatory compliance is to be sure to have the right set of Chinese patrons on one's side at all levels and regions and to have them, as partners, become the guarantors of legitimacy. There are, indeed, such a sufficient number of official Chinese denouncements of corruption that they provide a foreign company with cover. The foreign company should use this material as part of a stated policy to be a

"worthy guest" in China, while shifting the burden of ensuring that they are in full compliance to their Chinese partner. Frequently, foreign companies are at a disadvantage because they are ignorant of the many powerful official Chinese statements regarding their history of international dealings and their policies regarding corruption. I know only of Chinese policies condemning corruption, not advocating it. It makes strategic sense to use this material as the motivating force for avoiding corruption in China, rather than simply appealing to the FCPA as the motivation for one's actions.

For those companies truly desiring to be ethical, the problem is more complex, not the least is being "closed out" of deals, which are then snapped up by competitors willing to play the game.

As a general rule of thumb, a U.S. intelligence consultant, Kroll Associates (Asia) have suggested the following guidelines in choosing a local partner (Miles, 1995):

1. Investigate the backgrounds of local executives you place in charge of company matters. Did they do a good job for their previous company? Or did they leave after two years, taking the entire team with them? A common occurrence.
2. Ensure no one individual has total control over company matters.
3. Treat remarks such as "China is different" and "You shouldn't get involved" as a red light.
4. Establish regular and detailed auditing systems to ensure transparency.

To which I would add:

5. Be aware of the political standing of your counterparts and do not get caught in the cross fire of Chinese power struggles (*Economist*, 1995c).
6. Explain your difficulties to the Chinese side (deriving from the U.S. government, stockholders, competitors, . . .) and offer alternatives that are legitimate—especially something that addresses key Chinese policy objectives (e.g. technology transfer), the attainment of which will give leverage.
7. As much as possible use Chinese sources themselves as the basis for your unwillingness to do corrupt deals.
8. Rather than becoming entangled in a specific minor bribe, place the whole matter in a

broader context of negotiation. Rather than reactively saying "yes" or "no" to a specific bribe, proactively build up negotiating leverage and a viable set of alternatives at the outset.

This last point of building negotiating leverage is highly important. I conclude this article with a sketch of its basic elements. In the end, if one's objective is to attain "A," he/she should a) devise simultaneous and multiple means of doing so as well as b) build up negotiating leverage. This not only allows one's Chinese counterpart to save face by having a menu to consider, it secures effective freedom in negotiations.

It is difficult for a company to walk the moral path on its own. There are simply too many competitors willing to play the game and take the business away. Numerous attempts have been made to forge a common approach among OECD nations (Earle, 1996; Simons, 1966). Further, the U.S. government has urged American corporations to embrace a common code of conduct. On the one hand, this involves the Foreign Corrupt Practices Act (Givant, 1994) as well as Codes that go further in terms of human rights, intellectual property and other concerns. U.S. business people tend to reject such an approach (Gargan, 1994) for it would put them at a disadvantage with the multinationals from other countries. They feel that already too much business is lost due to side-stepping bribery and corruption (Greenberger, 1995; *Economist,* 1994).

Negotiation is an important part of strategy. Few things are "take it or leave it" and it is important to build and maintain latitude for creative imagination. Some important considerations are:

1. let the other side know your constraints (for example, an American company threatened by FCPA) and indicate what your "feasibility area" is;
2. offer alternatives that have a "legitimate business reason" (for example, explain that you cannot give cash but can provide training);
3. indicate that you are actively pursuing various partners; the competition within China between different companies, government ministries, and geographic regions is intense; let them know you have alternatives so as not to become boxed in or dependent;
4. let them know you are aware of their own official regulations and hint that exposure would

be embarrassing for everyone—everyone fears their own potential enemies

There are no hard and fast rules for such negotiations. However, it is clear that companies that have a product, technology or service critical to China have far more leverage than those companies for whom China can find easy substitutes. Further, a company that has other viable partners and alternatives also gains negotiating leverage. Overall, it makes sense for a company to primarily attend to three things: First, to diversify its Chinese partners as well as Asia Pacific partners so that it does not become boxed in by a single deal. Regionally, China is very diverse and it is possible to have a number of partners. At the same time it is important to form partnerships from the outside. In this way a particular deal becomes part of a China strategy but not the only viable option.

Second, it is important to offer one's Chinese counterparts alternatives that are both legitimate and that address important needs in Chinese development. Rather than simply paying a bribe, one can offer a local official help in marketing local products or special training (as Japanese trading companies are prone to do) and other consulting services.

Third, a company can gain leverage by presenting their approach in China's own terms. It should become familiar with China's internal documentation and processes regarding corruption and economic development. Rather than preaching from a Western pulpit—which Chinese find easy to counter—they should arm themselves with the ideals and procedures embedded in China's own development policies. China ardently desires to be an integral part of world commerce. The case should be made that standard international fair business practices are in its own economic interests.

Negotiating is not to be a frontal attack, but rather a strategy of creative imagination. Diversification of both partners and alternative courses of action bring (moral) freedom and reduces risk. Such a diversified negotiating context will set the stage for more creative solutions that are both morally right and strategically sound. In many ways the most difficult part of ethics is not denouncing what is wrong but the creative imagination and courage to craft something new. Diversified negotiation helps create the effective freedom to do just that.

References

Barmé, Geremie and Linda Jaivin: 1992, *New Ghosts, Old Dreams: Chinese Rebel Voices* (Random House Times Books, New York, NY).

Barnathan, Joyce: 1995, "The Gloves Are Coming Off in China: President Jiang's Crackdown on Corruption Could Unleash an All-out Power Struggle," *Business Week* (May 15), 60–61.

Barnathan, Joyce et al.: 1994, "China: Is Prosperity Creating a Freer Society?," *Business Week* (June 6), 94–99.

Barnathan, Joyce: 1993, "Now, Even Peasants Hate Beijing," *Business Week* (July 5), 47.

Bliss, Julia Christine and Gregory J. Spak: 1989. "The Foreign Corrupt Practices Act of 1988: Clarification or Evisceration?," *Law & Policy in International Business* 20(3), 441–469.

Borrus, Amy: 1995, "A World of Greased Palms," *Business Week* (November 6), 36–38.

Boulton, David: 1978, *The Grease Machine* (Harper and Row, New York, NY).

Brauchli, Marcus W.: 1993a, "Chaotic Change: Beijing's Grip Weakens as Free Enterprise Turns into Free-for-All," *New York Times* (August 26), A1, A7.

Brauchli, Marcus W.: 1993b, "Great Wall: As the Rich in China Grow Richer, the Poor are Growing Resentful," *New York Times* (October 9), A1, A8.

Cao Qingze: 1996, "Administrative Supervisory Department Fights Corruption," *Beijing Review* (April 1–7), 20–21.

Chen, Kathy: 1995, "As China Prospers, So Do the Children of Communist Leaders," *Wall St. Journal* (July 1), A1, A4.

Cheng Guoyou: 1994, "A Plain Discussion of Structural Corruption," *Shehui (Society)* 108 (January), 13–15; JPRS-CAR-94-019, pp. 32–33.

Clarke, Michael: 1990. *Business Crime: Its Nature and Control* (St. Martin's Press, New York, NY).

Clinard, Marshall B.: 1995, *Corporate Corruption: The Abuse of Power* (Praeger, New York, NY).

d'Andrade, Kendall, Jr.: 1985, "Bribery," *Journal of Business Ethics* 4, 239–240.

de Menthe, Boye: 1990, *Chinese Etiquette and Ethics in Business* (NTC Business Books, Lincolnwood, IL).

de Bary, William Theodore: 1991, *Learning for One's Self: Essay on the Individual in Confucian Thought* (Columbia University Press, Lincolnwood, IL).

Donaldson, Thomas: 1996, "Values in Tension: Ethics Away from Home," *Harvard Business Review* (September–October), 48–62.

Earle, Beverly: 1996, "The United States" Foreign Corrupt Practices Act and the OECD Antibribery Recommendation: When Moral Persuasion Won't Work, Try the Money Argument," *Dickinson Journal of International Law* 14(2), 207–231.

Economist, 1995a, "Business Ethics: Hard Graft in Asia" (May 27), 61.

Economist, 1995b, "The Politics of Corruption" (May 20), 33.

Economist,: 1995c, "The Perils of Connections" (February 25), 64–65.

Economist, 1994, "The Trouble with Caesar's Wife" (January 29), 37.

Embassy of the People's Republic of China: 1993, "Chinese President on China's Economic Development." *Newsletter* 14 (June 9), 3–4, Washington, DC.

Engardio, Pete: 1995, "China: Strife at the Top May Spark a War on Corruption," *Business Week* (March 6), 53.

Faison, Seth: 1995. "China's Anti-Graft Drive Grows; So Does Graft," *New York Times* (August 10), A3.

Gargan, Edward A.: 1996, "Family Ties That Bind Growth: Corrupt Leaders in Indonesia Threaten Its Future," *New York Times* (April 9), D1, D6.

Gargan, Edward A.: 1994, "Business Objects to a Code in China," *New York Times* (May 24), D2.

Givant, Norman: 1994, "The Sword that Shields," *China Business Review* (May–June), 29–31.

Gong, Xiaoxia (ed.): 1993, "Corruption and Abuses of Power During the Reform Era," *Chinese Sociology and Anthropology* (whole issue), 26(3) (Winter).

Greanis, George and Duane Windsor: 1982, *The Foreign Corrupt Practices Act: Anatomy of a Statute* (Lexington Books, Lexington, MA).

Greenberger, R. S.: 1995, "U.S. Firms Lost Business Due to Bribes, Report Says," *Wall St. Journal* (October 5), 2.

Hao, Yufan and Michael Johnston: 1995, "Reform at the Crossroads: An Analysis of Chinese Corruption," *Asian Perspective* 19 (Spring/Summer), 117–149.

He, Shougang: 1994, "Warning: Misplacement of Moral Concepts in Contemporary China," *Shehui (Society),* 110 (March), 93–94; JPRS-CAR-94-036, June 10, 49–50.

Hofstede, Geert: 1980, *Culture's Consequences: International Differences in Work-Related Values* (Sage Publications, Beverly Hills, CA).

Husted, Bryan W.: 1994, "Honor Among Thieves: A Transaction-cost Interpretation of Corruption in Third World Countries," *Business Ethics Quarterly* 4(1) (January), 17–27.

Jacoby, Neil H., Peter Nehemkis and Richard Eells: 1977, *Bribery and Extortion in World Business: A*

Study of Corporate Political Payments Abroad (MacMillan and Co., New York, NY).

Jiang Nanchun: 1995, "What is Causing Our Corruption Phenomenon?," *Zhenli de Zhuqiu (Pursuit of Truth)*, **10** (October 11), 23–26; FBIS-CHI-95-235, pp. 30–31.

Kolenda, Helena: 1990, "One Party, Two Systems: Corruption in the People's Republic of China and Attempts to Control It," *Journal of Chinese Law*, **4**(2), 189–232.

Kristoff, Nicholas D.: 1995, "Seoul Ex-President and 7 Businessmen Are Indicted for Bribery," *New York Times* (December 6), A7.

Kristoff, Nicholas D.: 1993, Kristoff, "Riddle of China: Repression as Standard of Living Soars," *New York Times* (September 7), A1, A10.

Legal Research Institute, Shanghai Academy of Social Sciences and Research Bureau, Shanghai Municipal People's Procuratorate: 1994, "Corruption and Bribery in Shanghai and Punishments Imposed to Counteract These Crimes," *Zhengzhi yu Falu (Political Science and Law)*, **70** (June 5), 4–11, JPRS-CAR-94-047, pp. 75–81.

Levy, Richard: 1995, "Corruption, Economic Crime and Social Transformation Since the Reforms: The Debate in China," *The Australian Journal of Chinese Affairs* **33** (January), 1–28.

Li, Ning: 1996, "Sharpening the Sword Against Corruption," *Beijing Review* (April 1–7), 16–19.

Liu, Amy: 1995, "Retired Leaders Urge Oversight of Top Officials," *Hong Kong Standard* (November 9), 6; FBIS-CHI-95-217, pp. 15–16.

Liu, Luoying and Xiong Guochang: 1994, "'Red Envelope' Phenomenon Analyzed in Context of Market Competition," *Faxue (Jurisprudence)*, **151** (June 10), 7–10; JPRS-CAR-94-048, pp. 74–75.

Melloan, George: 1995, "Political Corruption: The Good, Bad, Ugly," *Wall St. Journal* (November 13), A15.

Miles, Gregory L.: 1995, "Crime, Corruption and Multinational Business," International Business (July), 34–45.

Noonan, John T., Jr.: 1984. *Bribes* (MacMillan and Co., New York, NY).

Pearce, Frank and Laureen Snider (eds.): 1995, *Corporate Crime: Contemporary Debates* (University of Toronto Press, Toronto, CA).

Philips, Michael: 1984, "Bribery," *Ethics* **94,** 621–636.

Rocca, Jean-Louis: 1992, "Corruption and Its Shadow: An Anthropological View of Corruption in China," *China Quarterly* (June), 402–416.

Rosett, Claudia: 1989. "Japan's Recruit Scandal in Context," *Wall St. Journal* (April 10), A14.

Schwartz, Benjamin: 1985, *The World of Thought in Ancient China* (Harvard University Belknap Press, Cambridge, MA).

Simons, Marlise: 1996, "U.S. Enlists Rich Nations in Move to End Bribes," *New York Times* (April 12), A10.

Tsalakis, John: 1991, "A Comparison of Nigerian to American Views of Bribery and Extortion in International Commerce," *Journal of Business Ethics* **2,** 85–98.

Tsalakis, John and Michael S. LaTour: 1995, "Bribery and Extortion in International Business: Ethical Perceptions of Greeks Compared to Americans," *Journal of Business Ethics* **4,** 249–264.

Turow, Scott: 1985, "What's Wrong with Bribery?," *Journal of Business Ethics* **4,** 249–251.

Tyler, Patrick E.: 1995, "12 Intellectuals Petition China on Corruption," *New York Times* (February 26), 1, 6.

Tyler, Patrick: 1994, "Between Marxism and the Market, A Chinese Manager Finds Corruption," *New York Times* (May 25), D3.

Udoidem, Iniobong: 1987, "Tips in Business Transactions: A Moral Issue," *Journal of Business Ethics* **6,** 613–618.

Weisman, Steven R.: 1990, "Despite Scandal, 'Money Politics' Seems as Strong as Ever in Japan," *New York Times* (January 29), A1, A6.

Xinhua Domestic Service: 1995, "Ding Guangen on Spiritual Civilization Building," FBIS-CHI-95-217, pp. 16–18.

Xinhua Domestic Service: 1993, "Ending 12 Charges to Ease Peasant's Burden," FBIS-CHI-93-103, June 1, p. 69.

Young, Arthur and Company: 1978, *The Foreign Corrupt Practices Act of 1977—Toward Compliance with Accounting Provisions* (New York).

The Ethics of Slotting: Is This Bribery, Facilitation Marketing or Just Plain Competition?

ROBERT J. AALBERTS AND MARIANNE M. JENNINGS

I. Introduction

Finding "Bearwiches" on the cookie shelf in your grocery store will be a daunting task. Locating some "Frookies," a new line of fat-free, sugarless cookies, will take you on a journey through various aisles in the store, and you may find them at knee level in the health foods section. You can find packaged Lee's Ice Cream from Baltimore in Saudi Arabia and South Korea, but it will not be found on the grocery store shelves in Baltimore (Hetrick). The difficulty with finding these items is not that they are not good products. The manufacturers of these products cannot afford to buy shelf space. The shelf space in grocery stores is not awarded on the basis of consumer demand for Bearwiches or Frookies. Shelf space in grocery stores is awarded on the basis of the manufacturer's willingness to pay "slotting" fees. If manufacturers pay, they are given a space on the grocer's shelf. If the slotting fees are not paid, the product is not sold by the grocer.

Slotting fees are fees manufacturers pay to retailers in order to obtain retail shelf space.[1] The practice has been common in the retail grocery industry since 1987 (Aalberts and Judd). The origins of slotting fees are unclear with different parties in the food chain offering various explanations. Retailers claim slotting was started by manufacturers with the fees paid to retailers as an inducement to secure shelf space. Another theory of origin offered by retailers is that manufacturers use slotting fees to curtail market entrants. If a manufacturer buys more space with additional fees, the market can be controlled by existing manufacturers. Manufacturers claim slotting was started by retail grocers as a means of covering the bookkeeping and warehousing costs of the introduction of a new product. However, two things are clear. First, the practice of

affiliated fees for sale is expanding to other industries (Greenstein). The retail book industry, particularly the large chains, now demands fees from publishers for shelf slots and displays for their books. In malls, developers/ landlords now demand sums as large as $50,000 from tenants or prospective tenants before a lease can be negotiated or renegotiated. These fees for a position in the mall are referred to as "key money" or "negative allowances." (Interviews) In certain areas, home builders are demanding "access fees" or "marketing premiums" from appliance makers and other residential construction suppliers for use of their products in the builders' developments. (Interviews) In the computer software industry, the packaging of software programs with computers ensures sales and requires a fee. Even the display of programs in electronic stores is subject to a fee. (Interviews) The second clearly evolving trend in affiliated fees is that the practice is inconsistent and the purposes of the fees are unknown. Fees differ from manufacturer to manufacturer, from product to product and from retailer to retailer. This article discusses the nature and legalities of slotting fees and offers an ethical analysis of the practice.

II. How Slotting Works

Food manufacturers produce over 10,000 new products each year (Greenwald). However, store shelf space remains fixed. Because profit margins at grocery stores hover at very narrow levels of only one to two percent of sales,[2] additional shelf space would not increase profits nor produce guaranteed returns from the new products displayed there.

---

[1] "Slotting fees" actually pertain to obtaining space in the grocer's warehouse. "Shelf fees," which are fees for placement on the shelf, are also charged by some grocery retailers.

[2] Costs in the retail grocery industry are relatively fixed and cannot be readily reduced. Union wages and other unmanageable cost elements preclude effective efforts at increasing profit margins. Further, competition from the "club" stores (Cosco, Sam's Club, Price Club) is intense (BNA Policy Hearings).

From Journal of Business Ethics *20: 207–215, 1999. © 1999 Kluwer Academic Publishers. Printed in the Netherlands. Reprinted with permission.*

Additionally, grocers must assume the risk of allocating shelf space to a new product that would not sell at a level sufficient to provide even the narrow margins. Retail grocers must absorb the cost of warehousing the product, accounting for it in inventory, barcoding it and eventually stocking the shelves with it.[3] In many cases, particularly where the manufacturer is a small company, there has been little or no advertising of the product and the retail grocer must also incur the cost of advertising the product in some way or offer in-store coupons to entice customer purchases. To the retail grocer, the introduction of a new product and the allocation of precious shelf space is a high-cost risk. There are no guarantees that a new product will garner sales, and there is the downside of the loss of revenue from whatever product is displaced by the new product. To retail grocers, a slotting fee is a means of insulation from the risk of new product introduction and a means of advance recoupment of costs.

Within some retail grocery chains, slotting fees represent the net profits for the organization. Similar to the rental car industry in which earnings come from renters' fees for insurance, car seats and additional driver coverage, some retail grocers' profits come not from the sales of food but from the fees manufacturers pay for access (Greenwald).

The level and nature of slotting fees vary significantly. Some retailers have a flat fee of $5000 per product for introduction. Other retailers have a graduated fee schedule tied to the shelf space location. Eye-level slots cost more than the knee or ground-level slots. The prime spaces at the ends of grocery aisles bring premium slotting fees since those spaces virtually ensure customer attention.[4] Other stores require that a "kill fee" be paid when a product does not sell. One supermarket chain requires $500 just for a manufacturer to make an appointment to present a new product. Some retailers will not accept a new product even with a slotting fee. Small businesses often incur the cost of product development only to be unable to place the product with grocery stores (Hetrick).

Some stores charge a slotting fee, an additional fee if the product is new, and a "failure fee" on new products to cover the losses if the product fails to sell. A new fee, called the "staying fee," has also developed. A staying fee is an annual rent fee that prevents the retailer from giving a manufacturer's product slot to someone else (BNA). A 1988 survey found that 70% of all grocery retailers charge slotting fees with one retail store disclosing that its $15-per-store per product slotting fees bring in an additional $50 million in revenue each year.[5] Examples of various slotting fees paid and documented are found in Table I. The most typical slotting fee for a new product to be placed with a grocery retailer was $10,000. Slotting fees do not typically come down over time, even if the product sells well. At the retail level for CD-ROM sales, the producers pay a 20% fee per shipment, regardless of whether their product is in demand.

III. The Legal Issues Surrounding Slotting

The chairman of the board of a small food manufacturer in Ohio wrote to his Congressman and described slotting fees in this way: "This is nothing but a device to extort money from packers and squeeze all the independent and smaller processors off the shelves and out of business. We believe this is the most flagrant restraint of trade device yet conceived" (Gibson).

It is possible that a slotting fee might fall under the legally prohibited conduct of commercial bribery. However, for a successful prosecution for payment of a bribe, the conduct required must be that in which funds are paid by a seller to a buyer solely for the purpose of acquiring a contract or business opportunity (in the case of slotting, a space on the shelf). As noted earlier, however, the reality is that there are costs associated with awarding an item shelf space. If the funds are simply received by the retailer and used for general operating expenses which include advertising, bookkeeping and warehousing, then the notion that a slotting fee is commercial bribery does not fit

---

[3]The cost of shelving is that of the labor and materials involved in simply changing the shelf sign. Shelf fees are typically a minimal amount such as $50 (Hetrick).

[4]Referred to as "prime real estate" in the industry, slotting fees follow a graduated schedule for the locations. Amounts vary according to aisle space. Bread slotting fees are $500–$1000 per bread-type. Ice cream, with one small segment in frozen foods, brings $25,000 per flavor (Greenstein).

[5]No convenience store chains charge slotting fees. However, convenience stores do not warehouse inventory. Manufacturers deliver directly to the convenience stores (Gibson).

Table I. Slotting Fees: Amounts and Terms

Payor	Amount	Terms	Payee
Truzzolino Pizza Roll	$25,000	Chain-Wide	Safeway
Old Capital Microwave Popcorn	$86,000	Chain-Wide for $172,000 of Popcorn	Shoprite Stores
United Brands	$375,000	Frozen Fruit Juicebar	New York City Area Stores
Apple & Eve	$150,000	Fruit Punch Product	Limited Stores in Northeast
Frookies	50¢ per box (Increased Price from $1.79 to $2.29)	Sugar-Free Cookies	100 Stores (Various)
Frito-Lay	$100,000	New Product	Each Grocery Store Chain
Lee's Ice Cream	$25,000 per flavor	Ice Cream	Each Grocery

within the actus reus, or the required conduct, for criminal prosecution.[6]

Another possible question of legality centers around antitrust laws. The question federal or state regulators of anticompetitive behavior have considered is whether slotting fees actually inhibit competition either through the irregularity of the fees and possible price discrimination or through price increases that affect consumers because of these fee arrangements.

The Robinson-Patman Act, which is the federal statute governing issues of price discrimination, was passed in 1936 in response to complaints from suppliers and small, independent grocers about the power of large grocery store chains to exercise purchasing power over suppliers. The result of the purchasing power of the chains was that small, independent grocers paid substantially more for their inventory from suppliers than the large chains, and the suppliers were forced to offer large discounts to the powerful retail chains in order to retain them as customers. The impact on the marketplace was similar to the impact of slotting fees. Large grocery store retailers controlled which products were sold and the prices for the products. In those cases in which retailers refuse to carry a

new product even with slotting fees, a small business can be left with no market access and only the prospect of direct marketing.

The Robinson-Patman Act, enacted as an amendment to section 2 of the Clayton Act, prohibits a person engaged in interstate commerce from discriminating in price between different purchasers of commodities of like grade and quality. There are different categories of Robinson-Patman violations based on the distribution level of the competitor who claims injury. The most common categories are "primary-line" and "secondary-line" violations. Primary-line violations involve direct competitors of the seller who engage in price discrimination in selling to their customers. Secondary-line violations occur when competitors of favored purchasers who buy from the same seller are injured. There are also tertiary-line violations and violations at even more remote levels. Though rare, tertiary-line cases involve customers of the seller's customers. Violations at a fourth, or an even higher level, are possible where a distribution system utilizes four or more levels. While violations of the Robinson-Patman Act can be found at any level of distribution, these classifications are important because the ability to prove competitive injury becomes more difficult as the remoteness of the customer level increases (Aalberts and Juda).

[6]Again, it is important to note that a retailer may also charge an "advertising fee."

Two elements would be required to establish that the payment of differing slotting fees is a violation of Robinson-Patman. First, the federal government, through the Justice Department or Federal Trade Commission (FTC), would need to establish that different fees are charged different sellers by the grocery retailers to the various food manufacturers. Second, the federal government would be required to prove competitive injury at some level in the grocery store distribution chain. The injury in the case of slotting is not primary-line injury, it is either secondary- or tertiary-line injury depending upon whether a wholesaler was present between the manufacturer and the grocery retailer. In most situations, should the FTC decide to pursue a price discrimination case, the proof necessary would be that consumer prices are affected by slotting fees. In the case of the Frookies cookies example, owner Richard Worth has computed the cost figure for slotting fees as 50 cents added to the cost of each box of cookies in order to pay slotting fees.

Aside from the required establishment of the existence of price disparity, section 2(a) of the Robinson-Patman Act also requires that there be some kind of resulting competitive injury. The Act delineates three possible types of injury to competition: 1) a substantial lessening of competition; 2) a tendency to create a monopoly in any line of commerce; and 3) an injury to, or prevention or destruction of, competition with any person who either grants or knowingly receives the benefit of the discrimination, or with customers of either of them. Under the third category of possible injuries to competition, both the sellers who offer discriminatory prices and the preferred buyers who knowingly receive them are guilty of violating the Robinson-Patman Act (Aalberts and Judd).

The establishment of disparity in slotting fees is not sufficient to establish a Robinson-Patman Act violation because proof of the impact of the slotting fees on competition is required: does slotting reduce or eliminate competition? Assuming the government could establish a prima facie case of price discrimination, in the form of differing slotting fees, three defenses are possible. First, retailers could claim that there is a cost justification for the price differential. Second, retailers could argue that there has been a change in conditions and that the cost differential is due to changes in the market, obsolescence, or the perishable nature of the goods. Finally, the retailers could show a discriminatorily

lower price was charged to meet its competitors' price. The obvious defense for slotting differentials would be the explanation often advanced as to why Procter & Gamble and Campbell's soup pay no slotting fees: their advertising is pervasive and effective. (Interviews) The differentials in fees could also be tied to and justified by the amount of the manufacturer's ad budget. Nonetheless, it is clear that competition in the food manufacturing industry is lessening (Greenwald). The predominance of national products on the shelves is indicative of the power of those able to pay slotting fees.

One of Congress' original purposes in passing the Robinson-Patman Act was to regulate large retailers' promotional services. Prior to the Act's passage, retailers frequently used promotional schemes to shift to their vendors a substantial amount of their own advertising costs. Meanwhile, many smaller retail competitors, who did not have the market presence to make such demands on their vendors, were at a competitive disadvantage. Still, the defenses to Robinson-Patman permit cost-justified price disparity.

Robinson-Patman Act violations are not pursued aggressively, and when cases are litigated, they encounter a judicial environment which construes the antitrust statutes very narrowly. Perhaps the judicial precedent that comes closest to paralleling the slotting fee arrangement is *Grand Union Co. v. FTC*[7] in which ad fees varied for referrals.

In *Grand Union,* the defendant was a supermarket chain that entered into an agreement with an advertising firm. The agreement provided that Grand Union would lease space on a sign located on Broadway in New York's Times Square for a nominal fee. As part of the agreement, Grand Union was required to solicit several of its suppliers to advertise on the sign. In exchange for soliciting these suppliers, Grand Union received substantial cash payments and free advertising from the advertising firm. The court found that Grand Union's actions violated the Robinson-Patman Act and the Federal Trade Commission Act which prohibits generically unfair competition. The court reasoned that, in effect, the payments received by Grand Union lowered the cost of the supplies it purchased from the participating advertisers. Therefore, Grand Union received an unfair advantage over its retail competitors in direct contravention of the purpose of Robinson-Patman.

[7]300 F.2d 92 (2d Cir. 1962).

While the Justice Department is currently examining slotting fee practices, particularly as they relate to the market power of snack maker Frito-Lay, there is a hesitancy on the part of the FTC to get involved in the issue. When shown a video tape in which an entrepreneur was not even required to bring his product (barbecue sauce) for tasting by a grocery retailer but rather required only to pay a slotting fee, FTC official William Baer noted, "My job as a federal antitrust official is not to require supermarkets to taste barbecue sauce. The question is, do these slotting allowances really drive prices up for consumers? If they don't, and I'm saying I don't see any evidence that they do, although we're open to looking at it, then I'm not sure there's a problem" (Ross).

IV. *The Ethical Issues of Slotting*

With the complex legal issues and elements of proof required to establish criminal or antitrust violations in slotting it remains doubtful that there will be a legal resolution or regulation of the practice. However, the issue of whether slotting fees are ethical remains. To formulate an answer to that question, there are three impacts slotting fees have had that should be considered: the impact of slotting on the atmosphere of wholesale/retail interaction; the impact of slotting on market access; and the impact of slotting on consumers, both in the price they pay for the goods and in their perception of the fairness of these fee arrangements.

A. THE IMPACT OF SLOTTING ON THE ATMOSPHERE OF THE WHOLESALER/RETAILER RELATIONSHIP

Regardless of legalities, the use of slotting fees creates an atmosphere of mistrust and a breeding ground for other unethical and illegal conduct. It is unclear how slotting payments are made and where the payments are reported. Many small business owners report that the payments they make to grocery retailers must be made in cash (Ross). Some owners report that payments are made in cash to both the chain and to individual store managers. The atmospheric result is that there are large amounts of cash changing hands among sellers, managers and purchasers. The former CEO of Harvest Foods, a food retailer in the South, has been indicted on charges of bribery and other related offenses for the alleged receipt of hundreds of thousands of dollars in cash for slotting fees (Ross). If the grocery retailers' claims about costs and the need for advertising justify the slotting fees, then those fees should be paid legitimately and reflected on retailer's books as revenues offset by costs for those uses designated for that product such as inventory costs, advertising costs, and warehousing fees.

Because slotting fees are non-uniform and even non-universal, it is impossible to understand how the fee structure works, how much the fees should be, and whether the fees are actually related to the costs incurred by retailers in getting a new product to the shelf. The secretive and inconsistent nature of slotting fees and their payment in cash creates an atmosphere similar to that in drug trade.[8] Market entry rights are unclear, fees change, not everyone is permitted to buy into the system and the use and declaration of revenues is unknown. In at least four reports on the practice of slotting fees, parties on both sides referred to slotting as the grocery industry's "dirty little secret." Cost recoupment, the public airing of the fees, and public accounting disclosures should be a natural business function if the purposes the retailers offer as explanations for slotting are in fact a reality. The secrecy of the fees and the industry's unwillingness to discuss or disclose them raises the ongoing question of their legitimacy. Continued operation under the present rules invites the presence of an atmosphere of deceit, collusion and possible illicit activity.

B. THE IMPACT OF SLOTTING ON MARKET ACCESS

From the cost figures offered in Table I, it is safe to conclude that slotting fees could make market entry prohibitive for many small companies. In some instances, fees have gone beyond the initial slotting costs with some grocery chains now demanding up to $40,000 per year for a company to maintain just a square foot of retail space for its product. Even some of the larger companies have

---

[8]The authors could find only three manufacturers willing to discuss their personal experiences with slotting fees or industry practices. Retribution (i.e., denial of retail access) was cited as the reason for their reluctance. These three manufacturers spoke on condition of anonymity. Two other manufacturers, Richard Worth (Frookies) and Scott Garfield (Lee's Ice Cream) have been public in their discussion of slotting fees. Grocery retailers referred all questions to legal counsel or corporate officers who declined to be interviewed.

difficulty competing because of the large fees. Frito-Lay recently purchased Anheuser-Busch's Eagle Snacks after Anheuser had spent over $500 million trying to increase its 17% market share (Greenwald). Frito-Lay now holds 55% of the snack market and pays the largest slotting fees in the grocery industry. Borden ended its foray into the snack market in 1995, and barely survived before it did so. Nearly 30 regional snack companies have gone out of business in the last three years. A vice-president of Clover Club Foods, a Utah-based snack company, believes Frito-Lay's goal is to be the only salted-snack food company in the country (Gibson). The Independent Baker's Association has described the current situation with slotting fees as being "out of control" (BNA).

If Frito-Lay becomes the only salted-snack company in the United States because of "superior skill, foresight and industry" as the antitrust laws describe and as a capitalistic system encourages, then there are neither legal nor ethical issues. If, however, Frito-Lay becomes the only salted-snack company in the United States because it is best able to pay slotting fees or offers more in the way of slotting fees than any other company, then ethical, legal and economic questions emerge.

The practice of slotting in the grocery industry is symptomatic of the blurry lines used to distinguish bribes from "advertising fees," "access charges," or "facilitation payments." In various situations, payments that are perhaps a form of bribery have been statutorily sanctioned through sophisticated differentiations between true bribes and similar activities described in more artful terms such as facilitation payments or gratuities. Attempts to distinguish fees paid to buyers beyond the cost of the goods or services sold from bribes have been an ongoing exercise in the fields of law and ethics. For example, the Foreign Corrupt Practices Act (FCPA) makes "bribes" illegal but "grease payments" acceptable (FCPA).

Perhaps what is problematic about slotting fees is their ready acceptance as a way of doing business. In its handbook for stockholders in 1997, the international public accounting firm of Deloitte and Touche recommends that shareholders of food brokers, wholesalers and retailers ask the following series of questions at annual meetings.

> With respect to "shelving allowances" (money paid by vendors to obtain shelf space for products),

> . . . Are those allowances legal?
> . . . How much does the company realize from the allowance payments?
> . . . What has been done to maximize this income?

The sole criterion for evaluation is whether the payments are legal. Once that threshold test is satisfied, the company's goal, according to an audit firm, should be to maximize income from this activity. If the directive from those who audit public companies is to find ways for grocery retailers to increase slotting fees, the atmosphere within the industry takes on the characteristics a of market controlled by forces other than direct competition between products.

Manufacturers have experienced increased costs as a result of slotting fees. For consumers, the increased cost is not a guarantee of quality. The presence of products in stores is not a response to consumers' demands or even food manufacturers' (through advertising) created demand. Retailers are not necessarily offering those products most in demand or of highest quality. Retailers and manufacturers, through highly secretive bidding wars, determine both product availability and price. Product demand or quality is not part of the decision-making process; it is the ability to pay or pay more in fees that controls product availability.

It is impossible to determine the extent of the impact slotting fees have on small manufacturers and innovation. The ripple effect is likewise difficult to gauge. There are perceptions slotting fees create that are perhaps barriers to entry. The belief that there can be no new successful entrants into a particular industry or market has an impact on investment decisions. Further, marketing plans are based on the assumption that demand can fuel the product's presence on the shelf and eventually its sale. The fact that grocery retailers control a new entrant's success or failure is nearly a repeat of the monopolization era that preceded the federal antitrust laws.

Even the belief that a new and better product cannot be introduced without payment to buyers has an impact beyond just the product and consumer cost issues. A system in which payments control market access thwarts competition, encourages mediocrity and discourages innovation. Frito-Lay may have the best products on the market, but that conclusion should result from head-to-head competition and not from Frito-Lay's ability to pay retailers the highest fees in the industry. The eventual result in all industries in which fees beyond contract price are demanded is that large companies thrive while consumer choices are limited and their demands are less of a factor in the retailers' purchasing decisions.

C. THE IMPACT OF SLOTTING ON CONSUMERS

Apart from the higher prices consumers must pay in order for manufacturers to pay slotting fees, there is the problem of removal of the consumer from the loop. The principle of supply and demand is circumvented through a process controlled by the question, "What will it take to get and keep my shelf space?" It is no longer an issue of whether the consumer wants the product. Product availability is dictated by fees and consumers purchase what is available. With choices dictated, the market is controlled because consumers do not move from store to store looking for products. Substitution is a readily available solution for consumers in products with high frequency purchase rates. Elasticity of demand is high in most grocery store sale items and among grocery store shoppers. Further, prices for those items are then controlled by those who can pay the ever-increasing fees and still survive. In both choices and price, consumers are affected when slotting fees become the determinant of retail availability.

V. Conclusions and Recommendations

In January of 1996, grocery retailers formed an ethics committee for the first time in the organization's history. The charge to the committee was to review the industry practice of slotting fees. Many in the industry hold the belief that the fees do not present legal or ethical issues, but rather demonstrate that the most efficient marketers are able to capture shelf space and hence markets. Most grocery retailers continue to believe the fees are cost-based and cost-justified.

One suggestion offered for solving the need for slotting fees is to establish an improved system of test marketing. A product that is successful in testing would not require retailers to absorb risks or costs of failure. Such a system, however, is cum-

bersome and slow. Slotting fees are a much more manageable method of making product decisions as well as a means for shifting risk.

The industry practice of slotting introduces new questions into the dilemma of whether businesses have moral responsibilities. The traditional Friedman notion is that businesses should obey the law and make a profit and that any voluntary self-regulatory conduct beyond that is a violation of the corporate manager's responsibility to shareholders (Friedman, 1970). However, the additional question to be posed to this economics-based role of business is, what response should businesses have to conduct that is legal but that impairs market function? In the case of slotting fees, it is not immediately clear to market regulators that there is a statutory level violation, but economic theory would hold that market access is controlled by something other than quality or demand. Using Fieser's fairness principle, the control of access by the ability to pay slotting fees is unethical because it denies opportunities to businesses without review of the product (Fieser, 1996). In the more specific autonomy principle offered by Fieser, the use of slotting fees results in business infringement of "rationally reflective choices of people." Product choices are made not by consumer demand but by grocery retailer fee arrangements. Further, under either the contractarian or majority endorsement views of moral obligation, the beliefs of consumers 1) that they should have access to available goods, and 2) that their demand for those goods should dictate their availability are easily supportable. Slotting presents an issue of ethical uniqueness in business in that while we may differ on the absolute legal issues surrounding these fees, we may have agreement on the ethical issues because of their market impact.

Regardless of the cost and motivation issues, there are simple changes that could be made to eliminate the atmospheric and economic issues the secretive nature of slotting fees creates. First, the fees should be: 1) tied to cost; 2) published; and 3) uniform in application. The wide variances in fees and the failure to reveal those fees serve to create the atmosphere of distrust and contribute to the perception that innovation and new products cannot infiltrate the retail grocery industry. Second, the fees should not be accepted in cash and should be specifically accounted for on the books of retailers as advertising advances, posting fees, or in any other category of revenue for which the retailer is using the fees. Separate fees for slot maintenance or "dud" fees for products that fail should also be disclosed and specifically accounted for. If the costs associated with slotting a new product are legitimate, the disclosure of fees obtained should not be difficult or painful.

It is not unusual in the field of business ethics for disclosure to be the resolution of a dilemma. For example, a drug may be helpful in the treatment of a disease but may also have significant and perhaps painful side effects. It is not the sale of the drug that is unethical. It is the sale of the drug without disclosure of the side effects that presents the ethical violation. A system for slotting fees that is public and uniform would restore trust at both the customer and economic levels. Even one retailer's published schedule of fees would be preferable to the current market surreptitiousness.

Grocery shelf space might seem insignificant in the grand scheme of world economics. But it is symptomatic of the ever-growing tolerance of doing whatever it will take to do business. Market access based on bribes shakes the very foundations of free enterprise. The world of commerce might survive without Frookies and Lee's Ice Cream. But it cannot survive if Frookies is not given the chance to succeed or fail alongside Nabisco's Oreos, and Lee's can't compete side by side with Ben & Jerry's and Haagen-Daz.

References

Aalberts, R. J. and L. Lynn Judd: 1991, "Slotting in the Retail Grocery Business: Does It Violate the Public Policy Goal of Protecting Business Against Price Discrimination?" *DePaul Law Review* **40**, 397–416.

Deloitte Touche: 1997, Questions at Stockholders' Meeting.

Fiser, J.: 1996, "Do Businesses Have Moral Obligations Beyond What the Law Requires?" *Journal of Business Ethics,* April, 457–468.

Foreign Corrupt Practices Act: 1997, 15 U.S.C. § 78m(b).

Friedman, M.: 1970, "The Social Responsibility of Business Is to Increase Its Profits," *The New York Times Magazine,* Sept. 13, 32–33, 122–126.

Gibson, R.: 1988, "Supermarkets Demand Food Firms' Payments Just to Get on the Shelf," *Wall Street Journal,* Nov. 1, A1 and A14.

Grand Union v. FTC, 300 F.2d 92 (2d Cir. 1962).

Greenstein, J.: 1995, "Battle for Shelf Space Puts Publishers in Financial Bind," *Video Business* **15** (26), 42.

Greenwald, J.: 1996, "Frito-Lay Under Snack Attack," *Time,* June 30, 62–63.

Hetrick, Ross: 1995, "Ice Cream Firm Frozen," *Baltimore Sun,* Sept. 25, 13C.

Interviews with manufacturers and retailers conducted from 1995–1997. The authors pledged anonymity to these sources.

Laczniak, G.: 1983, "Business Ethics: A Managers' Primer," *Business,* Jan. 23–29.

"Policy Hearings Shift Focus to FTC Impact on Small Business": 1995, *BNA Antitrust and Trade Regulation Report* **69** (1738), 581.

Ross, B.: 1995, "Money Talks," *20/20,* Nov. 10, Transcript #1545.

Somervill, Sean: 1996, "High Price of Shelf Space," *Baltimore Sun,* 10 [sic], 4D.

Questions for Chapter 10

1. On what basis does Larmer distinguish between bribes and tips? Why does he view tips as morally unproblematic? Might there be moral problems associated with the practice of tipping? If so, what are they?
2. What is the difference between extortion and bribery?
3. How does Steidlmeier suggest one distinguish between a legitimate gift and an unacceptable bribe?
4. Discuss Steidlmeier's concept of "negotiating leverage." What practical considerations does he discuss in building such leverage?
5. In what sense, if any, is slotting unfair to the consumer?

6. Is it moral to use the willingness to pay large slotting fees as a means to crowd out smaller competitors? Defend your answer.

Case 10.1 A Fair Price for Tobacco?[1]

In the mid-1980s William Lamb and Carmon Willis, both tobacco growers in Kentucky, brought suit against Phillip Morris, Inc., and B.A.T. Industries, alleging that these companies had violated federal antitrust laws and the Foreign Corrupt Practices Act. The basis of their suit was that Phillip Morris and B.A.T., who buy tobacco not only from Kentucky growers but from foreign producers, had, through subsidiaries, entered into a contract with La Fundacion Del Nino (the Children's Foundation) of Caracas, Venezuela. The contract was signed by the Foundation's president, the wife of the then president of Venezuela, and under its terms the subsidiaries were to make periodic donations to the Children's Foundation totaling approximately $12.5 million dollars. In addition

to tax deductions for the donations, the subsidiaries received guarantees of price controls on Venezuelan tobacco, the elimination of controls on retail cigarette prices in Venezuela, and assurances that existing tax rates to tobacco companies would not increase. Lamb and Willis claimed that similar contracts had been arranged by Phillip Morris and B.A.T. in Argentina, Brazil, Costa Rica, Mexico, and Nicaragua. They asserted that such contracts amount to unlawful inducements designed to restrain trade and result in manipulation of tobacco prices to the detriment of domestic growers.

1. Is there anything immoral in companies signing contracts such as those signed by the subsidiaries of Phillip Morris, Inc., and B.A.T. Industries?

2. Would you classify such contracts as bribes? Why or why not?

[1]Based on Lamb v. Phillip Morris, Inc., as found in 915 *Federal Reporter,* 2nd series, 1024, (6th Cir. 1990).

Case 10.2 An Influential Friend[2]

In October 1986 Metropolitan Inc. was awarded a $38 million contract whereby it became the exclusive supplier of diesel fuel for the Chicago Transit Authority's (CTA's) vehicles. It won the contract by agreeing to give the CTA substantial discounts if fuel invoices were paid for within specified time periods and by agreeing to meet the CTA's Minority Business Requirement by employing a minority-run subcontracting firm.

Metropolitan entered into the contract believing that the CTA would not find it possible to pay its fuel bills promptly enough to entitle it to the agreed-upon discounts. Unfortunately for Metropolitan, this did not prove to be the case, and the company began losing money on its sales to the CTA. In an effort to remedy this, Metropolitan began to send the invoices late in order to prevent the CTA from taking advantage of the discount and, when this did not work, artificially inflated the invoices so that the CTA would still pay full price even after the discount had been applied.

[2]Based on United States v. Medley as found in 913 *Federal Reporter,* 2nd series, 1248 (7th Cir. 1990).

The CTA, becoming suspicious, launched an investigation. This alarmed Metropolitan's head, Brian Flisk, who then contacted Howard Medley, a member of the CTA's board of directors. During the subsequent conversation concerning the CTA investigation, Medley indicated to Flisk that he (Medley) would stand to gain a $300,000 commission if he were to sell a warehouse for some friends. Flisk indicated he was prepared to enter into negotiations for the warehouse, since Medley was helping him with the CTA investigation. At the time this took place a CTA ethics regulation explicitly prohibited board members from doing business with CTA vendors.

The CTA's investigation resulted in a report documenting Metropolitan's billing irregularities and raised questions about whether the subcontracting firm was a legitimate minority enterprise or a fraudulent pass-through corporation. Despite the fact that other board members spoke in favor of terminating Metropolitan's contract, and despite the fact that Metropolitan never satisfactorily answered the report's allegations,

Medley strongly defended Metropolitan and no action was taken by the board.

A short while later, a second investigation was undertaken by the CTA. The report arising from it indicated numerous problems with the quality of the diesel fuel being sold by Metropolitan. At Flisk's request, Medley again intervened and was again successful in preventing the termination of Metropolitan's contract.

1. Suppose Flisk thought the warehouse deal was a good deal entirely on its own merits, but was also aware that buying the warehouse would influence Medley's decisions in his favor. Would there be anything wrong in Flisk's pursuing the deal? Would pursuing the deal constitute offering a bribe?

2. Suppose Medley actively pursued Flisk and suggested that Flisk's problems could be solved through an appropriate "donation." Would Flisk be morally wrong to provide such a "donation?" Explain.

Further Readings for Chapter 10

Arnold Berleant, "Multinationals, Local Practice, and the Problem of Ethical Consistency," *Journal of Business Ethics,* 1(3), August 1982, pp. 185–193.

Tom Carson, "Bribery, Extortion, and the Foreign Corrupt Practices Act," *Philosophy and Public Affairs,* 14(1), Winter 1985, pp. 66–90.

John Danley, "Toward a Theory of Bribery," *Business and Professional Ethics Journal,* 2(3), pp. 19–39. (Note that *Business and Professional Ethics Journal,* 3(1), pp. 80–86, contained commentaries on Danley's article by Scott Turow and Kendall D'Andrade.)

INFOTRAC COLLEGE EDITION To learn more about the topics from this chapter, you can use the following words to conduct an electronic search on InfoTrac College Edition, an online library of journals. Here you will find a multitude of articles from various sources and perspectives: *www.infotrac-college.com/wadsworth/access.html*

bribery

extortion

slotting

Chapter 11

Advertising
and Marketing

Introduction

CHAPTER 11 MARKS A SHIFT in focus from the relationship between employer and employee to the relationship between business and consumer. We begin our examination of the ethical issues associated with this relationship by considering some of the ethical concerns associated with advertising and marketing.

Advertising is frequently defended on the grounds that the exchange of information is a necessary condition of an efficient free market. The free market, it is argued, provides optimal benefit to society. Customers will not buy unless they see the purchase as worthwhile and sellers will not sell unless they make a profit. Sellers who ask too high a price will find themselves undercut by competitors who realize they can sell the product for a cheaper price and still make a profit. At least in theory, this process goes on until the product is sold at the lowest possible price that still enables the seller to realize a profit.

In order for this process to work, there must be access to information. If advertising were not available, consumers would find it difficult to become aware of significant new products or compare the merits of competing products. One consequence would be that many new products would fail simply because there was no effective way for consumers to become aware of them. Another consequence would be that manufacturers would find it hard to capture large enough consumer bases to lower production costs.

The biggest problem with this argument is that it largely misses the point. However sound a defense of advertising as conveying information, it fails to address the issue that most advertising seems to be not primarily an attempt to present information, but rather an attempt to persuade or influence consumers. In many instances, little or no relevant information is presented to the consumer. Questions concerning the moral legitimacy of advertising must focus, therefore, not simply on the necessity of exchanging information in the marketplace, but on the techniques of persuasion advertisers typically employ.

Moving from advertising to marketing, we also meet ethical concerns. The principle of *caveat emptor,* that is, let the buyer beware, is widely appealed to, but how should this principle be understood and what is its application? Pointing to the responsibility of the purchaser to exercise due diligence scarcely resolves the question of what are the moral responsibilities of the seller. What, for instance, are the responsibilities of the salesperson in relation to informing the purchaser whether the product genuinely meets his or her needs? When does the legitimate practice of presenting a product in a positive light cross over into deception? These are not easy questions, but they are important concerns that cannot be resolved simply by appealing to the principle of *caveat emptor.*

What does seem clear, with regard to both advertising and marketing, is that these activities cannot be evaluated solely in terms of their effectiveness in generating sales. Both advertising and marketing depend on society's permission and support to occur. They are, therefore, at least to some extent, subject to the moral expectations of society. This means that in addition to their effect on the bottom line, they must also be evaluated in terms of the goals of the society in which they take place. At the very least, they must not be seen to subvert those societal goals. Given the value society places on individual autonomy, marketing practices that undermine the consumer's capacity to make free and informed decisions seem morally questionable.

Our first two selections by Tibor Machan and John Waide focus on moral questions raised by advertising's emphasis on persuasion. In his article "Advertising: The Whole or Only Some of the Truth?," Machan criticizes the assumption that advertising's primary purposes should be to convey information and provide help to consumers. He defends the doctrine of *caveat emptor,* suggesting that, so long as an advertiser does not deceive the customer, he or she has acted ethically. An advertiser has no duty to provide further information that will help the customer make a reasoned decision, for example, that the product is obsolete or the price has been grossly inflated.

Machan appeals to the concepts of rational expectations and essential properties in deciding what information must be revealed and what information may be withheld. In his view, a customer is entitled to expect that a product fulfill its function, for example, it is essential that an electric kettle be able to heat water. It would be deceptive for an advertiser or salesperson to withhold the information that a particular kettle or type of electric kettle was incapable of heating water. It is not, however, an essential property of an electric kettle that it be less expensive than other models or that it do as good a job at heating water. It would not, therefore, be deceptive to withhold the information that a particular kettle or type of kettle was more expensive or heated water less efficiently than its competitors.

In support of his view, Machan espouses a form of egoism that he terms classical. Appealing to Aristotle, he suggests that each individual should seek to promote his or her interests as a human being and an individual. He argues that we need not fear that such an egoism implies the permissibility of lying or cheating as sales practices, since such activities cannot be seen as fulfilling human nature and thus promoting one's interests as a human being.

In "The Making of Self and World in Advertising," John Waide criticizes the practice of marketing products by associating them with deep nonmarket desires (e.g., friendship) that they cannot possibly fulfill. He finds such associative advertising morally problematic on two counts. First, because the desire to sell the product is largely independent of a sincere concern to improve the life of the consumer, associative advertising undermines in its practitioners the concern and sympathy that are essential to moral virtue. Second, insofar as it is effective, it leads consumers to substitute market goods for the development of virtues. Associating friendship with the type of beer one drinks or the brand of mouthwash one uses devalues the development of virtues such as empathy and loyalty that are the true basis of friendship. In Waide's view, the central issue is not whether the consumer in some sense retains autonomy, but whether, in order to sell a product, it is morally desirable to encourage individuals to live lives in which the development of character and virtue is hindered or undermined. Although Waide makes no explicit reference to Aristotle, his emphasis on the development of character and virtue is certainly in the Aristotelian tradition. A question worth pondering is whether Waide's position is consistent with the *caveat emptor* approach taken by Machan, who also claims to find his inspiration in Aristotle, and, if not, which writer more accurately reflects Aristotle's ethical thinking.

Our final two articles focus on issues of sales, both at the level of corporate pricing of products and the level of decisions facing individual salespersons. In their article "Blind Man's Bluff: The Ethics of Quantity Surcharges," Omprakash Gupta and Anna Rominger explore the practice of charging higher unit prices for a larger rather than smaller quantity of the same brand and product. They note that, although various reasons are given for this practice, including human error, the demarketing of goods in scarce supply, and the effect of promotional specials, quantity surcharges are more likely to occur on products that are generally in demand and that consumers like to buy in larger packages. They also note that quantity surcharges are more apt to occur when it is difficult for the consumer to make price comparisons.

It is hard to avoid the conclusion that retailers are taking advantage of the belief that bigger is cheaper. Many products are in fact cheaper when bought in bulk, and consumers are aware that more resources and labor are required to produce and stock the same amount of product in smaller packages than in larger packages. Given that it costs the producer less to market larger quantities, the widespread assumption on the part of consumers is that it will be cheaper to buy in quantity.

At the present time, neither the Food and Drug Administration (FDA) nor the Federal Trade Commission (FTC) has attempted to regulate quantity surcharges. This means no civil suits for misrepresentation can take place. The fact that, at present, quantity surcharges pose no legal risks and that consumers generally remain unaware of their effect hardly settles the ethical questions that arise. Quantity surcharges occur over a wide range of goods and in some cases increase the unit price of the product by over 50 percent. On what basis can such price increases be ethically justified, and on what basis can retailers withhold information concerning the extent of such surcharges?

In our final reading, "Ethical Issues in Sales: Two Case Studies," Thomas Carson explores some of the ethical issues that arise at the individual level in sales. He does this by exploring two cases. The first case, that of a shoe salesperson, explores the issue of what constitutes deception and under what circumstances deception might be considered justified. The second case, that of an insurance salesperson, explores the question of what it means to employ proper and legitimate means in the selling of a product such as insurance. Both cases vividly illustrate the practical complexities of acting ethically.

Advertising: The Whole or Only Some of the Truth?

TIBOR R. MACHAN

WHEN COMMERCIAL ADVERTISING is criticized, often some assumption surfaces that should be explored more fully. I have in mind in particular the hidden premises that advertising is first and foremost a means for conveying information. Another assumption which lingers in the background of criticisms of advertising is that ethics requires that those who sell goods and services should first of all help customers.

My aim here is to defend the approach to advertising that does not require of merchants that they tell all. So long as merchants are honest, do not mislead or deceive, they are acting in a morally satisfactory manner. It is not good for them—and there is nothing in morality that requires it of them—to take up the task of informing consumers of the conditions most favorable to them in the market place, to aid them in their efforts to find the best deal.

The following passage will help introduce us to the topic. It illustrates the kind of views that many philosophers who work in the field of business ethics seem to find convincing.

> Merchants and producers have many ways of concealing truth from the customers—not by lying to them, but simply by not telling them facts that are relevant to the question of whether they ought to purchase a particular product or whether they are receiving full value for their money.[1]

[1]Burton Leiser, "Deceptive Practices in Advertising," in Tom L. Beauchamp and Norman Bowie (eds.), *Ethical Theory and Business* (Englewood Cliffs: Prentice-Hall, 1979), p. 479. Leiser's rendition of this view is perhaps the most extreme. Others have put the matter more guardedly, focusing more on the kind of suppression that conceals generally harmful aspects of products than on failure to inform the public of its comparative disadvantage vis a vis similar or even identical substitutes. Yet the general statements of the ethical point, in contrast to the examples cited, are very close to Leiser's own. See, e.g., Vincent Barry, *Moral Issues in Business* (Belmont: Wadsworth Publishing Company, 1983), Chapter 8. Barry chides advertisers for concealing "a fact . . . when its availability would probably make the desire,

The author goes on to state that "it is certainly unethical for (salesmen and businessmen) to fail to tell their customers that they are not getting full value for their money"[2] He cites David Ogilvy, a successful advertiser, admitting that "he is 'continuously guilty' of *suppressio veri,* the suppression of the truth."[3] In other words, what advertisers do ethically or morally wrong is to fail to tell all, the whole truth, when they communicate to others about their wares, services, goods, products, or what not.

Yet there is something unrealistic, even farfetched, about this line of criticism. To begin with, even apart from advertising, people often enough advance a biased perspective on themselves, their skills, looks, and so on. When we go out on a first date, we tend to deck ourselves out in a way that certainly highlights what we consider our assets and diminishes our liabilities. When we send out our resumes in our job search efforts, we hardly tell all. When we just dress for the normal day, we tend to choose garb that enhances our looks and covers up what is not so attractive about our whole selves.

Burton Leiser, the critic we have been using to illustrate the prevailing view of advertising, is not wholly unaware of these points, since he continues with his quotation from Ogilvy, who says, "Surely it is asking too much to expect the advertiser to describe the shortcomings of his product. One must be forgiven for 'putting one's best foot forward.'" To this Leiser exclaims, "So the consumer is *not* to be told all the relevant information; he is *not* to be given all the facts that would be of assistance in making a reasonable decision about a given purchase. . . ."[4] Nevertheless, Leiser does not tell us what is ethically wrong in such instances of *suppressio veri.* In fact, the claim that in all advertising one must present the whole truth, not just

purchase, or use of the product less likely than in its absence" (p. 278).
[2]Leiser, op. cit.
[3]Ibid., p. 484.
[4]Ibid., p. 479

be truthful about one's subject matter, presupposes the very problematic ethical view that one ought to devote oneself *primarily* to bettering the lot of other people. What commerce rests on ethically, implicitly or explicitly, is the very different doctrine of *caveat emptor* (let him [the purchaser] beware), which assumes that prudence is a virtue and should be practiced by all, including one's customers. I will argue here that the merchant's ethical stance is more reasonable than that of the critics.

I. The Vice of Suppressio Veri

Leiser and many others critical of business and sales practices assume that in commercial transactions persons owe others the whole truth and nothing but the truth. This is why they believe that merchants act unethically in failing to tell their customers something that customers might ask about if they would only think of everything relevant to their purchasing activities. Leiser gives a good example:

> Probably the most common deception of this sort is price deception, the technique some high-pressure salesmen use to sell their goods by grossly inflating their prices to two, three, and even four times their real worth. Again, there may be no "untruth" In what they say; but they conceal the important fact that the same product, or one nearly identical to it, can be purchased for far less at a department or appliance store. . . .[5]

Before I discuss the ethical points in these remarks, a word, first, about the alleged simplicity of learning whether some item for sale by a merchant is in fact available for purchase "for far less" elsewhere. The idea is, we may take it, that the customer will indeed obtain what he or she wants by purchasing this item from some other seller. This ignores the fact that it may be quite important for customers to purchase some items in certain places, in certain kinds of environments, even from certain types of persons (e.g., ones with good manners). Sheer accessibility can be crucial, as well as atmosphere, the merchant's demeanor, and so on. If it is legitimate for customers to seek satisfaction

from the market, it is also legitimate to seek various combinations of satisfaction, not simply product or price satisfaction.

Let us, however, assume that a customer could have obtained all that she wanted by going elsewhere to purchase the item at a price "far less" than what it costs at a given merchant's store. Is there a responsibility on the merchant's part (if she knows this) to make the information available to the customer? Or even more demandingly, is it ethically required that the merchant become informed about these matters and convey the information to potential customers?

The answer depends on a broader ethical point. What are the standards by which human beings should conduct themselves, including in their relationship to others? If something on the order of the altruist's answer is correct, then, in general, *suppressio veri* is wrongful. Telling the whole truth would help other people in living a good human life. Altruism here means not the ideal of equal respect for everyone as a human being, advocated by Thomas Nagel.[6] Rather it is the earlier sense of having one's primary duty to advance the interest of others.[7] A merchant need not be disrespectful toward his customers by not informing them of something that perhaps they ought to have learnt in the first place. By volunteering information that quite conceivably a customer should, as a matter of his personal moral responsibility (as a prudent individual), have obtained, a merchant might be meddling in matters not properly his own, which could be demeaning.

But an altruism in terms of which one is responsible to seek and obtain the well-being of his fellow human beings would render *suppressio veri* morally wrong. Such an altruism is certainly widely advocated, if not by philosophers then at least by political reformers. For example, Karl Marx states, in one of his earliest writings, that "The main

[5]Ibid., p. 481.

[6]Thomas Nagel, *The Possibility of Altruism* (Oxford: Clarendon Press, 1970).
[7]This is the sense of the term as it occurs in the writings of August Comte who reportedly coined it. Thus the *Oxford English Dictionary* reports that the term was "introduced into English by the translators and expounders of Comte," e.g., Lewes, *Comte's Philosophy*, Sc. 1. xxi. 224: "Dispositions influenced by the purely egotistic impulses we call popularly 'bad,' and apply the term 'good' to those in which altruism predominates" (1853), *The Compact Edition*, 65.

principle . . . which must guide us in the selection of a vocation is the welfare of humanity . . ." and that "man's nature makes it possible for him to reach his fulfillment only by working for the perfection and welfare of his society."[8] Here he states precisely the morality of altruism initially espoused by August Comte, who coined the term itself and developed the secular "religion" by which to promote the doctrine.[9]

Now only by the ethics of altruism does it follow unambiguously that a merchant who does not tell all "is certainly unethical." Neither the more common varieties of utilitarianism, nor Kant's theory, as it is often understood, implies this. If we are to live solely to do good for others, then when we have reason to believe that telling the whole truth will promote others' well-being (without thwarting the well-being of yet some other person), we morally ought to tell the whole truth to this person. So when a merchant has reason to believe that telling his customer about lower prices elsewhere (for goods which he sells at higher price) will benefit his customer, he ought morally to do so.

But for it to be established that this is what a merchant ought morally to do for any customer, and that not doing so "is certainly unethical," the sort of altruism Marx and Comte defended would have to be true. No other ethical viewpoint seems to give solid support to the above claim about what "is certainly unethical."

Still, might one perhaps be able to show the whole truth thesis correct by other means than depending on a strong altruistic moral framework? Not very plausibly.

Intuitionism, as generally understood, would not override the well entrenched belief that when one embarks on earning a living and deals with perfect strangers, one should *not* promote one's

weaknesses, one should *not* volunteer information detrimental to one's prospects. I doubt anyone would seriously advise job seeking philosophers to list on their C.V.s rejected articles and denied promotions—that would be counterintuitive.

It is also doubtful that most versions of utilitarianism would support a very strong general principle of self-sacrifice from which it can be shown that it "is certainly unethical" not to tell the whole truth. There could be many good utilitarian reasons to support at least a substantial degree of *caveat emptor* in the marketplace. For example, if the classical and neo-classical defenses—and the Marxian explanation of the temporary necessity—of the unregulated market of profit seeking individuals have any merit, it is for utilitarian reasons that the competitive, self-interested conduct of market agents should be encouraged. This would preclude giving away information free of charge, as a matter of what is right from a utilitarian perspective of maximizing the good of society, which in this case would be wealth.

Even a Kantian deontological ethics, as generally understood, advises against taking over what is very plausibly another person's moral responsibility, namely, seeking out the knowledge to act prudently and wisely. The Kantian idea of moral autonomy may not require seeking one's personal happiness in life, as the Aristotelian concept of the good moral life does, but it does 'require leaving matters of morality to the discretion of the agent. Meddling with the agent's moral welfare would conceivably be impermissibly intrusive. By reference to the categorical imperative it is difficult to imagine why one should invite commercial failure in one's market transactions, a failure that is surely possible if one is occupied not with promoting one's success but with the success of one's potential customers.

It seems then, that the altruist ethics, which makes it everyone's duty to further the interests of other people, is indeed the most plausible candidate for making it "certainly unethical" to suppress the truth in commercial transactions. Yet, of course, troubles abound with altruism proper.

When properly universalized, as all *bona fide* moralities must be, the doctrine in effect obligates everyone to refuse any help extended. Such a robust form of altruism creates a veritable daisy-chain of self-sacrifice. None is left to be the beneficiary of human action. Perhaps, therefore, what

---

[8]Loyd D. Easton and Kurt H. Guddat (eds.), *Writings of the Young Marx on Philosophy and Society* (Garden City: Anchor Books, 1967), p. 39. See, for a recent statement, W. G. Maclagan, "Self and Others: A Defense of Altruism," *The Philosophical Quarterly,* vol. 4 (1954), pp. 109–27. As Maclagan states it, "I call my view 'altruism' *assuming* a duty to relieve the distress and promote the happiness of our fellows." He adds that such a view requires "that a man may and should discount altogether his own pleasure or happiness as such when he is deciding what course of action to pursue" (p. 110).

[9]Wilhelm Windelband, *A History of Philosophy,* Vol. II (New York: Harper Torchbooks, 1968), pp. 650ff.

should be considered is a less extreme form of altruism, one which obligates everyone to be helpful whenever he or she has good reason to think that others would suffer without help.

Specifically, the altruism that might be the underpinning of the criticism of advertising ethics illustrated above should be thought of more along Rawlsian lines. According to this view we owe help to others only if they are found in special need, following the lead of Rawls's basic principle that "All social values—liberty and opportunity, income and wealth, and the bases of self-respect—are to be distributed equally unless an unequal distribution of any, or all, of these values is to everyone's advantage."[10]

But this form of moderate egalitarianism no longer supports the prevailing idea of proper business ethics.[11] In complying with this principle the merchant should, in the main—except when informed of special disadvantages of potential customers—put a price on his product that will sell the most of his wares at the margin. That is exactly what economists, who assume that merchants are profit maximizers, would claim merchants will do. And this is the kind of conduct that the merchant has reason to believe will ensure the equal distribution of values, as far as she can determine what that would be. The reason is that from the perspective of each merchant *qua* merchant it is reasonable in the course of commerce to consider potential customers as agents with equal status to merchants who are interested in advancing their economic interests. From this, with no additional information about some possible special disadvantage of the customer, merchants must see themselves as having equal standing to customers and as having legitimate motives for furthering their own interests.[12]

Thus, the Rawlsian egalitarian moral viewpoint will not help to support the doctrine that merchants owe a service to customers. Only the robust form of altruism we find in Marx and some others is a good candidate for the morality that, for example, Leiser assumes must guide our merchant. Ethical views other than altruism might support the view that the merchant ought to be extra helpful to special persons—family, friends, associates, even neighbors—but not to everyone. Even a narrow form of subjective 'ethical' egoism can lead merchants to regard it as their responsibility to be helpful toward *some* other people. For instance, a merchant might consider most of his customers close enough friends that the morality of friendship, which need not be altruistic and may be egoist, would guide him to be helpful even to the point of risking the loss of business. Or, alternatively, were it the case that having the reputation of being helpful leads to increased patronage from members of one's community, then in just such a community such a subjective egoist would properly engage in helping behavior, including now and then informing his customers of more advantageous purchases in other establishments.

II. The Morality of Caveat Emptor

In contrast to the assumption of altruism as a guide to business conduct, I wish to suggest a form of egoism as the appropriate morality in terms of which to understand commerce. I have in mind a form of egoism best called "classical" because, as I have argued elsewhere,[13] it identities standards of (egoistic) conduct by reference to the teleological conception of the human self spelled out in the works of classical philosophers, especially Aristotle, but modified in line with an individualism that arises from the ontology of human nature.[14] The idea, briefly put, is that each individual should seek to promote his interests as a human being *and* as the individual he is. . . . Classical egoism regards the individual person as the ultimate, though not

---

[10]John Rawls, *A Theory of Justice* (Cambridge, Mass.: Harvard University Press, 1971), p. 62.

[11]Because of the intimate association of ethics and altruism (self-sacrifice), some defenders of the value of commerce or business have settled for a total disassociation of business and morality. See, e.g., Albert Carr, "Is Business Buffing Ethical?" in Thomas Donaldson and Patricia H. Wethane (eds.), *Ethical Issues in Business* (Englewood Cliffs: Prentice-Hall, 1979), pp. 46–52.

[12]I [Tibor R. Machan] believe that this point about the compatibility of Rawlsian egalitarianism and the market economy has been argued in James Buchanan, "A Hobbesian Interpretation of the Rawlsian Difference Principle." *Kyklos*, vol. 29 (1976), pp. 5–25.

[13]Tibor R. Machan, "Recent Work in Ethical Egoism," *American Philosophical Quarterly*, vol. 16 (1979), pp. 1–15. See also T. R. Machan, "Ethics and the Regulation of Professional Ethics," *Philosophia*, vol. 8 (1983), pp. 337–348.

[14]*Nicomachean Ethics*, 119a 12. This point is stressed in W. F. R. Hardie, "The Final Good in Aristotle's *Ethics*," *Philosophy*, vol. 40 (1965), pp. 277–95.

sole, proper beneficiary of that individual's own moral conduct. The standards of such conduct are grounded on the nature of the individual *as a human being,* as well as that particular person, thus in a moral universe which is coherent there need be no fundamental conflict between the egoistic conduct of one person and the egoistic conduct of another.

Accordingly, in the case of our merchant, he should abide by the basic moral principle of right reason, and the more particular implication of this, namely the virtue of honesty, as he answers the questions his customer puts to him. He might, for example, even refuse to answer some question instead of either giving help or lying. It is a person's moral responsibility to promote his rational self-interest. And taking up the task of merchandising goods and services can qualify, for various individuals with their particular talents and opportunities in life, as promoting one's rational self-interest. So a merchant could be acting with perfect moral propriety in not offering help to a customer with the task of information gathering (especially when it is clear that competing merchants are doing their very best to publicize such information as would be valuable to customers). The responsibility of merchants is to sell conscientiously their wares, not to engage in charitable work by carrying out tasks that other persons ought to carry out for themselves.

It might be objected that if someone asks an informed merchant, "Is this same product available for a lower price somewhere else?" no other alternative but letting the customer know the answer exists—it could be rather strained to refuse to answer. But there are many ways to deflect answering that do not mark someone as a deceiver. Smiling at the customer, the merchant might quietly put a question in response to the question: "Well, do you actually want me to help you to take your business elsewhere?" Should it be clear to a merchant that the customer isn't going to be satisfied with the wares available in his or her establishment, it would make perfectly good sense to offer help—as indeed countless merchants do frequently enough. Thus, when one looks for shoes, one frequently finds that one merchant will guide a customer to another where some particular style or size is likely to be available. Both good merchandising and ordinary courtesy would support such a

practice, although it is doubtful that any feasible ethical system would make it obligatory!

In terms of the classical egoism that would seem to give support to these approaches to ethical issues in business, it does not follow that one would be acting properly by lying to avoid putting oneself at a competitive disadvantage. One's integrity, sanity, reputation, generosity and one's respect for others are more important to oneself than competitive advantage. Yet neither is prudence merely a convenience, and seeking a competitive advantage in the appropriate ways would indeed be prudent.[15]

Of course showing that this morality is sound would take us on a very long journey, although some work has already been done to that end.[16] As I have noted already, in numerous noncommercial situations human beings accept the form of conduct which characterizes ordinary but decent commercial transactions as perfectly proper. In introducing ourselves to people we have never met, for example, we do not advance information that would be damaging to the prospects of good relations. We do not say, "I am John Doe. When I am angry, I throw a fit, and when in a bad mood I am an insufferable boor." When we send an invitation to our forthcoming party, we do not say, "While this party may turn out to be pleasant, in the past we have had some very boring affairs that also set out to be fun." Innumerable noncommercial endeavors, including professional ones, are characterized by "putting but our best foot forward," leaving to others the task of making sure whether they wish to relate to us. The fields of romance, ordinary conversation, political advocacy, and so forth all give ample evidence of the widespread practice of putting our best foot forward and letting others fend for themselves. We do not lie, mislead or deceive others by not mentioning to them, unsolicited, our bad habits, our foibles. As suggested before, we are not lying or misleading others when in sending along our resumes or C.V.s we do not list projects that have been rejected.

[15]For more elaborate development of these points, see Tibor R. Machan, *Human Rights and Human Liberties* (Chicago: Nelson-Hall, 1975), Chapter 3.
[16]See., e.g., Eric Mack, "How to Derive Ethical Egoism," *The Personalist,* vol. 52 (1971), pp. 735–43.

The exceptions to this are those cases in which we have special obligations arising out of special moral relationships such as friendship, parenthood, collegiality, and so on. In these—as well as in contractual relationships where the obligations arise out of explicitly stated intent instead of implied commitments and promises—one can have obligated oneself to be of assistance even in competition or contest. Friends playing tennis could well expect one another to lend a hand when skills are quite uneven. Parents should not allow their children to fend for themselves, with limited information, as the children embark upon various tasks. And in emergency cases it is also reasonable to expect strangers to set aside personal goals that ordinarily would be morally legitimate.

Commercial relationships usually take place between strangers. The only purpose in seeking out other persons is for the sake of a good deal. Even here, sometimes further bonds emerge, but those are essentially beside the point of commerce. So the moral aspects of personal intimacy would not be the proper ethics for commercial relationships, anymore than they would be for sport or artistic competitions.

Some, of course, envision the good human community as a kind of large and happy family, the "brotherhood of man," as Marx did (not only early in his life but, insofar as his normative model of the ultimately good human society was concerned, for all of his career). For them the fact that some human beings interact with others solely for "narrow," "selfish" economic purposes will be a lamentable feature of society—to be overcome when humanity reaches maturity, perhaps, or to be tolerated only if out of such selfishness some public good can be achieved.[17]

But this alleged ideal of social life cannot be made to apply to human beings as they in fact are found among us. That vision, even in Marx, is appropriate only for a "new man," not the actual living persons we are (in our time). For us this picture of universal intimacy must be rejected in favor of one in which the multifaceted and multidimensional possibility of pursuing personal happiness—albeit in the tradition of Aristotle, not Bentham or

contemporary microeconomists—is legally protected (not guaranteed, for that is impossible). For them commercial interaction or trade does not place the fantastic burden on the parties involved that would be required of them if they needed to "be forgiven for putting one's best foot forward."

I have tried to offer some grounds for conceiving of trade in such a way that the unreasonable burden of having to tell others the whole truth, blemishes and all, need not be regarded as morally required. None of the above endorses cheating, deception, false advertising, and the like. It does recommend that we look at the practice of commercial advertising—as well as other practices involving the presentation of oneself or one's skills and wares in a favorable light—as morally legitimate, justified, even virtuous (insofar as it would be prudent).

III. Product Liability: Some Caution

One line of objection that has been suggested to the above approach is that failing to tell all about the features of a commercial transaction on the part of those embarking on it is like not telling someone about a defect in a product. When a merchant sells an automobile tire, if he is aware that this tire is defective, the mere fact that his customer does not explicitly inquire about defects does not appear to be, on its face, sufficient justification for suppression of the truth of the fact. But is this not just what my analysis above would permit, on egoistic grounds? And would that not be sufficient ground, as James Rachels argues[18] in another context against egoism, for rejecting the argument?

Without embarking on a full discussion of the topic of product liability, let me point out some possible ways of approaching the issues that are consistent with the moral perspective I have taken on truth telling. First, as in law, so in morality there is the "reasonable man" standard which can be appealed to in considering personal responsibility. After all, a merchant is selling an automobile tire and it is implicit in that act that he is selling something that will, to the best of available knowledge, function in that capacity when utilized in normal circumstances.

[17]The entire tradition of classical economics embodies this point, made most forcefully by Mandeville's *The Fable of the Bees* and Adam Smith's *The Wealth of Nations*.

[18]James Rachels, "Two Arguments Against Ethical Egoism," *Philosophia*, vol. 4 (1974), pp. 297–314.

One problem with this response is that it comes close to begging the question. Just what the reasonable expectation is in such cases of commercial transaction is precisely at issue. If it is true that *caveat emptor* is justified, then why not go the full distance and make the buyer beware of all possible hitches associated with the transaction?

The answer to that question introduces the second approach to handling the product liability issue. . . . I am thinking here of the need for a distinction between what is essential about some item and what is incidental or merely closely associated with it. And when we are concerned about truth telling—and I have not tried to reject the requirement of honesty, only that of telling everything that one knows *and* that may be of help to the buyer—it is more than likely that in the very identification of what one is trading, one commits oneself to having to give any information that is pertinent to the nature of the item or service at hand. Concerning automobile tires, their function as reliable equipment for transport on ordinary roads is a good candidate for an essential feature. So not telling of a defect in tires pertaining to this feature would amount to telling a falsehood, that is, saying one is trading x when in fact one is trading not-x (inasmuch as the absence of an essential feature of x would render whatever is identified as x a fake, something that would in the context of commercial transactions open the party perpetrating the misidentification to charges of fraud).

This is not to claim what is essential about items must remain static over time. The context has a good deal to do with the determination of essential attributes of items and services, and convention and practice are not entirely inapplicable to that determination. Here is where a certain version of the theory of rational expectations would be useful and may indeed already function in some instances of tort law. As J. Roger Lee puts it,

I have rights. They do not come out of agreements with others, being prior to and presupposed by such agreements. But standard relations with others, which I will call "rational expectations frameworks" fix the criteria of their application to situations in everyday life. And rational expectation frameworks are a guide to those criteria.

. . . For example, if I go into a bar and order a scotch on the rocks, then it is reasonable to expect that I'll get what I order and that neither it nor the place where I sit will be booby-trapped. There are countless examples of this.[19]

It is possible to show that from a robust or classical ethical egoist standpoint, *the truth about an item or service being traded should be told*. But this does not show that the whole truth should be told, including various matters associated with the buying and selling of the item or service in question—such as, its price elsewhere, its ultimate suitability to the needs of the buyer, its full value and so on. This perspective, in turn, does not imply that defective products or incompetent service are equally suitable objects of trade in honest transactions.[20, 21]

[19] J. Roger Lee, "Choice and Harms," in T. R. Machan and M. Bruce Johnson (eds.), *Rights and Regulations Economic, Political, and Economic Issues* (Cambridge, MA: Ballinger, 1983), pp. 168–69.

[20] For more on product liability, see Richard A. Epstein. *A Theory of Strict Liability* (San Francisco: Cato Institute, 1980). See, also, Tibor R. Machan, "The Petty Tyranny of Government Regulations," in M. B. Johnson and T. R. Machan (eds.), *Rights and Regulations op. cit.*

[21] This paper was presented to the American Association for the Philosophic Study of Society, San Francisco, California, March 27, 1987. I [Tibor R. Machan] wish to express my appreciation for the opportunity to give this paper to a very receptive and helpful audience at that meeting. I want also to thank the anonymous reviewer for the *Public Affairs Quarterly* for very helpful suggestions.

The Making of Self and World in Advertising

JOHN WAIDE*

IN THIS PAPER I will criticize a common practice I call associative advertising. The fault in associative advertising is not that it is deceptive or that it violates the autonomy of its audience—on this point I find Arrington's arguments persuasive.[1] Instead, I will argue against associative advertising by examining the virtues and vices at stake. In so doing, I will offer an alternative to Arrington's exclusive concern with autonomy and behavior control.

Associative advertising is a technique that involves all of the following:

1. The advertiser wants people[2] to buy (or buy more of) a product. This objective is largely independent of any sincere desire to improve or enrich the lives of the people in the target market.

2. In order to increase sales, the advertiser identifies some (usually) deep-seated non-market good for which the people in the target market feel a strong desire. By "nonmarket good" I mean something which cannot, strictly speaking, be bought or sold in a marketplace. Typical non-market goods are friendship, acceptance and esteem of others. In a more extended sense we may regard excitement (usually sexual) and power as non-market goods since advertising in the U.S.A. usually uses versions of these that cannot be bought and sold. For example, "Sex appeal" as the theme of an advertising campaign is not the market-good of prostitution, but the non-market good of sexual attractiveness and acceptability.

3. In most cases, the marketed product bears only the most tenuous (if any) relation to the non-market good with which it is associated in the advertising campaign. For example, soft drinks cannot give one friends, sex, or excitement

4. Through advertising, the marketed product is associated with the non-market desire it cannot possibly satisfy. If possible, the desire for the non-market good is intensified by calling into question one's acceptability. For example, mouthwash, toothpaste, deodorant, and feminine hygiene ads are concocted to make us worry that we stink.

5. Most of us have enough insight to see both
   a. that no particular toothpaste can make us sexy and
   b. that wanting to be considered sexy is at least part of our motive for buying that toothpaste.

Since we can (though, admittedly, we often do not bother to) see clearly what the appeal of the ad is, we are usually not lacking in relevant information or deceived in any usual sense.

6. In some cases, the product actually gives at least partial satisfaction to the non-market desire—but only because of advertising.[3] For example, mouthwash has little prolonged effect on stinking breath, but it helps to reduce the intense anxieties reinforced by mouthwash commercials on television because we at least feel that we are doing the proper thing. In the most effective cases of associative advertising, people begin to talk like ad copy We begin to sneer at those who own the wrong things. We all become enforcers for the advertisers. In general, if the advertising images are effective enough and reach enough people, even preposterous marketing claims can become at least partially self-fulfilling.

Most of us are easily able to recognize associative advertising as morally problematic when the

*An earlier draft of this paper was presented to the Tennessee Philosophical Association, 10 November 1984. I [John Waide] am indebted to that group for many helpful comments.

[1] Robert L. Arrington, "Advertising and Behavior Control," *Journal of Business Ethics* 1, pp. 3–12.

[2] I prefer not to use the term "consumers" since it identifies us with our role in a market, already conceding part of what I want to deny.

[3] Arrington, p. 8.

From Journal of Business Ethics 6, 1987. *Reprinted by permission of Kluwer Academic Publishers.*

consequences are dear, extreme, and our own desires and purchasing habits are not at stake. For example, the marketing methods Nestlé used in Africa involved associative advertising. Briefly, Nestlé identified a large market for its infant formula—without concern for the well-being of the prospective consumers. In order to induce poor women to buy formula rather than breastfeed, Nestlé selected non-market goods on which to base its campaigns—love for one's child and a desire to be acceptable by being modern. These appeals were effective (much as they are in advertising for children's clothing, toys, and computers in the U.S.A.). Through billboards and radio advertising, Nestlé identified parental love with formula feeding and suggested that formula is the modern way to feed a baby. Reports indicate that in some cases mothers of dead babies placed cans of formula on their graves to show that the parents cared enough to do the very best they could for their children, even though we know the formula may have been a contributing cause of death.[4]

One might be tempted to believe that associative advertising is an objectionable technique only when used on the very poorest, most powerless and ignorant people and that it is the poverty, powerlessness, and ignorance which are at fault. An extreme example like the Nestlé case, one might protest, surely doesn't tell us much about more ordinary associative advertising in the industrialized western nations. The issues will become clearer if we look at the conceptions of virtue and vice at stake.

Dewey says "the thing actually at stake in any serious deliberation is not a difference of quantity [as utilitarianism would have us believe], but what kind of person one is to become, what sort of self is in the making, what kind of a world is making."[5] Similarly, I would like to ask who we become as we

use or are used by associative advertising. This will not be a decisive argument. I have not found clear, compelling, objective principles—only considerations I find persuasive and which I expect many others to find similarly persuasive. I will briefly examine how associative advertising affects a. the people who plan and execute marketing strategies and b. the people who are exposed to the campaign.

a. Many advertisers[6] come to think clearly and skillfully about how to sell a marketable item by associating it with a non-market good which people in the target market desire. An important ingredient in this process is lack of concern for the well-being of the people who will be influenced by the campaign. Lloyd Slater, a consultant who discussed the infant formula controversy with people in both the research and development and marketing divisions of Nestlé, says that the R&D people had made sure that the formula was nutritionally sound but were troubled or even disgusted by what the marketing department was doing. In contrast, Slater reports that the marketing people simply did not care and that "those guys aren't even human" in their reactions.[7] This evidence is only anecdotal and it concerns an admittedly extreme case. Still, I believe that the effects of associative advertising[8] would most likely be the same but less pronounced in more ordinary cases. Furthermore, it is quite common for advertisers in the U.S.A. to concentrate their attention on selling something that is harmful to many people, e.g., candy that

---

[4]James B. McGinnis, *Bread and Justice* (New York: Paulist Press, 1979) p. 224. McGinnis cites as his source INFACT Newsletter, September 1977, p. 3. Formula is often harmful because poor families do not have the sanitary facilities to prepare the formula using clean water and utensils, do not have the money to be able to keep up formula feeding without diluting the formula to the point of starving the child, and formula does not contain the antibodies which a nursing mother can pass to her child to help immunize the child against common local bacteria. Good accounts of this problem are widely available.

[5]John Dewey, *Human Nature and Conduct* (New York: Random House, 1930), p. 202.

[6]This can be a diverse group including (depending upon the product) marketing specialists, sales representatives, or people in advertising agencies. Not everyone in one of these positions, however, is necessarily guilty of engaging in associative advertising.

[7]This story was told by Lloyd E. Slater at a National Science Foundation Chatauqua entitled "Meeting World Food Needs" in 1980–81. It should not be taken as a condemnation of marketing professionals in other firms.

[8]One could argue that the deficiency in compassion, concern, and sympathy on the part of advertisers might be a result of self-selection rather than of associative advertising. Perhaps people in whom these moral sentiments are strong do not commonly go into positions using associative advertising. I doubt, however, that such self-selection can account for all the disregard of the audience's best interests.

rots our teeth, and cigarettes. In general, influencing people without concern for their well-being is likely to reduce one's sensitivity to the moral motive of concern for the well-being of others. Compassion, concern, and sympathy for others, it seems to me, are clearly central to moral virtue.[9] Associative advertising must surely undermine this sensitivity in much of the advertising industry. It is, therefore, *prima facie* morally objectionable.

   b. Targets of associative advertising (which include people in the advertising industry) are also made worse by exposure to effective advertising of this kind. The harm done is of two kinds:

1. We often find that we are buying more but enjoying it less. It isn't only that products fail to live up to specific claims about service-life or effectiveness. More often, the motives ("reasons" would perhaps not be the right word here) for our purchases consistently lead to disappointment. We buy all the right stuff and yet have no more friends, lovers, excitement or respect than before. Instead, we have full closets and empty pocket books. Associative advertising, though not the sole cause, contributes to these results.

2. Associative advertising may be less effective as an advertising technique to sell particular products than it is as an ideology[10] in our culture. Within the advertising which washes over us daily we can see a number of common themes, but the most important may be "You are what you own."[11] The quibbles over which

beer, soft drink, or auto to buy are less important than the over-all message. Each product contributes its few minutes each day, but we are bombarded for hours with the message that friends, lovers, acceptance, excitement, and power are to be gained by purchases in the market, not by developing personal relationships, virtues, and skills. Our energy is channeled into careers so that we will have enough money to *be* someone by buying the right stuff in a market. The not very surprising result is that we neglect non-market methods of satisfying our non-market desires. Those non-market methods call for wisdom, compassion, skill, and a variety of virtues which cannot be bought. It seems, therefore, that insofar as associative advertising encourages us to neglect the non-market cultivation of our virtues and to substitute market goods instead, we become worse and, quite likely, less happy persons.

To sum up the argument so far, associative advertising tends to desensitize its practitioners to the compassion, concern, and sympathy for others that are central to moral virtue and it encourages its audience to neglect the cultivation of non-market virtues. There are at least five important objections that might be offered against my thesis that associative advertising is morally objectionable.

First, one could argue that since each of us is (or can easily be if we want to be) aware of what is going on in associative advertising, we must want to participate and find it unobjectionable. Accordingly, the argument goes, associative advertising is not a violation of individual autonomy. In order to reply to this objection I must separate issues.

   a. Autonomy is not the main, and certainly not the only, issue here. It may be that I can, through diligent self-examination, neutralize much of the power of associative advertising. Since I can resist, one might argue that I am responsible for the results—*caveat emptor* with a new twist.[12] If one's methodology in ethics is concerned about people and not merely their autonomy, then the fact that most people are theoretically capable of resistance will be less

---

[9]See Lawrence A. Blum, *Friendship, Altruism and Morality* (Boston: Routledge and Kegan Paul, 1980) for a defense of moral emotions against Kantian claims that emotions are unsuitable as a basis for moral judgement and that only a purely rational good will offers an adequate foundation for morality.

[10]I use "ideology" here in a descriptive rather than a pejorative sense. To be more specific, associative advertising commonly advocates only a part of a more comprehensive ideology. See Raymond Geuss, *The Idea of a Critical Theory* (Cambridge University Press, 1981), pp. 5–6.

[11]For an interesting discussion, see John Lachs, "To Have and To Be," *Personalist* 45 (Winter, 1964), pp. 5–14; reprinted in John Lachs and Charles Scott, *The Human Search* (New York: Oxford University Press, 1981), pp. 247–255.

[12]This is, in fact, the thrust of Arrington's arguments in "Advertising and Behavior Control."

important than the fact that most are presently unable to resist.

b. What is more, the ideology of acquisitiveness which is cultivated by associative advertising probably undermines the intellectual and emotional virtues of reflectiveness and self-awareness which would better enable us to neutralize the harmful effects of associative advertising. I do not know of specific evidence to cite in support of this claim, but it seems to me to be confirmed in the ordinary experience of those who, despite associative advertising, manage to reflect on what they are exposed to.

c. Finally, sneer group pressure often makes other people into enforcers so that there are penalties for not going along with the popular currents induced by advertising. We are often compelled even by our associates to be enthusiastic participants in the consumer culture. Arrington omits consideration of sneer group pressure as a form of compulsion which can be (though it is not always) induced by associative advertising.

So far my answer to the first objection is incomplete. I still owe some account of why more people do not complain about associative advertising. This will become clearer as I consider a second objection.

Second, one could insist that even if the non-market desires are not satisfied completely, they must be satisfied for the most part or we would stop falling for associative advertising. This objection seems to me to make three main errors:

a. Although we have a kind of immediate access to our own motives and are generally able to see what motives an advertising campaign uses, most of us lack even the simple framework provided by my analysis of associative advertising. Even one who sees that a particular ad campaign is aimed at a particular non-market desire may not see how all the ads put together constitute a cultural bombardment with an ideology of acquisitiveness—you are what you own. Without some framework such as this, one has nothing to blame. It is not easy to gain self-reflective insight, much less cultural insight.

b. Our attempts to gain insight are opposed by associative advertising which always has an answer for our dissatisfactions—buy more or newer or different things. If I find myself feeling let down after a purchase, many voices will tell me that the solution is to buy other things too (or that I have just bought the wrong thing). With all of this advertising proposing one kind of answer for our dissatisfactions, it is scarcely surprising that we do not usually become aware of alternatives.

c. Finally, constant exposure to associative advertising changes[13] us so that we come to feel acceptable as persons when and only when we own the acceptable, fashionable things. By this point, our characters and conceptions of virtue already largely reflect the result of advertising and we are unlikely to complain or rebel.

Third, and perhaps most pungent of the objections, one might claim that by associating mundane marketable items with deeply rooted non-market desires, our everyday lives are invested with new and greater meaning. Charles Revson of Revlon once said that "In the factory we make cosmetics; in the store we sell hope."[14] Theodore Levitt, in his passionate defense of associative advertising, contends that[15]

Everyone in the world is trying in his [or her] special personal fashion to solve a primal problem of life—the problem of rising above his [or her] own negligibility, of escaping from nature's confining, hostile, and unpredictable reality of finding significance, security, and comfort in the things he [or she] must do to survive.

Levitt adds: "Without distortion, embellishment, and elaboration, life would be drab, dull,

---

[13]I do not mean to suggest that only associative advertising can have such ill effects. Neither am I assuming the existence of some natural, pristine self which is perverted by advertising.

[14]Quoted without source in Theodore Levit, "The Morality (?) of Advertising," *Harvard Business Review* July–August 1970; reprinted in Vincent Barry, *Moral Issues in Business,* (Belmont, CA: Wadsworth Publishing Company, 1979), p. 256.

[15]Levitt (in Barry), p. 252.

anguished, and at its existential worst."[16] This objection is based on two assumptions so shocking that his conclusion almost seems sensible.

a. Without associative advertising would our lives lack significance? Would we be miserable in our drab, dull, anguished lives? Of course not. People have always had ideals, fantasies, heroes, and dreams. We have always told stories that captured our aspirations and fears. The very suggestion that we require advertising to bring a magical aura to our shabby, humdrum lives is not only insulting but false.

b. Associative advertising is crafted not in order to enrich our daily lives but in order to enrich the clients and does not have the interests of its audience at heart. Still, this issue of intent, though troubling, is only part of the problem. Neither is the main problem that associative advertising images somehow distort reality. Any work of art also is, in an important sense, a dissembling or distortion. The central question instead is whether the specific appeals and images, techniques and products, enhance people's lives.[17]

A theory of what enhances a life must be at least implicit in any discussion of the morality of associative advertising. Levitt appears to assume that in a satisfying life one has many satisfied desires—*which* desires is not important.[18] To propose and defend an alternative to his view is beyond the scope of this paper. My claim is more modest—that

it is not enough to ask whether desires are satisfied. We should also ask what kinds of lives are sustained, made possible, or fostered by having the newly synthesized desires. What kind of self and world are in the making, Dewey would have us ask. This self and world are always in the making. I am not arguing that there is some natural, good self which advertising changes and contaminates. It may be that not only advertising, but also art, religion, and education in general, always synthesize new desires.[19] In each case, we should look at the lives. How to judge the value of these lives and the various conceptions of virtue they will embody is another question. It will be enough for now to see that it is an important question.

Now it may be possible to see why I began by saying that I would suggest an alternative to the usual focus on autonomy and behavior control.[20] Arrington's defense of advertising (including, as near as I can tell, what I call associative advertising) seems to assume that we have no standard to which we can appeal to judge whether a desire enhances a life and, consequently, that our only legitimate concerns are whether an advertisement violates the autonomy of its audience by deceiving them or controling their behavior. I want to suggest that there is another legitimate concern—whether the advertising will tend to influence us to become worse persons.[21]

---

[16]Levitt (in Barry), p. 256.

[17]"Satisfying a desire would be valuable then if it sustained or made possible a valuable kind of life. To say this is to reject the argument that in creating the wants he [or she] can satisfy, the advertiser (or the manipulator of mass emotion in politics or religion) is necessarily acting in the best interests of his [or her] public." Stanley Benn, "Freedom and Persuasion," *Australasian Journal of Philosophy* 45 (1969); reprinted in Beauchamp and Bowie, *Ethical Theory and Business,* second edition (Englewood Cliffs, NJ: Prentice-Hall, 1983), p. 374.

[18]Levitt's view is not new. "Continual success in obtaining those things which a man from time to time desires—that is to say, continual prospering—is what men call felicity." Hobbes, *Leviathan* (Indianapolis: Bobbs-Merrill, 1958), p. 61.

[19]This, in fact, is the principal criticism von Hayek offered of Galbraith's argument against the "dependence effect." F. A. von Hayek, "The *Non Sequitur* of the 'Dependence Effect,'" *Southern Economic Journal,* April 1961; reprinted in Tom L. Beauchamp and Norman E. Bowie, *Ethical Theory and Business,* second edition (Englewood Cliffs, NJ: Prentice-Hall, 1983), pp. 363–366.

[20]Taylor R. Durham, "'Information, Persuasion, and Control in Moral Appraisal of Advertising," *The Journal of Business Ethics* 3, 179. Durham also argues that an exclusive concern with issues of deception and control leads us into errors.

[21]One might object that this requires a normative theory of human nature, but it seems to me that we can go fairly far by reflecting on our experience. If my approach is to be vindicated, however, I must eventually provide an account of how, in general, we are to make judgments about what is and is not good (or life-enhancing) for a human being. Clearly, there is a large theoretical gulf between me and Arrington, but I hope that my analysis of associative advertising shows that my approach is plausible enough to deserve further investigation.

Fourth, even one who is sympathetic with much of the above might object that associative advertising is necessary to an industrial society such as ours. Economists since Galbraith[22] have argued about whether, without modern advertising of the sort I have described, there would be enough demand to sustain our present levels of production. I have no answer to this question. It seems unlikely that associative advertising will end suddenly, so I am confident that we will have the time and the imagination to adapt our economy to do without it.

Fifth, and last, one might ask what I am proposing. Here I am afraid I must draw up short of my mark. I have no practical political proposal. It seems obvious to me that no broad legislative prohibition would improve matters. Still, it may be possible to make small improvements like some that we have already seen. In the international arena, Nestlé was censured and boycotted, the World Health Organization drafted infant formula marketing guidelines, and finally Nestlé agreed to change its practices. In the U.S.A., legislation prohibits cigarette advertising on television.[23] These are tiny steps, but an important journey may begin with them.

Even my personal solution is rather modest. *First,* if one accepts my thesis that associative advertising is harmful to its audience, then one ought to avoid doing it to others, especially if doing so would require that one dull one's compassion, concern, and sympathy for others. Such initiatives are not entirely without precedent. Soon after the surgeon general's report on cigarettes and cancer in 1964, David Ogilvy and William Bernbach announced that their agencies would no longer accept cigarette accounts and *New Yorker* magazine banned cigarette ads.[24] *Second,* if I am even partly right about the effect of associative advertising on our desires, then one ought to expose oneself as little as possible. The most practical and effective way to do this is probably to banish commercial television and radio from one's life. This measure, though rewarding,[25] is only moderately effective. Beyond these, I do not yet have any answers.

In conclusion, I have argued against the advertising practice I call associative advertising. My main criticism is two-fold:

a. Advertisers must surely desensitize themselves to the compassion, concern, and sympathy for others that are central emotions in a virtuous person, and

b. associative advertising influences its audience to neglect the non-market cultivation of our virtues and to substitute market goods instead, with the result that we become worse and, quite likely, less happy persons.

---

[22]The central text for this problem is *The Affluent Society* (Houghton Mifflin, 1958). The crucial passages are reprinted in many anthologies, e.g., John Kenneth Galbraith, "The Dependence Effect," in W. Michael Hoffman and Jennifer Mills Moore, *Business Ethics: Readings and Cases in Corporate Morality* (New York: McGraw-Hill, 1984), pp. 328–333.

[23]"In March 1970 Congress removed cigarette ads from TV and radio as of the following January. (The cigarette companies transferred their billings to print and outdoor advertising. Cigarette sales reached new records.)" Stephen Fox, *The Mirror Makers: A History of American Advertising and Its Creators,* (New York: William Morrow and Co., 1984), p. 305.

[24]Stephen Fox, pp. 303–4.

[25]See, for example, Jerry Mander, *Four Arguments for the Elimination of Television* (New York: Morrow Quill Paperbacks, 1977).

Blind Man's Bluff: The Ethics of Quantity Surcharges

OMPRAKASH K. GUPTA AND ANNA S. ROMINGER

1. Introduction

A CONSUMER IS SUBJECTED to a quantity surcharge when the unit price of a product packaged in a larger quantity is higher than the unit price of the same product and brand packaged in a smaller quantity. Ample empirical evidence, including a recent field study in Northwest Indiana documented by this article, indicates that merchants routinely charge quantity surcharges on groceries and other products. Shoppers who buy these goods often do so holding a contrary belief that the large economy size is a price value because they believe the unit price of goods packaged in larger quantities is less (Nason and Della Bitta, 1983). Since the practice of quantity discounting is so widespread, this belief that *bigger is cheaper* is amply demonstrated by the shopping behaviour of most shoppers. As pointed out by Dickson and Sawyer (1990), this may be one possible explanation why most consumers do not even make price comparison within a specific brand. Their study also showed that about half of the shoppers were not even aware of product prices. Granger and Billson (1972) study showed that in a randomly selected group of shoppers about eighty percent believed that the smaller size laundry products were more expensive than larger sizes. Quite obviously, when consumers buy larger packages thinking that such products are cheaper, they make costly decisions and suffer financial losses (Cude and Walker, 1984).

The disparity between actual retail practice and consumer knowledge and belief raises an important ethical question about such retail product pricing practice. The purpose of this article is to explore the ethical dimensions of quantity surcharges in the retail shopping environment. The organization of the rest of the paper as follows. In the next section, we review the existing literature relevant to quantity discount surcharge. The review will focus on studies on incidence of quantity surcharge, rationale for quantity surcharge and consumer deception. Section 3 is devoted to empirical findings of quantity surcharge in Northwest Indiana. In Section 4, we examine prevalent government regulations pertaining to the problems of pricing, packaging and labeling and investigate how they relate to the problem of quantity surcharge. In Section 5, we question and examine ethics of quantity surcharge in the context of a free enterprise system. Finally, we conclude the paper and suggest few possible ways to decrease, if not altogether eliminate, the problems associated with quantity surcharges.

2. Literature Review

Packaging is an important part of a product. As pointed out by Stern (1981), to consumers, the package and product are part of an entity; the product is the package and the package is the product. Though initially designed for product protection, packaging has played a major role in product promotion. The packaging industry has boomed to annual gross sales approaching $90 billion (Engel *et al.*, 1991, p. 562). The package is a vital form of communication with the consumers as it identifies brand, provides ingredients and directions, conveys information regarding price, quality, quantity, even warranties. Very often, with minimum human-service or even self-service, the package is the last form of promotion.

The producers and marketers very often package products in different quantities in order to meet needs of different types of consumers and also to provide a product variety. The large size economy packages are likely to appeal to heavy users whereas small size packages would attract those with lighter needs or those who wish to try the product. As pointed out by Adams *et al.* (1991), when merchants face a competitive environment in which it is difficult to raise the price of the product, reduction in package size without

From Journal of Business Ethics *15: 1299–1312, 1996. © 1996 Kluwer Academic Publishers. Printed in the Netherlands. Reprinted with permission of Kluwer Academic Publishers.*

lowering the price becomes an attractive and viable proposition.

INCIDENCE OF QUANTITY SURCHARGE

Probably the first serious study on existence of quantity surcharge was conducted by Widrick (1979a, 1979b) in two counties of New York. He had examined 970 and 2,177 brands in Oswego and Monroe counties, respectively. Though the incidence of surcharge varied from brand to brand and product to product, the average percentage of brands exhibiting quantity surcharge was 34 in Oswego County and 18 percent in Monroe County. A similar study was done by Nason and Della Bitta (1983) in Rhode Island during 1980 and 1981. A third study was done by Walker and Cude (1984) in a rural area in Illinois. Moore and Heeler (1992) did a similar study in Ontario, Canada, in 1991. Unlike three previous studies, this study focused on the existence of quantity surcharge in manufacturing firms. Agrawal *et al.* (1993) conducted a study in a large metropolitan area in western New York State. In addition to reporting incidence of quantity surcharge, they examined the supply and demand sides of the products that displayed quantity surcharge. The final reported study was done in Thessaloniki, Greece by Zotos and Lysonski (1993). The average percentage incidence of quantity surcharges found in these studies are displayed in Table I. These studies amply suggest that quantity surcharges are widespread, not only in the United States, but also in Canada and other foreign countries.

RATIONALE FOR QUANTITY SURCHARGE

In addition to documenting the existence of quantity surcharge, many researchers have investigated rationales for its existence. On the face of it quantity surcharges appear economically anomalous because they are not functionally related to production costs. More resources are required to produce two small containers than one larger one of equivalent volume (Widrick, 1985). Further, more labor is involved in handling, stocking, pricing and selling the two small containers compared to that

involved with the larger one. When manufacturers are interviewed about the purpose of quantity surcharges, most indicate familiarity with it, express surprise at the extent of its occurrence and attribute the practice to promotional specials (Widrick, 1979b). They also point out that quantity surcharges are aspects of retail pricing policy, because anti-trust laws prevent manufacturers from setting retail price.

Several scholars have addressed the marketing objectives of quantity surcharges by examining retail practice. In some cases, retailers use quantity surcharges as a valuable de-marketing tool to encourage the conservation of valuable resources such as oil and lumber (Widrick, 1979b). The ethics of using quantity surcharges as a de-marketing tool can be summarily resolved. If resources are scarce, pricing larger quantities at a premium is justified to conserve their use. As long as the higher unit price and the diminishing supply is publicized to the consuming public, quantity surcharges for this purpose do not raise ethical questions.

The use of quantity surcharges has not, however, been limited to goods in scarce supply. Researchers have interviewed retailers to determine why quantity surcharges persist as a part of their pricing policy when they are not needed to control supply. Retailers traditionally attribute the practice to one or more of three factors, i.e., promotional specials, human error in pricing or conscious pricing policy (Widrick, 1979b). Intrigued by the responses, Widrick tested the hypothesis that the practice is motivated by these three factors, namely: human error in pricing, the side effects of promotional specials or as a result of a conscious pricing policy. The empirical data he collected indicates that "quantity surcharges are more apt to occur when the ratio of brand sizes (larger divided by small) are not whole numbers, making it difficult for most consumers to make price comparisons." He therefore concluded that quantity surcharges are primarily caused by conscious pricing policy not pricing errors or promotional specials. If quantity surcharges are the result of conscious pricing policy, then an examination of potential to deceive is a relevant consideration in the ethics of this practice.

Researchers have also examined the existence of quantity surcharge with the conventional economics theory: the supply side and the demand side. Gerstner and Hess (1987) examined the problem

Table I. Average Percentage of Brands Exhibiting Quantity Surcharge

Study	Location	Percentage
1. Widrick (1979a, 1979b)	Monroe, New York	18
	Oswego, New York	34
2. Nason and Della Bitta (1983)	Rhode Island (1980)	25
	Rhode Island (1981)	29
3. Walker and Cude (1984)	Jackson, Illinois	19
4. Moore and Heeler (1992)	Ontario, Canada	12
5. Agrawal, Grimm, and Srinivans (1993)	Western N.Y. State	16
6. Zotos and Lysonski (1993)	Thessaloniki, Greece	18

from demand side and concluded that consumers with low storage cost prefer large size packages. They also observed many consumers prefer to buy a single large package rather than two small packages whose collective volume is significantly more than the large package. In their model, they made a serious assumption that the consumers are fully informed. This assumption is hardly a valid assumption as has been documented by many other studies. Salop (1977) concluded that merchants use quantity surcharge to discriminate shoppers with high *search cost*. The consumers who search less end up paying more for products in larger sizes. These studies, however, failed to provide any explanation to why significant variations among product types exist. Walden (1988) investigated the supply side to explain such variations. His study showed that the quantity surcharge often is a function of package cost, merchant's storage cost, and the product turnover rate. Heeler (1989) showed that quantity surcharges exist due to imperfections in market knowledge. Blattberg and Neslin (1990) argued that larger packages act as *stimulus* to buyers and hence merchants are encouraged to apply quantity surcharge. Agrawal *et al.* (1993) concluded that the merchants are more likely to impose quantity surcharge for products with greater demand in general and demand for larger packages in particular.

CONSUMER DECEPTION

Price is one of the most important considerations for consumers in making the selection of the package size. Consumer behavior studies indicate that consumers rate low prices and the labeling of unit prices extremely high in their selection of a grocery store. In one study, 92.5 percent of consumers rated all prices labeled and 87.7 percent rated unit pricing signs on the shelves as an extremely important consideration in their choice of a retail grocery (Anonymous, April 1992). If we assume consumers are rational actors who make reasoned choices, they would not generally purchase goods subject to a quantity surcharge. Then why do they do so?

Two reasons account for such consumer behavior. First, as we have indicated earlier, empirical evidence clearly indicates that the vast majority of consumers do not expect larger package sizes to carry higher unit prices because they are not even aware of the existence of quantity surcharge! Since the quantity discount practice is fairly common, the strong belief that *bigger is cheaper* is constantly perpetuated. This also discourages consumers from searching unit prices and making price comparisons. Singer *et al.* (1991) have argued that merchants tend to capitalize on this faulty cognitive consumer purchasing behavior and branded such practice as a framing technique. Widrick (1979b) argued that if a merchant exploits this belief, it essentially amounts to deceptive pricing. Gardner (1975) concluded that quantity surcharge has tremendous potential to deceive gullible consumers.

Secondly, pricing information is often inaccurate or missing, making value comparisons rather difficult. In the study done by Nason and Della Bitta (1983), it was found that in forty percent of the cases the unit price tags in the audited stores were either missing, mislocated or in conflict with an accurate calculation of the price. Further, Widrick's study indicated that quantity surcharges were more apt to occur when the ratio of package volumes (larger divided by smaller) were not whole numbers but complex fractions.

Murray and Raphel (1993) argued that consumers believe that an odd price is associated with value. When an odd price is associated with a larger quantity, that belief is strengthened. For example, they evidenced that the consumer response to changing the price of tomatoes from $0.33 a piece to $0.99 for three produced a 70 percent increase in sales. When coupled with data that indicates consumers make impulse decisions in about 65 percent of their purchases in supermarkets, this demonstrates quantity surcharges possess a large potential for misleading consumers in their selection of goods for purchase.

3. *Quantity Surcharge in Northwest Indiana*

Various previous studies, described in Section 2, clearly demonstrate the existence of quantity surcharge. These studies have, however, primarily focused on supermarkets and reported the existence of quantity surcharge. In this section, we briefly report results of a survey conducted in Northwest Indiana. The study was conducted from 1991 to 1993 in Lake and Porter counties, located in the northwest corner of the state of Indiana. This geographical region represents a conglomeration of urban and semi-urban population. There are two major cities, Gary and Hammond, and several small towns such as Merrillville, Portage, Munster, Hobart, Chesterton.

Unlike previous studies, our survey included drug stores (e.g. Osco Drug, Scot Drug, Walgreens), office supply stores (e.g. Office Max), nurseries (e.g. Four Season Landscape Nursery), and discounters (K-Mart, Wal-Mart, Venture) in addition to several large supermarkets. In addition to large corporate stores, we included small and medium size businesses with individual and family ownership. The scope of stores was enlarged to include merchants who constitute a significant part of the local economy and attract a wide array of consumers.

The primary data of this study was collected with the help of college students. These students, who resided in various communities of northwest Indiana, were explained the purpose of the study, asked to visit one or more neighborhood stores and to record the incidence of quantity surcharge. One of the plausible explanations for the existence of quantity surcharge is attributed to the fact that smaller packages are often temporarily put on sale, The students were, therefore, advised to exclude any data that indicated such promotional activity. Since neither the selection of stores, nor of the products was random, care should be taken in making any generalization from the reported data.

All previous studies essentially indicate the existence of quantity surcharge by reporting the percentage of products that exhibited such a characteristic. This approach, though useful, has limited utility. To a consumer, what would be perhaps more useful is not the existence of quantity surcharge, but the magnitude of such surcharge. In other words, a consumer not only would like to know that he/she may be paying more (per unit) while making a purchase in a large package, but also how much more that he/she is paying. Therefore, when a quantity surcharge was identified, we computed the percent surcharge. For example, the price of 6 cans of Coors Beer was $3.29, giving a unit price of $0.548 per can. The price of 24 cans of Coors Beer was $13.59 giving a unit price of $0.566 per can. Therefore the price per unit of the larger package is 3.27% higher than the smaller package. Table II gives a representative data of sixty products with quantity surcharges.

Table II shows that quantity surcharge varies tremendously and can even exceed 50 percent (e.g. Heinz Ketchup and Aqua Hair Spray). The average surcharge on products in this table is 17.79 percent. Because of the limitations of this study, care should be taken in making any generalizations. A case can, however, be made that the prevalent practice of quantity surcharge and its magnitude can have drastic effect on the consumer's pocketbook. This study also showed that quantity surcharges are widespread and include almost all types of products and merchants. In addition to grocery products, we found prevalence of surcharge in office supplies, health-care products, and nurseries. It is, therefore, imperative that a conscious consumer must be aware of not only the existence but also the extent of quantity surcharge irrespective of the type of the product and merchant.

Table II. Quantity Surcharge in Northwest Indiana

Product	Price ($)	Size	Price/Unit	Surcharge (in percent)
1. Coors Beer	3.29	6 can	0.548	
	13.59	24 can	0.566	3.27
2. Cuervo Gold Tequila	6.95	16 oz	0.434	
	21.99	48 oz	0.458	5.47
3. Baby Magic Baby Lotion	1.99	9 oz	0.221	
	3.99	16 oz	0.249	12.78
4. Enfamil Baby Milk	1.13	8 oz	0.141	
	2.03	13 oz	0.156	10.55
5. J & J Baby Shampoo	2.18	15 oz	0.145	
	3.08	20 oz	0.154	5.96
6. Brach's Candy	0.68	6 oz	0.113	
	1.69	12.5 oz	0.135	19.29
7. M & M Candy	1.99	8 oz	0.249	
	4.99	16 oz	0.312	25.38
8. Snicker's Candy	2.65	12.4 oz	0.214	
	3.25	14 oz	0.232	8.63
9. Brooks Chili	1.61	31 oz	0.052	
	2.19	40 oz	0.055	5.42
10. Brooks Mild Chili Beans	0.61	15.75 oz	0.039	
	1.73	40 oz	0.043	11.67
11. Bumble Bee Chunk Light Tuna	0.78	8.125 oz	0.096	
	1.53	12.25 oz	0.125	30.10
12. Campbell's Soup	2.00	5 can	0.400	
	2.99	6 can	0.498	24.58
13. Campbell's Veg Beef Soup	0.69	10.75 oz	0.064	
	1.25	19 oz	0.066	2.50
14. Chicken of Sea Chunk Light Tuna	0.65	6.125 oz	0.106	
	1.77	12.25 oz	0.144	36.15
15. Dole Pineapple Slice	0.49	8 oz	0.061	
	1.39	20 oz	0.070	13.47
16. Hormel Chili	1.09	22 oz	0.050	
	1.85	25 oz	0.074	49.36
17. Ivory Clear Dishwashing Liquid	0.97	22 oz	0.044	
	2.27	42 oz	0.054	22.58
18. Liquid Plumber	2.19	40 oz	0.055	
	3.79	64 oz	0.059	8.16
19. Pine-Sol Household Cleaner	2.99	32 oz	0.093	
	4.35	40 oz	0.109	16.39
20. Purex Laundry Detergent	4.39	47 oz	0.093	
	6.69	66 oz	0.101	8.52

Table II. (Continued)

Product	Price ($)	Size	Price/Unit	Surcharge (in percent)
21. Maxwell House Coffee	2.84	23 oz	0.123	
	6.59	39 oz	0.169	36.85
22. Heinz Ketchup	1.08	28 oz	0.039	
	1.89	32 oz	0.059	53.13
23. Henry's French Salad Dressing	1.25	8 oz	0.156	
	2.70	16 oz	0.169	8.00
24. Jiffy Peanut Butter	2.49	18 oz	0.138	
	5.69	40 oz	0.142	2.83
25. Kraft Parmesan Cheese	2.99	9.3 oz	0.322	
	6.29	16 oz	0.393	22.28
26. Open Pit Barbecue Sauce	1.49	18 oz	0.083	
	2.59	28 oz	0.093	11.74
27. Skippy Peanut Butter	1.89	18 oz	0.105	
	5.19	40 oz	0.130	23.57
28. Amour Lard	0.53	16 oz	0.033	
	2.49	64 oz	0.039	17.45
29. Gold Medal All Purpose Flour	1.59	5 lbs	0.318	
	3.29	10 lbs	0.329	3.46
30. Wesson Vegetable Oil	1.09	16 oz	0.068	
	1.75	24 oz	0.073	7.03
31. Aqua Hair Spray	0.72	10 oz	0.072	
	1.74	16 oz	0.109	51.04
32. Salon Selectives Shampoo	1.78	15 oz	0.119	
	2.97	22 oz	0.135	13.76
33. Everready Flashlight	1.99	1 light	1.990	
	4.99	2 lights	2.495	25.38
34. Bic Disposable Razors	1.13	6 units	0.188	
	2.13	10 units	0.213	13.10
35. Crest Toothpaste	1.56	6.4 oz	0.244	
	2.08	8.2 oz	0.254	4.07
36. Dial Soap	0.49	1 bar	0.490	
	2.09	3 bars	0.697	42.18
37. Irish Spring Soap	1.99	4 bars	0.498	
	4.99	8 bars	0.624	25.38
38. Listerine Cool Mint Mouthwash	2.22	24 oz	0.093	
	3.62	32 oz	0.113	22.30
39. Sure Unscented Deodorant	1.99	1.7 oz	1.171	
	3.89	2.7 oz	1.441	23.08
40. Arm & Hammer Baking Soda	0.49	1 lb	0.490	
	1.15	2 lbs	0.575	17.35

Table II. (Continued)

Product	Price ($)	Size	Price/Unit	Surcharge (in percent)
41. Ziplock Storage Bags	2.09	32 bags	0.065	
	3.69	50 bags	0.074	13.00
42. Benylin Cough Syrup	3.53	4 gms	0.883	
	7.23	8 gms	0.904	2.41
43. Faber Castell Erasers	0.39	1 unit	0.390	
	1.39	3 units	0.463	18.80
44. Aldi's Generic Bath Tissue	0.89	4 rolls	0.223	
	1.89	6 rolls	0.315	41.57
45. Brawny Paper Towel	0.79	1 roll	0.790	
	2.49	3 rolls	0.830	5.06
46. Charmin Bath Tissue	1.18	4 rolls	0.295	
	1.93	6 rolls	0.322	9.04
47. Jerky Dog Treats	0.46	1 oz	0.460	
	2.81	6 oz	0.468	1.81
48. Meow Mix Cat Food	2.99	3.5 lbs	0.854	
	6.40	7 lbs	0.914	7.02
49. Milk Bone Dog Biscuits	1.98	32 oz	0.062	
	4.29	64 oz	0.067	8.33
50. Jewel Mandarin Oranges	0.75	11 oz	0.068	
	1.29	16 oz	0.081	18.25
51. Potatoes	1.29	5 lbs	0.258	
	2.69	10 lbs	0.269	4.26
52. Mead Wireless Notebook	0.78	1 unit	0.780	
	2.39	3 units	0.797	2.14
53. Pepsi	1.59	6 can	0.265	
	3.99	12 can	0.333	25.47
54. V-8 Juice	0.59	11.5 oz	0.051	
	2.29	33 oz	0.069	35.26
55. Jewel Enriched Thin Spaghetti	0.67	16 oz	0.042	
	1.69	32 oz	0.053	26.12
56. La Preferida Enriched Rice	0.92	2 lbs	0.460	
	2.77	5 lbs	0.544	20.43
57. Miracaid Plant Food	4.49	24 oz	0.187	
	6.49	30 oz	0.216	15.63
58. Pringle's Potato Chips	1.29	7 oz	0.184	
	2.69	14 oz	0.192	4.26
59. Ultraslim Diet Mix Packets	2.29	6.96 oz	0.329	
	3.99	9.28 oz	0.430	30.68
60. Vigo Yellow Rice	0.65	5 oz	0.130	
	1.39	8 oz	0.174	33.65
Average percent surcharge				17.79

4. Quantity Surcharge and Government Regulations

The U.S. Food and Drug Administration (FDA) is charged with regulating fair packaging and labeling practices under the Fair Packaging and Labeling Act (FPLA).[1] The FPLA charges the FDA with the responsibility of monitoring food packages and labels to ensure the consumer is provided accurate information about the quantity of the contents to facilitate value comparisons.[2]

The FDA has implemented this responsibility in several ways, including prohibiting labels and packaging which relay veritable information in a misleading manner. For example, FDA regulations prohibit statements supplemental to accurate weight descriptions which exaggerate the amount of food such as *jumbo quart* and *full gallon*.[3] The FDA further requires food packages to use common or decimal fractions to represent measure. Packaging must limit fractional representations to those specified in the regulations unless there is a firmly established consumer use and trade custom employing different fractions.[4]

While quantity surcharges violate the spirit of the FPLA, because they multiply the complexity of value comparisons, they do not violate the letter of FDA regulations as long as the label and package pricing information is accurate and complete. As long as the FDA chooses not to regulate quantity surcharges, the consumer has no remedy under the FPLA because it does not authorize a private action for civil damages.

Civil suits for misrepresentation and false descriptions of products can be brought under the Lantham Act.[5] The Lantham Act prohibits unfair competition and protects intellectual property interests in trademarks. Business competitors who are injured by infringement and unfair competition may bring suit under the Lantham Act. The Act, however, does not authorize consumer suits and courts have held that retail purchasers of consumer goods do not have standing to bring an action under this Act against a seller who engages in mis-

representation or false advertising with regard to the characteristics of the good.[6] A competitor in a Lantham Act suit can only sue to protect its own interests, not those of consumers. The courts have held that a business competitor does not act as a vicarious avenger of the public's right to be protected, but solely to recover damages to its own commercial interests resulting from unfair competition.[7]

The Federal Trade Commission (FTC) can bring suits under the Lantham Act to regulate unfair competition and deceptive trade practices. In 1983, the FTC exercised its authority under the Act and issued a Deception Policy Statement which defined an act or practice as deceptive if there is a misrepresentation, omission or other practice that misleads a consumer, acting reasonably in the circumstances, to the consumer's detriment.[8] The FTC has not, however, seen it fit to identify quantity surcharges as a deceptive practice under this Deception Policy Statement.[9]

In conclusion, there is, at present, no private remedy available to consumers which will permit them to challenge quantity surcharges. Further, neither the FDA nor the FTC, under their authority to regulate deceptive practices, has seen it fit to identify quantity surcharges as a deceptive practice by regulation or investigative policy.

5. The Ethics of Quantity Surcharges

Quantity surcharges present two related ethical questions. The first question is whether quantity surcharges can be ethically justified as a conscious pricing policy choice. The second question concerns a truth-telling issue, i.e., can retailers ethically remain silent about the fact and incidence of quantity surcharges?

The first issue is a core issue about the ethics of imposing quantity surcharges as a conscious pricing policy on largely uninformed consumers. Any

---

[1] 15 U.S.C.A. Section 1451, *et. seq.*

[2] 15 U.S.C.A. Section 1451, 21 U.S.C.A. Section 331.

[3] 21 CFR Section 501.105(o).

[4] 21 CFR Section 501.105(d) and (j).

[5] *Grove Fresh Distributors v. Flavor Fresh Food, Inc.,* (N.D. Ill. 1989) 720 F. Supp. 714, 715.

[6] *Guarino v. Sun Co., Inc.* (D.C. N.Y. 1993) 8129 F. Supp. 405, 409.

[7] *Swartz v. Schaub* (N.D. Ill. 1993) 826 F. Supp. 274, 276.

[8] The Deception Policy Statement is appended to Cliffdal Associates, 103 F.T.C. 110, at 174–184, p. 183. See Ross D. Petty, *FTC Advertising Regulations: Survivor or Casualty of the Reagan Revolution?* 30 A.B.L.J 1–34 (1992) p. 10, note 47.

[9] *Id.*

consideration of the ethics of the practice will depend on what, if any, social responsibility business owes its customers. Free market defenders, such as Milton Friedman and his followers, contend that the one and only social responsibility of business is to increase profits, as long as the firm stays within the rules of the game, engages in free competition and avoids deception and fraud. Friedman (1970) contends that not only are business leaders ill-equipped to make social policy, they fail to serve the interests of their constituents in doing so. Managers who make social policy will not serve the interests of stockholders who can and will fire them if their investment falters. Employees will be disgusted with managers who make social policy because in effect the managers have depleted corporate funds which could have been used to increase wages. Finally, consumers will be disgruntled because social policy decisions may raise the price of goods to promote general social interests. Werner (1992) argued that what the free market defenders advocate is a Theory X approach. Under this approach, the corporation is not permitted to look beyond the profit motive; customers are merely sources of revenue whose social interests are not pertinent. The basic premise of the free market approach is that when managers go beyond the economic interest of the corporation in their decision-making, they become political agents with a social agenda. Using the market as a mechanism to accomplish political reform is regarded by Friedman as a threat to the very foundation of a free society.

Defenders of this approach would argue that the information needed to make a price comparison is available to the consumer in most cases with some investigative effort. The consumer has, however, failed to exercise diligence in the collection and evaluation of data which has skewed his operating beliefs and prevented accurate price comparisons. If the market will bear quantity surcharges, which it has for many years, then no further discussion is necessary. The market has and should determine the price.

The problem with this approach is that it does not deal with the market imperfections which occur when accurate and complete information is not available to the consumer. An error rate of over forty percent in the unit price labels on grocery shelves is more than a mere wrinkle of imperfection. Nor does the free market approach account for market imperfections which may occur when the consumer does not have the ability to rapidly process the information before making a selection.[10] There is empirical data that the persons for whom price is most important are the ones with the least ability to rapidly calculate unit price. The Shoemaker study (1978) indicated that those persons most likely to purchase larger package sizes are low income families and individuals with less formal education.

Even if corporate officers do not consciously make social policy decisions, corporate decisions do often have a powerful social impact (Spinello, 1992). Spinello asserted that the refusal to take consumer behavior data into account when setting prices is itself a moral and social decision. Thus, firms are social agents whether they intend to be or not.

Evan and Freeman (1993) recognized the limits of defining corporate purpose in solely economic terms and abandoned the traditional stockholder theory approach to corporate decision-making and proposed an alternative stakeholder theory to broaden corporate purpose. The stakeholder theory maintains that managers bear a fiduciary relationship to all stakeholders including supplies, customers, employees, stockholders and the local community. The purpose of the firm is to serve as a vehicle for coordinating all stakeholder interests, which may be economic, social and moral. They argue each of these stakeholder groups has a right to be treated in Kantian fashion as more than the means to some end. Each group of stakeholders has a role as participants in the firm, participants to whom management owes duties as a stakeholder group. For example, management owes a duty to customers to meet its social interest by providing accurate information about the products the company sells. Management owes a moral duty to its employees to provide a safe work place and wages commensurate with the cost of living. To its stockholders, business owes a duty to protect their economic interests by maximizing their investment.

[10]The State of Florida conducted a study of 13,000 high school juniors to determine their ability to handle routine everyday math computations. One of the questions on the test was "How much would you save on two pairs of jeans advertised as regularly $15, now one-third off?" More than three-quarters of these high school juniors with ten years of education could not figure out the correct answer.

Management owes a duty to each of the stakeholder groups individually but its greatest duty is to the whole. Management's primary duty is to keep the relationship between the various stakeholders in balance, not permitting one group to benefit at the expense of the other. In the case of quantity surcharges, the traditional stockholder theory would applaud them as profit generating. A stakeholder theory of corporate interests would view quantity surcharges through a different lens. According to this theory, management has a fiduciary duty to the stakeholders to act as their agent to safeguard the interests of each group and ensure the long-term survival of the organization.

By providing unit pricing information, retailers can serve both the interests of the stockholders and the consumers. The information will serve the consumers' interests by giving them the data needed to make value comparisons and informed pricing decisions. This practice will also serve the interests of the stockholders to protect their financial stake in the business. Industry statistics (Sansolo, 1992) show that one out of four shoppers shift grocery stores every year with forty-four percent giving lower prices as the reason. By giving customers accurate price information, retail grocers could promote higher levels of store loyalty. Sansolo further argues that, in the face of growing competition from clubs, mass merchandisers and deep-discounters, "supermarkets should return to their essential role of purchasing agent for the consumer."

The second ethical question raised by quantity surcharges is a truth-telling issue. Are retailers ethically justified in remaining silent about the incidence and frequency of quantity surcharges? An answer to this question depends on whether the practice is deceptive. While the practice is not a form of direct deception, i.e., it is not an intentional misrepresentation, some elements of indirect deception are apparent in the practice.

Immanuel Kant (1963) considered the question: could silence ever be a *falsiloquium* even in situations where people have no right to assume that the actor will express his/her thoughts? The example Kant gives is the case where he wishes his observers to assume that he is going on a journey. So he packs his luggage and wishes they will draw a conclusion that is not true. In Kant's analysis if the observers have no right to demand a declaration of his thoughts, then his actions are not unethical.

Quantity surcharges are in Kant's terms a *falsiloquium* or, in game playing terms, a bluff. Game playing analogies immediately bring to mind Alfred Carr's classic essay "Is Business Bluffing Ethical?" (1968). Carr used the poker analogy to argue that business ethics were different from private ethics because business operated in a different system. In business, like in poker, Carr thought bluffing is ethically justified by business standards which encourage the promotion of self-interest.

The use of quantity surcharges by retailers is very much like bluffing in poker. The retailer uses quantity surcharge to increase profit margins by relying on the consumers' mistaken belief in the volume discount heuristic. The bluff works if the consumer buys the goods packaged in larger quantities believing he/she is getting a better buy. If the consumer is informed, and can and does make a value comparison, he/she can call the retailer's bluff. The prevalence of this practice of pricing goods packaged in odd quantities makes the value comparison more difficult, and rates the odds in the retailer's favor. Further, certain disadvantaged groups, i.e., low income families and individuals with less education, are the primary victims of this practice.

Is this form of bluffing ethical? If the consumers are rational actors who make reasoned choices, they would not purchase goods packaged in larger quantities which bear a larger unit price, absent some other justifying factor. Accordingly, increased profits from this pricing policy depend on some level of consumer misinformation or mistake in failing to make value comparisons. Is it ethical to take advantage of consumer misinformation or mistake through this use of this pricing policy in a way which makes value comparisons complex?

The propriety of taking advantage of the unilateral mistake of another is covered by basic contract theory, which does not reward the behavior. Accordingly, whether the merchant has a duty to disclose the unit price can be addressed by asking whether there is a social contract between business and society which would impose such a duty. Thomas Donaldson (1983) proposed the development of such a contract based on the social contract between society and the state.

Because the state is created by society, its existence cannot be justified unless the state acts to protect human rights and the social welfare (Rawls, 1971). So, too, the corporation is created by the state which issues a charter to do business in that state. This grant gives the state the authority to regulate the conduct of business within the state.

Corporate existence is justified if the corporation serves society's interests by producing goods which consumers desire. Like government, large corporations are institutions which have tremendous influence on the lives of millions of people. Corporations continue to exist through the cooperation and commitment of society from which it draws its workers, to whom it sells its goods, which gives it status and from whom it draws its profits. The social contract justifies corporations as productive organizations not as corporations. Productive organizations make tradeoffs to maximize the welfare for both workers and consumer, but productive organizations must meet minimum standards of justice, i.e., they avoid deception or fraud, treat workers with respect as human beings and avoid any practice which systematically worsens the situation of a given group in society.

To John Rawls (1971), justice as fairness was part of the original social contract. In the original choice of terms, Rawls posits that two basic principles of justice would have been selected. The first rule requires equality in the assignment of basic rights and duties, the second holds that social and economic inequalities are just, only if they result in compensating benefits for everyone, particularly the least advantaged members of society. The first principle treats the parties as equals, disinterested observers, cloaked with a veil of ignorance over individual predispositions, who are considering whether the proposed practice would serve the good of their society. In the case of quantity surcharges, it is unlikely equals would choose a practice to promote their common society which operates to cloud the informed judgment of some of the parties.

The second principle holds that inequity in distribution of society's goods may be just, but only if all persons, including those on the lowest end of the distribution scale, are benefitted. When retailers use quantity surcharges to maximize profits, consumers do realize some benefits. Profits supply the funds to hire adequate staff so waits at the check-out are short and encourage frequent promotional specials which lower prices on some items. However, given the fact that the primary concern of consumers is lower prices and that lower price is of far greater concern to low income families who hold the volume discount heuristic most strongly, the benefits of quantity surcharges do not compensate the least advantaged member of society for their greater disadvantages.

6. *Discussion*

Empirical evidence amply demonstrates that quantity surcharge is widely practiced as a conscious pricing policy by business. The practice persists and has proven profitable because consumers are not only ignorant of its prevalence but they make purchasing decisions on a contrary assumption that the large volume purchase is the better buy.

As long as the practice is not regulated by government agencies, the only objections to its practice will come from a consideration of its ethics. The practice can only be justified by a resort to the traditional stockholder theory of business enterprise which posits firms act only to protect the investments of their owners. Under this theory, the pursuit of profit on behalf of the owners is not governed by the terms of private ethics but by another system of business ethics, which like the game of poker, assumes that all players are equals and will act in their self-interest, frequently and effectively bluffing the other players in order to win the pot.

While this narrow view of corporate responsibility has its defenders, many scholars question its singular focus on economic interests. A much broader role of corporate responsibility which not only accords all stakeholders an interest in the firm but weighs social, economic and moral interests in the balance has also been proposed.

The problems associated with quantity surcharge can be effectively reduced, if not altogether eliminated, by proper consumer education, appropriate price-labeling procedures, and modification of existing regulations. Consumer groups must make every possible effort to channelize the message that quantity surcharges are real and let the buyer beware!

Though consumers make inter-brand price comparisons, they do not make intra-brand comparisons due to their purchase discount heuristic. This can be corrected if stores adapt a more appropriate labeling procedure. In addition to the traditional display of the absolute price of a package, the store should also display the price per unit of the product. Though many stores do display per unit price, it is almost always displayed on shelf, individually with the product, making it difficult for shoppers to make intra-brand price comparison. As suggested by Russo *et al.* (1975), a more straightforward display may be more useful. We suggest that stores use a single display for a specific brand sold in different packages, indicating contents of each package, absolute price, and per unit price. All packages and the price display should be located in the same physical area making it convenient for shoppers to make price comparison. In addition, we also suggest that stores display several large warning signs showing that some large packages may have greater per unit prices until such time that consumers become aware of quantity surcharge practice.

As examined earlier, [since] existing government regulations do not expressly prohibit quantity surcharge, it is imperative that government, representing the interests of the society, act to reduce the incidence of this deceptive practice. We suggest that the concerned agencies examine this issue seriously and institute appropriate regulation.

Industry specialists themselves have been urging retailers to abandon the narrow focus on short term profits in favor of a more expansive role as the purchasing agent for the consumer. Ironically, quantity surcharges may not be in the economic self-interest of retailers. Long term benefits due to quantity surcharge pricing strategies are highly questionable. Consumers who become aware of quantity surcharge may abandon the store because of its deceptive pricing policy. In the end, the proof may be in the pudding.

References

Adams, A., A. di Benedetto and R. Chaudran: 1991, "Can You Reduce Your Package Size Without Damaging Sales?," *Long Range Planning* **24**, 86–96.

Agrawal, J., P. Grimm and N. Srinivasan: 1993, "Quantity Surcharges on Groceries," *The Journal of Consumer Affairs* **27**, 335–356.

Anonymous: 1992, "The Recessions Still Shapes Buying Habits," *Progressive Grocer 59th Annual Report,* 42–47.

Blattberg, R. and S. Neslin: 1990, *Sales Promotion: Concepts, Methods and Strategies* (Prentice Hall).

Carr, A.: 1993, "Is Business Bluffing Ethical?" in T. Donaldson and P. H. Werhane (eds.), *Ethical Issues in Business: A Philosophical Approach* pp. 90–97.

Cude, B. and R. Walker: 1984, "Quantity Surcharges: Are They Important in Choosing a Shopping Strategy?" *The Journal of Consumer Affairs* **18**, 287–295.

Dickson, P. and A. Sawyer: 1990, "The Price Knowledge and Search of Supermarket Shoppers," *Journal of Marketing* **54**, 42–53.

Donaldson, T.: 1982, *Corporations and Morality.*

Engel, J., M. Warsha and T. Kinnear: 1991, *Promotional Strategy* (Richard D. Irwin, Inc.)

Even, W. M. and R. E. Freeman: 1993. "A Stakeholder Theory of the Modern Corporation: Kantian Capitalism," in T. Donaldson and P. H. Werhane (eds.), *Ethical Issues in Business: A Philosophical Approach,* pp. 166–171.

Friedman, M.: 1970, "The Social Responsibility of Business Is to Increase Its Profits," *The New York Times Magazine* September 13, 1970, reprinted with permission in T. Donaldson and P. H. Werhane (eds.), *Ethical Issues in Business: A Philosophical Approach* (4th Ed. 1993), pp. 249–255.

Gardner, D.: 1975, "Deception in Advertising: A Conceptual Approach," *Journal of Marketing* **39**, 40–46.

Gerstner, E. and J. Hess: 1987, "Why Hot Dogs Come in Packs of 10 and Buns in 8s or 12s? A Demand-Side Investigation," *Journal of Business* **60**, 491–517.

Granger, C. W. J. and A. Billson: 1972, "Consumers' Attitudes Toward Package Size and Price," *Journal of Marketing Research* **9**, 239–248.

Greenberg, J. and R. Bies: 1992, "Establishing the Role of Empirical Studies of Organizational Justice in Philosophical Inquiries into Business Ethics," *Journal of Business Ethics* **11**, 443–444.

Heeler, R.: 1989, "On Quantity Discounts and Surcharges," *Proceedings of the 1989 European Marketing Academy,* pp. 1967–1980.

Kant, I.: 1963, "Ethical Duties Towards Others: Truthfulness," in *Lectures on Ethics,* trans. Louis Infield, reprinted with permission in T. Donaldson and P. H. Werhane (eds.), *Ethical Issues in Business: A Philosophical Approach* (4th Ed. 1993), pp. 84–89.

Moore, K. and M. Heller: 1992, "Knowledge of and Rationale for Quantity Surcharges: A Theoretical and Supply Side Perspective," *Proceedings of the 1992 European Marketing Academy,* pp. 857–867.

Murray and N. Raphel: 1993, "The Answer Is in Store," *Progressive Grocer* 1–22.

Nason, R. W. and A. J. Della Bitta: 1983, "The Incidence and Consumer Perceptions of Quantity Surcharges," *Journal of Retailing* **59,** 40–54.

Rawls, J.: 1971, *A Theory of Justice* (Harvard University Press, Cambridge).

Russo, J., G. Krieser and S. Miyashita: 1975, "An Effective Display of Unit Price Information," *Journal of Retailing* **39,** 11–19.

Salop, S.: 1977, "The Noisy Monopolist: Imperfect Information, Price Dispersion and Price Discrimination," *Review of Economic Studies* **44,** 393–406.

Sansolo, M.: 1992, "Is It Really That Bad?," *Progressive Grocer* 59th Annual Report, 8–9.

Shoemaker, R. W.: 1978, "Consumer Decisions on Package Size," *Research Frontiers in Manufacturing Dialogues and Directions,* American Marketing Association, 152–157.

Singer, A., S. Lysonski, M. Singer and D. Hayes: 1991, "The Ethical Myopia: The Case of Framing by Framing," *Journal of Business Ethics* **10,** 29–36.

Spinello, R. A.: 1992, "Ethics, Pricing and the Pharmaceutical Industry," *Journal of Business Ethics* **11,** 617–626.

Stern, W.: 1981, "Design Research: Beauty or Beast," *Advertising Age,* p. 43.

Walden, M.: 1988, "Why Unit Prices of Supermarket Products Vary," *The Journal of Consumer Affairs* **22,** 74–84.

Walker, R. and B. Cude: 1984, "The Frequency of Quantity Surcharges: Replication and Extension," *Journal of Consumer Studies and Home Economics* **8,** 121–128.

Werner, S. B.: 1992, "The Movement for Reforming American Business Ethics: A Twenty-Year Perspective," *Journal of Business Ethics* **11,** 61–70.

Widrick, S. M.: 1979a, "Measurement of Incidents of Quantity Surcharge Among Selected Grocery Products," *Journal of Consumer Affairs* **13,** 99–107.

Widrick, S. M.: 1979b, "Quantity Surcharge: A Pricing Practice Among Grocery Story Items— Validation and Extension," *Journal of Retailing* **55,** 47–58.

Widrick, S. M.: 1985, "Quantity Surcharge— Quantity Discount: Pricing as It Relates to Quantity Purchased," *Business and Society* **24,** 1–17.

Zotos, Y. and S. Lysonski: 1993, "An Exploration of the Quantity Surcharge Concept in Greece," *European Journal of Marketing* **27,** 5–18.

Ethical Issues in Sales: Two Case Studies

THOMAS L. CARSON

ETHICAL ISSUES IN SALES are an important and neglected topic in business ethics. Roughly 9% of the U.S. work force is involved in sales of one sort or another. But very little has been written about ethical issues in sales.

Case 1: Shoe Sales

The following case is taken from a paper that I received from a student. I am using this case with the student's permission. The student did not want me to use his/her name. I have made some minor stylistic and grammatical corrections, but other-wise, the description of this case is taken verbatim from the student's paper.]

My introduction to retail sales began at the age of seventeen in a small "stocks-to-suits" men's store. The old-timers I trained under endowed me with several pearls of wisdom that are universal to success in any sales: "don't make friends, make money" and "first you get their confidence, then you get their trust, then you get their money." In order to achieve the objective of making money the tactics employed are often morally question-able. Two examples may help to illustrate the type of tactics I am considering.

From Journal of Business Ethics 17: 725–728, 1998. © *1998 Kluwer Academic Publishers. Printed in the Netherlands. Reprinted by permission from Kluwer Academic Publishers.*

1) My present position as a women's shoe sales-man often necessitates the use of lying and decep-tion in order to make a sale. For example, it is useful to develop a sense of urgency or *need* on the part of the customer to buy a particular shoe. (It is easier to make the sale if they *need* a shoe rather than simply *want* it). Once a customer selects a specific shoe the salesman creates the urgency by stating, with much false sincerity and steady eye contact, "Ooh, that may be a tough one, there are only a few left." In fact, there may be several dozen in stock and in all sizes. It is now a simple matter to bring out other comparable shoes, all of a slightly higher price or those which management wants to "blow out," and extol their benefits. If the customer balks, or is visibly upset, a simple, "Let me double check," a short delay in the stock room, and the production of the first shoe, is almost a guarantee of a sale. Telling the truth, that there are several dozen in stock, will eliminate any sense of urgency on the part of the customer; she may decide to come back after her next paycheck as you have plenty. She may never come back, or if she does you may not be there, or she may wind up with another salesman. They waste your time, and on commission time *is* money.

2) Suppose that a customer *wants* a shoe that you do not have in *her* size. In this scenario she needs a size 7, but you only have a 6½ and a 7½. There are two ways to proceed, either of which achieves the same result, a successful sale. Since most women understate their size, I will only explain how to put them into the half size up (7½). While in the stock room lift up the inner sole of the 7½ and insert a foam "tap," apply a small amount of glue to the inner sole and put the inner sole back in place. This gives more cushion under the ball of the foot and takes up the extra space. Bring several shoes out including the 6½ and gimmicked 7½. Put the 6½ on them without telling her what size it is. [Since the customer asked to see a size 7, she will assume that the shoe she is trying on is a size 7.] The customer will of course say it is too tight at which point the salesman replies, "They all cut them a little differently, let's try the 7½." Put the 7½ on her, point out the mirror, and quickly box up the 6½, putting it to the side. Ask how it feels, et cetera, and close the sale. Without this deception it is almost *certain* that she will "walk" which means trouble from management and lost money.

QUESTIONS FOR DISCUSSION

1. The salesperson in this case suggests that the policies that he/she practiced were economi-cally advantageous to him/her. ("My present position as a women's shoe salesman often *Necessitates* [my emphasis] the use of lying and deception in order to make a sale.") Should we accept this? Will he/she make more money in the long run if he/she engages in such prac-tices? If the answer to this question is "yes" what, if anything, could store owners do to alter these incentives for engaging in lying and/or deception?

2. Is the salesperson lying in the two scenarios described here?

3. Assuming that the answer to question #2 is "yes," is the economic benefit to the salesper-son sufficient to justify lying?

4. Is the customer harmed or likely to be harmed in either of the two examples? If so, how? Would you knowingly purchase a pair of shoes that was a half size too large and fitted with a foam rubber tap? [These taps become flat-tened out rather quickly.]

Case 2: Health Insurance

[This is a true story drawn from my own experi-ence. I recently contacted Mr. Mokarem to obtain permission to use his name and to check his recol-lections of the facts.]

In 1980 I was teaching at Virginia Tech in Blacksburg, Virginia. At this time, I received a one year Fellowship from the National Endowment for the Humanities and took a leave of absence from Virginia Tech. The fellowship paid for my salary, but not my fringe benefits. I was surprised and annoyed to learn that the University would not pay for my medical insurance during the period of the fellowship. It seemed unjust to me that I was incurring additional expenses as a result of having won a fellowship which was supposed to be an honor. Immediately upon learning of this, I went to talk with someone in the benefits office at Virginia Tech. I was told that I had the option of continuing my health insurance (Blue Cross of Virginia) through the university, if I paid for the premiums out of my own pocket. The premiums seemed quite excessive to me and I was displeased with Blue Cross on other grounds (I had to fill out many forms in order to file claims and Blue Cross was slow in paying claims). I told the benefits person that this was a lousy deal and that I thought I could do better for myself by going to a private insurance company (I fear that I was rather rude to her.) I left the benefits office in state of agitation and walked off the campus where I saw a sign for a Prudential Insurance agent. I walked into the office and met the agent, Mr. A. O. "Ed" Mokarem. I told him that I was looking for a one-year medical insurance policy to cover me during the period of the fellowship and that, for all of my unhappiness with Blue Cross of Virginia, I planned to resume this policy in a year when I returned to teaching. (The university provided this policy free of charge to all faculty who were teaching.) He showed me a comparable Prudential policy which cost about half as much as the Blue Cross policy through the university. He took a good deal of time explaining the policy to me. I thought that it looked like a very good deal and I reasoned that the Prudential policy would probably involve less red tape in filing claims. I expressed considerable enthusiasm about the policy and asked him to fill out the forms so that I could purchase it. He then told me that there was a potential problem that I should consider. He said roughly the following:

> You will want to go back to Blue Cross next year since the university will give you the policy free of charge while you are teaching. The Prudential policy is a one-year terminal policy. If you develop any serious medical problems during the next year, Prudential will probably consider you "uninsurable" and will not be willing to sell you health insurance in the future. If you buy the Prudential policy, you may encounter the same problems with Blue Cross. Since you will be dropping your Blue Cross policy *voluntarily,* they will have the right to underwrite your application for re-enrollment. If you develop a serious health problem during the next year, their underwriting decision could be "Total Rejection," imposing some waivers and/or exclusions, or (at best) subjecting your coverage to the "pre-existing conditions clause," which would not cover any pre-existing conditions until you have been covered under the new policy for at least a year.

If I left Blue Cross for a year, I risked developing a costly medical condition for which no one would

be willing to insure me. That would have been a very foolish risk to take. So, I thanked him very much and swallowing my pride went back to renew my Blue Cross coverage through the university.

P.S. I never bought any insurance from Mr. Mokarem and never had occasion to send him any business. I did not speak with him again until 1995.

QUESTIONS FOR DISCUSSION

1. Did Mr. Mokarem have a moral duty to inform me of the problems that I might encounter if I purchased the Prudential policy? (More generally, do sales people have a duty to reveal problems with their products, even if doing so means running the risk of losing sales?)
2. Were his actions "above and beyond the call of duty"?
3. Did he violate his moral obligations to the Prudential Insurance Company by informing me as he did?
4. Is it a "good business practice" for insurance agents to act as he did? In the long run, will this kind of action help or harm him in business? Are morality and self-interest in conflict in this kind of case?
5. Would the principle of *caveat emptor* imply that it would have been (legally/morally) permissible for him to have withheld the information in this case?
6. Assess the following argument:

> In this case, the potential buyer should have asked about (or known about) the possibility of being turned down for medical insurance on account of pre-existing health problems. The buyer was foolish and imprudent not to have done so.
>
> Therefore, in this case the insurance agent had no duty to inform the buyer of the potential harm the buyer might suffer, even though it is likely that the buyer would have been seriously harmed by his purchase. The fault or blame for this harm would lie with the buyer, not the agent.

Postscript 1995. I had two long telephone conversations with Mr. Mokarem in May and June of 1995; we also corresponded by mail. He expressed the view that not informing me of the risks involved with purchasing the Prudential policy would have been legal but unethical. He also spoke to question #4. In this connection he stressed the importance of the distinction between a customer and a client. A client is someone with whom an insurance agent has a long-term relation and who is likely to refer friends and acquaintances to the agent. Agents who have clients and who act in the best interests of those clients will eventually find that their business is largely self-perpetuating. People will come to them and be willing to trust their judgment. On the other hand, agents who only care about making the next sale and disregard the interests of the people who come to them will not generally fare well in the insurance business. They will have few clients and will constantly need to be seeking out new customers. I asked Mr. Mokarem about his ethical views and principles as an insurance agent. He said that he always asks himself "if I were the client how would I want to be treated?—is this what I would want to be done to me if I were in the client's place?" He added that if insurance agents do this and make it a *policy* to *always give all information* and always think of the interests of the client then "people will see it and the sales will take care of themselves." In a letter to me, he wrote "I have always believed in and practiced the Principles and Covenants of 'The National Association of Life Underwriters'" (he included a copy of this in his letter to me). I include the complete statement of these principles below:

The National Association of Life Underwriters

I BELIEVE IT TO BE MY RESPONSIBILITY:

To hold my business in high esteem and strive to maintain its prestige.

To keep the needs of my clients uppermost.

To respect my client's confidence and hold in trust personal information.

To render continuous service to my clients and their beneficiaries.

To employ proper and legitimate means to persuade my clients to protect insurable obligations; but to rigidly adhere to the observance of the highest standards of business and professional conduct.

To perfect my skill and add to my knowledge through continuous thought and study.

To conduct my business on such a high plane that others emulating my example may help the standards of our vocation.

To keep myself informed with respect to insurance laws and regulations and to observe them in both letter and spirit.

To respect the prerogatives and cooperate with all others whose services are constructively related to ours in meeting the needs of our clients.

Questions for Chapter 11

1. Consider the practice of advertising prices as dramatic markdowns, for example, 50 or 75%, from "suggested retail prices" that are artificially inflated and are customarily charged. Would Machan feel such a practice is ethical? If so, why? If not, why not? Do you feel such a practice is ethical? How would you justify your view?

2. Compare Machan's approach to advertising with the position taken by Waide. Which do you find more defensible and why?

3. What does Waide mean by the term *associative advertising*?

4. Do you agree with Waide's claim that consumer autonomy is not the central issue in evaluating the morality of associative advertising? Why or why not?

5. Gupta and Rominger note that when merchants face a competitive environment in which it is difficult to raise the price of the product, a small reduction in package contents without lowering the price becomes an attractive and viable propo-

sition. Assuming the amount is clearly labeled, is such a practice morally problematic? Explain your answer.

6. Is the practice of imposing a quantity surcharge deceptive? Are marketeers ethically justified in imposing such surcharges on the basis of *caveat emptor?*

7. If a customer will not be harmed by a deception, and will remain unaware of the deception, is it morally wrong for the salesperson to use deception in order to make the sale? Why or why not?

8. If you were the insurance agent, would you have conducted yourself the way Mr. Mokarem did? Why or why not? If you were buying insurance, would you expect to be treated in the way he treats his clients?

Case 11.1 Selling Sugared Cereals[1]

On June 30, 1977, five organizations (The Committee on Children's Television, Inc., the California Society of Dentistry for Children, The American G.I. Forum of California, the Mexican-American Political Association, the League of United Latin American Citizens) brought a class action on behalf of California residents against General Foods, concerning General Foods' marketing of sugared cereals. These cereals (Alpha Bits, Honeycomb, Fruity Pebbles, Sugar Crisp, Cocoa Pebbles) contain from 38 to 50 percent sugar by weight.

One of the allegations of the plaintiffs was that these cereals are marketed on the basis of deceptive advertising. They charged that advertisements for these cereals are typically both implicitly and explicitly misleading. At the implicit level, the advertisements suggest that children who eat sugared cereals "are bigger, stronger, more energetic, happier, more invulnerable and braver than they would have been if they did not eat candy breakfasts." At the explicit

level they suggest that the cereals are healthful, nutritious grain products forming the most important element of a well-balanced breakfast. The plaintiffs also charged that the advertisements concealed the facts that there is no honey in Honeycomb, no fruit in Fruity Pebbles, and that sugared cereals contribute to tooth decay, as well as to more serious medical consequences. They also noted the failure of the advertisements to state that these cereals cost more per serving than do breakfast foods of greater nutritional value.

1. Does General Foods have any responsibility to reveal the fact that sugared cereals cost more per serving than breakfast foods of greater nutritional value? Explain.

2. Does the fact that there is no honey in a product called "Honeycomb" and no fruit in a product called "Fruity Pebbles" constitute deception? Why or why not? Does the fact that such products are marketed to children have any relevance to how this question should be answered? Why or why not?

3. How would you distinguish between "puffery" and "deception"? How would you describe the advertisements in question?

[1]Based on The Children's Committee on Television Inc. v. General Foods, as found in 673 *Pacific Reporter*, 2nd Series, 660 (Cal. 1983).

Case 11.2 The Bette Midler Soundalike[2]

In 1985, the Ford Motor Company and its advertising agency, Young and Rubicam Inc., promoted the Ford Lincoln Mercury by means of nineteen commercials. These commercials, known in the agency as "The Yuppie Campaign," attempted to make a favorable impression on Yuppies by bringing back college memories associated with popular songs of the seventies. The agency attempted to get the original artists responsible for popularizing the songs, but were only successful in nine cases. In the other ten cases, the songs were sung by "soundalikes."

One of the songs used was "Do You Want to Dance," a song associated with Bette Midler and her 1973 album "The Divine Miss M." The agency approached Midler, but she was not interested in doing the commercial. The agency then approached Ula Hedwig who had been a backup singer for Midler for ten years. Hedwig recorded the commercial, imitating Midler to the best of her ability.

So good was Hedwig's imitation that Midler was told by a number of people that it sounded exactly like her. Hedwig was told by friends that they thought it was Midler singing the commer-

[2]Based on Midler v. Ford Motor Co., as found in 849 *Federal Reporter*, 2nd series, 460 (1988).

cial and Ken Fritz, a personal manager in the entertainment business and not associated with Midler, testified in an affidavit that he thought Midler had done the singing.

The agency was careful to use neither Midler's name nor picture in the commercial and to obtain a license from the copyright holder to use the song. Nevertheless, Midler sued on the grounds that she had a right to protect her voice from imitation.

1. Given that Midler was offered first opportunity to sing, that the song was one she had previously sung, and that the product and commercial were attractive, would you agree that Midler was exploited?

2. In the course of the trial it was argued that

   [not] every imitation of a voice to advertise merchandise is actionable. . . . only . . . when a distinctive voice of a professional singer is widely known and deliberately imitated in order to sell a product, [have] the sellers . . . committed a tort. . . .

In view of the fact that there is little point to imitating a voice that is not widely known and associated with a famous individual, does this argument undermine the grounds on which it held Midler to be exploited?

Further Readings for Chapter 11

Robert Arrington, "Advertising and Behaviour Control," *Journal of Business Ethics* 1, 1982, pp. 3–12.

Tom Beauchamp, "Manipulative Advertising," *Business and Professional Ethics Journal* 3, Spring/Summer 1984, pp. 1–22.

Paul Camenisch, "Marketing Ethics: Some Dimensions of the Challenge," *Journal of Business Ethics* 10(4), 1991, pp. 245–248.

Roger Crisp, "Persuasive Advertising, Autonomy, and the Creation of Desire," *Journal of Business Ethics* 6, 1987, pp. 413–418.

Virginia Held, "Advertising and Program Content," *Business and Professional Ethics Journal* 3, 1983, pp. 61–76.

Robert Lippke, "Advertising and the Social Conditions of Autonomy," *Business and Professional Ethics Journal* 8(4), 1988, pp. 35–58.

INFOTRAC COLLEGE EDITION To learn more about the topics from this chapter, you can use the following words to conduct an electronic search on InfoTrac College Edition, an online library of journals. Here you will find a multitude of articles from various sources and perspectives: *www.infotrac-college.com/wadsworth/access.html*

false advertising

marketing ethics

Chapter 12

Corporate Responsibility

Introduction

INDIVIDUAL EMPLOYEES act as agents for their employers. As we have seen in our earlier discussion on whistleblowing (Chapter 7), this does not imply that the employee has the obligation to act immorally on behalf of his or her employer. Equally clear is the fact that the employer who asks an employee to perform an immoral action should be punished at least as harshly, and probably more harshly, than the employee who simply carries out the request.

This intuition that an employer who asks an employee to perform an immoral action is equally deserving of blame and punishment raises a number of very difficult, but important questions. We usually think that only genuine moral agents should be punished or blamed. I do not blame the donuts I bought ten minutes ago for being stale, but I may well blame the baker who sold them to me. Pretty obviously, the donuts do not qualify as a moral agent whereas the baker does. A problem we face in ascribing blame to employers, however, is that in many instances employees work for corporations. Is there any sense in which corporations can meaningfully be described as moral agents that can be held responsible for wrongdoing? It is to this important, but very challenging issue that we turn our attention in the first two articles of Chapter 12.

One of the classic and seminal works in this area is Peter French's "The Corporation as a Moral Person." French holds the view that corporations can be moral persons with all the rights, privileges and duties accorded to such persons. Put a little differently, French holds that it makes good sense to say that corporations, not just the individuals who work in them, can be held morally responsible. To talk of corporate responsibility, therefore, is not simply a shorthand way of referring to the responsibility of the individuals who work for the corporation. The corporation, quite apart from its component members, exists as a full-fledged moral person with its own responsibilities.

In his article "The Moral Status of the Corporation," R. E. Ewin, like French, addresses the very difficult conceptual problem of whether, and to what degree, corporations can be conceived as moral agents. Ewin is willing to grant that corporations can legitimately be conceived as moral agents, but the sense in which he holds this is true is not nearly so robust as in French. Ewin thinks it makes sense to talk of corporations as possessing rights and duties that cannot be reduced to the rights and duties of the component members of the corporation, but he does not think it makes any sense to talk of corporations as possessing virtues or vices. In his view, corporations are severely truncated persons who, although possessing rights and duties, remain merely instruments incapable of developing or exhibiting moral character. How well or how poorly a corporation behaves is a reflection not of the character of the corporation—it cannot have a character, since it is incapable of virtue or vice—but rather of the character of the full-blooded moral agents whose instrument it is.

Insofar as employees act as agents of their employer, it seems that any employer who commissions an employee to perform an immoral action is equally responsible for the wrongdoing that results. But what about instances where an employee, without the approval or knowledge of the employer, acts improperly? Does it make any sense to talk of the corporation or its senior executives having responsibility in such instances for the wrongdoing of its employees? Our final two articles in this chapter discuss this question.

In "The Moral Responsibility of Corporate Executives for Disasters," John D. Bishop explores the conditions under which senior executives can be held accountable for disasters. As is customary, he absolves executives of any blame resulting from disasters caused by "acts of God" or actions not performed on behalf of the corporation. Where he parts company with the standard view is his willingness to hold senior executives responsible in any instance in which the information necessary to prevent the disaster was possessed by company personnel. Usually it is thought that a senior executive is absolved of any responsibility for a disaster if, despite the executive's best efforts to obtain information that could have prevented the disaster, subordinates failed to convey that information. Bishop, relying on a concept he terms "professional responsibility," insists that executives have not only a moral responsibility to try to avoid disasters, but also a professional responsibility to be successful in their endeavors.

Robert Larmer, in "Corporate Executives, Disasters, and Moral Responsibility," criticizes Bishop on the basis that Bishop's position runs counter to our intuition that individuals should not be held responsible for events they have no way of anticipating or preventing. Larmer suggests that Bishop cannot escape this difficulty by invoking the notion of professional responsibility, since the notion of professional responsibility cannot ground his claim that we are justified in such instances in holding executives responsible based on moral considerations. Larmer goes on to argue that the notion of professional responsibility is itself open to ethical evaluation, and that its presumed authority ultimately derives from moral responsibility. This being true, Bishop is wrong to claim that senior corporate executives can be held responsible for events they had no way of anticipating or preventing.

The Corporation as a Moral Person

PETER A. FRENCH

I

IN ONE OF HIS *New York Times* columns of not too long ago Tom Wicker's ire was aroused by a Gulf Oil Corporation advertisement that "pointed the finger of blame" for the energy crisis at all elements of our society (and supposedly away from the oil company). Wicker attacked Gulf Oil as the major, if not the sole, perpetrator of that crisis and virtually every other social ill, with the possible exception of venereal disease. It does not matter whether Wicker was serious or sarcastic in making his charges (I suspect he was in deadly earnest). I am interested in the sense ascriptions of moral responsibility make when their subjects are corporations. I hope to provide the foundation of a theory that allows treatment of corporations as members of the moral community, of equal standing with the traditionally acknowledged residents: biological human beings, and hence treats Wicker-type responsibility ascriptions as unexceptionable instances of a perfectly proper sort without having to paraphrase them. In short, corporations can be full-fledged moral persons and have whatever privileges, rights and duties as are, in the normal course of affairs, accorded to moral persons.

II

It is important to distinguish three quite different notions of what constitutes personhood that are entangled in our tradition: the metaphysical, moral and legal concepts. The entanglement is clearly evident in Locke's account of personal identity. He writes that the term "person" is "a *forensic* term, appropriating actions and their merit; and so belongs only to *intelligent agents,* capable of law, and happiness, and misery."[1] He goes on to say that by consciousness and memory persons are capable of extending themselves into the past and thereby become "concerned and *accountable.*"[2] Locke is historically correct in citing the law as a primary origin of the term "person." But he is incorrect in maintaining that its legal usage somehow entails its metaphysical sense, agency; and whether or not either sense, but especially the metaphysical, is interdependent on the moral sense, accountability, is surely controversial. Regarding the relationship between metaphysical and moral persons there are two distinct schools of thought. According to one, to be a metaphysical person is to be a moral one; to understand what it is to be accountable one must understand what it is to be an intelligent or a rational agent and vice-versa; while according to the other, being an agent is a necessary but not sufficient condition of being a moral person. Locke holds the interdependence view with which I agree, but he roots both moral and metaphysical persons in the juristic person, which is, I think, wrongheaded. The preponderance of current thinking tends to some version of the necessary pre-condition view, but it does have the virtue of treating the legal person as something apart.

It is of note that many contemporary moral philosophers and economists both take a pre-condition view of the relationship between the metaphysical and moral person and also adopt a particular view of the legal personhood of corporations that effectually excludes corporations *per se* from the class of moral persons. Such philosophers and economists champion the least defensible of a number of possible interpretations of the juristic personhood of corporations, but their doing so allows them to systematically sidestep the question of whether corporations can meet the conditions of metaphysical personhood.[3]

---

[1] John Locke, *An Essay Concerning Human Understanding* (1960), Bk. II, Ch. XXVII.

[2] *Ibid.*

[3] For a particularly flagrant example see: Michael Jensen and William Meckling, "Theory of the Firm: Managerial Behavior, Agency Coats and Ownership Structure," *Journal of Financial Economics,* vol. 3 (1976), pp. 305–360. On

From American Philosophical Quarterly *16(3), 1979. Reprinted with permission.*

III

John Rawls is, to some extent, guilty of fortifying what I hope to show is an indefensible interpretation of the legal concept and of thereby encouraging an anthropocentric bias that has led to the general belief that corporations just cannot be moral persons. As is well known, Rawls defends his two principles of justice by the use of a thought experiment that incorporates the essential characteristics of what he takes to be a pre-moral, though metaphysical population and then "derives" the moral guidelines for social institutions that they would accept. The persons (or parties) in the "original position" are described by Rawls as being mutually self-interested, rational, as having similar wants, needs, interests and capacities and as being, for all intents and purposes, equal in power (so that no one of them can dominate the others). Their choice of the principles of justice is, as Dennett has pointed out,[4] a rather dramatic rendering of one version of the compelling (though I think unnecessarily complex) philosophical thesis that only out of metaphysical persons can moral ones evolve.

But Rawls is remarkably ambiguous (and admittedly so) regarding who or what may qualify as a metaphysical person. He admits into the category, in one sentence, not only biological human beings but "nations, provinces, business firms, churches, teams, and so on,"[5] then, perhaps because he does not want to tackle the demonstration of the rationality, etc., of those institutions and organizations, or because he is a captive of the traditional prejudice in favor of biological persons, in the next sentence he withdraws entry. "There is, perhaps, a certain logical priority to the case of human individuals: it may be possible to analyze the actions of so-called artificial persons as logical constructions of the actions of human persons. . . ."[6] "Perhaps" is, of course, a rather large hedge behind which to

hide; but it is, I suppose, of some significance that in *A Theory of Justice* when he is listing the nature of the parties in the "original position" he adds "c. associations (states, churches, or other corporate bodies)."[7] He does not, unhappily, discuss this entry on his list anywhere else in the book. Rawls has hold, I think, of an important intuition: that some associations of human beings should be treated as metaphysical persons capable on his account of becoming moral persons, in and of themselves. He has, however, shrunk from the task of exploring the implications of that intuition and has instead retreated to the comfortable bulwarks of the anthropocentric bias.

IV

Many philosophers, including, I think, Rawls, have rather uncritically relied upon what they incorrectly perceive to be the most defensible juristic treatment of collectivities such as corporations as a paradigm for the treatment of corporations in their moral theories. The concept of corporate legal personhood under any of its popular interpretations is, I want to argue, virtually useless for moral purposes.

Following many writers on jurisprudence, a juristic person may be defined as any entity that is a subject of a right. There are good etymological grounds for such an inclusive neutral definition. The Latin "*persona*" originally referred to *dramatis personae*, and in Roman law the term was adopted to refer to anything that could act on either side of a legal dispute. [It was not until Boethius' definition of a person: "*Persona est naturae rationabilis individua susbstantia* (a person is the individual subsistence of a rational nature)" that metaphysical traits were ascribed to persons.] In effect, in Roman legal tradition persons are creations, artifacts, of the law itself, i.e., of the legislature that enacts the law, and are not considered to have, or only have incidentally, existence of any kind outside of the legal sphere. The law, on the Roman interpretation, is systematically ignorant of the biological status of its subjects.

The Roman notion applied to corporations is popularly known as the Fiction Theory. Hallis characterizes that theory as maintaining that "the

---

p. 311 they write, "The private corporation or firm is simply one form of legal fiction which serves as a nexus for contracting relationships. . . ."

[4]Daniel Dennett, "Conditions of Personhood" in *The Identities of Persons* ed. by A. O. Rorty (Berkeley, 1976), pp. 175–196.

[5]John Rawls, "Justice as Reciprocity," in *John Stuart Mill, Utilitarianism,* ed. by Samuel Gorovitz (Indianapolis, 1971), pp. 244–245.

[6]*Ibid.*

[7]John Rawls, *A Theory of Justice* (Cambridge, 1971), p. 146.

personality of a corporate body is a pure fiction and owes its existence to a creative act of the state."[8] Rawls' view of corporate persons could not, however, be motivated by adherence to the Fiction Theory for two reasons. The theory does not demand a dichotomy between real and artificial persons. All juristic persons, on the theory, are creations of the law. The theory does not view the law as recognizing or verifying some pre-legally existing persons; it argues that the law creates its own subjects. Secondly, the theory, in its pure form at least, does not regard any juristic persons as composites. All things which are legislatively created as subjects of rights are non-reducible or, if you will, primitive individual legal persons. (It is of some note that the Fiction Theory is enshrined in English law in regard to corporate bodies by no less an authority than Sir Edward Coke who wrote that corporations "rest only in intendment and consideration of the law."[9])

The Fiction Theory's major rival in American jurisprudence and the view that does seem to inform Rawls' account is what I shall call "the Legal Aggregate Theory of the Corporation." It holds that the names of corporate bodies are only umbrellas that cover (but do not shield) certain biological persons. The Aggregate Theory treats biological status as having legal priority and corporate existence as a contrivance for purposes of summary reference. (Generally, it may be worth mention, Aggregate Theorists tend to ignore employees and identify corporations with directors, executives and stockholders. The model on which they stake their claim is no doubt that of the primitive partnership.) I have shown elsewhere[10] that to treat a corporation as an aggregate for any purposes is to fail to recognize the key logical differences between corporations and mobs. The Aggregate Theory, then, despite the fact that it has been quite popular in legislatures, courtrooms, and on streetcorners simply ignores key logical, socioeconomic and historical facts of corporate existence. [It might prove of some value in clarifying the dispute between Fiction and Aggregate theorists to mention a rather famous case in the English

law. (The case is cited by Hallis.) It is that of *Continental Tire and Rubber Co., Ltd.* vs *Daimler Co. Ltd.* Very sketchily, the Continental Tyre company was incorporated in England and carried on its business there. Its business was the selling of tires made in Germany, and all of its directors were German subjects in residence in Germany, and all but one of its shares were held by German subjects. The case arose during the First World War, and it turned on the issue of whether the company was an English subject by virtue of its being incorporated under the English law and independent of its directors and stockholders, and could hence bring suit in an English court against an English subject while a state of war existed. The majority opinion of The Court of Appeals (5–1) was that the corporation was an entity created by statute and hence was "a different person altogether from the subscribers to the memorandum or the shareholders on the register."[11] Hallis aptly summarizes the judgment of the court when he writes that "The Continental Tyre and Rubber Co., Ltd., was an English company with a personality at law distinct from the personalities of its members and could therefore sue in the English Courts as a British Subject."[12] The House of Lords, however, supporting the Aggregate Theory and no doubt motivated by the demands of the War, overturned the Court of Appeals. Lord Buckley wrote "The artificial legal entity has no independent power of motion. It is moved by the corporator. . . . He is German in fact although British in form."[13] This view has seen many incarnations since on both sides of the Atlantic. I take Rawls' burying of his intuition in the logical priority of human beings as a recent echoing of the words of Lord Parker who in the Continental Tyre case wrote for the majority in the House of Lords: ". . . the character in which the property is held and the character in which the capacity to act is enjoyed and acts are done are not *in pari materia*. The latter character is a quality of the company itself, and conditions its capacities and its acts and is attributable only to human beings. . . ."][14]

---

[8]Frederick Hallis, *Corporate Personality* (Oxford, 1930), p. xlii.
[9]10 *Co. Rep.* 253, see Hallis, p. xlii.
[10]"Types of Collectivities and Blame," *The Personalist*, vol. 56 (1975), pp. 160–169, and in the first chapter of my *Foundations of Corporate Responsibility* (forthcoming).

[11]"Continental Tyre and Rubber Co., Ltd. vs. Daimler Co., Ltd." (1915), K.B., p. 893.
[12]Hallis, p. xlix.
[13]"Continental Tyre and Rubber Co., Ltd. vs. Daimler Co., Ltd." (1915), K.B., p. 918.
[14](1916) 2 A.C., p. 340.

In Germanic legal tradition resides the third major rival interpretation of corporate juristic personhood. Due primarily to the advocacy of Otto von Gierke, the so-called Reality Theory recognizes corporations to be pre-legal existing sociological persons. Underlying the theory is the view that law cannot create its subjects, it only determines which societal facts are in conformity with its requirements. At most, law endorses the pre-legal existence of persons for its own purposes. Gierke regards the corporation as an offspring of certain social actions having then a *de facto* personality, which the law only declares to be a juridical fact.[15] The Reality Theory's primary virtue is that it does not ignore the non-legal roots of the corporation while it, as does the Fiction Theory, acknowledges the non-identity of the corporation and the aggregate of its directors, stockholders, executives and employees. The primary difference between the Fiction and Reality Theories, that one treats the corporate person as *de jure* and the other as *de facto,* however, turns out to be of no real importance in regard to the issue of the moral personhood of a corporation. Admittedly the Reality Theory encapsulates a view at least superficially more amenable to arguing for discrete corporate moral personhood than does the Fiction Theory just because it does acknowledge *de facto* personhood, but theorists on both sides will admit that they are providing interpretations of only the formula "juristic person = the subject of rights," and as long as we stick to legal history, no interpretation of that formula need concern itself with metaphysical personhood or agency. The *de facto* personhood of the Reality Theory is that of a sociological entity only, of which no claim is or need be made regarding agency or rationality etc. One could, without contradiction, hold the Reality Theory and deny the metaphysical or moral personhood of corporations. What is needed is a Reality Theory that identifies a *de facto* metaphysical person not just a sociological entity.

Underlying all of these interpretations of corporate legal personhood is a distinction, embedded in the law itself, that renders them unhelpful for our purposes. Being a subject of rights is often contrasted in the law with being an "administrator of rights." Any number of entities and associations can and have been the subjects of legal rights. Legislatures have given rights to unborn human beings, they have reserved rights for human beings long after their death, and in some recent cases they have invested rights in generations of the future.[16] Of course such subjects of rights, though they are legal persons, cannot dispose of their rights, cannot administer them, because to administer a right one must be an agent, i.e., able to act in certain ways. It may be only an historical accident that most legal cases are cases in which "the subject of right X" and "the administrator of right X" are co-referential. It is nowhere required by law, under any of the three above theories or elsewhere, that it be so. Yet, it is possession of the attributes of an administrator of rights and not those of a subject of rights that are among the generally regarded conditions of moral personhood. It is a fundamental mistake to regard the fact of juristic corporate personhood as having settled the question of the moral personhood of a corporation one way or the other.

V

Two helpful lessons however, are learned from an investigation of the legal personhood of corporations: (1) biological existence is not essentially associated with the concept of a person (only the fallacious Aggregate Theory depends upon reduction to biological referents) and (2) a paradigm for the form of an inclusive neutral definition of a moral person is provided: "a subject of a right." I shall define a moral person as the referent of any proper name or description that can be a non-eliminatable subject of what I shall call (and presently discuss) a responsibility ascription of the second type. The non-eliminatable nature of the subject should be stressed because responsibility and other moral predicates are neutral as regards person and person-sum predication.[17] Though we might say that The Ox-Bow mob should be held responsible for the death of three men, a mob is an

---

[15]See in particular Otto von Gierke, *Die Genossenschofts-theorie* (Berlin, 1887).

[16]And, of course, in earlier times animals have been given legal rights.

[17]See Gerald Massey, "Tom, Dick, and Harry, and All The King's Men," *American Philosophical Quarterly,* vol. 13 (1976), pp. 89–108.

example of what I have elsewhere called an aggregate collectivity with no identity over and above that of the sum of the identities of its component membership, and hence to use "The Ox-Bow mob" as the subject of such ascriptions is to make summary reference to each member of the mob. For that reason mobs do not qualify as metaphysical or moral persons.

VI

There are at least two significantly different types of responsibility ascriptions that should be distinguished in ordinary usage (not counting the lauditory recommendation, "He is a responsible lad.") The first-type pins responsibility on someone or something, the who-dun-it or what-dun-it sense. Austin has pointed out that it is usually used when an event or action is thought by the speaker to be untoward. (Perhaps we are more interested in the failures rather than the successes that punctuate our lives.)

The second-type of responsibility ascription, parasitic upon the first, involves the notion of accountability. "Having a responsibility" is interwoven with the notion "Having a liability to answer," and having such a liability or obligation seems to imply (as Anscombe has noted[18]) the existence of some sort of authority relationship either between people or between people and a deity or in some weaker versions between people and social norms. The kernel of insight that I find intuitively compelling, is that for someone to legitimately hold someone else responsible for some event there must exist or have existed a responsibility relationship between them such that in regard to the event in question the latter was answerable to the former. In other words, "X is responsible for y," as a second-type ascription, is properly uttered by someone Z if X in respect to y is or was accountable to Z. Responsibility relationships are created in a multitude of ways, e.g., through promises, contracts, compacts, hirings, assignments, appointments, by agreeing to enter a Rawlsian original position, etc. The right to hold responsible is often delegatable to third parties; though in the case of moral responsibility no del-

egation occurs because no person is excluded from the relationship: moral responsibility relationships hold reciprocally and without prior agreements among all moral persons. No special arrangement needs to be established between parties for anyone to hold someone morally responsible for his acts or, what amounts to the same thing, every person is a party to a responsibility relationship with all other persons as regards the doing or refraining from doing of certain acts: those that take descriptions that use moral notions.

Because our interest is in the criteria of moral personhood and not the content of morality we need not pursue this idea further. What I have maintained is that moral responsibility, although it is neither contractual nor optional, is not a class apart but an extension of ordinary, garden-variety, responsibility. What is needed in regard to the present subject then is an account of the requirements for entry into any responsibility relationship, and we have already seen that the notion of the juristic person does not provide a sufficient account. For example, the deceased in a probate case cannot be held responsible in the relevant way by anyone, even though the deceased is a juristic person, a subject of rights.

VII

A responsibility ascription of the second type amounts to the assertion of a conjunctive proposition, the first conjunct of which identifies the subject's actions with or as the cause of an event (usually an untoward one) and the second conjunct asserts that the action in question was intended by the subject or that the event was the direct result of an intentional act of the subject. In addition to what it asserts it implies that the subject is accountable to the speaker (in the case at hand) because of the subject's relationship to the speaker (who the speaker is or what the speaker is, a member of the "moral community," a surrogate for that aggregate). The primary focus of responsibility ascriptions of the second type is on the subject's intentions rather than, though not to the exclusion of, occasions. Austin wrote: "In considering responsibility, few things are considered more important than to establish whether a man *intended* to do A, or whether he did A

---

[18]G. E. M. Anscombe, "Modern Moral Philosophy," *Philosophy,* vol. 33 (1958), pp. 1–19.

intentionally."[19] To be the subject of a responsibility ascription of the second type, to be a party in responsibility relationships, hence to be a moral person, the subject must be at minimum, what I shall call a Davidsonian agent.[20] If corporations are moral persons, they will be non-eliminatable Davidsonian agents.

VIII

For a corporation to be treated as a Davidsonian agent it must be the case that some things that happen, some events, are describable in a way that makes certain sentences true, sentences that say that some of the things a corporation does were intended by the corporation itself. That is not accomplished if attributing intentions to a corporation is only a shorthand way of attributing intentions to the biological persons who comprise, e.g., its board of directors. If that were to turn out to be the case then on metaphysical if not logical grounds there would be no way to distinguish between corporations and mobs. I shall argue, however, that a *Corporation's Internal Decision Structure* (its CID Structure) is the requisite redescription device that licenses the predication of corporate intentionality.

Intentionality, though a causal notion, is an intentional one and so it does not mark out a class of actions or events. Attributions of intentionality in regard to any event are referentially opaque with respect to other descriptions of that event, or, in other words, the fact that, given one description, an action was intentional does not entail that on every other description of the action it was intentional. A great deal depends upon what aspect of an event is being described. We can correctly say, e.g., "Hamlet intentionally kills the person hiding in Gertrude's room (one of Davidson's examples), but Hamlet does not intentionally kill Polonius," although "Polonius" and "the person hiding in Gertrude's room" are co-referential. The event may be properly described as "Hamlet killed Polonius" and also as "Hamlet intentionally killed

the person hiding in Gertrude's room (behind the arras)," but not as "Hamlet intentionally killed Polonius," for that was not Hamlet's intention. (He, in fact, thought he was killing the King.) The referential opacity of intentionality attributions, I shall presently argue, is congenial to the driving of a wedge between the descriptions of certain events as individual intentional actions and as corporate intentional actions.

Certain events, that is, actions, are describable as simply the bodily movements of human beings and sometimes those same events are redescribable in terms of their upshots, as bringing about something, e.g., (from Austin[21]) feeding penguins *by* throwing them peanuts ("by" is the most common way we connect different descriptions of the same event[22]), and sometimes those events can be redescribed as the effects of some prior cause; then they are described as done for reasons, done in order to bring about something, e.g., feeding the penguins peanuts in order to kill them. Usually what we single out as that prior cause is some desire or felt need combined with the belief that the object of the desire will be achieved by the action undertaken. (This, I think, is what Aristotle meant when he maintained that acting requires desire.) Saying "someone (X) did y intentionally" is to describe an event (y) as the upshot of X's having had a reason for doing it which was the cause of his doing it.

It is obvious that a corporation's doing something involves or includes human beings doing things and that the human beings who occupy various positions in a corporation usually can be described as having reasons for *their* behavior. In virtue of those descriptions they may be properly held responsible for their behavior, *ceteris paribus*. What needs to be shown is that there is sense in saying that corporations, and not just the people who work in them, have reasons for doing what they do. Typically, we will be told that it is the directors, or the managers, etc., that really have the corporate reasons and desires, etc., and that although corporate actions may not be reducible without remainder, corporate intentions are always reducible to human intentions.

---

[19] J. L. Austin, "Three Ways of Spilling Ink" in *Philosophical Papers* (Oxford, 1970), p. 273.

[20] See for example Donald Davidson, "Agency," in *Agent, Action, and Reason,* ed. by Binkley, Bronaugh, and Marras (Toronto, 1971).

[21] Austin, p. 275.

[22] See Joel Feinberg, *Doing and Deserving* (Princeton, 1970), p. 134f.

IX

Every corporation has an internal decision structure. CID Structures have two elements of interest to us here: (1) an organizational or responsibility flow chart that delineates stations and levels within the corporate power structure and (2) corporate decision recognition rule(s) (usually embedded in something called "corporation policy"). The CID Structure is the personnel organization for the exercise of the corporation's power with respect to its ventures, and as such its primary function is to draw experience from various levels of the corporation into a decision-making and ratification process. When operative and properly activated, the CID Structure accomplishes a subordination and synthesis of the intentions and acts of various biological persons into a corporate decision. When viewed in another way, as already suggested, the CID Structure licenses the descriptive transformation of events, seen under another aspect as the acts of biological persons (those who occupy various stations on the organizational chart), to corporate acts by exposing the corporate character of those events. A functioning CID Structure *incorporates* acts of biological persons. For illustrative purposes, suppose we imagine that an event E has at least two aspects, that is, can be described in two non-identical ways. One of those aspects is "Executive X's doing y" and one is "Corporation C's doing z." The corporate act and the individual act may have different properties; indeed they have different causal ancestors though they are causally inseparable. (The causal inseparability of these acts I hope to show is a product of the CID Structure, X's doing y is not the cause of C's doing z nor is C's doing z the cause of X's doing y although if X's doing y causes event F then C's doing z causes F and *vice versa*.)

Although I doubt he is aware of the metaphysical reading that can be given to this process, J. K. Galbraith rather neatly captures what I have in mind when he writes in his recent popular book on the history of economics: "From [the] interpersonal exercise of power, the interaction . . . of the participants, comes the *personality* of the corporation."[23] I take Galbraith here to be quite literally

correct, but it is important to spell out how a CID Structure works this "miracle."

In philosophy in recent years we have grown accustomed to the use of games as models for understanding institutional behavior. We all have some understanding of how rules in games make certain descriptions of events possible that would not be so if those rules were non-existent. The CID Structure of a corporation is a kind of constitutive rule (or rules) analogous to the game rules with which we are familiar. The organization chart of a corporation distinguishes "players" and clarifies their rank and the interwoven lines of responsibility within the corporation. An organizational chart tells us, for example, that anyone holding the title "Executive Vice President for Finance Administration" stands in a certain relationship to anyone holding the title "Director of Internal Audit" and to anyone holding the title "Treasurer," etc. In effect it expresses, or maps, the interdependent and dependent relationships, line and staff, that are involved in determinations of corporate decisions and actions. The organizational chart provides what might be called the grammar of corporate decision-making. What I shall call internal recognition rules provide its logic.

By "recognition rule(s)" I mean what Hart, in another context, calls "conclusive affirmative indication"[24] that a decision on an act has been made or performed for corporate reasons. Recognition rules are of two sorts. Partially embedded in the organizational chart are procedural recognitors: we see that decisions are to be reached collectively at certain levels and that they are to be ratified at higher levels (or at inner circles, if one prefers that Galbraithean model). A corporate decision is recognized internally, however, not only by the procedure of its making, but by the policy it instantiates. Hence every corporation creates an image (not to be confused with its public image) or a general policy, what G. C. Buzby of the Chilton Company has called the "basic belief of the corporation,"[25] that must inform its decisions for them to be properly described as being those of that corporation. "The moment policy is side-

[23]John Kenneth Galbraith, *The Age of Uncertainty* (Boston, 1971), p. 261.

[24]H. L. A. Hart, *The Concept of Law* (Oxford, 1961), Ch. VI.
[25]G. C. Buzby, "Policies—A Guide to What a Company Stands For," *Management Record*, vol. 24 (1962), p. 5ff.

stepped or violated, it is no longer the policy of that company."[26]

Peter Drucker has seen the importance of the basic policy recognitors in the CID Structure (though he treats matters rather differently from the way I am recommending.) Drucker writes:

> Because the corporation is an institution it must have a basic policy. For it must subordinate individual ambitions and decisions to the *needs* of the corporation's welfare and survival. That means that it must have a set of principles and a rule of conduct which limit and direct individual actions and behavior. . . .[27]

X

Suppose, for illustrative purposes, we activate a CID Structure in a corporation, Wicker's favorite, the Gulf Oil Corporation. Imagine that three executives X, Y and Z have the task of deciding whether or not Gulf Oil will join a world uranium cartel. X, Y and Z have before them an Everest of papers that have been prepared by lower echelon executives. Some of the papers will be purely factual reports, some will be contingency plans, some will be formulations of positions developed by various departments, some will outline financial considerations, some will be legal opinions and so on. In so far as these will all have been processed through Gulf's CID Structure system, the personal reasons, if any, individual executives may have had when writing their reports and recommendations in a specific way will have been diluted by the subordination of individual inputs to peer group input even before X, Y and Z review the matter. X, Y and Z take a vote. Their taking of a vote is authorized procedure in the Gulf CID Structure, which is to say that under these circumstances the vote of X, Y and Z can be redescribed as the corporation's making a decision: that is, the event "XYZ voting" may be redescribed to expose an aspect otherwise unrevealed, that is quite different from its other aspects, e.g., from X's voting in the affirmative. Redescriptive exposure of a procedurally corporate aspect of an event, however, is not to be confused with a description of an event that

makes true a sentence that says that the corporation did something intentionally. But the CID Structure, as already suggested, also provides the grounds in its other type of recognitor for such an attribution of corporate intentionality. Simply, when the corporate act is consistent with, an instantiation or an implementation of established corporate policy, then it is proper to describe it as having been done for corporate reasons, as having been caused by a corporate desire coupled with a corporate belief and so, in other words, as corporate intentional.

An event may, under one of its aspects, be described as the conjunctive act "X did a (or as X intentionally did a) ε Y did a (or as Y intentionally did a) ε Z did a (or as Z intentionally did a)" (where a = voted in the affirmative on the question of Gulf Oil joining the cartel). Given the Gulf CID Structure, formulated in this instance as the conjunction of rules: when the occupants of positions A, B and C on the organizational chart unanimously vote to do something and if doing that something is consistent with, an instantiation or an implementation of general corporate policy and *ceteris paribus,* then the corporation has decided to do it for corporate reasons, the event is redescribable as "the Gulf Oil Corporation did j for corporate reasons f" (where j is "decided to join the cartel" and f is any reason (desire + belief) consistent with basic policy of Gulf Oil, e.g., increasing profits) or simply as "Gulf Oil Corporation intentionally did j." This is a rather technical way of saying that in these circumstances the executives voting is, given its CID Structure, also the corporation deciding to do something, and that regardless of the personal reasons the executives have for voting as they do and even if their reasons are inconsistent with established corporate policy or even if one of them has no reason at all for voting as he does, the corporation still has reasons for joining the cartel; that is, joining is consistent with the inviolate corporate general policies as encrusted in the precedent of previous corporate actions and its statements of purpose as recorded in its certificate of incorporation, annual reports, etc. The corporation's only method of achieving its desires or goals is the activation of the personnel who occupy its various positions. However, if X voted affirmatively purely for reasons of personal monetary gain (suppose he had been bribed to do so) that does not alter the fact that the corporate

[26]*Ibid.*
[27]Peter Drucker, *Concept of Corporation* (New York, 1964/1972), pp. 36–37.

reason for joining the cartel was to minimize competition and hence pay higher dividends to its shareholders. Corporations have reasons because they have interests in doing those things that are likely to result in realization of their established corporate goals regardless of the transient self-interest of directors, managers, etc. If there is a difference between corporate goals and desires and those of human beings it is probably that the corporate ones are relatively stable and not very wide ranging, but that is only because corporations can do relatively fewer things than human beings, being confined in action predominately to a limited socio-economic sphere. The attribution of corporate intentionality is opaque with respect to other possible descriptions of the event in question. It is, of course, in a corporation's interest that its component membership view the corporate purposes as instrumental in the achievement of their own goals. (Financial reward is the most common way this is achieved.)

It will be objected that a corporation's policies reflect only the current goals of its directors. But that is certainly not logically necessary nor is it in practice true for most large corporations. Usually, of course, the original incorporators will have organized to further their individual interests and/or to meet goals which they shared. But even in infancy the melding of disparate interests and purposes gives rise to a corporate long range point of view that is distinct from the intents and purposes of the collection of incorporators viewed individually. Also, corporate basic purposes and policies, as already mentioned, tend to be relatively stable when compared to those of individuals and not couched in the kind of language that would be appropriate to individual purposes. Furthermore, as histories of corporations will show, when policies are amended or altered it is usually only peripheral issues that are involved. Radical policy alteration constitutes a new corporation, a point that is captured in the incorporation laws of such states as Delaware. ("Any power which is not enumerated in the charter and the general law or which cannot be inferred from these two sources is *ultra vires* of the corporation.") Obviously underlying the objection is an uneasiness about the fact that corporate intent is dependent upon policy and purpose that is but an artifact of the socio-psychology of a group of biological persons. Corporate intent seems somehow to be a tarnished illegitimate offspring of human intent. But this objection is another form of the anthropocentric bias. By concentrating on possible descriptions of events and by acknowledging only that the possibility of describing something as an agent depends upon whether or not it can be properly described as having done something (the description of some aspect of an event) for a reason, we avoid the temptation to look for extensional criteria that would necessitate reduction to human referents.

The CID Structure licenses redescriptions of events as corporate and attributions of corporate intentionality while it does not obscure the private acts of executives, directors etc. Although X voted to support the joining of the cartel because he was bribed to do so, X did not join the cartel, Gulf Oil Corporation joined the cartel. Consequently, we may say that X did something for which he should be held morally responsible, yet whether or not Gulf Oil Corporation should be held morally responsible for joining the cartel is a question that turns on issues that may be unrelated to X's having accepted a bribe.

Of course Gulf Oil Corporation cannot join the cartel unless X or somebody who occupies position A on the organizational chart votes in the affirmative. What that shows, however, is that corporations are collectivities. That should not, however, rule out the possibility of their having metaphysical status, as being Davidsonian agents, and being thereby full-fledged moral persons.

This much seems to me clear: we can describe many events in terms of certain physical movements of human beings and we also can sometimes describe those events as done for reasons by those human beings, but further we can sometimes describe those events as corporate and still further as done for corporate reasons that are qualitatively different from whatever personal reasons, if any, component members may have for doing what they do.

Corporate agency resides in the possibility of CID Structure licensed redescription of events as corporate intentional. That may still appear to be downright mysterious, although I do not think it is, for human agency as I have suggested, resides in the possibility of description as well.

Although further elaboration is needed, I hope I have said enough to make plausible the view that we have good reasons to acknowledge the non-eliminatable agency of corporations. I have maintained that Davidsonian agency is a necessary and sufficient condition of moral personhood. I cannot further argue that position here (I have done so elsewhere). On the basis of the foregoing analysis, however, I think that grounds have been provided for holding corporations *per se* to account for what

they do, for treating them as metaphysical persons *qua* moral persons.[28]

[28]This paper owes much to discussions and comments made by J. L. Mackie, Donald Davidson and Howard K. Wettstein. An earlier version was read at a conference on "Ethics and Economics" at the University of Delaware. I also acknowledge the funding of the University of Minnesota Graduate School that supports the project of which this is a part.

The Moral Status of the Corporation

R. E. EWIN

PETER FRENCH'S PERSUASIVE ARGUMENTS to show that corporations[1] have rights and duties, and to that extent have a moral personality,[2] establish at best a Kantian sort of moral personality for them. His claim that ". . . corporations can be full-fledged moral persons and have whatever privileges, rights and duties as are, in the normal course of affairs, accorded to moral persons"[3] is misleading: the moral personality of corporations is severely limited. Corporations, as artificial persons, can have all sorts of rights and duties,[4] but they lack the emotional life without which there can be no possession of virtues and vices. The moral personality of a corporation can be no more than a Kantian moral personality, restricted to issues of rights and duties; it cannot be the richer moral life of generosity and courage, meanness and cowardice, that is lived by "natural" people. The moral

personality of a corporation is exhausted by its legal personality,[5] and that fact, taken together with the representative function of a corporation's management, places important limitations on what constitutes ethical behavior on the part of management. Those limitations are interesting because a common misunderstanding of them can lead ethical managers to behave in quite unethical ways and can lead members of the public to have quite improper expectations of corporations and management.

I. Acting on a Corporation's Behalf: Limitations

A corporation cannot act without some particular person acting on its behalf. That does not exclude it from being a moral person: there is a large range of things that the insane, the comatose, or babes in arms cannot do without some other person acting

[1]My [R. E. Ewin] concern in this paper is with ordinary listed corporations. An interesting project would be to consider different sorts of corporations with different sorts of points (an ordinary listed corporation, a private family company, Oxfam, a state-owned corporation, perhaps even the state) and what effects their different points have for the ethical requirements to be imposed on people acting for those corporations. That project must wait for another time.
[2]French (1979 and 1984).
[3]French (1979, p. 207).
[4]On the relationship between legal and moral rights, see Ewin (1987) *passim*.

[5]In arguing for this claim, I shall be both agreeing and disagreeing with the conclusion for which Peter A. French argues (on quite different grounds) in French (1979). His claim is that ". . . corporations can be full-fledged moral persons and have whatever privileges, rights and duties as are, in the normal course of affairs, accorded to moral persons" (p. 207). My claim is that corporations can have rights and duties, but that being a fully-fledged moral person involves substantially more.

From Journal of Business Ethics *10: 749–756, 1991. Reprinted by permission of Kluwer Academic Publishers.*

on their behalf, and people in those classes retain rights. It does, on the other hand, limit the sorts of actions that are open to corporations. In this section, I intend to examine those limitations and to show that they tend to restrict the moral concerns of corporations and their managers to matters of rights and duties.

On the face of it, corporations can act only through representatives and can do only those things that representatives can do. What representatives can do is work in terms of rights and duties.[6] Representatives can commit one to various things. In a democracy, our political representatives commit us to certain laws; by their actions on our behalf (even if not at our behest), they change what it is that we have a right or a duty to do. Somebody authorized by the corporation to buy bolts for the manufacture of tractors, by her actions, commits the corporation to paying the bill for the supply of bolts, that is, creates a duty for the corporation by her exercise of one of the corporation's rights that she has been authorized to exercise. If she decides also to buy flowers for her mother, then the corporation can properly require that she pay that bill from her private funds.

A representative exercises the rights of whomever he or she is representing. The control exercised by the represented might be quite direct: the buyer might be sent out to buy a certain number of bolts at a certain price from a certain supplier and authorized to do nothing else, so that unavailability of bolts at that price from that supplier means a wasted trip or phone call. The representative in such a case is nothing more than a delegate.

Some representatives become representatives without any authorization from the people they represent. As an example, it was not uncommon in colonial times for the colonial government to appoint somebody to represent the natives. The representative was appointed by the colonial governor, let us say, and in the standard case was certainly not appointed by the natives. Any authorization came from the government, not from the people represented. How, then, can this sort of representation be distinguished from simple

theft of rights? There is a limitation on what the representative can do with the rights of those he or she represents;[7] insofar as the rights and duties of the represented allow, the representative must act so as to further their interests. If I simply take over your rights and make them mine (perhaps I buy them from you, or you forfeit them as a penalty for something), then I can quite properly use them to further my own interests, since they have ceased to be your rights and have become mine. If, instead of taking over your rights and making them mine, I represent you with respect to those rights, then I must use them to further your interests rather than my own. We see the same sort of relationship between a guardian and an infant ward when the guardian must act as the infant's representative with respect to an inheritance the infant has received:[8] that the guardian is the guardian and thus the infant's representative is not a matter of authorization from the two-year-old, but, because of that, what the guardian can do in exercising the infant's rights is severely limited.

For the same reason, one would expect the same principle to hold when the authorization is a wide one so that the representative, though authorized, is much more than a mere delegate. There might be the further point here that the authorization could reasonably be taken to imply that sort of limitation. If the buyer is sent off to buy bolts, then *of course* she is expected not to pay a higher price for the same bolts that she could have bought for less, because she is supposed to be acting as a representative of the corporation and acting in its interests.[9]

The executive officers of a corporation are (at least, usually) elected by the shareholders or appointed by people who were elected by the shareholders. They do not attain their position in the same sort of way as does the colonial representative of native interests. But that is a matter of how they attain their positions as representatives, not of what it is to be a representative. The point about representation without consent is that it

---

[6]On the subject of representation, see A. Phillips Griffith (1960). My discussion of representation draws heavily on this paper.

[7]See Griffith.

[8]A similar analogy is used in introducing the explanation of the duties of directors and other officers in Ford (1986).

[9]Other things being equal, of course. It might be better to pay a higher price this time to retain good relations with that supplier because only that supplier can provide the bolts in times of shortage, or for some reason of that sort.

brings out what the job of a representative is. The point about voting or any other method of appointing representatives is that it goes on to the important question of who is to be the judge of the interests of the people represented. The function of the representative of a corporation is still that of furthering the interests of the members of the corporation as much as possible within the limitations imposed by their rights and duties.[10]

The guardian who has to look after the infant ward's inheritance may properly invest the money in something safe. If, as things turn out, the long-odds investments do pay off better, that is simply unfortunate; the infant will have to struggle through with less money than she might have had otherwise and, if the investments were reasonable, will not be able to sue the guardian for the difference. The ward, in the end, will have to live with the consequences of the guardian's proper action. If, on the other hand, the guardian uses the money to set up a fraud, even if he does so solely to further the ward's interests and with no thought of personal gain, then the *guardian* has to live with the consequences of that. Not everything done to further the interests of the represented is done in the capacity of representative, even if representatives should act so as to further the interests of those they represent; a representative can act as such only when acting within the limits imposed by the rights of the represented. It can be *my* act only if I could have authorized it, and I cannot hand over rights that I do not possess.

The ward, when she comes of age and takes over her inheritance, will have the rights to do all sorts of things with the money and may act in or against her own interests as she sees fit. The guardian, as we have seen, is more limited in what he can do. He is not precluded only from perpetrating fraud on his ward's behalf; he is not allowed to do various sorts of good on her behalf, either. When she takes over the inheritance, the ward can give it all to charity; the guardian cannot, when the ward is still two years old, give all her money to charity. But the law might allow a conservative imputation of authorization from a ward still too young to authorize anything: it might allow that the guardian, from the income on the inheritance,

make contributions to charity which the ward, if capable, might be expected to authorize if she is a decent person.

The basis of that imputed authorization would be that the ward could be expected to make it if she were capable of deciding such matters. Adult shareholders are quite capable of deciding such matters for themselves, so the same justification for doing good on behalf of those represented rather than pursuing their interests will not apply in the case of those representing the shareholders. For a corporation to be charitable, *prima facie,* is simply for some people (the executives of the corporation) to be "generous" with money belonging to other people (the shareholders), and that is a very dubious form of generosity. If those people who are being forced into "generosity" want to be generous with their own money, then they are quite capable of doing it for themselves and exercising their own judgment about which charitable enterprises are most worthy of support. There is no obvious ground here for a relaxation of the principle that the representative should act so as to further the interests of the represented as far as possible within the limits imposed by the rights and duties of the represented.[11]

Because corporations are legal persons, they have at least some moral personality: they can have rights and duties. Corporations, therefore, can act justly or unjustly. Beyond that, when it comes to such matters as acting generously or charitably, it looks as though there might be a problem. Corporations can act only through representatives, and representatives must act, so far as the rights and duties of the corporation allow, so as to further the interests of the corporation as far as possible. So it looks as though corporations might be logically locked into selfishness, which would leave

---

[10]This is an important limitation of which I shall not make much here. It deserves another paper.

[11]The sort of points that have been made will apply also when the issue that comes up is one of the relationship between the corporation's interest and the national interest. Except insofar as there is a specific duty to act in the national interest, a duty which would limit the actions that were open to the corporation, the job of the corporation will be to look after the shareholders' interests and leave them to concern themselves with whatever they think is the national interest to whatever extent they, personally, see fit. If the money is to be made in the domestic market, then corporations will be under no special obligation to try to produce export goods because the government has allowed a huge build-up of foreign debt.

them with a very limited and unsatisfactory moral personality. Of course, it might be very imprudent for them to *look* as though they were entirely selfish and might, with such a poor corporate image, have deleterious efforts on their trading performance, but that is not sufficient to defeat the point and solve the problem. All that shows is that an efficient firm would be *subtle* about its selfishness, considering what promoted its interests in the long run, and would employ a good advertising agency.

II. The Corporation's Inability to Exhibit Any Virtue or Vice

What matters with rights and duties is simply that the job be done and the requirements met, so I can employ somebody else to do the job for me in such cases. My debts are paid when they are paid, even if I pay them with very bad grace and only under the threat of legal penalty; I have then met the requirements of justice and done what justice requires, even if I have not shown myself to be a possessor of the virtue of justice. Duties can be carried out and rights recognized quite cold bloodedly. I can do my duty from any of many motivations: because I shall not be paid if I do not; because I want a reputation as a reliable person; because I think I owe it to others to do my duty; and so on. I can do my duty simply from habit and without thinking about it at all. In each of those cases, my duty has been done no matter what the motivation or lack of motivation. There is no problem at all about corporations doing their duties, and the same sort of point applies to corporations insisting on their rights. Corporations can behave justly or unjustly. What I shall proceed to show now is that, despite the possibility of their acting justly or unjustly, they cannot really exhibit any virtue or vice, including the virtue of justice. They lack the virtues and vices that make up the moral character of a natural person.

Corporations clearly have interests: it is those interests that the representatives who act for the corporation are supposed to serve. Since corporations have interests and can act, even if they act only through representatives, it at least looks as though they could be prudent or imprudent. Prudence is a virtue, so this might provide a move to a wider moral personality than seems to have been allowed for corporations so far.

It is not only the buying of bolts that corporations can do only through representatives or the activities of particular people. Decisions, too, must be made by particular people (or groups of people voting according to certain rules) if the corporation is to make any decisions at all, so what is considered in making those decisions will be considered by particular people and not by the corporation in some other form. There is, then, an important sense in which the corporation, as such, cannot think for itself; it can think only through the people who act for it. Hence, a corporation, as such, cannot give proper (or improper) consideration to its own interests. If the representatives of the corporation put the corporation's interests first, that might be selfless devotion rather than prudence on their part; if they do it because that will further their own personal interests in the long run, then that might be prudence on their part but is not prudence on the part of the corporation.[12]

This is a long way short of anything that would allow us to attribute the virtue of prudence to the corporation: the corporation, unlike its representatives, does not *care* about its interests, and possession of a virtue is a matter of what one cares about. Prudence is a matter of having a proper concern for one's interests; it requires a *concern*, though a proper concern that puts one's interests in the context of many other things and gives them only their proper importance. Corporations, as such, and as distinct from the people who act for them, have no feelings of that sort.

Virtues generally are a matter of caring about certain sorts of things,[13] so there is a general problem about whether a corporation can have any virtues (or any vices) if they cannot really care about things.[14] There might be no problem about whether corporations can *behave* justly or unjustly,

---

[12]Whether a corporation can exhibit virtues and vices by having (say) its executive officers do so when they act for it is an issue that I shall take up in Section III. Certainly one would often take reference to a corporation's virtues or vices as shorthand for reference to the virtues and vices of its officers when they act for it.

[13]On virtues generally, see Ewin (1981).

[14]We do read claims that certain corporations care. These might best be read as claims that the people who run those corporations care, or they might be more accurately read as expressing a desire that we should think well (no matter how confusedly) of the corporation so that we shall be more likely to buy its product or less likely to oppose its other activities.

but there is a real problem about whether they can *possess the virtue* of justice. If I pay what I recognize to be my debts, but do so with bad grace and only because I want to avoid time in jail, then I do what justice requires but I do not exhibit the virtue of justice. The just person does what justice requires *because justice requires it*[15] and because he or she cares about justice.

If I owe you $20 but am the irresponsible sort of person who regards his debts as being of no importance and consistently forgets them, and if I am also a good-hearted soul, then, when I see you sad because you lack the $20 you need to carry out some project that you have, I might give you the money to help you out. In fact, I shall then have repaid my debt and done what justice required, but if I exhibited a virtue at all it was a virtue something more like generosity than like justice because of what it was that moved me. I was moved by my concern for your well-being, not by any concern for justice. Had I owed the money to somebody else instead, to somebody who needed it but was not present so that their plight could touch my heart, then, being the sort of person I am in this story, I should have given you the money then, too, despite the injustice involved. I should have exhibited a sense of justice and the virtue of justice had I given you the money because I owed it to you, and only if I gave it to you for that reason.

The point is more obvious with something such as kindness. Kindness is quite clearly a matter of motivation, of performing the act because the other person is suffering or needs help and because one cares about that fact, not simply of performing a helpful act cold-bloodedly because it will help to win one a good reputation or another Boy Scout badge. A kind person, though the point needs a lot of qualifications to make it an accurate one,[16] is somebody who cares about the well-being of others and is therefore inclined to choose the well-being of others as an end for its own sake.

Corporations can give large donations to War on Want or Oxfam; there is no question that they can do what a kind person with their resources would do. Those resources are limited to the fairly impersonal: corporations can do helpful things such as providing a clean water supply or more beds for the hospital, but they cannot give a kind word or the personal touch that makes clear that somebody cares, and it is the kind word and personal touch that is really central to kindness. Nevertheless, there are actions that a kind person would perform which a corporation can also perform. Still, since the corporation cannot care, it cannot be exhibiting the virtue of kindness in performing those helpful acts. We regard the issue of motivation as crucial when we are concerned with the kindness of a natural person, and we should do the same when considering a corporation. Motivation is at the core of kindness.

Corporations, unlike the people who run them, have no emotional life. Corporations operate at the level of reason and requirement, but they do not get angry at being mistreated, they are not sickened by tales of the squalor in which some people have to live, and, generally, they simply do not have the emotional life required of a being that is to care about things as things must be cared about if one is to possess a virtue. Still, one might ask, does that matter so long as the corporation is run by people who do have that sort of emotional life and so long as the corporation is capable of performing helpful and other relevant sorts of actions?

III. The Corporation and Charitable Intentions

It might even be the case that a corporation was formed for charitable purposes—the Anti-Poverty Corporation, formed to raise money to lift some people from the squalor in which they are forced to live. That speaks well of the people who form and run such a corporation, no doubt, but it does not mean that the corporation itself possesses the virtue of charity. It does mean that the people running the corporation will have a fine chance to exercise their charitable instincts.

---

[15]Or, of course, some other version of that (because it was owed, because it was my duty, etc.) filling out the details of which would require reference to justice.

[16]A great many qualifications are needed: somebody who goes around helping willy-nilly, with no concern about what is his or her business and what is not, is an interfering busybody rather than a kind person. If help is needed and I care about that fact, it is still possible that I am not the right or best person to give the help; if your appendix has to be removed, it might be better if I wait for the surgeon. Helping might sometimes do no more in the long run than make people dependent; one needs good judgment about all sorts of things. And so on.

The more ordinary sort of corporation, one formed, say, to make a profit from the production of tractors, is not in the same position and does not give the same opportunity for those running it to exercise their charitable instincts. If the corporation is successful then the money will be there, and the board of directors might decide to give a lot of it to various worthy causes. Nevertheless, that is quite different from a case in which the Anti-Poverty Corporation does the same thing. The Anti-Poverty Corporation was formed for that purpose, advertises itself in those terms, and gives people a chance, by acting cooperatively, to raise money for anti-poverty projects that they could not raise if they were acting alone. The Big Red Tractor Corporation was formed to make profits by producing tractors and to give its shareholders a chance to make money for themselves that they could not have made by acting alone. They might then, of course, choose to donate that money to the Anti-Poverty Corporation, but that is a matter for them to decide.

Those who act for the Big Red Tractor Corporation have the job of furthering its interests insofar as they can do so while carrying out its duties and acting within the limitations of its rights. The interests of the corporation are determined by its point:[17] the point of the Big Red Tractor Corporation is to make the greatest possible return to its shareholders, so the people who act for the corporation have the job of making the greatest possible return to the shareholders and whatever will help them to do so will be in the interest of the corporation. The profit made by the corporation is, at first blush, the shareholders' money. The managers of the corporation are acting for the shareholders, as their representatives.

If those who act for the corporation have the duty of furthering its interests, and if that means that they have the duty of producing the greatest possible return to the shareholders, then they are in breach of their duty, and are therein acting unjustly, if they fail to make the best return to the shareholders that they can. That means that they can exercise their charitable instincts with the corporation's money only at the expense of acting unjustly.

Nor is it the case that they have a choice between generosity and justice, because the injustice infects the generosity. I can be generous only with what is *mine;* giving away what is somebody else's is merely irresponsible and does not show any willingness on my part to make myself worse off for the good of another.[18] If the profits belong to the shareholders, then those who act for the corporation, in exercising their charitable instincts, would be merely confused about charity and would be giving away what was somebody else's. The decision about whether to give it away should lie with the people who own it.[19]

The Anti-Poverty Corporation is not in a significantly different position from the Big Red Tractor Corporation as far as this point goes. If the executive officers, instead of putting the income of the corporation to charitable use, decide instead to raise their own salaries, then they have not merely been mean: they have failed to do their duty. The points about corporations apply to the Anti-Poverty Corporation, too; its officers deal in terms of doing their duties or failing to do so. It is simply that the duties of officers of the Anti-Poverty Corporation are different from those of the officers of the Big Red Tractor Corporation.

There is, of course, a quite separate point: if the Big Red Tractor Corporation gives large donations to good causes, that might give it a better image, give other people a more favorable attitude to it, and improve business so that profits were larger because of the money that was given away.[20] That

---

[17]Which leaves the interesting possibility that it might be in the interests of the Anti-Poverty Corporation to put itself out of business by removing everybody from squalor.

[18]The exception, of course, is when my giving what is somebody else's means my knowingly letting myself in for a lot of trouble. The generosity then lies in my taking that risk to make somebody better off.

[19]An interesting side-issue here is the extent to which these points apply to governments and their officers. Hobbes's sovereign was an artificial man, so my arguments seem to apply against what he says of the sovereign and charity (p. 387): "And whereas many men, by accident unevitable, become unable to maintain themselves by their labour; they ought not to be left to the Charity of private persons; but to be provided for, (as far-forth as the necessities of Nature require), by the Lawes of the Common-wealth. For as it is uncharitablenesse in any man to neglect the impotent; so it is in the Soveraign of a Common-wealth, to expose them to the hazard of such uncertain Charity."

[20]Or things might not work out that way. Cf. Michael Milken's remarks about owner-managership, quoted in Bruck (1988, p. 273). See Love (1986) for an account of a corporation that is confident that its involvement in community and charitable activities has paid off.

motivation has nothing to do with the motivation required for a case of generosity or charity; if it exhibited a virtue at all, it would be the virtue of prudence. What it is more likely to show is conscientiousness and careful planning on the part of those who act for the corporation.

The same sort of point applies if one considers other facts about the behavior of the corporation such as whether it adopts only environmentally friendly policies or whether it looks after its employees well. Such considerations might pay off in terms of corporate image, or they might show that the shareholders are jolly nice people who would rather give up some of their profits[21] than have the corporation pollute the air and the waterways;[22] it might lead to improved loyalty of employees, who are thus better motivated to do their duty when they could get away with doing less and might even be willing to do more,[23] thus improving corporate performance; but it will not show that the corporation as such cares about anything and will not show any virtue in the corporation. Such things might be good business practice, but they are not exhibitions of any moral virtue residing in the corporation itself.

People who run corporations can have virtues and vices just like anybody else, and they can show their virtues and vices in the work that they do in the corporation: they can be honest or corrupt; they can show fortitude or cowardice; they can show any of a range of virtues and vices. Corporations might behave much better when they are run by virtuous people, by people who consider such issues as the consequences of the corporation's activities and whether the shareholders have a right to inflict those consequences on others. But corporations themselves can possess no virtues; as far as that sort of consideration goes, they are merely instruments for others use. Shareholders can use them to raise money to give to the poor, which they can do whether the corporation be the Anti-Poverty Corporation or the Big Red Tractor Corporation, or they can use them to raise money to spend on riotous living. The morality is in the people who use the instrument, not in the instrument. And the managers are limited in the virtues that they can exhibit when acting on behalf of the corporation by the fact that they act as representatives of the shareholders: they do not act in their personal capacities, but in professional capacities, representing other people whose actions they are performing.

And that morality can, clearly, go wrong if the people using the instrument mistake their moral categories and take it that all the moral categories that apply to natural people also apply to corporations. It does not take ill-will to misuse the shareholders' money: good will might well be the explanation of why a corporate officer gives some of the corporation's money to charity, or provides excessive services to employees, or does a number of things that do not constitute acting in the interests of the shareholders as much as that can be done within the limits of their rights and duties. That corporations can come to be improperly accused of selfishness and other such vices is not the only problem arising from this sort of mistake about the moral categories that can appropriately be applied to corporations; it can also lead to corporate officers' failing to do their duties.

IV. Conclusion

If the morality is in the people who use the instrument and not in the corporation itself, then the corporation is rescued from the suggestion that it is logically tied into selfishness. The reason is plain: selfishness is not merely a matter of acting in one's own interests, as a corporation should do, but having an undue care for one's own interests at the

---

[21]Assuming unanimity amongst the shareholders, otherwise the problem about some giving away what belongs to others will arise again.

[22]There might be more to it than that. If the corporation executives are acting on behalf of the shareholders, acting as their representatives, then they must further the interests of those shareholders *insofar as they can do so while fulfilling the duties of the shareholders and acting within the limitations of their rights*. That leaves argument to be had about whether the shareholders have the right to pollute the air and the waterways; if they have not, then the executives may not do so on their behalf.

[23]But compare the judgment of Justice Plowman in *Parke v. Daily News Ltd.* ([1962] 1 Ch. 927) as reported in *Company Directors' Duties: Report on the Social and Fiduciary Duties and Obligations of Company Directors* by the Australian Senate Standing committee on Legal and Constitutional Affairs (Canberra: Australian Government Publishing Service, 1989), p. 11. The *Report*'s account of the case is: "In that case, directors of a company about to be wound up decided to pay compensation and other benefits to employees about to lose their jobs. The court held that according to law the directors were unable to do so. Their primary duty was to the shareholders."

expense of those of others. If corporations do not care, then they do not have an undue care for their own interests.

From all of this, it follows as well that descriptions of corporations as greedy are mistaken: that is not greed, it is the officers of the corporation doing their duty. If one objects to that, then one objects to the existence of corporations; presumably, shareholders do not so object. If greater profits are to be made by trading with South Africa, then that is what the officers of the corporation should do provided that it is not illegal for them to do so. On the other hand, in the normal run of things people have no duty to deal with any particular corporation. If people want to boycott that corporation so that trade with South Africa becomes unprofitable, then they are fully entitled to do so. Policies of ethical investing (as it has been called) attempt to exert that sort of pressure.

Because they are artificial people and not "natural" people, corporations lack the emotional makeup necessary to the possession of virtues and vices. Their moral personality is exhausted by their legal personality. Corporations can have rights and duties; they can exercise the rights through their agents, and they can in the same way fulfill their duties. If necessary, they can be forced to fulfill their duties. The moral personality of a corporation would be at best a Kantian sort of moral personality, one restricted to issues of requirement, rights, and duties. It could not be the richer moral life of virtues and vices that is lived by the shareholders, the executives, the shopfloor workers, the unemployed, and "natural" people in general.

The Moral Responsibility of Corporate Executives for Disasters

JOHN D. BISHOP

I. *Introduction*

WHEN LARGE CORPORATIONS are criticized for causing disasters, the senior executives of those corporations usually protest their personal innocence, and deny that they should bear any moral responsibility for the tragedy. They often protest that they were not given information which could have warned them of impending problems even though they made honest efforts to obtain such information. Subsequent investigations have sometimes revealed that others in the corporation (often engineers) knew of safety problems, but that this information failed to reach decision making executives. Examples of this phenomenon include the cargo door problem on the DC-10, and the explosion of the Challenger—both tragedies involving loss of life.

This denial of moral responsibility intuitively conflicts with the high remuneration that CEOs and other executives receive in return for being responsible for corporations. In particular, it conflicts with the bonus remuneration which they receive if the corporation performs well. If they benefit when the corporation flourishes, should they not accept responsibility when things go horribly wrong?

The denial also conflicts with the current trend in our society of holding senior executives more socially responsible (Brooks, 1989). To note a single example, a U.S. District Judge recently insisted that the CEO of Pennwalt Corp. should personally attend his court to enter a guilty plea on a toxic spill charge. Note that the judge was not making a legal point (corporate lawyers could have just as easily entered the plea), but a point about social responsibility (Globe and Mail, 1989).

This paper will analyse to what extent we can or should hold executives morally responsible for disasters. In particular, it will examine the case in which knowledge indicating impending problems

From Journal of Business Ethics *10: 377–383, 1991. Reprinted by permission of Kluwer Academic Publishers.*

is available to someone in the corporation, but has failed to reach decision making executives.

To help clarify the issues that the rest of the paper will deal with, the next section will eliminate some cases in which executives clearly are not responsible. Section III will elaborate on the reasons executives give for denying responsibility; in particular this paper concentrates on the case in which executives claim that they did not have and could not be expected to have had information vital to preventing the disaster. The reasons why apparently powerful executives cannot get information from their own corporation need to be examined carefully (Section IV) before moving on in the final two sections to analysing to what extent we are justified in holding executives morally responsible.

It perhaps should be made clear at the outset that moral responsibility, or the lack of it, does not have direct implications for legal liability. The legal aspects of this problem are complicated, especially when the tragedy is in one country, and the corporate head office is in another. Legal issues are not dealt with in this paper.

II. Limits on Executive Responsibility

It is commonplace in discussing morality that people should not be held responsible for events over which they have no influence or control. In this section, several types of events over which executives have no influence are eliminated from discussion. Executives cannot be held responsible for acts of God, nor, in their role as executives, for actions which are not performed on behalf of the corporation. Events not excluded in this section are not necessarily the moral responsibility of executives, but they are the actions which will be the basis of discussion in the rest of this article.

It can be accepted that executives are not responsible for obvious "acts of God." This does not mean that they should not be held accountable for the results of a natural event, for they may well be in a position to determine the outcome even when the event itself is inevitable. For example, suppose an earthquake causes a factory to collapse, killing several workers. Obviously, we cannot hold the executives of the company which owns the factory responsible for the earthquake itself; earthquakes are natural events which are beyond human control. However, we might hold the executives

responsible for the factory being built in an earthquake zone, or we might hold them responsible for the use of money saving construction methods which caused the building to collapse. In these cases, we would consider the executives at least partly responsible for the workers' deaths. The fact that a person has no influence or control over an event does not necessarily exempt him or her from responsibility for the consequences of that event. What we hold him or her responsible for are the actions which determined those consequences.

Corporate executives, in their role as executives, should also not be held responsible for events which are not the result of the corporation's activities. The concepts of the "executive's role" and of the "corporation's activities" both need explaining.

Executives, because they are people, have more responsibilities, as citizens, neighbours, parents. Such responsibilities, while not being denied, will not be discussed in this paper. The purpose of this present discussion is limited to the moral responsibility of executives in their role as executives. However, this should not be taken to mean that the moral principles that apply to persons acting in the role of executives are any different from those that apply in the rest of their lives. Although it is sometimes argued that the morality of professional activities differs from the morality of everyday life (Carr, 1968), that is a position which cannot be applied to executives without the most careful examination (Callahan, 1988-A; Gillespie, 1983; Nagel, 1978). I will not go into this debate here; since this paper does not discuss the actual moral duties of executives as executives, we need not discuss how they differ from their other duties.

The notion of "corporate activities" also needs expanding. It has been argued that corporations are moral entities in their own right, and that corporations can commit actions (French, 1977). This is a position which I reject for the sorts of reasons outlined in Danley (1980). However, in this paper I will avoid further discussion of this issue because it is not relevant to the current topic. Even if corporations are moral agents and as such are held responsible for corporate activities, this does not exempt the people in the corporation from also being held responsible for their role in those activities. Moral responsibility is not a fixed quantity; its assignment to one moral entity does not necessarily reduce the responsibility of other moral agents. Thus corporate executives can be held morally accountable to the same events for which the corporation is also accountable, though not necessarily to the same degree or for the same reasons. Because of this, I do not have to decide on corporate moral responsibility to discuss the issue of the responsibility executives [have] for their role in corporate actions.

"Corporate activities" can also refer to the actions of the corporation's employees which are done in their capacity as employees. Presumably, executives are in a position to influence such actions on the part of employees, and it is their responsibility for such actions that the rest of this paper will be concerned with. Executives may, for social reasons, be in a position to influence employee behaviour off the job, but the use of such influence does not concern us here. We will confine our examination to events which result from the actions of employees while on the job. To hold the executives responsible for such events (if we decide to do so) is to hold them responsible for the actions of others, but it is assumed that executives have some influence or control over the actions of employees. The question we need to discuss is to what extent the executive has such influence and control, and whether it extends only to actions the executive directly instigates, or to all actions and omissions of employees as employees.

Even though we will confine the discussion to executive responsibility for actions employees commit in their capacity as employees, for convenience' sake such employee actions will sometimes be referred to as the actions of the corporation. This should not be taken to imply that corporations can actually commit actions; the phrase is used as shorthand. Similarly, by employee actions, we mean only those committed as employees.

III. Why Executives May Not Be Morally Responsible

When things go horribly wrong, executives sometimes deny responsibility on the grounds that they did not know, and could not be expected to know, the information they needed to prevent the disaster. They maintain this even when some of the corporation's employees knew, or ought to have known, the relevant information.

Consider the case of DC-10 Ship 29, which crashed near Paris on March 3, 1974 when its cargo doors flew off. All 346 people aboard were killed. Subsequent investigations revealed that McDonnell-Douglas, the manufacturer of the aircraft, was aware of the cargo door problem, and that Ship 29 had been returned to the corporation for FAA ordered corrections to the door locking mechanism (French, 1984; Eddy *et al.*, 1976). These corrections were never made, though stamped inspection sheets indicated they had been. John Brizendine, President of the Douglas division of McDonnell-Douglas, denied all knowledge of this failure to fix the doors (French, 1982), though it is clear that at least some people in the company must have known. Since there is no reason to question Brizendine's honesty, we will assume that the information that could have prevented the disaster failed to reach him. (We will also assume that he would have acted on the information if he had received it.)

As a second example, consider the explosion of the Challenger space shuttle, again with loss of life. Engineers at Morton Thiokol, which manufactured the solid rocket booster, had repeatedly expressed concerns, in written memos and verbally, about possible failure of O-ring seals on cold weather launches (Grossman, 1988). These concerns failed to reach decision making management at NASA, who maintain that they would have stopped the launch had they been aware of the engineers' opinion (Callahan, 1988-B). Again, vital information that could have prevented disaster failed to reach executives responsible for the final decision.

I do not want to raise the issue of the honesty of the executives when they claim they did not know. It has transpired in some cases that executives knew more than they were willing to admit— such was the case in the Dalkon shield tragedy (Mintz, 1985), or the knowledge of tobacco executives about early cancer studies (White, 1988). However, it is clear that executives often do not know, and are not told even if others in the corporation have the information. The immorality of lying, and of being able to stop a disaster and not doing so, are beyond doubt; the responsibility (if any) of executives when they actually are not told is more problematic, and is the central topic of this paper. It will be assumed that in the cases cited (the

DC-10 cargo door problem and the Challenger disaster), executives were in fact in the dark about impending problems.

IV. Negative Information Blockage

Can executives be taken seriously when they claim that they cannot be expected to know about impending tragedy? After all, they have the authority to demand that information be given to them. And it is their job to know what is going on in their corporation. If someone in the company has or can get the information (which is the most interesting case), then why cannot the executives simply send a memo to all employees saying such information is to be sent directly to their attention? This question needs to be examined carefully if we are to determine whether executives are responsible when disaster strikes, or whether we should accept the claim that they did not know and could not have known the information needed to prevent the tragedy.

The problem with getting information to executives is a well-known phenomenon in corporate and other hierarchical organizations which I will call "negative information blockage." In brief, information regarding the riskiness of a corporation's plans is stifled at source or by intervening management, even when senior executives have demanded that such information be sent on to them. This phenomenon needs to be analysed further.

The notion of negative information requires the distinction between a corporation's objectives and its constraints. The objectives (or goals—I will use the two words interchangeably) of a corporation are what its senior executives are perceived as wanting to achieve. These objectives are, of course, the executive's, but it is convenient to refer to them as the corporation's. These goals may or may not be what the executives think they want to achieve, or what they say they want to achieve; corporate mission statements may not be honest or may not be believed. The actual goals of the executives (or the corporation) can only be identified by examining what sorts of behaviour the executives reward, as will be discussed below.

The constraints on a corporation are those facts which affect the pursuit of its goals, and which cannot be changed, at least in the short run. Some constraints are physical, and cannot be violated by anyone in the corporation even if they wanted to. For example, the cabins on jet aircraft need to be pressurized—that need is a fact which no manufacturer can do anything about. Other constraints are moral, legal, or mandated by safety. These constraints can be ignored by a corporation or its employees, and it is these sorts of constraints which interest us.

Objectives and constraints are very different concepts, though sometimes constraints are recognized in statements of a company's objectives. For example, the objective of an aircraft manufacturing corporation might be stated as: "To produce aircraft which can be safely operated." Here safety, which is a constraint, looks like it is part of the objective, but this appearance does not stand up to analysis. The objective is to produce operable aircraft; safety is actually a constraint on that goal because airplanes cannot be operated if they fall out of the sky. Safety is not a separate or secondary goal, but a condition of achieving the actual goal of making operable aircraft.

Within a corporation, goals and constraints are treated very differently. Rewards are given for employee behaviour which appears to help the company achieve its goals. Observing legal, moral, and safety constraints is seldom rewarded; it tends to be assumed that employees will observe such constraints without reward. Instead, employees in companies which enforce constraints are usually punished when violation of the constraint is discovered; they are not usually rewarded just for observing constraints. Complete failure of a corporation to enforce legal, moral or safety constraints raises obvious moral problems; this discussion will be centered on the more interesting case in which constraints are enforced by the corporation (i.e., by the executives), but ignored by some of the employees. Why they are ignored, even under the threat of punishment, has to do with the different ways in which executives encourage employees to pursue goals, and discourage them from violating constraints.

In general, employee behaviour which enhances corporate goals is rewarded, observing constraints is not. Hindering objectives is almost always punished. Constraints are constraints on the pursuit of the company's goals, and hence observing them can threaten an employee's rewards. In fact, observing constraints and asking one's management to do so as well may impede the company's goals to the point where the behaviour itself is punished. Surely this encourages violation of constraints.

There are other pressures on employees to put rewards for pursuing goals before the observance of constraints. Violation of constraints is only punished if one is caught; hence there is an element of gamble involved. The time factor also plays a major role; rewards are usually immediate, while discovery of violated constraints may be months or years away, by which time the employee has had his promotion and is safely elsewhere.

To complicate matters further, corporations are hierarchical. If an employee does resist temptation and observes constraints at the risk of losing rewards, his manager, or his manager's manager, may not. If getting a company to observe a constraint requires escalating concerns to the senior executive level (and this is the case we are concerned with in this article), then a single failure to resist temptation may block the concern from reaching the executives. This is the phenomenon of negative information blockage.

Since negative information blockage is inherent in the nature of goals, constraints, rewards and punishments, then to what extent can executives be held responsible for getting information past the blockage? The next section will consider two possible views on this topic.

V. Executive Responsibility and Negative Information Blockage

The first of the two views is that executives are responsible for doing whatever they can to prevent negative information blockage. They have a moral duty to structure the corporation to ensure that risks of disaster are discovered and made known to themselves (and then, of course, to act on the information). They have a moral responsibility to do as much as they can to prevent tragedy.

What exactly executives can do I will not discuss in detail; a few examples will suffice. They can offer rewards for information brought to them; they can keep an "open door" policy so junior employees can go around the blockages; they can set a personal example of concern for moral, legal, and safety constraints. These ideas are generally discussed in business ethics literature under the topic of whistleblowing, since whistleblowing is often the result of frustration with negative information blockage. (See, for example, Callahan, 1988-C.) Without going into further detail on what executives can do, we can summarize the first view of corporate executive responsibility by suggesting they should do whatever is reasonably possible to prevent knowledge of potential disasters from being blocked before it reaches them.

The second view is that executives, especially CEOs, are responsible for preventing tragedy, excepting only those cases, such as acts of God, which were discussed above in Section II. This view is radically different from the first; just how different can be seen if we consider how executives would be judged in the event of a tragedy. On the first view, the impartial spectator making moral judgements would inquire what steps the executives had taken prior to the tragedy to make sure information on the impending disaster had been conveyed to them. And, of course, they would ask whether the executives had acted on anything they knew. On the second view, the impartial spectator would hold the executive morally responsible for the failure to acquire sufficient information to prevent the tragedy, regardless of whether or not steps had been taken to circumvent negative information blockage. This view is essentially holding that since the tragedy happened, the steps taken were obviously not sufficient, and hence the executives are morally culpable.

It should be noted that on the second view, we are holding executives morally responsible even though they did not know the disaster might happen, and even though they may have taken some steps to acquire the knowledge. We are holding them morally responsible for the result, not the effort. The first view holds them responsible only for the effort.

There are many cases in life where people are held responsible for results rather than effort: it is one of the painful lessons we learn as children. For example, on examinations, students, especially in such subjects on medicine and engineering, are quite rightly marked on results, not the amount of effort they put into studying. And executives themselves do not hesitate to hold employees responsible for getting results.

Demanding results on the job, not just effort, is acceptable because it is necessary. When an engineer designs a bridge, it is important to society that it does not collapse. It is important to society that doctors are competent, not just that they are doing their best. We are often justified in holding people responsible for doing their job well.

If people fail in their jobs, they may or may not be held legally liable depending on the circumstances, but in any case their careers suffer, and they may lose their jobs. The fact that they are held responsible is reflected in the impact on their professional standing when they succeed or fail. To distinguish this type of responsibility from legal and moral responsibility, I will refer to it as professional responsibility.

The case of professional responsibility that best parallels the situation of executives is that of cabinet ministers in a parliamentary system. When things go wrong in an area of ministerial responsibility, the minister is held accountable and is expected to resign. They are not supposed to argue that they tried, that they have not been negligent, or that they are not legally liable. Thus Lord Carrington resigned when Argentina invaded the Falklands; he did not stay on protesting that it was not his fault (though it probably was not). The questions we must now deal with are: should we apply professional responsibility to executives? And secondly, how does professional responsibility relate to moral responsibility?

VI. Professional Responsibility

The concept of professional responsibility applies when the outcome of a professional activity is of great concern to a person or people other than the person doing the activity. It especially applies if the outcome is of concern over and above any contract the professional has with some other person, or if the outcome is of great concern to bystanders. Let me illustrate these points with an example.

When I buy a pair of shoes and find them faulty, I take them back to the shoe store and generally will be satisfied if I am given back my money. The responsibility is limited to reversing the contract. When I go to a doctor for an operation, I am not interested in hearing that he or she will refund me the cost of the operation if it goes wrong, especially if I die. We can say in this case that the doctor has a professional responsibility which goes beyond the "contract." It goes beyond because the consequences of failure go beyond the contract. Similarly, if an engineer designs a bridge that

collapses, then refunding the money he or she received for the design hardly helps those who were on the bridge when it collapsed. It helps so little that that course of action is seldom pursued. The engineer, in this case, has a professional responsibility.

Liability laws generally reflect the fact that responsibility can extend far beyond reversing the original contract, but this discussion is not an attempt to define legal liability. The point is that professional responsibility arises when the consequences of failure have effects on other people (customers or bystanders) which exceed the confines of the initial contract.

Clearly, this applies to executives. If they fail to create a corporate culture which overcomes negative information blockage and disaster results, it often involves the death of their customers (or of their customers' customers, as in the case of the DC-10s). It is clear that we are justified in holding executives professionally responsible when tragedy happens. In other words, we hold them professionally responsible for failing to obtain the information needed to prevent the disaster, whether or not they tried to.

But is holding executives professionally responsible different from holding them morally responsible? In the cases we have been examining, there is a close connection between the two.

Executives and everyone else have a moral responsibility to ensure that their activities do not result in the deaths of others if that result can be prevented. Executives, therefore, have a moral responsibility to do their best to obtain the information needed to prevent disasters. They have a professional responsibility, as we have seen, not just to do their best, but to actually succeed in preventing avoidable disasters. The latter grows out of the former in the sense that executives have a professional responsibility to succeed in fulfilling their moral responsibilities. (Of course, they also have professional responsibilities with other origins as well.) Thus, although normally a person only has a moral responsibility for trying to avoid immoral results, in this case (and in others) a person has a professional responsibility to succeed in fulfilling the underlying moral responsibility.

This conclusion has a major implication for judging executives; namely, when tragedy happens, we are justified in holding them responsible based on moral values. If they object that they did not have the information necessary to prevent the disaster and that they had made an honest effort to obtain that information, then we can accept that as individuals they have fulfilled their moral obligations. (We are assuming honesty.) But as professional executives, they have failed to fulfill their professional obligation to carry out moral requirements. We are still justified in holding them responsible based on moral considerations.

References

Brooks, L.J.: 1989, "Corporate Ethical Performance: Trends, Forecasts, and Outlooks," *Journal of Business Ethics* **8**, No. 1, pp. 31–8.

Callahan, J. C.: 1988-A, *Ethical Issues in Professional Life* (Oxford University Press, Oxford), pp. 49–50.

Callahan, J. C.: 1988-B, *Ethical Issues in Professional Life* (Oxford University Press, Oxford), p. 342.

Callahan, J. C.: 1988-C, *Ethical Issues in Professional Life* (Oxford University Press, Oxford), pp. 337–39.

Carr, A. Z.: 1968, "Is Business Bluffing Ethical?," *Ethical Issues in Professional Life*, C. Callahan, ed. (Oxford University Press, Oxford), pp. 69–72.

Danley, J. R.: 1980, "Corporate Moral Agency: The Case for Anthropological Bigotry," *Ethical Issues in Professional Life,* J. C. Callahan, ed. (Oxford University Press, Oxford), pp. 269–74.

French, Peter A.: 1977, "Corporate Moral Agency," *Ethical Issues in Professional Life,* J. C. Callahan, ed. (Oxford University Press, Oxford), pp. 265–69.

Gillespie, Norman Chase: 1983, "The Business of Ethics," *Ethical Issues in Professional Life,* J. C. Callahan, ed. (Oxford University Press, Oxford), pp. 72–6.

Globe and Mail: 1989, "Polluting firm's chairman hauled into court by U.S. judge," Associated Press, Globe and Mail, August 10 1989, p. B10.

Grosman, Brian A.: 1988, *Corporate Loyalty: A Trust Betrayed* (Penguin Books, Markham Ont.), pp. 177–79.

Mintz, Morton: 1985, *At Any Cost: Corporate Greed, Women, and the Dalkon Shield* (Random House, Inc., New York).

Nagel, Thomas: 1978, "Ruthlessness in Public Life," *Ethical Issues in Professional Life,* J. C. Callahan, ed. (Oxford University Press, Oxford), pp. 76–83.

White, Larry C.: 1988, *Merchants of Death: The American Tobacco Industry* (Beech Tree/Morrow, New York).

Corporate Executives, Disasters, and Moral Responsibility

ROBERT LARMER

IN A RECENT PAPER, John Bishop has explored the question of whether corporate executives can be held morally responsible for disasters.[1] His thesis is that they cannot be held responsible for acts of God, i.e. events which are beyond human control and could not reasonably be foreseen, and actions which are not performed on behalf of the corporation. They can be held responsible, however, both in instances in which they possessed the information needed to prevent the disaster, and in instances in which, although it was not personally

[1]John D. Bishop, "The Moral Responsibility of Corporate Executives for Disasters," *Journal of Business Ethics,* Vol. 10, 1991, pp. 377–83.

available, the necessary information was possessed by company personnel.

Bishop's claim that corporate executives should not be held accountable for "acts of God," nor for actions which are not performed on behalf of the corporation, seems uncontroversial, as does his claim that they should be held accountable in cases where they possessed the information needed to prevent the disaster but failed to act on it. What is controversial is his claim that corporate executives can be held accountable in instances where, although they did not personally possess the information needed to avert disaster, such information was in company hands. It is to this latter claim that

From Journal of Business Ethics 15: *785–788, 1996. Reprinted with permission.*

he devotes the bulk of his attention and upon which he focuses his argument.

Prima facie, the view that corporate executives can be held accountable for disasters, even in the absence of the information needed to prevent them, seems to run counter to Kant's commonly accepted dictum that *ought* implies *can.* It seems to make no sense to hold individuals responsible for preventing events they could not anticipate or forestall.

It might be replied that we often hold individuals responsible for fulfilling tasks they are incapable of performing. Intoxicated drivers, for example, are held morally culpable for failing to drive safely, even though it is clear they are incapable of doing so. Such cases however, do not refute the claim that ought implies can, since the only reason we hold the drunk driver morally culpable is that although it is not within his power to drive safely once intoxicated, it was within his power not to become intoxicated in the first place. The possibility is suggested that at least in some instances, we may legitimately hold corporate executives responsible for disasters they lacked the information to prevent, if the corporate executive was in a position to acquire the relevant information and could reasonably be expected to have done so.

I think this latter argument has merit and that it refutes the facile claim that a corporate executive's ignorance of the information needed to prevent a disaster is never morally culpable. It will not, however, serve Bishop's purposes. He wants to hold that so long as the necessary information was possessed by anyone within the company, the corporate executives of that company can be held accountable for the disaster. He further argues that it is not always reasonable to think that corporate executives are, or could be, in a position to obtain such information. He notes in this regard that the phenomenon of "negative information blockage," the stifling at the source or by intervening management of information regarding the riskiness of a corporation's plans, is characteristic of even well-run companies. He thinks that this phenomenon is inherent in any system of business and occurs even when senior executives have demanded that such information be brought to their attention.[2]

How then, does it make any sense to hold that even in the absence of the information needed to prevent a disaster, a corporate executive is always and inevitably to be held accountable so long as the requisite information was possessed by someone within the company? It is one thing to claim that a corporate executive's ignorance is no excuse in instances where she could reasonably be expected to have such information; it is quite another to suggest that she be held accountable even in instances where she could not reasonably be expected to have obtained it.

Bishop's answer is that we must distinguish between moral and professional responsibility. He notes that there are many instances where we hold individuals accountable not simply for doing their best, but for the success or failure of their efforts. Thus a cabinet minister may feel compelled to resign when a policy fails, even though he may be innocent of any negligence or moral laxness.[3]

He maintains that the concept of professional responsibility is relevant "when the outcome of a professional activity is of great concern to a person or people other than the person doing the activity [and] it especially applies if the outcome is of concern over and above any contract the professional has with some other person, or if the outcome is of great concern to bystanders."[4] He cites the example of an engineer designing a bridge, suggesting that the engineer's responsibilities go far beyond refunding her fee if the bridge collapses.[5]

Under these criteria, he argues we are justified in holding corporate executives professionally responsible for failing to obtain the information necessary to prevent disasters. The question of whether or not they tried to obtain the necessary information is pertinent to the issue of whether they are morally culpable, but irrelevant to questions of professional responsibility. He concludes that, since corporate executives not only have a moral obligation to seek to avoid disasters but a professional obligation to be successful in avoiding disasters, we are justified in holding them responsible on moral considerations.[6]

The concept of professional responsibility is interesting and deserves further explanation. It will not, however, bear the weight of Bishop's argument. There are at least three reasons this is so.

---

[2]Ibid., pp. 80–81.

[3]Ibid., pp. 381–82.
[4]Ibid., p. 382.
[5]Ibid., p. 382.
[6]Ibid., p. 382.

394 CHAPTER 12 Corporate Responsibility

First, if as Bishop insists, professional responsibility must be distinguished from both legal and moral responsibility,[7] it is difficult to see how invoking the notion of professional responsibility can support the conclusion that in cases where corporate executives are not morally culpable for lacking the information necessary to prevent a disaster, we are nevertheless "justified in holding them responsible based on moral considerations."[8] How, if the corporate executive is not morally culpable, do moral considerations enter the picture?

His answer is that, although professional responsibility must be distinguished from moral responsibility, part of a corporate executive's professional responsibility is to fulfill certain moral requirements. He comments that

> Executives . . . have a moral responsibility to ensure that their activities do not result in the deaths of others if that result can be prevented. . . . They have a professional . . . responsibility . . . not just to do their best, but to actually succeed in preventing avoidable disasters. The latter grows out of the former in the sense that executives have a professional responsibility to succeed in fulfilling their moral responsibilities.[9]

It may be agreed that one of a corporate executive's professional responsibilities is to fulfill certain moral obligations and that one of these is to do his best to avoid disasters. Let us suppose, however, that despite a corporate executive's best efforts, he is not successful in obtaining from company personnel information that could have prevented a disaster. On what grounds can we judge him as failing to fulfill his professional obligation? Certainly not on the grounds that he has failed to fulfill the moral requirements built into his professional responsibility, since all that morality requires is that he have done his best to avoid the tragedy.

Bishop insists that "although normally a person only has a moral responsibility for trying to avoid immoral results, . . . [in the case of a corporate executive] a person has a professional responsibility in fulfilling the underlying moral responsibility"[10] But what is required to fulfill this underlying moral responsibility? Bishop claims that it includes

actually preventing avoidable disasters. The problem is that what is avoidable by one person in a certain set of circumstances may be unavoidable by another, or even the same, person in a different set of circumstances. A disaster which is avoidable if certain information is passed on to a corporate executive may be unavoidable if that information never reaches her. Whether or not that information ever reaches her is, in many instances, beyond her ability to control. Her moral responsibility is to make every reasonable effort to be in possession of the information needed to prevent disasters; it is not actually to possess information she cannot obtain. Any judgement that she has failed to meet her professional obligation in such instances is grounded not in the fact that she has failed to meet the requirements of morality, but in the insistence that executives be successful in what they undertake. It is a mistake, therefore, to claim that moral considerations can justify the claim that so long as the information needed to avert a disaster was possessed by someone within the company, we can always hold its corporate executives responsible.

I have argued that any decision to hold corporate executives responsible for obtaining information they could not reasonably have been expected to gather must be based not on moral considerations, but on purely non-moral aspects of professional responsibility. This brings us to a second problem in Bishop's argument. The issue is not whether as a matter of fact we hold corporate executives legally or professionally responsible in certain situations, but whether we are morally justified in doing so. Put a little differently, our interest is in whether present notions of legal and professional responsibility need to be altered to fit the requirements of morality. Bishop's claim that corporate executives should be held professionally responsible for disasters, even in cases where they could not reasonably be expected to acquire the information needed to prevent the disaster, is a normative claim not about how in fact professional responsibility is presently understood, but how it *should* be understood. The understanding of professional responsibility it advocates should only be accepted if we find it acceptable to hold individuals morally responsible for events which they could not anticipate and over which they had no control.

The problem, as Bishop notes early in his paper, is that we do not hold people responsible for

[7]Ibid., p. 381.
[8]Ibid., p. 382.
[9]Ibid., p. 382.
[10]Ibid., p. 382.

events over which they have no influence or control. If there are instances in which individuals are held professionally responsible for events they could not reasonably be expected to have taken precautions against, this is an indication that we should reform our understanding of professional responsibility, not that we should abandon our basic moral intuitions.[11]

A third problem with Bishop's position is that, in the final analysis, the notion of professional responsibility is dependent upon the notion of moral responsibility. Initially, this does not seem the case: assignment of moral responsibility for a disaster can only occur if the individual was lax in taking efforts to avoid it; assignment of professional responsibility makes no such requirement. Things are not so simple, however. No one would want to hold corporate executives professionally responsible for disasters resulting from "acts of God," yet if professional responsibility does not require moral culpability why should such events be excluded? It seems clear that if no one could reasonably have been expected to have acquired the information necessary to have prevented a disaster we could never be justified in holding a corporate executive professionally responsible for its occurrence.

I suspect that what drives the notion of professional responsibility is that in complex situations it is very difficult to accurately judge degrees of moral culpability. Questions of whether all reasonable steps were taken to prevent a disaster and whose responsibility it was to take those various steps are notoriously hard to answer. Given the human tendency to pass the buck, it is useful to have a practical rule that in cases where it may possibly be doubted that he took all reasonable steps to prevent the disaster, a corporate executive be judged as failing in his professional duties, even though it is far from clear that he is actually morally culpable. Should it become clear, however, that he did take all reasonable steps to prevent the disaster and that he is in no way morally culpable, it also becomes clear that he cannot be held pro-

fessionally responsible. It cannot be denied, therefore, that professional responsibility derives from moral responsibility and that any assignment of professional responsibility for a disaster implies that there is at least the possibility of ascribing moral culpability for its occurrence. Contrary to Bishop, questions of professional responsibility cannot be treated independently of questions of moral responsibility.

I have been attacking Bishop's view that corporate executives can be held accountable for disasters so long as the information necessary to prevent the disaster was possessed by company personnel on the basis that it does not do justice to the fact that in many instances it is unreasonable to expect a corporate executive to obtain such information. My own view is that although it is often difficult to say whether a corporate executive could have done better in seeking to obtain the information necessary to prevent a disaster, we cannot sever the notion of professional responsibility from the notion of what can reasonably be expected. It is no easy matter to say what can reasonably be expected in the way of acquiring such information, but unless we attempt to do so the notion of professional responsibility becomes morally monstrous.

Two practical comments are in order. First, if we should be cautious to blame corporate executives for disasters, we should also be cautious to attribute a company's success to them. The idea that a company's success should automatically be attributed to its corporate executives and that this justifies extremely high salaries and bonuses strikes me as no more defensible than the suggestion that they should automatically be blamed if disasters occur. It seems far more likely that both the attribution of blame and credit should be spread more evenly through the corporation.

Second, there is a moral obligation on the part of corporate executives to know their capabilities and limitations. Even if one is doing one's best, one may be acting immorally if one insists on acting in an area where one knows oneself to be less qualified or competent than the job requires. A corporate executive is morally required to assess both the impact of her decisions and her competency in making decisions. A humble heart and a desire to act only in areas one knows oneself effective scarcely guarantee the avoidance of disasters, but they are a good beginning.

---

[11]Bishops slips very quickly from the observation that professional responsibility is often understood in a fashion that holds individuals accountable for events over which they had no control to the position that such a concept of professional responsibility is morally acceptable. The question of whether he has fallen victim to the naturalistic fallacy arises.

Questions for Chapter 12

1. Would French agree that corporate intentions are always reducible to human intentions? Explain why or why not.
2. What does French mean when he writes the following?

   [W]hen the corporate act is consistent with, an instantiation or an implementation of established corporate policy, then it is proper to describe it as having been done for corporate reasons, as having been caused by a corporate desire coupled with a corporate belief and so, in other words, as corporate intentional.

   Why does he wish to say this?

3. Ewin thinks that it is possible for corporations to possess rights and duties, but not virtues. Why? Does it make any sense to think that a corporation could be a person if it is incapable of ever exhibiting virtue or vice?
4. What is Ewin's argument for rejecting the claim that corporations are logically tied into selfishness?
5. On what basis does Bishop distinguish professional and moral responsibility?
6. Given that Bishop distinguishes professional and moral responsibility, does it make any sense to hold executives morally culpable in instances where they fail in their professional obligation to prevent disasters? Explain.
7. What does it mean to claim that "ought implies can"? Why does Larmer think that Bishop's claim runs counter to this principle?
8. Larmer suggests that questions of professional responsibility cannot be treated independently of questions of moral responsibility. What is his argument in support of this claim?

Case 12.1 How Safe a Gun?[1]

On June 19, 1983, during a trapshooting competition, the barrel of Robert Loitz's shotgun exploded, injuring his left hand and thumb. He subsequently brought suit against Remington, the manufacturer of his shotgun.

At issue was the safety of the Model 1100 12-gauge shotgun he had been using. This model, a semiautomatic gas-operated shotgun designed for hunting and target shooting and first marketed in 1963, had subsequent sales of over

three million. The particular gun used by Loitz was purchased secondhand in 1972 and had presented no problems prior to the explosion. Loitz, as is common with experienced competitors, was using shells he had reloaded.

Loitz alleged that the explosion was a result of Remington using unsuitable steel for the shotgun barrel. An expert witness, Dr. David Levinson, a professor of metallurgy at the University of Illinois, testified that, in his view, the gun barrel exploded in response to a normal-pressure shell as a result of metal fatigue. Levinson suggested that the high sulphur content of the steel used by Remington permitted the formation of fatigue

---

[1]Based on *Loitz v. Remington Arms Co., Inc.*, as found in 563 *Northeastern Reporter,* 2nd Series, 397 (Ill. 1990).

cracks that under repeated use could eventually cause the barrel to fail under normal pressure loads.

Remington alleged that the explosion was the result of an overloaded shell. Their expert witness, Dr. Richard Hertzberg, a professor of metallurgy at Lehigh University, testified that the explosion was probably the result of an overloaded shell. He based his view on his own tests of the strength of the steel used by Remington and on a comparison of Loitz's gun with guns that had been deliberately exploded by discharging overloaded shells. Hertzberg was not aware until trial that a Remington barrel had failed during proof-testing and was unable to explain why this could occur.

Testing of Loitz's unused reloaded shells revealed none that was overloaded. Evidence was also brought that, by the time of Loitz's accident, Remington had received reports of ninety-four other barrel explosions of Model 1100 barrels resulting in injury. In five of these cases, the persons involved claimed to be using factory-made ammunition. Remington maintained that, in all cases, the cause of the explosion was an overloaded shell. In addition, evidence was brought that, by 1979, Remington had received reports of over one hundred barrel explosions not resulting in injury.

1. Did Loitz deserve to receive damages? Why or why not?

2. To what degree, if any, do you regard Remington as morally culpable in regard to Loitz's accident? How would you justify your answer?

Case 12.2 The Untrustworthy Encyclopedia[2]

Wilhelm Winter and Cynthia Zheng enjoyed eating mushrooms. Wishing to harvest some of the edible wild varieties, they bought *The Encyclopedia of Mushrooms,* a reference guide on the habitat, collection, and cooking of mushrooms. This book was the work of two British authors and was originally published by a British firm. G.P. Putnam's Sons, an American publishing firm, later purchased copies of the book from the British firm and distributed it in the United States. Putnam played no part in the writing or editing of the book.

Relying on the *Encyclopedia*'s descriptions to determine which varieties were safe to harvest, Winter and Zheng went mushroom hunting. Unfortunately, after cooking and eating the mushrooms they collected, they both became critically ill. They subsequently required liver transplants.

Alleging that the *Encyclopedia* contained erroneous and misleading information with regard to identifying some of the most deadly species of mushrooms, they brought suit against Putnam on the grounds of product liability, breach of warranty, negligence, negligent misrepresentation, and false representation.

With regard to product liability, they argued that, although product liability is customarily held to extend only to tangible items, the *Encyclopedia* was analogous to aeronautical charts, which several jurisdictions had treated as "products" for the purposes of product liability. Their argument was that the *Encyclopedia* was analogous to aeronautical charts insofar as both represent natural features of the world and both are intended to be used while engaged in hazardous activity.

With regard to breach of warranty, negligence, negligent misrepresentation, and false representation, they argued that Putnam either had a duty to investigate the accuracy of the books it published or a duty to warn the consumer either that the information in the book cannot be relied on or that it had not investigated the text and cannot, therefore, guarantee its accuracy.

1. The court noted that computer software that fails to yield the result for which it was

[2]Based on Winter v. G.P. Putnam's Sons, as found in 938 *Federal Reporter,* 2nd Series, 1033 (9th Cir. 1991).

designed might be considered a "product" for the purposes of product liability. Might it be plausibly argued that the *Encyclopedia* is analogous to such software inasmuch as it, like the software, is designed, with proper use, to yield certain results?

2. Does a publisher have any moral, as opposed to legal, duty to try to ensure the accuracy of the works it publishes?

3. Should a publisher have a legal duty to ensure the accuracy of the books it publishes? What would be the implications of creating such a legal duty?

Further Readings for Chapter 12

Angelo J. Corlett, "Corporate Responsibility and Punishment," *Public Affairs Quarterly* 2(1), January 1988, pp. 1–16.

Peter French, "The Corporation as a Moral Person," *American Philosophical Quarterly* 3, 1979, pp. 207–215.

John Ladd, "Corporate Mythology and Individual Responsibility," *The International Journal of Applied Philosophy* 2, Spring 1984, pp. 1–21.

David T. Risser, "Punishing Corporations: A Proposal," *Business and Professional Ethics Journal* 8(3), 1988, pp. 83–91.

Jere Surber, "Individual and Corporate Responsibility," *Business and Professional Ethics Journal* 2(4), 1982, pp. 67–88.

INFOTRAC COLLEGE EDITION To learn more about the topics from this chapter, you can use the following words to conduct an electronic search on InfoTrac College Edition, an online library of journals. Here you will find a multitude of articles from various sources and perspectives: *www.infotrac-college.com/wadsworth/access.html*

corporate responsibility

corporate punishment

Chapter 13

Responsibilities of Professionals

Introduction

PROFESSIONALS SUCH AS DOCTORS, engineers, lawyers, and academics enjoy a great deal of power and prestige in society. Because of their specialized knowledge and their ability to affect basic issues of human life, they are commonly perceived as subject to more rigorous standards of conduct than nonprofessionals. Although it is no easy matter to say how a profession should be defined or precisely what distinguishes a profession from other occupations, we are accustomed to speaking of "professional ethics," meaning some special set of rules or guidelines designed to bring about moral conduct within a particular profession.

Without a doubt the notion of a professional ethic has played an important role in the development and self-understanding of the professions. It has, however, both a bright and dark side. At its best, a special set of rules or guidelines remind men and women of good will of their special responsibilities, and provides a repository of accumulated wisdom of what constitutes ethical practice within the profession. At its worst, such rules or guidelines may become a poor substitute for proper ethical motivation or represent the attempt of an elite group to escape public accountability.

The selections in the present chapter focus on the issue of what it means to be a professional and act ethically. They deal not with specific issues that arise in particular professions, but rather with the larger and more general question of how the concept of professional ethics is to be understood, internalized, and implemented.

In our first selection, "The Regulation of Virtue: Cross-Currents in Professional Ethics," Bruce Jennings examines three interrelated issues. The first concerns the dual emphasis that professional ethics must place on discerning both what is right and motivating right behavior. Although there are instances in professional life where it may be difficult to discern what is morally correct, there are many instances where the problem is not to understand what is right but rather to motivate individuals to do the right thing.

The second issue concerns the distinction between moral dilemmas inherent in the human condition and moral dilemmas created by institutional structures. Jennings observes that the first type are unavoidable, but that the second can often be avoided by altering institutional structures. An important part of professional ethics is to be open to the possibility of avoiding moral dilemmas by modifying the institutions within which professionals function.

The third issue concerns whether an emphasis on rules and regulations, which is typical of professional codes of conduct, undermines the emphasis on character and virtue that lies at the heart of professional ethics. Does an emphasis on regulations foster the perception on the part of professionals that adherence to rules is all it takes to act ethically? Is there a danger that simply following rules will become a substitute for good character and a commitment to service? The other side of the coin, of course, is whether a lack of emphasis on rules and regulation will encourage a lack of accountability on the part of professionals. It is easy to see how an issue arising out of this third concern is whether professionals should regulate themselves or be subject to external regulation.

In her article "Beyond Professional Ethics: Issues and Agendas," Beth Savan explores the role of what are sometimes called "ginger groups" within professional bodies. She notes that professional training often takes the form of an "apprenticeship," where success depends on the goodwill of senior members of the profession and where challenging the priorities or practices of the group is strongly discouraged. She further comments that this kind of training does not encourage, and may even discourage, a sense of responsibility to the larger community. She feels that this, combined with the fact that professionals typically occupy a high place in society and belong to powerful professional bodies that are largely autonomous, means that the self-interest of professionals tends to coincide with preserving the political and social *status quo*.

Savan is far from convinced that the vested interests of professionals can be counted on to correspond with the interests of the public whom they are pledged to serve. She considers it especially important that individuals within a profession who perceive a tension between the activities of their professional organizations and its stated commitment to serving public interest act as gadflies to their colleagues' consciences. These small "ginger" groups, usually at considerable cost to themselves, serve to prod the collective conscience of their professions.

Don Welch's "Just Another Day at the Office: The Ordinariness of Professional Ethics" discusses the frequently met claim that the moral standards for professionals should be substantially different from those for nonprofessionals. Welch views this claim as misleading on at least two grounds. First, although it may begin as a claim that professionals are held to a higher standard of morality than nonprofessionals, there is a lurking danger that, in the absence of any clear account of what "higher" amounts to, this claim amounts simply to saying that professionals should not be judged on the basis of what is considered moral for nonprofessionals. In practice, this can amount to an unjustified immunity for professionals to what we would otherwise morally require of them.

Second, Welch does not feel that the distinction between professionals and nonprofessionals can be made in such a way that it justifies the concept of a distinctively professional ethic. He argues that, although the context in which they encounter moral problems is different, both professionals and nonprofessionals experience and respond to ethical problems in the same way. In both cases, the fundamental issue is "that all of us, in all aspects of our lives, are subject to moral claims inherent in the roles we play." The fact that we all play a number of different roles and that these roles can be in tension or conflict means that we will all face competing duties. Put a little differently, the question is how do we balance competing priorities. This, Welch insists, is an issue for all of us and not simply professionals. To think, therefore, that professionals face a substantially different moral task than nonprofessionals is a mistake.

In his article "The Excuses That Make Professional Ethics Irrelevant," Banks McDowell notes that, in most instances, "the real problems facing professionals are not ones of learning, but of living up to the expectations of professional ethics." This means that we should focus not simply on the concept of what is required if one is to act ethically, but on the reasons that professionals give for failing in their professional duties. To what degree do these factors excuse a professional for failing to act ethically?

McDowell distinguishes four types of excuses that professionals give for failing in their duties. These are: (1) claims of ignorance, (2) transfer of responsibility, (3) irresistible pressure, and (4) technological failure. In assessing these, it is important to realize that an excuse can be either good or bad, that is, it can genuinely be a reason to think someone has a lessened responsibility for improper behavior, or it can fail to provide a reason for thinking someone should be held less responsible for such behavior. Of these four types of excuses, the claim of ignorance seems least likely to succeed as a valid reason for failure, since it is clearly the duty of professionals to know their ethical obligations. All the others, however, can, in certain circumstances, be seen as diminishing the guilt of someone who fails in his or her responsibilities.

A problem, of course, and one that McDowell does a good job of discussing, is that excuses are context-sensitive. In some circumstances these typical excuses are legitimate; in others they serve as mere rationalizations that should not be seen as mitigating guilt. This points to the fact that, until the fundamental problems masked by excuses are discerned and dealt with, their use by professionals to evade personal responsibility will be viewed with great suspicion by nonprofessionals.

The Regulation of Virtue:
Cross-Currents in Professional Ethics

BRUCE JENNINGS

PROFESSIONAL ETHICS is based on an optimistic wager best made by a subdued heart. The wager is that something of important ethical substance can be learned about the conduct of the professions in modern society from an interdisciplinary dialogue and, beyond that, ultimately from an even more inclusive public dialogue. The discourse of professional ethics is most successful when it achieves a public dimension—when it addresses matters of genuine public concern in a way accessible to the public at large. It is less successful when it is limited to professionals talking to other professionals about the ethics of their colleagues, and least successful of all when limited to philosophers talking

From Journal of Business Ethics *10(8), 1991. Reprinted by permission of Kluwer Academic Publishers.*

to other philosophers about the ethics of everybody else.

Now if the success of professional ethics rests upon its ability to cross boundaries, as it were, to be interdisciplinary and public, then it may be useful to step back and ask what must be the case in order for those boundaries to be crossed. What assumptions do we have to make in order for professional ethics to achieve "uptake" (as the ordinary language philosophers used to say)? What functions does discourse in professional ethics perform and whet keeps it meaningful or communicative? What keeps it from misfiring? For misfire it can, and often does—when it is hived off into an academic ghetto called "applied ethics," when it becomes an ideological *apologia* for professional domination and power, or when it is trivialized by an excessive concern with legal and financial issues so that most of the human moral drama inherent in professional practice—the drama of trust, dependency, vulnerability, fallibility, uncertainty, tragic choices—is overlooked.

I contend that professional ethics can and should be a medium through which we come to explore and to appreciate that moral drama richly. It can and should provide a forum for a critical and historical assessment of the social roles and influences of the professions in relation to the technologies and specialized knowledge the professions produce and reproduce. It can offer ethical critique and guidance by evaluating professional conduct in light of well reasoned and justified principles and rules. Finally, professional ethics can be a kind of ongoing conversation and renegotiation of the social contract between the professions and society.

One objection arises immediately. To say that this is a possible vision for what the discourse of professional ethics should aspire to be is to say that something like a public philosophy is still possible in what we euphemistically call our "pluralistic" society. Yet how can a rich public philosophy prosper in our divided, fragmented, Babelesque world, where increasingly small units of cultural cohesion can only communicate with one another in a *lingue franca* [i.e., any language serving as a medium of communication between different people] of interests and imperialistic rights-claims, and where, in order to avoid outright hostility, the most one can aspire to is an equilibrium of mutual avoidance, indifference, and the kind of toleration that signifies a desire not to be bothered oneself?

The present dispensation does not seem propitious for the emergence of a professional ethics nurtured by a public philosophy.[1]

The question of how professional ethics is possible is closely related to the question of what professional ethics is for. How are we to think about what can reasonably be expected from professional ethics? What framework of concepts and categories can we use to articulate its goals and purposes? In what follows I shall try to get a purchase on these questions by reflecting on three interrelated issues that tacitly inform and color much work in professional ethics. The first of these issues has to do with the difference (if there is one) between understanding and motivation. The second issue concerns how we interpret what I will call the situation of moral agency in the professions, and in particular whether the dilemmas moral agents face are somehow inherent in moral agency itself or are artifacts of specific institutional structures. The third issue involves the ambiguity captured in my title: it is the paradox that professional ethics regulation—i.e., general, rule-governed attempts to deter ethical misconduct and to encourage right conduct—must rely on a kind of motivation that is undermined by the very existence of the regulations that motivation is necessary to sustain. Professional ethics has not yet come to grips with this paradox because it has not really come to grips with the implications of the notion of moral virtue. And the reasons for this, in turn, lead us back to the problem of professional ethics as civic discourse.

Seeing the Right and Wanting to Do Right

Consider first the distinction between seeing the right versus motivating right conduct. What I have in mind is this. There are times in the moral life of professionals (and everybody else too) when it is absolutely clear what is right and what is wrong, and the problem is not knowing but acting; the problem is to get people to do what is right and to avoid doing what is wrong. At issue here is not really an ethical quandary or dilemma; the problem is more one of how to create the commitment to

[1]Sullivan, W: 1982, *Reconstructing Public Philosophy* (University of California Press, Berkeley).

the right thing within the psyches and self-identities of moral agents.[2] And outwardly, how do we structure our institutions in such a way that on the whole people acting without a policeman looking over their shoulder will do the right thing rather than the wrong thing? For no conceivable institution, not even the worst Gulag, can possibly police everyone all the time.

Seeing the right, on the other hand, is a problem that arises in those situations in life where reasonable people of good will look at the same circumstances and facts, but just don't know what is right and what is wrong. Reasonable people of good will can disagree about what the right thing to do is.

Both of these situations arise in professional practice. Professional ethics has to address the challenge of teaching professionals how to see the right, and it also has to figure out how to motivate right conduct. Many times professional ethics tends to err on the side of worrying excessively about motivating right conduct. This is scandal ethics; it is still probably the most publicly visible face of the discourse of professional ethics today. But one can go only so far with public ethical discourse in this mode. Talking about taking bribes is really not an interesting ethical question because there is no interesting argument in favor of taking bribes. There must be more to professional ethics than that.

At the same time, it is possible to be too idealistic and to forget about real world exigencies and demands. As students of professional ethics it is not open for us to say: "The only things I'm concerned about as an ethicist are the really interesting moral dilemmas of life. Don't bother me with the details about regulation and how to get people motivated. That's somebody else's problem; leave that to the educators or the psychologists or the lawyers or the bureaucrats. As an ethicist, as a philosopher, I am interested only in those moral dilemmas where we really have to agonize, balancing right versus right and figuring out how to choose the lesser of evils. My *metier* [i.e., trade or profession] is illumination and enlightenment, not moral police work; my task is to win through to some clarity and resolution in precisely those situations that initially present themselves to us as deep quandaries."

A great deal of time teaching, writing, and talking about professional ethics is quite properly spent in grappling with hard cases of precisely this kind. But so much time is spent in trying to sort out what the values are, what the rights and wrongs are, that no time is given over to figuring out how to change the world, how to actually affect professional behavior or how to make things better for clients, patients, or fellow citizens.

So we can err on both sides: a scandal ethics that is philosophically banal, or an exquisite, almost sublime brand of ethics that is essentially irrelevant to the actually existing world of professional practice. In my estimation, professional ethics has not yet decided which side it wants to err on, nor has it discovered how to cover moral understanding and moral motivation equally well.

The Situation of Moral Agency

A second important issue for professional ethics has to do with how we interpret the situation of the moral agent. What is the source of the moral dilemmas the agent faces, what is impinging on her range of moral choice, and what is the appropriate response to these dilemmas? Here it is useful to distinguish between what we might call "natural dilemmas" and "institutional dilemmas."

There are situations in the moral life where dilemmas flow just from the nature of things and from enduring features of what can only be called human nature. In any conceivable situation, in any conceivable institutional arrangement, human beings being what they are, they are bound to face certain kinds of moral choices and moral dilemmas. I simply cannot care for my ailing, elderly father and my six year old son in the same way, to the same degree, at the same time. In a completely just welfare state, neither my father in his nursing home nor my son in his day care center would be deprived of care and comfort. But it would be care and comfort from strangers, not from me, which is not the same, and the dilemma would remain.

On the other hand, we also face certain kinds of moral dilemmas that are just as clearly artifacts of a particular institutional arrangement. We face hard choices and tradeoffs figuring out how best to distribute burdens among people equitably because we are faced with artificial scarcity

[2]Pincoffs, E. L.: 1986, *Quandaries and Virtues* (University Press of Kansas, Lawrence).

imposed by the nature of our institutions or the nature of regulations and laws. A physician working in an intensive care unit, for example, is in a situation where someone else has made a determination that there are going to be ten beds in that unit, not eleven or twelve, and not fifteen. If you have eleven or twelve patients in need of those beds, you face a rationing or a triage ethical dilemma. But it is not inherent in the nature of things; it is an artifact of the health care system at a given time.

The distinction between natural dilemmas and institutional dilemmas has an important bearing on how we interpret what a moral agent is up against and what the appropriate response on her part would be. Professional practice is clearly embedded in a particular institutional and historical context. It is mostly contingent in the sense that the available resources, and even the very way the professionals view their reality and the choices they face, are best comprehended in relation to cultural and institutional patterns that are subject to deliberate, purposive change. For a professional as a moral agent to bow to the givens of the situation by appeal to these contingent conditions of his practice strikes us as an unduly accommodationist stance at best, or a kind of willful moral blindness at worst; and in any case as an exceedingly weak ethical justification for his conduct. Moral agents must not be too quick to interpret the situation of their moral agency as one in which it is necessary to embrace a tragic choice, or to settle for the lesser of two evils. Sometimes the proper response is to reject the limits and the choice, to reconstrue the situation of agency such that the givens are challenged and overthrown, not accepted. There are times when a solution to professional misconduct or ethical problems in professional life requires institutional change; at other times it requires some effort to change the people or attitudes that produce the (false) dilemma or tragic choice. Construing the situation of moral agency in this way does not put an end to moral problems and difficulties, to be sure. Very difficult matters of judgment and prudence remain, as do basic moral principles that should govern the means employed to bring about the morally requisite social change. But embracing these difficulties is surely preferable to the failure of moral nerve one commits when one accepts the intolerable as a given and tries to make the most of it.

The opposite error is somewhat harder to specify, but is just as morally problematic in its own way. It is characterized by a kind of moral hubris[i.e., pride], an unwillingness or an inability to see the limits and the tragic side to human life. Such a temperament is all too quick to sacrifice the interests of others in a vain quest for some kind of perfection in the human character or institutions that is not to be had. When professionals, in particular, are entrusted with the lives, resources, and interests of others, this kind of moral cowboy mentality is particularly reprehensible. We do not admire the crusading attorney who jeopardizes his client's freedom or assets in order to obtain a ruling that would be an important precedent, unless the client freely and knowledgeably consents to that legal strategy. Nor do we condone a physician who places a patient at greater risk than a standard therapy would in order to advance medical science, unless the benefit to the patient is proportionately great and the patient has given informed consent. In other words, there is something in the kind of moral agents that professionals are called to be, and something in the moral situation of professional practice that weighs heavily in favor of moral humility and even conservatism.

Beyond Regulatory Ethics

The paradox of the regulation of virtue lies at the heart of professional ethics. The paradox is that effective ethics regulation (that which deters improper conduct and encourages good conduct) may have to presuppose an underlying cultural ethos that cannot subsist in the face of regulation.[3] The notion of the regulation of virtue also suggests a kind of ambivalence that runs through much work in professional ethics these days, because both regulation and virtue are desirable things to promote, and professional ethics is unwilling or unable to do without either one.

It is not easy to have it both ways, however. Regulation talk and virtue talk inhabit two different universes of discourse, two different language games, two different ways of seeing the world and the moral life. Regulation talk has mostly behind it a model of rational self-interest on the part of

[3]Stone, C. D.: 1975, *Where the Law Ends: The Social Control of Corporate Behavior* (Harper and Row, New York).

actors. Regulation involves creating a structure of incentives or disincentives that will impact on the interests of individuals and will channel their behavior in one direction or another in accordance with some rational calculus that we presume agents do undertake. That is the essence of the notion, at least the modern notion, of regulation. The idea is that if you appeal to rational self-interest you can structure incentives in a way that will get people to orient their behavior in good ways rather than bad ways, in ways that serve the common welfare rather than in ways that are destructive and simply self-serving. Private vices, public virtues, as Mandeville put it.[4]

Now within this universe of discourse of regulation talk, there is a lowbrow version and a highbrow version. The lowbrow version of regulation talk is what you usually hear from economists; it is the straightforward kind of rational choice theory which many would say has very little to do with ethics at all. (This seems to me to be wrong because the entire tradition of utilitarianism is built along the same kind of theoretical and psychological lines.) But in any event, it is lowbrow in the sense that it does not require any highfalutin moral principles or motivation. As a planner or a regulator, you've got good old-fashioned self-interest and you use it; it's your tool, it's your raw material, it is the key to social control, the structuring of social order, and the achievement of good ends.

Highbrow regulation talk, by contrast, involves much of what we see today in the field of ethics and moral philosophy, particularly in its non-utilitarian variants—rights theory, neo-Kantianism, and deontological theory. John Rawls is probably the leading contemporary example of the perspective I have in mind. Highbrow regulation is regulation of and by moral principles. The goal is to use internalized moral commitments, what Rawls calls the sense of justice, much as the lowbrow regulators would use legal and economic incentives. The idea here is that human behavior is shaped by dint of the moral commitments moral agents make. If you internalize a commitment to justice, you will act as a just individual. And the principle is thereby made regulatory through this expanded conception of human motivation and psychology, expanded to include more than self-interest. A commitment to moral ideals and principles becomes a part of one's self-interest as an agent, a part of one's identity as a professional. This highbrow version of regulatory ethics is still within the universe of discourse of regulation talk, and I would still counterpoise it to virtue talk. Highbrow regulatory ethics, no less than the lowbrow version, is essentially concerned with the rewarding and punishing, the judging and guiding aspects of the rules and principles it develops.

Virtue talk stands in contrast to regulatory ethics mainly because it is as concerned with the agent's being as with his doing. Virtue talk involves notions of character, habit, disposition, inclination. It implies a way of being in the world, a general orientation toward the good on the part of the self in the living of a whole life. Alasdair MacIntyre relates virtues to goods that are internal to practices, and by practices he means activities such as we find professionals often engaged in.[5] Practices are structured, traditionbound kinds of activities that have a point to them, that have their own internal sets of rules, that can be done well or badly, according to criteria that people generally (or at least the members of the professional community generally) understand. The things that you get out of this kind of discipline—this living of your life according to these criteria and these notions of excellence and worth—are the goods that are internal to practices. You are not—or should not be—practicing medicine, say, or practicing law, just to get something external out of it, just to make money. You are doing it because it's a worthy way of life—because there's an intrinsic excellence in the doing of it.

Thus understood, virtue talk is less common in our moral vocabulary today than regulation talk. It is certainly less common in the idiom and discourse of professional ethics, but it is not absent altogether. In fact in the field of professional ethics right now there are interesting arguments and tensions between those who feel generally more comfortable working within the idiom of regulation talk, either highbrow or lowbrow, and those who feel more comfortable within the idiom of virtue talk. Among ethical theorists there are significant

[4]Hirschman, A. O.: 1977, *The Passions and the Interests* (Princeton University Press, Princeton).

[5]MacIntyre, A.: 1981, *After Virtue* (University of Notre Dame Press, Notre Dame), pp. 178ff.

and interesting philosophical debates taking place about whether a principle-based ethical theory or virtue ethics is more adequate and desirable as a philosophical framework.[6] Equally important, as one moves into the arena of applied ethics and professional practice, one finds some interesting splits there as well.

Generally, although there are many exceptions to this, the academic philosophers and ethicists tend to favor regulatory ethics while many practitioners, especially those of an older generation, favor virtue talk. They want their professional ethics to be channeled through the filter and the lens of concepts and categories such as virtue, character, excellence, and calling. That produces some very interesting arguments and tension within bioethics, for example, between philosophers and lawyers who want to talk about regulation and physicians who want to talk about the virtuous physician. It produces disagreements about the best approach to take to solve certain kinds of problems, such as the use of life-sustaining technology. Do we need more regulations, more hospital policies and protocols, more laws to clarify things? Or is the problem that we need more courage, more conviction, and more virtue among our physicians so that they would not be so hesitant to do the right thing. (Assuming that we know in those cases what the right thing to do is.)

So the arguments go back and forth. There's a certain kind of politics behind this line of argument. And the politics, of course, has to do with professional autonomy versus external control. Those are the stakes. In my reading of it, those who argue for an approach to professional ethics that relies on virtue talk are those who favor more internal autonomy by the profession; if not by the individual professional then at least self-regulation by the profession itself. Whereas those who look to a regulatory ethic usually tend to come up with notions of external regulation, legal accountability, administrative review, and the like. It is a very live question in our society today whether the professions are generally sufficiently accountable to the public, or whether they are overly regulated.

Toward a Civic Conception of Professional Ethics

However this question should be settled, one thing is clear. What we now see as the academic discourse of professional ethics has been—and remains—dominated by regulatory talk and regulatory ethics at the expense of virtue talk and virtue ethics, or some third alternative yet to be devised. Why is this so?

The answer seems to me to lie in the general orientation and stance of professional ethics. One of the reasons professional ethics has trouble appreciating virtue talk is that professional ethics has been characterized by a kind of judicial outlook.[7] By and large, professional ethics is the exercise of judicial reason. What I mean by that is as follows.

The task of judicial reason is the application of general moral principles to specific dilemmas and decisions arising in professional practice. Three ideas are central to this conception. First, in professional ethics, the primary unit of analysis is the activity of the individual professional practitioner rather than the collective practices of many practitioners or the traditions, norms and institutions of the profession as a whole. Professional ethics is concerned with individual moral agency, not communal moral practice. Second, the focus of professional ethics is not on professional activity in a broad sense, activity as a shape of a life, a pattern of conduct revealing character, a vocation, a practice of virtue and excellence. Instead the focus is on activity understood as decision making and choice. The moral agent envisioned by professional ethics generally is a weigher of options and a balancer of conflicting values and interests.

Finally, this conception of applying principles to choice situations is fundamentally juridical in method and spirit. The professional ethicist is supposed to stand in judgment on professional decision making, and the grounds of this evaluation is supposed to come from outside the field of knowledge of the profession itself. The principles applied by professional ethicists are both universal moral principles and principles of universal morality. As such their justification can come only from some exogenous or external standpoint of enlightened

---

[6]Cf. Clarke, S. G. and Simpson, E., eds.: 1989, *Anti-Theory in Ethics and Moral Conservatism* (State University of New York Press, Albany).

[7]Cf. Rorty, A. O.: 1988, "Three Myths of Moral Theory," in *Mind in Action* (Beacon Press, Boston), pp. 271–98.

reason. Indeed, professional ethics, at least during recent years, has been built on the assumption that endogenous sources of law and authority, internal sources of law and authority within the professions, are incapable of regulating the professions, or of providing the basis for the necessary evaluations and judgments we want to make of the professions. Thus the professional ethicist provides a moral view from afar. Even if professional ethics were to focus on a community of moral practice rather than individual acts of moral choice, according to the judicial conception of professional ethics, the ethicists as ethicist would be in, but not of that community.

The focus on individual decision making and choice, the notion that the unit of analysis is not a whole pattern of conduct but rather particular decisions and particular choices and the separation between the ethicist who judges and the professional practitioners who are being judged—these three things make it very difficult for the discourse of professional ethics to come to grips with notions of character and virtue. Still, an interesting question which the proponents of virtue ethics have not adequately answered would be what alternative model of professional ethics, and what alternative stance of the ethicist would be necessary in order to take virtue talk seriously? I think that at the very least what we would want to see is a less distanced and a less adversarial relationship between the ethicist and the principles and knowledge that the ethicist brings to bear, on the one side, and the profession and professionals, on the other.

I do not mean that ethicists should be uncritically immersed in the traditions, norms, and codes of the professions they are studying. One of the great liberating aspects of professional ethics in recent years is that it has gotten us beyond the generally banal and self-serving moral talk that is internal to so many professions. But we must be careful not to throw the baby out with the bath. In those segments of the professions that have been interested in ethics over the years, and in the record they left in professional journals and other internal professional sources going back into the nineteenth century in some cases, is revealed a kind of internal moral life and tradition. This is true in each one of our professions, I daresay; some richer and older than others, of course. But none of these occupations that we reasonably call a profession today is totally lacking in such an internal moral tradition.

Granting this, one may ask if this is of any philosophic value or interest?[8] And if the internal moral life and heritage of the professions are not in very good shape today, to what extent should we as ethicists be attempting to build upon it, to revitalize it, to reshape it? Or to what extent should we be saying: "Well, professions are not different from any other occupation because they have a kind of special tradition or a moral calling of their own. Let's just treat professionals like any other seller of services; let's just treat the professions as any other business enterprise or collective group that is trying to get its own way in society and pursue its own interest, and let's regulate it accordingly." The alternative as far as professional ethics is concerned then would also have to take stock of where it is the ethicist stands when she passes moral judgment. Where are we coming from when we talk about ethics? Are we coming from our own personal history? Are we coming somehow from practices and experiences that we ourselves have had in our society? Is ethics a kind of universal and timeless knowledge that some can gain and then apply to those who lack it?

These are fundamental questions that professional ethics at some point has to ask of itself. I think professional ethics by and large has taken those questions for granted. We have assumed that the principles that we argue with, and use come from someplace that is valid, that we do not have to scrutinize their theoretical basis or foundations, but we can just apply them without further ado. William May once made the following delightful characterization of a professional ethicist: "A professional ethicist is somebody who carries water from wells he had not dug, to fight fires he cannot find."[9] The professional ethicist is caught between the ethical theorist who comes up with the moral principles in the first place (digs the well), and professional practitioners who know from their practical experience what the problems are (where the fires are to be found). Professional ethicists have neither credential to bring to the enterprise. So wherein does our own legitimacy reside? Why

[8]Camenisch, P. F.: 1983, *Grounding Professional Ethics in a Pluralistic Society* (Haven Publication, New York).
[9]May, W. F.: 1980, "Professional Ethics: Setting, Terrain, and Teacher," in Daniel Callahan and Sissela Bok, eds.: 1980, *Teaching Ethics in Higher Education* (Plenum Press, New York), p. 239.

should anyone take us seriously? What's the payoff of doing professional ethics? What moral and even political authority ought it have in our culture?

An alternative to what I call the judicial model of professional ethics might be something that we can call professional ethics as civic discourse.[10] We have now returned to our starting point. Professional ethics should be a part of a broader dialogue in our society that takes place between professional elites and citizens. This dialogue should be about the role of the professions in this society, the nature, extent, and limits of professional power, and the social effects of those technologies the professions create and control and through them shape our entire way of life. That's what civic discourse is all about. It is about the kind of society we want to have and to build. How do we want to distribute power and authority? To what ends do we want to use technology and professional expertise?

This is a kind of conversation that professional ethics must be one voice in. Of course, ethicists are not the only participants in such a conversation. The professions have to have a voice in it. Citizens at large at the grassroots level have to have a voice in it. Other academic disciplines need to have a voice in it as well. Professional ethics would be greatly strengthened if we were able somehow to broaden and enrich the context within which we do our work in order to create something like a contribution to a broader civic discourse about those sorts of questions. We cannot regulate virtue in the professions unless we first nurture it, both there and in the wider civil society.

[10]I discuss this at greater length in "Bioethics and Democracy," *The Centennial Review* XXXIV (Spring 1990), pp. 207–225.

Beyond Professional Ethics: Issues and Agendas

BETH SAVAN

Introduction

IN GEORGE BERNARD SHAW's play *The Doctor's Dilemma,* Sir Patrick Cullen, an elderly doctor, declares that: "All professions are conspiracies against the laity."[1] This is, of course, an outrageous statement, now just as much as in 1906 when Shaw wrote his play. Indeed most professions have as their mottoes some maxim that urges their members to serve, protect, or defend their clients; and no doubt most professions do try to serve their clients as well as they can, according to their own particular lights.

But what Shaw's doctor points out is that the interests of the clients, or laity, and the vested interests of the professionals who set out to serve them may not be entirely consistent: in fact, Sir Patrick is suggesting that they are quite contrary.

It's clearly flippant and misleading to go as far as Shaw does, but it is certainly worthwhile to examine what the interests of the public or various publics are, and what exactly the interests of professionals and their organizations might be.

In this paper I briefly examine these interests, and then describe and discuss the efforts of various professional "ginger groups" to better serve the broad public interest. (For this purpose I define "the professions" as groups which apply special knowledge in the service of a client—Professor Stevenson's "Group B"—which I take to include academic "experts" working in fields relevant to public policy as well as doctors, lawyers, engineers, nurses, dentists, *et al.* I will concentrate primarily on activist groups in science, since this is where my background and interest lie.)[2]

[1]George Bernard Shaw: 1911 (rev. 1932), *The Doctor's Dilemma,* London: Constable and Co., Act I, p. 106.

[2]Jack Stevenson, "Reasonableness in Morals," in these proceedings.

From Journal of Business Ethics *8: 179–185, 1989. © 1989 Kluwer Academic Publishers. Printed in the Netherlands.*

As several speakers indicated during the Waterloo conference, most professional bodies now include committees or sub-groups devoted to encouraging the honest, decent, ethical delivery of professional services; they expect their clients' interests and more general concerns of social welfare to guide *how* their members work.[3] In some cases, though, these groups or others are also attempting to match *what* they do with the broader public interest. This is a much more profound and difficult demand, and can affect almost every aspect of professional practice. I will discuss some of the groups and individuals that have embarked on this path, and explain how it changes their careers and their working lives. Finally, I will conclude with a plea for better integration of the personal, political, and technical aspects of professional work.

Background

The professions are among the most respected groups in society. People with professional careers generally enjoy the unusual status and credibility reserved for those with specialized knowledge and mastery of a particular area essential to our well-being. Public credibility can lead to many advantages.

Partly because they are seen (and like to be perceived) as indispensable, professional groups have often established special positions for themselves in society—they have more independence in terms of practice, self-regulation, fees charged and range of services provided.

Professional training is gruelling, underpaid, stressful, and often exploitive, engendering alienation from clients and outsiders and encouraging a sense of group identity and common experience. Trainees form a sort of underclass, essential for the smooth operation of the profession. They perform many routine, arduous, but necessary tasks, such as carrying out most of the repetitive lab work in many fields of experimental science. This is justified as an essential learning experience. It forms part of the strict hierarchy existing in most professions, in which the senior members profit by the efforts of their more junior partners who are, in turn (provided they dutifully toe the

line) rewarded with good references and the support of their supervisor for their future career advancement.

I have described elsewhere the relationship between scientific research supervisors and their post-doctoral assistants as a kind of unwritten contract between the junior and senior scientist: the senior scientist secures the research funds, using his or her reputation to ensure generous grants to cover the cost of equipment, chemicals, and even the junior researcher's salary. In exchange, the junior investigator churns out data and drafts the papers, which he or she and the senior scientist co-author, to provide the senior scientist with proof that research funds are well spent. The senior researcher's reputation eases publication and also greatly enhances the job prospects of the junior researchers working in the lab.[4] In a system where promotion and success depend on an established group of prestigious individuals in the profession, challenging the priorities and/or practices of the group is strongly discouraged. This kind of isolated, stressful training does not encourage, and may even discourage, a sense of responsibility to the wider community.

Powerful professional bodies are largely autonomous—lawyers, doctors, dentists, and engineering groups operate with little outside scrutiny and negotiate (like powerful unions) directly with government to guarantee continued perks. Professionals contribute enormously to society but only on their own terms, as free agents, answerable directly to their internal governing bodies and with little contact, as individuals or as associations, with their client communities. As a result of these favourable arrangements professional groups are usually bulwarks of the status quo. As the recent brouhaha preceding the Province of Ontario's ban on extra-billing by doctors demonstrated, professionals will strenuously resist attempts to wrest control from their own internal hierarchies, and will insist on their nominal "self-employed" status. Professional bodies appear to feel responsible primarily to their peers rather than to the wider lay community that they serve.

Doctors, lawyers, nurses, and engineers, and various expert policy advisors, can have a strong influence and sometimes indirect power over the

---

[3]Note, for example, other papers in these proceedings by Mark Frankel and Leonard J. Brooks.

[4]Some of the above passage was taken from Chapter 5 of my book, 1988, *Science Under Siege,* Toronto: CBC Enterprises.

lives of their clients and the political and social choices affecting us all. An example is the medical profession's vigorous protection of its own turf in lobbying against giving more responsibility to nurses and midwives, and the recently established task force to investigate spiralling health-care costs set up by the Ontario government, with a membership composed mainly of doctors![5] Of course, it is inevitable that professional bodies will use their knowledge and influence to promote certain perspectives; but, because their self-interest usually coincides with the social and political status quo, and because the professionals themselves usually deny any bias at all, these subtle lobbying efforts can go unnoticed.

Not all professionals subscribe to the values and attitudes fostered by the official professional organizations. Many individual professionals lead double lives: in mainstream jobs, serving their bureaucratic masters; and surreptitiously blowing the whistle by smuggling out heavy brown paper envelopes containing confidential information on matters of public import, or gently discouraging the worst excesses of their colleagues.

More relevant to the theme of the conference at Waterloo are the various special-interest groups or splinter groups that have been formed with their own social, political, and moral perspectives. I will devote the rest of this paper to an exploration of these groups and their members, the mavericks in these professions: those who are willing to make their professional work in some way an extension of their personal convictions, and who may thereby sacrifice many of the benefits usually accruing to professionals. It is always more difficult to be in the minority, and groups which break ranks with the prevailing professional dogma—political, technical, or social—do so at considerable risk.

In the largely conservative professions, which pretend to maintain a certain reserve on social issues or a veneer of "objectivity," such activist groups stand out; their members can be isolated, labelled as "unprofessional" or "subjective," or seen as inappropriately using their status to promote personal interests. Movements to explore and act on the wider social responsibilities of pro-

fessionals can be seen as attempts to act separately from the larger, established professional hierarchy, to set up different rules governing professional practices, and to establish new links with the communities of clients. Ultimately this can lead to an effort to take some of the power and knowledge of the profession and pass it on to a larger lay group—to demystify the profession and undermine its status as the exclusive guardian of certain knowledge, judgements, and authority.

Issues and Agendas: What Is the Goal of the Activist Group?

Obviously, activist groups can have various goals, and each kind of coalition or committee of professionals can be useful. I will try to outline below some of the different ways I see such groups operating, and I will focus on those which encourage an integrated view of their values, their politics, and their professional endeavours. I have divided professional activist groups into two general categories: those dealing mainly with standards of professional practice, matters relevant primarily to persons *within* particular professions, and those which take professionals *beyond* their own practices to deal with political and social issues relevant to the larger milieu.

PROFESSIONAL STANDARDS GROUPS

This kind of group, which deals with activities within the discipline, is by far the most common and accepted form of professional ginger group. It would include the sub-committees of the American Association for the Advancement of Science (AAAS), the medical, engineering, and dental associations that deal with ethical professional practice. For example, the AAAS has an Office of Scientific Freedom and Responsibility, and it has sponsored workshops on whistle-blowing and a special project on professional ethics in scientific and engineering societies.[6] Many

---

[5] "OMA—Ministry of Health Task Force to analyze use of medical services," 12 February 1988 press release from the Ontario Ministry of Health.

[6] See, for example, 1981: *Agenda Book* of the Workshop on Whistle Blowing in Biomedical Research sponsored by the President's Commission for the Study of Ethical Problems in Medicine and Research, the American Association for the Advancement of Science Committee on Scientific Freedom

scientific or academic associations have developed conflict-of-interest and publishing guidelines that deal with such issues as plagiarism, republication of work, criteria for co-authorship, and measures for fairer and more effective peer review of publications by the professional association's journals.[7]

BEYOND PROFESSIONAL STANDARDS GROUPS

There are several sorts of activities relating a profession and its functions to the broader social or political context. These can be intended to benefit society as a whole, on matters of universal relevance, like nuclear war. Alternatively, an activist group may have goals which are geared to a segment of the population which is particularly needy or deprived of professional services. The range of projects undertaken by such a group can be divided into three categories: collective advocacy and action on single, focussed issues; support and assistance to individual professionals determined to make their careers socially constructive; and public education and empowerment, to enable lay clients to assume more power and responsibility in their dealings with professionals. These categories are somewhat artificial, and several professional groups engage in two or all of them; nonetheless it is useful to distinguish between these various endeavours in order to observe the evolution of particular groups and their members.

1. Many professional organizations take part in focussed, issue-oriented collective activities, like anti-nuclear lobbying (Science for Peace), lobbying against extra-billing (the Medical Reform Group), and medical and legal assistance to prisoners of conscience and torture victims (the Medical and Legal Networks of the Canadian branch of Amnesty International).

2. Several of these groups also provide important support for individuals devoting themselves to lines of professional work chosen on the basis of personal convictions. These include:

(a) **Not** doing work that is harmful (e.g., not accepting or applying for defence research contracts, and blowing the whistle on socially irresponsible activities in the profession); and

(b) **Doing** work which has as its goal some social or political goal grander than effective and ethical delivery of professional services (e.g., lawyers working with the poor and the disenfranchised, academics carrying out peace research as Anatol Rapoport advocates,[8] doctors working to return medical decisions to the patient in community health settings where the doctors are staff and not free agents).

In one of the rare commentaries on these ginger groups in science Dot Griffiths, John Irvine, and Ian Miles describe the evolution of the British groups advocating socially responsible science, from the view that scientists must merely avoid harmful work to a much stronger commitment to positive, socially constructive professional activity.[9] A rather broad range of concerned scientists established the British Society for Social Responsibility in Science (BSSRS) in 1969. Initially many members of this group articulated a use/abuse model of professional activity, arguing that science had the potential to be enormously beneficial but that it was often abused; and this abuse was the focus of their early efforts. Science and technology themselves were perceived as being either value-free or inherently good, and it was only those using (or abusing) the science who were to blame for the nasty outcomes of scientific work. Proponents of this view argued that individual professionals should produce honest "objective" work and should merely inform themselves on the uses to which it could be put. They actively avoided doing work which could be harmful.

More radical scientists, however, questioned this model, arguing that their work inevitably served social and political purposes and that the scientific bureaucracy itself reflected undesirable social and political assumptions. They supported

---

and Responsibility, and Medicine in the Public Interest, all in Washington, D.C.; and R Chalk, M. Frankel, and S. Chafer: 1980, *The AAAS Professional Ethics Project*, Washington: AAAS.

[7]See, for example, Mark Frankel's "Professional Codes: Why, How and with What Impact," also in these proceedings.

[8]Anatol Rapoport, "The Redemption of Science," in these proceedings.

[9]D. Griffiths, J. Irvine, and I. Miles: 1979, "Social statistics: Toward a Radical Science," in *Demystifying Social Statistics*, J. Irvine, I. Miles, and J. Evans, eds., London: Pluto Press.

the active pursuit of work which would directly benefit socially or politically deprived communities. This radical group gained control of the BSSRS, and the other, "liberal," group left to form the Council for Science and Society. Yet another group of British scientists and historians forms the Radical Science Collective, which argues that the very act of scientific inquiry must be political. They dispute the view that science can ever be "objective" or that it is only the products and applications of science that are political, and they suggest instead that the process of science inevitably incorporates the scientist's values, assumptions, and ideology.

3. Taken to its logical conclusion, professional activity which is devoted to social and political goals rather than merely the delivery of good-quality, non-harmful professional services can lead to public education and empowerment. Professional groups may share their knowledge and skills, making their expertise accessible to the public which needs it. This then places decisions in the hands of the public rather than in those of the professionals, and it allows the client groups to direct their professional employees and to participate in interpreting the results of professional intervention. Professional determination to share authority also leads to public education and to work with the media in order to correct the public view of the profession as a monolith with a uniform view of the world and itself. Professional groups with these goals operate, by necessity, outside the official professional bodies, trying to forge independent links with clients and client groups.

An excellent example of a professional body devoted to work which is explicitly useful to socially disadvantaged groups is the International Institute of Concern for Public Health (IICPH), based in Toronto. The IICPH is directed by Dr. Rosalie Bertell, a biometrician. She is assisted by a small administrative and support staff, and by various medical consultants who provide their services to the institute for a pittance. Collectively, they work with groups of radiation victims and residents of polluted communities on their agendas and concerns. The IICPH has a strong commitment to respecting the priorities of its clients, as was reflected in Dr. Bertell's speech accepting the Right Livelihood Award (termed the "Alternative Nobel Prize"), in December 1986. The quotations she used in that speech were not from respected experts, statesmen, or religious leaders, but from the words of a woman who was a non-fatal casualty of the 1979 reactor accident at Three Mile Island.

Current IICPH projects include an International Conference on Radiation Victims and assistance to people in Malaysia who are suing the Asian Rare Earth Company for careless dumping of radioactive and chemical toxic waste.[10] IICPH has also contributed to the Ontario Nuclear Safety Review and has assisted the Serpent River Indian Band in carrying out a local health survey. I discuss this last project at length below, as an example of the kind of interactive professional work which allows the client, rather than the professional, to retain authority over the expert work which is carried out

AN EXAMPLE OF CLIENT-PROFESSIONAL INTERACTION

In 1981 the IICPH was approached by the Serpent River Band, which has had more than the usual share of the hard times experienced by native people. Over the past decade members of this band have been particularly concerned about an abandoned acid plant on their reserve. Initially the IICPH developed a health questionnaire for them to administer to members of three bands on the north shore of Lake Huron: the Serpent River, Mississagi, and Spanish River bands. This survey established a very rough indication of the background level of health in these communities and provided a basis for more detailed medical examination of individual band members. Follow-up activities included screening clinics for high blood pressure and diabetes, and educational programs focussed on alcoholism and other public health problems. The project was very unusual in that only the band office had the lists which identified participating households: the band, and not the experts it had hired, retained control over the survey. The band then wanted to find out whether the abandoned acid plant site presented a health hazard or could safely be used for residential or commercial purposes. Dr. Bertell and her team carried out further investigations and concluded that the

[10]For more information contact International Institute of Concern for Public Health, 830 Bathurst Street, Toronto, Ontario M5R 3G1.

old acid plant indeed posed a health threat to band members, and that no homes or workplaces should be built on the site until the plant residue had been removed; they also recommended that further investigations were required to determine how best to protect public health now and during the cleanup.

This work helped the Band to press for cleanup of the plant site and compensation for past suffering and damage. Inevitably, however, given the sparse resources and records to which the IICPH team had access, its reports were not without weaknesses. Their summary of the report concluded that: "The limitation of this report is obviously its lack of clinical medical studies and its inability to quantify the extent of the medical problems identified as of concern to the Band. These aspects await further authorization and financial assistance from Health and Welfare Canada."[11] Clearly surveys like this one, carried out by non-experts and without external validation, are subject to serious reporting errors; nevertheless such preliminary indications of the nature and prevalence of local health problems can be the basis for subsequent more rigorous and expensive work.

Other cases, such as the work of Beverly Paigen on the health effects of Love Canal chemicals on local residents,[12] and that of Michael Rachlis (another participant in the "Activist Groups" session of the Waterloo conference) with the Environmental Health Committee of the South Riverdale Community Health Centre on local lead pollution,[13] offer further examples of sympathetic professionals putting their expertise at the service of community groups with the specific purpose of helping them improve their local situations. In these cases the professionals invest their time in the pursuit of agendas which have largely been set outside the profession; and goals for particular pieces

of work are developed interactively, with full participation of the lay clients.

A common pattern is revealed here: citizens raise an issue that intimately concerns them and their families and neighbours, and sympathetic experts and professionals respond to this concern, helping the citizens to study the problem, suggest remedies, and lobby to remove the cause. Sometimes the experts involved are criticized for employing "unscientific" or "unprofessional" methods, because the work is often carried out by volunteer citizens rather than by well-paid experts.[14] The fact remains that in many cases the citizen-instigated preliminary studies have indicated problems or alarming trends which have later been substantiated by government agencies with more time and resources. Of course, the government or agency officials rarely acknowledge their debt to the earlier studies; rather, they claim the hypotheses of those studies as their own. Official recognition and measurement of the problem may nonetheless then pave the way for action to remedy the situation or to compensate those who have suffered from it.

But there is another, more important, consequence of expert involvement in citizen advocacy. Ultimately, this kind of work encourages a critical public view of the role of the profession. It sows the seeds of a change in the popular perception of how professionals should behave. Experts dedicated to serving the broad public interest may be ignored or even ridiculed by their colleagues; but the public will take notice. Eventually other public groups will demand similar treatment from members of the profession and, whether they like it or

[11]R. Bertell, D. McLoughlin, and M. Stogre: 1986, *Serpent River Report* (unpublished), Toronto, International Institute of Concern for Public Health, p. 1.
[12]B. Paigen: 1982, "Controversy at Love Canal," *The Hastings Centre Report* 12:3 (June), pp. 29–37.
[13]South Riverdale Community Health Centre, *Submission from the Environmental Health Committee of the South Riverdale Community Health Centre to the Royal Society of Canada Commission on Lead in the Environment*, 13 June 1985 and 18 March 1986.

[14]The inadequacies in the resources and time available to lay groups attempting or assisting with professional work often lays them and their professional allies open to accusations of bias and lack of rigour; but these criticisms can also be seen as a difference in outlook, a difference in the values and priorities of the professionals involved. Advocates of "complete evidence" or "clear statistical significance" are sometimes more willing to risk being wrong in saying that a problem does *not* exist than the responsible professional may be to risk being wrong in saying that a problem *does* exist. In one case, the error involves mis-spent public funds; in the other, damaged human health. See, for example, B. Paigen: 1982, *op. cit.*, and N. Ashford: 1986, "Ethical Problems in Using Science in the Regulatory Process," *Natural Reserves and the Environment* 2:2 (Fall), a publication of the American Bar Association.

not, the more traditional professionals will have to alter their practices and their relationships with their clients.

It is no coincidence that the scientists or professional experts involved with citizen groups are often women. Women are likely to feel a greater responsibility to the lay communities to which they belong because they are usually more integrated into them: children ensure contacts with other parents in libraries, pools, community centres, schools, and daycares. This integration of the professional and the personal is important; it may be valued most by women, who often have to struggle to balance the demands of their careers and those of their families. Projects which combine these interests hold a natural appeal for many women.

Discussion and Conclusion

Women may deliberately seek a consonance between their professional and personal priorities, but there is a sense in which the values an individual holds most dear will unavoidably direct his or her career, whether this is welcome or not. I believe that professional behaviour is inescapably political, not in any partisan sense but because the choices that professionals make—in the work they pursue, the clients they cultivate, and the relationships they develop with their clients—inevitably reflect their values and the larger social goals they consider desirable. Indeed, professionals should recognize the responsibility they bear for the outcomes of their personal work, not merely in terms of traditional professional ethics but in terms of the goals and impacts of their particular professional practice on society. As individuals, or by participating in activist groups, they can give the public an alternative view of their profession and set the stage for public demand for more responsive, socially controlled professional practices.

This is an ambitious and demanding view of the social responsibilities of professionals and the groups to which they belong, but it is one which should, ultimately, be satisfying for those professionals adopting it. If professional work becomes more of an extension of the individual lives of the professionals, the professionals themselves become, in a sense, members of the communities that they also serve. And then they will never, in Shaw's words, "conspire against the laity."

Just Another Day at the Office: The Ordinariness of Professional Ethics

DON WELCH

MUCH OF THE WORK in professional ethics in recent years has focused on the distinctiveness of the ethics of the professions. Alan Goldman has described the view that professional duties must override what would otherwise be moral obligations because special norms and principles should guide a professional's conduct.[1] We've been told that professionalism embodies a standard of good conduct that is not the same as the norms of morality that ordinarily govern relations among persons.[2] Often the claim is not that professionals must meet the same moral standards as the rest of us and then go beyond those, but that their distinctive moral standards may conflict with the requirements of "ordinary morality."[3]

[1] Alan Goldman, *The Moral Foundations of Professional Ethics* (Totowa, N.J.: Rowman and Littlefield, 1980). Goldman himself finds these assertions unconvincing in most cases.

[2] Albert Flores, *Professional Ideals* (Belmont, CA: Wadsworth, 1988), p. 1.
[3] Rob Atkinson has described the distinction, "firmly ensconced in the literature," between legal professional

A prevailing assumption among many professionals is that they are called on to conform to ethical standards that are "higher" than those that apply to ordinary people.[4] Professional morality places its values "at a higher position in the ethical hierarchy. It gives them greater ethical importance than does ordinary morality."[5] On reflection, however, it is not at all clear what "higher" means. Consider one statement of the ethical meaning of professionalism:

> In ethical terms, to be a professional is to be dedicated to a distinctive set of ideals and standards of conduct. It is to lead a certain kind of life defined by special virtues and norms of character. And it is to enter into a subcommunity with a characteristic moral ethos and outlook.[6]

Because of these presumably distinctive ideals and standards, it is argued, professional ethics may sometimes justify, even require, a practitioner to do something different than what would otherwise be morally obligatory. This is an approach that "implies that the rules which decide what is ethical for ordinary people do not apply equally, if at all, to those with social responsibility."[7] These standards clearly establish a certain immunity for professionals from the moral requirements placed on "laypeople"; we shall return to the question of whether they are "higher."

The standards that are to govern the work of professionals are often written into canons or codes of professional ethics, which Michael Davis describes as conventions among professionals that are produced when an occupation becomes a profession. "What conscience would tell us to do *absent* a certain convention is not necessarily what conscience would tell us to do *given* that convention."[8] The existence of such professional codes, as well as conventions that take other forms, means that professionals are not permitted to engage in the weighing of the kinds of interests and factors that is allowed by ordinary morality.[9] Therefore, they are, to an extent, exempt from judgment based on moral standards outside the particular subcommunity that has its own distinctive moral ethos.

Given this heightened status that is accorded to professional ethics, it is understandable that entry into the club of professionalism is quite desirable. To the long-accepted entries of such occupations as law and medicine have been added such areas as engineering, accounting, nursing, social work, journalism, management, education, policy analysis and scientific research.[10] The insistence of many occupational groups that they too be recognized as "professionals" has lead one commentator to fear that the label "professional" is being threatened with evacuation of part of its meaning.[11]

Those who have been writing about the unique qualities and characteristics of professional ethics are themselves professionals. It is not surprising that, writing from their particular standpoints, they view their own moral dilemmas to be more noteworthy and different in kind from those faced by the masses. The sense one gets from reading much of the professional ethics literature is that, compared to the world of ordinary ethics, the demands placed on professionals are more compelling, the reasoning required of them is more sophisticated, and the compromises they make are morally superior. I am convinced, for the reasons stated below, that the distinctions are overdrawn.

Stephen F. Barker has attempted to establish the distinctiveness of professional ethics while avoiding

---

morality and ordinary morality in "Beyond the New Role Morality for Lawyers," *Maryland Law Review* 51 (1992): 855–860.

[4]Gerald J. Postema, "Moral Responsibility in Professional Ethics," *New York University Law Review* 55 (1980): 63.

[5]Benjamin Freedman, "A Meta-Ethics for Professional Morality," *Ethics* 89 (1978): 10.

[6]Bruce Jennings, Callahan and Wolf, "The Professions: Public Interest and Common Good," in "The Public Duties of the Professions," Special Supp., *Hastings Center Report* 17, no. 1 (1987): 5.

[7]Peter F. Drucker, "What Is 'Business Ethics'?" *The Public Interest* no. 63 (Spring 1981): 24.

[8]Michael Davis, "Thinking Like an Engineer: The Place of a Code of Ethics in the Practice of a Profession," *Philosophy and Public Affairs* 20, no. 2 (1991): 154–5.

[9]Ibid., p. 162.

[10]Some of these fields have been promoted from the ranks of "semi-professions," the term used for teachers, nurses and social workers in Amitai Etzioni (ed.), *The Semi-Professions and Their Organization* (New York: Free Press, 1969).

[11]Paul F. Camenisch, *Grounding Professional Ethics in a Pluralistic Society* (New York: Haven Publications, 1983), p. 4. John Kultgen has suggested the concept of professionalism should be relevant to all types of work in a modern industrial society in *Ethics and Professionalism* (Philadelphia: U. of Pennsylvania P., 1988).

the idea that professional obligations are more demanding and harder to comply with than those of nonprofessional occupations.[12] He identifies three features that distinguish the ethical ideology of a profession from nonprofessional ideology: (1) the ethical ideology of a profession does not stem merely from a business contract between employer and employee; (2) this professional ethical ideology involves requirements that those in the occupation have largely agreed to impose on themselves; and (3) this ideology includes an ethical ideal of service to society.[13]

A focus on the employer-employee contract, however, narrows the inquiry much too quickly. Certainly not all self-employed people are inherently more professional than all salaried people. It is true that professional obligations do not stem "merely" from an employer-employee business contract. But, as Barker recognizes, many professionals are employees and so some of their obligations *do* stem from such contracts. Further, it is also the case that all of the obligations of nonprofessionals cannot be traced to such an employer-employee contract.

Barker gives the following example, in his comparison of nonprofessional firefighters and professional physicians, to illustrate the distinctiveness of the non-contractual professional obligation: "[I]t will be unethical for the physician publicly to endorse medicines or treatments which have no proven medical value, though nonphysicians may do this blamelessly."[14] If one agrees with this conclusion, it is only because of the distinctive content of the practice of medicine, not because of some generalized sense of the distinctive nature of professional obligation. I would argue that a parallel obligation *does* apply to the firefighter: that it would be unethical for a firefighter who is making a presentation in an elementary school classroom during fire prevention week to endorse fire safety practices that are not safe.

We need to avoid taking the position that professionals impose upon themselves obligations to serve society in ways that nonprofessionals do not because the only ethical obligations nonprofessionals have is to adhere to their employee contract.

Confining the moral obligations of nonprofessionals to those embodied in such a contract is overly restrictive. Certainly there are firefighters, cafeteria workers, construction workers, secretaries, and a host of other nonprofessionals who, as members of those groups, have felt that they should respond to moral expectations that were not a part of a business contract.

Professionals do not have a monopoly on responding to the ideal of service to society. As Barker points out, many nonprofessionals are indeed called into service to society. Nor are professionals immune from employment arrangements that override a duty they have to service a larger community good. For example, physicians reject "bedside rationing" of scarce services for the good of society because of their obligation to the single patient before them; attorneys reject being drawn into seeking justice for the good of society because of their obligation to the single client before them. Of course service to an individual is one way in which a professional can be of service to society. But the same is true for nonprofessionals. One could reply that sometimes nonprofessionals act professionally, and sometimes professionals act in a nonprofessional manner. The question still remains whether it is appropriate to maintain such a generalized ideal of professionalism that calls for a different form of ethical analysis.

My point is that any claim for a stronger ethical content and a substantially different ethical structure for professional ethics is dubious. All of us, professionals and nonprofessionals, experience and respond to ethical problems in fundamentally the same way. The efforts to identify special concepts of morality for professionals create distracting distinctions that separate out pieces of the moral life that can be better understood as integral parts of a whole. I am *not* arguing that professionals do not have to respond to particular expectations that make a difference in the moral choices they make. Particular contexts do require particular kinds of ethical attention. My argument, rather, is that everyone is continuously engaged in exactly the same kind of process of moral deliberation.

Experts on professional ethics usually don't include truck drivers as members of the club. Let's consider a truck driver who is headed for El Paso, Texas, in June to deliver a load of furniture. Her intention is to drop off the furniture, then drive

[12]Barker, "What Is a Profession?" *Professional Ethics* 1 (Spring/Summer 1992): 73–99.
[13]Ibid., pp. 88–89.
[14]Ibid., p. 89.

empty 40 miles to Las Cruces, New Mexico, to pick up a load of onions to take back to Atlanta— or as close to Atlanta as she can get. A day out of El Paso our trucker needs to call ahead to Las Cruces to begin setting up the onion load.

Our truck driver has had a long and mutually satisfactory relationship with a truck broker who works out of Las Cruces in the summer. Over the years these two individuals have come to rely on the services each can provide the other, the trucker sometimes helping out the broker by taking a load that really didn't fit her own needs best, the broker sometimes giving the trucker special consideration in arranging loads with shippers. The trucker also knows that the dispatcher for the largest produce shipper in Las Cruces is willing to deal directly with truckers. A call to that dispatcher might produce a better load more quickly and save the trucker the brokerage fee. There is also a new truck broker who has just set up shop in Las Cruces who might have access to loads that are not available to the more established broker.

So the driver has to decide which people to call and what to say when she calls. She does not expect to arrive in Las Cruces until late Saturday afternoon. She knows that none of the shippers want to wait that late to load a truck on Saturday and they usually don't work on Sunday. She also knows that if she tells them she will be there Saturday morning and gets a commitment for a load on that basis, she will get loaded when she arrives late, even if it takes until midnight. Does she communicate her plans honestly, guaranteeing a two-day layover, or does she attempt to strike a deal based on a commitment she knows she can't keep?

She also knows that the probability of getting exactly what she wants—an 800-bag load with one drop in Atlanta for $1.85 per bag—is fairly low. One-drop loads to Atlanta are easy for brokers and shippers to cover. She can expect that the initial offers will be for loads to places like Dothan, Tallahassee and Chattanooga, with deliveries to be made at possibly three or four different places. While she knows she would accept one of these as a last resort, she doesn't want to give up too easily on more attractive possibilities. How honest should she be in her negotiations in terms of what she would be willing to accept?

Our driver knows that 790 fifty-pound bags of freshly loaded onions are all that she can carry within the legal weight limits of some states she'll

be crossing. An 800-bag load is standard, but onions dry out in transit and she can probably be within legal limits with an 800-bag load by the time she hits the first open scales. Even accepting a hard-and-fast 800-bag limit, however, may produce undesirable consequences as larger loads are not uncommon and the refusal to accept a larger load increases the difficulty of getting a load in a timely fashion. If the route offered is one that makes the probability of detection low enough to be worth the risk to her, should she be willing to accept a load that exceeds legal limits? Similarly, if an offered load has a delivery date that would require a driving schedule that exceeds the regulations on the number of hours per day that a trucker can drive, should that load be accepted?

In the course of these transactions, the driver will be under considerable pressure to (1) violate obligations incurred in a long-standing relationship, (2) make promises she can't keep, (3) be dishonest in negotiations with others, and (4) disobey the law. These seem to be some of the same kinds of moral dilemmas that pose the greatest problems for professionals. Further, while truck drivers may not have a written code of ethics that has been approved by a formal association, they do operate in a world of deeply entrenched mores and practices. To use Davis' term, *conventions* exist in the world of truckers, brokers and dispatchers that are recognized by all the participants. The driver makes these decisions in response to the expectations embodied in these customs and norms, not as an isolated individual simply pursuing her own self-interest.

The participants in this situation—the brokers, dispatchers, packing shed operators, other truckers—would not be surprised to find our truck driver making promises she could not keep or disobeying the law. The standard of practice in this occupation may well be to act in ways that would be deemed unethical in the abstract, or in ordinary circumstances. She may even be expected to act in such ways. My interest at this point is not in exploring whether it is wrong to follow vocational expectations that one be less than fully honest, but in asking whether that matter should be considered differently for professionals than for the rest of us.

The focus of the inquiry is to try to understand why "professional" conventions should receive greater moral weight than the conventions of the truckers—or the conventions of hundreds of other occupations or nonoccupational roles we play.

Quite apart from an analysis of the particular content of a code or an investigation of a specific situation, professional standards seem to have been accorded a special significance, simply because they are professional. Commentators have suggested many features that divide the professions from other pursuits.[15] The question is whether any of these features justify assigning greater moral weight to the norms that exist in professional subcultures. A consideration of four often-identified characteristics of a profession illustrates why I am doubtful that an adequate grounding exists for morally differentiated professional ethical analysis, as it is often described.

Most lists of features of the professions include something like the criteria mentioned earlier. One such feature is providing services that are important to society. In recent years we have seen many examples in other countries of people starving to death because of a lack of a food distribution system. Truck drivers provide this important service to society. Airplane mechanics, firefighters and farmers, to mention only a few others, also feel that they provide important services but find themselves on few lists of professionals. Even if service to society does provide a basis for separating the professions from other occupational pursuits, it seems that that feature would argue for less moral insularity, not more. The more crucial a service is to a community, the greater the community's stake is in seeing that the service is rendered in ways that are morally appropriate in light of prevailing societal standards.

Not unrelated to this first feature of the professions is a second characteristic: professionals are committed to some good larger than their own self-interest, e.g., the welfare of society. Accordingly, we expect morally superior behavior from those engaged in a profession. But it may well be that this self-proclaimed adoption of a higher calling was rooted in economic self-interest and a desire for social status, and a gap often exists between this vision and actual professional practice.[16] Indeed, the adoption of some ethical codes can be seen as ways of protecting professionals' self-interests by exempting them from the moral claims placed on the rest of us, rather than obligating them to higher moral aspirations in the service of the common good. And, since we're seeking distinctive features of the professions, it should be noted that we expect many others to be committed to some good larger than their own self-interest: mothers and fathers, United Way volunteers, scout masters and lay religious leaders, to name a few.

A third kind of feature often associated with the professions is the fact that they are often granted a degree of autonomy by society, sometimes including a societally granted monopoly for the services they render. This autonomy usually entails a judgment by peers, a certain insulation from lay judgment and control. Rather than providing grounds for the claimed moral distinctiveness, this feature seems to be a result of having found such distinctiveness. A measure of autonomy is granted because of a recognition that there is something distinctive about a profession that warrants this special treatment. The issue in this inquiry is not whether this degree of moral autonomy and insulation exists, nor whether additional responsibilities are generated by such a grant of autonomy; rather, the issue is why it is appropriate to separate out certain professions in this way.

A fourth feature of the professions also gives a basis for arguing for this autonomy and thus for moral distinctiveness: the nature of professional services requires skills and knowledge not possessed by the population at large. Professions entail extensive training with a significant intellectual component. The problems and moral dilemmas encountered by professionals simply cannot be accurately assessed by laypeople.

While this fourth feature seems on point, it is important that we not claim too much for it. This characteristic of professions may say much about *who* engages in moral assessments of professional behavior; it may say very little about *how* those people should make such assessments. Esoteric knowledge and specialized training may limit the number of people who can ably analyze a professional problem. These features, however, do *not* require that those able people analyze that problem using ethical modes of reasoning that are different from those of "ordinary morality."[17]

[15]See, for example, Michael Bayles, *Professional Ethics* (Belmont, CA: Wadsworth, 1981), pp. 7–11; Paul F. Camenisch, "On Being a Professional, Morally Speaking," in *Moral Responsibility and the Professions*, (eds.), Bernard Baumrin and Benjamin Freedman (New York: Haven Publications, 1983), pp. 42–61.

[16]Jennings, Callahan and Wolf, *op. cit.*, p. 5.

[17]In reaching this conclusion, I am agreeing with Mike W. Martin in his exchange of essays with Benjamin Freedman:

If I want to emphasize the continuities rather than the discontinuities, it is obviously important to identify what the truck driver has in common with the doctors and lawyers. In fact, at this point, I want to enlarge the conversation to address the continuities between the ethics of the professionals and those of every other person who plays a distinctive role in our community—which is all of us. So the discussion includes not only those driving trucks and engaged in other occupations, but also mothers and fathers, participants in political parties and neighborhood organizations, citizens, members of churches and synagogues. Davis is right that the conventions that exist among us affect our moral choices. We face such conventions, however, in every role we play.

In this regard, we should look at one other feature that is sometimes mentioned as being characteristic of the professions. Individuals incur certain obligations as they enter into a profession. They pledge to abide by a code of ethics, they covenant with others to uphold the standards of that profession, they agree to act in accordance with professional expectations. This kind of contracting among members of a profession creates limits on the extent to which one can act as an individual agent. Of course, our truck driver may have certain kinds of contractual obligations—to a company from which she leases the trailer or the bank that holds a note on the cab or the shipper who relies on a delivery. But it is important to look beyond these kinds of obligations that flow from formal arrangements. Agreements like bank loans and official codes of ethics are not the only sources for moral decision-making. Many of the professional conventions are matters of less formal expectations than those codified in rules and officially adopted standards. We are also subject to the conventions and expectations of family, friends and members of nonvocational groups, i.e., the expectations of ordinary morality.

The common thread, the source of the "ordinariness of professional ethics," is that all of us, in all aspects of our lives, are subject to moral claims inherent in the roles we play. The term "positional obligation" refers to the concept that holding a particular position or filling a particular role carries with it obligations that that person would not otherwise have.[18] This feature of role morality is not, of course, a new thought.[19] But the well-established insights of role morality render unremarkable the weaker claims of professional ethics—that professional roles entail obligations. Further, the insights of role morality cast doubt upon the stronger claims—that professional ethics require resort to moral norms and forms of moral reasoning that are different from that required by "ordinary" roles. Professional ethics conventions—in codes and in other forms—do create prima facie duties. We can only think about the ethical issues a professional confronts in the context of the conventions of that particular profession. But this insight applies to the conventions associated with all aspects of our lives. All of the other relationships that we establish create prima facie duties as well.[20] The difficult questions arise when we find ourselves subject to contradictory prima facie duties.

The inevitability of facing contradictory prima facie duties lies in the reality that each of us embraces multiple roles. We may be truck drivers or physicians. But at the same time we may also be mothers, citizens, church members and neighbors—to name only a few possibilities. Our continuing task is to respond to a variety of role expectations which inevitably conflict with one another from time to time. Insofar as professional obligations impose only prima facie duties and our response to these should be similar in character to our response to other prima facie duties, then we can avoid the danger Steven Salbu has identified as lurking in professional ethical standards: "A prefabricated, externally imposed code of ethics, taken literally to be what it pretends to be, suggests that the ethical issues have been addressed by the experts. The person who accepts the code at face value replaces the honest and difficult confrontation

Freedman, "A Meta-Ethics for Professional Morality," *Ethics* 89 (1978): 1–19; Martin, "Rights and the Meta-Ethics of Professional Morality," *Ethics* 91 (1981): 619–625; Freedman, "What Really Makes Professional Morality Different," *Ethics* 91 (1981): 626–30; Martin, "Professional and Ordinary Morality," *Ethics* 91 (1981): 631–33.

[18]Frederick Shauer, "The Questions of Authority," *Georgetown Law J.* 81 (1992): 97, using the term coined by Simmons in *Moral Principles and Political Obligations* (Princeton: Princeton U.P., 1979).

[19]See, for example, Dorothy Emmett, *Rules, Roles and Relations* (New York: St. Martin's, 1966).

[20]John H. Fielder, "Organizational Loyalty," *Business and Professional Ethics Journal* 11 (Spring 1992): 71–90.

of ethical questions with a mindless conformity to the rules."[21]

Recognizing that professional ethics is like other ethics, we can broaden the horizons of professionals engaged in moral reflection and moral decision-making. The insularity of professional ethics can give way to Bruce Jennings' model of "professional ethics as civic discourse," a call for a broader dialogue that is accessible to the public at large.[22] At the heart of such a model of professional ethics is the belief that ordinary people do have something worthwhile to contribute to a public discussions of professional morality.

The moral dilemmas faced by professionals are fundamentally the same as those we face in all arenas of life. The challenge raised by conflicting expectations in the professions is similar to the challenge raised in everyday life. How do we balance incompatible demands? How do we weigh competing priorities? How do we determine the appropriate answer to the question, "What ought I to do?"[23] I do not believe that the external demands of "ordinary morality" are always of secondary importance to the expectations that are generated by professional conventions. I cannot

accept a moral system that asserts that professional duty always overrides other duties such as the obligations accompanying one's role as a father or as a citizen.[24] Unless one is willing to make such a claim of unqualified preeminence for professional obligations, those obligations are recognized to be one set of moral expectations alongside others, to be responded to in the same way that we respond to ordinary moral expectations.

It does not follow that there is no such thing as professional ethics. We can recognize a particular ethic to be professional because it is marked by the realities of the relationships that exist in what we consider to be a professional setting—not by some distinctive structures for ethical reasoning. There is such a thing as professional ethics. There are also such things as parental ethics, political ethics, business ethics and religious ethics. In each case the distinctive character of the enterprise derives from the particular relationships and the content associated with particular contexts. These kinds of ethics do not call for different kinds of ethical reasoning than that called for by ordinary ethics. Rather, it is in ordinary ethics that we find the understandings of moral obligation that are common to all of these more particularized forms of ethics.

---

[21]Steven R. Salbu, "Law and Conformity, Ethics and Conflict," *Indiana Law Journal* 68 (1992): 106.

[22]Bruce Jennings, "The Regulation of Virtue," *J. of Business Ethics* 10 (1991): 567. See also Jennings, "Bioethics and Democracy," *Centennial Review* 34 (Spring 1990): 207–225.

[23]I have explored the approach suggested in this essay in greater depth in *Conflicting Agendas: Personal Morality in Institutional Settings* (Cleveland: Pilgrim Press, 1994).

[24]The "weight" that should be accorded to the conventions of a particular profession, or any other role, can be determined only through an analysis of the important ethical issues confronting practitioners in that profession. The relative priority given to internal professional conventions and "external," broader ethical norms will vary from case to case. Such an in-depth study of particular professions is, of course, beyond the scope of this article.

The Excuses That Make Professional Ethics Irrelevant

BANKS MCDOWELL

THERE IS WIDESPREAD AGREEMENT that we are facing a crisis in professional ethics. A common strategy for dealing with that crisis, or the perception that such a crisis exists, is to increase ethics instruc-

tion in the professional schools and to require continuing education programs devoted to ethics. The governing assumption seems to be that professionals must be taught what their ethical duties are.

From Professional Ethics Journal 3(3–4). © *Banks McDowell 1994. Reprinted with permission.*
The author explores this topic further in Ethics and Excuses *(Westport, CT: Quorum Books, 2000).*

The widely-held public perception that professionals are unethical does not appear, however, to be based on a belief that professionals, or their clients, are unclear about what ethical conduct is, but rather that professionals do not act ethically. It appears to be much more a problem of compliance than of incomplete knowledge.[1]

Professional groups claim that public perception is distorted, citing polls which have shown that while there is distrust of a profession as a whole, people like and trust their *own* doctors, lawyers, and accountants.[2] Most professionals certainly view themselves as good practitioners, rather than as one of the few bad apples causing rot in the barrel. Professions are using public-relations techniques in response to the public's perception. This approach can succeed only if the number of unethical actors is in fact relatively small. The public's perception, fueled by almost daily media reports of unethical actions by professionals,[3] is quite the reverse.

My analysis may be influenced by the fact I am a lawyer. Compliance problems are a lawyer's concern. Whenever the public feels actors are failing in their social and ethical responsibilities, there is a demand for the legal system to codify the duties and then use legal enforcement to compel obedience. This has happened in professional ethics not only with the Codes of Ethics, but also by means of specialized statutes defining ethical standards for professionals.[4] Professional ethics could well be analyzed as a sub-field of law where the norms function as legal rules, rather than as ethical principles. A distinguishing characteristic of law is that norm violation carries state-imposed sanctions. Suspension of licenses or probationary procedures by governmental agencies are examples of such sanctions. Malpractice actions in civil courts may also compel compliance with certain ethical precepts—in particular, that professionals meet acceptable levels of professional competence.

The interaction between ethics and law is complex. Not only does enacting legal norms based on ethical standards authenticate their social significance, but legal proceedings can then compel compliance. Statutory adoption of ethical norms followed by lax enforcement is a social signal that appearance, rather than compliance, is what matters. Repealing a legally-imposed norm so that it reverts to a nonenforceable ethical one signals even more clearly that society does not regard the standard as socially important.[5]

Legal processes have not been particularly successful in forcing compliance in a world corrupted by dysfunctional systems and bad organization. We have not minimized violent crime in inner city neighborhoods where unemployment is high, educational systems crumbling, and capital investment almost non-existent. Moving to social arenas more directly involving professionals, we have not minimized business fraud, political corruption, banker mismanagement, medicare fraud, insurance fraud, or lawyers pursuing frivolous suits.

If the real problems facing professionals are not ones of learning, but of living up to the expectations of professional ethics, we should focus more on the excuses offered and accepted for lapses from ethical standards.[6] "Excuse" carries different meanings. One, suggested by the word "alibi," is an attempt to *avoid responsibility* legitimately placed on the actor.[7] Another is a *justification* for

---

[1]The assumption of perfect compliance on which most ethical theories have been constructed avoids many of the real problems any effective system of applied ethics must deal with. See Michael Bayles, "Ethical Theory in the Twenty-First Century," in Joseph P. DeMarco and Richard M. Fox, (eds.), *New Directions in Ethics: The Challenge of Applied Ethics* (New York and London: Routledge & Kegan Paul, 1986), pp. 257–258.

[2]If they did not, they would normally find another professional to service their needs.

[3]Some of the more prominent examples are the activities of the lawyers in the Watergate cover-up, the activities of Clark Clifford in the B.C.C.I. scandal, medicare fraud by medical doctors and pharmacists, and conflict of interest problems raised by medical doctors in referring patients to hospitals and prescribing drugs sold by pharmacies in which they have a financial interest.

[4]An example of legislative regulation of a conflict of interest problem for professionals is 18 U.S.C.A. 207, a federal statute which makes it criminal for any former employee of the executive department or an independent federal agency

to appear as an agent or attorney in any matter about which he or she was engaged as a governmental employee for any party other than the U.S. for a specified period of time.

[5]There may be legitimate policy reasons for delegalizing a standard, such as rareness of occurrence, difficulty of establishing violations, or change in value positions in the society.

[6]The lawyer's cognate term relating to an excuse is a "defense."

[7]The classic analysis of excuses is J. L. Austin, "A Plea for Excuses," *Philosophical Papers,* 3rd. ed. (Oxford: Oxford U. P., 1979). Austin gives "justification and excuse" a different

being excepted from an otherwise applicable ethical obligation. "Excuse" may also refer to an *explanation* as to why the unethical conduct occurred. Such explanations are useful if one wants to change conduct.[8]

In his classic article, "A Plea for Excuses," J. L. Austin shows that one cannot fully understand responsibility, ethical or legal, without adding the realm of excuses to that of normative rules which specify duties. "If ordinary language is to be our guide, it is to evade responsibility, or full responsibility, that we most often make excuses. . . ."[9]

Four Types of Excuse

The excuses one hears, and perhaps uses, in professional practice fall into four groups: the claim of ignorance, the transfer of responsibility, the irresistible pressure, and the fault of machines. I will consider each in turn.

The Calm of Ignorance. One excuse often used is "I did not know what the ethical rules were." Such an excuse may be sincere, particularly among older professionals who were not required to take courses in professional ethics. Some ethical requirements are in fact counter-intuitive, such as the rigid requirement of confidentiality placed on lawyers even if the information in question is about harm being done to third parties. Required ethics courses undercut the legitimacy and persuasiveness of this excuse. As a practical matter, any system of regulatory standards with which people must or ought to comply has to reject this excuse. "Ignorance of the law is no excuse," and if professional ethics is not just law, but ethics, ignorance of ethics should fare no better.

I am skeptical about the factual accuracy in most cases of the claim of ignorance. How often does a professional acting unethically really do so out of ignorance or naivete? Even if the claim were true, however, it cannot in general be accepted as a valid excuse because it has to be the duty of a professional to know what his or her ethical obligations are.

To the extent that this excuse is sincere or widespread, increased instruction on the duty side of ethical responsibilities would be the appropriate response.

The Transfer of Responsibility. Perhaps the most common excuse is that a particular ethical breach was not the agent's responsibility, but someone else's. Much ethical analysis is built on a two-person model—the autonomous professional and the client. In such a simple model, it is difficult for professionals to evade or escape responsibility for injuries their professional activities cause a client or third parties. That model misses the reality of contemporary professional practice. As Christopher Lasch has observed,

> [t]he prevalent mode of social interaction today is antagonistic cooperation (as David Riesman called it in *The Lonely Crowd*), in which a cult of teamwork conceals the struggle for survival within bureaucratic organizations.[10]

Most professional practice today is in large groups—law firms, accounting firms, or medical clinics and hospitals—which are bureaucratic in style and organization, and where professionals are both competing with and cooperating with each other. There are always superiors, rivals for promotion, other members of the team, often junior professionals or staff, who can be blamed for lapses. From childhood on, it seems almost instinctive to pass blame to someone else. Harry Truman's famous statement, "The buck stops here," is striking because it seems an unusual assumption of responsibility for a contemporary person to take. A more representative figure is Ross Thomas's fictional con-man, Otherguy Overby. The nickname "Otherguy" came from his often-used and almost

---

meaning than I do. The situation where an actor admits that he acted in a certain way, but claims it was a good thing is what he means by justification. In contrast, the situation where the actor admits that he acted in a wrong way, but offers an explanation to partly or totally escape responsibility is what he means by "excuse." I am more concerned with distinguishing between persuasive and unpersuasive excuses. The person to be persuaded may be an objective observer, the professional or legal institution which can impose a sanction, or the actor himself.

[8]I do not here distinguish between a completely persuasive excuse, a partial excuse, and a totally invalid excuse. These important distinctions which control the degree of responsibility an actor has fall outside the focus of this article.

[9]Austin, *supra* note 7 at 181.

[10]Christopher Lasch, *The Culture of Narcissism: American Life and Age of Diminishing Expectations* (New York: Warner Books, 1979), p. 209.

always successful excuse, "The other guy did it."[11]

Not only are specialized professional groups today the dominant mode of practice for many professions, but elite autonomous professionals are increasingly integrated into large corporate organizations. Major corporations, private or governmental, will have legal departments, medical clinics, accounting departments, engineering departments, etc. Blame can often be transferred onto the other types of professionals.[12] This is not always overt and conscious evasion of responsibility. It may be factually difficult to determine individual responsibility for ethical lapses in complex professional operations.

An individualist ethics which permits the transfer of responsibility around the ring of participants in group activity poses two difficult problems. The first problem is developing some method for fixing responsibility of a team activity onto some particular member either because he or she was the director of the team or else was the actor who most closely related causally to injuries caused a client. The legal system which has faced this problem for decades, if not centuries, has moved in many contexts to theories of absolute, or non-fault liability, as a way of avoiding this problem.[13]

The second difficult problem is that of collective responsibility or guilt. This is an old issue in ethics, but one that is as interesting as it is important. There way be different types or degrees of unethical conduct. Not only the most casually significant actor bears ethical responsibility, but the members of a team or group who observe the unethical activity of some members and do not take whatever action is available to them to prevent the activity must bear ethical responsibility, as well. This has been most discussed. In connection with the responsibility of the German people during the Nazi period in regard to the holocaust, but it is a issue that must be faced in any group or professional activity where some actors are unethical. Others cannot ethically turn their heads away and disavow responsibility.

The Irresistible Pressure. Another kind of excuse is that the professional does not have the power to act ethically or that the cost of ethical behavior is too high. Most professionals regularly feel pressure to act unethically. In assessing the responsibility of a particular professional under pressure, one must distinguish the following excuses:

(a) "I had to do it to keep up with competitors, either inside or outside the professional working group I belong to." There is a widespread cynical belief that acting ethically places one at a competitive disadvantage. It is difficult to prove or disprove the truth of that belief. A variant of this excuse is the claim: "If I don't do the unethical act and earn the reward, someone else will." Or, the claim: "If that person is unlikely to suffer penalties, why should be or she have the reward rather than I?"[14]

(b) "I had to do it because my employer told me to or expected me to." In the real world, it is often unnecessary for an employer to *explicitly* order an employee to act in ways that are questionable

[11]The character appears in Ross Thomas's popular set of novels, *Chinaman's Chance, Out on the Rim,* and *Voodoo, Ltd.*
[12]One well-known example of this problem was the Hyatt Regency disaster in Kansas City, Missouri, where on July 17, 1981, a skywalk in the lobby collapsed, killing 114 people and seriously injuring scores of others. There were ongoing disputes about whether the collapse was the fault of the owners, the architects, the design engineers, the general contractor, sub-contractors, or suppliers. The liability to injured parties ran into the tens of millions of dollars. See *Firestone v. Crown Center Redevelopment Corporation,* 693 S.W.2d 99 (Sup. Ct. of Mo, en banc, 1985).
[13]Perhaps the best example is the liability imposed an manufacturers for injuries caused to consumers by defective products. An influential statement of the theory is found in the *American Law Institute, Restatement of the Law of Torts,* Second, § 402A: Special Liability of Seller of Product for Physical Harm to User or Consumer.
(1) One who sells any product in a defective condition unreasonably dangerous to the user or consumer or to his property is subject to liability for physical harm thereby caused to the ultimate user or consumer, or to his property if
   (a) the seller is engaged in the business of selling such a product, and

   (b) it is expected to and does reach the user or consumer without substantial change in the condition in which it is sold.
(2) The rule stated in Subsection (1) applies although
   (a) the seller has exercised all possible care in the preparation and sale of his product, and
   (b) the user or consumer has not bought the product from or entered into any contractual relation with the seller.
[14]The childhood variant of this excuse is "My friend did the same thing and was not punished by his parents, so it is unfair for you to punish me."

because of the widely-held cynical view that this is what is expected.

(c) "'Loyalty to the group requires that I participate in unethical activity even if I have reservations." This is a well-recognized ethical dilemma when group loyalty seems to conflict with duties owed to others. It raises the whistle-blower's problem with all its moral conflicts. The power of peer pressure is real and often seems irresistible if one desires to remain a member of the group.

(d) "Financial pressures compel unethical behavior." Large organizations of professionals have substantial fixed overhead costs, large investments in technology and in the education of individual professionals, and today even marketing costs.[15] These costs plus adequate compensation for the professionals represent an income floor the organization cannot fall below without going bankrupt. This may not appear to be a serious moral dilemma, because ethical professionals presumably would accept bankruptcy or leave the profession if the only way to continue practicing were to pad expenses or provide unnecessary services.[16] A poll of candid professionals would, I suspect, show that not many would agree that bankruptcy was preferable to some degree of overcharging.[17]

---

[15]Until recently, it was a violation of ethics for many professions to advertise or solicit clients. The total ban on advertising was invalidated by the Supreme Court as violating the First Amendment in *Bates v. State Bar of Arizona,* 433 U.S. 350 (1977). States can only restrict advertising that is false and misleading. *Zauderer v. Office of Disciplinary Counsel,* 471 U.S. 6236 (1985). The ban on soliciting was invalidated in *Shapero v. Kentucky Bar Association,* 486 U.S. 466 (1988). That has created substantial financial pressure on professionals to spend money on marketing to meet competition.

[16]This problem of overcharging was a central subject of Banks McDowell, *Ethical Conduct and the Professional's Dilemma: Choosing between Service and Success* (Westport, CT: Quorum Books, 1991).

[17]One can always argue that the true cost to a client requires paying the fixed overhead and other costs of practice, and spreading this among the clients is not unethical. When the number of clients falls below an acceptable number to bear the costs, the ethical dilemma of leaving the profession or overcharging is present. Competitive pressures could in theory prevent overcharging, but this requires sophisticated customers who shop among professionals and can make sound decisions about the value of services, conditions which I feel are seldom present when a client hires a professional.

Financial pressure can also lead to overwork so that the best level of performance cannot be maintained. A well-known example is that of medical interns and residents who are expected to be on duty for tours of 36 hours or more with little opportunity to rest.[18]

There are two broad ways to deal with seemingly irresistible pressures that professionals claim push them into unethical activity: either (1) to demand that all professionals be strong enough to resist the pressure or, (2) to redesign social structures and the way professional services are delivered in ways that minimize such pressures. It is obviously easier and less disruptive to select the first alternative and to expect professionals to be strong enough ethically to resist such pressures. That may, however, be unrealistic, which forces us to consider the second alternative more seriously.

The Fault of Machines. Another way of evading responsibility is to blame it on technological failure. Almost all professional activity today makes use of complex technology, consisting of machinery and the techniques for using it. Malfunctions can occur in machinery, in communication systems, in techniques, or in integrating the work of various professionals who are masters of specialized technology. One can always argue that the professional is responsible for all the technology used in handling a client, but technology today is so complex that one must rely on technical experts when the system malfunctions. For example, medical doctors, even though trained in chemistry and pharmacology, rely heavily on drug manufacturers for information about appropriate drugs, side-effects, dosages, etc.

We have been conditioned to think that machines can be made to work perfectly. They are not supposed to possess the human capacity for error. When machines and technology break down, there is the same diffusion of individual responsibility we talked about above. Was it the designer, the manufacturer, the wholesaler, the installer, the repairperson, or the user who committed the human error which led to the machine's malfunction? In both ethical and legal theory we still try to identify particular individuals who must bear the

---

[18]See Joseph Berger, "The Long Days and Short Life of a Medical Student; Relatives Say Fatigue May Have Had a Role in the Car Crash That Killed Frank Ingulli," *N.Y. Times,* Sunday, May 30, 1993, Sec. 1, p. 39, Col. 2.

responsibility for technological failure, but that effort seems artificial and unrealistic. No single person can be responsible for the functioning of incredibly complex and integrated technological systems. To select any single one or a small group to bear that responsibility raises the difficult issue of whether it is ethically defensible to ascribe responsibility to a person who has no real control or ability to prevent such malfunctioning.

The Fallibility of Human Beings

An additional excuse used by all professionals who view themselves as decent people is that we are all fallible and a certain level of ethical wrongdoing as unavoidable and tolerable. Defendants in malpractice suits routinely describe their misconduct as only a minor error and blame greedy lawyers and ungrateful clients for suing. The error is not seen as something the professional should be held responsible for, so it is unnecessary to alter conduct, except defensively to be prepared for the next lawsuit.

This common claim made by professionals who have injured their clients in some way has three distinguishable elements. One element is whether the professional was acting in good faith, i.e. without the intent to harm. Carelessness, a middle position between intentional and accidental injuring, has gradually become for lawyers, who label it negligence, the most important aspect of civil liability.

The second element is the amount of harm caused by the wrongdoing. While one can argue that the degree of injury is not relevant to the question of wrongdoing, in the practical world it makes an enormous difference. One example comes from G. J. Warnock: "If I knock over the pepper-pot inadvertence will get me off the hook, but not if I knock over your Sevres vase."[19] Another example is the everyday experience of driving a car. I am more likely to drive with great care on a street crowded with pedestrians than when I am on an empty highway.

The third aspect is that some tolerance for the inherent fallibility of the human actor needs to be built into any ethical system. Much ethical discussion still assumes that the ethical human being should not have such lapses. This is not a weak

excuse because we all, however competent and decent, cannot go through a professional life without some professional misjudgments or ethical lapses.[20] The problem is that of determining what degree of mistakes made in good faith is acceptable. The difficulty, of course, is that once this excuse is accepted, intentionally unethical professionals can always *claim* their actions were of this intermittent good faith quality.

These excuses are sophisticated versions of excuses regularly used by children. My secretary, Leslie Vigus, who has two teenage daughters told me she always hears "You didn't *tell* me I wasn't supposed to do that" or "My sister did it."[21] Courses in professional ethics are often expected to undo or reverse ethical training that has been going on for two or more decades from parents, peers and teachers, and that has frequently tolerated such avoidance of responsibility.[22]

Implications for Professional Ethics

These various excuses are not always conscious efforts to avoid ethical responsibility. They reflect the reality of the way professions are organized and the way in which they function, with the consequent constraints and pressures on individual professionals. Teachers of professional ethics must help students understand and adapt to that reality in ways consistent with both the individual's ethics and to the ethics of the profession. Otherwise, there will be enormous guilt carried by profession-

[19]G. J. Warnock, *J. L. Austin* (London and New York: Routledge, 1991), p. 79.

[20]See Bernd Guggenberger, *Das Menschenrect auf Irrtum* (Munich and Vienna: Carl Hanser Verlap, 1987). Guggenberger, a well-known German social theorist, argues that the modern complex world makes human error much more devastating and yet human error is not only necessary but also a valuable happening, since it is only through trial and error that we make progress. He argues that we must develop a mistake-friendly environment in which errors are expected and do not do irreparable damage.

[21]Ms. Vigus has granted permission to attribute this statement to her.

[22]After reading a draft of this article, George Hole commented that an important problem is why parents or teachers tolerate such excuses. That question is outside the scope of this paper, but it does raise two interesting problems: (1) to what extent are excuses a matter of social or cultural convention, and (2) can professional ethics require conduct substantially more demanding than the accepted codes of ethics that control the more general population.

als and little change in the conduct of the profession as a whole.

Legalizing professional ethics as a set of quasi-minimal requirements leaves aspirational ethics out in the cold. Furthermore, even those fairly remote boundary lines may appear insignificant because effective sanctions are rarely used.

Should the common excuses employed by professionals for actions of questionable morality be thought of as mere alibis or as genuine justifications? For the great range of ethical questions, this must be determined by the actor. If the professional feels the excuse is appropriate, whether from rationalization, ignorance, or on valid grounds, he or she then feels free to act against the standard.[23] The reality testing of that judgment might be the reaction of peer professionals. However, many, if not most, professionals are reluctant to criticize their peers' actions, partly out of professional courtesy and partly as a protective device, believing that refraining from criticizing other professionals will encourage others to abstain from criticizing them. Another reality test—at least at the borderlines where professional codes of ethics are at work—might be whether some professional or legal sanction is sought. For those amoral professionals whose only concerns are about consequences,[24] that likelihood is not great enough to effectively inhibit self-interested justifications even for gross violations of ethical standards.

If one feels, as I am inclined to do, that the problematic excuses are more likely the result of

bad institutional structure than of consciously immoral actors, then one major task of ethical study and education must be to help professionals identify the pressures that push them toward unethical action, to realize when they have gone past acceptable or tolerable limits, to realize that *excuses are often a way of avoiding these tough choices,* and to survive in that difficult world where one is often uncomfortable with the choices one is forced to make.

A list of acceptable excuses coupled with our well-known capacity to rationalize action in accordance with self-interest could combine to trivialize the operation of ethics in professional practice. We seem to have produced in professionals a fair amount of anxiety and guilt without the inner strength or institutional support that leads to personal or systemic change which would relieve the gulf between ideal and practice. The psychological price professionals pay and the social price clients pay is still excessively high.

Conclusion

Looking at professional ethics through the lens of the excuses offered when a professional has not complied with a putative obligation raises a series of questions that ought to be addressed by specialists in professional ethics. Under what circumstances is an excuse a mere alibi for unethical conduct and when is it a genuine justification? If an excuse relies on the individual's position in professional organizations, should we not criticize the way the profession is organized and suggest structural changes that might reduce the number of situations in which problematic excuses are required? To what extent should we assist each other to adjust to what some regard as a corrupt system and to what extent should we encourage each other to be agents of change inside that system?[25]

The analysis of professional ethics which says that the problem is lack of knowledge of pure ethical duties, the assumption that individual professionals always have the option to act in accordance with those duties, and the definition of

---

[23]To the extent that the actor represses awareness that he or she is performing an unethical act, it raises serious questions of self-awareness. See John J. McDermott, "Pragmatic Sensibility: The Morality of Experience," in DeMarco and Fox, *supra* note 3, at 122:

> The moral question which dogs us in our human activity is forever sullied if we live a life of self-deception. To the contrary, the task is to face up to the deepest paradox in our lives, namely, that our decisions are of paramount importance, though they have no ultimate future to sanction them.

[24]Here I am utilizing Oliver Wendell Holmes, Jr.'s famous "bad man" analysis. "If you want to know the law and nothing else, you must look at it as a bad man, who cares only for the material consequences which such knowledge enables him to predict, not as a good one, who finds his reasons for conduct, whether inside the law or outside of it, in the vaguer sanctions of conscience." Holmes, "The Path of the Law," 10 *Harvard Law Review* 459 (1897).

[25]This has been a question which has bothered me since my earliest days as a teacher. For my analysis then, which I still stand by, see McDowell, "The Dilemma of a (Law) Teacher," 52 *Boston University Law Review* 147 (1972).

ethics as establishing ethical borderlines prevent us from dealing with the really difficult issues. Such ethical analyses appear theoretical and irrelevant to students and professionals who know or intuit that the most important moral issues they will meet are how to avoid or come to terms with systemic pressures, that is, to develop some defensible way of adjusting personal and professional ideals with financial and competitive pressures to compromise.

In "A Plea for Excuses,"[26] J. L. Austin recognized that he had only opened up the subject of "excuses" and that a much more detailed study would enlighten the entire area of responsibility

[26]See Austin, *supra* note 7.

and what it means to act or not to act.[27] In the professional arena, fundamental problems that are masked by excuses still need to be addressed. The use of excuses to evade personal responsibility contributes to the marginalization of professional ethics. Until we deal more forthrightly with the existence of a ready and acceptable set of excuses, the current emphasis on professional ethics will remain largely a public relations gambit rather than a real improvement in professional integrity.

[27]According to G. J. Warnock, *J. L. Austin*, pp. 65–66, Austin was compressing into some 30 pages a whole series of classes or seminars. The discussion of necessity had to be compact, focusing on important questions and leaving much of the complexity, some of the answers and almost all of the reasons for the answers out of the presentation.

Questions for Chapter 13

1. What does Jennings mean when he claims that contemporary professional ethics has not come to grips with the notions of character and virtue? Do you agree? Why or why not? Does an emphasis on rules and regulations inevitably undermine an emphasis on character and virtue? Explain your answer.

2. Which do you take to be the bigger problem in professional ethics: discerning what is right or motivating people to do what is right? Defend your view.

3. Savan distinguishes between two types of "ginger groups," each of which functions with different goals. What are these two types and what are their goals?

4. On what grounds does Savan think that the training and practice of professionals encourage a sense of responsibility primarily to their peers rather than to the wider public interest? Do you agree with her analysis? Why or why not?

5. Welch claims that "efforts to identify special concepts of morality for professionals create distracting distinctions that separate out pieces of the moral life that can be better understood as integral parts of a whole." What does he mean by saying this? Do you agree? How do you justify your agreement or disagreement?

6. Welch argues that the fact that specialized training may limit the number of people who can analyze a professional problem does not imply that those people analyze the problem using ethical modes of reasoning that are different from those of nonprofessionals. Do you agree? How would you defend your answer?

7. In what sense do excuses make professional ethics irrelevant?

8. McDowell claims there are two broad ways to deal with seemingly irresistible pressure that professionals claim push them into unethical activity. What are these two broad ways? Which do you think is liable to be more effective?

Case 13.1 Medical Research and the Interests of the Patient[1]

On October 5, 1976, shortly after being diagnosed as having a rare disease known as hairy-cell leukemia, John Moore traveled from Seattle to the UCLA Medical Center to confirm the diagnosis. At the time, Dr. David W. Golde, the physician who attended Moore at the UCLA Medical Center, confirmed the accuracy of the original diagnosis. On October 8, 1976, Golde informed Moore that Moore had reason to fear for his life and recommended the removal of Moore's spleen to slow down the progress of the disease. On Golde's advice, Moore gave written consent authorizing a splenectomy. The operation was performed on October 20, 1976. During the period between November 1976 and September 1983, Moore traveled from his home in Seattle to the UCLA Medical Center several times. On each of these visits, Golde took samples of blood, blood serum, skin, bone marrow aspirate, and sperm. Moore made these trips on the understanding that they were essential for his health and that the procedures involved should only be performed under Golde's supervision.

What Golde did not reveal to Moore was the large commercial value of Moore's blood and bodily substances and Golde's plans to benefit financially from his exclusive access to Moore's cells. Golde, along with Shirley G. Quan, a researcher employed by the University of California, planned, using recombinant DNA technology, to use Moore's cells to help them produce lymphokines, that is, proteins that regulate the immune system. Golde and Quan made arrangements prior to the removal of Moore's spleen to obtain portions of it following Moore's splenectomy, so that it would provide them with material for research. Neither Golde nor Quan informed Moore of these plans or requested his permission to perform research. Moore alleges that, in reply to his subsequent inquiries about whether his cells might be of financial value, Golde repeatedly informed him they had no commercial value and actively discouraged him from further investigation.

Sometime prior to August 1979, Golde and Quan were successful in establishing what is called a cell line from Moore's T'lymphocytes. On January 30, 1981, the University of California applied for a patent of the cell line, listing Golde and Quan as its inventors. Royalties were to be shared by Golde, Quan, and the university. With the university's assistance, Golde negotiated agreements for commercial development of the cell line. Through an agreement with Genetics Institute Inc., Golde became a paid consultant and acquired 75,000 shares of common stock. Genetics Institute also agreed to pay Golde and the university at least $330,000 over three years. On June 4, 1982, Sandoz Pharmaceuticals Corporation was added to the agreement and the compensation payable to Golde and the university was increased by $110,000.

Upon becoming aware of these developments, Moore sued on thirteen grounds. Among these were lack of informed consent, a breach of fiduciary duty, fraud and deceit, and unjust enrichment.

1. Golde held that Moore had no cause for complaint, inasmuch as the research activities in no way affected the quality of his medical treatment. Supposing Moore's medical treatment was in no way compromised, are Golde's actions justified?

2. What moral responsibilities, if any, did Quan, the university, and the companies have with respect to Moore?

3. Is Moore morally entitled to a share of the profits from products developed from his cells?

[1]Based on Moore v. Regents of the Univ. of Cal. as found in 793 *Pacific Reporter,* 2nd series, 479 (Cal. 1990).

Case 13.2 A Lawyer Whistleblows²

Robert W. Herbster was employed as chief legal officer and vice-president in charge of the legal department for North American Company for Life and Health Insurance, under an oral contract terminable at will. In 1984, Herbster brought a suit for retaliatory discharge against North American. According to Herbster, he had been discharged for failing to remove or destroy documents in North American's files that had been requested in lawsuits pending in the federal court in Alabama against North American. These documents tended to support allegations of fraud in the sale of annuities by North American. Herbster also claimed that if he had not refused to remove or destroy these documents, he would have defrauded the federal court of Alabama and violated his Code of Professional Responsibility.

North American claimed that there was no cause of action for retaliatory discharge by an attorney terminated by his client, that Herbster was discharged because of the inferior quality of his work, and that they had never directed Herbster to destroy or remove any discovery information.

1. Can you think of safeguards that would protect the special attorney-client relationship, yet protect lawyers from retaliation by employers who ask them to perform unethical actions?

2. How would you have acted in Herbster's circumstances?

²Based on Herbster v. North American as found in 501 *Northeastern Reporter,* 2nd series, 343 (Ill. App. 2d Dist. 1986).

Further Readings for Chapter 13

J. C. Callahan, ed., *Ethical Issues in Professional Life* (New York: Oxford University Press, 1988).

Michael Davis, "Professional Responsibility: Just Following the Rules?," *Business and Professional Ethics Journal* 18, 1999, pp. 65–87.

A. Flores and D. G. Johnson, "Collective Responsibility and Professional Roles," *Ethics* 93, April 1983, pp. 537–545.

Karl J. Mackie, "Business Regulation, Business Ethics and the Professional Employee," *Journal of Business Ethics* 8, 1989, pp. 607–616.

INFOTRAC COLLEGE EDITION To learn more about the topics from this chapter, you can use the following words to conduct an electronic search on InfoTrac College Edition, an online library of journals. Here you will find a multitude of articles from various sources and perspectives: *www.infotrac-college.com/wadsworth/access.html*

professional ethics

professional codes

Chapter 14

Affirmative Action and Comparable Worth

Introduction

THE TOPICS OF AFFIRMATIVE ACTION (sometimes called reverse discrimination) and comparable worth (sometimes known as pay equity) generate heated debate. Many proponents argue that programs of affirmative action and comparable worth are the only way to bring about a more just society, but critics just as vigorously contend that such programs undermine any attempt to make society more just.

What makes it possible for men and women of good will to disagree so vehemently on these issues? The explanation lies, I think, in the fact that both affirmative action and pay equity programs pose a host of complicated, intertwined factual and moral questions. It is no easy matter, for example, to determine the factual question of to what degree occupational and wage differences between men and women are the result of sex discrimination, rather than other causal factors. Thus it is possible to hold that discrimination on the basis of sex is morally wrong, yet remain unconvinced that occupational and wage differences between the sexes are the result of sex discrimination. Equally, it is no easy matter to resolve the moral question of how far we may depart from what seem to be just procedures of hiring or promotion (procedural justice) in the interests of what seems to be a just result (substantive justice) of placing minority members in positions from which they have been historically excluded. Thus it is possible for someone to agree that it is morally desirable to see minority members begin to occupy positions from which they have been historically excluded, without thereby agreeing that just procedures of hiring and promotion should be circumvented in order to achieve this result. It is important, therefore, in approaching the topics of affirmative action and comparable worth, to discern whether disagreements are a result of weighing moral values differently, holding different factual beliefs, or some combination of both.

The title of the first selection, "What Is Wrong with Reverse Discrimination?," by Edwin C. Hettinger is misleading, inasmuch as it seems to suggest that he does not think programs of affirmative action can be morally justified. Hettinger supports affirmative action, defined as the hiring or admitting of a slightly less well qualified woman or black, rather than a slightly more qualified white male, for the purpose of helping to eradicate sexual and/or racial inequality or for the purpose of compensating women and blacks for the burdens and injustices they have suffered due to past and ongoing sexism and racism. He attempts to support his position by first arguing that a number of common objections to affirmative action have no force. He dismisses as irrelevant the objections that (1) affirmative action is equivalent to racism and sexism, (2) race and sex are morally arbitrary and irrelevant characteristics that should have no role in hiring or promotion, (3) affirmative action involves unjustified stereotyping, and (4) failing to hire the most qualified person is unjust.

Hettinger takes more seriously the objection that affirmative action is unjust because it judges people on the basis of involuntary characteristics, for example, an individual's being born male, and the objection that affirmative action unfairly burdens white males. He feels that these objections have some force, that it is unfortunate that programs of affirmative action have the consequence that white males may be passed over in consideration for a job simply on the basis of their gender, and that white males personally innocent of any sexism or discrimination are nevertheless involuntarily forced to make uncompensated sacrifices of their job and promotion prospects. In his view, however, these are minor evils easily outweighed by the good accomplished by such programs in promoting an egalitarian society.

Louis P. Pojman comes to quite a different conclusion than Hettinger. In his article "The Moral Status of Affirmative Action," Pojman examines the history of affirmative action and the arguments both for and against affirmative action programs of preferential treatment. He concludes that, despite being well-intentioned, such programs are morally unjustified and pragmatically ineffective. He examines seven arguments for affirmative action, these being: (1) that minority role models are needed, (2) that racial and sexist stereotypes need to be broken, (3) that a just society should have equal numbers in proportion to each group in the workplace, (4) that preferential treatment is owed to those wronged by past injustice, (5) that those who have innocently profited by past injustice should pay compensation, (6) that preferential policies are an important means of achieving diversity in a pluralist society, and (7) that the best qualified person is not entitled to the job. He finds all of these arguments deficient to some degree. He then develops seven arguments against affirmative action. These are: (1) that affirmative action unfairly discriminates against young white males, (2) that affirmative action perpetuates the victimization syndrome, (3) that affirmative action encourages mediocrity and incompetence, (4) that affirmative action policies tend to shift the burden of proof in that disproportional representation in an employer's workforce is automatically viewed as evidence of discrimination, (5) that jobs should be awarded on the basis of merit, (6) that affirmative action policies can lead to a slippery slope whereby almost any minority group can claim the need for special treatment, and (7) that there is mounting empirical evidence that preferential policies do not result in a less discriminatory or more egalitarian society. In his view, all of these arguments against affirmative action policies must be taken very seriously.

Programs of comparable worth are based on the claim that women's jobs are consistently undervalued. Proponents of such programs point to the undeniable fact that women, on the average, make far less money than men. They suggest that the explanation of this fact is systematic discrimination against women, resulting in women being paid less than men in comparable jobs, and that justice requires intervention to ensure equal remuneration.

Opponents of comparable worth tend to object either on the basis that it is not clear that the primary cause of wage differences between men and women is sex discrimination or on the basis that, even if it can be shown that sex discrimination is the primary cause of the wage differences between men and women, policies of comparable worth are an ineffective way of dealing with the problem. Those who object for the first reason point out that we cannot simply assume that the fact that women on the average earn less than men is the result of discrimination. It has been argued, for example, that as early as 1971, single women in their thirties who had worked continuously since leaving school earned slightly more than single men of the same age, and that female academics who never married earned more than male academics who never married.[1] On this view, most of the income differences between men and women turn out to be differences between married women who interrupt their working career and all other categories. Those who object for the second reason claim that imposing artificial structures to inflate women's wages simply will not be effective and that it would be far better to find some other means of addressing society-enforced gender difference.

Our third and final reading of this chapter, "Comparable Worth: An Economic and Ethical Analysis," is written by Laura Pincus and Bill Shaw. These authors present a history of comparable worth and discuss the arguments both for and against comparable worth. The article is interesting in that it is a joint effort of two colleagues who disagree, and are unlikely to reach agreement, on the wisdom of implementing programs of comparable worth.

[1]See, for example, Walter Block, "Economic Intervention, Discrimination and Unforeseen Consequences," in *Discrimination, Affirmative Action, and Equal Opportunity* (Vancouver: The Fraser Institute, 1982), pp. 51 and 112.

What Is Wrong with Reverse Discrimination?

EDWIN C. HETTINGER*

MANY PEOPLE THINK it obvious that reverse discrimination is unjust. Calling affirmative action reverse discrimination itself suggests this. This discussion evaluates numerous reasons given for this alleged injustice. Most of these accounts of what is wrong with reverse discrimination are found to be deficient. The explanations for why reverse discrimination is morally troubling show only that it is unjust in a relatively weak sense. This result has an important consequence for the wider issue of the moral justifiability of affirmative action. If social policies which involve minor injustice are permissible (and perhaps required) when they are required in order to overcome much greater injustice, then the mild injustice of reverse discrimination is easily overridden by its contribution to the important social goal of dismantling our sexual and racial caste system.[1]

By "reverse discrimination" or "affirmative action" I shall mean hiring or admitting a slightly

*I thank Cheshire Calhoun, Beverly Diamond, John Dickerson, Jasper Hunt, Glenn Lesses, Richard Nunan, and Martin Perlmutter for helpful comments.

[1]Thomas Nagel uses the phrase "racial caste system" in his illuminating testimony before the Subcommittee on the Constitution of the Senate Judiciary Committee, on June 18, 1981. This testimony is reprinted as "A Defense of Affirmative Action" in *Ethical Theory and Business*, 2nd edition, ed. Tom Beauchamp and Norman Bowie (Englewood Cliffs, NJ: Prentice-Hall, 1983), pp. 483–487.

From Business and Professional Ethics Journal *6(3), 1986. Reprinted with permission.*

less well qualified woman or black, rather than a slightly more qualified white male,[2] for the purpose of helping to eradicate sexual and/or racial inequality, or for the purpose of compensating women and blacks for the burdens and injustices they have suffered due to past and ongoing sexism and racism.[3] There are weaker forms of affirmative action, such as giving preference to minority candidates only when qualifications are equal, or providing special educational opportunities for youths in disadvantaged groups. This paper seeks to defend the more controversial sort of reverse discrimination defined above. I begin by considering several spurious objections to reverse discrimination. In the second part, I identify the ways in which this policy is morally troubling and then assess the significance of these negative features.

Spurious Objections

1. REVERSE DISCRIMINATION AS EQUIVALENT TO RACISM AND SEXISM

In a discussion on national television, George Will, the conservative news analyst and political philosopher, articulated the most common objection to reverse discrimination. It is unjust, he said, because it is discrimination on the basis of race or sex. Reverse discrimination against white males is the same evil as traditional discrimination against women and blacks. The only difference is that in this case it is the white male who is being discriminated against. Thus if traditional racism and sexism are wrong and unjust, so is reverse discrimination, and for the very same reasons.

But reverse discrimination is not at all like traditional sexism and racism. The motives and intentions behind it are completely different, as are its consequences. Consider some of the motives underlying traditional racial discrimination.[4] Blacks were not hired or allowed into schools because it was felt that contact with them was degrading, and sullied whites. These policies were based on contempt and loathing for blacks, on a feeling that blacks were suitable only for subservient positions and that they should never have positions of authority over whites. Slightly better qualified white males are not being turned down under affirmative action for any of these reasons. No defenders or practitioners of affirmative action (and no significant segment of the general public) think that contact with white males is degrading or sullying, that white males are contemptible and loathsome, or that white males—by their nature—should be subservient to blacks or women.

The consequences of these two policies differ radically as well. Affirmative action does not stigmatize white males; it does not perpetuate unfortunate stereotypes about white males; it is not part of a pattern of discrimination that makes being a white male incredibly burdensome.[5] Nor does it add to a particular group's "already overabundant supply" of power, authority, wealth, and opportunity, as does traditional racial and sexual discrimination.[6] On the contrary, it results in a more egalitarian distribution of these social and economic benefits. If

---

[2]What should count as qualifications is controversial. By "qualifications" I refer to such things as grades, test scores, prior experience, and letters of recommendation. I will not include black skin or female sex in my use of "qualification," though there are strong arguments for counting these as legitimate qualifications (in the sense of characteristics which would help the candidate achieve the legitimate goals of the hiring or admitting institution). For these arguments see Ronald Dworkin, "Why Bakke Has No Case," *The New York Review of Books,* November 10th, 1977.

[3]This paper assumes the controversial premise that we live in a racist and sexist society. Statistics provide immediate and powerful support for this claim. The fact that blacks comprise 12% of the U. S. population, while comprising a minuscule percentage of those in positions of power and authority, is sufficient evidence that our society continues to be significantly racist in results, if not in intent. Unless one assumes that blacks are innately less able to attain, or less desirous of attaining, these positions to a degree that would account for this huge under-representation, one must conclude that our social organizations significantly disadvantage blacks. This is (in part) the injustice that I call racism. The argument for the charge of sexism is analogous (and perhaps even more persuasive given that women comprise over 50% of the population). For more supporting evidence, see Tom Beauchamp's article "The Justification of Reverse Discrimination in Hiring" in *Ethical Theory and Business,* pp. 495–506.

[4]Although the examples in this paper focus more on racism than on sexism, it is not clear that the former is a worse problem than is the latter. In many ways, sexism is a more subtle and pervasive form of discrimination. It is also less likely to be acknowledged.

[5]This is Paul Woodruff's helpful definition of unjust discrimination. See Paul Woodruff, "What's Wrong with Discrimination," *Analysis,* vol. 36, no. 3, 1976. pp. 158–160.

[6]This point is made by Richard Wasserstrom in his excellent article "A Defense of Programs of Preferential Treatment,"

the motives and consequences of reverse discrimination and of traditional racism and sexism are completely different, in what sense could they be morally equivalent acts? If acts are to be individuated (for moral purposes) by including the motives, intentions, and consequences in their description, then clearly these two acts are not identical.

It might be argued that although the motives and consequences are different, the act itself is the same: reverse discrimination is discrimination on the basis of race and sex, and this is wrong in itself independently of its motives or consequences. But discriminating (i.e., making distinctions in how one treats people) on the basis of race or sex is not always wrong, nor is it necessarily unjust. It is not wrong, for example, to discriminate against one's own sex when choosing a spouse. Nor is racial or sexual discrimination in hiring necessarily wrong. This is shown by Peter Singer's example in which a director of a play about ghetto conditions in New York City refuses to consider any white applicants for the actors because she wants the play to be authentic.[7] If I am looking for a representative of the black community, or doing a study about blacks and disease, it is perfectly legitimate to discriminate against all whites. Their whiteness makes them unsuitable for my (legitimate) purposes. Similarly, if I am hiring a wet-nurse, or a person to patrol the women's change rooms in my department store, discriminating against males is perfectly legitimate.

These examples show that racial and sexual discrimination are not wrong in themselves. This is not to say that they are never wrong; most often they clearly are. Whether or not they are wrong, however, depends on the purposes, consequences, and context of such discrimination.

2. RACE AND SEX AS MORALLY ARBITRARY AND IRRELEVANT CHARACTERISTICS

A typical reason given for the alleged injustice of all racial and sexual discrimination (including affirma-

tive action) is that it is morally arbitrary to consider race or sex when hiring, since these characteristics are not relevant to the decision. But the above examples show that not all uses of race or sex as a criterion in hiring decisions are morally arbitrary or irrelevant. Similarly, when an affirmative action officer takes into account race and sex, use of these characteristics is not morally irrelevant or arbitrary. Since affirmative action aims to help end racial and sexual inequality by providing black and female role models for minorities (and non-minorities), the race and sex of the job candidates are clearly relevant to the decision. There is nothing arbitrary about the affirmative action officer focusing on race and sex. Hence, if reverse discrimination is wrong, it is not wrong for the reason that it uses morally irrelevant and arbitrary characteristics to distinguish between applicants.

3. REVERSE DISCRIMINATION AS UNJUSTIFIED STEREOTYPING

It might be argued that reverse discrimination involves judging people by alleged average characteristics of a class to which they belong, instead of judging them on the basis of their individual characteristics, and that such judging on the basis of stereotypes is unjust. But the defense of affirmative action suggested in this paper does not rely on stereotyping. When an employer hires a slightly less well qualified woman or black over a slightly more qualified white male for the purpose of helping to overcome sexual and racial inequality, she judges the applicants on the basis of their individual characteristics. She uses this person's sex or skin color as a mechanism to help achieve the goals of affirmative action. Individual characteristics of the white male (his skin color and sex) prevent him from serving one of the legitimate goals of employment policies, and he is turned down on this basis.

Notice that the objection does have some force against those who defend reverse discrimination on the grounds of compensatory justice. An affirmative action policy whose purpose is to compensate women and blacks for past and current injustices judges that women and blacks on the average are owed greater compensation than are white males. Although this is true, opponents of affirmative action argue that some white males have been more severely and unfairly disadvantaged than

---

National Forum (The Phi Kappa Phi Journal), vol. viii, no. 1 (Winter 1978), pp. 15–18. The article is reprinted in *Social Ethics*, 2nd edition, ed. Thomas Mappes and Jane Zembaty (New York: McGraw-Hill, 1982), pp. 187–191. The quoted phrase is Wasserstrom's.

[7]Peter Singer, "Is Racial Discrimination Arbitrary?" *Philosophia*, vol. 8 (November 1978), pp. 185–203.

some women and blacks.[8] A poor white male from Appalachia may have suffered greater undeserved disadvantages than the upper-middle class women or blacks with whom he competes. Although there is a high correlation between being female (or being black) and being especially owed compensation for unfair disadvantages suffered, the correlation is not universal.

Thus defending affirmative action on the grounds of compensatory justice may lead to unjust treatment of white males in individual cases. Despite the fact that certain white males are owed greater compensation than are some women or blacks, it is the latter that receive compensation. This is the result of judging candidates for jobs on the basis of the average characteristics of their class, rather than on the basis of their individual characteristics. Thus compensatory justice defenses of reverse discrimination may involve potentially problematic stereotyping.[9] But this is not the defense of affirmative action considered here.

4. FAILING TO HIRE THE MOST QUALIFIED PERSON IS UNJUST

One of the major reasons people think that reverse discrimination is unjust is because they think the most qualified person should get the job. But why should the most qualified person be hired?

---

[8]See, for example, Robert Simon, "Preferential Hiring: A Reply to Judith Jarvis Thomson," *Philosophy and Public Affairs,* vol. 3, no. 3 (Spring 1974).

[9]If it is true (and it is certainly plausible) that every black or woman, no matter how fortunate, has suffered from racism and sexism in a way in which no white male has suffered from racism and sexism, then compensation for this injustice would be owed to all and only blacks and women. Given this, arguing for affirmative action on the grounds of compensatory justice would not involve judging individuals by average features of classes of which they are members. Still it might be argued that for certain blacks and women such injustices are not nearly as severe as the different type of injustice suffered by some white males. Thus one would have to provide a reason for why we should compensate (with affirmative action) any black or woman before any white male. Perhaps administrative convenience is such a reason. Being black or female (rather than white and male) correlates nicely with the property of being more greatly and unfairly disadvantaged, and thus race and sex are useful rough guidelines for determining who most needs compensation. This does, however, involve stereotyping.

a. Efficiency. One obvious answer to this question is that one should hire the most qualified person because doing so promotes efficiency. If job qualifications are positively correlated with job performance, then the more qualified person will tend to do a better job. Although it is not always true that there is such a correlation, in general there is, and hence this point is well taken. There are short term efficiency costs of reverse discrimination as defined here.[10]

Note that a weaker version of affirmative action has no such efficiency costs. If one hires a black or woman over a white male only in cases where qualifications are roughly equal, job performance will not be affected. Furthermore, efficiency costs will be a function of the qualifications gap between the black or woman hired, and the white male rejected: the larger the gap, the greater the efficiency costs.[11] The existence of efficiency costs is also a function of the type of work performed. Many of the jobs in our society are ones which any normal person can do (e.g., assembly line worker, janitor, truck driver, etc.). Affirmative action hiring for these positions is unlikely to have significant efficiency costs (assuming whoever is hired is willing to work hard). In general, professional positions are the ones in which people's performance levels will vary significantly, and hence these are the jobs in which reverse discrimination could have significant efficiency costs.

While concern for efficiency gives us a reason for hiring the most qualified person, it in no way explains the alleged injustice suffered by the white male who is passed over due to reverse discrimination. If the affirmative action employer is treating the white male unjustly, it is not because the hiring policy is inefficient. Failing to maximize efficiency does not generally involve acting unjustly. For instance, a person who carries one bag of groceries at a time, rather than two, is acting inefficiently, though not unjustly.

It is arguable that the manager of a business who fails to hire the most qualified person (and thereby sacrifices some efficiency) treats the owners

---

[10]In the long run, however, reverse discrimination may actually promote overall societal efficiency by breaking down the barriers to a vast reservoir of untapped potential in women and blacks.

[11]See Thomas Nagel, "A Defense of Affirmative Action," p. 484.

of the company unjustly, for their profits may suffer, and this violates one conception of the manager's fiduciary responsibility to the shareholders. Perhaps the administrator of a hospital who hires a slightly less well qualified black doctor (for the purposes of affirmative action) treats the future patients at that hospital unjustly, for doing so may reduce the level of health care they receive (and it is arguable that they have a legitimate expectation to receive the best health care possible for the money they spend). But neither of these examples of inefficiency leading to injustice concern the white "male victim" of affirmative action, and it is precisely this person who the opponents of reverse discrimination claim is being unfairly treated.

To many people, that a policy is inefficient is a sufficient reason for condemning it. This is especially true in the competitive and profit oriented world of business. However, profit maximization is not the only legitimate goal of business hiring policies (or other business decisions). Businesses have responsibilities to help heal society's ills, especially those (like racism and sexism) which they in large part helped to create and perpetuate. Unless one takes the implausible position that business' only legitimate goal is profit maximization, the efficiency costs of affirmative action are not an automatic reason for rejecting it. And as we have noted, affirmative action's efficiency costs are of no help in substantiating and explaining its alleged injustice to white males.

b. The Most Qualified Person Has a Right to the Job.
One could argue that the most qualified person for the job has a right to be hired in virtue of superior qualifications. On this view, reverse discrimination violates the better qualified white male's right to be hired for the job. But the most qualified applicant holds no such right. If you are the best painter in town, and a person hires her brother to paint her house, instead of you, your rights have not been violated. People do not have rights to be hired for particular jobs (though I think a plausible case can be made for the claim that there is a fundamental human right to employment). If anyone has a right in this matter, it is the employer. This is not to say, of course, that the employer cannot do wrong in her hiring decision; she obviously can. If she hires a white because she loathes blacks, she does wrong. The point is that her wrong does not consist in violating the right some candidate has to her job

(though this would violate other rights of the candidate).

c. The Most Qualified Person Deserves the Job. It could be argued that the most qualified person should get the job because she deserves it in virtue of her superior qualifications. But the assumption that the person most qualified for a job is the one who most deserves it is problematic. Very often people do not deserve their qualifications, and hence they do not deserve anything on the basis of those qualifications.[12] A person's qualifications are a function of at least the following factors:

a. innate abilities,
b. home environment,
c. socio-economic class of parents,
d. quality of the schools attended,
e. luck, and
f. effort or perseverance.

A person is only responsible for the last factor on this list, and hence one only deserves one's qualifications to the extent that they are a function of effort.[13]

It is undoubtedly often the case that a person who is less well qualified for a job is more deserving of the job (because she worked harder to achieve those lower qualifications) than is someone with superior qualifications. This is frequently true of women and blacks in the job market: they worked harder to overcome disadvantages most (or all) white males never faced. Hence, affirmative action policies which permit the hiring of slightly less well qualified candidates may often be more in line with considerations of desert than are the standard meritocratic procedures.

The point is not that affirmative action is defensible because it helps ensure that more deserving

---

[12]This is Wasserstrom's point. See "A Defense of Programs of Preferential Treatment," in *Social Ethics,* p. 190.

[13]By "effort" I intend to include (1) how hard a person tries to achieve certain goals, (2) the amount of risk voluntarily incurred in seeking these goals, and (3) the degree to which moral considerations play a role in choosing these goals. The harder one tries, the more one is willing to sacrifice, and the worthier the goal, the greater are one's deserts. For support of the claim that voluntary past action is the only valid basis for desert, see James Rachels, "What People Deserve," in *Justice and Economic Distribution,* ed. John Arthur and William Shaw (Englewood Cliffs, NJ: Prentice-Hall, 1978), pp. 150–163.

candidates get jobs. Nor is it that desert should be the only or even the most important consideration in hiring decisions. The claim is simply that hiring the most qualified person for a job need not (and quite often does not) involve hiring the most deserving candidate. Hence the intuition that morality requires one to hire the most qualified people cannot be justified on the grounds that these people deserve to be hired.[14]

d. The Most Qualified Person Is Entitled to the Job. One might think that although the most qualified person neither deserves the job nor has a right to the job, still this person is entitled to the job. By "entitlement" in this context, I mean a natural and legitimate expectation based on a type of social promise. Society has implicitly encouraged the belief that the most qualified candidate will get the job. Society has set up a competition and the prize is a job which is awarded to those applying with the best qualifications. Society thus reneges on an implicit promise it has made to its members when it allows reverse discrimination to occur. It is dashing legitimate expectations it has encouraged. It is violating the very rules of a game it created.

Furthermore, the argument goes, by allowing reverse discrimination, society is breaking an explicit promise (contained in the Civil Rights Act of 1964) that it will not allow race or sex to be used against one of its citizens. Title VII of that Act prohibits discrimination in employment on the basis of race or sex (as well as color, religion, or national origin).

In response to this argument, it should first be noted that the above interpretation of the Civil

Rights Act is misleading. In fact, the Supreme Court has interpreted the Act as allowing race and sex to be considered in hiring or admission decisions.[15] More importantly, since affirmative action has been an explicit national policy for the last twenty years (and has been supported in numerous court cases), it is implausible to argue that society has promised its members that it will not allow race or sex to outweigh superior qualifications in hiring decisions. In addition, the objection takes a naive and utopian view of actual hiring decisions. It presents a picture of our society as a pure meritocracy in which hiring decisions are based solely on qualifications. The only exception it sees to these meritocratic procedures is the unfortunate policy of affirmative action. But this picture is dramatically distorted. Elected government officials, political appointees, business managers, and many others clearly do not have their positions solely or even mostly because of their qualifications.[16] Gives the widespread acceptance in our society of procedures which are far from meritocratic, claiming that the most qualified person has a socially endorsed entitlement to the job is not believable.

5. UNDERMINING EQUAL OPPORTUNITY FOR WHITE MALES

It has been claimed that the right of white males to an equal chance of employment is violated by affirmative action.[17] Reverse discrimination, it is said, undermines equality of opportunity for white males.

If equality of opportunity requires a social environment in which everyone at birth has roughly the same chance of succeeding through the use of his or her natural talents, then it could well be argued that given the social, cultural, and educational disadvantages placed on women and blacks,

---

[14]It would be useful to know if there is a correlation between the candidate who is most deserving (because she worked the hardest) and the one with the best qualifications. In other words, are better qualified candidates in general those who worked harder to achieve their qualifications? Perhaps people who have the greatest natural abilities and the most fortunate social circumstances will be the ones who work the hardest to develop their talents. This raises the possibility, suggested by John Rawls, that the ability to put forward effort is itself a function of factors outside a person's control. See his *A Theory of Justice* (Cambridge, MA: Harvard University Press, 1971), pp. 103–104. But if anything is under a person's control, and hence is something a person is responsible for, it is how hard she tries. Thus if there is an appropriate criterion for desert, it will include how much effort a person exerts.

[15]See Justice William Brennan's majority opinion in United Steel Workers and Kaiser Aluminum v. Weber, United States Supreme Court, 443 U.S. 193 (1979). See also Justice Lewis Powell's majority opinion in the University of California v. Bakke, United States Supreme Court, 483 U.S. 265 (1978).

[16]This is Wasserstrom's point. See "A Defense of Programs of Preferential Treatment," p. 189.

[17]This is Judith Thomson's way of characterizing the alleged injustice. See "Preferential Hiring," *Philosophy and Public Affairs*, vol. 2, no. 4 (Summer 1973).

preferential treatment of these groups brings us closer to equality of opportunity. White males are full members of the community in a way in which women and blacks are not, and this advantage is diminished by affirmative action. Affirmative action takes away the greater than equal opportunity white males generally have, and thus it brings us closer to a situation in which all members of society have an equal chance of succeeding through the use of their talents.

It should be noted that the goal of affirmative action is to bring about a society in which there is equality of opportunity for women and blacks without preferential treatment of these groups. It is not the purpose of the sort of affirmative action defended here to disadvantage white males in order to take away the advantage a sexist and racist society gives to them. But noticing that this occurs is sufficient to dispel the illusion that affirmative action undermines the equality of opportunity for white males.[18]

Legitimate Objections

The following two considerations explain what is morally troubling about reverse discrimination.

1. JUDGING ON THE BASIS OF INVOLUNTARY CHARACTERISTICS

In cases of reverse discrimination, white males are passed over on the basis of membership in a group they were born into. When an affirmative action employer hires a slightly less well qualified black (or woman), rather than a more highly qualified white male, skin color (or sex) is being used as one criterion for determining who gets a very important benefit. Making distinctions in how one treats people on the basis of characteristics they cannot help having (such as skin color or sex) is morally problematic because it reduces individual autonomy. Discriminating between people on the basis

of features they can do something about is preferable, since it gives them some control over how others act towards them. They can develop the characteristics others use to give them favorable treatment and avoid those characteristics others use as grounds for unfavorable treatment.[19]

For example, if employers refuse to hire you because you are a member of the American Nazi party, and if you do not like the fact that you are having a hard time finding a job, you can choose to leave the party. However, if a white male is having trouble finding employment because slightly less well qualified women and blacks are being given jobs to meet affirmative action requirements, there is nothing he can do about this disadvantage, and his autonomy is curtailed.[20]

Discriminating between people on the basis of their involuntary characteristics is morally undesirable, and thus reverse discrimination is also morally undesirable. Of course, that something is morally undesirable does not show that it is unjust, nor that it is morally unjustifiable.

How morally troubling is it to judge people on the basis of involuntary characteristics? Notice that our society frequently uses these sorts of features to distinguish between people. Height and good looks are characteristics one cannot do much about, and yet basketball players and models are ordinarily chosen and rejected on the basis of precisely these features. To a large extent our intelligence is also a feature beyond our control, and yet intelligence is clearly one of the major characteristics our society uses to determine what happens to people.

Of course there are good reasons why we distinguish between people on the basis of these sorts of involuntary characteristics. Given the goals of basketball teams, model agencies, and employers in general, hiring the taller, better looking, or more intelligent person (respectively) makes good sense.

---

[18]If it is true that some white males are more severely disadvantaged in our society than are some women and blacks, affirmative action would increase the inequality of opportunity for these white males. But since these individuals are a small minority of white males, the overall result of affirmative action would be to move us closer toward equality of opportunity.

[19]James Rachels makes this point in "What People Deserve," p. 159. Joel Feinberg has also discussed related points. See his *Social Philosophy* (Englewood Cliffs, NJ: Prentice-Hall, 1973), p. 108.

[20]He could work harder to get better qualifications and hope that the qualifications gap between him and the best woman or black would become so great that the efficiency cost of pursuing affirmative action would be prohibitive. Still he can do nothing to get rid of the disadvantage (in affirmative action contexts) of being a white male.

It promotes efficiency, since all these people are likely to do a better job. Hiring policies based on these involuntary characteristics serve the legitimate purposes of these businesses (e.g. profit and serving the public), and hence they may be morally justified despite their tendency to reduce the control people have over their own lives.

This argument applies to reverse discrimination as well. The purpose of affirmative action is to help eradicate racial and sexual injustice. If affirmative action policies help bring about this goal, then they can be morally justified despite their tendency to reduce the control white males have over their lives.

In one respect this sort of consequentialist argument is more forceful in the case of affirmative action. Rather than merely promoting the goal of efficiency (which is the justification for businesses hiring naturally brighter, taller, or more attractive individuals), affirmative action promotes the non-utilitarian goal of an egalitarian society. In general, promoting a consideration of justice (such as equality) is more important than is promoting efficiency or utility.[21] Thus in terms of the importance of the objective, this consequentialist argument is stronger in the case of affirmative action. If one can justify reducing individual autonomy on the grounds that it promotes efficiency, one can certainly do so on the grounds that it reduces the injustice of racial and sexual inequality.

2. BURDENING WHITE MALES WITHOUT COMPENSATION

Perhaps the strongest moral intuition concerning the wrongness of reverse discrimination is that it is unfair to job-seeking white males. It is unfair because they have been given an undeserved disadvantage in the competition for employment; they have been handicapped because of something that is not their fault. Why should white males be made to pay for the sins of others?

It would be a mistake to argue for reverse discrimination on the grounds that white males

deserve to be burdened and that therefore we should hire women and blacks even when white males are better qualified.[22] Young white males who are now entering the job market are not more responsible for the evils of racial and sexual inequality than are other members of society. Thus, reverse discrimination is not properly viewed as punishment administered to white males.

The justification for affirmative action supported here claims that bringing about sexual and racial equality necessitates sacrifice on the part of white males who seek employment. An important step in bringing about the desired egalitarian society involves speeding up the process by which women and blacks get into positions of power and authority. This requires that white males find it harder to achieve these same positions. But this is not punishment for deeds done.

Thomas Nagel's helpful analogy is state condemnation of property under the right of eminent domain for the purpose of building a highway.[23] Forcing some in the community to move in order that the community as a whole may benefit is unfair. Why should these individuals suffer rather than others? The answer is: Because they happen to live in a place where it is important to build a road. A similar response should be given to the white male who objects to reverse discrimination with the same "Why me?" question. The answer is: Because job-seeking white males happen to be in the way of an important road leading to the desired egalitarian society. Job-seeking white males are being made to bear the brunt of the burden of affirmative action because of accidental considerations, just as are homeowners whose property is condemned in order to build a highway.

This analogy is extremely illuminating and helpful in explaining the nature of reverse discrimination. There is, however, an important dissimilarity that Nagel does not mention. In cases of property condemnation, compensation is paid to the owner. Affirmative action policies, however, do not compensate white males for shouldering this burden of moving toward the desired egalitarian society. So

---

[21]For a discussion of how considerations of justice typically outweigh considerations of utility, see Manuel Velasquez, *Business Ethics* (Englewood Cliffs, NJ: Prentice-Hall, 1982), Chapter Two.

[22]On the average, however, white males have unfairly benefited from the holding back of blacks and women, and hence it is not altogether inappropriate that this unfair benefit be removed.

[23]Nagel, "A Defense of Affirmative Action," p. 484.

affirmative action is unfair to job-seeking white males because they are forced to bear an unduly large share of the burden of achieving racial and sexual equality without being compensated for this sacrifice. Since we have singled out job-seeking white males from the larger pool of white males who should also help achieve this goal, it seems that some compensation from the latter to the former is appropriate.[24]

This is a serious objection to affirmative action policies only if the uncompensated burden is substantial. Usually it is not. Most white male "victims" of affirmative action easily find employment. It is highly unlikely that the same white male will repeatedly fail to get hired because of affirmative action.[25] The burdens of affirmative action should be spread as evenly as possible among all the job-seeking white males. Furthermore, the burden job-seeking white males face—of finding it somewhat more difficult to get employment—is inconsequential when compared to the burdens ongoing discrimination places on women and blacks.[26] Forcing job-seeking white males to bear an extra burden is acceptable because this is a necessary step toward achieving a much greater reduction in the unfair burdens our society places on women and blacks. If affirmative action is a necessary mechanism for a timely dismantlement of our racial and sexual caste system, the extra burdens it places on job-seeking white males are justified.

Still the question remains: Why isn't compensation paid? When members of society who do not deserve extra burdens are singled out to sacrifice for an important community goal, society owes them compensation. This objection loses some of its force when one realizes that society continually places undeserved burdens on its members without compensating them. For instance, the burden of seeking efficiency is placed on the shoulders of the least naturally talented and intelligent. That one is born less intelligent

(or otherwise less talented) does not mean that one deserves to have reduced employment opportunities, and yet our society's meritocratic hiring procedures make it much harder for less naturally talented members to find meaningful employment. These people are not compensated for their sacrifices either.

Of course, pointing out that there are other examples of an allegedly problematic social policy does not justify that policy. Nonetheless, if this analogy is sound, failing to compensate job-seeking white males for the sacrifices placed on them by reverse discrimination is not without precedent. Furthermore, it is no more morally troublesome than is failing to compensate less talented members of society for their undeserved sacrifice of employment opportunities for the sake of efficiency.

Conclusion

This article has shown the difficulties in pinpointing what is morally troubling about reverse discrimination. The most commonly heard objections to reverse discrimination fail to make their case. Reverse discrimination is not morally equivalent to traditional racism and sexism since its goals and consequences are entirely different, and the act of treating people differently on the basis of race or sex is not necessarily morally wrong. The race and sex of the candidates are not morally irrelevant in all hiring decisions, and affirmative action hiring is an example where discriminating on the basis of race or sex is not morally arbitrary. Furthermore, affirmative action can be defended on grounds that do not involve stereotyping. Though affirmative action hiring of less well qualified applicants can lead to short run inefficiency, failing to hire the most qualified applicant does not violate this person's rights, entitlements, or deserts. Additionally, affirmative action hiring does not generally undermine equal opportunity for white males.

Reverse discrimination is morally troublesome in that it judges people on the basis of involuntary characteristics and thus reduces the control they have over their lives. It also places a larger than fair share of the burden of achieving an egalitarian society on the shoulders of job-seeking white males without compensating them for this sacrifice. But these problems are relatively minor when

---

[24]It would be inappropriate to extract compensation from women or blacks since they are the ones who suffer the injustice affirmative action attempts to alleviate.

[25]This is a potential worry, however, and so it is important to ensure that the same white male does not repeatedly sacrifice for the goals of affirmative action.

[26]Cheshire Calhoun reminded me of this point.

compared to the grave injustice of racial and sexual inequality, and they are easily outweighed if affirmative action helps alleviate this far greater injustice.[27]

[27]Of course one must argue that reverse discrimination is effective in bringing about an egalitarian society. There are complicated consequentialist arguments both for and against this claim, and I have not discussed them here. Some of the questions to be addressed are: (1) How damaging is reverse discrimination to the self-esteem of blacks and women? (2) Does reverse discrimination promote racial and sexual strife more than it helps to alleviate them? (3) Does it perpetuate unfortunate stereotypes about blacks and women? (4) How long are we justified in waiting to pull blacks and women into the mainstream of our social life? (5) What sorts of alternative mechanisms are possible and politically practical for achieving affirmative action goals (for instance, massive early educational funding for children from impoverished backgrounds)?

The Moral Status of Affirmative Action

LOUIS P. POJMAN

HARDLY A WEEK GOES BY but that the subject of Affirmative Action does not come up. Whether in the guise of reverse discrimination, preferential hiring, non-traditional casting, quotas, goals and time tables, minority scholarships, or race norming, the issue confronts us as a terribly perplexing problem. . . .

There is something salutary as well as terribly tragic inherent in this problem. The salutary aspect is the fact that our society has shown itself committed to eliminating unjust discrimination. Even in the heart of Dixie there is a recognition of the injustice of racial discrimination. Both sides of the affirmative action debate have good will and appeal to moral principles. Both sides are attempting to bring about a better society, one which is color-blind, but they differ profoundly on the morally proper means to accomplish that goal.

And this is just the tragedy of the situation: good people on both sides of the issue are ready to tear each other to pieces over a problem that has no easy or obvious solution. And so the voices become shrill and the rhetoric hyperbolic. . . .

In this paper I will confine myself primarily to Affirmative Action policies with regard to race, but much of what I say can be applied to the areas of gender and ethnic minorities.

I. Definitions

First let me define my terms:

Discrimination is simply judging one thing to differ from another on the basis of some criterion. "Discrimination" is essentially a good quality, having reference to our ability to make distinctions. As rational and moral agents we need to make proper distinctions. To be rational is to discriminate between good and bad arguments, and to think morally is to discriminate between reasons based on valid principles and those based on invalid ones. What needs to be distinguished is the difference between rational and moral discrimination, on the one hand, and irrational and immoral discrimination, on the other hand.

Prejudice is a discrimination based on irrelevant grounds. It may simply be an attitude which never surfaces in action, or it may cause prejudicial actions. A prejudicial discrimination in action is immoral if it denies someone a fair deal. So discrimination on the basis of race or sex where these are not relevant for job performance is unfair. Likewise, one may act prejudicially in applying a relevant criterion on insufficient grounds, as in the case where I apply the criterion of being a hard worker but then assume, on insufficient evidence, that the black man who applies for the job is not a hard worker.

From Public Affairs Quarterly 6(2), 1992. Reprinted with permission.

There is a difference between *prejudice* and *bias.* Bias signifies a tendency towards one thing rather than another where the evidence is incomplete or based on non-moral factors. For example, you may have a bias towards blondes and I towards red-heads. But prejudice is an attitude (or action) where unfairness is present—where one *should* know or do better, as in the case where I give people jobs simply because they are red-heads. Bias implies ignorance or incomplete knowledge, whereas prejudice is deeper, involving a moral failure—usually a failure to pay attention to the evidence. But note that calling people racist or sexist without good evidence is also an act of prejudice. I call this form of prejudice "defamism," for it unfairly defames the victim. . . .

Equal Opportunity is offering everyone a fair chance at the best positions that society has at its disposal. Only native aptitude and effort should be decisive in the outcome, not factors of race, sex or special favors.

Affirmative Action is the effort to rectify the injustice of the past by special policies. Put this way, it is Janus-faced or ambiguous, having both a backward-looking and a forward-looking feature. [In Roman mythology, *Janus* was a god with two faces.] The backward-looking feature is its attempt to correct and compensate for past injustice. This aspect of Affirmative Action is strictly deontological. The forward-looking feature is its implicit ideal of a society free from prejudice; this is both deontological and utilitarian.

When we look at a social problem from a backward-looking perspective we need to determine who has committed or benefited from a wrongful or prejudicial act and to determine who deserves compensation for that act.

When we look at a social problem from a forward-looking perspective we need to determine what a just society (one free from prejudice) would look like and how to obtain that kind of society. The forward-looking aspect of Affirmative Action is paradoxically race-conscious, since it uses race to bring about a society which is not race-conscious, which is color-blind (in the morally relevant sense of this term).

It is also useful to distinguish two versions of Affirmative Action. *Weak Affirmative Action* involves such measures as the elimination of segregation (namely the idea of "separate but equal"), widespread advertisement to groups not previously represented in certain privileged positions, special scholarships for the disadvantaged classes (e.g., all the poor), using underrepresentation or a history of past discrimination as a tie breaker when candidates are relatively equal, and the like.

Strong Affirmative Action involves more positive steps to eliminate past injustice, such as reverse discrimination, hiring candidates on the basis of race and gender in order to reach equal or near equal results, proportionate representation in each area of society.

II. A Brief History of Affirmative Action

1. After a long legacy of egregious racial discrimination the forces of civil justice came to a head during the decade of 1954–1964. In the 1954 U.S. Supreme Court decision, *Brown v. Board of Education,* racial segregation was declared inherently and unjustly discriminatory, a violation of the constitutional right to equal protection, and in 1964 Congress passed the Civil Rights Act which banned all forms of racial discrimination.

During this time the goal of the Civil Rights movement was equal opportunity. The thinking was that if only we could remove the hindrances to progress, invidious segregation, discriminatory laws, and irrational prejudice against blacks, we could free our country from the evils of past injustice and usher in a just society in which the grandchildren of the slave could play together and compete with the grandchildren of the slave owner. We were after a color-blind society in which every child had an equal chance to attain the highest positions based not on his skin color but on the quality of his credentials. In the early '60s when the idea of reverse discrimination was mentioned in civil rights groups, it was usually rejected as a new racism. The Executive Director of the NAACP, Roy Wilkins, stated this position unequivocally during congressional consideration of the 1964 civil rights law. "Our association has never been in favor of a quota system. We believe the quota system is unfair whether it is used for [blacks] or against [blacks]. . . . [We] feel people ought to be hired because of their ability, irrespective of their color. . . . We want equality,

equality of opportunity and employment on the basis of ability."[1]

So the Civil Rights Act of 1964 was passed outlawing discrimination on the basis of race or sex.

> Title VII, Section 703(a) Civil Rights Act of 1964: It shall be an unlawful practice for an employer—(1) to fail or refuse to hire or to discharge any individual or otherwise to discriminate against any individual with respect to his compensation, terms, conditions, or privileges of employment, because of such individual's race, color, sex, or national origin; or (2) to limit, segregate, or classify his employees or applicants for employment in any way which would deprive or tend to deprive any individual of employment opportunities or otherwise adversely affect his status as an employee because of such individual's race, color, religion, sex, or national origin. [42 U.S.C.2000e-2(a)].
>
> . . . Nothing contained in this title shall be interpreted to require any employer . . . to grant preferential treatment to any individual or to any group . . . for account of an imbalance which may exist with respect to the total numbers or percentage of persons of any race . . . employed by any employer . . . in comparison with the total or percentage of persons of such race . . . in any community, State, section, or other areas, or in the available work force in any community, State, section, or other area. [42 U.S.C.2000e- 2(j)].

The Civil Rights Act of 1964 espouses a meritocratic philosophy, calling for equal opportunity and prohibits reverse discrimination as just another form of prejudice. The Voting Rights Act (1965) was passed and Jim Crow laws throughout the South were overturned. Schools were integrated and public accommodations opened to all. Branch Rickey's promotion of Jackie Robinson from the minor leagues in 1947 to play for the Brooklyn Dodgers was seen as the paradigm case of this kind of equal opportunity—the successful recruiting of a deserving person.

2. But it was soon noticed that the elimination of discriminatory laws was not producing the fully integrated society that leaders of the civil rights movement had envisioned. Eager to improve the situation, in 1965 President Johnson went beyond equal opportunity to Affirmative Action. He issued the famous Executive Order 11246 in which the Department of Labor was enjoined to issue government contracts with construction companies on the basis of race. That is, it would engage in reverse discrimination in order to make up for the evils of the past. He explained the act in terms of the shackled runner analogy.

> Imagine a hundred yard dash in which one of the two runners has his legs shackled together. He has progressed 10 yds., while the unshackled runner has gone 50 yds. How do they rectify the situation? Do they merely remove the shackles and allow the race to proceed? Then they could say that "equal opportunity" now prevailed. But one of the runners would still be forty yards ahead of the other. Would it not be the better part of justice to allow the previously shackled runner to make-up the forty yard gap; or to start the race all over again? That would be affirmative action towards equality. [President Lyndon Johnson 1965 inaugurating the Affirmative Action Policy of Executive Order 11246.]

In 1967 President Johnson issued Executive Order 11375 extending Affirmative Action (henceforth "AA") to women. Note here that AA originates in the executive branch of government. Until the Kennedy-Hawkins Civil Rights Act of 1990, AA policy was never put to a vote or passed by Congress. Gradually, the benefits of AA were extended to Hispanics, native Americans, Asians, and handicapped people.[2]

---

[1]Quoted in William Bradford Reynolds, "Affirmative Action Is Unjust" in D. Bender and B. Leone (eds.), *Social Justice* (St. Paul, MN, 1984), p. 23.

[2]Some of the material in this section is based on Nicholas Capaldi's *Out of Order: Affirmative Action and the Crisis of Doctrinaire Liberalism* (Buffalo, NY, 1985), chapters 1 and 2. Capaldi, using the shackled runner analogy, divides the history into three stages: a *platitude stage* "in which it is reaffirmed that the race is to be fair, and a fair race is one in which no one has either special disadvantages or special advantages (equal opportunity)"; a *remedial stage* in which victims of past discrimination are to be given special help in overcoming their disadvantages; and a *realignment stage* "in which all runners will be reassigned to those positions on the course that they would have had if the race had been fair from the beginning" (p. 18f).

The phrase "An Equal Opportunity/Affirmative Action Employer" ("AA/EO") began to appear as official public policy. But few noticed an ambiguity in the notion of "AA" which could lead to a contradiction in juxtaposing it with "EO," for there are two types of AA. At first AA was interpreted as, what I have called, "Weak Affirmative Action," in line with equal opportunity, signifying wider advertisement of positions, announcements that applications from blacks would be welcomed, active recruitment and hiring blacks (and women) over *equally* qualified men. While few liberals objected to these measures, some expressed fears of an impending slippery slope towards reverse discrimination.

However, except in professional sports—including those sponsored by universities—Weak Affirmative Action was not working, so in the late '60s and early '70s a stronger version of Affirmative Action was embarked upon—one aimed at equal results, quotas (or "goals"—a euphemism for "quotas"). In *Swann v. Charlotte-Mecklenburg* (1971), regarding the busing of children out of their neighborhood in order to promote integration, the Court, led by Justice Brennan, held that Affirmative Action was implied in *Brown* and was consistent with the Civil Rights Act of 1964. The NAACP now began to support reverse discrimination.

Thus began the search for minimally qualified blacks in college recruitment, hiring, and the like. Competence and excellence began to recede into second place as the quest for racial, ethnic, and gender diversity became the dominant goals. The slogan "We have to become race conscious in order to eliminate race consciousness" became the paradoxical justification for reverse discrimination.

3. In 1968 the Department of Labor ordered employers to engage in utilization studies as part of its policy of eliminating discrimination in the work place. The office of Federal Contract Compliance of the U.S. Department of Labor (Executive Order 11246) stated that employers with a history of *underutilization* of minorities and women were required to institute programs that went beyond passive nondiscrimination through deliberate efforts to identify people of "affected classes" for the purpose of advancing their employment. Many employers found it wise to adopt policies of preferential hiring in order to preempt expensive government suits.

Employers were to engage in "utilization analysis" of their present work force in order to develop "specific and result-oriented procedures" to which the employer commits "*every good-faith effort*" in order to provide "relief for members of an '*affected class,*' who by virtue of *past discrimination* continue to suffer the present effects of that discrimination." This self-analysis is supposed to discover areas in which such affected classes are underused, considering their availability and skills. "*Goals and timetables* are to be developed to guide efforts to correct deficiencies in the employment of affected classes people in each level and segment of the work force." Affirmative Action also calls for "rigorous examination" of standards and criteria for job performance, not so as to "dilute necessary standards" but in order to ensure that "arbitrary and discriminatory employment practices are eliminated" and to eliminate unnecessary criteria which "have had the effect of eliminating women and minorities" either from selection or promotion.[3]

4. In 1969 two important events occurred. (a) The Philadelphia Plan—The Department of Labor called for "goals and time tables" for recruiting minority workers. In Philadelphia area construction industries, where these companies were all white, family run, businesses, the contractor's union took the case to court on the grounds that Title VII of the Civil Rights Act prohibits quotas. The Third Circuit Court of Appeals upheld the Labor Department, and the Supreme Court refused to hear it. This case became the basis of the EEOC'S aggressive pursuit of "goals and time tables" in other business situations.

(b) In the Spring of 1969 James Forman disrupted the service of Riverside Church in New York City and issued the Black Manifesto to the American Churches, demanding that they pay blacks $500,000,000 in reparations. The argument of the Black Manifesto was that for three and a half centuries blacks in America have been "exploited and degraded, brutalized, killed and persecuted" by whites; that this was part of the persistent institutional patterns of first, legal slavery and then, legal discrimination and forced segregation; and that through slavery and discrimination whites had procured enormous wealth from black labor with

---

[3]Wanda Warren Berry, "Affirmative Action Is Just" in D. Bender, *op. cit.,* p. 18.

little return to blacks. These facts were said to constitute grounds for reparations on a massive scale. The American churches were but the first institutions to be asked for reparations.[4]

5. The Department of Labor issued guidelines in 1970 calling for hiring representatives of *underutilized* groups. "*Nondiscrimination* requires the elimination of all existing discriminatory conditions, whether purposeful or inadvertent . . . *Affirmative action* requires . . . the employer to make additional efforts to recruit, employ and promote qualified members of groups formerly excluded" (HEW Executive Order 22346, 1972). In December of 1971 Guidelines were issued to eliminate underutilization of minorities, aiming at realignment of job force at every level of society.

6. In *Griggs v. Duke Power Company* (1971) the Supreme Court interpreted Title VII of the Civil Rights Act as forbidding use of aptitude tests and high school diplomas in hiring personnel. These tests were deemed presumptively discriminatory, employers having the burden of proving such tests relevant to performance. The notion of *sufficiency* replaced that of excellence or best qualified, as it was realized (though not explicitly stated) that the social goal of racial diversity required compromising the standards of competence.

7. In 1977, the EEOC called for and *expected* proportional representation of minorities in every area of work (including universities).

8. In 1978 the Supreme Court addressed the *Bakke* case. Alan Bakke had been denied admission to the University of California at Davis Medical School even though his test scores were higher than the 16 blacks who were admitted under the Affirmative Action quota program. He sued the University of California and the U.S. Supreme Court ruled (*University of California v. Bakke,* July 28, 1978) in a 5 to 4 vote that reverse discrimination and quotas are illegal except (as Justice Powell put it) when engaged in for purposes of promoting diversity (interpreted as a means to extend free speech under the First Amendment) and restoring a situation where an institution has had a history of prejudicial discrimination. The decision was greeted with applause from anti-AA quarters and dismay from pro-AA quarters. Ken Tollett

lamented, "The affirmance of *Bakke* would mean the reversal of affirmative action; it would be an officially sanctioned signal to turn against blacks in this country. . . . Opposition to special minority admissions programs and affirmative action is anti-black."[5]

But Tollett was wrong. The *Bakke* case only shifted the rhetoric from "quota" language to "goals and time tables" and "diversity" language. In the '80s affirmative action was alive and well, with preferential hiring, minority scholarships, and "race norming" prevailing in all walks of life. No other white who has been excluded from admission to college because of his race has even won his case. In fact only a year later, Justice Brennan was to write in *U.S. Steel v. Weber* that prohibition of racial discrimination against "any individual" in Title VII of the Civil Rights Act did not apply to discrimination against whites.[6]

9. Perhaps the last step in the drive towards equal results took place in the institutionalization of grading applicants by group related standards, race norming. Race norming is widely practiced but most of the public is unaware of it, so let me explain it.

Imagine that four men come into a state employment office in order to apply for a job. One is black, one Hispanic, one Asian and one white. They take the standard test (a version of the General Aptitude Test Battery or VG-GATB). All get a composite score of 300. None of them will ever see that score. Instead the numbers will be fed into a computer and the applicants' percentile ranking emerges. The scores are group-weighted. Blacks are measured against blacks, whites against whites, Hispanics against Hispanics. Since blacks characteristically do less well than other groups, the effect is to favor blacks. For example, a score of 300 as an accountant will give the black a percentile score of 87, an Hispanic a percentile score of 74 and a white or oriental a score of 47. The black will get the job as the accountant. See Table 1.

This is known as race norming. Until an anonymous governmental employee recently blew the whistle, this practice was kept a secret in several state employment services. Prof. Linda Gottfredson

[4]Robert Fullinwider, *The Reverse Discrimination Controversy* (Totowa, NJ, 1970), p. 25.

[5]Quoted in Fullinwider, *op. cit.,* p. 4f.
[6]See Lino A. Graglia, "'Affirmative Action,' the Constitution, and the 1964 Civil Rights Act," *Measure,* no. 92 (1991).

Table 1. Percentile Conversion Tables

Jobs are grouped into five broad families: Family I includes, for example, machinists, cabinet makers, and tool makers; Family II includes helpers in many types of agriculture, manufacturing, and so on; Family III includes professional jobs such as accountant, chemical engineer, nurse, editor; Family IV includes bus drivers, bookkeepers, carpet layers; Family V includes exterminators, butchers, file clerks. A raw score of 300 would convert to the following percentile rankings:

	I	II	III	IV	V
Black	79	59	87	83	73
Hispanic	62	41	74	67	55
Other	39	42	47	45	42

Sources: Virginia Employment Commission: U.S. Department of Labor. Employment and Training Administration, Validity Generalization Manual (Section A: Job Family Scoring).

of the University of Delaware, one of the social scientists to expose this practice, has since had her funding cut off. In a recent letter published in the *New York Times* she writes:

> One of America's best-kept open secrets is that the Employment Service of the Department of Labor has unabashedly promulgated quotas. In 1981 the service recommended that state employment agencies adopt a race-conscious battery to avoid adverse impact when referring job applicants to employers. . . . The score adjustments are not trivial. An unadjusted score that places a job applicant at the 15th percentile among whites would, after race-norming, typically place a black near the white 50th percentile. Likewise, unadjusted scores at the white 50th percentile would, after race-norming, typically place a black near the 85th percentile for white job applicants. . . . [I]ts use by 40 states in the last decade belies the claim that *Griggs* did not lead to quotas.[7]

[7]Linda Gottfredson, "Letters to the Editor," *New York Times,* Aug. 1, 1990 issue. Gender-norming is also a feature of the proponents of Affirmative Action. Michael Levin begins his book *Feminism and Freedom* (New Brunswick,

10. In the *Ward Cove, Richmond,* and *Martin* decisions of the mid-80s the Supreme Court limited preferential hiring practices, placing a greater burden of proof on the plaintiff, now required to prove that employers have discriminated. The Kennedy-Hawkins Civil Rights Act of 1990, which was passed by Congress last year, sought to reverse these decisions by requiring employers to justify statistical imbalances not only in the employment of racial minorities but also that of ethnic and religious minorities. Wherever underrepresentation of an "identified" group exists, the employer bears the burden of proving he is innocent of prejudicial behavior. In other words, the bill would make it easier for minorities to sue employers. President Bush vetoed the bill, deeming it a subterfuge for quotas. A revised bill is now in Congressional committee.

Affirmative Action in the guise of underutilized or "affected groups" now extends to American Indians, Hispanics—Spaniards (including Spanish nobles) but not Portuguese, Asians, the handicapped, and in some places Irish and Italians. Estimates are that 75% of Americans may obtain AA status as minorities: everyone except the white non-handicapped male. It is a strange policy that affords special treatment to the children of Spanish nobles and illegal immigrants but not the children of the survivors of Russian pogroms or Nazi concentration camps. . . .

III. *Arguments for Affirmative Action*

Let us now survey the main arguments typically cited in the debate over Affirmative Action. I will briefly discuss seven arguments on each side of the issue.

1987) with federal Court case *Beckman v. NYFD* in which 88 women who failed the New York City Fire Department's entrance exam in 1977 filed a class-action sex discrimination suit. The court found that the physical strength component of the test was not job-related, and thus a violation of Title VII of the Civil Rights Act, and ordered the city to hire 49 of the women. It further ordered the fire department to devise a special, less-demanding physical strength exam for women. Following EEOC guidelines if the passing rate for women is less than 80% of that of the passing rate of men, the test is presumed invalid.

1. NEED FOR ROLE MODELS

This argument is straightforward. We all have need of role models, and it helps to know that others like us can be successful. We learn and are encouraged to strive for excellence by emulating our heroes and role models.

However, it is doubtful whether role models of one's own racial or sexual type are necessary for success. One of my heroes was Gandhi, an Indian Hindu, another was my grade school science teacher, one Miss DeVoe, and another was Martin Luther King. More important than having role models of one's own type is having genuinely good people, of whatever race or gender, to emulate. Furthermore, even if it is of some help to people with low self-esteem to gain encouragement from seeing others of their particular kind in leadership roles, it is doubtful whether this need is a sufficient condition to justify preferential hiring or reverse discrimination. What good is a role model who is inferior to other professors or business personnel? Excellence will rise to the top in a system of fair opportunity. Natural development of role models will come more slowly and more surely. Proponents of preferential policies simply lack the patience to let history take its own course.

2. THE NEED OF BREAKING THE STEREOTYPES

Society may simply need to know that there are talented blacks and women, so that it does not automatically assign them lesser respect or status. We need to have unjustified stereotype beliefs replaced with more accurate ones about the talents of blacks and women. So we need to engage in preferential hiring of qualified minorities even when they are not the most qualified.

Again, the response is that hiring the less qualified is neither fair to those better qualified who are passed over nor an effective way of removing inaccurate stereotypes. If competence is accepted as the criterion for hiring, then it is unjust to override it for purposes of social engineering. Furthermore, if blacks or women are known to hold high positions simply because of reverse discrimination, then they will still lack the respect due to those of their rank. In New York City there is a saying among doctors, "Never go to a black physician under 40," referring to the fact that AA has affected the medical system during the past fifteen years. The police use "Quota Cops" and "Welfare Sergeants" to refer to those hired without passing the standardized tests. (In 1985 180 black and Hispanic policemen, who had failed a promotion test, were promoted anyway to the rank of sergeant.) The destruction of false stereotypes will come naturally as qualified blacks rise naturally in fair competition (or if it does not—then the stereotypes may be justified). Reverse discrimination sends the message home that the stereotypes are deserved—otherwise, why do these minorities need so much extra help?

3. EQUAL RESULTS ARGUMENT

Some philosophers and social scientists hold that human nature is roughly identical, so that on a fair playing field the same proportion from every race and gender and ethnic group would attain to the highest positions in every area of endeavor. It would follow that any inequality of results itself is evidence for inequality of opportunity. John Arthur, in discussing an intelligence test, Test 21, puts the case this way.

> History is important when considering governmental rules like Test 21 because low scores by blacks can be traced in large measure to the legacy of slavery and racism: segregation, poor schooling, exclusion from trade unions, malnutrition, and poverty have all played their roles. Unless one assumes that blacks are naturally less able to pass the test, the conclusion must be that the results are themselves socially and legally constructed, not a mere given for which law and society can claim no responsibility.
>
> The conclusion seems to be that genuine equality eventually requires equal results. Obviously blacks have been treated unequally throughout US history, and just as obviously the economic and psychological effects of that inequality linger to this day, showing up in lower income and poorer performance in school and on tests than whites achieve. Since we have no reason to believe that differences in performance can be explained by factors other than history, equal results are a good benchmark by which to measure progress made toward genuine equality.[8]

[8]John Arthur. *The Unfinished Constitution* (Belmont, CA, 1990), p. 238.

The result of a just society should be equal numbers in proportion to each group in the work force.

However, Arthur fails even to consider studies that suggest that there are innate differences between races, sexes, and groups. If there are genetic differences in intelligence and temperament within families, why should we not expect such differences between racial groups and the two genders? Why should the evidence for this be completely discounted?

Perhaps some race or one gender is more intelligent in one way than another. At present we have only limited knowledge about genetic differences, but what we do have suggests some difference besides the obvious physiological traits.[9] The proper use of this evidence is not to promote discriminatory policies but to be *open* to the possibility that innate differences may have led to an over-representation of certain groups in certain areas of endeavor. It seems that on average blacks have genetic endowments favoring them in the development of skills necessary for excellence in basketball.

Furthermore, on Arthur's logic, we should take aggressive AA against Asians and Jews since they are over-represented in science, technology, and medicine. So that each group receives its fair share, we should ensure that 12% of the philosophers in the United States are Black, reduce the percentage of Jews from an estimated 15% to 2%—firing about 1,300 Jewish philosophers. The fact that Asians are producing 50% of Ph.Ds in science and math and blacks less than 1% clearly shows, on this reasoning, that we are providing special secret advantages to Asians.

But why does society have to enter into this results game in the first place? Why do we have to decide whether all difference is environmental or genetic? Perhaps we should simply admit that we lack sufficient evidence to pronounce on these issues with any certainty—but if so, should we not be more modest in insisting on equal results? Here is a thought experiment. Take two families of different racial groups, Green and Blue. The Greens decide to have only two children, to spend all their resources on them, to give them the best education. The two Green kids respond well and end up with achievement test scores in the 99th percentile. The Blues fail to practice family planning. They have 15 children. They can only afford 2 children, but lack of ability or whatever prevents them from keeping their family down. Now they need help for their large family. Why does society have to step in and help them? Society did not force them to have 15 children. Suppose that the achievement test scores of the 15 children fall below the 25th percentile. They cannot compete with the Greens. But now enters AA. It says that it is society's fault that the Blue children are not as able as the Greens and that the Greens must pay extra taxes to enable the Blues to compete. No restraints are put on the Blues regarding family size. This seems unfair to the Greens. Should the Green children be made to bear responsibility for the consequences of the Blues' voluntary behavior?

My point is simply that Arthur needs to cast his net wider and recognize that demographics and childbearing and -rearing practices are crucial factors in achievement. People have to take some responsibility for their actions. The equal results argument (or axiom) misses a greater part of the future.

4. THE COMPENSATION ARGUMENT

The argument goes like this: blacks have been wronged and severely harmed by whites. Therefore white society should compensate blacks for the injury caused them. Reverse discrimination in terms of preferential hiring, contracts, and scholarships is a fitting way to compensate for the racist wrongs.

This argument actually involves a distorted notion of compensation. Normally, we think of compensation as owed by a specific person *A* to another person *B* whom *A* has wronged in a specific way *C*. For example, if I have stolen your car and used it for a period of time to make business profits that would have gone to you, it is not enough that I return your car. I must pay you an amount reflecting your loss and my ability to pay.

[9]See Philip E. Vernon's excellent summary of the literature in *Intelligence: Heredity and Environment* (New York, 1979) and Yves Christen "Sex Differences in the Human Brain" in Nicholas Davidson (ed.), *Gender Sanity* (Lanham, 1989) and T. Bouchard, *et al.,* "Sources of Human Psychological Differences: The Minnesota Studies of Twins Reared Apart," *Science*, vol. 250 (1990).

If I have only made $5,000 and only have $10,000 in assets, it would not be possible for you to collect $20,000 in damages—even though that is the amount of loss you have incurred.

Sometimes compensation is extended to groups of people who have been unjustly harmed by the greater society. For example, the United States government has compensated the Japanese-Americans who were interred during the Second World War, and the West German government has paid reparations to the survivors of Nazi concentration camps. But here a specific people have been identified who were wronged in an identifiable way by the government of the nation in question.

On the face of it the demand by blacks for compensation does not fit the usual pattern. Perhaps Southern states with Jim Crow laws could be accused of unjustly harming blacks, but it is hard to see that the United States government was involved in doing so. Furthermore, it is not clear that all blacks were harmed in the same way or whether some were *unjustly* harmed or harmed more than poor whites and others (e.g. short people). Finally, even if identifiable blacks were harmed by identifiable social practices, it is not clear that most forms of Affirmative Action are appropriate to restore the situation. The usual practice of a financial payment seems more appropriate than giving a high level job to someone unqualified or only minimally qualified, who, speculatively, might have been better qualified had he not been subject to racial discrimination. If John is the star tailback of our college team with a promising professional future, and I accidentally (but culpably) drive my pick-up truck over his legs, and so cripple him, John may be due compensation, but he is not due the tailback spot on the football team.

Still, there may be something intuitively compelling about compensating members of an oppressed group who are minimally qualified. Suppose that the Hatfields and the McCoys are enemy clans and some youths from the Hatfields go over and steal diamonds and gold from the McCoys, distributing it within the Hatfield economy. Even though we do not know which Hatfield youths did the stealing, we would want to restore the wealth, as far as possible, to the McCoys. One way might be to tax the Hatfields, but another might be to give preferential treatment in terms of

scholarships and training programs and hiring to the McCoys.[10]

This is perhaps the strongest argument for Affirmative Action, and it may well justify some weak versions of AA, but it is doubtful whether it is sufficient to justify strong versions with quotas and goals and time tables in skilled positions. There are at least two reasons for this. First, we have no way of knowing how many people of group *G* would have been at competence level *L* had the world been different. Secondly, the normal criterion of competence is a strong *prima facie* consideration when the most important positions are at stake. There are two reasons for this:

1. society has given people expectations that if they attain certain levels of excellence they will be awarded appropriately and
2. filling the most important positions with the best qualified is the best way to ensure efficiency in job-related areas and in society in general.

These reasons are not absolutes. They can be overridden. But there is a strong presumption in their favor so that a burden of proof rests with those who would override them.

At this point we get into the problem of whether innocent non-blacks should have to pay a penalty in terms of preferential hiring of blacks. We turn to that argument

5. COMPENSATION FROM THOSE WHO INNOCENTLY BENEFITED FROM PAST INJUSTICE

White males as innocent beneficiaries of unjust discrimination of blacks and women have no grounds for complaint when society seeks to rectify the tilted field. White males may be innocent of oppressing blacks and minorities (and women), but they have unjustly benefited from that oppression or discrimination. So it is perfectly proper that less qualified women and blacks be hired before them.

The operative principle is: He who knowingly and willingly benefits from a wrong must help pay for the wrong. Judith Jarvis Thomson puts it this

---

[10]See Michael Levin, "Is Racial Discrimination Special?" *Policy Review*, Fall issue (1982).

way. "Many [white males] have been direct beneficiaries of policies which have down-graded blacks and women . . . and even those who did not directly benefit . . . had, at any rate, the advantage in the competition which comes of the confidence in one's full membership [in the community], and of one's right being recognized as a matter of course."[11] That is, white males obtain advantages in self-respect and self-confidence deriving from a racist system which denies these to blacks and women.

Objection. As I noted in the previous section, compensation is normally individual and specific. If *A* harms *B* regarding *x, B* has a right to compensation from *A* in regards to *x.* If *A* steals *B*'s car and wrecks it, *A* has an obligation to compensate *B* for the stolen car, but *A*'s son has no obligation to compensate *B.* Furthermore, if *A* dies or disappears, *B* has no moral right to claim that society compensate him for the stolen car—though if he has insurance, he can make such a claim to the insurance company. Sometimes a wrong cannot be compensated, and we just have to make the best of an imperfect world.

Suppose my parents, divining that I would grow up to have an unsurpassable desire to be a basketball player, bought an expensive growth hormone for me. Unfortunately, a neighbor stole it and gave it to little Lew Alcindor, who gained the extra 18 inches—my 18 inches—and shot up to an enviable 7 feet 2 inches. Alias Kareem Abdul Jabbar, he excelled in basketball, as I would have done had I had my proper dose.

Do I have a right to the millions of dollars that Jabbar made as a professional basketball player— the unjustly innocent beneficiary of my growth hormone? I have a right to something from the neighbor who stole the hormone, and it might be kind of Jabbar to give me free tickets to the Laker basketball games, and perhaps I should be remembered in his will. As far as I can see, however, he does not *owe* me anything, either legally or morally.

Suppose further that Lew Alcindor and I are in high school together and we are both qualified to play basketball, only he is far better than I. Do I deserve to start in his position because I would have been as good as he is had someone not cheated me as a child? Again, I think not. But if being the lucky beneficiary of wrongdoing does not entail that Alcindor (or the coach) owes me anything in regards to basketball, why should it be a reason to engage in preferential hiring in academic positions or highly coveted jobs? If minimal qualifications are not adequate to override excellence in basketball, even when the minimality is a consequence of wrongdoing, why should they be adequate in other areas?

6. THE DIVERSITY ARGUMENT

It is important that we learn to live in a pluralistic world, learning to get along with those of other races and cultures, so we should have fully integrated schools and employment situations. Diversity is an important symbol and educative device. Thus preferential treatment is warranted to perform this role in society.

But, again, while we can admit the value of diversity, it hardly seems adequate to override considerations of merit and efficiency. Diversity for diversity's sake is moral promiscuity, since it obfuscates rational distinctions, and unless those hired are highly qualified the diversity factor threatens to become a fetish. At least at the higher levels of business and the professions, competence far outweighs considerations of diversity. I do not care whether the group of surgeons operating on me reflect racial or gender balance, but I do care that they are highly qualified. And likewise with airplane pilots, military leaders, business executives, and, may I say it, teachers and professors. Moreover, there are other ways of learning about other cultures besides engaging in reverse discrimination.

7. ANTI-MERITOCRATIC (DESERT) ARGUMENT TO JUSTIFY REVERSE DISCRIMINATION: "NO ONE DESERVES HIS TALENTS"

According to this argument, the competent do not deserve their intelligence, their superior character, their industriousness, or their discipline; therefore

---

[11]Judith Jarvis Thomson, "Preferential Hiring" in Marshall Cohen, Thomas Nagel and Thomas Scanlon (eds.), *Equality and Preferential Treatment* (Princeton, 1977).

they have no right to the best positions in society; therefore society is not unjust in giving these positions to less (but still minimally) qualified blacks and women. In one form this argument holds that since no one deserves anything, society may use any criteria it pleases to distribute goods. The criterion most often designated is social utility. Versions of this argument are found in the writings of John Arthur, John Rawls, Bernard Boxill, Michael Kinsley, Ronald Dworkin, and Richard Wasserstrom. Rawls writes, "No one deserves his place in the distribution of native endowments, any more than one deserves one's initial starting place in society. The assertion that a man deserves the superior character that enables him to make the effort to cultivate his abilities is equally problematic; for his character depends in large part upon fortunate family and social circumstances for which he can claim no credit. The notion of desert seems not to apply to these cases."[12] Michael Kinsley is even more adamant:

> Opponents of affirmative action are hung up on a distinction that seems more profoundly irrelevant: treating individuals versus treating groups. What is the moral difference between dispensing favors to people on their "merits" as individuals and passing out society's benefits on the basis of group identification?
>
> Group identifications like race and sex are, of course, immutable. They have nothing to do with a person's moral worth. But the same is true of most of what comes under the label "merit." The tools you need for getting ahead in a meritocratic society—not all of them but most: talent, education, instilled cultural values such as ambition—are distributed just as arbitrarily as skin color. They are fate. The notion that people somehow "deserve" the advantages of these characteristics in a way they don't "deserve" the advantage of their race is powerful, but illogical.[13]

It will help to put the argument in outline form.

1. Society may award jobs and positions as it sees fit as long as individuals have no claim to these positions.
2. To have a claim to something means that one has earned it or deserves it.
3. But no one has earned or deserves his intelligence, talent, education or cultural values which produce superior qualifications.
4. If a person does not deserve what produces something, he does not deserve its products.
5. Therefore better qualified people do not deserve their qualifications.
6. Therefore, society may override their qualifications in awarding jobs and positions as it sees fit (for social utility or to compensate for previous wrongs).

So it is permissible if a minimally qualified black or woman is admitted to law or medical school ahead of a white male with excellent credentials or if a less qualified person from an "underutilized" group gets a professorship ahead of a far better qualified white male. Sufficiency and underutilization together outweigh excellence.

Objection. Premise 4 is false. To see this, reflect that just because I do not deserve the money that I have been given as a gift (for instance) does not mean that I am not entitled to what I get with that money. If you and I both get a gift of $100 and I bury mine in the sand for 5 years while you invest yours wisely and double its value at the end of five years, I cannot complain that you should split the increase 50/50 since neither of us deserved the original gift. If we accept the notion of responsibility at all, we must hold that persons deserve the fruits of their labor and conscious choices. Of course, we might want to distinguish moral from legal desert and argue that, morally speaking, effort is more important than outcome, whereas, legally speaking, outcome may be more important. Nevertheless, there are good reasons in terms of efficiency, motivation, and rough justice for holding a strong *prima facie* principle of giving scarce high positions to those most competent.

The attack on moral desert is perhaps the most radical move that egalitarians like Rawls and company have made against meritocracy, but the ramifications of their attack are far-reaching. The

[12]John Rawls, *A Theory of Justice* (Cambridge, 1971), p. 104. See Richard Wasserstrom "A Defense of Programs of Preferential Treatment," *National Forum* (Phi Kappa Phi Journal), vol. 58 (1978). See also Bernard Boxill, "The Morality of Preferential Hiring," *Philosophy and Public Affairs,* vol. 7 (1978).
[13]Michael Kinsley, "Equal Lack of Opportunity," *Harper's,* June issue (1983).

following are some of its implications. Since I do not deserve my two good eyes or two good kidneys, the social engineers may take one of each from me to give to those needing an eye or a kidney—even if they have damaged their organs by their own voluntary actions. Since no one deserves anything, we do not deserve pay for our labors or praise for a job well done or first prize in the race we win. The notion of moral responsibility vanishes in a system of levelling.

But there is no good reason to accept the argument against desert. We do act freely and, as such, we are responsible for our actions. We deserve the fruits of our labor, reward for our noble feats and punishment for our misbehavior.

We have considered seven arguments for Affirmative Action and have found no compelling case for Strong AA and only one plausible argument (a version of the compensation argument) for Weak AA. We must now turn to the arguments against Affirmative Action to see whether they fare any better.[14]

[14]There is one other argument which I have omitted. It is one from precedence and has been stated by Judith Jarvis Thomson in the article cited earlier:

> Suppose two candidates for a civil service job have equally good test scores, but there is only one job available. We could decide between them by coin-tossing. But in fact we do allow for declaring for *A* straightaway, where *A* is a veteran, and *B* is not. It may be that *B* is a non-veteran through no fault of his own. . . . Yet the fact is that *B* is not a veteran and *A* is. On the assumption that the veteran has served his country, the country owes him something. And it is plain that giving him preference is not an unjust way in which part of that debt of gratitude can be paid (p. 379f).

The two forms of preferential hiring are analogous. Veteran's preference is justified as a way of paying a debt of gratitude; preferential hiring is a way of paying a debt of compensation. In both cases innocent parties bear the burden of the community's debt, but it is justified.

My response to this argument is that veterans should not be hired in place of better qualified candidates, but that benefits like the GI scholarships are part of the contract with veterans who serve their country in the armed services. The notion of compensation only applies to individuals who have been injured by identifiable entities. So the analogy between veterans and minority groups seems weak.

IV. Arguments Against Affirmative Action

1. AFFIRMATIVE ACTION REQUIRES DISCRIMINATION AGAINST A DIFFERENT GROUP

Weak Affirmative Action weakly discriminates against new minorities, mostly innocent young white males, and strong Affirmative Action strongly discriminates against these new minorities. As I argued in III.5, this discrimination is unwarranted, since, even if some compensation to blacks were indicated, it would be unfair to make innocent white males bear the whole brunt of the payments. In fact, it is poor white youth who become the new pariahs on the job market. The children of the wealthy have no trouble getting into the best private grammar schools and, on the basis of superior early education, into the best universities, graduate schools, managerial and professional positions. Affirmative Action simply shifts injustice, setting blacks and women against young white males, especially ethnic and poor white males. It does little to rectify the goal of providing equal opportunity to all. If the goal is a society where everyone has a fair chance, then it would be better to concentrate on support for families and early education and decide the matter of university admissions and job hiring on the basis of traditional standards of competence.

2. AFFIRMATIVE ACTION PERPETUATES THE VICTIMIZATION SYNDROME

Shelby Steele admits that Affirmative Action may seem "the meagerest recompense for centuries of unrelieved oppression" and that it helps promote diversity. At the same time, though, notes Steele, Affirmative Action reinforces the spirit of victimization by telling blacks that they can gain more by emphasizing their suffering, degradation and helplessness than by discipline and work. This message holds the danger of blacks becoming permanently handicapped by a need for special treatment. It also sends to society at large the message that blacks cannot make it on their own.

Leon Wieseltier sums up the problem this way.

> The memory of oppression is a pillar and a strut of the identity of every people oppressed. It is

no ordinary marker of difference. It is unusually stiffening. It instructs the individual and the group about what to expect of the world, imparts an isolating sense of aptness. . . . Don't be fooled, it teaches, there is only repetition. For that reason, the collective memory of an oppressed people is not only a treasure but a trap.

In the memory of oppression, oppression outlives itself. The scar does the work of the wound. That is the real tragedy: that injustice retains the power to distort long after it has ceased to be real. It is a posthumous victory for the oppressors, when pain becomes a tradition. And yet the atrocities of the past must never be forgotten. This is the unfairly difficult dilemma of the newly emancipated and the newly enfranchised: an honorable life is not possible if they remember too little and a normal life is not possible if they remember too much.[15]

With the eye of recollection, which does not "remember too much," Steele recommends a policy which offers "educational and economic development of disadvantaged people regardless of race and the eradication from our society—through close monitoring and severe sanctions—of racial and gender discrimination.[16]

3. AFFIRMATIVE ACTION ENCOURAGES MEDIOCRITY AND INCOMPETENCE

Last Spring Jesse Jackson joined protesters at Harvard Law School in demanding that the Law School faculty hire black women. Jackson dismissed Dean of the Law School, Robert C. Clark's standard of choosing the best qualified person for the job as "Cultural anemia." "We cannot just define who is qualified in the most narrow vertical academic terms," he said. "Most people in the world are yellow, brown, black, poor, non-Christian and don't speak English, and they can't wait for some White males with archaic rules to appraise them."[17] It might be noted that if Jackson is correct about the depth of cultural decadence at

Harvard, blacks might be well advised to form and support their own more vital law schools and leave places like Harvard to their archaism.

At several universities, the administration has forced departments to hire members of minorities even when far superior candidates were available. Shortly after obtaining my Ph.D. in the late '70s I was mistakenly identified as a black philosopher (I had a civil rights record and was once a black studies major) and was flown to a major university; only to be rejected for a more qualified candidate when it was discovered that I was white.

Stories of the bad effects of Affirmative Action abound. The philosopher Sidney Hook writes that "At one Ivy League university, representatives of the Regional HEW demanded an explanation of why there were no women or minority students in the Graduate Department of Religious Studies. They were told that a reading or knowledge of Hebrew and Greek was presupposed. Whereupon the representatives of HEW advised orally: "Then end those old fashioned programs that require irrelevant languages. And start up programs on relevant things which minority group students can study without learning languages."[18]

Government programs of enforced preferential treatment tend to appeal to the lowest possible common denominator. Witness the 1974 HEW Revised Order No. 14 on Affirmative Action expectations for preferential hiring: "Neither minorities nor female employees should be required to possess higher qualifications than those of the lowest qualified incumbents."

Furthermore, no test may be given to candidates unless it is *proved* to be relevant to the job.

> No standard or criteria which have, by intent or effect, worked to exclude women or minorities as a class can be utilized, unless the institution can demonstrate the necessity of such standard to the performance of the job in question.
>
> Whenever a validity study is called for . . . the user should include . . . an investigation of suitable alternative selection procedures and suitable alternative methods of using the selection procedure which have as little adverse impact as possible. . . . Whenever the user is shown an alternative selection procedure with

15Quoted in Jim Sleeper, *The Closest of Strangers* (New York, 1990), p. 209.
16Shelby Steele, "A Negative Vote on Affirmative Action," *New York Times,* May 13, 1990 issue.
17*New York Times,* May 10, 1990 issue.

18Nicholas Capaldi, *op. cit.,* p. 85.

evidence of less adverse impact and substantial evidence of validity for the same job in similar circumstances, the user should investigate it to determine the appropriateness of using or validating it in accord with these guidelines.[19]

At the same time Americans are wondering why standards in our country are falling and the Japanese are getting ahead. Affirmative Action with its twin idols, Sufficiency and Diversity, is the enemy of excellence. I will develop this thought below (IV.6).

4. AFFIRMATIVE ACTION POLICIES UNJUSTLY SHIFT THE BURDEN OF PROOF

Affirmative Action legislation tends to place the burden of proof on the employer who does not have an "adequate" representation of "underutilized" groups in his work force. He is guilty until proven innocent. I have already recounted how in the mid-eighties the Supreme Court shifted the burden of proof back onto the plaintiff, while Congress is now attempting to shift the burden back to the employer. Those in favor of deeming disproportional representation "guilty until proven innocent" argue that it is easy for employers to discriminate against minorities by various subterfuges, and I agree that steps should be taken to monitor against prejudicial treatment. But being prejudiced against employers is not the way to attain a just solution to discrimination. The principle: innocent until proven guilty, applies to employers as well as criminals. Indeed, it is clearly special pleading to reject this basic principle of Anglo-American law in this case of discrimination while adhering to it everywhere else.

5. AN ARGUMENT FROM MERIT

Traditionally, we have believed that the highest positions in society should be awarded to those who are best qualified. . . . Rewarding excellence both seems just to the individuals in the competition and makes for efficiency. Note that one of the most successful acts of integration, the recruitment of Jackie Robinson in the late '40s, was done in just this way, according to merit. If Robinson had been brought into the major league as a mediocre player or had batted .200 he would have been scorned and sent back to the minors where he belonged.

Merit is not an absolute value. There are times when it may be overridden for social goals, but there is a strong *prima facie* reason for awarding positions on its basis, and it should enjoy a weighty presumption in our social practices.

In a celebrated article Ronald Dworkin says that "Bakke had no case" because society did not owe Bakke anything. That may be, but then why does it owe anyone anything? Dworkin puts the matter in Utility terms, but if that is the case, society may owe Bakke a place at the University of California/Davis, for it seems a reasonable rule-utilitarian principle that achievement should be rewarded in society. We generally want the best to have the best positions, the best qualified candidate to win the political office, the most brilliant and competent scientist to be chosen for the most challenging research project, the best qualified pilots to become commercial pilots, only the best soldiers to become generals. Only when little is at stake do we weaken the standards and content ourselves with sufficiency (rather than excellence)—there are plenty of jobs where "sufficiency" rather than excellence is required. Perhaps we now feel that medicine or law or university professorships are so routine that they can be performed by minimally qualified people—in which case AA has a place.

But note, no one is calling for quotas or proportional representation of *underutilized* groups in the National Basketball Association where blacks make up 80% of the players. But if merit and merit alone reigns in sports, should it not be valued at least as much in education and industry?

6. THE SLIPPERY SLOPE

Even if Strong AA or Reverse Discrimination could meet the other objections, it would face a tough question: once you embark on this project, how do you limit it? Who should be excluded from reverse discrimination? Asians and Jews are overrepresented, so if we give blacks positive quotas, should we place negative quotas to these other groups? Since white males, "WMs," are a minority which is suffering from reverse discrimination, will we need a New Affirmative Action policy in the

[19]Ibid.

21st century to compensate for the discrimination against WMs in the late 20th century?

Furthermore, Affirmative Action has stigmatized the *young* white male. Assuming that we accept reverse discrimination, the fair way to make sacrifices would be to retire *older* white males who are more likely to have benefited from a favored status. Probably the least guilty of any harm to minority groups is the young white male—usually a liberal who has been required to bear the brunt of ages of past injustice. Justice Brennan's announcement that the Civil Rights Act did not apply to discrimination against whites shows how the clearest language can be bent to serve the ideology of the moment.[20]

7. THE MOUNTING EVIDENCE AGAINST THE SUCCESS OF AFFIRMATIVE ACTION

Thomas Sowell of the Hoover Institute has shown in his book *Preferential Policies: An International Perspective* that preferential hiring almost never solves social problems. It generally builds in mediocrity or incompetence and causes deep resentment. It is a short term solution which lacks serious grounding in social realities.

For instance, Sowell cites some disturbing statistics on education. Although twice as many blacks as Asians students took the nationwide Scholastic Aptitude Test in 1983, approximately fifteen times as many Asian students scored above 700 (out of a possible 800) on the mathematics half of the SAT. The percentage of Asians who scored above 700 in math was also more than six times higher than the percentage of American Indians and more than ten times higher than that of Mexican Americans—as well as more than double the percentage of whites. As Sowell points out,

in all countries studied, "intergroup performance disparities are huge" (108).

There are dozens of American colleges and universities where the median combined verbal SAT score and mathematics SAT score total 1200 or above. As of 1983 there were less than 600 black students in the entire US with combined SAT scores of 1200. This meant that, despite widespread attempts to get a black student "representation" comparable to the black percentage of the population (about 11%), there were not enough black students in the entire country for the Ivy League alone to have such a "representation" without going beyond this pool—even if the entire pool went to the eight Ivy League colleges.[21]

Often it is claimed that a cultural bias is the cause of the poor performance of blacks on SAT (or IQ tests), but Sowell shows that these test scores are actually a better predictor of college performances for blacks than for Asians and whites. He also shows the harmfulness of the effect on blacks of preferential acceptance. At the University of California, Berkeley, where the freshman class closely reflects the actual ethnic distribution of California high school students, more than 70% of blacks fail to graduate. All 312 black students entering Berkeley in 1987 were admitted under "Affirmative Action" criteria rather than by meeting standard academic criteria. So were 480 out of 507 Hispanic students. In 1986 the median SAT score for blacks at Berkeley was 952, for Mexican Americans 1014, for American Indians 1082 and for Asian Americans 1254. (The average SAT for all students was 1181.)

The result of this mismatching is that blacks who might do well if they went to a second tier or third tier school where their test scores would indicate they belong, actually are harmed by preferential treatment. They cannot compete in the institutions where high abilities are necessary.

Sowell also points out that Affirmative Action policies have mainly assisted the middle class black, those who have suffered least from discrimination. "Black couples in which both husband and wife are college-educated overtook white couples of the same description back in the early 1970s and continued to at least hold their own in the 1980s" (115).

[20]The extreme form of this New Speak is incarnate in the Politically Correct Movement ("PC" ideology) where a new orthodoxy has emerged, condemning white, European culture and seeing African culture as the new savior of us all. Perhaps the clearest example of this is Paula Rothenberg's book *Racism and Sexism* (New York, 1987) which asserts that there is no such thing as black racism; only whites are capable of racism (p. 6). Ms. Rothenberg's book has been scheduled as required reading for all freshmen at the University of Texas. See Joseph Salemi, "Lone Star Academic Politics," no. 87 (1990).

[21]Thomas Sowell, *op. cit.*, p. 108.

Sowell's conclusion is that similar patterns of results obtained from India to the USA wherever preferential policies exist. "In education, preferential admissions policies have led to high attrition rates and substandard performances for those preferred students . . . who survived to graduate." In all countries the preferred tended to concentrate in less difficult subjects which lead to less remunerative careers. "In the employment market, both blacks and untouchables at the higher levels have advanced substantially while those at the lower levels show no such advancement and even some signs of retrogression. These patterns are also broadly consistent with patterns found in countries in which majorities have created preferences for themselves . . ." (116).

The tendency has been to focus at the high level end of education and employment rather than on the lower level of family structure and early education. But if we really want to help the worst off improve, we need to concentrate on the family and early education. It is foolish to expect equal results when we begin with grossly unequal starting points—and discriminating against young white males is no more just than discriminating against women, blacks or anyone else.

Conclusion

Let me sum up. The goal of the Civil Rights movement and of moral people everywhere has been equal opportunity. The question is: how best to get there. Civil Rights legislation removed the legal barriers to equal opportunity, but did not tackle the deeper causes that produced differential results. Weak Affirmative Action aims at encouraging minorities in striving for the highest positions without unduly jeopardizing the rights of majorities, but the problem of Weak Affirmative Action is that it easily slides into Strong Affirmative Action where quotas, "goals," and equal results are forced into groups, thus promoting mediocrity, inefficiency, and resentment. Furthermore, Affirmative Action aims at the higher levels of society—universities and skilled jobs—yet if we want to improve our society, the best way to do it is to concentrate on families, children, early education, and the like. Affirmative Action is, on the one hand, too much, too soon and the other hand, too little, too late.

Martin Luther said that humanity is like a man mounting a horse who always tends to fall off on the other side of the horse. This seems to be the case with Affirmative Action. Attempting to redress the discriminatory iniquities of our history, our well-intentioned social engineers engage in new forms of discriminatory iniquity and thereby think that they have successfully mounted the horse or racial harmony. They have only fallen off on the other side of the issue.[22]

[22] I am indebted to Jim Landesman, Michael Levin, and Abigail Rosenthal for comments on a previous draft of this paper. I am also indebted to Nicholas Capaldi's *Out of Order* for first making me aware of the extent of the problem of Affirmative Action.

Comparable Worth: An Economic and Ethical Analysis

LAURA PINCUS AND BILL SHAW

The Egyptians do practically everything backwards from other people, in their customs and laws—among which the women go to market and make deals, whereas the men stay at home and weave; and other folk weave by pushing the weft upwards, but the Egyptians push it down. Men carry burdens on their heads, whereas women do it on their shoulders. The women piss standing up, and the men sitting down.

> *Herodotus, Histories, 2.35–36 (cited in Elizabeth Wayland Barber,* Women's Work: The First 20,000 Years *185 (1994))*

From Journal of Business Ethics *17: 455–470, 1998. © 1998 Kluwer Academic Publishers. Printed in the Netherlands. Reprinted with permission of Kluwer Academic Publishers.*

I. Introduction

PAY EQUITY is a concept that encompasses both equal pay and comparable worth. Comparable worth is the more controversial of the two measures, but the thrust of both these efforts is to narrow, if not eliminate, wage disparity across gender lines.[1] In context with other measures of equity in the workplace, comparable worth addresses the wage effects of labor market segregation, while affirmative action and "color gender/ethnic blind" civil rights programs address the problem of segregation itself.[2]

In its initial effort to address pay equity, Congress passed the Equal Pay Act.[3] This act requires that men and women working in equivalent positions receive equal compensation. The wage-gender disparity, however, turned out to be a persistent one notwithstanding the effect of the Equal Pay Act. This led some legal scholars to contend for a stronger antidote—comparable worth.[4]

Comparable worth addresses the wage gap by objectively comparing dissimilar jobs in order to determine the relative worth of those jobs to the achievement of the firm's objectives. The contention is that equal contribution merits equal compensation even if the jobs are dissimilar.[5] Workers in traditionally female-dominated professions are compensated at lower rates than workers in traditionally male-dominated professions and, it is contended, this discrepancy is based, not on the contribution of the job to the goals and objectives of the firm, but on discriminatory biases instead.[6]

In order to correct this market failure,[7] comparable worth proponents argue that the value of these jobs—specifically the contribution that these jobs make to the success of the firm—should be closely tied to employee compensation. To phrase the matter differently, comparable worth advocates pose an ethical question—why should women be expected to subsidize employers with their time, effort, and skill while men, who contribute no more to the firm's success, are compensated at a higher rate.

The primary attack on comparable worth is based on economic efficiency. In a free market, it is argued, fairness follows from efficiency. Supporters of comparable worth contend that it will lend

---

[1]"Pay equity" and "comparable worth" are used interchangeably in Canada. Canada also uses the term "employment equity" to refer to affirmative action legislation.

[2]George Rutherglen, *The Theory of Comparable Worth as a Remedy for Discrimination* **82** Geo. L. J. 135, 142–146 (1993).

[3]29 U.S.C. sec. 206(d)(1) (1988).

[4]Deborah Rhode, *Occupational Inequality,* 1988 Duke L. J. 1207. The extent of the disparity remains a controversy. While some researchers contend that the difference in wages between men and women is as much as thirty cents per dollar, Francine Blau & Andrea Beller, *Trends in Earnings Differences by Gender* **41** Indus. & Lab. L. Rev. 513, 514 (1988), other data evidences a much smaller gap. B. Orris, *Comparable Worth, Disparate Impact and The Market Rate Salary Problem: A Legal Analysis and Statistical Application* **71** Cal. L. Rev. 730 (1983). Elaine Sorensen, using 1991 Population Survey Data, finds an inverse relationship between the hourly earnings of women in an occupation and the proportion of workers in the occupation that are women. Specifically, women who work in a female-dominated job earn $3.88 per hour less than women, with the same amount of education, who work in a male-dominated job. Elaine Sorensen, Comparable Worth: Is It a Worthy Policy? 9 (1994). When single women without children are compared to their male counterparts, the difference becomes as small as seven cents per dollar. U.S. Bureau of the Census, Current Population Reports, Series P-60, No. 174, 112–18 (1992); Nicholas Mathys & Laura Pincus, *Is Pay Equity Equitable? A Perspective That Looks Beyond Pay* **44** Lab. L. J. 351, 354 (1993).

[5]Judge Richard A. Posner explains comparable worth as follows: "Comparable worth is not a legal concept but a shorthand expression for the movement to raise the ratio of wages in traditionally women's jobs to wages in traditionally men's jobs." American Nurses Assn. v. State of Illinois, 783 F.2d 716, 719 (7th Cir. 1986).

[6]Sorensen, *supra* note 4, at 10–13.

[7]It is not a matter of controversy that the conditions of an efficiently operating free market are as follows: (1) buyers and sellers can freely enter and leave the market and are so numerous that no individual or firm can impact the price or quantity of goods sold, (2) that all parties to economic transactions have full and free information, (3) that all costs (including social costs) are paid by producers, and (4) the government does not control or regulate prices. Relevant to this inquiry is the common understanding that markets fail when, over time, business does not cover all of its costs (e.g., product safety cost, environmental pollution cost, non-relevant job discrimination costs). Government interventions that compel business to absorb these costs, (e.g., product safety standards, the Clean Air Act, Title VII) are efforts to correct market failures and restore, or establish, free and efficient markets. The object of these interventions is to prevent business firms from imposing these costs, in the form of negative externalities, on the general public.

effective support to the effort of title VII in combatting discrimination against women, and that the elimination of gender-based discrimination will enhance both the distributional fairness and efficiency of the market system. Comparable worth advocates believe that they are addressing a market failure and that, in conjunction with other such efforts, comparable worth advances an approach to wage determination that is preferable to the current market-based approach.

This paper explores legal, economic and ethical arguments for and against the doctrine of comparable worth. The authors contend for conflicting positions in order to bring the perspective of advocates to a issue of enduring controversy.

II. The Legal Status of Comparable Worth

Legal efforts to eliminate the historical wage gap between men and women began at the state level.[8] It moved to the federal level in 1942 when the War Labor Board issued an order requiring changes to equalize "the wages or salary rates paid to females with the rates paid to males for comparable quality and quantity of work on the same or similar operations."[9] Congress eventually addressed the wage discrepancy in 1963 with the passage of the Equal Pay Act[10](EPA). The EPA provides that an employer must provide workers of both sexes equal pay for equal work, and provides four affirmative defenses for pay differentials.[11] Although the EPA's "equal work" requirement has been interpreted as requiring equal pay for "substantially equal" work,[12] this standard is not wide enough to encompass a comparable worth evaluation of dissimilar jobs.

At the same time that courts were interpreting the parameters of the EPA, wage differences began

to be addressed under Title VII of the Civil Rights Act of 1964. A preliminary question arose between the interaction of the EPA and Title VII. The Bennett amendment attempted to address these questions by allowing pay differentials under Title VII if payment was based on the affirmative defenses found in the EPA.[13] The question remained however, whether a comparable worth claim was actionable under Title VII. The Ninth Circuit Court of Appeals seemed to answer this question affirmatively in the case of *Gunther v. County of Washington*.[14]

The issue in *Gunther* was whether workers could bring a suit under Title VII alleging sex-based wage discrimination for jobs that were not equal. The court of appeals held that Title VII did not preclude such a claim.[15] The Supreme Court affirmed holding that the Bennett Amendment merely incorporated the EPA's four affirmative defenses, and that it did not preclude claims of sex-based wage discrimination under Title VII where the jobs at issue are not equal.[16] However, the majority carefully avoided the comparable worth issue, stating that the respondent's claim was not based on the "controversial concept of 'comparable worth.'"[17]

After *Gunther*, lower courts were reluctant to extend Title VII to include comparable worth claims, and the Ninth Circuit's decision in *AFSCME v. State of Washington*,[18] dealt a crippling blow to comparable worth. In *AFSCME*, the Ninth Circuit held that plaintiffs cannot bring a Title VII comparable worth claim under the disparate impact theory.[19] The court found that reliance on the market to set wages "does not constitute a single practice that suffices to support a claim under disparate impact theory."[20] Judge (now Justice) Kennedy dismissed the plaintiff's disparate treatment claims as well saying that dis-

---

[8]Karen J. Maschke, *Litigation, Courts, and Women Workers* (1989).

[9]*Id.,* citing General Order No. 16, as amended, reprinted in Wartime Wage Control Dispute Settlement 135 (1945).

[10]029 U.S.C. 206(d) (1988).

[11]*Id.* The four defenses are pay differentials due to (1) a seniority system, (2) a merit system, (3) a system measured by a quality or quantity of production, and (4) a system based on any factor other than sex.

[12]Schultz v. Wheaton Glass Company, 421 F.2d 259, 265 (3rd Cir. 1970).

[13]42 U.S.C. 2000e–s(h)(1988).

[14]602 F.2d 882 (9th Cir. 1979). *See also,* IUE v. Westinghouse, 631 F.2d 1094, 1105 (3rd Cir. 1980) (in accord); *but see,* Lemons v. City and County of Denver, 620 F.2d 228, 229 (10th Cir. 1980).

[15]*Id.*

[16]County of Washington v. Gunther, 451 U.S. 161, 166 (1981).

[17]*Id.*

[18]770 F.2d 1401 (9th Cir. 1985).

[19]*Id.,* at 1405–1406.

[20]*Id.*

criminatory intent could not be inferred from the fact that the state's comparable worth study revealed a wage disparity between genders. Thus, after *AFSCME,* the only theory a comparable worth plaintiff may rely on is disparate treatment, and proving discriminatory intent is made extremely difficult. Accordingly, subsequent courts have been unwilling to allow comparable worth claims. Instead, most of the impetus for comparable worth policies has come at the state and local level and in the private sector.

III. Arguments Supporting the Doctrine of Comparable Worth

Opponents of comparable worth base their critique on economic theory. They claim that the labor market currently sets an employee's economic worth. Part III of this article will contend that economic theory ignores the historical and societal causes of the wage discrepancy, that it incorrectly assumes a high level of economic efficiency in the market, that market-advocates fail to adequately explain the enduring discrepancy between wages in male and female job categories and that the market is not self-correcting in any reasonably foreseeable time period, and that there are good reasons to believe that government intervention makes sound public policy.

THE HISTORICAL AND SOCIETAL BIAS

Economic analysis disregards the historical and societal basis for the wage differential between men and women. While the key factor for the wage differential is gender segregation in the labor market (i.e., that men and women do different jobs), economic theories fail to take into account that most women were "channelled" into certain jobs by social expectations of what was "appropriate" work for women.[21] Such channelling may take the form of an increased emphasis on the appropriate skills for women to learn, by implicit "signals" in traditionally male-dominated fields that women should not join, or by overt harassment and intimidation when women attempt to join the particular profes-

sion (e.g., intimidation/sexual harassment by co-workers in the construction industry).

The problem with the economic theorists' reliance on "choice" is that they consider it to be radically free—in the mold of some disembodied, existential choice—rather than one structured by the societal and historical factors of the labor market. These theorists proceed as if choice is a matter to be determined in a vacuum, or at least in a setting no more problematic than a multiple choice quiz in Economics 101. They too easily ignore the choices that flesh-and-blood women have to make in a real world. Rosemary Hunter expressed her contempt for the inability of economic models to capture the complexity of the gender gap as follows:

> Moreover, a great many women in the labor market today were, as girls, educated to perform "women's work"—primarily so that they would become good wives and mothers, and incidentally so that they could participate in the labor market if necessary. Families did not invest in girls' education to the same extent as boys'. Schools taught boys a range of useful market skills, while girls were taught sewing and domestic science. Girls' aspirations to careers were actively dampened and deflected. To label all of this as women's rational "choices" about investment in human capital is repugnant. Indeed, the attractive-sounding concepts of "choice" and "preference" in economic models obscure the operations of a patriarchal . . . social system. . . . Human capital and individual choice theories allow white males to ignore the fact that they are the beneficiaries of the most thorough and effective affirmative-action program ever known.[22]

It seems that very few people within the business community would challenge Professor Hunter's position. In fact, much of what she claims could easily be conceded-cultural conditioning operating on males and females from an early age has indeed imposed upon them certain roles and preferences that affect their job choices. The response to Professor Hunter could continue then as follows: given the current spectrum of legal measures and social pressures that have opened job opportunities without regard to sex, it is through

[21]Rosemary Hunter, *A Feminist Response to Gender Gap in Compensation Symposium* **82** Geo. L. J. 147 (1993).

[22]*Id.,* at 150–151.

no fault of the business community that males and females select divergent career paths.[23]

This argument fails to excuse the complicity of the business community in perpetuating measurable and significant wage discrimination however. It presupposes that the business community has no role in shaping the perceptions of young women and men, that it is really not an active player in the culture that molds and conditions young people today. In this view, business has no leadership role but a passive one only. It further assumes that, unless and until there is some form of government intervention, business has no obligation to address this heavily documented wage disparity.

For all practical purposes, arguments along these lines exempt the business community from any responsibility in the matter. In the name of "individual preference" and "free choice," most business firms seem willing to accept a subsidy—a virtual windfall—at the expense of their female employees who are not being compensated in proportion to their contribution to profits. What needs to be emphasized, however, and clarified for business people and for citizens and voters as well, is that this argument is unsupported by the very business ideology to which it subscribes.

The business ideology is that of a free and efficient market, but such a market presupposes that business is covering its full share of costs, including social costs. Since it is not covering those costs—and, just as importantly, since business is "in denial" that it is implicated in shaping the choices of women and men—it is not acting responsibly and it is not acting consistently with its own ideology.

THE MARKET EFFICIENCY HYPOTHESIS

Comparable worth supporters assert that women's jobs are undervalued by the marketplace because they are traditionally performed by females. This claim is supported by the observation that when women enter traditionally male-dominated positions, pay rates have fallen.[24]

Economists reply that sex discrimination in the market is self-defeating because it gives non-discriminating firms a competitive disadvantage over discriminating firms. Nobel laureate Gary Becker notes three sources of employment discrimination: co-worker discrimination, customer discrimination, and employer discrimination.[25] While economists generally believe that customer and co-worker discrimination will be eliminated by market mechanisms, this view needs to be reconsidered according to Professor Jane Friesen.[26] Friesen reaches this conclusion based on the work of scholars who have found that customer boycotts[27] and the discriminatory tastes of co-workers[28] defeat the efforts of non-discriminatory employers to "swim against the tide." In other words, the conventional economic wisdom that "discrimination does not pay" and that it will be rooted-out by opportunistic, non-discriminating employers does not stand up under scrutiny.

Employer discrimination, noted by Becker, is frequently cited by economists as implausible. The high costs of implementing one's discriminatory tastes are said to be the obstacle that will prevent employers from imposing a wage tax on women

---

[23]Jennifer Roback, *The Gender Gap in Compensation: Beyond Equality* **82** Geo. L. J. 121, 123–124 (1993) (arguing that the documented wage gap is not a real cause for concern because money income is a poor indicator of utility or happiness and that we can infer next to nothing by comparing the income of one person with another).

[24]For example, in Litigation, Courts, and Women Workers, *supra* note 8, Karen J. Maschke observes that male secretaries and clerks were paid more than women who entered the jobs after they had been held by men.
[25]Gary S. Becker, The Economics of Discrimination 8 (1957).
[26]Jane Friesen, *The Gender Gap in Compensation: Alternative Economic Perspectives on the Use of Labor Market Policies to Redress the Gender Gap in Compensation* **82** Geo. L. J. 31 (1993).
[27]*Id.* at 34, citing George A. Akerlof, *Discriminatory, Status-based Wages Among Tradition-oriented, Stochastically Trading Coconut Producers* **93** J. Pol. Econ. 265 (1985).
[28]Friesen, *supra* note 26, at 34.
[29]Becker, *supra* note 25 (defining a "taste for discrimination" as the willingness "to forfeit income in order to avoid certain transactions"). Kenneth J. Arrow argues that, in a constant or decreasing cost industry, a nondiscriminatory employer could produce at lower costs than a discriminating employer by employing more members of the disadvantaged class. *See generally*, Kenneth J. Arrow, *The Theory of Discrimination*, in Discrimination in Labor Markets 3 (Orley Ashenfelter & Albert Rees, eds., 1973). This argument depends, however, on the plausibility of certain assumptions—constant costs, long-run elasticity of supply factors, and the number of

(and minorities).[29] The persistence of the wage gap, however, belies the force of Becker's "discriminatory taste" hypothesis. Even if the Becker hypothesis explains the gap, it can serve as no justification. At best it can explain the segregation of women into job categories that remove them from contact with discriminating customers or co-workers.[30]

Several explanations have been set forth for the continuing discrepancy between male and female wages. Wage differentials attributable to superior training and education evoke little argument. Models based on individual choice are more problematic however.[31] For example, women are said to freely choose jobs that provide more flexibility since they are more likely to leave the job market or have job interruptions because of family requirements (having a baby, etc.). Women who anticipate work interruptions are predicted to choose more flexible, presumably lower-paying, jobs. Evidence of this hypothesis is, however, very weak.[32] A more plausible explanation of why women's skills tend to be undervalued is because they are not seen as skills at all, hence, they have no market value.[33]

Further studies have looked to the effect that marriage and children have had upon the wages of men and women. Where marriage has a large positive effect on men's wages, it has a smaller, but positive, effect on women's wages when controlled for occupation, experience, tenure, and schooling.[34] Becker concludes that this data supports the proposition that it is more efficient to have men at work and women at home.[35] The marriage premium, however, may simply be evidence of favoritism towards married men,[36] or it may show nothing more than that the same qualities that make some men economically productive are also the qualities that make them good candidates for marriage.[37]

The specialization argument implies that the division of labor along gender lines is more efficient, thus better. Clearly this begs the question in favor of efficiency and leaves one to wonder why, of all the world's goods, efficiency is advanced as paramount. With no articulated foundation for efficiency as the paramount good, economists will be unable to rebut the feminist claim that economic independence "trumps" efficiency and that top priority should be given to strategies that will secure women's economic independence rather than having such a high proportion of the female population depending on transfer payments from a

---

nondiscriminating firms in the industry. *See* Glen G. Cain, *The Economic Analysis of Labor Market Discrimination: A Survey*, in 1 Handbook of Labor Economics 693 (Orley Ashenfelter & Richard Layard, eds., 1986).

[30]Cain, *supra* note 29, at 719. Friesen, *supra* note 26, at 32.

[31]Friesen, *supra* note 26, at 36.

[32]Charles Brown, *Equalizing Differences in the Labor Market* 64 Q. J. Econ. 113 (1980); Robert S. Smith, *Compensating Differentials and Public Policy: A Review*, 32 Indus. & Lab. Rel. Rev. 339 (1979); Randall K. Filler, *Male-Female Wage Differentials: The Importance of Compensating Differentials* 38 Indus. & Lab. Rel. Rev. 426 (1985).

[33]Elinor Lenz & Barbara Myerhoff, The Feminization of America, 75–95 (1985) (description of the home as the feminine domain and workplace as the domain of the husband); The Worth of Women's Work, sec. II (Anne Statham *et al.* eds., 1988); Marilyn Waring, Counting for Nothing (1988); Nancy S. Barrett, *Women in the Job Market: Occupations, Earnings, and Career Opportunities*, in The Subtle Revolution: Women at Work, 46–54 (Ralph E. Smith ed., 1979) (economic harm to women caused by job segregation which permits employers to circumvent equal pay principles).

[34]Friesen, *supra* note, at 38. *See generally,* David Neumark & Sanders Korenman, Sources of Bias in Women's Wage Equations, 24–26 (National Bureau of Economic Research Working Paper No. 4019, 1992).

[35]*See generally,* Gary S. Becker, *Human Capital, Effort, and Division of Labor* 3 J. Lab. Econ. 533 (1985) (hypothesizing that women's greater responsibility for child care and housework will lead to less commitment to business careers, less energy for demanding managerial positions, but that marriage provides men with the opportunity to specialize, which leads to greater productivity and higher earnings).

[36]Martha Hill, *The Wage Effects of Marital Status and Children* 14 J. Hum. Resources 579 (1979).

[37]Robert Nakosteen & Michael Zimmer, *Marital Status and Earnings of Young Men* 14 J. Hum. Resources 223 (1987).

[38]*Cf.,* Rosemary Hunter, *The Gender Gap in Compensation: Afterword—A Feminist Response to the Gender Gap in Compensation Symposium* 82 Geo. L. J. 147 (1993). Lest one view with dismay what may seem to be a deconstructionist tactic (a tactic sometimes attributed to Jacques Derrida and to Stanley Fish) to undermine one account with another which is no more, or less, credible than that which it is intended to rebut, *see* Martha Nussbaum, *Skepticism About Practical Reason, in Literature and the Last,* 107 Harv. L. Rev. 714–43 (1994), this section is stocked with good reasons supporting the why, the how, and the impact of government intervention.

spouse or from the government.[38]

Given the continuing existence of an unexplainable difference in wages, the party opposing a change towards more equitable pay rates should bear the burden of showing that the current wage differentials are efficient or acceptable. In the traditional disparate impact approach to Title VII discrimination, since it is often difficult (if not impossible) to prove discriminatory intent on behalf of an employer, an employee is given the opportunity to show an inference of discrimination and require the employer to explain the reasons for the discriminatory impact.

It seems only fair that burden shifting should apply as well in the comparable worth debate. Given that there remains some unexplained wage difference, the party opposing comparable worth should be required to bear the burden on this issue. If women's jobs pay less precisely because they are performed by women, then comparable worth would appear to be a viable alternative. Waiting for the market to correct itself, if it ever does, may take many years. Conservative estimates for a gender balanced work force, at the current rate of change, range from 75–100 years.[39]

DISPARATE WAGES AS A MARKET FAILURE

The weight of the evidence suggests that the wage disparity between men and women amounts to a market failure and that the magnitude of the failure justifies government intervention. Edward McCaffrey notes that many labor markets fail at a basic level because of the inability of employers to pay employees at their marginal productivity (MP).[40] Transaction costs prevent employers from designing a labor contract that matches an employee's wage to her MP.[41] Therefore, most employers use a linear wage structure where an employee is initially paid at a wage above her MP (assuming training is required) and subsequently paid at a wage beneath her MP. Since employers must overpay initially and depend on subsequent underpayment to recoup costs, *ex ante* predictions about an employee's tenure are crucial.

Incomplete and asymmetric information prevents employers from accurately distinguishing tenure between short-term and long-term women employees.[42] In response, employers tend to view *all* woman employees as "potential mothers" and underestimate the *average* tenure for women employees. Women are offered lower initial wages or are excluded from an occupation altogether. Women who wish to receive comparable wages must "act like men" by convincing potential employers of their commitment to the job.

In McCaffrey's view, employers are acting "rationally" in a "second-best" market, but he attacks the practice as highly inefficient. As he states, "the market, deeply flawed, has been dictating choices instead of accommodating them, as liberal theory (of efficiency) would have it."[43] Further, he stresses that doing nothing (letting the market be) lets transaction costs and incomplete information perpetuate market failure and high inefficiency. Government intervention, then, can provide an appropriate remedy for the failure of the labor market to cure gender discrimination.[44]

IMPLICATIONS OF PUBLIC SECTOR SUCCESSES

Implementation of comparable worth has primarily taken place in the public sector.[45] To this extent, several case studies examine the effects of wage adjustments by state governments on the wage and employment levels of women and men.

Elaine Sorensen documented the economic effects of comparable worth salary adjustments made by the Minnesota state government from 1983 to 1987.[46] First, Sorensen noted that prior to comparable worth adjustments in 1983, women working for the state earned 72% as much

---

[39]Rhode, *supra* note 4, at 1209.

[40]Edward McCaffrey, Slouching Toward Equity **103** Yale L. J. 595 (1993).

[41]These costs include the difficulty (time, effort, expense) of measuring a Worker's MP at any one time.

[42]*Id.,* at 610.

[43]*Id.,* at 674.

[44]*Id.,* at 656.

[45]By 1989, 20 states had provided comparable worth adjustments to at least some state employees.

[46]Elaine Sorensen, Comparable Worth: Is It a Worthy Policy? 191 (1994).

as men. After four years of comparable worth implementations, women's relative pay increased 9 percentage points, to 81 percent.[47] To isolate the effects of comparable worth, Sorensen employed a fixed-effects regression model, using panel data consisting of employees with repeated observations over time. Controlling for age, tenure, and change in education, Sorensen found that Minnesota's comparable worth policy increased women's pay by 15%, relative to what would be expected on the basis of current trends. Men's relative pay, during the same period, increased by 2.8%. Moreover, comparable worth increased women's pay in "targeted" jobs 23.6% while women in non-targeted jobs received a 0.5% increase as a result of comparable worth adjustments.[48]

Next, Sorensen estimated the labor demand functions for targeted and non-targeted jobs to isolate the effect of comparable worth on employment levels. She found that comparable worth did slow the overall growth of female employment in the state sector, as economic theory predicts, but only by a small amount. Male employment growth was similarly limited by comparable worth, but, on balance, the project was a successful one in Sorensen's estimation.[49]

One limitation of Sorensen's analysis was that she ignored the "substitution effects" caused by comparable worth. Sorensen assumed that once the wages of targeted jobs are increased, the employer does not substitute away from targeted jobs to the relatively cheaper non-targeted positions.[50] Shulamit Kahn acknowledges this economic prospect in her analysis of comparable worth adjustments made by the city of San Jose, California.[51] Using personnel data, Kahn investigates the effects of wage adjustments made to female government jobs from 1981 to 1986.

Like Sorensen, Kahn found that comparable worth increased the wages in targeted female jobs, relative to non-targeted jobs. This wage increase remained significant even after controlling for natural growth in California, Silicon Valley, and San Jose.[52] Unlike Sorensen, Kahn did not find that comparable worth slowed down the growth of either male or female government employment. Instead, male and female San Jose government jobs grew at a faster rate than similar jobs in 13 of California's 14 largest cities.[53] Moreover, Kahn did not find that San Jose substituted away from targeted government jobs to the relatively cheaper non-targeted positions. Employment grew faster in targeted jobs than in non-targeted jobs, controlling for the growth of targeted jobs, growth of the San Jose government, and shifts in government management.[54] Kahn, like Sorensen, concluded that the positive economic impacts of comparable worth outweigh its negatives.

Unfortunately, Sorensen and Kahn investigate the economic effects of comparable worth within the vacuum of one specific governmental body. Both concede that a comparable worth regime may not work as well outside of the governmental body which they analyze. Douglas Ehrenberg fills this analytical gap by evaluating evidence provided by studies of the empirical consequences of comparable worth in several states.[55] Ehrenberg compared, critiqued, and synthesized each of these studies to locate general equilibrium wage and employment effects of comparable worth. In

---

[47] *Id.*

[48] *Id.*, at 107.

[49] *Id.*, at 112. Comparable worth slowed the growth rate from 20% to 17.2% and 3.9% to 2.9% for female and male employment respectively.

[50] Sorensen, *supra* note 46, at 113. Sorensen acknowledged this limitation at the end of her analysis.

[51] Shulamit Kahn, *Economic Implications of Public-sector Comparable Worth: The Case of San Jose, California* **31** Ind. Rel. 2 (70).

[52] *Id.*, at 275–277, 286.

[53] *Id.*, at 278.

[54] *Id.*, at 284.

[55] Ronald Ehrenberg, Econometrics Analysis of the Empirical Consequences of Comparable Worth: What Have We Learned? (National Bureau of Economic Research 1988). Specifically, Ehrenberg synthesizes Kahn and Killingsworth's studies of San Jose, Orazem & Matilla's study of Iowa, and Killingsworth's study of Minnesota. One should note as well the evidence of Australia's adoption of comparable worth. The Australian system was phased in between 1969 and 1975. Women's wages compared to men's increased from 65% to 86%. Employment for women continued to rise, but at a rate 1/3 less than was expected (unemployment among women was up by 0.5%). Robert G. Gregory & Robert C. Duncan, *Segmented Labor Market Theories and the Australian Experience of Equal Pay for Women,* Journal of Post Keynesian Economics, 403–428 (1981).

the final analysis, he concluded that "comparable worth's direct effects will be to reduce the overall female/male gap modestly and that this reduction will be achieved at a cost of only small female employment."[56]

All of these case studies suggest that comparable worth is a legitimate and potentially effective tool with which to reduce wage disparity between women and men in certain job sectors. Since opponents to comparable worth fail to fully explain the wage disparity or offer a basis for market neutrality, their stand-still policy on comparable worth is scarcely tenable.

IV. Arguments in Opposition to Comparable Worth

THE PROCESS ARGUMENT

Part IV of this article will advance the primary argument in opposition to the imposition of a comparable worth system on the American work force. This argument is based on a theory of market efficiency. Opponents to comparable worth contend that artificially inflated wage rates are not the answer, no matter what is the cause of the wage gap.[57] Traditional economic theories hold that supply and demand efficiently determine the appropriate price for any good or service. Therefore, if women in traditionally female-dominated professions are financially compensated less than men in traditionally male-dominated professions, this disparity reflects either the inherent comparative values of those professions to society or the intrinsic rewards which might be offered by the lower paying positions. Comparable worth proponents argue that the disparity is evidence of market imperfections that devalue certain positions merely because they are performed by females. To the contrary, it is precisely this gap which supports the claim that the market is efficient and that the market merely reflects disparate decisions made by men and women in our society, as well as mirrors the free choices of labor consumers.[58]

Both men and women reach difficult, if "wrenching," job-choice decisions, subject to an array of pressures both from societal sources as well as personal and familial sources. Others would resolve these societally-enforced gender differences by imposing an artificial structure on the labor market, as discussed in Part III, rather than by addressing the true gender-based problems of our society. An artificial (non-market-induced) inflation of wages in female-dominated professions will only channel more women into occupations which may not be valued highly by society, ignoring the societally-created differences between the employment needs of men and women and creating an imbalance in the labor supply and the needs of consumers of that labor.

In addition, artificial inflation of wages in traditionally female-dominated professions will serve to attract men to those professions. In doing so, the competition for these positions, which initially attracted women because of the intrinsic rewards they held out to women (greater flexibility, less time/energy commitment, less investment in human capital), becomes greater. Women, who on average entered the work force more recently than men, may not have the requisite experience with which to compete once men enter that market. Accordingly, some women will be foreclosed from jobs taken over by men.

The flaw in comparable worth analysis is the determination of the "worth" of any position. Under market theory, the worth of an employment position is equal to the amount agreed upon by someone willing to pay for a certain service and someone willing to sell her or his services. Where the demand of the labor users/employers is high and the supply of labor is low, as is the case in certain male-dominated professions, the worth of a certain position increases. Likewise, where the demand of the employer is relatively low and the supply of labor is increasing, the worth of a certain position may decrease. On the other hand, comparable worth theorists contend that there exists some intrinsic value to a position, regardless of

---

[56]*Id.,* at 24.

[57]*See infra* notes 58–61, and accompanying text. *See also* Spaulding v. University of Washington, 740 F.2d 686, 706–707; American Federation of State, County and Municipal Employees (AFSCME) v. Washington, 770 F.2d 1401 (9th Cir. 1985), American Nurses Assn. v. State of Illinois, 783 F.2d 716, 719 (7th Cir. 1986).

[58]Ellen Paul, Equity and Gender, 47 (1989).

what someone is willing to pay for that position. Yet, they offer no effective means by which to determine this value.

For instance, as stated in earlier arguments in favor of comparable worth, as discrimination becomes less tolerated and minority and female workers become more accepted in the labor force, the market becomes more efficient with the elimination of discrimination. The elimination of discrimination comes from increased exposure to women and minorities and increased awareness through education. Accordingly, no artificial mechanism is necessary to boost wages in certain occupations to a "true" level. In fact, Becker found that discrimination was less in competitive industries than in monopolistic ones, evidencing the critical effect of free market competition on wages.[59]

Comparable worth advocates should also be required to specify what is meant by a "true" level. If the market is deemed inefficient, is the "true" level the rate at which men are being paid in equivalent positions? How does one determine which positions are equivalent? These quandaries have plagued comparable worth proponents for years. Comparable worth has understandably been described as "a fallacious notion that apples are equal to oranges and that the price for both should be the same."[60]

An illuminating example of the problems inherent in the presumption that wage differences are due to discrimination is offered by economist Sharon Smith:

Consider an employer with only two jobs:

French-English translator and a Spanish-English translator. *A priori*, it would seem that neither job involves more skill, effort or responsibility than the other; and they would presumably entail the same working conditions. The jobs would therefore be determined to be comparable and, hence, to merit the same pay. If the French translators were predominantly male and better paid than the Spanish translators who, let us suppose, are predominantly female, is this not convincing evidence of discrimination? Perhaps, but now add one more "fact" to this hypothetical example: suppose the employer in question is located in Miami. Is there still any reason to suppose that (even) if the firm does not discriminate, it would necessarily pay the two groups of translators the same wage? Clearly not.[61]

In fact, it would be difficult without more facts to determine which group would be better paid. Discrimination is not the only, much less the obvious explanation for a wage differential in this example; and artificial modification of the wages offered would lead to an inefficient allocation of resources, an imbalance between the services offered and the demand for those services. It is not clear that, in the absence of discrimination, these positions would command the same wages. Wages should, undoubtedly, be based on the value of the position and its contribution to the success of the firm. Unfortunately, however, the computation of that value is subjective and prejudiced by perception. The flaw, which the market must be left to correct, is in this *perceived* value of the position to the firm (male-dominated positions are perceived to be more valuable). Apparently, the fundamental assumptions which underlie comparable worth are flawed and misguided as they fail to distinguish the actual causes of wage disparity.[62]

[59]Gary S. Becker, The Economics of Discrimination, 159 (1957).

[60]Helen Remick and Ronnie Steinberg, *Comparable Worth*, in Gertrude Ezorsky (ed.), Moral Rights in the Workplace, 249 (1987). It is interesting to note that, in fact, Nancy Perlman of the National Committee on Pay Equity did try to compare apples and oranges during Congressional hearing in 1983, or at least contended that it was relevant that oranges were better. She attempted to equate comparable worth and the nutritional evaluation of fruit. For instance, if an orange were nutritionally better for a person, it would warrant a higher price. U.S. Congress, House of Representatives, Pay Equity: Equal Pay for Work of Comparable Value, Parts I & II, Serial No. 97-53, Committee on Post Office and Civil Service, Subcommittees on Human Resources, Civil Service, Compensation and Employee Benefits, 69 (1983).

[61]Michael Gold, A Dialogue on Comparable Worth, 43–44 (1983).

[62]Judge Richard Posner explains that "unless employers forbid women to compete for the higher paying, traditionally men's jobs—which would violate federal law—women will switch into those jobs until the only difference in wages between the traditionally women's jobs and traditionally men's jobs will be that necessary to equate the supply of workers in each type of job to the demand." American Nurses Assn. v. State of Illinois, 783 F.2d 716, 719 (7th Cir. 1986).

THE CAUSE ARGUMENT: GENDER ROLE SOCIALIZATION AS THE PRIMARY CATALYST TO DISPARITY

In order to reach an efficient and effective solution regarding the gender wage gap, it is critical to determine the cause of the gap. Comparable worth proponents are quick to blame the wage discrepancy on the discriminatory channelling of women into certain, lower paying professions, disregarding both the possibility that women seek different rewards in the work place as well as the distinction between supply-side societal discrimination and demand-side employer discrimination.[63]

An additional element in the channelling argument is the contention that women in male-dominated professions are overtly harassed and intimidated when they attempt to join that profession.[64] However, the United States offers women an intricate web of protection from such harassment in the form of Title VII and related caselaw.[65] Therefore, in lieu of upsetting the labor market by requiring higher wages than the market can naturally support, barriers to free movement within the labor market must be attacked; women must be educated regarding their legal rights in connection with self-protection against employer discrimination, and societal discrimination through gender role socialization must be destroyed. As a consequence, there will be no need for greater equality of wages between professions because women will be as free as men to enter professions which pay higher wages.

Further, research evidences a trend towards equality of wages. The wage gap between men and women ages 55 to 64 remains at thirty-five cents per dollar, while the wage gap for incoming professionals (ages 20 to 24) is only eleven cents per dollar.[66] The wide gap for older workers may be attributed to the fact that women bear much of the child rearing responsibilities and consequently may have to leave the work force to care for children, resulting in pay erosion over time.[67] On the other hand, the narrowing of the gap for incoming professionals may be the result of a growing awareness among younger workers of their rights to equal pay as well as an emerging balance of family responsibilities between the genders.[68] Between 1970 and 1988, the number of married women entering the work force doubled, raising the labor supply for certain positions, resulting in an equivalent decline in wages for those positions.[69] This logical consequence is not, as proponents of com-

---

[63]Nicholas Mathys & Laura Pincus, *supra* note 4 (discussing gender differences in connection with intrinsic rewards sought in the work place); Mark Killingsworth, The Economics of Comparable Worth, 45 (1990).

[64]Contardo v. Merrill Lynch, Pierce, Fenner & Smith, Inc., 753 F. Supp. 406, 410–412 (D.Ma. 1990).

[65]42 U.S.C. 2000e–s(h) (1988). For a general discussion of the capability of the law to redress wage-based discrimination, *see, e.g.,* Isabelle Pinzler & Deborah Ellis, *Wage Discrimination and Comparable Worth: A Legal Perspective* 45 J. Soc. Iss. 51 (1989). On the other hand, courts have systematically rejected application of comparable worth in the courtroom. *See, e.g.,* Spaulding v. University of Washington, 740 F.2d 686, 706–707 (9th Cir. 1984); Lemons v. City and County of Denver, 620 F.2d 228 (10th Cir. 1980); Christensen v. Iowa, 563 F.2d 353 (8th Cir. 1977); American Federation of State, County and Municipal Employees (AFSCME) v. Washington, 770 F.2d 1401 (9th Cir. 1985).

[66]Nicholas Mathys & Laura Pincus, *Is Pay Equity Equitable? A Perspective That Looks Beyond Pay* 44 Lab. L. J. 351, 354 (1993). *See also* June O'Neill, *The Shrinking Pay Gap,* Wall St. J., October 7, 1994, at A10.

[67]*See e.g.,* Joni Hersch, *Male-Female Differences in Hourly Wages: The Role of Human Capital, Working Conditions and Housework* 44 Indus. & Lab. Rel. Rev. 746 (1991); Gary Becker, *Human Capital, Effort and The Sexual Division of Labor* 3 J. Lab. Econ. 533 (1985); American Nurses Assn. v. State of Illinois, 783 F.2d at 719 ("Economists have conducted studies which show that virtually the entire difference in the average hourly wage of men and women, including that due to the fact that men and women tend to be concentrated in different types of jobs, can be explained by the fact that most women take considerable time out of the labor force in order to care for their children. As a result, they tend to invest less in their 'human capital' (earning capacity); and since part of any wage is a return on human capital, they tend therefore to be found in jobs that pay less"). *See also* Brigitte Berger, *Comparable Worth at Odds with American Realities,* in Comparable Worth: Issue for the 80's, A Consultation of the U.S. Commission on Civil Rights, V. 1, at 69 (1984), cited in Ellen Paul, Equity and Gender: The Comparable Worth Debate, 49 (1989).

[68]E. Erlich, *The Mommy Track,* 3096 Business Week, 123 Mar. 20, 1989 at 126 (discussing a growing trend at firms to offer paid extended leave, flexible scheduling, flextime, job sharing and telecommuting).

[69]Catherine Ross, John Mirowsky and Karen Goldsteen, *The Impact of the Family on Health,* in Alan Bloom, ed., Contemporary Families, Looking Forward, Looking Back (1991).

parable worth would contend, the result of a generic devaluation of traditionally female-dominated positions, but instead a market consistent effect of an increase in supply.

Proponents of comparable worth argue that the remaining wage gap is evidence of employer discrimination against women. Contrary to this contention, lingering wage discrepancies between the genders may be the result of a societal "residue of tradition"[70] which has held women primarily responsible for care of the family and home, notwithstanding whether they hold positions outside of the home.[71] Indeed, marriage has been shown to increase a man's participation rate in the labor force while marriage reduces women's participation in the labor force.[72] Until such time as society accepts a gender-neutral home environ-

ment, women may have greater demands placed on them than men, which in turn will affect their job choices as well as job performance.[73] A continuing evolution of the work force toward a greater understanding of the varying needs of men and women is evident from the growing attention to diversity programs in the work place. Employers are realizing that the only means by which to achieve competitiveness and efficient use of human resources is to take advantage of the differences between male and female workers, instead of disparaging them. Discrimination is eliminated where workers are considered on the basis of the quality of their work, as opposed to their genders. The employer who continues to reach discriminatory employment decisions on the basis of gender will fall out of the competitive market.[74]

Indeed, Becker found that discrimination by an employer reduces the employer's income as well as that of the victim of the discrimination. Discrimination therefore does not yield a benefit to the discriminating party.[75] Economist Robert Higgs offers additional support for this theory: "The most effective way to eliminate discrimination is to make all markets as competitive as possible. Competitive markets place costs of discrimination on discriminators far more readily than any other alternatives, certainly far more readily

---

[70]Donna Berardo, *et al.*, *A Residue of Tradition: Job, Careers and Spouses' Time in Housework* **49** Marriage & Fam. 381 (1987). *See also,* Deborah Rhode, *Occupational Inequality,* 1988 Duke L. J. 1207. For a general discussion of gender role socialization, *see, e.g.,* Paula England & George Farkas, Households, Employment and Gender: A Social, Economic and Demographic View, 153–154 (1986).

[71]Sarah Berk, The Gender Factory: The Apportionment of Work in American Households (1985); Joseph Pleck, Working Wives, Working Husbands (1985). In addition, researcher June O'Neill finds support for the contention that men and women approach work differently. Her research shows that, while men work continuously throughout their lives, women work only during 60% of their lives. June O'Neill, *The Trend in the Male-Female Wage Gap in the United States* **3** J. Lab. Econ. S91, S113–115 (1985) and *An Argument Against Comparable Worth,* Comparable Worth: Issue for The 80's, A Consultation of the U.S. Commission on Civil Rights, V. 1 at 179 (1984), cited in Ellen Paul, *supra* note 67, at 47. O'Neill also cites research which shows that only 77% of women between the ages of 35 and 29 expect to work at all. June O'Neill, *Role Differentiation and the Gender Gap in Wages Rates,* in L. Larwood, Women and Work, 64–66 (1985). *See also* Michele Wittig & Rosemary Lowe, *Comparable Worth Theory and Policy* **45** J. Soc. Iss. 1, 4 (1989).

[72]W. Bowen & T. Finegan, The Economics of Labor Force Participation, 40–41, 197–199 (1969); David Neumark & Sanders Korenman, Sources of Bias in Women's Wage Equations, 24–26 (National Bureau of Economic Research Working Paper No. 4019) (1992) cited in Jane Friesen, *Alternative Perspectives on The Use of Labor Market Policies to Redress the Gender Gap in Compensation* **82** Geo. L. J. 31, 39 (1993) (finding a positive effect of marriage on men's wages and an insignificant effect of marriage on women's wages). The socialization of these disparate gender roles may begin when the individual is as young as two years old.

H. B. Lewis, Psychic War on Men and Women (1976). A separate study reports that 54% of girls in 2nd, 4th, and 6th grades planned to be nurses, teachers, housekeepers, secretaries or waitresses, while only 1% of the boys shared the same aspirations. Fifty-seven percent of the boys planned to be fire fighters, police officers, car mechanics, construction workers, or involved in a sports-related position. Gloria Nemerowicz, Children's Perceptions of Gender and Work Roles (1979).

[73]Linda Jackson argues that the pressures may not be based entirely on external stimulation. Her research demonstrates that many women are equally satisfied with less pay than men and do not perceive a discrepancy between the pay they want and the pay they receive. Linda Jackson, *Relative Deprivation and the Gender Wage Cap* **45** J. Soc. Iss. 117, 120–121 (1989). One may argue, however, that this distinction, itself, is societally-encouraged.

[74]Richard A. Posner, The Economics of Justice, 352 (1983). For a general economic analysis of discrimination, *see, e.g.,* Gary Becker, The Economics of Discrimination, 159 (1957); Richard A. Posner, *The Efficiency and the Efficacy of Title VII* **136** U. Pa. L. Rev. 513 (1987); Richard A. Posner, Economic Analysis of Law, §27.1 (1986).

[75]Becker, *supra* note 74, at 19, 21.

than a political alternative."[76]

In addition, raising wages in traditionally female-dominated professions will encourage women to remain in those professions. If the reason that certain women chose that specific profession was because of discriminatory social channelling,[77] artificially increasing wages in those professions will only serve to further support the female professional ghetto and gender-based job segregation.[78] Women would suffer problems in perception similar to the individual under a quota system who is *perceived* to have been awarded a job solely on the basis of their race. They would be considered weaker and more dependent on the state for assistance, rather than the objectivity of the free market.[79] If in fact it is society or educational institutions or some other force which "channels" women into certain professions against their "will" or desires, then emphasis should be placed on relieving women of those areas of pressure, rather than artificially inflating the market for their employment.

THE EFFECT ARGUMENT

While it is therefore accepted that a (financially-based) wage discrepancy exists as a result of differences in gender role socialization, it is inappropriate and destructive to the labor market to impose the cost of this gender role socialization and segregation on employers. Economists Fischel and Lazear explain the inconsistency: "[t]here is no connection between the injury (discrimination by society as a whole) and the remedy (sanctions against particular employers who by definition have not engaged in discrimination)."[80] Employers have neither benefitted from nor perpetuated the disparity in wages; instead they are merely reacting to market forces. To claim that wage disparity has provided a benefit to employers would be to ignore employers in traditionally male-dominated professions. These employers would argue that they have been victims of the wage disparity and gender role socialization because male employees cost them more than females, and females do not seem to be interested in their open positions.

Comparable worth proponents argue that, as men have historically reaped the benefit of higher wages, there is no inherent inequity in imposing comparable worth wage increases which, in turn, may result in fewer positions.[81] As with an increase in minimum wage, comparable worth wage increases will render some workers better off, and others less so. In fact, from an economic perspective, there are two reasons why the level of employment will contract overall. First, as the price of lower-paying positions increases (pursuant to a comparable worth wage increase), the difference in price between hiring a higher-paid worker and a lower-paid worker decreases and employers have less reason to hire the lower priced worker where the two can be substituted. Second, the increase in the price of human resources (otherwise considered a tax on employment of persons in traditionally female-dominated positions) will force the employer to scale back in other ways, such as decreasing the size of its work force or charging consumers a greater price for goods or services.[82] Those who are kept in the remaining positions may have higher wages, while fewer people are employed. A critical judgment of the result depends on whether the increase in wages offsets the losses from reduced employment.[83]

---

[76]"Discrimination and the Marketplace: An Interview with Robert Higgs," in *Comparable Worth: Will It Close the Pay Gap?* **4** Manhattan Rep. 9 (1984), cited in Ellen Paul, Equity and Gender: The Comparable Worth Debate, 44 (1989).

[77]*See supra* notes 63, 64, and accompanying text.

[78]Ellen Paul, *supra* note 76, at 51–52.

[79]*Id.*

[80]Daniel Fischel & Edward Lazear, *Comparable Worth: A Rejoinder* **53** U. Chi. L. Rev. 950, 950 (1986).

[81]Research has shown through analogies to the effects of Title VII that imposition of comparable worth wage increases will result in employment losses for men. Andrea Beller, *The Economics of Enforcement of Antidiscrimination Law: Title VII of the Civil Rights Act of 1964* **21** J. L. & Econ. 359 (1978).

[82]Epidemiological studies in Minnesota, San Jose and Australia evidence a direct correlation between comparable worth wage increases and a decrease in the employment rate in traditionally female-dominated positions. Mark Killingsworth, The Economics of Comparable Worth, 280–281 (1990).

[83]Hartmann instead contends that "once unequal pay [for jobs of comparable worth] is understood as sex-based wage *discrimination*, even arguments that redress would be costly or might lead to some unemployment won't hold up against the basic issue of fairness and the importance of removing

The entire burden of correcting for the time lag of women entering the educational institutions and the work force should fall on the shoulders of neither the male employee nor the employer. Such a result is untenable as the system would not be penalizing those specific individuals who are the actual causes of the disparity; rather it would penalize those who are most capable of effecting change.

In fact, no one need bear the cost of the wage discrepancy. Through greater efforts at educating women as to their legal rights, women who believe that they are being undervalued in their present occupations may consider moving to a different, higher paying field. On the other hand, women who enjoy the intrinsic benefits of lower paying positions (such as flexible working hours, greater autonomy, and other factors) may choose to remain in those positions as a result of the increased benefits found there, paying for those benefits with lower wages. If the supply of workers demanding higher paying positions increases as a result of the influx of women in those fields, the salaries will correspondingly decrease and some may return to their previous positions. In the end, those workers who value higher wages will be drawn to those positions where the compensation is predominantly financially based, while other workers with different priorities may find themselves drawn to positions with lower pay but greater intrinsic rewards.

Opponents of comparable worth believe that the imposition of this measure could prove disastrous to the labor market. It would allow, and even encourage, an inefficient allocation of human and financial resources to occupations which, in truth, society does not value as highly as others. The price of these human resources would be artificially inflated, out of balance with the benefit to the employer/user of the resource. Accordingly, the employer would not be able to afford the same number of workers and would be forced to lay off workers who would have been employed. On the other hand, without comparable worth, those employees who are dissatisfied with the compensation received in their present position may choose to leave that job and search for a different job with higher wages, whether in a male- or female-dominated industry. Resources are therefore allocated in the most efficient manner, with the higher paying positions going to those who value that extrinsic benefit, and the lower paying positions going to those who value intrinsic benefits. Freedom of contract and free choice are preserved and the market is successful. "If this be struck down or arbitrarily interfered with, there is a substantial impairment of liberty in the long-established constitutional sense. The right is as essential to the laborer as to the capitalist, to the poor as to the rich. . . ."[84]

V. Beyond Economic Efficiency

An alternative analysis to the problem of a continuing wage difference is to look beyond the pure economic aspects of the job market and look at the problem from an ethical perspective. Comparable worth provides fairness in the job market by ensuring that residual discrimination (that which is not addressed by Title VII and related statutes) is not tolerated. Women are given the opportunity to earn wages commensurate with the effort and value of their work, instead of an artificially depressed wage which they currently face in many sectors. Further, comparable worth would help change society's view of the inherent worth of women in the marketplace, giving women true equality in the marketplace. The changing societal view would also extend towards the elimination of channelling that discourages women (and men) from entering certain professions. While opponents may assert that comparable worth is reverse discrimination against men, the remedial effects of comparable worth are necessary given the history of depressed female wages and sex segregation in the work force. Similarly, comparable worth should not be considered "discriminatory" if it merely sets wages at the level they would be set absent the initial discrimination against women. The resulting equity of having one's wage rate reflect one's work

---

discrimination." Heidi Hartmann, *Pay Equity for Women: Wage Discrimination and the Comparable Worth Controversy,* in Robert Fullinwider & Claudia Mills (eds.), The Moral Foundations of Civil Rights, 175 (1986). However, Hartmann does not consider the possibility that the wage differential is not due to discrimination. Accordingly, the ends may not justify the means.

[84]Coppage v. Kansas, 236 U.S. 14, 17 (1914).

value, and the elimination of discrimination, are desirable goals. This basic sense of fairness justifies placing the cost of a comparable worth policy on the beneficiaries of a lower wage rate for women. Accordingly, the burden also rests on those who have actually perpetuated the discrimination against women. In any event, any substantial burdens should fall on parties other than women, a more equitable result. Thus, there are substantial non-economic benefits that comparable worth policies provide.

On the other hand, while its proponents claim that comparable worth promotes fairness in the job market, they present us with a problematic sense of fairness. Fairness in the job market might also be seen as the outcome of free choices by men and women to reach independent decisions regarding their career orientation. Without legal restraint, men and women are free to choose their profession based on extrinsic factors such as pay, promotion opportunities, and fringe benefits, as well as intrinsic factors such as (autonomy, challenge, and variety.[85] Restraint comes instead only in the form of socialization.

Contrary to the arguments of the proponents, it is an environment free from comparable worth which allows women the opportunity to earn wages commensurate with the effort and value of their work. The market determines the value of these positions through the concepts of supply and demand, and the individual determines the effort expended. Ellen Paul notes, in her critique of comparable worth, that the meaning of the term "value" depends on whether one is using moral language or economic language. Economists consider value to mean the price for which something will trade in a free market exchange. Ethicists, on the other hand "are looking for some higher order moral principle that, irrespective of the market, can compare the work of the plumber to the tree-trimmer. . . . Within our society, there is no agreement about higher order moral principles. . . . How can we expect individuals in society to agree about how particular jobs con-

tribute to ends, when those ends themselves are in dispute?"[86] The market-defined value of a position is therefore the only objective valuation possible.

The supply of labor is the result of the socialization process which is where the changes may be first effectuated. Accordingly, efforts at modifying the valuation of women's work should begin, not with the artificial inflation of compensation, but instead much earlier during the growth and culturalization process of girls and boys, men and women. In fact, if the price of women's work were artificially inflated, an incorrect message would be sent to girls and women that they are lesser market players, incapable of exerting individual market power, and needy of assistance.

VI. *Conclusion*

This article has been the joint effort of two colleagues who are not likely ever to agree on the wisdom of implementing a program of comparable worth on the national, state, or local level. Clearly it is a matter of means, not ends, that separates us. Both writers are committed firmly to the goal of eliminating sexual bias in the marketplace both because it undermines the productive contribution that women are capable of making and because it is unfair and degrading to women. Beyond that, we are at odds on how best to achieve our mutual objective, and we offer this essay in the hope of contributing something of value to those who have not examined the issue and who, upon examination of this and other sources, can suggest better ways of eliminating this harmful sexual bias in the workplace.

---

[85]Nicholas Mathys & Laura Pincus, *Is Pay Equity Equitable? A Perspective That Goes Beyond Pay* 44 Lab. L. J. 351, 360 (1993).

[86]Ellen Paul, *supra* note 76, at 115. Paul suggests that it would be an unpleasant world if people did, in fact, agree about objective valuation. For example, she offers, if Michael Jackson earned a million dollars for a performance and an emergency room nurse earned twenty dollars for her work over the same two hours, a world of objective valuation would consider that he was actually worth 50,000 times as much as the nurse. One would know her or his intrinsic value simply by looking to her or his salary. Instead, in a free market, moral worth and value are different than price and salary. *Id.*, at 115–116.

Questions for Chapter 14

1. Hettinger argues for strong affirmative action (reverse discrimination) on the basis that, although it is to some degree undesirable, it is nevertheless justified inasmuch as it is required to achieve the important goal of dismantling our sexual and social caste system. What moral theory appears to underlie this claim?

2. Do you agree with Hettinger's claim that failing to compensate job-seeking white males for the sacrifices placed on them by reverse discrimination is no more morally troublesome than failing to compensate less talented members of society for their undeserved sacrifice of employment opportunities for the sake of efficiency? Why or why not?

3. What is "race norming"? Is it morally justified? Why or why not?

4. How does Pojman respond to the argument made by Hettinger and others that, since qualifications for a job are largely undeserved, that is, not based on merit, there is no sense in which the most qualified candidate deserves the job?

5. Shaw argues against comparable worth on the basis that "artificially inflating" women's wages will not successfully address the problem of sex discrimination in the workplace. Pincus argues for comparable worth on the basis that women's wages have been "artificially depressed." What is the basis of their disagreement on this matter and who do you think is right? What argument can you give in support of your view?

6. Are there factors other than sex discrimination that help to explain the wage gap between men and women? If so what are they? The wage gap has narrowed, even in the absence of policies of comparable worth. Does this suggest that such policies are not needed?

Case 14.1 Group Composition, Discrimination, and Hiring Practices[1]

Jobs at Ward's Cove Packing Company's Alaskan salmon cannery fall into two general categories: lower-paying unskilled "cannery" jobs which are predominantly filled by nonwhites, and higher-paying skilled "noncannery" jobs predominantly filled by white workers. The cannery is in operation only during the salmon runs in the summer; the rest of the time it is inoperative and unstaffed. Every year, a few weeks before the salmon runs, workers filling noncannery jobs arrive to prepare the plant for canning opera-

tions. When the salmon runs begin, the workers who operate the cannery lines arrive and remain as long as there are fish to can. Upon completion of the runs, these cannery positions are terminated, the workers leave, and the plant is shut down and winterized by the noncannery workers. Due to the fact that the location is remote and the work intense, both groups of workers are housed at the cannery and have their meals provided by the company. The two groups live in separate dormitories and eat in separate mess halls.

In 1974, a group of nonwhite cannery workers brought action against Ward's Cove alleging that, among other things, separate hiring channels, a

[1]Based on Ward Cove Packing Co., Inc. v. Atonio, as found in 109 *Supreme Court Reporter* 2115 (1989).

lack of objective hiring criteria, and the practice of not promoting from within, had produced a racially stratified workforce in which they were denied skilled noncannery jobs on the basis of race.

1. Approximately 17 percent of Ward Cove's new hires for medical jobs at the cannery were nonwhite and approximately 15 percent of the new hires for office worker positions were nonwhite. Supposing it to be the case that less than 15 to 17 percent of applicants for these jobs were nonwhite, would this indicate that Ward's Cove is nondiscriminatory in its employment practices? Would the question of whether the minorities represented in the noncannery jobs are the same as the minorities represented in the cannery jobs have any relevance to your decision? Explain your answer.

2. Is Ward's Cove policy of housing noncannery and cannery workers in separate dormitories and mess halls defensible? Why or why not?

Case 14.2 Affirmative Action and Seniority[2]

In the early 1980s, certain job classifications at Brass Craft Canada Ltd. were exclusively occupied by men and others by women, even though most of the jobs could be performed equally well by either sex. This pattern of employment had given rise to separate seniority lists for male and female employees. As a result, it would sometimes happen that a female employee with less seniority than a male might be called back to work earlier. The reverse would also sometimes happen. The union was well aware of this practice and had never raised any objection.

The situation changed after a recession caused a layoff more extensive than any formerly experienced. At the end of the layoff, the company hired four additional female employees into a traditionally female classification. At this point, all the employees on the female seniority list had been recalled, but three employees on the male seniority list had not. The four female employees had previously been employed as replacement workers during an earlier strike. When the strike ended, Brass Craft had terminated their employment in compliance with the Collective Agreement, but, because the Agreement did not forbid rehiring such persons, felt it was permitted to rehire them.

Initially, the union complained on the grounds that it violated the "spirit" of the return-to-work agreement to expect union members to work alongside "scabs" who had filled their jobs during a strike. They later grieved on the basis that segregated seniority lists had unfairly discriminated against the three male employees who had not been recalled.

Brass Craft responded by retaining its four new female employees and requested the three male employees who remained on layoff to signify in writing their willingness to take jobs traditionally classified as female. They then assigned them jobs as they became available, whether those jobs were in male or female classifications. Brass Craft also agreed, after discussion, to integrate their seniority lists. They did not feel, however, that compensation was owed to these workers for the interval of time between the four new hires and the opening of positions those laid off eventually filled.

1. Are there instances in which segregated seniority lists are more fair than nonsegregated lists?

2. Given the union had made no objection to segregated lists in the past, should Brass Craft have been obligated to pay compensation to the three laid-off male employees?

3. Would Brass Craft have been justified in terminating the four new female employees in order to meet the demands of the union as regards the three laid-off male employees?

[2]Based on Brass Craft Canada, Ltd. and the International Association of Machinists and Aerospace Workers, Local 2446 (1983), as found in 11 *Labour Arbitration Cases*, 3rd Series, p. 236.

Further Readings for Chapter 14

Tanis Day, "Pay Equity: Some Issues in the Debate." Background paper for the Canadian Advisory Council on the Status of Women, March 1987, pp. 1–17.

Sidney Hook, "Rationalizations for Reverse Discrimination," *New Perspectives* 17, Winter 1985, pp. 9–11.

William Shaw, "Affirmative Action: An Ethical Evaluation," *Journal of Business Ethics* 7, 1988, pp. 763–770.

Laurie Shrage, "Some Implication of Comparable Worth," *Social Theory and Practice* 13(1), Spring 1987, pp. 77–102.

Thomas Sowell, *Preferential Policies: An International Perspective* (New York: William Morrow, 1990).

Richard Wasserstrom, "A Defense of Programs of Preferential Treatment," *National Forum: The Phi Kappa Phi Journal* 58(1), Winter 1978, pp. 15–18.

INFOTRAC COLLEGE EDITION To learn more about the topics from this chapter, you can use the following words to conduct an electronic search on InfoTrac College Edition, an online library of journals. Here you will find a multitude of articles from various sources and perspectives: *www.infotrac-college.com/wadsworth/access.html*

affirmative action

reverse discrimination

employment equity

comparable worth

pay equity

Chapter 15

Business and the Family

Introduction

CHAPTER 15 EXPLORES the relation between business and the family. Although there is a wide interest on the part of psychologists and sociologists concerning the interrelation of family and work, those in the field of business ethics have paid comparatively little attention to this topic. This is unfortunate. One of the most persistent problems many face is how to juggle work family and work responsibilities. These two domains interpenetrate one another to a remarkable degree, and questions of their relation cannot fail to raise important issues concerning not only prioritizing employment and family responsibilities, but also how work and family institutions are to be structured. This topic raises important ethical issues at both the social and personal level.

In our first reading, "Men and the Politics of Gender," a selection from chapter 10 of her book *No Man's Land,* Kathleen Gerson argues that there has been a decline of cultural consensus on the meaning of manhood. As a result, there is a great diversity of parenting models from which men must choose. She suggests that we should accept this diversity and not make the mistake of insisting there is only one correct model of male parenting. She also argues that if men are to have a genuine opportunity to be equally involved in parenting, this implies a reorganization of the workplace, since the current structure of the workplace makes it difficult for a parent, regardless of gender, to combine employment and parenting.

Our next two readings address questions of the place of the family in modern industrial society and its relation to capitalism. In his article "Business and 'Family Values,'" George Randels, Jr. suggests that families adopt the standard of mutuality for career and domestic responsibilities. Rejecting the view that the husband should function as the primary breadwinner and that the wife should assume the majority of domestic duties, he advocates that a family's structure should be oriented to the family's common good. He argues that such an understanding of family structure, and the flexibility of roles it allows each member, escapes an unexamined acceptance of rigid traditional roles without falling into the trap of radical individualism.

Randels also argues there is no necessary link between capitalism and patriarchy. Despite criticism by Marxist and feminist thinkers who suggest that capitalism is irrevocably linked to the subordination of women within both the workplace and the family, he argues that capitalism is not inherently oppressive. In place of neoclassical capitalism with its controlling assumption that individuals act simply as self-interested autonomous agents, he advocates a form of capitalism that emphasizes that individuals do not simply act autonomously, but as members of larger groups, for example, families, that should be seen as legitimate stakeholders in capitalist enterprises.

Like Randels, Domènec Melé, in his article "Organization of Work in the Company and Family Rights of the Employees," repudiates neither capitalism nor the contemporary family. He argues that the organization of work within a capitalist system must recognize a number of family rights. In his view, although family duties fall primarily upon members of the family itself, employers have an ethical obligation to take into account the family responsibilities of their employees. Put a little differently, employers have a duty to recognize the duties of employees to their families, by organizing the workplace in such a manner that they do not hinder employees in their attempt to carry out these duties. He suggests that employers must recognize the following family rights in organizing the workplace.

1. The right to find the necessary social support to consolidate the unity and stability of the family so that it may carry out its specific task.

2. The right to socioeconomic conditions that enable it to carry out its duties with respect to the procreation and upbringing of children.

3. The right to working hours and periods necessary to devote to the other spouse, the children, and to just being together.

4. The right to quality of work life that does not affect the workers' genetic heritage nor their physical or mental health nor the necessary attention to their respective families.

5. The right to a sufficient compensation to start and maintain a family.

In our final selection, "Work and Family: Should Parents Feel Guilty?" Lynn Sharp Paine explores the issue of parental guilt as regards entrusting children to caregivers in order to pursue careers. Paine argues that many discussions of this issue are superficial inasmuch as they simply assume that these absence-related guilt feelings are irrational and inappropriate. This is to ignore the possibility that these feelings of guilt might be appropriate. She goes on to argue that the guilt feelings of many parents are a rational response to falling short of what they have good reason to regard as their parental responsibilities. She suggests that parents who feel guilty should not be treated as neurotic or mistaken. Rather, they should be encouraged, along with employers, to seek patterns of employment compatible with fulfilling what they understand to be their parental duties.

Men and the Politics of Gender

KATHLEEN GERSON

WE ARE IN A PERIOD of sustained and deeply rooted diversity in men's lives—one in which breadwinners, involved fathers, and single and childless men are contending for economic and social support. This transformation extends well beyond the confines of the so-called underclass or other minorities pursuing "alternative lifestyles." The fundamental social and economic changes propelling this revolution have affected most men, and especially those under the age of forty. Even if they have not personally experienced declining economic fortunes or been involved with work-committed women, men have felt the ripple effects of changes that have spread outward in unforeseeable ways.

Men are facing new dilemmas as well as new choices. Those who withdraw from work or share economic obligations with a woman face being labeled inadequate providers. Those who decide not to have children are seen as irresponsible or selfish. Those who become primary breadwinners confront the charge that they are male chauvinists. Diversity has thus generated ambivalence and disagreement about the appropriate obligations and legitimate rights of men. It is time for the national debate to address the cultural, political, and social policy implications of changes in men's lives.

. . .

Men's Parenting and Social Policy

The decline of male breadwinning poses significant dangers, but it also offers an unprecedented opportunity to bring greater equality to family and work life while expanding men's and women's range of choice and enhancing the well-being of children. Accomplishing these ends, however, requires more than the efforts of ordinary men. Just as individuals develop strategies to respond to unavoidable change, so must societies. While changes in the organization of the economy, marriage, and child rearing make the decline of breadwinning inevitable, social policies can help shape the forms that emerge to take its place. We have seen how opportunities and barriers at work and in the home can either thwart or encourage men's family involvement. Since men's choices are shaped by social circumstances, the challenge is to build social institutions that support the best aspects of change (such as the expansion of equality, choice, and family involvement) and discourage the worst (such as the abandonment of children and the overburdening of women). In the best American tradition, we need to build policies that respect diversity, encourage responsibility, and create equal opportunity.

Diversity in men's choices is here to stay. A new cultural consensus on the meaning of manhood appears no more imminent than the emergence of a new dominant pattern of behavior. In light of these new realities, we need to avoid replacing one dogma with another. Tolerance for diversity is central to American political culture. On the other hand, a cultural politics of division and blame draws attention away from the social challenge to adapt to inevitable change. It is time to abandon the search for one, and only one, correct pattern for all men. It is time not only to accept diversity but to respect it.

In rejecting rigid definitions of manhood, we need to include new responsibilities along with an expanded range of choice. Among men who retain a breadwinning identity, there is a difference between those who are actually supporting nonemployed wives and those who refuse to admit that their wives are breadwinners, too. Among men who have moved away from parenthood, there is a difference between those who have decided that the responsible choice is to remain childless and those who have abdicated responsibility for their children. Among involved fathers, there is a difference between those who have accepted equal responsibility for domestic work and those who remain helpers. Clearly, some choices are more responsible than others.

We can uphold the ideal of diversity and choice without sacrificing responsible standards of behavior. In a world where marital and parenting commitments have become fragile, this does not mean that everyone should get married or have children. It does, however, mean that choosing marriage or parenthood implies assuming serious responsibilities and making necessary sacrifices. If a man chooses to marry, he is agreeing to uphold the principles of justice and fairness. If he chooses to become a father, he is making a lifelong commitment to caring for his children.

Upholding standards of justice and sharing in personal commitments is neither a punishment nor an unmitigated loss to men. We have seen that men have much to gain from more equal relationships with women and more caring connections to children. Economic and social changes may require men to relinquish some long-standing privileges, but they also offer men a chance to claim new rights and surrender old burdens. No longer held solely responsible for the economic health of their families, men can look forward to sharing the obligations of breadwinning and enjoying the pleasures of care. Moreover, if men become more involved in the care of their children, they gain the moral authority to fight for parental rights inside and outside of marriage. Not only do involved fathers have a greater claim to parental rights in the event of divorce, but they are also less likely to abandon their children.[1] If marriage becomes more just and equal, then so can divorce. On the

other hand, if men want parental rights, they must earn them the way women do—by being responsible, caring, sharing parents who meet their children's needs in myriad ways every day.

Institutions can foster or discourage responsible choices. If we want men to behave responsibly, then we must build social policies that support and encourage such an outcome. Effective social supports could transform men's family involvement from a latent, incipient possibility to expected, unremarkable behavior. Given the growing proportion of women struggling to balance work and family obligations and the growing proportion of children living without the economic or emotional contributions of men, men's commitment to care and equality has become greatly needed as well as morally desirable. Such a profound transformation in men's lives will require equally fundamental changes in the organization of the workplace and the economic opportunities available to women.

Women's movement into the labor force has made it clear that the home and the workplace are interacting rather than separate spheres. Yet conflicts between work and family have typically been viewed as a woman's problem. The current organization of the workplace makes it difficult for any parent, regardless of gender, to combine employment and parenting. Work also poses obstacles to men's family involvement, and to ignore these obstacles is to leave the problem unfairly resting on women's shoulders.

In addition, the historical bargain between employers and families has broken down. When employers paid their male workers enough to support a homemaking wife, they could argue that children's needs were not their concern. Since employers are now less likely to pay men a family wage that subsidizes female caretakers, the time has come to admit that most families depend on either two earners or one parent. These revolutionary changes in gender and family life require a new bargain between employers and workers based on the principle that parenthood is a right, not just a privilege, for all.

What does this mean in practical terms? At the least, it means no longer penalizing employed fathers or mothers for providing the care and attention that children require. Even more, it means offering workers greater flexibility in how they choose to balance work and family contributions over the course of the week, the year, and the career.

---

[1]Numerous studies have noted that when divorced fathers are estranged from their children or from making decisions about their children's lives, they are likely to withhold or withdraw economic support as well. By allowing and encouraging fathers' participation, we increase the chances that children will also receive economic support. [See the following:

Hanson, Shirley, M. H. 1986. "Father/Child Relationships: Beyond Kramer v. Kramer." In Men's Changing Roles in the Family, pp. 135–50. Edited by Robert A. Lewis and Marvin B. Sunnar. New York: Haworth Press.

McLurahan, Sara, Judith Seltzer, Tom Hannon and Elizabeth Thomson. 1992. "Child Support Enforcement and Child Well-Being: Greater Security or Greater Conflict?" Paper presented at the Annual Meeting of the American Sociological Association (August), Pittsburgh.

Wallerstein, Judith S. and Sarah Blakerlee. 1989. Second Chances: Men, Women, and Children a Decade After Divorce. New York: Tickner and Fields.

Weitzman, Lenore J. 1985. The Divorce Revolution: The Unexpected Social and Economic Consequences for Women and Children in America. New York: Free Press.]

Caretaking demands ebb and flow in unpredictable ways that cannot be addressed via rigid work schedules and career tracks. We need to create a more flexible boundary between family and work. Yet only about 3,500 companies address family policy issues at all, and most do so in a piecemeal fashion. Only about 50 companies have developed fully integrated work/family benefits, including appointing someone with designated responsibility to develop and oversee a package of policies.[2]

Bringing the workplace into a new partnership with family life will require more than the goodwill of employers, most of whom are unlikely to institute change unless compelled to do so. And it will require more than *de jure* policies that formally allow family involvement but informally penalize those who choose it. If involved parenting remains a formal option that few feel entitled to take without great sacrifice to their careers, the most ambitious among us—women as well as men—will resist involved parenthood and reject the programs that exist on paper but punish those who utilize them.[3] Instead, we need "family support" policies that allow involvement for all parents. If men and women unite to fight for the parental rights of all

workers, then the conflicts between work and family may begin to dissolve.

Creating genuine family support policies to replace the patchwork of company-initiated programs that now exist will require political and legislative action. The federal family leave law that requires larger firms to offer their workers three months of unpaid leave in the event of a child's birth or a family medical emergency is certainly an important start, but it needs to become the floor on which we build more fundamental programs rather than the ceiling above which family policies cannot rise. Sweden, for example, guarantees all workers six weeks of paid vacation each year, three months paid leave when children are sick, the right to work part-time without losing one's job until one's children are seven years old, and eighteen months of parental leave to fathers as well as mothers. A quarter of Swedish fathers take paternity leave.[4] To move beyond family leave to secure the broader range of parental rights that many Europeans now take for granted may ultimately depend on a "parents' movement" comparable to the movements for workers' rights that once secured limits on the length of the work week, safer working conditions, and minimum wage guarantees. This means bringing men into the fight that women have pioneered in pursuit of a more family-supportive workplace.

A reorganized workplace is necessary, but not sufficient, to bring men into family life. Men's family involvement also depends on equal economic opportunities for women. Women's economic resources give them the leverage to insist that men parent more. They also make it possible for men to work less. A father's involvement depends on economic opportunities for his female partner. Thus, policies that promote economic opportunity for women also promote men's parental involvement.

Of course, economic opportunity and family obligation are related. Women cannot enjoy equal

[2]These estimates are based on a study by the Families and Work Institute reported in Smith et al., 1990. Smith et al., 1990, and Schor, 1992, argue that social policies need to redress the time imbalance caused by "greedy" work institutions.

To imagine a more flexible integration of family and work, we need only look to the world before the advent of industrialism, when work and family were more closely integrated and parenthood was not rigidly divorced from other productive activities. (See Stacey, 1990 and 1991, on the "postmodern family" and Hochschild with Machung, 1989, on modern women as "urbanized peasants.")

[3]Schwartz, 1989, proposed that employers offer women a "mommy track." By relegating mothers, and mothers only, to a second tier in the managerial structure of organizations, this proposal provides a remarkably regressive response to new family dilemmas. It allows employers to avoid addressing the twin dilemmas of gender inequality and work/family conflicts; it reinforces an unequal division of labor between women and men; it forces women, but not men, to make wrenching decisions between employment and parenting; and it maintains the historic obstacles to male parental involvement. In other words, the idea of a mommy track perpetuates the idea that work and parenthood are in conflict and that caring for children is an indication of low work commitment. As Capek (1990: 1) notes: "The issues for a viable, competitive workforce—ultimately the same issues for a viable, competitive American economy—are not 'mommy tracks' hut managing diversity: not 'letting in a few

women without rocking the boat,' but radically rethinking the future American workplace in an increasingly multiracial, multicultural global economy." Other critiques of the mommy-track approach include Smith et al., 1990, and Rodgers and Rodgers, 1989.

[4]Hobson (1991: 846–48). Studies that document the comparative lack of family and child-care policies in the United States include Hofferth, 1990; Hofferth and Phillips, 1987; Kamerman and Kahn, 1987; Moen, 1989; and Pleck, 1989 and 1993.

employment opportunities until men shoulder equal family obligations, and men are not likely to become equal parents until women enjoy equal economic opportunities. Indeed, when parenthood becomes as costly to men's work careers as it is to women's, then men, too, will have a stake in reducing the economic and social penalties for taking care of children.[5]

Equal opportunity and a reorganized workplace will be difficult to achieve, and the struggle to achieve them will surely remain politically controversial.[6] But the costs of *not* creating family-friendly workplaces, equal economic opportunities for women, and equal family opportunities for men will be much worse. Even if these were not worthy goals in themselves, our economic and social health depends on achieving them. The costs of a system that has put parenthood, along with women and children, last have already proved to be far too high.[7]

Why should men support institutional changes that respect diversity and promote responsibility and equality? Because policies that offer men an equal opportunity to parent and offer women an equal opportunity to support their families will reduce the dilemmas and expand the range of choices for all. Even more important, the long-run fates of men, women, and especially children will depend on how our political and social institutions respond to the spreading dilemmas of family life that have been created in no small measure by changes in the lives of men.

Revolutionary change has produced confusion and disagreement among men and dilemmas for which there are few clear resolutions. Some men are opposing challenges to their power and privilege, labeling them threats to the social order and moral fabric. Others are welcoming the chance to escape the narrow and stringent demands of twentieth-century masculinity. Inevitably, conflicts are emerging between those who see change as a threat and those who see it as an opportunity, and between those for whom opportunity means more freedom and those for whom it means more sharing. As new conflicts develop among men, new alliances may also develop between men and women who share a similar vision of the future they would like to create.[8] Indeed, men and women face a historic opportunity to forge new alliances based on their common ground as parents and workers.

Will future generations of men—the children of those who have created and coped with the current transformation—emulate, rebel against, or ignore the choices made by this one? Will they steadfastly declare themselves to be the only breadwinners and breadwinners only, even as they watch their female friends and partners build strong work commitments? Will they eschew family obligations in ever-rising numbers, deciding not to father children or to care for those they have? Or will they join with women to create a more equal and flexible balance between family and work, caretaking and breadwinning? These are all ways for men to claim the no man's land created by social change. Which vision becomes predominant in reality depends on which alternatives men are offered. Either we create the conditions for equality and caring or we live with the consequences of failing to do so.

[5]Okin, 1989, argues that our notions of justice should encompass themes of both care and abstract rights. For women, care has all too often meant relinquishing rights and becoming dependent on men within marriage. Since marriage can no longer offer women economic security, the philosophy of individual rights must encompass women and the obligation to care for others must include men.

[6]Some feminists have expressed discomfort with those aspects of change that require women to forfeit some privileges in order to obtain other rights. For example, Smart and Seven-Huijsen, 1989, and Chesler, 1988, argue that women should retain priority in child custody decisions, even though redefining men's and women's parental rights is a logical consequence of the movement toward gender equality (Kingson, 1988). Other feminists have argued that equality requires recognizing diversity among men and women rather than perpetuating a principle based on gender difference. See Vogel, 1990.

[7]The heavy social costs of *not* implementing family support policies have been well documented by Edelman, 1987; Folbre, 1987; Hewlett, 1991; and Sidel, 1986 and 1990. Less obvious is the mounting evidence that companies also incur higher costs by denying family support, such as parental leave, than by offering it. See Spalter-Roth and Hartmann, 1990, and Roel, 1991.

[8]The development of political divisions among men may also involve the emergence of coalitions between men and women who share similar world views. Numerous studies have found that a "marriage gap" in voting behavior is larger than the more highly publicized gender gap. Breadwinners and homemakers tend to vote in similar ways, while single men and women also show similar voting patterns. See Brackman and Erie, 1986; Fleming, 1988; Gerson, 1987a; Goertzel, 1983; Greenberg, 1985; Kingston and Finkel, 1987; Klein, 1985; Luker, 1984; Mansbridge, 1985 and 1986; Mason and Lu, 1988; and Weisburg, 1987.

Business and "Family Values"

GEORGE D. RANDELS, JR.

The perfect fund manager is the guy who can't pick his kids out in a police lineup.[1]
    —Michael Stolper, investment consultant

I refuse to buy into the traditional role of motherhood.[2]
    —Marie Holman-Rao, divisional president,
        The Limited

FOR FAMILIES THAT only need one income, the mother's working outside the home "becomes similar to an illicit pleasure, almost akin to having an affair."[3] So states a recent *New York Times* "Business Day" article. Normative notions of the traditional family apparently continue to reign, undaunted by the approaching millennium. Even women at the top of their profession feel that the pressure to balance home and career falls primarily on their shoulders, as evidently was the case for Pepsi-Cola North America CEO Brenda Barnes, who resigned last September to spend more time with her three children.[4] Gender roles remain strong at home and in the workplace, in spite of Barnes's rising above the glass ceiling to the executive suite.

These conditions contribute to an on-going theme in the literature of religious ethics. Quite rightly, feminist (and other) theologians and ethicists reject the normative nature of traditional gender roles as unjust, and even part of a sinful social order. In its place, they advocate mutuality and alternative anthropologies. I find much of this work compelling. Yet, in the process of promoting a progressive social agenda, these scholars often go on to reject capitalism as endemic to the old sex-

ual-political order. We can see this rejection in Christine Gudorf's relatively recent, *Body, Sex, and Pleasure,*[5] although it admittedly plays only a minor role. It is much more prominent, however, in the work of Mary Hobgood and Beverly Harrison, whose analyses Gudorf accepts in this regard, as well as others, such as Rosemary Radford Ruether. Although I have much sympathy with these scholars and others regarding their concern for social justice and desire to reconstruct social ethics, historical analysis and many contemporary cases illustrate the need for a more fine-grained analysis regarding business and its possibilities. Gudorf and Hobgood apparently have an overly narrow understanding of business, and base their critique upon that image. Harrison's account is more sophisticated, but is also too narrow inasmuch as it focuses primarily on neoclassical economic theory as providing "the ideological boundaries of capitalism."[6] While these critiques contain much validity, these scholars make the same mistake as their right-wing opponents by assuming that they discern the essential nature of business. I contend that no such essential nature exists, and so their critiques pertain only to a particular manifestation of business in a larger, patriarchal social structure. Capitalism may bring its own set of problems, but any economic system would be skewed under such conditions.

For the sake of clarity, I should note here at the outset my understanding of the traditional family and its acceptable alternatives, as well as capitalism and business. At base, the traditional family is the ideal of modern nuclear family, consisting of husband, wife, and children, with the husband as the bread-winner through work done outside of the house and the wife as the domestic worker. This ideal is most often not met but is still controlling

---

[1]Quoted in *The Chicago Tribune* (21 March 1993): 4–3; cited by Todd David Whitmore, "Children and the Problem of Formation in American Families," *Annual of the Society of Christian Ethics* (1995): 272.
[2]Quoted in Reed Abelson, "When Waaa Turns to Why: Mom and Dad Both Work? Sure. But What to Tell the Children?" *New York Times* (11 November 1997): C6.
[3]Ibid.
[4]Ibid.

[5]Christine Gudorf, *Body, Sex, and Pleasure: Reconstructing Christian Social Ethics* (Cleveland: Pilgrim Press, 1994).
[6]Beverly Harrison, *Making the Connections: Essays in Feminist Social Ethics* (Boston: Beacon Press, 1985), 68.

From The Annual of the Society of Christian Ethics *1998 (Washington, D. C.: Georgetown University Press).*
Reprinted with permission.

when the wife's role is expanded beyond that of homemaker. She may also work outside of the home in support of her husband's income, or perhaps just for something to do. What she brings in may be more than "pin money"—indeed, it may be crucial for the family's well-being—but it remains supplemental income, and does not free her from her domestic responsibilities. The husband's role remains as the primary bread-winner, and the wife's as primary domestic worker, even when they deviate from these roles to various degrees.

Rejection of the traditional family model as a normative concept that assigns women and men rigid roles does not mean that all other possible arrangements are therefore morally acceptable. A more liberal conception of family rejects both rigid traditional roles and radical individualism. Instead, it invokes mutuality as the standard for career and domestic responsibilities. Gudorf and other feminist theologians have been instrumental in making the case for mutuality as opposed to self-sacrifice as the ideal for familial and other relations,[7] and I support this shift. Mutuality is not an exact science, however, and particular democratized families could determine that traditional roles or their reversal are best. Mutuality will not necessarily lead to perfectly equal roles. As Don S. Browning, et al., contend, mutuality should not devolve into individualistic reciprocity.[8] A family's structure should be oriented to the family's common good, not strictly to any individual's separate good. Moreover, nothing in this formulation excludes same sex couples and parents.

Besides family, two other crucial concepts for this paper are capitalism and business. While any dictionary will provide several definitions for business, in its collective sense it is almost interchangeable with capitalism, as well as with free market. These all can refer to a particular type of economic system. What is capitalism? Typically, it is understood as an exploitative economic system focused on self-interested—often understood as selfish—pursuit of wealth. Profit is king and acqui-

sition is the chief good. Many neo-classical economists extend this point in an attempt to explain not only capitalism, but also much of human behavior.

But just as the traditional family model does not articulate the essential nature of men, women, or family, this typical understanding of capitalism fails to articulate the essential nature of business. I submit that there is no one way to conduct business, no one form of capitalism. One can reject particular forms of capitalism and economic theory without rejecting free enterprise. Likewise, one can reject the normative rigidity of the traditional family structure and roles without rejecting free enterprise. In fact, one can accept much of the Marxist-feminist critique, albeit with some question regarding capitalism's historic support of the traditional family. I see vulgar capitalism, or what R. Edward Freeman calls "cowboy capitalism,"[9] and neoclassical economic theory as rejecting the traditional family in favor of radical individualism.

In contrast, I would advocate the type of capitalism that can converse with theological ethics, and that would support families—not *the* family—more broadly conceived. This type of capitalism would reject both the rigid traditional family roles that denigrate women, and the radical individualism that undermines family. It would more clearly serve the common good, not a narrowly conceived individual good at the expense of the larger community.

Harrison contends that "to provide justice for women under advanced capitalist economies would require fundamental political and economic change."[10] Perhaps we are in the process of such change, although not fundamental in the revolutionary sense that she envisions. Instead of rejecting capitalism per se, we can reject business as usual in favor of progressive forms of capitalism. This revisioning would not merely provide female access to a "male-defined" activity, but would also address the concerns of women and diminish the hyper-individualism that negatively impacts families.

---

[7]See, e.g., Christine E. Gudorf, "Parenting, Mutual Love, and Sacrifice." *Women's Consciousness, Women's Conscience,* ed. Barbara Hilkert Andolsen, Christine E. Gudorf, and Mary D. Pellauer (Minneapolis: Seabury, 1985).
[8]Don S. Browning, et al, *From Culture Wars to Common Ground: Religion and the American Family Debate* (Louisville, KY: Westminster John Knox Press, 1997), 47.

[9]R. Edward Freeman, *Ethics Digest* 1 (1989), quoted in Robert C. Solomon, *Ethics and Excellence: Cooperation and Integrity in Business* (New York: Oxford University Press, 1992): 65.
[10]Harrison, 52–53.

Patriarchy and Capitalism

When examining western culture and its economics, secular and theological feminists generally argue that home and work are divided into separate spheres, the former being the domain of the woman, and the latter being the domain of the man, with the man dominant in both. This radical separation and its associated patriarchy are unjust. At the same time, many of these same scholars make a "bleeding spheres" argument, contending that these spheres reinforce one another.[11] Hobgoods thesis is that in the dominant U.S. culture, "sexual and capitalist ideologies work in tandem to impoverish human relationships within and outside marriage."[12] So far, so good for Hobgood's argument, because there is much evidence that the traditional ideologies have had that effect. Hobgood gets into trouble, however, when she claims that "traditional marriage is essential to capitalism"[13] and so reinforced by it. She distinguishes five particular ways in which she contends this is so. All of them are problematic, but I will focus on only one of them here: the necessity for gender inequality in the labor market. Hobgood contends that the gender system of the traditional family relegates women to "a secondary labor sector of lower-paying, low-benefit, dead-end jobs." Domestic roles serve "capitalism by making people assume that segmented public labor is natural. Wage differentials . . . between men and women make a tremendous amount of profit for individual capitalists and are essential to their survival in the economic system."[14] In a statement that supports several of these items, Harrison contends that "advanced industrial technological systems of production, developed under the aegis of private capital, weaken women's social role while supporting and strengthening ideologies of women's 'special nature' and 'special place' because those ideologies

serve the smooth workings of these economic systems."[15] Both scholars' positions coincide with that of Marxist-feminist Iris Young, who claims that the "*marginalization of women and thereby our functioning as a secondary labor force is an essential and fundamental characteristic of capitalism.*"[16]

Clearly these scholars raise issues that have been and continue to be problems for capitalist societies. Two recent studies of pay for male executives find that men with stay-at-home wives earn significantly more than men whose spouses work,[17] and women, on average, continue to receive lower pay and status, although there has been some improvement in recent years.[18] Men continue to work long hours and neglect their families, reinforcing the husband's role strictly as a provider. While fewer office parties include strippers, sexual harassment in the workplace remains alive and well. Although most members of U.S. society no longer expect that women should aspire to be only homemakers and mothers, social pressure nevertheless remains on working women to hold primary responsibility for the domestic life. When nominated for U.S. Attorney General, Zoe Baird was condemned not only for her nanny problems, but at least implicitly for having one at all, indicating that she neglected her children. Her high-salaried position was not a matter of economic necessity for her family, and so its time demands made her suspect as a mother.

Nevertheless, the more-or-less essentialist argument regarding capitalism's necessary subordination of women in both domestic life and the workplace is problematic on both historical and theoretical grounds. It is a historically contingent subordination, not an essential one. As Harriet Bradley notes, "it is misleading to detach an analy-

---

[11]Thanks to Ann Mongoven for supplying the term "bleeding spheres" during the discussion at the annual meeting to characterize this argument.

[12]Mary E. Hobgood, "Marriage, Market Values, and Social Justice: Toward an Examination of Compulsory Monogamy," *Redefining Sexual Ethics: A Sourcebook of Essays, Stories, and Poems,* ed. Susan E. Davies and Eleanor H. Haney. (Cleveland: Pilgrim Press, 1991), 116.

[13]Ibid., 119.

[14]Ibid.

[15]Harrison, 42.

[16]Iris Young, "Beyond the Unhappy Marriage: A Critique of the Dual Systems Theory," *Women and Revolution: A Discussion of the Unhappy Marriage of Marxism and Feminism,* ed. Lydia Sargent (Boston: South End Press, 1981), 58 (emphasis in the original).

[17]Associated Press, "Men Earn Less When Wives Work;" available from C-ap@clarinet.com; accessed 27 October 1994. Having a wife to take primary responsibility for domestic matters enables men to devote more time and energy to their careers.

[18]Federal Glass Ceiling Commission, *Good for Business: Making Full Use of the Nation's Human Capital* (Washington, DC, 1995).

sis of sex relations at work from an understanding of sex relations in the society as a whole and their historical evolution."[19] Patriarchy clearly predates capitalism. Long before Adam Smith sketched his "system of natural liberty," men dominated the political, legal, and economic systems, including the sexual division of labor. Early capitalism was highly dependent on these antecedent practices and traditions for its own gender arrangements. Law, medicine, and academia all share this same historical, patriarchal background with capitalism. Each one has perpetuated this background in its own way, developing particular role structures for men and women that only relatively recently have begun to erode.[20] Arguments regarding them, however, generally call for only reforming the institutions, rather than eliminating them in favor of something else.

Like the rest of these practices, capitalism does not require a gender hierarchy for its internal structure nor the traditional family standard as an external support, in spite of inheriting those things at its inception. To avoid repetition, I will leave discussion of capitalism's internal structure for the next section of this paper, and now will address the notion of traditional family as a necessary external support. Historically, this role is quite problematic, because during the vulgar capitalism of the industrial revolution, the use of female and child labor prompted the complaint that capitalism was undermining the traditional family. (Religious and moral conservatives raise similar complaints today about working mothers without condemning capitalism in the process.) This complaint came not just from social conservatives, but also from Marx and Engels. In the *Communist Manifesto,* they contended that the bourgeoisie "has put an end to all feudal, patri-archal, idyllic relations. . . . [It] has torn away from the family its sentimental veil, and has reduced the family relation to a mere money relation."[21] They viewed the condition as even worse for the proletarians "in the practical absence of the family." For them, "all family ties . . . are torn asunder, and their children transformed into simple articles of commerce and instruments of labor."[22] In *Das Kapital,* Marx wrote that the workman previously sold only 'his own labour power, which he disposed of nominally as a free agent. Now he sells wife and child. He has become a slave dealer."[23]

In a somewhat different vein, Engels contended in his later writing that capitalism's impact on women would be at least somewhat salutary because it would begin the process of abolishing the patriarchal family as the economic unit of society.[24] According to Heidi Hartmann, Engels held that "women's participation in the labor force was the key to their emancipation. Capitalism would abolish sex differences and treat all workers equally. Women would become economically independent of men and would participate on an equal footing with men in bringing about the proletarian revolution." Capitalism would erode patriarchal relations.[25] Large-scale industry thus provides a means for the wife to escape her domestic servitude, but also creates the modern work-family dilemma. "[W]hen she fulfills her duties in the private service of her family, she remains excluded from public production and cannot earn anything; and when she wishes to take part in public industry and earn her living independently, she is not in a position to fulfill her family duties."[26]

[19]Harriet Bradley, *Men's Work, Women's Work: A Sociological History of the Sexual Division of Labour in Employment* (Minneapolis: University of Minnesota Press, 1989), 171.

[20]To take a relatively recent example from academia, Vassar College was harshly criticized by a federal judge for consistent prejudice against married women in the hard sciences. U.S. District Court Judge Constance Baker Motley wrote that Vassar's Biology Department operated under the stereotype "that a married woman with an active and ongoing family life cannot be a productive scientist and therefore, is not one despite much evidence to the contrary." Gail Appleson, "Judge Rules Against Vassar in Discrimination Case," Reuters, available at clarinews@clarinet.com; accessed 23 May 1994.

[21]Karl Marx, *The Communist Manifesto, The Marx-Engels Reader* (2nd ed.), ed. Robert C. Tucker (New York: W.W. Norton Co., 1978, 1972), 475–476.
[22]Ibid., 487–488.
[23]Karl Marx, *Capital* (vol. 1), Karl Marx and Frederick Engels, *Collected Works* (vol. 35) (New York: International Publishers, 1996), 399.
[24]Friedrich Engels, *The Origin of the Family, Private Property, and the State, The Marx-Engels Reader* (2nd ed.), ed. Robert C. Tucker (New York: W.W. Norton Co., 1978, 1972), 744.
[25]Heidi Hartmann, "The Unhappy Marriage of Marxism and Feminism: Towards a More Progressive Union," *Women and Revolution: A Discussion of the Unhappy Marriage of Marxism and Feminism,* ed. Lydia Sargent (Boston: South End Press, 1981), 4.
[26]Engels, 744.

Of course, traditional families fared somewhat better than Marx and Engels predicted, and Jane Humphries argues that they may have taken on a role radically different than the one that Hobgood describes. Humphries' Marxist perspective leads her to claim that proletarian families can survive and even thrive under capitalism, but not as a support of the system. Humphries contends that the working class family is not "an essential component of the conditions of existence of the capitalist mode of production." Working class families have resisted alternatives to the traditional family structure, viewing its erosion as "a threat to its standard of living and ability to engage in class struggle."[27] Furthermore, "the family does not merely respond to capitalism, or worse still, reflect capitalism; it also shelters working people from capitalist oppression and—most neglected function of all—plays a crucial role in their struggle against capitalism and toward a better life."[28] Maintenance of the traditional family, then, may be a revolutionary act, rather than a supporting one. Although I would not argue that all or even most families fit the role that Humphries articulates, her argument along with others suggests that a much more complicated landscape exists regarding the relation between traditional families and capitalism than one of simple support.

Furthermore, if bleeding indeed occurs between the domestic and economic spheres, then changes in the traditional gender structure of families should influence changes in corporate structures. Likewise, improvements for women in the economic sphere should influence changes in the domestic sphere.[29] Changes in both spheres would indicate that an essentialist understanding of gender roles in a capitalist system is just as flawed as an essentialist view of the traditional family.

I now turn to the internal structure of capitalism, which is often associated with neoclassical economic theory. While not the essence of capitalism—indeed, there is no such thing—neoclassical

economics clearly has been strongly influential and has provided a forcefully articulated framework that claims to articulate that essence.

Neoclassical Economic Theory

Neoclassical Economic Theory posits atomistic individuals with narrowly self-interested outlooks. As economist Julie Nelson notes, "The subject of the economist's model world is an individual who is self-interested, autonomous, rational, and whose active choices are the focus of interest, as opposed to one who would be social, other-interested, dependent, emotional, and directed by an intrinsic nature."[30] Nelson calls it a gendered "male" perspective that pays no heed to family or affective relationships, ignores much productive human activity, and too often neglects the common good. Neo-classical theorists would reject the gender-specific charge, claiming that all humans seek to maximize their individual utility, whatever that might be. The rational individual weighs the cost of obtaining these desired goods against their perceived benefits.

Harrison rightly rejects neoclassical economic theory as inadequate for the task of theological ethics. She is too hasty, however, in acquiescing to the commonly held belief among economists and others that ethics falls outside of the realm of economic theory and business activity.[31] Milton Friedman, whom Harrison and many others cite as the primary spokesperson for this school of thought, himself provides a normative framework for capitalism. When Friedman assails the notion of corporate social responsibility, he expounds his conception of business ethics in the process. Friedman holds that managers have a fiduciary duty to the stockholders to maximize profits within variously articulated limits, such as avoiding deception and fraud.[32] Not attending to stockholder interests is unethical, and so is engaging in deception and fraud, even in the pursuit of profit.

[27]Jane Humphries, "The Working Class Family: A Marxist Perspective," *The Family in Political Thought,* ed. Jean Bethke Elshtain (Amherst, MA: University of Massachusetts Press, 1982), 199–200.
[28]Ibid., 222 (emphasis in the original).
[29]On this latter point, see Scott Coltrane, *Family Man: Fatherhood, Housework, and Gender Equity* (New York: Oxford University Press, 1996).

[30]Julie A. Nelson, *Feminism, Objectivity, & Economics* (New York: Routledge, 1996), 22.
[31]Harrison, 69.
[32]Milton Friedman, *Capitalism and Freedom* (University of Chicago Press, 1962, 1982); and "The Social Responsibility of Business Is to Increase Its Profits." *New York Times Magazine* (Sept. 13, 1970).

Friedman thus presents a normative argument, attempting to persuade the reader how individuals and corporations should operate in a free and democratic society. Friedman's vision is, of course, too narrow for the marketplace, let alone for other spheres of life. It provides a minimalist ethic for a libertarian worldview, with no guidance for what to do with one's freedom. Even its version of commutative justice is impoverished. Within Friedman's narrow "rules of the game," the sole yardstick for measuring one's actions is that of profitability. Yet, while far from satisfactory, this yardstick nevertheless provides a small starting point for addressing and rejecting traditional, segmented, subordinate roles for women.

Because of the mandate to maximize profit, neoclassical economic theory is forced to reject the glass ceiling for women and the pigeon-holing of them into traditional roles. Refusal to develop and utilize their talent runs contrary to the theory—if good employees are not developed and allowed to succeed, then financial performance will be less than optimal. At least one study shows that among the Standard and Poor 500 companies, those with better records regarding various equity issues outperform the ones with the worst records by a better than 2-to-1 margin.[33] There is every indication that female-friendly and family-friendly businesses outperform their rivals. Contrary to standard business ideology, doing right by the employees in this way can, and often does, improve the bottom line.[34] Organizations and businessmen that fail on these fronts fail to maximize profits, and put themselves at a competitive disadvantage with their rivals. Family-friendly corporations provide additional motivation, improving productivity, and find it easier to recruit and keep good employees. Research by the Families and Work Institute and the University of Chicago provides evidence that employees who have access to, and take advantage of, family-oriented programs such as day care and flex hours are more productive. They do not feel compelled to choose between work and family, because they can have both. Similarly, *Working Mother* magazine says of AT&T, its top firm for

women: "When the company goes out of its way to accommodate employees' family needs, they feel obliged to go out of their way for AT&T."[35]

A conversation with neoclassical economics regarding the rejection of traditional family roles and in support for children is thus possible, but the results are only partially satisfactory because of the approach's strict focus on profit maximization as its sole good, validating nearly anything that serves this goal. The limited conversation provides sufficient evidence, however, against Hobgood's bald claim that the traditional family is essential to capitalism, or the claim that capitalism cannot address women's and family issues. The problem, then, is not capitalism per se, but that the larger culture and particular—even most—capitalist practices, corporate cultures and business people are prisoners of a problematic ideology.[36]

Alternative Theories for Capitalism

With the rejection of cowboy capitalism and the inadequacy of neoclassical economic theory comes the need for new theory. As a replacement, Harrison proposes a neo-Marxian "radical political economic" theory that she claims correlates far better with theological ethics, and so provides a richer conversation. The four points of overlap between this radical political economic theory and theological ethics are: 1) the attention to concrete conflict and suffering: 2) the understanding of political economy as a transformable sociohistorical reality; 3) the acceptance of "responsibility for concretely illuminating the experiences of everyday life"; and 4) the recognition that "all economic activity is intrinsically and directly related to the overall cultural and institutional matrix of human social life." Contrary to the capitalist framework, says Harrison, human life does not exist in isolated, unrelated spheres (e.g., economics, politics, morality, and religion), nor are all spheres subsumed

---

[33]Federal Glass Ceiling Commission, 14.
[34]Jay Mathews, "Easing an Employee's Family Strains Reaps Benefits for Employers Too," *Washington Post* (May 2, 1993): H2.

[35]Reuters, "ATT, Xerox among top firms for mothers," available from C-reuters@clarinet.com; accessed 13 Sept 1994.
[36]I say "business people" and not "businessmen" here because some businesswomen can be part of the problem. In her summer internship, my former research assistant, Jennifer Dellapina, witnessed ostracism of a lesbian manager by other female managers, as well as by male managers.

under the neo-classical rubric. Harrison's proposed theory would address these issues.[37]

I agree that all four features of Harrison's radical theory are crucial to an ethically superior economic theory; clearly Harrison rightly rejects the notion of isolated spheres in favor of an integrated view. I would argue, however, that a "kinder, gentler" capitalism can also converse with theological ethics on these same four points. Interestingly, unlike Hobgood, Harrison leaves the door slightly ajar for retaining capitalism. Following Marx, she holds that capitalism's successes create the conditions for economic democracy. She also claims that "radical political economists do not treat capitalism as irrevocably evil, but they do insist that its pattern of exploitation must be transcended historically."[38] Nevertheless, the tenor of her writings indicates a rejection of this prospect, except as a logical possibility.

One reason that Harrison may find capitalism's prospects dubious at best is her reading of the business ethics literature. She criticizes it as "boring" and, along with corporate responsibility ethics, inadequate as an economic ethics, because it remains tied to the assumptions of neoclassical economic theory and preoccupied with questions regarding its relevance because of those assumptions.[39] While that critique may have been true enough twelve years ago when she published *Making the Connections,* much has happened since then that makes business ethics look more like the radical theory and feminist theory that she espouses, blurring the distinction between reform and revolution. Most business ethics scholars are not Chamber of Commerce cheerleaders or lacking in conceptual resources, but engage in critical reflection on the traditional assumptions of capitalism and problems with its practice. They develop alternative visions that can connect with theological ethics, providing a basis for much richer conversation.

This is not to say, however, that nothing interesting and important was going on in the management literature to challenge the assumptions of neoclassical economics. For example, in a 1960 issue of *California Management Review,* Keith Davis argued that "it is hardly possible to separate economic aspects of life from its other values. Business deals with a *whole* man in a *whole* social structure, and all aspects of this situation are interrelated."[40] And in 1954, management guru Peter Drucker maintained that the business enterprise has an economic responsibility to strengthen society, but doing so "in accordance with society's political and ethical beliefs," which he recognized would change over time.[41]

Nevertheless, it was probably R. Edward Freeman's 1984 publication of the revolutionary *Strategic Management: A Stakeholder Approach* that began a marked shift not only in the business ethics literature, but also in management textbooks. In this work, Freeman builds on this earlier thread in the management literature, rejecting the stockholder theory of the firm—the notion that managers' purpose is to maximize stockholder value (an offshoot of neoclassical economics). In its place, Freeman expounds the first systematic account of "stakeholder theory," contending that managers are responsible to a larger and diverse constituency who can affect, or are affected by, a firm's actions. Managers must create value not only for stockholders, but also for employees, consumers, suppliers, local communities, and so forth. When stakeholder interests conflict, managers must balance the competing claims.[42]

Stakeholder theory has proved to be a popular model, and it has been developed in several directions. Freeman and various co-authors have also refined the theory several times. In one article, he and co-author William Evan characterize it as "Kantian Capitalism." They claim that no stakeholder group may serve as mere means to the ends of others; all deserve respect, and each has a legitimate claim on the firm. "The very purpose of the firm is . . . to serve as a vehicle for coordinating stakeholder interests." Moreover, each stakeholder group must participate in the decisions that substantially affect its welfare.[43] More recently,

---

[37]Harrison, 76–77.
[38]Ibid., 77.
[39]Ibid., 69.

[40]Keith Davis, "Can Business Afford to Ignore Social Responsibilities?" *California Management Review* 2/3 (1960): 74 (emphasis in the original).
[41]Peter Drucker, *The Practice of Management* (New York: Harper & Bros., 1954), 35.
[42]R. Edward Freeman, *Strategic Management: A Stakeholder Approach* (Boston: Pitman, 1984).
[43]William M. Evan and R. Edward Freeman, "A Stakeholder Theory of the Modern Corporation: Kantian Capitalism,"

Freeman and co-authors Andrew C. Wicks and Daniel R. Gilbert, Jr. provide a feminist reinterpretation of the stakeholder concept that attempts to integrate individual and community. This view holds that "the corporation is constituted by the network of relationships, which it is involved in with the employees, customers, suppliers, communities, businesses and other groups who interact with and give meaning and definition to the corporation."[44] Other authors have gone further, arguing that notions of justice and rights provide insufficient grounding for stakeholder theory, but feminist theory and its ethic of care supply the necessary elements.[45] Rather than merely providing access for women, these versions provide a complete revisioning of the firm and its relationship to the larger society. Instead of a single theory, it might be better to say that Freeman, his co-authors, and many other scholars have developed several theories that utilize the stakeholder concept.

Besides the work in stakeholder theory, much other recent work in the field "makes the connections," employing virtue theory, narrative theory, and moral imagination, among other things, in their discussions of business and ethics.[46] More importantly, however, we can see these connections in business practice. Tom Chappell, founder

and CEO of Tom's of Maine, explicitly adopts stakeholder principles in the management of his company. He explicitly connects them to lessons from Buber, Jonathan Edwards, and Kant learned from his days at Harvard Divinity School. From Buber, Chappell learned the value of developing I-Thou rather than I-It relationships with his customers and employees. From Edwards's notion of being-as-relation, he learned that one's identity comes from a sense of connection with others and accountability to them. Being an individual does not mean being isolated from others. Chappell applied this lesson not only to himself, but also to his company. Tom's of Maine's statement of beliefs, mission statement, and, crucially, its day-to-day operations show that the firm is not driven exclusively by the profit-motive as per neoclassical economics, but rather integrates profit-making with other values, such as environmental concern, respect for others, and sharing wealth with the local community through donations and on-the-payroll volunteer work.[47] It also has a Leadership and Career Development Program for women, who make up 45% of the employees, 50% of the managers, and 33% of the board of directors.[48]

Although we might expect such attitudes to reside exclusively at small firms, we can find larger examples of what Tom Peters calls "excellent corporations." Robert Haas, CEO of Levi Strauss, is an outspoken advocate of stakeholder theory. Haas has changed Levi's ethical focus from mere legal compliance to a values-oriented approach. Six ethical principles serve as its basis: honesty, promise-keeping, fairness, respect for others, compassion, and integrity. Like Chappell, Haas seeks to link good ethics with good business by empowering employees through participatory management, and aspiring to a range of values. Deserving special mention are Levi's Global Sourcing Guidelines, which ban the use of child labor, and how its reaction to discovering that a few of their contractors were violating those guidelines. Rather than fire the children, whose loss of income would harm their families, or violate its principles, Levi decided to pay wages and send the children to school full time.[49]

Ethical Theory and Business (4th edition), ed. Tom Beauchamp and Norman Bowie (Englewood Cliffs, NJ: Prentice-Hall, 1993), 82.

[44]Andrew C. Wicks, Daniel R. Gilbert Jr., and R. Edward Freeman, "A Feminist Reinterpretation of the Stakeholder Concept," *Business Ethics Quarterly* 4/4(1994): 483.

[45]Brian K. Burton and Craig P. Dutton, "Feminist Ethics as Moral Grounding for Stakeholder Theory," *Business Ethics Quarterly* 6/2 (1996). See also Jeanne M. Liedtka, "Feminist Morality and Competitive Reality: A Role for an Ethic of Care," *Business Ethics Quarterly* 6/2 (1996); John Dobson and Judith White, "Toward the Feminine Firm," *Business Ethics Quarterly* 5/3 (1995); and Robbin Derry, "Toward a Feminist Firm: Comments on John Dobson and Judith White," *Business Ethics Quarterly* 6/1(1996).

[46]See, e.g., Robert C. Solomon, *Ethics and Excellence: Cooperation and Integrity in Business* (New York: Oxford University Press, 1992); Daniel R. Gilbert Jr., "A Critique and A Retrieval of Management and the Humanities," *Journal of Business Ethics* 16 (1997); and Patricia Werhane, "Moral Imagination and the Search for Ethical Decision-making in Management," *The Ruffin Lectures in Business Ethics* (Charlottesville, VA: The Darden School, University of Virginia, 1994).

[47]Tom Chappell, *The Soul of a Business: Managing for Profit and the Common Good* (New York: Bantam, 1993).

[48]Federal Glass Ceiling Commission, 179.

[49]Robert D. Haas, "Ethics—A Global Business Challenge," *Vital Speeches of the Day* 60(1 June 1994): 507–508.

Stakeholder theory clearly overlaps with theological ethics. Chappell's use of Buber and Edwards nicely dovetails with the feminist emphasis on mutuality in human relationships. It also connects with Pope John Paul II's vision of the firm's purpose as

> not simply to make a profit, but . . . as a community of persons who in various ways are endeavoring to satisfy their basic needs, and who form a particular group at the service of the whole society. Profit is a regulator of the life of a business, but it is not the only one; other human and moral factors must also be considered which, in the long term, are at least equally important for the life of a business.[50]

It would seem, then, that stakeholder theory can manifest itself in concrete ways that can dialogue with theological ethics on the same four points as Harrison's radical economic theory. Freeman's various versions of stakeholder theory and Chappell's and Haas's practical applications concur with Harrison's insights that we should not attempt to separate business from other spheres of life, and that the connections should be based on mutuality and the common good, rather than patriarchy and hyper-individualism.

Business, Family, and Values

The autonomy-supporting element of the Kantian capitalism version of stakeholder theory rejects the rigid traditional family structure as normative for business practice. It allows for a range of possible family and career structures and rejects discrimination based on such things as gender and sexual orientation. The feminist reinterpretations highlight community and mutuality, more clearly rejecting the atomistic individualism of neoclassical economics in favor of recognizing that we exist in a larger social framework, with responsibilities to others. Business is not an isolated sphere of activity but is intimately connected with everything else that we do. Further, corporations themselves ought to be communities, their members

holding common values and working together to achieve goals that fit with the larger community. To hold both liberty and community as important values means that corporations themselves need to be liberal communities.

A modified "family values" version of stakeholder theory would recognize that not only are individual employees stakeholders, but so also are their families. Many employees join organizations not strictly as individuals, but as members of families, or they may form families during their tenure. Families reap various benefits from business enterprises but also bear certain risks and burdens (e.g., time and work pressures that negatively impact domestic life), both clearly giving them a stake in the business. Catholic social thought has long viewed families as stakeholders, although not using the term itself, in its call for organizations to pay a "living wage" to male heads of households sufficient to support their families. My modified family values version of stakeholder theory would reject the traditional family model associated with the living wage idea, but uphold its recognition that employer obligations reach beyond individual employees.

In rejecting the traditional family model as normative, corporations must reject the automatic association of men with career and women with family, and all of the trappings that go along with this association, such as rewarding men with stay-at-home wives. The traditional family is, of course, one possibility, but with increasing opportunities for women and a decline in "family wage" manufacturing jobs for men, it is a choice that is decreasing in incidence with less than 30% of all families meeting its ideal standard. The alternative is not the creation of two tracks—a career track for women who want to join the traditional male model and a second-tier "mommy track" for women who also want families, as proposed by Felice Schwartz[51]—but various tracks. Or better yet, no tracks. Instead, corporations can and should provide room for all employees to attend to family and other projects, providing them with necessary institutional support. The principle of subsidiarity thus should be applied to the firm.

---

[50]Pope John Paul II, *Centesimus Annus* (Washington, DC: United States Catholic Conference, 1991) 69.

[51]Felice N. Schwartz, "Management Women and the New Facts of Life," *Harvard Business Review* 67 (Jan–Feb 1989).

Possible ways to implement that principle include allowing flex-time (77% of Fortune 1000 companies have some form of it already), day care (13% of the same companies), job-sharing, tele-commuting, and parental leave. It is difficult to specify in the abstract the upper and lower limits of institutional support that must be provided, or the particular forms they should take. The principle of subsidiarity would reject undue interference in family life, and the standard of mutuality would indicate that conversation must take place to determine what is appropriate in a particular context.

Control Data Corporation CEO Lawrence Perlman testified before Congress in support of the Family and Medical Leave Act, because of Control Data's success with a similar policy of its own. Although Perlman rejects a federal solution for every workplace problem, he sees this act as one that "can make a real difference in the quality of employees' lives and in the quality and efficiency of businesses. Family and medical leave . . . responds to fundamental changes in the composition of the American workforce and recognizes that each employee is a whole person with a life that extends beyond the workplace."[52]

Perlman, then, advocates the type of capitalism that can converse with theological ethics. Rather than dictating a particular family structure, capitalism can support various potential family structures. That is precisely what Apple Computer did, in spite of opposition from a Texas community where it sought to locate a facility. According to Apple spokeswoman Lisa Byrne, "We don't feel that we're in the business of defining what a family is. But we want to treat all our employees with respect and fairness" regarding their families.[53] Other imperfect but important exemplars like Hewlett-Packard provide female-friendly programs like leadership development and mentoring, family-friendly programs like job flexibility and dependent care, and benefits for domestic partners. This is a type of capitalism theological ethics can and should support.

[52]Christopher Dodd, et al., "Should the Congress Approve the Family and Medical Leave Act," *Congressional Digest* (April 1991): 18.

[53]Associated Press, "Apple Gets Offer After Rejection," *St. Petersburg Times* (5 December 1993): 91.

Organization of Work in the Company and Family Rights of the Employees

DOMÈNEC MELÉ

BUSINESSMEN ARE WELL AWARE of the marked relationship between family affairs of employees and their behavior in the company. The organization of work and activities in the company considerably affect family life. Some work setups can lead to family problems, and family problems, in turn, affect employee performance in the company. This intrinsic relationship between the family and organization of work makes it a subject of great concern to both employees and managers.

In countries such as Spain, where the family is a deep-rooted institution, the family-company relationship arouses considerable concern. According to a survey recently conducted by IESE among two hundred Spanish managers, the study of the family-work relationship came out as one of the four or five most important subjects that must be taught in the business ethics courses.[1]

Until now, very little attention has been given to the study of the relationship between the organization of work in the company and the family rights and duties of the employee. However, a number of interesting works are available, albeit

[1]It will be published.

From Journal of Business Ethics 8: 647–655, 1989. *Reprinted by permission of Kluwer Academic Publishers.*

focussed only on some particular problems and referring specifically to American society.[2]

Some people consider that the family, by being a part of the employee's personal life, has no bearing on the company. Thus, any interference by the company in the employee's family life, is seen as an intrusion into the personal life of the employee. As such, it must be avoided. But in doing so, companies fail to take into account the importance of the family as the basic unit of society and its corresponding rights.

Others consider that it is sufficient to have flexible agreements between the company and its employees concerning family issues. In this situation, the rights of the family are taken into account only if the negotiating parties are conscious of them. Many times the family duties of the employees are viewed only as interests which are in conflict with the company's interests. They fail to realize, however, that the family is a source of real rights.

It must be pointed out that in the "Universal Declaration of Human Rights" and in the "International Agreement of Civil and Political Rights," it is categorically stated that "the family is the natural and fundamental unit of society and is entitled to the protection of society and the State."[3] Other international texts on human rights are couched in similar terms,[4] showing the existence of a wide international consensus on the intrinsic value of the family. In addition, a detailed Charter of the Rights of Family[5] was published by Roman Catholic Church in 1983 and a European Charter of Family Rights is being prepared at the moment.[6]

Nevertheless, some family rights can easily be infringed upon as a result of the organizational work within the company. These rights can be enumerated as follows:

a. The right to find the necessary social support to consolidate the unity and stability of the family so that it may carry out its specific task.

b. The right to socio-economic conditions that enable it to carry out its duties with respect to the procreation and upbringing of children.

c. The right to working hours and periods necessary to devote to the other spouse, the children and to just being together.

d. The right to a quality of work life that does not affect the workers' genetic heritage nor their physical or mental health nor the necessary attention to their respective families.

e. The right to a sufficient compensation to start and maintain a family.

The following discussion deals with some aspects of work organization connected with the above-mentioned family rights illustrated in several scenarios taken from cases that have been published or that the author has direct knowledge of.

---

[2]Such as those by Cfr. R. M. Kanter: 1977, "Work and Family in the United States" (Russell Suge, New York).

R. Bailyn: 1978, "Accommodations of Work to Family" in *Working Couples* ed. by R. Rapoport and R. N. Rapoport (Harper and Row, New York).

J. P. Fernández; 1986, *Child Care and Corporation Productivity: Resolving Family/Work Conflicts.* (Lexington Books, Lexington).

A. C. Michalos: 1986, "Job Satisfaction, Marital Satisfaction and the Quality of Life: A Review and a Preview" in, *Research and the Quality of Life,* ed. by F. M. Andres (University of Michigan Press, Ann Arbor Michigan), pp. 57–83.

[3]U.N.O.: *Universal Declaration of Human Rights,* art. 16,3 (Paris, 12.10.1948); *International Agreement of Economic, Social and Cultural Rights,* Art. 10,1 and Art. 23,1, adopted by the General Assembly of the UN in its resolution 2200 A (XXI) on 11.16.1966. Came into effect on 12.30.1976.

[4]*American Declaration of Human Rights* (1948), Art. 6; *European Social Charter* (1961), Art. 16; *American Convention of Human Rights* (1969), Art. 17, 1. Recommendation 2018 (XX) adopted by the General Assembly of the UN on 12.1.1965; *Declaration on Social*

Progress and Development proclaimed by the General Assembly of the UN in its resolution 2542 (XXIV) on 12.11.1969.

[5]Holy See: 1983, *Charter of the Rights of the Family* (London, Catholic Truth Society). In 1981, Pope John Paul II pointed out some basic family rights and committed the Holy See to prepare a Charter on the Rights of the Family (Exh. Apost. *Familiaris consortio,* n. 46. London, Catholic Truth Society). This Charter has been the first monographic international document on the rights of the family.

[6]This European Charter of Family Rights was proposed by Mr. Oreja, the Secretary General of the Council of Europe in his address to the 20th Conference of European Ministries responsible for the family. (Allocution du Secrétaire Général pour la 20c Conférence des Ministres Européen chargés des Affaires familiaires. Brussels, May 19, 1987).

Business and Working Environment Must Favor Marital Unity and Stability

Company policy on work organization may attack the family's unity and stability in a variety of situations such as those illustrated in the following scenarios:

A. BRIBERY OR EXTORTION USING EXTRA-MARITAL SEXUAL RELATIONS

The use of sexual favour is a well known way of bribery or extortion.

> Scenario 1: A company invites several managers from client companies to a convention at which its latest products will be presented. The reception includes all kinds of entertainment, including callgirls, which are supposed to smooth the way for sales to the potential buyers.

B. SEXUAL HARASSMENT

Sexual harassment within the company is, of course, another form against the unity and stability of marriage. It usually happens with extortion from someone superior.

> Scenario 2: A male supervisor sexually harasses a female subordinate. The subordinate is aware of the unfavorable consequences that would result from rejecting the supervisor's advances: loss of promotion, misleading information on her performance to their superiors, effect on salary increases, and perhaps, dismissal in a future restructuring.

C. SITUATIONS THAT FAVOR SEXUAL ATTRACTION IN THE COMPANY

Moreover, some company practices—work arrangement, business trips, etc.—can also lead to immoderate sexual attraction among employees, although, these company practices are not conceived to lead to such consequences.

> Scenario 3: A fast-moving finance company specialising in high-risk loans wishes to recruit a recent Harvard MBA graduate. On his first visit to the company, the young MBA realised

that most of the women in the office were young and very attractive. In fact, he had never seen so many pretty women in one place before. Later he learned that the company's vice-president (only him?) usually had some employee accompany him on his business trips, suggesting that they sleep together to "save the firm the price of a second room."

The executives earned a lot of money but if they wanted to get to the top they had to work Saturdays and Sundays. With all this, it is not surprising that the company's divorce rate was somewhat high.[7]

In all these situations, in addition to damaging the family, the business organization itself will suffer adverse consequences: distorted communications, hostile self-interests that go against the company's interest, impairment of the work unit's reputation, greater slowness in decision-taking, etc.

D. DUAL CAREERS AND PROLONGED SEPARATION OF SPOUSES

In cases where both husband and wife work, a good working opportunity which requires relocation to another city may come to either of the two. The overall success, however, can only be guaranteed if the other spouse can be permitted to relocate to the same city. Otherwise, the family may suffer temporary separation or the professional life of one may suffer to give in to the other.

A better alternative can be found if firms could take into account the family issues in dual careers.

> Scenario 4: A large group of companies has recruited Antonio to turn around one of its ailing companies near Barcelona. Antonio is then asked to do the same in another company in the south of Spain. It is planned that he will spend three to five years in the new company. Antonio may have a very good career before him in this group of companies but he must be prepared to accept all the changes the company requires.
>
> Antonio is married with three children aged less than 14. His wife Montse is an architect and works for the regional government. Her

---

[7]C. P. Dredge and V. Sathe, *Mike Miller (A)*, Case Study of Harvard Business School, ICCM 9.482.061.

career prospects are also good. Montse also takes an active part in political life and knows a lot of people in the Barcelona area. Their children are happily enrolled in a school in Barcelona. Montse and Antonio also think that such a dramatic cultural change would not be good for the children. Antonio's bosses have pressured him alot on this change and have made him understand that if he does not accept their demands, he can expect little future in the company. Antonio faces a dilemma and fears that he would not be able to find such a good job in another company.

It is hard to say just how much a company can pressure its employees in defense of its legitimate interests but it is clear that if it does not act with a certain consideration for family circumstances, it will be favoring the breakup of the family. Also, the prolonged separation of spouses gives rise to a lot of problems, especially when this separation is accompanied by frequent dealings with people of the other sex for work or social reasons, which may also undermine the unity and stability of the family.

On this point, the comment made by R. Quinn[8] is interesting in that he states that in 74% of the love affairs that occur at work, the man holds a higher position than the woman and, in almost half of the cases, the woman involved is his secretary.

In all these scenarios, of course, the person involved is free to refuse the proposition of infidelity but the company's policy, the work environment or the behaviour of its managers may significantly influence the preservation of the unity and stability of the marriage.

The company can make it easier to fulfill the duties of marital unity and stability by acting in the following areas:

1. Forbidding its employees to use all forms of bribery including the exploitation of the sexual instincts of potential customers.
2. Penalizing those who take advantage of their power by extorting people in exchange for sexual gratification.
3. Taking steps to prevent sexual harassment between employees, especially those occurring

from the abuse of power. It should be borne in mind that, according to the Merit System Protection Board, sexual harassment has little to do with mutual physical attraction, provocative behaviour or even sex.[9] It is above all an expression of dominance and nonreciprocal behaviour directed by the strongest at the weakest.

4. Acting with care in the design of work organization and avoiding, as much as possible, forms of business activity that may easily result in thoughtless sexual provocation among its employees.
5. Creating an appropriate atmosphere within the company in order to avoid sexual harassment and to encourage managers to exercise care in their relations with the people with whom they work the most.
6. Taking into account the effects of dual careers on the families, avoiding the considerable pressure on the employees resulting in discrimination.
7. Avoiding as much as possible prolonged separations of spouses.

Compatibility of Work with the Obligations of Parenthood

Attention given to the family, and especially to the bringing up of children, can be unacceptably low as a result of the ineffective work organization in the company. The organization itself can hinder, and in some cases, even prevent the parents from freely choosing the type of education their children should receive. Here are a few situations:

A. MOVING EMPLOYEES OR MANAGERS TO ANOTHER CITY OR COUNTRY

This may affect the professional or social interests of the concerned spouse or of the rest of the family, as well as affecting the children's education (change of school, educational system or culture).

Scenario 5. A leading leather tanning factory in Valencia (Spain) opened a factory in Indonesia.

[8]R. E. Quinn: March 1977, "Coping with Cupid: The Formation, Impact and Management of Organizational Romance," in *Administrative Science Quarterly*.

[9]Merit System Protection Board: 1981, "Sexual Harassment in the Federal Workplace" (U.S. Government Printing Office).

The factory had to be managed by someone trusted by the company, who knew the tanning process and the leather-tanning trade well. The company management was convinced that this person had to be one of its employees. However, moving the employee with his family not only meant having to live in a different country and culture but also the impossibility of finding a school that would educate his children in accordance with his wishes. In fact, in spite of the promotion and the good pay, there was no-one willing to accept the position and relocate.

The company saw two alternatives: pressure the person concerned in various ways until he was persuaded to move or find alternative solutions that respect the family rights. The final solution was to appoint two managers who would work alternately on three month periods in Indonesia and Valencia.

B. BUSINESS TRIPS THAT EXCESSIVELY SHORTEN THE AMOUNT OF TIME AVAILABLE TO THE FAMILY

Scenario 6. A Barcelona company is in the turnkey business of building and selling ceramic and earthenware plants. It has projects all over the world. Part of its staff of 1,500 employees work on the assembly and start-up of the new plants and, where necessary, on repairing those already existing.

These travelling workers spend from six months to two years away from their city (normally abroad). Their allowances are not excessive and they are not given more vacation time than their non-travelling colleagues. If necessary, the return from one country is tied up with the departure for an assignment in another country; as a result the worker is hardly able to spend any time with his family. Of course, his employment contract includes the obligation to travel as often as necessary.

On occasions, especially when the stay is going to be long, the workers take their families with them. The educational problems that arise are heightened by the cultural and religious differences in the customer-countries, some of which have communist governments.

The trips abroad are organized without any consideration for the worker's personal situation.

Obviously, moving away is not equally distressing for all employees. Consider the case of a bachelor, or of a man whose children are already grown up or of a man whose children are of school age. It does not seem reasonable to exclude an employee's family situation unless no consideration is made of the personal aspect of work.

A totally liberal approach would argue that business trips and work abroad are within the contractual provisions and previously freely agreed upon. However, such circumstances harm family rights. And because family rights are natural rights, they must obviously come before any other kinds of commitment, including working commitments.

On the other hand, contracts that contain elements of coercion may lead one to question their fairness. This would be the case of a contract that did not respect the worker's family rights if the freedom of choice was reduced, as occurs, for example, in situations of excess supply of labor.

C. RIGIDITY IN WORKING HOURS AND THE POSSIBILITY OF WORKING AT HOME

It is becoming increasingly common for both wife and husband to work outside the home. In the USA, more than two-fifths of the work force (47 million employees) are composed of spouses in working households.[10] In Europe, the proportion of this kind of people could vary widely according to the country but is important enough to pay attention to.[11]

Rigid working hours adversely affect mothers who wish or need to work out of home, especially when the children are still young. This is perhaps one of the most pressing problems for many young families. The problems that usually arise when both parents work are well known: the care of small children, the mismatch between work and school vacations and working hours, the care of

---

[10]Conference Board: 1985, "Corporations and Families: Changing Practices and Perspectives," Report No. 868 (Conference Board, New York).

[11]On the employment of women by age group in different European countries: *vid.* 1986, "Year Book of Labour Statistics," 46th Issue, pp. 35–42. (International Labour Office, Geneva).

children when they fall ill and above all, the deficiencies in upbringing that usually arise because of lack of time and the parents being too tired to give enough attention to their children.

There seems to be no doubt that the best solution to these problems is to spend more time working at home, especially when the children are very young. However, this is not always possible for a number of reasons.

Some companies have proposed various solutions ranging from locating kindergartens and schools next to companies to flexible working hours. They are solutions that each have their pros and cons and respond rather to a compromise of interest than to a social recognition of the rights and duties of parents, foremost among which is the care and upbringing of their children.

On the other hand, working outside of home with a reasonable degree of flexibility may also provide very suitable solutions.[12]

Nancy R. Pearcy, a writer resident in Canada and a former feminist, advocates work in the house and not just housework. This would be compatible with the mother's important task of bringing up her children. She thinks that women who work at home can have the best of both worlds: earn a living while being able to freely organize their working hours, in accordance with the number and age of their children.[13] The idea is interesting and even feasible in some situations; however, when there is no appropriate labor legislation, there may be companies that take advantage of conscientious and hard-working mothers to exploit them using the well-known practices of the underground economy:

> Scenario 7. An imitation jewelry firm contracts out assembly work to homeworkers. Without any employment contract, social security, abnormally low piece rates and tax avoidance, this firm is able to make large profits while the workers—mothers with small children in almost all cases—are able to look after their offspring while working at home but with a ridiculously low pay.

[12]K. Ropp: 1987, "Case Studies" in *Personnel Administrator*, Vol. 32, No. 8, pp. 72–79.
[13]Cfr. N. R. Pearcey: 1987, "Why I Am Not a Feminist (Any More)," *The Human Life Review*, New York, March, pp. 80–88.

It does not seem fair that labor legislation prevents flexible working schedule or home-working. Perhaps this justifies some forms of black economy but, in any case, business ethics demands that abuses be avoided and that alternatives be devised to solve this problem which, for many families, has serious effects.

D. EXCESSIVE WORKING HOURS AND LACK OF VACATION PERIODS WHICH HINDER FAMILY LIFE AND ESPECIALLY THE CARE OF CHILDREN

Inflexible and prolonged working hours and rigidity at work in general (prohibition of part-time working, vacation periods dictated by the company, etc.) all too often affect family duties, especially those of mothers who work out of home. This situation largely depends on the company management. Even though working hours can be influenced by labor legislation, companies usually still have ample room for maneuver.

> Scenario 8. Arturo Garcia, the managing director of a Spanish firm employing 90 people, usually has his lunch outside of the office and, after a long rest, returns to his office at about 5:30. He then starts to work at a feverish pace. He wants his immediate subordinates to extend their working day until very late to help him. One of his secretaries, who is an excellent worker, has stated her desire not to extend her working hours beyond the normal time because she must go to fetch her children from school. This attitude has upset Mr. Garcia who is not prepared to promote that person nor increase her salary beyond that stated in the collective agreement because, according to him, "she can't be counted on."
>
> Arturo Garcia places his convenience and habits before the legitimate rights of his employees. Mr. Garcia could probably organize his work without interfering with the family rights of his employees.

E. OVERWORK TO THE DETRIMENT OF FAMILY LIFE

In some occasions, temporary increases in the workload make it necessary to do a lot of overtime work. And this at times becomes a habit and the person is forced to do overtime work on a regular basis. Without guidance, he may lose sight of the fact that work is not an end in itself.

> Scenario 9. Juan is a top executive in a Spanish automobile company. He is married and has three children aged 6, 8 and 11. He leaves home at 6:30 a.m. and gets back exhausted at about 10 p.m. when the children are already in bed. He also goes to the office on many weekends or takes work home. His job requires frequent travel. In order to make the best use of time, he often starts his trips on a Sunday.
>
> Juan earns a lot of money which he uses to try to satisfy all his wife's and children's desires. His wife, Maria, often complains that she has everything except a husband. The few times she is with her husband to talk about their children, she tries to explain to him that he cannot delegate to her his part of the children's upbringing. Juan justifies himself by saying that the amount of work he has to do is due to the pace set by the company's president and that he has to work as hard as the president does to maintain his position, earn enough money and maintain the, admittedly high, standard of living of his family.

In the situation of overwork shown in the previous situation, the initial responsibility lies with the employee. Juan should reconsider his scale of values, his duties as father and husband, his behavior towards his family and the organization of his own work. However, the company may also be partly responsible. Could Juan alone change the situation without giving up his job? Perhaps, but the management style imposed by the president no doubt has a significant influence.

Working Conditions in Relation to Family Duties

Hygiene and safety conditions at work primarily affect the worker. However, working conditions may have effects that go beyond the individual worker, involving his family life.

The following two situations, while not intended to be exhaustive, illustrate two types of inadequate working conditions and their relation to family rights.

A. PHYSICAL, CHEMICAL OR PSYCHOLOGICAL CONDITIONS THAT AFFECT THE EMPLOYEE'S HEALTH

This obviously affects to a greater or lesser extent the real possibilities of carrying out family activities.

> Scenario 10. In Spain, as in other countries, in the mid-'60s there was no protection against the deafening noise in the cement factory mills. The people who worked there ended up completely deaf. In exchange, the company paid them a bonus for dangerous work. It is not difficult to imagine the problems of oral communication that occur in the family.

Today, this situation has been overcome in most industrialized countries by thick insulating walls and remote control. It is a point that is usually well protected by legislation in industrialized countries. The problem lies in the enforcement of this legislation and, above all, in the working conditions in certain developing nations.

B. LACK OF PROTECTION OF FERTILITY AND GENETIC HERITAGE OR INADEQUATE WORKING CONDITIONS FOR PREGNANT MOTHERS

The protection of the transmission of life derives from the right of the new being already conceived to life or the genetic heritage which may be altered as a result of the action of certain substances present at the place of work. It also derives from the inalienable right of parents to responsibly transmit life, which should not be harmed by working conditions.

> Scenario 11. AT&T detected a high rate of miscarriages among the female workers in the chip manufacturing lines. Consequently, in 1986, AT&T decided to transfer those pregnant workers who were working on the semiconductor production lines.[14]

[14]Cfr. *La Actualidad Electrónica*, Barcelona, January, 1987, p. 20.

Respect of Independence and Family Privacy

The company, as also the rest of society, should not interfere in family privacy nor in its future prospects. Nor should it pressure or discriminate due to:

a. the status of the spouse and the number of children
b. the type of education or school chosen by the parents
c. the family's moral or religious values

> Scenario 12. In 1978, the American Cyanamid Company in Willow Island (West Virginia) had a dye production plant which used lead chromate, a feto-toxic substance. Eight women worked in this section. As a result of legislation, the company drew up a series of safety regulations which included removing women from this section unless they could certify they were sterile. In fact, of the eight women employed in the lead dye section, five had themselves surgically sterilized. This drastic decision was probably influenced by the poor economic conditions in the area, the small size of the Willow Island facilities and the non-existence of jobs available for the women in the immediate short term. In subsequent lawsuits, the company argued that it had tried to dissuade the five women from sterilizing themselves and that it had offered them suitable alternatives in the form of jobs of similar rank and pay. If this is true, the offer was either not convincing or the regulations made did not take into account sufficiently the logical consequences in those female workers who destroyed all possibility of having children in order to keep their jobs.[15]

In cases such as this, the organization of work may violate family privacy and one of the most important family rights: the right of responsible procreation. This type of situation shows the inadequacy of a system of ethics that does not take into account the foreseeable consequences.

Sufficient Compensation for a Decent Family Life

Paying unjustly low wages is another way of violating family independence. It is well-known that remuneration for work done is the principle means of living for most employees.

If real pay is insufficient to bring up a family, then a basic right is trampled under foot which, to a large extent, conditions all the rest.

> Scenario 13. A Spanish company employs 60 workers. Its financial situation is good. Most of the workers hold positions that require little skill or experience. However, wages are scaled above all according to years of service (for historical reasons and union pressure) and to date, very few benefits have been given to workers and their families. Unfortunately, economic protection of the family in Spain is one of the lowest in Europe (an annual allowance of 2000 pesetas per child and tax deduction of 16,000 pesetas per child, in 1987).
>
> Some of the workers in this company with large families are in serious financial difficulties. Others see in the current pay system an effective coercion tool against procreation. Obviously, these problems affect the working atmosphere.
>
> Management is considering restructuring wage rates taking into account not only production but also the worker's family situation.

In several international human rights documents, the need has been stated to provide economic protection for the family.[16] John Paul II, following a long tradition of social teaching by the Roman Catholic Church, insists in the encyclical *Laborem exercens* on the need for a sufficient level of remuneration to enable the employee to lead a decent family life.[17]

The State, mainly through welfare benefits and tax deductions, can provide a certain economic protection for the family. However, the company cannot remain aloof from the economic rights of

---

[15]Cfr. J. B. Matthews, K. E. Goodpaster and L. L. Nash: 1985, *Policies and Personas. A Casebook in Business Ethics* (McGraw-Hill, New York) pp. 72ff.

[16]Cfr. U.N.O. *Universal Declaration of Human Rights,* art. 23.3; *European Social Charter,* art. 4.1; U.N.O. *International Agreement on Human Rights,* art. 11.1, etc.
[17]John Paul II, Enc. *Laborem exercens,* No. 19 (Boston: St Paul Press, 1981).

its employees' families, especially when State aid is insufficient. This consideration gives rise to two statements:

a. The wages paid should not be less than those required by an average family to live a decent life within the context of the time and place concerned.
b. The benefits granted by the company to its workers should cover all members of their families. These benefits should be greater the lesser the protection given by society in general to families. It is not always easy to give these family-weighted benefits. It requires a lot of solidarity not only from the company with respect to its employees, but also among the individual employees, taking into consideration the overall financial capability of the firm to grant the benefits.

Efforts should also be made to prevent a particular company from being excessively affected by the size of its workers' families.

Also, those workers with large families may be discriminated against. It therefore seems advisable to create special funds for families from certain groups of companies or economic sectors. Thus, it would be possible to better respect the economic rights of the family without resorting to the State or overburdening individual companies.

Conclusion

The narrow attitude towards work which separates the worker from his family life should be dispelled.

The worker is not just "labor" but a person who has family duties of crucial importance for himself and for society.

Family duties fall primarily upon the members of the family itself but, by being natural rights of all those who have chosen marriage and family, they should be respected and even promoted by the firm to ensure social justice in employer-employee relations.

It is one of the company's ethical obligations to organize work, taking into account the family duties of its employees and their subsequent compliance.

The idea is that the loose agreement between employee and employer is insufficient, and unjust without the explicit consideration of the rights of the family. When the negotiating parties do not have the same power or there exists the need to work, family rights and other rights may be disregarded in the name of freedom of negotiation.

Family rights must be enforced with care and not just as a mere legalism in the organization or work in the firm. By doing so, the efforts to respect family rights will lead to corresponding improvements in labor relations.

Finally, when employees feel hindered to comply with their family duties because of excessive work, they become unmotivated and less efficient. Hence, the organization is worse off.

Work and Family: Should Parents Feel Guilty?

LYNN SHARP PAINE

MANY WORKING PARENTS feel guilty about the time they spend away from their children.[1] Until recently, judging from media coverage, career-minded women seemed to be the primary sufferers.

---

[1] In testimony before the Senate Subcommittee on Children, Family, Drugs, and Alcoholism, Dana B. Friedman of the Conference Board reported that "Millions of men and women are going to work, each day carrying in their lunch pails and briefcases, the right amount of private guilt, the proper level of subdued expectation, and the perfect amount of stress which serves as the fulcrum for what is called 'balancing work and family life.'" Hearing on S. 1985, The Act for Better Child Care Services, March 15, 1988.

From Public Affairs Quarterly *5(1), 1991. Reprinted by permission.*

It is increasingly clear, however, that fathers, too, feel conflict and guilt about their children's care.[2] A recent Stanford University study found that among couples whose members both hold graduate business degrees, husbands have *more* anxiety about the children than their wives.[3] Advertisers have discovered that parental guilt is a theme with sales potential, and entrepreneurs have discovered that it is a source of economic opportunity.[4]

Employers are concerned about the effects of parental guilt on productivity. "Executive Guilt: Who's Taking Care of the Children?" appeared recently as a cover story for *Fortune* magazine.[5] The article, which describes corporate responses to employees' child-care problems, quotes Dr. Lee Salk, professor of psychology and pediatrics at New York Hospital-Cornell Medical Center. Says Salk, "Guilt is what parents are coming to talk to me about."[6]

What, exactly, do these parents feel guilty about? According to these articles and studies, many parents believe they are not giving their children enough personal time and attention. Many who aspire to traditional careers in the professions and business, or to high levels of achievement in other fields, entrust their young children to caretakers for most of the child's waking hours. As a result, some parents carry with them a nagging sense of guilt.[7] Even when their children appear to be developing normally and have the best child

care money can buy, some parents feel they are not fulfilling their parental responsibilities.

Are such feelings appropriate? Is it reasonable for parents to feel guilty about their absences when their children are well cared for by others?[8] The thrust of the popular literature on parental guilt is that absence-related guilt feelings are generally irrational and inappropriate.[9] This view, I will argue, rests on failure to acknowledge the moral foundations of guilt feelings and on a very narrow conception of parents' obligations. On a different conception of parental obligations and values, a conception I will elaborate, absence-related guilt can be seen to be a morally fitting response to the situation of working parents.

My ultimate aim is practical. I want to know how parental guilt feelings are best dealt with. But to answer this practical question we must understand the basis of these feelings. If parental guilt is a neurosis with no rational basis, as suggested by some commentators, counseling or psychiatric treatment may be called for. But if, as I argue, guilt is a morally fitting response to the situation of working parents, efforts to address the situation, not simply the feelings, will be in order.

I. Morality and Guilt Feelings

Concerned about employment opportunities for women, many popular writers have urged mothers to dismiss their feelings of guilt. Perhaps they fear that acknowledging the possible legitimacy of guilt will cause mothers to flee the workplace and justify employers in refusing to hire them.[10] One approach to undermining the seriousness of guilt feelings is to

[2]E.g., Cathy Trost, "Men, Too, Wrestle with Career-Family Stress," *Wall Street Journal* (November 1, 1988), p. B1, col. 3; David Wessell, "Working Fathers Feel New Pressures Arising from Child-Rearing Duties," *Wall Street Journal* (September 7, 1984), p. 29, col. 4

[3]Fern Schumer Chapman, "Executive Guilt: Who's Taking Care of the Children?" *Fortune* (February 16, 1987), p. 30.

[4]The idea behind upscale daycare, according to one investor, is "to rid white-collar executives of the guilt of leaving their children." Lawrence Ingrassia, "Day-Care Business Lures Entrepreneurs," *Wall Street Journal* (June 3, 1988), p. 21, col. 3.

[5]Chapman, "Executive Guilt."

[6]Ibid.

[7]Take the New York executive described in the *Fortune* magazine article mentioned earlier For a time, when his one-year-old daughter was spending eleven hours a day in a child-care center, he was profoundly unhappy. His feelings of guilt overwhelmed his ability to concentrate on his work, and he considered quitting to stay home with his child. When his parents moved next door and took over as babysitters, he found that he could focus on his work again, but even in those circumstances, his guilt feelings did not completely disappear.

[8]One may, of course, be guilty without feeling guilty and feel guilty without being guilty. However, in the standard case involving violations of generally accepted and justifiable ethical standards one hopes that objective attributions of guilt and subjective feelings of guilt coincide. The words "guilt" and "parental guilt" are used throughout this paper to mean "guilt feelings."

[9]See, e.g., Sandra Scarr, *Mother Care/Other Care* (New York: Basic Books. Inc., 1984); Gloria Norris and Joann Miller, "Motherhood and Guilt," *Working Woman* (April 1984), p. 159.

[10]Hostility to the idea that absence-related guilt feelings may be morally appropriate is understandable. Historically, the idea that children need the personal attention of their parents has serves as a rationale for keeping women in the home and out of the workplace, since mothers have traditionally been assigned the role of custodial parent. And research on

redescribe them as non-moral feelings—as unhappiness, regret, or anxiety, for example.[11] Another is to explain them as vestiges, like the human appendix, which no longer serve any identifiable function but survive as a reminder of the past.[12] Both approaches are ultimately unsatisfying because they neglect essential attributes of guilt feelings, attributes such as the self-criticism and sense of moral failure that are part of feeling guilty. The truth that these accounts fail to acknowledge is that guilt feelings are moral feelings. They cannot be understood apart from the unsatisfied moral imperative or unrealized moral ideal underlying them.

For example, one commentator redescribes guilt as excessive anxiety. The author of a *Glamour* magazine piece asserts that "guilt is nothing but good, healthy, loving concern taken a step too far."[13] This account, however, neglects the element of self-criticism implicit in guilt feelings.[14] When I am anxious about my children, I am concerned about *them*. I imagine what they may do or what may happen to them, and I may take steps to assure myself that they are all right. It is entirely possible for me to feel anxious about my children even if I am confident that I have made the right decision to, for example, permit them to bicycle to school. Anxiety may exist quite independently of guilt. When I feel guilty, I may also be anxious, but more importantly and, in addition, I believe I have fallen short morally. Perhaps I have failed to teach

the children bicycle safety, or I have neglected to warn them about a dangerous crossing. When I feel guilty my concern focuses on *me* as well as on them. Any explanation of guilt that leaves out the element of moral self-criticism is conceptually inadequate. Excessive anxiety can, of course, be destructive in its own right. But it is quite a different thing from guilt.[15]

Disregard for the moral basis of guilt feelings is also seen in other attempts to explain maternal guilt. One psychologist, for example, attributes mothers' guilt to "a mismatch between the current realities of family life and ideas about motherhood and children that suited the late-nineteenth and early-twentieth centuries."[16] The author argues that today's mothers suffer guilt because they are not living up to the nineteenth-century ideal of exclusive attachment between mother and child.[17]

This account of maternal guilt is unsatisfactory for many reasons. Besides leaving fathers' guilt untouched, its historical accuracy is questionable. Among the Victorian middle and upper classes, children were often looked after by relatives, nannies, wet nurses, and various domestics, while their mothers attended to the myriad aspects of household management and family and social life.[18] But setting aside historical accuracy, the account fails to explain why the ideal of exclusive attachment should persist while other nineteenth-century ideals have been abandoned with changing circumstances. Moreover, if parents were only clinging wistfully to out-moded conceptions of parenthood, why would they describe themselves as feeling guilty rather than nostalgic or regretful?

The answer is found by noticing the moral imperative implicit in the governing ideal of

---

maternal deprivation has been misused to show that full-time maternal care is essential to children's well-being. See generally Ann Daily, *Inventing Motherhood. The Consequences of an Ideal* (New York: Schocken Books, 1982), p. 162. See also Michael Rutter, *Maternal Deprivation Reassessed* (Hammondsworth, England: Penguin Books, Ltd., 1972).

[11]For a discussion of the difference between regret and moral feelings, see R. M. Hare, *Moral Thinking* (New York Oxford University Press. 1981), pp. 28–30.

[12]See, e.g., the following comment by a pediatric psychologist: "For so many years there was this ethic that if you don't care for your own child, you're doing something wrong. Although that has dissipated considerably, many mothers still carry remnants of that in their heads." Diane Granat, "Are You My Mommy?" *Washingtonian* (October 1988), p. 182.

[13]Louise Lague, "The Good News About Working Moms and Guilt," *Glamour* (May 1984), p. 234.

[14]Gabrielle Taylor emphasizes the element of self-assessment in her account of guilt in *Pride, Shame and Guilt* (Oxford: Claren don Press, 1986), pp. 85–107.

[15]Herbert Morris, too, makes the point that guilt cannot be reduced to anxiety. See "The Decline of Guilt," *Ethics,* vol. 99, no. 1 (October 1988). pp. 66–67.

[16]Sandra Scarr, *Mother Care/Other Care*, p. 54.

[17]Ibid.., p. 105.

[18]Scarr, by her own account, seems to confuse Victorian with Freudian ideas about motherhood. See ibid, pp. 81–105. Jerome Kagan gives a contrasting account of nineteenth-century attitudes toward the mother-child relationship. He attributes the emphasis on the child's attachment to the mother to Freud and, more recently, to John Bowlby. See Jerome Kagan, *The Nature of the Child* (New York: Basic Books, Inc., 1984). pp. 50–63. See also Ann Dally, *Inventing Motherhood: The Consequences of an Ideal,* pp. 104–42, for a historical account different from Scarr's.

parenthood. Parents feel guilty because they see themselves as failing to be the kind of parent they believe they *ought* to be, not simply the kind of parent they would *like* to be. Unlike nineteenth-century ideals of entertaining or landscaping which are also impractical in today's world, the purportedly nineteenth-century ideal of motherhood has a moral dimension which is ignored by the vestige theory of maternal guilt. Once we notice this dimension, we cannot simply discard the ideal as impractical and inconvenient. We must look more deeply at its foundations and its relationship to human well-being.

"Guilt" is a popular and perhaps overused word. No doubt, some parents mistakenly describe as guilt," feelings that are more accurately described as "regret," or "sadness," arising from missing their children. Some parents may falsely report feeling guilty when, in fact, they are relieved to spend most of their time in a professional environment in the company of adults. Some reports of guilt may reflect simple hypocrisy driven by the desire to present oneself as a dutiful parent. Still, the existence of spurious claims does not eliminate the problem. Parents who feel guilty about not seeing enough of their children are expressing feelings of moral inadequacy. If these feelings are genuine, they cannot be resolved by redescriptions and explanations of the sort commonly found in the popular literature. Fashioning a suitable and effective response to parents' guilt feelings requires that we take them seriously and acknowledge their moral foundations.

II. Resolving Feelings of Guilt

Guilt is not altogether a bad thing. A testament to our commitment to important values, guilt feelings have a positive role in moral life. They can lead to conduct that affirms important moral standards, restores human relationships, and improves the well-being of others. Guilt feelings aroused by the contemplation of forbidden conduct can sometimes deter it. But unresolved guilt can have a destructive effect on personality and on the ability to function effectively. Gnawing guilt can interfere with concentration and with the self-esteem and hope necessary to forge ahead with one's projects and daily activities. In extreme cases, it can lead to personality disorders involving obsessive behavior

and even to madness.[19] It is thus understandable that many people are concerned about parental guilt and would like to reduce its frequency.

The first step toward a fitting and effective resolution of parental guilt is to assess its moral appropriateness. The goal is not simply to eliminate guilt feelings—an objective which could probably be achieved in many cases through a program of belief or behavior modification—but to do so while acknowledging guilt's positive role in upholding morality. This more complex aim demands that morally appropriate guilt be resolved in a way that affirms the moral standards at stake. Affirmation may take many forms: an apology, a change in behavior, reparation or compensation for harm done, confession, acceptance of punishment.[20] Even a symbolic affirmation may be fitting. The important point is that the suitability of a resolution depends on the nature of the moral deficiency in question.

Fashioning an effective resolution thus depends centrally on correct identification of the moral standards and factual beliefs behind the feelings. Failure to appreciate the full range of parents' moral concerns, is, I suggest, another problem with much of the mass-media advice and many employer-sponsored child-care programs intended to help parents.[21] The prevailing assumption seems to be that parental guilt is driven by a moral principle of avoiding harm to children, where harm is thought of narrowly in terms of children's present interests in physical, intellectual, social, or emotional health, and is measured by the degree of departure from some standard of normalcy.

---

[19]For an enlightening discussion of the effects of guilt, see Taylor, *Pride, Shame and Guilt,* pp. 93–7.

[20]Guilt need not be linked with liability to punishment or the possibility of reparation, as argued by Anthony O'Hear in "Guilt and Shame as Moral Concepts." *Proceedings of the Aristotelian Society,* vol. 77 (1976–77), pp. 73–86. Guilt feelings that arise from forgetting a promise to a friend, for instance, do not typically involve liability to punishment or even necessarily, the possibility of reparation.

[21]I have in mind corporations that have responded to parental concerns by providing financial or other assistance in securing child care rather than restructuring work so that parents can be more involved with their children's upbringing. According to Chapman. "Executive Guilt," p. 33, some 3000 companies offer subsidized daycare centers, financial assistance for child care or child-care referral services.

The assumption that parents' central concern is their children's interests in "normal" or "average" development along these discrete dimensions is implicit in much popular advice. One writer, for instance, instructs that, "Reality guilt is when you have neglected or abused your children. Neurotic guilt is the conflict you feel between what you want to do and what you feel you have to do."[22] Other commentators reassure parents by pointing to studies showing "that children in quality daycare don't suffer any cognitive loss or feel any less attached to their parents."[23] The same assumption influences the direction of child-care research, which tends to focus on finding out whether daycare is harmful to children's physical, cognitive, or socio-emotional development.[24] Studies typically test hypotheses about the intellectual achievement and ability, or the emotional and social development of daycare children as compared to non-daycare children.

Assumptions about the moral norms behind guilt feelings affect our assessment of their appropriateness and shape our approach to resolving them. If we assume that parental guilt is based on concerns about children's physical, intellectual, and socio-emotional development, its appropriateness becomes an empirical question to be resolved, at the general level, by social scientists. On the evidence to date, a case can be made that the guilt feelings we are exploring here—absence-related guilt felt by parents whose children enjoy high-quality substitute care—are simply inappropriate. Research on the effects of daycare is inconclusive in many respects, and much debate centers on its effects, especially the effects of infant daycare.[25]

But, as yet, it does not appear that children cared for by parent substitutes suffer identifiable cognitive, physical, social, or emotional deficiencies.[26] Children looked after in quality daycare centers perform as well, and sometimes better, than non-daycare children on the chosen dimensions.[27]

Within this moral framework, the central, perhaps the only, issue is the quality of substitute care. Guilt felt by parents whose care arrangements lead to sub-normal child development is seen as appropriate and suitably resolved by improving the quality and availability of substitute care. On the other hand, guilt feelings of parents whose children are developing normally along the defined dimensions are regarded as inappropriate and best dealt with through reasoning, counseling, or therapy. Such parents are advised to recognize how others—their parents, doctors, and children—"make them" feel guilty.[28] They are exhorted to examine the scientific studies showing that daycare is not harmful and can actually enhance their children's social skills. Their guilt feelings come to be seen as psychological aberrations rather than morally appropriate feelings calling for an affirmation of their moral ideals.[29]

---

[22]Lague, "The Good News About Working Moms and Guilt," p. 234.

[23]Bettye M. Caldwell, quoted in Chapman, "Executive Guilt," p. 36.

[24]See, for example, Bengt-Erik Andersson, "Effects of Public Day-Care: A Longitudinal Study," *Child Development,* vol. 60 (1989), pp. 857–66. For reviews of research on daycare, see, for example, Alison Clarke-Stewart, *Daycare* (Cambridge, MA: Harvard University Press, 1982), pp. 63–77; Thomas J. Gamble and Edward Zigler, "Effects of Infant Day Care: Another Look at the Evidence," *American Journal of Orthopsychiatry,* vol. 56 (January 1986), pp. 26–42.

[25]See K. Alison Clarke-Stewart, "Infant Day Care Maligned or Malignant?" *American Psychologist,* vol. 44 (February 1989), pp. 266–273; Gamble and Zigler, "Effects of Infant Day Care."

[26]See T. Berry Brazelton, "Issues for Working Parents," *American Journal of Orthopsychiatry,* vol. 56, n. 1 (January 1986), at p. 23. ("Most studies to date have not found negative consequences, but these studies tend to be biased in one of several ways.") See also, Clarke-Stewart, *Daycare,* pp. 63–77. Of course, much depends on the operative conception of harm and how it is measured, and some researchers claim that certain types of group arrangements do have undesirable effects such as increasing children's aggressiveness and assertiveness. Certainly, particular care arrangements can have detrimental effects on the cognitive and emotional development of the children involved. Even the most ardent critics of maternal guilt reluctantly acknowledge that "If your child is truly suffering under your present child care arrangements, perhaps you should consider lowering your life-style and paying for better care." Norris and Miller, "Motherhood and Guilt," pp. 159–60.

[27]See, e.g., Bengt-Erik Anderson, "Effects of Public Day-Care"; Clarke-Stewart, *Daycare,* pp. 63–77; and research reported in Ruth J. Moss, "Good Grades for Day-Care," *Psychology Today* (February 1987), p. 21.

[28]Norris and Miller, "Motherhood and Guilt," pp. 159–60.

[29]The observation of Dr. Salk, quoted above, indicates the extent to which parents are seeking psychological help with their feelings of guilt. See Chapman, "Executive Guilt." p. 30.

Some parents may find this line of reasoning comforting. For a variety of reasons, others will find it interesting but unsatisfying. The evidence—the long-term evidence—is not really "in." We know little about the effects of child-rearing practices on adult development. Perhaps, the social, emotional, or cognitive harms will show up later. Many parents feel that parental obligation goes beyond protecting children from harm—that is, protecting them from falling below a minimal standard defined by statistical averages—and requires the positive promotion of each child's cognitive, physical, and social capabilities. Even those with a more minimal conception of parental obligation may continue to be concerned about the possibly harmful effects, not of daycare in general, but of the particular arrangements they have devised for their children.

Still other parents will find this line of reasoning largely irrelevant because it rests on a faulty assumption about the moral standard at issue. For these parents, guilt persists in the face of excellent substitute care not because of concerns about their children's cognitive, physical, or socio-emotional health, but because they have a moral ideal of parenthood that calls for greater personal involvement with their children. Departures from this ideal are problematic not because of the effects typically measured in studies of substitute care, but because of the moral harm involved—moral harm to both children and their parents. On this alternative conception of the underlying moral imperative, I suggest, parental guilt feelings are a very appropriate response to a situation in which parents have little time to spend with their children. I will explain, the persuasiveness of this suggestion depends on the strength of the case for the ideal.

III. *Morally Appropriate Guilt*

Guilt feelings can fail to be appropriate in one of two ways.[30] They may be inappropriate because based on a moral standard for which there is no reasonable justification. Or they may be inappro-

priate because based on beliefs about, among other things, the consequences of conduct, the availability of morally preferable alternatives, or the degree of fault. As we have seen, one line of reasoning about parental guilt treats it as inappropriate because based on false beliefs about the effects of substitute care.

Assessing the appropriateness of guilt feelings thus requires inquiry into both the relevant facts and the underlying moral standards. This assessment may sometimes be a straightforward, though not necessarily simple, matter of ascertaining the truth of critical beliefs and matching conduct against moral requirements, as the legal model of criminal guilt might suggest. But in other cases, perplexing problems attend our judgments about the moral standards to which we hold ourselves. There is, for instance, the problem of conflicting obligations. Sometimes I have no choice but to violate some general moral obligation, even though, after careful consideration, I decide that I ought, all things considered, to take one course of action rather than another. Are my feelings of guilt appropriate if I have done the best I can?

A similar problem arises when I am forced by others to do something which is morally wrong. I may not be culpable, strictly speaking, but I have nevertheless done something which ought not be done. Should I feel guilty? The best response is that guilt is understandable even though perhaps inappropriate under the specific circumstances. My character is such that I have an aversion to doing things that generally I ought not do, and feel guilty when I do those things even for a good reason. A little extra guilt may be the price of a good character. Of course, if I have arranged things in a way that makes it likely that conflicts will arise, my feelings of culpability are more appropriate.[31]

Problematic cases aside for the moment, feeling guilty is sometimes clearly appropriate: if, for example, I knowingly lie about my qualifications to gain an advantage in a job competition. My subsequent feelings of guilt are perfectly appropriate because, very simply, I did what I ought not to have done under the circumstances—namely, lie.

[30]Herbert Morris discusses the ways guilt can fail to be appropriate. His concern is to argue that guilt can be appropriate despite the absence of moral culpability. See Herbert Morris, "Nonmoral Guilt," in *Responsibility, Character, and the Emotions,* ed. by Ferdinand Schoeman (New York: Cambridge University Press, 1987), pp. 222–25.

[31]Ruth Barcan Marcus argues that we ought to conduct our lives and arrange our institutions so as to minimize situations of moral conflict. See Ruth Barcan Marcus, "Moral Dilemmas and Consistency," *Journal of Philosophy,* vol. 77, no. 3 (1980), p. 121.

The conclusion that guilt is appropriate is unproblematic in this case. The link between the breach of a morality and the feelings of guilt is straightforward. The general prohibition against lying is widely accepted and easily justifiable by almost any standard of moral justification. Even the most minimal morality contains a prohibition on lying. The case involves no factual questions and there appear to be no factors mitigating blameworthiness. My lie was not an act of desperation intended to secure the only available opportunity for a livelihood for my dependents. It was simply a means of capturing for myself an advantage over similarly situated competitors.

More difficult are questions about the appropriateness of guilt in cases involving standards that are not so widely accepted because they are thought to be supererogatory or simply different. For example, some people believe they are obligated to contribute a tenth of their income to charity and may feel guilty when their contributions fall below this standard. Others would regard such a standard as far too onerous. Some people are more inclined than others to impose moral requirements on themselves. It is very likely that these people will more frequently see themselves as falling short and thus carry a heavier burden of guilt than those who demand less of themselves.[32]

This example resembles the case of parental guilt: both involve moral standards that are far from universally accepted. Unlike the principle of honesty or fidelity to promises, for example, the standards seem somewhat optional. How are we to assess the appropriateness of guilt in this sort of case? Herbert Morris has suggested that we ask

1. whether there is common acceptance of the reported feeling without a corresponding widespread inclination to seek some explanation other than that offered by the person; and
2. whether there is widespread respect for the moral ideal underlying the feeling.[33]

Morris's recommendation is not very helpful in the case of parental guilt. This case is problematic just because there is no consensus on the ideal underlying the feelings. Knowing that there is no general agreement on the ideal will not help us

determine whether guilt is appropriate. More importantly, Morris's approach is unsatisfying for the same reasons that all relativistic theories are unsatisfying: there is no way to distinguish what is accepted from what ought to be accepted. We must, instead, examine the basis for the underlying moral ideal and decide whether it makes sense to hold oneself to such a standard.

IV. Parental Love and Parental Presence

Feelings of guilt associated with parental absence can be explained by a moral ideal of parenthood calling for attentive love and personal engagement with one's children. This ideal has a variety of closely related sources. As I will elaborate, it flows from parents' responsibilities for their children's moral education and their obligations as fiduciaries for their children's interests. It also has roots in the needs and interests of adults and the community. But it rests fundamentally on a judgment that deep personal commitments, relationships of love involving personal engagement with other human beings, have intrinsic moral value. A life with such relationships, and the joys and hardships they entail, is morally better than a life without them.

Relationships of love offer the most thoroughgoing experience of sympathetic identification with another that we are likely to encounter. These relationships are enriching, enlarging, a source of unique joy. They are onerous, trying, and a source of unique pain. But they are our link with other human beings as ends in themselves and in this respect have intrinsic moral worth. The giving of oneself and the appreciation of the other at the core of these relationships are the sources of their moral value. Although parental love lacks the mutuality of love between friends or spouses, it is based, like other love relationships, on concern for the other for his own sake. The very absence of mutuality is perhaps a reason to see in parental love greater moral value than in relationships between equals.

Insofar as the ideal of parenthood outlined here depends upon the intrinsic moral value of personal relationships of love, there can be no substitute for some degree of personal interaction between parent and child. Parents cannot delegate to others the responsibility for providing love and attention as they delegate the responsibility for providing

[32]See Herbert Fingarette, "Feeling Guilty," *American Philosophical Quarterly* vol. 16. no. 2 (April 1979), p. 159.
[33]Morris, "Nonmoral Guilt," p. 224.

transportation, medical care, or music education. For the parent, the moral value of personal involvement lies not just in bringing about a certain result for the child but also from the giving of himself and actively caring for the child. Only through direct involvement can the parent enjoy this moral good.[34]

Personal involvement also has instrumental moral value for parents. By testing and enhancing their capacity to care deeply and continuously for others, parenthood can propel adults into a new phase of their own moral development. Parents who take seriously their role as moral example and teacher are bound to experience moral growth through the reassessment of moral beliefs and commitments that goes with personal involvement in child care. Moreover, personal involvement enhances parents' performance as fiduciaries for their children. Without a substantial core of shared experience, it is doubtful that parents could know their children well enough to make intelligent decisions in their behalf.

These are compelling reasons to think that personally caring for one's children can be a source of great moral value for a parent. There are also reasons to think that the moral good for children is promoted by personal involvement with their parents. These reasons can be seen by looking more closely at some tasks of parenthood.

One of the central tasks of parenthood is to prepare children for life by nurturing the ties and interests that will permit them to flourish when no longer dependent on their parents. A great deal has been made of the centrality of autonomous decision-making.[35] In this connection, the ability to relate to others and moral behavior are equally important. The capacity to participate in intimate relations of love later in life[36] and the capacity to engage in moral thought and action appear to be closely linked, both causally and conceptually, with

each other[37] and with the experience of being loved by one's parents.[38]

For children, the moral importance of parental love rests not only on its causal role in contributing to dispositions to be honest and responsible and to trust others, but also on its role as exemplar. A child's conception of what it is to love another has its earliest roots in the experience of being the recipient of parental love and an observer of the love between her parents. Besides being the child's first sustained love relationship, the parent-child relationship provides a uniquely intimate commitment. The importance of parental love as an example—positive or negative—of what love requires may only surface in adulthood.

A parent's engagement with this child is not only an expression of love for the child, it is also an indication of how much the parent values intimate relationships. Parents' choices reflect their conception of the good and provide children with an example of how diverse goals and values—love, self, work, achievement, money, morality—can and should be integrated into a coherent life.[39] In

---

[34]I was advised by a partner in the law firm where I worked before the birth of my second child not to take a long maternity leave. Otherwise, he said, "I would begin to love the baby."

[35]Several writers treat the capacity for autonomous choice as the central capacity parents should be concerned with. See, for example, Jeffrey Blustein, *Parents and Children: The Ethics of the Family* (New York: Oxford University Press, 1982), pp. 120–36. Blustein devotes only a brief paragraph to the capacity to develop deep personal relationships.

[36]E. H. Enkson, *Childhood and Society* (New York: W. W. Norton, 1963).

[37]I am grateful to Joseph Fletcher for bringing to my attention the following quotation from R. M. Hare: "To think that love and morality have different languages, so that the one can be at variance with the other, is a mistake often made by those to whom love means sex, and morality means a book of rules the reasons for which everyone has forgotten. But in truth morality is love. For the essence of morality is to treat the interests of others as of equal weight with one's own." "Community and Communication," in *Applications of Moral Philosophy* (London: Macmillan, 1972), p. 115. See also Annette Baier, "Trust and Antitrust," *Ethics*, vol. 96 (1986), pp. 231–60.

[38]Psychologists have said that family affection is an important factor in the development of children's sense of honesty, responsibility, and moral courage. See, e.g., the following works cited in Michael Schulman and Eva Mekler, *Bringing up a Moral Child* (Reading, Mass: Addison-Wesley Publishing Company, Inc., 1985), p. 132; Brown, A. W. Morrison J., and Couch, G. B., "Influence of Affectional Family Relationships on Character Development," *Journal of Abnormal and Social Psychology* (1947), pp. 422–28; McCord, W., McCord, J., and Howard, A., "Familial Correlates of Aggression in Non-Delinquent Male Children," *Journal of Abnormal and Social Psychology* (1961), pp. 62, 79–93.

[39]Of course, one cannot simply "read off" values from choices. The constraints under which certain choices are made may make them quite unreflective of the agents actual values. This seems to be the case for many parents who entrust their children to the care of others in order to work.

many cases, parents are the only adults to whom children can look for such an example, for they are the only adults children know well enough. Others—teachers, doctors, family members, friends—are seen only in their particular roles or seen too infrequently to provide useful examples of how life might be lived. It is not surprising that absence-related guilt seems to afflict career-oriented professionals whose work, while perhaps socially valuable, is also a source of self-gratification and for whom the giving up of work-related opportunities may require self-sacrifice. At the margin—after fulfilling legitimate material requirements—the decision to take on more work rather than to attend to one's children may reflect the choice of a lesser moral good over a greater one, and the choice of self-interest over the interests of others. For the parent who subscribes to the ideal of parenthood I have described, all-consuming work may be a source not only of absence-related guilt but of guilt related to the discrepancy between professed moral values and conduct.

A certain amount of parental presence is necessarily required for parental love to fulfill the functions outlined here. If parental love is to serve as an example of a relationship of love, it must be accessible to the child and the child must perceive it to be such a relationship. Parents' personal involvement is also important if parental love is to fulfill its causal role in strengthening moral dispositions and preparing children for participation in later love relationships. This is, quite simply, because what matters from the child's perspective is not only that she is loved, but that she also believes herself to be loved.[40]

Unfortunately, a child can feel unloved and quite alone at the same time his parents see themselves as deeply loving. The discrepancy may arise because of the child's level of cognitive and emotional development. He may not be able to appreciate the depth of a parent's abstract love or impersonal expressions of concern: the trouble a parent may take, for instance, in finding a daycare provider. Children's limited knowledge of the world, their shorter time horizons, and their emerging conceptions of self—all affect their perceptions of their parents' love and concern. There is a risk that impersonally expressed concern for a child's well-being will be inadequate to support the child's belief that she is loved.

The importance of parental presence is not due exclusively to children's limited cognitive capacities, however. Most of us, children and adults alike, feel loved and valued by those who seek out our companionship, take our perspectives and problems seriously, give us a high priority in their scheme of things, and support us even in difficult times. Aristotle's idea that loving entails caring for another for that person's sake captures an important motivational element in genuine love: it must proceed from concern for the beloved and not from the lover's concern for herself. Our belief that we are loved depends on our perception of the lover's motives and on the presence of certain expressions of love. I will not believe you love me if your attentions appear to be a means to your own advantage. Nor will I believe you love me if you show insufficient interest in me as a person.

An example may be helpful. Suppose, while assuring me of his love, my husband regularly arranges to have his personal agent or substitute join me for dinner or evenings out, counsel me on problems, and perhaps occasionally even spend the night. At some point, no matter how carefully and efficiently he manages the coming and going of his substitutes, no matter how much I like them, and no matter how much he protests that he really loves me, I will begin to doubt him. I will begin to think his excuses of responsibilities at work are bogus or that he loves his work first and foremost. Or I may think his attentions to me spring from some source other than love of me.

These same difficulties are present when parents delegate to others too much of the responsibility for providing their children with loving care and attention. The child's understanding of his parents' reasons for delegating his care is very important. The child who realizes that the family's very livelihood depends on his parents' being away from home is quite likely to feel differently from the child who sees his parents' absence as selfish expressions of their desire for self-fulfillment. It is impossible to assess the effects of parental absence without including the motives and perceived motives of parents. The precise amount of personal attention

[40]For discussion of the importance of the partiality parents show their children, see Elizabeth Newson. "Unreasonable Care: The Establishment of Selfhood," in *Human Values,* ed. by Godfrey Vesey (Atlantic 'Highlands, NJ: Humanities Press, Inc., 1976), pp. 1–26. She argues that parent partiality is important for the development of self-esteem.

required to sustain a child's trust in the parent's love is probably quite variable since it depends in part on the child's ability to comprehend and interpret the parents' conduct and motives as well as on the child's conceptual maturity. As the child's capacity for abstract thought matures, the amount of personal attention required could be expected to diminish. Nevertheless, as with adult love, there would appear to be some minimum amount of personal attention necessary for a parent to love his child in a way that the child recognizes as love.

As noted, delegating too much of the responsibility to give children love and attention may jeopardize their trust in their parents' love. But one might wonder why parents' love should matter so much if children believe they are loved by the nannies, daycare providers, and other caregivers hired by parents. The difficulty with all these parent surrogates is the very limited nature of their love and commitment.[41] The employment relationship is a tenuous foundation for bonds of love. This is especially true given the low pay, high turn-over, and low morale characteristic in today's child-care and domestic labor markets. The more serious problem, however, stems from fundamentals of the employment relationship.

Except in extraordinary cases, the child's welfare occupies quite a different position in a parent's and an employee's scheme of priorities. Usually, no matter how much an employee loves her charges, her attachment is contingent on receipt of adequate compensation. Assisting the child—as teacher, nanny, babysitter—is a job and must be seen in that context. Employment mobility and the needs of the employee's own family limit the commitment most are willing to make. If fulfilling parental responsibilities requires a stable, constant and relatively permanent attachment, all non-family parent substitutes suffer a comparative disadvantage.[42] The parents' affection for the child and the relative permanence of the parent/child attachment give parents a stake in the child's welfare much greater than the stake any employee could be expected to have. This differential, coupled with the other factors noted, may translate into less rigorous protection and promotion of the child's interests.[43] While the caretaker may well be affectionate, she probably will not and should not be expected to demonstrate the level of personal commitment normally associated with a love relationship.

If the child does become attached to the parent substitute, the substitute's departure for a better job may be that much more problematic. The consequences for the child's self-esteem must be considered but also his developing conception of love hangs in the balance. What sort of love can be so easily withdrawn? The serious question is how much of the responsibility for giving children love and attention can be delegated to others without unacceptably distorting the love. It is perfectly possible to hire someone to give a child affection and attention within the confines of an employment relationship. The risk is that this form of limited love will provide an inadequate foundation for a conception of fully committed love, and that the parents more permanent, but less involved, expressions of love will be inadequate, too. There may be no one the child perceives as fully committed and from whom he learns what it means to love.

Instrumental justifications for spending time with one's children must not obscure this basic value judgment: that relationships of love are intrinsically valuable as elements of a morally good and satisfying life. Acceptance of this judgment is perhaps the central, though not the only, reason many parents both want and feel they ought to spend more time with their children than their jobs and professional commitments permit.

V. Conceptions of the Family

Guilt associated with parental absence rests centrally on parents' obligation to give their children

---

[41]The problem of limited commitment would seem more acute in some situations than others. Child care provided by extended family members whose involvement with the child is likely to be relatively permanent would nor pose the problem I discuss here.

[42]See Newson, "Unreasonable Care," for discussion of distinctive characteristics of the parent-child relationship important for the child's well-being. She focuses on its long-term nature and the shared history behind continuing interactions.

[43]Rousseau argued against delegating parental responsibilities for education on the grounds that no hired teacher would be sufficiently dedicated to the child's interests. *Emile,* trans. by Allan Bloom (New York: Basic Books, 1979), pp. 49–50.

love. But it is also linked to a conception of the family as the primary source of the individual's sense of self-worth and sense of morality. Within such a conception, parents have a special responsibility to show children they are valued for themselves and not just for the role they fulfill or for their achievements.[44] In contrast, for example, to business firms in which individuals are valued primarily for their contribution to the firm's goals, the family is a place where ideally they are also valued for themselves and for their personal qualities. Parents communicate this sense of individual worth through the love and friendship they extend to their children and through their attitudes toward themselves and their roles in the family. To the extent that parents willingly delegate parental responsibilities to others, they reflect a view of themselves as replaceable functionaries rather than uniquely important members of the family unit.

No less important is the family's special responsibility for moral education. The fundamental moral capacities for trust and for caring, as well as the dispositions to respect certain basic principles of honesty and fidelity to one's word must be nurtured from the beginnings of life. Given the existing structure of social institutions, there is no practical alternative to the family for this basic grounding in morality. The family is the only organization in which membership is sufficiently permanent to provide the constancy and consistency conducive to the development of these basic moral capacities and dispositions. Ideally, of course, morality will be reinforced by other social institutions. But it is doubtful that other institutions can make up for the family's failures in moral education.

In summary, the connections among parental love, parental involvement, and morality are multifaceted. Insofar as morality rests on willingness to care for others for their own sake, it rests on an attitude of love which receives its earliest nurturing through parental example. To the extent that morality involves dispositions to act in certain ways and not others, it is nurtured through the example, instruction, and consistent discipline provided by parents over the long term. Insofar as morality raises questions about how to live and what is valuable, parents can be children's greatest resource.

Parental involvement is essential if the family is to fulfill its role as the primary source of the individual's self-worth and sense of morality. Within this conception, the parent is both a source of love and a moral teacher, and as such, cannot be replaced. While these particular parental responsibilities are not delegable in the ways that many others are, they are not in principle inconsistent with parents' roles as breadwinners, household managers, overseers of childrens' education and health, or with parents' roles outside the family. But they depend on a personal commitment of time that may in practice conflict with the demands of other roles and responsibilities.

A managerial conception of parenthood which appears to be taking hold among some parents permits an easier reconciliation of these competing demands.[45] Unlike the ideal outlined here, the managerial ideal is, in principle, consistent with the delegation of all parental responsibilities.[46] The parental role becomes that of a manager who delegates, coordinates, and monitors performance. Inconsistent with commitment to the intrinsic value of love, the managerial conception also reflects an instrumental view of the individual. Good management dictates that every member of an organization be regarded as replaceable and that substitution of one individual for another not affect its functioning.

Managing children's activities is a very essential task of parenthood, but it is not the only one. If

___

[44]See generally Newson, "Unreasonable Care."

[45]Women in management compare running their families with running their companies. One mother quoted in the *Washingtonian* article cited earlier notes that supervising the care of her children "requires as much management as running my own company." Diane Granat, "Are You My Mommy?" p. 168. The similarities between parents and executives are discussed by Kenneth Keniston and the Carnegie Council on Children in *All Our Children* (New York: Harcourt Brace Jovanovich, 1977), pp. 17–18.

[46]Cynthia Fuchs Epstein concludes from her study of women lawyers that "The women who seemed to thrive the most on the challenge of managing multiple roles were those who experienced the least guilt about delegating duties at work and at home. . . . These women did not tend to brood about the amount of time they spent with their children, but rather defined circumscribed times with children as adequate. . . . "Cynthia Fuchs Epstein, "Multiple Demands and Multiple Roles: The Conditions of Successful Management," in *Spouse, Parent, Worker* ed. by Faye J. Cosby (New Haven: Yale University Press, 1987). pp. 23–43 at 30.

parents come to see themselves primarily as managers of their children's upbringing, not involved personally but only as higher-order supervisors, there is a danger that the distinctive competencies and roles of the family will be lost—that the family will come to be just another organization and the parent, just another functionary.[47] Adopting the managerial conception of parenthood may lead to a reduction in the guilt experienced by parents who spend little time with their children, but it may also lead to morally diminished quality of life for children, parents, and society.[48] To the extent parental love provides the foundation for the moral community in which we live as adults, widespread adoption of the managerial conception of parenthood is a threat to that community.[49]

If this argument is correct, employment practices incompatible with family life must be reassessed. We must recognize that the economic benefits yielded by these practices are won at considerable moral and social expense. Insofar as the operation of the economy depends on the moral fabric of the community, we must consider whether these practices may not be ultimately self-defeating, even from an economic point of view.

VI. Practical Implications: Resolving Parental Guilt

I have outlined a case for the moral ideal of parenthood which I believe lies behind the guilt feelings reported by middle-class professionals. Many parents who are experiencing guilt may not have articulated for themselves these ideals and responsibilities, so pervasive is the view that guilt feelings are irrational and inappropriate. I have tried to show not only that these ideals are not irrational, but that there are strong arguments in their favor. There appear to be very good reasons to regard some parental responsibilities as non-delegable and to support parents who believe that they ought to spend more time with their children. Guilt-plagued parents should not be treated as neurotic or mistaken and sent for counseling to overcome their guilt. Instead, they should be encouraged to reorganize their lives to give expression to deeply held and important familial values and to speak up for patterns of employment that are compatible with fulfilling parental responsibilities as they see them.[50]

From a social point of view, serious reconsideration must be given to the organization of work and to the usual child-care benefits offered by government and private employers. Birth leave, tax breaks through "cafeteria" benefit plans, full-time child-care services, employer-sponsored referral services, sick leave for children's illnesses—the usual benefits discussed—will do nothing to assuage the guilt aroused by regular day-to-day parental absences. That will be dealt with only by rather radical changes in patterns of work and career development. Opportunities for part-time work, self-directed work, job-sharing, and career breaks represent path-breaking steps in the right direction, but these practices must become more widely available and fully institutionalized as normal and acceptable if they are to make a significant contribution to the problem of parental guilt.

The nation's child-care policy must include support for daycare for the many families that need it. However, a policy that focuses only on daycare will not resolve the guilt problem discussed here. This problem will require public policy initiatives that encourage employers to accommodate variable work commitments as well as insurance and benefit plans that do not rigidly exclude part-time workers. It will require employers to take the lead

---

[47]I would agree with philosopher Michael Phillips who notes in passing in his article, "Bribery," ". . . many of us are uncomfortable thinking of the family as just another organization and thinking of a parent as just another functionary." *Ethics* (July 1984), p. 625.

[48]Epstein cites the correspondence between reduction of guilt and willingness to delegate in "Multiple Demands, Multiple Roles."

[49]Annette Barer is quoted as observing that "Rawls' theory like so many other theories of obligation, in the end must take out a loan . . . on the natural virtue of parental love . . . if the just society is to last beyond the first generation." See Owen Flanagan and Kathryn Jackson, "Justice, Care, and Gender: The Kohlberg-Gilligan Debate Revisited," *Ethics*. vol. 97 (1987), pp. 622–37; see p. 630.

[50]Herbert Morris notes that the desire to minimize social disruption is a powerful forte behind the tendency to devalue guilt in contemporary society. Parents should realize that resistance to changing the workplace to accommodate the needs of parents and children may account for ready acceptance of the idea that parental guilt is irrational in today's world. See generally Morris, "The Decline of Guilt," p. 73.

in creating and permitting their employees to create new career patterns. Ultimately, however, such initiatives will succeed only if there is widespread recognition of the moral importance of the parent-child relationship and the value of parents' involvement with their children.

Given the various factors involved in each family situation, it is impossible to say, in general, just how much time it takes to satisfy the parental ideal I have described.[51] However, there is no reason to think that being a good parent takes just the amount of time left over after work is finished or even after normal working hours as conventionally defined in today's business world. Ideological blinders and women's desires to enter the professional and managerial workforce on a par with men have made the issue of time for children a taboo topic. Now that women's competence is no longer in question and now that men are taking on more parental responsibilities, we can perhaps give this matter the attention it deserves.[52]

---

[51]Graduate students at the University of Virginia's Darden School of Business Administration were asked how much time parents should spend with pre-school children each week. The most popular response was 31–50 hours, the answer selected by 47% of the male respondents and 69% of the female respondents. A third of the men and 16% of the women indicated that children should have more than 50 hours a week with a parent. Memorandum, "Results of Survey on Family and Career Issues," Center for the Study of Applied Ethics (now The Olsson Center). The Darden School, Charlottesville, Virginia (May 4, 1984).

[52]Earlier versions of this paper were presented at the 1986 annual meeting of the Society for Applied Philosophy and the March 15, 1988, Scholars Luncheon at Georgetown University's Kennedy Institute of Ethics. I want to thank members of both groups for their criticisms and helpful suggestions. In particular, I am grateful to Henry Richardson for urging me to reconsider the relationships between the intrinsic and instrumental value of parental love. I also appreciate the valuable comments I received from Judith Areen, Norman Bowie, Sidney Callahan, Joseph Fletcher, Kenneth Goodpaster, R. M. Hare, Joel Kupperman, Dennis Thompson, and this journal's anonymous referee.

Questions for Chapter 15

1. Gerson suggests that we recognize the legitimacy of a number of different styles of male parenting. Do you agree that all these different styles are equally legitimate? Explain.

2. Gerson argues that we need effective social supports that can transform men's family involvement from a latent, incipient possibility to expected, unremarkable behavior. Would such policies discriminate against families that have chosen to structure themselves on the "male as breadwinner" model? Do you agree with the claim that if the male is the sole or primary breadwinner he cannot be deeply involved in his family? Why or why not?

3. What does Randels mean by the term *cowboy capitalism?* How does it differ from *Kantian capitalism?*

4. What is Randels's argument for suggesting that capitalism is not irrevocably linked to patriarchy?

5. What does Melé mean when he asserts that the family is a source of real rights? Can a family possess rights or can rights only be possessed by particular individuals?

6. What does Melé think are the rights of the family as regards employment? Do you agree that these are genuine rights? Why or why not?

7. Paine suggests that personal involvement in child-rearing has instrumental moral value for parents. What does she mean and what is her argument in support of this claim?

8. What is Paine's criticism of the prevailing assumption that parental guilt is driven by a moral principle of avoiding harm to children?

Case 15.1 Men and Child-rearing Leave[1]

Gerald Schafer, a teacher, was employed by the Board of Public Education of the School District of Pittsburgh, Pennsylvania, from August 1978 until December 14, 1981. In the early fall of 1981, Schafer requested an unpaid leave of absence for the 1981–1982 school year so that he might pursue child-rearing. Although female employees were routinely granted such leaves, Schafer was advised that males were never granted child-rearing leaves and was told to apply for a ninety-day unpaid emergency leave. Schafer applied for the emergency leave and also for a child-rearing leave to take effect at the end of his emergency leave. He was granted an emergency leave but, toward its end, informed that no child-rearing leave would be forthcoming. On November 30, 1981, Schafer submitted a letter of resignation in which he stated that, in light of his inability to obtain appropriate child care or

[1]Based on Schafer v. Board of Public Education of the School District of Pittsburgh, PA, 903 *Federal Reporter,* 2nd series, 243 (3rd Cir. 1990).

child-rearing leave, he was forced to resign in order to care for his son.

Near the end of December 1981, Schafer did locate day care for his son, but did not at that time request reinstatement. He alleges that this is because he did not believe he had the option to return to his former job. On June 23, 1982, he wrote the Board requesting that the Board reconsider its denial of his leave so he could return to work in September 1982. The Board responded that he was no longer an employee.

Schafer filed a charge of discrimination against the Board. The Board subsequently introduced a policy of granting male employees child-rearing leave on the same basis as it is granted to female employees, but refused to grant Schafer reinstatement and back pay.

1. Should child-rearing leaves be legislated or a matter or negotiation between employers and employees? Justify your answer.
2. Are men equally entitled to child-rearing leaves as women? Why or why not?

Case 15.2 Family Responsibilities and Career Advancement

Large law firms have high overhead costs and, as a consequence, often expect employees to produce high billable hours. Employees are encouraged to put in long hours and to make commitment to work their first priority. This frequently results in employees, especially those beginning their careers, experiencing tension between work and family responsibilities. Typically, part-time work is not encouraged,

since there is a perception that the overhead applicable to a part-time lawyer is only slightly less than a full-time position, but the billable hours produced by a part-timer are far less than those produced by a full-time employee. Those employees who choose part-time work do not tend to be promoted as quickly or advance as far as those who work full-time.

A recent report entitled *Touchstones for Change,*[2] prepared by the Canadian Bar Association Task Force on Gender Equality, challenges a number of common assumptions. It argues that, given the high cost of recruiting and retraining, it makes good sense to facilitate more job flexibility, explore work sharing, and provide greater opportunity for part-time employees to be promoted. It also argues that models of compensation other than billable hours be considered, such as client satisfaction, quality of work, or area of specialization. One of its more controversial suggestions is that lawyers with child-rearing responsibilities should receive reductions of 20 percent or more in hours of work with no reduction in salary. Specifically, it recommends "that law firms provide parental leave benefits and that an employee's entitlement to or eligibility for consideration for available raises, compensation benefits, seniority, admission to partnership and other advancement not be affected while they are on paid parental leave."[3] A further recommendation was that law firms recognize the need for alternate work arrangements for all lawyers with parental responsibili-

[2]*Touchstones for Change: Equality, Diversity and Accountability,* Report of the Canadian Bar Association Task Force on Gender Equality in the Legal Profession (Ottawa, Ontario: The Canadian Bar Association, August 1993).
[3]*Touchstones for Change,* p. 100.

ties and that they provide emergency backup child care for their employees.

1. The Task Force felt that its recommendations would be beyond the ability of small firms or the legal profession to support economically and suggested that the government provide support either through tax exemption or direct subsidy. Does society, through government, have an obligation to provide such support? Is such government support practical if we extend the report's suggestions to other occupations? In light of government deficits, is such support desirable?

2. The Task Force noted that men are taking an increasingly greater role in family responsibilities and recognized that male lawyers are also concerned about balancing their professional and family responsibilities. It argued, however, that women typically bear the lion's share of family responsibilities and that, therefore, the emphasis in the short term should be on altering workplace policies to accommodate women with family responsibilities. Do you agree? Why or why not?

3. Do you feel that it is fair to suggest that a single man or woman who has devoted his or her time and energy to his or her career should enjoy no advantage in career advancement over someone who has chosen to work part-time? Explain your answer.

Further Readings for Chapter 15

Loren Falkenberg and Mary Monachello, "Dual-Career and Dual-Income Families: Do They Have Different Needs?," *Journal of Business Ethics,* 9, 1990, pp. 339–351.

J. H. Greenhaus and N. J. Beutell, "Sources of Conflict Between Work and Family Roles," *Academy of Management Review* 10, 1985, pp. 76–88.

Rosanna Hertz, *More Equal Than Others: Women and Men in Dual-Career Marriages* (Berkeley: University of California Press, 1986).

Kathleen B. Jones, "Socialist-Feminist Theories of the Family," *Praxis International* 8, October 1988, pp. 284–300.

Eva Kittay, "Taking Dependency Seriously: The Family and Medical Leave Act Considered in Light of the Social Organization of Dependency Work and Gender Equality," *Hypatia* 10, 1995, pp. 8–29.

Ian Maitland, "Community Lost," *Business Ethics Quarterly* 8, 1998, pp. 655–670.

Peter Moss and Nickie Fonda, eds., *Work and the Family* (Great Britain: Maurice Temple Smith Ltd., 1980).

INFOTRAC COLLEGE EDITION To learn more about the topics from this chapter, you can use the following words to conduct an electronic search on InfoTrac College Edition, an online library of journals. Here you will find a multitude of articles from various sources and perspectives: *www.infotrac-college.com/wadsworth/access.html*

parental leave

flex time

daycare

Chapter 16

Business
and the Community

Introduction

IN CHAPTER 16 THE ISSUE of the social responsibility of business is explored. Although the term *social responsibility of business* is widely used, its meaning is not entirely clear. In a very general sense, almost any of the ethical constraints upon the pursuit of profit can be viewed as a social responsibility of business. Thus, for instance, fair and honest advertising seems a social responsibility of business. Construed in this way, the term should not be taken to refer to a specific issue, but rather to any obligation arising out of business's interactions with society. When the term is understood in this general sense, discussion of the social responsibility of business focuses on the extent of the ethical constraints on business's pursuit of profit. Some theorists claim that business will fulfill its obligations if it avoids causing harm, or makes reparation for any harm it causes. Other theorists think business has additional obligations, suggesting that these further constraints on the pursuit of profit are grounded in an implicit social contract between business and society.

In a narrower sense, some take the term not to refer to ethical constraints upon the pursuit of profit, but rather to business's presumed obligation to pursue certain social goods independently of seeking profit. Understood in this way, the term *social responsibility of business* generally refers to questions of whether business should act philanthropically and to what degree.

We need, therefore, to distinguish two types of questions in discussing the issue of the social responsibility of business. The first concerns the type and extent of the ethical constraints that govern business's pursuit of profit; the second whether business has moral responsibilities beyond pursuing profit in an ethical manner. Our first two articles deal with the concept of social responsibility defined in what I have called the general sense, that is, questions of what are the ethical constraints upon business's pursuit of profit. Our third article discusses the issue of corporate philanthropy.

In our first selection, Milton Friedman argues that the only social responsibility of business is to achieve profits through open and free competition without deception or fraud. He emphatically rejects any notion of social responsibility defined in what I have called the narrow sense, that is, pursuing social goods independently of seeking profit. In Friedman's view, executives of a company who pursue objectives other than profit act immorally. The money they spend amounts to a tax on the shareholders, and the policies they implement have not been authorized by the democratic process. In effect, they impose taxes and social policy for which they have no mandate.

Robert L. Lippke, in his article "Setting the Terms of the Business Responsibility Debate," contrasts Friedman's view with a conflicting view which holds that there exists a social contract between business and society, requiring business to do more than maximize profits while avoiding deception or fraud. Lippke finds neither view satisfactory. He proposes what he considers a viable compromise. On the one hand, he sides with Friedman in insisting that business should not implement social policy, but rather pursue profits in a principled way. On the other hand, he sides with the social contract approach in insisting that business's unique position in society generates special duties. His basic claim is that we cannot conceive of agents abstractly in discussing their moral responsibilities. In Lippke's view, Friedman is correct to insist that the sole goal of business is to pursue profit through free and open competition. Where Friedman goes wrong, according to Lippke, is in conceiving employer and employee as rough equals in terms of their abilities to affect one another. This may sometimes be the case, but often it is not. When it is not the case, the more powerful party should take into account that there is more to preserving another's autonomy, that is, the ability to take part in free and open competition, than simply avoiding violence or deception.

George Brenkert, in his article "Private Corporations and Public Welfare," argues that the suggestion that business has moral responsibilities beyond pursuing profit in an ethical manner fails to take account of important considerations in the setting of public policy. The basic problem he points to is that those receiving corporate aid typically lack any constitutional voice in the organization helping them. This tends to undermine the democratic setting of public policy, since the policies that are being pursued are not set by individuals who may be voted in or out of office, but rather by private corporations with an agenda that may not reflect the public will.

The Social Responsibility of Business Is to Increase Its Profits

MILTON FRIEDMAN

WHEN I HEAR BUSINESSMEN speak eloquently about the "social responsibilities of business in a free-enterprise system," I am reminded of the wonderful line about the Frenchman who discovered at the age of 70 that he had been speaking prose all his life. The businessmen believe that they are defending free enterprise when they declaim that business is not concerned "merely" with profit but also with promoting desirable "social" ends; that business has a "social conscience" and takes seriously its responsibilities for providing employment, eliminating discrimination, avoiding pollution and whatever else may be the catchwords of the contemporary crop of reformers. In fact they are—or would be if they or anyone else took them seriously—preaching pure and unadulterated socialism. Businessmen who talk this way are unwitting puppets of the intellectual forces that have been undermining the basis of a free society these past decades.

The discussions of the "social responsibilities of business" are notable for their analytical looseness and lack of rigor. What does it mean to say that "business" has responsibilities? Only people can have responsibilities. A corporation is an artificial person and in this sense may have artificial responsibilities, but "business" as a whole cannot be said to have responsibilities, even in this vague sense. The first step toward clarity in examining the doctrine of the social responsibility of business is to ask precisely what it implies for whom.

Presumably, the individuals who are to be responsible are businessmen, which means individual proprietors or corporate executives. Most of the discussion of social responsibility is directed at corporations, so in what follows I shall mostly neglect the individual proprietor and speak of corporate executives.

In a free-enterprise, private-property system, a corporate executive is an employee of the owners of the business. He has direct responsibility to his employers. That responsibility is to conduct the business in accordance with their desires, which generally will be to make as much money as possible while conforming to the basic rules of the society, both those embodied in law and those embodied in ethical custom. Of course, in some cases his employers may have a different objective. A group of persons might establish a corporation for an eleemosynary [charitable] purpose—for example, a hospital or a school. The manager of such a corporation will not have money profit as his objective but the rendering of certain services.

In either case, the key point is that, in his capacity as a corporate executive, the manager is the agent of the individuals who own the corporation or establish the eleemosynary institution, and his primary responsibility is to them.

Needless to say, this does not mean that it is easy to judge how well he is performing his task. But at least the criterion of performance is straightforward, and the persons among whom a voluntary contractual arrangement exists are clearly defined.

Of course, the corporate executive is also a person in his own right. As a person, he may have many other responsibilities that he recognizes or assumes voluntarily—to his family, his conscience, his feelings of charity, his church, his clubs, his city, his country. He may feel impelled by these responsibilities to devote part of his income to causes he regards as worthy, to refuse to work for particular corporations, even to leave his job, for example, to join his country's armed forces. If we wish, we may refer to some of these responsibilities as "social responsibilities." But in these respects he is acting as a principal, not an agent; he is spending his own money or time or energy, not the money of his employers or the time or energy he has contracted to devote to their purposes. If these are "social responsibilities," they are the social responsibilities of individuals, not of business.

What does it mean to say that the corporate executive has a "social responsibility" in his capacity as businessman? If this statement is not pure rhetoric, it must mean that he is to act in some way that is not in the interest of his employers. For example, that he is to refrain from increasing the price of the product in order to contribute to the social objective of preventing inflation, even though a price increase would be in the best interests of the corporation. Or that he is to make expenditures on reducing pollution beyond the amount that is in the best interests of the corporation or that is required by law in order to contribute to the social objective of improving the environment. Or that, at the expense of corporate profits, he is to hire "hard-core" unemployed instead of better-qualified workmen to contribute to the social objective of reducing poverty.

In each of these cases, the corporate executive would be spending someone else's money for a general social interest. Insofar as his actions in accord with his "social responsibility" reduce returns to stockholders, he is spending their money. Insofar as his actions raise the price to customers, he is spending the customers' money Insofar as his actions lower the wages of some employees, he is spending their money.

The stockholders or the customers or the employees could separately spend their own money on the particular action if they wished to do so.

The executive is exercising a distinct "social responsibility," rather than serving as an agent of the stockholders or the customers or the employees, only if he spends the money in a different way than they would have spent it.

But if he does this, he is in effect imposing taxes, on the one hand, and deciding how the tax proceeds shall be spent, on the other.

This process raises political questions on two levels: principle and consequences. On the level of political principle, the imposition of taxes and the expenditure of tax proceeds are governmental functions. We have established elaborate constitutional, parliamentary and judicial provisions to control these functions, to assure that taxes are imposed so far as possible in accordance with the preferences and desires of the public—after all, "taxation without representation" was one of the battle cries of the American Revolution. We have a system of checks and balances to separate the legislative function of imposing taxes and enacting expenditures from the executive function of collecting taxes and administering expenditure programs and from the judicial function of mediating disputes and interpreting the law.

Here the businessman—self-selected or appointed directly or indirectly by stockholders—is to be simultaneously legislator, executive and jurist. He is to decide whom to tax by how much and for what purpose, and he is to spend the proceeds—all this guided only by general exhortations from on high to restrain inflation, improve the environment, fight poverty and so on and on.

The whole justification for permitting the corporate executive to be selected by the stockholders is that the executive is an agent serving the interests of his principal. This justification disappears when the corporate executive imposes taxes and spends the proceeds for "social" purposes. He becomes in effect a public employee, a civil servant, even though he remains in name an employee of a private enterprise. On grounds of political principle, it is intolerable that such civil servants—insofar as their actions in the name of social responsibility are real and not just window-dressing—should be selected as they are now. If they are to be civil servants, then they must be selected through a political process. if they are to impose taxes and make expenditures to foster "social" objectives, then political machinery must be set up to guide the assessment of taxes and to

determine through a political process the objectives to be served.

This is the basic reason why the doctrine of "social responsibility" involves the acceptance of the socialist view that political mechanisms, not market mechanisms, are the appropriate way to determine the allocation of scarce resources to alternative uses.

On the grounds of consequences, can the corporate executive in fact discharge his alleged "social responsibilities"? On the one hand, suppose he could get away with spending the stockholders' or customers' or employees' money. How is he to know how to spend it? He is told that he must contribute to fighting inflation. How is he to know what action of his will contribute to that end? He is presumably an expert in running his company—in producing a product or selling it or financing it. But nothing about his selection makes him an expert on inflation. Will his holding down the price of his product reduce inflationary pressure? Or, by leaving more spending power in the hands of his customers, simply divert it elsewhere? Or, by forcing him to produce less because of the lower price, will it simply contribute to shortages? Even if he could answer these questions, how much cost is he justified in imposing on his stockholders, customers and employees for this social purpose? What is his appropriate share and what is the appropriate share of others?

And, whether he wants to or not, can he get away with spending his stockholders', customers' or employees' money? Will not the stockholders fire him? (Either the present ones or those who take over when his actions in the name of social responsibility have reduced the corporation's profits and the price of its stock.) His customers and his employees can desert him for other producers and employers less scrupulous in exercising their social responsibilities.

The fact of "social responsibility" doctrine is brought into sharp relief when the doctrine is used to justify wage restraint by trade unions. The conflict of interest is naked and clear when union officials are asked to subordinate the interest of their members to some more general social purpose. If the union officials try to enforce wage restraint, the consequence is likely to be wildcat strikes, rank-and-file revolts and the emergence of strong competitors for their jobs. We thus have the ironic phenomenon that union leaders—at least in the

U.S.—have objected to Government interference with the market far more consistently and courageously than have business leaders.

The difficulty of exercising "social responsibility" illustrates, of course, the great virtue of private competitive enterprise—it forces people to be responsible for their own actions and makes it difficult for them to "exploit" other people for either selfish or unselfish purposes. They can do good—but only at their own expense.

Many a reader who has followed the argument this far may be tempted to remonstrate that it is all well and good to speak of government's having the responsibility to impose taxes and determine expenditures for such "social" purposes as controlling pollution or training the hard-core unemployed, but that the problems are too urgent to wait on the slow course of political processes, that the exercise of social responsibility by businessmen is a quicker and surer way to solve pressing current problems.

Aside from the question of fact—I share Adam Smith's skepticism about the benefits that can be expected from "those who affected to trade for the public good"—this argument must be rejected on grounds of principle. What it amounts to is an assertion that those who favor the taxes and expenditures in question have failed to persuade a majority of their fellow citizens to be of like mind and that they are seeking to attain by undemocratic procedures what they cannot attain by democratic procedures. In a free society, it is hard for "good" people to do "good," but that is a small price to pay for making it hard for "evil" people to do "evil," especially since one man's good is another's evil.

I have, for simplicity, concentrated on the special case of the corporate executive, except only for the brief digression on trade unions. But precisely the same argument applies to the newer phenomenon of calling upon stockholders to require corporations to exercise social responsibility (the recent G.M. crusade, for example). In most of these cases, what is in effect involved is some stockholders trying to get other stockholders (or customers or employees) to contribute against their will to "social" causes favored by the activists. Insofar as they succeed, they are again imposing taxes and spending the proceeds.

The situation of the individual proprietor is somewhat different. If he acts to reduce the returns of his enterprise in order to exercise his "social responsibility," he is spending his own money, not someone else's. If he wishes to spend his money on such purposes, that is his right, and I cannot see that there is any objection to his doing so. In the process, he, too, may impose costs on employees and customers. However, because he is far less likely than a large corporation or union to have monopolistic power, any such side effects will tend to be minor.

Of course, in practice the doctrine of social responsibility is frequently a cloak for actions that are justified on other grounds rather than a reason for those actions.

To illustrate, it may well be in the long-run interest of a corporation that is a major employer in a small community to devote resources to providing amenities to that community or to improving its government. That may make it easier to attract desirable employees, it may reduce the wage bill or lessen losses from pilferage and sabotage or have other worthwhile effects. Or it may be that, given the laws about the deductibility of corporate charitable contributions, the stockholders can contribute more to charities they favor by having the corporation make the gift than by doing it themselves, since they can in that way contribute an amount that would otherwise have been paid as corporate taxes.

In each of these—and many similar—cases, there is a strong temptation to rationalizes these actions as an exercise of "social responsibility." In the present climate of opinion, with its widespread aversion to "capitalism," "profits," the "soulless corporation" and so on, this is one way for a corporation to generate goodwill as a by-product of expenditures that are entirely justified in its own self-interest.

It would be inconsistent of me to call on corporate executives to refrain from this hypocritical window-dressing because it harms the foundations of a free society. That would be to call on them to exercise a "social responsibility"! If our institutions, and the attitudes of the public make it in their self-interest to cloak their actions in this way, I cannot summon much indignation to denounce them. At the same time, I can express admiration for those individual proprietors or owners of closely held corporations or stockholders of more broadly held corporations who disdain such tactics as approaching fraud.

Whether blameworthy or not, the use of the cloak of social responsibility, and the nonsense spoken in its name by influential and prestigious businessmen, does clearly harm the foundations of a free society. I have been impressed time and again by the schizophrenic character of many businessmen. They are capable of being extremely farsighted and clear-headed in matters that are internal to their businesses. They are incredibly short-sighted and muddle-headed in matters that are outside their businesses but affect the possible survival of business in general. This short-sightedness is strikingly exemplified in the calls from many businessmen for wage and price guidelines or controls or incomes policies. There is nothing that could do more in a brief period to destroy a market system and replace it by a centrally controlled system than effective governmental control of prices and wages.

The short-sightedness is also exemplified in speeches by businessmen on social responsibility. This may gain them kudos in the short run. But it helps to strengthen the already too prevalent view that the pursuit of profits is wicked and immoral and must be curbed and controlled by external forces. Once this view is adopted, the external forces that curb the market will not be the social consciences, however highly developed, of the pontificating executives; it will be the iron fist of Government bureaucrats. Here, as with price and wage controls, businessmen seem to me to reveal a suicidal impulse.

The political principle that underlies the market mechanism is unanimity. In an ideal free market resting on private property, no individual can coerce any other, all cooperation is voluntary, all parties to such cooperation benefit or they need not participate. There are no "social" values, no "social" responsibilities in any sense other than the shared values and responsibilities of individuals. Society is a collection of individuals and of the various groups they voluntarily form.

The political principle that underlies the political mechanism is conformity. The individual must serve a more general social interest—whether that be determined by a church or a dictator or a majority. The individual may have a vote and a say in what is to be done, but if he is overruled, he must conform. It is appropriate for some to require others to contribute to a general social purpose whether they wish to or not.

Unfortunately, unanimity is not always feasible. There are some respects in which conformity appears unavoidable, so I do not see how one can avoid the use of the political mechanism altogether.

But the doctrine of "social responsibility" taken seriously would extend the scope of the political mechanism to every human activity. It does not differ in philosophy from the most explicitly collectivist doctrine. It differs only by professing to believe that collectivist ends can be attained without collectivist means. That is why, in my book *Capitalism and Freedom,* I have called it a "fundamentally subversive doctrine" in a free society, and have said that in such a society. "there is one and only one social responsibility of business—to use its resources and engage in activities designed to increase its profits so long as it stays within the rules of the game, which is to say, engages in open and free competition without deception or fraud."

Setting the Terms of the Business Responsibility Debate

ROBERT L. LIPPKE

THERE ARE TWO APPROACHES to determining the limits of business moral responsibility that are quite prevalent in the literature of business ethics.

One of these approaches, initially suggested by Milton Friedman, and recently rejuvenated by Douglas J. Den Uyl, involves conceiving of business

From Social Theory and Practice *11(3), Fall 1985. Reprinted with modifications by permission of the author* and Social Theory and Practice.

people as constrained to deliberate and act in ways that are only minimally demanding.[1] So long as business people avoid harming others in certain traditional and obvious ways, and live up to their agreements, nothing else is (morally) required of them. The second approach, advocated by Thomas Donaldson and Norman Bowie, shares certain basic tenets both historically and logically with the first approach.[2] However, utilizing the device of a social contract, the second approach adds responsibilities commensurate with the economic, social, and political power of business people. Hence, on the second approach, the responsibilities of business people are held to exceed those of moral agents in other contexts.

After sketching the logic of these two approaches, I will argue that the first approach is more defensible than the second. Then, I will contend that the real debate over the limits of business moral responsibility is between the first approach and a third approach, the outlines of which I will also sketch. While retaining the normative moral principles of the first approach, this third approach builds in a concern for the considerable power and influence of some agents (for example, business people) that the second approach acknowledges, but fails to incorporate adequately. In addition to indicating the plausibility of this third approach as a model for the analysis of business moral responsibility, I will show why the debate between it and the first approach turns on a solution to issues like the moral status of property rights and the nature of economic justice. While I will not try to address these difficult ethical issues in this paper, I do hope to show that they cannot be sidestepped in determining the limits of business moral responsibility.

The first and second approaches both have their origins in the writings of classic liberals like Hobbes, Locke, and Mill. Both approaches are predicated on what might be termed an "abstract individuals" conception of moral agency. This involves initially conceiving of moral agents independently of the more concrete social, economic, and political relations they have to one another. Put another way, agents are conceived of independently of the specific causal chains they are in a position to initiate. So conceived, agents are seen as rough equals in terms of their abilities to affect one another. This conception is then combined with some traditional liberal ethical assumptions:

> . . . individuals are in an important sense "ends in themselves." On this theory, to be an "end in oneself" means that no one's purposes are subservient to or a means to the purposes of other individuals or groups. Each person is free to pursue his or her own ends provided those ends do not prevent others from being able to formulate purposes of their own.[3]

An emphasis on freedom and autonomy is at the heart of both general approaches. This emphasis, along with the commitment to the equal moral worth of persons, yields a familiar set of moral constraints on action. The constraints prohibit killing, violence, coercion, fraud, and deception, and thereby secure persons from the sorts of harms and interferences that might defeat their freedom (understood in terms of the range and quality of options effectively open to them) and their autonomy (understood in terms of their ability to form and execute a rational life-plan).

Importantly, these constraints, if generally observed, can be seen as making possible a free enterprise system where persons engage in only those business transactions they freely and rationally choose to engage in. Often, those in the classic liberal tradition wrap individuals in moral rights that are seen as the basis or ground of these moral constraints. Hence, depending on the author, one will find an emphasis on rights to freedom and autonomy rather than on obligations to not interfere with freedom and autonomy. Little seems to turn on these differences in emphasis, though as we will see, some might wish to argue otherwise.

Further moral constraints on action derive from the voluntary agreements of persons. The operative notion is that of *consent*. Persons are the rightful possessors of their time, energy and efforts. As

---

[1]Milton Friedman, *Capitalism and Freedom* (Chicago: The University of Chicago Press, 1962), see especially the Introduction and Chapter 1. Douglas J. Den Uyl. *The New Crusaders: The Corporate Social Responsibility Debate* (Bowling Green State University: The Social Philosophy and Policy Center, 1984), pp. 24–26.
[2]Thomas Donaldson, *Corporations and Morality* (Englewood Cliffs, NJ: Prentice-Hall, Inc., 1982), pp. 18–57. Norman Bowie, "Changing the Rules," in Tom L. Beauchamp and Norman E. Bowie, (eds.), *Ethical Theory and Business* (Englewood Cliffs, NJ: Prentice-Hall, Inc., 1983), pp. 103–106.

[3]Den Uyl, *New Crusaders,* p. 24.

such, these resources can only be construed as under moral constraint where persons themselves have placed them under constraint by consent.[4] Putting all of this together, we get the first approach to the limits of business moral responsibility, as neatly summarized by DeGeorge:

> Providing its actions do not harm anyone, and providing its transactions are fair, the corporation is a morally acceptable kind of entity. . . .[5]

The transactions of business people will be fair so long as they are reached through "free and open competition, without deception or fraud."[6]

Additionally, those attracted to this first approach revolt at the suggestion of any responsibility on the part of business people to serve non-contracted-to noneconomic ends. Friedman is famous for thumbing his nose at such proposals, stressing the fiduciary role of management vis-à-vis the property rights of the stockholders.[7] In keeping with the logic of this first approach, Narveson sweepingly rejects the idea of corporate responsibility to aid the less fortunate in society by citing the lack of any agreement "struck on terms of mutual self-interest" between business people and the less fortunate.[8]

Up to this point, the moral responsibilities of business people supported by the first approach, though not insignificant, are nonetheless quite modest. Let us call this approach the "Abstract Individuals Approach" (*AIA*). Aware that the effects of business activity often outstrip those wrought by ordinary agents, some writers have sought to utilize the notion of a *social contract* to add responsibility beyond those the *AIA* supports. The "Social Contract Approach" (*SCA*) initially conceives of individual moral agents abstractly, but employs the time-honored notion of *consent* to add constraints on business activity commensurate with the social and economic power and influence of business. Donaldson and Bowie both contend that the *ground* of these further responsibilities (for example, minimizing pollution and the depletion

of natural resources) is a social contract between business and society.[9]

The *SCA* is an extension of the logic of the *AIA*. This extension immediately runs into serious problems when the nature of this contract is queried, as one supporter of the *AIA* has pointed out.[10] Is this contract supposed to be an actual or explicit contract! Bowie cites the existence of the corporate charter as evidence of the reality of this contract. Ostensibly, the claim is that by obtaining a charter, those who form a corporation agree to do more than simply avoid malfeasance and honor their business contracts. Yet, as Hessen shows, the articles of incorporation require no such promise or agreement on the part of those who form a corporation.[11] In the main, certain kinds of factual information are all that is required, and Hessen claims that where that information is given, the relevant state official has little or no discretionary power:

> He cannot demand any additional information; he cannot extract any oath of corporate allegiance to the public interest; he cannot even refuse to certify the corporate charter.[12]

If these claims are correct any argument that relies on the existence of the corporate charter to expand the responsibilities of business people beyond those implied by the *AIA* seems most unpromising.

Moreover, the move to an *implied* contract is laden with difficulties.[13] A thorough investigation of the conditions under which an individual can properly be said to *imply* her agreement to something would take us well beyond the scope of this article. This much is clear, however. In order for an agreement to be implied by a set of circumstances, the agents involved must be in a position to have a fairly determinate idea of what the provisions of the agreement are. It is primarily on this point that the implied *SCA* surely flounders. Are those who apply for a corporate charter supposed to be aware that they are to serve the "public interest," whatever that is? Or, are they supposed to recognize (and

[4]Ibid., pp. 24–25.
[5]Richard T. DeGeorge, *Business Ethics* (New York: Macmillan Publishing Co., Inc., 1982), p. 133.
[6]Friedman, *Capitalism and Freedom,* p. 133.
[7]Ibid., p. 135.
[8]Jan Narveson, "Justice and the Business Society," in Beauchamp and Bowie, *Ethical Theory and Business,* 613–21, p. 617.
[9]Donaldson, *Corporations and Morality,* pp. 41–49, Bowie "Changing the Rules," p. 103.
[10]Den Uyl, *New Crusaders,* pp. 12–19. Den Uyl makes further damaging criticisms of the *SCA.*
[11]Robert Hessen, *In Defense of the Corporation* (Stanford, CA: Hoover Institution Press, 1979), pp. 25–26.
[12]Ibid., p. 25.
[13]Bowie, "Changing the Rules," p. 105.

how, exactly?) that their responsibilities do not end with those supported by the *AIA,* or by existing norms and practices? Are these matters we could hold any normal business person knows (or has reason to know) the forms and limits of?[14] I think not.

In the political-legal domain, the notion of implied consent has often been used to ground obligation to the law on the part of citizens. However, even if we grant the cogency of such an argument in that domain, carrying it over to the business domain is no easy matter.[15] At least in the political-legal domain, citizens can pretty straightforwardly find out what they have "agreed" to, by consulting constitutions, positive law, and case law. But there seem to be no comparable sources for business people to rely on in order for them to apprise themselves of the provisions of their implied agreement. Indeed, debate about what the "public interest" consists in, or about what business people have implied their agreement to, is likely to be protracted, and for that reason, the implied *SCA* seems unattractive.

Donaldson is not averse to employing the notion of an "abstract" contract between society and what he calls "productive organizations."[16] The difficulty with such a move has been forcefully pressed by Dworkin.[17] While an actual or implied agreement might bind agents (if made under certain conditions), it is not clear what independent obligatory force an abstract or hypothetical agreement has. At best, the notion of an abstract agreement seems a device to call attention to an independent argument of some kind. What is that argument in this case? It cannot involve the existence of the corporate charter for the reasons already cited. Neither will it do to cite corporate use of society's infrastructure. Corporations pay taxes to cover that use, so why should their responsibilities extend beyond those of other taxpayers?

Nor will it suffice to simply invoke the idea that property is "society's" to divide up, dole out, and determine the legitimate uses of. For one thing, there is a long, venerable tradition against this interpretation of property rights. But even if there were not, it is far from clear how such a premise can aid in establishing the conclusions of those who opt for the *SCA.*[18]

My suggestion is that the use of *consent* in attempting to ground responsibilities should be kept within strict limits. Actual or implied consent may establish specific responsibilities for agents, or may release agents from responsibilities that would otherwise be binding on them. Once one starts to invoke consent to ground more open ended or vague responsibilities (for example, to serve the public interest), the argument becomes problematic. Fairness requires that agents have some determinate idea of what they have or have not consented to. When this is not the case, consent becomes a device for adding (or subtracting) responsibilities on the whims of those who can offer no substantial argument as to why such an addition (or subtraction) is justified.

Though I have sided with supporters of the *AIA* against supporters of the *SCA,* I think the latter are onto something of considerable importance. Those who favor the *SCA* are aware that many business people (especially those situated in large corporate power structures) have access to resources, technology, and labor power on a scale that no adequate accounting of their responsibilities should ignore. Yet, if the *SCA* is defective, what is to replace it?

In its place I want to offer a model for analyzing the responsibilities of business people that I will call the "Social Niche Approach" (*SNA*). According to the *SNA,* it is usually a mistake to conceive of persons abstractly in attempting to delineate their moral responsibilities. Persons always have a social niche, that is, a set of concrete social, economic, political, and historical relations to other persons. In a variety of ways, and with varying magnitudes, these relations determine persons' abilities to affect others' lives and interests. As we have seen, on the *AIA,* violence, deception,

---

[14]For instance, if at one time it was common practice, as it likely was, to expose employees to unsafe working conditions, would an implied contract oblige employers to act in a way that was contrary to such an established practice?

[15]Even in the political-legal sphere, the presence of factors like poverty, language-barriers, etc., raises questions about whether one who has continued to live under a political-legal system can unproblematically be said to have implied her consent to abide by its laws and institutions.

[16]Donaldson, *Corporations and Morality,* pp. 41–42.

[17]Ronald Dworkin, *Taking Rights Seriously* (Cambridge, MA: Harvard University Press, 1977), p. 151.

[18]It is also not at all clear how the privileges gained by incorporation (namely, entity status, perpetual duration, and limited tort liability for stockholders) establish any sort of obligation to serve wider interests.

and fraud are taken to pretty much exhaust wrongful interference. This, I think, ignores many of the more subtle ways in which positions of power and influence are used to initiate causal chains that affect the freedom and autonomy of others. The *SNA* fastens on relevant differentials in power, influence, and ability, and tailors an agent's moral responsibilities accordingly.[19]

In other words, the *SNA* spells out the theoretical underpinnings of the notion that increased power brings with it increased responsibility, but without grounding that increased responsibility in *consent*. Building on the normative moral principles of the *AIA* (namely, principles requiring respect for the freedom and autonomy of individuals), the *SNA* draws attention to the real world of concretized agents that the *AIA* ignores. Of course, these moral principles could be challenged as well, but doing so would take me beyond the scope of the paper. My aim is to propose the *SNA* as a plausible alternative model for analyzing the responsibilities of business people. Thus, the *SNA,* like the *SCA,* can be seen as a development of the *AIA.*

The idea behind the *SNA* is the following: if the function of moral constraints on action is to secure the freedom and autonomy of persons, then the *SNA* can be understood as requiring that we consider the social niche of agents in determining what constraints are applicable to their decisions and actions. Attention to the social niche of agents prevents moral responsibility from being reduced to lowest common denominator terms—that is, to the ways in which abstract individuals are constrained to act toward others. According to the *SNA,* it is inappropriate to characterize an agent's responsibilities independently of an empirical investigation of that agent's social niche.[20]

The implications of the *SNA* can best be illustrated by considering some examples of the ways in which the social niche of some agents determines their ability to affect others in morally significant ways: (1) Some business people routinely make decisions about what natural resources to develop and at what rates. Obviously, these decisions may affect the range and quality of options open to both present and future persons, as well as their ability to execute rational life-plans. In the case of future persons, the limitations of the *AIA* are especially apparent. Conceived abstractly, agents are not likely to be seen as able to significantly affect the life-prospects of many future persons. To object here that the ramifications of any single decision by a business person in this area are slight and perhaps unforeseeable no doubt raises an important point. In some cases (though not all), it is the aggregate effects of many decisions that are significant. But this may only show that what is needed is a framework of public policy to funnel these decisions in a direction conducive to minimizing the adverse effects of decisions made on the basis of a business's self-interest. In such cases, the responsibility of business persons is to support (or at least not resist) the implementation of such a public policy, and to abide by it once it is implemented. (2) Decisions about what technology to use in the production of goods and services may have significant adverse implications for the freedom and autonomy of employees. The concerns expressed by Donaldson and others about the dulling or stifling of initiative and creativity, and the loss of a sense of responsibility or of a sense of self-worth, can all be accommodated by the *SNA.* The ability to form and execute a rational life-plan is surely threatened by the atrophy of abilities brought about by some working conditions. It is also threatened by an agent's loss of the sense that it is important to control his own destiny, or by his loss of the sense that he is able to do so. Also, exposing employees to hazardous chemicals, or to noise and pollution whose effects take years to manifest themselves threatens their freedom, if we assume that being diseased or disabled limits the range and quality of options open to them. All of these more subtle effects are less likely to be seen as morally significant if the *AIA* is uncritically adhered to.

---

[19]The *SNA* has certain affinities to the approach to business moral responsibility articulated by David Braybrooke in *Ethics in the World of Business* (Totowa, NJ: Rowman and Allanheld, 1983), see especially pp. 145–46.

[20]Instead of attributing responsibilities to organizations like corporations, I prefer to attribute them to individuals *within* such organizations. It is within the context of such an organization that agents have access to resources, technology, and labor power. That agents within an organization must often share responsibilities with superiors and subordinates complicates attributions of responsibility a bit. It seems reasonable to say that one of the responsibilities of business people will be to ensure that procedures and mechanisms necessary to fulfill their shared responsibilities are established and maintained within a corporation. On this, see Kenneth E. Goodpaster, "The Concept of Corporate Responsibility," *Journal of Business Ethics Vol. 2* (1983): 1–22.

(3) The use of sophisticated advertising techniques, and what Braybrooke refers to as the "aggregate and cumulative effects" of advertisements, raise serious questions about the ability of persons to resist the self-serving and in many cases arguably harmful messages promulgated.[21] The sorts of non-rational persuasion used by advertisers would likely be seen as objectionable if used by political regimes out to promote their interests—especially in the absence of countervailing information. Yet, why not raise the same objections to the increasing use of corporate resources to affect the thought-processes and emotional responses of consumers? Again, the access to resources and the sheer volume of advertisements this makes possible seem to outstrip the confines of the *AIA*. (4) Relevant here also are decisions about plant closings or the automation of jobs long held by persons. It can be argued that in making decisions about these matters, business people have an obligation to take into account the effects of their actions on the range and quality of options left open to employees.[22] The *SNA* brings this argument into sharper focus. That business people may find such moral requirements unusual may only show their allegiance to existing moral standards, or to the *AIA*. Also, that an agent's social niche has historical dimensions serves to reinforce the contention that the symbiotic relationship that develops between a plant and a community is morally relevant to closing decisions. The unilateral termination of such a relationship, especially when this occurs without warning and without efforts to ameliorate its effects, seems a type of ingratitude that is condemnable. The sense that employees and other members of the community *deserve* better than this can be accounted for in terms of the idea that those who make plant closing decisions in this manner fail to return the sort of treatment that has been the reciprocal *status quo*.

While the preceding examples illustrate some of the implications of adopting the *SNA*, much needs to be said by way of further elaborating on and defending it. Let me undertake these tasks by considering several counterarguments to the *SNA*.

One likely response by supporters of the *AIA* will be predicated on the notion that the adverse effects of business activity that the *SNA* calls attention to are not ones that persons have moral rights protecting them from. Or, supporters of the *AIA* might concede that persons have moral rights in these areas, but insist that the property rights of stockholders outweigh such rights. Neither of these objections is conclusive in the absence of solutions to some more fundamental normative ethical problems.

The first objection leads us to consider the *basis* or *ground* of moral rights. On this, a variety of normative ethical approaches is available. Regardless of which one is chosen, it is hard to imagine how the kinds of effects mentioned in the preceding examples can be in principle distinguished from the effects of more traditional harmful actions (for example, violence, deception, fraud). It will not do for supporters of the *AIA* to maintain that because such affects are unusual (especially if one conceives of matters via the *AIA*) they are not right-protected. For why should their unusualness matter?[23]

The second objection admits the moral relevance of these adverse effects, and perhaps their overridingness in other contexts, but throws up property rights as a trump card to sweep all such considerations aside. As Den Uyl rightly points out, critics of business cannot simply assume that the property rights of stockholders must yield to demands for greater corporate responsibility.[24] However, supporters of the *AIA* equally cannot assume that property rights inevitably outweigh other rights. One notorious difficulty with rights-talk is that many who resort to it offer little guidance as to how moral rights are to be ranked—or if one prefers—qualified in ways that render them congruent with one another. This is something that it seems any adequate ethical theory must do, and given the enormity of the undertaking, something supporters of the *AIA* might be excused for having failed to do. Nonetheless, the point remains that invoking property rights at this juncture is, at best, the beginning of an argument against the implications of the *SNA*, nothing more. Whatever considerations may be offered in support of prop-

---

[21] Braybrooke, *Ethics,* pp. 327–28.

[22] John P. Kavanagh, "Ethical Issues in Plant Relocation," in Beauchamp and Bowie, *Ethical Theory and Business,* pp. 106–14.

[23] See William T. Blackstone, "Ethics and Ecology," in Beauchamp and Bowie, *Ethical Theory and Business,* pp. 411–18. Blackstone argues that the right to a livable environment emerged with an awareness of the impact of potentially damaging technology.

[24] Den Uyl, *New Crusaders,* p. 33.

erty rights will have to be systematically examined and weighed against the considerations supporting other rights.[25]

Once all of these considerations are taken into account, it is far from clear that property rights will prevail over the other rights the *SNA* calls attention to. This is especially true in the case of stockholders' property rights. In some cases, the money they invest is arguably surplus property—that is, property over and above what they require to meet their basic needs or promote their most vital interests. Also, it is part of the commonly accepted ideology of the stockmarket that there is risk involved. Presumably, those who invest often have other (perhaps less lucrative) options open to them that are less risky, and in this way they differ from employees or other members of the community who may be harmed by business activities.[26]

However, leaving the two preceding points aside, there are other reasons why it is surely not inevitable that the stockholders' rights will prevail. The adverse effects the *SNA* focuses attention on are far from insignificant. The loss of a sense of self-worth, damage to one's health, interference with one's capacity to make rational, autonomous choices, and so on, all seem more significant, morally speaking, than what may only amount to a decline in the value of one's investments. Why this is so is not hard to discover. The former sorts of effects undercut the capacity to work at all, and thus acquire property. Or, they injure a person's ability to use and enjoy whatever property he or she has managed to acquire. Even where a sizeable portion of stockholder investments are of things like pension funds, which do affect investors' most vital interests, it is important to not exaggerate the conflict that must be theoretically resolved. It will generally not be the case that accommodating the rights of employees and members of the public will require that stockholders' investments be wholly jeopardized. Rather, stockholders may simply have

to accept somewhat less in earnings if the rights of others are to be respected.

It will also not do for supporters of the *AIA* to contend that most persons have consented to suffering the sorts of adverse effects not prohibited by the *AIA*. For one thing, this contention has the familiar ring of open-ended (and therefore indeterminate) consent, and thus suffers from the defects noted earlier. Second, while we cannot embark here on an examination of the difficult matter of stating the conditions under which persons can be said to freely undertake risks, the following points are pertinent: (1) Those to be adversely affected must know of the dangers or it must be reasonable to say they should have known. It seems likely that there will be (and have been) many cases of harmful business activity of the sort the *SNA* calls attention to where this epistemic condition is not satisfied. (2) Those to be adversely affected must have other options open to them that it is reasonable for them to choose so as to avoid suffering the effects. Notice that with respect to the agreements or contracts of business people, the contrast between the *AIA* and the *SNA* is informative. Because of the sometimes enormous differences in power that exist between business persons and those they deal with, the former are able to gain agreements on terms highly favorable to their interests at the expense of others' interests. Where all agents are conceived abstractly, they appear as rough equals, with none in a position to force or hold out for extremely favorable terms. The differentials in power that the *SNA* calls attention to raise questions about the voluntariness of certain exchanges. In cases where business people are in a position to determine the range and quality of options open to those they deal with, the issue whether an agreement is made under duress must be considered. For instance, if a firm threatens to close a plant unless concessions on working conditions are made by the employees' union, it is relevant to assessing the voluntariness of such an agreement to consider the other options open to the employees. Suppose that short of unemployment and its attendant hardships, there are none, and that the concessions on working conditions render the work significantly more dangerous. Can we say simply that the employees have "consented" to suffering such adverse effects if they make the concessions? It seems we cannot. After all, if the adverse effects are ones that persons have a right not to suffer, then an "agreement" forged under such

---

[25]If one conceives of property only in terms of individuals' personal effects (for example, houses, automobiles, clothes), the moral constraints of the *AIA* may appear sufficient. However, the employment of property as means of production has consequences that outstrip the confines of the *AIA*. [26]Admittedly, some assumptions made by investors would have to be changed under the *SNA* because of the greater constraints on business activity the approach supports. However, I see no reason to believe that people would refuse to invest where such constraints are taken seriously.

conditions is surely morally suspect. Perhaps the firm cannot fairly be held responsible for the lack of other viable options open to the employees. This may be a matter on which collective social action is necessary and appropriate. But, it does seem plausible to say that the situation is one that the firm is not morally at liberty to exploit.[27] (3) Related to the preceding, the inability to prevent the suffering of adverse effects should not be taken as equivalent to consenting to them. Employees or members of the general public may know that industries hire lobbyists to promote exclusively industry interests, but lack the resources to effectively counter such activities on the part of business persons.

A third objection to the potentially demanding responsibilities of the *SNA* receives impetus from an alleged crucial difference between types of moral requirements. The constraints supported by the *AIA* might be seen as defensible ones because they are largely negative in character, requiring agents simply to refrain from harming or interfering with others (plus honoring their agreements). The constraints do not require agents to invest their time, energy, or other resources in efforts to aid others. As we have seen, Friedman and others will insist that it is not appropriate for management to use corporate resources to pursue social causes of management's (perhaps idiosyncratic, or worse, objectionable) choosing. Better, so the argument goes, that business people refrain from harming others and attend to safeguarding the property rights of the stockholders.

This line of reasoning involves a number of confusions and unargued for assumptions. First, it tries to draw a distinction between what some have called "negative injunctions" and "affirmative duties," and then suggest that the former can be satisfied by doing nothing.[28] However, the inaction/action distinction is not the same as the negative injunction/affirmative duty distinction. In reality, adherence to even the negative injunctions will require agents to do things—to allocate time, energy, and resources in some ways rather than others. For instance, treating employees with only minimal respect will require business people to pay them adequately, deal with unsafe working conditions, institute fair evaluation procedures, and the like. Similarly, avoiding fraud or deception may require business persons to advertise and sell their products in some (perhaps more costly) ways than others.

The negative injunction/affirmative duty distinction is actually aimed at capturing the difference between adverse effects that an agent himself causes (or might cause) and ones that are caused in other ways, but regarding which an agent could do something to help lessen or alleviate. It may be that any plausible ethical theory will seek to restrict the range of affirmative duties agents have lest they become overburdened by moral demands on their time, energy, and resources.[29] But that is different from requiring agents to concern themselves with effects that they themselves cause. In essence, the *SNA* calls attention to the unusual and varied range of causal chains that some agents are in a position to initiate.[30]

Also, though management's fiduciary role poses serious obstacles to attempts to apply the concept of affirmative duties to business people, it is important to note the larger issue that lurks just beneath the surface. We might admit that if the property rights of stockholders always withstand moral scrutiny, then Friedman's argument is compelling. However, that is certainly a problematic "if." It seems clear that property holdings are greatly influenced by factors that are largely beyond any

---

[27]Even where duress is not present, and so the issue of consent is not directly relevant, a further question about the fairness of contracts can be raised. Courts have held that a contract may be "unconscionable." The reasoning behind such cases seems in part to be that the terms of an agreement may be so substantively unfair to one of the parties that the agreement should be considered void. Such agreements seem more likely to occur between parties of unequal economic (or other) power. Though relevant to my discussion, the philosophical problems unconscionability raises are too complex to attempt an analysis of here. For a discussion that is somewhat crucial of the courts' decisions, see Charles Fried, *Contract as Promise* (Cambridge, MA: Harvard University Press, 1981), pp. 103–109.

[28]On this, see John G. Simon, Charles W. Powers, Jon P. Gunneman, "The Responsibilities of Corporations and Their Owners," in Beauchamp and Bowie, *Ethical Theory and Business,* pp. 86–93.

[29]Simon, Powers, Gunneman, "Responsibilities of Corporations," pp. 88–90.

[30]Importantly, my acceptance of the distinction between negative injunctions and affirmative duties indicates one reason why the *SNA* does *not* rely on a "can implies ought" inference. Also, I admit that where those who suffer adverse effects on their freedom and autonomy have consented to risk such effects, agents responsible for initiating the relevant causal chains have no obligation to refrain from doing so, though they can refrain from doing so.

given individual's control. Factors such as a person's native talents, socioeconomic starting point, and the occurrence of past injustices may all have a significant effect on property acquisitions. Also, it is apparent that collective efforts can be undertaken to modify the influence of these factors. The question then is whether justice requires such collective efforts, and to what extent, or are we simply to allow such factors to have their full impact on property holdings? Property holdings determine both the range and quality of options open to persons, and influence their ability to execute effectively rational life-plans. These effects on freedom and autonomy, combined with the seeming moral arbitrariness of allowing such factors to determine life-prospects, makes it plausible to contend that some collective efforts are warranted.

Of course, any such changes in public policy, or in the structuring of the basic institutions in society, are matters that go well beyond the responsibilities of business people. On this point, Friedman is certainly correct when he warns against asking business people to be the agents of social change. Still, there will be one very important responsibility of business people if justice requires some modification of property holdings—namely to refrain from using their considerable power (perhaps at the stockholders' behest) to undermine or obstruct such collective efforts. Admittedly, it is hard to be optimistic that such a responsibility is one that will be fondly embraced by business people.

There is one further counterargument that I will only briefly deal with. It might be alleged that by requiring business people to observe only the constraints of the *AIA,* greater benefits will accrue to all persons over the long term. This rather crude teleological argument suffers from a number of defects. Chief among them is that there is no attempt to demonstrate that those who suffer in some way because only minimal constraints are adhered to are the ones who subsequently receive some of the allegedly greater benefits. It is reasonable in some cases to ask an individual to accept a loss in the short term if that loss will be outweighed by a future benefit. Yet, where there is no such linkage of short-term losses with long-term benefits, the imposition of a loss seems unjustifiable. By contrast, the *SNA* secures all individuals from losses in a more certain and equal fashion.

In conclusion, I have tried to establish the *SNA* as a legitimate contender with the *AIA* in the debate over the limits of business moral responsibility. I have also suggested that resolution of that debate will force us to focus squarely on a variety of fundamental issues in ethics and social philosophy. It seems to me that supporters of the *AIA* and the *SCA* have tried in different ways to sidestep those difficult issues. If the arguments I have offered are sound, then it is precisely to issues like the ground of moral rights and the nature of economic justice that the business responsibility debate must turn.[31]

---

[31]I am grateful to the referees who read this paper for making some valuable suggestions about how to improve it.

Private Corporations and Public Welfare

GEORGE G. BRENKERT

I

THE DOCTRINE OF corporate social responsibility comes in many varieties.[1] Its most developed version demands that corporations help alleviate "public welfare deficiencies," by which is understood problems of the inner city, drug problems, poverty, crime, illiteracy, lack of sufficient funding for educational institutions, inadequate health care delivery systems, chronic unemployment, etc.

In short, social responsibility, it is contended, requires that corporations assume part of the

---

[1]"Private corporation" will be used to refer exclusively to private corporations engaged in the production of goods and services for profit.

From Public Affairs Quarterly 6(2), April 1992. *Reprinted by permission.*

responsibility for the basic prerequisites of individual and social life within a community or society. Social responsibility demands this even though, it is claimed, corporations are not causally responsible for these conditions and doing so may not enhance their profits.

In response, corporations today provide job training for the hard-core unemployed, help renovate parks, sponsor clean-up programs, establish manufacturing plants in ghetto areas, offer seminars to high school students on how effectively to seek employment, support minority business adventures, provide educational films as well as additional instructors and tutors to public schools (i.e. "adopt" schools), etc.[2]

Such projects have, seemingly, met with a great deal of approval. Indeed, during a time when the welfare of many is deficient, one wonders how anyone could object to such activities. It might seem that any objections to such corporate behavior would stem not from their participating in these activities, but from their not participating even more.

Nevertheless, a number of objections to corporations engaging in such activities have been raised and are well-known. Many of these criticisms are not very good and will not be reviewed here. There is, however, one objection that is much more interesting, even if it is rarely developed. The essence of this objection is that corporate social responsibility to produce directly the public welfare involves the illegitimate encroachment of private organizations into the public realm. There is much greater merit to it than might appear at first glance.

II

This objection takes various forms. Theodore Levitt, for example, claims that the essence of free enterprise is the production of high-level profits.

Private business corporations tend to impose this narrowly materialistic view on whatever they touch. Accordingly, corporate responsibility for welfare threatens to reduce pluralism and to create a monolithic society.[3] George C. Lodge similarly maintains that "the demand that business apply itself to problems which government is finding it increasingly difficult to comprehend or affect . . . is . . . absurd. Corporations, whatever else they may be, are not purveyors of social assistance."[4] Unelected businessmen, he claims, have "neither the right nor the competence" to define or establish the goals and the criteria by which society should repair or remake itself.[5] Finally, Richard DeGeorge claims that

> there is great danger in expecting corporations to take upon themselves the production of public welfare, because they already have enormous power and are not answerable for its use to the general public. Politicians are elected by the public and are expected to have the common good as their end. We should not expect corporations to do what they are neither competent nor organized to do. . . .[6]

These criticisms question the right as well as the competence of corporations to contribute directly to the public welfare. Further, they challenge the influence which corporations in so acting may gain over society. Both increased corporate power and a decrease of social pluralism are feared results.[7]

Unfortunately, these criticisms are, more often than not, simply noted, rather than elaborated upon. In particular, the suggestion implicit within them that the provision of public welfare by private corporations runs afoul of an important distinction between what is public and what is private has not been discussed in recent literature. It is this point which requires greater attention.

The argument offered here is that corporate responsibility for public welfare threatens to reduce, transform, and in some cases eliminate

---

[2]Sandra L. Holmes reports in a study of how executives perceive social responsibility that 78% of the executives surveyed either strongly agreed or agreed more than they disagreed with the statement that "Business possesses the ability and means to be a *major* force in the alleviation of social problems" (pp. 39–40). It is clear from the context that by "social problems" is meant the kinds of problems listed in the text under "public welfare." Cf. Sandra L. Holmes, "Executive Perceptions of Corporate Social Responsibility," *Business Horizons* (June, 1976).

[3]Theodore Levitt, "The Dangers of Social Responsibility," *Harvard Business Review,* vol. 36 (September–October, 1958), pp. 44–47.
[4]George C. Lodge, *The New American Ideology* (New York: Alfred A. Knopf, 1975), p. 189.
[5]Ibid., p. 190. Cf., also p. 218.
[6]DeGeorge, *Business Ethics,* 3rd ed. (New York: Macmillan Publishing Co., 1986), p. 171.
[7]Cf. Levitt, "The Dangers of Social Responsibility."

important public dimensions of social life. For this reason we must be wary of it and reluctant to accept it in its present forms. Several characteristics of this argument should be noted at the outset. First, it does not pretend to show that all corporate measures that address public welfare deficiencies are (by themselves or individually) wrong, mischievous, or mistaken. Still, we must not be overly impressed by particular instances and thereby miss the systematic and general implications that are thereby promoted. It is not uncommon for individually rational actions to lead to collectively irrational or morally problematic results.

Second, this argument does not address corporate social responsibilities with regard to damages that corporations may themselves directly cause to the environment, employees, members of society, etc. For all these harms it is reasonable to believe that corporations do have responsibilities. The question this paper addresses concerns the implications of demanding that corporations go beyond correcting the damages they have brought about and assume responsibility for public welfare deficiencies for which they are not causally responsible.

Finally, if we could identify the harms that corporations directly *and* indirectly cause, then the arena of responsibilities that corporations have to society might significantly increase and the deficiencies in public welfare (assuming corporations fulfilled their responsibilities) might correspondingly decrease. This paper presupposes that, even in such a situation, there would remain public welfare deficiencies for which corporations are said to be socially responsible and for which they are neither directly nor indirectly causally responsible.[8]

The present argument has four parts. To begin with, it is important to highlight the different relation that exists between an individual (or group) who is aided by a private corporation, and the relation between such an individual (or group) and

public attempts to aid their welfare. The differences in these relations will, in practice, often be insignificant—especially when things go well. However, when problems arise theoretical and practical differences can be important. Surely cases could be identified in which corporations have successfully enhanced the public welfare. However, it is not to be expected that corporations will always act so successfully or so clearly in accord with public needs.

The point here is not that corporations may act in misguided ways so much as what happens in those instances where there are problems. Obviously appeals and complaints can be made to the corporation. However, the fact remains that appeals to the corporation tend to be appeals from external constituencies. Inasmuch as those aided by the corporation are not members of the corporation, they have no standing, as it were, within the corporation other than the one the corporation decides to give them. They have no "constitutional" rights against corporations as they do against public endeavors. They are not "citizens" of the corporation. Thus, they have, in principle, no internal access to the corporation's decision-making processes. They are part of that process only if the corporation allows it. Those who make the decisions to undertake various programs cannot be voted out of office—there is no political, and little legal control, over them. Accordingly, to advocate corporate provision of, and responsibility for, public welfare is to advocate that the basic requisites for human well-being are to be provided by institutions whose deliberations, at least at present, do not in principle include representation of those whose interests are affected. Those deficient in welfare lack formal control or power over those agencies from whom they obtain their welfare. Further, since those deficient in welfare tend to be those who are (in general) powerless, the advocacy of corporate responsibility for welfare tends to continue their powerlessness. Corporate social responsibility, in excluding any formal relation between those who are recipients of corporate aid and the corporation, maintains a division between the powerless and the powerful. A democratic society, one would suppose, would seek to moderate, rather than increase, the inequality presupposed in this division.

This situation contrasts with the state or other public bodies which provide, as part of their

---

[8]The importance of indirect causal factors and the resulting responsibility of corporations has been defended by Larry May in his comments, "Corporate Philanthropy and Social Responsibility," given on an earlier version of this paper, before the Society for Business Ethics meeting in Boston, MA, on December 28, 1990. How we might determine for which harms corporations are directly or indirectly causally responsible is not addressed in this paper. Both topics, but especially the latter, raise significant problems.

nature, various forms of administrative, legal and political redress.[9] The state's activities on behalf of its citizenry are hemmed in (at least in principle) by safeguards and guarantees (voting, representation, public hearings, sunshine laws, etc.) which are not imposed on corporations. Indeed, such public forms of access and standing are generally said to be contrary to the corporation's private status. Accordingly, whenever people outside the private corporation are granted such access it is simply due to the benevolence of the corporation.

Now this different relation between individuals and the agencies (private or public) which provide support for them is particularly crucial when that support concerns their basic welfare, i.e. items to which one might reasonably claim a right: e.g., minimal health care, educational opportunities, physical security, shelter, and food. Surely various private institutions such as corporations, churches, etc. may appropriately give aid to those who are deficient in such welfare, when this occurs on an occasional or special basis. Accordingly, private institutions may aid the welfare of their members (those who have access and voice within the organization) as well as non-members (those who do not have such access and voice).

However, those who advocate that this become the normal situation are (implicitly at least) also advocating a condition that places the recipients in a tenuous position vis-à-vis the granting agencies. Though recipients may receive various goods and/or services they need from private corporations, not only are such individuals dependent on those agencies for the aid they receive, but they also lose any formal or "constitutional" voice in the agency which purports to aid them. In effect, any right they have to such welfare is degraded to an act of benevolence on the part of the contributing organization. They can no longer insist or demand that they be treated in various ways, but must play the role of supplicants.

It is in this kind of situation that the view attributed to Andrew Carnegie can arise unchecked by formal mechanisms to control it: "In the exercise of his trust he was responsible only to his own conscience and judgment of what was best for the community."[10] Recipients of such aid lack means of redress which, in matters of basic importance such as welfare, are terribly significant.

Furthermore, when the institutions (i.e. large business corporations) involved in providing welfare are not themselves dedicated to the welfare of others but primarily focused on their own self-interested economic ends, and when these organizations are extremely large and powerful, then we must reflect on the implications of the lack of membership, and hence the lack of redress and voice, within those organizations. Specifically, we need to consider whether these needs ought not to be met by organizations which will grant those receiving such aid the voice and access which has traditionally protected people who are dependent upon others.

In short, when corporations are asked to undertake public welfare on an ongoing basis, the welfare they give is privatized in a manner that eliminates an important relation for those receiving such welfare. To the extent that it formalizes a relation between the powerful and the powerless, it exposes the recipients of such aid to abuses of power. At the same time, the equality that democracy implies is also jeopardized.[11]

Second, a variation on the preceding point concerns the standards by which decisions on the nature and means of implementing corporate welfare measures are made. Again, this might not appear to be a significant problem with regard to the construction or reconstruction of an inner-city park, a neighborhood clean-up campaign, or reading tutors in the schools.[12] Surely corporations

---

[9]Even if this is not true in any particular case, it is still appropriate to demand such access and forms of redress of present (i.e., democratic or republican) forms of government.

[10]Robert H. Bremner, *American Philanthropy* (2nd ed.; Chicago: The University of Chicago Press, 1988), p. 101.

[11]This argument allows that other private organizations, such as churches, etc., may legitimately contribute to individuals' welfare needs. The smaller the organization, the more individual the contribution, and the greater the identity of the organization is bound up with promoting the public good, the less there is a problem. On the other hand, some organizations, such as churches, run into problems (e.g., First Amendment issues and attempts to convert others rather than simply aid them) that other private groups do not.

[12]Even the park example is not all that simple. There are questions that need to be asked before the park can be built or renovated: what will be the nature and form of the park? Who will maintain it (will anyone?)? Will trash containers be put out and regularly emptied (by whom?)? Is the construction of this park likely to require increased police patrols? Are additional burdens being placed on the city recreational

will, by and large, consult with the people involved to get their ideas and approval. On other occasions, the people involved will seek out a corporation to aid them. But this does not lay the issue to rest since the standards the corporation seeks to follow may be primarily private in nature, rather than public or general.[13]

Suppose, for instance, that the welfare measures which the corporation seeks to provide (and to which their recipients agree) are of questionable constitutionality. They agree, perhaps, on educational films with a religious or a racist message for the public schools. Or, suppose they agree on an educational program but the corporation liberally sprinkles the presentation with its corporate logo, mascot, jingle, and the like. Suppose that in training of the hard-core unemployed they aim at white, rather than black or Hispanic, populations. The point at issue concerns the legitimacy of these decisions.

The standards according to which the public welfare is fulfilled must be a matter for the public (through its representatives) to determine, not the private corporation.[14] Two reasons lie behind this

claim. Such welfare concerns what is common among the citizens, what holds the members of a society together, and what is the nature of their basic prerequisites. It constitutes a statement about how we, as a community or society, believe that we should live. Fulfillment of welfare deficiencies for some that manifests prejudice against other groups, or works to their disadvantage, requires special justification and close public scrutiny, if it is allowed to stand.

In addition, to the extent that corporate contributions to public welfare are tax deductible, the foregone tax revenues constitute a public contribution to itself, through the agency of the corporation. Since public monies are committed through such contributions, the public has a right to assure itself that the standards according to which such monies are expended meet its (minimal) standards.[15]

Accordingly, the legitimacy of the decisions the private corporation makes regarding public welfare cannot be judged simply according to its own

---

department, trash department, police department? If so, who decides and upon what basis? Admittedly, these questions must be faced whether the city *or* a corporation builds the park. However, the important point is that when corporations aid public welfare many important questions remain to be answered. The city or the public is not suddenly let off the hook.

[13]The problem is even more complex since those individuals the corporation addresses in the public forum may themselves primarily hold private values. That is, their vision of themselves and society may have lost any sense of the public. Bellah et al document the degree to which "Americans . . . are genuinely ambivalent about public life" (Bellah et al, *Habits of the Heart* [Berkeley: University of California Press, 1985], p. 250).

[14]Similarly for a host of other projects there are questions which demand social or public decision, which only the public through the government can legitimately give. For example, it might be asked whether it is really so bad for corporations to provide tutors for secondary schools to help with basic reading skills. But are these tutors trained in teaching? Do they serve to justify inadequate teaching staffs? Do they undercut the demands of teachers for adequate social commitment for education? What programs are they trained to teach? Do they constitute an influx of business oriented courses rather than humanity courses, or science courses? These are serious issues which need to be addressed on the social and public level, not simply on the private corporation level.

Likewise, it might be asked whether it is wrong for corporations (e.g., McDonald's) to start drives for houses for relatives of the seriously ill to stay in while at the hospital. But again, supposing that the rest of the community contributes the preponderant amount, why should the community not get the credit for the house? Why doesn't the name of the house reflect public values or ideals?

We need not assume that public answers to all these questions may be easily arrived at. However, if corporations (or other private groups) simply operate on their own standards, the public discussion which may lead to public standards and agreement will be short-circuited. As a result, the public will be impoverished.

[15]This claim applies to similar contributions that come from other private groups, e.g., churches, the Audubon Society, etc. When such contributions come from small and numerous groups, there is less reason for concern since they may counterbalance each other. It is reasonable for a society to encourage such contributions. Nevertheless, society may legitimately review the nature of their contributions, given that their contributions are tax deductible and they enjoy (where applicable) tax-exempt status.

This issue is particularly of concern, however, when such contributions come from large corporations which can bring significant power and resources to bear. Similarly, when churches or other private groups become large and their powers significant, the consideration raised in the text applies as well. In short, when the contributions of private groups are supported by the public through tax deductions and when those contributions may in particular cases have a significant effect on the public, the public may legitimately review the standards according to which the contributions are made.

private standards. Thus, if the corporation tries to impose its own view and standards, it is crossing an important line between the private and the public. It is naive, then, simply to argue that people's welfare is the responsibility of corporations, without providing for social determination and direction of the activities which corporations undertake.[16]

In those instances in which corporate contributions are of a charitable (or prudential) nature *and* the objects of their actions are wholly private, it would seem that corporations might legitimately give to those individuals or organizations which promote their own values and ideas. In this way, their gifts may reflect their own idiosyncratic standards. Accordingly, some object to business giving to private universities whose faculty advocate ideas opposed to capitalism.[17] However, in contrast, the direction and satisfaction of public welfare according to private standards is not appropriate, since the public welfare is not to be determined simply by this or that individual corporation's ideas and values, but by a political process and, ideally a community dialogue, on what those values should be.[18]

Finally, if corporations are said to be responsible for remedying certain deficient levels of public welfare, but are not given control (both in terms of applicable standards and practical direction) over how such remedies are to be emplaced, then when these measures fail the corporation can hardly be held accountable. Nevertheless, since they will be associated with such efforts, they will often be faulted for their lack of success. Hence, if corpora-tions are required to engage in social responsibility efforts, there will be an understandable tendency for them to seek control over the situations in which they participate. This means, however, supplanting (or reducing) public control and substituting their own judgments and standards for those of the public. Consequently, the demand for corporate social responsibility is a demand that encourages the substitution of private standards, authority and control for those of the public.

III

Third, the demand for corporate social responsibility arises, it has been assumed, due to deficient public welfare, which stems, at least in part, from inadequate public funding. Corporate opposition to higher taxes has played a contributing role to this situation, since taxes are viewed as coercive takings of corporate property.[19] The lower the taxes the greater the return on investment corporations make and the greater the flexibility corporations have to use their resources as they choose. Part of the appeal of corporate social responsibility for public welfare is that the aid that is given is voluntary. Provision of such aid heads off higher taxes, government regulation and hence coercion. In short, behind the demand for corporate social responsibility is a view that holds that the public realm and the state constitute a sphere of coercion, while the private realm and the actions it takes are voluntary.[20]

---

[16]For example, Control Data's program, called "City Venture," which sought to write blueprints for economic rebirth of down-and-out city neighborhoods had to be withdrawn: "A bossy, 'we know what's best' attitude offended prickly independent community groups in Minneapolis and Miami, forcing City Venture to be withdrawn" (Neil R. Peirce, "To Corporate Social Involvement," *The Knoxville Journal*, 1982, p. A4).

[17]Robert H. Malott, "Corporate Support of Education: Some Strings Attached," *Harvard Business Review*, vol. 56 (1978), pp. 133–8.

[18]This is not to say that corporations, or anyone, must (or should) give to causes they believe to be wrong-headed. Rather, if corporations (or other organizations) are given responsibility for public welfare, they may not simply apply their own idiosyncratic standards. This allows, of course, that they could choose, from a range of public welfare needs, to support those compatible with their own views. Since the issue concerns basic deficiencies from which people suffer, this should not be impossible.

[19]Similarly Levitt argues: "American capitalism also creates, fosters, and acquiesces in enormous social and economic cancers. Indeed, it fights against the achievement of certain forms of economic and social progress, pouring millions into campaigns against things which people have a right to expect from their government . . . (Levitt, "The Dangers of Social Responsibility," p. 48).

[20]Since corporate social responsibility is, usually, viewed either as charitable or as prudential in nature, corporations can make their own, voluntary choices as to when, what and how much they will do. The alternative is to have the public (the state or the government) take more from them in order to fulfill the public welfare needs. Because this restricts their choices—their freedom (as they would see it)—they argue against state action here. In short, corporate social responsibility is an expression of the liberal view of society. It is also an expression of an individualistic view: "utilitarian individualism" and "expressive individualism" (Bellah et al, *Habits of the Heart*, p. 27ff). These views contrast with what they call "civic republicanism."

This is illustrated in Friedman's comment that "the political principle that underlies the political mechanism is conformity. . . . It is appropriate for some to require others to contribute to a general social purpose whether they wish to or not."[21] Corporate social responsibility, then, explicitly seeks to reduce the realm of the public, by reducing the area within which coercion and force might be used.

Now if the public were simply a realm of coercion, such a view would seem unexceptionable. On the contrary, however, such a view arguably distorts the realm of the public. Corporate social responsibility implies that the public is simply an area within which individual prudential interests are worked out and coercion imposed by the state. Both eliminate an important sense of the public.

The public is also the area within which general and common interests are articulated. It is what binds people together, in contrast to the private realm within which people are separated from each other and view each other as limitations upon their freedom.[22] Accordingly, it is the realm of the "we," rather than the "you" or "I." It is what is done in all our names, and not just yours or mine. It is the area, some have even held, within which freedom is only possible.[23] There is (or can be) a different sense of accomplishment when the community builds or creates something rather than simply this or that private organization. Conversely, there is a different sense of loss when a public figure, a President or Prime Minister dies, rather than the head of a private corporation.

Now charity is an extension of the private into this public realm. It is personal, self-given, and can't be demanded in particular cases. It need not be based on political discussion or compromise so much as on one's own willingness to aid others. Those who receive do not have grounds upon which they can demand or negotiate beyond which the charitable organization allows. Charity does not necessarily involve any political or public process by which recipient and contributor are bound together. Thus, Hannah Arendt comments,

"The bond of charity between people . . . is incapable of founding a public realm of its own. . . ."[24] In short, charity cannot be the basis of a public or political dimension between people.

As such, corporate social responsibility drives out the political and the public. The appeal to corporate responsibility is a confession that the public or political realm has broken (or is breaking) down. It is an unwitting manifestation of liberal individualism extending the realm of the private to encompass the public.

Consequently, Friedman is quite wrong when he complains that the doctrine of social responsibility "taken seriously would extend the scope of the political mechanism to every human activity."[25] This is plausible only in that case when the corporation and its executives both engage in social responsibility activities *and*, as a result, become subject to political election procedures since they are viewed as "civil servants."[26] On the other hand, if this does not happen (and there is little present evidence that it will), then the doctrine of social responsibility extends the nature of private activities to many activities in the public or political realm. In short, quite the opposite of what Friedman contends, it extends the scope of the private "to every human activity."

The problem with this approach is that it is implausible to treat society as simply an example of an ideal market situation. This is implied by the above comments on the nature of the public. Not all public (or private) values can be produced or sustained by market exchanges. Friedman slips from discussion of market activities to talk of society without argument. Thus, after he portrays the voluntary nature of the ideal free market, he immediately goes on (without argument) to equate such exchanges with society itself.[27] However, it does not follow (and it is not plausible) to think of society as itself simply an ideal free market. Once again, then, corporate social responsibility involves views and demands which question legitimate distinctions between the private and the public.

[21]Milton Friedman, "The Social Responsibility of Business Is to Increase Its Profits," in Milton Snoeyenbos, Robert Almeder, James Humber (eds.), *Business Ethics* (Buffalo, New York: Prometheus Books, 1983), p. 78.
[22]Ibid., pp. 245, 248.
[23]Nancy L. Schwartz, "Distinction Between Public and Private Life," *Political Theory,* vol. 7 (1979), p. 245.

[24]Hannah Arendt, *The Human Condition* (Chicago: The University of Chicago Press, 1958), p. 53.
[25]Milton Friedman, "The Social Responsibility of Business Is to Increase Its Profits," in Milton Snoeyenbos, Robert Almeder, James Humber (eds.), *Business Ethics* (Buffalo. New York: Prometheus Books, 1983), p. 79.
[26]Friedman, "The Social Responsibility of Business Is to Increase Its Profits, p. 75.
[27]Ibid.

IV

Finally, though the relation of the public and the private is a shifting relation, we must guard against collapsing one—either one—term of this relation into the other. The view that the public is simply the arena in which individual actions affect others without their voluntary approval impoverishes the notion of the public.[28] As noted above, the public is more and different than this. The public is what binds a people together and relates them to each other.[29] It is what is done in their common name; it is what makes them a people, rather than simply a random collection of individuals. It embodies the values, norms and ideals we strive towards even if we fail fully to achieve them. It is the responsibility of public agencies (the state or its government) to foster (at least) the minimal conditions under which the public may exist. To be a citizen is to owe allegiance to the government as it works to realize these principles and values.

Now suppose that the government does not fulfill its responsibilities to individuals for basic welfare. The demand that private corporations—rather than the government—dispense public welfare is a step in the privatization of the public realm. The benefits that individuals receive from the government have long been thought to play an important role in their obligations to the state and, hence, their citizenship within the state.[30] If these benefits come from private groups, rather than the state, then one would expect loyalties and obligations to be modified accordingly.

Consequently, if a corporation provides training for the hard-core unemployed, renovates the local park, or provides the house which shelters the sick, it is to the corporation that those aided will be grateful and indebted, not to the community or society of which they are members.[31] It is the corporation to which one's loyalties will be turned, and not to the city or state of which one is a citizen. Indeed, the very notion of citizenship thereby becomes impoverished. The grounds upon which the state has been said to acquire the obligations of its citizenry have been narrowed. In its place develop isolated (groups of) individuals beholden to private institutions of which they are not members (or citizens) and over which they have no formal control.

Surely in these days of popular advertising, the corporation may seem more personal, less abstract, than the community or the state. Through logos, jingles and mascots corporations seek to get people to identify with them and their products. And through corporate measures to aid their welfare, individuals would have concrete reason to be indebted to them, even if not members or citizens of them. But to accept or promote this situation, and the view of the individual's relations to private and public institutions which it involves, merely reveals the state of poverty to which our notions of the public and citizenship have come. Such corporations encourage us to seek a common identity rather than to foster our common (public) interests.[32] We are invited to replace the realm of the public which unavoidably involves impersonality with a personal and privatized realm. We transform a realm laden with political meanings into a private and psychologized realm.[33]

However, the danger here does not simply stem from the implications of the altered identifications and loyalties that characterize citizens. The increasing privatization of the public realm that we see in shopping malls, corporate housing developments, the suburban environment, and corporate attempts

---

[28]Cf. John Dewey, *The Public and Its Problems* (Chicago: Gateway Books, 1946).

[29]Cf. Hannah Arendt, "The public realm, as the common world, gathers us together and yet prevents our falling over each other, so to speak"; *The Human Condition* (Chicago: The University of Chicago Press, 1958), p. 52.

[30]Cf. A. John Simmons, *Moral Principles and Political Obligations* (Princeton: Princeton University Press, 1979), pp. 157–90.

[31]The following comes from a letter to an editor from a mother of a child in a school adopted by IBM. She was responding to objections that others had raised because children in the school were preparing posters and having assemblies to thank IBM for adopting their school. She argues: "to say that this is taking away from the children's learning time is not true. What better learning experience is there than to teach our children what's going on in their schools and to have them have a special program to thank these companies? . . . I believe it is very important that these adopting companies realize, by way of parents and children, that we are honored and grateful that they are willing to help 'our' children with their education" (Letters to the Editor, *The Knoxville News-Sentinel*, November 28, 1986).

[32]Cf. Richard Sennett who complains that as part of the end of public culture "the pursuit of common interests is destroyed in the search for a common identity" (p. 261); *The Fall of Public Man* (New York: Vintage Books, 1976).

[33]Cf. Sennet, Ibid.

to establish their own identity and role models within the schools carry other consequences to which we must be keenly sensitive. For example, in private shopping malls people may be prevented from political speech; in corporate housing developments, they may be prohibited from having children and remaining in their home; and cultural exhibits may be skewed to suit corporate purposes.[34] Rights which all citizens share may be, wittingly or unwittingly, foregone through private efforts uninformed by public reflection and participation. In short, the public values and interests of a society can be threatened not simply by an authoritarian government but also by self-interested, though well-meaning, private groups and institutions which lack a sense of the significance of the public realm and the meaning of citizenship.

V

In conclusion, several comments are appropriate. First, it may be allowed that many objections which can be brought against corporate attempts to secure public welfare can also be brought against government or public attempts. Thus, both government and corporations may be inflexible, insensitive, impersonal, noninnovative, as well as hard to move or get through to. They may produce programs which are misconceived, uncoordinated, and/or precipitously stopped, leaving people in the lurch. The production of such programs may increase their power, size and influence; they may also deal paternalistically with those they seek to aid. One would be tempted to abandon all attempts to aid those deficient in welfare were it not for the fact that many people continue to suffer grievously from inadequate welfare. Thus, the question is a complex and messy one. There is no easy and neat answer.

Second, large corporations, however, will continue to be part of our social and political landscape. Their significant economic and political

power are obvious. In this situation, the thrust of the public/private argument is two-sided. It can be taken to urge the separation of private corporations and public institutions. This is fraught with all the problems of bureaucratization, distant government, powerful but indifferent corporations, and failed efforts to satisfy public welfare needs. This is not to say that these problems could not be overcome within a fairly strict separation of the private and the public.[35] Still, this would involve a recommitment (and rediscovery!) of the public realm that might be difficult in countries such as the U.S.

On the other hand, the above argument can also be taken to recommend that we require such large corporations be made more fully public, social organizations. Indeed, many argue that large corporations are no longer simply private organizations. George C. Lodge, for example, comments that "it is now obvious that our large public corporations are not private property at all. . . . The best we can say," he continues, "is that the corporation is a sort of collective, floating in philosophic limbo, dangerously vulnerable to the charge of illegitimacy and to the charge that it is not amenable to community control."[36] Thus, that corporations increasingly are called to participate in the production of public welfare is not so surprising given their present, quasi-public nature. The further claim that has been made is that this quasi-public nature needs to be institutionalized so as to make it amenable to greater public control and direction. This direction, however, is one that others violently oppose.

Thus, we stand at a crossroads. This juncture is part and parcel of that "tension between self-reliant competitive enterprise and a sense of public solidarity espoused by civic republicans" that some have identified as "the most important unresolved problem in American history."[37] If one rejects the view that corporations must more fully take on the

---

[34]IBM, for example, "barred the display of computer-art works designed for the equipment of a major business competitor, Macintosh, in the company's heretofore prestigious IBM Gallery of Science and Art in midtown Manahattan"; Susan Davis, "IBM Nixes Macintosh," *Art in America*, vol. 76 (1990), p. 47. The works barred were part of a touring show organized by the Walker Art Center. IBM, which finances its namesake galleries, "bars its competition 'as a matter of policy'" (*Ibid.*, p. 47).

[35]It would not, for example, prohibit linking education and business in various ways. Various courses of study in schools might be coordinated with job opportunities in private business, without corporations providing for those courses or other educational needs. Public and government welfare measures would have to be tied much more closely to local needs and allowed much greater flexibility in resolving those needs.

[36]Lodge, *The New American Ideology*, p. 18.

[37]Bellah et al, *Habits of the Heart*, p. 256.

character of public institutions, then demands for corporate social responsibility for public welfare should be seriously curtailed.

The preceding arguments do not show conclusively that corporations ought never to aid public welfare. They are one set of considerations which might, in some circumstances, be overridden. However, they do indicate important reasons why we should be more reluctant to proceed down the path that many have been encouraging us to take.

When we are repeatedly told that the sight of corporate social responsibility is so lovely, and that the prospects of corporate responsibility for public welfare are so rosy, one may rightfully come to suspect that we are being led down the garden path.[38]

[38]I am indebted to John Hardwig, W. Michael Hoffman, Larry May, Richard Nunan, and an anonymous referee for their perceptive and helpful comments on earlier versions of this paper.

Questions for Chapter 16

1. What does Friedman mean when he says, "In a free society, it is hard for 'good' people to do 'good,' but that is a small price to pay for making it hard for 'evil' people to do 'evil'"? Do you agree or disagree, and why?

2. Many commentators feel that Friedman's position implies ethical egoism. Do you agree? Why or why not?

3. Why does Lippke characterize Friedman's approach as the Abstract Individuals Approach (AIA)? How does it differ from what he calls the Social Contract Approach (SCA)?

4. Could Friedman accept Lippke's Social Niche Approach (SNA)? If not, what criticisms do you think he would make of it?

5. Brenkert claims, "The appeal to corporate responsibility is a confession that the public or political realm has broken (or is breaking) down." Do you agree? Why or why not?

6. Does Brenkert's argument demonstrate that corporations should not act philanthropically? How would Brenkert respond to the suggestion that businesses have an obligation to act philanthropically, but that the standards that govern their actions should be set politically?

Case 16.1 Socially Responsible Loans

It is well known that major banks are wary of making loans in low-income neighborhoods. Loans are available from second-mortgage companies, but at a much higher rate of interest. Federal and state governments have shown little interest in regulating these companies, and as a consequence, there are few limits on what interest rates they can charge. Rates of 20 or 30 per-

cent are not uncommon, and service fees often further inflate the cost of borrowing. In many instances, elderly homeowners in low-income neighborhoods are actively targeted. Such homeowners frequently receive telephone calls from mortgage brokers wishing to lend them money. Recipients of such telephone calls are well advised to think very carefully before borrowing, since the number of people who have lost their homes through such second mortgages is remarkably high. For example, a study by a Boston community group revealed that over 80 percent of the homeowners who took out mortgages with the second-mortgage lender Resource Financial Group lost their homes or were facing foreclosure. Even more revealing was the fact that 90 percent of Resource's loans were in low-income minority neighborhoods where the mainstream banks are reluctant to make loans.[1]

What is less well known is that many banks lend second-mortgage companies money for operating expenses and frequently purchase home equity loan contracts from these compa-

nies. From 1990 until 1991, the number of big banks buying home equity loans on the secondary market grew from 12.5 percent to 20.9 percent.[2] The banks disclaim any responsibility for the sometimes shady practices of mortgage brokers on the basis that these companies are entirely separate businesses and that they, the banks, have no way of knowing when abuses have taken place. Critics urge that banks are at least partially responsible for the problem inasmuch as they have denied mainstream credit to low-income communities.

1. Do banks have any responsibility to lend money in low-income communities?

2. Should the amount of interest that can be charged on a loan be regulated? If it should be, then by whom?

[1]Michael Hudson, "Loan Scams That Prey on the Poor," *Business and Society Review*, 84, Winter 1993, pp. 11–15, p. 12.

[2]Hudson, p. 13.

Case 16.2 Business and Public Education

In a time when there is increasing concern over the ability of government to provide adequate funding of the public school system, many are suggesting that corporate sponsors play a role in schools. In Toronto, Ontario, the school board recently signed an agreement with Pepsi-Cola. Under the agreement, Pepsi gets exclusive sales access to vending machines selling pop and juice to the student population. The agreement also includes the distribution of promotional videos featuring celebrities speaking on topics such as drug abuse and "Pepsi student of the month awards" in which students win Pepsi clothing and have their names inscribed on plaques donated by Pepsi.[3] Nor is this an isolated incident. In return for television news-and-advertising packages involving the loan of a

satellite dish and television sets for each classroom, many school boards in the United States require their students to watch advertising provided by corporate sponsors. One popular contract stipulates that 90 percent of the children in a school must watch the program 90 percent of the times it is shown and that each program must be watched in its entirety, that is, the show cannot be interrupted and the teacher does not have the right to turn it off.[4] Inasmuch as students are required by law to be in school and the schools are obliged to honor the contract, advertisers are assured of an audience. An even bigger role for business may be in the offing. Burger King has opened a number of accredited high schools,

[3]*Globe and Mail*, January 15, 1994, p. A1.

[4]Jonathan Kozol, "Kids as Commodities: The Folly of For-Profit Schools," *Business and Society Review*, 84, Winter 1993, pp. 16–20, p. 16.

and many other corporations are considering opening profit-making schools as alternatives to publicly funded institutions.

1. Some shareholders have expressed concern that they pay taxes to support education and that corporate donations to education constitute a second tax they ought not to have to pay. Do you agree or disagree, and why?

2. Critics of corporate sponsorship have expressed concern that corporate donations are so heavily tied to advertising. Should corporate sponsors be allowed to tie their donations to advertising? Why or why not?

3. Are corporately backed alternative, for-profit schools a good idea? Defend your answer.

Further Readings for Chapter 16

David Crossley, "Paternalism and Corporate Responsibility," *Journal of Business Ethics* 21, 1999, pp. 291–302.

Thomas Donaldson, "Constructing a Social Contract for Business" in his *Corporations and Morality* (Englewood Cliffs, NJ: Prentice-Hall, 1982), pp. 18–35.

Krzysztof Klincewicz, "Ethical Aspects of Sponsorship," *Journal of Business Ethics* 17, 1998, pp. 1103–1110.

John Kultgen, "Donaldson's Social Contract for Business," *Business and Professional Ethics Journal* 5(1), 1985, pp. 28–50.

Theodore Levitt, "The Dangers of Social Responsibility," *Harvard Business Review* 36, September/October 1958, pp. 41–50.

Fred D. Miller, Jr. and John Ahrens, "The Social Responsibility of Corporations" in *Commerce and Morality,* ed. Tibor R. Machan (Totowa, NJ: Rowman & Littlefield, 1988), pp. 140–160.

Thomas Mulligan, "A Critique of Milton Friedman's Essay 'The Social Responsibility of Business Is to Increase Its Profits,'" *Journal of Business Ethics* 5, 1986, pp. 265–269.

INFOTRAC COLLEGE EDITION To learn more about the topics from this chapter, you can use the following words to conduct an electronic search on InfoTrac College Edition, an online library of journals. Here you will find a multitude of articles from various sources and perspectives: *www.infotrac-college.com/wadsworth/access.html*

corporate philanthropy

social responsibility of business

corporate sponsorship

Business and the International Community

Introduction

IN CHAPTER 17 we consider some of the many ethical issues that arise in the course of doing business internationally. In considering this topic, we do well to remember that most of the ethical issues we discuss in this text can be raised not only in a domestic but also in an international context. That there are specific issues that arise in the international context that do not arise domestically cannot be denied, for example, the issue of child labor discussed in our fourth reading. In most instances, however, doing business in foreign markets does not present us with new issues, but rather with familiar problems that must be addressed in an unfamiliar context. In our present chapter, our first three readings on intellectual property, pollution, and gender equality present us with ethical issues examined elsewhere in the text, only in an international setting. While it is true that these are in one sense very familiar issues, it is equally true that the international context makes these already very complicated issues even more difficult.

In his article "The Moral Legitimacy of Intellectual Property Claims: American Business and Developing Country Perspectives," Paul Steidlmeier takes up the topic of intellectual property that we discussed in Chapter 9. He notes the increasing tension between developed and developing countries over the issue of intellectual property claims. Developed countries with strong business cultures view intellectual property as private property and argue that it deserves strong protection in the interests of encouraging research and development. Less developed countries tend to view intellectual property as a form of common property that should be accessible to all. There exists, therefore, a debate over whether the monopoly claims of patents and copyrights asserted by the businesses of developed countries are legitimate.

Steidlmeier goes on to note several factors that complicate the debate, among them the fact that property is understood differently at different times and in different cultures, and the tension between individual and social values.

Although he avoids drawing firm conclusions concerning how the debate should be resolved, he seems unconvinced that intellectual property rights can be justified in their present form. He appears open to viewing intellectual property as primarily a form of common property that may take limited private forms.

In "Business Ethics and the International Trade in Hazardous Wastes," Jang B. Singh and V. C. Lakhan discuss the growing tendency of industrialized countries to export hazardous wastes to third-world countries. Although the practice of transporting and dumping hazardous wastes in lesser developed countries may in many instances be legal, there can be little doubt that it poses a major threat to both the environment and human health in those countries. On what grounds and under what conditions can the exporting of hazardous waste be justified?

Singh and Lakhan claim that it is especially difficult to provide any moral justification of shipping such waste to lesser developed countries. They argue that to export wastes to countries that do not benefit from the industrial processes which produce these wastes and whose citizens do not have lifestyles that lead to the production of such wastes is unethical. They also argue that decisions to import hazardous wastes are often made by governments that hold power by force and have no democratic mandate to expose their populations to the risks involved.

In "Ethics and the Gender Equality Dilemma for U.S. Multinationals," Don Mayer and Anita Cava explore the difficulties of applying American views on gender and racial equality in foreign markets. They attempt to avoid both cultural relativism, that is, simply adopting the practices of the culture in which one finds oneself, and ethnocentrism, that is, imposing one's own cultural practices in a foreign setting. They suggest that there are minimum universal principles that can be legitimately broadened to include gender and racial equality. It is useful to compare their treatment of this issue with Mary Midgley's general treatment of cultural relativism ("Trying Out One's New Sword") in Chapter 2.

In "Cross-Cultural Ethics and the Child Labor Problem," Hugh Hindman and Charles Smith address the issues raised by child labor. They note that child labor tends to be the result of the early stages of industrialization. Children certainly work in preindustrial societies, but in such societies the household is generally the site of production. This means that the household tends to function in such a way that it provides an apprenticeship similar to that provided by skilled craftsmen in small workshops. In the early stages of industrialization and mass production, this teaching aspect of childrens' work is lost: children are hired for the most menial of tasks and never receive the opportunity to acquire greater skill. That child labor is the result of the early stages of industrialization is evidenced not only by the fact that child labor is presently concentrated most heavily in developing countries throughout Asia, Africa, and Latin America, but also by the fact that countries such as Great Britain and the United States passed through a stage of child labor in the process of becoming industrialized.

In Hindman and Smith's view, child labor is not only morally repugnant, but is also economically inefficient and injurious. Child laborers, because they receive insufficient schooling and little or no vocational training, do not grow up to be productive workers. In the long run, child labor is always a poor bargain, mortgaging the future in order to pay the present. Thus, although it should certainly be opposed on moral grounds, it can reasonably be expected that, as countries advance in industrial and economic development, the use of child labor will be abandoned as economic and moral factors converge to show its unacceptability.

The Moral Legitimacy of Intellectual Property Claims: American Business and Developing Country Perspectives

PAUL STEIDLMEIER

I. The Growing Debate over Intellectual Property

IN INTERNATIONAL TRADE and development circles a battle is raging over intellectual property. The term intellectual property generally covers patents, copyrights, trademarks and trade secrets. The essence of the current debate is whether such items should be protected by governments on a global scale and, if so, to what extent.

The theoretical positions on intellectual property rights vary widely as do the practical prospects for actually protecting anything at all in particular regions. Nowhere is the difference more sharp than between the developed and developing countries. The developed countries argue that strong protection of intellectual property is essential to provide incentives for future innovations and to ensure the competitive profitability of companies that spend on research. The developing countries are more interested in the diffusion of technology and generally support only very weak protection of intellectual property. This paper reviews the positions adopted by each side in deciding whether intellectual property rights are really rights rather than privileges and outlines the conditions to be met by an international intellectual property regime if it is to possess moral validity. In what follows I first clarify the notion of property and then review the claims put forth by developed and developing countries to legitimate their views.

II. Intellectual Property and Private, Common and Public Forms of Property

Ownership of property is

1. a *right* that people have regarding
2. a (commercial) *resource*
3. over *time* (Munzer, 1990; Reeve, 1986).

The modern Western notion of property (derived principally from John Locke and Adam Smith) recognizes the property owner as the one having the *greatest possible interest* in a thing (consistent with a fair legal system). That is, from the start the property owner is recognized as the *principal stakeholder* but not the only stakeholder in the product or process which is denominated as property. The rights of owners over such assets consist in the power to use, obtain income from and exchange the assets, while denying such determinative power to other parties. At the same time, property owners must be mindful of the legitimate rights of third parties. Third parties have a stake in another's private property rights if they are affected by the consequences of the owner's property decisions (Freeman, 1984). Legal examples are provided by zoning regulations and the granting of rights of way. The rights of these other stakeholders are defined in terms of the property owner's *duties*. The moral question is this: with respect to a particular asset what constitutes a fair set of reciprocal rights and duties between all stakeholders, defined as those with a legitimate interest in a resource or asset denominated as property?

Even when something is recognized as property, however, there are different approaches to specifying its nature in terms of

1. *private* individual,
2. *common* and
3. *public* (government) forms of property.

Common property differs from private individual property in that under common property access is granted to all, although some individuals may enjoy specific use-rights. For example, in most of Sub-Saharan African agriculture land is considered *common property* while clans, families and individuals are granted use-rights. Also, in the United States, most sources of water are common property which are publicly administered through the grant of use-rights. Public property differs from common property in that the government is the

From Journal of Business Ethics *12, 1993. Reprinted by permission of Kluwer Academic Publishers.*

owner (of forest land in the U.S., for example) and the decision-making authority regarding the property is vested in government acting in a fiduciary capacity on behalf of all the people. The people themselves, however, hardly exercise any property rights as such (in terms of allocation and exchange of property).

Western business increasingly views "not yet specifically applied" technology as

1. a commodity with commercial value—expressed in direct sales, licensing, and contracts for technical, management and engineering assistance—and
2. as private property.

Developing countries tend to view such technology as non-commercial scientific knowledge and, therefore, as a sort of a "common property" transferable to them without payment to the discoverer(s). In the intellectual property debate, therefore, U.S. business interests are claiming private property rights while developing countries assert that such property—if indeed it can be "property"—is common or public property.

The principal questions for ethical research which emerge from this discussion are

1. what counts as property, and
2. to what extent may owners establish exclusive claims over it.

The debate is complicated by the fact that the words "ownership" and "property" have different meanings in various social and historical settings. "Property" in Aristotle, the Bible, Aquinas, Kant, Locke or Marx does not represent an univocal concept. This for two reasons. First, what counts as property changes historically. In many areas two hundred years ago, for example, slaves and even women represented socially legitimate property. In the twentieth century Western world they do not. Even the defense of something like land as private property is not unambiguous. For example, land as private property in the middle ages meant feudal institutions of property; in much of Latin America today it may mean institutions of landed estates (*latifundiae*). It emerges that "property" is a tremendously dynamic and fluid reality both in *concept* and *historical sociological form*. It is inseparable from cultural values and legal traditions.

While an asset such as land has almost universally counted as property, an intellectual discovery generally has not. Something resembling patents existed in sixteenth century Italy and in seventeenth century England. The first set of completely formalized procedures only appeared in 1790 [in the United States] (Congressional Quarterly, 1990). In the rest of Western Europe patent law was very much a nineteenth century development which has been subject to almost continual modification of conditions. To patent scientific ideas and information as property is a very new development in human history indeed. Traditionally, intellectual ideas have been treated as part of the public domain—much like the alphabet or nuclear physics. While applications, such as a particular keyboard or a nuclear plant design, might be patented or copyrighted the idea itself could not be.

This scenario is further complicated when one adds the dimensions of the *exclusion of others* and *time*. Time not only raises the issues of inheritance but of the limits of monopoly power associated with patents and copyrights. One point put forward by developing countries in the intellectual property debate calls for restricting the period of patent monopoly, rather than granting patent holders generous monopolies of seventeen years or more. Exclusion of others is especially called into question when the property owner does little or nothing with the property for the public good. The alleged failure to productively exploit patents has led Brazil and India to adopt the policy of compulsory licensing and even the loss of patent rights (Gadbaw and Richards, 1988, pp. 4, 167, 203).

In what follows I discuss in turn the approaches to intellectual property rights put forth by American business interests and the counter position articulated by the Government of India (1989) in the context of the current Uruguay round of the General Agreement on Tariffs and Trade (GATT) negotiations. India has emerged as the principal voice of the developing countries.

III. Legitimating What Counts as Property and Providing for Exclusion

Property rights are a deeply philosophical issue—the thorniest point being the legitimation of a set of property claims. Claims to property are rationalized in a variety of ways. The most absolute legitimation is theological where God's will, providence and "manifest destiny" are appealed to as having conferred these rights upon the chosen. Such arguments have been brought to bear to justify colonialism; they are also put forth by parties who wish to settle land in the Middle East. In today's pluralistic world, however, theological reasoning does not find widespread acceptance across creeds and cultures and people are seeking a more secular philosophical rationale. It is not all that clear that intellectual property rights are really "rights." In the intellectual property debate it is often forgotten that the property rights advocated by American companies are primarily based upon modern Western values and culture. I say modern, because many contemporary capitalists have forgotten the way Adam Smith linked property rights to distributive justice, not just to self interest (Johnson, 1989). Furthermore, Islamic cultures, which stretch from Morocco to Indonesia and account for almost a quarter of the world's population, articulate a coherent, sophisticated and distinctively non-Western view of property rights (Behdad, 1989). Buddhism (Pryor, 1990; 1991) also possesses a long and nuanced tradition regarding economics and property rights. Hinduism (Uppal, 1986), which forms the backdrop for the Indian position, has definite implications for patterns of economic development. The end result is that while intellectual property rights are a global issue, it is notoriously difficult to establish a global basis for their legitimation.

Granting this complexity and the meta-ethical issues it raises, in what follows I confine myself to three general sets of philosophical arguments which are often cited to legitimate a set of property rights:

1. liberty and self-realization;
2. rights to livelihood; and
3. rights to the fruit of one's labor and effort.

All of these rights are associated with efficiency, social benefits and the common good. In what follows I examine in turn the U.S. business and developing country positions.

THE BUSINESS ARGUMENTS

The arguments put forth by U.S. companies in favor of tightening up international intellectual property law and enforcement reflect the legal position set forth in Article I, Section 8, of the U.S. Constitution which granted to Congress the power:

> To promote the progress of science and useful arts, by securing for limited times to authors and inventors, the exclusive right to their respective writing and discoveries.

This Constitutional orientation has spawned six different regimes of U.S. intellectual property law, including copyright, patent, semiconductor chip and trademark protection at the Federal level and trade secret and misappropriation of other information at State levels (Besen and Raskind, 1991).

Incentives and rewards form the centerpiece of the American heritage regarding the purpose of an intellectual property protection system. Yet the rationale of intellectual property protection is based on more fundamental principles that lead proponents to argue that intellectual property claims are based on rights, not mere privileges.

A moral right identifies an interest which any individual should be free to pursue as s/he chooses. Furthermore, the free pursuit of such interests cannot be subordinated to the interests of others. In discussing whether intellectual property is such a fundamental interest a number of reasons come to the fore.

The first major argument advanced for private property in general is tied to the right of liberty and a correlative view of the creative self-fulfillment of the person. According to this philosophical position the possession of property confers a degree of freedom and self-determination upon the possessor. Rather than being subjected to others for their sustenance, property confers upon people the possibility of being subjects of their own destiny. Property ownership enables people to decide some of the details of their lives for themselves. In this context, property rights are an expression of liberty and linked to the innovative process in terms of creative liberation of human potential. The free creative process is cumulative. In general business wants the inventive process to be as free as possible. Business interests have been very active in trying to get the government to remove antitrust regulations which might affect cooperative research and exchange of information.

The second general argument put forth by business for the protection of intellectual property advances from reflections upon the free, creative processes of property creation to rights to the fruit of one's labor. Intuitively, people have argued for centuries that those who work and make an effort have a right to the fruits of their labor. This argument was formalized by John Locke in his famed example of the hunter going into the forest to hunt a deer (Locke, 1965). Locke's argument assumes plentiful natural resources as well as conditions of fair access—assumptions of questionable realism. The point is that labor creates assets and the value of those assets accrues to the laborer.

U.S. business presents the "fruits of labor" argument collectively in terms of the enterprise. The pharmaceutical industry, for example, claims that on average it costs over $100 million to develop a new drug and bring it to market (Pfizer, 1989). Pharmaceuticals are easily cloned and the industry is one of the more seriously affected by pirating (U.S. International Trade Commission, 1989). Cloning, it is asserted, unjustly robs the company of the fruit of its labor.

The third principal argument of U.S. business is based upon incentives to innovate. Many American businesses spend on average 5% to 10% of their sales on research (U.S. Patent and Trademark Office, 1990). Business leaders argue that if the fruits of their expenditures on research and development are not effectively protected, then incentives to innovate will perish. In the long-run, a decline in innovation will lead to stagnation of the economy and significant social harm in terms of lost jobs, the erosion of community tax-bases, and the decline in general well-being which continued innovation proffers. This argument is more utilitarian in nature and claims that strong protection of intellectual property rights will lead to the most beneficial social consequences. The point is set in the context of efficient use of property and the overall social benefits generated thereby. The future welfare of humanity sorely depends upon technological innovation. It will not be forthcoming at the desired rate unless it is protected. This position reflects a view of human motivation suggested by Adam Smith when he argues that people will manage best when they have a personal stake in the outcome. This view of human psychology and economic activity led to his belief in the greatest social utility being produced by the invisible hand of property owners and entrepreneurs interacting in a climate of fair competition. Transposed to the modern context, the argument is that protecting intellectual property rights creates incentives which, in turn, will induce greater overall efficiency and welfare in the economy.

DEVELOPING COUNTRY ARGUMENTS

Developing countries have generally taken a different approach to property claims (Deardorff, 1990). The fact that property is so linked to liberty and self-actualization is an argument developing countries employ for destroying rather than bolstering monopoly powers in property. At issue here are points such as negotiating the time of patent protection (with reference to a fair return on investment), compulsory licensing, the removal of trade barriers, access to credit, and measures to create new instruments of technology transfer.

In discussing the pressure exerted by the United States on South Korea regarding intellectual property, the (then) Ambassador to the United States, Mr. Kyung-Won Kim (1986) wrote:

> Historically, Koreans have not viewed intellectual discoveries or scientific inventions as the private property of their discoverers or inventors. New ideas or technologies were "public goods" for everybody to share freely. Cultural esteem rather than material gain was the incentive for creativity.

Mr. Kim raised the question of whether intellectual property is not, after all, common property. Mr. Kim criticized the exercise of monopoly power with reference to intellectual property rights. In essence he was suggesting that the set of intellectual property rights proposed by the Untied States and other OECD countries was illegitimate. In this he found lots of company of the likes of Brazil, India, Taiwan, Singapore, Mexico, China and others. His argument counters the individualist argument by placing liberty and creativity in a more communitarian framework. The emphasis is upon the liberty and creativity of a people not just an individual. As Joseph Needham (1981) has shown in his exhaustive studies of China, such cultural frameworks can provide the basis for tremendous innovation.

If, indeed, intellectual property is a right, it is one conferred by society and is a secondary right. The Government of India (1989, p. 1) makes the case that intellectual property rights are necessarily relative:

The essence of the [intellectual property protection] system is its monopolistic and restrictive character; its purpose is not to "liberalise," but to confer exclusive rights on their owners. Recognising the extraordinary implications of the system, international conventions on this subject incorporate, as a central philosophy, the freedom of the member states to attune their intellectual property protection system to their own needs and conditions. This fundamental principle should inform and guide all of the discussions in the Negotiating Group on the intellectual property protection system.

The reason India argues for the freedom of member states to set the fundamental conditions for intellectual property rights is that it believes that any principles or standards which govern intellectual property should be true to the socioeconomic, developmental, technological and public interest priorities and needs of developing countries. Very specific concrete policies follow from the Indian position: patents must be fully worked (or exploited) in the host country, licensing of rights may be made compulsory, and certain areas (such as food, pharmaceuticals, agricultural chemicals, and biogenetic innovations) may be excluded from patentability altogether. India's position finds great sympathy in developing countries on both developmental and moral (fairness) grounds (Lepp, 1990; Rapp and Rozek, 1990; Siebeck, 1990).

In essence, therefore, developing countries argue that individual claims on intellectual property are subordinated to more fundamental claims of social well-being. Unlike inalienable rights, intellectual property rights can be subordinated to greater interests; in this case the right of a people to livelihood. In this view, intellectual property is primarily a form of common property which may take some limited private forms.

The developing country position regarding rights to livelihood follows from the above. Attention must be paid to the logic of the development position. For people to be able to live they must be able to either produce what they need or be able to purchase it. In agrarian societies having some land is directly linked to livelihood. This point assumes importance in terms of setting forth a comprehensive set of property rights for all *peoples and persons*. Developing countries implicitly reject the "trickle down theory" of development

and limited technology transfer linked to private intellectual property rights. They shift priorities and define property rights first in a social and, then, in a private way. The argument contends that the "right to livelihood" (read development) takes precedence over other claims upon which property rights are based. In essence, therefore, such a position presents essentially the same arguments which would be put forth in arguing for radical land reform: the present system of intellectual property rights violates the (cultural) norms of distributive justice. The needs of the poor take priority over the wants of the rich. To this end the Government of India (1989, pp. 7) argues:

> It is relevant to note that the food, pharmaceutical and chemical sectors have been accorded a different treatment in the patent laws of developing countries because of the critical nature of these sectors to their socioeconomic and public interests.

Developing countries are arguing that the rights of people to development take a certain priority over private property claims (Government of India, 1989). The statement goes on to link patent monopolies to predatory pricing in pharmaceutical and agro-chemical sectors and concludes (p. 8):

> Every country should therefore be free to determine both the general categories as well as the specific products or sectors that it wishes to exclude from patentability. . . .

The argument of developing countries is that while people may have a right to the fruit of their labor, they have a duty to reward society which practically made the very fruitfulness of labor possible. The historical patterns of interdependence (if not dependence) between peoples evokes a concern for the equitable sharing of benefits and bearing of costs. Some Third World countries voice the argument that the R&D infrastructure enjoyed in the first world was built off the labor of the poor and extracted by the Monroe doctrine, European colonialism and other rationalizations of "manifest destiny." That is, the historical conditions which have given rise to the opportunity set enjoyed by first world intellectual labor is not a moot point. For the private fruits of innovative labor were only made possible by the common property of research and development (R&D) infrastructure. To the extent that this infrastructure was historically built from developing country resources, developing countries have a claim on the results. The costs which developing countries have borne may be measured not only by riches taken out but also by policies and practices which internally disrupted their proper development if not creating their underdevelopment. To put it bluntly, they claim that Third World labor has not always been equitably rewarded by First World business concerns. There are residual claims to be taken into account.

Regarding economic efficiency, developing countries argue that the marginal productivity of new technologies, when employed in the Third World, is far greater than in the first. The marginal argument means that the developed countries are already saturated in new technologies. While concentration of technologies in the developed world will continue to lead to productive growth, that growth is far smaller than the level of growth which would be unleashed if these technologies were introduced to the developing world where they are absent. To take an example from agriculture, Japan applies over 380 kilograms (kg) of fertilizer to a hectare (ha) of farmland. Additional applications of fertilizer will not significantly increase farm output at the margin. But that same fertilizer applied to farmland in a developing country where less than 20 kg/ha are now used, would dramatically increase output (Steidlmeier, 1987). It is for such a reason that India will not grant patents in agricultural technologies. This point suggests a utilitarian theme: that global redistribution of property rights would most benefit the majority, especially the world's poor who are struggling to meet basic needs.

IV. Dilemmas

Most observers agree that new international institutions of intellectual property are needed to tap the innovative creativity of peoples and persons and to adequately diffuse the fruits of such innovation. New arrangements are needed both in terms of building up R&D infrastructures as well as in terms of enterprise policies. This argument is important not so much for dividing up existing technologies as for generating new ones and diffusing them around the globe. There are a number of ethical problems related to prospective intellectual property regimes. I discuss three points: utilitarianism, rights and distributive justice.

Intellectual property rights restrict the diffusion of a particular technology for 17 to 20 years. Business frequently advances the position that intellectual property rights spur innovation, the production of greater wealth and improved well-being. Frequently, however, the utilitarian argument of business is based upon a narrow set of stakeholders—those within national boundaries and with direct ties to the company in question. Developing countries also use a utilitarian argument but with a very significant change: the world's poor become the principal stakeholders. The greatest utilitarian benefits are seen in an intellectual property regime which makes for the development of entire peoples. The greatest happiness of the greatest number is demographically weighted by the masses of the world's poor. In essence they argue that the greatest happiness of the greatest number would ensue if there were far greater diffusion of technology rather than greater protection of private property rights. Precisely for this reason both India and Brazil demand that a patent be fully worked and that, in many cases, licensing be made compulsory. Business people are suspect of the rhetoric. They point to local elites within developing countries who argue redistribution of property on the international level but give little attention to distributive justice within their own borders. In effect, business contends, these people are just out for themselves.

Secondly, almost without exception business argues intellectual property rights in collective terms. The important issue of the property rights of individual researchers working for the firm is passed over (Anawalt, 1988). The structure of modern science has been transformed dramatically over the past century. The Edisons of the world have been largely supplanted by Bell Labs and other research laboratories. Researchers engaged in such labs are contractually forced to cede all personal property claims to their discoveries. While management does deserve some return for the provision of a research infrastructure—without which many scientists would not be able to function—it is questionable whether it is legitimate to make the ceding of property claims a condition of employment. What happens in practice is that the fruits of scientific labor are passed to management and to owners. The rights of inventors have not been delineated; indeed, they are forced to forego them.

Aside from the comparative rights of inventors versus a company's rights, the rights of a people versus a company must be considered. In this context, developing countries consistently assert that the priority of the right of a people to their livelihood and development takes precedence over rights of private property. For this reason India restricts pharmaceuticals and agricultural chemicals from patents altogether. Furthermore, when patents are granted for items which are of crucial importance for people to meet their basic needs, many restrictive conditions are imposed.

Social rules which govern intellectual property raise many questions of distribution. The first area of distribution regards what is owed society for the bountiful research infrastructure which is supplied from *both* domestic and international sources. The right of property carries with it duties toward those who make the enjoyment of that right possible. If the labs make it possible for the scientist to function, it is the social infrastructure which makes it possible for the labs to function. Even granting Locke's assumptions about the hunter, labor does not confer absolute property rights; for labor takes place within a social milieu, whether the natural bounty of creation or the public infrastructure of knowledge, which serves as the basis for creative labor. The argument of what is owed society also surfaces in the discussion of compulsory licensing and the full working of patents. Both measures emphasize the distributive rights of society to a stream of benefits for the bountiful infrastructure it provides.

The structure of international research also raises the issue of the distributive fairness of initial conditions. In the intellectual property arena, people's access to education and R&D is widely uneven across countries and is further complicated by the brain drain. Thus, the ability to innovate is itself impaired.

The distributive issues are by far the most difficult to handle in the intellectual property debate. On a utilitarian basis, the developing countries would prevail unless business interests could show that strict protection of private intellectual property rights would lead to greater overall productivity. To date, historical evidence does not support such a contention (World Bank, 1991). An argument based on rights is even more difficult. If need has priority over effort or merit (in this context, what one is owed for innovativeness and bril-

liance), then the developing country argument prevails. If that order is reversed, then business interests would prevail.

If disputes over intellectual property are to be resolved, change must take place in three areas: the socio-ethical legitimation of the property rules which govern action, transformation of management towards a global stakeholder model, and the building up of a coherent international public policy process. This will be a long historical process, if for no other reason than that technology continually outpaces arrangements set up to manage it.

References

Anawalt, H. C.: 1988, *Ideas in the Workplace: Planning for Protection* (Carolina Academic Press, Durham, NC).

Behdad, S.: 1989, "Property Rights in Contemporary Islamic Economic Thought: A Critical Perspective," *Review of Social Economy* Vol. 47(2), pp. 185–211.

Besen, S. M. and L. J. Raskind: 1991, "An Introduction to the Law and Economics of Intellectual Property," *Journal of Economic Perspectives* Vol. 5(1), pp. 3–27.

Brown, C. G. and F. W. Rushing: 1990, "Intellectual Property Rights in the 1990s: Problems and Solutions," in F. W. Rushing and C. G. Brown (eds.), *Intellectual Property Rights in Science, Technology and Economic Performance* (Boulder, CO, Westview Special Studies in Science, Technology and Public Policy).

Congressional Quarterly: 1990, "Is the U.S. Patent System Out of Date?," *Editorial Research Reports* Vol. 1(19), May 18.

Deardorff, A. V.: 1990, "Should Patent Protection Be Extended to All Developing Countries?," *The World Economy* Vol. 13(4), pp. 497–506.

Freeman, R. E.: 1984, *Strategic Management: A Stakeholder Approach* (Pitman Publishing Co., Boston, MA).

Gadbaw, R. M. G. and T. J. Richards: 1988, *Intellectual Property Rights—Global Consensus, Global Conflict?* (Westview Press, Boulder, CO).

Government of India: 1989, "Paper Presented by India in Uruguay Round Multilateral Talks" (Indian Embassy, Washington, D.C.) (Xerox).

Hazarika, S.: 1989, "India and U.S. Disagree on Patents," *New York Times,* April 17, p. D-10.

Hoffman, G. M.: 1990, "Piracy of Intellectual Property—A Report of the International Piracy Project," *Bulletin of the American Society for Information Science,* pp. 9–11.

Johnson, R. D.: 1989, "Adam Smith's Radical Views on Property, Distributive Justice and the Market," *Review of Social Economy* Vol. 47(3), pp. 247–271.

Kim K. W.: 1986, "A High Cost to Developing Countries," *New York Times*, October 5, p. D2.

Lepp, A. W.: 1990, "Intellectual Property Rights Regimes in Southeast Asia," *Journal of Southeast Asia Business*, Vol. 6(11), pp. 28–40.

Locke, J.: 1965, *Two Treatises on Civil Government* (Mentor Books, New York).

Munzer, S. R.: 1990, *A Theory of Property* (Cambridge University Press, New York, NY).

Needham, J.: 1981, *Science in Traditional China: A Comparative Perspective* (Harvard University Press, Cambridge, MA).

Pfizer, Inc.: 1989, Interview with General Patent Counsel.

Pryor, F. L.: 1991, "A Buddhist Economic System— In Practice," *American Journal of Economic and Sociology* Vol. 50(1), pp. 17–32.

Pryor, F. L.: 1990, "A Buddhist Economic System— In Principle," *American Journal of Economic and Sociology* Vol. 49(3), pp. 339–349.

Rapp, R. J. and R. P. Rozek: 1990, "Benefits and Costs of Intellectual Property Protection in Developing Countries," *Journal of World Trade* Vol. 24, pp. 75–102.

Reeve, A.: 1986, *Property* (Humanities Press International, Atlantic Highlands, NJ).

Siebeck, W., R. E. Evenson, W. Lesser, and C. A. Primo Braga: 1990, *Strengthening Protection of Intel- lectual Property in Developing Countries. A Survey of the Literature* (World Bank, Washington, DC).

Steidlmeier, P.: 1992, "China's Most Favored Nation Trading Status: Activists' Attempts to Reform China and U.S. Business Prospects" (State University of New York, School of Management Working Paper, Binghamton, NY).

Steidlmeier, P.: 1987, *The Paradox of Poverty: A Reappraisal of Economic Development Policy* (Ballinger Publishing Co., Lexington, MA).

U.S. Patent and Trademark Office, National Technical Information Service: 1990, "Industrial Patent Activity in the United States" (Washington, D.C.).

U.S. International Trade Commission: 1989, *Foreign Protection of Intellectual Property Rights and the Effect on U.S. Industry and Trade* (USITC Publication 2065, Washington, D.C.).

Uppal, J. S.: 1986, "Hinduism and Economic Development in South Asia," *International Review of Economics and Ethics* Vol. 1(1), pp. 20–33.

World Bank: 1991, *World Development Report*, 1990 (Washington, D.C.).

Business Ethics and the International Trade in Hazardous Wastes

JANG B. SINGH AND V. C. LAKHAN

THE EXPORT OF HAZARDOUS WASTES by the more developed countries to the lesser developed nations is escalating beyond control. The ethical implications and environmental consequences of this trade in hazardous wastes highlight the need for international controls and regulations in the conduct of business by corporations in the more developed countries. In the late 1970s, the Love Canal environmental tragedy awakened the world to the effects of ill conceived and irresponsible disposal of hazardous by-products of industries. Today, the media focuses its attention on the alleged illegal dumping of hazardous wastes in the lesser developed countries (see Barthos, 1988, and Harden, 1988). The most recent dramatic case so far is that of Koko, Nigeria where more than eight thousand drums of hazardous wastes were dumped, some of which contained polychlorinated biphenyl (PCB), a highly carcinogenic compound and one of the world's most toxic wastes (Tifft, 1988). The government of Nigeria has detained a number of Nigerians in connection with the incident and President Babangida has indicated that they may face a firing squad if found guilty of

From Journal of Business Ethics 8(8), 1989. *Reprinted by permission of Kluwer Academic Publishers.*

illegal dumping. Previous to this was the media documentation in the spring of 1987 of an American barge laden with 3000 tonnes of garbage being turned back to the United States by the Mexican navy. The barge had already tried, unsuccessfully, to dump its noxious cargo in North Carolina, Alabama, Mississippi and Louisiana. The Mexican navy action was aimed at preventing the barge from dumping its cargo in Mexico.

The three cases cited above serve as disturbing examples of the international trade in hazardous wastes. Not all of the activities involved in this trade are illegal. In fact, governments are often directly involved in the business of hazardous wastes. This paper examines various characteristics of the international trade in hazardous waste and discusses the ethical implications of such business activity.

The International Trade in Hazardous Wastes and Attendant Problems

Miller (1988) defined hazardous waste as any material that may pose a substantial threat or potential hazard to human health or the environment when managed improperly. These wastes may be in solid, liquid or gaseous form and include a variety of toxic, ignitable, corrosive, or dangerously reactive substances. Examples include acids, cyanides, pesticides, solvents, compounds of lead, mercury arsenic, cadmium, and zinc, PCB's and dioxins, fly ash from power plants, infectious waste from hospitals, and research laboratories, obsolete explosives, herbicides, nerve gas, radioactive materials, sewage sludge, and other materials which contain toxic and carcinogenic organic compounds.

Since World War II, the amount of toxic by-products created by the manufacturers of pharmaceuticals, petroleum, nuclear devices, pesticides, chemicals, and other allied products has increased almost exponentially. From an annual production of less than 10 million metric tonnes in the 1940s, the world now produces more than 320 million metric tonnes of extremely hazardous wastes per year. The United States is by far the biggest producer, with "over 275 million metric tonnes of hazardous waste produced each year" (Goldfarb, 1987). The total is well over one tonne per person. But the Untied States is not alone. European countries also produce millions of tonnes of hazardous wastes each year (Chiras, 1988). Recent figures reported by Tifft (1988) indicate that the twelve countries of the European Community produce about 35 million tonnes of hazardous wastes annually.

The problems associated with hazardous wastes started to gain world-wide attention after 1977 when it was discovered that hazardous chemicals leaking from an abandoned waste dump had contaminated homes in a suburban development known as Love Canal, located in Niagara Falls, New York. This event triggered a frantic search for new ways and places to store hazardous wastes, and an introduction of new environmental regulations to store, handle, and dispose of hazardous wastes. With the "not in my backyard" (NIMBY) syndrome in the developed societies, the manufacturers and creators of hazardous wastes began to escalate the practice of dumping their wastes in the lesser developed countries.

Table 1 mainly provides an extensive list of companies which are exporting various toxic wastes to the lesser developed countries. The United States and certain European countries are now turning to areas in Africa, Latin America, and the Caribbean to dump their wastes. Historically, the trade in wastes has been conducted among the industrialized nations: A major route involving industrialized nations is that between Canada and the United States. The movement of wastes from the United States into Canada is governed by the Canada-U.S.A. Agreement on the Transboundary Movement of Hazardous Waste which came into effect on November 8, 1986 (Environment Canada). In 1988, the United States exported 145,000 tonnes. Of this amount, only one third was recyclable, leaving approximately 96,667 tonnes of hazardous organic and inorganic wastes such as petroleum by-products, pesticides, heavy metals, and organic solvents and residues for disposal in the Canadian environment. Of interest is the fact that Canada restricts the import of nuclear waste, but not toxic, flammable, corrosive, reactive, and medical wastes from the United States.

Most of the United States hazardous wastes are shipped from the New England states, New York and Michigan and enter Ontario and Quebec which in 1988 received approximately 81,899 and 62,200 tonnes respectively. The neutralization and disposal of the imported hazardous wastes are done by several Canadian companies, with the two largest being Tricil and Stablex Canada Inc. Tricil

Table 1. Identification of Actual Waste Shipments and Active Proposals

Importing Country	Name of Firm	Point of Export	Type of Waste
1. Argentina	American Security International	Florida, U.S.A.	Solvents/Chemical Sludge
2. Benin	Sesco Ltd.	Gibraltar	Non-Nuclear Toxic Waste
3. Benin	Government of France	France	Radioactive Wastes
4. Brazil	Applied Technologies	U.S.A.	Unspecified Toxic Wastes
5. Brazil	Ashland Metal Co.	Pennsylvania, U.S.A.	N/A
6. Brazil	Delatte Metals Inc.	California, U.S.A.	N/A
7. Brazil	Astur Metals Inc.	Puerto Rico, U.S.A.	N/A
8. Canada	Over 400 Firms	Mainly points in New England, New York and Michigan	Petroleum by-products, Pesticides, Heavy Metals and organic solvents and residues
9. Dominican Republic	Arbuckle Machinery	Texas, U.S.A.	PCB Wastes
10. Dominican Republic	Franklin Energy Resource	New York, U.S.A.	Refuse
11. Dominican Republic	World Technology Co.	Italy	Toxic Liquid Wastes
12. Equatorial Guinea	Unspecified British	U.K.	Chemical Wastes
13. Gabon	Denison Mining	Colorado, U.S.A.	Uranium Tailing Wastes
14. Guinea	Bulkhandling Inc.	Philadelphia, U.S.A.	Toxic Incinerator Ash
15. Guinea-Bissau	Hamilton Resources	U.K.	N/A
16. Guinea-Bissau	B/S Import-Export Ltd.	U.K.	Pharmaceutical Industrial Wastes
17. Guinea-Bissau	Hobday Ltd.	U.K.	Pharmaceutical Industrial Wastes
18. Guinea-Bissau	Intercontrat S.A.	Switzerland	Pharmaceutical Industrial Wastes
19. Guinea-Bissau	Lindaco Ltd.	Michigan, U.S.A.	Pharmaceutical Industrial Wastes
20. Guyana	Pott Industries	California, U.S.A.	Industrial Oil Wastes
21. Guyana	Teixeria Farms International	California, U.S.A.	Paint Sludge
22. Haiti	Palino and Sons	Philadelphia, U.S.A.	Toxic Incinerator Ash
23. India	Jack & Charles Colbert	U.S.A.	Lead Tainted Hazardous Wastes
24. Mexico	Arm Co. Steel	Missouri, U.S.A.	N/A
25. Mexico	Border Steel Mills	Texas, U.S.A.	N/A
26. Mexico	Chapparral Steel	Texas, U.S.A.	N/A
27. Mexico	Nucor Steel, Nebraska	Nebraska, U.S.A.	N/A
28. Mexico	Nucor Steel, Texas	Texas, U.S.A.	Furnace Dust
29. Mexico	Nucor Steel, Utah	Utah, U.S.A.	Furnace Dust
30. Mexico	Razorback Steel	Arkansas, U.S.A.	N/A
31. Mexico	Sheffield Steel Corp.	Oklahoma, U.S.A.	N/A
32. Mexico	Federated Metal	New Jersey, U.S.A.	Lead Wastes
33. Mexico	B.F. Goodrich	Texas, U.S.A.	PCB's, Mercury Cinders
34. Mexico	Diamond Shamrock	Texas, U.S.A.	PCB Wastes
35. Mexico	Bayou Steel Corp.	Louisiana, U.S.A.	Furnace Dust
36. Nigeria	Jack & Charles Colbert	U.S.A.	Lead Tainted Hazardous Wastes
37. Paraguay	American Securities Int.	Florida, U.S.A.	Solvents/Chemical Sludge
38. Peru	American Securities Int.	Florida, U.S.A.	Solvents/Chemical Sludge
39. Senegal	Intercontrat, S.A.	Switzerland	N/A
40. South Africa	American Cyanimid	New Jersey, U.S.A.	Mercury-Laced Sludge
41. South Africa	Quanex	Texas, U.S.A.	PCB Wastes
42. South Korea	Jack & Charles Colbert	U.S.A.	Lead Tainted Hazardous Wastes
43. Surinam	Mine Tech International	Netherlands	PCB Wastes
44. Tonga	Omega Recovery	California, U.S.A.	Hazardous Wastes
45. Uruguay	American Security Int.	Florida, U.S.A.	Solvents/Chemical Sludge
46. Zimbabwe	Jack & Charles Colbert	U.S.A.	Lead Tainted Hazardous Wastes

This table includes information mainly on actual waste shipments and active proposals for shipments from Europe and the United States to less developed countries.
Source: Klatte *et al.,* 1988.

with several locations in Ontario, imports wastes from more than 85 known American companies which it incinerates and treats in lagoons and landfill sites. Stablex Canada imports a wide variety of hazardous wastes from more than 300 U.S. companies. It uses various disposal methods, including landfills and cement kilns which burn not only the components needed for cement but also hazardous waste products. With the established Canada-U.S. Agreement on the Transboundary Movement of Hazardous Waste companies like Tricil and Stablex may increase their importation of hazardous wastes generated in the United States. As it stands, the Untied States Environmental Protection Agency estimates that over 75% of the wastes exported from the U.S. is disposed of in Canada (Vallette, 1989). This estimate will likely have to be raised in the near future. Canada-United States trade in hazardous wastes is not a one-way route. It is believed that all of the hazardous wastes imported by the Untied States (estimated at 65,000 tonnes in 1988) is generated in Canada (Ibid).

An especially controversial trend in the international trade in hazardous wastes is the development of routes between industrialized and "lesser developed countries." For example, according to the United States Environmental Protection Agency there have been more proposals to ship hazardous wastes from the United States to Africa during 1988, than in the previous four years (Klatte *et al.*, 1988).

African nations have recently joined together to try to completely ban the dumping of toxic wastes on their continent. They have referred to the practice as "toxic terrorism" performed by Western "merchants of death." Some African government officials are so disturbed by the newly exposed practices that they have threatened to execute guilty individuals by firing squad. Recently, Lagos officials seized an Italian and a Danish ship along with fifteen people who were associated with transporting toxic wastes in the swampy Niger River delta, into Nigeria. This occurred shortly after the discovery of 3800 tonnes of hazardous toxic wastes, which had originated in Italy. Local residents immediately became ill from inhaling the fumes from the leaking drums and containers which were filled with the highly carcinogenic compound PCB, and also radioactive material.

Companies in the United States have been responsible for sending large quantities of hazardous wastes to Mexico. Although Mexico only accepts hazardous wastes for recycling, which is referred to as "sham re-cycling," there are numerous reports of illegal dumping incidents. Two Californian companies have proposed the shipping of 62,000 tonnes of hazardous wastes each year to Guyana for incineration. They are also close to concluding a deal with the Guyana Government "to build a giant toxic waste incinerator in that country." The companies have suggested that "the incinerator ash be sold as fertilizer and building materials" (Morrison, 1988, p. 8). Guyana is one of a large number of developing countries whose economic plight makes it willing to accept proposals such as this, despite the long term human and environmental costs (Ibid., p. 9).

Given the fact that hazardous wastes are:

1. toxic;
2. highly reactive when exposed to air, water, or other substances that they can cause explosions and generate toxic fumes;
3. ignitable that they can undergo spontaneous combustion at relatively low temperatures;
4. highly corrosive that they can eat away materials and living tissues;
5. infectious; and
6. radioactive;

Miller (1988) has, therefore, emphasized correctly that the proper transportation, disposal, deactivation, or storage of hazardous wastes is a grave environmental problem which is second only to nuclear war.

The practice of transporting and dumping hazardous wastes in lesser developed nations, where knowledge of environmental issues is limited is causing, and will pose, major problems to both human health and the environment. Several comprehensive studies have outlined the detrimental impacts which hazardous waste can have on humans and natural ecosystems. Epstein *et al.*, (1982) have provided a thorough and dramatic coverage of the impacts of hazardous wastes, while Regenstein (1982), in his book *"America the Poisoned,"* gives a good overview of the implications of hazardous wastes. Essentially, hazardous wastes not only contaminate ground water, destroy habitats, cause human disease, contaminate the soil, but also enter the food chain at all levels, and eventually damage genetic material of all living things. For instance, when hazardous wastes enter water bodies, they are taken up by Zoo plankton, which single cell fish ingest while feeding. Other higher-level organisms also accumulate these substances, so that tissue concentrations become higher at higher levels of the food chain. The accumulation and biological magnification which occurs exposes organisms high on the food chain to highly dangerous levels of many chemicals. Understanding toxic chemical repercussions is still barely out of the dark ages, but it is known that metals present in water are toxic for fish. The metals irritate their gills and cause a mucus to build up on them, which eventually causes the fish to suffocate (Chiras, 1988). When hazardous wastes are deposited in the soil they are taken up by food crops, which eventually affect livestock as well as humans. When the ash enters the air, it also has the ability to cause pollution. Even though air is a finite resource capable of cleansing itself, it cannot entirely get rid of all pollutants. Besides causing respiratory problems in the local inhabitants, air pollution will damage the crops and reduce the yields. The rate of photosynthesis will be decreased with harmful effects on animal respiratory and central nervous systems (Miller, 1988.)

The hazardous wastes can also directly threaten human health through seeping into the ground and causing the direct pollution of aquifers, which supply "pure" drinking water. Today, in the United States, a long list of health related problems are caused by hazardous chemicals from "leaking underground storage tanks" (LUST). Investigations now show that human exposure to hazardous wastes from dumpsites, water bodies, and processing and storage areas can cause the disposed synthetic compounds to interact with particular enzymes or other chemicals in the body, and result in altered functions. Altered functions have been shown to include mutagenic (mutation-causing), carcinogenic (cancer-causing), and teratogenic (birth-defect causing) effects. In addition, they may cause serious liver and kidney dysfunction, sterility and numerous lesser physiological and neurological problems (see Nebel, 1987).

The Ethical Implications

The very notion of dumping one's wastes in someone else's territory is repulsive. When the Mexican navy turned back an American barge laden with garbage one Mexican newspaper columnist commented that "the incident serves to illustrate once again the scorn that certain sectors of U.S. society feel toward Mexico in particular and Latin America in general" (Mexico Sends Back, April 27, 1987, p. F9). Others have pointed to the export of wastes as an example of neo-colonialist behaviour. An official of an environmental organization expressed this view in the following manner: "I am concerned that if U.S. people think of us as their backyard, they can also think of us as their outhouse" (Porterfield and Weir, 1987, p. 343). In addition to arousing emotions such as those described above, the international trade in hazardous wastes raises a number of ethical issues. The rest of this paper examines some of these.

THE RIGHT TO A LIVABLE ENVIRONMENT

The desire for a clean, safe and ecologically balanced environment is an often expressed sentiment. This is especially so in industrialized countries where an awareness of environmental issues is relatively high—a fact that is gaining recognition in political campaigns. However, expression of the desire for a clean, safe environment is not the same as stating that a clean, safe environment is the right of every human being. But the right of an individual to a livable environment is easily established at the theoretical level. Blackstone (1983) examines the right to a livable environment from two angles—as a human right and as a legal right. The right to a clean, safe environment is seen as a human right since the absence of such a condition would prevent one from fulfilling one's human capacities.

> Each person has this right qua being human and because a livable environment is essential for one to fulfill his human capacities. And given the danger to our environment today and hence the danger to the very possibility of human existence, access to a livable environment must be conceived as a right which imposes upon everyone a correlative moral obligation to respect.
>
> (Blackstone, 1983, p. 413)

Guerrette (1986) illustrates this argument by reference to the Constitution of the United States. He proposes that people cannot live in a chemically toxic area, they cannot experience freedom in an industrially polluted environment and they cannot be happy worrying about the quality of air they breathe" or the carcinogenic effects of the water they drink (Guerrete, 1986, p. 409). Some even argue (e.g., Feinberg, 1983) that the right to a livable environment extends to future generations and that it is the duty of the present generation to pass on a clean, safe environment to them.

Establishing the right to a livable environment as a human right is not the same as establishing it as a legal right. This requires the passing of appropriate legislation and the provision of a legal framework that may be used to seek a remedy if necessary. Such provisions are more prevalent in the industrialized countries and this is one of the push factors in the export of hazardous wastes to the lesser developed countries. This points to the need for a provision in international law of the right to a decent environment which with accompanying policies to save and preserve our environmental resources would be an even more effective tool than such a framework at the national level (Blackstone, 1983, p. 414). As ecologists suggest, serious harm done to one element in an ecosystem will invariably lead to the damage or even destruction of other elements in that and other ecosystems (Law Reform Commission of Canada, 1987, p. 262) and ecosystems transcend national boundaries. The need for international law in this area has not led to the formulation of the same. However, there have been campaigns to stop the flow of hazardous wastes across national boundaries. In a current campaign, the international environmental group, Greenpeace, is calling for a global ban on the transboundary movement of wastes. Greenpeace is basing its appeal on Principle 21 of the 1972 Declaration of the United Nations Conference on the Human Environment which declares that each state is responsible for ensuring that activities within their jurisdiction or control do not cause damage to the environment of other states or of areas beyond the limits of their own national jurisdiction (Klatte *et al.,* 1988, p. 3).

A more direct harmful effect of the international trade in hazardous wastes is the damage to the health of workers involved in the transportation and disposal of these toxic substances. For example, prolonged exposure to wastes originating in Italy and transported by a ship called Zanoobia is suspected of causing the death of a crew person and the hospitalization of nine others (Klatte *et al.,*

1983, p. 12). Whereas worker rights in work-place health and safety are gaining wider recognition in many industrialized nations this is not so in the "less developed" countries which are increasingly becoming the recipients of hazardous wastes. Widespread violation of workers' right to a clean, safe work environment should therefore be expected to be a feature of the international trade in hazardous wastes.

RACIST IMPLICATIONS

The recent trend of sending more shipments of hazardous wastes to Third World countries has led to charges of racism. *West Africa,* a weekly magazine, referred to the dumping of toxic wastes as the latest in a series of historical traumas for Africa. The other traumas cited by the magazine were slavery, colonialism and unpayable foreign debts. An article in another African magazine viewed the dumping of wastes in Koko, Nigeria as follows:

> That Italy did not contemplate Australia or South Africa or some other place for industrial waste re-echoes what Europe has always thought of Africa: A wasteland. And the people who are there, waste beings.
>
> (Brooke, 1988, p. A10)

Charges of racism in the disposal of wastes have been made before at the national level in the United States. A study of waste disposal sites found that race was the most significant among variables tested in association with the location of commercial hazardous wastes facilities. The findings of this national study which were found to be statistically significant at the 0.0001 level showed that communities with the greatest number of commercial hazardous wastes facilities had the highest concentration of racial minorities (Lee, 1987, pp. 45–46). The study found that although socio-economic status appeared to play a role in the location of commercial hazardous wastes facilities, race was a more significant factor.

In the United States, one of the arguments often advanced for locating commercial waste facilities in lower income areas is that these facilities create jobs. This is also one of the arguments being advanced for sending wastes to poor lesser developed countries. An examination of Table 1 would reveal that nearly all the countries receiving hazardous wastes have predominantly coloured populations. This is the reason why charges of racism are being made against exporters of wastes. However, it must be noted that even though the trend of sending wastes to countries such as those listed in Table 1 has recently gained strength, the bulk of the international trade in hazardous wastes is still within industrialized Europe and North America which have predominantly noncoloured populations.

For example, the United States Environmental Protection Agency estimates that as much as 75% of the wastes exported from the U.S. is disposed of in Canada (Klatte *et al.,* 1988, p. 9). Another striking example is that a dump outside Schonberg, East Germany, is the home of well over 500,000 tonnes of waste a year from Western Europe (Rubbish Between Germans, March 1, 1986, p. 46). Thus, while charges of racism in the export of hazardous wastes are being made by some Third World leaders, figures on the international trade in such substances do not substantiate these claims.

CORPORATE RESPONSIBILITY

The international trade in hazardous wastes basically involves three types of corporations—the generators of wastes, the exporters of wastes and the importers of wastes. These entities, if they are to act in a responsible manner, should be accountable to the public for their behaviour.

> Having a corporate conscience means that a company takes responsibility for its actions, just as any conscientious individual would be expected to do. In corporate terms, this means that a company is accountable to the public for its behaviour not only in the complex organizational environment but in the natural physical environment as well. A company is thus responsible for its product and for its effects on the public.
>
> (Guerrette, 1986, p. 410)

Using Guerrette's definition of corporate responsibility, it seems clear that a corporation involved in the international trade in hazardous wastes is not likely to be a responsible firm. The importer of hazardous wastes is clearly engaged in activities that will damage the environment while the exporter being aware that this is a possibility, nevertheless, sends these wastes to the importer. However, it is the generator of hazardous wastes that is the most culpable in this matter. If the

wastes are not produced then obviously their disposal would not be necessary. Therefore, in view of the fact that virtually no safe method of disposing of hazardous wastes exists, a case of corporate irresponsibility could easily be formulated against any corporation involved in the international trade in these substances.

GOVERNMENT RESPONSIBILITY

Why do countries export wastes? A major reason is that many of them are finding it difficult to build disposal facilities in their own countries because of the NIMBY syndrome mentioned earlier. Other reasons are that better technologies may be available in another country, facilities of a neighboring country may be closer to a generator of waste than a site on national territory and economies of scale may also be a factor. However, to these reasons must be added the fact that corporations may be motivated to dispose of waste in another country where less stringent regulations apply (Transfrontier Movements, March 1984, p. 40). It is the responsibility of governments to establish regulations governing the disposal of wastes. In some countries these regulations are stringent while in others they are lax or non-existent. Moreover, some countries have regulations governing disposal of wastes within national boundaries as well as regulations relating to the export of hazardous wastes. For example, companies in the United States that intend to export hazardous wastes are requested to submit notices to the Environmental Protection Agency (EPA) and to demonstrate that they have the permission of the receiving country (Porterfield and Weir, 1987, p. 341). However, the effectiveness of these controls is in question. The General Accounting Office has found that "the E.P.A. does not know whether it is controlling 90 percent of the existing waste or 10 percent. Likewise it does not know if it is controlling the wastes that are most hazardous" (Ibid.). Moreover, there is evidence indicating that other U.S. government agencies are encouraging the export of hazardous wastes. The Navy, the Army, the Defense Department, the Agriculture Department and the Treasury Department are some government agencies that have provided hazardous wastes to known exporters. Also, major U.S. cities, sometimes with the approval of the State Department, have been suppliers to the international trade in hazardous wastes (Porterfield and Weir, 1987, p. 342).

While more stringent regulations, higher disposal costs, and heightened environmental awareness are pushing many companies in industrial countries to export hazardous wastes, it must be, nevertheless, realized that the governments of lesser developed countries are allowing such imports into their countries because of the need for foreign exchange. These governments are willing to damage the environment in return for hard currency or the creation of jobs. One must assume that on the basis of cost-benefit analysis these governments foresee more benefits than harm resulting from the importation of hazardous wastes. However, these benefits go mainly to a few waste brokers while the health of large numbers of people is put at risk. In some cases decisions to import wastes are made by governments which hold power by force and fraud. For example, Haiti which has imported wastes (see Table 1) is ruled by a military dictatorship and Guyana which is actively considering the importation of industrial oil wastes and paint sludge is ruled by a minority party which has rigged all elections held in that country since 1964. The ethical dilemma posed by this situation is that of whether or not an unrepresentative government of a country could be trusted to make decisions affecting the life and health of its citizens. In fact, a larger question is whether or not any government has the right to permit business activity that poses a high risk to human life and health.

Generally, governments of waste generating countries, in reaction to political pressure, have imposed stringent regulations on domestic disposal and some restrictions on the export of hazardous wastes. However, as the examples above illustrate, the latter restrictions are not strictly enforced, hence, indicating a duplicitous stance on the part of the generating countries. The governments of importing countries, in allowing into their countries, wastes that will disrupt ecosystems and damage human health, deny their citizens the right to a livable environment

Conclusion

Hazardous wastes are, in the main, by-products of industrial processes that have contributed significantly to the economic development of many countries. Economic development, in turn, has led to lifestyles which also generate hazardous wastes. To export these wastes to countries which do not benefit from waste generating industrial processes or whose citizens do not have lifestyles that generate such wastes is unethical. It is especially unjust to send hazardous wastes to lesser developed countries which lack the technology to minimize the deleterious effects of these substances. Nevertheless, these countries are increasingly becoming recipients of such cargoes. The need for stringent international regulation to govern the trade in hazardous wastes is now stronger than ever before. However, this alone will not significantly curb the international trade in hazardous wastes. International regulation must be coupled with a revolutionary reorganization of waste-generating processes and change in consumption patterns. Until this is achieved the international trade in hazardous wastes will continue and with it a plethora of unethical activities.

References

Barthos, G.: 1988, "Third World Outraged at Receiving Toxic Trash," *Toronto Star,* June 26, pp. 1, 4.

Blackstone, W. T.: 1983, "Ethics and Ecology" in Beauchamp, T. L. and Bowie, N. E. (Eds), *Ethical Theory and Business* 2nd. edition (Prentice-Hall, Inc., Englewood Cliffs, New Jersey) pp. 411–424.

Brooke, J.: 1988, "Africa Fights Tide of Western Wastes," *Globe and Mail,* July 18, p. A10.

Chiras, D. D.: 1988, *Environmental Science* (Benjamin Commings Publishing Co. Inc., Denver).

Environment Canada: 1986, *Canada-U.S.A. Agreement on the Transboundary Movement of Hazardous Waste* (Environment Canada, Ottawa).

Epstein, S. S., Brown, L. O., and Pope, C.: 1982, *Hazardous Waste in America* (Sierra Club Books, San Francisco).

Feinberg, J.: 1983, "The Rights of Animals and Unborn Generation," in Beauchamp, F. L. and Bowie, N. E. (Eds), *Ethical Theory and Business,* 2nd. edition, (Prentice-Hall Inc., Englewood Cliffs, New Jersey) pp. 428–436.

Goldfarb, T. D.: 1987, *Taking Sides: Clashing Views on Controversial Environmental Issues* (Dushkin Publishing Co. Inc., Connecticut).

Guerrette, R. H.: 1986, "Environmental Integrity and Corporate Responsibility," *Journal of Business Ethics* Vol. 5, pp. 409–415.

Harden, B.: 1988, "Africa Refuses to Become Waste Dump for the West," *Windsor Star,* July 9, p. A-6.

Klatte, E., Palacio, F., Rapaport, D., and Vallette, J.: 1988, *International Trade in Toxic Wastes: Policy and Data Analysis* (Greenpeace International, Washington, D.C.).

Law Reform Commission of Canada: 1987, "Crimes Against the Environment" in Poff, D. and Waluchow, W., *Business Ethics in Canada* (Prentice-Hall Canada Inc., Scarborough), pp. 261–264.

Lee, C.: Summer 1987, "The Racist Disposal of Toxic Wastes," *Business and Society Review* Vol. 62, pp. 43–46.

Miller, T.: 1988, *Living in the Environment* (Wadsworth Publishing Co., California).

Montreal Gazette: April 27 1987, "Mexico Sends Back U.S. Barge Filled with Tonnes of Garbage," p. F9.

Morrison, A.: 1988, "Dead Flowers to U.S. Firms That Plan to Send Waste to Guyana," *Catholic Standard,* Sunday, May 8.

Nebel, B. J.: 1987, *Environmental Science* (Prentice-Hall, Inc., New Jersey).

OECD Observer: March 1984, Transfrontier Movements of Hazardous Wastes: Getting to Grips with the Problem," pp. 39–41.

Porterfield, A. and Weir, D.: 1987, "The Export of U.S. Toxic Wastes," *The Nation,* Vol. 245, Iss. 10 (Oct. 3), pp. 341–344.

Regenstein, L.: 1982, *America the Poisoned* (Acropolis Books, Washington, D.C.).

The Economist: March 1 1986, "Rubbish Between Germans," p. 46.

Tifft, S.: 1988, "Who Gets the Garbage," *Time* July 4, pp. 42–43.

Vallette, J.: 1989, *The International Trade in Wastes: A Greenpeace Inventory (Fourth Edition)* (Greenpeace International, Luxembourg).

Ethics and the Gender Equality Dilemma for U.S. Multinationals

DON MAYER AND ANITA CAVA

We hold these truths to be self-evident: that all men are created equal, and endowed by their creator with certain rights—life, liberty, and the pursuit of happiness.

U.S. Declaration of Independence, 1776

All human beings are born free and equal in dignity and rights.

United Nations Universal Declaration of Human Rights, 1948

JUDGING FROM THE U.S. Declaration of Independence, gender equality was not self-evident in 1776. By 1948, however, the Universal Declaration of Human Rights took care not to exclude women from the ambit of declared rights. Since then, while gender equality has come a long way in the United States, many difficult and divisive issues remain unresolved. After completing a global inventory of attitudes on gender equality, Rhoodie (1989) concluded that many nations give only "lip service" to the goals of gender equality articulated in international conventions and declarations such as the U.N. Declaration of Human Rights (1948). Given the uneven progress of gender and racial equality in the world, it is inevitable that multinational enterprises (MNEs) encounter uneven ethical terrain.

Recently, the U.S. Congress and the Supreme Court have differed markedly over how the principles of non-discrimination in Title VII of the Civil Rights Act of 1964 (Title VII) should be applied by U.S. MNEs in their overseas activities. Both Congress and the Court recognized that U.S. non-discrimination laws may create difficulties for U.S. companies doing business in host countries where racial and/or gender discrimination is a way of life. But Congress, having the last word, decided in the Civil Rights Act of 1991 that Title VII protects

From Journal of Business Ethics *12(9), 1993. Printed by permission of Kluwer Academic Publishers.*

U.S. citizens from employment discrimination by U.S. MNEs in their overseas operations.[1]

In so doing, Congress effectively reversed the Supreme Court, which only a few months earlier had decided that Title VII did not apply "extraterritorially" (*E.E.O.C. v. Aramco,* 1991).[2] According to the Court, to apply U.S. laws abroad might cause "unintended clashes between our laws and those of other nations which could result in international discord." The majority of the Court wanted Congress to be entirely clear about its intent before imposing the ethical values inherent in Title VII on the activities of a U.S. company in a foreign country.

This reluctance is understandable. It seems logical to assume that companies would prefer not to have two personnel policies, one for U.S. citizens and one for host country nationals and others. Human resource directors indicate a preference for following the laws and customs of the host country while doing business there, but a concern for furthering human rights values in the U.S.[3] Such a preference corresponds to other observed realities, since the recent history of law and business ethics shows that a number of U.S. MNEs would engage in bribery in foreign countries, if that should be the custom, in order to remain "competitive." Similarly, many U.S. MNEs were willing to acquiesce to *apartheid* in South Africa, despite the fact

that such behavior would not be tolerated in the United States.

The multinational that adopts such a policy of moral neutrality follows what Bowie (1977) has identified as moral relativism. The approach of a moral relativist is characterized as—"When in Rome, do as the Romans do." This prescription has its arresting aspects. If Rome existed today as a commercial power, would U.S. corporate executives entertain one another by watching slaves battle to the death, attending Bacchanalian orgies, or cheering while faithful but hapless Christians were being mauled by lions? While such practices do not have overt current counterparts, there are nonetheless substantial differences among cultures in matters of gender equality (Rhoodie, 1989).

How does the MNE deal ethically with such contrasts? Bowie suggests that while ethical relativism cannot support business ethics in the global economy, neither can we afford to be "ethnocentric" and assume that "our" way is the one "right way." Bowie uses the term "ethnocentric" to describe a view that "when in Rome, or anywhere else, do as you would at home" (Bowie, 1988; Wicks, 1990). Essentially, it was this concern that animated the Supreme Court's decision in *Aramco,* which explicitly worried about "unintended clashes" between U.S. law and Saudi Arabian law. Further, it is this concern about "ethnocentrism" that fuels speculation that applying Title VII's equal opportunity provisions in countries like Japan is a recipe for corporate noncompetitiveness and perhaps even a form of cultural imperialism.

This article explores some of the difficulties faced by U.S. multinationals in complying with Title VII as applied abroad and examines the ethical arguments surrounding achieving the goal of gender equality. Part 1 discusses the current dilemma for international human resource managers and their employees, as well for citizens of host countries. We focus on Japan as a model of a country in transition and consider the extreme situation of the Islamic countries as a counterpoint in the analysis. The emphasis is on practical and legal considerations. Part II returns to the issues of ethical relativism and cultural imperialism, and suggests that U.S. multinationals should not opt for moral relativism by deferring entirely to cultural traditions in countries such as Japan, traditions that may be contrary to declared international standards

---

[1]Civil Rights Restoration Act of 1991, P. L. 102–166, Nov. 21, 1991, 105 Stat. 1071. For the purposes of this discussion, a U.S. MNE is an enterprise with operations in one or more foreign countries.

[2]*E.E.O.C. v. Aramco, Boureslan v. Aramco,* 111 S. Ct. 1227 (1991).

[3]The authors mailed a survey entitled "Use of U.S. Employment Discrimination Law Abroad" to human resource directors of 120 companies identified as multinational enterprises. In part, the questionnaire solicited information about whether or not the company felt it wise to apply Title VII abroad. The eight responses that were received provide anecdotal, as opposed to statistically significant, information. Six respondents indicated it would be "unwise" to attempt to apply Title VII to U.S. citizens working abroad. The reasons given appear predictable: it would be "difficult"; it is the "local manager's responsibility"; we "do not attempt" to impose our norms on others. Two respondents believed it would be wise to implement such a policy despite the obstacles discussed in this paper. Nonetheless, all respondents indicated that the policy is appropriately enforced in the U.S. and two believed it would be wise to do so abroad as well.

for gender and racial equality and contrary to apparent global trends.

I. Perspectives on the Current Dilemma

Human resource managers, employees, and host country nationals will have varying perspectives on the application of U.S. civil rights statutes for the promotion of gender equality in the foreign workplace. Each merits consideration in order to understand the framework within which an ethical analysis can be applied.

A. THE MNE MANAGERIAL PERSPECTIVE

For a MNE whose operations cover the U.S., Europe, Asia, and the Middle East, the differing cultural norms with respect to equal opportunity in the workplace are a bit unreal. Despite strong movements for gender equality in the Scandinavian countries and, to a lesser extent, in the U.S. and Europe, the basic condition of women worldwide is largely "poor, pregnant, and powerless" (Rhoodie, 1989). The differences among various nations span a continuum from cultures with a strong commitment to gender equality in the workplace to those with strong commitments to keeping women out of the workplace entirely (Mayer, 1991).

For the MNE trying to "do the right thing," the situation suggests a kind of ethical surrealism, where reality retreats before an unreal mix of elements—social, cultural, legal, and philosophical. It seems natural that companies doing business abroad would want to follow host country laws and customs. Obviously, following U.S. law only for U.S. employees poses a dual dilemma. First, assuming that gender discrimination is culturally accepted and legally tolerated in many foreign countries, what should be the MNE personnel policy? The MNE has the option of designing a single non-discriminatory policy for all workers or creating a two-track system, protecting the legal rights of U.S. nationals while accommodating the host country's norms for their nationals and others. Second, where the MNE has adopted a Code of Ethics for global application and the Code specifically refers to equal opportunity, can the MNE honor its commitment in a principled way?

Strict compliance with an ethical position would suggest a simple solution to this conundrum: Adopt an equal opportunity program, educate all employees, and enforce it consistent with Title VII's mandates across the board. Admittedly, however, following U.S. law worldwide, for all employees, is surely "ethnocentric" and may also be unworkable. In some host countries, such as Saudi Arabia, the legal conflicts may be pronounced. In others, such as Japan, the cultural conflicts may undermine consistent enforcement of Title VII-oriented policies throughout the workforce.

Taking Japan as an example, the U.S. MNE doing business in Tokyo is confronted with a patriarchal society in which women are expected to manage household work while men dominate the other forms of work (Lebra, 1984). Although men and women receive comparable educations through the high school level, women are expected to marry by age 25. Employment after that age is generally discouraged (Prater, 1981). There is seldom, if ever, a managerial track for Japanese women: if employed by a major Japanese company, they are often given positions largely designed to make the office environment more comfortable (such as by serving tea and appearing "decorative"), and are not taken seriously as career office workers (Seymour, 1991).

For a U.S. MNE to announce a policy of equal opportunity for Japanese operations, tie that policy to Title VII enforcement, and expect no negative results would require a supposition that the overwhelmingly male population of Japanese customers, suppliers, and government officials would treat U.S. women and Japanese women equally. But, in fact, the sensitivity of Japanese males to sexual harassment issues is only dawning (Ford, 1992; Lan, 1991), and some other forms of overt discrimination are likely. Assuming, as seems warranted, that the MNEs' female employees will be adversely affected to some degree by prevailing male attitudes in Japan, how would the company find that balanced approach that yields the least friction and the best results?

Such a question suggests that a utilitarian analysis, or some pragmatism, may be entirely appropriate here. It is well beyond the scope of this paper to suggest how absolute adherence to Title VII and equal opportunity principles should be tempered to achieve greater harmony with the host country culture, but a few observations are in order. First, Title VII's dictates may need to be culturally adjusted. An "appropriate" response to repeated incidents of Japanese males looking up female employees' skirts may be more educational than admonitory, at least for the first transgressions. Second, companies should be wary of any utilitarian or pragmatic approaches that predict a "non-competitive" result unless business hews to some perceived cultural norms. This point needs further elaboration.

In a country such as Saudi Arabia, the cultural norms and the sacred law, or *Shari'a,* are fairly congruent. The winds of change are not, seemingly, as strong as in other parts of the world. Japan, on the other hand, has demonstrated its willingness to adopt some "Western ways" in order to be part of the global economy, and there is considerable evidence that Japanese pragmatism has already created some new opportunities for women in the workplace (Prater, 1991). Moreover, legislation exists which purports to promote gender equality in the workplace, though some critics have questioned its efficacy (Edwards, 1988). In short, the "downside" of promoting equal opportunity in Japan because of cultural norms may easily be overstated; while Japanese males are not as sensitive to sexual harassment issues, for example, there are signs that they are becoming so (Lan, 1991).

For a host country culture that is less in flux, and whose culture and laws present a unified force against social change, the ethical issues change somewhat. This is because Title VII expressly allows discrimination in certain instances through the *bona fide* occupational qualification (BFOQ)[4] exception. The BFOQ exception provides that it will not be illegal to discriminate "on the basis of . . . religion, sex, or national origin in those certain instances where religion, sex, or national origin is a *bona fide* occupational qualification reasonably necessary to the normal operation of that particular business or enterprise."

In *Kern v. Dynalectron,*[5] for example, a company in the business of flying planes into the holy city of Mecca advised potential employees that Saudi Arabian law prohibited the entry of non-Muslims into the holy area under penalty of death.

One pilot took instruction in the Muslim religion, but was Baptist at heart, and rescinded his "conversion." Returning to the U.S., he sued under Title VII for employment discrimination based on religion. The federal appeals court ultimately determined that Title VII applied but that being Muslim was, in this situation, a "*bona fide* occupational qualification" and not discriminatory.

It remains to be seen how gender qualifications may be raised and litigated for alleged discrimination overseas. But if those qualifications have the force of law, and are not the result of cultural preferences only, the most serious ethical dilemma is whether or not to do business in that country at all. To take an example based on racial classification, if South African law prohibited blacks from being hired by MNEs, the MNEs' only ethical choices would be to

1. do business in South Africa and comply with the law,
2. refuse to do business in South Africa, or
3. do business there and hire blacks anyway.

How are these three options analyzed from a perspective of ethics and the law? Option (3) may certainly be seen as an ethical policy, though probably of the "ethnocentric" variety, yet few ethicists and even fewer business executives would counsel such a course. Option (1) is well within the mainstream of ethical relativism, and, we would argue, is less ethical than choosing option (2). But again, *cultural* conflicts do not create such choices; legal mandates do. And countries whose cultural values are colliding with the values of "outsiders" may choose, at least temporarily, to preserve their culture through legal mandates. Saudi Arabia has laws which prohibit women from travelling alone, working with men, working with non-Muslim foreigners, and these laws apply to foreign women as well as host country women (Moghadam, 1988).

Even without such explicit laws of prohibition, MNEs and their human resource managers may hesitate to violate unwritten or cultural laws, and taking moral relativism's approach to the problem of gender equality in other countries may seem prudent. But such an approach seems to depend on a rather sketchy kind of utilitarian analysis: Engaging in overt equal opportunity policies will result in cultural condemnation, loss of customer and client contacts, and eventual unprofitability of the entire overseas enterprise. But in host countries

---

[4]42 U.S.C. § 2000e-1 (1988).
[5]577 F. Supp. 1196, *affirmed* 746 F.2d 810 (1984).

whose culture is tied to the mainstream of world business, long-held attitudes will be difficult to maintain, and the negative impact of "doing things differently" should not be overestimated, nor should the definite benefits and opportunities of pursuing gender quality be overlooked (Lansing and Ready, 1988).

In this context, a comment about the employee's perspective seems appropriate. It might be difficult to generalize here because individual perspective often differs, depending upon personal ideology, situation, and career opportunities. However, from the viewpoint of a female manager in a U.S. MNE, we will assume that the greatest good would be a business world safe for gender equality and supportive of same. Adler and others have noted the difficulty of persuading MNEs that women managers can succeed in many countries whose cultures actively promote gender inequality (Adler, 1984). Certainly, a U.S. female manager's inability to obtain firsthand experience in dealing with Japanese businesses comes close to being a career handicap, and for Japanese women, the existence of opportunities outside the home may safety be regarded as benefits.

Ultimately, most American citizen employees of MNEs will test any policy by asking whether or not they are personally adversely affected. Companies that take care to structure career advancement opportunities such that experience in countries hostile to a protected class may find themselves with few employee complaints. However, MNEs not able to finesse the mandate of Title VII and the reality of certain foreign cultures will find themselves facing a similar set of choices described above with respect to apartheid. Now, however, a decision to accommodate host country norms must be accompanied by a fund out of which to pay judgments in Title VII litigation.

B. THE HOST COUNTRY'S PERSPECTIVE

From the overall Japanese societal perspective, the changes contemplated by a mandate of gender equality may indeed be troubling. The social structure that has built up over centuries, which has "worked" to achieve stability and a degree of consensus and comfort, could crumble if more and more women leave household work to obtain work

in the "business world." Who will do the careful packing of lunches, the guidance for "cram courses" after school, tending to the children and dinner and bedtime while spouse is engaged in the obligatory socializing with office mates after hours? While Japanese men may now be undertaking more domestic duties, the differences are still staggering. One recent estimate suggested that Japanese women put in four to five hours of domestic work daily, while their husbands put in eight minutes (Watanabe, 1992).

Any change in the prescribed social order is bound to seem disruptive, and, therefore, negative. As one Islamic man declared to a National Public Radio correspondent during the Persian Gulf war, if women are allowed in the workplace, the forces of social decay would soon send the divorce and crime rates skyrocketing. This argument, a kind of utilitarian "parade of horribles,[6] overtly trades on fear of change, is not empirically rigorous, and assumes that changes in the U.S. over a fifty year period represent the ultimate result of mindless social tampering. For the Islamic, this particular proponent of gender inequality in the workplace has a back-up argument, the *Qur'an*.

By appeal to divine, or infinite wisdom, we find an argument more akin to natural law or universalism. The argument may even suppose that not only Islamic society, but all other societies, would be well advised to follow this divinely decreed social ordering. What is manifest to the Islamic mind is contrary, it would seem, to "Western" notions of gender equality. This conflict pits two "objective" or "universal" truths against one another: the "truth" of the *Qur'an* and the "truth" of the Universal Declaration of Human Rights. Is the moral relativist right, after all?

II. Ethical Relativism and Ethical Ethnocentrism: A Synthesis for Overseas Gender Discrimination Issues

In general terms, the theory of moral relativism holds that different moral standards are "equally

---

[6]George Christie, of Duke University Law School, coined this phrase in reference to attorneys, who learn to see the dark possibilities issuing from any proposed action and are prone to recite a "parade of horribles" to their clients.

valid or equally invalid," and there are no "objective standards of right and wrong or good and evil that transcend the opinions of different individuals or different societies."[7] At the opposite extreme of the continuum is the objective approach, which is premised on the notion that there are "transcultural" norms that are universally valid.

Bowie (1988) suggests that the proper view is a point closer to the latter position. Although he stops short of embracing universalism, Bowie believes there are minimum ethical principles that are universally evident such as "do not commit murder" and "do not torture." These principles, clearly, can be enforced without imposing ethnocentric (or imperialistic) views upon a host country. To these minimum universal principles, Bowie adds the "morals of the marketplace," which are required to support transactions in the business world. These include honesty and trust. The combination of these two strands of quasi-universalism is as far as Bowie will go in staking his claim on the continuum.

Consider again the dilemmas faced by a U.S. MNE doing business in Japan, trying to integrate a tradition and practice of equal opportunity into a tradition and practice of unequal opportunity. One strategy for "blending in" with the Japanese market might be to adopt a thoroughly Japanese outlook and approach. That would include differing pay scales for men and women, actively discouraging women past the age of 25 from working with the company, and pointedly not inviting women employees to the after-five work/social functions that seem to play such an important part in an employee's successful corporate bonding.

Other than outright moral relativism, the social contract approach would appear to be the most likely proponent of such assimilation. Social contract theory examines the ethical foundations of societies by the relationships that exist within and between people, organizations, and groups. In an article on "extant social contracts," Dunfee (1991) explains and defends this communitarian approach to ethics, which appears grounded in relativism, but he also appears to offer an escape clause by way of a "filtering" device using utilitarian or deontological approaches. Dunfee would apparently recognize that racial discrimination is more widely condemned, and that gender discrimination is more widely tolerated, and conclude that perpetuating gender discrimination is less unethical than perpetuating racial discrimination. In a subsequent article, Dunfee and Donaldson (1991) retreat somewhat from the relativism approach and appear to suggest some dimensions of gender equality qualify as a "hypernorm," that is, a norm "recognized as core or foundational by most humans, regardless of culture." The example they give, however, is that of Saudi Arabia prohibiting women from driving, a rule that violates hypernorms of freedom of movement and rights of self-realization. Obviously, this issue does not approach the complexity posed by the international application of gender equality in the workplace.

In essence, what seems problematic for social contract theory is the substantial variance between the almost universally professed ideals of gender equality and the globally pervasive policies of gender inequality. If one looks to social practice for guidance as to what is ethical, gender inequality becomes relatively more ethical; yet if one looks to professed ideals and principles of equality, many existing forms of gender inequality (dowry deaths, female infanticide, widow-burning, and abortion based on male preference) (Howe, 1991) seem inexcusable. Ethical guidelines, apart from legal obligations, seem to require more explicit direction.

Bowie rejects relativism and argues for recognition of minimum universal principles and morals of the marketplace, an essentially deontological approach. He suggests that the latter may even control over the former where completely foreign agents meet to do business. Bowie draws upon democratic theory, torture and genocide, and examples based on bribery, apartheid, and political-economic values to make his point. He is, however, silent on gender discrimination. One wonders whether Bowie would view this issue as primarily social or as a political-economic priority on a plane with his other examples.

We take the position that neither relativism nor extant social contract theory are much help to MNEs in a host country whose values run counter to the company's ethical code or the laws and traditions of its country of origin. Instead, the concepts of minimum universal principles and morals of the marketplace legitimately can be broadened

[7]Van Wyk, *Introduction to Ethics*, St. Martin's Press, New York (1990), p. 15.

to embrace gender equality. Support for this position is evident in the increasingly international consensus on this point.

For example, as Frederick (1991) has pointed out, the United Nations Universal Declaration of Human Rights, the OECD Guidelines for Multinational Enterprises, and the International Labor Office Tripartite Declaration all give support to "nondiscriminatory employment policies" and the concept of "equal pay for equal work." Note that neither of these policies is widespread in Japan. The United Nations Convention on the Elimination of All Forms of Discrimination Against Women (1979) was ratified by a large number of nations, both industrialized and developing. The European Community has passed a number of Council directives aimed at promoting gender equality in employment (Weiner, 1990).

We believe that by following policies which generally promote gender equality, without slavish adherence to all U.S. judicial opinions on Title VII and with good faith adjustments where cultural conditions require, a U.S. MNE in Japan can maintain its own code of ethics without the "inevitable" loss of "competitiveness." Moreover, it can do so without being "ethnocentric" or "imperialist," and by doing so it can avoid a kind of ethical balkanization that adherence to moral relativism would require. After all, a dozen different cultural traditions might require a dozen different HRM policies, each geared to the host country's dominant yet often changing traditions.

. . . In going to a traditional culture where gender inequality is the norm, the MNE must be aware that there is another community emerging, one whose shape is as yet dimly perceived, but a community where goods, services, and information are traded with ever-increasing speed. Included in the information exchange is the communication of different values, and while these values are not being passed along in traditional ways, their transmission is inevitable. In this exchange of values and ideas, the ideals of equality are manifest in many ways. Any MNE, whatever the cultural norms it confronts in a particular country, would be wise to pay attention.

References

Adachi, K.: 1989, "Problems and Prospects of Management Development of Female Employees in Japan," *Journal of Management Development* Vol. 8(4), 32–40.

Adler, N.: 1984, "Women in International Management: Where Are They?," *California Management Review* Vol. 26, 78–89.

Bassiry, G. R.: 1990, "Business Ethics and the United Nations: A Code of Conduct," *SAM Advanced Management Journal* (Autumn), pp. 38–41.

Bellace, J.: 1991, "The International Dimension of Title VII," *Cornell International Law Journal* 24, 1–24.

Bowie, N.: 1988, "The Moral Obligations of Multinational Corporations," in Luper-Fay (ed.), *Problems of International Justice* (Westview Press, New York), pp. 97–113.

Bowie, N.: 1977, "A Taxonomy for Discussing the Conflicting Responsibilities of a Multinational Corporation," in *Responsibilities of Multinational Corporations to Society* (Arlington, Va.: Council of Better Business Bureau), pp. 21–43.

Carney, L. and O'Kelly: 1987, "Barriers and Constraints to the Recruitment and Mobility of Female Managers in the Japanese Labor Force," *Human Resource Management* Vol. 26(2), 193–216.

Daimon, S.: 1991, "'Karoshi' Phenomenon Spreading to Female Workforce," *Japan Times Weekly* (Intl. Ed.), Sept. 30–Oct. 6, p. 7.

Donaldson, T. and T. Dunfee: 1991, "Social Contracts in Economic Life: A Theory," No. 91–156 (revised) Working Paper Series, Department of Legal Studies, The Wharton School, University of Pennsylvania, pp. 27–32.

Dunfee, T.: 1991, "Extant Social Contracts," *Business Ethics Quarterly* Vol. 1, 22–37.

Edwards, L.: 1988, "Equal Employment Opportunity in Japan: A View from the West," *Industrial and Labor Relations Review* 41(2), 240–250.

Ford, J.: 1992, "Sexual Harassment Taken for Granted," *Japan Times Weekly* (Intl. Ed.), Feb. 10–16, p. 4.

Frederick, W.: 1991, "The Moral Authority of Transnational Corporate Codes," *Journal of Business Ethics* Vol. 10, 165–177.

Gundling, E.: 1991, "Ethics and Working with the Japanese: The Entrepreneur and the Elite Course," *California Management Review* Vol. 33(3), 25–39.

Howe M.: 1991, "Sex Discrimination Persists, According to a U.N. Study," *New York Times* June 16, p. A4, col. 1.

Lan, S.: 1991, "Japanese Businessman Produces Video to Prevent Lawsuits," *Japan Times Weekly* (Intl. Ed.), Nov. 11–17, p. 8.

Lansing, P. and K. Ready: 1988, "Hiring Women Managers in Japan: An Alternative for Foreign

Employers," *California Management Review* 30(3), 112–121.

Lebra, D.: 1984, *Japanese Women: Constraint and Fulfillment* (University of Hawaii Press, Honolulu).

Mayer, D.: 1991, "Sex Discrimination Policies for U.S. Companies Abroad," in Sanders, W. (ed), *Proceedings of the Council on Employee Responsibilities and Rights* (forthcoming).

Moghadam, V.: 1988, "Women, Work, and Ideology in the Islamic Republic," *International Journal of Middle East Studies* Vol. 20, 221–243.

Neff, R.: 1991, "When in Japan, Recruit as the Japanese Do—Aggressively," *Business Week* June 24, p. 58.

Prater, C.: 1991, "Women Try on New Roles; but Hopes Can Still Collide with Tradition," *Detroit Free Press* November 27, p. 1 (5th in a series, later published in the *New York Times*).

Rhoodie, E.: 1989, *Discrimination Against Women: A Global Survey of the Economic, Educational, Social and Political Status of Women* (London, U.K., McFarland and Company).

Seymour, C.: 1991, "The Ad-business: Talented Women Need Not Apply," *Japan Times Weekly* (Intl. Ed.), Dec. 9–15, p. 7.

Simon, H. and F. Brown: 1990/91, "International Enforcement of Title VII: A Small World After All?," *Employee Relations Law Journal* Vol. 16(3), 281–300.

United Nations: 1979, *Convention of the Elimination of All Forms of Discrimination Against Women*, U.N. Doc. A/34/36 (Dec. 18, 1979).

Watanabe, T.: 1992, "In Japan, a 'Goat Man' or No Man; Women Are Gaining More Clout in Relationships," *Los Angeles Times* Jan. 6, A1, col. 1.

Weiner, M.: 1990, "Fundamental Misconceptions About Fundamental Rights: The Changing Nature of Women's Rights in the EEC and Their Application in the United Kingdom," *Harvard International Law Journal* Vol. 31(2), 565–574.

Wicks, A.: 1990, "Norman Bowie and Richard Rorty on Multinationals: Does Business Ethics Need 'Metaphysical Comfort'?," *Journal of Business Ethics* Vol. 9, 191–200.

Cross-Cultural Ethics and the Child Labor Problem

HUGH D. HINDMAN AND CHARLES G. SMITH

IN 1995, BASED ON LIMITED statistical evidence from 100 countries, the International Labour Organization (ILO) estimated there were 73 million child workers between the ages of 10 and 14 worldwide in 1995. One year later, based on a closer scrutiny of the problem, the ILO estimated, in 1996:

> In the developing countries alone, there are at least 120 million children between the ages of 5 and 14 who are fully at work, and more than twice as many (or about 250 million) if those for whom work is a secondary activity are included (ILO, 1996).

The 120 million children fully at work comprise a labor force roughly equivalent to that of the United States. The 250 million for whom work constitutes at least a secondary economic activity comprise a labor force as large as our entire population.

Today, the use of child labor is concentrated most heavily in the developing countries throughout Asia, Africa, and Latin America:

> 61% (of child workers) are found in Asia, 32% in Africa, and 7% in Latin America. Although Asia has the largest number of child workers, Africa has the highest incidence at around 40% of children between 5 and 14 years old (ILO, 1996).

Children today, as they always have, work predominantly in agricultural and domestic labor, and in informal economic sectors. While much of this work is done within household systems of production, it is increasingly intersecting the channels of global commerce. Agricultural export (DOL, 1995), global tourism (Black, 1995), and organized trafficking in children (ILO, 1996) all connect directly to global markets.

Further, as children are drawn to industrial employment as their nation industrializes, their

From Journal of Business Ethics *19: 21–33, 1999.* © 1999 Kluwer Academic Publishers. Printed in the Netherlands. *Reprinted by permission of Kluwer Academic Publishers.*

work necessarily affects, and is affected by, global commerce. In textiles, apparel, and sporting goods, reports of sweatshop conditions, often involving children, have become so common place and embarrassing that leading global producers and distributors have felt compelled to respond (DOL, 1996). But even where children are drawn to industrial production for local and regional markets (such as mining, construction, or brick-making), it is invariably not far removed from the influence of global markets.

Why It Hurts: Economics of Child Labor

We aim to demonstrate the moral repugnance of-child labor by making the not so astonishing case that it is, in fact, economically inefficient and injurious. Ultimately, we aim to develop models of economic cause and effect that can serve as practical and empirical guideposts dealing with issues related to child labor. In this paper, we attempt to begin sketching the conceptual-theoretical framework for our project.

THE ECONOMIC FRAMEWORK

We intend to show that child labor is inefficient and injurious, in both the short run and the long run, to workers, nations, and the world economy—that it is so counterproductive as to be injurious to society itself—in short, that it is at odds with established precepts of economic theory. We begin by attending to effects of child labor at the level of the national economy. Inter-twined in national effects are the effects of child labor on the children themselves and others in the labor market and so, they are examined as well.

Our framework is grounded in economic theory dating to Adam Smith (1776). According to Smith, the principal determinants of the wealth of any given nation are:

1) the proportion of the population engaged in productive labor, and,
2) the relative productivity of that labor force.

Robert Reich (1991) argues that Smith's propositions are more important in today's global economy than they were in Smith's time of merchant capitalism. Reich stresses the importance of Smith's maxims to advanced economies such as the United States. He notes that when information, financial capital, technology, and goods and services themselves, can flow freely worldwide, few corporations will remain fully contained within national borders. Corporations will remain connected to consumer markets in the advanced economies, while they work to develop consumer markets elsewhere. But production can take place anywhere in the world. Thus, Reich argues that the only major economic resource that remains relatively fixed within a nation's borders is its labor force.

The importance of Smith's propositions can be extended to the developing nations as well. Where global investments in production flow freely to wherever the highest rate of return is anticipated, the well-being of the labor force largely determines the well-being of the nation. Natural resources and supportive infra-structure may assist in attracting investment. But where investment is based on returns to investors residing elsewhere, the only created wealth with any real assurance of remaining within the nation's borders is whatever the labor force generates through their wages.

There are two major advantages to grounding our work in the theories of Adam Smith (aside from the legitimacy derived from leaning on the Father of Economic Thought). First, it has stood the test of time. Grounded in Britain's period of merchant capitalism when industrialism was just beginning to emerge, the model should be equally suitable for the analysis of historical data and contemporary data. Second, its emphasis on the role of labor in economic development (given our interest in child labor). While numerous additional factors have been identified as important to a nation's development, including the quantity and quality of real capital, the level of technological sophistication, the availability of natural resources, and various other sociocultural and political influences, all economists recognize the fundamental importance of labor force characteristics.

DEPENDENT VARIABLES

Following Smith, the ultimate dependent variable of interest is national wealth. Other important dependent variables include economic growths, efficiency, and the distribution of wealth. As dependent variables, these measures can be viewed as important goals of national economies.

1) National Wealth—Represented by Gross. National (Domestic) Product per Capita. This is the total volume of goods and services produced divided among the population. It shows the average volume of goods and services per person.

2) Economic Growth—This is the increase in per capita output or the total volume of output for a society (Kindleberger and Herrick, 1977). It is measured by the rate or real increase in output or income over time.

3) Efficiency—The extent to which a society is effective in utilizing its available resources so that consumption and production cannot be reordered to increase the satisfaction of some without decreasing the satisfaction of others (Bator, 1957).

4) Wealth and Income Distribution—Once the total National Wealth (or Income) is known, examination of its distribution enables assessment of the relative well-being of various segments of the population (e.g., the rich vs. the poor). Judgments regarding "fairness" can be made. That is, a "fair" distribution of wealth/income occurs when the rewards of work are distributed to the producers of work in a fashion sufficient to secure a stable and increasing standard of living.

INDEPENDENT VARIABLES

Two broad sets of independent variables are required under Adam Smith's theoretical framework: 1) variables associated with the proportion of the population engaged in productive labor; and 2) variables associated with the relative productivity of the labor force. To the extent possible, data should be partitioned in such a way as to allow assessment of independent effects of child labor vs. adult labor.

PROPORTION OF POPULATION WORKING

Appropriate variables include estimates of the productive labor force as a percentage of the total population along with estimates of hours worked. Since the focus of the research is on child labor, data should be partitioned to distinguish between child workers and adult workers. To assess longer term trends, it will be useful to include projections of population growth.

RELATIVE PRODUCTIVITY

Productivity is measured by output per unit of labor. National productivity indices can be constructed by dividing total output (GNP) by total labor input (# of workers × average hours). The most important short-run determinant of productivity is technology, measured by capital (or investment) per worker. The most important long-run determinant of productivity is human capital accumulation, measured by schooling and employer provided training. Productivity growth rates and productivity of children relative to adults are additional measures to consider.

INEFFICIENCIES OF CHILD LABOR

Evaluation of child labor under Smith's first proposition, that national wealth increases as a function of the proportion of the population at work, presents a conceptually and empirically tractable challenge. At first blush, pulling all the children out of the labor force, would have the obvious effect of removing that proportion of the population from the productive side of the economic ledger. This is the obvious first effect on the family—the loss of the child's income; and the obvious first effect on the nation—the loss of the children's share of gross national product.

But the total effects of the loss of child labor remain theoretically indeterminate. They depend on the effects of the loss of child labor on adult employment; they depend on the extent to which child labor effectively substitutes for adult labor, and the extent to which child labor complements adult labor.

Where children are effective substitutes for adults (i.e., where they are, economically speaking, "small adults"), employment of children has zero to negative total effects. Thus, eliminating child labor should have no discernible effect on national wealth and may improve national well-being. Where more children are employed, fewer adults work. Conversely, eliminating child labor would make more jobs available for adults. Such a circumstance would exist, for example, in textiles where, if children were not employed as doffers and sweepers, someone would have to do the work of doffing and sweeping. The rate of substitution would depend on the relative productivity of children and adults. Thus, if adult productivity was twice that of children, eliminating a fixed number of child workers would provide jobs for half that number of adults; but total output would remain constant. Further, if both children and adults are paid a constant proportion of their marginal productivity, then costs to the employer should be neutral. If however, children's wages are below even their meager productivity, as many would suggest though the evidence is unclear (Nardinelli, 1990), then use of child labor introduces inefficiencies into the market (even though eliminating it would be costly to employers).

Under other circumstances, child labor augments adult labor. Where mothers have no alternatives for child care, sending the children to work, either alongside the mother or in separate enterprises, can enable the mother to work. Under these conditions, elimination of child labor would be unequivocally bad for the mothers who could no longer work. The reduced supply of adult workers should operate to reduce total output, raise adult wages, or both.

In the short-run, then, elimination of child labor, or merely reducing the hours worked by children, would reduce national wealth by reducing the proportion of the population engaged in productive labor. But this considers only the first of Smith's two propositions; productivity considerations will also weigh heavily.

In the long-run, it seems clear that heavy use of child labor in industrial or other settings harmful their development would, for the next generation of adult workers, reduce the proportion of the population working. Where children grow up stunted, malnourished, poisoned, mangled, or otherwise abused through their labor, some portion of them are likely to be unable to work as adults; another portion of them will be less productive adults than they would have otherwise been. As Fuller (1922) noted regarding the period of American industrial child labor:

> Most of the adult unemployed are themselves graduates of child labor. They went to work at too early an age, received insufficient schooling and no special vocational training, and joined the ranks of the marginal laborers, the last to be hired and the first to be fired (p. 64).

Thus, heavy use of child labor will tend to perpetuate poverty into the next generation. It serves as a drag on long-run growth in the wealth of the nation.

Relative productivity of the labor force is clearly the more important determinant of the wealth of the nation. Consider that, among advanced industrialized nations, when hours of work were reduced from 60+ per week in early industrial stages to 40 or less in later periods, wealth tended to increase dramatically. This can only be explained by productivity growth.

The most important determinant of short-run productivity is the tools and technology workers use in their labor. This can be estimated by the dollar value of capital or investment per worker. On this score, there is no doubt that heavy use of child labor is associated with low productivity work systems. Children, themselves, generally perform among the most menial tasks with few tools. For any given establishment, the higher the proportion of the work force made up by children, the lower the capital/worker ratio (Marvel, 1977). Thus, heavy use of child labor distorts allocation away from capital and toward labor, taking its toll on both productivity and efficiency. Employers simply do not entrust the operation of expensive and sophisticated machinery to children. Whether as cause or effect, higher productivity work systems are clearly associated with the elimination of child labor.

The most important determinant of long-run productivity is human capital accumulation. Basic human resource policy identifies four challenges involved in the creation of a productive workforce: 1) development; 2) allocation; 3) utilization; and 4) conservation (Parnes, 1984). Development is the acquisition of skills necessary to become a productive worker. Allocation is the market process used to match trained people to available jobs. Utilization is how employees are used at the work site. And, conservation is the maintenance of these employees in their productive and retired lives. Sound policy choices in all these areas improve worker productivity and increase the overall well-being of society.

Central to the development, allocation, utilization and conservation of human resources is the improvement in employee human capital. Government and firm actions directed at increasing employee stock in their own capabilities will heighten the productive output of employees and so increase the wealth of the nation itself. Employees acquire human capital through education, training, health care, migration, and job search. The most important of these are schooling and training.

Children who work in industrial employments rarely attend school even where schooling is available. Where schooling is not available, removing children from the workplace can clearly make them worse off if, as a consequence, they are forced to turn to prostitution, rag-picking, or other less desirable employments.

There is an association between the rise of industrialism and availability of schooling, even if the causal connection is remote and unclear. It may be that industrialism creates demand for better-skilled workers and, thus, schooling (demand that continued employment of children suppresses); or it may simply be a function of the shift from household based production to enterprise based production (where the household is no longer able to attend effectively to the child's learning).

Whatever the relationship, it is clear that industrial employment suppresses schooling and that the effect is much more pronounced than that associated with other forms of employment. In the North American South around 1910 when schooling was finally becoming widely available, the likelihood that children employed in traditional agricultural pursuits also attended school was 0.79 (after controlling for effects of family resources and such) while the likelihood that industrial child workers attended school was only 0.30 (Walters and Briggs, 1993). In Britain, where regulations required that work be coupled with schooling, it is widely understood that many employers flagrantly disregarded the educational requirements.

Thus, premature industrial work acts as a more serious barrier to human capital acquisition than other forms of work. In the advanced economies, returns to a year of schooling, both in terms of the stream of lifetime earnings and in improved productivity, far outweigh the returns to an additional year of work experience. While the magnitude of the respective returns may differ in developing nations, there is no basis for suspecting that the basic relationship would not hold.

Clearly the assignment of children into the production process is inefficient because it denies society the current benefits of more mature workers with superior human capital and, more importantly, because it prohibits the future development of human capital skills, thus, perpetuating an underclass of uneducated workers.

CHILD LABOR AND THE HISTORY OF INDUSTRIAL DEVELOPMENT

If child labor is both inefficient and injurious, then it remains to be explained why it is so prevalent today, and why it has been so prevalent throughout history. The answers are simultaneously simple and complex. On the supply side, two factors play a predominant role: 1) poverty—not just being poor, as in having just enough to get by and no more—but crushing poverty, where continued survival remains in perpetual doubt; and 2) lack of available alternatives, most notably education. On the demand side, where demand for labor is derived from demand for the products and services produced by that labor, the only major factor is the perceived advantage of children over adults.

Ethics Across Time

Every advanced industrialized nation has gone through a period of heavy use of industrial child labor. Indeed, it is a hallmark characteristic of advanced (i.e., "civilized") nations that they have, by and large, passed through this stage of development. The prescription for developing nations is clear: pass through this stage of development as quickly as possible.

As David L. Lindauer, Professor of Economics, Wellesley College, observes:

> We know of no case where a nation developed a modern manufacturing sector without first going through a "sweat shop" phase. How long ago was it that children could be found working in the textile factories of Lowell, Massachusetts, of Manchester, England, or of Osaka, Japan? Should the developing economies of today be any different? If child labor is a necessary evil of industrialization, then a nation should be judged on how quickly it passes through this phase (cited in Nichols, 1993).

LESSONS FROM BRITISH AND AMERICAN HISTORY WITH CHILD LABOR

Britain was the inventor of the Industrial Revolution and the first to go through it. Consequently, it was the first nation to experience those forms of child labor most closely associated with industrialism. The consensus among economic historians of the period is that "the well being of several generations of children was sacrificed to make Great Britain wealthy" (Nardinelli, 1990, p. 3). While Nardinelli argues the emphasis on industrial child labor was overblown, he notes that:

> Child labor has come to be regarded as a ghastly by-product of the industrial revolution. The cruelty described in much of the historical literature has made the employment of children the industrial revolution's most despised feature (p. 2).

The classical era considered to be Britain's Industrial Revolution is generally considered to be 1760–1830. While there were many forces that signified the maturation of British industrialism, the Factory Act of 1833, that embarked on a course of regulating child labor and other abuses of industrialism, signaled the end of the revolutionary era of unregulated capitalism.

By the 1830s and the Factory Act, there were roughly 56,000 children between 10 and 13 working in textiles, the focal industry for public condemnation. Children under 15 comprised 20% of the textile workforce. While children worked in other industrial enterprises, especially mining, metals, machinery, and pottery—further, industrial employment was dwarfed by traditional employment in agriculture and services (only about 1/3 of child workers were in industrial settings)—conditions in textile manufacturing aroused public sentiment against child labor (Nardinelli, 1990).

While American industrialization occurred later, similar patterns, both in employment of children and in the public condemnation thereof, were observed. At the time of the formation of the National Child Labor Committee in 1904:

> Ten-year old boys were commonly found in the blinding dust of coal breakers, picking slate with torn and bleeding fingers; thousands of children sweltered all night for a pittance in the glare of the white-hot furnaces of the glasshouses. Young girls toiled in damp, dust-laden cotton mills for long hours, six days a week. Unsanitary factories and tenement sweatshops, canneries, and the street trades, including the night messenger service, all took their toll from the home, the schoolhouse, and the playground while most Americans looked on with

approval or indifference. Child labor had effective opponents (Trattner, 1970, p. 11).

Both Britain and America had prominent advocates for the use of child labor. In Britain, it was the likes of Andrew Ure who, in his *Philosophy of Manufactures* (1835) portrayed working children as "lively elves" engaged in "sport," arguing that most children were better off in factories than at home. In America, Alexander Hamilton (*Report on Manufactures,* 1791) and the forerunners of the U.S. Chamber of Commerce advocated use of women and children to fuel industrialization of the New Nation.

But what was it about industrial child labor that provoked such public condemnation? After all, children had always been employed in agricultural and domestic work, often under equally arduous conditions. The key is in the historic shift from production within the household to production outside the household. Prior to industrialization, the household was the basic unit of both production and consumption. With industrialization, the enterprise became the basic unit of production. In early industrialization, then, it was only natural that the entire household, children and all, would hire itself out for productive employment. Initially, children worked alongside their parents in one family unit. Over time, however, under the dual logics of division of labor and systematic management, children came to be separated from their parents, working under overseers and foremen, often in entirely different enterprises from where their parents worked. But it was much more than parental supervision and oversight that was lost. In the household system of production, time could be taken for learning and training. The household was the site of production, but it was also the site of human capital acquisition. Under this combination of work and learning, the household often provided a virtual apprenticeship similar to that provided by skilled craftsmen in small workshops. But that was lost in industrial employment. Because they performed the most menial tasks, the only training most children received was on-the-job work experience itself. When coupled with the long hours of work, there was often no time in the child's day set aside for learning anything new. The child's work became just that—work, and nothing more.

In both Britain and the United States, an organized movement eventually undertook the social and political project of eliminating child labor.

568   CHAPTER 17   Business and the International Community

Organized opposition did not emerge, however, from among parents or relatives of child workers. Many historical sources portray parents as willing accomplices to the industrial subjugation of their children. Besides, economic circumstances rendered most families powerless to protest the conditions of their subsistence.

Organized opposition obviously did not emerge from the employers of child labor, themselves. While it is true that technologically advanced manufacturers sometimes found it in their interest to support restrictions on child labor to maintain competitive advantage over their less advanced competitors (Marvel, 1977), there is no case where industrialists led the charge against child labor.

Finally, and perhaps more curiously, organized opposition to child labor did not originate with labor organizations, who might have most reasonably construed child labor as a competitive menace to the conditions of adult labor. Organized labor, when pressed to take a position on the question of child labor, generally opposed it; but more generally, did not place the issue of child labor high on its agenda. During the early period of industrialism, when industrial child labor was most prevalent, organized labor remained concentrated among the skilled craftsmen and artisans of the day. Industrial unionism would not come into being for several generations. Further, many among the craft unionists of the day had acquired their skills and training through an indentured apprenticeship during their own youth.

In both countries, organized opposition to industrial child labor emerged among groups tending toward the wealthy, the "progressive," and the detached. For example, in the United States, it was organizations like the National Child Labor Committee, led by zealots such as Alexander McElway (see Appendix 1) and supported by the likes of social photographer Lewis Hine, that worked for the abolition of child labor:

> Motivated by pity, compassion, and a sense of patriotism, they argued that, for the child, labor was a delusion; for industry it was a fallacy; and for society, a menace. Child labor meant the spread of illiteracy and ignorance, the lowering of the wage scale and hence the standard of living, the perpetuation of poverty, an increase in adult unemployment and crime, the disintegration of the family, and, in the end, racial degeneracy (Trattner, 1970, p. 12).

MR. COBBETT'S ASTONISHING DISCOVERY

Whenever restrictions were proposed on the use of child labor, the business community could be counted to object. The general contours of the objection were predictable: 1) tinkering with the free market is unwise—employers and children (or their parents or masters) should enjoy freedom of contract; 2) restrictions would increase employment costs, resulting in reduced employment and threatened competitiveness. Employer objections were generally accompanied by dire predictions of economic ruin. When the original British Factory Legislation of 1833 proposed abolishing labor of children under 9 and restricting children 9 to 14 to a mere 48 hours per week, employers worried that the withdrawal of this labor from British textiles would place the industry at a competitive disadvantage with, especially, German textiles. Mr. Cobbett, a Member of Parliament, was prompted to an astonishing discovery. He was quite surprised to learn that, while many had presumed the power of the British Empire to be attributable to its banks, its navy, its colonies, or the monarchy itself, the truth of the matter had now been exposed. The strength of the British Empire rested on the shoulders of 30,000 working girls in Lancashire. So great was the empire's dependence on these girls that a mere reduction in their hours to 48 per week, coupled with the loss of the labor of girls under 9, doomed the empire to economic collapse.

And so it goes; ever since Mr. Cobbett made his astonishing discovery, the business community has predictably railed against every regulatory impulse that threatens to increase labor costs (but encourages regulation that promotes competitive advantage). From child labor to minimum wages and maximum hours to workplace safety and health, the business community has aggressively advocated the rights of the worst elements of their own community: employers who wished to be free to exploit labor; employers who sought competitive advantage by driving down labor costs; the lowest common denominator among employers.

The British approach was to regulate child labor, rather than to seek an outright abolition as was the case in the U.S. The Factory Act established modest restrictions on child labor. Children 9–12 were restricted to 9 hrs per day or 48 hrs per week and were required to attend school (when children on that kind of work schedule might attend school was not clearly addressed). The only outright prohibition was on employing children under 9 in textiles. Perhaps the most significant aspect of the Factory Act was its provision for a labor inspectorate. For the first time, officials of the government would have access to the manufactories to observe conditions of both child and adult labor.

As a consequence of their regulatory approach, use of child labor did not peak until 1874. By that time, over 200,000 children from 10–14 (8.4% of the population of 10–14 year olds) were employed in industry (and these comprised no more than 1/3 of child workers as agriculture and domestic services continued to dominate the labor market for children). By that time, however, the long hours associated with earlier regimes had long passed. Children were now on government regulated 1/2 work, 1/2 schooling programs and, while many regarded the schooling programs that were offered as shams, the heaviest period of child exploitation had passed.

In contrast with the British, American opponents of child labor tended to seek outright abolition of the practice. As a result of their stridency, their efforts to cultivate support in legislative halls and courts were slow to bear fruit. For example, the legislative history of the Keating-Owen Act of 1916 (the first major federal prohibition, banning the use of child labor in goods entering interstate commerce) dates to 1907. Likewise, the movement had to endure numerous defeats in the courts. It was not until the constitutionality of the Fair Labor Standards Act was upheld in 1941 that abolition of child labor became the law of the land. By that time, child labor was already well on the way out.

Which was most effective? The British reformist approach or the American abolitionist approach? The answer is not altogether clear. In the long run, it appears that either approach will lead to a general eradication of child labor. Or, as many others will argue, no regulation was necessary at all. Both economies simply outgrew their need for child labor as they became economically advanced.

Ethics Across Place

Advanced nations—those that have passed through their period of heaviest use of child labor—tend to unanimously condemn child labor and to argue for application of universal (Western) standards. In the United States, whenever a major retailer or brand-name manufacturer is discovered to have relied on child labor (or other forms of exploited labor), a national revulsion is predictable. Any number of accounts can be cited from Kathy Lee Gifford's public embarrassment and subsequent conversion to the cause, to Doonesbury's Nike chronicles, to the Pakistani Soccer Ball squabble, to the Department of Labor's NO Sweat Campaign.

The problem is, with their cultural blinders of smug self-righteousness and moral superiority, advanced nations often do more harm than good. Nowhere is this clearer than in the case of the Harkin Bill, introduced into Congress in 1992, which would have prohibited import of products made by children under 15. Mere discussion of the bill panicked the garment industry of Bangladesh, 60% or $900 million of which was exported to the U.S., into the summary and massive dismissal of child workers, many of whom were only forced into more hazardous work for even lower pay; significant numbers were forced into prostitution (UNICEF, 97). That our smug self-righteousness so often results in worsening conditions for the very children we pity is, by itself, a persuasive argument that we really do not understand global child labor.

In addition, our apparent blindness to the existence of child labor within our own economies subjects us to deserved approbation for applying a global double-standard. Never mind our convenient loss of memory about our own history (conditions of working children in British and American textiles were arguably much worse than conditions of children working in textiles in developing nations today). In the United Kingdom today, for instance, it is currently estimated that between 15 and 26% of 11-year-olds and between 36 and 66% of 15-year-olds are working. In the United States, the General Accounting Office reports a 250% increase in child labor violations from 1983 to 1990 (GAO, 1992), and in a three-day sting operation, the Department of Labor discovered more than 11,000 children working illegally (cited in UNICEF, 1997, p. 20).

THE ROLE OF BUSINESS

Consumers in advanced industrialized economies can be counted on for vocal expressions of repugnance when they learn that products they are asked to buy have been produced by children or other exploited labor. At least some proportion of consumers have little tolerance for complicity in the exploitation of children and adults. The problem is that consumers have little capacity to know who makes their products and under what conditions they are made. Their only real sources of such information are the media and the firms that produced the goods in the first place. If businesses are not to be continually buffeted by public relations crises caused by the media's discovery of exploited labor, then business itself has a business interest, quite apart from its social responsibility, to take a lead in addressing the problems of child labor. When corporate social responsibility is then factored in, it simply becomes imperative that business act responsibly.

Many firms are taking action, even if only for public relations purposes. In the late 1980s and early 90s, many firms adopted ethical codes of conduct that included prohibitions on child labor in overseas plants and contract operations. While there are many concerns over the vigor of implementation and enforcement efforts, anecdotal evidence suggests that the mere adoption of a code has significant effects on employment of children in developing nations (DOL, 1996).

But just what kinds of actions can and should businesses be expected to take?

CULTURAL RELATIVISM VS. UNIVERSAL HUMAN RIGHTS

An interminable debate over the nature of corporate social responsibility rages between proponents of teleological and deontological perspectives. Utilitarian ethicists, the teleologists—or ethical relativists, are more inclined to grant legitimacy to local cultural, social, religious, political and economic differences when applying their moral calculus. While such a position immunizes them from charges of "moral imperialism," the utilitarians are vulnerable to endorsement of practices in the developing nations that are considered morally repugnant by advanced Western cultural norms. Deontologists, by contrast, establish, with moral certitude, a process for extending universal moral truths to cultures alien to Western logics and mores. They are the moral imperialists—the ethnocentrists. While the dispute between the teleologists and the deontologists rages in seminar halls and academic conferences, the business practi-

tioner is left without syllabus or program, let alone a moral compass . . . maturing of a moral code applicable to international business behaviors.

Donaldson (1989) has developed an ethical system which fuses the disparate positions of teleological and deontological thinkers. His approach enables global business to embrace and remain true to Western morality without falling prey to ethnocentrism; and also to recognize cultural diversity without falling prey to ethical relativism.

His moral system or "algorithm" provides participants a framework for applying sound ethical reasoning to new and often difficult choices posited by international business considerations. Central to the process is a comparison of home country ethical practices to host country ethical practices. If a disparity exists between the host and home countries, then the task is to "tolerate cultural diversity while drawing the line on moral recklessness" (p. 103). Guidance is provided by the answers to the following two questions:

> Is it possible to conduct business in the host country successfully without undertaking the objectionable practice (e.g., employing children). If the answer is "yes" then do something acceptable to both cultures. For example, hire only adults and provide support to local host country educational institutions.
>
> Is the practice in clear violation of a fundamental international human right? If so, avoid the practice.

The advance made by this ethical system is its applicability across disparate cultures. The framework becomes even more compelling if the world is converging toward a similar culture based on the logic of industrialism. For then, child labor is no longer defensible even when based on unique national experiences or cultural mores.

GLOBAL CONVERGENCE VS. LOCAL EXCEPTIONALISM

The question is, "Is a global culture developing?" Culture is a complex whole comprised of arts, law, knowledge, morals, customs, and "other capabilities and habits acquired by man as a member of society" (Kerr, Dunlop, Harbison and Myers, 1960, p. 77). And while the concept of culture must be taken as a whole comprising more than the sum of its parts, it nevertheless can be evaluated in terms of its constituent parts. These include the family system, class and race, religion and ethical valuations, legal structure, and the concept of the nation state. As nations progress economically, these cultural dimensions are changing to adopt to the new logic of industrialization. And while these dimensions maintain a national or cultural identity they are in fact being pulled toward one and other.

We argue that, as the world develops under the logic of industrial capitalism, and the correspondent temptations of consumerism, formerly disparate cultures are inexorably converging, creating a global culture founded in Western political economy. Of course we could be wrong: the world could be converging on an Eastern model of political economy. Whichever, East and West are now inextricably intertwined in the global economy. The point is, economies converge: they follow more or less predictable patterns of development; and over time, they increasingly come to resemble one another. Further, the degree of "convergence" influences not only issues of child labor, but other policy choices of enormous importance for business and government decision-makers. For example, firms must determine the extent of operational centralization and sensitivity to local markets and conditions as well as the advisability of establishing a single corporate culture based on global involvement (Bartlett and Ghoshal, 1991). Similarly governments policies directed at economic growth and wealth distribution are moderated by the extent to which the nation state has internationalized.

The more generalizeable patterns of economic, political and social development are—that is, stronger the trends toward convergence—the stronger the argument for universality of human rights in general, and the rights of children in particular. The more development is characterized by local exceptionalism, the stronger the rebuttal favoring cultural relativism in development of rights. While we are persuaded by the former, strong cases can be made supporting both of the debate.

Movements in international and national law would seem to indicate a trend toward convergence around a consensual condemnation of child labor. The United Nations, principally through its United Nations Childrens Fund (UNICEF) and the International Labour Organization's (ILO) International Programme on the Elimination of Child Labour (IPEC) has worked to focus global attention on the problem. The United Nations Declaration of Universal Human Rights contains several provisions bearing on child labor, including the right to an education and freedom from exploitive labor. More significantly, in 1989, the United Nations adopted the Convention on the Rights of the Child which has now been ratified by all but six member states (interestingly, the United States is among the six), making it the most widely ratified treaty on human rights in world history. Now, 96% of the world's children live in states that have accepted a legal obligation to protect the rights of children (UNICEF, 1997).

More specific instruments aimed directly at child labor are gaining widespread acceptance. ILO Convention 138, adopted in 1973, is the most comprehensive regulation of minimum ages for child labor. It establishes a global standard that the minimum age for child labor is 15 years, or the age limit for compulsory education, whichever occurs later. The convention also contains numerous flexibility clauses permitting deviation from the global standards where warranted by local exceptions. While only 46 member states have ratified Convention 138 so far, 130 of 170 states have ratified either Convention 138 or one of the various conventions addressing minimum age for child labor that were adopted prior to 1973 (ILO, 1995). Finally, nearly all nations on earth, even those such as the United States that have not ratified global conventions, have established national legislation restricting child labor; minimum ages are a near-universal feature of those laws.

These trends, taken together, suggest an unmistakable trend, at least in the political and legal spheres, toward convergence on global condemnation of child labor.

However, despite these relatively recent efforts, global child labor continues to flourish. The movement toward convergence in law seems strangely detached from everyday experience. Because it is illegal almost everywhere, child labor remains largely a hidden phenomenon, confined to the back channels and informal sectors of many economies, including advanced economies. The simple fact that child labor remains widespread would seem to belie any convergence of global sentiment around its eradication. The sheer magnitude of the problem suggests a movement in law quite divergent from plain reality. The gross dimensions of the problem provide alarming support for the conclusion that cultural relativism may be prevailing—that local exceptionalism may dominate over convergent trends.

But examination of the history of child labor in advanced economies brings the argument full circle. While it can be argued that use of child labor is particular to a nation's current stage of economic development (a relativist argument), it also appears to be true, in the main, that advanced nations, always and everywhere, have grown beyond their heavy reliance on child labor and, thus, every nation should eventually be expected to do so (a universalist argument). When the debate is shifted in this way, the relevant question becomes: is heavy reliance on child labor necessary to economic development? We have shown that it is not; that it has always been economically inefficient and injurious.

The Immorality of Child Labor

Child labor is inappropriate because, first, it is (or will come to be seen as) morally reprehensible and, second, it is economically inefficient and injurious. Case closed.

Appendix 1: Declaration of Dependence by the Children of America in Mines and Factories and Workshops Assembled

WHEREAS, We, Children of America, are declared to have been born free and equal, and

WHEREAS, We are yet in bondage in this land of the free; are forced to toil the long day or the long night, with no control over the conditions of labor, as to health or safety or hours or wages, and with no right to the rewards of our service, therefore be it

RESOLVED, I—That childhood is endowed with certain inherent and inalienable rights, among which are freedom from toil for daily bread; the right to play and to dream; the right to the normal sleep of the night season; the right to an education, that we may have equality of opportunity for developing all that there is in us of mind and heart.

RESOLVED, II—That we declare ourselves to be helpless and dependent; that we are and of right ought to be dependent, and that we hereby present the appeal of our helplessness that we may be protected in the enjoyment of the rights of childhood.

RESOLVED, III—That we demand the restoration of our rights by the abolition of child labor in America.

> Alexander J. McKelway, 1913—cited in
> Trattner (1970)

References

Bartlett, Christopher A. and Sumantra Ghoshal: 1991, *Managing Across Borders: The Transnational Solution* (Harvard Business School Press, Boston MA).

Bator, F. M.: 1957, "The Simple Analytic of Welfare Maximization," *American Economic Review* **47**, 22–59.

Black, Maggie: 1995, *In the Twilight Zone: Children in the Hotel, Tourism and Catering Industry* (Geneva, ILO).

Donaldson, Thomas: 1989, *The Ethics of International Business* (Oxford University Press, NY).

Fuller, Raymond G.: 1922, *The Meaning of Child Labor* (A.C. McClure & Co., Chicago).

Hamilton, Alexander: 1791, "Report on Manufactures," in Samuel McKee (ed.), *Papers on Public Credit, Commerce and Finance* (The Liberal Arts Press, NY), 1957, pp. 175–276.

ILO: 1995, "Governing Body Document on Child Labour: Committee on Employment and Social Policy" (GB.264/ESP/1).

ILO: 1997, *Child Labour: Targeting the Intolerable* (Geneva).

Kerr, Clark, John T. Dunlop, Frederick H. Harbison and Charles A. Myers: 1960, *Industrialism and Industrial Man* (Harvard University Press, Cambridge MA).

Kindleberger, C. P. and B. Herrick: 1977, *Economic Development*, 3rd Edition (McGraw-Hill, New York).

Marvel, Howard P.: 1977, "Factory Regulation: A Reinterpretation of Early English Experience," *The Journal of Law and Economics* **20**(2) (Oct), 379–402.

Nardinelli, Clark: 1990, *Child Labor and the Industrial Revolution* (Indiana University Press, Bloomington).

Nichols, Martha: 1993, "Third-World Families at Work: Child Labor or Child Care?," *Harvard Business Review* (Jan–Feb), #93105.

Parnes, Herbert S.: 1984, *People Power: Elements of Human Resource Policy* (Sage Publications, Beverly Hills CA).

Reich, Robert: 1991, *The Work of Nations: Preparing Ourselves for 21st Century Capitalism* (Vintage Books, New York).

Smith, Adam: 1776, *An Inquiry into the Nature and Causes of the Wealth of Nations* (Oxford University Press, Oxford, 1993).

Trattner, Walter I.: 1970, *Crusade for the Children: A History of the National Child Labor Committee and Child Labor Reform in America* (Quadrangle Books, Chicago).

UNICEF: 1997, *State of the World's Children: 1997* (Oxford University Press, Oxford, UK).

U.S. Department of Labor: 1995, *By the Sweat & Toil of Children (Vol. II): The Use of Child Labor in U.S. Agricultural Imports & Forced and Bonded Child Labor* (Washington, Bureau of International Labor Affairs).

U.S. Department of Labor: 1996, *The Apparel Industry and Codes of Conduct: A Solution to the International Child Labor Problem?* (Washington, Bureau of International Labor Affairs).

U.S. General Accounting Office: 1992, *Child Labor: Information on Federal Enforcement Efforts* (HRD-92-127FS).

Ure, Andrew: 1835, *The Philosophy of Manufactures* (Frank Cass, London, 1967), p. 301.

Walters, Pamela B. and Carl M. Briggs: 1993, "The Family Economy, Child Labor, and Schooling: Evidence from the Early Twentieth-Century South," *American Sociological Review* **58** (April), 163–181.

Questions for Chapter 17

1. On what basis does Steidlmeier distinguish between common and public property?

2. How do you think Steidlmeier would respond to Paine's (Chapter 9) defense of trade secrets?

3. What do Singh and Lakhan mean when they note that "expression of the desire for a clean, safe environment is not the same as stating that a clean safe environment is the right of every human being"?

4. Suppose a country with high unemployment and few natural resources decides to build a state-of-the-art disposal facility for processing hazardous wastes. If such a facility is economically viable and environmentally responsible, can it still be argued that to export "wastes to countries which do not benefit from waste generating industrial processes or whose citizens do not have lifestyles that generate such wastes is unethical"? In such an instance, would it be true that the importer was not benefiting from the waste generating industrial processes?

5. Does the view that there are transcultural moral truths imply ethnocentrism, that is, that the moral views of one's own society are those transcultural truths? Explain.

6. Mayer and Cava suggest that, with regard to gender equality, American multinationals should not slavishly adhere to all U.S. judicial opinions and should be prepared to make good faith adjustments where cultural conditions require. Is this too great a concession to ethical relativism? How does this advice differ in essence from the cultural relativist's advice "when in Rome do as the Romans do"?

7. On what basis do Hindman and Smith argue that "higher productivity work systems are clearly associated with the elimination of child labor"?

8. Hindman and Smith argue that child labor is both inefficient and injurious. What reasons do they give to explain why it is so prevalent today and why it has been so prevalent throughout history?

Case 17.1 Discrimination or Job Requirement[1]

Wade Kern, a helicopter pilot, was hired by Dynalectron Corporation on August 17, 1978. Through a subcontract, Dynalectron provided Kawasaki Heavy Industries Limited with pilots to work in Saudi Arabia. The duties of these pilots involved flying helicopters over crowds of Muslim pilgrims retracing Muhammad's path to Mecca. These flights were designed to protect pilgrims against any violent outbreaks and to help fight the fires that frequently resulted from cooking fires being started too close to pilgrims' tents.

The pilots were stationed at three bases: Jeddah, Dhahran, and Riyadh. Due to the fact that the pilots stationed at Jeddah were required to fly into Mecca and that Saudi Arabian law, in accordance with Islamic religion, forbids non-Muslims to enter Mecca on pain of beheading, Kern, who was to be stationed in Jeddah, was required by Kawasaki to convert to Islam.

[1]Based on Kern v. Dynalectron Corp. as found in 577 *Federal Supplement* 1196 (1983).

Kern, a Baptist Christian, initially agreed to convert. He attended a course on the Islamic faith held in Tokyo, chose his new Islamic name, and signed a certificate of conversion. At this point he changed his mind, returned to Fort Worth at his own expense, and informed Dynalectron of his decision. Dynalectron offered him a job as a member of the air crew, a position that would not require his conversion, but Kern declined. Kern subsequently sued Dynalectron on the basis that he had been discriminated against because of his religious beliefs.

1. Do you agree that, in these circumstances, being Muslim is a legitimate occupational qualification?
2. Suppose the Saudis were to insist not only that the pilots be Muslim, but also male. Would it be legitimate for Dynalectron to hire only male pilots in such circumstances?
3. Would there have been anything wrong in Kern taking the course and signing a certificate of conversion, but only pretending that his conversion was genuine?

Case 17.2 Conflicting Rights?[2]

In 1981, female secretarial employees of Sumitomo Shoji America, Inc. brought a class action suit against their employer, claiming that its policy of hiring only male Japanese nationals for management positions was in violation of Title VII of the Civil Rights Act of 1964 which forbids discrimination on the basis of age, nationality, race, or sex. In reply, their employer argued that under the provisions of the Treaty

[2]Based on Avigliano v. Sumitomo Shoji America, Inc. as found in 638 *Federal Reporter,* 2nd series, 552 (1981).

of Friendship, Commerce and Navigation between Japan and the United States it is permitted to engage executive personnel of its choice and hence should be considered exempt from the requirements of Title VII of the Civil Rights Act.

1. Sumitomo Shoji further argued that there should be no difference in treatment between a parent Japanese company operating in the United States and a U.S. incorporated subsidiary such as Sumitomo Shoji. Do you agree? Why or why not?

2. How would you respond to the argument that Sumitomo Shoji is not discriminating on the basis of sex, and thus violating Title VII of the Civil Rights Act, but simply exercising its acknowledged treaty right to appoint Japanese citizens in executive roles?

3. Is Title VII of the Civil Rights Act consistent with the provisions of treaties that allow foreign companies operating in the United States to engage personnel of their choice? Why or why not?

Further Readings for Chapter 17

Thomas Donaldson, "Multinational Decision-Making: Reconciling International Norms," *Journal of Business Ethics* 4, 1985, pp. 357–366.

Michael Hoffman, Ann Lange, and David Fedo, eds., *Ethics and the Multinational Enterprise* (New York: University Press of America, 1986).

John Kline, *International Codes and Multinational Business* (Westport, CT: Quorum Books, 1985).

Louis Turner, *Multinational Companies and the Third World* (New York: Hill & Wang, 1973).

INFOTRAC COLLEGE EDITION To learn more about the topics from this chapter, you can use the following words to conduct an electronic search on InfoTrac College Edition, an online library of journals. Here you will find a multitude of articles from various sources and perspectives: *www.infotrac-college.com/wadsworth/access.html*

cultural relativism

intellectual property

gender equity

sexual harassment

environmental ethics

hazardous waste disposal

child labor

Chapter 18

Business and the Environment

Introduction

THERE ARE SOME REMARKABLE similarities between the development of business ethics and the development of environmental ethics. Both have come into prominence in the latter half of the twentieth century and both have moved from the status of minor branches of applied ethics to the status of major subdisciplines in the field of ethics. This being the case, it is somewhat naive to include a single chapter entitled "Business and the Environment." Nevertheless, it is important to say something, however brief and preliminary, about what it means for those engaged in business to take their ethical responsibilities regarding the environment seriously.

A problem we immediately face is that, while most ethicists would agree that we need to take environmental issues seriously, there is disagreement over what is required in order to do this. Some more radical thinkers insist that we must abandon the anthropocentrism characteristic of traditional ethical thinking; others working within a more traditional framework maintain that we can satisfactorily address environmental concerns without abandoning the view that humans are preeminently valuable in the natural order.

The form this debate generally takes is whether entities other than humans have what is called "intrinsic" value, as opposed to "extrinsic" or "instrumental" value. An example will serve to make this distinction clear. My wife is valued by me not on the basis of whether she can be an effective instrument of supper preparation, but simply on the basis of who she is. She has what ethicists call "intrinsic" worth. A frying pan, on the other hand, has only "instrumental" or "extrinsic" worth, inasmuch as I value it only as a means to an end.

The more radical environmental ethicists tend to argue for an egalitarianism in which nonhuman individuals or communities can be seen as having equal worth as human individuals or communities. Those working within a more traditional framework tend to argue that an adequate environmental ethic can be developed, even if nonhuman entities are only valued instrumentally. My own view, but one which I will not attempt to develop here, is that both sides in this debate err by not examining the possibility that there may exist degrees of intrinsic worth. There seems to be no reason why one might not simultaneously hold that human beings are preeminently valuable, yet deny that other entities simply have instrumental value.

I have included four readings in this chapter. The first is by Thomas Heyd and was specially written for this text. He provides us with an essay that is designed to serve as an introductory survey of the theoretical and practical aspects of environmental ethics. He begins by making some suggestions as to how individuals come to recognize that they have ethical responsibilities with regard to the natural environment. He goes on to provide an overview of various ethical theories regarding our responsibilities to the environment. Turning from the theoretical to the practical, he makes some observations and suggestions on the opportunities and limitations for taking environmental responsibilities seriously in the workplace. He concludes by noting the significance that taking personal responsibility for the interests of the environment has for oneself as well as for nature.

Mark Sagoff's article "Zuckerman's Dilemma: A Plea for Environmental Ethics" explores the distinction between intrinsic and extrinsic value. Using the well-known childrens' story *Charlotte's Web,* he explores the consequences of valuing nature only extrinsically and argues that any adequate environmental ethic must understand that the natural environment has intrinsic value. In his view, nature is to be valued in and of itself, independently of whether it can be used as an instrument to further human interests.

Sagoff is aware that this raises the problem that if nature is to be preserved and valued for its own sake, how far may we go in using nature instrumentally? How can we balance our need to use nature instrumentally with our recognition of its intrinsic value? His suggestion is that, although there are no hard-and-fast rules, we should, as in our dealings with other individuals, never treat nature solely as a means to an end. The natural environment may serve our ends, but it should not be valued simply on that basis.

Our third article, "Environmentalism and Economic Freedom: The Case for Private Property Rights," focuses on the question of whether protection of the environment is best accomplished within a free market capitalist economy or an interventionist socialist economy. Its author, Walter Block, argues that, although environmentalists tend to be drawn toward socialism, protection of the environment is more likely to take place under a free enterprise system that takes private property rights seriously. In his view, the primary reason for environmental damage is that the government fails to acknowledge and protect property rights.

Block attempts a practical demonstration of his view by considering the problems of air pollution and waste disposal as test cases. He argues that these problems arise not because there is too little government regulation and intervention, but because there is too much. If private property rights were acknowledged and strictly enforced, and if those polluting or disposing of wastes were forced to pay the true costs of polluting or waste disposal, the market would function in such a way that people, out of their own self-interest, would choose what is environmentally correct.

Our final selection is the article "Ecological Marketing Strategy for Toni Yogurts in Switzerland." In it Thomas Dyllick describes a successful attempt by Toni, a Swiss firm producing yogurt, to combine environmental concerns and effective marketing. Dyllick suggests that economic goals do not necessarily collide with environmental responsibility, though he also believes that economic goals do not, by themselves, provide sufficient motivation for developing and maintaining a long-term commitment to environmental responsibility. In his conclusion, he attempts to distill and generalize some of the lessons that can be learned from Toni's successful venture.

Environmental Ethics and the Workplace: A Call to Action

THOMAS HEYD

Introduction: From Alienation to Personal Involvement

NEARLY EVERYONE AGREES that there are serious environmental problems in our world, such as the increase in the size and frequency of storms, speeded up desertification and loss of coastal areas due to the greenhouse gas effect, and nearly everyone might agree that decisions made and activities undertaken in the workplace contribute in a large way to these problems. But, if asked what role environmental ethics has in the workplace, most people tend to think merely in terms of paper recycling, or perhaps of conserving energy by turning off the lights after leaving the office. For many individuals, it is difficult to envisage how a deeper concern for environmental ethics can be implemented in the workplace.

In this essay I have a number of aims. I propose to discuss the various ways in which personal responsibility for one's impact on the natural environment may come about, and how this responsibility applies to individuals even in the workplace.[1] I then provide an overview of some important crit-

ical perspectives on our behaviour regarding the natural environment. I follow this with an analysis of what it would mean for individuals in the workplace to take their ethical responsibilities in the context of environmental degradation seriously, while noting the special limitations as well as opportunities that their special situation implies. Finally, I conclude by noting the significance that taking personal responsibility for the integrity of the natural environment has for oneself, as well as for nature.[2]

Environmental Responsibilities, Critical Perspectives, and the Workplace

Ethics, we might say, is reflection on appropriate attitudes and action with regards to significant others.[3] In ordinary life we may perceive that we have certain responsibilities arising out of the relationships in which we are engaged with other human

---

[1]My proposals here are not intended to convey the impression that the goodwill of individuals in the workplace may be sufficient to alleviate the rapid rush toward environmental degradation in which we presently find ourselves. Communities will have to take concerted action through strictly legislated limits on the exploitation of common goods, such as air, water, forests, and open spaces, and on their use as waste sinks; on the dissemination of toxins and genetically modified organisms; on the generation of radioactive wastes; etc., if the integrity of the environment is to be even minimally protected.

[2]By "integrity of the natural environment" I mean the condition of the environment that allows for its normal functioning as the site for the flourishing of various species of living beings, as are commonly found there unless human interventions have impeded their presence. By "environmental degradation" I mean the processes that diminish the integrity of the natural environment, as well as the resulting condition.
[3]Although the terms *ethics* and *morality* usually are used interchangeably today, I propose to primarily use the term *ethics* for *reflection* on the correctness of attitudes concerning, and actions affecting, significant others, reserving *morality* for the set of attitudes and actions themselves, insofar as they may be subject to praise or censure and may characterize a person's character.

Printed by permission of Thomas Heyd.

beings. We may realize a responsibility for the return of an item we have borrowed, for payment when purchasing a good, or for caring for an elderly relative. We perceive these responsibilities because we have entered into relationships with someone as a borrower, as a purchaser, or as a younger relative, respectively. For us, who are involved in them, these relationships generate particular normative relations, which in turn may generate a *sense* of responsibility or a feeling of obligation when we realize that the relevant relationship of being a borrower, a purchaser, or a younger relative is instantiated.[4]

It may be argued that, even in the absence of a *sense* of responsibility, relationships, such as being a borrower or a purchaser, *set* us certain responsibilities, such as returning the item and paying for the good obtained. That is, moral responsibility is not just a subjective but also an *objective* matter. Moreover, even if demands to take responsibility for certain actions may arise from within a specific society and its particular culture, this is not to say that the norms explicitly or implicitly contained in such demands are "merely" relative to a culture. Rather, on reflection we may well find sufficient reasons for the view that the norms in question should be held transculturally, or by any rational being. That is, we may find sufficient *arguments* for the conclusion that a certain responsibility applies to anyone in similar circumstances.

Environmental ethics, as do biomedical ethics, legal ethics, and so on, concerns reflection on appropriate action with regard to significant others as considered within a specific context. So, while biomedical ethics focuses on human actions within the context of biological research and medicine, environmental ethics does similarly regarding actions considered within the context of the natural environment. Just as some actions assessed from within the medical setting may be considered ethically correct or incorrect, some actions assessed within the context of the natural environment similarly may be a matter of moral praise or censure.

Environmental morality, therefore, is to consider how we ought to act insofar as we affect things that surround us. Although the term *environment* strictly speaking also encompasses humanly made or artifactual things and spaces surrounding us, generally, when discussion focuses on environmental ethics, the "environment" of concern is the natural environment. This is not to say that the humanly made environment is inconsequential from the point of view of ethics. Rather, the reason for the focus in environmental ethics on the *natural* environment, in contrast to the artifactual environment, is that the former more fundamentally constitutes a condition for the flourishing of a great variety of human and non-human beings. The natural environment, dramatically affects *us* in a variety of ways through the goods that it offers us on a regular basis, whether they be perceived as of narrow biological importance, such as air or water, or as of aesthetic significance, such as the limpid transparency of the skies on a clear day or the ever-present but always changing sound of the sea's surf. The natural environment may also, of course, affect us through the harms that it may cause through events such as storms or diseases. Furthermore, *we* affect the natural environment through certain actions, the extremes of which may be described as pollution and overexploitation, on the one hand, and as protection and restoration, on the other.

TAKING RESPONSIBILITY: FROM ANTHROPOCENTRISM TO GAIA-CENTRISM

In environmental ethics discussion sometimes is carried out in terms of a thing's intrinsic value as contrasted with its extrinsic value. That is, it is proposed that we can distinguish the value of a thing considered *independently of* its usefulness from the

---

[4]The point of view on ethics developed here is indebted to Mary Midgley's "Duties Concerning Islands" in Donald VanDeVeer and Christine Pierce, *People, Penguins and Plastic Trees* (Wadsworth, *1st edition*, 1986), 156–64, and Val Plumwood's "Nature, Self and Gender: Feminism, Environmental Philosophy, and the Critique of Rationalism" in Christine Pierce and Donald VanDeVeer (eds.), *People, Penguins and Plastic Trees* (Wadsworth, *2nd edition*, 1995), 197–213. It is to be noted that we cannot derive values from facts. Our experience, however, is *not* neatly divided into values and facts. Our experience, which is heavily dependent on the modes of knowing and valuing particular to our culture, rather, acquaints us with the world in value-laden ways. We may, of course, on reflection, critique the values that we initially were caught up in; this is how we rid ourselves of problematic prejudices. But we may also, on reflection, come to the conclusion that we need to deepen our commitment to certain of our value configurations.

value *due to* its usefulness. We may note, for example, that each person considers her- or himself as having a value independently of her or his usefulness to others, while forks or computers or turbans may have little or no value in cultures that do not use these items. To indicate that some being has intrinsic and not just extrinsic or instrumental value, and hence ought to be accorded consideration from the moral point of view, I speak of a morally significant being.[5]

Although the nonphilosopher initially may have the impression that normative theories in ethics are intended to generate new ethical knowledge, careful study of the classics, such as Immanuel Kant's *Grounding of the Metaphysics of Morals,* shows that these theories have the more modest goal of providing systematic reflection on the basis of the morality that is *already* current in her or his culture.[6] Kant's is intended to reflect a principle of concern *common* within our culture, namely, respect for each person's autonomy.[7] For example, since stealing makes the individual stolen from less capable of leading the life she or he would want to, such actions are morally impermissible. The foundation of the principle is straightforward since each individual values her or his autonomy, and hence can see the sense in not acting in ways that undermines a person's autonomy.

Similarly, a rival theory, contractarianism, proposes that we need to respect the implicit as well as the explicit agreements that make society possible, since society is useful to each individual that belongs to it.[8] This reflects a principle based on the *common* notion of reciprocity and mutual beneficence. For example, since truth telling is the foundation of all agreements in society, we each need to respect the injunction against lying and deceit if we choose to belong to, and benefit from, society.

Both the principle of respect for autonomy and the principle of respect for contractual relationships exclusively focus on relationships with other *human* beings, though they tacitly suppose that at least some nonhuman beings need to be treated with care because of the relationships that some human beings have with them. For example, my respect for the autonomy of a human being who has befriended a certain bird may mean that I should not harm that bird. Similarly, although according to the contractarian principle I have no reason to respect trees (with which I cannot enter into agreements since they cannot negotiate with me), my at least implicit agreement with other human beings to respect *their* interests means that I should not harm nonhuman beings, such as certain trees, that are significant to them. In other words, even anthropocentric or human-centered ethics supposes that we may have *indirect* responsibilities with regard to certain nonhuman beings.

Within the European traditional cultures, utilitarianism is the first major theory of ethics that outrightly leaves the door open for *direct* consideration of the interests of nonhuman beings, insofar as utilitarianism seeks to represent the common notion that acting rightly is acting in such a way as to bring about happiness and to diminish unhappiness for the aggregate of those concerned.[9] This way of rendering the content of morality includes all sentient beings (those capable of feeling pleasure and pain) among the morally significant. In other words, according to this perspective, we ought to count very many of the animals (at least those with a developed nervous system) among those to be considered from the moral point of view.

[5]There are beings, of course, with whom we have both morally significant *and* instrumental relationships, as in the case of one's spouse who is also one's business partner. To speak of a morally significant being is equivalent to speaking of a being with "moral standing"; this latter term, and the criteria for attributing moral standing to some being, are discussed at some length by Christine Pierce and Donald VanDeVeer in their second edition of *People, Penguins and Plastic Trees,* pp. 6–14; they propose that "[some being] has moral standing if and only if the existence of [that being] or its interests in well-being have positive moral weight" (p. 7).
[6]Notably Kant repeatedly praises common moral reason. See Immanuel Kant, *Foundations of the Metaphysics of Morals,* translated by Lewis White Beck (Bobbs-Merrill, 1959).
[7]I do not claim that ethics merely is a descriptive matter. What I am proposing, rather, is that when ethics concerns itself, among other things, with normative relations, its intended aim is the systematization and deepening of our understanding of the prescriptive claims of common morality. This does not mean that upon reflection we cannot reject the norms of common morality. The idea simply is that ethics, if it is to go beyond abstractions, will have a link with the norms that guide us in the prephilosophical stage.

[8]For a summary discussion, see, e.g., "The Idea of a Social Contract" in James Rachels, *The Elements of Moral Philosophy* (Random House, 1999), 143–61.
[9]Regarding utilitarianism, as defended by John Stuart Mill, see, e.g., "Utilitarianism," in this volume. For a summary account of the significance of this perspective for our treatment of nonhuman animals, see Rachels, "The Utilitarian Approach," in his *Elements,* 96–106.

Although the *application* of the utilitarian principle to situations involving nonhuman animals generally is neglected in today's industrialized societies fed by factory farms,[10] one may argue that the moral consideration of sentient beings reflects a common value, though this value is only applied to selected animals with whom special ties have been developed (e.g., the squirrel that feeds in front of someone's window or the pet pig bought for one's child's amusement).

While it is true that as highly culture-dependent social beings we mostly are preoccupied with the relationships that we entertain with other human beings, on reflection we may admit an affinity with all living beings. It is this relationship with all living things that according to biocentric ethics leads to a generalized "reverence for life" and a respect for living things insofar as they are "teleological-centers-of-life."[11] That is, we may take note that the basis of our caring for living things is constituted by the fact that, in their various intricate ways, they are goal-directed, and, more specifically, directed toward goals with which we can empathize: survival, general flourishing of their own sort, reproduction. Respect for living things requires that one allow these beings spaces in which they *can* flourish. In fact, those spaces themselves, teeming as they are with various life forms, may be seen as analogous to organisms that are similarly composed of many organic and cellular subunits. People often do show appreciation for areas of land or sea that represent especially good environments for certain living things such as caribou or salmon. Frequently their appreciation for those areas is mingled with self-interest, insofar as they represent valuable procurement places to satisfy human needs and desires, but, interestingly, individuals can also feel that the relationships with those areas of land or sea warrant a certain care for their own sake.

This notion of responsibility for ecologically significant areas of land, sea, and more generally,

ecosystems to which we also belong, finds expression in Aldo Leopold's call for a Land Ethic. Leopold proposed that we take note of the community and organic unity constituted by the complex natural environments in which human beings are mere citizens and participants. Being in community, and forming an organic unity, with the land and its inhabitants, however, supposes certain responsibilities for their care and a respect for their flourishing. Consequently, Leopold advised that one

> Examine each question in terms of what is ethically and esthetically right, as well as what is economically expedient. A thing is right when it tends to preserve the integrity, stability, and beauty of the biotic community. It is wrong when it tends otherwise.[12]

A variant of this appreciation for living things as part of, and dependent on, wholes larger than single organisms, is expressed in calls for the protection of species from extinction. Individuals in our cultures, that through relationship with certain kinds of living things have developed a sense of responsibility for them, may develop a concern for the continued existence of beings *of that kind* which may issue in what Holmes Rolston calls "duties to species."[13] Respect for complex parts of our natural environment, such as ecosystems or species, may be called "ecocentric."

Taking this view further, it is sometimes suggested that people may develop a relationship with the planet as a whole. Though this may seem too abstract to be a realistic proposition, one may note that, given our increasing understanding of the global interconnections of geological, meteorological, and biological processes, there is a certain basis in experience for this view. The idea that such a relationship with the globe should lead to a kind of responsibility for its well-being has found expression in connection with the "Gaia Hypothesis" which argues that, since the planet as a whole in many ways appears to function as an organism, we ought to accord it care similar to the

---

[10]On the use of nonhuman animals in our society and the moral problems that this poses, see, e.g., Peter Singer, *Animal Liberation* (Random House, *2nd edition*, 1990).

[11]On reverence for life, see Albert Schweitzer, *Civilization and Ethics* (London: A.&C. Black, 1946). On living things as teleological centers of life see Paul Taylor, "The Ethics of Respect for Nature," and also John Rodman, "Ecological Sensibility," both in VanDeVeer and Pierce, 1st edition, 169–84 and 165–68, respectively.

[12]See Aldo Leopold. "The Land Ethic," in Pierce and VanDeVeer, 2nd edition, 142–51, reprinted from Aldo Leopold, *Sand County Almanac* (Oxford University Press, 1981).

[13]See Holmes Rolston III, "Duties to Endangered Species," in Pierce and VanDeVeer, 2nd edition, 314–25.

care that we would accord to individual living things.[14]

II. CRITICAL PERSPECTIVES AND ACTION

1. Moral Critiques. The view that we may expect individuals to "take responsibility"' for their actions, implies that ethics attains a role beyond merely private reflection. Thus, ethics obtains a publicly critical role capable of developing important critiques of the activities that generate the present environmental degradation. Even purely anthropocentric approaches, such as the Kantian or the contractarian perspectives, may appeal to the duties *regarding* the natural environment that accrue to us because of our duties *to* other human beings. This critical approach has been further developed in various ways. It has been argued, for example, that each individual has a right to a livable environment.[15] Hence, those who are degrading the environment, for example, through the spraying of fields or vineyards with substances that may be hazardous to people's health, may be unjustifiably interfering with certain individuals' rights.[16]

Moreover, to impose certain important environmental impacts, as represented by the dissemination of genetically modified organisms in our environment or the delivery of toxic materials into our communities, on the supposition that these activities are justified by the economic benefits generated, is to impose health risks for which usually no informed consent has been obtained or compensation is provided.[17] One response to this problem has been to demand the application of the precautionary principle in a wide range of cases. In other words, in order to protect citizens from un–agreed-to risks it is proposed that no activities be undertaken until it has been shown that they will not increase the risks to which individuals are already subject.

Furthermore, although the moral status of future generations of human beings is a matter of debate,[18] various arguments may be offered to the effect that we do have responsibilities to them and that those responsibilities are being neglected by serious environmental degradation. These arguments can be supported by Kantian and contractarian approaches, since the status of future human beings as autonomous and as potential contractors, respectively, is being overlooked if our own generation degrades the environment that they will come to inherit. Since utilitarianism enjoins us to consider the effects of our actions on all those affected, given environmental degradation that lasts beyond our life spans, responsibilities for future human generations also become an issue from this perspective.

These arguments have attained further specification through the idea of sustainable development. The notion of sustainable development implies that we have a duty to meet humanity's "current needs *without* compromising the ability of future generations to meet their own needs."[19] A similar idea is behind the notion that the present generation has a duty of stewardship with regard to the Earth's natural environment in the light of the needs of both present and future generations.[20]

---

[14]See James Lovelock, *The Ages of Gaia* (New York: Norton. 1988).

[15]See William T. Blackstone, "Ethics and Ecology," in William T. Blackstone (ed.), *Philosophy and Environmental Crisis* (Athens, Georgia: University of Georgia Press, 1974).

[16]We are talking of a *moral* right and not of a legal right. Legal rights may constitute important ways of ensuring decent treatment of certain beings, but are independent of moral rights. For an interesting argument in support of legal rights for nonhuman parts of nature, see Christopher D. Stone, "Should Trees Have Standing? —Toward Legal Rights for Natural Objects," in Pierce and VanDeVeer, 2nd edition, 113–25.

[17]With regard to the traffic of toxic materials and the moral implications that this has, see, e.g., Jang B. Singh and V. C. Lakhan, "Business Ethics and the International Trade in Hazardous Wastes," in this volume. The export of such materials to impoverished areas inhabited by racial minorities also poses issues of environmental racism; see, e.g., Karl Grossman, "Environmental Racism" in Pierce and VanDeVeer, second edition, 39–44.

[18]For an introductory review of the debate, see, e.g., Joseph R. Des Jardins, "Ethics, Energy, and Future Generations" in Joseph R. Des Jardins, *Environmental Ethics* (Wadsworth, 1993), 69–98.

[19]Emphasis added; The World Commission on Environment and Development, *Our Common Future* (Oxford University Press, 1990), p. 8.

[20]Besides its justification through various forms of anthropocentric ethics, the idea of stewardship for future generations also receives backing from diverse forms of religious ethics that demand conscientiously good management of the Earth because of our duty to a higher being.

Both a duty to limit our activities to those that are sustainable in this sense and a duty of stewardship for the sake of future generations have their foundation in the idea that future human beings and their needs deserve the same kind of concern as present human beings and their needs.

One way to interpret the demand that our activities be sustainable and take into account a duty of stewardship toward future generations is to insist on the *internalization* of all costs. Practically this means that, if in the process of doing business there is a significant generation of possibly polluting materials or a relatively important decimation of resources, the producer of the environmental degradation should take on the costs for reparation or "making whole" again. That is, the producer of the pollutants is not to *externalize* these costs, in which case present and future generations would have to pay for them.[21]

According to nonanthropocentric perspectives, besides duties *regarding* the various nonhuman beings in our natural environment (based on our duties *to* human beings), we may be said to have duties *to* them. Specifically, from the point of view that focuses on the continuity of sentience (which includes the capacity to suffer) between human beings and a large class of nonhuman animals, human beings accrue a responsibility for those activities that hinder the full flourishing of, and cause suffering to, sentient nonhuman animals. Thus, this perspective provides grounds for critique not only of species decimations through hunting and fishing but also for the human degradation, through water pollution, clear felling, or urbanization among others, of the ecosystems on which sentient nonhuman animals depend.

From the point of view of biocentric and ecocentric ethics we accrue responsibilities for interferences in the flourishing of all living things, and of ecosystems and species, respectively. This means that we should be morally concerned, among other things, about the death of many of our lakes and rivers, the rapid disappearance of tropical and temperate rain forests, the proliferation of toxins in water systems and food chains, the production and uncontrolled diffusion of genetically modified organisms, and the ultimate effect on ecosystems of nuclear wastes that will be emitting radiation for hundreds of thousands of years.

2. Social Critiques. The attempt of individuals to take responsibility for the impact of their actions on the natural environment may largely be ineffectual if essentially contrary trends prevail in society. Such contrary trends are generally expressed in both a practice and a set of ideas or conceptual structure. Since there has been considerable concern in European and North American countries about these matters at least since the 1970s, we may come to wonder why the rate at which our environment suffers serious degradation continues, nonetheless, to increase. Part of the answer may be found in various analyses that focus on social and cultural factors.

For example, ecological feminism (ecofeminism), argues that the abusive use of the natural environment and the oppression of women have similar causes. Specifically, this is a critique of social practices that are based on a belief system which assigns women and nature to a subordinate moral category in relation to men and culture or society, and, furthermore, operates on the assumption that the morally superior is entitled to dominate the morally inferior. Ecofeminists point out that, since there is no basis either for that belief system or for that assumption, it is difficult to see how social structures that facilitate the oppression of women and the degradation of the natural environment may be justified.[22] Many ecofeminists argue that traditional ethics is deficient by its abstract appeal to reason. They argue that in environmental matters, as in other areas of life, attention needs to be placed on the relationships that individuals, as embodied and embedded beings, have developed with particular parts of their lived-in world, since such relationships are the basis for an ethics of care. They suggest that such an approach would prove to be both sympathetic to the point of view of women and helpful to the development of a conceptual reconstruction of our place in relation to nature as other.[23]

---

[21]For a summary defense of the importance of internalizing private costs of production, see, e.g., Velasquez, 238–41.

[22]This is Karen Warren's way of summarizing the ecofeminist critique. See her "The Power and Promise of Ecological Feminism," in Pierce and VanDeVeer, 2nd edition, 213–27.
[23]See Val Plumwood. She also critiques deep ecology for the alleged failure to perform the necessary historical analysis of its conceptual baggage. A number of critiques of the

An independent, but related, critique has been presented by the approach called social ecology. In this view the degradation of the natural environment is the result of generalized structures of hierarchical domination in modern, European cultures. Such structures are held responsible for the inequality in our societies, and also for misguided attempts to control nature through interventions such as the introduction of chemical pesticides in agriculture, large hydroelectric projects, nuclear power generating stations, and so on.[24]

Closely related to ecofeminist and social ecology critiques is the analysis of our present environmentally pernicious trends as due to the prevalence of technological rationality. This perspective, developed initially by Herbert Marcuse of the Frankfurt School, argues that in modern, industrialized societies instrumental reason is applied to all beings, including humanity and nonhuman nature.[25] Instrumental reason, or "means-ends rationality," is the application of reason to the attainment of ends or goals without careful assessment of the value of the goals pursued. The result is a variety of techniques (commonly referred to as "technologies") that focus our attention on the extrinsic value of things.[26] Thus, whereas formerly a person's visit to the marketplace was a manner of keeping in touch with one's community while acquiring some necessities, instrumental rationality turns it into a mere occasion for the maximization of the respective interests of producers and con-sumers in an increasingly mechanized and staffless "supermarket." Such a rationality approaches ancient forests simply as sites for the application of sophisticated "labor-saving" machinery facilitating lumber extraction management regimes, and sea shores and lakes are seen solely in terms of tourism development and water extraction.

3. Cultural Critiques. Although the social critiques noted in the previous section implicitly call for a rethinking of the conceptual framework supportive of our society's collusion with patriarchy, its patterns of hierarchical domination, and its technological rationality, very little is usually said about what is to replace the practices and belief systems in question. The movement known as deep ecology has made an attempt to speak to this latter aspect.

Deep ecology critiques "shallow" attempts merely to reform the activities that cause environmental degradation. It critiques, for example, the introduction of various techniques and devices that allow us to continue treating the rest of nature as a *mere resource* for human desires. Deep ecology proposes that we need to think "deeply" about our relationship with the natural environment by noting that human beings are *fundamentally* connected to the rest of nature.[27]

For example, although introducing electrically powered vehicles may at first seem like an improvement on current air pollution–causing conditions, their introduction might prove problematic since it would allow, and maybe encourage, the further expansion of roads and urbanization into the remaining natural environment. In light of the interconnectedness of all things, deep ecology suggests that we reconsider the special place attributed to human beings in our thinking. As a part of nature, we should be pleased if the rest of nature flourishes and have little reason to favor narrow human interests over the flourishing of the eco-sphere as a whole.

contemporary discourse on nature have also issued from writers influenced by postmodernist and poststructuralist perspectives. See, e.g., Jane Bennett and William Chaloupka (eds.), *In the Nature of Things* (University of Minnesota Press, 1993).

[24]On social ecology, see, e.g., Murray Bookchin, "Remaking Society: Pathways to a Green Future," in Pierce and VanDeVeer, 2nd edition, 227–33.

[25]See Herbert Marcuse, *One-Dimensional Man* (Boston: Beacon Press, 1991), and *Eros and Civilization* (Boston: Beacon Press, 1955).

[26]For further work on the "rationality" and politics built "into" technology, see, e.g., Albert Borgmann, *Technology and the Character of Contemporary Life: A Philosophical Inquiry* (University of Chicago Press, 1984), and Langdon Winner, *Autonomous Technology: Technics-out-of-control as a Theme in Political Thought* (Cambridge: MIT Press, 1986). Regarding the politics of "formal technologies," see Susan Leigh Star, "Layered Space, Formal Representations and Long-distance Control: The Politics of Information," *Fundamenta Scientiae*, Vol. 10, No. 2 (1989), 125–54.

[27]See Arne Naess, for example, "Self Realization: An Ecological Approach to Being in the World' in Pierce and VanDeVeer, 2nd edition, 192–97. There are a number of other proposals aimed at creating the conditions for rethinking our place in the greater environment. Some appeal to the example provided by various Native and traditional cultures. Others, like Anthony Weston's "Enabling Environmental Practice," in Pierce and VanDeVeer, 2nd edition, 463–69, propose that we begin by becoming acquainted, through a new "environmental practice," with our natural surrounds.

4. Summation. While moral critiques of our present activities focus on the responsibilities that may accrue to us as individuals who are in particular relationships with various beings or larger parts of our environment, social critiques point to some of the underlying structural features that need to be changed and, hence, call for cooperation among individuals, if we are to avoid further environmental degradation. Cultural critiques attempt to provide positive alternatives to traditional conceptions of our relation to nature by envisioning a different place for human beings *within* nature. Even if we only agree with *some* of the critiques offered by environmental ethicists, the urgency of stemming the degradation of our natural environment suggests we have strong reasons to take action. The question that concerns us next is the applicability of environmental ethics from within our role in the workplace.

III. ENVIRONMENTAL RESPONSIBILITY IN THE WORKPLACE: IMPACTS, LIMITATIONS, AND OPPORTUNITIES

Is it realistic to suppose that in the workplace one can act on one's moral responsibility concerning environmental matters? I propose that, though there are objections to the idea that ordinary morality may be relevant at the workplace, they can be addressed. Furthermore, even if particular work situations impose specific limitations on one's freedom to act, ultimately there remain considerable opportunities for action on one's environmental responsibilities in most workplaces.

1. The Workplace as a Special Place and Its Environmental Impacts. The workplace is a very special place in present European civilization.[28] In contrast to the situation in many other societies, and in European societies at other times, for us the place and the circumstances in which we gain our livelihood are mostly *separate* from the places and circumstances in which we enjoy the rewards of our labors. Under these circumstances, although certain values such as the desire for achievement may be recognized as useful in the maximization of productivity, generally speaking, values expressive of affective ties are treated as irrelevant or as problematic in the workplace. It is assumed that values that suppose other than instrumental relationships with human beings, nonhuman animals, place, or a particular manner of working, should be put aside so as not to interfere with the effectiveness and efficiency of work processes and their objectives. This perspective is often expressed by the phrase "business is business."

We may note, however, that the supposition that a separate set of values is appropriate in the business workplace depends on its actual separateness from the rest of life. Someone may quite reasonably say that the rules of common courtesy do not apply when engaged in a wrestling match, but the question remains whether the workplace really *is* as isolated from the rest of life as to warrant a very different set of values, that is, values superordinate to those otherwise current in society.

A very strong case can be made for the view that the workplace is not isolated from the rest of life, since it does *interact* with it in very many and thoroughgoing ways. On the one hand, work absorbs a great proportion of each citizen's waking time, intelligence, and energy, in other words, part of our lives. On the other, most work activities affect other people in society and, ultimately, require considerable quantities of materials from the natural environment, that is, the environment in which we all live and on which we all depend. So, individuals in the workplace actually are in *especially* direct and close relationships and interactions with the world around them.

Further, the impact of the workplace on the natural environment often is very negative. Many, if not most, of today's environmental problems are attributable to activities in, or emanating from, the workplace, especially from large corporate businesses. Examples discussed in the media, such as the Exxon Valdez oil spill, readily come to mind. Nearby industry smoke stacks or the sight of industry effluents entering a neighboring creek, moreover, remind us of the importance of business in the despoliation of our home ground.

Attributing a significant share of environmental destruction to the business workplace may engender

---

[28]I refer to the civilization prevalent in modern, industrialized North America, Australia, Europe, and other places, such as South Africa, as "European" because it has its origin in Europe. In other words, I use the term *European* somewhat in the way that *Western* has been used recently, but reject this use of the latter term because of its geographical inaccuracy. (Judging by the shortest distances, Europe is west of Asia but *east* of the Americas; Australia seems both east *and* west, while South Africa is *south,* of Europe.)

certain objections. It may be suggested that if there are environmental impacts arising in the workplace, ultimately these are to be blamed on citizens viewed as consumers, since they create the demand for products that otherwise would not be made. This overlooks the fact that for most products on the market, there was no demand *at all* until industry made them available and known through advertising campaigns. Further, even if much workplace activity is attributable to consumer demand, this will not suffice to exonerate the role of the workplace in environmentally degrading changes, since this would be a case of blame shifting when the appropriate reaction should be blame sharing.[29]

Another response to the claim that the business workplace is responsible for much environmental destruction is that the economies of industrialized countries are turning more and more toward the supposedly "clean" service and the high technology sectors. Such comments overlook, however, that many parts of the service sector such as, for example, banking or insurance, ultimately are involved in the industrial sectors by way of the direct funding of new mining, manufacturing, or infrastructure projects, and the strictly profit-guided manipulation of stocks. The latter leads to an exacerbation of the pursuit of profit within corporations, with a consequent readiness to cut corners on important environmental concerns. The high technology sector, furthermore, has its own growing set of plants, satellites launches, and mobile telephone towers, all of which may have harmful effects on the integrity of the natural environment.

In summary, we may conclude that there is no reason to suppose that a different, special set of values should be applied to the workplace than to the rest of society. Rather, we should conclude that it is of great urgency to seek the application of ethical principles in the workplace.

2. Limitations and Opportunities. In one sense we may admit that the workplace indeed is a special place, since for most of us it is the place on which we primarily depend for our livelihood, and where we often focus on our realization as creative, productive persons. This circumstance limits the extent to which one can carry through on one's ethical responsibilities, be they concerning the state of the natural environment or otherwise. But, as noted, the workplace *is* connected to the rest of life. Hence, one should suppose that at the very least the principle not to cause harm must be acknowledged, even if there may be little room for beneficence.

In other words, although there may be little opportunity to *promote* the integrity of the natural environment, it is appropriate for individuals to be concerned about environmental *degradation* originating in their workplace. This is especially so because the workplace also is a place at which there is available *special knowledge* about the impacts on the environment of various courses of action. Since greater knowledge commonly supposes both greater capacity to act *and* greater accountability, the role of the workplace in the prevention of environmental degradation becomes very important. Practically this means considering both the impacts of the workplace on the immediate environment in which work is carried out, and the impacts that happen at a distance in either space or time.

Presently many workplaces have instituted recycling programs for paper and other materials, but the possibilities for action in the proximal environment are much wider than that.[30]

The question remains *who* in the workplace may be expected to take on responsibility to halt environmental degradation, given that the workplace is mainly directed toward the securement of livelihood (if not toward the maximization of profit). It would seem unrealistic to suppose that the average

---

[29]Even if one may determine the individual who has primary responsibility for an untoward event, this does nothing to absolve others who contributed to the event, even if only passively. We can imagine many examples. For instance, even if their is only one arsonist who sets fire to a house, there can be indefinitely many others who would share the blame for the ruination of the house by not notifying the firefighters or considering other ways to subdue the flames. On sharing and shifting responsibility, see, e.g., James L. Muyskens, "The Nurse as a Member of a Profession," in Callahan, 290–95.

[30]Some possibilities of action that may be available, to name only a few, are the reduction of commutes by moving within walking or pedaling distance, the reduction of air travel by scheduling fewer face-to-face meetings out of town, reduction of the toxicity of materials used in the workplace, and reduction of the material used in packaging.

employee of a large corporation could afford to risk her or his job for the sake of possibly negligible impacts on the total degradation of the natural environment. It is relevant, however, that workplaces are not all alike, and that some individuals in some workplaces enjoy more autonomy than some others. We may note the following diversity in workplace situations:

1. The self-employed, including individuals who sell and make goods as well as fishers and farmers. These individuals have great leeway to direct their workplace in such a way that it is in agreement with their responsibility for the integrity of the natural environment.

2. Employees in cooperative enterprises. In a cooperative, employees usually are also owners who have a say on the board of directors themselves or through their representatives. Oftentimes they also have a say in the day-to-day management of their workplaces.[31] In such employment situations, there is almost as much opportunity to pursue well-defined goals of low impact on the integrity of the natural environment as there is for the self-employed.

3. Professionals. This class includes lawyers and physicians, but also dentists, accountants, teachers, and nurses.[32] Although professionals are subject to a certain degree to regulations arising from their associations, to state legislation, and to their employers if not self-employed, on the whole they enjoy a degree of autonomy not generally shared by ordinary employees. Consequently, they also have substantial opportunities for acting on their environmental responsibilities.

4. Managers, including CEOs, and other employees in situations that allow at least some degree of participation in workplace decision making. These individuals have opportunities to at least modify present prac-

tices to make them more agreeable to the aims of safeguarding environmental integrity.[33]

5. Employees who are members of a union or association. As such they may be able to obtain special protection from the employer for employees who make suggestions, or lodge complaints, regarding environmental matters. Alternatively, it might be possible to institute within the workplace the position of environmental ombudsperson, who would have leeway to alert publicly the employer about ways to avoid contributing to environmental degradation.

6. Political representatives at all levels, federal, provincial or state, municipal, and so on. Though contrary to the platform of some political parties, in today's political climate the pursuit of a "healthier" natural environment is a goal that generally will bring politicians public support. Anyone with political office usually has excellent opportunities to put into place programs that will combine her or his stated platform with the satisfaction of her or his ethical responsibilities concerning the integrity of the natural environment.

7. Investors in productive enterprises. Although not directly involved in the workplace, investors are (co-)owners of whatever workplace they invest in, and hence play a role in the objectives pursued there. Investors can (co-)determine the charters under which businesses will operate by taking part in General Meetings. They can also make the choice of which investments they make in terms of the explicit aims and practices, and the compatibility of those aims and practices with the integrity of the natural environment, of the enterprises under consideration.

The effectiveness of action from the workplace will vary depending on specific circumstances. In this context it is important to remember that, generally speaking, moral responsibility is commensurate to the urgency of the situation, but also to one's capacity. Nevertheless, it seems clear that any viable environmental ethic depends primarily on our individual and collective *conscience,* that is, our sense of responsibility for the environment and our readiness to act on that responsibility.

---

[31]On the opportunities for democratic participation in cooperatives, see, e.g., Jaques and Ruth Kaswan, "The Mondragan Cooperatives," *Whole Earth Review* (Spring 1989), 8–17.

[32]For an enlightening discussion of what it is to be a professional, and the ethical repercussions this has, see Michael D. Bayles, *Professional Ethics* (Wadsworth, 1989).

[33]Note the example of the CEO of Toni Yogurts in Dyllick's paper in this volume.

Zuckerman's Dilemma: A Plea for Environmental Ethics

MARK SAGOFF

E. B. WHITE's *Charlotte's Web* serves as an environmental parable for our time. As we reflect on our relationship with nature, we might consider the three ways in which Wilbur the pig was valued in White's story. His instrumental value cashes out in ham hocks and sausage. His aesthetic value earns him a ribbon at the county fair. His moral value is the value he has in and of himself, and Charlotte the spider loves him for it. We can value nature the way Charlotte valued Wilbur, or we can, as the farmer Zuckerman did at first, see the natural world only in terms of the pork chops it provides.

Many of us recall from childhood—or from reading to our own children—E. B. White's story of the spider Charlotte and her campaign to save Wilbur, a barnyard pig.[1] Charlotte wove webs above Wilbur's sty proclaiming the pig's virtues in words—"TERRIFIC, . . . RADIANT," and "HUMBLE"—she copied from newspaper advertisements salvaged by a helpful rat. Wilbur won a special prize at the county fair. Moved by these events, Zuckerman, the farmer who owned Wilbur, spared him from being sent to market. Charlotte saved Wilbur's life.

"Why did you do all this for me?" the pig asks at the end of *Charlotte's Web*. "I don't deserve it. I've never done anything for you."

"You have been my friend," Charlotte replied. "That in itself is a tremendous thing. I wove my webs for you because I liked you. After all, what's a life, anyway? We're born, we live a little while, we die. A spider's life can't help being something of a mess, what with all this trapping and eating flies. By helping you, perhaps I was trying to lift up my life a little. Heaven knows, anyone's life can stand a little of that" (p. 164).

The Varieties of Goodness

Charlotte's Web illustrates three ways we value nature. First, nature benefits us. Nature is useful: it serves a purpose, satisfies a preference, or meets a need. This is the instrumental good. Traders have this kind of value in mind when they bid on pork belly futures. Price is the usual measure of the instrumental good.

Second, we may value nature as an object of knowledge and perception. This is the aesthetic good.[2] While the basis of instrumental value lies in our wants and inclinations, the basis of aesthetic value lies in the object itself—in qualities that demand an appreciative response from informed and discriminating observers. The judges who awarded Wilbur a prize recognized in him superb qualities—qualities that made him a pig to be appreciated rather than a pig to be consumed.

Third, we may regard an object (as Charlotte did Wilbur) with love or affection. Charlotte's love for Wilbur included feelings of altruism, as we would expect, since anyone who loves a living object (we might include biological systems and communities) will take an interest in its well-being or welfare. Love might also attach to objects that exemplify ideals, aspirations, and commitments that "lift up" one's life by presenting goals that go beyond one's own welfare. We might speak of "love of country" in this context. Objects of our love and affection have a moral good, and, if they are living, a good of their own.

Aesthetic value depends on qualities that make an object admirable of its kind; when these qualities change, the aesthetic value of the object may change with them. With love, it is different. Shakespeare wrote that love alters not where it alteration finds, and even if this is not strictly true, love still tolerates better than aesthetic appreciation changes that may occur in its object.

Although love is other-regarding in that it promotes the well-being of its object, it does not

---

[1] E. B. White, *Charlotte's Web* (New York: Harper & Row, 1952).

[2] In defining the instrumental and aesthetic good, I follow the analysis of Georg Henrik von Wright, *The Varieties of Goodness* (London: Routlege & Kegan Paul, 1963), pp. 19–40. Von Wright, however, uses the term *technical good* where I use the term *aesthetic good*.

From Hastings Center Report *21(5), 1991. Reprinted with permission.*

require actions to be entirely altruistic. Only saints are completely selfless, and it is hardly obvious that we should try to be like them.[3] Nevertheless, anyone's life can stand some dollop of idealistic or altruistic behavior, as Charlotte says.

When we regard an object with appreciation or with love, we say it has intrinsic value, by which we mean that we value the object itself rather than just the benefits it confers on us. This essay concerns the intrinsic value of nature in its relation to environmental policy. The two forms of intrinsic value—aesthetic and moral—differ in important ways, as one would expect, since moral value arises in the context of action, while aesthetic value has to do with perception. I shall touch on these differences, but I do not have space to explicate them here.

The Value of Nature

Those of us who wish to protect estuaries, forests, species, and other aspects of nature may give any of three kinds of arguments—instrumental, aesthetic, or moral—to support our conviction. We might argue on instrumental grounds, for example, that we should save species for their possible medicinal applications, or rain forests because they add to global oxygen budgets. An aesthetic argument, in contrast, would point to the magnificent qualities a ten-thousand-year-old forest or estuary may possess. In nature we find perhaps for the last time in history objects commensurate with our capacity to wonder.

A moral argument describes obligations we have toward objects of nature insofar as we regard them with reverence, affection, and respect. Such an argument may contend that humanity confronts a great responsibility in learning to share the world with other species. Love of or respect for the natural world increases our stature as moral beings, and it may teach us to be critical of and to change our preferences and desires. By taking an interest in the welfare of some creature beside herself, Charlotte too found there is more to life than "all this trapping and eating flies."

Within the next decade or two, we shall decide the fate of many estuaries, forests, species, and other wonderful aspects of the natural world.

How can we justify efforts to protect them? Will instrumental or prudential arguments do the trick? If not, how will we justify the sacrifices we must make to save our evolutionary and ecological heritage?

Why Save the Whales? Consider, as a real-world example, whales. Two centuries ago, whale oil fetched a high price because people used it in lamps. Whales had instrumental value. Electric lights are better and cheaper than oil lamps; accordingly, there is little or no market for whale oil today.

Why, then, do so many people care about saving whales? Is it for instrumental reasons? Are they concerned about maintaining a strategic reserve of blubber? Do they worry that the seas might fill up with krill? No; as whales have lost their instrumental value, their aesthetic and moral worth has become all the more evident.

Whale oil has substitutes in a way that whales do not. We get along easily without whale oil because electricity lights our lamps. The extinction of whales, in contrast, represents an aesthetic and moral loss—something like the destruction of a great painting or the death of a friend. Life goes on, of course, but we mourn such a loss and, if we caused it, we should feel guilty or ashamed of it. No one cares about the supply of whale oil, but we do care about the abundance of whales. Aesthetic and moral value attaches to those animals themselves rather than to any function they serve or benefit they confer on us. When they perish, all that was valuable about them will perish with them.

Fungibility as the Mark of the Instrumental. Insofar as we care about an object for instrumental reasons, we would accept a substitute—for example, ballpoint pens in place of quills—if it performs the same function at a lower cost. The market price of any object should in theory not exceed that of the cheapest substitute.

With intrinsic value, it is different. When we see, for example, a Jacques Cousteau film about the ability of humpback whales to communicate with each other over hundreds of miles, we are properly moved to admire this impressive species. That we can fax junk mail faster and farther is irrelevant. We admire the ability of these whales to do what they do. It is this species we admire; its qualities demand admiration and attention.

[3]See Susan Wolf, "Moral Saints," *Journal of Philosophy* 79 (1982): 419–39.

Similarly, love is not transferable but attaches to the individuals one happens to love. At one time, people had children, in part, because they needed them as farmhands. Today, we think the relation between parents and children should be primarily moral rather than instrumental. One can purchase the services of farmhands and even of sexual partners, but our relationship to hired labor or sex is nothing like our relationship to children or spouses. We would not think of trading a child, for example, for a good tractor.

Technology, though still in its infancy, promises to do for many aspects of nature what it has done for whales and for children, namely, to make us economically less dependent on them. This need not concern us. That we no longer require whales for oil or children for tending bobbins does not imply that we cease to value them. The less we depend on nature economically, the more we may find that the reasons to value species, forests, estuaries, and other aspects of nature are not instrumental but aesthetic and moral.

Why Protect the Natural Environment? We undertake many environmental programs primarily to protect the well-being of nature, even if we defend them as necessary to promote the welfare of human beings. Why, for example, did the Environmental Protection Agency ban DDT in the 1970s? The pesticide killed pelicans and other wildlife; that was the reason to prohibit its use. EPA banned it, however, as a human carcinogen—which it is not.[4] Today we should make no such pretense.[5] The new Clean Air Act undertakes an expensive program to control acid rain. The law does not pretend that acid rain causes cancer. It answers directly to moral and aesthetic concerns about what coal-burning power plants are doing to trees and fish.

We environmentalists often appeal to instrumental arguments for instrumental reasons, that is, not because we believe them, but because we think that they work. I submit, however, that advances in technology will continue to undermine these arguments. The new biotechnologies, for example, seem poised to replace nature as the source of many agricultural commodities. As one environmentalist observes: "In the years to come, an increasing number of agricultural activities are going to be taken indoors and enclosed in vats and caldrons, sealed off from the outside world."[6]

When machinery replaced child labor in mills and mines, people did not stop raising children. Society found it possible to treat children as objects of love rather than as factors of production. As biotechnology industrializes agriculture, we may protect farmland for its aesthetic and symbolic value rather than for its products. We may measure wealth not in terms of what we can consume but in terms of what we can do without—what we treasure for its own sake.

Poverty is one of today's greatest environmental and ecological problems. This is because people who do not share in the wealth technology creates must live off nature; in their need to exploit the natural commons, they may destroy it. Analogously, in an urban context, poor people have had to send their children to work in sweat shops—to survive. The problem, of course, is not that poor people have the wrong values. Extreme and deplorable inequalities in the distribution of wealth lead to the mistreatment of children and to the destruction of the environment.

---

[4]During the early 1970s an enormous investment in research led to completely inconclusive findings based on animal studies, although one prominent pharmacologist summed up the available evidence by saying that at then-current levels DDT was not a human carcinogen. For documentation, see Thomas R. Dunlap, "DDT," *Scientists, Citizens, and Public Policy* (Princeton: Princeton University Press, 1981), esp. pp. 214–17. Oddly, there have been few epidemiological studies during the 1980s, but those that were done show no clear link between DDT exposure and cancer risk. For a review with citations, see Harold M. Schmeck, Jr., "Study Finds No Link Between Cancer Risk and DDT Exposure," *New York Times,* 14 February 1989, reporting a decade-long study of nearly 1,000 people with higher than average exposure to DDT; it found no statistically significant link between the amount of DDT in their bodies and the risk of death by cancer.

[5]Scholars argue correctly, I believe, that "in the 1970s, the prevention of cancer risks was accepted as a proxy for all environmental damage." A. Dan Tarlock, "Earth and Other Ethics: The Institutional Issues," *Tennessee Law Review* 56, no. 1 (1988): 63 (citing the DDT controversy as an example). See also, *Regulating Pesticides, National Academy of Sciences* (Washington, D.C.: NAS Press, National Research Council, 1980), pp. 18–28.

[6]Jeremy Rifkin, *Biosphere Politics: A New Consciousness for a New Century* (New York: Crown, 1991), p. 69.

Accordingly, I question the adequacy of the argument environmentalists often make that we must protect nature to provide for the welfare of human beings. I think it is also true that we must provide for the welfare of human beings if we are to protect the natural environment.

Zuckerman's Dilemma

Zuckerman faced a dilemma. He had to choose whether to butcher Wilbur (the slaughterhouse would have paid for the pig) or on moral and aesthetic grounds to spare his life.

What reasons have we to preserve biodiversity, protect rain forests, and maintain the quality of lakes, rivers, and estuaries? I should like to suggest that we confront Zuckerman's dilemma with respect to many of the most wonderful aspects of nature. As we come to depend on nature less and less for instrumental reasons, we may recognize more and more the intrinsic reasons for preserving it.

Water Pollution. Consider, as an example, the problem of water pollution. The question I wish to ask here is whether instrumental arguments would justify the expenditure of the roughly $200 billion Americans invested between 1970 and 1984 in controlling water pollution.[7] Did this investment pay off in terms of our health, safety, or welfare? Could we conclude that, in this instance, instrumental as well as intrinsic values justify the protection of the environment?

I think it fair to say that the large public investment in water pollution control cannot be justified on instrumental grounds alone. The same money put into public clinics, education, or antismoking campaigns might have led to greater improvements in public safety and health. This is true in part because the major uses of water—commercial, industrial, agricultural, and municipal—are not very sensitive to water quality. Drinking water can be treated very cheaply and thus can tolerate many common pollutants. "Much of what has been said about the need for high quality water supplies," two experts write, "is more a product of emotion than logic. . . . [A] plant at Dusseldorf, Germany, withdraws water from the Rhine River, which is of far lower quality than the Delaware, the Hudson, or the Missouri, treats it . . . and produces quite potable drinking water."[8]

The Value of an Estuary. In the Chesapeake Bay, as in other prominent aquatic ecosystems, pollution must concern us deeply for moral and aesthetic reasons. It is not clear, however, that the harm pollution does to nature translates into damage to human health, safety, or welfare. Indeed, more pollution might be better from a strictly instrumental point of view.

The reason is that the major uses of the Bay are fairly insensitive to water quality. The Chesapeake possesses instrumental value as a liquid highway (Baltimore is a major port), as a sewer (tributaries drain several major cities), and as a site for a huge naval base (Norfolk). These uses affect but are not greatly affected by water quality or, for that matter, by the biological health, integrity, richness, or diversity of the Chesapeake ecosystem.

How does pollution affect the health of commercial and recreational fisheries in estuaries? Consider rockfish (striped bass). Environmentalists for many years deplored the pollution of the Hudson off Manhattan; they pronounced that portion of the estuary—one of the most degraded in the world—biologically dead. Developers of the Westway Project, who wished to fill the offshore waters to build condos, hired scientists who confirmed that rockfish did not and probably could not visit the polluted lower Hudson.

Environmentalists were able to stop the project, however, by arguing in the nick of time that even though the "interpier" area may be the most polluted ecosystem in the world, it functions as perhaps the most important, healthy, and thriving hatchery for rockfish on the Atlantic coast. The well-being of fish populations—at least as we view it—can have more to do with politics than with pollution.[9]

---

[7]Office of Policy Analysis, EPA, *The Cost of Clean Air and Water, Executive Summary* (1984), p. 3. For an overview of the disappointing results of water quality protection, see William Pedersen, "Turning the Tide on Water Quality," *Ecology Law Quarterly* 15 (1988): 69–73.

[8]A. Kneese and B. Bower, *Managing Water Quality: Economics, Technology, Institutions* (Baltimore: Johns Hopkins Press, Resources for the Future, 1968), p. 125.
[9]For details about the Westway Project, see *The Westway Project: A Study of Failure of Federal/State Relations,* Sixty-Sixth Report by the Committee on Government Operations,

In the Chesapeake, rockfish populations rebounded after a moratorium on fishing. One might surmise, then, that while fisheries have been hurt by overharvesting, the effects of pollution are harder to prove. Bluefish, crabs, and other "scavengers" abound in polluted waters, including the Chesapeake. And organic pollutants, primarily compounds of nitrogen and phosphorus, could support oysters and other filter feeders if their populations (depleted by overfishing and natural disease) returned to the Bay.

Maryland's former director of tidal fisheries, recognizing the benefits of genetic engineering, argued that the Chesapeake Bay "should be run more like a farm than a wilderness."[10] He believed that the state should subsidize efforts to fabricate fish the way Frank Perdue manufactures chickens. Many experts agree that industrial mariculture, by pushing fish populations far beyond the carrying capacity of ecosystems, will render capture fisheries obsolete.[11]

Pollution at present levels hardly bothers boaters, which is why there are so many "stinkpots" out there. Even in a "sick" estuary, a 347 Evinrude outboard gives people what they apparently want: plenty of noise and plenty of wake. Many recreational fish remain plentiful, and biotechnologists are engineering others to withstand pollutants to which they now succumb. They have perfected a nonmigrating rockfish that need not transit the anoxic stem of the Bay. (They have also perfected an acid-tolerant trout that does well in acidified lakes.) It may not be efficient to regulate pollution to accommodate species. It may be cheaper to regulate species to accommodate pollution.

Since a nasty jellyfish occurring naturally in the Bay makes swimming too painful, recreational interest in the Chesapeake is limited in any case. Most vacationers experience the Bay from bridges, where they sit in terrific traffic jams on their way to resorts on the Atlantic shore. They seem willing to pay a lot to visit the Ho Jos, discos, go gos, peep shows, and condos that stretch from Atlantic City to Virginia Beach. If you are looking for recreational benefits people are willing to pay for, look for them there.

Why Not Pollute? We may find acts of environmental destruction to be aesthetically and morally outrageous even if they do no damage to human health, safety, or welfare. News reports tell us that Prince William Sound, now "sparkling with sea life and renewed health," has produced a record salmon catch a little more than a year after the tragic Valdez spill.[12] From a strictly instrumental point of view, that spill was not nearly so detrimental as many environmentalists thought. The immediate victims, more than 36,000 waterfowl, at least 1,016 sea otters, and 1,144 bald eagles, have no commercial value. Populations of wildlife will be detrimentally affected probably forever. These animals have enormous aesthetic and moral—but little instrumental—worth.

I do not mean to suggest that water pollution, especially when it is illegal or careless, is anything but morally and aesthetically outrageous. I do not mean to minimize the harm it does. I am arguing only that pollution may represent a failure in aesthetic appreciation and moral responsibility without representing a market failure, that is, without impairing any of the uses we make of an estuary. The Chesapeake will perform its major economic tasks: to function as a sewer, a liquid highway, and a place for boating. If it were only the beneficial use rather than the intrinsic value of the Bay that concerned us, controlling pollution further might not be worth the cost.

98th Cong. 2d Sess., HR 98-1166, Washington, D.C., U.S.G.P.O., 1984. See also *Action for a Rational Transit v. West Side Highway Project,* 536 F. Supp. 1225 (S.D.N.Y. 1982); *Sierra Club v. U.S. Army Corps of Engineers,* 541 F. Supp. 1327 (S.D.N.Y. 1982) and 701 F.2d 1011 (2d Cir. 1983). For another case history exemplifying the same point farther up the Hudson, see L. W. Barnhouse et al., "Population Biology in the Courtroom: The Hudson River Controversy," *BioScience* 34, no. 1 (1984): 14–19.

[10]George Krantz is quoted in the *Washington Post,* 26 September 1984.

[11]See, for example, Harold Webber, "Aquabusiness," in *Biotechnology and the Marine Sciences,* ed. R. Colwell, A. Sinskey, and E. Pariser (New York: Wiley, 1984), pp. 115–16. Webber believes we depend on traditional fisheries only because the "results of recent research an development in the biotechnological science have not yet been integrated into the broader context of large scale, vertically integrated, high technology, centrally controlled, aquabusiness food production systems." He calls the substitution of industrial for "natural" methods of fish production in aquatic environments "Vertically Integrated Aquaculture (VIA)."

[12]Jay Mathews, "In Alaska, Oil Spill Has Lost Its Sheen," *Washington Post,* 9 February 1991.

The Problem of Scale

"What's wrong with this argument," a reader might object, "is that it leaves out the question of scale. We can get away with polluting an estuary here and there if elsewhere healthy ecosystems support the global processes essential to life. At a local scale, an instrumental calculus may argue for industrializing a particular environment. The problem, though, is that when we apply the same calculus to every ecosystem, we end up by destroying the crucial services nature provides."

This argument has weight with respect to activities that affect the atmosphere. Scientists have shown a connection between the use of CFCs and changes in stratospheric ozone. Likewise, the excessive combustion of coal and oil threatens to change the world's climate. That we should follow policies that prudence recommends, I have no doubt. The Montreal Protocol concerning CFCs represents an important first step. Prudence also recommends that we reach similar international agreements to decrease the amount of fuel we burn and, perhaps, to increase our reliance on those forms of energy that do not involve combustion.

While it is urgent that we limit atmospheric pollution, this does not give us a reason to protect intrinsically valuable species or ecosystems. The pollution, degradation, and exploitation of the Chesapeake Bay, for example, has no cognizable effect on global biochemical processes. One may argue, indeed, that the more eutrophic the Bay becomes, the more carbon it will store, thus helping to counter the "greenhouse" effect. By solving the problems of the Chesapeake, we do little to solve the problems of the atmosphere. The two sets of problems arise from different causes, involve different sorts of values, and require different solutions.

Rain Forests. Consider the rain forests, which seem doomed by economic progress. One can argue persuasively that humanity has no more important ethical or aesthetic task than to keep these magnificent ecosystems from being turned into particle boards and disposable diapers. Popular arguments to the effect that rain forests store net carbon or add to global oxygen budgets, however, may not be convincing.

Since rain forests are climax ecosystems, they absorb through the cold burning of decay as much oxygen as they release through respiration; thus the popular belief that these forests add to global oxygen budgets betrays a naivete about how climax ecosystems work.[13] One way to get a rain forest to store net carbon may be to chop it down and plant instead of trees fast-growing crops genetically designed to do very nicely in the relevant soil and climatic conditions. (The biologist Dan Janzen has described this dreadful possibility.)[14] The trees could be used to make disposable diapers which, after use, would go to landfills where they would store carbon nearly forever.

Biodiversity. Anyone with any moral or aesthetic sense must agree that another of humanity's greatest responsibilities today is to arrest shameful and horrendous rates of extinction. Yet one is hard pressed to find credible instrumental arguments for protecting endangered species in their habitats. The reason that we produce Thanksgiving turkeys by the millions while letting the black-footed boobie become extinct is that one bird has instrumental value while the other has not. The boobie had no ecological function; it was epiphenomenal even in its own habitat. Its demise in no way contributed, for example, to the loss of stratospheric ozone or to the "greenhouse" effect.

[13]For discussion, see T. C. Whitmore, "The Conservation of Tropical Rain Forests," in *Conservation Biology: An Evolutionary Perspective,* ed. M. Soule and B. A. Wilcox (Sunderland, Mass.: Sinauer, 1980), p. 313: "The suggestion, sometimes made, that atmospheric oxygen levels would be lowered by the removal of tropical rain forests rests on a mistaken view of climax ecosystems."

[14]See William Allen, "Penn Prof Views Biotechnology as Potential Threat to Tropical Forests," *Genetic Engineering News* 7, no. 10 (1987): 10. The article quotes a letter by Janzen: "Tropical wildlands and most of the earth's contemporary species still exist because humanity has not had organisms capable of converting all tropical land surfaces to profitable agriculture and animal husbandry. Within one to three decades, organisms modified through genetic engineering will be capable of making agriculture or animal husbandry, or both, profitable on virtually any land surface. Agricultural inviability, the single greatest tropical conservation force, will be gone."

Some commentators have speculated that transpiration from rain forests may play some role in the atmosphere. Since more than 85 percent of water absorbed into the atmosphere comes from the oceans, however, the marginal difference—if any—in transpiration between natural and biotech species in rain forests is unlikely to be consequential.

Environmentalists, to justify their efforts to protect biological diversity, sometimes speculate that exotic species might prove useful for medical purposes, for instance. No public health professional, as far as I know, has vouched for this proposition. Pharmaceutical companies are not known for contributing to the Nature Conservancy or for otherwise encouraging efforts to preserve biodiversity. They are interested in learning from folk medicine, but they cannot even think of tracking down, capturing, and analyzing the contents of millions of species (many of them unidentified) each of which may contain thousands of compounds.

If pharmaceutical companies wanted to mine exotic species, they would not preserve them in their habitats. They might trap and freeze them or sequence their genes for later reconstruction. Seed companies would likewise store germ tissue in banks, not leave it in the wild. Capturing and freezing specimens, not preserving habitats, would be the way to go, to make biodiversity benefit us.

Even a single endangered species enlists our respect and admiration, since (as one observer has said) it would require another heaven and earth to produce such a being. The grand diversity of life, particularly the existence of rare and exotic species, presents a profound moral obligation for civilization, which is to share the earth peaceably with other species. This obligation exists whether or not we can defend the preservation of species on grounds of self-interest rather than morality. The destruction of biodiversity may be immoral, even sinful, without being irrational or imprudent.

A Plea for Environmental Ethics

In an old movie, a character played by W. C. Fields, having, it appears, negligently killed a baby, confronts its hysterical mother. Eyeing her youthful figure, he says: "No matter, madam; I would be happy to get you with another."

What we find chilling in this scene is Fields's appeal wholly to instrumental value. He sees nothing wrong with killing a baby as long has he can "get" its mother with another child who, one day, will be equally capable of supporting her in her old age. To Fields, objects have only instrumental value; we can evaluate all our actions in terms of costs and benefits. They have no other meaning.

Moral Value—A Benefit or Cost? The scene in the movie might remind us of the way the EXXON Corporation dealt with public outrage over the recent unpleasantness in Prince William Sound. The corporation assured everyone that the salmon fishery would bounce back. If anyone was out of pocket, EXXON would lavishly compensate them. EXXON said to the outraged public: "No matter, madam; we will be happy to make you at least as well off."

From the point of view of instrumental value alone, both Fields and EXXON were correct. They could replace whatever was lost with equally beneficial or useful substitutes. Another baby could grow up to plow land or tend bobbins as well as the first. The mother's income in old age would not decrease. EXXON too would make up lost income. Isn't it irrational, then, for people to complain when children are killed or wildlife is destroyed? From the point of view of instrumental value, they aren't worth much. They may have meaning, but they confer few benefits on us. They make demands on us. They are mostly costs.

Indeed, raising children, preserving nature, cherishing art, and practicing the virtues of civil life are all costs—the costs of being the people we are. Why do we pay these costs? We can answer only that these costs are benefits; these actions justify themselves; these virtues are their own reward.

I wonder, therefore, whether we environmentalists do well to argue for environmental protection primarily on instrumental rather than on moral and aesthetic grounds. Are the possible medicinal or agricultural uses of rare and endangered species really what we care about? We might as well argue that we should protect whales for the sake of their oil or sea otters to harvest their teeth. I think the destruction and extinction of wildlife would horrify us even if we knew sea otters, murres, and eagles would never benefit us. How do we differ from Charlotte, then, who saved Wilbur even though he did nothing for her?

Preference Versus Judgment. "The distinction between instrumental and intrinsic value," someone may object, "lies beside the point of environmental policy, since a cost-benefit analysis, based in willingness-to-pay estimates, can take both sorts of preferences into account. Whether people are willing to pay to protect wildlife for moral, aesthetic, or self-interested reasons (hunting, for example) is their business; all the policy maker needs to know is what their preferences are and how much they are willing to pay to satisfy them."

This objection misses the crucial importance of the way we choose to make decisions. Consider, for example, how we determine whether a person is innocent or guilty of a crime. We might do this by sending questionnaires to a random sample of citizens to check off whether they prefer a guilty or innocent verdict and, perhaps, how much they are willing to pay for each. This method of reaching a verdict would be "rational" in the sense that it aggregates "given" preferences (data) according to mathematical principles laid down in advance. The method is also "neutral" in that it translates a data set into a social choice without itself entering, influencing, or affecting the outcome.

On the other hand, we may trust the finding of innocence or guilt to juries who are steeped in the evidence, who hear the arguments, and then, by deliberation, reach a collective judgment. This procedure, since it involves discussion and even persuasion, would not proceed from "given" preferences according to rules laid down in advance. The process or method itself is supposed to affect the result.

Which model would be most appropriate for environmental policy? Consider erosion. Public officials must assess instrumental reasons for protecting soil: they must determine how much arable land we need for crops, how much we are losing, and how best to conserve what we have. They also weigh intrinsic values, for example, what soil and its protection expresses about us or means to us as a community. Our policy, presumably, should be based not on the revealed or expressed preferences of a random sample of people, no matter how rigorous our techniques of sampling and aggregating may be, but on the judgment of responsible authorities after appropriate public consideration and debate.

Similarly, policies for civil rights, education, the arts, child labor, and the environment depend on judgment—often moral and aesthetic judgment—concerning facts about the world and about ourselves, that is, about our goals and intentions as a community. People who believe we ought to save the whales, for example, do not tell us simply what they prefer; rather, they call for the reasoned agreement or disagreement of others. That is why public policy is always argued in public terms—in

terms of what we ought to do, not what I happen to want.

With respect to aesthetic experience, anyone can tell you what he or she likes, but not everyone can tell you what is worth appreciating. A person judges aesthetically not for himself or herself only but on the basis of reasons, arguments, or ideas that he or she believes would lead others to the same conclusion. Knowledge, experience, sensitivity, discernment—these distinguish judgments of taste from expressions of preference.

To be sure, we enjoy objects we appreciate, but we do not value these objects because we enjoy them. Rather, we enjoy them because we find them valuable or, more precisely, enjoyment is one way of perceiving their value. To enjoy ecological communities aesthetically or to value them morally is to find directly in them or in their qualities the reasons that justify their protection. This is not a matter of personal preference. It is a matter of judgment and perception, which one might believe correct or mistaken, and thus argue for or against, within an open political process.

The contrast I have drawn between instrumental and intrinsic value borrows a great deal, of course, from Kant, who summed up the distinction as follows: "That which is related to general human inclination and needs has a market price. . . . But that which constitutes . . . an end in itself does not have a mere relative worth, i.e., a price, but an intrinsic worth, i.e., a dignity."[15] Kant believed that dignity attaches to objects because of what they are and, therefore, how we judge them. The discovery of what things are—whether it is their moral, aesthetic, or scientific properties—has to do with knowledge. Like any form of knowledge it is intersubjective: it represents not the preference of individuals but the will, the perception, or the considered opinion of a community.

Are Values Relative? While many Americans may share an environmental ideology—the United States has been described as Nature's Nation[16]—this does not apply everywhere. Even if the love of nature belongs to most cultures, moreover, it

[15]Immanuel Kant, *Foundations of the Metaphysics of Morals,* ed. R. P. Wolff, trans. L. W. Beck (Indianapolis: Bobbs-Merrill, 1959), p. 53. Emphasis in original.
[16]Perry Miller, *Nature's Nation* (Cambridge, Mass.: Harvard University Press, 1967).

might express itself in different ways. The Japanese may not experience whales as we do; Moby Dick is one of our classics. Italians, who treasure their artistic heritage, might as soon eat as listen to a song bird. How can we expect other cultures to respond to nature in the ways we do?

This kind of question may lead environmentalists to suppose that instrumental arguments for protecting nature have a universality that intrinsic arguments do not. Yet instrumental arguments depend on interpretations of fact—models of climate change, for example—that invite all kinds of disagreement. And ethical issues arise, moreover, even when instrumental concerns are paramount, such as when determining how much industrialized and developing nations should cut back combustion to counter global warming. It may be easier to persuade, attract, or cajole other nations to cooperate (if not agree) with our moral and aesthetic concerns than with our reading of prudence or self-interest. The process of reaching agreement is the same, however, whether instrumental or intrinsic values are at stake.

Living with Nature. I have argued that we ought to preserve nature for its sake and not simply our benefit. How far, however, should we go? The Chesapeake Bay commends itself to us for intrinsic but also for instrumental reasons. How can we balance our need to use with our desire to protect this ecosystem?

We confront this kind of question, I believe, also in relation to people whom we love and whose freedom and spontaneity we respect but with whom we have to live. Children are examples. We could treat our children—as we might treat nature—completely as means to our own ends. We would then simply use them to take out the empties, perform sexual favors, tend bobbins, or whatever it is that benefits us. This would be despicable as well as criminal. We know that morality requires that we treat our children as ends in themselves and not merely as means to our own ends.

At the same time, we have to live with our kids, and this allows us to make certain demands on them, like not to wake us up too early in the morning, no matter how much we love them for their own sake. While we insist on protecting our children's innate character, independence, and integrity, we have to socialize the little devils or they will destroy us and themselves. I think this is

true of nature: we can respect the integrity of ecosystems even if we change them in ways that allow us all to share the same planet.

No clear rules determine how far one should go in disciplining one's children or in modifying their behavior; socialization may have fairly broad limits. But there are limits; we recognize child abuse when we see it. Have we such a conception of the abuse of nature? I think we need one. At least we should regard as signs of environmental abuse the typical results of egregious assaults on ecosystems, such as eutrophication, pandemic extinctions, and so on. We might then limit changes we make in nature by keeping this notion of ecological health—or disease—in mind.

Zuckerman's Response

William Reilly, administrator of the Environmental Protection Agency, recently wrote: "Natural ecosystems . . . have intrinsic values independent of human use that are worthy of protection." He cited an advisory scientific report that urged the agency to attach as much importance to intrinsic ecological values as to risks to human health and welfare. Mr. Reilly added: "Whether it is Long Island Sound or Puget Sound, San Francisco Bay or the Chesapeake, the Gulf of Mexico or the Arctic tundra, it is time to get serious about protecting what we love. Clearly we do love our great water bodies: . . . They are part of our heritage, part of our consciousness. Let us vow not to let their glory pass from this good Earth."[17]

In 1991 the State of Maryland offered anyone registering an automobile the option of paying $20 (which would go to an environmental fund) to receive a special license plate bearing the motto: "Treasure the Chesapeake." A surprising number of registrants bought the plate. How many of us would have ponied up the $20 for a plate that read: "Use the Chesapeake Efficiently" or "The Chesapeake: It Satisfies Your Revealed and Expressed Preferences"?

To treasure the Chesapeake is to see that it has a good of its own—and therefore a "health" or "integrity"—that we should protect even when to do so does not benefit us. "Why did you do all this

[17]William K. Reilly, "A Strategy to Save the Great Water Bodies," *EPA Journal* 16, no. 6 (1990): 4.

for me?" Wilbur asked. "I've never done anything for you." Even when nature does not do anything for us—one might think, for example, of the eagles and otters destroyed in Prince William Sound—we owe it protection for moral and aesthetic reasons. Otherwise our civilization and our lives will amount to little more than the satisfaction of private preferences: what Charlotte described as "all this trapping and eating flies."

In this essay, I have proposed that we may lift up our lives a little by seeing nature as Charlotte did, not just as an assortment of resources to be managed and consumed, but also as a setting for collective moral and aesthetic judgment. I have also suggested that our evolutionary heritage—the

diversity of species, the miracle of life—confronts us with the choice Zuckerman had to make: whether to butcher nature for the market or to protect it as an object of moral attention and aesthetic appreciation.

If Zuckerman had not learned to appreciate Wilbur for his own sake, he would have converted the pig to bacon and chops. Likewise, if we do not value nature for ethical and aesthetic reasons, then we might well pollute and degrade it for instrumental ones. If a spider could treat a pig as a friend, however, then we should be able to treat a forest, an estuary, or any other living system in the same way.

Environmentalism and Economic Freedom: The Case for Private Property Rights

WALTER BLOCK[1]

I. Introduction

This paper shall attempt to reconcile environmentalism and economic freedom.

Before making this seemingly quixotic endeavor, we must be sure we are clear on both concepts. Environmentalism may be noncontroversially defined as a philosophy which sees great benefit in clean air and water, and to a lowered rate of species extinction. Environmentalists are particularly concerned with the survival and enhancement of endangered species such as trees, elephants, rhinos and whales, and with noise and dust pollution, oil spills, greenhouse effects and the dissipation of the

ozone layer. Note, this version of environmentalism is a very moderate one. Moreover, it is purely goal directed. It implies no means to these ends whatsoever. In this perspective, environmentalism is, in principle, as much compatible with free enterprise as it is with its polar opposite, centralized governmental command and control.

Economic freedom also admits of a straightforward definition. It is the idea that people legitimately own themselves and the property they "capture" from nature by homesteading,[2] as well as the additional property they attain, further, by trading either their labor or their legitimately owned possessions.[3] Sometimes called libertarian-

[1]The author wishes to thank Jonathan Adler of CEI, Dianna Reinhart, Jane Shaw and Rick Stroup of PERC, P. J. Hill of Wheaton College and Jan Leek of NCPA for bibliographical and other help. None are responsible for the content of this paper. The author wishes also to thank two anonymous referees for very substantive help in the rewriting of this essay. Without their assistance this article would have been a far less cogent one.

[2]For a critique of homesteading, see Stroup (1988). For a rejoinder, see Block (1990b); for another defense of homesteading, see Hoppe (1993).

[3]For a general explication of the private property based free enterprise system, see Rothbard (1973), Hoppe (1989). For political economic perspectives that are sometimes confused with this vision, see Hayek (1973), Nozick (1974). For a rebuttal of these, see Rothbard (1982b).

From Journal of Business Ethics *17: 1887–1899, 1998.* © *1998 Kluwer Academic Publishers. Printed in the Netherlands. Reprinted by permission of Kluwer Academic Publishers.*

ism, in this view the only improper human activity is the initiation of threat or force against another or his property. This, too, is the only legitimate reason for law. To prevent murder, theft, rape, trespass, fraud, arson, etc., and all other such invasions is the only proper function of legal enactments.

At first glance the relationship between environmentalism and freedom would appear direct and straightforward: an increase in the one leads to a decrease in the other, and vice versa. And, indeed, there is strong evidence for an inverse relationship between the two.

For example, there is the Marxist and even communist background of some advocates of environmental concerns.[4] People like these come to the ecological movement with an axe to grind. Their real interest is with power: running the lives of others, whether for their own good, for the good of society, or for the good of the unstoppable "forces of history." They were doing pretty well on this score for decades in Russia and Eastern Europe. Thanks to them, this vast part of the globe was marching in lock step toward the Marxist vision of all power to the "proletarians." But then, in 1989, thanks to the inner contradictions of communism (Mises, 1969), their world turned topsy turvy. Some shifted their allegiances to the only fully communist systems remaining: Cuba, North Korea. As for the others, nothing daunted, they just switched horses on the same old wagon: instead of formal socialism, these people adopted environmentalism as a better means toward their unchanged ends. They can best be characterized as "watermelons," in that while they are green on the outside they are still red on the inside.

Then, there are the real greens. They see environmentalism not as a means toward an end, but as the very goal itself. The most radical of them are very forthright. They see man as the enemy of nature, and would, if they could, destroy the former to save the latter. States Graber (1989, p. 9), who is a U.S. National Park Service research biologist: "Until such time as Homo sapiens should decide to rejoin nature, some of us can only hope for the right virus to come along." In the view of Foreman (1990, p. 48), who is co-founder of Earth First![5] and former lobbyist for the Wilderness Society, "We are a cancer on nature." And here is how Mills (1989, p. 106) describes the other members of her own species: "Debased human protoplasm."[6]

Some are only slightly less radical. They do not yearn for virtually the end of the human race. Instead, they merely hold that animals have rights, that trees have rights, that microscopic organisms have rights. It is reputed that Ghandi, for instance, sometimes went around wearing a surgical mask, so that he would not inadvertently kill a microorganism by inhaling it. If so, that practice would certainly be in keeping with this philosophy.

Stepping down a peg in the extremism of the ecologically concerned, there are those who merely blame markets, free enterprise, capitalism, for the ruination of the planet. In their view, what is needed is to curb these vicious appetites, and to return to a "kinder, gentler" version of governmental interventionism. For example, with regard to contaminated New York City beaches, the Commissioner of Health from the Big Apple stated on Canadian Public Television (30 July 1988):

> I think the motivation is greed, you know, non-caring about the planet, non-caring about the ocean, and not caring about the people who live on the planet and want to use the ocean—greed.

In the view of environmentalist Renate Kroisa regarding pulp mill operators (CTV Report, 15 March 1989):

> They would rather rape the environment and make a lot of money for themselves than not rape the environment, clean up, and later on . . . stay competitive. The mills are here to make a lot of profit, and they're making a lot of profit at the cost of our environment.[7]

---

[4]Names which come to mind in this regard include Tom Hayden, Jane Fonda, Helen Caldicott, Jeremy Rifkin, Kirkpatrick Sale and E. F. Schumacher. For discussions of this phenomenon, see Horowitz (1991), Bramwell (1989), Rubin (1994) and Kaufman (1994).

[5]This is the group that urges tree spiking; placing a metal spike in trees so that when the chain saw of the lumberman encounters it, his injury or even death will result. Their rallying cry slogan is "Back to the Pleistocene."

[6]These views were cited in Goodman, Stroup et al. (1991, p. 3).

[7]Reported in "On Balance," Vol. II, No. 9, 1989, p. 5.

And states Commoner,[8]

The origin of the environmental crisis can be traced back to the capitalist precept that the choice of production technology is to be governed solely by private interest in profit maximization.

Other statements of this ilk include Porrit and Winner. (1988, p. 11): "The danger lies not in the odd maverick polluting factory, industry or technology, but in . . . industrialism itself"; Bookchin (1970, p. 14): "The plundering of the human spirit by the marketplace is paralleled by the plundering of the earth by capital"; and free markets "take the sacredness out of life, because there can be nothing sacred in something that has a price" (Schumacher, 1973, p. 45).[9]

Then there are those who oppose not only market competition in general, but also want to ban particular products made possible by this system. For instance, there are calls to prohibit 747 airplanes (Rifkin, 1980, p. 216), automobiles (Sale, 1989, p. 33), eyeglasses (Mills, 1989, p. 106), private washing machines (Bookchin, 1989, p. 22), tailored clothing (Schumacher, 1973, pp. 57–58), toilet paper (Mills, 1989, pp. 167–168).

Paradoxically, there is a very limited but possible sense in which it is rational to prefer the reds to the greens. True, the former, not the latter, killed millions upon millions of people (Conquest, 1986, 1990). But at least their goal, their purpose, their aim, their end, was to *help* human beings. Yes, they picked a tragically erroneous way of going about this, a philosophy from which the entire world's peoples are still reeling. However, it must be conceded, they were not traitors to their species.[10] This, unfortunately, cannot be said of some of the greens, particularly the more radical ones. Nor can it be denied, that at least so far, with the exception of a few unfortunate loggers, the greens have not killed nor hurt very many people. But if their own publicly articulated intentions are to be believed,

given the power they might be a greater danger to the human race than even the communists.[11]

This, in short, is the case for believing there to be an inverse relationship between environmentalism and freedom. However, it is not a direct and straightforward one: an increase in the one does not always lead to a decrease in the other, and vice versa.

What are the exceptions? How can environmentalism and economic freedom be reconciled?[12] Simple. By showing that free enterprise is the best means toward the end of environmental protection. This appears a daunting task at the outset, given the emphasis placed by most environmentalists on socialism, and their hatred for capitalism. But a hint of the solution may be garnered by the fact that laissez-faire capitalism, as adumbrated above, strenuously opposes invasions, or border crossings, and that many environmental tragedies, from air pollution to oil spills, may reasonably be interpreted in just such a manner. The reason for environmental damage, then, is the failure of government to protect property rights (omissions) and other state activity which either regulates private property, or which forbids it outright (commissions). Let us consider a few test cases.

II. Air Pollution

According to the mainstream economic analysis, libertarianism is wrong. The problem of airborne pollutants is not due to a failure of government to protect private property rights. Instead, this comes about because of "market failure," a basic flaw in free enterprise. Pigou (1912, p. 159) gives the classic statement of this view:

> Smoke in large towns which inflicts a heavy loss on the community . . . comes about because there is no way to force private polluters to bear the social cost of their operations.

Samuelson (1956, 1970) conveys the same sentiment in terms of the divergence between private

---

[8]Cited in DiLorenzo (1990).

[9]Cited in Goodman, Stroup et al., 1991, p. 4.

[10]It is on this ground that the Communists may be preferred to the Nazis. For apart from members of the Aryan nations, the Nazis actually did intend to, and actually succeeded in, killing massive numbers of people. In terms of actual numbers of people killed, however, the reverse is the case.

[11]Of course, actions speak louder than words, and on this basis the greens do not even deserve to be mentioned in the same breath. On the other hand, even though intentions are less important than actual deeds, the former are not morally irrelevant.

[12]For a book that attempts to do just this, see Block, 1990a.

and social costs. Lange and Taylor (1938, p. 103) are yet additional socialists who make a complementary point:

> A feature which distinguishes a socialist economy from one based on private enterprise is the comprehensiveness of the items entering into the socialist price system.

In other words, for some strange dark mysterious reason, capitalists, under laissez faire, are excused from even considering the physical harm they do to the property of others through the emissions of their smoke particles. Under socialism, in contrast, the central planner of course takes this into account, nipping the problem of pollution in the bud.

There is so much wrong with this scenario it is hard to know where to begin a refutation. Perhaps we may best start with an empirical observation. If this criticism of the market were true, one would expect that, even if the Soviets couldn't successfully run an economy, they could at least be trusted as far as the environment is concerned. In actual point of fact, nothing could be further from the truth.

Exhibit "A" is perhaps the disappearance of the Aral and Caspian Seas, due to massive and unchecked pollution, overcutting of trees, and consequent desertification. Then there is Chernobyl, which caused hundreds, if not thousands of deaths.[13] For ferry boats in the Volga River, it is forbidden to smoke cigarettes. This is not for intrusive paternalistic health reasons as in the west, but because this river is so polluted with oil and other flammable materials that there is a great fear that if a cigarette is tossed overboard, it will set the entire body of water on fire. Further, under Communism, there was little or no waste treatment of sewage in Poland, the gold roof in Cracow's Sigismund Chapel dissolved due to acid rain, there was a dark brown haze over much of East Germany, and the sulfur dioxide concentra-

tions in Czechoslovakia were eight times levels common in the U.S. (DiLorenzo, 1990).

Nor was it a matter merely of the absence of democracy in the U.S.S.R. The ecological record of the U.S. government, where democracy is the order of the day, is none too savory. The Department of Defence has dumped 400,000 tons of hazardous waste, more than the five largest chemical corporations combined. The Rocky Mountain Arsenal carelessly disposed of nerve gas, mustard shells, the anticrop spray TX, and incendiary devices. And this is to say nothing of the infamous Yellowstone Park forest fire, which the authorities refused to put out, citing ecological considerations;[14] nor the TVA's 59 coal fired power plants; nor the underpricing and overuse of land administered by the Bureau of Land Management; nor the fact that the government subsidizes forest overcutting by building logging roads.

These are not examples of market failure. Rather, they are instances of government failure: direct controls and inability or unwillingness to uphold private property rights.

But what of Pigou and Samuelson's charge of the misallocative effect of negative externalities, or external diseconomies? This, too, is erroneous.

Up to the 1820s and 1830s, the legal jurisprudence in Great Britain and the U.S. was more or less predicated upon the libertarian vision of non-invasiveness (Coase, 1960, Horwitz, 1977). Typically, a farmer would complain that a railroad engine had emitted sparks which set ablaze his haystacks or other crops. Or a woman would accuse a factory of sending airborne pollutants to her property, which would clean laundry hanging on a clothesline. Or someone would object to the foreign matter imposed in one's lungs without permission. Almost invariably, the courts would take cognizance of this violation of plaintiff's rights.[15] The usual result during this epoch was injunctive relief, plus an award of damages.

Contrary to Pigou and Samuelson, manufacturers, foundries, railroads, etc., could *not* act in a vacuum, as if the costs they imposed on others were of

---

[13]True, there is the U.S. counterpart nuclear meltdown at Three Mile Island. But a popular bumper sticker puts this into some sort of perspective. It stated: "More people died at Chappaquidick than at Three Mile Island." ("Chappaquidick" refers to the death of a single individual, Mary Jo Kopechne, while being driven by Senator Ted Kennedy.) The point is, of course, that no one, not a single solitary individual, lost his life at Three Mile Island.

[14]Forest fires, it turns out, are "natural," and nothing must be done which interferes with nature.

[15]Called at the time "nuisance suits," we can with hindsight see them as environmental complaints.

no moment. There *was* a "way to force private pollsters to bear the social cost of their operations": sue them, make them pay for their past transgressions, and get a court order prohibiting them from such invasions in future.

Upholding property rights in this manner had several salutary effects. First of all, there was an incentive to use clean burning, but slightly more expensive anthracite coal rather than the cheaper but dirtier high sulfur content variety; less risk of lawsuits. Second, it paid to install scrubbers, and other techniques for reducing pollution output. Third there was an impetus to engage in research and development of new and better methods for the internalization of externalities: keeping one's pollutants to oneself. Fourth, there was a movement toward the use of better chimneys and other smoke prevention devices. Fifth, an incipient forensic pollution industry was in the process of being developed.[16] Sixth, the locational decisions of manufacturing firms were intimately effected. The law implied that it would be more profitable to establish a plant in an area with very few people, or none at all; setting up shop in a residential area, for example, would subject the firm to debilitating lawsuits.[17]

But then in the 1840s and 1850s a new legal philosophy took hold. No longer were private property rights upheld. Now, there was an even more important consideration: the public good. And of what did the public good consist in this new dispensation? The growth and progress of the U.S. economy. Toward this end it was decided that the jurisprudence of the 1820s and 1830s was a needless indulgence. Accordingly, when an environmental plaintiff came to court under this new system, he was given short shrift. He was told, in effect, that of course his private property rights were being violated; but that this was entirely proper, since there is something even more impor-

tant than selfish, individualistic property rights. And this was the "public good" of encouraging manufacturing.[18]

Under this legal convention, all the economic incentives of the previous regime were turned around 180 degrees. Why use clean burning, but slightly more expensive anthracite coal rather than the cheaper but dirtier high sulfur content variety? Why install scrubbers, and other techniques for reducing pollution output, or engage in environmental research and development, or use better chimneys and other smoke prevention devices, or make locational decisions so as to negatively impact as few people as possible? Needless to say, the incipient forensic pollution industry was rendered stillborn.

And what of the "green" manufacturer, who didn't want to foul the planet's atmosphere, or the libertarian, who refused to do this on the grounds that it was an unjustified invasion of other people's property? There is a name for such people, and it is called "bankrupt."[19] For to engage in environmentally sound business practices under a legal regime which no longer requires this is to impose on oneself a competitive disadvantage. Other things equal, this will guarantee bankruptcy.

From roughly 1850 to 1970, firms were able to pollute without penalty. *This* is why "there is no way to force private polluters to bear the social cost of their operations" a la Pigou; *this* is why there was a Samuelsonian "divergence of social and private costs." This was no failure of the market. It was a failure of the government to uphold free enterprise with a legal system protective of private property rights.

---

[16]It is only because murder and rape were illegal that there was a call for a forensic industry, capable of determining guilt based on semen, blood, hair follicles, DNA, etc. If these activities were legal, these capabilities would not have developed. Similarly, when one can sue for pollution, it is of the utmost importance to determine guilt or innocence; hence, the establishment of environmental forensics.

[17]Of course, "coming to the nuisance" was not deemed acceptable. That is, one could not build a residential abode in an area first homesteaded by pollution emitters, and then sue for pollution. On this see Rothbard (1982a, 1990).

[18]As a sop to the plaintiffs, the law and judicial practice was altered so as to require very high minimum heights for smokestacks. In this way the local perpetrator of invasive pollution no longer negatively impacted the local plaintiff. But of course this did no more than sweep the problem under the rug, or, rather, into the clouds. For if polluter A no longer affected complainant A, he affected others. And polluters B, C, D, . . ., who previously did not harm A, now began to do so.

[19]This is the exact opposite of Adam Smith's (1776) "invisible hand." Ordinarily, in laissez faire capitalism, selfish seeking of profit leads to the public good. For example, one invests in a good which is in very short supply, and hence most needed by the populace, and earns the greatest possible profit. Here, instead, if a person acts in an environmentally responsible manner, he goes broke.

In the 1970s a "discovery" was made: the air quality was dangerous to human beings and other living creatures. Having caused the problem itself, the government now set out to cure it, with a whole host of regulations which only made things worse. There were demands for electric cars, for minimal mileage per gallon for gasoline, for subsidies to wind, water, solar and nuclear[20] power, for taxes on coal, oil, gas and other such fuels, for arbitrary cutbacks in the amount of pollutants into the air. The nationwide 55 mile per hour speed limit was not initially motivated by safety considerations, but rather by ecological ones. "Rent seeking" played a role in the scramble, as eastern (dirty burning sulfur) coal interests prevailed over their western (clean burning anthracite) counterparts. The former wanted compulsory scrubbers, the latter wanted the mandated substitution of their own coal for that of their competitors.

And what was the view of the supposedly free market oriented Chicago School? Instead of harking back to a system of private property rights, they urged the "more efficient" statist regulations. Instead of a command and control system, they urged the adoption of tradeable emissions rights (TERs). In this system (Hahn, 1989, Hahn and Stavins, 1990, Hahn and Hester, 1989), instead of forcing each and every polluter to cut back by, say, one third, they would demand of all of them together that this goal be attained. Why is this beneficial? It might be difficult and expensive for some firms to reduce pollution from 150 to 100 tons, and easy and cheap for others. Under TERs, some could reduce the pollution levels by less than 1/3 (or even increase them), while they would in effect pay others to reduce theirs by more than this amount. The means through which this would be accomplished would be a system of "rights to pollute," and an organized market through which these could be bought and sold.

The implications of this scheme for freedom are clear. States Anderson (1990):

> Fortunately, there is a simple, effective approach available—long appreciated but under used. An approach based solidly on . . . private property rights.

[20]The Price Anderson Act—protecting firms from legal responsibility for accidents—is the most egregious case of the latter.

At its root all pollution is garbage disposal in one form or another. The essence of the problem is that our laws and the administration of justice have not kept up with the refuse produced by the exploding growth of industry, technology and science.

If you took a bag of garbage and dropped it on your neighbor's lawn, we all know what would happen. Your neighbor would call the police and you would soon find out that the disposal of your garbage is your responsibility, and that it must be done in a way that does not violate anyone else's property rights.

But if you took that same bag of garbage and burned it in a backyard incinerator, letting the sooty ash drift over the neighborhood, the problem gets more complicated. The violation of property rights is clear, but protecting them is more difficult. And when the garbage is invisible to the naked eye, as much air and water pollution is, the problem often seen is insurmountable.

We have tried many remedies in the past. We have tried to dissuade polluters with fines, with government programs whereby all pay to clean up the garbage produced by the few, with a myriad of detailed regulations to control the degree of pollution. Now some even seriously propose that we should have economic incentives, to charge polluters a fee for polluting—and the more they pollute the more they pay. But that is just like taxing burglars as an economic incentive to deter people from stealing your property, and just as unconscionable.

The only effective way to eliminate serious pollution is to treat it exactly for what it is—garbage. Just as one does not have the right to drop a bag of garbage on his neighbor's lawn, so does one not have the right to place any garbage in the air or the water or the earth, if it in any way violates the property rights of others.

What we need are tougher clearer environmental laws that are enforced—not with economic incentives—but with jail terms.

What the strict application of the idea of private property rights will do is to increase the cost of garbage disposal. That increased cost will be reflected in a higher cost for the products and services that resulted from the process that produced the garbage. And that is how it should be. Much of the cost of disposing of waste material is already incorporated in the price of the goods and services produced. All of it should be. Then only those who benefit from the garbage made will pay for its disposal."[21]

Economic freedom thus implies a movement back to the legal status of pollution in the earlier epoch. Nor need we fear undue economic hardship and dislocation because of adjustment problems. For apart from obvious and blatant pollution, which has already been curtailed through command and control regulations, it will take at least a few years for environmental forensics to develop to the point where industry will have to make more basic changes.

There are of course objections to "turning the clock back" to the 1820s. For one thing, there is the fear that if we allow anyone to sue anyone else for pollution, that will mean the end of industry altogether. And not only of industry and other accoutrements of modern civilized life. This would also bring the curtain down on life itself, as, strictly speaking, even exhaling (carbon dioxide) could be seen as a pollutant, and thus forbidden. Fortunately, this scenario is not tenable. First of all, although industry up to the 1830s was no great shakes compared to the modern era, it was not as nonexistent as implied by this objection either. Secondly, there is a reason for this: the burden of proof is on the plaintiff, so only the more egregious cases of pollution were in effect actionable, and *de minimis* was in operation, so that frivolous lawsuits, or ones alleging only tiny amounts of pollution were disregarded.[22]

Another objection, a more reasonable one, is that if allowing pollution lawsuits again will not bring industry to a screeching halt, it will at least greatly disorganize it. Perhaps it might be better to allow for a 10 year waiting or warning period, so that industry could adjust, before imposing so draconian a set of measures.

This option does indeed sound more pragmatic, but there are problems with it. We have said that pollution amounts to an invasion. Suppose that someone had the authority to immediately end an invasion, say, for example, slavery, and refused to do so for 10 years on the grounds that this would be too "disruptive" or "impractical." Say what you

will about such a decision on pragmatic grounds, it cannot be maintained that it enhances freedom.

Fortunately, we can have our cake and eat it too in the present context. That is, we can allow environmental lawsuits immediately, but also have a "waiting period" of perhaps 10 years or so in any case. This can be accomplished because of the 150 year gap, from approximately 1845 to 1995, when environmental forensics could have developed, but did not, thanks to a legal regime which was not conducive to it.[23] The point is, had environmental forensics been developing over these last 150 years, but for some reason not implemented, and we were to suddenly allow environmental lawsuits for the first time at present, this would indeed drive industry to an abrupt halt. For the plaintiff's burden of proof would be easy to satisfy, under these assumptions. Moreover, there would be plenty of invasive pollution around to find people guilty of perpetrating.

For with emissions strictly controlled (in the early period), development would have proceeded along non pollution intensive lines. In contrast, with carte blanche on emissions (the later period), industry would have developed in a pollution intensive manner. Moving from a system where pollution was all but legal (1845–1970), to one where it was strictly controlled (as it was before 1845), would thus have called for a basic restructuring of industry.

Let me try to make this point in another way. There is a difficulty which the private property rights theory of environmental protection must wrestle with: if we institute such a system abruptly, especially if we did so, say, in the 1960s before these concerns had captured the public imagination, we ran the risk of halting industry dead in its tracks, something to be resisted at the very least on pragmatic grounds. On the other hand, if we offered, for example, a ten year waiting period before environmental lawsuits could be undertaken,

---

[21]For another critique of tradeable emissions rights, see McGee and Block, 1994.
[22]On this see Rothbard, 1982a (1990).

[23]From 1845 to 1970, approximately, polluters had a free run of the atmosphere, other people's property and their lungs. From roughly 1970 to 1995, and counting, there was concern for invasive air and water borne pollutants, but only command and control (and in the last few years tradeable emissions rights schemes) regulations. Provision for environmental lawsuits is still, as of this 1995 writing, virtually nonexistent. See Horwitz (1977), Block (1990, pp. 282–285).

then we are complicit in violations of the libertarian code during this decade. Happily we can avoid this dilemma. First, we allow lawsuits as soon as we have the power to do so, thus escaping from the second (disrupting industry) horn of the dilemma. We escape from the first, too, because of the fact that for the plaintiff to be successful in his lawsuit he must prove beyond a reasonable doubt that a specific particular polluter is responsible for invading his person or property. But to do so, given the sad sorry state of environmental forensics at least at the time of this writing, will take time, plausibly, as much time as it will take for industry to end the error of its ways without any great disruption. That is, suppose it takes 10 years for industry to adjust to the legal dispensation of the 1830s. This will not be as harmful to the economy as might be supposed because it might take a similar amount of time to figure out precisely who is polluting whom.[25]

III. Waste Disposal

The brou-ha-ha over paper vs plastic and styrofoam wrappers also has implications for economic freedom.

In the late 1980s, a McDonald's restaurant opened its doors in Moscow. In some ways, this was no great shakes. Ray Kroc's burger emporia had by that time been doing business in hundreds other countries. But in other ways, this was a very big deal indeed. For at that time Russia was still under the control of Communism. Allowing a private firm to do business in the heart of the beast thus showed a weakness in the totalitarianism of the U.S.S.R. What could be a greater chink in the armor than a popular restaurant intimately tied to western capitalism?

McDonald's is a reasonable example of a capitalist enterprise. It employs thousands of people, particularly young persons, minority members, immigrants. It brings joy to millions of customers, and has sold, almost unbelievably, in the billions of burgers. It is an indication of quality. You can travel practically the world over, and be assured of the same kind of meal they serve in "Kansas." This chain (and other imitators) has been a boon to the poor. Before its birth, it was difficult for the poor to enjoy a restaurant meal; thanks to this initiative, away from home dining has become a commonplace for those with modest means. All in all, McDonald's was not a poor choice as a chip in the high stakes gambling with the Communists over the future of the world's political economy.

But at about the same time that Ronald McDonald was taking up residence behind the Iron Curtain, back at home, in "the land of the free and the home of the brave," he was running into entry restrictions and other barriers. Dozens of town councils, all across this great land of ours, were refusing to give McDonald's permission to open up new stores. Why? A takeover of Soviet fifth columnists? A communist revolution in the good old U.S. of A? Not a bit of it. Instead, it was all due to left wing environmentalism.

Why were the local greens so bitterly opposed to more quarter pounder outlets? Because they came wrapped in styrofoam and other plastic packaging, and if there is one thing practically guaranteed to drive an environmentalist to apoplexy, it is precisely these materials.

Let us assume, merely for the sake of argument, that everything any ecologist has ever said about plastic and styrofoam is true. That compared to paper, these substances are not environmentally friendly, they are not biodegradable, they are not recyclable, they are not reusable, they cannot be returned to nature. On the contrary, when buried in the ground, they come back to haunt us in the future as hazardous wastes. And that as a result, anyone foolish enough to dispose of them ruins his land for subsequent farming, housing, factories, shopping malls, etc.

Under these conditions, let us enquire into the ability of the market place to transmit this knowledge (paper, good; plastic, bad) so that it is taken into account by the economy. After all, this is precisely what the price system is presumably designed to do. Prices, after all, are like street signs. Just as the latter guide us around geographical space,[26]

---

[24]If a legal theory is to be a robust one, it must not rely on the accidents of time or place. That is, it must be applicable at any epoch in history. Since I claim that libertarianism fits this bill, it is incumbent upon me to show how it would apply not only when environmental concerns have been incorporated into the law, but also when they were not.

[25]I am grateful to an anonymous referee for forcing me to clarify my presentation of this point.

[26]In the days of yore when a city was faced with a besieging army, one of the defensive measures they would take was to tear down the street signs. They did so on the ground that

the former are supposed to impose direction on the economy.

At first glance it would appear that while prices might accomplish their task in the general economy, they are a dismal failure when it comes to environmental concerns. Picture yourself at the supermarket checkout counter. You have just selected your groceries, and the clerk has charged you for them. After paying, you are asked that inevitable, fateful $64,000 question: paper or plastic bag?

Under these circumstances, the only reason for picking the environmentally sound paper, and eschewing the toxic plastic, is benevolence. For let us assume that the cost to you is $0.01 for each. In some cases, this is explicit. You pay a penny for either one. In other cases, it is only implicit: you don't pay for the bag, paper or plastic; rather, it is included in the price of the groceries, in much the same manner as the lighting, or cleaning, or advertising of the store. Benevolence for the planet, or for your fellow creatures is your only possible motivation for choosing the paper; for by stipulation the economic considerations are equal. One penny for each.

But we all know what Smith (1776) said about benevolence. It is not from benevolence, but rather from a keen appreciation of self interest, that the butcher, the baker and the candlestick maker share with us their wares. Given the evils of plastic, benevolence is a weak reed indeed upon which to base our hopes for its elimination. Nor is it a question of benevolence versus selfishness. Given the importance of ridding the planet of these noxious substances, it behooves us to mobilize *both* motivations, not just one of them.

Benevolence is far from sufficient. For suppose that half of all industrialists had the personality of a liberarian Mother Teresa, and refused to pollute, even though allowed to do so by law. What would happen to them? They would go bankrupt, for they would give themselves a competitive disadvantage. If all industrialists are roughly of equal ability, but some pollute and others spend money on smoke prevention devices, it is clear that the invisible hand will be choking us, not helping us. No, the only solution is to change the law to one

which upholds property rights, so that trespassers do not continue to be privileged.

Why has the price system seemingly failed? Is this intrinsic to capitalism, one of the "market failures" that socialist economists are always prattling on about? Not at all. The failure stems not from laissez faire, but from state prohibition. Specifically, the government has nationalized, or municipalized, the industry of solid waste management.

Right now, we do not pay a red cent for garbage disposal. Instead, we are forced by government to disburse tax money for this purpose, and are then given these services for "free." In other words, this service is run along the lines of socialized medicine. There, too, services are provided for "free," courtesy of our tax dollars.

These systems have several disadvantages.[27] For one thing, there is the phenomenon of "moral hazard." Charge people a very low or zero price, and they will buy much more than at normal prices. Further, they will "waste" the good or service.[28] This is seen in the fact that socialized medicine is a hypochondriac's dream come true, and that consumers purchase items which are promiscuously wrapped. Given that the housewife doesn't have to pay to dispose of package coverings, it is no wonder that the manufacturer has little incentive to economize on containers.[29]

How would a private market in garbage disposal function? Everything would be privatized. The trucks would make pickups from the homeowner as well as the dump sites themselves. There would be no mandatory recycling nor bottle deposit requirements;[30] there would only be laws against trespassing: disgorging waste material onto other people's private property.

---

[27]Apart, that is, from the immorality of forcing people, whether by democratic vote or no (Spooner, 1870, 1966), to pay for things they have no desire to purchase.

[28]If we ran a socialized milk program as we do garbage disposal and medical care, people would probably have "milk gun" (instead of water gun) fights, was their cars with milk, and take milk baths.

[29]In addition to excessive amounts of wrappings, our zero price policy has also led to the combination of different materials in them, such as paper, plastic, tin and other metals, cardboard, etc. All of this makes it more expensive to recycle.

[30]Which are but further infringements upon economic freedom.

---

this would hardly much disaccommodate long time citizens, but would play havoc with the invader's ability to travel around town.

How would prices be established? Assume that burying inoffensive paper costs only a penny per bag, but that the plastic variety is so harmful that each one does $5.00 worth of damage[31] to the land in which it is placed. Given competition, no dump site owner will be able to charge more than $5.00 for burying a plastic bag, lest the additional profits earned thereby attract new entrants into the industry. In like manner the price cannot fall below this amount, since if it does, it will bankrupt all who agree to it. For example, if a private dump site owner were to accept $4.00 compensation for agreeing to permanently store a plastic bag on his land, he would lose $1.00 on that transaction. Multiply this by a few truckloads of this substance, and he will no longer be able to continue in business.[32]

Now let us return to our supermarket checkout scenario. Only this time, under full privatization, we make an entirely different economic calculation than before.

	Purchase Cost	Disposal Cost	Total
Paper	$0.01	$0.01	$0.02
Plastic	$0.01	$5.00	$5.01

Previously, there was no impetus to choose either paper or plastic. Each cost $0.01, and that was the end of it. Now, however, matters are very different. For we are called upon not merely to purchase the bag material, but also to dispose of it

later on at our own expense. Given disposal costs of one penny for paper and five dollars for plastic, our total costs are readily calculated: two cents for paper, and five dollars and one cent for plastic.

Is there any doubt that the whole problem would disappear in one fell swoop under these economic conditions? Virtually no consumer in his right mind would choose environmentally unfriendly plastic. The costs would simply be prohibitive. Everyone would "do the right environmental thing" and select paper.

This does not mean, of course, that plastic bags would be totally banned by economics. They would still be utilized, but only when their value to the user was greater than $5.01. For example, blood, intravenous solution and other medical fluids might still employ plastic containers.

Thus, thanks to the "magic of the market," we can again have our cake and eat it too. Under a full private property rights regime, there is no reason to legislatively ban McDonald's. If plastic and styrofoam are truly hazardous to the health of the planet, they will impose tremendous costs on dump site owners. These will be passed on to consumers. If McDonald's continued to insist upon use of plastic and styrofoam, this firm would lose out to other competitors (Burger King, Wendy's, Pizza Hut, Taco Bell, A&W, etc.) who were more greatly concerned for their customer's pocketbooks. Under present assumptions, there is simply no need to reduce freedom in order to protect the planet. The two work in tandem.

But it is now time to question our assumptions about the relative harm to the planet of plastic and styrofoam. According to "garbologist"[33] Rathje (1989), plastic is not so much a hazard to the globe as it is inert. If there is anything dangerous to the planet it is paper; not in the form of bags, but rather telephone books. After many years of burial, these release methane gas, and other dangerous substances. If so, perhaps paper and plastic will be able to compete with one another on a somewhat more equal footing.

This is an empirical question, which cannot be decided on the basis of armchair economic theorizing. It may safely be left in the hands of the

---

[31]Science cannot at present precisely determine the amount of damage that might be caused. (I owe this point to an anonymous referee.) However, this presents no philosophical challenge to entrepreneurship. Those dumpsite owners whose predictions are the closest to reality will prosper, at least compared to their colleagues furthest away, given ceterus paribus conditions. But make no mistake about it; given the assumptions on the basis of which we are now operating, storing paper most certainly *will* harm the dumpsite itself, at the very least in terms of economics. For, to reiterate, we are presuming that buried plastic and styrofoam has much the same effect as a toxic waste. Those dumpsite owners who allow storage of these items under their land will reduce its economic value after the landfill is complete, and alternative uses (housing, farms, etc.) are contemplated.
[32]I am here implicitly assuming that the present discounted (dis)value of burying a single plastic bag is $5.00. Obviously, to charge only $4.00 for this service would be to lose money on the deal.

[33]A garbologist is to mounds of waste material as is an archeologist to ancient ruins. Each years to "get to the bottom" of their respective subject matters. Each analyses them from their own perspective.

private dump site owning industry, for these entrepreneurs, unlike environmental bureaucrats, stand to lose their own personal fortunes if their prices are not consonant with actual harm to their property, and hence to the environment in general.

IV. Conclusion

I have tried to show that in at least two cases, air pollution and waste disposal, the concerns of environmentalists and those who favor economic freedom can be reconciled. However, there might appear to be what one anonymous referee called a "basic structural flaw in the development of (my) argument" in that the public policy conclusions in each of these two cases appear to be very different. "On the one hand," continues this referee, "(I) applaud . . . the existence of a pre-1850 legal system which enforced private property rights. But in (my) final argument for letting the market control waste disposal there is no clear indication of what *if any* role environmental law would play."

I am tremendously grateful to this referee in that he has given me an opportunity to further explicate libertarian environmentalist theory. The seeming contradiction in how I handle the two ecological issues can be reconciled in this way. In the case of air pollution, the violation of economic freedom and private property rights was that polluters were allowed by law to in effect trespass on other people's land, to say nothing of their lungs. In the case of waste disposal, the breach of economic freedom and private property rights is no less apparant, although it takes an altogether different form. Here, the infraction consists of the nationalization (e.g., municipalization) of what would otherwise be private dumpsites. But in both cases there is a transgression of the free enterprise ethic. Therefore, in each, the capitalist oriented environmentalist will advocate a return to market principles. In the one case this consists of an end to legal trespass, in the other of privatization of garbage dumping. Thus, there is no "structural flaw," or indeed, any inconsistancy whatever, in this analysis.

Let me make this point in a different way. Egalitarian socialists oppose both income disparities and private medicine. For the former they advocate wealth redistribution; for the latter, socialized medicine. Now these are two very distinct things. Seemingly, they are incompatible with one another. But not really, since both are aspects of an underlying vision.

It is the same in the present case. Laws prohibiting trespass of smoke particles, and privatizing dumpsites are superficially very different. In actual point of fact they are but opposite sides of the same coin, in that they both emanate from the same philosophical principle.

One last point. The typical way of treating pollution in the literature is as an "externality." By now it should be clear that I totally reject this approach. An external diseconomy is defined as a harm perpetrated by A on B, one for which B can neither collect damages nor halt through injunction. But *why* is B so powerless? It is my contention that the victim of pollution finds himself in this precarious position solely because of inadequacies in the law. Previous to 1850, for example, *there was no* pollution externality. This came about due to a "government failure" to uphold the law against trespass, not because of any alleged "market failure" such as externalities.

References

Anderson, Martin: 4 January 1989, *The Christian Science Monitor*, p. 19, reprinted in Block, 1990a.

Block, Walter: 1990b, "Earning Happiness Through Homesteading Unowned Land: A comment on 'Buying Misery with Federal Land' by Richard Stroup," *Journal of Social Political and Economic Studies* 15(2) (Summer), 237–253.

Block, Walter (ed.): 1990a, *Economics and the Environment: A Reconciliation* (The Fraser Institute, Vancouver).

Bookchin, Murray: 1989, "Death of a Small Planet," *The Progressive* (August).

Bookchin, Murray: 1970, "Toward and Ecological Solution," *Ramparts* (May).

Bramwell, Anna: 1989, *Ecology in the 20th Century* (Yale University Press, New Haven).

Coase, Ronald H.: 1960, "The Problem of Social Cost," *Journal of Law and Economics* 3, 1–44.

Commoner, Barry: 1990, *Making Peace with the Planet* (New York Pantheon Books).

Conquest, Robert: 1986, *The Harvest of Sorrow* (Oxford University Press, New York).

Conquest, Robert: 1990, *The Great Terror Edmonton* (Edmonton University Press, Alberta).

DiLorenzo, Thomas: 1990, "Does Capitalism Cause Pollution?," St. Louis, Washington University:

Center for the Study of American Business, Contemporary Issues Series 38.

Foreman, David: 1990, "Only Man's Presence Can Save Nature," *Harpers* (April).

Goodman, John C. and Richard L. Stroup et al.: 1991, *Progressive Environmentalism: A Pro-Human, Pro-Science, Pro-Free Enterprise Agenda for Change* (National Center for Policy Analysis, Task Force Report, Dallas, TX).

Graber, David M.: 1989, "Mother Nature as a Hothouse Flower," *Los Angeles Times Book Review* (22 October).

Hahn, Robert W.: 1989, "Economic Prescriptions for Environmental Problems: How the Patient Followed the Doctor's Orders," *Journal of Economic Perspectives* **3**(2) (Spring), 95–114.

Hahn, Robert W. and Gordon L. Hester: 1989, "Where Did All The Markets Go? An Analysis of EPA's Emissions Trading Program," *Yale Journal on Regulation* **6**(1) (Winter), 109–153.

Hahn, Robert W. and Robert N. Stavins: 1990, "Incentive-Based Environmental Regulation: A New ERA from an Old Idea?," Harvard University Energy and Environmental Policy Center Discussion Paper, June 26.

Hayek, F. A.: 1973, *Law, Legislation and Liberty* (The University of Chicago Press, Chicago).

Hoppe, Hans-Hermann: 1993, *The Economics and Ethics of Private Property: Studies in Political Economy and Philosophy* (Kluwer, Boston).

Hoppe, Hans-Hermann: 1989, *A Theory of Socialism and Capitalism: Economics, Politics and Ethics* (Dordrecht, Boston).

Horowitz, David: 1991, *Deconstructing the Left* (Second Thoughts Books, Lanham, MD).

Horwitz, Morton J.: 1977, *The Transformation of American Law, 1780–1860* (Harvard University Press, Cambridge).

Kaufman, Wallace: 1994, *No Turning Back: Dismantling the Phantasies of Environmental Thinking* (Basic Books, New York).

Lange, Oscar and Fred M. Taylor: 1938, *On the Economics Theory of Socialism* (University of Minnesota Press, Minneapolis).

McGee, Robert and Block, Walter: 1994, "Pollution Trading Permits as a Form of Market Socialism, and the Search for a Real Market Solution to Environmental Pollution," *Fordham University Law*

and Environmental Journal **VI**(1) (Fall), 51–77.

Mills, Stephanie: 1989, *Whatever Happened to Ecology?* (Sierra Club Books, San Francisco).

Mises, Ludwig von: 1969, *Socialism* (Liberty Fund, 1981, Indianapolis).

Nozick, Robert: 1974, *Anarchy, State and Utopia* (Basic Books Inc., New York).

Pigou, Arthur: 1912, *Wealth and Welfare* (MacMillan, London).

Porrit, Jonathan and Winner, David: 1988, *The Coming of the Greens* (Fontana, London).

Rathje, William L.: 1989, "Rubbish!," *Atlantic Monthly* (December), 99–109.

Rifkin, Jeremy: 1987, "Time Wars: A New Dimension Shaping Our Future," *Utne Reader* (September).

Rifkin, Jeremy: 1980, *Entropy: A New World View* (Bantam, New York).

Rothbard, Murray N.: 1982a, "Law, Property Rights, and Air Pollution," *Cato Journal* **2**(1) (Spring), reprinted in Walter Block (ed.), *Economics and the Environment: A Reconciliation* (The Fraser Institute, Vancouver), 1990.

Rothbard, Murray N.: 1973, *For a New Liberty* (Macmillan, New York).

Rothbard, Murray N.: 1982b, *The Ethics of Liberty* (Humanities Press, Atlantic Highlands, NJ).

Rubin, Charles T.: 1994, *The Green Crusade: Re-Thinking the Roots of Environmentalism* (McMillan Free Press, New York).

Sale, Kirkpatrick: 1989, "Presidential Matters," *Resurgence* **132** (January–February).

Samuelson, Paul A.: 1970, *Economics*, 8th ed. (McGraw-Hill, New York).

Samuelson, Paul A.: 1956, "Social Indifference Curves," *Quarterly Journal of Economic* **70**(1) (February), 1–22.

Schumacher, E. F.: 1973, *Small Is Beautiful* (Harper and Row, New York).

Smith, Adam: 1776/1965, *An Inquiry into the Nature and Causes of the Wealth of Nations* (Modern Library, New York).

Spooner, Lysander: 1966, *No Treason* (Larkspur, Colorado (1870)).

Stroup, Richard: 1988, "Buying Misery with Federal Land," *Public Choice* **57**, 69–77.

Ecological Marketing Strategy for Toni Yogurts in Switzerland

THOMAS DYLLICK

I. Ecological Problems and Company Responsibility

IT WAS THE UNSETTLING MESSAGE of the first report to the Club of Rome, "The limits to growth," that exponential growth of the population and its consumption would inevitably lead to a depletion of natural resources and a degradation of the environment, that convinced Walter Regez, a practicing Christian who should become Toni's CEO a few years later, of his company's ecological responsibility. In 1972 he gave orders to look into ways in which his organization, a milk producers' cooperative in the Zurich area, could contribute in its own domain to solve the ecological problems of the time. Their interest was soon focused on the question of packaging for their yogurt products. They had followed the general trend in the industry in the fifties, by substituting the formerly used heavy glass containers with the cheaper plastic cups, thereby contributing to the coming of a wasteful "throw-away-society." Towards the end of 1972, he demanded to prepare for the reintroduction of returnable glass containers for Toni's yogurt products. Looking back some years later, he summarized his motives for this decision in the following way:

> We tried to accept our responsibilities in our own domain of action, where we actually could contribute on our part. Growing amounts of waste, the depletion of natural resources, the degradation of the environment and energy shortages were reason enough to change our views and to include the ecology in our company's philosophy and strategy.[1]

One of his ambitions was to show that economic goals did not have to collide necessarily with ecological constraints, moreover, that there was a way to combine the company's goals with the preservation of the environment. The strategy developed, therefore, had to be *economically acceptable* on the one hand, but it had to be *ecologically reasonable* at the same time. Three ecological goals were stated explicitly:

1. Reducing the amount of resources and energy needed
2. Involving actively a number of external groups, mainly the consumers, the retailers, and the packaging industry
3. Strengthening and developing ecological consciousness among the population in general

What Toni had to experience in implementing this strategy was the fact that good ecological intentions alone are not a sufficiently reliable basis to build its strategy upon. The inclusion of ecological goals into its marketing strategy needed an effective implementation at an operative level as well to make it a success, finally.

II. The Toni Cooperative and the Swiss Yogurt Market

The Toni cooperative is the largest of 13 milk producers' cooperatives serving the different regions of Switzerland. Together they form the Swiss Milk Producers' Association (SMPA), a national self-help organization founded in 1907 to represent the interests of the many small milk producers. Although the SMPA is organized in the form of a private corporation, it has been charged with a number of public duties: organizing for an orderly and cost-effective distribution of milk in the whole country, assuring the income of the milk producers, controlling milk production, assuring a high level of product quality by training the producers and providing them with technical assistance. Over and above these political functions, the SMPA plays a central role in the marketing of all milk products as well. They engage in market research,

[1] Walter Regez, Die Rolle unternehmerischen Handelns beim Schutz der Umwelt., Speech given at Toni's press conference on February 5, 1985, in Zürich, mim., p. 3.

From Journal of Business Ethics 8(8), 1989. *Reprinted by permission of Kluwer Academic Publishers.*

product development, product design, advertisement, sales promotion, and partly distribution as well. As one of their functions, they are offering to their members a national yogurt brand, Cristallina, to allow for a successful marketing of a nationally distributed brand. While product design, product development, and advertisement is done centrally by the SMPA, the actual production and distribution of the yogurt is done by the regional cooperatives. The national brand, offered by the SMPA, had come under increasing internal competition by private label brands, however, sold by some of the larger regional cooperatives, Toni being one of them. In general, the regional cooperatives are held not to intrude into the others' area, even though enforcement mechanisms are weak.

Toni, seated in Winterthur near Zurich, is the largest milk producers' cooperative within the SMPA. It operates in the central and eastern region of Switzerland, encompassing the Zürich metropolitan area, the most densely populated area of Switzerland. Its members include some 800 local milk and cheese cooperatives, adding up to some 11,000 individual milk producers, whose milk it is obliged to take. It operates 6 dairies in different locations and runs 120 local shops and milk businesses. It employs 1100 people, and processes 15% of the total Swiss milk production. Its total sales in 1986/87 reached 675 Million Swiss Franks. Yogurt amounts to somewhat more than 10% of total sales.

The sales of the swiss *yogurt market* in 1986 amount to 10% or 440 Million Franks, being the fifth largest segment within the total milk products market. At the same time it is a particular interesting segment within a stagnant and heavily regulated industry, showing the highest growth rate and above average returns. For this reason most competitors concentrate on the yogurt segment of the market. The market is heavily concentrated, typical of the Swiss food retail market in general. The leading brand, a private label yogurt of gigantic Migros, had 45% of the market in 1974 by itself, when Toni started its returnable glass project. The two leading brands had 65%, while Toni didn't have more than 1.8% of the market. Concentration is even heavier looking at the retail market. The two dominating food retailing chains in Switzerland, Migros and Coop, both being a cooperative themselves, captured more than 70% of the market. The yogurt market was characterized by very little product dif-

ferentiation. Competition was focused on the price of the product alone.

III. The Ecological Context

Problems of resource scarcity, energy shortage, and deterioration of the natural environment have been on top of the political agendas since the mid seventies in most industrial nations. In particular this has been true for Switzerland. While the Swiss population has grown by 19% within the past 20 years, household waste has tripled within this period. The tremendous increase in per capita waste production is reflected in the corresponding figures: 150 kg p.c. in 1960 jumped to 375 kg p.c. in 1983. While this growth seemed to level off in the mid seventies, it resumed its continued growth and will be reaching 400 kg p.c. soon. Household waste makes up for some 30% of total waste production in Switzerland, a considerable part of it, around 40%, coming from packaging materials alone.

The use of plastic materials has been increasing enormously since the 1950s, thanks to its useful features and its wide applicability. Per capita plastic consumption increased from 47 to 75 kg between 1971 and 1983. Roughly one quarter is used for packaging purposes alone. Plastic materials are based on non-renewable oil and gas as their primary resources, and two thirds end up in the household waste. The recycling of plastic materials is only just beginning in Switzerland. Not more than 5% of total plastics consumption is being reused today, compared to more than 70% of total glass production. The rate of per capita glass recycling in Switzerland has reached more than 20 kg recently, a figure not reached anywhere else in the world.

IV. Yogurt Packaging

Four criteria are mainly used in evaluating different ways of yogurt packaging: protection (product safety, safety of the user and the environment, quality preservation, hygiene, durability), favorability (for transportation, storage, handling, rationing), ecology (energy usage, resource usage, pollution, waste production), and cost (packaging material, packaging, transport, storage, recycling). These criteria demand very different qualities from any concrete form of packaging. Any single form of packaging will be better with respect to some criteria, and worse with respect to others. The mix of advantages on the one hand, and cost on the other hand is very different in the case of different forms of yogurt packaging, too.

Since the 1950s plastic cups sealed with aluminum foil have been introduced successively to become quickly the dominant form of yogurt packaging. Its advantages are economical: low price, little weight, and efficiency in transport because the empty cups can be stacked. Its disadvantages are mainly ecological: use of nonrenewable fossil fuels and waste production. Glass packaging, on the contrary, has some ecological advantages: no waste, provided it is returned and reused, resource and energy savings, but it has qualitative advantages, as well. It preserves the quality of the contents better than any other form of packaging. Its disadvantages are mainly economical: price, cost of transportation, and storage of empty glasses. The difference in cost of packaging was at nearly 5 Rappen per piece, constituting some 7% of its retail price. The rate of glasses returned plays a critical role, reducing the difference in cost. But cost parity is impossible to be reached, even if 100% of glasses are returned. Plastic cups were used for nearly all yogurts sold in 1974, when Toni started its recyclable glass project. Only some yogurts were sold in non-recyclable glasses, accounting probably for as little as 1% of the market.

V. Realizing the Project and Crisis in 1981

The realization of Toni's project, named "Take care of the environment," started early in 1974 with a test run among Zürich's consumers. Toni proposed to them to decide themselves on the reintroduction. It announced to introduce Toni yogurt in a recyclable glass container and to invest half a million Franks for a washing machine, if the consumers would return more than 30% of the glasses sold within a 6-month-period. 30% was considered to be the economically justifiable lower boundary for the project. The experts polled were very negative about the outcome of this test. They estimated that no more than 5–10% of the glass containers would be returned, mainly due to the fact that they were to be sold without a deposit. When Toni announced that 40.2% of the glasses had been returned, the surprise was considerable.

The press hailed the company for taking a bold step in the right direction, giving them free public relations. The consumer organizations and the ecologists supported the project as well. Toni subsequently installed a washing machine in its new Zürich dairy, where all the recycled glass containers were washed before being reused.

In the beginning, the Toni yogurt "in the glass" was sold mainly in the Zürich metropolitan area, while Toni's other dairies decided not to switch to the glass packaging right away. It was a high quality yogurt, sold at a premium price primarily by the small milk shops, the traditional retail outlet of the milk producers' cooperatives. The quality aspect of the yogurt dominated the sparsely used market communication, while the ecological aspect of the packaging was part of Toni's PR-campaign.

After modest initial increases, Toni's yogurt sales were stagnant the following years. In the beginning of 1981 the whole project was in a deep *crisis*. The signs of this crisis were:

- decreasing market share, while the total market was expanding.
- decreasing rates of glasses recycled: while they had reached 50% in the mid-seventies, by 1980 they were down to 35%, less than in 1974 when the project was started.
- increasing uneasiness on the part of the retailers, because of the cost of handling the returned glass containers.
- it was still mainly distributed by the small milk shops, while the dominating retail chains did not carry Toni because of the handling problems.
- a competitor, Emmi, another regional milk producers cooperative, had introduced a glass container for their yogurts as well, although it was not recycled.
- the aluminum cap showed some leaking problems, as aluminum technically could not be fastened close enough to a glass surface.

But Toni was challenged on ecological grounds as well: a study on the comparative ecological advantage of the glass packaging, commissioned by Toni's competitors, came to the conclusion that the plastic cup was ecologically equivalent to the glass container, if not better, looking at the total energy balance over the whole life cycle of the packaging material. Although the study was criticized for looking at energy usage alone, not taking into consideration resource usage and waste production, it was a blow to Toni's ecological marketing strategy.

VI. Marketing Actions Taken to Counter the Crisis and Success in the Market

Toni was not willing to give up on the recyclable glass packaging. They studied the situation and came up with a number of *marketing actions* that were implemented after 1981. They included the following:

- the substitution of the aluminum cap by a reclosable plastic cap, that could be recycled and reused (for a different purpose) as well, improving the ecological motive of the packaging.
- development of a special crate for depositing the empty glass containers in front of the retailers' by the consumers themselves, freeing the retailers from any handling of the empty containers, while being a highly visible promotional device at the same time.
- a fresh and very original advertising campaign, based on a new corporate identity, that was to become a classic. It was based on the quality image of the yogurt, using the slogan: "Toni Yogurt in the glass, because for quality nothing is too good." The more valuable packaging material was suggested as tangible proof of the higher quality of the product.
- promotional discounts were offered to support the marketing offensive.

Sales took off rapidly beginning in 1982, after these actions had been implemented. The *economic results* are clearly demonstrating the great success of the actions taken. They consisted of:

- a tripling of sales within a three year period (1982–1985).
- a tripling of market share within a four year period (1981–1985), bringing Toni up to third place from fifth place.
- an expansion of the total market by 13%, 80% of which went to Toni.
- a number of retail chains was forced to include Toni in their assortments, due to consumer demand, allowing for a better national distribution.

- awards for their original and effective advertising campaign, which has become a classic. Its best pieces are sold today as a collector's item.
- a massive good will on part of the consumers in favor of the Toni brand and the whole organization.

VII. Results Concerning the Ecology

But what are the results of Toni's marketing strategy concerning the ecology? With Toni's success in the market, its competitors were forced to react. What started then can be best characterized as an *ecological head-on race,* with Toni's competitors trying to match its ecological strategy. Hirz, the No. 4 in the market, that suffered from Toni's success, switched to a newly developed more ecological packaging, using 50% recycled paper. Emmi and Christallina were forced to introduce a recyclable packaging as well. Migros, the market leader, evaluated the decision to switch to a recyclable glass packaging, but decided negatively. Instead, it had improved on its plastic packaging steadily, reducing the amount of energy, resources, and waste by more than 40% between 1972 and 1982.

Toni reacted to this ecological head-on race with an increased ecological activity. It commissioned a new study in 1983, which pointed to the weight of the glass container and the rate of recycling as the critical factors in improving the ecology of its glass packaging. Its *ecological actions,* implemented in 1985, therefore included:

- the development and introduction of a new glass container with 25% less weight, to save resources and energy.
- the foundation of a Toni foundation named "Take care of the environment" to spur recycling of their glass containers and ecological activity in society in general. They organized yearly glass returning campaigns, and promised to pay 1 Rappen to the foundation for every glass container returned. The foundation in turn financed a "Toni prize," which is awarded yearly to the organization found to have contributed most significantly to the betterment of the ecology. The board of the foundation includes, among other publicly known personalities, a former minister as its chairman.

The *ecological results* of these activities are considerable as well. They consist of:

- a more than doubling of the rate of recycled glasses, from 32% in 1981 up to an incredible 70% in 1985.
- a tripling of the share of glass packaging in the whole 180 g market, bringing it to 17% in 1985 up from 6% in 1980.
- two awards for their recycling idea.
- the successful introduction of an ecological focus in marketing yogurts in Switzerland forced *all* competitors to improve on the ecology of their packaging as well, thereby reducing the amount of resources and energy wasted.
- the enhancement of the ecologic consciousness of the Swiss public in general, while offering a practical option to contribute personally to improving the ecological condition.

As a consequence of the ecological improvements of its glass packaging, Toni announced at a press conference in early 1985, without any doubt its packaging now could be considered the most ecological packaging available, even when looking at its energy balance alone. But as ecological performance, being a multi-dimensional construct, cannot be measured and judged unambiguously and as all its competitors are improving their ecological performance constantly as well, what has been aptly termed as a "war of beliefs" over the most ecological yogurt packaging will go on without any definite result. Trying to evaluate the ecological success of Toni's strategy, therefore, it will not be sufficient to judge Toni's comparative success on its own. Its real success has to be seen in the *collective ecological improvements* by the whole industry, brought about by Toni's bold move to integrate the ecology into its marketing strategy. By pushing ecologically ahead, it succeeded in shifting the main competitive focus of the industry from price to ecology. Toni, being only a minor competitor with some 2% market share in the mid-seventies, was able to change the strategic rules of the game to its own advantage, thereby causing all competitors to improve on the ecology of their packaging as well. This has to be considered the true ecological success of Toni's strategy.

Lessons to Be Learned

The *lessons* learned from the Toni case are telling in five respects, at least:

1. Value changes in society-at-large have changed the shape of consumer demand and created a new market for ecological goods and ecological arguments. This market offers new opportunities for active and creative competitors, that is only beginning to be realized. Within this domain of ecological values and demand it has become possible to reach economic objectives in terms of market share and ecological goals of society-at-large at the same time.

2. The Toni case, however, demonstrates the difficulties encountered in making an ecological marketing strategy work as well. Good ecological intentions alone are not sufficient. It takes stamina and all the marketing expertise used for any other commercial good as well to make it a successful innovation. In the Toni case it needed 8 years of collective learning and adaptation before sales finally took off.

3. Toni developed a new type of strategy particularly adequate for its ecological focus: a *collective* marketing strategy that includes external groups like consumers, retailers, packaging manufacturers, consumer organizations, ecological organizations, and the media.

4. It shows, too, how the competitive focus of a consumer product can be shifted successfully to ecology without any state intervention, if a committed competitor should decide to go ahead. The result may be, as in the Toni case, ecological improvements of all competitors, to the benefit of society.

5. Marketing thinking alone may be too weak as a motivation for embarking on an ecological strategy, although in the Toni case the strategy followed could be explained *ex post facto* as nothing else but good long term marketing thinking. What it needs to develop an ecological marketing strategy early enough, and what it needs to pull it through all the difficulties in realizing and adapting the strategy over time is a commitment to ecological goals as well. And this is where economic thinking does not reach far enough. For this it needs an ethical commitment as well.[2]

[2]For more cases and a thorough conceptual treatment of the topic "Managing the corporate external environment" see: Thomas Dyllick, Management der Umweltbeziehungen. Öffentliche Auseinandersetzungen als Herausforderung, Gabler Verlag, Wiesbaden 1989.

Questions for Chapter 18

1. Discuss the ways in which Heyd suggests that we may come to recognize that we have moral responsibilities to the environment.
2. Heyd describes what is known as the Gaia Hypothesis. What is this hypothesis and how does it function as a foundation for thinking about environmental responsibility? Do you agree with this hypothesis?
3. Sagoff suggests that things other than humans have intrinsic worth. Do you agree? Do all natural things, including the Ebola and AIDS viruses, have intrinsic worth?
4. Sagoff appeals to the notion of "ecological health" in his discussion of how we should treat nature. If asked to describe what you think "ecological health" is, what would you say?
5. Block mentions the phenomenon of "moral hazard." What is this moral hazard and why does Block feel that a free market system will escape it?
6. Block does not consider the question of whether nonhuman entities can be considered to have intrinsic value. Does this in any way undermine his argument?
7. Why does Dyllick suggest that marketing thinking alone may be too weak a motivation for embarking on an ecological strategy?
8. What does Dyllick mean when he suggests that to evaluate the ecological success of Toni's strategy, it is not sufficient to judge Toni's comparative success on its own?

Case 18.1 Ski Pants and the Environment[1]

Patagonia Ltd. is a successful outdoor-wear company with aspirations to conduct business in an environmentally responsible way. It recently undertook an environmental audit to investigate its impact on the environment. Concerns raised by the audit include: that the use of polyester contributes to the depletion of petroleum, a nonrenewable resource; that the use of cotton contributes to the use of highly toxic pesticides; and that the use of wool involves the destruction of fragile ecosystems by large flocks of sheep. As a preliminary response, Patagonia has decided to drop approximately one-third of its product line and seek out suppliers that grow only "organic" cotton. In the catalog describing product lines, company president Yvon Chouinard tells potential customers that "Last fall, you had a choice of five ski pants, now you may choose between two. This is, of course, un-American, but two styles of ski pants are all that anyone needs." He goes on to state that his ultimate goal is to halt further growth of Patagonia.[2]

Reactions to Patagonia's policy vary widely. Many commentators praise Chouinard's decision. Tom Turner, a staff writer for the Sierra Club Legal Defense Fund, calls Chouinard's message

[1]This case study is based on "Can Slower Growth Save the World?," *Business and Society Review,* Spring 1993, No. 85, pp. 10–20.

[2]"Can Slower Growth Save the World?," p. 10.

glorious and sees the policy adopted by Patagonia as an important step in the voluntary restraint producers and consumers must adopt if we are to move toward environmentally benign technologies.[3] Hazel Henderson, an advisor to the Calvert Social Investment Fund, calls Chouinard a rare combination of clever entrepreneur and informed social conscience. In her view, he has anticipated the inevitable move to a more sustainable economy and is ahead of competitors in adapting Patagonia to the marketplace of the future. She suggests that "He may well end up with a jackpot: awards from social and environmental groups, a more desirable, higher-markup product line, plus a more manageable and highly valued company."[4] In a similar vein, J. H. Foegen, a professor of business, Frank Tsai, a financial consultant, and Alan Parker, director of shareholder relations and special projects at Ben & Jerry's Homemade Inc., suggest that Chouinard has anticipated the future in his emphasis on the limits to growth and applying environmentally benign technology.[5]

There are many other commentators, however, who feel that Patagonia's policy is misguided. Doug Bandow, a senior fellow at the Cato Institute, agrees with Chouinard's claim that consumers should not be spending simply for the sake of spending, but suggests that Chouinard errs in viewing pollution as a moral evil, rather than as an unfortunate cost to be limited as far as possible. He suggests what is important is that we ensure that the benefits of processes that cause pollution outweigh the costs of pollution they generate. He argues that, in order for this to occur, it is important that a commodity, for example, cotton, be priced to reflect its full costs of production. In his view, the problem is not economic growth, but political processes that skew the marketplace by artificially encouraging destructive and uneconomic growth.[6]

Jonathan Adler, an environmental policy analyst at the Competitive Enterprise Institute, comments that Chouinard confuses environmental impact with environmental damage. He notes, for example, that pesticide use has had environ-

mental benefits as well as disbenefits. He argues that human action invariably impacts the environment, but that to equate environmental impact and environmental damage leads to the conclusion that primitive societies are preferable to ours, even though they have dramatically shorter life expectancies and, in many respects, lower qualities of life. He raises the question of whether Chouinard's views imply not simply that we should limit the different styles of ski pants produced, but that we should not manufacture ski pants at all.[7]

Michael Silverstein, a writer and commentator on environmental economics, criticizes Chouinard on the basis that he tends to foster the view that we must choose between the environment and economic growth. This, Silverstein argues, has the consequence not of creating an ecologically sound marketplace, but of condemning underdeveloped nations to poverty in the name of saving nature. What is required, Silverstein suggests, is not that we attempt to restore nature to some pristine purity untouched by human intervention, but that we meld prolific consumption and economic well-being with environmental health.[8]

1. Among other criticisms of Patagonia's policies, Bandow suggests that it is the quantity produced rather than the variety offered that is the basic cause of pollution. On this basis, he suggests that Patagonia should be concentrating not on reducing the variety of styles offered, but on reducing sales. Do you agree? What would be the implications of taking such an approach?

2. What definition would you give of the term *pollution?* Adler wants to distinguish between environmental damage and environmental impact. Is this distinction a valid one? If so, how would you go about making it?

3. Chouinard suggests that "Third World resources are close to exhaustion." Is this consistent with the fact that the price of these resources has declined on world markets? Why or why not?

[3]"Can Slower Growth Save the World?," p. 12.
[4]"Can Slower Growth Save the World?," pp. 16, 17.
[5]"Can Slower Growth Save the World?," pp. 17–19.
[6]"Can Slower Growth Save the World?," pp. 14, 15.
[7]"Can Slower Growth Save the World?," p. 15.
[8]"Can Slower Growth Save the World?," p. 16.

Case 18.2 Bankruptcy, Pollution, and Social Obligation[9]

William Kovacs was the chief executive officer and stockholder of Chem-Dyne Corporation which operated an industrial and hazardous waste disposal site in Hamilton, Ohio. In 1976, the state of Ohio sued Kovacs for maintaining a nuisance, polluting public waters, and causing fish kills. In 1979, Kovac settled the lawsuit by agreeing to pay $75,000 dollars to compensate the State for injury to wildlife, to remove specified wastes from the property, to bring no additional industrial wastes to the site, and to cause no further pollution of the air or public waters.

When Kovacs failed to comply with this agreement, the State obtained permission for a receiver to take possession of Kovacs's property and implement a cleanup of the Chem-Dyne site. The receiver had taken possession of the site, but had not completed a cleanup, when Kovacs filed

[9]Based on Ohio v. Kovacs as found in 105 *Supreme Court Reporter* 705 (1985).

a personal bankruptcy petition. In his petition he argued that, since cleanup costs arose from a statutory violation rather than a contractual breach, these costs were dischargeable in bankruptcy and he had no obligation to pay them.

The State took the position that the costs of the cleanup were not dischargeable in bankruptcy and filed a complaint in Bankruptcy Court.

1. Would Kovacs, even in the absence of a legal obligation to pay for the costs of a cleanup, nevertheless have a moral obligation to pay those costs?

2. Should the company that produces a pollution problem always be solely responsible for the costs of cleanup?

3. Suppose a problem of pollution is not detected, indeed could not have been detected or anticipated, until some years after the site has changed hands. Who should have the responsibility of paying for cleanup costs?

Further Readings for Chapter 18

Terry Anderson and Donald Leal, *Free Market Environmentalism* (San Francisco: Westview Press, 1991).

W. Michael Hoffman, Robert Frederick, and Edward S. Petry, Jr., eds., *Business, Ethics and the Environment* (New York: Quorum Books, 1990).

Lisa Newton and Catherine Dillingham, *Watersheds* (Belmont, CA: Wadsworth, 1994).

Tom Regan, ed., *Earthbound: New Introductory Essays in Environmental Ethics* (New York: Random House, 1984).

Charles Rubin, *The Green Crusade: Rethinking the Roots of Environmentalism* (New York: Free Press, 1994).

INFOTRAC COLLEGE EDITION To learn more about the topics from this chapter, you can use the following words to conduct an electronic search on InfoTrac College Edition, an online library of journals. Here you will find a multitude of articles from various sources and perspectives: *www.infotrac-college.com/wadsworth/access.html*

deep ecology

environmental ethics

environmentalism

Writing Article Summaries and Critical Essays

Writing Article Summaries

THE AIM OF THIS TEXT is not simply to introduce a body of material, but to engage the student and provoke critical analysis. The skills needed to detect, analyze, and respond to arguments are especially important for philosophers, but they will stand all of us in good stead in our day-to-day activities. I have provided, therefore, some practical hints that will help beginners develop these skills.

One of the first things to keep in mind is to distinguish your own view from the view of the person you are reading. Put a little differently, it is very important to get clear what a person is saying before you begin to respond to her. Otherwise, you run the risk not only of misrepresenting her argument, but of responding to something quite different from what was actually said.

This seems straightforward, but it is easier said than done, even for professional philosophers. All of us read or listen with certain opinions and views already in place, and these often make it hard for us to be clear on what is actually said. Just as you might mistake a piece of cardboard on the highway for a dead rabbit if you were expecting to see a dead rabbit rather than a piece of cardboard, so it is easy to misconstrue a person's argument if you were expecting him to say something else.

It is essential, therefore, to examine a person's argument carefully, before you respond to it. A great aid to doing this is to construct an article summary. There are many ways in which this may be done, but all good summaries will have certain essential elements in common.

Most importantly, the summary should make clear the main claim or claims of the article. This is, in effect, the bottom line, the conclusion the writer wishes you to accept. Usually it can be stated very briefly in a sentence or two. This is especially true of well-written articles.

The summary should also make clear what arguments the author uses to support her main claim. It is important to discern the number and structure of the arguments given for accepting the conclusion, that is, the main claim. This is not always easy, but it is essential. Remember that critical analysis cannot take place until we first become clear what the arguments we are critically analyzing are. As in the case of understanding the main claim, you will find that the better-written an article is, the easier it is to discern the arguments used to establish its conclusion.

If an author has done his job well, he will also consider counterarguments to his position and indicate how he answers or would go about answering these counterarguments. You should include in your summary any objections the author considers and the replies he makes to them.

These are the essential elements of an article summary. It is sometimes useful to include a brief synopsis of the problem the author is considering or to provide some background information to set the context, but these are generally optional. I suggest, therefore, that the beginning student consider organizing her article summaries under four headings: (1) Main Claim (Thesis), (2) Supporting Arguments, (3) Objections Considered, and (4) Author's Reply to Objections.

This is a suggestion only. It is often possible, for example, to consider an author's supporting arguments and replies to objections under one heading, since a successful counterargument is frequently also a supporting argument. The important thing to grasp is that you should seek to discern these four characteristic activities of stating a main claim, defending it by supporting arguments, considering objections, and replying to objections, in the articles you examine. To give some idea of how this works in practice, I have provided two sample summaries at the end of this appendix.

Writing Critical Essays

The same headings that provide a framework upon which to construct a summary can guide the writing of a critical essay. Although these headings will usually not appear in the essay, it is essential to state clearly your main claim, the arguments in support of it, the objections to it, and your reply to objections. The essential difference between writing an article summary and a critical essay is that, whereas in an article summary you are simply aiming to be as accurate as possible in describing someone else's argument, in a critical essay you are formulating and developing an argument of your own. In practice, of course, the two processes intermingle, since in formulating and defending your own position you will generally find it necessary to respond to the views of others.

Several pitfalls need to be avoided by those beginning to write critical essays. One of the most common is making the main claim too broad. In a short paper where it is not possible to discuss all facets of a complex moral problem, it is usually better to focus on a specific claim than on a very general one. For example, a student writing on the topic of abortion will probably write a better paper if she focuses on a specific issue, such as whether abortion is justified in instances of rape, than if she tries to address all the problems associated with the issue of abortion. It is better to do a good job of discussing one issue than a mediocre job of discussing several. This is not to suggest that it is not important to develop a broad perspective and to examine whether what you say on one issue is consistent with what you say on another. Rather, it is to be realistic about what can and cannot be accomplished in a short essay.

Another pitfall to be avoided is underestimating the strength of the arguments of those with whom you disagree. It is important that you be fair in your treatment of objections to your position. Do not misdescribe counterarguments and do not select for discussion only the weakest arguments against your view. Your goal should be to refute the strongest arguments against your position, since if you can accomplish this you have nothing to worry about. Refuting only weak objections accomplishes little, since it is always open to your critic to reply that much bigger artillery can be brought to bear.

A useful way of accomplishing this is to think of yourself as possessing two hats: one is labeled "thesis," the other "antithesis." When wearing the "thesis" hat, you formulate and defend your main claim. When wearing the "antithesis" hat, you consider the ways in which an intelligent critic might attack your main claim and its supporting arguments. If, when you are writing a critical essay, you take time to change hats every so often, it will prove a great aid to not underestimating the strength of objections to your position.

Another trap to be avoided is that of reinventing the wheel. Taking the time to do some reading on a topic to see what has already been said will help not only to clarify your position, but also to avoid mistakes and dead ends previously detected by others. It is also an aid to not underestimating objections to your position, since you become aware of some of the common arguments against your point of view. Do not, however, make the mistake of thinking that you must read everything that has ever been written on a topic before you can write a critical essay. All that is required is that you begin to get a grasp of the important arguments for and against the position you wish to defend.

It is important in this regard to give credit where credit is due. It is one thing to put into your own words an argument that has been used by another writer; it is quite another to appropriate it with few or no changes and characterize it as your own. It is important when you are using another author's words to indicate this to the reader. Failure to do so is called plagiarism and has very serious academic penalties if detected. A further reason why it is important to indicate when you are making use of another author's words is that it then becomes possible for your readers to determine whether you have quoted that author accurately and in context.

We learn by doing. You will find that as you write article summaries and critical essays, their quality will improve and they will not be so hard to produce. Writing them can never be a purely mechanical process, but it is a skill that can be fairly easily mastered if you pay attention to the basics I have described.

Sample Summary

Article summary of Albert Carr's **"Is Business Bluffing Ethical?"**

Main Claim

The ethics of business are impersonal game ethics. No one should condemn business because its standards of right and wrong differ from the prevailing traditions of morality in society.

Arguments in Support of Main Claim

1. Just as the ethics of ordinary morality are suspended in games, so they are suspended in business. A business person is not, therefore, immoral if she does not follow ordinary morality in the course of doing business.
2. It is impossible to be successful in business if one applies the ethical standards of private life. Therefore business people are entitled to conduct business on a different standard of morality.

Objection Considered

1. A person might have serious qualms about some of the seemingly immoral activities associated with business and not be able to reconcile the activities that take place in business with his personal beliefs.

Reply to Objection

1. The morality of business practices cannot be judged on the standards of private morality. As long as a business practice is legal and produces a profit, it is morally acceptable.

Sample Summary

Article summary of Mary Midgley's **"Trying Out One's New Sword"**

Main Claims

Moral isolationism, i.e., cultural relativism, fails as: (1) the best explanation of cultural diversity, (2) a foundation for tolerance and respect of other cultures, and (3) a consistent theory of morality.

Arguments in Support of Main Claims

1. Moral isolationists (cultural relativists) commonly make the claim that we cannot understand any culture except our own well enough to make judgments about it. This implies, however, several claims that moral isolationists do not usually acknowledge. These are: (1) that other cultures cannot criticize us, (2) that it is impossible to ever praise another culture, (3) that anthropologists will be unable to understand other cultures, and (4) that we cannot judge our own culture.
2. Moral isolationism, when carefully thought through, results in moral nihilism, since it reduces *all* moral judgments to trivial local quirks of one's own culture.
3. It is impossible to respect something that is entirely unintelligible. To the degree that one insists that other cultures must be respected and tolerated, one must deny moral isolationism.
4. There is no such thing as separate, unmixable cultures, and hence the view that, in principle, it is impossible to understand and evaluate cultures other than our own must be mistaken.

Latin Phrases and Their Meanings

a posteriori–behind, after

a priori–in advance, before

ab initio–from the beginning

ad hoc–this specific thing (in context it often refers to an argument that is not well justified)

bona fide–genuine

caveat emptor–let the buyer beware

de minimus–minimum

ex ante–from before (prior)

ex hypothesi–by hypothesis

ex nihilo–out of nothing

in foro interno–an internal forum or debate

ipso facto–therefore

iura fictus–derivative rights

mens rea–guilty mind (criminal purpose)

per se–essentially

persona ficta–fictious (artificial) person

prima facie–initial presumption

qua–as

quid pro quo–something in return for something

res gestae–accomplishments or results

status quo–present order or standing

suppressio veri–suppression of the truth

via media–middle way

vice versa–to invert an order or relation

CREDITS

Chapter 1. 4: From *Harvard Business Review* 46(1), 1968. Reprinted by permission of *Harvard Business Review*. Copyright © 1968 by the President and Fellows of Harvard College; all rights reserved. 10: From *Journal of Business Ethics* 16: 1447-1452. © 1997 Kluwer Academic Publishers. Printed in the Netherlands. Reprinted with permission from Kluwer Academic Publishers.

Chapter 2. 21: From Mary Midgley, *Heart and Mind*. Copyright © 1981 Mary Midgley. Reprinted with permission of St. Martin's Press. 24: Reprinted with permission of George Williamson. 29: Reprinted from Aristotle's *Nichomachean Ethics*, trans. W. D. Ross, © 1925 Oxford University Press. 32: From Immanuel Kant, *Grounding for the Metaphysics of Morals*, 3rd ed., 1993, trans. James W. Ellington, p. 7-15, p. 34-37 (edited). Reprinted by permission of Hackett Publishing Company, Inc. All rights reserved. 35: From John Stewart Mill, *Collected Works of John Stewart Mill, Vol. 10, Essays on Ethics, Religion and Society*, ed. J. M. Robson. Toronto: University of Toronto Press, © 1969. 38: From *Journal of Social Philosophy* 20 (1-2) (Spring-Fall 1989). Reprinted by permission of the *Journal of Social Philosophy*.

Chapter 3. 55: From *Journal of Business Ethics* 15: 475-485. © 1996 Kluwer Academic Publishers. Printed in the Netherlands. Reprinted with permission from Kluwer Academic Publishers. 64: From *Journal of Business Ethics* 15: 495-508. © 1990 Kluwer Academic Publishers. Reprinted with permission from Kluwer Academic Publishers. 77: From *Business and Professional Ethics* 4, 1985. Reprinted by permission. 84: From *Journal of Business Ethics* 21: 125-135. © 1999 Kluwer Academic Publishers. Reprinted with permission from Kluwer Academic Publishers.

Chapter 4. 101: From *Business and Professional Ethics* 6(3), 1986. Reprinted by permission. 111: From *Journal of Business Ethics* 17: 1805-1815, 1998. © 1998 Kluwer Academic Publishers. Reprinted with permission from Kluwer Academic Publishers. 121: From *Public Affairs Quarterly* 7(1), 1993. Reprinted by permission. 127: From *Journal of Business Ethics* 19: 355-362. © 1999 Kluwer Academic Publishers. Reprinted with permission from Kluwer Academic Publishers.

Chapter 5. 140: From *Public Affairs Quarterly* 5(4), 1991. Reprinted by permission. 150: From *Journal of Social Philosophy* 24 (1), 1993. Reprinted by permission of the *Journal of Social Philosophy*. 162: From *Public Affairs Quarterly* 13(1), 1999. Reprinted with permission.

Chapter 6. 185: From *Business and Professional Ethics Journal*. Reprinted by permission. 193: From *Journal of Business Ethics* 5: 129-136, 1986. © 1986 Kluwer Academic Publishers. Reprinted with permission from Kluwer Academic Publishers. 200: From *Moral Rights in the Workplace*, ed. Gertrude Ezorsky (Albany: State University of New York Press, 1987). Reprinted by permission.

Chapter 7. 208: From *Business and Professional Ethics Journal*, 8(4), 1988. Reprinted with permission. 216: From *Journal of Business Ethics* 11: 125-128. © 1992 Kluwer Academic Publishers. Reprinted with permission from Kluwer Academic Publishers. 220: From *Journal of Business Ethics* 17: 1517-1527, 1998. © 1998 Kluwer Academic Publishers. Reprinted with permission from Kluwer Academic Publishers.

Chapter 8. 235: From *Journal of Business Ethics* 8: 841-845, 1989. © 1989 Kluwer Academic Publishers. Reprinted with permission from Kluwer Academic Publishers. 239: From *Public Affairs Quarterly* 10(2), 1996. Reprinted with permission. 244: From *Journal of Applied Philosophy* 10(2), 1993. Reprinted by permission of Society for Applied Philosophy, 1993. Blackwell Publishers, 108 Cowley Road, Oxford, OX4 IJF. UK and 3 Cambridge Center, Cambridge, MA 02142, USA.

Chapter 9. 260: From *Philosophy and Public Affairs* 18 (1989), 31-52. © The Johns Hopkins University Press. Reprinted by permission of The Johns Hopkins University Press. 271: From *Philosophy and Public Affairs* 20(1991), 247-263. © The Johns Hopkins University Press. Reprinted by permission of The Johns Hopkins University Press. 281: From *Business & Professional Ethics Journal* 10(2), Summer 1991. Reprinted with permission. 293: From *Business and Professional Ethics Journal* 6, 1997, p. 102-109. Reprinted with permission.

Chapter 10. 306: From *Encyclopedia of Applied Ethics*, Vol. 2. Copyright © 1998 by Academic Press. All rights of reproduction in any form reserved. 312: From *Journal of Business Ethics* 20: 121-132, 1999. © 1999 Kluwer Academic Publishers. Reprinted with permission from Kluwer Academic Publishers. 323: From *Journal of Business Ethics* 20: 207-215, 1999. © 1999 Kluwer Academic Publishers. Reprinted with permission from Kluwer Academic Publishers.

Chapter 11. 336: From *Public Affairs Quarterly* 1(4), 1987. Reprinted with permission. 343: From *Journal of Business Ethics* 6, 1987. Reprinted by permission from Kluwer Academic Publishers. 349: From *Journal of Business Ethics* 15: 1299-112, 1996. © 1996 Kluwer Academic Publishers. Printed in the Netherlands. Reprinted by permission from Kluwer Academic Publishers. 361: From *Journal of Business Ethics* 17: 725-728, 1998. © 1998 Kluwer Academic Publishers. Printed in the Netherlands. Reprinted by permission from Kluwer Academic Publishers.

Chapter 12. 370: From *American Philosophical Quarterly* 16(3), 1979. Reprinted with permission. 379: From *Journal of Business Ethics* 10: 749-756, 1991. Reprinted by permission from Kluwer Academic Publishers. 386: From *Journal of Business Ethics* 10:77-383, 1991. Reprinted by permission from Kluwer Academic Publishers. 392: From *Journal of Business Ethics* 785-788, 1996. Reprinted with permission.

Chapter 13. 401: From *Journal of Business Ethics* 10(8): 561-568. Reprinted by permission of Kluwer Academic Publishers. 408: From *Journal of Business Ethics* 10(8): 561-568. Reprinted by permission of Kluwer Academic Publishers. 414: From *Professional Ethics Journal* 2(3-4). © Don Welch 1993. Reprinted with permission. 420: From *Professional Ethics Journal* 3(-4). © Banks McDowell 1994. Reprinted with permission.

Chapter 14. 432: From *Business & Professional Ethics Journal* 6(3), 1986. Reprinted with permission. 441: From *Public Affairs Quarterly* 6(2), 1992. Reprinted with permission. 456: From *Journal of Business Ethics* 17: 455-470, 1998. © 1998 Kluwer Academic Publishers. Printed in the Netherlands. Reprinted by permission of Kluwer Academic Publishers.

Chapter 15. 476: From Kathleen Gerson, *No Man's Land*, p. 277-316. Copyright © 1993 by Basic Books. Reprinted by permission of Basic Books, a member of Perseus Books, L. L. C. 480: From *The Annual of the Society of Christian Ethics* 1998 (Washington, D.C.: Georgetown University Press). Reprinted with permission. 489: From *Journal of Business Ethics* 8: 647-655. Reprinted by permission of Kluwer Academic Publishers. 497: From *Public Affairs Quarterly* 5(1), 1991. Reprinted with permission.

Chapter 16. 514: From *New York Times Magazine*, September 13, 1970, p. 32-33, 122-126. Copyright © 1970 by The New York Times Company. Reprinted by permission. 518: From *Social Theory and Practice* 11(3), Fall 1985. Reprinted with modifications by permission of the author and *Social Theory and Practice*. 526: From *Public Affairs Quarterly* 6(2), April 1992. Reprinted with permission.

Chapter 17. 540: From *Journal of Business Ethics* 12, 1993. Reprinted by permission of Kluwer Academic Publishers. 547: From *Journal of Business Ethics* 8(8), 1989. Reprinted by permission of Kluwer Academic Publishers. 555: From *Journal of Business Ethics* 12(9), 1993. Reprinted by permission of Kluwer Academic Publishers. 562: From *Journal of Business Ethics* 19: 21-33, 1999. © 1999 Kluwer Academic Publishers. Printed in the Netherlands. Reprinted by permission of Kluwer Academic Publishers.

Chapter 18. 578: Printed by permission of Thomas Heyd. 588: From *Hastings Center Report* 21(5), 1991. Reprinted by permission. 597: From *Journal of Business Ethics* 17: 1887-1899, 1998. © 1998 Kluwer Academic Publishers. Printed in the Netherlands. Reprinted by permission of Kluwer Academic Publishers. 609: From *Journal of Business Ethics* 8(8), 1989. Reprinted by permission of Kluwer Academic Publishers.